BUSINESS

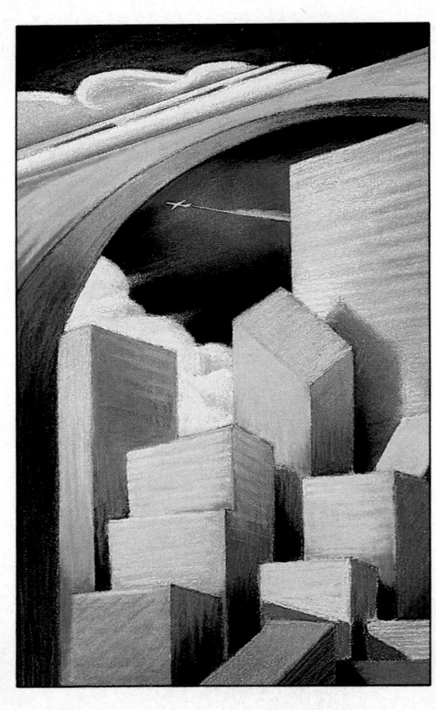

BUSINESS

THIRD EDITION

SAMUEL C. CERTO
The Roy E. Crummer Graduate School of Business
at Rollins College

STEWART W. HUSTED
Lynchburg College in Virginia

MAX E. DOUGLAS
Indiana State University

with the assistance of
ROBERT J. HARTL
University of Southern Indiana

ALLYN AND BACON
Boston London Sydney Toronto

To — Mimi, Trevis, Matthew, Sarah, and Brian
— Kathy, Ryan, and Evan
— Roseanne, Mark, Jason, William, Kathryn, and Blake

Series editor: *Jack Peters*
Developmental editors: *Allen Workman and Hannah Rubenstein*
Senior Editorial Assistant: *Carol Alper*
Production Assistant: *Lisa Feder*
Cover Administrator: *Linda Dickinson*
Composition Buyer: *Linda Cox*
Manufacturing Buyer: *Bill Alberti*
Editorial-Production Service: *York Production Services*
Text Designer: *Stuart Paterson for York Production Services*
Photo Researcher: *Laurel Anderson/Photosynthesis*
Production Administrator: *Mary Beth Finch*

Library of Congress Cataloging-in-Publication Data

Certo, Samuel C.
Business / Samuel C. Certo, Stewart W. Husted, Max E. Douglas with the assistance of Robert J. Hartl.—3rd ed.
p. cm.
Includes bibliographical references.
ISBN 0–205–12080–6
1. Management. 2. Business enterprises—United States. I. Husted, Stewart W. II. Douglas, Max E. III. Title.
HD31.C412 1990
658—dc20 89–39245
CIP

Printed in the United States of America.
10 9 8 7 6 5 4 3 2 1 94 93 92 91 90 89

The credits and acknowledgements for figures, tables, boxes, and cases begin on p. xx. They should be considered an extension of the copyright page.
Cover and p. ii illustration: Paul Schulenburg © 1989.
Part Opening illustrations by Richard A. Goldberg.

Photo Credits

p. 6: Courtesy of Turner Broadcasting Inc. p. 9: Michael L. Abramson/Woodfin Camp & Assoc. p. 22: Courtesy of Cincinnati Milacron. p. 23: Larry Keenan Jr. p. 25: Christian Simonpietri/Sygma. p. 34: Jim Brown/Offshoot. p. 40: Comstock. p. 44: Jim Brown/Offshoot. p. 54: George Gersler/Comstock. p. 55: Shepard Sherbell/Picture Group. p. 68: Courtesy of Levi Strauss Company. p. 79: Richard Howard/Offshoot. p. 81: Russ Schleipman/Offshoot. p. 87: Picture Group. p. 100: Hartman-Dewill/Comstock. p. 102: David Dempster/Offshoot. p. 107: Duomo. p. 110: Richard Howard/Offshoot. p. 128: Courtesy of Wally Amos. p. 130: Richard Howard/Offshoot. p. 137: JP Laffont/Sygma. p. 150: Rob Nelson/Picture Group. p. 166: Richard Howard/Offshoot. p. 169: Sepp Seitz/Woodfin Camp & Assoc. p. 177: John Troha/Black Star. p. 181: Richard Howard/Offshoot. p. 199: Richard Howard/Offshoot. p. 205: Courtesy of Allen-Bradley. p. 208: Gabe Palmer/The Stock Market. p. 222: Courtesy of Apple Computer Company. p. 228: Richard Howard/Offshoot. p. 234: Courtesy of IBM Corp. p. 241: David Dempster/Offshoot. p. 252: Courtesy of Toyota Corp. p. 257: Martha Everson/Picture Group. p. 265: Claudia Parks/The Stock Market. p. 268: Richard Howard/Offshoot. p. 269: Ted Cordingley/Offshoot. p. 280: Cara Lise Metz/ILGWU. p. 282: The Library of Congress. p. 285: Andrew Popper/Picture Group. p. 295: D. Goldberg/Sygma. p. 308: Courtesy of Maytag. p. 316: Courtesy of Allen-Bradley. p. 317: Richard Howard/Offshoot. p. 329: Steve Dunwell/The Image Bank. p. 331: Courtesy of Harley-Davidson. p. 344: Vail Cart Tyler/Offshoot. p. 348: Courtesy of Scandinavian Airlines System. p. 350: John Curtis/Offshoot. p. 354: David Dempster/Offshoot. p. 375: Richard Howard/Offshoot. p. 379: Kenneth Jarecke/Contact Press Images. p. 386: Ted Cordingley/Offshoot. p. 419: Russ Schleipman/Offshoot. p. 422: John Curtis/Offshoot. p. 432: Picture Group. p. 440: Larry Lawfer/Offshoot. p. 441: Courtesy of New England Telephone. p. 444: John Curtis/Offshoot. p. 469: Fred Ward/Black Star. p. 470: Fred Ward/Black Star. p. 473: P. Robert Garvey/The Stock Market. p. 478: Ken Straiton/The Stock Market. p. 490: Gabe Palmer/The Stock Market. p. 500: Gabe Palmer/The Stock Market. p. 517: Gabe Palmer/The Stock Market. p. 526: Courtesy of Bethlehem Steel. p. 530: Richard Howard/Offshoot. p. 534: Mark Gibson/The Stock Market. p. 542: Russ Schleipman/Offshoot. p. 558: Courtesy of Reginald Lewis. p. 560: Frank Siteman/The Picture Cube. p. 568: Peter Morgan/Picture Group. p. 571: Andrew Popper/Picture Group. p. 574: Gabe Palmer/The Stock Market. p. 603: Jim Brown/Offshoot. p. 604: Mark Richards/Picture Group. p. 606: Tom Pich/Sygma. p. 609: Peter Marlow/Sygma. p. 610: C. Simonpietri/Sygma. p. 633: Russ Schleipman/Offshoot. p. 634: Michael A. Keller/The Stock Market. p. 637: Dan McCoy/Rainbow. p. 641: Courtesy of Burlington Industries. p. 659: Richard Howard/Offshoot. p. 662: Courtesy of The American Cancer Society. p. 663: Edward Pieratt/Comstock. p. 676: Koch-Contrasto/Picture Group. p. 685: Comstock. p. 686: Courtesy of Heinz Company. p. 693: Russ Schleipman/Offshoot.

BRIEF CONTENTS

PART

PART

PART

PART

PART

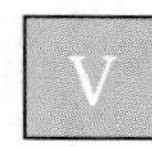

PART

CONTENTS

PART II

STARTING UP A BUSINESS 96

CHAPTER 4

SELECTING A FORM OF BUSINESS OWNERSHIP 98

CHAPTER 5

SMALL BUSINESS AND ENTREPRENEURSHIP 126

PART

MANAGING ORGANIZATIONS 160

CHAPTER 9

HUMAN RESOURCE MANAGEMENT 250

CHAPTER 10

LABOR-MANAGEMENT RELATIONS 278

CHAPTER 11

PRODUCTION AND OPERATIONS MANAGEMENT 306

PART

MARKETING FOR TODAY'S CONSUMER 340

CHAPTER 12

CHAPTER 13

CHAPTER 14

CHAPTER 15

PROMOTING GOODS AND SERVICES 430

PART

FINANCING BUSINESS VENTURES 462

CHAPTER 16

MONEY AND THE BANKING SYSTEM 464

CHAPTER 17

ACCOUNTING: UNDERSTANDING THE LANGUAGE OF BUSINESS 496

PREFACE

FEATURES OF THIS TEXT

As with previous editions, the purpose of this text is to provide students with a realistic introduction to the world of business. Business today is far more than theoretical concepts. It is excitement, hard work, and challenge! The focus of this book is to give students a thorough understanding of important business principles as well as an appreciation for the overall environment in which they are practiced.

The acceptance and support of our ideas and concepts contained in the first two editions has served as both inspiration and motivation in designing and implementing this revision. *Business* and its ancillaries represent the fulfillment of the stringent standards we set for ourselves during the revision process. In developing this edition, we had three main objectives: (1) to provide students with an appropriate body of business concepts; (2) to present these concepts in a way that would be interesting and yet help students to learn what they read, and (3) to provide instructors with valuable support materials that could be used to enrich individual learning environments.

We were fortunate to receive many thoughtful comments from both instructors and students who had firsthand experience using these support materials. Our personal experiences in teaching introduction to business supplemented these comments. Based upon this feedback and personal experience we laid out an ambitious and innovative revision for the third edition.

A REVISION TO REFLECT CURRENT BUSINESS PRACTICE

The text of the new third edition of *Business* is designed to strengthen the features of earlier editions, both with new teaching features and new coverage of current business principles and practice. Through a series of focus groups, a careful evaluation of course objectives was made for the new edition to insure that the text's coverage of business topics was comprehensive, precise, well-balanced, and up-to-date.

Building on an already complete system of learning aids, the third edition introduces several new learning resources and makes a renewed commitment to a concise presentation of key business concepts. Both in the text discussion and in the new *margin notes* placed beside these discussions, key definitions are clearly stated to help reinforce student understanding of terms and concepts. To strengthen comprehensive and balanced coverage, many new topics have been added or amplified to reflect the current practice of today's business. Users of earlier editions will find several areas of new coverage: in the management areas of motivation, leadership, organization, and human resources; in the financial areas of corporate finance, fundraising, and investment; and in every functional area, new coverage of services and especially of global influences on the competitiveness of U.S. business.

Above all, in its examples and topic coverage, this third edition provides students with a thoroughly current view of business practice by focusing on several new themes:

- *Entrepreneurship and innovation* as key ingredients in the U.S. business scene. This theme is reinforced throughout the text, appearing in the introductory "Business Practice Example" cases (starting with the entrepreneur Ted Turner) and the "Highlights in Business Practice" boxes in all twenty-three chapters.
- *The rise of a global economy and its impact on the competitive position of U.S. business enterprises.* In addition to a chapter on International business, nearly every chapter features a major topic, key example, or box, to highlight and remind students of the influence of global competition on current business practice.
- *The pursuit of excellence as a necessary ingredient in the competitive power of U.S. business.* More than half of the Business Practice Examples and video interviews (discussed below) focus on the components of excellence in overcoming challenges in each functional area of management, marketing, and finance. This theme lends itself particularly well to classroom exploration of real-world examples provided by the taped video interviews from CNN Broadcast News. These twenty taped interviews with key people in American business have been packaged *especially for integrated instructional use,* specifically illustrating and amplifying the major concepts and examples that appear in the text.

THE BUSINESS PRACTICE EXAMPLE CONCEPT

The Business Practice Example cases provide superior reinforcement of text material for the student. The reason for this is both the basic form and the execution of this feature, which begins as an introductory case ("Business Practice Example") and then continues three times within the chapter ("Business Practice Example Continues"). Each chapter begins with an example of a current business practice, which raises key issues and introduces students to the significance of the topics that will be covered in the chapter. "Business Practice Example Continues" sections are placed at three strategic points within each chapter, reinforcing the business concepts discussed within the chapter through the extension of the Business Practice Example. In this way, students can see concepts illustrated in the context of a well-known, real-world company. Our teaching and feedback from adopters have convinced us that these continuing examples help students better organize the many concepts they learn in Introduction to Business. They also make chapters more interesting to students, and this usually results in increased learning.

All of the examples of business practice are new to this edition and focus on real, undisguised companies. For instance, in Chapter 3, "Social Responsibility and Ethics," students learn that the Levi Strauss Company is one of the world's foremost corporate practitioners of social responsibility. As the chapter progresses, individual "Business Practice Continues" segments illustrate Levi Strauss's specific social responsibility practices. These practices are concrete evidence of material introduced in the text and serve to both broaden and strengthen student comprehension.

HIGHLIGHTS IN BUSINESS PRACTICE

Highlights in Business Practice boxes provide additional real-world examples of business practices. Two to three highlights appear in each chapter, on topics ranging from Merck Pharmaceutical's donation to third world nations of a drug to cure river blindness (Chapter 3, "Social Responsibility and Ethics"); to management consultant Tom Peters' newest thinking of organizational competitiveness (Chapter 7, "Motivation and Leadership in Organizations"); to a comparison of real purchasing power around the globe (Chapter 1, "Entrepreneurial Excellence in the American Economy").

ADDITIONAL LEARNING AIDS IN THE TEXT

Chapter Outlines. Each chapter is introduced with a chapter outline. This outline can help students keep chapter content in perspective while reading as well as help them both preview and review chapter information.

Learning Objectives. Each chapter is introduced through a set of learning objectives. These objectives direct the student to key study areas and provide a framework for self-learning.

Key Terms. Each chapter's key terms are boldfaced and defined upon introduction to help ensure that students note important concepts. A list of key terms, cross-referenced to the page number on which they first appear, is provided at the end of each chapter.

Margin Definitions. Key terms are fully defined in margin notes, helping students focus on important concepts and aiding significantly in student review of chapter material. This feature is new to this edition.

Summaries. Each chapter contains a concise summary of the important points discussed in the chapter.

Check Your Learning. Each chapter includes a self test. Students respond to several objective questions that directly relate to the learning objectives stated at the beginning of the chapter. By answering these questions, the students actively focus on and review key concepts. An answer key with referenced page numbers is provided at the end of the chapter.

Questions for Review and Discussion. Each chapter ends with several questions. Some simply focus on reviewing chapter material. Others are more loosely tied to chapter content and are intended to stimulate critical thinking for classroom discussion.

Concluding Case. Each chapter ends with a short concluding case that asks students to analyze contemporary business practices as they relate to the operation of a specific organization. Business practices at companies such as Digital Equipment Corporation, Safeway Stores, and AT&T are explored.

Glossary. Key business terms and their definitions appear at the end of the text. Because students may need more than a definition to gain a full understanding of the term, each term is followed by page numbers where related discussion can be found.

ADDITIONAL STUDENT LEARNING AIDS

Study Guide
Best of Business Readings
Stock Market Practice Set
Software Packages

INSTRUCTOR'S RESOURCE MATERIAL

Annotated Instructor's Edition
Test Bank
Computerized Test Bank
Transparencies
Detailed Chapter Outline
Ready-to-Duplicate Materials
CNN Videotapes
Allyn and Bacon Business Line

ACKNOWLEDGEMENTS

The compliments and congratulations that we have received over the years concerning *Business* have been very satisfying. In reality, many of these positive comments have resulted from and are based upon the work of a number of our colleagues. We appreciate this opportunity to "set the record straight" by giving credit to the many professionals who have made significant contributions to this text and its ancillaries.

Robert Hartl, Indiana State University, has played an important role in the development of this text. Professor Hartl served as a special reviewer and contributor for the finance chapters. His contribution in updating and generally improving the finance material has been invaluable.

We are pleased to see that the package of ancillaries that accompanies this new edition is indeed outstanding! It is important to keep in mind that the development of these ancillaries did not occur by chance. Several talented introduction to business instructors from across the country have spent many long, hard hours developing and producing these ancillaries.

In particular, Michael Kauffman, Director of Business Development, Santa Barbara Community College prepared the Instructor's Manual and annotations for this edition. We would again like to thank James B. Pettijohn, Southwest Missouri State University, for his work on the Lecture Enrichment Items in the Instructor's Manual. The Test Bank was prepared by Max E. Douglas, Indiana State University, and Philip Weatherford, Embry-Riddle Aeronautical University. Nathan Himmelstein of Essex Community College prepared the Detailed Chapter Outline, provided in a separate supplement. Finally, the Study Guide was written by business communications/training specialist Stewart Husted, and Janet A. Fye, Indiana Vocational Technical College.

We would like to thank each of these ancilliary authors for the valuable contribution he or she has made to this new edition of *Business.*

Reviewer comments were invaluable in the development of this project. Insights that reviewers furnished were of significant help in refining concepts and improving overall project quality. We owe special thanks to the following project reviewers for their commitment and professionalism:

John Bowdidge
Southwest Missouri State

Judith Bulin
Monroe Community College

Thomas Haynes
Illinois State

Robert Ketchum
Northeastern University

James Pettijohn
Southwest Missouri State University

Lee Rose
Central State University

Al Travers
Indiana Vocational Tech College

Larry Waldorf
Boise State University

Phillip Weatherford
Embry Riddle University

The publishing professionals at Allyn and Bacon were very helpful and empathetic in guiding our author team through all phases of the publishing process. Personal involvement and support for our project occurred at all levels. We were extremely pleased that John Isley, the president of Allyn and Bacon, has been personally involved in various stages of project planning and implementation. Enthusiasm, direction, and control for our project were a constant and valuable contribution made by Bill Barke, vice-president and editorial director. Editorial advice was ably provided by Jack Peters, Senior Editor. Our developmental editors/writers, Hannah Rubenstein and Allen Workmen, are simply the best in the business. Our production editor, Mary Beth Finch, could not have done a better job. We could always count on Carolyn Harris, Marketing Manager for Business, to get things done that "couldn't be done."

We would also like to extend our thanks to our colleagues for the support and encouragement they have shown us during the development of this new edition. In particular, we acknowledge the support Dean Martin Schatz of the Crummer Graduate School of Business at Rollins College, Dean Roy Savoian, School of Business at Lynchburg College, and Acting Dean Herbert Ross, School of Business, Indiana State University. Outstanding clerical assistance was provided by Susan Crabill and Debbie Shake.

Lastly, our families deserve a very special thanks. Without their enthusiasm, this project could never have been completed.

Samuel C. Certo
Stewart W. Husted
Max E. Douglas

TEXT AND ILLUSTRATION CREDITS

Chapter 1

Business Practice Example: Gwenda Blair, "Once More with Cheek," *Business Month,* July–August 1988, pp. 30–38; "Turnaround Ted," *Forbes,* January 9, 1989, p. 111; Ernest Leiser, "The Little Network That Could," *New York Times Magazine,* March 20, 1988; Subrata N. Chakravarty, "He's a Constitutional Monarch Now," *Forbes,* September 5, 1988; Maggie Mahar, "Captain Courageous and the Albatross," *Barron's,* July 11, 1988. **Table 1.1:** *U.S. Statistical Abstract,* 1988, p. 496. **Figure 1.2:** Data from *U.S. Statistical Abstract,* 1989. **Figure 1.4:** *Retail Prices in Moscow and Four Western Cities in October 1986,* Keith Bush, Radio Free Europe/Radio Liberty. © 1987 The NFIB Foundation. All rights reserved. Reprinted by permission. **Figure 1.5:** Reprinted from *U.S. News & World Report* issue of May 9, 1983. Copyright, 1983, U.S. News & World Report. **Highlight in Business Practice (p. 16):** Lee Smith, "The Wealth of Nations: The World Is Getting Richer," *Fortune,* September 14, 1987, p. 35; Gene Koretz, "Economic Trends: The Price of Being a City Dweller from Chicago to Calcutta," *Business Week,* November 7, 1988, p. 24; Shawn Tully, "The Good Life Costs Princely Sums Abroad," *Fortune,* April 13, 1987, p. 29; NFIB Foundation and Keith Bush (Radio Free Europe), "What's the Difference? Retail Prices in Moscow and Four Western Cities in October, 1986," poster published by the National Federation of Independent Business, P.O. Box 7515, San Mateo, CA, 1987. **Highlight in Business Practice (p. 21):** Emily T. Smith, "Are You Creative?" *Business Week,* September 30, 1985; Roger von Oech, "Creative Whacks," in *Whack on the Side of the Head* (New York: Warner Books, 1988). **Highlight in Business Practice (p. 23):** Gene Bylinski, "Genentech Has a Golden Goose," *Fortune,* May 9, 1988, pp. 52–62; Joan O. Hamilton, "Genentech Gets a Shot at the Big Time," *Business Week,* October 28, 1985, p. 108; Joan O. Hamilton, "Biotech's First Superstar," *Business Week,* April 14, 1986, pp. 68–72. **Concluding Case:** Sarah Bartlett, "The Crash," *Business Week,* April 18, 1988, p. 55; Christopher Farrell, "Where Was the Invisible Hand during the Crash?" *Business Week,* April 18, 1988, p. 65.

Chapter 2

Business Practice Example: Holman Jenkins, Jr., "Rising Interest in Exodus Insurance," *Insight,* March 21, 1988, pp. 34–37; June Kronholtz, "Few in Hong Kong Still Trust Promises of British and China," *Wall Street Journal,* April 13, 1987, p. 1; "The Future of Hong Kong," *Business Week,* March 5, 1984, pp. 50–64; James P. Sterba, "Although Hong Kong Reverts to China Soon, U.S. Influence Prevails," *Wall Street Journal,* October 6, 1985, p. 1; Emily MacFarquhar and Frank Ching, "China Lays Down the Law for Hong Kong," *U.S. News & World Report,* May 16, 1988, pp. 34–35. **Figure 2.4:** Basic data from U.S. Department of Labor. Data appeared in figure "Growing Work Force," *U.S. News & World Report,* August 29–September 5, 1988, p. 103. **Highlight in Business Practice (p. 42):** Stewart Toy, "Doctor Hammer is 90—and the Road Show Keeps Rolling On," *Business Week,* May 5, 1988, pp. 49–52; J. Cook, "A Lunch with Armand Hammer," *Forbes,* April 9, 1984, pp. 51–52; Bob Considine, *The Remarkable Life of Doctor Armand Hammer* (New York: Harper & Row, 1975). **Figure 2.5:** Reprinted from the *U.S. News & World Report* issue of May 1, 1978. Copyright U.S. News & World Report. **Figure 2.6:** Data from *1989 Britannica Book of the Year* (Chicago: Encyclopaedia Britannica, 1989), p. 725. **Figure 2.7:** U.S. Department of Commerce, Bureau of Economic Analysis, *Business Conditions Digest.* **Figure 2.8:** U.S. National Center for Education Statistics. **Figure 2.9:** Reprinted from *U.S. News & World Report* issue of September 17, 1984. Copyright, 1984, U.S. News & World Report. **Figure 2.10:** Adapted from Joseph A. Pechman, Brookings Institution, appearing in *Insight,* May 16, 1988, p. 45. **Highlight in Business Practice (pp. 54–55):** Sources: Dusko Doder, "Beijing Gives Life to an Ancient Curse," *U.S. News & World Report,* April 18, 1988; Dusko Doder, "China's Me-Generation," *U.S. News & World Report,* December 12, 1988; "Changing Communism," *World Press Review,* January 1988; "Free Market Communism," *U.S. News & World Report,* February 4, 1985; Christopher S. Wren, "Breaking Out," *New York Times Magazine,* August 14, 1988; Kathy Wilhelm, "Beijing Says Lucrative Sectors of Ailing Economy Will Be Taxed," *Boston Globe,* March 22, 1989. **Figure 2.11:** "Lure of Capitalism," adapted from *U.S. News & World Report* issue of February 4, 1985. Copyright, 1985, U.S. News & World Report. **Figure 2.12:** Adapted from Fig. 1.3 (p. 12) in *Getting into Business* by Wylie A. Walthall. Copyright © 1979 by Wylie A. Walthall. Reprinted by permission of Harper & Row, Publishers, Inc. **Highlight in Business Practice (p. 59):** Louis Kraar, "Japan's Gung-Ho U.S. Car Plants," *Fortune,* January 30, 1989, pp. 98–108; "Japan's Clout in the U.S.," *Business Week,* July 11, 1988, pp. 64–75; Jerry Buckley, "How Japan Is Winning Dixie," *U.S. News & World Report,* May 9, 1988, pp. 43–57. **Figure 2.13:** Basic data from U.S. Bureau of Economic Analysis, appearing in "Japan's Growing Stake in America," *U.S. News & World Report,* May 9, 1988, p. 59. **Concluding Case:** Data and quotation from Mitchell Zuckoff, "Minimum Wage Changes," *Terre Haute (Ind.) Tribune-Star,* January 17, 1988, p. F4.

Chapter 3

Business Practice Example: "Levi Strauss & Co. Makes Sense of Informational Reform," *Personnel Journal,* June 1988, p. 17; Rod Willis, "The Levi Strauss Credo: Fashion and Philanthropy," *Management Review,* July 1986, pp. 51–54; Levi Strauss & Co. fact sheets and informational literature. **Table 3.1:** From R. Joseph Mansen, Jr., "The Social Attitudes of Management," in Joseph W. McGuire, *Contemporary Management,* © 1974, p. 616. Reprinted by permission of Prentice-Hall, Inc., Englewood Cliffs, New Jersey. **Figure 3.1:** Adapted with permission from a presentation by Keith Davis, "The Reasons for and against Business's Acceptance of Social Responsibility," Conference on Social Issues, University of California, Los Angeles, August 4, 1971. **Figure 3.3:** From Sandra L. Holmes, "Executive Perceptions of Corporate Social Responsibility," *Business Horizons,* June 1976. Copyright, 1976, by the Foundation for the School of Business at Indiana University. Reprinted by permission. **Highlight in Business Practice (p. 78):** Stephen Budinsky, "An Act of Vision for the Third World," *U.S. News & World Report,* November 2, 1987; Ellen Schultz, "America's Most Admired Corporations," *Fortune,* January 18, 1988; "Miracle Worker: Cure for River Blindness," *Time,* November 2, 1987; John Walsh, "Merck Donates Drug for River Blindness," *Science,* October 30, 1987, p. 610. **Figure 3.4:** Adapted with permission from Bernard Butcher, "Anatomy of a Social Performance Report," *Business and Society Review,* Autumn 1973. Copyright © 1973, Warren, Gorham & Lamont, Inc., 210 South Street, Boston, MA 02111. All rights reserved. **Figure 3.5:** "The Pressure to Compromise Personal Ethics," p. 107. Reprinted from the January 31, 1977, issue of *Business Week* by special permission, © 1977 by McGraw-Hill, Inc. **Figure 3.6:** Reprinted by permission of the *Harvard Business Review.* An exhibit from "Product Liability: Manufacturers Beware!" by Lawrence A. Benningson and Arnold I. Benningson (May-June 1974). Copyright © 1974 by the President and Fellows of Harvard College; all rights reserved. **Figure 3.7:** Courtesy of Whirlpool Corporation. **Highlight in Business Practice (pp. 85–86):** Brian Houlden, "The Corporate Conscience," *Management Today,* August 1988, pp. 80–84; "Businesses Are Signing Up for Ethics 101," *Business Week,* February 15, 1988, pp. 56–57; Todd Bakrett, "Business Ethics for Sale," *Newsweek,* May 9, 1988, p. 56. **Table 3.2:** National Oceanic and Atmospheric Administration, appearing in "A Witch's Brew of Pollutants," *Newsweek,* August 1, 1988, p. 45. **Table 3.3:** From Meg Cox, "Snap, Crackle, Give," *Wall Street Journal,* May 13, 1988, p. 20R. Reprinted by permission of the *Wall Street Journal,* © Dow Jones & Company, Inc., 1988. All rights reserved. **Concluding Case:** *Competition Guidelines,* March 1984, pp. 3, 4. Courtesy of AT&T.

Chapter 4

Business Practice Example: Milton Moskowitz, *The Global Marketplace* (New York: Macmillan, 1987), pp. 248–251; and direct mail items sent to Hard Rock International shareholders: R. J. Barry Cox, "Hard Rock Cafe Interim Results Chairman's Statement," February 16, 1988, and "Recommended Proposal for the Acquisition by Pleasurama PLC . . . of Hard Rock International," August 13, 1988. **Figure 4.1:** U.S. Bureau of the Census, *Statistical Abstract of the United States,* 108th ed., 1988. **Highlight in Business Practice (p. 107):** Keith H. Hammonds, "For Celtic Fans, It's Wait Till Next Year," *Business Week,* June 27, 1988, p. 89; Hal Lancaster, "Timeout: Despite Success of Celtic Sale, Doubts Remain about Sports Offerings," *Wall Street Journal,* May 8, 1987, p. 17; "Administration Targets New Partnerships," *Insight,* July 27, 1987, p. 47; Laurie P. Cohn and Bryan Burrough, "Master Limited Partnerships Take Off, but Some May Fall Short of Promise," *Wall Street Journal,* December 12, 1985, p. 19. **Figure 4.2:** Reprinted by permission from "Fortune 500," *Fortune,* April 24, 1989, p. 354. © 1989 Time Inc. All rights reserved. **Highlight in Business Practice (pp. 116–117):** Vivian Brownstein, "Where All the Money Comes From," *Fortune,* January 2, 1989, pp. 75–80; Lori Ioannou, "Foreigners Rush to Buy into the U.S.," *Euromoney,* May 1988, pp. 41–42; Stephen Kindel, "The American Way," *Financial World,* October 4, 1988, pp. 28–30; Richard I. Kirkland, "Merger Mania Is Sweeping Europe," *Fortune,* December 19, 1988, pp. 157–167; Lester C. Thurow, "Speaking Out," *Business Month,* September 1988, p. 98. **Unnumbered table (p. 117):** Basic data reprinted by permission from Salomon Brothers, Inc., appearing in Jack Eagan, "Let's Make a Deal Goes Global," *U.S. News & World Report,* February 22, 1988, p. 67.

Concluding Case: Judith H. Dobrznski, "Whose Company Is It, Anyway?" *Business Week,* April 25, 1988, pp. 60–61; Stratford P. Sherman, "Pushing Corporate Boards to Be Better," *Fortune,* July 18, 1988, pp. 58–67.

Chapter 5

Business Practice Example: Gail Buchalter, "Happier Cookie," *Forbes,* March 10, 1986, p. 178; "Famous Amos among Ten Rags-to-Riches Inductees," *Jet,* March 30, 1987, p. 6; Andrea Adelson, "New Famous Amos Owner Wants Bigger Market Share," *New York Times,* May 2, 1988, p. D3; CNN Cable News Network, "Pinnacle" interview, September 24, 1988. **Figure 5.1:** Small Business Administration, appearing in *USA Today,* May 9, 1988, p. E1. **Figure 5.2:** Reprinted by permission from NFIB Foundation, *Small Business Primer,* p. 6. Estimates developed from data in *Enterprise Statistics, County Business Patterns,* and *The State of Small Business,* 1984. **Figure 5.3:** Data reprinted from the October, 1985, issue of *Venture,* for Entrepreneurial Business Owners & Investors, by special permission. © 1985 Venture Magazine, Inc., 521 Fifth Avenue, New York, NY 10175. **Figure 5.5:** Adapted from U.S. Small Business Administration, "Checklist for Going into Business," *Small Marketers' Aids.* **Table 5.1:** Reprinted by permission of *Black Enterprise Magazine,* appearing in Constance Mitchell, "Some Blacks Plunge into Business Mainstream in Creating a Business," *Wall Street Journal,* May 11, 1988, p. 1. **Figure 5.6:** Data from *Statistical Abstract of the United States,* 1986. Figure reprinted by permission from NFIB Foundation, *Small Business Primer,* p. 63. **Table 5.2:** Reprinted by permission of Cicco and Associates, appearing in Steven Galante, "Are Money and Status Losing Their Allure?" *Wall Street Journal,* January 12, 1988, p. 31. **Highlight in Business Practice (p. 142):** Pete Engardio, "The Peace Corps' New Frontier," *Business Week,* August 22, 1988, pp. 62–63; Peace Corps literature. **Highlight in Business Practice (p. 140):** Yohannan T. Abraham and Kathawala Yunus, "The Big Brother—Incubator Synergy in Organizing and Operating a Small Business," in *Small Business Entrepreneurship Proceedings,* ed. Ralph B. Weller (Chicago: Midwest Business Administration Program, 1986), pp. 45–52; and John R. Schermerhorn, Jr., and Harold P. Welsch, "Interorganizational Strategies for the Performance Effectiveness of Small Business Incubators," unpublished paper presented to the Midwest Business Administration Association, Chicago, March 1988. **Figure 5.7:** (a) Reprinted by permission of Dun & Bradstreet Corp., appearing in "Out of Business: Failures in 1986," *Wall Street Journal,* April 2, 1987, p. 24. (b) Reprinted by permission of Comprehensive Accounting Corp., from survey of 203 firms, appearing in "USA Snapshots: Why Businesses Fail," in "Careers," (annual special section), *USA Today,* May 1987, p. 10. **Highlight in Business Practice (p. 146):** Rita Stollman, "The New Entrepreneurial Woman," *Business Week Careers, 1987,* p. 91. Reprinted by special permission, © 1987 McGraw-Hill, Inc. **Table 5.3:** Reprinted by permission from *Black Enterprise* magazine, September 1988, appearing in Buck Brown, "Minority Franchisees Allege Redlining by the Big Chains," *Wall Street Journal,* October 26, 1988, p. B1. **Figure 5.8:** Data from "Fastest Growing Franchises," *Venture,* March 1988, pp. 44–47. **Figure 5.9:** Data from "Franchise 100," *Venture,* November 1988. **Concluding Case:** Steven Golob, "Export Expertise," *Nation's Business,* January 1988, pp. 26–30; James Abnor, "Heading into the 21st Century," *Barron's,* May 9, 1988, pp. 39, 47.

Chapter 6

Business Practice Example: Carol Davenport, "America's Most Admired Corporations," *Fortune,* January 30, 1989, pp. 68–71; "Wall Street Transcript Names Award Winners—Drug Industry," *Wall Street Transcript,* February 1, 1988, pp. 188–189; Stephen W. Quickel, "Merck & Company—Sheer Energy," *Business Month,* December 1988, p. 36; "Managers Rate Merck Best in U.S.," *Pensions and Investment Age,* May 2, 1988; Ellen Schultz, "America's Most Admired Corporations," *Fortune,* January 18, 1988, pp. 32–37. **Table 6.1:** "Who Made the Most and Why," p. 51. Reprinted from the May 2, 1988, issue of *Business Week* by special permission, © 1988 by McGraw-Hill, Inc. **Figure 6.1:** Frank Allen, "Chief Executives Typically Work 60-Hour Weeks, Put Careers First," *Wall Street Journal,* August 19, 1980, p. 31. Reprinted by permission of the *Wall Street Journal,* © Dow Jones & Company, Inc., 1980. All rights reserved. **Table 6.2:** (a) and (b) based on E. Meadows, "How Three Companies Increased Their Productivity," *Fortune,* March 10, 1980, pp. 92–101. (c) based on William B. Johnson, "The Transformation of a Railroad," *Long-Range Planning,* December 1976, pp. 18–23. **Figure 6.2:** From Thomas L. Martin, *Malice in Blunderland* (New York: McGraw-Hill, 1973). Format reprinted by permission of General Tire & Rubber Company, Akron, Ohio. **Highlight in Business Practice (p. 176):** Buck Rodgers, "Creating Customer Commitment," American Management Association video, 1988. Reprinted by permission of American Management Associations. **Highlight in Business Practice (p. 180):** Ronaleen R. Roha, "Seven Mistakes That Can Kill Your Business, and How to Avoid Them," *Changing Times,* August 1988, pp. 47–50; Carol Hymowitz, "Five Main Reasons Why Businesses Fail," *Wall Street Journal,* May 21, 1988, p. 21; Kenneth Labich, "The Seven Keys to Business Leadership," *Fortune,* October 24, 1988, pp. 58–66. **Figure 6.8:** Joseph L. Massie, John Douglas, *Managing: A Contemporary Introduction,* 3d ed., © 1981, p. 251. Reprinted by permission of Prentice-Hall, Inc., Englewood Cliffs, N.J. **Figure 6.9:** Paul Hersey, Kenneth H. Blanchard, *Management of Organizational Behavior: Utilizing Human Resources,* 4th ed., © 1982, p. 6. Adapted by permission of Prentice-Hall, Inc., Englewood Cliffs, N.J. **Figure 6.10:** Paul Hersey, Kenneth H. Blanchard, *Management of Organizational Behavior: Utilizing Human Resources,* 4th ed., © 1982, p. 6. Adapted by permission of Prentice-Hall, Inc., Englewood Cliffs, N.J. **Figure 6.11:** Paul Hersey, Kenneth H. Blanchard, *Management of Organizational Behavior: Utilizing Human Resources,* 4th ed., © 1982, p. 6. Adapted by permission of Prentice-Hall, Inc., Englewood Cliffs, N.J. **Concluding Case:** Data from studies by National Federation of Independent Businesses and *Business Week.*

Chapter 7

Business Practice Example: Interview with J. Patrick Barrett, Avis CEO, "Pinnacle," CNN News Broadcast, March 27, 1987; Jeremy Main, "Companies That Float from Owner to Owner," *Fortune,* April 28, 1986, p. 36; "Is Avis Moving into the Passing Lane?" *Business Week,* May 9, 1988, pp. 100–101. **Figure 7.2:** Data for diagram based on hierarchy of needs in "A Theory of Human Motivation" from *Motivation and Personality,* second edition, by Abraham H. Maslow. Copyright © 1970 by Abraham H. Maslow. Reprinted by permission of Harper & Row, Publishers, Inc. **Figure 7.3:** From Douglas McGregor, *The Human Side of Enterprise.* © 1960 McGraw-Hill Book Company. Reprinted by permission of McGraw-Hill, Inc. **Figure 7.4:** William Ouchi, *Theory Z,* © 1981, Addison-Wesley, Reading, Massachusetts. Adapted material. Reprinted with permission. **Figure 7.6:** Reprinted by permission of the *Harvard Business Review.* An exhibit from "How to Choose a Leadership Pattern" by Robert Tannenbaum and Warren H. Schmidt, (May/June 1973). Copyright © 1973 by the President and Fellows of Harvard College; all rights reserved. **Highlight in Business Practice (pp. 206–207):** Geoffrey Holmes, "Accounts Who Thrive on Chaos," *Accountancy,* May 1988; Joseph M. Queenan, "In Search of Non-Excellence: Tom Peters, You're in Big Trouble," *Barron's,* October 5, 1987; James Traub, "No More Trumpets," *Business Month,* May 1988. **Figure 7.7:** Reprinted by permission of the artist, Seymour Chwast, from "The 21st Century Executive," *U.S. News & World Report,* March 7, 1988, p. 49. **Table 7.1:** Reprinted by permission of the *Harvard Business Review.* An exhibit from "One More Time: How Do You Motivate Employees?" by Frederick Herzberg (September/October 1987). Copyright © 1987 by the President and Fellows of Harvard College; all rights reserved. **Table 7.2:** Reprinted by permission of the *Harvard Business Review.* An exhibit from "One More Time: How Do You Motivate Employees?" by Frederick Herzberg (September/October 1987), p. 114. Copyright © 1987 by the President and Fellows of Harvard College; all rights reserved. **Highlight in Business Practice:** Adapted by permission from Dale Keiger, "John G. Smale: Chairman & CEO of the Procter & Gamble Company," *Sky,* November 1987, pp. 52–59. **Figure 7.9:** Reprinted by permission of the *Harvard Business Review.* An exhibit from "Breakthrough in Organization Development" by Robert R. Blake, Jane S. Mouton, Louis Barnes, and Larry Greiner (November/December 1964). Copyright © 1964 by the President and Fellows of Harvard College; all rights reserved. **Concluding Case:** Michael Meyer, Carl Robinson, and Jeanne Gordon, "Capitalism's Last Frontier," *Newsweek,* May 16, 1988, pp. 52, 54. Copyright 1988 by Newsweek, Inc. All rights reserved. Reprinted by permission.

Chapter 8

Business Practice Example: Brian O'Reilly, "Apple Finally Invades the Office," *Fortune,* November 9, 1987, pp. 52–64; John Scully with John A. Byrne, *Odyssey* (New York: Harper & Row, 1987); Brian O'Reilly, "Growing Apple Anew for the Business Market," *Fortune,* January 4, 1988, p. 37. **Highlight in Business Practice (p. 229):** Excerpted from Robert Johnson, "McDonald's Combines a Dead Man's Advice with a Lively Strategy," *Wall Street Journal,* December 18, 1987, p. 1. Reprinted by permission of the

Wall Street Journal, © Dow Jones & Company, Inc., 1987. All rights reserved. **Figure 8.9:** All but matrix organization authority reprinted with permission of Macmillan Publishing Company from *The New Management* by Robert M. Fulmer. Copyright © 1974 by Robert M. Fulmer. **Highlight in Business Practice (p. 240):** Ronald Alsop, "Consumer-Product Giants Relying on Intrapreneurs in New Ventures," *Wall Street Journal,* April 22, 1988, p. 19. Reprinted by permission of the *Wall Street Journal,* © Dow Jones & Company, Inc., 1988. All rights reserved. **Concluding Case:** Leslie Helm, John W. Verity, Geoff Lewis, Thane Peterson, and Johnathan B. Levine, "What's Next for Digital?" pp. 88–89. Reprinted from the May 16, 1988, issue of *Business Week* by special permission, © 1988 by McGraw-Hill, Inc.

Chapter 9

Business Practice Example: Mack Chrysler, "Its 'Mondai Nai' When East Meets West," *Ward's Auto World,* August 1988, pp. 54–55; "Toyota Goes It Alone," *Automotive News OEM Edition,* September 5, 1988; Richard Koenig, "Toyota Takes Pains, and Time, Filling Jobs at Its Kentucky Plant," *Wall Street Journal,* December 1, 1987, pp. 1, 31. **Highlight in Business Practice (p. 260):** Excerpted by permission from Susan G. Strotner, "Some Workers Behind in Reading, Math," *Central Florida Business,* July 11–17, 1988, p. 5. **Table 9.3:** Adapted from Leslie W. Rue and Lloyd L. Byars, *Management: Theory and Application,* © 1977 Richard D. Irwin, Inc., Homewood, IL. Reprinted by permission. **Text section "Employee Compensation":** Based on David J. Cherrington, *Personnel Management: The Management of Human Resources,* 2d ed. (Boston, Allyn & Bacon, 1987), pp. 338–459. **Figure 9.6:** U.S. Department of Commerce. **Highlight in Business Practice (p. 268):** Reprinted by permission from Dinah Wisenberg, "Stride Rite Chief: Day Care Working," *Boston Globe,* February 23, 1989, p. 31. **Figure 9.7:** Gene E. Burton, Dev S. Pathak, and David B. Burton, "Equal Employment Opportunity: Law and Labyrinth," *Management World,* September 1976; reprinted with permission from the Administrative Management Society, Willow Grove, PA 19090. **Concluding Case:** Excerpted from Harry Hurt III, "The Aerospace Labor Crunch," *Newsweek,* July 18, 1988, p. 45. Copyright 1988 by Newsweek, Inc. All rights reserved. Reprinted by permission.

Chapter 10

Business Practice Example: Michael Powell, "Babes in Toil-Land," *New York Newsday,* January 8, 1989; Peter Kwong and JoAnn Lum, "How the Other Half Lives," *Nation,* June 18, 1988, pp. 858–860; James Leung, "Sweatshops Thriving in Bay Area," *San Francisco Chronicle,* December 5, 1988; Cynthia B. Costello, *Home Based Employment: Implications for Working Women* (Washington, D.C.: Women's Research and Education Institute, 1987); ILGWU informational literature. **Figure 10.1:** Reprinted by permission of American Federation of Labor and Congress of Industrial Organizations. **Figure 10.2:** Reprinted by permission of American Federation of Labor and Congress of Industrial Organizations. **Table 10.1:** Report of the AFL-CIO Executive Council, 1988. **Highlight in Business Practice (pp. 286–287):** Laxmi Nakarmi, "Lorean Labor's New Voice Is Saying: 'More,'" pp. 45–46. Reprinted from the May 2, 1988, issue of *Business Week* by special permission, © 1988 by McGraw-Hill, Inc. **Figure 10.3:** "State Labor Legislation Enacted in 1989," *Monthly Labor Review,* U.S. Department of Labor, 1989. **Figure 10.4:** From Wendell French, *The Personnel Management Process,* 5th ed., © 1982 Houghton Mifflin Company, Boston. Used by permission of Houghton Mifflin Company. **Figure 10.6:** Reprinted with permission of Macmillan Publishing Company from *Personnel,* 2d ed., by Dale S. Beach. Copyright © 1970 by Dale S. Beach. **Figure 10.7:** From *Personnel Management: The Utilization of Human Resources* by H. J. Chruden and A. W. Sherman, Jr. Copyright © 1980 South-Western Publishing Company. Reprinted by permission. **Figure 10.8:** Reprinted with permission of Macmillan Publishing Company from *Personal and Industrial Relations,* 3d ed., by John B. Miner and Mary Green Miner. Copyright © 1977 by Macmillan Publishing Company. **Figure 10.9:** U.S. Department of Labor, Bulletin number 2120 (August 1982). **Figure 10.10:** U.S. Department of Labor, Bureau of Labor Statistics, 1988–1989 data, in U.S. Department of Labor, *Occupational Outlook Handbook,* 1988–1989 ed., p. 10. **Figure 10.11:** U.S. Department of Labor, Bureau of Labor Statistics, in U.S. Department of Labor, *Occupational Outlook Handbook,* 1988–1989 ed., p. 10. **Concluding Case:** Adapted from Albert R. Karr, "Labor Unions' Chance for Gains in 1988 Hits a Wall of Resistance," *Wall Street Journal,* June 29, 1988, pp. 1, 17. Reprinted by permission of the *Wall Street Journal,* © Dow Jones & Company, Inc., 1988. All rights reserved.

Chapter 11

Business Practice Example: *Wall Street Transcript,* January 4, 1988, p. 87.933; *Dun's Business Month,* April 30, 1984, pp. 67–69; Carol J. Loomis, *Fortune,* April 30, 1984, pp. 78–82; *Appliance Manufacturer,* November 1987, pp. 27–55; *Appliance,* March 1984, pp. M15–M39; Andrea Chancellor, "Maytag Running at Full Cycle," *Journal of Commerce,* p. 13A. **Figure 11.2:** From a brochure handed out during a tour of Kellogg's (Battle Creek, Michigan). **Highlight in Business Practice (p. 313):** Dyan Machan, "Great Hash Browns, but Watch Those Biscuits," *Forbes,* September 19, 1988, pp. 192–196; Fanny Moser, "The McDonald's Mystique," *Fortune,* July 4, 1988, pp. 112–116; Peter Nulty, "How McDonald's Keeps the Profits Sizzling," *Fortune,* February 1, 1988, pp. 100, 102; "TWST Names Award Winners Restaurant Industry," *Wall Street Transcript.* **Figure 11.3:** Information based on U.S. Department of Labor and Conference Board data, appearing in "Workers around the World," *U.S. News & World Report,* December 28–January 4, 1988, p. 114. **Figure 11.4:** Reprinted by permission from Joel Dreyfuss, "Networking: Japan's Latest Computer Craze," *Fortune,* July 7, 1986, p. 95. © 1986 Time Inc. All rights reserved. **Figure 11.5:** Adapted with permission from E. S. Groo, "Choosing Foreign Locations: One Company's Experience," *Columbia Journal of World Business,* September-October 1971, p. 77. **Table 11.1:** Adapted by permission from E. S. Groo, "Choosing Foreign Locations: One Company's Experience," *Columbia Journal of World Business,* September-October 1971, p. 77. **Figure 11.7:** William C. House, "Environmental Analysis: Key to More Effective Dynamic Planning," reprinted with permission of the Planning Executives Institute from the January-February 1977 issue of *Managerial Planning,* p. 27. **Figure 11.8:** Reprinted by permission from Richard B. Chase and Nicholas J. Aquilano, *Production and Operations Management: A Life Cycle Approach,* 4th ed., p. 5., © 1985 Richard D. Irwin, Inc., Homewood, Illinois. **Table 11.2:** Reprinted by permission from James B. Dilworth, *Production and Management: Manufacturing and Nonmanufacturing,* pp. 173–174. Copyright © 1979 by Random House, Inc. **Figure 11.10:** Reprinted by permission of the Sperry Corporation. **Highlight in Business Practice (p. 331):** Adapted by permission from Jay Heizer and Barry Render, *Production and Operations Management* (Boston: Allyn & Bacon, 1988), pp. 242a–d. **Figure 11.12:** Adapted by permission from Naoto Sasaki and David Hutchins, *The Japanese Approach to Product Quality: Its Applicability to the West* (Oxford, England: Pergamon Press, 1984), p. 68. **Concluding Case:** Michael Walcholz, "How Hospitals Use Data," *Wall Street Journal,* December 17, 1987, p. 33. Reprinted by permission of the *Wall Street Journal,* © Dow Jones & Company, Inc., 1987. All rights reserved.

Chapter 12

Business Practice Example: "Timberland Introducing New Line," *Advertising Age,* August 22, 1988, p. 51; Steven Flax, "Boot Camp," *Inc.,* September 1987, pp. 99–104; Fox Butterfield, "Shoes That Sell—Made in America," *New York Times,* August 18, 1985; Rebecca Fannin, "How to Upgrade a Working Boot," *Marketing and Media Decisions,* November 1983; Stanley W. Angrist, "Betting the Company," *Forbes,* April 25, 1983, pp. 109, 110; Timberland annual reports, 1987, 1988. **Highlight in Business Practice (p. 348):** Adapted by permission from Karl Albrecht and Ron Zemke, *Service America* (Homewood, Ill.: Richard D. Irwin, 1985), pp. 20–26. **Figure 12.3:** Data from Joel Kotkin, "Selling to the New American," *Inc.,* July 1987, pp. 44–52. **Table 12.1:** Philip Kotler, *Marketing Management: Analysis, Planning, and Control,* 6th ed., © 1988, p. 287. Reprinted by permission of Prentice-Hall, Inc., Englewood Cliffs, NJ. **Figure 12.4:** From Eugene Carlson, "Population Density Remains Primary Factor for Retailers," *Wall Street Journal,* November 8, 1984, p. 33. Reprinted by permission of the *Wall Street Journal,* © Dow Jones & Company, Inc., 1984. All rights reserved. **Figure 12.5:** Adapted by permission from "After-Tax Income on the Rise," *USA Today,* June 19, 1987, p. 3A; data from U.S. Census Bureau. **Figure 12.6:** Data from SAMI, reprinted by permission from "No. 1 Markets for Selected Products," *Fortune,* September 16, 1985, p. 65. © 1985 Time Inc. All rights reserved. **Figure 12.7:** "Inside the Consumer's Mind," *Newsweek,* December 30, 1985, p. 7. Copyright 1985 by Newsweek, Inc. All rights reserved. Reprinted by permission. Data from SRI International and Simmons Market Research Bureau, 1985. Illustration by Scott MacNeill-Newsweek. **Concluding Case:** Brian Dumaine, "Who's Gypping Whom in TV Ads," *Fortune,* July 6, 1987, pp. 78–79; Bill Abrams, "TV 'Sweeps' May Not Say Much, but for Now That's All There Is," *Wall Street Journal,* February 28, 1985, p. 31; Sally Bedell Smith, "Changin' Times," *Terre Haute Tribune-Star,* January 4, 1985, p. D2; Harry F. Waters, "A Ratings Revolution," *Newsweek,* September 14, 1987, p. 76.

Chapter 13

Business Practice Example: Eric Gelman, "Ford's Idea Machine," *Newsweek,* November 24, 1986, pp. 64–66; Bruce Nussbaum, "Smart Design," *Business Week,* April 11, 1988, pp. 102–118; Stephanie McDonald, "Looking Good: More Firms Place Higher Priority on Product Design," *Wall Street Journal,* January 22, 1987, p. 31; Stephanie McDonald, "As Awareness of Industrial Design Grows, Firms Start to Use It as a Marketing Tool," *Wall Street Journal,* February 23, 1987, p. 21; John Bussey, "Did U.S. Car Makers Err by Raising Prices When the Yen Rose?" *Wall Street Journal,* April 18, 1988, p. 1; Russell Mitchell, "How Ford Hit the Bull's Eye with Taurus," *Business Week,* June 30, 1986, pp. 66–70; Ann Fisher, "Ford Is Back on Track," *Fortune,* December 23, 1985, pp. 18–21. **Table 13.1:** Classifications by the U.S. Department of Commerce, appearing in Samuel C. Certo, *Marketing: Practices and Principles* (New York: McGraw-Hill, 1986), p. 181. **Figure 13.1:** Reprinted by permission of the *Harvard Business Review.* An exhibit from "Strategy Is Different in Service Businesses," by Dan R. E. Thomas (July/August 1978). Copyright © 1978 by the President and Fellows of Harvard College; all rights reserved. **Table 13.2:** W. Earl Sasser, R. Paul Olsen, and D. Daryl Wyckoff, *Management of Service Operations: Text, Cases and Readings,* © 1978. Reprinted by permission of Allyn & Bacon, Inc. **Figure 13.4:** Data reprinted by permission of the Conference Board, appearing in "New Products: How Companies Get Ideas," *Terre Haute Tribune-Star,* February 8, 1987, p. F3. **Highlight in Business Practice (p. 387):** Susan Chandler, "A Taste for Success Sends NutraSweet against Sugar," *Chicago Sun-Times,* March 8, 1987, p. 9; Wendy L. Wall, "Marketing NutraSweet in Leaner Times," *Wall Street Journal,* May 7, 1987, p. 32; NutraSweet Company promotional materials. **Highlight in Business Practice (p. 393):** Christopher Power and Todd Vogel," Air Fares Have a Ticket to Rise," *Business Week,* December 12, 1988, pp. 30–31; Christopher Powell et al., "The Frenzied Skies: Tén Years after Deregulation, the Airlines Are Still in the Throes of Change," *Business Week,* December 19, 1988, pp. 70–80; Nancy R. Gibbs, "Come Fly the Costly Skies: The Airlines Jack Up Prices Just in Time for the Holidays," *Time,* November 28, 1988, p. 87; Clemens P. Work and Robert J. Morse, "Better Buys, Crowded Skies," *U.S. News & World Report,* October 31, 1988, pp. 50–52. **Figure 13.7:** Adapted with permission of *Inc.* magazine from "The Economics of Bottled Water," *Inc.,* March 1986, p. 70. Copyright © 1986 by Goldhirsh Group, Inc., 38 Commercial Wharf, Boston, MA 02110. **Concluding Case:** Steven M. Sack, "Price Advice: Keep It Fair," *Sales & Marketing Management,* May 1986, pp. 53–55; Robert E. Weigand, "Is It Time to Retire Robinson-Patman?" *Wall Street Journal,* June 20, 1986, p. 20; Stephan Wermiel and Barbara Rosewicz, "High Court Eases a Use of Antitrust Law, Freeing Firms in Dealing with Retailers," *Wall Street Journal,* May 3, 1988, p. 4.

Chapter 14

Business Practice Example: Alice LaPlante and Roberta Furger, "Compaq Vying to Become the IBM of the '90s," *InfoWorld,* January 23, 1989, pp. 1, 5; Stuart Gannes, "America's Fastest-Growing Companies," *Fortune,* May 23, 1988, pp. 28, 30; Erik Larson, "The Best-Laid Plans," *Inc.,* February 1987, pp. 60–61; Brian O'Reilly, "Compaq's Grip on IBM's Slippery Tail," *Fortune,* February 18, 1985, pp. 74–76; CNN Business News "Inside Business" interview with Rod Canion, aired October 4, 1987. **Figure 14.1:** Reprinted by permission from Glos, Steade, and Lowry, *Business,* p. 143. Copyright © 1980 by South-Western Publishing Company. **Table 14.1:** "Shopping by Catalog," *Wall Street Journal,* January 7, 1988, p. 19. Reprinted by permission of the *Wall Street Journal,* © Dow Jones & Company, Inc., 1988. All rights reserved. Data from Krupp/Taylor USA; Yankelovich, Skelly & White/Clancy, Shulman Inc. **Highlight in Business Practice (p. 423):** Lawrence H. Kaufman, "How Business Worldwide Is Profiting from Air Cargo" an ad appearing in *Business Week,* 1986 [no specific date given] (New Hope, Penn.: Loving Associates, 1986); "Cadillac's Bill for Air Mailing Allantes May Be $20 Million," *Auto Week,* December 30, 1985, p. 4. **Concluding Case:** Amy Dunkin, William C. Symonds, Todd Mason, and Kathleen Deveny, "Why Some Benetton Shopkeepers Are Losing Their Shirts," *Business Week,* March 14, 1988, pp. 78–79; Teri Agins, "Handshake Deals: Benetton Is Accused of Dubious Tactics by Some Store Owners," *Wall Street Journal,* October 24, 1988, pp. 1, A4; Jennet Conant, Janet Huck, and Karen Brailsford, "The Age of McFashion," *Newsweek,* September 28, 1987, pp. 66–68.

Chapter 15

Business Practice Example: Scott Hume, "Pepsi Rises to Top Ad-Recall Spot," *Advertising Age,* January 30, 1989; Patricia Winters, "Pepsi Gets the Joke," *Advertising Age,* February 6, 1989; Gary A. Hemphill, "A Firm Grip," *Beverage Industry,* March 1988; Larry Jabbonsky, "Pepsi: Usurps Authority," *Beverage World,* August 1988; Wayne Walley, "Conner Takes Bow in Pepsi's Next Ad 'Event,'" *Advertising Age,* September 5, 1988; Gary A. Hemphill, "Tidmore's March across the South," *Beverage Industry,* October 1988. **Figure 15.1:** Data reprinted by permission from National Association of Broadcasters 1987 survey of 187 stations, appearing in "And Now, This Message," *USA Today,* June 30, 1987, p. D1. **Figure 15.2:** Expenditure data reprinted with permission from "U.S. Advertising Volume," in Robert J. Coen, "Ad Spending Outlook Brightens," *Advertising Age,* May 15, 1989, p. 24. Copyright 1989 Crain Communications, Inc. All rights reserved. Table prepared for *Advertising Age* by Robert J. Coen, McCann-Erickson. **Figure 15.3:** Courtesy of Television Bureau of Advertising. **Figure 15.4:** Courtesy IBM Corp. **Table 15.1:** Reprinted with permission from *Advertising Age,* September 28, 1988. Copyright 1988 Crain Communications, Inc. All rights reserved. **Figure 15.5:** Data reprinted courtesy of Ogilvy & Mather, appearing in "Advertising Attitudes," *Terre Haute Tribune-Star,* July 15, 1985, p. D5. **Highlight in Business Practice (p. 443):** "Bad Translations Turn Ads from Mild to Spicy," *Inc.,* November 1986, p. 18; "Now Are They the Ones That Wear Kimonas?" *Wall Street Journal,* March 13, 1988, p. 27; John Wall, "Minorities Slice the Advertising Pie," *Insight,* March 9, 1987, pp. 46–47. **Figure 15.6:** Reprinted from "Clip File," *U.S. News & World Report,* December 5, 1988, p. 93. Copyright 1988 U.S. News & World Report, Inc. Data from Manufacturers Coupon Control Center, Newspaper Advertising Bureau, Inc. **Concluding Case:** Pete Engardo, "Fast Times on Avenida Madison," *Business Week,* June 6, 1988, pp. 62–67; John Wall, "Minorities Slice the Advertising Pie," *Insight,* March 9, 1987, pp. 46–47.

Chapter 16

Business Practice Example: CNN Business News, "Inside Business," interview with Robert Steele, CEO of Dollar Dry Dock Bank, October 2, 1988; Lynn Brenner, "Finding a Niche in New York City: Dollar Dry Dock Airs TV Spots in Korean, Russian, Spanish," *Consumer Financial Services,* December 15, 1988, p. 1; Judith Graham, "Bank Enlists Help for Vet Card," *Advertising Age,* January 11, 1988, p. 2. **Figure 16.2:** Data from U.S. Treasury Department, Financial Management Service; appearing in *World Almanac and Book of Facts, 1988* (New York: Newspaper Enterprise Association, 1987), p. 105. **Figure 16.3:** Federal Reserve System. **Table 16.1:** Federal Reserve System. **Figure 16.4:** Data reprinted by permission from IBCA Banking Analysis Ltd., as reported in "International Bank Scoreboard," *Business Week,* June 27, 1988, p. 77. **Highlight in Business Practice (pp. 479–480):** Gary Hector, "How to Rescue the S&L Industry," *Fortune,* December 19, 1988, pp. 143–149; Howard Rudnitsky, Allan Sloan, and John R. Hayes, "Is Anybody Really Fooled?" *Forbes,* July 11, 1988, pp. 74–76; Howard Rudnitsky and Allan Sloan, "Blackballing Bass," *Forbes,* October 3, 1988, pp. 38–39; William E. Sheeline, "The Big Names in S&L Buyouts," *Fortune,* September 26, 1988, p. 10; Gary A. Shilling, "Let the Government Make You Rich," *Fortune,* October 10, 1988, pp. 167–168. **Unnumbered figure (p. 479):** Data from Federal Deposit Insurance Corporation, reported in *Wall Street Journal,* November 11, 1987, p. 10. **Figure 16.6:** Federal Reserve System. **Table 16.4:** Federal Reserve System. **Concluding Case:** "Bank Fees Rise—So Do Gripes by Consumers," *U.S. News & World Report,* April 1, 1985, pp. 74–75; Walt Bogdanich, "Banks' New Services Prompt Higher Fees and a Need for Consumers to Shop Around," *Wall Street Journal,* August 6, 1984, p. 19.

Chapter 17

Business Practice Example: Adapted from Daniel Akst and Lee Berton, "Accountants Who Specialize in Detecting Fraud Find Themselves in Great Demand," *Wall Street Journal,* February 26, 1988, p. 17. Reprinted by permission of the *Wall Street Journal,* © Dow Jones & Company, Inc., 1988. All rights reserved. **Table 17.2:** Reprinted by permission from C. Dwayne Dowell and Patrick B. Dorr, "CPA Licensing Requirements to Begin the 80's," *Collegiate News and Views,* Winter 1980–1981, pp. 1, 3–6; and from "CMA Certificate in Management Accounting," Institute of Management Accounting, Ann Arbor, Michigan, 1982–1983. **Highlight in Business Practice (p. 504):** Tom Cassidy, transcript of "Pinnacle," Cable News Network, April 18, 1987; Price Waterhouse, *Expect More from Us,* publication 714700 (New York: Price Waterhouse, n.d.), pp. 1–48. **Concluding Case:** John A. Byrne, "Curious about the Crash," *Business Week,* April 11, 1988, p. 66; Lee Burton, "Firms' Annual Reports Are Short on Candor, and May Get Shorter," *Wall Street Journal,* September 9, 1987, p. 1.

Chapter 18

Business Practice Example: Carol Davenport, "America's Most Admired Corporations," *Fortune,* January 30, 1989, p. 75; "Inside Business" interview with Walter Williams, CNN Business News, May 8, 1988; Ellen Shultz, "America's Most Admired Corporations," *Fortune,* January 18, 1988, p. 39; Peter Scolieri, "Bethlehem Steel to Spend $45M," *American Metal Market,* September 23, 1988, p. 7; Tom Balcerek, "Bethlehem Steel Plans to Sell Wire Rope Division," *American Metal Market,* October 4, 1988, p. 5; "Company Briefs," *New York Times,* January 28, 1988, p. D3. **Highlight in Business Practice (p. 535):** Reprinted by permission from Gene Woolsey, "On Doing Good Things and Dumb Things in Production and Inventory Control," *Interfaces,* May 1975, pp. 65–67. Copyright 1975, The Institute of Management Science. **Figure 18.7:** Federal Reserve Bulletin. **Concluding Case:** "Getting In on the Ground Floor," p. 13, adapted from the April, 1985, issue of *Venture,* for Entrepreneurial Business Owners & Investors, by special permission. © 1985 Venture Magazine, Inc., 521 Fifth Avenue, New York, NY 10175.

Chapter 19

Business Practice Example: Andrew Kupfer, "The Newest Member of the LBO Club," *Fortune,* January 4, 1988, pp. 32–33; Peter Flinch, "Reg Lewis Hits the Big Time—and Takes It in Stride," *Business Week,* August 24, 1987, p. 27; B. Austin, "Beatrice Unit Gets Lewis' TLC Mark," *Advertising Age,* August 24, 1987, p. 37; Lois Therrien, "How Sweet It Is to Be Out from Under Beatrice's Thumb," *Business Week,* May 9, 1989, pp. 98–99; "Pinnacle" interview with Reginald Lewis, CNN Business News, August 20, 1988. **Figure 19.8:** Reprinted by permission of Standard & Poor's.

Chapter 20

Business Practice Example: David B. Hilder, "Risky Business," *Wall Street Journal,* July 10, 1985, pp. 1+; David Sellers, "Too Many Hot Seats on the Boards," *Insight,* February 2, 1987, pp. 40–41; Bill Powell, "Is It Safe to Go Back in the Boardroom?" *Newsweek,* May 4, 1987, pp. 45–46. **Figure 20.1:** Based on Insurance Checklist for Small Businesses from *Entrepreneurship and Venture Management: Text and Cases* by Kenneth W. Olm and George E. Eddy, pp. 230–235. Copyright 1985 Merrill Publishing Co., Columbus, Ohio. Reprinted by permission of the publisher. **Table 20.1:** *Life Insurance Fact Book* (Washington, D.C.: American Council of Life Insurance, 1988), pp. 112–113. **Figure 20.2:** Social Security Administration. **Highlight in Business Practice (p. 609):** Ronald Henkoff, "Lloyd's Names Aren't Game," *Newsweek,* June 3, 1985, p. 55; Stewart Powell, "Lloyd's of London: Modern Risks the Old Fashion Way," *U.S. News & World Report,* December 3, 1984, pp. 48–49; George Anders, "Money, Prestige Draw Wealthy Investors to Lloyd's of London Despite Big Risks," *Wall Street Journal,* April 19, 1985, p. 23. **Concluding Case:** H. J. Ullmann, "Money Talk," *Saturday Evening Post,* December 1984, p. 112.

Chapter 21

Business Practice Example: Business Practice Example adapted from Ralph King, Jr., "Made in the U.S.A.," by permission of *Forbes* Magazine from the May 16, 1988, issue, pp. 108–112. Business Practice Example Continues are from Thomas K. Theodore and Lou Bronson, "Achieving Competitive Advantage: A Holistic Approach to Management," *Management Review,* June 1987, p. 52; Jay Heizer and Barry Render, *Production and Operations Management: Strategies and Tactics* (Boston: Allyn & Bacon, 1988), p. 256; Kae H. Chung, *Management: Critical Success Factors* (Boston: Allyn & Bacon, 1987), pp. 528–553. **Figure 21.1:** Illustration by Harold Smelcer from William J. Cook, "Truck 54, Where Are You?" *U.S. News & World Report,* March 21, 1988, p. 64. **Highlight in Business Practice (p. 625):** Excerpted with permission of *Inc.* magazine from Sara Glazer, "Technology and Managing People: John McCormack on Improving People Management with the Help of Computers," *1988 Inc. Office Guide,* pp. 48–49. Copyright © 1988 by Goldhirsh Group, Inc., 38 Commercial Wharf, Boston, MA 02110. **Figure 21.2:** From "Parts of the Personal Computer and What They Do," *Time,* January 3, 1983, p. 39. Copyright 1982 Time Inc. All rights reserved. Reprinted by permission from *Time.* **Figure 21.7:** Reprinted by permission from Joel Dreyfuss, "Catching the Computer Wave," *Fortune,* September 26, 1988, p. 78. © 1988 Time Inc. All rights reserved. **Figure 21.8:** Reprinted by permission from Joel Dreyfuss, "Catching the Computer Wave," *Fortune,* September 26, 1988, p. 82. © 1988 Time Inc. All rights reserved. **Concluding Case:** Reprinted by permission from Susan Dillingham, "Computers Altering the Dining Experience," *Insight,* February 29, 1988, p. 47.

Chapter 22

Business Practice Example: Michael Brody, "When Products Turn to Liabilities," *Fortune,* March 3, 1986, pp. 20–24; Harry Bacas, "Liability: Trying Times," *Nation's Business,* February 1986, pp. 22–27; Paul M. Barrett, "Tort Reform Fight Shifts to State Courts," *Wall Street Journal,* September 19, 1988, p. 27; James E. Ellis, "Monsanto and the Copper-7: A 'Corporate Veil' Begins to Fray," *Business Week,* September 26, 1988, p. 50; Paul M. Barrett, "Suit against Aetna in Robins Case Presses Right to Shun Class Actions," *Wall Street Journal,* November 90, 1988, p. B10. **Highlight in Business Practice (p. 652):** Mark Magnier, "Counter-Attack on Prop 103," *Terre Haute Tribune-Star,* November 13, 1988, p. F1; Richard B. Schmitt, "California's Voters Shake Up Insurers," *Wall Street Journal,* November 10, 1988, p. B1; *Newsweek,* March 27, 1989, p. 34; *Money,* January 1989, pp. 17–18. **Table 22.2:** 1987 Annual Report of the Director of the Administrative Office of the United States Courts, appearing in Paul M. Barrett, "Court May Have to Lead Product-Liability Reform," *Wall Street Journal,* October 10, 1988, p. B1. **Concluding Case:** "Used-Car Shoppers Get Help Beginning Today," *Terre Haute Tribune-Star,* May 9, 1985, p. A15; Melinda G. Gurles, "Used Car Buyers Get a Little More Protection," *Wall Street Journal,* May 12, 1988, p. 25.

Chapter 23

Business Practice Example: James E. Ellis, "Tower to McDonnell: Turbulence Ahead," *Business Week,* May 23, 1988, pp. 117–118; James E. Ellis, "McDonnell-Douglas Tries More Butter and Fewer Guns," *Business Week,* April 28, 1986, pp. 84–86; Milton Moskowitz, Michael Katz, and Robert Levering, *Everybody's Business* (New York: Harper & Row, 1980); Richard G. O'Lone, "Airframe Manufacturers Seek Sales Opportunities in Eastern Bloc," *Aviation Week & Space Technology,* February 15, 1988, pp. 112. Louis Kraar, "How One Man Landed China's 1 Billion Order," *Fortune,* August 18, 1986, p. 46. **Table 23.1:** Adapted by permission from "America's Leading Exporters," *Fortune,* July 18, 1988, p. 71. © 1988 Time Inc. All rights reserved. **Figure 23.1:** Data for 1982–1987 from *1989 Britannica Book of the Year* (Chicago: Encyclopaedia Britannica, 1989), p. 726. Used by permission. **Table 23.2:** William Holstein and Brian Bremmer, "The Little Guys Are Making It Big Overseas," p. 64. Reprinted from the February 27, 1989, issue of *Business Week* by special permission, © 1989 by McGraw-Hill, Inc. Data from company reports. **Table 23.3:** William Holstein and Brian Bremmer, "The Little Guys Are Making It Big Overseas," p. 66. Reprinted from the February 27, 1989, issue of *Business Week* by special permission, © 1989 by McGraw-Hill, Inc. Data from The Exporter, Census Bureau. **Figure 23.2:** Illustration by Richard Gage; basic data from Gary C. Hufbauer, Diane T. Berliner, and Kimberly A. Elliot; from "The Fallout from Protectionist Measures," *U.S. News & World Report,* March 21, 1988, p. 51. **Highlight in Business Practice (p. 686):** Gregory L. Miles, Frank J. Comes, and Ellen Wallace, "Heinz Squares Off against Its Archrival," p. 58. Reprinted from the December 12, 1988, issue of *Business Week* by special permission, © 1988 by McGraw-Hill, Inc. **Table 23.4:** Reprinted by permission from "The Top 25 Multinational Corporations," *Fortune,* August 1, 1988, p. D3. © 1988 Time Inc. All rights reserved. **Concluding Case:** Mark M. Nelson, "Unilever Aims to Bolster Lines in U.S.," *Wall Street Journal,* June 19, 1987, p. 6; Andrew C. Brown, "Unilever Fights Back in the U.S.," *Fortune,* May 26, 1986, pp. 32–38.

BUSINESS

PART

FOUNDATIONS OF OUR BUSINESS SYSTEM

CHAPTER

1

Entrepreneurial Excellence in the American Economy

CHAPTER

2

The Free Enterprise System in a Global Economy

CHAPTER

3

Social Responsibility and Ethics

CHAPTER

1

ENTREPRENEURIAL EXCELLENCE IN THE AMERICAN ECONOMY

LEARNING OBJECTIVES

After reading this chapter you should be able to:

1. Explain the importance of business to the American economy and distinguish among the three major types of economic activities.
2. Explain the major purpose of business and the interrelationship of its two major objectives.
3. List the four major uses of profits.
4. Discuss the role of profits in our economy.
5. Compare and contrast mercantilism with Adam Smith's philosophy of free trade.
6. Discuss the business and economic highlights of early American history.
7. Explain the importance of creativity and discuss why it is often the key ingredient in a successful business.

OUTLINE

Business Practice Example: Ted Turner: Media Entrepreneur

The Importance of Business

- Types of Economic Activities
- Purpose and Objectives of Business

Why Are Profits Important?

- Profit and Loss System
- Uses of Profits
- Economic Survival

The Role of Profits in Our Economy

- Expansion of the Economy
- Efficient Use of Resources
- Higher Quality of Life and Prosperity
- The Role of Competition
  - Types of Competition
- Free-Market Concept
  - Supply and Demand in the Free Market

The Roots of the Modern American Economy

- The Mercantile System and Adam Smith
- The Industrial Revolution and the Nineteenth Century
- Business Creativity and the Twentieth Century
  - Science and Technology
  - Information-Processing Explosion
  - Shift from a Production Era to a Marketing Era
  - Return to the Entrepreneurial Spirit
  - Service Revolution

Summary

Key Terms

Check Your Learning

Review and Discussion

Concluding Case: The Invisible Hand versus the 1987 Crash

Notes

Check Your Learning Answer Key

Highlight in Business Practice: Purchasing Power

Highlight in Business Practice: Tips on Creativity

Highlight in Business Practice: Genentech: Entrepreneurial Excellence Right from the Start

BUSINESS PRACTICE EXAMPLE

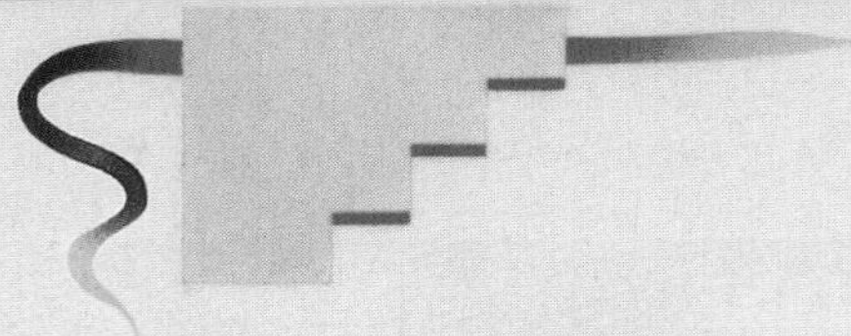

Ted Turner: Media Entrepreneur

He's been called "Captain Courageous," a visionary, a madcap, and more. He's an entrepreneur in the classic mold—sharing with earlier Americans such as Henry Ford of the Ford Motor Co. and William Paley, founder of CBS, the credit for founding an industry (cable television). His name is Ted Turner, and he's the Chairman of the Board and President of Turner Broadcasting System, Inc. (TBS). The Atlanta-based company owns and operates, among other properties, four television networks, including Cable News Network (CNN), HEADLINE NEWS, SuperStation TBS, and Turner Network Television (TNT). Turner owns more television networks than any of his competitors, now, or ever.

Turner was born in 1938 and grew up in Georgia. After turning around his father's outdoor advertising business, he bought a small, run-down UHF television station in Atlanta—against the advice of nearly everyone. Few people could watch the channel because its assigned frequency could not be picked up by most television sets. At that time, cable TV was a rudimentary system intended to improve reception of existing channels only. Turner discovered that he could broadcast by satellite to other cable systems around the country. In 1976, he established the first "superstation," a television station that distributes its signal to a wide area by means of satellites.

It's fine and well to own a television station, and even better to be able to transmit nationwide, but you need something to transmit. Programming is the name of the game. Initially, WTCG carried retread sitcoms and, after Turner purchased a basketball and a baseball team, Atlanta Hawks and Atlanta Braves games. Still, viewers were pleased with the station, and within four years, the superstation, renamed WTBS, was getting national advertising and rising revenues.

In 1980, Turner created the first all-news network, CNN. At first the object of much derision from his colleagues in broadcasting, CNN grew steadily more successful as the staff gained experience, and larger and larger audiences came to rely on the station. By 1985, CNN went in the black, where it has stayed ever since. By 1988, more than 41 million homes received CNN. And while this cable network's audience is growing, the "Big Three" broadcast networks' audience has declined by more than 15 percent in the past eight years. The New York Times called CNN "the most innovative development in television news in the quarter century."

Not content to leave success well enough alone, Ted Turner has risked the farm more than once since his success with CNN and HEADLINE

NEWS. In 1985, he attempted and failed a hostile takeover of CBS, losing $21 million in the process. And in 1986, he purchased MGM, with its huge library of over 3,300 films (including such classics as *Gone with the Wind*) for an astonishing $1.2 billion. He ultimately had to sell back MGM's studios and other properties—all but the film library—and add a consortium of cable operators as part owners and board members of Turner Broadcasting System to pay for the purchase. Again, the industry predicted his downfall. And, once again, they were wrong.

WHAT'S AHEAD

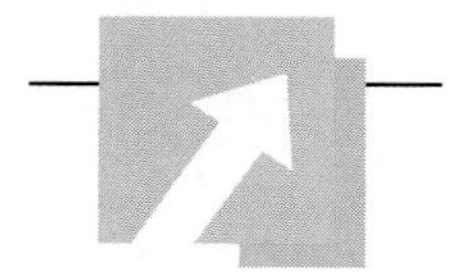

As the introductory example unfolds, it will become clear that Turner Broadcasting System, like any other business, must serve the public by satisfying customer needs and wants. Any business that fails to do so will have a difficult time making a profit. This chapter will explain why profits are important to business and why business is important to the American economy. It will also survey the economic highlights of early American business, which laid the foundation for our current standard of living—one of the highest standards in the world.

Nearly every American dreams of starting a business that one day will bring the riches and fame of a Henry Ford or a John D. Rockefeller. Few ever do it, of course, but every year witnesses new, innovative business ideas that show substantial potential. And every day more and more Americans are venturing into the world of business—a world of excitement, and hope, and many, many surprises.

In the nineteenth century and much of the twentieth century, business leaders built their successes on products such as oil, textiles, communications, transportation, and steel. As we near the twenty-first century, many new types of businesses and industries are forming, as well as a new breed of entrepreneurs.

THE IMPORTANCE OF BUSINESS

Calvin Coolidge once said that "the chief business of the American people is business." What is business? How important are businesses to the American economy? To answer the second question first, very important. Businesses are the core of our economic system. Their actions, or lack of action, have an important effect on our daily lives. Can you imagine watching the nightly news or reading a newspaper without seeing and hearing about inflation, employment, the stock market, the cost of living, and a multitude of other everyday business topics? Has a day ever gone by that you haven't been exposed to an advertisement? Where would you work if there were no businesses? Obviously, if we look at

Table 1.1 Many types of businesses can be found in the American economy.

Types of businesses	
Services	6,220,000
Finance, insurance, real estate	2,272,000
Retailing	2,763,000
Construction	1,758,000
Transportation, public utilities	721,000
Manufacturing	622,000
Agriculture, forestry, fishing	560,000
Wholesaling	550,000
Mining	251,000
Total	15,717,000

Details may not add to totals because of rounding.

numbers only, as displayed in Table 1.1, we can see that business is everyone's business.

The next section will address our first question: What exactly do we mean by the term *business?*

Types of Economic Activities

A ***business*** is an organization that is created to earn a profit for providing needed goods and services to society.

Profit is revenue that exceeds expenses in a business.

Our economy is composed of three major types of economic activities: agriculture and mining (extraction), manufacturing, and services (see Figure 1.1). It is the total of these economic activities that makes up American business. Within each activity, individuals own and operate businesses. A **business** is an organization that is created to earn a **profit** (revenue that exceeds expenses) for providing needed goods and services to society. For example, Toys-R-Us and Panasonic are businesses. In contrast, *nonprofit organizations* such as the Boy Scouts, the Red Cross, Big Brother–Big Sister, and churches do not attempt to earn a profit for the goods and services they provide.

Agriculture includes not only the thousands of farms that dot the U.S. countryside but also other industries involving natural resources, such as forestry and fishing. Closely related to agriculture is the extraction industry of mining. Amax Coal Company, a business involved in the extraction of coal for commercial and consumer use, is owned by many stockholders. Coal from Amax fires the giant furnaces and turbines of large manufacturing businesses. In the manufacturing sector, USX Corporation and Digital Equipment Corporation (DEC) manufacture products ranging from steel and pipe (USX) to mainframe computers and software (DEC). Manufacturing also includes the business of producing tangible consumer goods such as VCRs, toys, and grocery items.

Other businesses specialize in service activities such as distributing, transporting, storing, and selling steel and countless other manufactured goods. Service

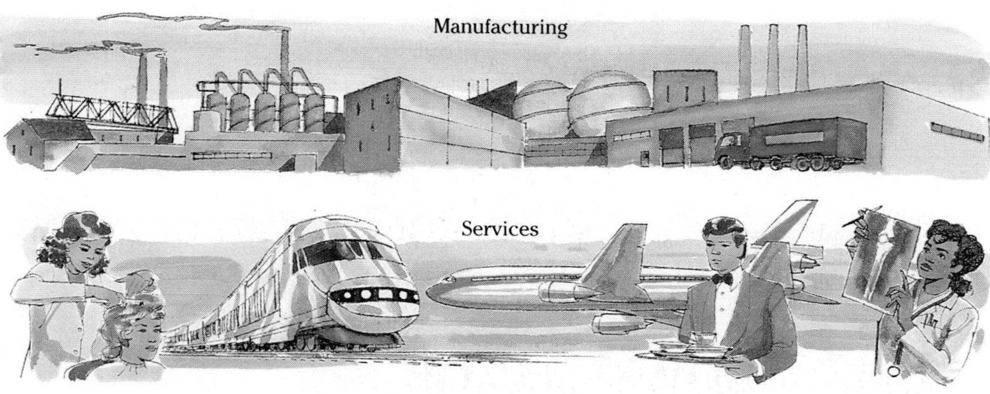

Figure 1.1
The American economy is composed of three major economic activities.

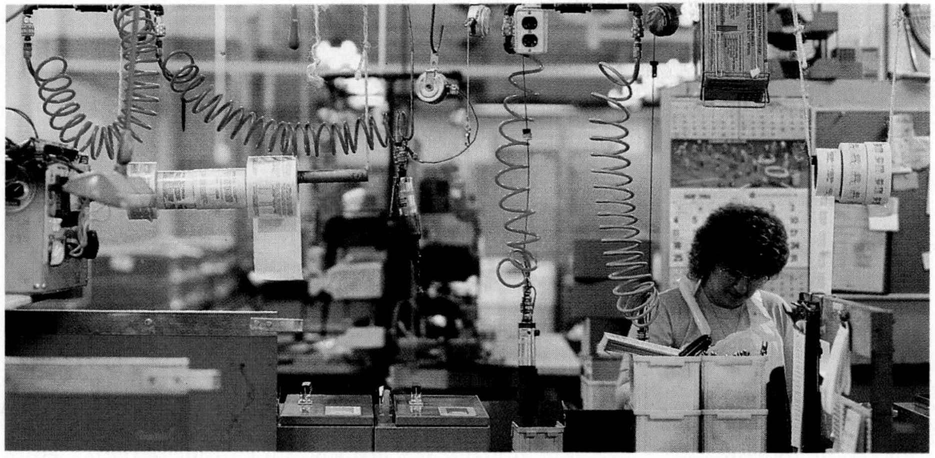

Our economy is composed of three major types of economic activities: agriculture and mining, manufacturing, and service. Allen-Bradley, a U.S. manufacturer of industrial control devices is shown here.

businesses, though they do not produce goods directly, are extremely important to our economy. Today the service industries—including finance, trade, transportation, and public utilities—generate over half of all the business activity in our economy. Of all consumer spending, 46 percent is in the service area; and over three-fourths of all jobs are now in the service industries—more than twice the number in agriculture and manufacturing. According to the Coalition of Service

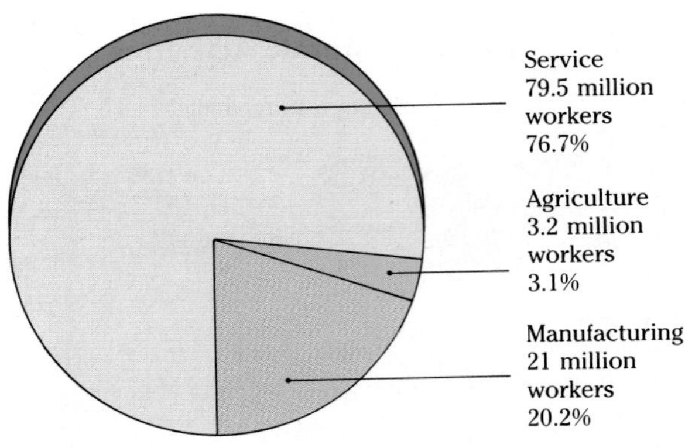

Figure 1.2
Three-quarters of the nation's workers are employed in service industries.

Industries, over 95 percent of 25 million new jobs created since 1970 have been in services. Furthermore, since 1945, the service sector has created an average of fifteen new jobs for each new manufacturing job. Ours is increasingly a service-oriented economy (see Figure 1.2).[1]

Purpose and Objectives of Business

Why do businesses exist? Above all, to serve the public. Any business that does not serve the public will not exist for long. However, if a business is to thrive and grow, it must do more. Generally, business owners will strive to accomplish two major objectives. First, they will try to provide specific goods or services that will satisfy human needs and wants. For example, a local clothing store will sell consumer goods such as coats, pants, and other articles of clothing—products that people need and want for everyday use. Second, owners will strive to operate at a profit. In other words, they will try to generate income that exceeds expenditures such as salaries, rent, taxes, and the cost of goods—and to generate that income at a rate that will compensate them for taking the risk of operating the business.

WHY ARE PROFITS IMPORTANT?

Profit and Loss System

Americans must remember that ours is a profit and loss system. In his book *Economics,* Nobel laureate Paul Samuelson states, "Profits are the carrots held out as an incentive to efficiency, and losses are the sticks that penalize using inefficient methods or devoting resources to uses not derived by spending consumers."[2]

Entrepreneurs are individuals who assume the risk of starting their own businesses.

Without such "carrots," early American inventors would have had little reason to take the risks they did. We might never have had automobiles, airplanes, movies, radios, or computers—all of which brought large profits to those willing to assume the risk of loss. These risk takers are referred to as **entrepreneurs.** The greater the risk, the greater must be the prospective profit to compensate for it. For example, entrepreneur Bill Gates III risked a great deal when he dropped out of Harvard in 1975 at the age of nineteen to team up with Paul Allen in founding Microsoft Corporation. Gates is now chairman of Microsoft, one of the world's largest software producers. Its major products include BASIC, MS-DOS, Word, Windows, and the operating software for the Apple Macintosh. In 1986, Gates took the company public (sold shares of ownership in it). By doing so he became the computer industry's first billionaire.[3]

Uses of Profits

Profits have a number of uses beyond that of giving a reward to risk-taking entrepreneurs:

- One major use is for *reinvestment in the company* to improve its competitive position through better production capacity. The company's money is used for newer equipment, expanded facilities, and, often, more jobs.
- A second use of profits is to provide *tax funds in support of government services.* Income taxes are not deducted as business expenses but are always paid from profits. (Business income taxes range from 20 to 34 percent of income.)
- In a third use, profits may be *donated to charities or contributed to community projects or political parties.* In one year, IBM alone gave $188.4 million to charitable organizations.
- Finally, after profits have been put to work in these capacities, the final payoff is available to those who hold ownership shares in the company—the stockholders—*as payments in the form of dividends.* These dividends benefit many Americans; there are approximately 26 million stockholders in the United States, and even more in the rest of the world, who are sharing profits from American businesses.

Economic Survival

By now it should be clear that *profit* is not a dirty word. Each of us has some stake in healthy levels of profits (the average profit margin for American businesses is approximately 5 percent), both to support public services and to maintain our high standard of living. Without the profit motive, our society would face a downward spiral: (1) Businesses would be unable to renovate or expand their operations to face worldwide competition, and thus they would often fail. (2) Failed businesses would severely decrease the jobs and money available to individuals. (3) If people had no money, the nation's standard of living would decrease. (4) As more people got hurt in this cycle, they would demand action, usually from the government. This could result in the kind of emergency regulation, taxation, and other kinds of intervention that most people would find unwelcome.

THE ROLE OF PROFITS IN OUR ECONOMY

Profits affect the entire society. This section examines how they help ensure a smoothly running economy.

BUSINESS PRACTICE EXAMPLE Continues

As an entrepreneur, Ted Turner has taken tremendous risks throughout his career. Establishing the first superstation was a risk. Establishing the first all-news network was an even greater risk. These and other risks have paid off for Turner, who owns three 5,000-acre plantations, a large island off the coast of South Carolina, a beach house in Big Sur, and a 10,000-acre ranch in Montana. But Turner's main use of profits has been for reinvestment in the Turner Broadcasting System. CNN was originally housed in a less than elegant building. His original equipment was nearly all second-hand, purchased from local stations. In 1981, the first year of operation, CNN spent $40 million but lost $11 million. It was not until 1985 that it turned a modest profit. But by 1987, profits soared to about $61 million. Turner then purchased a modern news center with state-of-the-art electronic hardware.

Turner has also used profits in support of world peace and the protection of the environment. In 1985, he was one of a group that founded The Better World Society, a nonprofit organization dedicated to the production and international distribution of television programming on issues of critical importance to the survival of the planet. In the same year, Turner organized the Goodwill Games, an off-year Olympics-style competition held for the first time in Moscow in 1986.

Expansion of the Economy

Capital is the funds used to modernize and expand businesses and to purchase machinery and other resources.

The *multiplier effect* is the change in the rate of spending that causes a chain reaction throughout the economy.

Profits are necessary if business and society are to advance and grow. For example, it is estimated that in many manufacturing industries $200,000 in new capital is required to create just one new job. **Capital** is the funds used to modernize and expand, as well as to purchase the equipment and other resources needed to create wealth. The profits at one General Motors plant can be used to construct a new plant in another location, which in turn creates new jobs for people in the second community and for suppliers and others as well.

At work here is the **multiplier effect**—the change in the rate of spending that causes a chain reaction throughout the economy, because spending by one business results in income for others. As Figure 1.3 shows, each round of spending to run a company (ABC Corporation in the figure) adds to the total funds invested in the company. As time goes on, more and more money is concentrated in the company and less is required to keep it growing. Since the same effect occurs

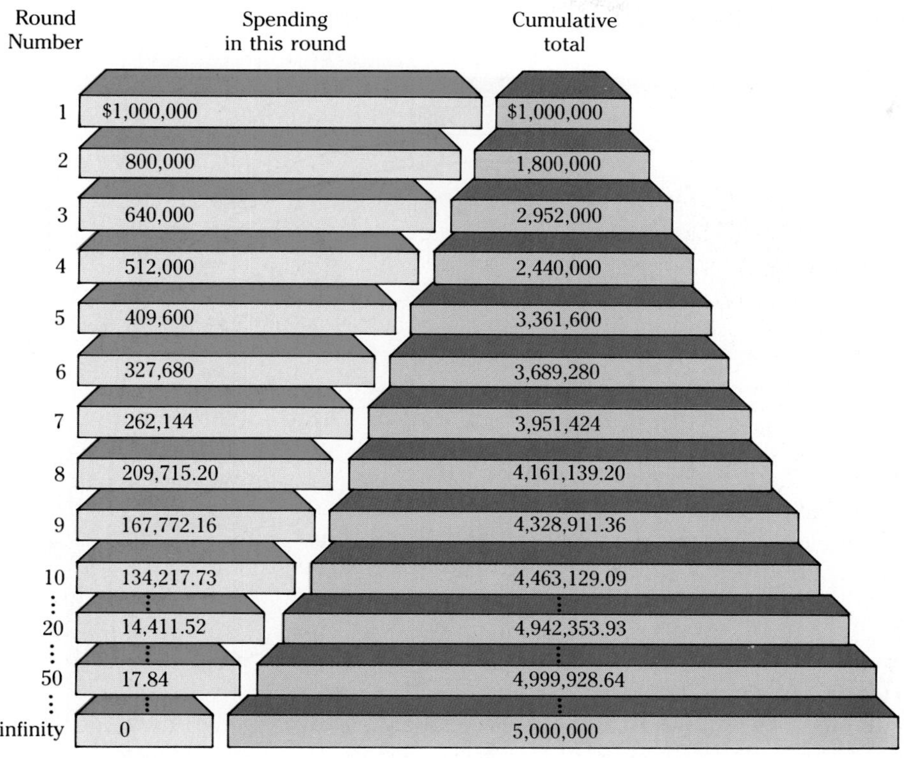

Round Number
Spending in this round
Cumulative total
1 $1,000,000 $1,000,000
2 800,000 1,800,000
3 640,000 2,952,000
4 512,000 2,440,000
5 409,600 3,361,600
6 327,680 3,689,280
7 262,144 3,951,424
8 209,715.20 4,161,139.20
9 167,772.16 4,328,911.36
10 134,217.73 4,463,129.09
20 14,411.52 4,942,353.93
50 17.84 4,999,928.64
infinity 0 5,000,000

Figure 1.3
The multiplier spending chain for ABC Corporation forms when cumulative spending builds up value in the firm. Eventually ABC's economic power has a multiplier effect on other companies.

in millions of companies, a rapid buildup of business activity can occur in the whole economy in a short time. Unfortunately, the multiplier effect can work in reverse too. If many businesses drastically slow down their spending, the chain reaction can create a slowdown for the entire economy.

Efficient Use of Resources

The desire of a business to make a profit usually encourages the efficient use of both human and natural resources in an effort to keep costs down. Holly Farms, for example, produces chickens for food. It also uses them for fertilizer and for down for pillows and comforters.

The concept *efficient resource allocation* holds that "any reallocation of resources that makes some individuals in the economy better off in their own estimation while not worsening the lot of anyone else is an improvement in the functioning of the economy. Any allocation of resources that takes advantage of every opportunity is called an efficient allocation."[4] Certainly companies motivated by profit will try to take advantage of every opportunity.

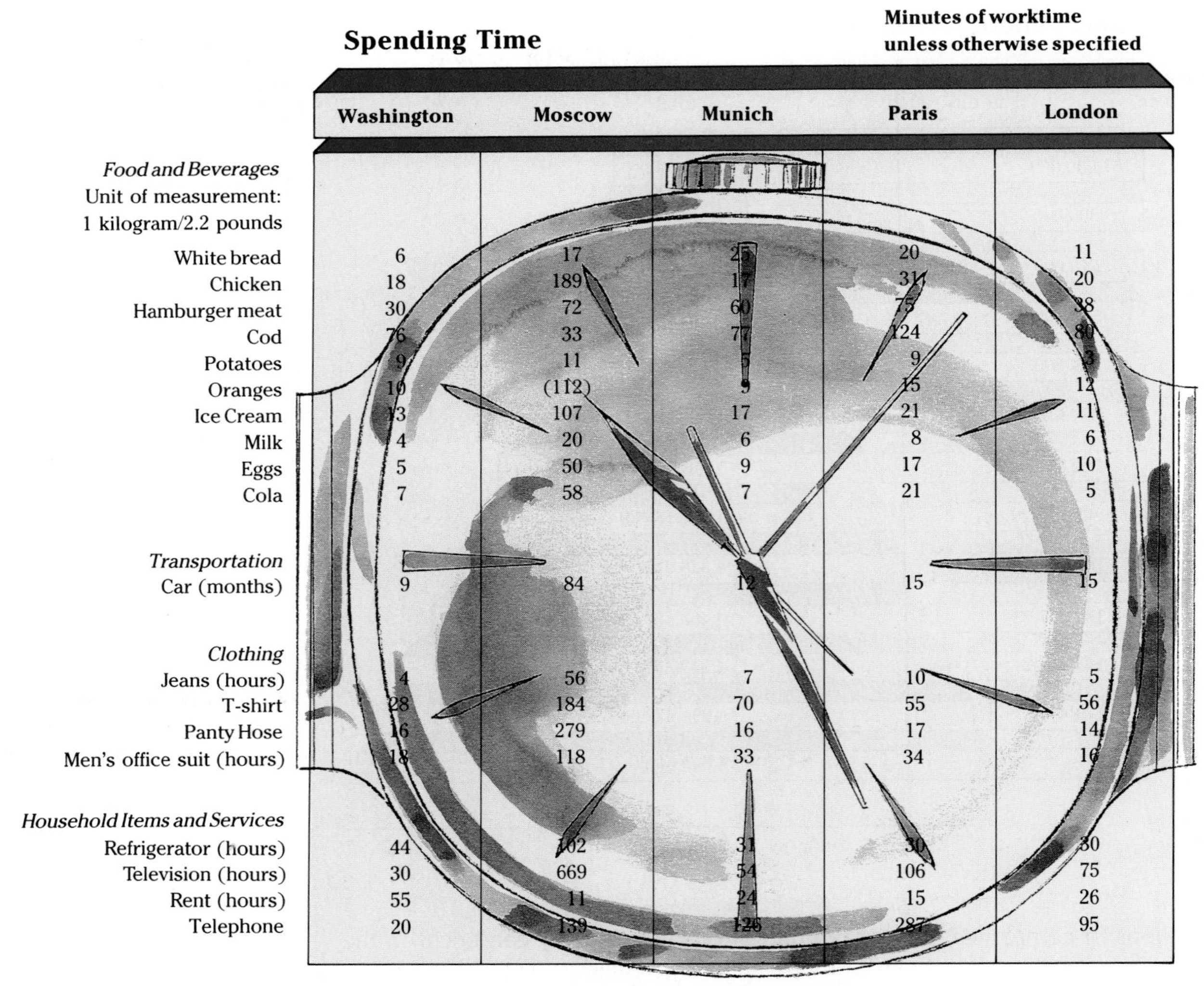

Spending Time — Minutes of worktime unless otherwise specified

	Washington	Moscow	Munich	Paris	London
Food and Beverages Unit of measurement: 1 kilogram/2.2 pounds					
White bread	6	17	25	20	11
Chicken	18	189	17	31	20
Hamburger meat	30	72	60	75	38
Cod	76	33	77	124	80
Potatoes	9	11	5	9	3
Oranges	10	(112)	9	15	12
Ice Cream	13	107	17	21	11
Milk	4	20	6	8	6
Eggs	5	50	9	17	10
Cola	7	58	7	21	5
Transportation					
Car (months)	9	84	12	15	15
Clothing					
Jeans (hours)	4	56	7	10	5
T-shirt	28	184	70	55	56
Panty Hose	16	279	16	17	14
Men's office suit (hours)	18	118	33	34	16
Household Items and Services					
Refrigerator (hours)	44	102	31	30	30
Television (hours)	30	669	54	106	75
Rent (hours)	55	11	24	15	26
Telephone	20	139	126	287	95

Figure 1.4 Real income, or the value of income in terms of its purchasing power, can vary greatly from city to city and nation to nation.

Higher Quality of Life and Prosperity

The ***standard of living*** in a nation is its quality of living.

Real income is the value of a person's income in terms of its purchasing power.

The incentive to earn a profit is the mainstay of the American economy. The success of an economy can be measured by its **standard of living,** or quality of living. The best measure of standard of living is **real income**—the value of a person's income in terms of its purchasing power (see Figure 1.4). According to a survey by the Union Bank of Switzerland, real income in the United States is anywhere from 10 to 30 percent higher than it is in Canada, Australia, and the wealthier nations of Europe.[5] Real income in other countries lags even further behind.

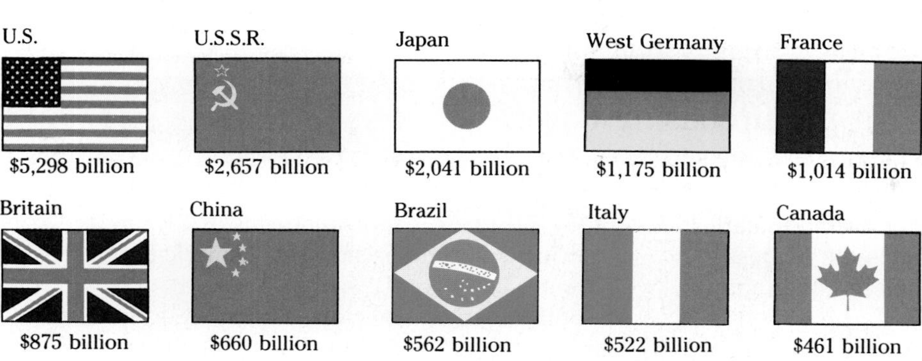

Figure 1.5
The United States is predicted to continue having the world's largest economy in the year 2000.

Many people are convinced that the United States will remain at the top of the list in the years immediately ahead. But it is expected that in the long run the huge edge the United States holds will narrow appreciably and perhaps even disappear. The fact that real income in the United States has recently declined supports that claim. Some economists predict that if our real income continues to decline, we may not be on top by the year 2000.[6]

Another measure of standard of living includes per capita GNP. **Gross national product (GNP)** is the sum of all goods and services produced per year. It provides us with a measure of the size of our economy. See Figure 1.5 for a projection of GNP outputs for the year 2000.

Gross national product (GNP) is the sum of all goods and services produced per year.

Per capita GNP is the average amount of goods and services produced per person annually. Per capita GNP in the United States was $18,367 in 1987. Although the United States no longer has the highest per capita GNP in the world, our standard of living remains quite high. Americans, on a per capita basis, still consume more goods and services than people in any other country.

Regardless of how we measure standard of living, its implications for the American economy are important. A decrease in the standard of living can bring increased social and political tensions and an economic slowdown. Among the indicators of such a decrease are higher unemployment, fewer construction starts, weak consumer spending, less production, and a declining money supply. Fortunately, Americans have the economic and political freedoms that enable them to work toward avoiding a lower standard of living.

The Role of Competition

Operating under competitive pressures, the profit motive determines largely how goods and services are produced. Competition is good for the economy, benefiting both businesses and consumers. The pressure of competition motivates businesses to cut costs and lower prices. It also forces them to try to provide better service and more choice than their competitors. Consumers get new and improved products and great efficiency in a competitive environment.

HIGHLIGHT IN BUSINESS PRACTICE

Purchasing Power

Purchasing power for average salaries in the U.S. is perhaps the highest in the world. Nonetheless, other countries are catching up.

Just what is purchasing power? Purchasing power is *real income,* or what an individual's or nation's money can actually purchase in the way of goods and services. Purchasing power is one of the best measures of a country's standard of living, but country to country comparisons are difficult. Even within one country purchasing power can vary widely. Someone living in Los Angeles, for example, has 33% to 55% more purchasing power than someone with the same salary living in New York or Houston. The variation between countries is even greater.

Alan Heston and Robert Summers, two economists from the University of Pennsylvania, have come up with a system to compare the purchasing power parity (PPP) of citizens of different countries. Heston and Summers give the U.S. an index score of 100. By comparison, West Germany gets a score of 84 and Japan, 77. With their money, therefore the average West German can purchase about 84% of the goods and services that Americans can, and the average Japanese, 77%.

But while the average West German and Japanese have less purchasing power than Americans, their standards of living have risen far more dramatically than ours. In 1950, the PPP for West Germany was 40%, while that for Japan was only 17%. Now, 57% of Japanese households have air conditioners (Americans, 60%), 71% have cars (Americans, 87%), and 99% have color television sets (Americans, 88%).

Still, American executives continue to have it far better than their European or Japanese counterparts. Chief executives of major U.S. corporations can earn $1 million or more in salary. Japanese executives, in comparison, earn around $250,000, while European executives often earn half that amount. And, as we've just seen, these smaller salaries also have far less purchasing power. Although European and Japanese firms supplement their employees' salaries with elaborate perks—cars, free medical services, large entertainment allowances, and country club memberships—these do not help employees build up assets of their own.

Other Asian countries have also shown amazing increases in purchasing power. Now Hong Kong (PPP 58), Singapore (46), Taiwan (36) and Korea (31) have middle classes that can afford to take family vacations and send their children to U.S. colleges.

Unfortunately, the purchasing power of the Latin American nations is declining. In the 1960s and 1970s, the standard of living in these countries rose, mainly as the result of foreign borrowing. Now foreign debt is forcing the standard of living down again. The worst situation in terms of purchasing power is seen in Africa, where repressive governments have driven down crop prices so far that farmers no longer take part in the cash economy. The PPP in Zaire, for example, is only 2.5.

Types of Competition

There are four basic types of competition in our economy: pure competition, monopolistic competition, oligopoly, and monopoly. Every business belongs to one of these categories, the basis being the nature of specific industries.

Pure competition is competition that results when there are so many small businesses in an industry that no single business can influence the price charged on a fairly uniform product. Thus price is established by supply and demand. The classic example of a purely competitive industry is agriculture, where there are so many farmers selling such similar products as corn, wheat, and soybeans that no single farmer can set the price.

Pure competition is the competition that results when there are so many small businesses in an industry that no single business can influence the price charged on a fairly uniform product.

Monopolistic competition is competition occurring in industries where there are a large number of businesses but where the products are often differentiated from those of competitors by nonprice factors. For example, several businesses manufacture baseball bats; however, there is only one Louisville Slugger brand. Each manufacturer offers different types and sizes of bats, both wooden and aluminum, at different prices. This type of competition gives each business some power over the prices it charges.

Monopolistic competition is competition occurring in industries where there are a large number of businesses but where the products are often differentiated from those of competitors by nonprice factors.

An **oligopoly** is an industry in which there are few competitors. The most obvious American oligopolies are the automobile and steel industries. In an oligopoly, the products can be similar (steel) or different (automobiles). However, in either case, the oligopolist has considerable control over the product's price.

An ***oligopoly*** is an industry in which there are few competitors.

A **monopoly** is a market situation in which there is no competition. To many people, the lack of competition is un-American. In this country, monopoly is prohibited by the Sherman and Clayton acts, except when regulated by the government. Regulated monopolies include the local telephone, natural gas, and electric utilities. In these industries, the government's regulatory body sets prices and profits.

A ***monopoly*** is a market situation in which there is no competition.

Free-Market Concept

In the United States, we enjoy what is called a free-market system, which is sometimes referred to as economic voting. The **free-market concept** is the economic concept that how consumers spend their money determines which products and businesses will survive in the market. Every purchase made is a "vote" for the producer of the good or service. The system is democratic in that the majority rules; the producer that gets the most votes can make the most profit.

The ***free-market concept*** is the economic concept that how consumers spend their money determines which products and businesses will survive in the market.

Supply and Demand in the Free Market

In theory, each individual in the market is free to sell goods or services at any price to anyone willing to pay that price. Supply and demand regulate the system; the quantity supplied will increase as the demand increases.

The amount of a good or service offered for sale at a specific price is **supply.** It includes only the amount available for sale at a specific time. For example, grain held back by farmers who are hoping for a price increase is not part of supply.

Supply is the amount of a product for sale at a specific price.

The quantity of a good or service that consumers are willing to purchase at different prices is **demand.** Only when the goods and services can actually be sold at a given price does a demand for them exist. You may want to purchase a new Corvette or stereo, but unless you have the purchasing power to buy it, your demand for those products does not exist.

Demand is the quantity of a product that consumers are willing to purchase at different prices.

In practice, supply and demand work to balance each other, as chapter 2 will show in detail. If a high-priced product offered for sale is not met with customers willing to pay the price, the supplied product does not sell; it is not in balance with demand. If the supplier does not adjust the price to fit demand, a competitor with a lower price is likely to turn up and make the sale. In this way, successful competitors will eventually drive unsuccessful ones out of business, and society as a whole will benefit from the market-regulated pricing and efficient production.

In the American economy, the supply and demand system is remarkably responsive to what people want. Performance—not promises—is what pays off in the free market, and every day is an election day for consumers.

THE ROOTS OF THE MODERN AMERICAN ECONOMY

What has made America the land of opportunity—a country where the greatest freedom and prosperity has existed for the widest range of people? To answer this question, let's examine the economic birth of our nation in 1776 and follow it through over two hundred years of business leadership. As we will see, the passions for personal profit and religious escape contributed greatly to transforming America from an agrarian and heavily industrialized society into the sophisticated consumer society that exists today.

BUSINESS PRACTICE EXAMPLE Continues

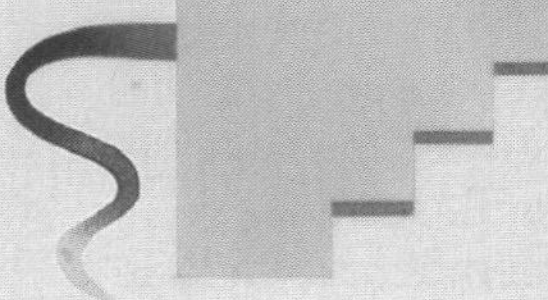

Until Ted Turner established the first superstation in 1976, the television industry was an oligopoly, in which the three major networks, ABC, NBC, and CBS, controlled the airwaves. Today, the broadcast industry operates in an environment that is becoming more and more competitive. It is now much closer to being a pure competitive market.

The pressure of competition posed by Turner's networks, and by the many other cable broadcast stations, has deeply affected the industry, especially the "Big Three" networks. The size of a network's audience determines its ratings, which in turn affects how much advertising it can attract, and what price it can charge for air time. While many cable broadcasters collect subscriber fees as well as advertising revenues, ABC, CBS, and NBC must rely on advertising revenues exclusively.

The amount of revenues a network can collect in turn will determine how much it can spend on programming. Competition in the broadcast industry has provided the consumer with a wider range of programming choices. Viewers can now subscribe to college sports, home shopping, religious, and a variety of other networks for small monthly fees.

The Mercantile System and Adam Smith

In 1776, America was a British colony that was heavily influenced by European mercantilist philosophy. **Mercantilism** is an economic system based on colonizing new territories and exploiting their natural resources. European nations extracted raw materials from their colonies and shipped them to the home countries. There they were made into finished goods, which in turn were sold to the colonies at exorbitant prices.

Mercantilism is an economic system based on colonization and the exploitation of natural resources.

In 1776, the year of the American Revolution, a Scottish former professor of moral philosophy, Adam Smith, published *The Wealth of Nations.*[7] This book was meant to serve not as a text but as a policy-guiding document for his peers to use in the conduct of government. *The Wealth of Nations* presented a persuasive argument for a new approach to economic policy.

The book revolutionized the world of economics. In it, Smith argued that the free market is an ingenious mechanism that is regulated through supply and demand. Smith's institutional framework did not call for extensive government regulation. Instead it supported the **laissez-faire** (French for "let alone"), or hands off, approach to business by government. Smith believed that when individuals are allowed to promote their own interests, an effective supply and demand system will regulate the economy. As he put it, an *invisible hand* will automatically promote the well-being of society as well.

Laissez faire is a hands off approach to business by government.

What Smith meant by the invisible hand was competition. It is competition that brings us lower prices, more efficient service, and a better quality and variety of goods and services. Thus, it is easy to see why Adam Smith is considered the father of free-market economics.

The Industrial Revolution and the Nineteenth Century

After gaining its independence, America continued to be populated by strong, adventurous, self-sufficient, and courageous people who harnessed vast reserves of natural resources.

Early business was centered around **cottage industries,** in which most items were made in the homes (cottages) of the settlers. America has always been blessed with enterprising immigrants. Among them was Samuel Slater, a young British apprentice mechanic, who, disguised as a farmer, immigrated to America in 1789. In Britain, Slater had memorized the plans for constructing a water-powered spinning machine—an invention that became the key to England's **Industrial Revolution** (the shift from cottage industries to a factory system of manufacturing). In Rhode Island, Slater reconstructed this powerful piece of equipment from memory. He then set up a complete mechanized factory for cotton spinning, thereby initiating America's Industrial Revolution. From this beginning, American business activity shifted into the factory system of production that dominated the nineteenth century.

Cottage industries are industries that rely on most items being made in homes.

The ***Industrial Revolution*** is the shift, originating in England, to a factory system of manufacturing.

During America's dynamic era of growth, mechanized industrial production made possible the accumulation of vast fortunes by early tycoons. J. P. Morgan made a fortune reorganizing and consolidating railroads. John D. Rockefeller incorporated the Standard Oil Company of Ohio in 1870. By the turn of the century, he controlled 90 percent of American oil-refining capacity and had an annual income of $45 million. Steel magnate Andrew Carnegie was twenty when he made his first investment, in 1856: he bought ten shares of railroad stock for $50 a share. Cornelius Vanderbilt began building steamboats in 1829 with $30,000 he had saved. Twenty-five years later, he acknowledged he was worth $11 million.

Driven by the profit motive and by the power of industrialized production, entrepreneurs took daring business risks. They brushed aside competitors to take more and more of the market, and their business methods helped America become the most productive economy of the nineteenth century. Their initiative plus the skills and energy of a rapidly growing labor force built the world's largest industries. America developed immense transportation, agriculture, steel, communications, banking, and oil industries, which became the backbone of twentieth century success in these areas.

Business Creativity and the Twentieth Century

Creativity is another term for innovation.

The **creativity** (innovation) unleashed by a competitive free market and the profit motive has been a major factor in the continuing success of America in the past ninety years. Nobel Prize winner Dr. Albert Szent-Györgyi identified a key ingredient when he said, "Creativity is seeing what everyone else sees, but thinking what no one else thinks." This ability was at work in the businessperson who first looked at a pile of sawdust and thought, "This could be fuel if we compressed it into a fire log." The energy for technological advances comes from this kind of creativity combined with risk-taking enterprise.

Creativity is fostered in many ways. At McDonald's international headquarters in Oak Brook, Illinois, a think tank shaped like a flying saucer sits in the middle of the open-design offices. The think tank is open to all McDonald's employees. One section is an enclosed room containing a large circular waterbed and a stereo system. McDonald's executives claim many of their creative, award-winning commercials have been thought up in this environment.

Creativity has been responsible for at least five areas in which the United States has been expanding and developing as the world's leader in business. The areas are science and technology, information processing, the shift to marketing, the return to entrepreneurship, and the service revolution.

Science and Technology

Many of the scientific developments of the 1800s and early 1900s produced technologies that evolved into some of our largest industries and corporations. Henry Ford's Greenfield Village in Dearborn, Michigan, is a testimony to American scientific efforts in the past. This museum, alongside the Ford headquarters, includes the actual laboratories and factories used by Alexander Graham Bell, Thomas Edison, the Wright brothers, John and Horace Dodge, and other famous American inventors.

Automation is the substitution of machines for human labor.

In more recent times, Americans have taken a step beyond mechanization to add computers to machines. The computers have been able to eliminate much of the drudgery of handwork operations. The increasing use of computers with machines produces **automation,** which lets machines not only do the work but also control and check it. For example, automated robots have largely replaced humans in checking the quality of automobiles on the assembly line. As factories become automated, many labor costs are eliminated and there is a gain in efficiency, cost-effectiveness, and safe working conditions. Automation has also brought rapid changes in people's jobs. It can be painful when old jobs are lost,

HIGHLIGHT IN BUSINESS PRACTICE

Tips on Creativity

Creativity is key to the entrepreneurial spirit. Fortunately, the latest research shows that people can be taught to be more creative. Many companies are now eagerly applying techniques to foster creativity that are being taught by leading management consultants.

One such consultant is Roger Von Oech, who has provided his services to over 25,000 professionals, and has written a best-selling book called *A Whack on the Side of the Head.* Von Oech holds a Ph.D. from Stanford in the history of ideas, a degree that he proposed to the university and of which he is the sole recipient.

Von Oech has identified some common inhibitors of creativity, and how to overcome them. The following is some free advice, courtesy of Von Oech:

To Err Is Creative. "He who never made a mistake," said Samuel Smiles, "never made a discovery." What were the three biggest errors or failures you have had in the past three years? Look closer. What were the benefits? What did you discover? What new opportunities were created by your mistakes?

Ask "What If." Set aside time each day to ask "what if" questions. What if animals became more intelligent than people? What if highway blacktop came in "bluetop" or "redtop" depending on the speed limit? What if men had babies? Such questions will stretch your imagination and lead to new ideas.

Look for Lots of Ideas. "The best way to get a good idea," recommends chemist Linus Pauling, "is to get lots of ideas." The next time you have a problem, don't stop with the first acceptable answer: How do you keep a fish from smelling? Cook it when you catch it. Throw it back. Keep a cat nearby. Burn incense. Cut its nose off.

Break the Rules. Napoleon broke the rules on the proper way to conduct a military campaign. Beethoven broke the rules on how a symphony should be written. Most advances in science, art, cooking, design, and medicine have come when someone challenged the rules and tried another approach. What rules can you break?

and it may take time to create new ones or to retrain people to fit the new technology of an automated factory.

Since World War II, the United States has introduced atomic energy, plastics, electronics, and thousands of other inventions for use by the modern consumer. Science and technology continue to advance through the 1990s; approximately 60 percent of the products on the market today were not available ten years ago. American industry also faces an increasing challenge from the creative energy of foreign competitors. Research and development teams in Japan and Europe, backed by government support, have developed basic inventions and industrial applications at a rate that will challenge American supremacy.

America has often benefited from foreign competition, as in the 1950s, when we were challenged by the Soviet Union's entry into space with Sputnik. In order

The increasing use of computers with machines produces automation, which lets machines not only do the work but also control and check it. Here, an automated robot has been programmed to laser-trim an auto dashboard while simultaneously monitoring the quality.

to compete, the United States started a new billion dollar space industry, which put the first man on the moon, in 1969. By the early 1990s, Americans will be shuttled into space for prolonged periods of time for work and, in the future, perhaps even for recreation. As a result of new space exploration, newer technology and business will be required—all creating new jobs. As with space technology, American research teams will increasingly be forced to combine resources to develop competitive technology for the twenty-first century.

Information-Processing Explosion

In all major industries, automated production increasingly has shifted input away from physical labor and materials and toward information and knowledge. Since the development of the first computer (in 1939, by George Stibitz of Bell Telephone Laboratories), computers and data processing have turned the business world inside out. Computers are used to plot target ranges in tanks, make hotel and airline reservations, edit text, and measure gasoline and drinks. They also have hundreds of other sophisticated uses that make our lives more enjoyable. An increasing number of individuals use computers to keep financial records and play games.

Computers are also used for a variety of business applications. For example, computers electronically keep track of a firm's expenses, revenues, equipment, and inventory. Computers assist sales managers in tracking sales and in forecasting potential sales. In addition, they may be used to keep payroll records, or to produce elaborate reports using desktop publishing.

Shift from a Production Era to a Marketing Era

In 1913, Henry Ford, with his mass-produced, low-cost Model T automobile and his $5-a-day minimum wage for workers, provided the catalyst for the most drastic change in America's economic history. However, at General Motors, the innovative Alfred P. Sloan competed successfully with the seemingly impregnable Model T by introducing yearly model changes, a variety of colors, installment credit, and modern marketing techniques. GM, along with other marketing pioneers, such as General Electric, emphasized satisfying consumers' needs and wants. This effort, called the *marketing concept,* created many new jobs.

HIGHLIGHT IN BUSINESS PRACTICE

Genentech: Entrepreneurial Excellence Right from the Start

In 1975, Robert A. Swanson and Herbert W. Boyd each invested $500 seed money in a genetic engineering business venture they named Genentech. Just fifteen years later, Genentech realized sales of $230 million. Today, Genentech is the fourth largest pharmaceutical company in the United States and is running full steam ahead toward a projected $1 billion in sales for 1990. Its story is an impressive example of successful entrepreneurial risk-taking.

Of the thirty drugs produced in the United States that generate sales of over $100 million, Genentech has produced three, all through genetic engineering. The firm first produced a genetically engineered human protein, a gene-spliced version of a brain hormone called somotostatin; this was developed under Boyd's direction at three separate laboratories in California, as the company had not generated the capital necessary to set up its own laboratory.

Only one year after marketing this major breakthrough, Swanson and nine scientists were able to set up shop in a warehouse, and there they created Genentech's second success, a clone of a human growth hormone called protropin. Eli Lilly now holds the license for this important drug. Protropin enabled Genentech to realize its first profits.

Continued on next page

HIGHLIGHT IN BUSINESS PRACTICE

Genentech: Entrepreneurial Excellence Right from the Start *(Continued)*

Most recently, Genentech engineered its third success: a drug called t-Pa, which Genentech marketed under the name Activase. The drug can dissolve blood clots that cause heart attacks, and as such is a long-awaited weapon in the battle against heart disease, the number one killer in the industrialized world.

In 1987, Genentech's profits totaled $42 million, much of which it earned on t-Pa. A dose of the drug initially cost $2200, from which the company earned a gross profit of about $1800. As supply was low and demand high, Genentech could charge high prices for t-Pa because it was the only firm manufacturing it.

As Genentech's earnings grew, the company's work force expanded to 2000. Using a "junior" stock program set up early in the company's growth, many of these 2000 employees were able to purchase stock at the heavily discounted price of $35 per share. The stock quickly rose to $72 per share, making millionaires of many employees. Presently twenty-five percent of Genentech's stock is owned by employees.

Genentech's success has spawned a new industry—biotechnology—and thousands of other jobs.

Swanson and Boyd took full advantage of the private enterprise system to build a successful and profitable venture. Drug research and experimentation are very expensive and involve an enormous amount of risk-taking; if, after spending billions on the development of a drug, the FDA denies the company approval of the drug, all of the money spent on its development is lost. The risk-taking, creativity, initiative, and business acumen of the people at Genentech have made it the world's foremost research organization in commercial biotechnology.

Return to the Entrepreneurial Spirit

Creativity has also spawned the ideas for many small businesses. A recent trend in our economy is a return to the entrepreneurial spirit of the nineteenth century. More and more Americans are starting their own businesses. The number of self-employed Americans has increased 50 percent since 1970—this despite all the hard work required, the problems encountered, and the realization that over 60 percent of all new businesses will fail within five years. In 1986, over 700,000 new corporations and countless other small businesses were started, 30 percent of them by women and minorities. This is nearly twice the number in 1975.

Most entrepreneurs are driven by the freedom to be their own boss and the incentive of earning a profit. Others are motivated by the opportunity for achievement and the challenge of successfully running a company. While most entrepreneurs are sole proprietors, more and more companies are being founded by

entrepreneurial teams. These teams are groups of experienced business managers and professionals who join together to create new companies. Some of the best teams are composed of individuals with different backgrounds (engineering, finance, marketing, management, law) and areas of expertise.

Entrepreneurial teams are groups of experienced business managers and professionals who join together to create new companies.

The creative entrepreneurial spirit hasn't gone unnoticed by larger corporations. Realizing that money is not always the key motivator for entrepreneurs, many companies have explored the concept of **skunkworks**—entrepreneurial units operating within a company. The term, which originated in the L'il Abner comic strip, was first given this meaning by Lockheed California Company when it formed a special entrepreneurial team to create a new aircraft. The creative and motivated team produced a workable aircraft in 143 days.

Skunkworks are entrepreneurial units operating within a company.

Entrepreneurial teams and skunkworks have been used several times by Apple Computer. The company was founded by the entrepreneurial team of Stephen Jobs, Steve Wozniak, and Mike Markkula. Later a skunkworks environment was used by Jobs to create the Macintosh computer. From then on, Apple was committed to broadening the team approach to include **intrapreneurship**—giving individuals with entrepreneurial skills a chance to create and produce new products in a variety of in-company settings. Using this concept, the company gains new human, financial, and physical resources to accomplish its mission. Apple allowed intrapreneur William Campbell to create Claris, a software branch of the company whose mission was to produce software for the Macintosh. Apple gave Claris millions of dollars in seed money, a staff of experienced managers, and eighty-five programmers.[8] The division introduced its first product, an engineering drawing program, in late 1988.

Intrapreneurship is the concept of allowing those with entrepreneurial skills to operate separate units within companies for the purpose of producing innovative new products.

Service Revolution

One area in which creativity and entrepreneurship have thrived is the service industries, the current driving force of our economy. From services, value is created not through goods but through intangible tasks. Services have generated 25 million new jobs since 1970, and this boom is expected to add 21 million more new jobs by the year 2000. However, we have a complex, interrelated economy. Services, high-tech industry, basic manufacturing, and agriculture all depend on and enhance one another. Much of the service sector's output supports the production of goods. For example, financial institutions provide the capital necessary for industrial expansion. Furthermore, many high-tech manufacturers derive 30 to 60 percent of their revenues from service activities. Service industries generate over 25 percent of American merchandise exports.

The Coalition of Service Industries has this to say about services:

> Far from diminishing the vitality of the goods-producing sector, the dynamic growth of service supports and enhances it. Information processing, telecommunications, marketing, finance, and other services offer manufacturing and agriculture the economies of scale and greater efficiencies that come from specialized division of labor. The inseparable link between services and the rest of our economy means that new developments and innovations everywhere can raise productivity, lower costs, and increase U.S. competitiveness in all economic areas.[9]

Nearly one-third of Americans who start their own businesses are women and minorities. Marsha Broderick started her own all-female "Pink Lady" Construction Company in Northridge, California.

BUSINESS PRACTICE EXAMPLE Continues

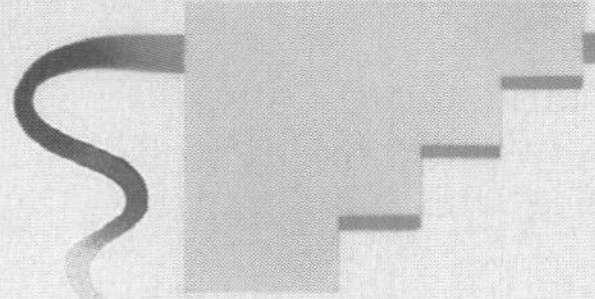

In October of 1988, Turner Broadcasting System launched its fourth network, Turner Network Television (TNT). TNT represents Ted Turner's most direct attempt to compete with the "Big Three" networks, and with media magnate Rupert Murdoch's Fox network. According to Forbes Magazine, "TNT may well become cable's answer to the broadcast networks." Designed to become basic cable's star channel, plans call for TNT to air classic films from Turner's enormous film library, major sporting events, exclusive children's programs and made-for-TNT movies and miniseries. Turner ultimately hopes to provide more hours of original programming than the "Big Three" networks. And he claims he'll take the high road in terms of programming content.

The widely criticized purchase of the expensive MGM film library is now proving to be a boon to Turner, who has been able to garner large revenues from domestic and foreign syndication rights. Just as important, the film library is providing programming for TNT. And the fact that Turner had to sell part of his company to 31 cable system operators to pay for the MGM purchase is also proving to be positive. TNT was launched with 17 million subscribers in place, thanks in part to his new board members.

Is Ted Turner going to slow down at all now that he's over 50? Perhaps. "I was an entrepreneur for a good number of years, and I enjoyed it immensely," Turner said in 1988. But, he said, "I don't have to take risks any more. When we were small, I had to take risks, move fast and scratch and fight. . . . I think we can grow now with safety."

Issues for Discussion

1. Discuss how Ted Turner turned adversity into opportunity in establishing the first "superstation" in 1976.
2. Describe five ways that Ted Turner has used the profits generated from his networks.
3. How can the "Big Three" networks—ABC, NBC, and CBS—expand their viewer base and remain competitive in the face of the cable networks?
4. Describe some opportunities for young entrepreneurs in the cable industry today.

SUMMARY

The U.S. economy is made up of three types of economic activities: agriculture and mining (extraction), manufacturing, and services. These activities are what American business is all about.

Businesses are organizations created to earn a profit. They also exist to serve the public. Without the incentive of profits, there would be few entrepreneurs. Of course, profits have a number of other uses as well—for example, they are spent on reinvestment, taxes, charitable contributions, pension funds, and dividends.

For the economy as a whole, profits ensure expansion. The profits used by one company can have a multiplier effect on the economy. Also, the desire to make a profit encourages the efficient use of human and natural resources. An economy's success can be measured by people's standard of living, which itself is measured by real income and per capita gross national product.

Next to profits in its effect on the economy is competition. Our economy encompasses four types of competition: pure competition (so many small businesses in an industry that no single one can influence the price of most products), monopolistic competition (industries in which nonprice factors differentiate products, so each business has some power over prices), oligopoly (industries with few competitors and considerable control over prices), and monopoly (a market in which there is no competition).

The United States enjoys a free-market system, a form of economic voting. Supply and demand are its regulators.

The modern American economy has its roots in the passions for personal profit and religious freedom. The British who started the early colonies were influenced by mercantilism—colonizing new territories and exploiting their natural resources. In 1776, however, Adam Smith, in his *Wealth of Nations,* argued for what he termed the invisible hand (of competition)—the free-market system.

After gaining independence, the United States centered its economy in cottage industries. However, in 1789, a British mechanic brought to America the plans for a water-powered spinning machine, which led to America's Industrial Revolution. This revolution made possible the accumulation of vast amounts of wealth by early tycoons.

In the twentieth century, creativity has been a major factor in the success of the American economy. Five areas in which creativity has helped us expand and develop are science and technology (including automation), information processing (particularly the development of computers), the shift to marketing (with its emphasis on satisfying consumers' wants and needs), the return to entrepreneurship (including an increase in the number of small businesses as well as intrapreneurship in larger companies), and the service revolution (the dynamic growth of services in today's economy).

KEY TERMS

Automation p. 20
Business p. 8
Capital p. 12
Cottage industries p. 19
Creativity p. 20
Demand p. 17
Entrepreneurial teams p. 25
Entrepreneurs p. 10
Free-market concept p. 17
Gross national product (GNP) p. 15
Industrial Revolution p. 19
Intrapreneurship p. 25
Laissez faire p. 19
Mercantilism p. 19
Monopolistic competition p. 17
Monopoly p. 17
Multiplier effect p. 12
Oligopoly p. 17
Profit p. 8
Pure competition p. 17
Real income p. 14
Skunkworks p. 25
Standard of living p. 14
Supply p. 17

CHECK YOUR LEARNING

Reread the following learning objectives. Each objective is followed by a few questions. Answering these questions accurately will help you retain the most important concepts discussed in this chapter. After answering each question, check your answer with the key at the end of this chapter. (*Hint:* If you have doubt regarding the correct response, consult the page whose number follows the answer.)

Circle:

A. Explain the importance of business to the American economy and distinguish among the three major types of economic activities.

T F 1. Business is the sum total of all economic activity.

T F 2. The core of our economic system is business, which makes our country thrive.

a b c d 3. Which of the following businesses is involved primarily in service: (a) Amax Coal Company; (b) Ford Motor Company; (c) Macy's Department Store; (d) Indiana Farm Co-op.

B. Explain the major purpose of business and the interrelationship of its two major objectives.

T F 1. The major purpose of business is to make a profit.

T F 2. Profits are affected by the degree of satisfactory service provided by a business.

C. List the five major uses of profits.

a b c d 1. Profits are used for all of the following except: (a) taxes; (b) salaries; (c) reinvestment; (d) stockholder dividends.

D. Discuss the role of profits in our economy.

a b c d 1. The profit motive provides: (a) jobs; (b) highest standard of living; (c) less waste; (d) all of the above.

T F 2. Profits are necessary for our economy to survive.

a b c d e 3. The automobile and steel industries are examples of what type of competition: (a) monopoly; (b) pure competition; (c) oligopoly; (d) monopolistic competition; (e) none of the above.

E. Compare and contrast mercantilism with Adam Smith's philosophy of free trade.

a b c d 1. Adam Smith believed in: (a) laissez faire; (b) negative income tax; (c) invisible hand; (d) a and c.

T F 2. Mercantilism included the common European practice of taking raw materials from the colonies and forcing the colonies to buy them back as finished products.

F. Discuss the business and economic highlights of early American history.

T F 1. Eli Whitney brought the Industrial Revolution to America in 1789.

T F 2. Alfred Sloan of GM was one of the first executives to introduce the marketing concept.

G. Explain the importance of creativity and discuss why it is often the key ingredient in a successful business.

T F 1. Creativity is characterized by curiosity and an open mind.

a b c d 2. All of the following are factors centered around creativity that have helped make America great in the twentieth century, except: (a) demographics; (b) science; (c) service revolution; (d) entrepreneurial spirit.

QUESTIONS FOR REVIEW AND DISCUSSION

1. Define the key terms listed at the end of this chapter.
2. What do you think Calvin Coolidge meant when he said that "the chief business of the American people is business"?
3. Name and define the four types of economic activities. Make a list of five businesses in your home or college community that are involved primarily in each one of these activities (for a total of twenty businesses).
4. Think of a business you used to patronize that went bankrupt or of a product that is no longer being made. Why do you think the business went bankrupt or the product is no longer being made?
5. Take various quarterly reports from corporations discussed in the chapter and graph their profit or loss for a two-year period. Do these graphs give you a clearer picture of whether these businesses are truly earning a fair profit? Explain. How have these companies fared since 1987?
6. Why do many people think that profit is a dirty word? Ask four people what they think is the average profit earned by corporations (after taxes). Ask them what they believe is a fair profit. How do their answers compare with the national average profit of 5 percent?
7. Evaluate this statement by Nobel Prize winner Albert Szent-Györgyi: "Creativity is seeing what everyone else sees, but thinking what no one else thinks." Can you think of some products on the market that illustrate the statement?
8. Ask three local entrepreneurs how they came up with the ideas for their businesses. Write a report on your findings.

CONCLUDING CASE

The Invisible Hand versus the 1987 Crash

October 19, 1987, is a day a lot of people will never forget. On that day, the stock market dropped 508 points, or, as some people say, it crashed. The crash brought a wave of dire predictions. Among them was the prediction that our economy would sharply slow down and the good times would suddenly end. Fortunately these predictions have not come true.

Congress, however, reacted by calling for more regulation to prevent future crashes. This was a reversal of laissez-faire government policy during recent years. The laissez-faire philosophy was made popular by a group of economists from the University of Chicago. As *Business Week* explained (April 18, 1988, p. 65), "They converted a lot of economists and policymakers to their view that interventionist government policies, instead of being a balancing wheel, are themselves the source of economic instability. The competitive market is superior, they argued, because it seeks a comforting stability on its own by quickly balancing the needs of rational buyers and sellers."

After the crash, many economists revised their views. They now believe that the free-market model, built around a belief in individual rationality, market equilibrium, and pure competition, does not always work. They argue that investors and other market participants (especially those who trade stocks and bonds by computer) do not always act rationally, or on good information. Furthermore, they believe that there are some gaping holes in the free-market model.

Issues for Discussion

1. Do you believe there are "gaping holes" in the free-market model? Explain.
2. Discuss whether the crash was a market correction or a catastrophe.
3. Explain how the "invisible hand" either worked or didn't work during the crash.

NOTES

1. Stanley Ginsberg and Robert D. Hamrin, "Services: The New Economy," Coalition of Service Industries, 1986.
2. Irwin Ross, "What's a 'Healthy Profit'? *Reader's Digest,* November 1979, pp. 107–111.
3. Bro Uttal, "A Computer Jock's $550-Million Jackpot," *Fortune,* January 5, 1987, pp. 84–85.
4. William J. Baumol and Alan S. Blinder, *Economics: Principles and Policy* (New York: Harcourt Brace Jovanovich, 1979), p. 593.
5. "It Still Pays to Be a U.S. Wage Earner," *Business Week,* October 11, 1982, p. 16.
6. "Family Income Doubles, but Buying Power's Less," *Indianapolis News,* July 27, 1981, p. 31.
7. Adam Smith, *The Wealth of Nations* (1776; New York: Modern Library, Random House, 1937).
8. Richard Brandt, "Apple's Software Branch May Be Headed for a Fall," *Business Week,* August 15, 1988, p. 84.
9. Ginsberg and Hamrin, "Services."

CHECK YOUR LEARNING ANSWER KEY

A. 1. T, *p. 7*
2. T, *p. 7*
3. c, *p. 9*

B. 1. F, *p. 10*
2. T, *p. 10*

C. 1. b, *p. 11*

D. 1. d, *pp. 12–14*
2. T, *p. 11*
3. c, *p. 17*

E. 1. d, *p. 19*
2. T, *p. 19*

F. 1. F, *p. 19*
2. T, *p. 23*

G. 1. T, *p. 20*
2. a, *p. 20*

CHAPTER

2

THE FREE ENTERPRISE SYSTEM IN A GLOBAL ECONOMY

LEARNING OBJECTIVES

After reading this chapter you should be able to:

1. Explain how consumers, producers, and the government make our economic system work.
2. List the four factors of production and explain how they are essential to our economy.
3. Explain how the U.S. government promotes a balanced economy.
4. Describe the important characteristics of the private enterprise system.
5. Compare capitalism, socialism, and communism.
6. Discuss why the U.S. economic system is an integral part of the global economy.

OUTLINE

Business Practice Example: Hong Kong . . . Capitalism or Communism?

The Economy

Why the American Economy Works

- Consumers
  - The Demand Curve
  - The Supply Curve
  - The Equilibrium Price
- Producers
  - Factors of Production
  - Productivity
- The Roles of Government in the American Economy
- Promoting a Balanced Economy
  - Leading Economic Indicators
  - Monetary Policy
  - Fiscal Policy
  - Inflation
  - Employment

World Economic Systems

- The Private Enterprise System
  - Benefits of the Private Enterprise System
  - Some Criticisms of the Private Enterprise System
- Planned Economies in Socialist Systems
- Communist Planned Economic Systems
- Changes in Planned Economic Systems
- Mixed Economic Systems

The Global Economy

Summary

Key Terms

Check Your Learning

Review and Discussion

Concluding Case: Minimum-Wage Increase—A Small-Business Perspective

Notes

Check Your Learning Answer Key

Highlight in Business Practice: Armand Hammer—Entrepreneur for a Peaceful Future

Highlight in Business Practice: China's Rocky Road to Economic Reform

Highlight in Business Practice: Japan Wins Hearts in Tennessee

BUSINESS PRACTICE EXAMPLE

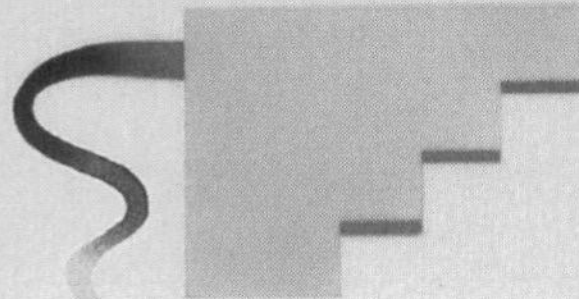

Hong Kong . . . Capitalism or Communism?

Hong Kong, a British colony located off the southern coast of China's Kwangtung Province, has been under British rule for over 150 years. The island was won in the first Opium War (1839–42), and was later expanded to include Kowloon and the New Territories, which are located on mainland China. In 1898 the Chinese formally leased the New Territories for 99 years to the British.

Probably no other country operates a more laissez-faire version of capitalism than Hong Kong. The city-nation of 5.5 million people has a market economy based on light industry and thriving international trade. The GNP has experienced steady growth, totaling $31.9 billion (U.S.). Hong Kong exports more than $19 billion in goods and is the 18th largest trading power. It is the third largest container port and financial center in the world. Over 800 U.S. companies employ 50,000 nonunion workers in industries such as textiles, electronics, toys, and chemicals. On July 1, 1997, however, the 99-year lease expires. All this commercial activity could change when the British colony once again becomes part of communist China.

Despite a 1984 Chinese-British agreement designed to allow the private enterprise climate of Hong Kong to continue for another 50 years, some are skeptical that this will occur. James McGregor, director of the Hong Kong Chamber of Commerce, has commented: "I don't believe that a communist country can successfully become responsible for a free enterprise trade territory and keep its hands off. It won't work." But others don't believe the Chinese will want to destroy the prosperity of Hong Kong. After all, a healthy Hong Kong brings China $7 billion in foreign trade annually, representing fully 40 percent of China's hard currency.

For China, it will be important to avoid cutting off the producers of so many golden eggs. The main drive toward prosperity has been the profit motive as an incentive to entrepreneurs. In the late 1980s the managers and risk-takers here began to react to the uncertain state of Hong Kong's future by emigrating in increasing numbers. Unless China can build confidence that a capitalist economy will continue, it may lose the chance to benefit from the power of the economic engine in its front yard.

WHAT'S AHEAD

Unlike the citizens of Hong Kong, you probably won't need to choose another country in which to live. If you did have to make a choice, however, you would want to examine each country's economic system. Then you would realize how complex each economic system is. As you will

see in this chapter, no economic system is perfect, and each has advantages and disadvantages. The American economic system of private enterprise and capitalism is believed by many people to be the best. This is evidenced by the thousands of immigrants who choose to come to the United States each year.

THE ECONOMY

This chapter examines how the world's economic systems allocate scarce resources in the production and distribution of goods and services for consumption. The study of this field is known as **economics.** Economics has traditionally been divided into two fields: macroeconomics and microeconomics.

Macroeconomics is the study of the behavior of entire economies, no matter how small. At this level, economists are interested in how an economic system develops patterns of price levels, rates of unemployment, and rates of inflation. Each of these elements will be discussed later in the chapter.

The study of the behavior of organizations or individuals in the economy is called **microeconomics.** Economists, marketers, and consumers find information related to the decision making of these units to be invaluable. Especially relevant is information related to the prices of goods and services in the marketplace. Producers like to predict how much of a product consumers will buy and at what price. Then they try to supply an amount equal to demand at that price. As chapter 1 showed, it is this interaction of supply and demand that determines the prices people pay for products in a free-market system. Supply and demand will be further discussed later in the chapter.

Economics is the study of how economic systems allocate scarce resources in the production and distribution of goods and services for consumption.

Macroeconomics is the study of the behavior of entire economies.

Microeconomics is the study of the behavior of organizations or individuals.

WHY THE AMERICAN ECONOMY WORKS

As we saw in chapter 1, the American economy operates as a free-market system. It gives each of us the power to make many economic decisions. Key economic decisions are made by three groups: consumers, producers, and the government. Although you may think of yourself as a consumer only, most people are part of all three groups. This section will explore in detail the roles of consumers, producers, and governments and will show how everyone is involved in each of these roles.

Consumers

Almost two-thirds of the total U.S. economic output consists of goods and services bought by individuals and households for personal use. These individuals are called **consumers.** The remaining one-third is bought by businesses and governments. Thus, it is easy to see why ours is a consumer economy.

Consumers are the ultimate users of products.

Each of us has an economic vote. We exercise this vote every day when we make decisions to buy or not to buy. These decisions directly affect the economy.

Our willingness and ability to spend money for certain goods and services constitutes the demand for those things. This demand is influenced by the prices and quality of goods and services. When the price of something rises, we might decide to buy less of it or to buy something else. If the price goes down, we might buy more. Our income also affects our demands. The more we earn, the more likely we are to choose expensive items or simply to purchase more. We purchase cheaper or fewer items when our income is decreased.

The Demand Curve

Businesses often ask the question: How many will we be able to sell? A precise answer can never be given. The answer depends on a series of quantities demanded, with each quantity corresponding to a different price. The quantity demanded also depends on a number of other variables. It may depend on the weather, the size of the market, consumer incomes, and even the price of substitute goods and services.

A ***demand curve*** illustrates graphically the relationship between price and quantity demanded at each price for a specific period of time.

A graphic representation of demand is shown in Figure 2.1. The **demand curve** in the figure shows the relationship between price and quantity demanded for video tapes sold during a specific time period. If a store offers a quality video tape but prices it high, say at $20, demand for it will probably be 0. At a lower price, say $15, a relatively small market of affluent buyers will emerge, and 8 tapes will be sold. At a relatively low price, say $4, the market will become considerably larger, and 45 units will be sold. Used in this way, the curve can, in theory,

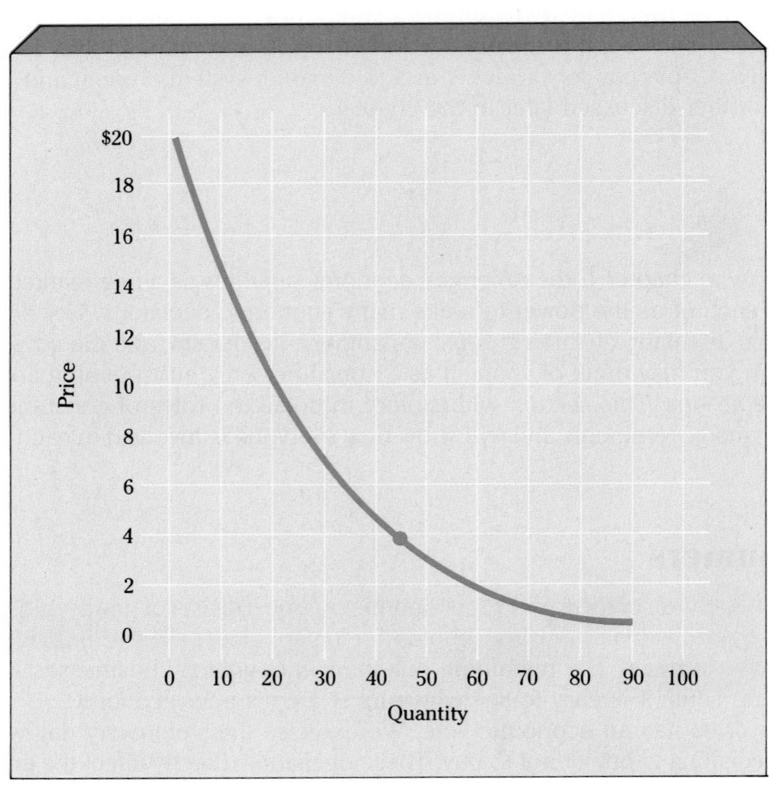

Figure 2.1
Demand curve for video tape. The demand curve shows the relationship between price and quantity demanded. If video tapes are priced at $4 each, then 45 units can be sold.

determine the number of these video tapes demanded at any price during a specific period of time.

The Supply Curve

A related question asked by businesses is: How many do we want to produce? Again, the answer is not a single number. It depends on a series of prices, each related to a different quantity sold.

The **supply curve** of a company or industry illustrates graphically the quantities of a good or service that will be offered for sale during a specific period of time at each of the prices prevailing during that period. Like the amount demanded, the amount supplied might vary on the basis of such factors as taxes, weather, and technology. Products priced too low, however, do not allow the seller to recover costs or to earn a profit. Therefore, at very low prices, no products will be produced. In Figure 2.2, at the price of $3, it will pay to produce some video tapes. The higher the price, the more tapes will be produced.

A ***supply curve*** illustrates graphically the quantities of a product that will be offered at each price for a specific period of time.

The Equilibrium Price

Figure 2.3 offers a clear picture of the relationship of suppliers and demanders. Figures 2.1 and 2.2 revealed that price is the most important factor in determining

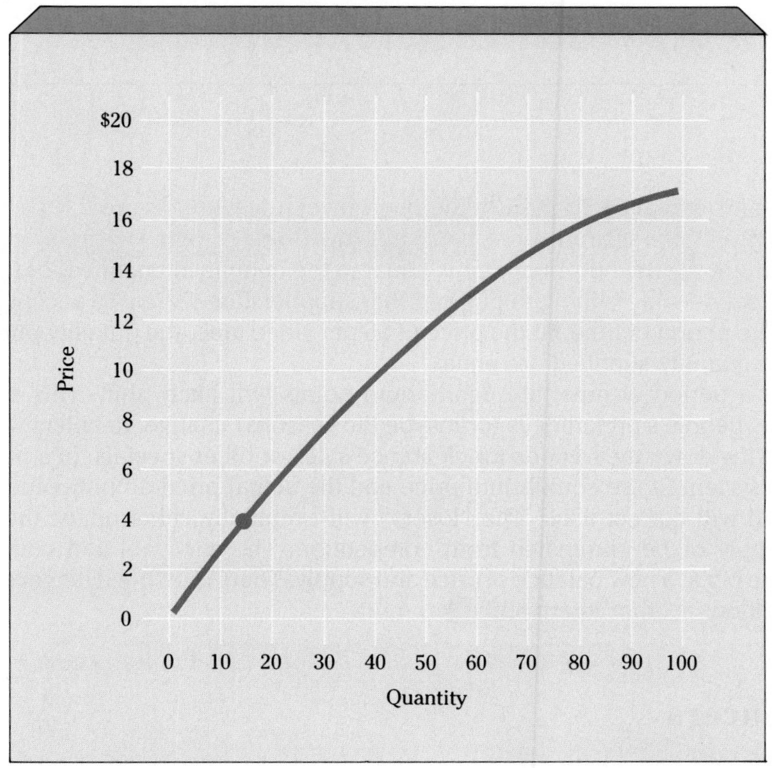

Figure 2.2
Supply curve for video tape.

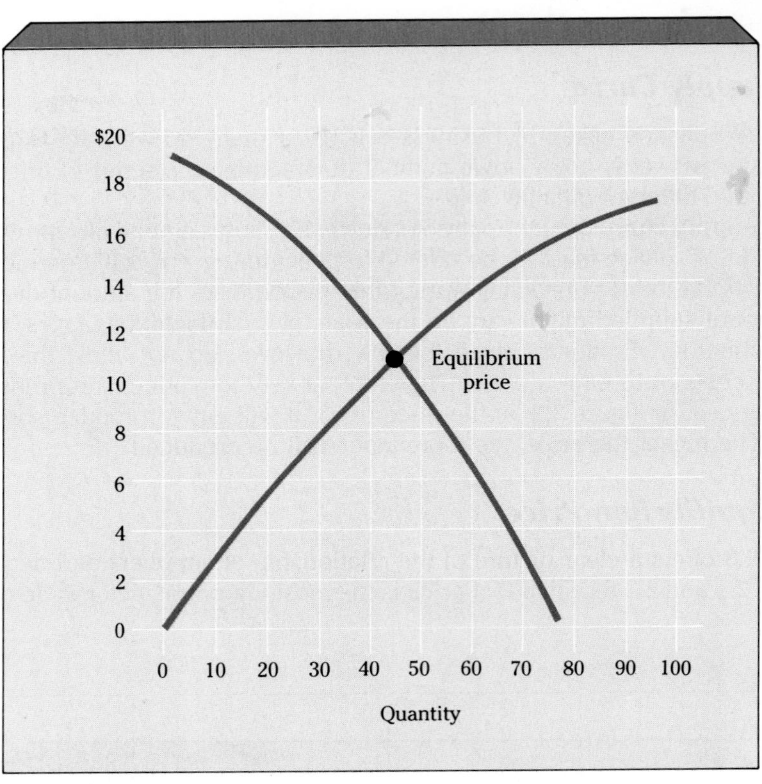

Figure 2.3
Equilibrium price for video tape.

The ***equilibrium price*** is the price at which the quantity supplied during a specific time period is equal to the quantity demanded during that period.

supply and demand. By putting the two curves together, Figure 2.3 shows that the point of intersection represents the **equilibrium price.** This price is the point where the quantity supplied is equal to the quantity demanded, or the price that demanders are willing to pay and that suppliers are willing to accept, during a specific period of time. At the price of $6 per video tape, the quantity purchased and the quantity supplied are equal.

Over a period of time, the equilibrium points will likely shift. This shift will occur as people's preferences (or maybe the seasons) change. Retailers will react by marking down their goods for clearance sales or other specials. In a pure free-market system, if the equilibrium price and the actual price do not coincide, the situation will correct itself. The "losers" will eventually either adjust their price and supply or be eliminated from competition. The survivors will continue to compete but at a new balance of price and supply. There is no need for government intervention or other interference.

Producers

The people who work by themselves or in groups to provide goods and services are *producers.* They include workers, managers, investors, and entrepreneurs.

Factors of Production

For the goods and services to be produced, four *factors of production* must be present: land, labor, capital, and entrepreneurs.

Land, which is one of America's most valuable resources, includes property and its natural resources—for example, factories and the places to locate them. The economic reward for the use of land is rent.

Labor is both workers and managers—about 119 million people in the United States. The labor supply grew rapidly in the late 1970s and 1980s, as more and more women and teenagers entered the work force. (See Figure 2.4.) A well-trained labor force is essential to the creation of goods and services. The economic reward for labor is wages.

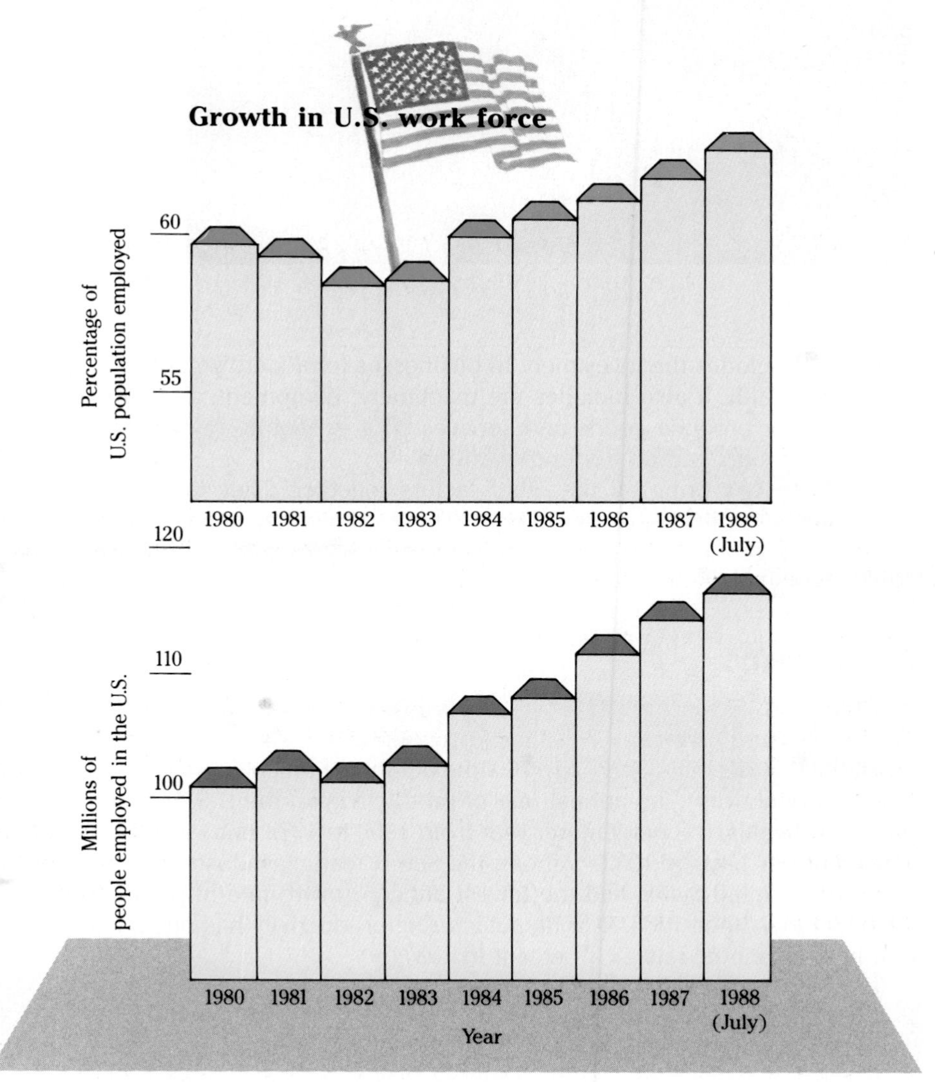

Figure 2.4
Growth in U.S. work force.

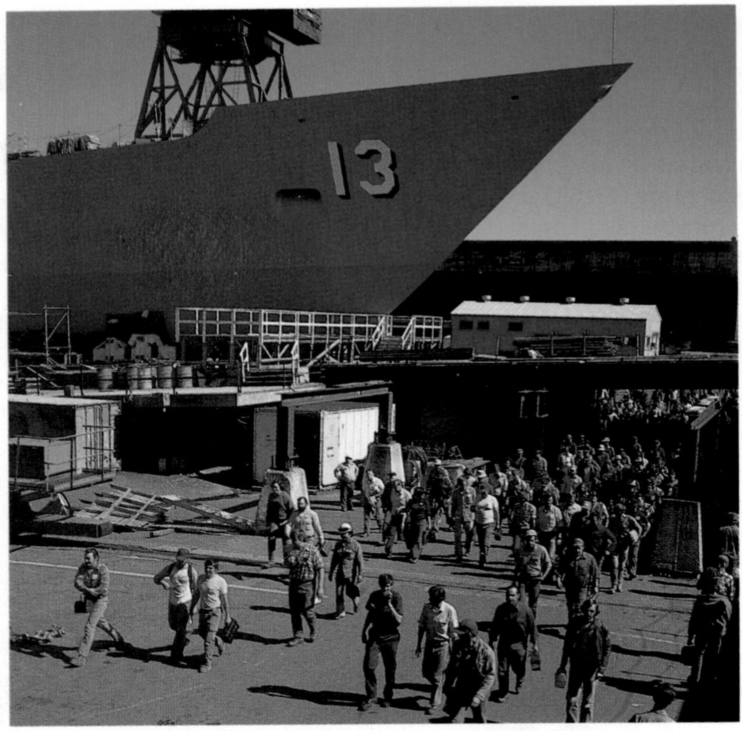

These shipyard workers and the shipyard where they work comprise two of the four factors needed to produce goods and services: labor and land.

Capital includes the investment in businesses to modernize and expand them to create wealth. It also includes the machinery, equipment, and supplies used to help labor produce goods and services. The economic reward for capital is interest or profits earned from production.

Entrepreneurs bring all the other factors together. They take the risks and assemble the capital to start businesses. They may actively manage the businesses or hire managers to take over this responsibility. The economic reward for entrepreneurs is profits.

Productivity

Productivity is the measure of output of products and services in relation to the input of capital, raw materials, land, and labor.

An important part of the U.S. economy is **productivity**—the measure of output of products and services in relation to the input of capital, raw materials, land, and labor (all factors of production). More output per unit of input gives a favorable rate of productivity. The annual rate of productivity in the U.S. private economy grew at a healthy 1.8 percent per year from 1950 to 1972 but sagged to less than 1 percent per year by 1982.[1] Among the seven leading industrial nations of the world, the United States had the lowest annual growth rate in productivity from 1970 to 1985. Since 1985, U.S. manufacturing productivity has once again grown at a healthy annual rate (3.3 percent in 1987).

The historically higher productivity growth rate in the United States was a key to the increases in the U.S. standard of living up to the 1970s. At the 1.8 percent growth rate, the standard of living doubled about every generation. In the 1980s, however, it stayed about the same, instead of growing. Increasing productivity is the only way to raise a nation's real income.

The rise and fall of productivity rates in any economy is affected by how much productive effort goes into manufacturing and how much into services. Manufacturing makes intensive use of land resources and of capital—the money and machinery that goes into production. As manufacturing activity grows, capital is reinvested in new, more efficient machinery and technologies, which produce more and more output for each hour of productive time. By stepping up its manufacturing efficiency, Japan has experienced the world's highest growth in the rate of productivity.

The production of services makes much more intensive use of labor than of machinery. To gain in productivity, a worker must produce more per hour this year than last year. Each $1 per hour raise for the worker must produce more than $1 in valuable services. Hard work and entrepreneurship help labor become more efficient. But increasing productivity in services is much more complex than it is in manufacturing. Thus the United States—a predominantly service economy—has not gained as much in productivity as Japan, which is primarily a manufacturing economy. As the U.S. economy grows and wages increase, productivity problems may continue to haunt us.

BUSINESS PRACTICE EXAMPLE Continues

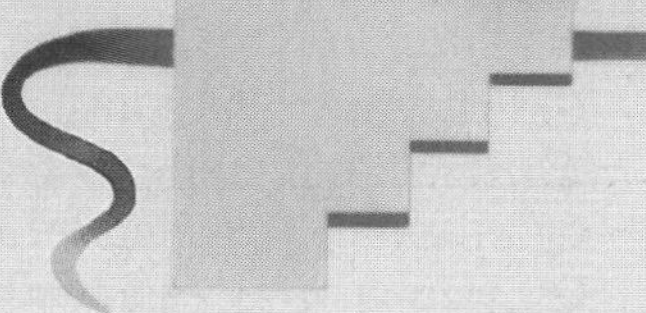

The uncertain future of the free-market economy in Hong Kong created a great uneasiness in the city's most important asset—the entrepreneurs who make the system work. In the late 1980s, the middle managers and civil servants began to look elsewhere for a future with more reliable opportunity. In 1987, three percent of the middle managers left the colony, double the rate in 1986. Since nearly three-quarters of these people were college-educated, this amounted to a serious brain drain for the city. Today the trend continues, with thousands of middle-class Hong Kong residents fleeing to Australia, Canada, and the U.S. (The threat of a harsh mainland Chinese government imposing itself on Hong Kong has only added fuel to this exodus.) Estimates reveal that as many as 150,000 residents may be leaving annually. As local businesses outbid one another to replace lost workers, wages and costs go up and Hong Kong producers lose some of their competitive advantage. Unless this trend can be reversed, the colony could lose the labor, capital, and entrepreneurship that make up its greatest resources.

HIGHLIGHT IN BUSINESS PRACTICE

Armand Hammer—Entrepreneur for a Peaceful Future

Few people in history have come closer than Dr. Armand Hammer to bridging the gap between capitalism and communism. Dr. Hammer was the first American to facilitate trade with Communist Russia, starting just after the Russian Revolution in 1921 and continuing on to the present.

At 90-plus years, Hammer serves as CEO of Occidental Petroleum, the eighth largest oil company in the United States. He has also served as a "freelance diplomat" for many decades. He was the only Western businessman invited by the Soviets to Moscow during the 1988 Reagan-Gorbachev summit. His efforts to gain a pullout of Soviet troops from Afghanistan and to persuade Soviet leader Mikhail Gorbachev to recognize Israel, along with his enormously helpful hand in the Chernobyl nuclear accident, led to his nomination for the Nobel peace prize.

While he attended the Columbia University Medical School, Hammer joined his father's faltering pharmaceutical business. He managed both to make the company a success and to achieve excellence as a medical student. One of his first business coups was cornering the market on tincture of ginger, an alcoholic beverage that temporarily escaped Prohibition laws. He also correctly forecast that the price and demand for drugs would increase after World War I. At the same time as his competitors were laying off chemists and pharmacists, Hammer was adding both staff and outlets. He became a millionaire while still in school.

When he graduated, Hammer decided to please his father, a member of the communist Socialist Labor party, by traveling to Russia to help fight a typhoid epidemic. Armed with a WWI surplus field hospital, an ambulance, and the $2 million he made from the sale of his company, Hammer booked passage.

Hammer arrived in Russia at the time of the Great Famine of 1921. Everywhere he visited Russians were starving. On one tour, to Ekaterinburg, local officials took him first to the sick and dying, and then showed him stocks of platinum, emeralds, semiprecious stones, mineral products, and thousands of furs. Due to a blockage in Europe, Russia was unable to export these goods in exchange for food. Using his personal fortune, Hammer offered to trade a million bushels of U.S. wheat for furs and other goods. Such a deal needed the approval of Lenin, which Hammer received, along with an invitation to meet the communist leader. Lenin told Hammer that Russia had plenty of physicians. What the country really needed was foreign capital. He offered to make Hammer the first foreign concessionaire (in asbestos) in post civil-war Russia.

Since that first meeting with Lenin, Hammer has engineered countless deals between Russia and the United States. In the 1920s (Hammer lived in Russia until 1930), he was the exclusive agent for Ford, U.S. Rubber, Allis-Chambers, Parker Pen, Ingersoll-Rand, and Underwood Typewriter. In 1974, he struck a $20 billion bartering agreement involving fertilizer. His latest venture is a plan to build a $1.2 billion petrochemical plant.

In addition to his many arrangements with the Russians, in 1979 Hammer signed a deal with the Chinese to jointly develop the world's largest open pit coal mine. A pioneer in the global economy, Armand Hammer will certainly go down in history as one of the world's great entrepreneurs and ambassadors of goodwill.

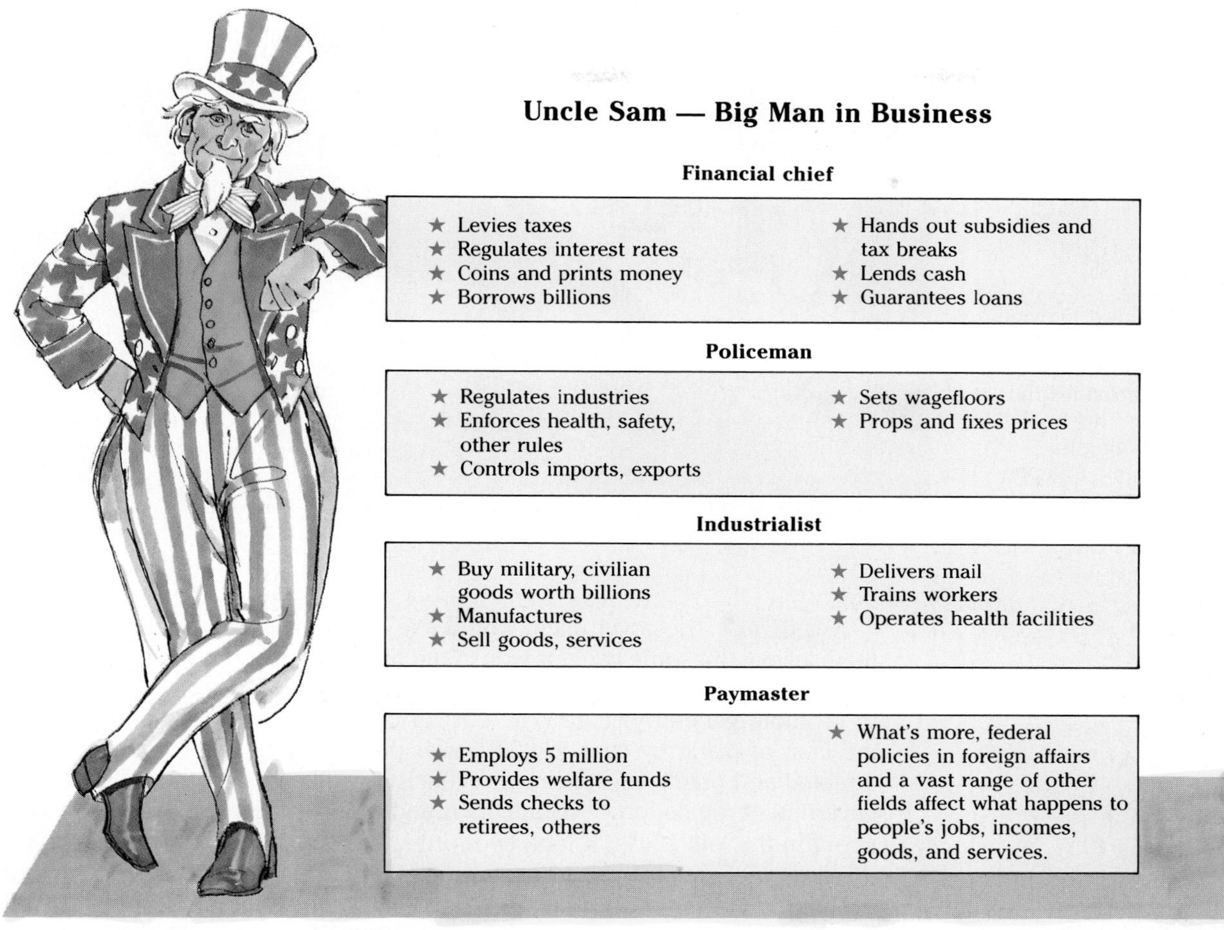

Uncle Sam — Big Man in Business
Financial chief
★ Levies taxes
★ Regulates interest rates
★ Coins and prints money
★ Borrows billions
★ Hands out subsidies and tax breaks
★ Lends cash
★ Guarantees loans
Policeman
★ Regulates industries
★ Enforces health, safety, other rules
★ Controls imports, exports
★ Sets wagefloors
★ Props and fixes prices
Industrialist
★ Buy military, civilian goods worth billions
★ Manufactures
★ Sell goods, services
★ Delivers mail
★ Trains workers
★ Operates health facilities
Paymaster
★ Employs 5 million
★ Provides welfare funds
★ Sends checks to retirees, others
★ What's more, federal policies in foreign affairs and a vast range of other fields affect what happens to people's jobs, incomes, goods, and services.

Figure 2.5 The roles of the U.S. government have grown considerably since the founding fathers first outlined them, in 1787.

The Roles of Government in the American Economy

The Preamble to the Constitution (1787) established very limited economic roles for American government. But as the United States grew, so did the roles of government. Today, government has five major roles: regulation, the promotion of growth and self-development, protection, competition, and support (see Figure 2.5).

Adam Smith believed individuals and businesses should be free to advance their interests as long as what they did advanced the welfare of the whole society. In the American private enterprise system, the government acts as an umpire, calling foul on the few who hurt the entire economy (society) for their personal gain.

Adam Smith believed individuals and businesses should be free to advance their interests as long as their activities did not harm society. This boat craftsman is pursuing his dreams of economic independence and artistic satisfaction.

Deregulation is the removal or softening of government regulation of industries.

Regulation. The government would like individuals and groups to regulate themselves. But some can't or won't, and these the government must regulate by using laws and agencies to protect public safety, health, and morals and to promote general welfare. The cost of complying with regulations boosts the cost of living by over $2,000 a year per family of four.[2] When properly directed and practiced, however, regulation can be of benefit to all. The first government regulation of competition and other commercial activities came about in the late 1800s. It took two forms: the regulation of industry and the enactment of statutes concerning competition. Regulated industries include securities, mining, public utilities, insurance, and others. However, in the early 1980s there was a trend toward **deregulation**—the removal or softening of government restraints affecting various industries. The aim of deregulation is to encourage competition and to reduce the cost of compliance. Deregulated industries include airlines, communications, railroads, and trucking. Despite this trend, regulation is still a major role of the government. There are 54 federal regulating agencies with 118,000 full-time employees. Later chapters will discuss regulatory statutes and the agencies required to enforce them.

Promotion. The second important role of government is promoting the growth and development of business. This role can be accomplished in a variety of ways. For example, the federal government provides millions of dollars in urban renewal funds to cities to redevelop their downtown business districts. The Small Business Administration provides direct, guaranteed loans to businesses and farmers. The Joint Training Partnership Act (JTPA) provides jobs and training for hundreds of thousands of Americans. The Army Corps of Engineers maintains American harbors. The Department of Defense provides national defense and promotes business by being a customer for many products. The Department of Transportation funds the interstate highways. The Federal Aviation Administration controls airport traffic. And the Department of Commerce encourages foreign trade.

Protection. Businesses are protected by various laws that guarantee exclusive ownership of inventions or written works, and there are federal agencies to enforce these laws. For example, the Federal Trade Commission places tariffs on foreign imports to protect and promote domestic producers.

Competition. The federal government serves as a competitor to businesses in certain industries. During the Great Depression, it established the Tennessee Valley Authority (TVA) to produce electrical power for certain parts of the rural South where businesses were unwilling to risk the investment. Today the federal government operates Amtrak, a nationwide passenger rail service. Amtrak was established by the Rail Passenger Act of 1970 after private railroads decided to discontinue passenger service. Amtrak competes most heavily with interstate buses. In addition, the U.S. Postal Service competes with such firms as United Parcel Service and Federal Express.

Support. The final role of government is to provide direct support to individuals who cannot meet their own minimum needs because of such special circumstances as retirement and lack of employment. The federal government provides such support in part through social security and veterans' programs. Most Americans accept the principle that an affluent society must do what it can to prevent hunger and misery, to provide retirement benefits, and to offer equality of opportunity. To accomplish these major goals, the federal government spent about $4,306 per person in 1988 (compared with $1,075 in 1976). These support-related expenditures account for the greatest portion of the federal budget. Figure 2.6 illustrates the cost of federal spending and its relationship to federal receipts.

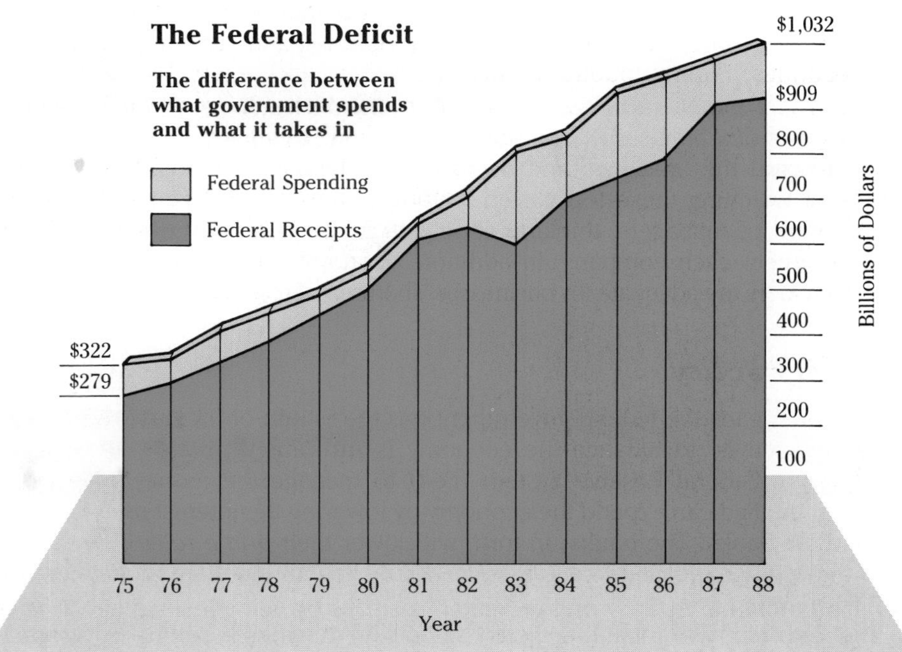

Figure 2.6
The federal government spends more dollars than it receives from taxes and other income. Congress has ordered this practice to end by 1991.

It takes many people and much money to ensure that government will fulfill its roles. Approximately one out of every six workers is employed by local, state, and federal governments. The annual cost of maintaining the federal government is $1 trillion (see Figure 2.6). This amount is financed by taxes and by borrowing, and many economists consider it highly inflationary. The federal government has operated at a deficit for thirty-two of the years between 1956 and 1990.

Promoting a Balanced Economy

The federal government is required by the Employment Act of 1946 "to promote maximum employment, production, and purchasing power" for the nation. Yet, in our economy, these things are not under government control. Our free-market system allows the forces of supply and demand a maximum chance to operate. It is these forces in the market that determine the levels of industrial production, financial stability, and employment. However, the government tries to promote the nation's economic well-being with limited action to encourage a balance among economic forces.

The first step in promoting economic balance is developing reliable information to monitor our roles as consumers, national and international spenders, producers, and employees. Using this information, legislators and officials negotiate specific policy actions to balance the economy—tax changes, trade agreements, banking regulations, and occasional government interventions in the market. Certain key aspects of the economy are of special national concern. They include leading economic indicators, monetary policy, fiscal policy, inflation, and employment.

Leading Economic Indicators

A common role of government is to develop accurate information about the levels of economic activity within the national system. The federal government measures levels of industrial production as well as employment and other activities. These measurements taken together are called *leading economic indicators.* The most famous set of indicators is the *Composite Index of Leading Indicators (CILI).* It is composed of a time series of economic data that, by their nature and content, tend to signal the upswings and downswings of economic behavior. A major benefit of watching these top eleven leading indicators (see Figure 2.7) is the organization of managers' thinking about the future course of events and how they will affect each company. In addition, economists generally maintain that most indicators are adequate for businesses' short-run analyses and policy making.

Monetary Policy

Monetary policy is the process used by the Federal Reserve System to manage the money supply.

One of the means the federal government has to restrain or increase the pace of economic activity to balance the economy is **monetary policy**—the process used by the Federal Reserve System (Fed) to manage the money supply. For example, the Fed can expand the economy by lowering the interest rates on loans it makes to banks. The banks, in turn, will lower their *prime rates* (the interest rates they charge their best customers), thereby generating more money for consumer spending.

The Fed can also alter the money supply by buying or selling government securities or changing reserve requirements (the amount of funds that banks belonging to the Federal Reserve System are required to keep with the Fed). (See

Components of the Composite Index of Leading Indicators

Average weekly hours of production or nonsupervisory workers, manufacturing (hours)

Average weekly initial claims for unemployment insurance, state programs (thousands—inverted scale)

Manufacturers' new orders in 1982 dollars, consumer goods and materials industries (billions of dollars)

Vendor performance, percent of companies receiving slower deliveries (percent)

Contracts and orders for plant and equipment in 1982 dollars (billions of dollars)

New private housing units authorized by local building permits (index: 1967 = 100)

Change in manufacturing and trade inventories on hand and on order in 1982 dollars, smoothed (annual rate, billions of dollars)

Change in sensitive materials prices, smoothed (percent)

Stock prices, 500 common stocks (index: 1941 – 43 = 10)

Money supply M2 in 1982 dollars (billions of dollars)

Change in business and consumer credit outstanding (annual rate, percent)

Figure 2.7
Key economic indicators assist in the prediction of economic trends.

chapter 16 for a more detailed discussion of our federal banking systems.) The Fed also controls the circulation of all coins and currency, plus accounts of individuals.

Fiscal Policy

The federal government generally allows the market economy to operate freely. At the same time, however, it exercises economic power through taxation and spending on government projects. A government's use of taxation and spending to help influence the economy according to a national economic plan is **fiscal policy.** These two tools can be used to create a desired influence on *aggregate demand* (the total amount that government, business, and consumers are willing to spend). A major exercise of fiscal policy was recommended by the economist John Maynard Keynes during the Great Depression of the 1930s. Keynes believed that government spending on public works projects, training for the jobless, and other related types of tax-based programs would stimulate the economy.

Fiscal policy is the government's use of spending or taxation to influence the economy according to a national economic plan.

In 1981, a new direction in fiscal policy was undertaken by the president and Congress. The new policy was guided by the ideas of *supply-side economics*—the view that government should concentrate on helping stimulate the nation's productive capacity. Legislation under this policy called for reduced taxes (as a way to stimulate spending and production), along with cuts in government spending and attempts to balance the federal budget. In the late 1980s, the government continued this policy—attempting to lower tax rates while broadening the tax base by allowing fewer loopholes and tax shelters. The result was a stimulated economy but insufficient tax revenues to cover continued government spending on social and military programs. By 1986, spending had exceeded income by $220 billion, creating a very large **federal deficit,** or debt.

The ***federal deficit*** is the negative difference between the government's revenues and spending.

In order to curb this debt and the continuing pattern of spending, Congress in 1986 passed the Gramm-Rudman Act, a law mandating a balanced federal budget by 1991. The law requires Congress to cut $50 billion from military and domestic spending. Targeted for possible elimination are Amtrak, the Appalachian Regional Commission, the Interstate Commerce Commission, and a host of other agencies, grants, and subsidies. Because of the political perils involved, progress toward the goal of a balanced budget will be slow. Few expect the target year of 1991 to be met.

However, by 1987, the annual federal deficit had been lowered to approximately $145 billion, and many members of Congress believed it could be lowered to $50 billion by 1995. That would be a reduction of debt from 5 percent of total national spending to less than 1 percent. If such a policy were carried out, government spending as a percentage of total national spending would fall from 24.5 percent to 22 percent by 1995. Programs to reduce federal deficits would aim to cut government borrowing, hold interest rates down, and minimize inflation.

Inflation

A sustained increase in an economy's overall level of prices is *inflation.* It creates a decline in the purchasing power of money. If the amount of money available in the economy is in excess of the available supply of goods and services, the result is **demand-pull inflation.** If the cost of labor, machinery, fuel, or other materials goes up rapidly, the economy may react with **cost-push inflation.** Either way, the result is a general rise in prices and a reduction in what we can purchase with our dollars. Although the inflation rate reached 18 percent in 1980, it was down to 4 percent by the late 1980s. (Figure 2.8 illustrates the effect of inflation on the cost of a college education.)

Demand-pull inflation is a decline in the purchasing power of money.

Cost-push inflation is inflation caused by increased production expenses.

Employment

Government policy also affects employment. When the economy is operating below its long-term potential, it can grow more rapidly than usual until it reaches what economists call **full employment**—the point where further declines in unemployment would unleash steep inflation. At the full employment level, any unemployment that occurs is called the *natural rate of unemployment,* or joblessness; it stems from seasonal layoffs and voluntary job changes rather than from recessions.

Full employment is the point where further declines in unemployment would unleash steep inflation.

Recession is officially defined as a decline in total national spending for two consecutive quarters. However, a better definition is "periods of decline in total output, income, employment, and trade usually lasting six months to a year and marked by widespread contradictions in many sectors of the economy."[3]

A ***recession*** is a decline in total national spending for two consecutive quarters.

A recession usually brings about national unemployment of approximately 8 percent, but many cities and states suffer a higher rate. For example, unemployment in many rural and urban areas is at depression levels of 17 percent or more. (A **depression** is an extended economic slump with very high unemployment.) Although at one time economists believed the low unemployment rate of the 1950s and 1960s (2 to 4 percent) was the natural rate, most experts consider 5 to 6 percent to be the nation's long-term underlying jobless rate.[4] Figure 2.9 illustrates the relationship of joblessness and **business cycles**—alternating periods of prosperity and recession.

A ***depression*** is an extended economic slump with very high unemployment.

Business cycles are alternating periods of prosperity and recession.

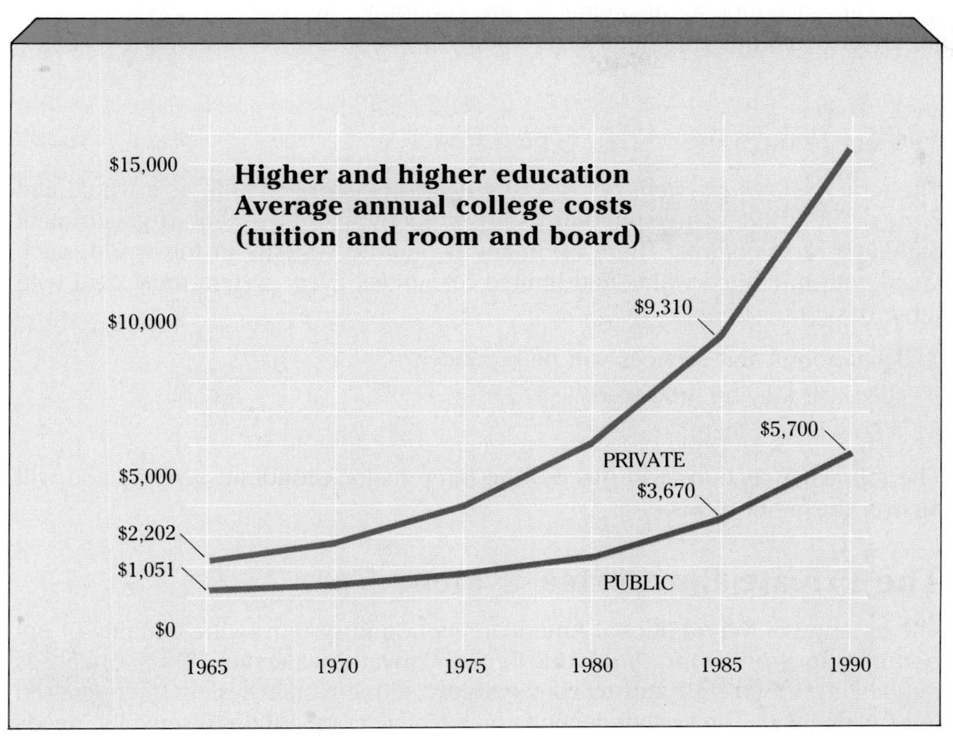

Figure 2.8 In 1990, yearly costs will average more than $5,700 at public colleges and almost $16,000 at private colleges.

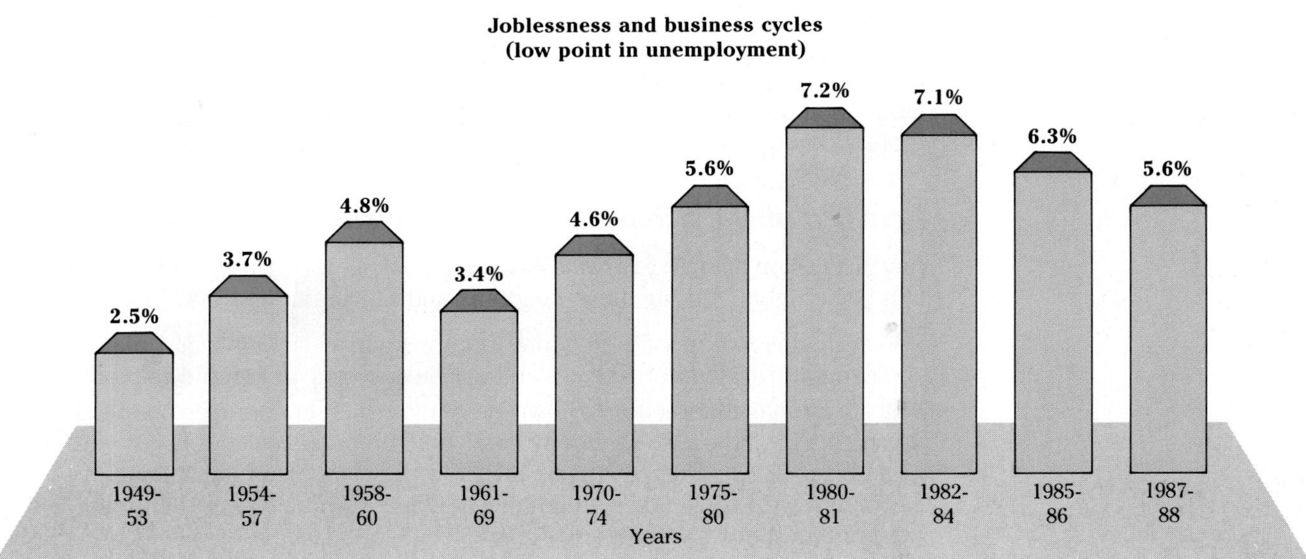

Figure 2.9 With each economic recovery in recent decades, the low point in unemployment has tended to be higher.

By now, no doubt, you've realized that balancing the economy is a complex task. The government can influence the economy, but federal policies must be timely or economic problems can multiply.

WORLD ECONOMIC SYSTEMS

The term *economic system* refers to the nature of economic life as a whole and particularly to the ownership and use of property and the extent of government regulation and control. There are many economic systems in the world, each faced with unlimited wants and limited resources. Every system must deal with three basic questions:

1. What goods and services will be produced?
2. How will they be produced?
3. Who will use them?

The following sections will discuss the three major economic systems and will answer these questions.

The Private Enterprise System

The *private enterprise system* is a free-market system.

Capitalism is the economic system in which the bulk of capital is owned by individuals and corporations.

The essence of the traditional American economic system is the equality of opportunity to profit from hard work through private ownership. This equality is provided by the **private enterprise system**—a free-market system often referred to as capitalism. The system depends on effective competition to serve the needs of society. It is modified only by laws and regulations.

In **capitalism,** the bulk of a nation's capital is privately owned by individuals and corporations rather than being owned by the government. Among the capitalist nations, besides the United States, are Hong Kong, Japan, Kenya, Singapore, South Korea, Switzerland, Taiwan, and West Germany. The citizens of these nations are often termed capitalists, because they use their capital to create more wealth. However, you do not have to be wealthy to be a capitalist. For example, people who put money into savings accounts or who own stock—regardless of how little—qualify as capitalists, because they are using their money (capital) to make more money. Both business owners and farmers are considered capitalists.

Benefits of the Private Enterprise System

Any discussion of the U.S. private enterprise system must revolve around freedoms and basic rights. Among these freedoms and rights are the following:

- Every individual has the freedom to choose an occupation and place of employment. This freedom creates enthusiasm for work and promotes productivity.
- Everyone has the freedom to own property, which encourages people to save, work hard, and use the property efficiently. Property is also a major part of the tax base. Towns that have a great deal of industry also have a large tax base, which lowers local taxes. In addition, people take better care of property they own than they do of property they rent.
- Competition is a basic right in the U.S. private enterprise system. It is regulated by the government to prevent unethical competition designed to eliminate businesses.

- Every American has the right to start or discontinue a business and to incur the risk for all capital owned or borrowed to start the business. The owner must have a business license, and the firm must operate within the legal limits of the law. For example, a plumber can start a business simply by securing enough capital and obtaining a business license. Most localities, however, would not issue a license to an entrepreneur who wanted to start a brothel, a gambling hall, or any other illegal operation.
- Businesspeople in the United States have the right to make their own decisions. There is no master plan for the economy. Therefore, every business is allowed to purchase what it wants, hire whomever it wishes, expand or contract at will, and make similar decisions.
- Goods and services in the United States are sold at a price based on supply and demand. Prices determined in a free market are a gauge for making future production plans.
- Americans have the right to bargain collectively. *Collective bargaining* helps labor obtain fair wages and reasonable working conditions, which in turn help increase purchasing power and standards of living.
- Americans are free to influence taxation. Traditionally, Americans have protested taxes in one form or another. In 1986, the Tax Reform Act was passed to provide a new system of taxation. This U.S. example established a standard for a worldwide reduction in taxes.

Some Criticisms of the Private Enterprise System

Critics of the private enterprise system bring a variety of charges against the system. A summary of the charges follows:

- Capitalism perpetuates grave inequities of wealth and extravagantly rewards success. Father Theodore Hesburgh, former president of the University of Notre Dame, said: "The real threat to capitalism is the maldistribution of wealth across the globe. We cannot hope for world peace when 20 percent of the people in the world have 80 percent of the goods."[5] Indeed, the United States, with 5 percent of the world's population, produces 40 percent of the world's goods and services; and 20 percent of its population earns 46 percent of the income.
- The capitalist drive for profits has warped people, making them overly competitive and aggressive.
- Private enterprise values wasteful private consumption more than needed public services, according to economist John Kenneth Galbraith.

As summed up by economist Robert Heilbroner,[6] many of the issues regarding capitalism can be reduced to two questions: Does capitalism work? Does it work well enough?

The first question can be answered with a strong yes, especially when capitalism is compared with economic systems that stress government planning. The second question addresses some of the criticisms of private enterprise and is much more complex.

So far, the U.S. private enterprise system has worked well enough to feed a majority of its citizens and to avoid being overthrown. It has surprised critics with its ability to survive severe crises, especially during the 1930s and 1940s. However, criticism since the early 1800s has centered on the question of whether most of the people can be supported as well as they should be.

BUSINESS PRACTICE EXAMPLE Continues

For over 150 years Hong Kong operated as a colony of Great Britain, a parliamentary democracy. Despite this, the colony has never had a strong democratic history. In 1843, Sir Henry Pottinger, the first governor, decided the colony should have a legislature, so he appointed one. The governor still handpicks most of the legislature, writes the laws and controls the budget. While the colony had no formal democratic government, the British Parliament did insure that it had freedom and that large scale socialist programs were created. The government's social welfare system provides benefits for unemployment, disability, and old age. It also offers low-cost medical care through public hospitals and free public education through the primary grades.

Now unless mainland China acts otherwise, Hong Kong will have a new government. In order to get Hong Kong back, China had to pledge that Hong Kong would remain capitalist for 50 years, and that its social and economic systems would remain unchanged. The China-British declaration of 1984 stated categorically that mainland laws would not apply to Hong Kong, except those concerning defense or foreign affairs. In 1988, the Chinese released the first draft of Hong Kong's postcolonial constitution, called the "Basic Law." Loopholes in the law allow China to decide which of its laws would apply in Hong Kong, and the Basic Law follows the colony's present authoritarian structure. In the meantime, would-be democrats are calling for a revision of the Basic Law and for immediate elections.

As noted by critics, competitive systems can produce a visible waste of effort as well as unequal distribution of wealth. Also, over the last century, some large-scale social problems, including recent environmental problems, have emerged. These problems have left people unwilling to wait and see if things will work themselves out.

Such severe conditions often force economic planners and politicians to try running their economies according to a "better plan." The result is that in the last century several nations have assigned a strong role to government planning, in the hope of a more efficient and more equal distribution of wealth. (In the next few sections, we will examine some major *planned economies.*) Yet, after less than a century and many disappointments, several of these economies seem to have recognized that there are serious limitations to government planning. In fact, there seems to be a worldwide trend toward modifications in favor of a free-market system.

Planned Economies in Socialist Systems

Socialism is the general term for any economic system in which the government has heavy control over economic planning decisions and also owns and controls key resources and industries. Socialism can therefore be a matter of degree, depending on how large the role of government is in planning and ownership. In some nations, such key industries as communications, transportation, utilities, and heavy manufacturing are government owned. Sweden, India, Italy, and Norway are examples. In other countries, the degree of government ownership has varied. In Great Britain and France, it has recently been reduced. Nations that have tried socialist planning are often democratic in the area of individual freedoms, including the freedom to invest money in businesses at home or abroad. Socialism as an economic system has been tried in many developing Third World nations.

Socialism is the general term for any economic system that depends heavily on the government to make economic planning decisions and to own and control key resources and industries.

In recent years, Great Britain has moved steadily away from a socialist economic system.[7] A pattern of heavy government ownership in the 1960s and 1970s has been made over to become what some have called "popular capitalism." Under its long-term prime minister, Margaret Thatcher, the British government has sold more than 40 percent of its nationalized industry to businesses and over 1 million public housing units to their tenants. Key public companies sold were in the automotive, aerospace, and telecommunications industries. The government sale included, among others, British Airways, Rolls Royce, British Gas, Jaguar, and British Telecom. This trend toward privatization and deregulation is also strong in France, Mexico, Brazil, India, and many Third World nations.

In addition, Great Britain and many other nations with planned economies have followed the U.S. lead in dramatically lowering personal income taxes (see Figure 2.10). In Great Britain, taxes have been lowered twice in recent years. The top rate has been slashed from 60 percent to 40 percent, and the basic rate has been sliced from 27 to 25 percent (and will eventually be lowered to 20 percent). Other socialist nations that have lowered their tax rates include Canada, France, Jamaica, Denmark, and Sweden. The tax cuts are intended to stimulate the economy and to create new jobs.[8]

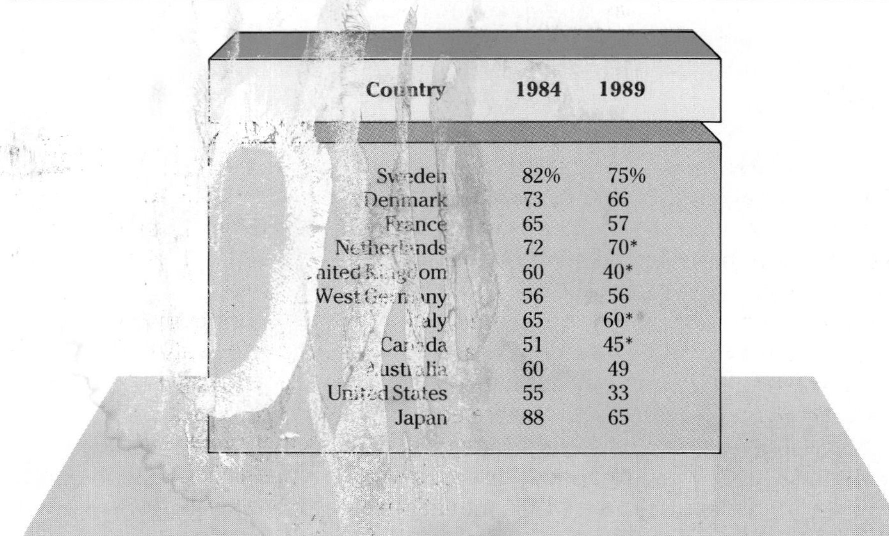

Country	1984	1989
Sweden	82%	75%
Denmark	73	66
France	65	57
Netherlands	72	70*
United Kingdom	60	40*
West Germany	56	56
Italy	65	60*
Canada	51	45*
Australia	60	49
United States	55	33
Japan	88	65

Figure 2.10
Many countries are reducing individual income tax rates, particularly top brackets, and compressing the number of brackets. (National and local taxes are combined here.)

*Proposed.

HIGHLIGHT IN BUSINESS PRACTICE

China's Rocky Road to Economic Reform

A decade of economic reform in Communist China has created a new "me generation" of Chinese consumers. Many of China's youth now have dreams of fast cars, high fashion, and electronic gadgets that their Maoist parents and Confucian-minded grandparents never will understand. The economic climate in China today is one of private enterprise and joint ventures with Americans and Europeans. This is very different from only 11 years ago when China was just emerging from Mao's crippling Cultural Revolution.

The credit for fanning the flames of materialism belongs to China's Premier Deng Xiaoping, who in 1978 set about revamping China's moribund economic system. Deng's economic changes began with rural reform. Eight hundred million peasants (four-fifths of the population) were offered the opportunity to grow the crops of their choice and to keep all but 15%, which was reserved as the state's quota. As a result of rural reform, China's food production doubled and the income of a typical Chinese peasant tripled. This success paved the way for even more economic reforms.

Urban reforms—those in business and industry—have been slower to take hold because the central bureaucracies are reluctant to change their socialist ways. Nevertheless, since 1979, free market principles have helped to create 70 million new jobs and have encouraged private owners to start four-fifths of the new businesses opened. Deng offered factory managers wide latitude in deciding what products to make and how to manage the companies. He levied taxes on businesses instead of

requiring that all the profits be returned to the state. Prices, which had traditionally been set by central committees, were decontrolled. Managers were encouraged to purchase their raw materials on the free market. Some state-owned businesses were even leased to private entrepreneurs. Chinese people are now encouraged to work for themselves as a way of creating jobs or services. As a result, over 20 million Chinese workers (of a population of a billion) now work in the private sector.

The economic transformation of China has not been without problems. The growing demand for consumer goods and record economic growth has spurred inflation to 36 percent annually. The 20 percent industrial growth has overtaxed the country's energy supply and transportation networks. In September,

1988, an austerity program aimed at slowing the economy was ordered, including cutbacks in construction, loans, and luxury spending. Not enough localities complied with the program, so in March, 1989, even more controls were implemented by the National People's Congress. In addition to the previous measures, wages are strictly controlled and importation of goods that could be produced domestically were restricted or barred. The most productive sectors of the economy—private business, rural factories, and free-market farming bore the brunt of new taxes as the screws were tightened on the economic growth.

Economic reform has not transformed China from a socialist to a capitalist country. However, Western influenced economic reform has changed the way China carries out its development and has opened the door for new ideas and methods.

Communist Planned Economic Systems

Communism is based on the economic and political doctrines of Karl Marx, whose goal was to create a more equitable distribution of wealth than capitalist systems. The term **communism** describes a totally planned economy, ruled by a single political party, whose industries and resources are all owned by the government. In contrast to capitalism and socialism, communist systems of total control usually offer individuals few economic freedoms. Marx believed that an equitable distribution of wealth would result in a classless society. However, communist economies have established their own "new class," which enjoys special privileges. Those who belong to the new class are members of the Communist party. In the Soviet Union, only a reported 7 percent of the population has been selected for such membership.[9]

Communism is the term used to describe a totally planned economy, ruled by a single political party, whose industries and resources are all owned by the government.

The Soviet Union, China, Cuba, Angola, Poland, Hungary, Yugoslavia, and Vietnam are communist nations. Since World War II, nations have entered the communist bloc as the result of revolution rather than election. However, some noncommunist nations, including France and Italy, have strong Communist parties that claim they will eventually transform the countries into communist nations through elections. Communism in those free, capitalistic nations is called *Eurocommunism.*

Communists believe their system is superior to others because it uses centralized government planning and control. The government decides what is made, how much is made, and who gets it. Most communist nations use five-year plans. The first such plan was put into operation in 1929 in the Soviet Union, the world's largest planned economy. Communists believe a planned economy yields less waste than the competitive private enterprise system. However, this belief is beginning to be modified, even in the Soviet Union. That country has never been able to claim a standard of living comparable with that in the U.S. (See Figure 2.11.)

In a communist planned economic system, all of the industries and resources are owned by the government and decisions are made based upon the priorities of the government and not the marketplace.

Changes in Planned Economic Systems

Do planned economies work? In communist societies, planned economies regularly have produced insufficient agricultural output, inadequate and substandard

Living standards— U.S. versus Soviet Union	U.S.	Soviet Union	Soviet percentage of U.S. total
Daily calorie supply (per person)	3,450	3,328	97%
Grain production (pounds per person)	1,960	1,405	71
Meat production (pounds per person)	236	130	55
Automobiles (per 1,000 persons)	538	35	7
Refrigerators (per 1,000 persons)	349	268	77
Telephones (per 1,000 persons)	791	84	11
Physicians (per 1,000 persons)	2	4	200
Infant Mortality (deaths per 1,000 births)	11	32	294
Life expectancy at birth (years)	75	69	92

Figure 2.11 Americans enjoy a higher standard of living than do citizens of the Soviet Union.

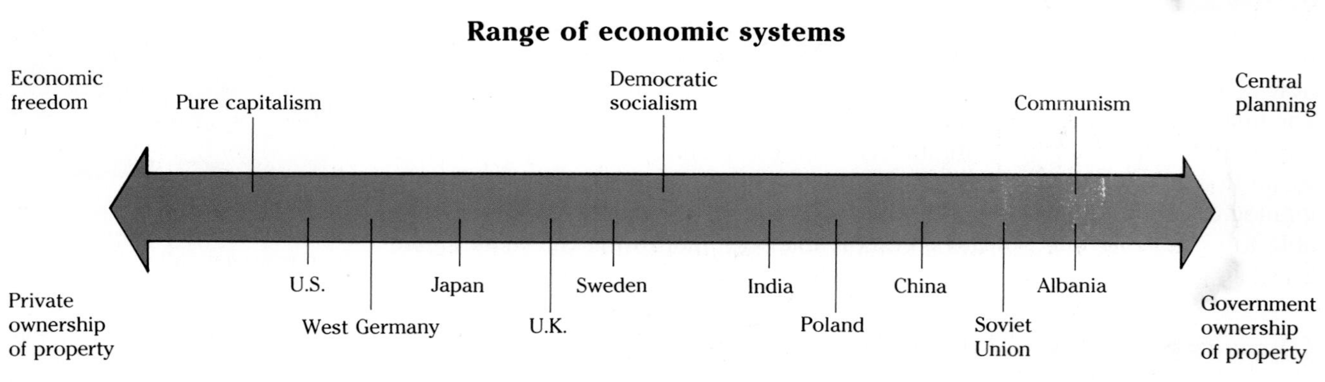

Figure 2.12 Most nations have mixed economies rather than pure capitalism, pure socialism, or pure communism.

consumer products, and few personal freedoms. Realizing that most of their people could benefit from some of the economic freedoms found in free-market nations, many communist nations are instituting radical reforms. The reform movement was started by China in 1979. By using free-market principles, the Chinese were able to raise their employment (70 million new jobs between 1979 and 1987) and productivity.

Noting China's success, the Soviet Union, under the leadership of Mikhail Gorbachev, decided in 1986 to implement an economic restructuring policy called *perestroika*. In 1987, the country's Supreme Soviet passed laws to "promote a nationwide discussion of important questions of state life." These laws and the policy behind them, called *glasnost*, encouraged openness, individual responsibility, and competition within state enterprises. At the same time, the policy envisioned the strengthening of central planning in regard to strategic and macroeconomic issues.[10] This vision was evident at the 1987 session of Comecon (the communist equivalent of the European Community). Soviet leaders encouraged member nations to follow the Soviet lead in restructuring their economies and integrating them more closely with those of other member nations and with the European Community.

Mixed Economic Systems

Few nations are purely capitalist, socialist, or communist. The term **mixed economy** has been used to describe economies that are a mix of socialism and private enterprise—that is, economies in which a combination of market and government forces regulates the distribution of resources. In nominally socialist Sweden, for example, 90 percent of production is carried on by private enterprise. And the basically capitalist United States can be considered a mixed economy because some public utilities—for example, the TVA—are government owned. (See Figure 2.12 for a range of economic systems and Table 2.1 for a comparison of economic rights under each major system.)

A ***mixed economy*** is an economy that combines socialism and private enterprise.

As economies develop in mixed forms, they are able to establish better trade relationships. Poland, a communist country, has had a long-standing trade relationship with the United States. The United States has opened up a lively trade with China and recently also with the Soviet Union. In general, world trade has the effect of breaking down economic barriers between nations.

THE GLOBAL ECONOMY

Today, most people's lives are touched by companies whose headquarters are in a country other than their own. Never before have so much money and so many goods and people crossed national borders so rapidly or in such high volume. A totally free and unrestricted global marketplace is far from reality. However, most companies now must think and act in international terms. As more and more companies sell worldwide, brand names such as Coca-Cola, Bic, Panasonic, IBM, Nissan, and hundreds of others link people together in an integrated world economy.

Americans are becoming more aware of the world economy as we become more dependent on foreign companies for our products and, in many cases, our

Table 2.1 Comparisons of economic rights under three major economic systems.

Basic Economic Rights	U.S. Private Enterprise	Socialism	Communism
Freedom to choose jobs	Individuals have the right to choose their occupation and place of employment.	Individuals are free to select occupations and place of employment within the state-controlled economy.	Limited freedom is allowed in the selection of occupations and place of employment. Nearly everyone works for the state.
Freedom to own property	Private ownership of business and industry is encouraged and sanctioned by the Constitution.	Major utilities and transportation, mining, and communications industries are owned by the government. A mixture of private and public ownership exists.	All industries and virtually all farms are owned by the state.
Freedom to compete	Competition is encouraged by the state. Monopolies are forbidden unless they are government regulated.	Competition is encouraged in smaller businesses but is usually restricted in major key industries (usually owned by the state).	Competition is nonexistent because the government owns and controls all businesses and industries.
Freedom to make business decisions	No appeal to higher authority is necessary regarding business decisions.	Management of major key industries must follow government plans.	A master plan is used to make major economic/business decisions.
Freedom to buy and sell in a free market	Goods and services are sold at prices based on supply and demand. A wide assortment is available.	Goods and services are sold at prices based on supply and demand. A wide assortment is available.	The choice of consumer goods is limited. Prices (higher) are determined by the state.
Freedom to bargain collectively	Large-scale union participation is allowed, with the right to bargain collectively.	Large-scale union participation is allowed, with the right to bargain collectively.	Labor unions are forbidden. No collective bargaining is allowed.
Freedom to influence taxation	Medium taxes are levied, with the right to influence by vote.	Heavy taxes are levied, with the right to influence by vote.	Heavy taxes, in the form of sales tax and large cost margins, are levied.
Freedom to make a profit	All net profits can be kept by individuals incurring risk in a business.	Profits earned by non-state-owned businesses are encouraged within limits.	All "profits" (margins) go to the state.

jobs. For example, most VCRs, cameras, TVs, and other electronic goods come from Japan. Where would Americans be without their Sony Walkman radios? What kind of Christmas would millions of children and adults have if it weren't for toys and clothes from South Korea, Taiwan, and Hong Kong? The popular Reebok athletic shoes are owned by the British and made in South Korea. From Brazil and Spain we import most of our leather dress shoes and from Italy the popular

HIGHLIGHT IN BUSINESS PRACTICE

Japan Wins Hearts in Tennessee

From Sharp TV sets and microwave ovens made in Memphis, to Bridgestone tires produced in Lavergne, and Nissan cars and trucks made in Smyrna, the Japanese are becoming an impressive presence in Tennessee. Twenty-nine Japanese companies have set up shop in twenty-one Tennessee communities and are employing over 10,000 people in the state. Some 20,000 more workers are employed in Tennessee businesses that rely on the Japanese companies. Together, their paychecks total $500 million a year, helping to bring Tennessee from the 45th ranked state in per capita income (in 1979) to 38th.

The Japanese influence is seen in the community, from Japanese newspapers in the newsstands to the names of Japanese companies printed on Little League uniforms. The grocery stores have begun stocking more fresh fish and other favorite Japanese staples, and video stores rent Japanese-language videos. For many Americans the change has meant having a foreign boss, adjusting to different attitudes in the work place, taking business trips to Japan, and socializing with Japanese coworkers and neighbors. For the Japanese families in America for the first time it has meant a lonely and frustrating adjustment to a new culture. Many Tennessee communities are helping to bridge the culture gap by establishing Japanese cultural centers, English classes, and special Saturday schools to help Japanese children maintain their Japanese culture.

Americans are finding that along with the paychecks and job security offered by the Japanese firms come social stresses and costs. The Japanese high standards of quality and efficiency in the work place have meant higher pressure and stress on the workers. In order to lure the companies to their towns, the state and municipal governments offered expensive incentives that have cost taxpayers $11,000 per job created since Nissan first set up shop in Smyrna. New industry in a community means higher property values and taxes, increased traffic through town, strains on all the municipal services, and a change in life style from the small town atmosphere residents once knew. To competing American businesses, a Japanese presence means having to pay higher wages and benefits to attract good workers.

In all, the Japanese investors have won the hearts of Tennessee workers who can find work at home instead of having to move on. There are even enough jobs to attract workers from neighboring states.

Benetton sweaters. And our most popular ice cream brand, Baskin-Robbins, is owned by the British. Indeed, we live in a global village, with people from around the world using and enjoying the same products.

Partly because of all this consumption of foreign goods, the United States has accumulated huge trade and budget deficits. In order to finance them, we have had to attract large sums of foreign investment. In the past few years, foreign

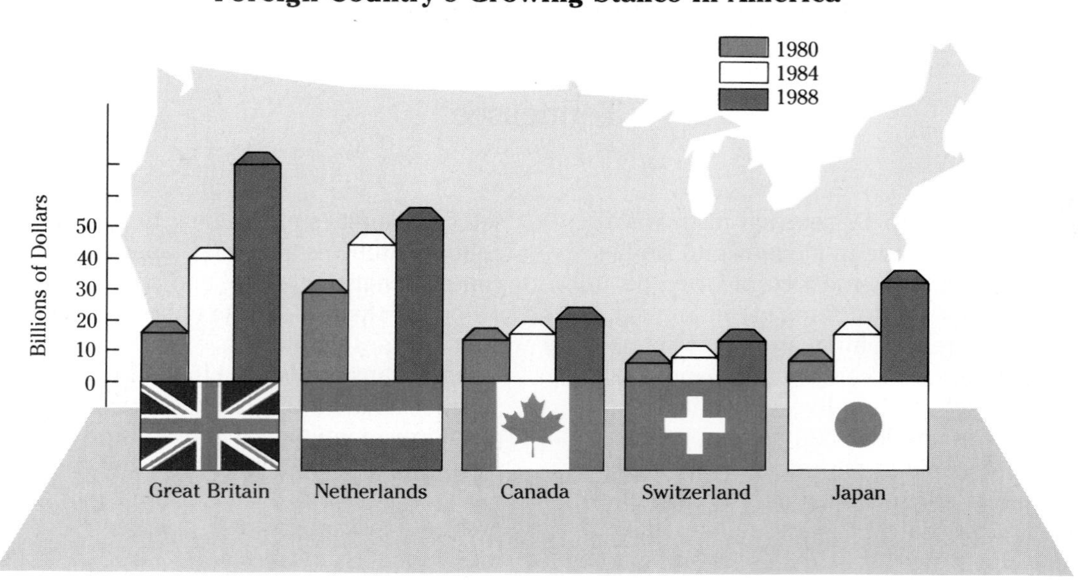

Figure 2.13 Foreign countries with the highest direct investments in the United States.

investors have been able to purchase over $1.7 trillion in U.S. assets, including stocks, bonds, real estate, and whole companies. (The breakdown by country appears in Figure 2.13.) In addition, foreign investors have bought a sixth of the U.S. debt by purchasing Treasury securities. By investing in the United States, they help finance the country's growth, since Americans are not saving enough to satisfy the nation's investment needs.

Other forms of investment, such as plant construction (by Honda, Michelin, and Sony, to name but a few), are creating new jobs and wealth. Many Americans in the United States are now working for West German, Japanese, British, French, and Dutch employers. The balance of foreign-controlled ownership of American industry has become a lively topic for public discussion.

Foreign companies are having an impact on our lives in other ways too. As the Japanese and others invest heavily in the United States, they are providing many Americans with a taste of their culture. Just as we gave the Japanese baseball, they are giving us the martial arts, tree miniaturization, sushi bars, and new styles of management. To win over their employees and improve their image with local citizens, many foreign companies are increasingly playing a philanthropic role in the United States. For example, Honda gave $50,000 to a black nursery school in Harlem. Japanese companies so far have given $140 million to U.S. causes in order to become accepted as a "good neighbor."[11] The long-term effects of large-scale foreign investment on America's material and psychic health remain to be seen.

BUSINESS PRACTICE EXAMPLE Continues

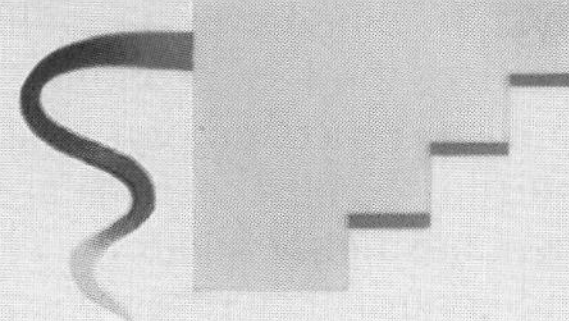

The U.S. is Hong Kong's largest trading partner. U.S. businesses have sunk over $6 billion into the Hong Kong economy, and the U.S. is Hong Kong's second largest market after China. Exports include most clothes labeled Calvin Klein, Ralph Lauren, Bill Blass, and Perry Ellis, many popular toys, and electronic gadgets. Furthermore, Hong Kong businessmen poured $567 million into U.S. businesses in 1986. For example, seeking a favorable climate for their money, Hong Kong textile magnates have bought plants in North Carolina and Maine.

To many, Hong Kong looks more like an American colony than a British one. Today the more than 14,000 Americans living there and the half-million U.S. visitors find themselves right at home. The colony has over 700 fast food restaurants (including 26 McDonalds owned by a Chinese with a Ph.D. from the University of Illinois), 26 branches of Citibank, over 600 U.S.-style supermarkets, and even a Harvard Club. Whether all of this American-style capitalism can continue is anyone's guess. In the end Hong Kong's prospects of remaining a capitalist enclave will be as good as China's word.

Issues for Discussion

1. Do you believe that China can successfully operate its "one country, two systems" policy? Explain your answer.
2. Explain why Hong Kong is experiencing its current brain drain.
3. Compare and contrast the differences between present Hong Kong and what you believe it will be like in 2000 under communist rule.

SUMMARY

Economics is the study of how economic systems allocate scarce resources. It is divided into macroeconomics (the study of the behavior of entire economies) and microeconomics (the study of the behavior of organizations or individuals in an economy). Key economic decisions are made by consumers, producers, and governments.

Consumers buy goods and services for personal use. Their willingness and ability to buy them constitute the demand curve. At high prices, the quantity demanded is low, and at low prices the quantity demanded is high. Supply operates much the same way, but in reverse. If businesses can sell goods at a high price, they will produce many of them. If the price they are offered is very low, they'll stop producing them. The price at which supply equals demand is the equilibrium price.

Producers work to provide the goods and services. They include workers, managers, investors, and entrepreneurs. To produce anything, four factors of production are needed: land, labor, capital, and entrepreneurs. An important part of the economy is productivity—the measure of output in relation to input.

Government has five major economic roles: regulation (the trend lately has been deregulation), promotion of the growth and development of businesses, protection of businesses, competition (in that the government operates certain "businesses," such as the post office and Amtrak), and support to individuals who can't meet their minimum needs (social security, for example).

Certain key aspects of the economy are of major concern to government: leading economic indicators (measures of economic activity), monetary policy (management of the money supply), fiscal policy (taxation and spending), inflation (a sustained increase in overall prices), and full employment (the point where further declines in unemployment would create steep inflation). Recessions are responsible for major drops in the employment rate. Alternating periods of recession and prosperity are called business cycles.

There are three major economic systems: The private enterprise system is a modified free-market system. It characterizes the U.S. economy, which relies on capitalism (private ownership of a nation's capital). Planned economies in socialist systems are systems in which the government has heavy control over economic planning and owns and controls key resources and industries. Communist planned economies are totally planned economies, ruled by a single political party, whose industries and resources are all owned by government. A fourth system is mixed economies (economies in which a combination of market and government forces regulate the distribution of resources).

Today, we exist in a world economy. Many of our goods come from other countries, and many U.S. companies sell their goods throughout the world. Some U.S. companies are even owned by foreign firms.

KEY TERMS

Business cycles p. 48
Capitalism p. 50
Communism p. 55
Consumers p. 35
Cost-push inflation p. 48
Demand curve p. 36
Demand-pull inflation p. 48
Depression p. 48
Deregulation p. 44
Economics p. 35
Equilibrium price p. 38
Federal deficit p. 48
Fiscal policy p. 47
Full employment p. 48
Macroeconomics p. 35
Microeconomics p. 35
Mixed economy p. 57
Monetary policy p. 46
Private enterprise system p. 50
Productivity p. 40
Recession p. 48
Socialism p. 53
Supply curve p. 37

CHECK YOUR LEARNING

Reread the following learning objectives. Each objective is followed by a few questions. Answering these questions accurately will help you retain the most important concepts discussed in this chapter. After answering each question, check your answer with the key at the end of this chapter. (*Hint:* If you have doubt regarding the correct response, consult the page whose number follows the answer.)

Circle:

A. Explain how consumers, producers, and the government make our economic system work.

a b c d — 1. Key decisions in the American economy are made by all of the following except: (a) consumers; (b) military; (c) producers; (d) government.

T F — 2. The American economy is often described as a "consumer economy."

T F 3. The law of supply and demand makes the American economy work.

T F 4. Managers, investors, and entrepreneurs are not considered to be producers.

a b c d 5. When the government provides various programs and policies that help business, it is providing: (a) regulation; (b) protection; (c) support; (d) promotion.

B. List the four factors of production and explain how they are essential to our economy.

a b c d e 1. All of the following are factors of production except: (a) land; (b) water; (c) labor; (d) capital; (e) entrepreneurship.

T F 2. Land includes the factory for production and a place to put it.

C. Explain how the U.S. government promotes a balanced economy.

T F 1. Sometimes the government competes with private enterprise.

T F 2. The greatest portion of the federal budget is spent on defense.

a b c d e 3. Which of the following factors affects our overall economy: (a) fiscal policy; (b) employment; (c) inflation; (d) monetary policy; (e) all of the above.

D. Describe the important characteristics of the private enterprise system.

T F 1. In recent years, Americans have successfully influenced the rate of taxation.

a b c d e 2. Which of the following is a freedom characteristic of the private enterprise system: (a) to bargain collectively; (b) to make a profit; (c) to compete; (d) to choose an occupation and a job; (e) all of the above.

a b c d 3. Competition in the private enterprise system is regulated by: (a) business and industry; (b) the market; (c) the government; (d) consumers.

E. Compare capitalism, socialism, and communism.

a b c d 1. The electricity industry would be owned by the government in all of the following nations except: (a) England; (b) Japan; (c) Sweden; (d) Soviet Union.

T F 2. There are few privately owned businesses in socialist countries.

T F 3. Competition is freely encouraged in Cuba.

T F 4. Communist nations use planned economies.

T F 5. Citizens of socialist nations are heavily taxed.

F. Discuss why the U.S. economic system is an integral part of the global economy.

a b c d e 1. Which of the following nations is not a leading employer of Americans: (a) West Germany; (b) Canada; (c) France; (d) Holland; (e) none of the above.

T F 2. Foreign investors own more than $1 trillion in U.S. assets.

QUESTIONS FOR REVIEW AND DISCUSSION

1. Define the key terms listed at the end of this chapter.
2. Explain how consumers, producers, and the government make the key decisions in our economic system.
3. Do you think that government has overstepped its role as prescribed in the Preamble of the American Constitution? Discuss what you believe the role of government should be in our economy.
4. Do you think that competition serves a useful purpose in our economy? Do you think you would benefit personally if competition were eliminated? Explain.
5. Evaluate this statement by Winston Churchill: "The inherent vice of capitalism is the unequal sharing of blessings; the inherent virtue of socialism is the equal sharing of miseries."
6. Explain why the private enterprise system is the best system available. Do you believe that mixed economies are an answer to less than perfect economic systems? Explain.
7. Why is socialism becoming less popular in many traditional socialistic nations? What did Milton Friedman mean by "There is no such thing as a free lunch"?

8. Do businesses in communist nations make a profit? If so, what happens to those profits? How is this different from the handling of profits under capitalism and socialism?
9. Review the American economy for the previous year and explain the effect fiscal policy, monetary policy, inflation, and employment had on the overall health of the economy for that year.

CONCLUDING CASE

Minimum-Wage Increases—A Small-Business Perspective

Mandated in 1938 by the Fair Labor Standards Act, the minimum wage has been gradually increased, from 25 cents to $3.35 per hour. By 1990, new legislation could create a minimum wage that might rise over a three-year period to $4.65 an hour, after which it might be indexed to inflation.

U.S. Labor Department figures show that most minimum-wage employees work part time and that 60 percent are between sixteen and twenty-four years old. Women make up a majority of minimum-wage earners, and most of them are not heads of households.

Many employers oppose the increase in the minimum wage. For example, managers at Burger King claimed that the rise in labor costs would result in layoffs of young employees who work in positions that do not require specialized skills or training. According to many small-business owners, unskilled minority youths and college students would lose many job opportunities. One small-business owner stated, "We'll stop hiring, raise prices, and even shrink the number of jobs." Another major concern is that current employees making above the minimum wage will want automatic increases to justify their skill level. Much appears at stake for small-business employers if the minimum wage moves upward.

Issues for Discussion

1. Explain the economic reasoning behind an employer's statement that a higher minimum wage will mean massive layoffs, or that lower wages will promote more employment. What nongovernment factors might cause the lowest wages to be raised?
2. According to the Bureau of Labor Statistics, 4.7 million workers earn the minimum wage or less. If employers are forced to reduce their labor force, what types of jobs will most likely be eliminated? How might consumers be adversely affected?
3. Give at least two reasons for increasing the minimum wage.

NOTES

1. "Business Productivity Up in 1987," *Terre Haute Tribune-Star,* February 5, 1988, p. C5.
2. Mary Paul, "Is a Regulatory Revolt Next?" *Nation's Business,* October 1978, p. 29.
3. Sylvia Nasar, "How to Spot a Recession," *Fortune,* March 28, 1988, pp. 63–68.
4. "The 'Full Employment' Flash Point Seems to Be Shifting," *Business Week,* July 25, 1988, p. 14.
5. "Capitalism: Is It Working?" *Time,* April 21, 1980, p. 54.
6. Robert Heilbroner, "Reflections: The Triumph of Capitalism," *New Yorker,* January 23, 1989, pp. 98–109.
7. Richard I. Kirkland, Jr., "The Death of Socialism," *Fortune,* January 4, 1988, pp. 64–71.
8. Holman Jenkins, Jr., "More Nations Warm to Tax Reform," *Insight,* May 6, 1988, pp. 44–45.
9. Bruce Steinberg, "Reforming the Soviet Economy," *Fortune,* November 25, 1985, pp. 90–96.
10. Barry Newman, "Russians Want Stuff to Spend Money On, or Perestroika's a Flop," *Wall Street Journal,* June 17, 1988, p. 1.
11. William J. Holstein, "Japan's Clout in the U.S.," *Business Week,* July 11, 1988, pp. 64–66.

CHECK YOUR LEARNING ANSWER KEY

A. 1. b, *p. 35*
2. T, *p. 35*
3. T, *p. 38*
4. F, *p. 38*
5. d, *p. 44*

B. 1. b, *p. 39*
2. T, *p. 39*

C. 1. T, *p. 45*
2. F, *p. 45*
3. e, *pp. 45–46*

D. 1. T, *p. 51*
2. e, *pp. 50–51*
3. c, *p. 50*

E. 1. b, *p. 53*
2. F, *p. 53*
3. F, *p. 55*
4. T, *p. 55*
5. T, *p. 53*

F. 1. b, *p. 60*
2. T, *p. 60*

CHAPTER

3

SOCIAL RESPONSIBILITY AND ETHICS

LEARNING OBJECTIVES

After reading this chapter you should be able to:

1. Discuss the role of social responsibility in modern management.
2. Outline the arguments for and against an organization performing social responsibility activities.
3. Define and discuss the importance of social audits.
4. Describe several different socially responsible business practices.

OUTLINE

BUSINESS PRACTICE EXAMPLE

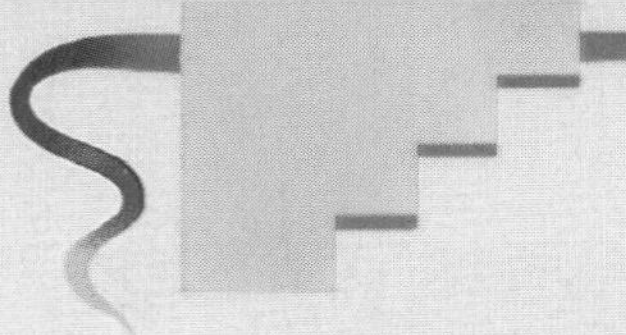

Levi Strauss: The Company with a Conscience

As the cover of one of the company's informational brochures claims, "Everyone knows his first name." Indeed, the "Levi" of Levi Strauss is known worldwide, to millions of people who don't know a word of English, but who do know a good pair of jeans. What many people don't know is that for years Levi Strauss has been a recognized leader in corporate social responsibility. The company has tackled illegal immigration, AIDS in the workplace, and a host of other social problems through its innovative programs.

Based in San Francisco, Levi Strauss patented his first jeans—then called "waist high overalls"—in 1873 and sold them to gold miners. With their indestructible brown canvas and riveted pockets made to support the weight of gold nuggets, the jeans were an instant success. By the 1890s, the company began assigning "lot numbers" to each of its clothing products, a practice that continues today. The waist-high overall was given the number "501."

In addition to overseeing the growth of his business, Levi Strauss became involved in many philanthropic causes, including, in 1897, the establishment of 28 scholarships at the University of California. His death in 1902 was mourned by the entire city. Never married, Levi Strauss left the company to four nephews, and today, the company is privately held by descendants of the Strauss family and by firm employees.

In the United States, Levi Strauss & Co. has production, finishing, and distribution facilities in 12 states and employs approximately 24,000 people. Internationally, the company has separate divisions serving Europe, Canada, Latin America, and the Asia/Pacific region and sells its products directly in more than 70 countries. Additional countries have licensing agreements with the company to make and sell Levi's branded products. Nearly 90 percent of all Levi's products sold in the U.S. are made in the U.S. The company generally manufactures goods in the countries or regions in which they will be sold.

The Levi Strauss Foundation, the philanthropic arm of the company, was established in 1952. In 1968 the company created a Community Affairs Department, with 26 staff members who coordinate efforts with company facilities worldwide. The philosophy behind the company's corporate social responsibility programs is the idea that while giving money is important, time and effort are perhaps the greatest gifts. It was out of this philosophy that the pioneering Community Involvement Teams program, or "CITs," was established. Any group of three or more employees who share an interest in a community project can form a CIT. Grants from the Levi Strauss Foundation help many of the programs succeed, and assistance in securing other sources of funding is provided by the staff of the Community Affairs Department.

Today, there are scores of CITs worldwide, and approximately 8,000 employees participate. Levi Strauss employees have formed CIT groups to focus on children, AIDS, public schools, immigration, and the homeless. CITs looking for volunteers advertise in the *Volunteer Hotline,* a regularly published newsletter put out by the department. In 1984, the White House honored this program and presented the company with the President's Volunteer Action Award for Corporate Volunteerism.

WHAT'S AHEAD

The above Business Practice Example traces some social responsibility activities which Levi Strauss has been involved with over the years. Social responsibility encompasses many individual issues, from product and environmental control to external relations with society. This chapter offers arguments for and against a company like Levi Strauss performing social responsibility activities and will discuss socially responsible practices, including ethical actions, consumer-oriented actions, and environmental protection. It will also show how to measure social responsibility.

FUNDAMENTALS OF SOCIAL RESPONSIBILITY

- An electric space heater is accidentally overturned by a young child. Instead of clicking off, as promised by the manufacturer, it stays on. The heat builds up, and soon the carpet is on fire.
- The residents of a small midwestern town cannot drink their tap water because wastes from an underground dump, illegally created by a local manufacturer, have seeped into the town's water supply.
- A new drug to treat high blood pressure is dramatically successful. Ten years later, a study finds that a large proportion of patients who used the drug developed a serious form of kidney disease.
- A man with AIDS finds his insurance cancelled, even though he has paid his premiums regularly for years. He faces his catastrophic illness without the means to pay for it.

The situations just described dramatically illustrate a few of the many issues in social responsibility that managers face. Although the term **social responsibility** can be defined in a number of ways, here we will define it as the managerial

Social responsibility is the managerial obligation to take action that will protect and improve not only the interests of the organization but also the welfare of society as a whole.

obligation to take action that will protect and improve not only the interests of the organization but also the welfare of society as a whole.[1] Today, people are paying a great deal of attention to social responsibility. Environmental hazards such as the greenhouse effect and acid rain have made many people realize that the actions of industries can affect everyone. The actions of businesses have both helped us and hurt us. The same industry that gave us the polio vaccine also gave us thalidomide, a drug that caused deformities in infants. The industry that moved us out of the horse and buggy age and, later, into high-speed highway travel also unintentionally caused the banks of smog over our nation's freeways.

Areas of Social Responsibility Involvement

As shown in Table 3.1, there are many areas in which business can act to protect and improve the welfare of society. Three areas that receive constant public attention are the following:

1. *External relations (community development, government relations, and international relations).* Should a construction firm, for example, build profitable luxury condominiums or less profitable moderately priced, badly needed accommodations for senior citizens? What partnerships, if any, should businesses form with government? Is the company commitment to employee safety and quality control as stringent in foreign plants as in the home country's?
2. *Product control.* What responsibilities do the manufacturers of products have in ensuring their products' safety? For example, how far should a drug manufacturer go to ensure that its products won't cause harm to consumers?
3. *Environmental control.* Matters relating to air, water, noise, and land pollution are part of environmental control. Strip mining, for instance, is the fastest and cheapest way to provide supplies of coal for our energy needs, but the process ravages the earth, stripping away topsoil and leaving gaping pits. What responsibility does a strip-mining company have to the land and its occupants?

Views on Social Responsibility

Arguments for It

The most common argument in support of businesses engaging in social responsibility activities is that since businesses form a significant part of society, they should be responsible for helping maintain and improve societal welfare. After all, society asks no less of its individual citizens.

Proponents of business involvement in social responsibility often argue that social responsibility and profit maximization actually go hand in hand.[2] Many recognize that social responsibility activities can enhance a corporation's public image. Del Monte, for example, garnered a good deal of favorable publicity when it became the first national packer to itemize nutritional contents on its labels.

Arguments against It

The free-market economist Milton Friedman has argued that to make business managers simultaneously responsible for reaching profit objectives and enhancing societal welfare represents a conflict of interest. For Friedman, a business's sole objective should be to pursue profits. He explains:

Table 3.1 Major social responsibility areas in which business can become involved.

Categories of Social Responsibility Issues

Product Line

Internal standards for product
- Quality, e.g., does it last?
- Safety, e.g., can it harm users or children finding it?
- Disposal, e.g., is it biodegradable?
- Design, e.g., will its use or even "easy" misuse cause pain, injury, or death?

Average product life comparisons versus
- Competition
- Substitute products
- Internal standards or state-of-the-art regular built-in obsolescence

Product performance
- Efficacy, e.g., does it do what it is supposed to do?
- Guarantees/warranties, e.g., are guarantees sufficient, reasonable?
- Service policy
- Service availability
- Service pricing
- Utility

Packaging
- Environmental impact (degree of disposability; recycleability)
- Comparisons with competition (type and extent of packaging)

Marketing and Sales Practices
- Legal standards
- "Undue" pressure (a qualitative judgment)

Credit practices against legal standards

Accuracy of advertising claims—specific government complaints

Consumer complaints about marketing practices
- Clear explanation of credit terms
- Clear explanation of purchase price
- Complaint answering policy
  - —Answered at all
  - —Investigated carefully
  - —Grievances redressed (and cost)
  - —Remedial action to prevent future occurrences

Adequate consumer information on
- Product use, e.g., dosage, duration of use, etc.
- Product misuse

Fair pricing
- Between countries
- Between states
- Between locations

Packaging

Employee Education and Training

Policy on leaves of absence for
- Full-time schooling
- Courses given during working hours

Dollars spent on training
- Formal vocational training
- Training for disadvantaged worker
- OJT (very difficult to isolate)
- Tuition (job-related versus non-job-related)
- Special upgrading and career development programs
- Compare versus competition

Special training program results (systematic evaluations)
- Number trained in each program per year
- Cost per trainee (less subsidy)
- Number or percent workers still with company

Plans for future programs

Career training and counseling

Failure rates

Extend personnel understanding
- Jobs
- Skills required later
- Incentive system now available
- Specific actions for promotion

Corporate Philanthropy

Contribution performance
- By category, for example:
  - —Art
  - —Education
  - —Poverty
  - —Health
  - —Community development
  - —Public service advertising
- Dollars (plus materials and work hours, if available)
  - —As a percent of pretax earnings
  - —Compared to competition

Selection criteria for contributions

Procedures for performance tracking of recipient institutions or groups

Programs for permitting and encouraging employee involvement in social projects
- On company time
- After hours only
- Use of company facilities and equipment
- Reimbursement of operating units for replaceable "lost" time
- Human resource support
  - —Number of people
  - —Work hours

Extent of employee involvement in philanthropy decision making

Environmental Control

Measurable pollution resulting from
- Acquisition of raw materials
- Production processes
- Products
- Transportation of intermediate and finished products

Violations of government (federal, state, and local) standards

Cost estimates to correct current deficiencies

Extent to which various plants exceed current legal standards, e.g., particulate matter discharged

Resources devoted to pollution control
- Capital expenditures (absolute and percent)
- R & D investments
- Personnel involved full time, part time
- Organizational "strength" of personnel involved

Competitive company performance, e.g., capital expenditures

Effort to monitor new standards as proposed

Continued on next page

Table 3.1 *(Continued)*

Categories of Social Responsibility Issues

Programs to keep employees alert to spills and other pollution-related accidents

Procedures for evaluating environmental impact of new packages or products

External Relations

Community Development

Support of minority and community enterprises through
- Purchasing
- Subcontracting

Investment practices
- Ensuring equal opportunity before locating new facilities
- Identifying opportunities to serve community needs through business expansion (e.g., housing rehabilitation or teaching machines)
- Funds in minority banks

Government Relations

Specific input to public policy through research and analysis

Participation and development of business/government programs

Political contributions

Disclosure of Information/ Communications

Extent of public disclosure of performance by activity category

Measure of employee understanding of programs such as:
- Pay and benefits
- Equal opportunity policies and programs
- Position on major economic or political issues (as appropriate)

Relations/communications with constituencies such as stockholders, fund managers, major customers, and so on

International

Comparisons of policy and performance between countries and versus local standards

Employee Relations, Benefits, and Satisfaction with Work

Comparisons with competition (and/or national averages)
- Salary and wage levels
- Retirement plans
- Turnover and retention by level
- Profit sharing
- Day care and maternity
- Transportation
- Insurance, health programs, and other fringes
- Participation in ownership of business through stock purchases

Comparisons of operating units on promotions, terminations, hires against breakdowns by
- Age
- Sex
- Race
- Education level

Performance review system and procedures for communication with employees whose performance is below average

Promotion policy—equitable and understood

Transfer policy

Termination policy (i.e., how early is "notice" given)

General working environment and conditions
- Physical surroundings
  - —Heat
  - —Ventilation
  - —Space/person
  - —Lighting
  - —Air conditioning
  - —Noise
- Leisure, recreation, cultural opportunities

Fringe benefits as a percent of salary for various salary levels

Evaluation of employee benefit preferences (questions can be posed as choices)

Evaluation of employee understanding of current fringe benefits

Union/industrial relations
- Grievances
- Strikes

Confidentiality and security of personnel data

Minority and Women Employment and Advancement

Current hiring policies in relation to the requirements of all affirmative action programs

Specific program of accountability for performance

Company versus local, industry, and national performance
- Number and percent minority and women employees hired in various job classifications over last five years
- Number and percent of new minority and women employees in last two or three years by job classification
- Minority and women and nonminority turnover
- Indictments for discriminatory hiring practices

Percent minority and women employment in major facilities relative to minority labor force available locally

Number of minority group and women members in positions of high responsibility

Promotion performance of minority groups and women

Specific hiring and job upgrading goals established for minority groups and women
- Basic personnel strategy
- Nature and cost of special recruiting efforts
- Risks taken in hiring minority groups and women

Programs to ease integration of minority groups and women into company operations, e.g., awareness efforts

Specialized minority and women career counseling

Special recruiting efforts for minority groups and women

Opportunities for the physically handicapped
- Specific programs
- Numbers employed

Arguments for Social Responsibility

1. It is in the best interest of the business to promote and improve the communities where it does business.
2. Social actions can be profitable.
3. It is the ethical thing to do.
4. It improves the public image of the firm.
5. It increases the viability of the business system. Business exists because it gives society benefits. Society can amend or take away its charter. This is the "iron law of responsibility."
6. It is necessary to avoid government regulation.
7. Sociocultural norms require it.
8. Laws cannot be passed for all circumstances. Thus business must assume responsibility to maintain an orderly legal society.
9. It is in the stockholder's best interest. It will improve the price of stock in the long run because the stock market will view the company as less risky and open to public attack.
10. Society should give business a chance to solve social problems that government has failed to solve.
11. Business, by some groups, is considered to be the institution with the financial and human resources to solve social problems.
12. Prevention of problems is better than cures — so let business solve problems before they become too great.

Arguments against Social Responsibility

1. It might be illegal.
2. Social actions cannot be measured.
3. It violates profit maximization.
4. Cost of social responsibility is too great and would increase prices too much.
5. Business lacks social skills to solve societal problems.
6. It would dilute business's primary purposes.
7. It would weaken U.S. balance of payments because price of goods will have to go up to pay for social programs.
8. Business already has too much power. Such involvement would make business too powerful.
9. Business lacks accountability to the public. Thus the public would have no control over its social involvement.
10. Such business involvement lacks broad public support.

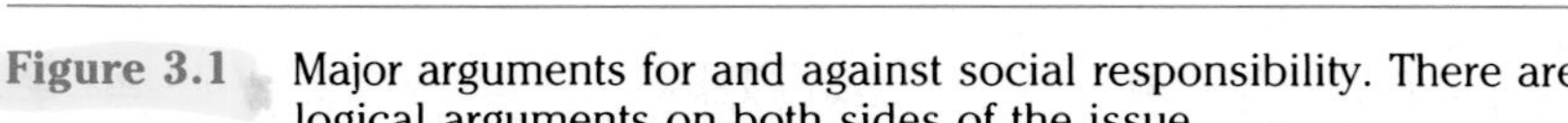

Figure 3.1 Major arguments for and against social responsibility. There are logical arguments on both sides of the issue.

> In a free enterprise, private property system, a corporate executive is an employee of the owners of the business. He has direct responsibility to his employers. That responsibility is to conduct the business in accordance with their desires, which generally will be to make as much money as possible while conforming to the basic rules of society, both those embodied in law and those embodied in ethical custom. . . . Insofar as his actions reduce returns to the stockholders, he is spending their money. Insofar as his actions raise the price to customers, he is spending the customers' money.[3]

Figure 3.1 lists some of the prominent arguments for and against business social responsibility.

THE DAVIS MODEL OF SOCIAL RESPONSIBILITY

The ***Davis model of social responsibility*** is five propositions that describe why and how business should take corrective action that protects and improves its welfare and the welfare of society as well.

A widely accepted model of social responsibility has been developed by Keith Davis.[4] The **Davis model of social responsibility** consists of five propositions that describe why and how business should take action that protects and improves its own welfare and the welfare of society as well.

Proposition 1: Social responsibility arises from social power. This proposition explains why business should assume social responsibility. It is based on the premise that business has a significant amount of influence and power over such critical social issues as minority employment and environmental pollution. In essence, it is mainly the action of business—in concert with legislation—that determines the composition of the work force and the condition of the environment. Building on this premise, Davis reasons that since business possesses this power over society, society can and must hold business responsible for its actions. Davis explains that no more is expected from business than the established legal system of society expects of each citizen who exercises individual power.

Proposition 2: Business shall operate as a two-way open system with open receipt of input from society and open disclosure of its operation to the public. This proposition explains how social responsibilities should be met. Davis suggests that there must be continuing honest and open communication between business and society's representatives if the welfare of society is to be maintained or improved. Each must listen to the other.

Proposition 3: Both social costs and benefits of an activity, product, or service shall be thoroughly calculated and considered in order to decide whether or not to proceed with it. This proposition furnishes specific guidelines about how social responsibilities should be met. It stresses the fundamental notion that technical feasibility and economic profitability are not the only factors that should influence business decisions. Business must also consider both the long- and short-term social consequences before it undertakes any activity.

Proposition 4: Social costs related to each activity, product, or service shall be passed on to the consumer. This proposition makes the point that business cannot be expected to finance completely activities that, while socially advantageous, hurt the company, and thus the shareholders, economically. Therefore, the costs should be passed on to the consumer through pricing of the goods or services involved. At Anheuser-Busch's Merrimack, New Hampshire, plant, for example, water treatment costs that the brewery must pay to the town have increased from 11 cents per 1,000 gallons to 70 cents. Merrimack wants the plant, but it also wants clean water. The company wants to help but must also maintain its profit and price structure. Who pays for its social responsibility activities?

Proposition 5: Business institutions, as citizens, have the responsibility to become involved in certain social problems that are outside of their normal area of operation. This proposition makes the point that if a business possesses the expertise to solve a social problem with which it may not be directly associated, it should be held responsible for helping society solve that problem. It should do this, Davis reasons, because business will eventually share increased profit from a generally improved society.

SOCIAL RESPONSIBILITY IN PRACTICE

We have seen that there are arguments for and against social responsibility in business. If you are a manager, however, you probably will not have the luxury

BUSINESS PRACTICE EXAMPLE Continues

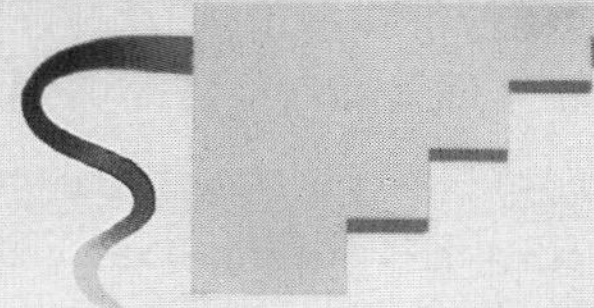

Levi Strauss is clear on where it stands on corporate social responsibility. As company president and CEO Robert Haas has said, "It's simply the way we feel a corporation should be run. . . . It's simply better business to find ways to simultaneously serve all our constituencies' needs and interests." In 1982, just as the AIDS epidemic was striking the U.S., San Francisco employees asked for and received support from senior management to educate employees and raise funds. Eventually Levi Strauss & Co.'s "AIDS Initiatives" program was created, offering employee education sessions, counseling and referral, grants and contributions to support public education and patient care, and public policy initiatives. In 1987, the company, along with a dozen other San Francisco Bay area organizations, joined the United Way to implement an AIDS education program for the Bay area. Corporations nationwide and internationally have asked for help from Levi Strauss in setting up similar programs, and CEO Haas is in strong demand as a speaker by both business schools and corporations. In 1989 the company received yet another award—this time, Harvard University's prestigious George S. Dively Award for leadership in corporate public initiative.

of supporting one side or the other. First, some social responsibility activities are legally required. There is no choice but to perform them. Second, some social responsibility activities may help you accomplish the organization's goals. These you might do voluntarily, although they are not required legally. As a manager, you must inform everyone in the organization of your managerial direction in this area. We will examine each of these considerations in the following sections.

Performing Required Activities

Certain social responsibility activities are federally legislated. Businesses must hire and promote the most worthy candidates, for example, whether those candidates are young or old, male or female, black or white, Protestant or Jewish. This is the law.

Specific pieces of legislation that govern socially responsible business activities include the Equal Pay Act of 1963, the Federal Water Pollution Control Act amendments of 1972, the Clean Air Act amendments of 1977, and the Highway Safety Act of 1978. In 1988, the Economic Dislocation and Worker Adjustment Assistance Act became law, providing services to help workers adjust to plant closings and

Federal Agency	Primary Agency Activities
Equal Employment Opportunity Commission	Investigates and conciliates employment discrimination complaints based on race, sex, and creed.
Office of Federal Contract Compliance Programs	Ensures that employers holding federal contracts grant equal employment opportunity to people regardless of race or sex.
Environmental Protection Agency	Formulates and enforces environmental standards in such areas as water, air, and noise pollution.
Consumer Product Safety Commission	Strives to reduce consumer inquiries related to product design, labeling, etc.
Occupational Safety and Health Administration	Regulates safety and health conditions in nongovernment workplaces.
National Highway Traffic Safety Administration	Attempts to reduce traffic accidents through the regulation of transportation-related manufacturers and products.
Mining Enforcement and Safety Administration	Attempts to improve safety conditions for mine workers by enforcing mine safety and equipment standards.

Figure 3.2 Federal agencies and social responsibility legislation. The federal government has agencies whose primary function is to develop business-related legislation and make sure the laws are followed.

relocations. Several government agencies exist not only to develop such business-related legislation but to make sure that the legislation is followed. Figure 3.2 lists several of these agencies and their major functions.

Performing Voluntary Activities

Legislated activities represent the bare minimum in social responsibility. How far beyond these minimum standards should any manager attempt to go?

Given our definition of *social responsibility* as the managerial obligation to take action that will protect and improve not only the interests of the organization but also the welfare of society as a whole, managers must assess both the positive and negative outcomes of socially responsible actions over the short term and the long term. Then they must undertake the activities that will maximize organi-

Positive Outcomes	Percent Expecting
Enhanced corporate reputation and goodwill	97.4
Strengthening of the social system in which the corporation functions	89.0
Strengthening of the economic system in which the corporation functions	74.3
Greater job satisfaction among all employees	72.3
Avoidance of government regulation	63.7
Greater job satisfaction among executives	62.8
Increased chances for survival of the firm	60.7
Ability to attract better managerial talent	55.5
Increased long-run profitability	52.9
Strengthening of the pluralistic nature of American society	40.3
Maintaining or gaining customers	38.2
Investor preference of socially responsible firms	36.6
Increased short-run profitability	15.2

Negative Outcomes	Percent Expecting
Decreased short-run profitability	59.7
Conflict of economic or financial and social goals	53.9
Increased prices for consumers	41.4
Conflict in criteria for assessing managerial performance	27.2
Disaffection of stockholders	24.1
Decreased productivity	18.8
Decreased long-run profitability	13.1
Increased government regulation	11.0
Weakening of the economic system in which the corporation functions	7.9
Weakening of the social system in which the corporation functions	3.7

Figure 3.3

Positive and negative outcomes of social responsibility activities. The most positive outcomes, as seen by executives, are enhanced corporate reputation and goodwill.

zational success while contributing to the maintenance or improvement of society's welfare. While this may sound easy, studies indicate it is not.

In an attempt to assess the positive and negative outcomes expected by firms as a result of their social responsibility activities, Sandra L. Holmes surveyed the top executives of 560 major firms.[5] Represented were such industries as commercial banking, life insurance, transportation, and utilities. Figure 3.3 lists the projected outcomes and indicates the percentage of executives who expected to experience them. On the plus side, over 97 percent expected their corporate reputation to be enhanced. On the minus side, over 59 percent expected their short-term profits to decrease.

Although the information in Figure 3.3 may provide managers with some helpful insights into how socially involved their organizations should become, it does not provide hard and fast answers. Managers must gauge positive and negative outcomes based on their understanding of their firms.

Communicating the Degree of Involvement

It should be clear by now that determining the extent to which a business should be socially responsible is not a cut-and-dried process. Nevertheless, managers must have well-defined positions in this vital area. Furthermore, they must communicate their positions to all the organization members. They must also establish social responsibility objectives and set realistic guidelines for implementation, since everyone in the organization must behave consistently. As in so many other areas, communication is important.

HIGHLIGHT IN BUSINESS PRACTICE

Social Responsibility and Philanthropy: High Marks for Merck

In 1987 and 1988, *Fortune* magazine judged Merck to be the top company in the United States. All companies reviewed were judged in ten comprehensive categories, ranging from "quality of management" to "quality of social responsibility." Merck received near-perfect scores in almost every area in which it was examined.

Merck & Co., Inc. researches, develops, and distributes drugs designed to prevent or cure disease or illness. This giant in the pharmaceutical industry broke important ground recently with its introduction of two cholesterol-reducing agents, Mevacor and Zocor. These substances are welcome solutions to a very dangerous health problem.

To Merck, social responsibility has a far greater value than being merely a legally mandated aspect of doing business. In 1987, the firm donated one of its drugs, Mectizan, to 18 million Africans and, in doing so, gave the recipients hope for a brighter economic future. Mectizan cures onchocerciasis—river blindness—in the 18 million Africans who are afflicted with it.

River blindness is caused by a parasite that breeds around some of Africa's potentially most fertile—but until now uninhabitable—riverbank land. Human beings are the parasite's host, and the parasite's microscopic offspring eventually invade the eyes of the host and cause blindness. This disease permanently blinds 500,000 Africans per year and partially blinds all others who become infected.

Mectizan is based on Merck's veterinary drug ivermectan, which is used to treat animals infected with worm parasites. Mectizan has been tested for two years in humans. There have been few or no side effects reported, which makes it an even more powerful ally for those humans so badly in need of it.

Merck chairman Dr. P. Roy Vagelos indicated that his company's donation of the drug was based on the company's knowledge that the people most in need of this breakthrough cannot buy it. The World Health Organization will monitor its use and success and will review applications from other countries seeking a free supply of the drug.

Dr. Vagelos does not sit back and reflect on his corporation's achievements. Granted, Merck may have found some important solutions to critical world problems, but as far as he's concerned, there's too much work left to do. His is one corporation that takes social responsibility to heart.

MEASURING SOCIAL RESPONSIBILITY

Once managers have decided on a company's social responsibility objectives and have communicated that level of involvement to the employees, it becomes useful to measure the company's performance in achieving the objectives. The specific areas in which individual companies take such measurements will vary, of course, depending on the objectives each has set. However, all companies should probably measure certain areas. The results of real measurements in these areas indicate that business has invested much money and effort to ensure product safety, safe working conditions, and a clean environment.

Areas of Measurement

The four major areas for social responsibility measurement are economic function, quality of life, social investment, and problem solving.[6]

The Economic Function Area

The part of measuring a company's social responsibility activity that gauges the economic impact on society is the **economic function area.** This measurement focuses on such issues as whether the organization is producing goods and services that people need, creating jobs for society, paying fair wages, and ensuring worker safety. The measurement indicates the economic contribution made by the organization to benefit society.

The ***economic function area*** is the part of measuring a company's social responsibility activity that gauges the economic impact on society.

The Quality-of-Life Area

The part of measuring a company's social responsibility activity that gauges the improvement or maintenance of a desirable quality of life for individuals or society is the **quality-of-life area.** Such practices as producing high-quality goods, dealing fairly with employees and customers, and making an effort to preserve the natural environment could all be indicators that the organization is upholding or improving the general quality of life in society.

The ***quality-of-life area*** is the part of measuring a company's social responsibility activity that gauges the improvement or maintenance of a desirable quality of life for individuals or society.

Companies can improve the quality of life for their employees by offering benefits such as day care. This worker enjoys lunch with children at the Stride Rite Day Care Center in Boston.

The Social Investment Area

The part of measuring a company's social responsibility activity that gauges the contribution of money and other resources to help solve community social problems is the **social investment area.** Company involvement in programs such as United Way is one example. All forms of company-sponsored cooperation with community organizations lie within this area of measurement.

The ***social investment area*** is the part of measuring a company's social responsibility activity that gauges the contribution of money and other resources to help solve community social problems.

The Problem-Solving Area

The part of measuring a company's social responsibility activity that gauges the degree to which the company actively solves social problems is the **problem-solving area.** Involvement in long-range community planning, devoting company resources to pinpoint social problems, and creating products that solve social problems belong to the problem-solving area.

The ***problem-solving area*** is the part of measuring a company's social responsibility activity that gauges the degree to which the company actively solves social problems.

The Social Audit: A Progress Report

The summary of an organization's social responsibility activities is called its **social audit.** It is actually the process of taking social responsibility measurements.[7] The purpose of a social audit is to provide managers with an assessment of organizational performance in the social responsibility area. The audit can be performed either by staff or by outside consultants.

Figure 3.4 (p. 82) presents part of a sample social audit prepared by a major bank in San Francisco.[8] The figure is not meant to illustrate a standard format to be used for compiling the results of a social audit. In fact, probably no two organizations conduct and present the results of a social audit in exactly the same way.

The ***social audit*** is a summary of an organization's social responsibility activities.

SOCIALLY RESPONSIBLE BUSINESS PRACTICES

The actions taken by managers that contribute to the attainment of organizational objectives while enhancing the welfare of society are **socially responsible business practices.** We can classify the major areas of such practices as follows: (1) code-of-conduct business practices, (2) consumer-oriented business practices, (3) environmental protection business practices, and (4) philanthropic business practices.

Socially responsible business practices are actions taken by managers that contribute to the attainment of organizational objectives while enhancing the welfare of society.

Code-of-Conduct Business Practices: Ethics[9]

The term *ethics* has many definitions. The one provided by humanitarian Dr. Albert Schweitzer seems to capture the essence of many others. According to Schweitzer: "**Ethics** is a code of behavior which a society considers moral and appropriate for guiding the way in which its members deal with one another. We feel an obligation to consider not only our personal well-being, but also that of other humans." Essentially, ethical behavior is behavior consistent with the golden rule: Do unto others as you would have them do unto you. The following statement, made by a senior vice president of Gulf Oil Corporation, stresses the importance of ethics in business: "We've learned that honesty *does* count, integrity *is* important, that fair dealing, open dealing, and straightforward dealing are the only

Ethics is a code of behavior that a society considers moral and appropriate for guiding the way in which its members deal with one another.

BUSINESS PRACTICE EXAMPLE Continues

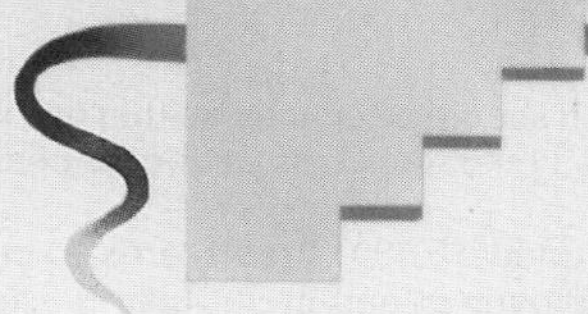

In 1986 Levi Strauss & Co. created a "Special Projects Division" within the Corporate Affairs Department, charging it with writing a "report card"—another phrase for "social audit"—to target areas where the company could improve as a corporate citizen. Areas that have received attention as a result of these social audits include increasing purchases from minority-owned businesses and more closely monitoring advancement opportunities for women and minority employees.

Levi Strauss is obviously extremely sensitive to all four areas of measurement described in the text. For instance, in 1984, faced with the too-strong dollar and declining international sales, the company closed 32 of its 100 facilities and laid off 7,500 employees. Aware of the economic impact this loss created for many of the small towns in which the targeted facilities were located, Levi Strauss extended full medical benefits to all employees from three months to a year (depending on length of service), provided extensive job retraining and outplacement, and gave laid-off workers priority in hiring at other company plants.

In the problem-solving area, Levi Strauss established a Special Emphasis grants program, the purpose of which is to "enhance the economic options and opportunities of economically disadvantaged population groups, including the poor and others at risk of slipping into poverty."

kinds of dealings that pay off in the long run. . . . We have noticed no material loss of business either here or overseas because of our strengthened ethical standards."

Many corporations seriously strive to be ethical in their behavior. However, survey results reported by *Business Week* indicate that there is pressure in some organizations to sacrifice personal ethics for the good of the organization.[10] As Figure 3.5 shows, 59 percent of managers surveyed at Pitney-Bowes, a manufacturer of business equipment, and 70 percent of the managers surveyed at Uniroyal Tire believed there was pressure in their organizations to compromise personal ethics to achieve corporate goals.

The right to safety is one of the consumer's four basic rights. Safety testing of automobiles helps to ensure this right.

Consumer-Oriented Business Practices

Socially responsible business practices are often consumer oriented. Consumer advocate Ralph Nader is generally acknowledged as the main force behind the birth and growth of **consumerism**—the social movement that seeks to strengthen the rights and powers of buyers in relation to sellers. Consumers argue that they have four basic rights[11]:

Consumerism is the social movement that seeks to strengthen the rights and powers of buyers in relation to sellers.

Social Performance Report • Part 1 • Mainstream Issues

Priority • Consumer Issues

Issue • Discrimination in Credit • Minorities

Potential — New legislation pending in Congress, which should be enacted within two years. Growing public awareness due to increased press coverage. Class actions a possibility.

Progress — New guidelines instituted for small loans (under $5,500), credit cards. Race no longer part of the application, emphasis on employment and credit history. No automatic restrictions.

Problems — No progress in increasing applications from minorities.

Position — Keeping pace with the competition. Better advertising of new policies would help generate new business.

Issue • Complaints and Errors

Potential — Most stated reason for customer choosing another bank is errors. Three percent reduction in closed accounts would be the equivalent of increased profits of $320,000. This could be dramatically increased if complaints were handled more quickly.

Progress — Instituted toll-free line to handle complaints. Feedback has been positive. Cost: $50,000. New manager hired in checking. Instituted a system whereby all checks are double-processed. Errors down 18%. Cost: $80,000.

Problems — No progress in ridding checking and savings account statements of errors.

Position — Perception in the marketplace regarding our service is improved. Substantial reduction in closed accounts (7%).

Priority • Employee Development

Issue • Affirmative Action

Potential — Continued close monitoring by government. Potential liability by class actions now $1 million to $10 million. Program to upgrade underutilized talent in bank (especially women) could significantly increase productivity, as well as decrease recruitment costs. Growing number of qualified minorities in area increase pool of qualified candidates.

Progress — Strong minority program instituted during the year with goals, time-tables, and mechanisms for enforcement. The recent record is good: 1985, 18.3 percent of employees minority; 1986, 19.9 percent; 1987, 23.7 percent; 1988 goal is parity. Plans to institute a similar program are underway for 1990.

Problems — Minorities and women still concentrated in the lower ranks:

Percent of Bank Officers Who Are:	1985	1986	1987	1990 Goal
Minority	4.3%	5.8%	7.1%	10.8%
Women	16.9%	19.7%	22.0%	30.0%

To reach 1990 goals, we must concentrate on developing programs to identify and train potential candidates for promotion.

Position — The above effort is largely required. It will offer no competitive advantage or disadvantage, since it is mandated industry-wide.

Figure 3.4 Portion of sample social audit report.

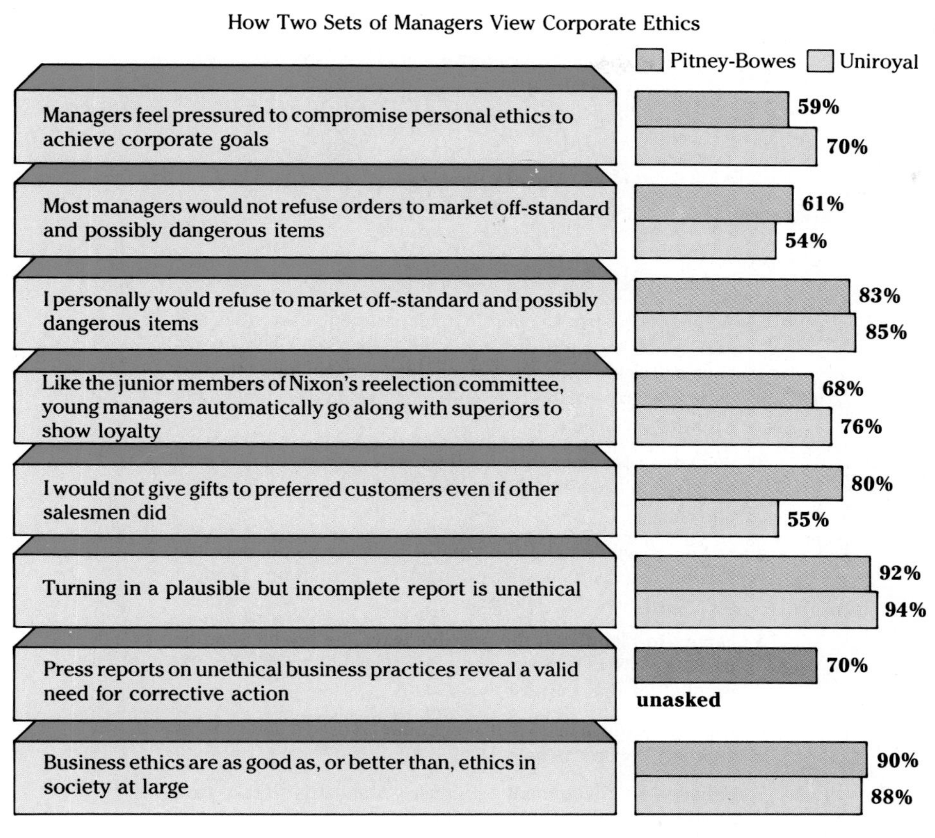
How Two Sets of Managers View Corporate Ethics
Pitney-Bowes
Uniroyal
Managers feel pressured to compromise personal ethics to achieve corporate goals
59%
70%
Most managers would not refuse orders to market off-standard and possibly dangerous items
61%
54%
I personally would refuse to market off-standard and possibly dangerous items
83%
85%
Like the junior members of Nixon's reelection committee, young managers automatically go along with superiors to show loyalty
68%
76%
I would not give gifts to preferred customers even if other salesmen did
80%
55%
Turning in a plausible but incomplete report is unethical
92%
94%
Press reports on unethical business practices reveal a valid need for corrective action
70%
unasked
Business ethics are as good as, or better than, ethics in society at large
90%
88%

Figure 3.5
Ethical behavior is sometimes sacrificed as managers bow to organizational pressure.

1. The **right to safety**—the right to purchase products that are not dangerous. Toys, appliances, and automobiles are examples of products that have at one time or another violated this consumer right. Are the eyes of a child's doll small buttons that can be pulled off and eaten? With extensive use, will an electric toaster overheat and cause a fire? When parked on an incline, will an automobile slip out of gear and roll backward? Figure 3.6 lists several business practices that can result in dangerous products.

The ***right to safety*** is the right to purchase products that are not dangerous.

2. The **right to be informed**—the right to know what a product is, what precautions must be taken during its use, and what ingredients it contains. Does a packaged food contain any substance that might cause an allergic reaction? Must a paint be used only in a well-ventilated room? The right to be informed generally focuses on how business should advertise, label, and market its products.

The ***right to be informed*** is the right to know what a product is, what precautions must be taken during its use, and what ingredients it contains.

3. The **right to choose**—the right to select a product from a number of competing ones in a competitive marketplace. Such a marketplace assures that consumers are paying fair prices for products.

The ***right to choose*** is the right to select a product from a number of competing ones in the marketplace.

4. The **right to be heard**—the right to be listened to by business. Consumers should have an effective means of communicating to business their likes, dislikes, and grievances.

The ***right to be heard*** is the right to be listened to by business.

Figure 3.6
Situations in which business practices can result in dangerous products. To a great extent, consumerism is the reaction to business practices that have created dangerous products.

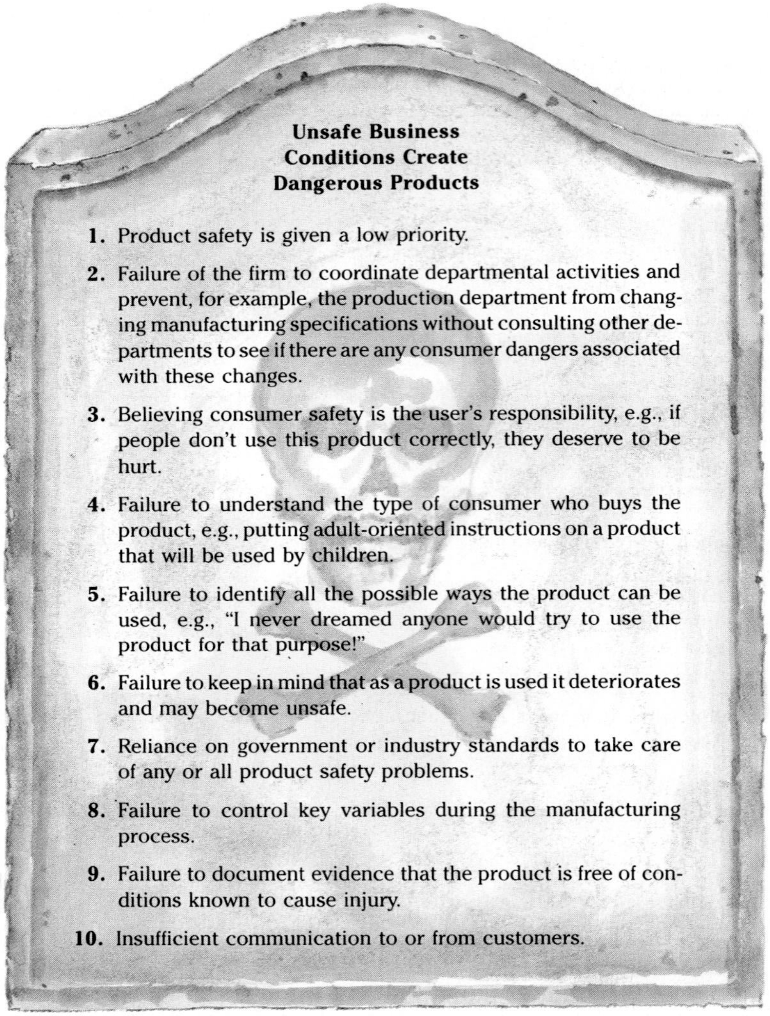

Unsafe Business Conditions Create Dangerous Products

1. Product safety is given a low priority.
2. Failure of the firm to coordinate departmental activities and prevent, for example, the production department from changing manufacturing specifications without consulting other departments to see if there are any consumer dangers associated with these changes.
3. Believing consumer safety is the user's responsibility, e.g., if people don't use this product correctly, they deserve to be hurt.
4. Failure to understand the type of consumer who buys the product, e.g., putting adult-oriented instructions on a product that will be used by children.
5. Failure to identify all the possible ways the product can be used, e.g., "I never dreamed anyone would try to use the product for that purpose!"
6. Failure to keep in mind that as a product is used it deteriorates and may become unsafe.
7. Reliance on government or industry standards to take care of any or all product safety problems.
8. Failure to control key variables during the manufacturing process.
9. Failure to document evidence that the product is free of conditions known to cause injury.
10. Insufficient communication to or from customers.

Figure 3.7, a Whirlpool advertisement, indicates how the company has responded to consumerism.

More and more, modern managers are finding that in order to reach organizational goals they must respect and protect the rights of consumers. The ability to uphold consumer rights has become a valuable management skill.

Environmental protection is the conducting of business in a fashion that assists the company in reaching its objectives but does not damage the natural surroundings.

Environmental Protection Business Practices

Business practices that protect the environment are generally considered socially responsible. **Environmental protection** is the conducting of business in a

Lesson from a dying breed.

Extinction is a dreadful word. Like Donne's bell, it doesn't ring. It tolls. And it's tolling for the eagle now, which puts us in danger, too.

We're in danger of losing the living symbol of our highest standards: Pride. Honor. Honesty. To lose the eagle would be sad. To forget him would be tragic.

At Whirlpool we believe it's our duty to remember. Remember what these standards mean to us. In our lives. And in our business.

We start with pride. To make something of quality is a challenge these days. An appliance is either quality built or it isn't. And if it isn't good enough for us, we know it's not good enough for you.

The test of honor and honesty comes after the sale. We believe a customer should always be treated like a customer. Now, or years from now. With this in mind, we've developed several ways of extending our services for as long as anyone needs them.

For example, we have Cool-Line® service. A toll-free telephone number you can call with any problem or question. Try it. We're always glad when people do. (800) 253-1301. In Michigan, (800) 632-243.

And if you ever do need service, just call Tech-Care® service. It's our nationwide franchised service . . . from a group of service technicians who know what they're doing. And who will be happy to come out and help your whenever you need them. They're in the Yellow Pages.

Or our warranty. It's written clearly, simply. It can be read, understood and used with confidence. We feel that's the way a warranty should work.

These services are really extensions of our way of thinking. Our way of life. They represent our standards: Pride. Honor. Honesty.

They may be in danger. They may be impractical. But at Whirlpool, we believe it's our duty to keep them very much alive.

Figure 3.7
How the Whirlpool Corporation has reacted to consumer rights.

fashion that assists the company in reaching its objectives but does not damage natural surroundings. Over all, environmental protection focuses on the elimination of **pollution**—the contamination of the environment caused by human activities. The following sections discuss three kinds of pollution: air, water, and land.

Pollution is the contamination of the environment caused by human activities.

HIGHLIGHT IN BUSINESS PRACTICE

Business Ethics Gets a Tryout

Since the Wall Street insider trading scandal of 1987, in which arbitrageurs Ivan Boesky, Dennis Levine, and others were caught illegally trading inside information for huge profits, the business community has paid a great deal of attention to business ethics. Most business schools now require coursework on ethics. A new industry of consultants on ethics has emerged, charging top dollar to counsel corporations on establishing ethics policies and procedures. Employees have responded to all of this activity with a mixture of enthusiasm and cynicism, largely depending on whether they feel their companies truly believe in ethical behavior or are just practicing good public relations.

Continued on next page

HIGHLIGHT IN BUSINESS PRACTICE

Business Ethics Gets a Tryout *(Continued)*

"There's no question that all sorts of people are feasting at the trough called ethics," says Mark Past, director of the business ethics center at Arizona State University. But while some companies do seem to be paying lip service to ethics by hiring expensive consultants and then ignoring their suggestions, many other companies have demonstrated a firm commitment to ethical practices.

The fact that a company has a written code of ethics does not in itself guarantee that it practices what the code preaches. Companies with extensive codes but with little or no enforcement can fare as poorly as, or worse than, companies with no code at all. In a study conducted by former Washington State University professor Marilynn Cash Mathews, 350 firms were surveyed to determine how effective their ethics programs were. Results showed that those with written ethics policies were more often charged with wrongdoing than those without such formal policies. Included in those companies that had detailed ethical policies was the Northrop Corp., a Los Angeles-based defense contractor. Just months after forming an extensive ethics "initiative," Northrop was accused of several wrongdoings, including overcharging the government for the Stealth bomber program and improprieties in the MX missile program. On the other hand, companies with superior business ethics practices, such as the Xerox Corp. and General Mills, Inc., have written ethical codes *and* strict enforcement.

There is nearly unanimous agreement that involvement of top management in creating an ethics program is the single most important thing a company can do to ensure an ethical environment. "You need a culture and peer pressure that spells out what is acceptable and what isn't and why. It involves training, education, and follow-up," says Andrew C. Sigler, chairman of Champion International Corp. and a member of a task force on ethics established by the Business Roundtable. The Roundtable report made several recommendations, including greater commitment of top management to ethics programs, written codes that clearly communicate management expectations, implementation programs, and monitoring mechanisms.

Air Pollution

Air pollution is the contamination of the air we breathe.

The contamination of the air we breathe is **air pollution.** The automobile industry, for example, has been closely monitored and pressured to ensure that its vehicles do not release poisonous gases into the air as they are being driven. Chemical companies, steel mills, and many other manufacturers are being pressured to stop pouring poisonous gases into the air through their smokestacks.

Another serious pollutant is acid rain, rain containing large amounts of sulphur released into the atmosphere by certain industries and by power plants. Acid rain causes great harm to the environment, particularly to trees and forests. The issue of an entire country's social responsibility to another country has arisen in the case of this serious pollutant. Acid rain falling in Canada was found to come from industrial emissions in the United States. As a result, the United States accepted a proposal by Canada to clean up emissions along the border between the two countries. The cost of this project to the United States is over $5 billion.[12]

Water Pollution

The contamination of lakes, rivers, and oceans is **water pollution.** Discharge from mills and smelters in Puget Sound, for instance, has inundated surrounding waterways with heavy metals and toxic chemicals. The result is grave danger to all kinds of marine life in the area. Another example is Boston Harbor, which, like many other major city harbors, has been seriously contaminated by industrial waste and inadequate sewage treatment. Boston's fifty-square-mile harbor has been turned into a cesspool. Fish suffer from fin rot and tumors.[13] Table 3.2 lists several pollutants that are presently contaminating our water.

Water pollution is the contamination of lakes, rivers, and oceans.

Land Pollution[14]

The contamination of the ground is **land pollution.** Perhaps the most widely discussed pollutant of land is hazardous waste. This waste consists of the by-products of manufacturing; people who come in contact with it can become seriously ill, receive genetic damage, and may even die. Commonly observed hazardous waste pollutants include the electrical insulating compound polychlorinated biphenyl (PCB), various pesticides, and heavy metals such as mercury and lead. Unfortunately, only about 10 percent of hazardous wastes are safely dumped each year. The remainder are discarded recklessly and often cause serious damage to the people living near the dump sites.

Land pollution is the contamination of the ground.

To encourage a nationwide cleanup of hazardous waste dumps, Congress passed the Comprehensive Environmental Response, Compensation, and Liability Act in 1980. This act became popularly known as the "superfund" law, since it established a $1.6 billion fund to help pay for the cleanup effort. In 1986, Congress authorized over a fivefold increase in the superfund, to a five-year total of $9

Industrial accidents pose an enormous danger to our environment. These workers are attempting to contain the water pollution from the Valdez oil spill in Prince William Sound, Alaska.

Table 3.2 Water pollution today.

Pollutant	Source	Effects
Nutrients	Fertilizers, sewage.	Algae blooms, marine life destruction.
Chlorinated hydrocarbons: pesticides, DDT, PCBs	Agricultural runoff, industrial waste.	Contaminated and diseased fish and shellfish.
Petroleum hydrocarbons	Oil spills, industrial discharge, urban runoff.	Ecosystem destruction.
Heavy metals: arsenic, cadmium, copper, lead, zinc	Industrial waste, mining.	Diseased and contaminated fish.
Particulate material	Soil erosion, dying algae.	Smothering of shellfish beds, blockage of light needed by marine plant life.
Plastics	Ship dumping, household waste, litter.	Strangling and mutilation of wildlife, destruction of natural habitats.

billion. It was to be financed by a broadly based tax on corporations as well as special taxes on chemical producers and crude oil producers.

Today, environmental protection is of grave concern worldwide. Although pollution is a natural danger resulting from various kinds of manufacturing processes, it must be studied and dealt with in the most socially responsible manner possible. Business has been and will continue to be pressured on this score, both by legislation and by public-interest groups.

Philanthropic Business Practices

Philanthropy is the active effort to help humanity that typically is demonstrated by donations of money, property, or labor.

Philanthropy is the active effort to help humanity that is typically demonstrated by the donation of money, property, or labor. One prominent business philanthropy is the Kellogg Foundation, established by W. K. Kellogg, the founder of the Kellogg Company. This foundation has made over $60 million in donations since 1931 in three areas: agriculture, health, and education. Table 3.3 illustrates the types of grants the foundation makes.

Business philanthropic donations are commonly made with two motives in mind: helping society and helping the organization become more successful. For example, Japanese companies commonly combat image problems by setting up U.S. foundations. Six large Japanese corporations have formed such foundations in the last five years. The reason is partly to reverse the growing trend of anti-

Table 3.3 Kellogg's largest grants in 1987 (in millions of dollars)

Grant Recipient	Amount and Duration of Grant	Purpose
University of Michigan (Ann Arbor)	$5.0 (5 years)	Encouragement of interdisciplinary scholarship.
	$5.0 (2 years)	Funding for a chemical science building.
	$2.1 (5 years)	Computerized database of libraries in Michigan.
City of Battle Creek, Mich.	$4.1 (2 years)	Recreational and cultural facilities.
Binder Park Zoological Society (Battle Creek, Mich.)	$2.1 (5 years)	Educational exhibits, including replacement of "zoo mobile."
Michigan State University (East Lansing)	$2.0 (3 years)	Health-related activities and projects that encourage a healthy life-style.
Maternity Center Association (New York City)	$1.9 (2 years)	Birthing centers in two low-income, minority communities.
University of Missouri (Columbia)	$1.7 (3 years)	Development of services to help the elderly remain at home.
National Academy of Sciences (Washington, D.C.)	$1.5 (5 years)	Development of programs at the Institute of Medicine.
International Fertilizer Development Center (Muscle Shoals, Ala.)	$1.5 (3 years)	Fertilizer center in Africa.
United Way of America (Alexandria, Va.)	$1.4 (3 years)	Development of programs to boost minority leadership.

Japanese sentiment in the United States because of widespread Japanese takeovers of American businesses. Most of the Japanese companies' grants are awarded to education-related projects. One such grant was to finance a day-care center for the children of women who are on welfare.[15]

BUSINESS PRACTICE EXAMPLE Continues

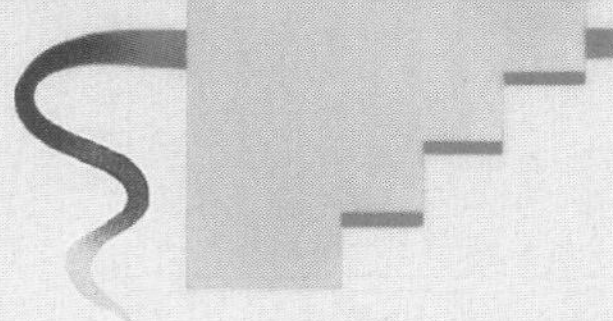

This section of text highlights socially responsible business practices which focus on environmental protection, consumerism, philanthropy, and ethics. Levi Strauss has received a lot of attention lately because of the ethical manner in which it has dealt with immigrant employees.

Under the Immigration Reform and Control Act of 1986, certain undocumented immigrants who had lived in the United States since 1982 were able to become legal residents under a temporary "amnesty" program in effect between May, 1987 and May, 1988. Unfortunately, many undocumented immigrants who could potentially benefit from this amnesty period did not understand all of the requirements they had to fulfill, and/or did not have the family application fee of $420.00. Levi Strauss conducted free, confidential immigration counseling sessions in 18 facilities in Texas and New Mexico. Experts in immigration law provided employees a summary of the law, an explanation of the requirements of the application process, and referrals to local community agencies assisting individuals seeking legal residency. In addition, the company offered loans of up to $1000 to help employees and their dependents pay the costs of the application process.

Issues for Discussion

1. How does Levi Strauss & Co.'s social responsibility activities, such as its counseling sessions for immigrants and its Community Involvement Teams, also help the company?
2. Are business practices at Levi Strauss consistent with the Davis model of social responsibility? Discuss.
3. Describe how Levi Strauss fulfills the four areas of measurement discussed in the text—the economic function, quality-of-life, social investment, and problem-solving areas.

SUMMARY

Social responsibility is the managerial obligation to take action that will protect and improve the interests of the organization and the welfare of society. Three major areas of social responsibility involvement are external relations, product control, and environmental control.

Among the arguments supporting social responsibility

activities are (1) that businesses form a significant part of society and therefore should help maintain and improve it and (2) that the public image of companies will be enhanced. One of the arguments against such activities is that they decrease short-term profitability.

The Davis model of social responsibility offers five propositions describing how and why businesses should perform social responsibility activities: (1) social responsibility arises from social power; (2) businesses should openly receive input from society and openly disclose their operations to the public; (3) social costs and benefits should be calculated before a business proceeds with an activity; (4) social costs should be passed along to the consumer; and (5) businesses, as citizens, should become involved in social problems outside their normal area of operation.

Some social responsibility activities are required by law, and some are voluntary. Managers must communicate their company's position on social responsibility to all organization members.

Social responsibility activities are measured in four areas: (1) economic function (the economic impact of an activity on society); (2) quality of life (the extent to which an activity improves or maintains the desirability of living in a society); (3) social investment (solving community social problems); and (4) problem solving (the degree to which a company actively works to solve social problems). The summary of an organization's social responsibility activities is called a social audit.

There are four major areas of socially responsible business practices (those that contribute to the attainment of organizational objectives while enhancing society's welfare): (1) code-of-conduct practices (ethical behavior); (2) consumer-oriented practices (which observe consumers' right to safety, right to be informed, right to choose, and right to be heard); (3) environmental protection practices (avoiding damage to natural surroundings and eliminating pollution of the air, water, and land); and (4) philanthropic practices (actively helping humanity by donating money, property, or labor).

KEY TERMS

Air pollution p. 86
Consumerism p. 81
Davis model of social responsibility p. 73
Economic function area p. 79
Environmental protection p. 84
Ethics p. 80
Land pollution p. 87
Philanthropy p. 88
Pollution p. 85
Problem-solving area p. 80
Quality-of-life area p. 79
Right to be heard p. 83
Right to be informed p. 83
Right to choose p. 83
Right to safety p. 83
Social audit p. 80
Social investment area p. 80
Socially responsible business practices p. 80
Social responsibility p. 69
Water pollution p. 87

CHECK YOUR LEARNING

Reread the following learning objectives. Each objective is followed by a few questions. Answering these questions accurately will help you retain the most important concepts discussed in this chapter. After answering each question, check your answer with the key at the end of this chapter. (*Hint:* If you have doubt regarding the correct response, consult the page whose number follows the answer.)

Circle:

A. Discuss the role of social responsibility in modern management.

T F 1. Social responsibility focuses on obligations.

T F 2. Attention by managers to the area of social responsibility focuses on product control and not environmental control.

T F 3. Social responsibility protects society and organizations.

B. Outline the arguments for and against an organization performing social responsibility activities.

1. Arguments *for* managers performing social responsibility activities include: (a) it is ethical to do; (b) social action cannot be measured; (c) business lacks skill to solve social problems; (d) a and b. a b c d
2. Because of certain laws, some social responsibility activities must be performed by business. T F
3. Arguments relating to specific organizations performing social responsibility activities usually include positive but not negative results of performing the activities. T F

C. Define and discuss the importance of social audits.

1. Social responsibility measurements are involved in social auditing. T F
2. As with accounting, social auditing follows well-defined procedures. T F

D. Discuss several different socially responsible business practices.

1. It is safe to say that there is little or no pressure on managers to sacrifice their personal ethics for the good of the organization. T F
2. Consumers are fighting for the right to: (a) be informed; (b) be safe; (c) be heard; (d) all of the above. a b c d
3. Environmental pollution can involve: (a) air pollution; (b) water pollution; (c) land pollution; (d) all of the above. a b c d
4. Philanthropy is a business practice followed only by companies with headquarters in the United States. T F

QUESTIONS FOR REVIEW AND DISCUSSION

1. Define the key terms listed at the end of the chapter.
2. Do you think business should or should not perform social responsibility activities? Explain.
3. Choose an organization in your community and discuss its involvement in social responsibility activities. If possible, interview managers in that organization in order to develop a more comprehensive answer.
4. What major characteristics do you think society will have ten years from now? How will these characteristics influence the operation of businesses?
8. As a consultant, how would you advise a manager to deal with consumerism? Why would you advise the manager as you did?
9. Give three examples of ethical behavior and three of unethical behavior by a drug manufacturer.
10. From personal experience, would you say that business is trying to protect the environment? Give examples.
5. What problems could arise if management does not communicate to other employees the degree of social responsibility involvement that their organization will exercise?
6. In which of these four areas would it be most difficult to take social responsibility measurements: the economic function area, quality-of-life area, social investment area, or problem-solving area? Explain.
7. Conduct a social audit on an organization of your choice. What are the conclusions of your audit?
11. Suppose the Metropolitan Opera is having a fund drive to raise $100 million and a Fortune 500 company decides to donate $1 million to the drive. How should the company's board of directors justify this act to stockholders who want higher dividends, consumers who want a lower price, and employees who want higher wages?

CONCLUDING CASE

A Letter to AT&T Employees

DEAR FELLOW EMPLOYEE:

Although our just-completed reorganization has not changed our fundamental competitive policies, our new business environment requires more careful attention than ever to competitive obligations. It is therefore appropriate at this time to reissue and amplify AT&T's competition guidelines.

AT&T is committed to a policy of vigorous, lawful, and ethical competition. This policy rests upon three fundamental principles of competitive behavior:

• First, success in the marketplace must be achieved solely by our own competitive efforts. Arrangements or understandings with our competitors that might reduce or restrain competition between us must be avoided.

• Second, our competitive efforts must rely upon the merits of our products and services. We must concentrate upon anticipating and satisfying the needs of our customers. We should not seek to limit the competitive opportunities of our rivals.

• Third, we must avoid, to the extent possible, even the appearance of improper competitive practices or improper business purposes.

Whenever a question involving compliance with these Guidelines does arise, it will call for careful and informed judgment. It is entirely possible that the exercise of this judgment—*your* judgment—will be questioned at a later time in an antitrust or regulatory proceeding. Therefore, you should discuss the matter directly and confidentially with your Legal Department in order to assure informed and responsible management decision-making and compliance with our competition policy.

By observing these Guidelines and consulting counsel whenever questions arise, we can ensure that our policy of lawful and ethical competition will be effective.

C. L. Brown
Chairman

Issues for Discussion

1. Why should a company such as AT&T be concerned with ethical issues in business?
2. Give an example of an unethical business practice that could be implemented at AT&T. Discuss why the practice is unethical.
3. The AT&T letter states: "Our competitive efforts must rely upon the merits of our products and services." Is this an ethical position for AT&T to take? Explain.

NOTES

1. Frederick D. Sturdivant, *Business and Society: A Managerial Approach* (Homewood, Ill.: Richard D. Irwin, 1985).
2. R. E. Freeman and D. R. Gilbert, *Corporate Strategy and the Search for Ethics* (Englewood Cliffs, N.J.: Prentice-Hall, 1989).
3. Milton Friedman, "Does Business Have Social Responsibility?" *Bank Administration,* April 1971, pp. 13–14.
4. Keith Davis, "Five Propositions for Social Responsibility," *Business Horizons,* June 1975, pp. 19–24.
5. Sandra L. Holmes, "Executive Perceptions of Corporate Social Responsibility," *Business Horizons,* June 1976, pp. 34–40.
6. Frank H. Cassell, "The Social Cost of Doing Business," *MSU Business Topics,* Autumn 1974, pp. 19–26.
7. Archie B. Carroll, *Business and Society* (Boston: Little, Brown, 1981), pp. 365–383.
8. Bernard Butcher, "Anatomy of a Social Performance Report," *Business and Society Review,* Autumn 1973, pp. 26–32.
9. This section is based on *Ethics Resource Center Bulletin* (Chapel Hill, N.C.: American Viewpoint, n.d.); and Larue Tone Hosmer, *The Ethics of Management* (Homewood, Ill.: Richard D. Irwin, 1987).
10. "The Pressure to Compromise Personal Ethics," *Business Week,* January 31, 1977, p. 107.
11. Philip Kotler, "What Consumerism Means for Marketers," *Harvard Business Review,* May–June 1972, pp. 48–57.

12. William Brown, "Hysteria about Acid Rain," *Fortune,* April 14, 1986, pp. 125–126.
13. Tom Morganthau, Mary Hager, Lisa Brown, Ted Kennedy, and Lisa Drew, "Don't Go Near the Water," *Newsweek,* August 1, 1988, pp. 42–48.
14. This section is based on William C. Frederick, Keith Davis, and James E. Post, *Business and Society: Corporate Strategy, Public Policy, Ethics* (New York: McGraw-Hill, 1988), pp. 432–433.
15. M. Cox, "Business Bulletin," *Wall Street Journal,* June 30, 1988, p. 1.

CHECK YOUR LEARNING ANSWER KEY

A. 1. T, *p. 69*
2. F, *p. 70*
3. T, *p. 70*

B. 1. a, *p. 73*
2. T, *p. 73*
3. F, *p. 73*

C. 1. T, *p. 80*
2. F, *p. 80*

D. 1. F, *p. 81*
2. d, *p. 83*
3. d, *p. 85*
4. F, *p. 88*

PART

STARTING UP A BUSINESS

CHAPTER

Selecting a Form of Business Ownership

CHAPTER

Small Business and Entrepreneurship

CHAPTER

4

SELECTING A FORM OF BUSINESS OWNERSHIP

LEARNING OBJECTIVES

After reading this chapter you should be able to:

1. Compare and contrast sole proprietorships, partnerships, and corporations and list the advantages and disadvantages of each.
2. Distinguish among secret, silent, dormant, and nominal partners.
3. Distinguish among domestic, foreign, and alien corporations.
4. Discuss current trends in the composition of corporate boards of directors and the role of today's board members.
5. Discuss corporate growth trends of the twentieth century and distinguish among the various types of mergers.
6. Compare and contrast the alternate forms of ownership.

OUTLINE

Business Practice Example: The Hard Rock Cafe

Sole Proprietorships

- Advantages
  - Tax Structure Simplicity
  - Ease of Establishment and Dissolution
  - Flexibility
  - Ownership of Profits
  - Secrecy
- Disadvantages
  - Unlimited Liability
  - Limited Life
  - Size and Capital Limitations
  - Lack of Employee Opportunities
  - Limited Managerial Skills

Partnerships

- Advantages
  - Legal Status
  - Employee Retention and Motivations
  - Ease of Establishment and Organization
  - Specialized Management
  - Personal Interest
- Disadvantages
  - Unlimited Liability
  - Limited Life
  - Frozen Investment
  - Owner Conflicts
  - Size and Capital Limitations

Corporations

- Forming a Corporation
- Corporate Governance
- Advantages
  - Limited Liability
  - Continuous Life
  - Ownership Transferability
  - Specialized Management
  - Ease of Expansion
- Disadvantages
  - Difficulty of Creation
  - Double Taxation for Owners
  - Lack of Secrecy
  - Government Regulation
  - Lack of Personal Interest by Employees
- Corporate Ownership Trends
  - Mergers and Acquisitions
  - Other Ownership Trends

Alternate Forms of Ownership

- Cooperatives
- Joint Ventures
- Nonprofit Organizations

Summary

Key Terms

Check Your Learning

Review and Discussion

Concluding Case: Balancing the Boardroom

Notes

Check Your Learning Answer Key

Highlight in Business Practice: The Boston Celtics: A Master Limited Partnership

Highlight in Business Practice: The Global Merger Boom

BUSINESS PRACTICE EXAMPLE

The Hard Rock Cafe

The Hard Rock Cafe is the world's largest international sitdown restaurant chain. The company, founded in 1971 in London, England, earns $5 million annually on $26 million in sales. Today Hard Rock Cafes are located in London, New York, Los Angeles, Dallas, Chicago, Washington, D.C., Houston, San Francisco, Boston, Tokyo, Stockholm, Amsterdam, Bombay, Cancun, and Manila. Although all have a common name, they are not owned and operated by the same people.

The restaurant chain was started by two rich young Americans, Isaac Tigrett and Peter Morton. Tigrett and Morton, both 22 years old at the time, hatched the idea and opened the first restaurant on June 14, 1971, with money largely borrowed from their parents. The entrepreneurs' concept had a number of components. It was a throwback to the old malt shop, featuring a variety of sundaes and shakes, along with hard liquor from a well-stocked bar. The menu had a decidedly American flavor: steaks, burgers, barbequed ribs, corn-on-the-cobb, and apple pie. It had pinball machines and raucous rock and roll music. It was purposely brash, like a highway truck stop. And it had an outrageous decor based on memorabilia from the world of rock and roll music. Among the artifacts that adorn Hard Rock Cafes today are Elvis Presley's motorcycle and original tour jacket, Chubby Checker's "Checkerboard Boots," Bo Diddley's box guitar, and Ringo Starr's autographed snare drum.

Location was important. Morton wanted a place accessible to both natives and tourists. Tigrett, a little turned off by the British class structure, wanted to make a statement, and he was therefore delighted to put a swinging, informal cafe that served hamburgers and didn't have a dress code on Park Lane, a posh street in Mayfair. The Hard Rock turned out to be handy to entertainers who were staying at the nearby Mayfair hotels. Steven Speilberg had a hamburger there every day while he was filming Raiders of the Lost Ark in London. The place became a hangout for young people and entertainers. Restauranteurs don't make money, however, on people who just hang out. After consulting with a sound engineer at Muzak, Tigrett and Morton turned the decibel level so high that people had to shout to talk. People also ate faster to escape the noise. In London, turnover increased fivefold after the sound level was raised. The Hard Rock Cafe was a smash hit!

WHAT'S AHEAD

As the owners of the Hard Rock Cafe discovered, choosing the best form of business ownership is not always easy. It requires careful review and analysis of many different business characteristics. As times change, so do the needs of businesses. Many businesses that start as small sole proprietorships will grow to be large multinational corporations. Thus, the decision about the form of ownership is influenced by both current and projected circumstances.

In this chapter, we will examine the three basic forms of private ownership: sole proprietorship, partnership, and corporation. The examination will include the characteristics, advantages, and disadvantages of each. In addition, we will look into several alternate forms of ownership. When you have completed this chapter, you should be able to recognize the strengths and weaknesses of each form of private ownership and to recommend the best ownership choice on the basis of current and projected circumstances.

Every entrepreneur who strives to own and operate a successful business must carefully evaluate the various forms of business ownership. Selecting a form of ownership is a major step in establishing a business. The right choice can mean profitability, stability, continuity, and perhaps even an advantage over the competition.

There are three major forms of business ownership. The first, **sole proprietorship**—a business owned by own person—is the most common, since entrepreneurs tend to own and operate their businesses by themselves. A **partnership,** by contrast, has two or more owners, who may or may not actively manage the business. The final form of ownership is the **corporation**—a legal entity with the authority to act on its own and with liability separate from that of its owners. This form of ownership accounts for the largest amount of business receipts. Figure 4.1 gives a breakdown of the forms of business ownership in the United States.

A ***sole proprietorship*** is a business owned by one person.

A ***partnership*** is an association of two or more individuals to carry on as co-owners of a business.

A ***corporation*** is a state-chartered legal entity with the authority to act on its own and with liability separate from that of its owners.

SOLE PROPRIETORSHIPS

A sole proprietorship has special appeal to a person just starting in business because it provides a form of ownership in which the proprietor can own and operate a business for personal profit. Sole proprietors own and manage such businesses as restaurants, drugstores, beauty parlors, construction firms, and farms.

About 70 percent of all American businesses are sole proprietorships. Of these, approximately 70 percent have total sales of less than $25,000 per year. Less than 0.3 percent of these sole proprietorships earn over $1 million a year in sales.[1] The largest number of sole proprietorships, accounting for over 29 percent of total sales, are personal service companies. Wholesale and retail trade (increasing) and construction (decreasing) also account for a large number of sole proprietorships.

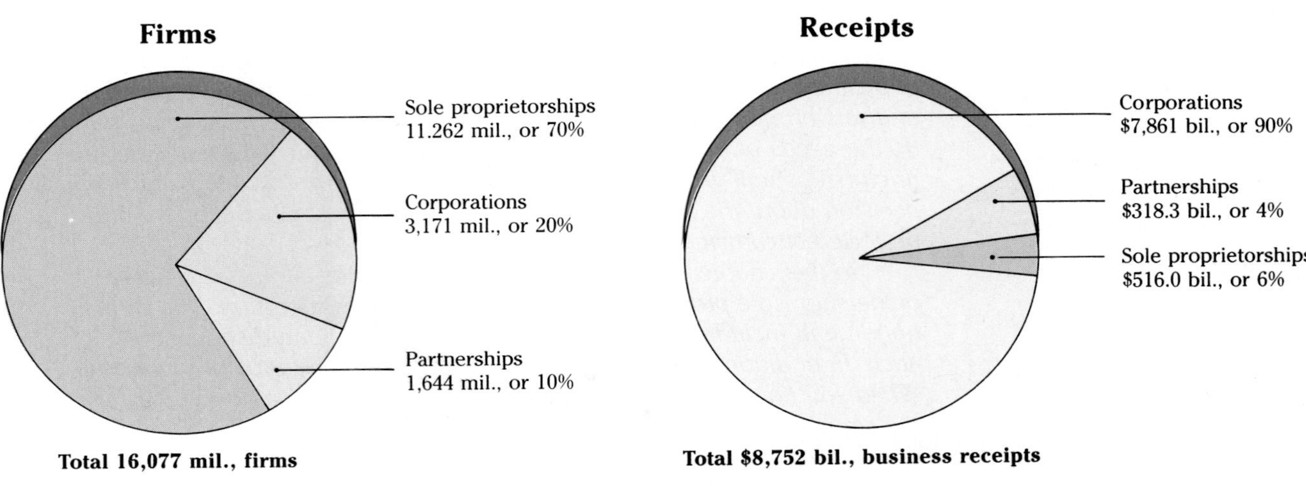

Figure 4.1 Sole proprietorships are the largest form of business ownership in the United States. However, corporations account for 90 percent of revenues.

Advantages

Sole proprietors enjoy many advantages. Following are some of the reasons the sole proprietorship has become the major form of business ownership.

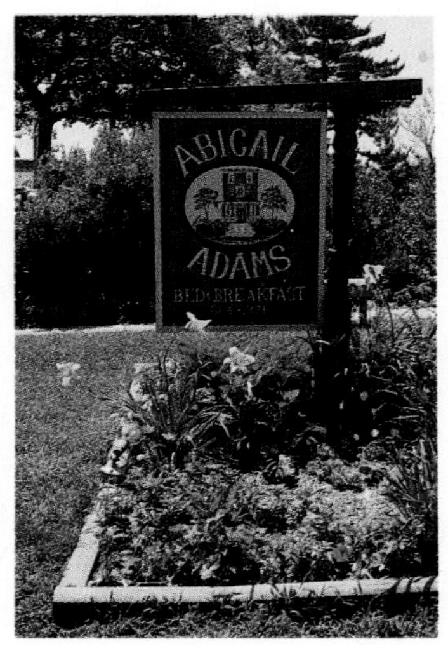

A sole proprietorship exists when one individual owns and operates a business, such as this bed and breakfast inn, for personal profit.

Tax Structure Simplicity

Sole proprietorships operate under the tax structure for individuals. Thus they avoid the often higher and more complex state and federal corporate taxes. The Federal Income Tax Reform Bill of 1986 allows small businesses earning less than $50,000 a year to be taxed at a 15 percent rate. A graduated rate is used until income exceeds $75,000, at which point the corporate maximum rate of 34 percent is applied. Furthermore, the sole proprietor is also eligible to establish a tax-exempt retirement account (Keogh plan).

Ease of Establishment and Dissolution

Except for having to obtain state and local licenses or permits, there are few requirements for establishing most legal businesses. Organizing a sole proprietorship is relatively simple and inexpensive and seldom requires outside help. Just as easy are the steps required for dissolution. The only requirement is to ensure that all debts are paid.

Flexibility

The sole proprietor is able to decide when to operate, when to take a vacation and for how long, when to expand or open a new store, which people to hire, what merchandise to purchase, and so on. This flexibility gives the sole proprietor a good deal of freedom.

Ownership of Profits

All after-tax profits are for the exclusive use of the sole proprietor. This strong motivator helps increase the satisfaction of working for oneself. Sole ownership of profits makes the usual hard work and long hours bearable.

Secrecy

The sole proprietorship offers the most confidential method of operation. Since there are no stockholders and no board of directors, there is no need for annual reports or for the routine sharing of information with others. In addition to this financial secrecy, operational secrecy is also provided. Thus it is difficult for competitors to copy the proprietor's strategies.

Disadvantages

There are relatively few disadvantages for a sole proprietorship, although those that do exist are important.

Unlimited Liability

In a sole proprietorship, all assets, both business and personal, are subject to the claims of creditors. This condition, called **unlimited liability,** is an advantage when a sole proprietor wants a bank loan. But it is a distinct disadvantage during bankruptcy. A large percentage of small businesses fail each year, and the owners often lose their personal assets along with their businesses. Unlimited liability is the main disadvantage of sole proprietorships.

Unlimited liability is the condition that allows both the business and personal assets of a sole proprietor or a partner to be subject to the claims of creditors.

Limited Life

A sole proprietorship is not permanent. When the owner dies, the business is automatically dissolved. If the business is to be passed on to family members, a new proprietorship (or partnership) must be formed. Sickness or a serious accident on the part of the owner could also create operational problems, forcing the dissolution of the proprietorship. In addition, sole proprietorships are very vulnerable in times of recession. During the 1981–1983 recession, record numbers of small businesses failed because of inflation, tight credit policies, and poor management.

Size and Capital Limitations

The sole proprietorship is limited in size by the amount of capital that can be raised by the owner. Large growth, requiring millions of dollars, is next to impossible. The lack of capital may also cause operational disadvantages. The proprietorship may have to locate in poor areas, it may not be able to make full payment for merchandise and supplies, and it may not be able to attract top-notch employees. For these reasons, a business requiring a large amount of capital should not be organized as a sole proprietorship.

Lack of Employee Opportunities

In a sole proprietorship, employees are limited in many ways. Wages and salaries are often low, and there is little room for advancement. Therefore, it is common for good employees to "jump ship" and go to work for larger competitors or to start their own businesses.

Limited Managerial Skills

Most new sole proprietors know their product and how to service it but are not competent managers. They often lack skills in pricing, buying, promotion, sales, personnel, and finance. Larger businesses, whether partnerships or corporations, have many specialists to make decisions in these areas. Sole proprietors do everything themselves. Often they must rely on outside consultants or seek additional training.

PARTNERSHIPS

Since partnerships are unincorporated, they are very similar to sole proprietorships, offering some of the same advantages and disadvantages. The Uniform Partnership Act adopted by most states defines *partnership* as an association of two or more partners to carry on as co-owners of a business for profit. (Approximately 80 percent of partnerships have only two owners.) Of all types of ownership, partnerships represent the smallest number of businesses, and their number is decreasing. In 1988, they accounted for only 10 percent of the total number of businesses and only 4 percent of the total profits earned.[2]

Partnerships are not well suited for large businesses. Historically, they have best served lawyers, doctors, accountants, and other providers of professional services. Currently, however, finance, real estate, and insurance firms rank first

BUSINESS PRACTICE EXAMPLE Continues

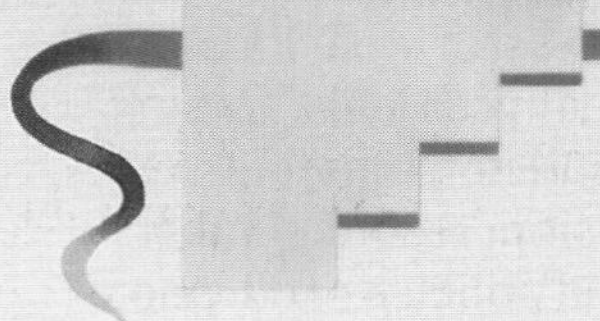

Before Tigrett and Morton became partners in their popular business, each operated his own sole proprietorship. Morton, who hails from an old Chicago restaurant family, operated an American-style restaurant in Chelsea. He called it the Great American Disaster. It was an instant hit. Then he met Tigrett, the son of a wealthy Tennessee financier, John B. Tigrett, who had moved his family to England when Isaac was 15. Isaac went to private school in Lugano, Switzerland. One of his enterprises was buying used Rolls-Royces and reselling them to Americans.

in the total number of partnerships; and wholesale and retail businesses rank second.

Partnerships are classified as either general or limited. The **general partnership** is the more common of the two. It is owned by general partners—partners who are usually active in the business and who must assume unlimited liability for all business debts. The **limited partnership** contains at least one general partner (who must assume unlimited liability for business debts) but can have many limited partners—partners who are forbidden by law to participate in management but who usually provide capital to the partnership. The liability of limited partners is limited to their investment. Limited partnerships offer general partners the possibility of raising additional capital without giving up managerial control. They offer limited partners a place in which to invest their money without the need for active management.

A ***general partnership*** is a partnership owned by general partners, who are usually active in the business and who must assume unlimited liability of all business debts.

A ***limited partnership*** is a partnership in which at least one general partner must assume unlimited liability for all business debts and one or more other partners have liability limited to their investment.

Partners—both general and limited—can choose to be secret, silent, dormant, or nominal. The choice depends largely on the degree of involvement the individual wants in the partnership or the types of expertise the person brings to it.

Secret partners are active in the business but are not known to the general public. By law, they are general partners, since limited partners cannot be active in the management of the business.

Silent partners are known to the public but are not active in the management of the business. Often they are local or national celebrities.

Dormant partners are neither active in management nor known to the public. They are usually limited partners and tend to be investors seeking a tax shelter.

Nominal partners do not invest capital in the partnership and thus are not true partners. What they provide are nonmonetary factors of value to the partnership—for example, experience in the type of business or special skills. They give the impression of being part owners of the business.

Partners of whatever type should draw up **articles of partnership**—a legal document containing the provisions of ownership, including an outline of the monetary and managerial responsibilities of each partner. This document is required in most states. Among the more common provisions in it are the names of the partners and the amounts of their investment, the distribution of profits and losses, the duties and salaries of each partner, and the method of withdrawal from or dissolution of the partnership.

Articles of partnership are a legal document containing the provisions of ownership for a partnership, including an outline of the monetary and managerial responsibilities of each partner.

Advantages

Partnerships share many of the advantages of sole proprietorships.

Legal Status

Because the articles of partnership are required or accepted in most states, partnerships have a definite legal status. Enough cases involving partnerships have been tried in court that legal precedence has been established. As a result, solving the legal problems of partnerships is relatively simple in comparison to solving the problems of other types of ownership.

Employee Retention and Motivation

Partnerships are usually larger than sole proprietorships, so they tend to do better at retaining and motivating good employees. One excellent way of keeping good employees is to make them partners. This practice is common in law firms and some other professional service businesses. Outstanding employees may be promoted to junior partnerships and eventually be allowed to buy in as senior partners.

Ease of Establishment and Organization

Establishing a partnership requires little more than drawing up the articles of partnership. Organizing a partnership is inexpensive, and there are few government restrictions or taxes.

Specialized Management

Partnerships can recruit partners with expertise in various areas of business operations. When important decisions must be made, partners can combine their managerial talents to seek the best solution. Furthermore, partners have a wider range of freedom in making decisions than do corporate managers.

Personal Interest

When individuals work for themselves and are thus able to retain the profits they generate, personal interest and incentives are greater. Partners usually share the profits according to the amount of time or capital they invest in the operation.

Disadvantages

The fact that only a small number of partnerships exist suggests that there are some major disadvantages to them.

Unlimited Liability

Each general partner shares jointly in the liability of the business. All the assets, of each partner, both business and personal, are subject to claims. If one partner cannot pay off the debts, then the others are responsible for them. Only limited partners have limited liability. For example, if a physician in a medical partnership is sued for malpractice, each partner is liable for any financial losses, including legal expenses and increased insurance rates.

Limited Life

Of the three types of ownership, partnerships have the shortest life. Many circumstances—death, insanity, bankruptcy, and withdrawal, for example—may terminate a partnership. The uncertainty about the life of the partnership can cause problems in long-range planning and in development or capital accumulation programs.

Frozen Investment

It is much easier to form a partnership than to pull out of one. This becomes obvious when a partner decides to withdraw. Finding a replacement who can meet such partnership requirements as capital investment, managerial experience

HIGHLIGHT IN BUSINESS PRACTICE

The Boston Celtics: A Master Limited Partnership

Master limited partnerships are a relatively new (1981) hybrid investment vehicle. Created initially for investments in the oil and gas industry, companies see the partnerships as a way to keep shareholders happy, raise capital, and sometimes highlight assets they believe are undervalued in the market. There are two types of master limited partnerships: the "roll out," in which a company spins off assets to shareholders, and the "roll up," in which dozens of private partnerships are exchanged for publicly traded units. In both cases the sponsor becomes the general partner and continues to manage the company.

In master limited partnerships, shareholders receive tax deductions usually reserved for corporations that own depleted assets. This does not sit well with many in Congress, who are attempting to eliminate this form of partnership. They believe revenue should be taxed like that of corporations and not as income to individual partners.

In 1983, Don F. Gaston, Alan N. Cohn and Paul R. Dupee formed a partnership and purchased the Boston Celtics for $15 million. In December of 1986, the partners joined the rush to master limited partnerships and sold 40 percent of the team through an offering of limited partnership units on the New York Stock Exchange. Without giving up control of the team, the general partners grossed $46.8 million on 2.6 million shares (opened at $18.38 per unit) sold to 60,000 investors. For their investment, shareholders were guaranteed a dividend of $1.40 a unit plus an extra amount determined

by play-off earnings in 1988. Tickets to Celtics home games are another thing. Even shareholders must join the 15-year waiting list.

While everyone agrees the general partners made a killing on the public offering, many experts question the partners' ability to manage the team assets—five super starters and their alternates. All but one of the starters is over 30 years old. To make matters worse, the Celtics selected 24th out of 25 NBA teams in the draft. Each year as the team gets older, the odds of competing in the play-offs decrease. In 1988, play-off revenue was an estimated additional $4.2 million (down $1 million from 1987 when the Celtics went to the final series). At this point the team needs to rebuild to replace Larry Bird and company when they retire. And what do the limited partners have to say about the way the general partners manage the company? Nothing! Unlike corporations, master limited partners have no voting rights.

and skills, dedication, and the approval of the remaining partners is not an easy task. Often, when one partner withdraws, the most likely buyers are the remaining partners.

Owner Conflicts

Many partners were originally friends who later found out that friends do not necessarily make good business associates. Most disagreements in partnerships revolve around divided authority. For example, one partner may want to fire an employee, while the other partner doesn't.

Size and Capital Limitations

Like sole proprietorships, partnerships are limited to the amount of capital invested or borrowed by the partners. Even if a partnership has an excellent credit rating, it would have a hard time borrowing the large sums of money needed to operate and maintain a major national business. To help alleviate this potential problem, Congress passed the Small Business Innovation Research Act to provide an additional source of borrowed capital. Legislators predict a positive impact on future innovation and the creation of new jobs.

CORPORATIONS

What unique attributes make corporations such a powerful factor in the economy? Most important is probably the fact that they exist as legal entities. Since 1819, they have been viewed as artificial individuals apart from any real people who may own or work for them. This means that corporations can be legally immortal;

BUSINESS PRACTICE EXAMPLE Continues

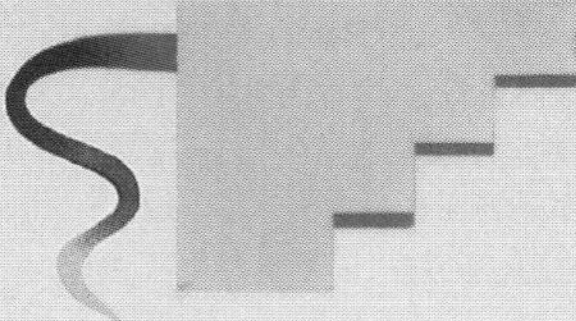

Tigrett and Morton formed a partnership in order to create the large financial base necessary to launch the Hard Rock Cafe. Several years later, Tigrett and Morton had a falling out and went their separate ways. However, each wanted his share of the Hard Rock Cafes. After legal squabbles, they agreed on a division of the spoils. In October 1982, Morton opened a Hard Rock Cafe in Los Angeles with backing from several show business investors: Steven Spielberg, Barry Diller, Henry Winkler, Willie Nelson, and John Denver. Two years later, Tigrett opened his Hard Rock Cafe in New York City, with comedian Dan Aykroyd as his new partner.

The ex-partners divided the country in half, with Morton getting the West and Tigrett the East. While this all may sound a little confusing, it doesn't get any better. Morton got his hometown of Chicago, and while Tigrett has Dallas, Morton was assigned Houston. Outside the U.S., Morton has rights for Australia, Brazil, Israel, and Vancouver, Canada. Tigrett has the rest of the world, except for the unofficial imitators in Amsterdam, Bombay, and Bangkok.

Company	Millions of dollars in sales
1. General Motors	$121,085.4
2. Ford Motor	92,445.6
3. Exxon	79,557.0
4. International Business Machines	59,681.0
5. General Electric	49,414.0
6. Mobil	46,198.0
7. Chrysler	35,472.7
8. Texaco	33,544.0
9. E. I. DuPont de Nemours	32,514.0
10. Philip Morris	25,860.0

Figure 4.2
The top ten U.S. corporate giants, 1987.

they can continue to exist long after their founders are dead. Because corporations are artificial, they are made up only of what their owners have contributed; they cannot lose any more than the owners put in. Corporations thus have the economic power of many contributors while reducing the contributors' financial risk and outliving them all.

Forming a Corporation

It can be complex and difficult to form a corporation. All corporations except financial institutions, government corporations, and some financial corporations are chartered under state laws. Depending on where the corporation is incorporated, it can be considered domestic, foreign, or alien. **Domestic corporations** are corporations that do business in the state in which they are chartered. **Foreign corporations** are corporations that do business outside their chartered state. **Alien corporations** are corporations organized in a foreign country but operating in the United States. General Motors, for example, was incorporated in Delaware and is a domestic corporation in that state, but it is a foreign corporation in the other states in which it operates. Toyota, Nissan, and Mazda are all alien corporations because they were organized in Japan.

Once a new corporation is organized and promoted, it must pay an incorporation fee and file **articles of incorporation**—a legal document explaining the purpose of the corporation, the number of shares issued, the names of the officers and directors, the bylaws, and other information—with the appropriate state office (usually the secretary of state). If the articles do not violate state laws, the state grants the corporation a **charter**—a document authorizing the corporation to operate.

Domestic corporations are corporations that do business in the state in which they are chartered.

Foreign corporations are corporations that do business outside their chartered state.

Alien corporations are corporations organized in a foreign country but operating in the United States.

Articles of incorporation are a legal document explaining the purpose of the corporation, the number of shares issued, the names of the officers and directors, the bylaws, and so on.

A ***charter*** is a document authorizing a corporation to operate in a given state.

Corporate Governance

Many states require corporations to have a minimum of three **stockholders** (the owners of the corporation). For each share of common stock owned, a stockholder is entitled to one vote. Voting normally takes place at the annual meeting. Only

Stockholders are the owners of a corporation. They are also referred to as shareholders.

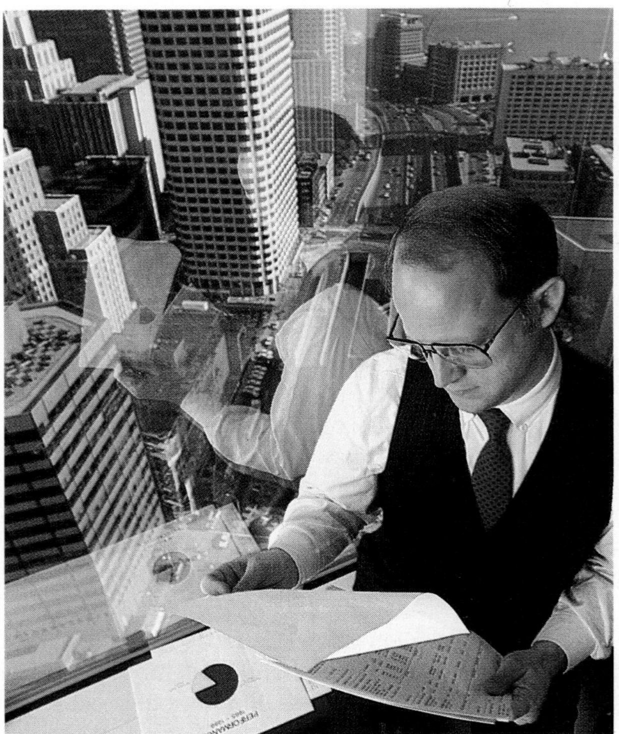

A corporation's chief executive officer oversees the day-to-day operations of the firm as well as establishes and reviews corporate policies.

A ***proxy*** is a written authorization that transfers a stockholder's voting rights to a corporate board member or other appointed person.

The ***board of directors*** is the people elected by the stockholders to govern a corporation.

The ***chief executive officer (CEO)*** is the corporate officer who runs the day-to-day operations of a corporation.

a small percentage of stockholders attend annual meetings, however. The others sign a **proxy**—written authorization that gives a board member or other appointed person the right to cast their votes. Stockholders may vote for board members and on amendments to the charter, mergers, general policies, and any appropriate resolution proposed by another stockholder at the annual meeting.

Because of changing societal demands and preferences, there is an increasing public interest in corporate governance. Most of this interest centers on the **board of directors**—the people elected by stockholders to govern a corporation. According to a General Motors Public Interest Report, the major responsibility for ensuring that a corporation achieves a balance between its response to society's interests and its own economic concerns rests with its board of directors.

The board has four major responsibilities:

1. To be loyal, to avoid conflicting and competing interests concerning purchase and sale of control, deduction of dividends, and the diversion of a corporate opportunity.
2. To exercise proper business judgment and to avoid gross negligence.
3. To comply with securities laws.
4. To represent the interests of the stockholders, employees, and consumers.[4]

It is also the board's responsibility to elect its officers, including the chairman of the board, the president of the corporation, the vice president, the secretary, and the treasurer. The board also chooses the corporation's **chief executive officer (CEO)**—the corporate officer who runs the day-to-day operations of the firm. The CEO is usually either the chairman of the board or the president.

In addition, board members (directors) must vote on the declaration of dividends and serve on standing committees that establish and review policy relating to finances, nominations, the public, audits, bonuses and salaries, and so on. According to a survey by Arthur D. Little, Inc., the average director each year spends over 150 hours on board business. Boards tend to meet nine to ten times per year.[5]

The average Fortune 1000 corporate board is composed of fourteen members. However, big corporations may have more. General Motors, for example, has twenty-four. Most board members are **outside directors**—directors not employed by the corporation. They are usually selected for their broad experience in business, finance, or administration. In 1989, the National Association of Security Dealers began requiring member companies to have at least two outside directors. The Securities and Exchange Commission is studying a proposal to require all 10,000 SEC-registered companies to have two outside directors on their audit committees.[6] **Inside directors** are board members employed by the corporation and are often officers of the corporation.

Outside directors are board members who are not employed by the corporation.

Inside directors are board members employed by the corporation.

Directors are supposed to have the time to serve on the board and should be free of all legal impediments to serving. According to a survey by Heidrick and Struggles, 87.6 percent of all corporations use outside directors, and 55 percent of these directors have no ties (such as family ties) with the corporations. The average salary range for outside directors of U.S. corporations is $17,000 to $22,000 a year.[7] Forty-three percent of corporations have women, and minorities are represented on 30 percent of corporate boards.[8] According to a recent survey by Heidrick and Struggles, white female participation on boards has increased from 3.3 percent in 1982 to 4.8 percent (expressed as a percent of total board seats available). Blacks have increased from 1.2 to 2.4 percent since 1982.[9]

Advantages

There are many advantages to incorporation.

Limited Liability

Unlike sole proprietors and partners, stockholders are not liable for company losses. In 1988, Texaco reported a $4.4 billion loss. However, no stockholder was held liable for money lost in that quarter or at any other time. If a corporation goes bankrupt, its creditors can claim the assets of the corporation but not the assets of the owners. Thus the stockholders can lose only the money they invested in the company.

Continuous Life

In the 1819 *Dartmouth College v. Woodward* Supreme Court decision, Chief Justice John Marshall gave corporations perpetuity, or unlimited life, unless their state charter indicated otherwise. When perpetuity is not granted, the state usually gives corporations a thirty-five-year charter, after which the charter may need to be renewed. Thus, if any officers or stockholders die, quit, or sell, the corporation continues to exist.

Ownership Transferability

It is easy to buy or sell ownership in a corporation. This is one reason corporations have many owners. Buying or selling ownership in a corporation is simply a matter of calling a stockbroker, who can, within minutes, buy or sell stock listed on a stock exchange. The ease of this transfer will be discussed in greater detail in chapter 19.

Specialized Management

In larger corporations, management can employ specialists in every area. In a sole proprietorship or partnership, one or a small number of people must perform the management functions. In small businesses, there is little capital to employ specialists for areas such as accounting and research. The corporation's ability to hire specialists leads to improved efficiency. In addition, corporations usually have more funds available to employ outside management consultants if special problems arise.

Ease of Expansion

Corporations have the potential to raise large sums of capital by selling stocks or bonds (securities). That capital can be used to build new facilities, purchase new equipment, employ more people, or expand research and development efforts. In addition, corporations are able to borrow large sums of money because their valuable assets can be used for collateral. Furthermore, financial institutions normally lend money to financially strong corporations at a low interest rate (called the *prime interest rate*).

Disadvantages

Several major disadvantages to incorporation must be considered when the form of ownership is being determined. Table 4.1 lists a number of advantages and disadvantages to all three forms of ownership.

Difficulty of Creation

Incorporation can be both expensive and complex. Costs vary, but each state charges a fee for the charter and additional annual fees to renew it. Many corporations obtain their charters in Delaware because its requirements are less complex and expensive than those of other states.

Double Taxation for Owners

Corporations normally pay higher taxes than individuals—20 to 34 percent of earnings. In addition, corporate profits are in effect doubly taxed. Because the corporation is treated as a separate individual, its profits on earnings are taxed. The balance is left as dividends paid to the stockholders or for reinvestment in the firm. However, the stockholders, as individuals, are also separately taxed. Thus their corporate earnings are taxed twice. The business earnings of sole proprietors and partners are taxed only once, since their profits are treated as personal income.

Table 4.1 Advantages and disadvantages of major forms of business ownership.

Characteristic	**Sole Proprietorship**	**Partnership**	**Corporation**
Taxes	Operates under simplest tax structure afforded individuals and often avoids higher state and federal taxes.	Taxed on individual earnings of each partner.	Taxed at 20–34% of earnings; double taxation.
Establishment and dissolution	Few requirements other than state and local licenses; debt must be paid to dissolve.	Requires articles of partnership; difficult to dissolve.	Requires state charter; usually difficult and expensive to establish and dissolve.
Secrecy	Excellent.	Good.	Fair.
Lifetime	Dissolved on death of owner.	Dissolved on death or withdrawal of any partner; shortest life of all forms of ownership.	Continues regardless of death of stockholders or company officers.
Liability	Owner liable for all debts.	Partners liable for all debts.	Stockholders not liable for debts.
Size and capital limitations	Limited to owner's capital on hand and loans.	Limited to partners' capital on hand and loans.	Stocks or bonds can be sold; money can be borrowed for expansion.
Employee benefits and opportunities	Usually lower wages and fewer benefits; impossible to get to top without buying company.	Promising employees can become partners.	Usually better salaries and benefits; good advancement possibilities.
Management skills	Owner/manager must be a jack-of-all-trades.	Each partner can specialize.	Many specialized managers and consultants available.
Transfer of ownership	Can be sold to any buyer who meets sales terms.	Must have agreement of all partners.	If listed on stock exchange, ownership is easy to sell.

Many states allow the formation of **S corporations,** small corporations with a limited number of stockholders (thirty-five or fewer). These corporations are taxed as partnerships but maintain all the advantages of incorporation—for example, limited liability. The Internal Revenue Service expects 1,013,900 S corporations to file annual tax returns in 1992—22 percent of the total number of corporate returns. Chapter S status can be revoked under certain circumstances—for example, if more than 25 percent of the corporation's gross receipts are interest on investments.

S corporations are small corporations with a limited number of stockholders; they are taxed as partnerships.

S corporations themselves generally pay no income taxes, but the stockholders pay individual taxes on their share of earnings, whether or not the earnings are distributed. Only a limited amount of earnings can be retained and reinvested by the corporation. Losses also flow through to stockholders, who can use them to offset personal income. This feature makes S corporations particularly useful for setting up new businesses, since such businesses usually show losses in their first few years. When a company turns profitable, the business can be changed to the regular corporate form—the *C corporation*. This form allows the owners to retain and invest earnings.[10]

Lack of Secrecy

Sole proprietorships and partnerships are not required to make public the financial position of the business. However, corporations must publish an annual report for their stockholders and must periodically release statements on executive salaries, expansion plans, new product development, plant closings, and many other items that can be kept secret in other forms of ownership.

Government Regulation

Corporations, the most heavily regulated form of business ownership, are restricted to activities included in their state charters. Although corporate charters can be amended with state approval, most charters define their purposes in broad enough terms to avoid later amendment. Corporations are also required to keep volumes of records for the government and stockholders. These records report how the corporations are complying with various regulations, such as those involving the environment and affirmative action.

Lack of Personal Interest by Employees

Employees of corporations may lack the personal motivation that sole proprietors and partners have. Many corporate employees believe that management does not care about their personal welfare. Also, employees often do not take much interest in their work because they cannot see how they are directly affected by an increase or decrease in profits. Furthermore, the stockholders usually are little interested in management. Thus, corporations often have an air of impersonality.

Corporate Ownership Trends

Mergers and Acquisitions

An ***acquisition*** is the purchase of a controlling share in a corporation by another corporation.

A ***merger*** is the combining of two companies.

An **acquisition** occurs when one company, usually a conglomerate, purchases a controlling share in another company. The acquired company is still managed separately. The combining of two companies in related industries is called a **merger.** In a merger, the companies are often combined to form a new corporation. The twentieth century has been a time of many mergers and acquisitions. For example, from 1955 to 1980, *Fortune* magazine's core group of 262 corporations (those appearing in both the 1955 and the 1980 list of the top 500 corporations in the United States) purchased 4,500 other companies.[11]

In the early 1980s, mergers began to increase dramatically. In 1987, over 3,450 companies, worth a total of almost $150 billion, were bought by other companies (see Figure 4.3).[12] During the Reagan presidency, the early leaders were oil and chemical companies, which took advantage of relaxed antitrust policies. Furthermore, many corporations felt the need to insulate themselves against the general environment of business uncertainty.[13] For example, the 1984 merger of the chemical giant Socal (Chevron) with Gulf Oil occurred because Socal wanted to ensure against any disruptions in its basic fuel stock supply. Today, mergers

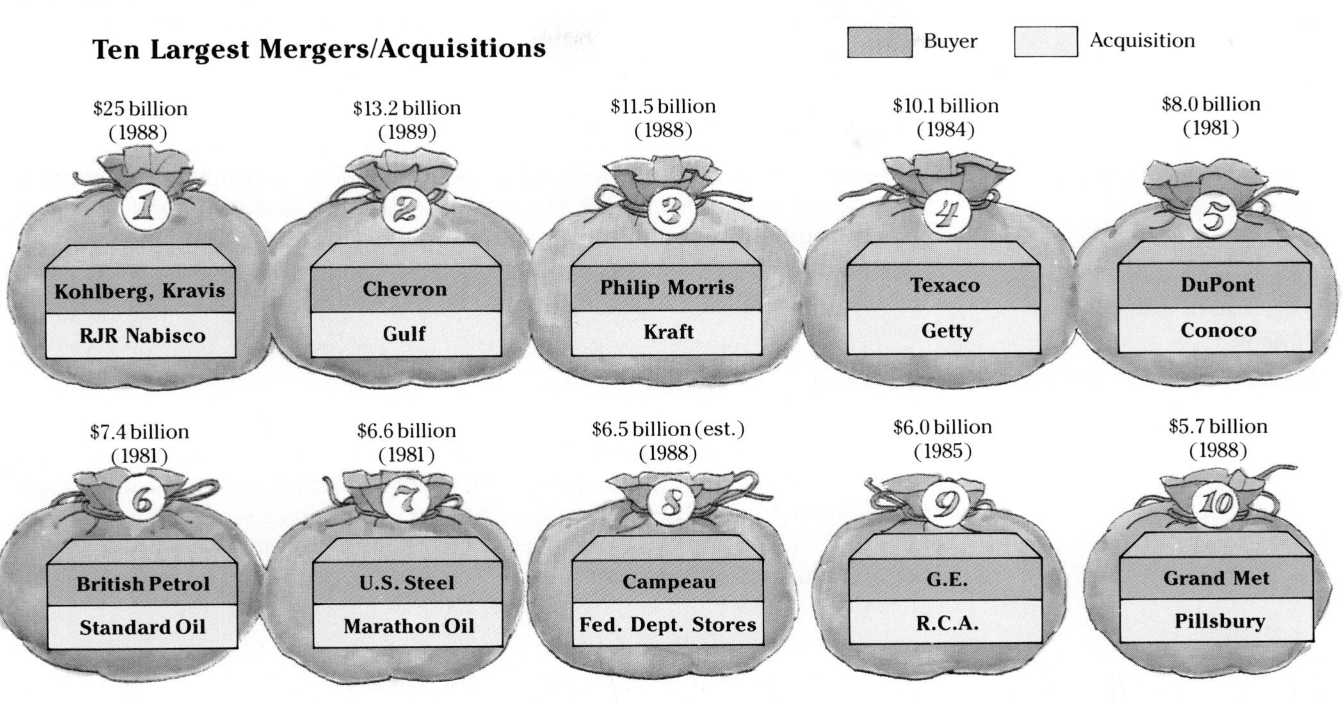

Figure 4.3 The ten largest mergers/acquisitions. Scarce resources, advancing technology, changing markets, and a probusiness administration are accelerating the trend toward large-scale mergers and acquisitions.

are likely to occur because of an attraction to a company's strong cash flow or its well-known brands (to avoid the high cost of trying to develop new brands) or perhaps because of greed on the part of private investors.

There are several types of mergers. A **horizontal merger** involves the combination of competing companies that perform the same function. In the early part of the twentieth century, many horizontal mergers occurred. A classic example is the acquisition of competing oil companies by Standard Oil. However, horizontal mergers that prevent other companies from competing were outlawed by antitrust legislation. Nonetheless, in 1988, the U.S. attorney general approved the merger of Knight-Ridder's *Detroit Free Press* and Gannett's *Detroit News,* which included a unique *joint operating agreement (JOA).* Under the JOA, the newspapers merged their business operations, divvied up the market, fixed prices and advertising rates, and pooled their profits.[14]

A ***horizontal merger*** is the combining of competing companies performing the same functions.

In the 1920s, vertical mergers were popular. A **vertical merger** occurs when a major corporation purchases one of its suppliers or the supplier purchases the corporation. For example, General Motors purchased the Delco battery company; CNN purchased MGM/UA Entertainment, a major supplier of old movies; and PepsiCo over the years has purchased Taco Bell, Kentucky Fried Chicken, and Pizza Hut. (Of course, each of these fast-food chains is stocked with plenty of Pepsi.)

A ***vertical merger*** is a merger that occurs when a major corporation purchases one of its suppliers or the supplier purchases the major corporation.

An ***amalgamation*** is the merger of two corporations that creates a third corporation in which neither company is dominant.

A ***conglomerate merger*** is the joining together of unrelated corporations.

A ***parent company*** is a corporation that owns all or the majority of stock in another company.

Subsidiaries are companies owned by corporations.

Amalgamation occurs when the merger of two corporations creates a third corporation in which neither company is dominant. A classic amalgamation is the 1917 merger of Buick, Oldsmobile, Cadillac, and Pontiac to form General Motors. A more modern one is the merger of Burroughs and the Sperry Corporation to form United Information Service (UNISYS).

Lately, corporate growth patterns have shown a trend toward the **conglomerate merger,** the joining together of unrelated corporations. For example, Paramount Communications is the **parent company** (owning all or the majority of stock) of several **subsidiaries** (the companies owned in this way). Paramount Communications' subsidiaries include the New York Rangers and Knicks, Paramount Productions, Madison Square Garden, and Allyn and Bacon, the publisher of this textbook.

Foreign Mergers and Acquisitions Many companies invest their surplus money in foreign mergers and acquisitions. Such was the case of two recent acquisitions: Grand Metropolitan (England) bought Pillsbury, and Campeau (Canada) bought Federated Department Stores. By owning a piece of a U.S. company, foreign companies can expand their employment base and increase their opportunity to export large sums of profits from the stable U.S. political and economic environment to their home countries.

HIGHLIGHT IN BUSINESS PRACTICE

The Global Merger Boom

The merger boom, which started in the U.S. 15 years ago, has now reached overseas. Now any company, no matter how large or significant, is vulnerable. In Europe, Societé Général de Belgique, a conglomerate that holds interests in 1,200 companies world-wide and accounts for one-third of the Belgian economy, was the $4.5 billion take-over target of Italy's Olivetti. The goal of Olivetti's Chairman Carlo De Benedetti was to form a pan-European company large enough to compete against American and European multinationals.

This "strength-through-merger" strategy was similarly used by the large Swedish electrical engineering firm Asea, which recently arranged a friendly merger with its Swiss competitor Brown Boveri, creating a single giant with combined sales of $18 billion. Although this particular merger was amicable, the CEO of Asea, Percy Barnevik, encourages more aggressive merger and acquisition activities among European companies. "We're so far away from where the U.S. is today that we should stop worrying so much about pushing harder in this area," Barnevik says. "We need more hostile takeovers."

To cope with competition in their midst, some European corporations have begun to invest aggressively in the U.S. market. Sulzer Brothers, a Swiss manufacturing firm that has specialized in heavy machinery and marine diesel engines, has invested $1 billion in the U.S. in the past 5 years. A hostile takeover attempt by the Swiss financier Tito Tettamonti caused a major restructuring of Sulzer. "To get return on equity into the 7% range, we have to move to faster-growing businesses and faster-growing markets," says CEO Fritz Fahrni. This return is impossible in Switzerland, so Sulzer has turned to the U.S. So far Sulzer has purchased Intermedics, a major manufacturer of pacemakers and heart valves; Bingham International, a heavy pumps and paper machinery manufacturer; and a controlling interest in Techmedia. "The only thing that will keep this company from facing another serious threat in the future," says Fahrni, "is at least doubling profits in the next few years."

The devaluation of the dollar and the fall in stock prices since the 1987 Crash have made U.S. companies and real estate increasingly attractive to foreign investors. In the period from the crash to mid-March 1988, 118 foreign firms made bids of $38.1 billion to buy U.S. firms. The plastics, steel, and general manufacturing industries are prime targets because many foreign exporters to the U.S. now find it cheaper to establish production facilities in the U.S. Foreign investment in real estate has also increased 30% since the crash, and Japanese investments alone reached $10 billion in 1988.

Although some foreign acquisitions have been friendly—for example, Sony's cash purchase of CBS Records—others have been aggressively opposed by U.S. firms. Eastman Kodak paid $5.1 billion for Sterling Drug to fend off the Swiss firm F Hoffman-LaRoche. Despite occasional opposition, however, given constricted growth opportunities abroad and their need for expansion, more foreign corporations with high cash savings will continue to consider U.S. acquisitions. Furthermore, as long as the United States runs a deficit, it will need recourse to foreign cash. Corporate reorganizations in the U.S., reacting to these global merging trends, will be more active and volatile than ever.

Recent high-priced international mergers and acquisitions.

Buyer	Seller	Price
ASEA (Sweden)	Brown Boveri (Switzerland)	$15.0 bil.
British Petroleum (Britain)	Standard Oil (U.S.)	$ 7.40 bil.
Amoco (U.S.)	Dome Petroleum (Canada)	$ 4.18 bil.
Unilever (Netherlands)	Chesebrough-Pond's (U.S.)	$ 3.10 bil.
American Hoechst (West Germany)	Celanese (U.S.)	$ 2.72 bil.
JMB Realty (U.S.)	Cadillac Fairview (Canada)	$ 2.00 bil.
Hanson Trust (Britain)	Kidde (U.S.)	$ 1.80 bil.
Groupe Bruxelles & Tractebel (Belgium)	Imperial Continental Gas Association (Britain)	$ 1.62 bil.
Rupert Murdoch (U.S.)	Herald & Weekly Times (Australia)	$ 1.54 bil.
Blue Arrow (Britain)	Manpower (U.S.)	$ 1.34 bil.

Other Ownership Trends

Today's business world is in a topsy-turvy state. While many corporations are buying other corporations, others are selling, going private (buying up their outstanding company stock), or being bought out by management or other employees. These megadeals are having a profound effect on the American economy. Their most troubling effect is the creation of large amounts of debt. To finance the megadeals, companies are draining billions of dollars in stock from their treasuries and replacing them with IOUs.

A ***leveraged buyout (LBO)*** is an acquisition technique that involves the use of large amounts of borrowed funds to purchase a company.

Often companies are purchased through **leveraged buyouts (LBOs)**—the use of large sums of borrowed money to buy out a company. The king of LBOs is Kohlberg Kravis Roberts & Company, the second largest conglomerate in the United States. Thus far, KKR has put together four of the largest leveraged buyouts in history. Through its partnerships, KKR controls twenty-four companies, including Duracell, Motel 6, Red Lion Inns, Safeway, Stop & Go, and Owens-Illinois. In late 1988, KKR, through a leveraged buyout, purchased RJR Nabisco for $25 billion. This deal came about when the chief executive officer of RJR Nabisco attempted to take the company private with another record bid—$17.6 billion.[15]

Sometimes, in order to finance a deal, a corporation decides to *divest* itself of (sell) one or more of its companies. For example, in 1985, KKR acted as a partner with management in a record $6.2 billion leveraged buyout of Beatrice Companies. This attempt to take the company private eventually caused management to lose the company, when it was forced to sell various subsidiaries, one by one, to pay its debt. Two years later, in 1987, the company was sold again, in another leveraged buyout, to the TLC Group (see profile of Reginald Lewis). The TLC Group also divested three of Beatrice's subsidiaries.[16]

ALTERNATE FORMS OF OWNERSHIP

Thus far, we have examined the three main types of business ownership—sole proprietorship, partnership, and corporation. Other forms of ownership also exist, although they are not commonly used. Each fills a specific need. Three of the better-known alternate forms of ownership are cooperatives, joint ventures, and nonprofit organizations.

Cooperatives

Cooperatives are groups of individuals who voluntarily act together for a common benefit.

Popularly referred to as co-ops, **cooperatives** are groups of individuals who voluntarily act together for a common benefit. In the United States, there are over 40,000 co-ops, and they have an estimated 60 million members.[17] Cooperatives are incorporated under state charters. Their members have one vote apiece, regardless of the number of shares they own. The members elect their boards of directors. Since cooperatives are not established to earn a profit, sometimes their board members and employees are volunteers. Whatever profits are earned are usually returned to the shareholders as dividends, which are applied toward the reduction of membership costs.

The three most common types of cooperatives are farm co-ops, consumer co-ops, and credit unions. *Farm co-ops* are organized principally to purchase farm supplies such as seed, fuel, and fertilizer and to sell the resulting produce. By trading in volume, farmers are able to eliminate middlemen and save money. Among the many farm co-ops are Sunkist-Agway, Land O' Lakes, Ocean Spray, Sun Maid, and Gold-Kist.

Many farm co-ops are thinly capitalized and therefore have little money to spend on ever-increasing marketing and developmental projects. For this reason, two of them—Gold-Kist (a poultry co-op) and Land O' Lakes (a dairy co-op)—recently went public, selling shares of stock to raise additional money.[18]

Consumer co-ops are retail outlets owned by their customers. East Lansing, Michigan, is home to a popular co-op primarily for the Michigan State University biking population. Members of the co-op, by working a certain number of hours each month, become eligible for free bike repairs and can buy parts at cost. The largest consumer co-op is REI (Recreational Equipment, Inc.) Co-op, which has over 1.5 million members. Each member pays a membership fee to join. REI has returned dividends to members for over forty years.

Credit unions are most commonly found at government offices and private companies around the country. More than 36 million people in the United States belong to credit unions. (This type of co-op is discussed more fully in chapter 17.)

Joint Ventures

A **joint venture** exists when two or more people or companies join together to undertake a specific, limited, usually short-term project. The joint venture is taxed as a partnership, and each person or company has unlimited liability during its existence. The management of the venture is often assigned to one individual or company; thus a common complaint about joint ventures is divided authority.

A ***joint venture*** is two or more people or companies who have joined together to undertake a specific, limited, usually short-term project.

Real estate developments are the most common form of joint venture. In addition, according to a Conference Board survey, 40 percent of all industrial corporations with annual sales of more than $100 million now have at least one international joint venture.[19] General Motors, for example, launched a joint venture with a Japanese company to build a plant in Michigan to manufacture robots. Joint ventures are an increasingly common way for foreign companies to enter new markets.

Nonprofit Organizations

In the past, most Americans worked for profit-making businesses or for the government. Today, however, a third sector of our economy is growing rapidly. This sector is composed of nonprofit organizations. In 1987, the Internal Revenue Service reported that over 850,000 nonprofit organizations were operating in the United States. These organizations are classified under twenty-one categories of tax-exempt entities. All escape paying taxes so long as they do not pass tax-free earnings on to individuals in any form other than reasonable salaries.

A business needs profits in order to operate at maximum production and efficiency. Nonprofit organizations—which include, among others, churches, hospitals, and foundations—do not generate profits to operate. The needed funds come instead from government, philanthropic foundations, and corporations. In 1987, corporations alone gave $4.6 billion to nonprofit organizations.

In recent years, however, government grants have decreased and corporate giving has not taken up the slack. The answer to declining grants, according to many nonprofit organizations, is to act entrepreneurially. Most nonprofit organizations are at least implementing sound business techniques. Many are also selling products closely tied to their purpose. Museums, for example, sell replicas of some of their displayed items. Cause-related campaigns sponsored by nonprofit organizations are adding as much as $100 million annually to their coffers.[20]

BUSINESS PRACTICE EXAMPLE Continues

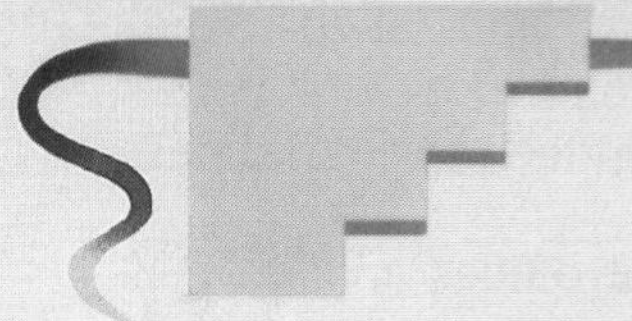

Tigrett took his Hard Rock clubs public by incorporating in 1984. In the beginning he sold a small number of shares over-the-counter in London. Toward the end of 1986, you could have become a stockholder of Hard Rock Cafe Plc by purchasing a share for $1.20. In 1987, Drexel Burnham Lambert sold another small piece of the company to American investors in a $40 million offering. The shares came out at $16 per share and quickly plunged to $10. The money raised by the offering was earmarked for new Hard Rock Cafes in Boston and Washington, D.C.

The prospectus for the U.S. offering disclosed that the Hard Rock does not live by food and drink alone. Each restaurant sells merchandise such as T-shirts, jackets, hats, and watches featuring the Hard Rock logo. These sales account for 46 percent of revenues. A separate store is planned in New York City to sell the popular Hard Rock merchandise.

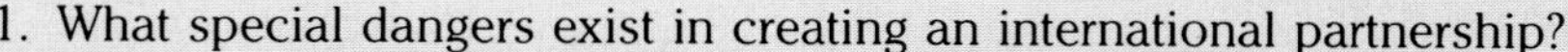

Issues for Discussion

1. What special dangers exist in creating an international partnership?
2. How can Tigrett and Morton protect themselves against the unauthorized use of the Hard Rock idea, name, and logo in other worldwide locations?
3. Why do you believe that partners frequently have disagreements? What protects partners when dividing up the assets?
4. What were the advantages of Tigrett taking his Hard Rock Cafes public? Why do you think Morton decided to remain a partnership?
5. Which form of ownership, in general, do you favor? Explain your answer.

SUMMARY

There are three major forms of business ownership: sole proprietorship (a business owned by one person), partnership (a business with two or more owners, who may or may not actively manage it), and corporation (a legal entity with authority to act on its own and liability separate from that of its owners).

Among the advantages of sole proprietorships are tax structure simplicity, ease of establishment and dissolution, flexibility, profits belonging only to the one person, and confidentiality. Among the disadvantages are unlimited liability, limited life, limitations on size and capital, lack of employee opportunities, and limited managerial skills.

Partnerships are classified as general and limited. General partnerships are owned by partners who are active in the business and who have unlimited liability for all business debts. Limited partnerships are owned by at least one general partner, who has unlimited liability for debts; and limited partners, who are forbidden to participate in management, who usually provide capital, and whose liability is limited to their investment.

Partners can be secret (not known to the general public), silent (not active in management), dormant (neither active nor known to the public), and nominal (not true partners but giving the impression of being partners).

Articles of partnership outline the partners' responsibilities. Partnerships have the following advantages: legal status, better retention and motivation of employees than in sole proprietorships, ease of establishment and organization, specialized management, and personal interest. Disadvantages are unlimited liability of general partners, limited life, frozen investment, owner conflicts, and size and capital limitations.

Corporations can be public (open—selling stock to the public) or private (closed—usually owned by only a few stockholders and not selling stock to the public). Domestic corporations do business in the state in which they are chartered, foreign corporations do business outside their chartered state, and alien corporations are organized in a foreign country but operate in the United States.

Each corporation files articles of incorporation, and the state then grants it a charter. Corporations are governed by the stockholders, the board of directors, and the chief executive officer. Boards may include outside directors and inside directors.

The advantages to incorporation are limited liability, continuous life, ownership transferability, specialized management, and ease of expansion. The disadvantages are difficulty of creation, double taxation for owners (except in the case of chapter S corporations—small corporations with a limited number of stockholders—which are taxed as partnerships), lack of secrecy, government regulation, and lack of personal interest by employees.

Mergers are the combining of two companies. Horizontal mergers combine competing companies that perform the same function. Vertical mergers occur when a corporation purchases one of its suppliers, or vice versa. Amalgamation occurs when the merger creates a third corporation in which neither company is dominant. Conglomerate mergers join together unrelated corporations. Many foreign companies have been buying U.S. corporations. Leveraged buyouts are the purchase of companies with large sums of borrowed money.

Alternate forms of ownership are cooperatives (groups of people who voluntarily act together for a common benefit), joint ventures (companies or people joined together to undertake a specific, limited, usually short-term project), and nonprofit organizations (organizations that rely on government, corporate, and charitable funding and that do not earn a profit).

KEY TERMS

CHECK YOUR LEARNING

Reread the following learning objectives. Each objective is followed by a few questions. Answering these questions accurately will help you retain the most important concepts discussed in this chapter. After answering each question, check your answer with the key at the end of this chapter. (*Hint:* If you have doubt regarding the correct response, consult the page whose number follows the answer.)

Circle:

A. Compare and contrast sole proprietorships, partnerships, and corporations and list the advantages and disadvantages of each.

a b c d — 1. All of the following are basic forms of business ownership except: (a) partnership; (b) cooperative; (c) corporation; (d) sole proprietorship.

a b c d — 2. All of the following are advantages of sole proprietorships except: (a) tax advantages; (b) secrecy; (c) flexibility; (d) unlimited liability.

a b c d — 3. All of the following are disadvantages of partnerships except: (a) credit standing; (b) unlimited liability; (c) limited life; (d) owner conflicts.

B. Distinguish among secret, silent, dormant, and nominal partners.

T F — 1. Nominal partners are not true partners.

T F — 2. Silent partners are known but are not active.

C. Distinguish among domestic, foreign, and alien corporations.

T F — 1. Foreign corporations are those that operate in foreign countries.

T F — 2. Corporations are allowed to do business only in the state in which they are chartered.

D. Discuss current trends in the composition of corporate boards of directors and the role of today's board members.

T F — 1. The average Fortune 1000 board of directors is composed of fourteen members.

T F — 2. Most board members are inside directors.

T F — 3. Women and minorities are continually gaining more seats on corporate boards.

E. Discuss corporate growth trends that have occurred in the twentieth century and be able to distinguish among the various types of mergers.

a b c d — 1. When two similar corporations join together, the merger is called a(n): (a) vertical merger; (b) horizontal merger; (c) conglomerate merger; (d) amalgamation merger.

T F — 2. Recently there has been a trend toward conglomerate mergers.

F. Compare and contrast the alternate forms of ownership.

T F — 1. A joint venture is an example of an alternate form of incorporated ownership.

a b c d — 2. All of the following are examples of cooperatives except: (a) farm co-ops; (b) consumer co-ops; (c) mutual co-ops; (d) credit unions.

QUESTIONS FOR REVIEW AND DISCUSSION

1. Define the key terms listed at the end of the chapter.
2. Design a chart to compare the major strengths and weaknesses of sole proprietorships, partnerships, and corporations.
3. Name the four different types of partners and explain the differences among them. Why do these different types exist? For example, why would a partner want to be active in a business but not be known?
4. Discuss why corporate boards of directors are electing more and more outside directors and why there is a trend toward more minorities and women serving as board directors.

5. Explain how the role of today's board director has changed from that role in the past.
6. Explain why many companies charter their corporations in Delaware.
7. Trace the changes in merger patterns in twentieth century America. What do you believe has caused the recent trend toward huge conglomerates?
8. Visit a local credit union and one other form of cooperative. Find out the membership requirements of each and report your findings to the class.
9. Interview a successful sole proprietor and make a list of the characteristics that you believe have made this individual a success. If this sole proprietor ever considered forming a partnership or incorporating, ask why the person chose not to change the present form of ownership.

CONCLUDING CASE

Balancing the Boardroom

Never in the history of American corporations has the corporate boardroom been in such turmoil. Convinced by corporate raiders that U.S. firms are poorly managed, activist shareholders are demanding and getting a greater say in the way companies are run. While protests by shareholders over such issues as divesting in South Africa are nothing new, today's stockholder wants more power in the boardroom decision-making process. In the past, this was next to impossible, because most shareholder voting was done by proxy. Thus, management controlled the nonsecretive vote and the way corporations were operated.

Stockholder resolutions are aimed at two major issues: confidential voting and shareholder access to the proxy statement. These two issues hold the key to controlling boardroom balance. In the past, proxy votes were normally won by management, which controls the process as inside directors. For this reason, among others, stockholders at Amoco, Chevron, and Unocal are asking that shareholders with investments of at least $1 million in a company be given the right to comment on management proposals, including board nominations, in the proxy statement. Honeywell, Lockheed, and Loral stockholders are seeking to require management to end open voting and to hire independent outsiders to tabulate secret voting of proxies. The resolution at Honeywell is sponsored by the New York City Employee's Retirement System (NYCERS). Their goal is to end manager influence on voting.

Proxy soliciters (usually outside firms) are working hard to obtain enough proxies to win for management at companies such as USAir, Dayton Hudson, and J. C. Penney. In April 1988, Gillette stockholders used their proxies to vote in a proposal to prohibit future buy-back payments to would-be acquirers.

It appears that corporations are finally beginning to honor the legal principle that directors and managers must be accountable to shareholders. The roles of stockholders, managers, and directors are shifting. Ultimately, this will lead to a change in the way corporations are managed.

Issues for Discussion

1. Are outside directors responsible to management or to stockholders? Explain.
2. Do you think the common practice of having the CEO serve as chairman of the board is a good one? Explain.
3. If someone makes a serious offer for a company, who should decide whether to accept? Management? Stockholders? Both? Explain.

NOTES

1. U.S. Bureau of the Census, *Statistical Abstract of the United States,* 108th ed. (Washington, D.C.: Government Printing Office, 1988), p. 496.
2. Ibid.
3. Ibid.
4. Cleaveland D. Miller, "The Fiduciary Duties of a Corporate Director," *Practical Accountant,* January–February 1980, p. 63.
5. "Inside Look at Life in the Corporate Board Room," *U.S. News & World Report,* January 28, 1985, p. 71.

6. Harriet C. Johnson, "Women Find Reward at the Top," *USA Today,* February 29, 1988, p. 18.
7. "On Corporate Boards, It's Still a White Male World," *Wall Street Journal,* December 12, 1988, p. 1.
8. Amanda Bennett, "Losing Ground? Surveyed Firms Report Fewer Women Directors," *Wall Street Journal,* January 17, 1987, p. 17.
9. "On Corporate Boards, It's Still a White Male World."
10. "Going into Business Yourself," *U.S. News & World Report,* September 3, 1984.
11. Milton Moskowitz, Michael Katz, and Robert Levering, *Everybody's Business* (New York: Harper & Row, 1980), p. 824.
12. Louis Rukeyser, *Business Almanac* (New York: Simon & Schuster, 1988), p. 260.
13. "Is Business Getting Too Big?" *Newsweek,* July 20, 1981, p. 53.
14. Holman Jenkins, Jr., "A Push to Put Two Presses Together," *Insight,* September 7, 1987, p. 46.
15. Mark N. Vamos, "For KKR, Here Comes the Grunt Work," *Business Week,* December 19, 1988, pp. 28–29.
16. Ford S. Worthy, "Beatrice's Sell-off Strategy," *Fortune,* June 23, 1986, pp. 44–49.
17. Andrea Rock, "Co-ops Can Feed, Finance, Doctor and Bury You," *Money,* May 1985, p. 198.
18. Corie Brown, "Why Farm Co-ops Need Extra Seed Money," *Business Week,* March 21, 1988, p. 96.
19. Mark N. Dodesh, "Foreign Earnings of U.S. Multinationals Are Down and Should Stay There Awhile," *Wall Street Journal,* February 13, 1981, p. 38.
20. Zachary Schiller, "Doing Well by Doing Good," *Business Week,* December 15, 1988, pp. 53–57.

CHECK YOUR LEARNING ANSWER KEY

A. 1. b, *p. 101*
2. d, *p. 103*
3. a, *p. 108*

B. 1. T, *p. 105*
2. T, *p. 105*

C. 1. F, *p. 109*
2. F, *p. 109*

D. 1. T, *p. 111*
2. F, *p. 111*
3. T, *p. 111*

E. 1. b, *p. 115*
2. T, *p. 116*

F. 1. F, *p. 119*
2. c, *p. 118*

CHAPTER

5

SMALL BUSINESS AND ENTREPRENEURSHIP

LEARNING OBJECTIVES

After reading this chapter you should be able to:

1. List the common criteria used to define *small business.*
2. Discuss key facts that help explain the contribution of small business to the economy.
3. List the basic steps involved in starting a small business.
4. Identify the main behavioral traits possessed by successful entrepreneurs.
5. List and explain the pros and cons of small-business ownership.
6. Describe the SBA's role in assisting small businesses.
7. Analyze the advantages and disadvantages of franchise ownership.
8. Identify the procedures to follow in analyzing a franchise opportunity.

OUTLINE

Business Practice Example: The Famous Amos Chocolate Chip Cookie—This Cookie Hasn't Crumbled

Small Business Is Here to Stay

- Definition of *Small Business*
- Small Business and American Capitalism

Operating a Small Business—A Closer Look

- Developing a Business Plan
- Financing the Business
- Entrepreneurial Traits
- Entrepreneurship Opportunities for Women and Minorities
  - Female Entrepreneurs
  - Minority Entrepreneurs
- Entrepreneurship around the World
- Advantages of Small-Business Ownership
  - Owner as Key Decision Maker
  - Control of Profits
  - Personal Contact with Employees and Customers
  - Sense of Self-Pride
  - Work Satisfaction
- Disadvantages of Small-Business Ownership
  - Customers as the Real Boss
  - Lack of Specialization
  - Sole Responsibility for Decisions
  - Competition with Big Business
  - Risk of Failure
- Minimizing Risk: Buying a Successful Business

Helping Entrepreneurs Succeed—Functions of the Small Business Administration

- Financial Programs
- Management Counseling
- Procurement Assistance
- Seminars and Publications
- Small Business Investment Companies
- Minority Assistance Programs

Opportunities in Franchising

- Definition of *Franchising*
- Advantages of Franchising
  - Name Recognition
  - Proven Management Methods
  - National Promotion
  - Standardized Products
  - Financial Assistance
- Disadvantages of Franchising
  - Franchise Fees and Profit Sharing
  - Strict Compliance with Standardized Operations
  - Restricted Product Mix
  - Inventory Purchasing Requirements

Choosing the Right Franchise

Mixing Small Business and Franchising

Summary

Key Terms

Check Your Learning

Questions for Review and Discussion

Concluding Case: Federal Government Encourages Small-Business "Exportese"

Notes

Check Your Learning Answer Key

Highlight in Business Practice: Peace Corps Trains Third-World Entrepreneurs

Highlight in Business Practice: Incubators for New Entrepreneurs

Highlight in Business Practice: The New Entrepreneurial Woman

BUSINESS PRACTICE EXAMPLE

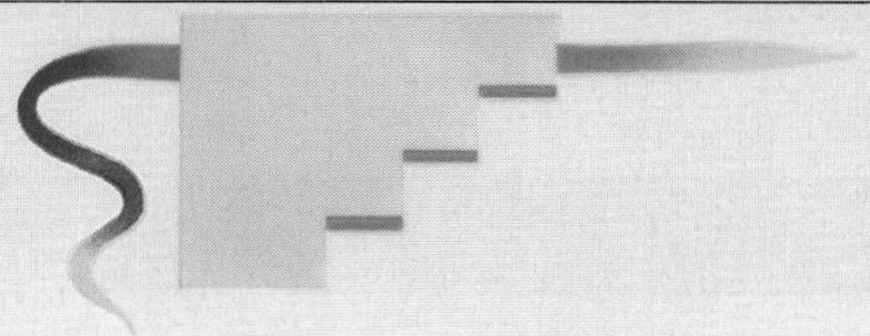

The Famous Amos Chocolate Chip Cookie—This Cookie Hasn't Crumbled

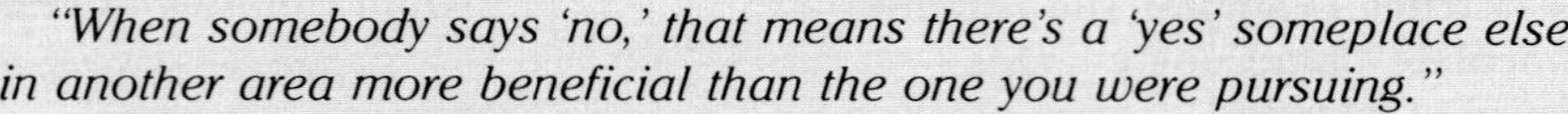

"When somebody says 'no,' that means there's a 'yes' someplace else in another area more beneficial than the one you were pursuing."

"Entrepreneurs cannot do everything well, so they need to look at what their strengths are and then surround themselves with people to plug in the other areas."

"I've always felt that life is like dancing. When you get in step with it, when you're synchronized, it's beautiful. When you're not in harmony, you look like a clod. . . ."

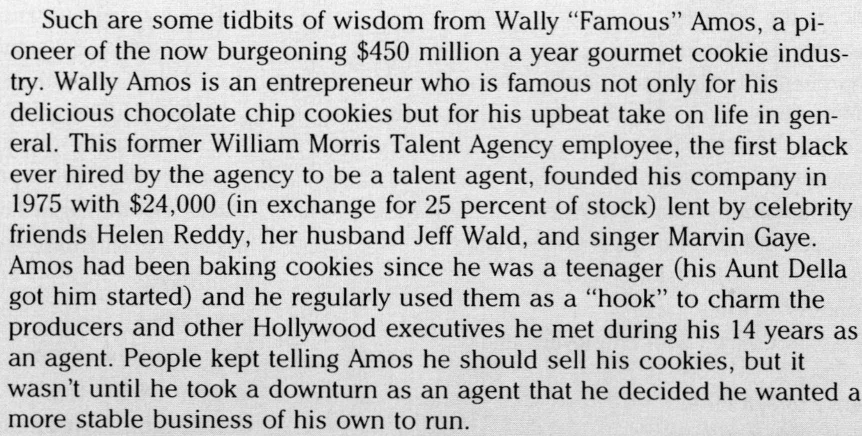

Such are some tidbits of wisdom from Wally "Famous" Amos, a pioneer of the now burgeoning $450 million a year gourmet cookie industry. Wally Amos is an entrepreneur who is famous not only for his delicious chocolate chip cookies but for his upbeat take on life in general. This former William Morris Talent Agency employee, the first black ever hired by the agency to be a talent agent, founded his company in 1975 with $24,000 (in exchange for 25 percent of stock) lent by celebrity friends Helen Reddy, her husband Jeff Wald, and singer Marvin Gaye. Amos had been baking cookies since he was a teenager (his Aunt Della got him started) and he regularly used them as a "hook" to charm the producers and other Hollywood executives he met during his 14 years as an agent. People kept telling Amos he should sell his cookies, but it wasn't until he took a downturn as an agent that he decided he wanted a more stable business of his own to run.

Amos opened his first store, which an artist friend designed, on Sunset Boulevard. He traded in his tailored suits for Hawaiian-style shirts, baggy pants, and a panama hat. Then he had himself photographed and put on each package of Famous Amos cookies. For the opening, he sent out 2,500 invitations to the press, and, as a band played, poured champagne and dispensed cookies to his willing publicity pawns. By the next morning, lines formed outside his door as people tried to purchase part of L.A.'s latest media event.

The Famous Amos Chocolate Chip Cookie Company quickly grew to stores in Santa Monica and Hawaii. The company grossed $300,000 in its first year, $4 million in 1979, and $10 million in 1987. Today, there are 27 "fresh-baked" retail outlets across the country, and Famous Amos cookies line the shelves of thousands of grocery stores and supermarkets worldwide.

WHAT'S AHEAD

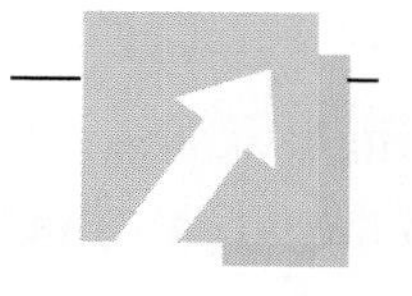

Small business has been called the last frontier. Entrepreneurs, like Wally Amos, accept challenge and risk in return for the possibility of significant profit, but many of these risk takers do not survive in business.

This chapter will discuss the role of entrepreneurship in the American economy, the pros and cons of small-business ownership, and the function of the Small Business Administration. It will also examine franchising as an alternate way of starting a small business from scratch.

SMALL BUSINESS IS HERE TO STAY

Thousands of goods and services are provided every day through the dedication and hard work of small-business professionals. Clothing, food, appliances, lawn-care service, and day-care centers are just a few examples. The merchant philosophy of the early colonial period continues to energize today's free-enterprise system.

Your first entrepreneurial experience may have been a lemonade stand. Some of you may have participated in student business programs such as Junior Achievement or sold candy to make extra money for your school or church. In any of these situations, you likely experienced challenges and frustrations similar to those faced by the millions of owners of small businesses throughout the country. Individuals who assume the risk of starting their own businesses are known as **entrepreneurs.**

Entrepreneurs are individuals who take the risk of starting their own businesses.

Small ventures often mature into large enterprises. In 1886, for example, a twenty-three-year-old railroad agent named Richard Warren Sears bought a consignment of watches that a local jeweler had refused. He offered these watches for sale to other agents through mail orders and cash on delivery. Sears made $5,000 in six months and quit his job to go into business in Minneapolis. The next year, he hired a watchmaker named Alvah C. Roebuck. This particular small venture grew into America's largest retail chain.

The capitalistic system thrives on the profit incentive as an encouragement to start businesses. An examination of entrepreneurial drive will help clarify the role of American small business.

Definition of *Small Business*

We commonly think of local restaurants, beauty shops, florists, and television repair shops as small businesses. Indeed, these types of businesses do follow a common small-business pattern. They often employ fewer than twenty-five people, are independently owned, and offer their service or product in a limited geographical area.

A ***small business*** is an independently owned and managed business that serves a limited geographic area and is not dominant in its industry.

Official definitions of *smallness* are provided by two government agencies. The first, the Committee on Economic Development, states that a firm is a **small business** if it meets two or more of the following criteria:

1. Management is independent. (Managers are usually the owners.)
2. Venture capital is supplied and ownership is controlled by an individual or small group.
3. The area of operation is mostly local.
4. The firm is small when compared to relative size in its industry.

The ***Small Business Administration (SBA)*** is a federal agency whose main purpose is to provide financial and managerial assistance to small American firms.

The second agency, the **Small Business Administration (SBA),** exists to provide financial and managerial assistance to small firms. According to the SBA, a firm is small if it is "one which is independently owned and operated and not dominant in its field of operation."

Both definitions stress independent ownership and management. In a narrow sense, they would exclude chain stores and franchises. In addition, both agencies consider the size of the firm in comparison to others in the industry. Of course, size is commonly determined by sales, profits, or number of employees. The obvious question is, how small is small? Included under the SBA definition, for example, are retail operations that gross between $3.5 and $13.5 million a year and manufacturing firms with as many as 1,500 employees.[1] In this chapter, we will assume that a business is small if either set of criteria is met.

Small Business and American Capitalism

The following facts about small businesses will help us understand their economic impact.[2]

- 99 percent of nonfarm businesses are considered small.
- Approximately 50 percent of small businesses are classified as full-time operations.
- Small businesses employ 48 percent of the private work force, contribute 42 percent of all sales, and are responsible for 38 percent of the gross national

This migratory bee colony is an example of a small business in the production sector.

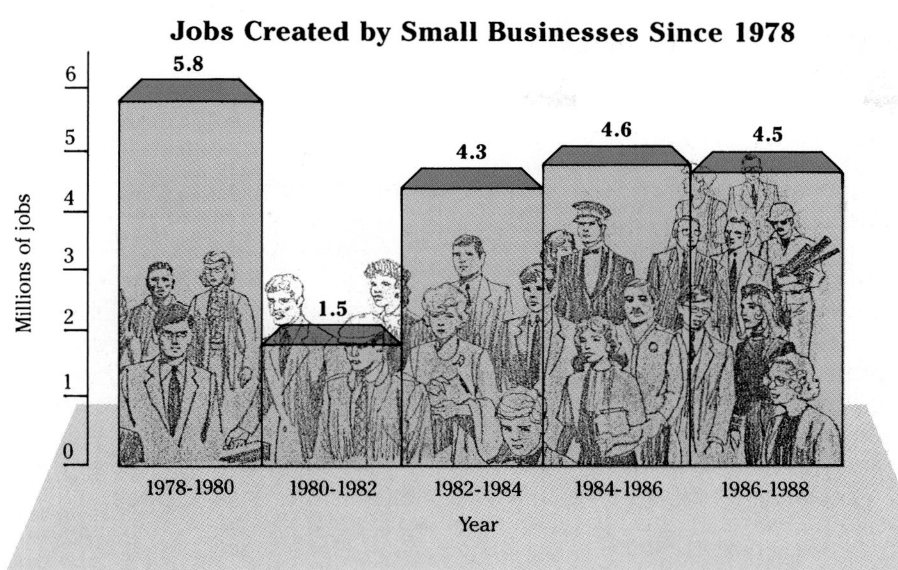

Figure 5.1
Jobs created by small businesses since 1978.

product. In the period 1986–1988, small businesses employed an estimated 4.5 million people (see Figure 5.1).

- Two-thirds of new jobs are created by businesses that employ fewer than five hundred people and that are less than five years old.[3]
- Most young people learn their basic job skills working for small businesses.

Figure 5.2 shows the industry concentrations of small firms. As expected, the service and retail industries dominate the small-business arena, while the production sector plays an important but less significant role. Since the service sector is the fastest-growing part of the U.S. economy, small businesses have good reason to be optimistic about the future.

OPERATING A SMALL BUSINESS—A CLOSER LOOK

As chapter 4 explained, most small businesses start out as sole proprietorships. But successful entrepreneurship involves more than just setting up a particular form of business. Let's take a look at how an entrepreneur creates a business.

Developing a Business Plan

First, an entrepreneur must conduct preliminary market studies to determine if potential customers exist for the product or service to be offered. If the initial research is positive, a business plan is developed. A **business plan** is a comprehensive written proposal that describes the business and its specific goals and objectives. It is essential for convincing lenders and investors to finance the business. Business plans usually include at least the following:

A ***business plan*** is a comprehensive written proposal that describes a business and its specific goals and objectives.

1. A summary to provide an overview of the plan and to attract the investor's interest.

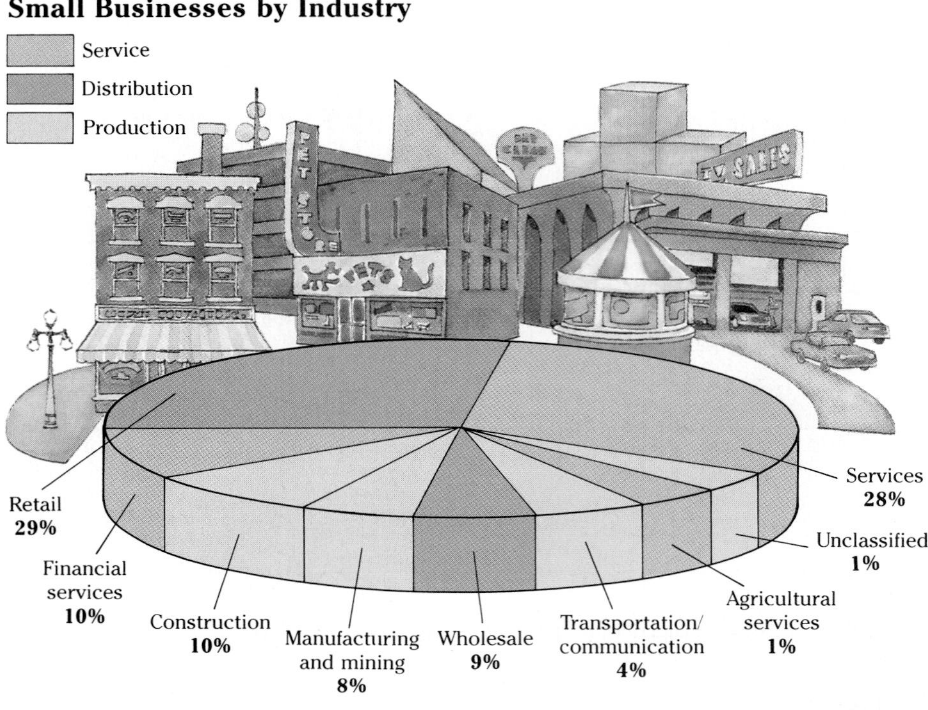

Figure 5.2
Small businesses by industry. Most small businesses are in the retail and service sectors.

2. A concise explanation of the company's proposed business and a statement about what makes it unique. The explanation should also contain an industry analysis and profile.
3. A market analysis describing the company's product or service and the target market as well as a marketing plan depicting pricing, promotion, distribution, and product strategies.
4. Financial statements projecting profit and loss positions as well as cash-flow estimates for the first two to five years and including a detailed budget.
5. A management profile describing the experience and background of each employee, including resumes, letters of recommendation, and other evidence that the borrower is of good character and has the ability to pay back the loan.

Financing the Business

Venture capital is start-up money used to finance a new business or expand one that shows potential.

Venture capitalists are investment specialists seeking to invest in potentially high-growth new companies.

After the business plan is finished, the entrepreneur must secure capital. **Venture capital** is start-up money used to finance a new business or expand one that shows potential. It is often difficult to obtain because the survival rate of small firms is poor. Although there are many sources of start-up money, Figure 5.3 shows that personal resources provide more than half of venture capital. Banks are the second largest source of capital. In order to earn a reasonable profit, most banks like to lend no less than $25,000.

Companies anticipating high growth may look to **venture capitalists**—investment specialists who seek promising new businesses that will pay high returns

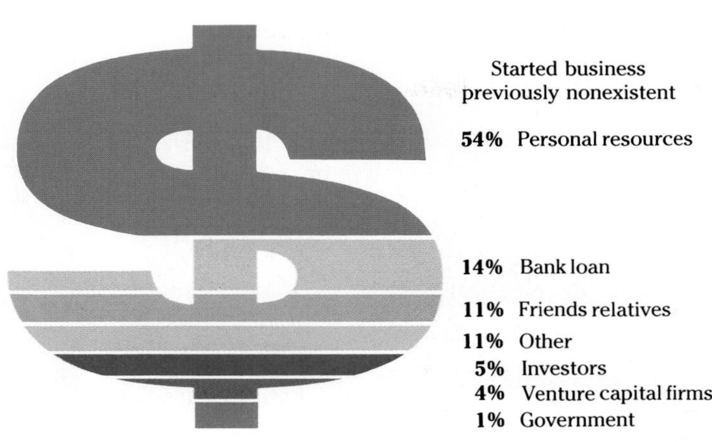

Figure 5.3
Sources of capital for new small businesses. Personal resources are by far the most common source of venture capital for small businesses.

on their investment. It is a common practice for venture capitalists to be active in the management of a firm. Once the company has prospered, the venture capitalists can sell their shares for a substantial profit.

Entrepreneurial Traits

Several studies have attempted to identify common entrepreneurial traits. Figure 5.4 presents a behavioral profile of successful small-business people. Obviously, successful entrepreneurs must be high achievers, with enough inner drive to meet the daily challenges and frustrations of running small firms. Most entrepreneurs are not gamblers, but they are willing to assume moderate risks, and they are very aware of potential failure. Successful entrepreneurs are goal oriented, which is important because a new venture must have a well-designed planning system.

Many entrepreneurs start their own firms because their jobs with other firms do not allow for individual creativity (keen mental ability and analytical thinking combined with a high level of innovation). In addition to thinking creatively, small-business owners must communicate effectively with customers and employees. The crucial link in the communication process is the ability to empathize—to put oneself in someone else's position. Finally, successful entrepreneurs must understand their products or services. Constant study and training are often required of entrepreneurs if they wish to remain technically competent.

Several tests exist to help people determine if they would succeed as entrepreneurs. Figure 5.5 provides a set of questions and a key with which you can evaluate your own entrepreneurial potential.

Entrepreneurship Opportunities for Women and Minorities

Countless opportunities exist in small-business ownership for women and minorities. While both groups are taking increasing advantage of these opportunities, neither has a significant share of business ownership.

Figure 5.4
Traits of successful entrepreneurs. Research studies have indicated that there are six common entrepreneurial traits among successful small-business people.

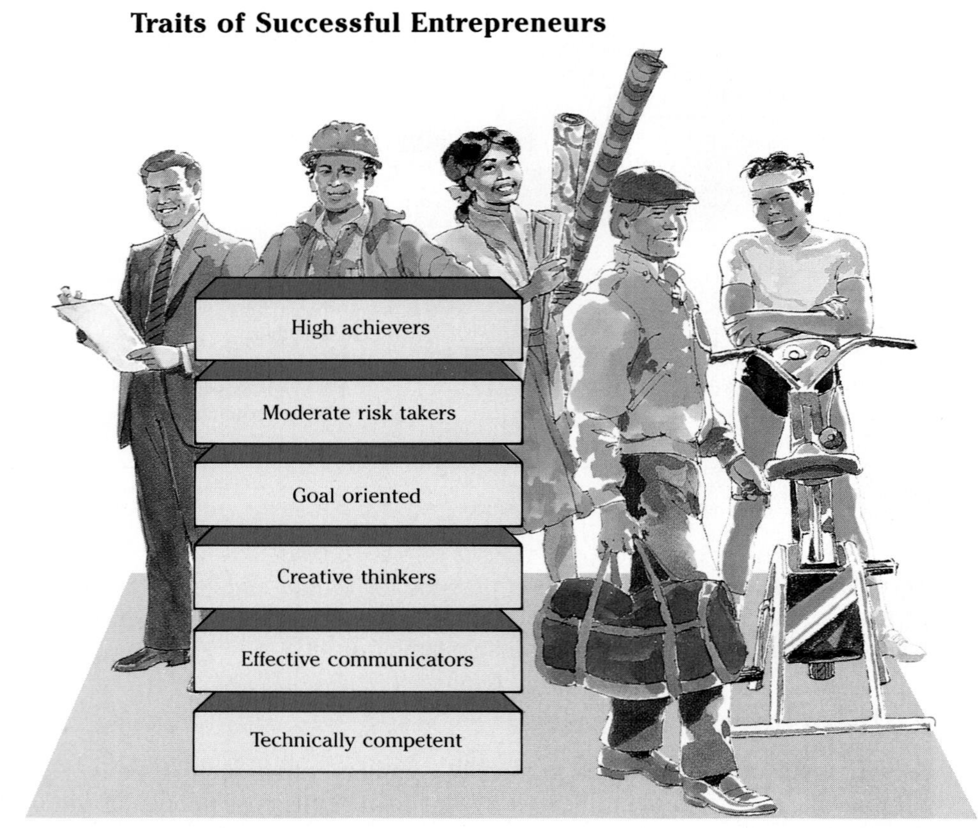

Traits of Successful Entrepreneurs
High achievers
Moderate risk takers
Goal oriented
Creative thinkers
Effective communicators
Technically competent

Female Entrepreneurs

Women-owned businesses are playing an increasingly vital role in the U.S. free-enterprise system. Government statistics indicate that women started new businesses at three times the rate men did between 1974 and 1984. The Bureau of Labor Statistics reports that 2.6 million full-time firms (one-third of the total number) had female owners in 1984. In the prior decade, women owned 26 percent of small businesses.

Who are these new risk takers? Some women develop business expertise through volunteer work and apply what they learn to profit-making ventures. Others climb the corporate ladder but become disenchanted by bureaucracy and by limited opportunities for career development. A growing number of female entrepreneurs have advanced college degrees in areas such as telecommunications, aerospace, marketing, accounting, and biomedical engineering.

According to a 1985 presidential report to Congress, *The State of Small Business,* 91 percent of women-owned sole proprietorships were in service industries

Under each question, check the answer that says what you believe or comes closest to it. Be honest with yourself.	
Are you a self-starter?	I do things on my own. Nobody has to tell me to get going. If someone gets me started, I keep going all right. Easy does it. I don't put myself out until I have to.
How do you feel about other people?	I like people. I can get along with just about anybody. I have plenty of friends — I don't need anyone else. Most people irritate me.
Can you lead others?	I can get most people to go along when I start something. I can give the orders if someone tells me what we should do. I let someone else get things moving. Then I go along if I feel like it.
Can you take responsibility?	I like to take charge of things and see them through. I'll take over if I have to, but I'd rather let someone else be responsible. There's always some eager beaver around wanting to show how smart he is. I say let him.
How good an organizer are you?	I like to have a plan before I start. I'm usually the one to get things lined up when the group wants to do something. I do all right unless things get too confused. Then I quit. You get all set and then something comes along and presents too many problems. So I just take things as they come.
How good a worker are you?	I can keep going as long as I need to. I don't mind working hard for something I want. I'll work hard for awhile, but when I've had enough, that's it. I can't see that hard work gets you anywhere.
Can you make decisions?	I can make up my mind in a hurry if I have to. It usually turns out OK too. I can if I have plenty of time. If I have to make up my mind fast, I think later I should have decided the other way. I don't like to be the one who has to decide things.
Can people trust what you say?	You bet they can. I don't say things I don't mean. I try to be on the level most of the time, but sometimes I just say what's easiest. Why bother if the other fellow doesn't know the difference.
Can you stick with it?	If I make up my mind to do something, I don't let anything stop me. I usually finish up what I start — if it goes well. If it doesn't go well, I quit. Why beat your brains out?
How good is your health?	I never run down! I have enough energy for most things I want to do. I run out of energy sooner than most of my friends seem to.
Now count the checks you made.	How many checks are there beside the first answer to each question? How many checks are there beside the second answer to each question? How many checks are there beside the third answer to each question?
If 8 or more of your checks are beside the first answers, you probably have what it takes to run a business. If not, you're likely to have more trouble than you can handle by yourself. Better find a partner who is strong on the points you are weak on. If 5 or more checks are beside the third answer, not even a good partner will be able to shore you up.	

Figure 5.5
Small-business readiness test. Certain questions should be answered before the decision to start a business is made.

such as real estate, health care, data processing, leisure, retail trade, communications, and insurance. These industries are usually labor-intensive small-scale operations that require small amounts of capital.

BUSINESS PRACTICE EXAMPLE Continues

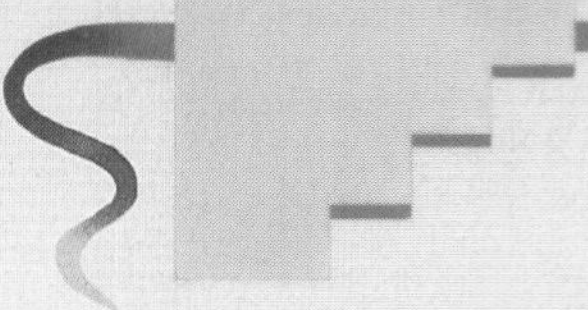

The Famous Amos Chocolate Chip Cookie Company began with venture capital loaned by friends of Wally Amos. "I put together a proposal to show what I was going to do, how I was going to do it, and why," Amos said. First Amos took the plan to conventional financing sources, such as the Small Business Association, but none were enthusiastic about his idea.

Others, however, were. According to investor Jeffrey Wald, "I was impressed with the proposal. It was thoroughly investigated; Wally wasn't going out there blindly. The idea was well thought out and based on the premise that everybody likes chocolate chip cookies." Today, Wald's original investment of $10,000 is worth well over one million dollars.

Wally Amos exemplifies the entrepreneurial traits needed for success. He was always a high achiever, as seen by his success as a path-breaking talent agent who discovered singers such as Simon and Garfunkel. He started his cookie company because his job didn't allow him to be as creative as he wished. He is a master of promotion and of communicating effectively with customers and employees. So much so, in fact, that he uses himself instead of advertising campaigns to sell his product, traveling across the country extolling the message that anyone can do anything he or she wants in life. "Wherever I show up," Amos has said, "it's an advertisement for cookies." Finally, Amos understands his product inside and out. After all, he perfected the recipe!

How do female entrepreneurs compare to their male counterparts? In many ways they are similar. Both are high achievers, dislike bureaucracy, and enjoy making their own decisions. In short, male and female entrepreneurs desire results.

Minority Entrepreneurs

There are approximately 840,000 minority-owned businesses; they are 1.8 percent of the U.S. minority population. This compares to 6.4 percent for the nonminority population. Almost all minority-owned firms (94 percent) are sole proprietorships, whereas only 69 percent of nonminority businesses are sole proprietorships. Of the three main minority groups—Asians, blacks (African-Americans), and Hispanics—Asians are the most likely to own businesses. Compared to the general business-owning population, minorities own more service and retail businesses

Native American Michael Nelson's Western-style shoe store is one of the approximately 840,000 minority-owned businesses in the U.S.

and fewer manufacturing and finance firms.[4] (Table 5.1 lists the largest black-owned industrial and service companies.) Minority entrepreneurs can receive special help from the federal government. (The material on minority assistance programs appears in the SBA section of the chapter.)

In recent years, the number of minority entrepreneurs entering business through franchises has greatly increased. Organizations such as Jesse Jackson's Operation PUSH have helped by encouraging franchise companies (Coca-Cola and Anheuser-

Table 5.1 Largest black-owned industrial and service companies.

Name and Location	Chief Executive	1987 Sales (in millions)
TLC Group (New York)	Reginald F. Lewis	$1,800.0
Johnson Publishing (Chicago)	John H. Johnson	201.5
Phila. Coca-Cola Bottling	J. Bruce Llewellyn	166.0
H.J. Russell (Atlanta)	Herman J. Russell	141.9
Motown Industries (Los Angeles)	Berry Gordy	100.0
Soft Sheen (Chicago)	Edward Gardner	81.3
Trans Jones (Monroe, Michigan)	Gary White	79.3
Systems Mgmt Amer. (Norfolk, Va.)	Herman Valentine	62.7
Maxima (Rockville, Md.)	Joshua Smith	56.1
M&M Products (Atlanta)	Cornell McBride	47.3

Busch, for example) to sell franchises to black investors. A 1985 survey reported 9,147 minority-owned franchises, an increase of 13 percent over a similar 1984 survey. (Further information about black-owned franchises appears later in the chapter.)

Although black-owned businesses are only a small segment of all businesses, current financial trends indicate that by 1998 there will be a noticeable change in the size and strength of the average black company. For example, many new black business owners are using leveraging techniques to buy, rather than build, companies. The largest black-owned multinational company, TLC Group, purchased Beatrice Companies in 1987 for $985 million. Previously TLC had purchased the McCall Pattern Company for around $1 million and sold it for $90 million three years later. Deals of this sort are landmark business cases; they illustrate that today's black-owned businesses are mainstream American businesses.

Entrepreneurship around the World

Across the globe, nations are relying on entrepreneurs to support their sagging economies, create native-owned industrial bases, slow the "brain-drain" of educated people leaving the country, and, in some less-developed countries, feed the poor. Examples from around the world follow.[5] (Figure 5.6 compares the small-business output of the United States with the total output of several countries.)

Taiwan. Some Taiwanese entrepreneurs are secretly taking advantage of China's low labor costs by using Taiwan's industrial technology, investment capital, and marketing expertise to illegally produce "knock-offs" (imitations

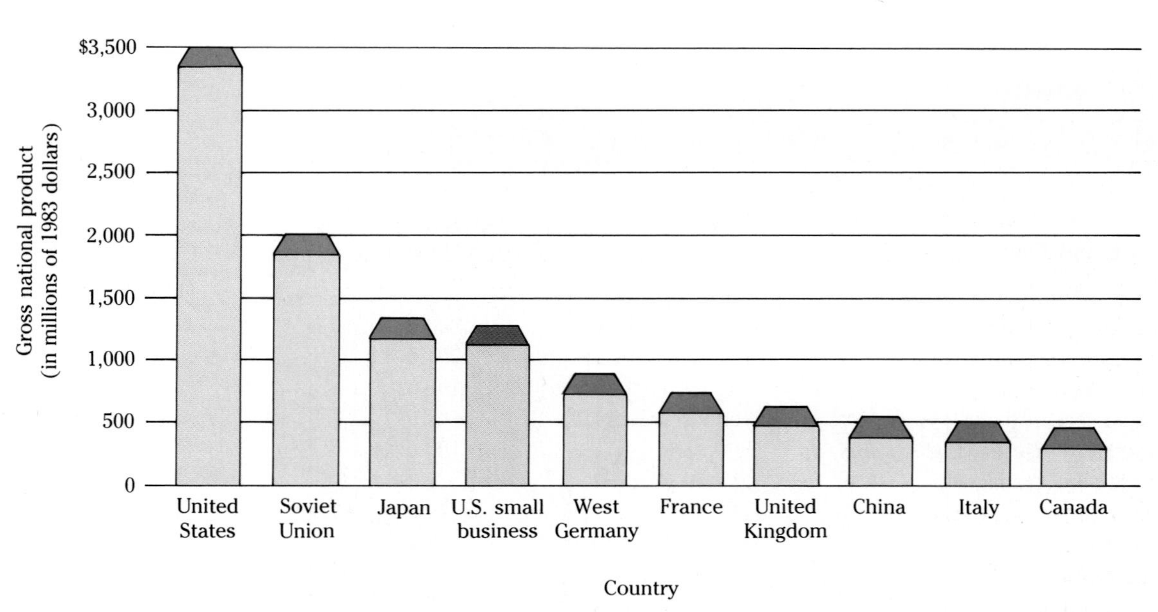

Figure 5.6 Output of small businesses in the United States compared with output of the world's largest countries.

sold as the real thing) of such products as Reebok athletic shoes. Other entrepreneurs are taking advantage of Taiwan's subsidized industrial space and tax exemptions to start up legal high-tech electronics businesses.

Ireland. The Irish have created several organizations to spur entrepreneurial growth and the country's emerging economy. In addition, the nation offers generous tax breaks for foreign entrepreneurs willing to relocate in Ireland. The hope is that the entrepreneurial spirit will rub off on local Irish.

France. The French, who have traditionally displayed a great disdain for the self-made rich, are now desperately trying to create an entrepreneurial ethic. The government is encouraging private startups by providing entrepreneurs with low-interest loans, tax credits, and grants. The government has also authorized employees to take sabbaticals from jobs to create new companies. Sectors in which newer ventures are doing well include pharmaceuticals, food processing, and upscale textiles and clothing.

Kenya. After years of foreign domination by entrepreneurs from Britain, India and Pakistan, native Kenyans have begun to invest in major local businesses. Indians in Kenya have emerged as the leading entrepreneurs; they have started building shopping malls.

Advantages of Small-Business Ownership

Many incentives exist for the owners of small firms. Table 5.2 ranks the most important sources of satisfaction for small-business owners.

Table 5.2 Small-business benefits.

Surveyed small-business owners rank pride in product as their most important source of satisfaction. The rankings:

1	Pride in product/service
2	Control
3	Freedom
4	Flexibility
5	Self-reliance
6	Customer contact
7	Income
8	Employee contact
9	Recognition
10	Privacy
11	Security
12	Status

HIGHLIGHT IN BUSINESS PRACTICE

Peace Corps Trains Third-World Entrepreneurs

The Peace Corps is getting down to business. Founded in 1961 by President John F. Kennedy, this U.S. agency, once known for its volunteers in education, health and agriculture (60 percent of whom were liberal arts majors), is now promoting small business development in Third World nations. The current director, Loret M. Ruppe, is credited with turning the Peace Corps around and making its brand of volunteerism chic. Today the Peace Corps has five applications for every opening.

Capitalism is currently "hot" around the globe as the best way to run an economy, and Congress is pursuing many avenues to help Third World nations develop their economies. One very successful approach has been to provide "microenterprise" loans and experienced business professionals to countries requesting assistance. In order to accomplish this goal, in 1985 Congress authorized the Peace Corps to double its volunteers to 10,000. In 1988 the Corps budget had grown to $146 million.

Volunteers are given great latitude in finding projects. For example, projects have been created to help vendors set up sidewalk donut and shoeshine shops, to teach bookkeeping and marketing skills to fishermen, and to assist local artisans in buying raw materials and selling their products. One such project, in Ecuador, used an initial $5,000 grant from the Inter-American Development Bank to train and establish 1,200 artisans for a straw market. Another project, headed by two volunteers in the Dominican Republic, loaned $1.2 million to 4,674 microenterprises that created 6,000 jobs.

If a sense of doing good for others, gaining valuable experience, and promoting your economic system interest you, why not explore the opportunities available overseas? In addition to the Peace Corps, churches, private charities such as CARE, and other U.S. agencies are always seeking volunteers. One easy way to find out if volunteerism is for you is to try a two-week work project during Christmas or Spring break. Many church-affiliated organizations on campus regularly send teams of students overseas. For example, De Paul University students have built housing in Panama and schools in Liberia. Other students have assisted volunteer doctors and dentists in the Dominican Republic and other Third World nations. Try it! You'll like it!

Owner as Key Decision Maker

Entrepreneurs want to make decisions independently. Small-business owners can implement new ideas with a minimum of red tape. Feedback on their decisions is fast. Most small-business people cherish the independence of being their own boss.

Control of Profits

A definite plus in owning a business is the control of profits. The profits derived from the operations of the firm serve as one of the primary incentives for successful business entrepreneurs. Owners can decide how much to reinvest in the business and how much to use for living expenses. Profits allow the business to grow and thus provide great satisfaction for the owner.

Personal Contact with Employees and Customers

Today, many customers perceive big business as impersonal and indifferent to their needs. Employees of large corporations frequently voice similar feelings of alienation. Small-business owners can provide a warm and friendly place, where customers are often known on a first-name basis and treated as part of the "family." Employees have direct contact with the owners and can express their thoughts openly. This rapport often encourages harmonious working relationships among employees. Frequently, the boss works alongside the employees, so a team environment is established. Small-firm owners who recognize the value of greater personalization can greatly enhance the success of their businesses.

Sense of Self-Pride

As mentioned earlier, small-business owners are high achievers and goal setters. Many owners dream of having the business mature and continue for generations. Entrepreneurs take great pride in having made it on their own, often through considerable sacrifice and hard work. It is common for successful entrepreneurs to encourage their children to take over the family business because of personal pride.

Work Satisfaction

Some small-business owners work long hours even though they could earn more money working for someone else. Most of them feel greatly enriched by shouldering the responsibility for their own destiny. Working for someone else frequently results in a routine and unchallenging position, but being in business for oneself constantly challenges innovative and creative talents. Watching dreams and ideas become reality is a rewarding experience.

Disadvantages of Small-Business Ownership

Owners of small firms must be aware of certain limitations, however.

Customers as the Real Boss

Some entrepreneurs quickly learn that the independence they sought in establishing their own firm is soon lost to a demanding public. Many small-business owners left secure forty-hour-a-week jobs in which they reported to one immediate supervisor. When they entered the world of small business, they became accountable to their customers. And a customer whose water pump stops working on Sunday morning wants instant service. As a result, many entrepreneurs, especially those in repair businesses, work seventy to eighty hours per week. The independence so deeply cherished by entrepreneurs may be more myth than reality.

HIGHLIGHT IN BUSINESS PRACTICE

Incubators for New Entrepreneurs

To help foster economic development and create new jobs, private and public sponsors have experimented with a business incubator program. An incubator is a facility with flexible space that is rented to small businesses at reduced rates. Incubators allow the tenants to share common facilities and support services such as meeting rooms, secretarial and accounting services, research libraries, and computer time. Financial assistance and management or technical assistance is frequently available. State agencies, public universities, and large private corporations commonly serve as sponsors.

The incubator program is designed to help new ventures get off the ground by reducing certain barriers. According to Carlos Morales, founder and Executive Director of the National Business Incubation Association (NBIA), 80 percent of incubated businesses are still around five years after start-up. Morales feels that this success rate is because the incubator concept addresses some of the most common reasons for business failure. Examples of some of the benefits provided by incubators include the following:

1. Entrepreneurs rent facilities and services at below market rates.
2. Building maintenance responsibilities rest with the incubator sponsor.
3. Locating with other new entrepreneurs provides an opportunity for sharing ideas, thereby reducing start-up anxiety.
4. Tenants have access to equipment, facilities, and managerial services that normally would be unavailable or unaffordable.
5. New ventures receive increased visibility because of sponsor publicity.

Ann Kuznicki, owner of ATB Enterprises, Inc., a computer software company in Montgomeryville, Pennsylvania, is one example of how an incubator can reduce expenses. Kuznicki rents 400 square feet of space in the Montgomeryville Technology Enterprise Center. Her $300 monthly rent also covers utilities and the use of a conference room. She pays an additional $110 a month for phones and an in-house answering service.

Most incubator sponsors limit the amount of time that a new enterprise can lease space—usually two to five years. After a firm has completed its incubation period, it "graduates" to a new location and operates on its own.

The number of business incubators operating in the U.S. mushroomed from half a dozen in 1979 to over 300 in 1987. The business incubator program tries to allow a gestation period that results in a higher level of new venture successes.

Lack of Specialization

Large companies have the financial resources to hire specialists for their many positions. Owners and employees of small businesses frequently must wear many hats. It is not uncommon for the owner to assume the role of production supervisor, marketing representative, personnel specialist, and accountant, as needs arise. Because entrepreneurs assume so many roles, they frequently become preoccupied with short-term planning. This type of crisis management may result in business failure. To whatever extent is possible, small-business owners should assign selected responsibilities to key employees so that they can devote adequate time to longer-range planning.

Sole Responsibility for Decisions

The saying "a leader's life is a lonely life" is applicable to entrepreneurs. Their decisions determine the fate of the enterprise. Large corporations hire specialists to help managers make difficult decisions. Entrepreneurs rely on limited skills and information. If the decision is good, the owner gets all the recognition; if the decision is bad, the owner must be willing to assume the entire blame.

Competition with Big Business

Large firms have economies of scale that allow them to offer goods and services at lower prices than can smaller firms. For example, the owner of a local men's clothing store must compete with Sears, Penney's, and other nationally known companies. As a result, the owner may decide to stress such nonprice variables as service, expertise, and friendliness, capitalizing on many customers' opposition to a cold, no-frills business environment. Entrepreneurs must recognize and market their environment if they are to remain competitive with big business.

Risk of Failure

As chapter 1 pointed out, the capitalistic system is a profit and loss system. The ultimate risk faced by any business owner is bankruptcy, the price that entrepreneurs must pay for making poor decisions.

In fact, the survival statistics for new businesses are less than encouraging. Analysts agree that the smaller and newer the enterprise, the more likely it is to fail. For example, over 55 percent of the firms that go out of business annually have been in existence for five years or less (see Figure 5.7, which also describes the reasons for failure).[6]

Nearly 98 percent of business failures involve inadequate management.[7] For example, one entrepreneur may have general business experience but lack the specific skills needed for a particular venture. Others may be skilled technically but lack the management skills of planning, organizing, and directing operations. An unbalanced perspective can also be a detriment to success. Business owners must view the business as a set of interrelated activities. Those who look only at the financial aspects will find that their marketing and production areas suffer.

More than half of all business failures are a result of general incompetence. Many entrepreneurs become overly optimistic about a new idea and do not do the research required to determine whether it is feasible. This blind optimism can quickly result in failure.

Minimizing Risk: Buying a Successful Business

Often it makes more sense to buy an existing business than to build one from scratch. For example, a recent graduate of a veterinary school who wants to start a practice will find it difficult to go it alone. The costs of capitalizing a new practice are often prohibitive, and there is also the problem of establishing a client base. One way around this obstacle is to work for an established veterinarian

Figure 5.7 Failures of new businesses. (a) Business failures in 1986 by age of business (preliminary figures). (b) Reasons for business failures. Most small-business failures can be blamed on bad management, according to a survey of owners of U.S. firms with annual sales of $300,000 or less.

who wishes to retire and sell the business, or at least to allow a partner to buy into it. An arrangement could be made to allow the retiring veterinarian to take home a decreasing rate of the profits for an agreed-upon time period.

There are several significant advantages to buying a successful business. They include the following:

1. Risk is reduced when a successful business is purchased. The previous owner has already found a proven market segment and has developed an established clientele.
2. It is easier to plan for the financial and marketing aspects of the business because of the historical records that come with it. The data will enable the buyer to build on the company's strengths and avoid possible pitfalls.
3. Profits will be accrued much faster than they would with a new business. How much faster will depend on how smooth the transition is.
4. A new business may require capitalization in the form of loans, trade credit, or other financial transactions. The purchase of an established business usually takes only one financial transaction.

If you have the opportunity to purchase an existing business, be sure to do your homework. It is the buyer's responsibility to ensure that the business is indeed successful—or can be made successful. At a minimum, the buyer should investigate the physical facilities to make sure they are adequate, the inventory to ensure that it is of agreed-upon value, and current leases and policies to ensure that there will be no surprises down the road. By considering these issues, the buyer is likely to minimize the risk and to pay a reasonable price for the business.

BUSINESS PRACTICE EXAMPLE Continues

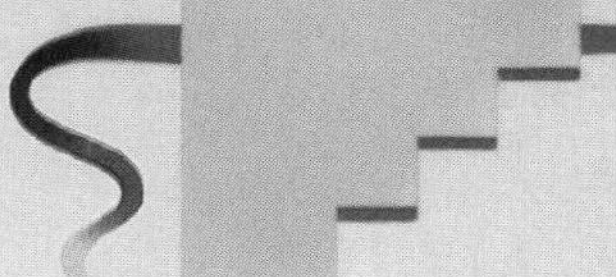

By 1987, the Famous Amos Chocolate Chip Cookie Company had sales of $10 million, but the company posted a loss of $300,000. Claiming his real strength was in promotion and not management, Amos sold the company to Denver real estate investors and entrepreneurs Jeffrey and Ronald Baer. Wally Amos remains a director and shareholder. "I would rather have a small part of a strong team than 100 percent of nothing," Amos said at the time. "I'll continue what I do best for the company, which is to promote."

(Another way of minimizing risk is to purchase a franchise. A later section of the chapter discusses this method of small-business ownership.)

HELPING ENTREPRENEURS SUCCEED—FUNCTIONS OF THE SMALL BUSINESS ADMINISTRATION

The Small Business Administration was created by Congress in 1953 as an advocate for small businesses. In this supportive role, it has provided both prospective and established entrepreneurs with financial assistance, management counseling, and training. It has also advised small firms about their eligibility for government procurement contracts.

During the late 1980s, the SBA as a separate government agency was targeted for proposed budget cutbacks. Nevertheless, the programs described here were strongly supported in Congress and would likely continue in other government units if the SBA's funds were cut back.

Financial Programs

The SBA has offered a wide variety of loan programs to small firms. The purpose of these programs is to help small businesses that are unable to borrow money at reasonable interest rates from conventional lenders.

Most SBA financial assistance has been in the form of **guaranty loans**—loans made by banks or other private lenders that are guaranteed up to 90 percent by the SBA. That is, the SBA will pay the lender up to 90 percent of the value of the loan if the borrower defaults. The maximum guaranty loan is $750,000, with maturity up to twenty-five years. The average guaranty loan is $17,500, and the

Guaranty loans are loans made by banks or other private lenders that are guaranteed up to 90 percent by the SBA.

HIGHLIGHT IN BUSINESS PRACTICE

The New Entrepreneurial Woman

If she didn't enjoy making money so much, Graciela Chichilnisky is convinced she would "have to be a masochist."

In the past two years she has worked 14-hour days, shuttling between offices in Manhattan and London. And everytime she gets to sleep, someone calls from the other side of the globe. She has raised about $7.5 million in equity capital, no small undertaking. But the most difficult job, she says, is managing the egos of 43 employees.

A GLOBAL FINANCIAL INFORMATION SERVICE

Now that the first product in her newly minted enterprise is in place, Chichilnisky, 41, is thriving on the feeling that she has created something unique. On Dec. 17, 1986, her company, Financial Telecommunications Ltd., officially introduced EQUINET™, a telecommunications network designed to speed international securities transactions.

The system is currently up and running in New York, Boston, Chicago, San Francisco, London, Brussels and Tokyo. In essence, it records details of an international stock or bond trade and automatically communicates that information to all the parties involved around the world. Clients can access the network with almost any equipment, including an IBM-PC.

Her gold-chip client list, she says, already includes such financial service firms as Salomon Brothers, Merrill Lynch, Wells Fargo, First Chicago, and Shearson, American Express. By year end, she expects annual sales of close to $2 million and about $8 million by 1988.

EQUINET is designed to replace a cumbersome series of telephone and telex calls that until now followed every international equity deal. According to Chichilnisky, 40% of those deals go awry because there are so many parties involved. People end up disagreeing over just what has been sold to whom and by whom.

A native of Argentina, Chichilnisky is busy developing two more international telecommunication products: EXNET, for foreign-exchange trades, was introduced in June; EQUILOAN, for the borrowing and lending of securities, will be introduced before the end of the year.

average maturity is about eight years. Congress authorized loans totaling up to $478 million for 1989.[8]

In addition to its regular loan program, the SBA has administered a number of financial assistance programs. Among the loans authorized by the SBA are the following:

1. Loans to small businesses suffering substantial economic injury as a result of shortages of energy and fuel.
2. Loans to physically handicapped small-business proprietors.

3. Loans to small firms experiencing substantial economic loss because of a new federal law or regulation.
4. Loans to businesses and individuals whose property was destroyed in a natural disaster.

Management Counseling

The SBA places special emphasis on its management counseling for small businesses. SBA staff specialists, known as management assistance officers, provide advice and consultation on specific problems. Additional counsel is available from two other groups: The **Service Corps of Retired Executives (SCORE)** is an SBA-sponsored volunteer group of retired executives who give advice and consultations to small businesses. The **Active Corps of Executives (ACE)** is another SBA-sponsored volunteer group, this time of active business executives who give advice and consultations to small businesses.

A closely related program is **Small Business Institutes (SBIs)**—SBA- and university-sponsored programs that allow qualified seniors and graduate students in business schools the opportunity to provide on-site managerial consulting to small businesses. Students are usually assigned to a consulting team and are supervised by faculty advisers and SBA personnel. Over five hundred universities participate in this program.

Another campus-centered program, located at fifty-two universities, is **Small Business Development Centers (SBDCs).** These centers draw from federal, state, and local resources to provide managerial and technical assistance, research studies, and other types of specialized assistance to small businesses. SBDCs in forty-five states use university faculty to support and nurture these activities.

The ***Service Corps of Retired Executives (SCORE)*** is an SBA-sponsored volunteer group of retired business executives who give advice and consultation to small businesses.

The ***Active Corps of Executives (ACE)*** is an SBA-sponsored volunteer group of active business executives who give advice and consultation to small businesses.

Small Business Institutes (SBIs) are SBA- and university-sponsored programs that allow qualified seniors and graduate students in business schools the opportunity to provide on-site managerial consulting to small businesses.

Small Business Development Centers (SBDCs) are university-managed centers that provide faculty and others to give small businesses research, technical, and managerial assistance.

Procurement Assistance

Through the help of the SBA's federal procurement specialists, small businesses are assisted in contracting for government business. The SBA has counseled businesses on how to prepare bids, secure government contracts, and get their company names on bidders' lists.

To facilitate the matchup of small businesses and federal contracts, a computerized system, the **Procurement Automated Source System (PASS),** was developed. This system lists the names and capabilities of small companies so federal procurement officers can efficiently assign work to them. PASS computer terminals are available at more than one hundred government and industrial locations. About a hundred thousand small businesses are listed in this government data bank.[9]

The ***Procurement Automated Source System (PASS)*** is a computerized system for matching small businesses and federal government contracts.

Seminars and Publications

Short workshops in small-business management have frequently been cosponsored by the SBA and local colleges and universities. These workshops have usually been designed for established entrepreneurs and have covered such topics as cash management, business forecasting, and marketing. Prebusiness workshops have also been offered for prospective business owners. In addition, the SBA has distributed technical publications on hundreds of topics dealing with small-business operations. Most of these management assistance aids can be obtained free from the SBA.

Small Business Investment Companies

Small Business Investment Companies (SBICs) are licensed by the SBA to lend money to small business ventures.

Because money is hard to obtain for relatively risky investments, the SBA has licensed, regulated, and provided financial assistance to privately owned and operated **Small Business Investment Companies (SBICs).** These investment groups have provided funds for small businesses through straight loans and by investments that give the SBIC actual or potential ownership of a portion of the equity of the businesses. Approximately five hundred SBICs have provided seed money and management assistance to the small businesses they finance. Since 1953, SBICs have loaned around $6 billion to some 70,000 businesses.

Minority Assistance Programs

The SBA organized the Office of Minority Small Business and Capital Ownership Development to assist minority groups wanting to start their own firms or expand existing ones. Field representatives from this office have worked with local business development organizations and have explained to potential minority entrepreneurs how the SBA's services and programs can contribute to their success.

The SBA also has licensed specialized SBICs to help small businesses owned and managed by socially or economically disadvantaged people. These SBICs used to be known as Minority Enterprise Small Business Investment Companies (MESBICs) and more recently were termed the SBA 301(d) program.[10] Another minority program has allowed qualified companies to sidestep normal bidding procedures to be named primary suppliers in certain government contracts. Under this "set-aside" program (Small Business Act, Section 8a), $3 billion in 4,200 contracts were awarded in 1987. These contracts can only be awarded to minority-owned businesses. Minority-owned companies have been counseled about government contracts not only by the SBA but also by the Commerce Department's **Minority Business Development Agency (MBDA).** This agency has conducted surveys, provided credit assistance, and awarded grants to organizations sponsoring minority enterprises. MBDA assistance has gone to companies with the greatest potential for employing large numbers of minority workers. It is possible that the functions of this agency will be merged with others in the SBA during the 1990s.

The ***Minority Business Development Agency (MBDA)*** is a Commerce Department agency that conducts surveys, provides credit assistance, and awards grants to organizations sponsoring minority enterprises.

OPPORTUNITIES IN FRANCHISING

Many Americans spend thousands of dollars a year purchasing the products or services of franchises. Franchises such as McDonald's, Wendy's, and Pizza Hut seem to have always been around. But, in fact, the growth of franchised food establishments over the past quarter century has been phenomenal. The franchise concept has also been extended to real estate services. Century 21, ERA, and Coldwell-Banker are all franchises. Lawn-care services, legal services, computer stores, day-care centers, and tanning shops are all available through franchise arrangements. In total, according to the U.S. Department of Commerce, there are over two thousand different franchises available.

Table 5.3 Black-owned franchises.

Following is the number of black-owned franchises, according to a survey of more than 2,000 franchise companies.

Company	Black Units	Total Units	Percent
McDonald's	395	7,591	5.2
Burger King	175	4,756	3.7
Popeye's	150	715	21.0
Kentucky Fried Chicken	120	3,400	3.5
Southland	110	3,064	3.6
Subway Sandwiches	89	2,300	3.9
Wendy's	64	2,571	2.5
Church's Fried Chicken	56	386	14.5
Mister Softee	48	612	7.8
Baskin-Robbins	35	2,500	1.4

Franchising accounts for nearly one-third of all retail sales in the United States. About 42 percent of all eating places are franchises. This percentage includes more than 20,000 hamburger, 12,000 pizza, and 10,000 chicken outlets.[11]

These facts indicate that there are growing opportunities for entrepreneurs in the field of franchise ownership. However, operating a franchise does not guarantee success. Careful planning and research and a close examination of the franchise concept is necessary prior to the signing of a contract with a franchise owner.

Many franchise operations are minority-owned businesses. See Table 5.3 for a list of ten franchises some of whose units have black owners.

Definition of *Franchising*

Franchising is the creation of an agreement under which the owner-franchisor of a product, service, or method grants a license to a buyer-franchisee to distribute the owner's product or service or to use the owner's method. The major trade association in this field, the International Franchise Association, defines *franchising* as "a continuing relationship in which the franchisor provides a license privilege to the franchisee to do business plus assistance in organizing, training, merchandising and management in return for consideration from the franchisee."[12]

The **franchisor,** of course, is the owner-supplier of the license, the training, the merchandise, and the managerial assistance. The **franchisee** is the purchaser of the franchise (the business).

Franchising is the creation of an agreement under which the owner-franchisor of a product, service, or method grants a license to a buyer-franchisee to distribute the owner's product or service or to use the owner's method.

A ***franchisor*** is the owner-supplier of a franchise who provides the license, training, merchandise, and managerial assistance necessary for a franchisee to do business.

A ***franchisee*** is the purchaser of a franchise.

Pizza Hut accounts for many of the more than 12,000 franchised pizza outlets in the U.S.

The franchise agreement outlines the responsibilities of each party. Franchisees are permitted to use predesigned logos and trademarks, preselected store layouts, and other standardized products and services. In return, they agree to comply with certain uniform practices outlined in the agreement. Franchisors are usually obligated to provide a host of services to franchisees. Among them are site analysis for store location, special training programs, national advertising, and centralized purchasing.

The ten fastest-growing franchises are shown in Figure 5.8. Domino's Pizza heads the list, having opened 650 new stores in 1987.

Advantages of Franchising

Franchising often gives entrepreneurs the advantages of business ownership but with a somewhat reduced risk.

Name Recognition

One advantage of franchising is name recognition. Holiday Inn, Hertz Rent A Car, Long John Silver's, and McDonald's are household words. Consumer recognition and acceptance of certain logos and slogans give the franchisee extra drawing power. The fact that Ronald McDonald may rival Santa Claus in name recognition among children is testimony to the benefits of franchising. Customers expect courteous service, consistency in food quality, and cleanliness when visiting a McDonald's. A franchise operation that fulfills these expectations affirms the quality behind the name.

Proven Management Methods

Many well-known franchisors require new operators to undergo extensive training before opening their stores. The most famous training center is McDonald's Ham-

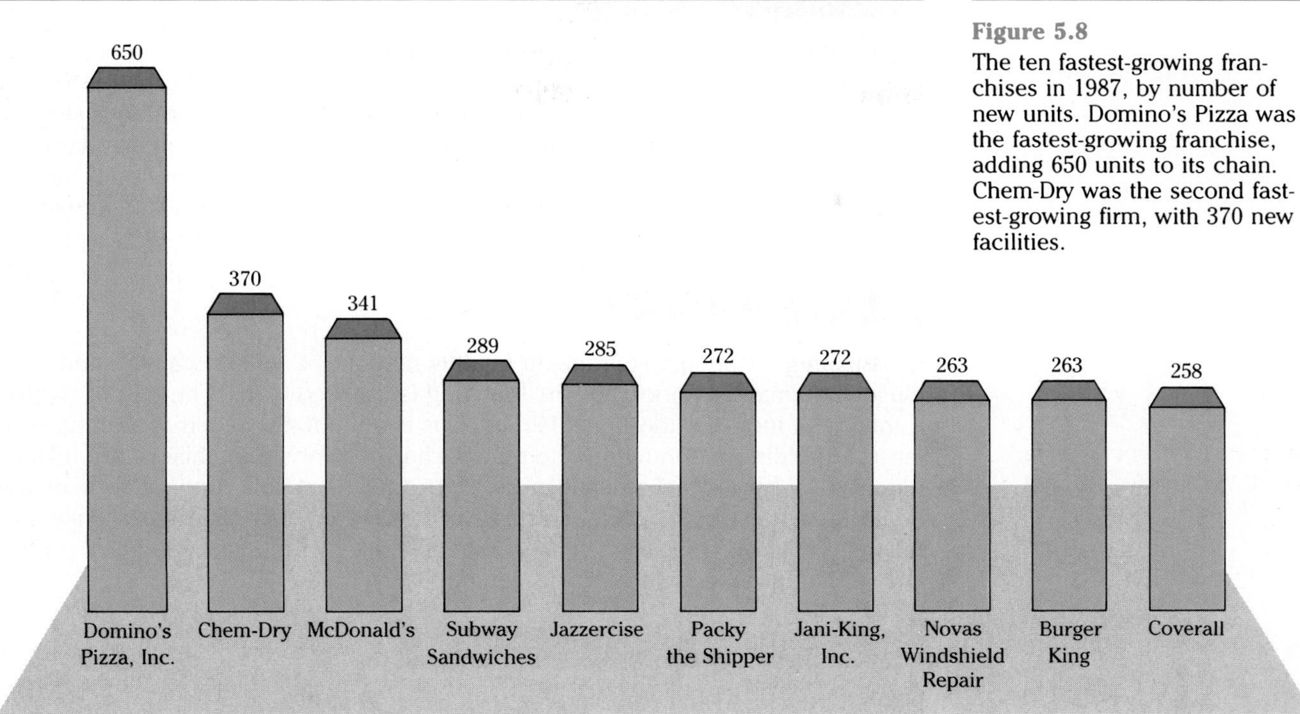

Figure 5.8
The ten fastest-growing franchises in 1987, by number of new units. Domino's Pizza was the fastest-growing franchise, adding 650 units to its chain. Chem-Dry was the second fastest-growing firm, with 370 new facilities.

burger University in Oak Brook, Illinois. New owners of McDonald's franchises attend an intensive two-week course that covers every aspect of operating a franchise, including store management, sales strategy, finance, advertising, and purchasing agreements.

Many franchisors provide experienced help during the opening of a new store. Furthermore, management training of owners and employees continues after the franchise begins operation.

National Promotion

A constant media blitz reminds the public of the quality products and services available at selected franchises. Ronald McDonald is featured on national billboards, and in numerous magazine ads, and he frequently appears in special concerts sponsored by the corporation. Century 21 Real Estate assures its customers on television that moving a family to a new location can be an enjoyable experience.

The cost of these national advertising campaigns is shared by the franchisor and the franchisees. Usually, franchisees pay the franchisor a stated percentage of monthly sales or a flat monthly fee. The advertising is prepared by a large professional agency and is uniformly aired throughout the market area. To complement the national promotion, franchisees are often required to run ads in their own market area. Staff specialists from the franchise headquarters provide help in planning and designing local ads.

Standardized Products

McDonald's constantly reminds consumers that each hamburger is 100 percent pure ground beef. Wendy's promises that its sandwiches are freshly cooked—never placed in a warming bin. Hertz Rent A Car promises fast, courteous service, even at the busiest airports. These examples point out the value of standardized products and services. Customers expect the same quality and courteous service regardless of the location of the dealer. Compliance with uniform standards benefits all the members of the franchise network.

Financial Assistance

Establishing a franchise requires a healthy amount of venture capital, and franchisors often assist franchisees in arranging for needed loans. The cost of starting a franchise includes the franchise fee plus the amount needed to purchase or lease a building and buy the equipment and inventory. Franchisees are usually required to have cash assets equal to 20 percent of this amount to start the business. Once the franchise is established, the franchisor provides a system of financial control. This service allows the franchisee to maintain inventory control and prepare the necessary accounting and tax records.

Disadvantages of Franchising

Like all business ventures, franchising has inherent limitations.

Franchise Fees and Profit Sharing

It is common for franchisors to charge a one-time fee for the use of their name by the franchisee. According to Figure 5.9, Dairy Queen/Brazier's franchising fee is $30,000. In addition, the franchisee may be required to share a percentage of profits based on monthly or quarterly sales. Dairy Queen/Brazier collects a 4 percent royalty fee based on gross sales. This charge is in addition to the advertising fee of 3 to 5 percent of gross sales. Entrepreneurs must weigh the value of these outlays before signing franchise agreements.

Strict Compliance with Standardized Operations

Entrepreneurial freedom is somewhat limited under a franchise arrangement. Each outlet must comply with certain quality control standards. Corporate staff members visit the outlets frequently to ensure uniformity of operations. Failure to meet quality and cleanliness standards, for example, can result in the termination of the franchise.

Restricted Product Mix

Experimenting with the types of products or services offered by a franchise is usually forbidden. Pizza Hut, for example, has claimed that its focus on a limited menu allows for specialization, which contributes to franchise profits. Other fast-food franchises have expanded their product mixes. For example, salad bars have been added at most fast-food operations. However, changes are decided on by headquarters personnel. These types of management controls must be accepted by the franchisee.

Figure 5.9
Franchise highlights. Key variables should be evaluated when franchise investment opportunities are compared.

Dairy Queen/Brazier
Location: Minneapolis, Minnesota
Number of franchises: 4,928
Fee: $30,000
Additional investment: $82,000–$278,000
Financing by franchisor: Yes, equipment only
Training by franchisor: Yes
Royalty on profits: 4% of gross sales
Advertising fee: 3–5% of gross sales

Century 21
Location: Irvine, California
Number of franchises: 6,726
Fee: $8,000–$17,000
Additional investment (approx.): $3,000–$20,000
Financing by franchisor: No
Training by franchisor: Yes
Royalty on profits: 6%
Advertising fee: 2% of gross sales

7-Eleven
Location: Dallas, Texas
Number of franchises: 7,012
Fee: $42,700
Additional investment (approx.): $30,400–$109,000
Financing by franchisor: Yes
Training by franchisor: Yes
Royalty on profits: Takes 52–63% of gross profit
Advertising fee: No national fee

McDonald's Corporation
Location: Oak Brook, Illinois
Number of franchises: 7,263
Fee: $22,500
Additional investment: $340,000–$415,000
Financing by franchisor: Yes
Training by franchisor: Yes, 2 weeks at Hamburger University
Royalty on profits: 12% of gross sales
Advertising fee: No national fee

Postal Instant Press
Location: Los Angeles, California
Number of franchises: 1,149
Fee: $40,000
Additional investment: $25,000–$146,000
Financing by franchisor: Yes
Training by franchisor: Yes
Royalty on profits: 6–8%
Advertising fee: 1% of gross sales

Inventory Purchasing Requirements

Under the terms of some contracts, the franchisee is required to purchase merchandise from the franchisor or from suppliers licensed by the franchisor. This type of policy limits the options available to the franchisee and results in higher inventory costs if independent suppliers can offer similar merchandise at lower prices.

CHOOSING THE RIGHT FRANCHISE

Franchise success stories abound. As Figure 5.10 suggests, however, an entrepreneur must carefully weigh the pros and cons of franchising before signing any formal agreement. Anyone who decides to seriously pursue a franchise opportunity should read the following suggestions:

1. Investigate the franchise thoroughly. A quick profile of the company can be obtained in the *Franchise Opportunities Handbook* published by the Department of Commerce. Be sure to write the franchisor and request a detailed explanation of the history and business experience of the firm.
2. Comparison shop. Write other franchisors in the same industry and compare their offerings.
3. Visit with company representatives. Request a full disclosure statement highlighting all the pertinent information about the franchisor.
4. Ask specific questions about the present number of franchises and their locations, the projected number and locations of franchises, the success of the franchise units, and the number of stores repurchased from franchisees.
5. Visit with current holders of franchises, preferably those who have been in business two years or more.
6. Have a lawyer examine all documents before signing them.

Certainly, this list is not all-inclusive. Franchising, like all business arrangements, involves a degree of risk. However, a step-by-step evaluation procedure may help in the choice of the best franchise.

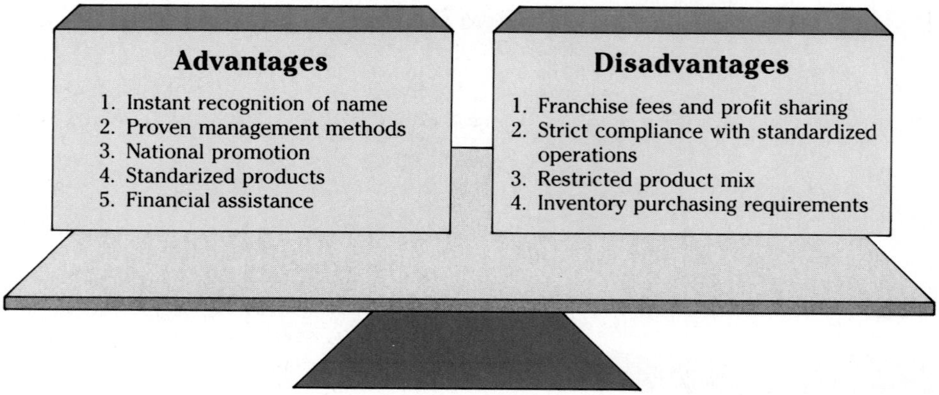

Figure 5.10
Advantages and disadvantages of franchising. Successful franchising is not accomplished by chance. Before making a franchise decision, a person should thoroughly investigate the franchise and weigh the advantages and disadvantages.

Advantages
1. Instant recognition of name
2. Proven management methods
3. National promotion
4. Standarized products
5. Financial assistance
Disadvantages
1. Franchise fees and profit sharing
2. Strict compliance with standardized operations
3. Restricted product mix
4. Inventory purchasing requirements

MIXING SMALL BUSINESS AND FRANCHISING

We have seen that franchising can give the entrepreneur many of the advantages of larger companies while allowing a reasonable degree of independence. A number of franchises started as independent concerns. Colonel Sanders's Kentucky Fried Chicken grew from a family-operated restaurant in Corbin, Kentucky, to one of the top five fast-food franchises in the world. The same growth pattern occurred with McDonald's. Ray Kroc, the founder, purchased a hamburger joint from the McDonald family in San Bernardino, California, and parlayed it into a franchising empire. Although free-enterprise purists claim that a franchise holder is not a true entrepreneur, the difference is often a matter of degree. Both independent small businesses and franchises offer ownership opportunities to thousands of businesspeople.

As the American family becomes more dual-career oriented, free time for both spouses will be more limited. Eating out is already part of American life—over one-third of our food dollars are spent in restaurants. Fast-food restaurants, leisure businesses, tax-preparation firms, lawn-care services, day-care centers, and other service-oriented businesses seem to have a bright future indeed.

BUSINESS PRACTICE EXAMPLE Continues

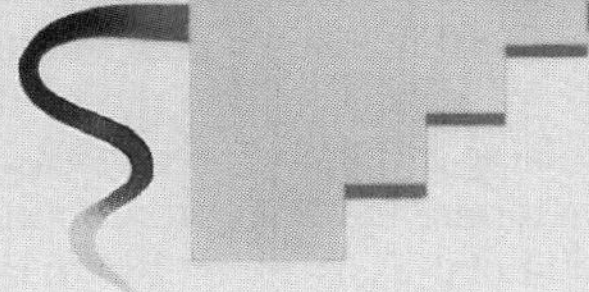

Until 1983, Famous Amos cookies were sold exclusively through its own retail outlets and in department stores and supermarkets. In 1983, the company launched its franchise operations, and by 1985 the company had 42 franchised stores in eleven states. Famous Amos franchisees reported net earnings of 25 to 30 percent of gross sales.

By 1989, however, the Famous Amos franchises stood at just 20 domestically and 15 internationally. The company's strategy is to grow in the wholesale market, which it is doing by leaps and bounds. Its distribution network continues to grow as it seeks ever more shelves on which to place its product. While Wally Amos no longer has a controlling interest in the company, he is still the company's greatest promotional tool, touring the country with his message of happiness and hope for generations of future entrepreneurs.

Issues for Discussion

1. What entrepreneurial characteristics does Wally Amos possess?
2. Discuss the methods of financing used by Wally Amos.
3. What advantages did financing offer Famous Amos Chocolate Chip Cookies?

SUMMARY

People who start their own businesses are entrepreneurs, and the businesses they start tend to be small. According to the Small Business Administration (SBA), small businesses are independently owned and operated and are not dominant in their field of operation. The SBA is a government agency that provides financial and managerial help to small businesses.

To create a small business, the entrepreneur should develop a business plan (a written proposal that describes the business and its objectives) and secure venture capital (start-up money), often through venture capitalists (investment specialists looking for new businesses that offer high returns).

Successful entrepreneurs have six traits: high achievement, moderate risk taking, goal orientation, creativity, ability to communicate, and technical competence. Opportunities for female and minority entrepreneurs have recently increased. Many minority entrepreneurs enter business through franchises. Entrepreneurship is increasing throughout the world.

Among the advantages to small-business ownership are independence in decision making, control of profits, personal contact with employees and customers, self-pride, and work satisfaction. Among the disadvantages are long work hours, lack of specialization, sole responsibility for decisions, competition with big business, and risk of failure. Sometimes it is better to buy a successful business. Among the advantages are reduced risk, easier financial and marketing planning, faster profit accrual, and less capitalization.

The SBA has offered small businesses financial programs, including guarantee loans (loans made by private lenders that are guaranteed up to 90 percent by the SBA). It also has offered management counseling, including additional counsel from related groups and programs—the Service Corps of Retired Executives, the Active Corps of Executives, Small Business Institutes, and Small Business Development Centers.

It has provided procurement assistance through the Procurement Automated Source System, and it has offered seminars and publications on small-business management. It also has provided financial assistance to privately owned and operated Small Business Investment Companies—groups that lend money to small businesses or invest in them.

The SBA also organized the Office of Minority Small Business and Capital Ownership Development and has licensed certain Small Business Investment Companies to help businesses owned and managed by socially or economically disadvantaged people. Finally, the Commerce Department has created the Minority Business Development Agency to conduct surveys, provide credit assistance, and award grants to organizations sponsoring minority enterprises.

Franchising is the creation of an agreement under which the owner-franchisor of a product, service, or method licenses a buyer-franchisee to distribute the product or service or use the method. The advantages of franchising are name recognition, proven management methods, national promotion, standardized products, and financial assistance. The disadvantages are franchise fees and profit sharing, compliance with standardized operations, restricted product mix, and inventory purchasing requirements.

To choose the right franchise, one should investigate franchises thoroughly, comparison shop, visit with company representatives, ask questions about current and projected franchises, visit with current franchisees, and have a lawyer examine all documents.

KEY TERMS

CHECK YOUR LEARNING

Reread the following learning objectives. Each objective is followed by a few questions. Answering these questions accurately will help you retain the most important concepts discussed in this chapter. After answering each question, check your answer with the key at the end of this chapter. (*Hint:* If you have doubt regarding the correct response, consult the page whose number follows the answer.)

Circle:

A. List the common criteria used to define *small business.*

a b c d

1. Small businesses usually: (a) are independently owned; (b) are franchised operations; (c) market goods on a local basis; (d) both a and c.

T F

2. One common criterion used to determine the size of a business is the number of employees.

B. Discuss key facts that help explain the contribution of small business to the economy.

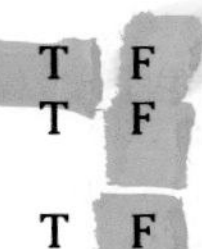

T F

1. Using the SBA definition, 99 percent of nonfarm businesses are defined as small firms.

T F

2. Small businesses generate approximately 60 percent of the GNP.

T F

3. Unfortunately, the small-business sector contributes only a small number of new jobs for the economy.

C. List the basic steps involved in starting a small business.

a b c d

1. Most venture capital for new businesses is provided by: (a) government; (b) banks; (c) personal savings; (d) friends.

T F

2. An analysis of the market potential of a product or service takes place after the business is formed.

D. Identify the main behavioral traits possessed by successful entrepreneurs.

a b c d

1. A successful entrepreneur is: (a) creative; (b) an effective planner; (c) a high achiever; (d) all of the above.

a b c d

2. Which one of the following attributes would *least* describe a successful small-business person: (a) high risk taker; (b) innovative; (c) independent; (d) goal oriented.

E. List and explain the pros and cons of small-business ownership.

a b c d

1. Choose one that may be a key disadvantage of small business ownership: (a) control of profits; (b) independence in decision making; (c) being your own boss; (d) personal sense of pride.

a b c d

2. Owning their own business usually allows entrepreneurs to: (a) determine their own hours; (b) work less than forty hours a week; (c) rely on employee expertise; (d) maintain a closer personal relationship with employees and customers.

T F

3. The biggest cause of small-business failure is poor management.

F. Describe the SBA's role in assisting small businesses.

a b c d

1. The SBA: (a) guarantees small-business loans; (b) provides management assistance to small firms; (c) helps small companies procure government contracts; (d) all of the above.

T F

2. SCORE gives college students the opportunity to counsel small-business owners.

T F

3. Minorities receive minimal assistance from the SBA.

G. Analyze the advantages and disadvantages of franchise ownership.

a b c d

1. Which is *not* an advantage of franchise ownership: (a) name recognition; (b) royalty fees; (c) proven management methods; (d) standardized product lines.

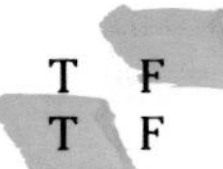

2. Franchisees have the same independence in decision making as any other small-business owner.
3. McDonald's is an example of a fast-food franchise.

H. Identify the procedures to follow in analyzing a franchise opportunity.

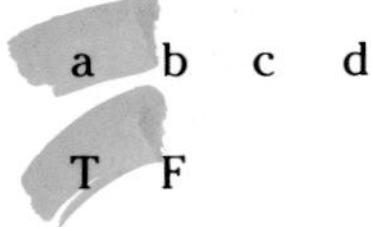

1. Before signing a franchise agreement, the franchisee should: (a) investigate the franchise; (b) visit with franchisees who just started their operations; (c) minimize legal costs; (d) secure a partner.
2. It is a good practice to have your lawyer examine the franchise agreement before you sign it.

T F

QUESTIONS FOR REVIEW AND DISCUSSION

1. Define the key terms listed at the end of the chapter.
2. What two agencies have suggested criteria for defining *small business?* What are some common characteristics of small firms?
3. Cite some specific economic contributions made by small companies.
4. Discuss the advantages and disadvantages of small-business ownership with a local entrepreneur. Does the entrepreneur agree with those discussed in the text? What new ones were mentioned by the entrepreneur?
5. "Small business owners enjoy being their own boss." Agree or disagree with this statement and explain your position.
6. What services does the SBA offer to help firms succeed?
7. An alternative to starting a business from scratch is buying a franchise. What are the advantages of owning a franchise? What are the disadvantages?
8. Suggest some steps to follow in analyzing a franchise opportunity.
9. "Franchising is really big business." Do you agree or disagree? Explain.
10. Examine the real estate signs in your hometown or college town. How many realty firms are affiliated with large franchise networks? Visit with a sales representative of one of the franchisors and discuss its franchise agreement.
11. Arrange for an interview with a manager or owner of a fast-food franchise. Find out the terms of the franchise agreement and ask the person to comment about the arrangement. Report your findings to the class.
12. Visit your library and look up key facts about one franchise in each of the following areas: auto transmission repair, fast print-shops, pizza parlors, convenience stores, and motel chains. The *Franchise Opportunities Handbook* should contain much of the needed information. *Venture* magazine is another good source.

CONCLUDING CASE

Federal Government Encourages Small-Business "Exportese"

According to James Abnor, former administrator of the SBA, small businesses must recognize they exist in a global economy. During the next decade, they will experience a complete redefinition of their markets. They will be less tied to the fairly stable and geographically restricted markets of the past, and they will find themselves competing more in highly volatile international markets. Expanding sales into foreign marketplaces actually strengthens the domestic economy. For example, $1 billion worth of goods and services sold in export markets generates 25,000 new jobs in the United States.

In an effort to help small businesses learn the nuts and bolts of exporting, the SBA joined forces with private enterprise and more than a dozen cabinet-level departments and federal agencies. With the financial support of American Telephone & Telegraph Company, it prepared the *Exporter's Guide.* In 1988, AT&T and the SBA sponsored a series of seminars across the United States to help small businesses learn about exporting. Many of the seminars were taught by SCORE volunteers with international trade experience.

Another innovative program is Matchmaker delegations. In cooperation with the Commerce Department, the SBA has sponsored trade missions that match U.S. exporters with overseas buyers of specific products. Lastly, the SBA has cooperated with the Office of International Trade in sponsoring regional international trade forums as well as hundreds of smaller workshops.

Two books published by the Commerce Department are highly recommended for the novice exporter. The first, *A Basic Guide to Exporting,* has addresses and phone numbers for the 194 Commerce offices and for over 500 other public and private groups dealing in international trade. The guide explains the steps involved in exporting, from making the first export sales contact to collecting the cash for the goods or services; and it shows the relationships among all the intermediaries involved and explains their functions. The second book is *Partners in Export Trade,* a state-by-state directory that provides information on 4,500 export brokers, including banks that finance exporters; companies, manufacturers, and service organizations that are exporters; and management companies, research firms, and others that assist exporters.

As one successful small-business exporter warned: "You can be selling in the United States and be fat and happy—then have some foreign competition come in. In order to remain viable, it is very important to learn other markets."

Issues for Discussion

1. What are some major obstacles small businesses must overcome in exporting to foreign markets?
2. How could video tapes, satellite communications, and other high-tech options be used to promote small-business products in an overseas market?
3. Suggest other creative programs that the federal government could develop to encourage small-business exporting.

NOTES

1. U.S. Small Business Administration, "Fact Sheet Regular Loan Program," September 1988.
2. U.S. Small Business Administration, "Fact Sheet 40," January 1988, p. 1.
3. David Birch, *Job Creation in America,* Free Press, 1987.
4. *The State of Small Business: A Report of the President,* 1987, pp. 24–27.
5. Sabin Russell, "Now It's the World's Turn," *Venture,* September 1984, pp. 48–61.
6. "Out of Business," *Wall Street Journal,* April 2, 1987, p. 29.
7. Dun & Bradstreet, *Business Failure Record,* 1982–1983.
8. U.S. Small Business Administration, "Fact Sheet Regular Loan Program," September 1988.
9. U.S. Small Business Administration, "Your Business and the SBA," February 1987.
10. Teri Agins, "Owning Franchises Has Pluses, but Wealth Isn't Guaranteed," *Wall Street Journal,* October 22, 1984, p. 29.
11. U.S. Department of Commerce, *Franchise Opportunities Handbook* (Washington, D.C.: Government Printing Office, 1984), p. 27.

CHECK YOUR LEARNING ANSWER KEY

A. 1. d, *p. 130*
   2. T, *p. 130*
B. 1. T, *p. 130*
   2. F, *p. 130*
   3. F, *p. 131*
C. 1. c, *p. 132*
   2. F, *p. 131*
D. 1. d, *p. 133*
   2. a, *p. 133*
E. 1. b, *p. 143*
   2. d, *p. 141*
   3. T, *p. 143*
F. 1. d, *p. 145–147*
   2. F, *p. 147*
   3. F, *p. 148*
G. 1. b, *p. 152*
   2. F, *p. 152*
   3. T, *p. 150*
H. 1. a, *p. 154*
   2. T, *p. 154*

PART

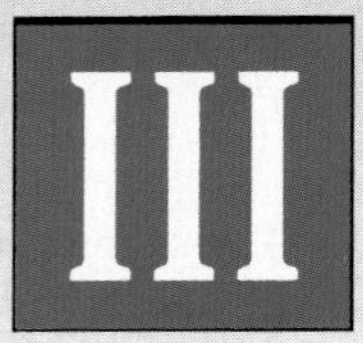

MANAGING ORGANIZATIONS

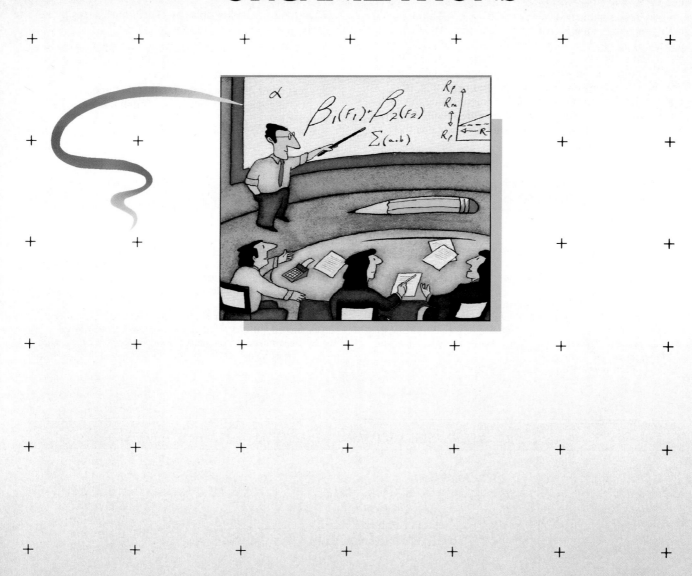

CHAPTER

6

Management Fundamentals

CHAPTER

7

Motivation and Leadership in Organizations

CHAPTER

8

Organizing a Business

CHAPTER

9

Human Resource Management

CHAPTER

10

Labor-Management Relations

CHAPTER

11

Production and Operations Management

CHAPTER

6

MANAGEMENT FUNDAMENTALS

LEARNING OBJECTIVES

After reading this chapter you should be able to:

1. Define *management.*
2. Explain the purpose of management.
3. List the four basic management functions and describe the relationships among them.
4. Discuss the implications of decision making, effectiveness, and efficiency for managers.
5. Discuss the role of objectives and the hierarchy of objectives in the management process.
6. Outline the skills and functions appropriate for various levels of management.
7. Explain the term *universality of management.*

OUTLINE

Business Practice Example: Management Effectiveness at Merck

The Importance of Management

The Definition of *Management*

Management and Objectives

The Process of Management

- Planning
  - Strategic Planning
  - Tactical Planning
  - Coordinating Strategic and Tactical Planning
  - Three Planning Tools
- Organizing
- Directing
- Controlling
  - Measuring Performance
  - Comparing Performance to Standards
  - Identifying Deviations and Their Causes
  - Taking Corrective Action
- Reaching Objectives through Management Functions

Management and Decisions

- What Is a Decision?
- Types of Decisions
- The Decision-Making Process

Managers and Resources

- Managerial Effectiveness and Efficiency

Types of Organizational Objectives

- A Hierarchy of Objectives

Levels of Management

- Management Levels and Skills
- Management Levels and Functions

The Universality of Management

Summary

Key Terms

Check Your Learning

Questions for Review and Discussion

Concluding Case: Managers of Large and Small Businesses—Some Differences

Notes

Check Your Learning Answer Key

Highlight in Business Practice: Buck Rodgers on Creating Customer Commitment

Highlight in Business Practice: Tips for Managerial Success

BUSINESS PRACTICE EXAMPLE

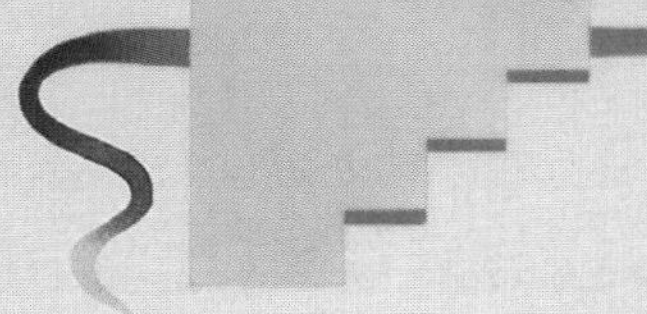

Management Effectiveness at Merck

Top awards for managerial excellence have been coming year after year to the management team at Merck & Co., the world's largest drug company. Signs of its success are its high sales, high earnings per share, and continued product innovation. A sales increase of 18.5% for 1988 was close to Merck's record increase of 22.6% for the previous year, and share values rose 37.7% in 1987 followed by 36% in 1988. By 1989 Merck had 14 drugs that were bringing in $100 million a year in revenues, five of these introduced since 1985.

Roy Vagelos, who has been the CEO of Merck since 1985, is widely recognized as responsible for the drug company's dramatic success. Top awards from *Fortune* and *Business Month* for managerial innovativeness can be traced to Vagelos' strategy: innovative expansions in Merck's worldwide market through aggressive efforts both in product development and in opening up new markets.

An admirer inside Merck said of top management: "They have vision. . . . Vagelos came all the way up . . . from the research side, built that part of the company, and that's what's driving it right now. The reason he's where he is, is because the products have succeeded." Vagelos himself speaks of innovation in product development as "a strategy game. You pick out the areas where you can do some good, where real innovation is possible, and put money into them." Merck currently invests more money in research than any other drug company, $650 million in 1988. "It's a high-risk business," says Vagelos. "We recognize that most of the research we do and most of the drugs we come up with will fail. But we challenge our people to get into new fields, and we tell them that the objective is to make a drug, not just to discover facts and publish in trade journals."

Merck has also devoted energy to improving its access to worldwide markets. Its drug Vasotec, a vascular drug used to treat high blood pressure, marked up a record $1 billion in sales in 1988. A market leader in the U.S., Canada, and Australia, the company gets half its revenues from abroad. During the late '80s Merck targeted Europe and Japan for its newest push. One Merck employee praised top management's efforts to open new markets: "They have been innovative all across the board, in terms of how they want to spend their money and where. The purchase [of a new facility] in Japan was very long vision, but has turned out to be very successful for them, especially now that products are coming through." Still, Vagelos is not satisfied with Merck's record-breaking progress in reaching world markets. "This isn't enough," he said of Merck's top awards for excellence in performance from *Fortune* and other major business magazines. "Sure, we're now number one in the world," he tells his managers, "but our market share is a puny 4.4%. We need at least twice that much before we can feel comfortable."

WHAT'S AHEAD

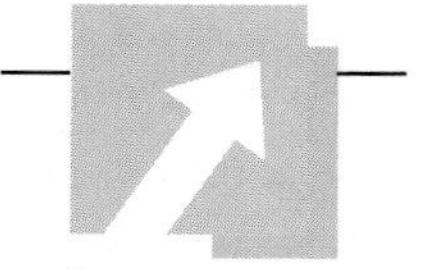

The Business Practice Example discusses management at Merck & Co. From Merck's example we can see that management is an important element in our society. This chapter will explain what management is and will describe its objectives. It will then discuss the management process, which includes planning, organizing, directing, and controlling. An essential part of management at a company like Merck is decision making, and the chapter will cover that process as well. It will continue with a discussion of other critical management issues at Merck like managerial resources, organizational objectives, the levels of management, and of the universality of management.

THE IMPORTANCE OF MANAGEMENT

Managers influence all phases of modern organizations. A quick look at the jobs section in the classified advertisements of any major newspaper confirms this through its description of many different types of management activities. Plant managers, for example, run manufacturing operations that produce clothes, food, and automobiles. Sales managers maintain sales forces that market goods. Personnel managers provide organizations with competent and productive workers.

Good managers are important both to society and to the individuals within it. To exist and to improve, society needs a steady stream of managers to guide its organizations. Management is important to individuals because many of them earn their living by being managers.

Some managers earn a good living indeed. Table 6.1 lists the annual compensation for the ten best-paid chief executives in the United States. According to a

Table 6.1 The ten highest-paid chief executives in the United States.

	Company	1987 Salary and Bonus	Long-Term Compensation	Total Pay
		Thousands of Dollars		
1. Jim P. Manzi, Chmn.	Lotus	$ 941	$25,356	$26,297
2. Lee A. Iacocca, Chmn.	Chrysler	1,740	16,156	17,896
3. Paul Fireman, Chmn.	Reebok Intl.	15,424	—	15,424
4. Phillip B. Rooney, Pres.	Waste Mgt.	950	13,326	14,276
5. Richard M. Furlaud, Chmn.	Squibb	1,405	12,480	13,885
6. Donald F. Flynn, Sr. V-P	Waste Mgt.	640	12,577	13,217
7. John F. Welch Jr., Chmn.	General Electric	2,057	10,574	12,631
8. Harold A. Poling, Vice-Chmn.	Ford Motor	2,809	7,746	10,555
9. Jack G. Clarke, V-P	Exxon	787	8,887	9,674
10. Eugene R. White, Vice-Chmn.	Amdahl	683	8,163	8,846

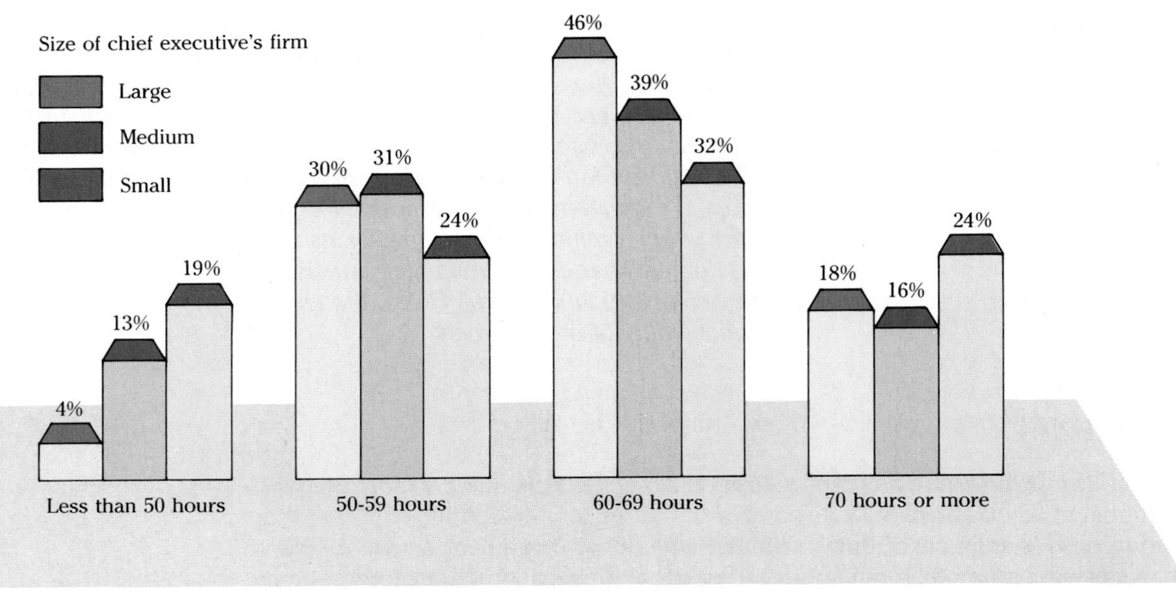

Figure 6.1 Executive work loads. Few executives work a typical forty-hour workweek.

survey reported in *Business Week* in 1988, the top amount is over $26 million. Although the amounts in the table are surprising, they are probably justified. These executives must make decisions that involve many millions of dollars and affect vast numbers of people. Their actions can have a significant impact on the economy. Being a manager is very rarely a "nine-to-five" proposition. As Figure 6.1 indicates, in this country's largest firms, 46 percent of the executives work from sixty to sixty-nine hours a week.

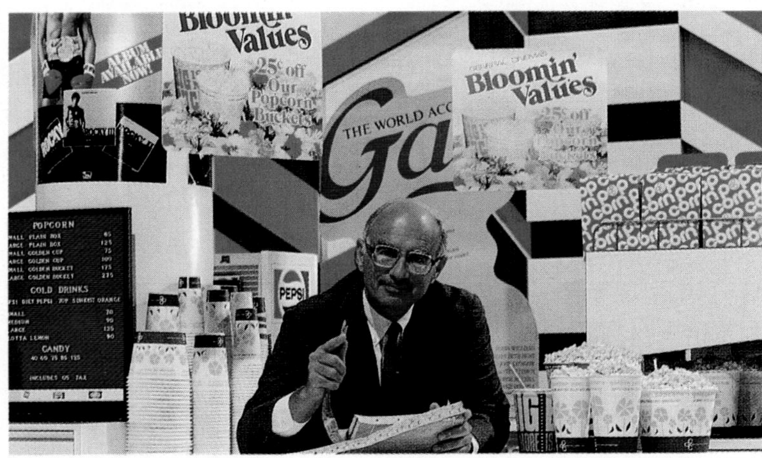

Richard A. Smith is the CEO of the General Cinema Corp. Like other CEO's worldwide, Smith earns a high salary for his efforts.

THE DEFINITION OF *MANAGEMENT*

Management is the process of working with and through people and other organizational resources to reach organizational objectives.[1] Three separate elements in this definition can be isolated as characteristics of management:

Management is the process of working with and through people and other organizational resources to reach organizational objectives.

1. Management concentrates on reaching organizational objectives.
2. Management involves coordinating a series of continuing and related activities.
3. Management works with and through people and other organizational resources.

MANAGEMENT AND OBJECTIVES

The fundamental purpose of management is to guide organizations toward accomplishing their objectives. All organizations exist to accomplish certain objectives. **Organizational objectives** are the targets an organization is attempting to hit. One objective of a school, for example, is to promote learning. One objective of a police department is to capture law breakers. One objective of a prison is to rehabilitate law breakers.

Organizational objectives are the targets an organization is attempting to hit.

Two primary objectives of any business, as chapter 1 emphasized, are to provide a product or service that will satisfy the needs and wants of its customers and to make a profit. A business that fails to satisfy consumer needs and wants—and profitably—will soon be out of business. Managers exist to combine and use organizational resources in ways that help organizations achieve these primary objectives.

If properly developed, organizational objectives reflect the purpose of the organization. The primary purpose of a hospital, for example, may be to provide high-quality medical assistance to the community. Its organizational objectives would focus on ways to provide this assistance. If an organization is accomplishing its objectives, it is simultaneously accomplishing its mission, or purpose, thereby justifying its reason for existence. Of course, organizations have differing purposes and thus differing types of organizational objectives.*

Managers move organizations toward achieving their objectives by designing activities and assigning them to organization members, who then perform them. If these activities are designed well, the production of each worker will help the organization achieve its objectives. Managers strive to encourage worker activity that helps the organization reach its objectives and to discourage activity that hinders it.

THE PROCESS OF MANAGEMENT

Management involves coordinating a series of continuing and related activities. The coordination process includes four basic activities—planning, organizing, directing, and controlling.

*It is common for management theorists as well as practicing managers to use the terms *objectives* and *goals* interchangeably. Although this text usually uses the term *objective* to refer to an organizational target, *goal* is also sometimes used.

Planning

Planning is determining the tasks to be performed in achieving organizational objectives, setting guidelines on how to perform them, and indicating when they should be performed.

Determining the tasks to be performed in achieving organizational objectives, setting guidelines on how to perform them, and indicating when they should be performed are all encompassed in the term **planning.** Planning begins with an analysis of organizational objectives. Through plans, managers outline exactly what the organization must do to be successful. Planning is frequently discussed at two levels—strategic and tactical.

Strategic Planning

Strategic planning is long-range planning that focuses on the organization as a whole.

Long-range planning that focuses on the organization as a whole is **strategic planning.** Top-level managers analyze the organization as a complete unit and ask themselves what must be done to reach organizational objectives. They consider factors such as the competitive environment and the company's resources. *Long range* is usually defined as a future period of about three to five years or longer. During strategic planning, managers are trying to decide in the present what must be done to ensure organizational success in the future.

A ***strategy*** is a set of actions designed to help a company outperform the competition and reach its long-range objectives.

Strategic planning results in formulating strategies and, ultimately, in reaching goals. A **strategy** is a set of actions designed to help a company outperform the competition and reach its long-range objectives. All organizations need the guid-

Table 6.2 Examples of organizational objectives and related strategies for three organizations in different business areas.

Company	Type of Business	Sample Organization Objectives	Strategy to Accomplish Objectives
(a) Ford	Automobile manufacturing	1. Regain market share lost to General Motors. 2. Regain quality reputation damaged because of Pinto gas tank explosions.	1. Resize and down-size present models. 2. Continue to produce subcompact, intermediate, standard, and luxury cars. 3. Emphasize use of programmed combustion engines instead of diesel engines.
(b) Burger King	Fast food	Increase productivity.	1. Increase people efficiency. 2. Increase machine efficiency.
(c) Illinois Central Gulf Railroad	Transportation	1. Continue company growth. 2. Continue company profits.	1. Modernize. 2. Develop valuable real estate holdings. 3. Complete an appropriate railroad merger.

ance of strategies. For a strategy to be worthwhile, however, it must be consistent with organizational objectives. Table 6.2 illustrates this desired consistency by presenting sample organizational objectives and strategies for three well-known businesses.

Examples of strategic plans include mergers and acquisitions, the addition or divestiture of product lines, and the expansion of markets into new geographic areas. On the international front, a growing sense of worldwide competition is causing managers to consider business threats and opportunities throughout the world. As a result, managers are becoming increasingly involved in internationally oriented strategic plans. One strategy they are using is the **license agreement,** a right granted by one company to another to use its brand name or technology. Ohio Mattress Company, for example, has purchased the right from Sealy to make and sell Sealy mattresses in Puerto Rico.

A ***license agreement*** is a right granted by one company to another to use its brand name or technology.

Another example of an internationally oriented strategy commonly used by modern managers focuses on joint ventures. (As chapter 4 showed, a joint venture is a partnership formed by two or more companies for the purpose of undertaking some mutually desirable, limited business venture.) Renault, for example, created a joint venture to buy diesel engines from Fiat, gasoline engines from Volvo, and gearboxes from Volkswagen.

Tactical Planning

Short-range planning that focuses on current operations of various parts of the organization is **tactical planning.** *Short range* is defined as a period of time extending only about a year into the future. Over all, tactical plans can be made in such organizational areas as production, marketing, and personnel. They emphasize what the organization must do to be successful at some point a year or less into the future.

Tactical planning is short-range planning that focuses on current operations of various parts of the organization.

Tactical or short range planning focuses decisions relating to the current operations of an organization.

BUSINESS PRACTICE EXAMPLE Continues

Observers of the drug industry can see a clear strategy in action at Merck & Co., as summed up by one analyst: "Their strategy is flawless. It's further penetration of international markets where they're weak, and generation of new pharmaceutical products to expand their future. They basically are just continuing the strongest development program possible." The need for a long-range strategic plan centered around development was probably a major reason why Roy Vagelos, a successful research & development product developer, was promoted to become Merck's CEO in 1985. As Vagelos himself characterized his strategic plan for product development, "The trick is not doing it one year or two years. The trick is to take advantage of the fact that we have numerous new products doing well, to lay the foundation for long-term growth of the corporation."

However, implementing such a strategic plan called for some critical work on short-range tactical plans in two stages. According to one analyst, "When Vagelos took over, the first thing he did was make a major commitment to accelerate the earnings growth. They had to get the stock price up; it had been a poor stock for a dozen years before that. Then they brought all these new products into the market and very successfully have been marketing them." A key tactic in getting the new products to market was getting critical clearances through government safety regulations at the Food and Drug Administration. Under Vagelos's management, tactical plans for expediting this lengthy process were put into practice. Soon Merck's products were gaining FDA approval and getting to market more than 10 months earlier than the average for other drug companies. The new drug Mevacor won FDA approval in a record 9½ months.

Coordinating Strategic and Tactical Planning

Strategic planning focuses on the longest period of time worth considering, whereas tactical planning focuses on the shortest period of time worth considering. Both types of planning are necessary, and they complement each other. Tactical planning outlines what should be done in the short term to reach the goals at which strategic planning aims.

Table 6.2 illustrates how strategic and tactical planning should complement each other. Assume that Burger King, a fast-food company, has the objective of increasing productivity and that its strategic planning has resulted in the plan to increase the efficiency of its employees by a certain amount in about three to five years. Related tactical plans should focus on what should be done in the short term to increase this efficiency. Issues such as how to hire more qualified employees, how to improve training programs, and how to acquire better equipment would all be appropriate short-range planning issues addressed during Burger King's tactical planning.

Three Planning Tools

Managers commonly use three planning tools: rules, policies, and budgets. A **rule** is a planning tool that designates a specific required action. In essence, it indicates what an organization member should or should not do. It precisely outlines the desired action, allowing no room for interpretation. The following directives are examples of rules: All employees must begin work promptly at 9 o'clock. No employee shall eat at his or her desk. Each employee will be eligible for a paid vacation only after completing a year of employment.

A ***rule*** is a planning tool that designates a specific required action.

Unlike a rule, which is specific, a **policy** is general in nature. It is a planning tool that furnishes broad guidelines for channeling management thinking in certain directions. It is essentially a general expression of management intent concerning what action should be taken to achieve organizational objectives. For example, an organizational policy relating to personnel might be worded as follows: Our organization will strive to recruit only the most talented employees. This statement offers managers only general direction for recruiting personnel. It is intended to display the importance management has attached to hiring competent people.

A ***policy*** is a planning tool that furnishes broad guidelines for channeling management thinking in certain directions.

The third common planning tool is the **budget**—a financial plan that covers a specified length of time. It details how funds will be spent on items such as labor, raw materials, and capital goods. In addition, it shows how the funds for these expenditures will be obtained.

A ***budget*** is a financial plan that covers a specified period of time.

Each of these planning tools is intended to outline what has to be done to achieve organizational objectives. Other planning issues, such as labor scheduling and plant site selection, will be discussed in chapter 11.

Organizing

The process that managers use to best combine people, equipment, materials, and all other resources to carry out organizational plans and reach organizational objectives is **organizing.** In general, organizing involves assigning to various workers the tasks that were identified during planning. More specifically, organizing includes activities such as determining what jobs need to be performed in order to reach organizational objectives, establishing departments or divisions for the organization, outlining how many and which employees a manager should supervise, and hiring and training employees to perform jobs. These and other aspects of organizing are discussed in more detail in chapter 8.

Organizing is the process that managers use to best combine people, equipment, materials, and all other resources to carry out organizational plans and reach organizational objectives.

Through organizing, plans are put into action. If an organization is well organized, the output of individual workers will contribute to the success of the departments. This in turn contributes to the success of the divisions and ultimately to the overall success of the organization.

Directing

Directing is guiding the actions of organization members toward the attainment of organizational goals.

An important aspect of the manager's role is **directing**—guiding the action of organization members toward the attainment of organizational goals. Generally, the ultimate purpose of directing is to increase productivity. Because directing is accomplished largely through motivating and leading people, it is considered a complex skill.

How—and how much—managers use this function depends on their position. Presidents of companies spend little time directing employees. Department supervisors, on the other hand, spend practically all their time on this management function. The many aspects of directing are discussed in detail in chapter 7.

Controlling

Controlling is the process of evaluating the organization's performance and taking corrective action, where necessary, to ensure that objectives are met.

The process of evaluating the organization's performance and taking corrective action, where necessary, to ensure that objectives are met is **controlling.** Quite simply, controlling means making something happen the way it was planned to happen. As this definition implies, planning and controlling are virtually inseparable, so much so that they have been called the Siamese twins of management.

Figure 6.2 is a newsletter sent to General Tire Company employees by the firm's corporate personnel office. Although the newsletter is essentially a lighthearted discussion of Murphy's law, it does make the serious point that managers should continually control activities to make sure that plans remain on course.

Figure 6.3 illustrates the steps of the controlling process: (1) measuring performance, (2) comparing performance to standards or objectives, (3) identifying deviations and their causes, and (4) taking corrective action.

Measuring Performance

In order to measure performance, the manager must first establish some unit of measure and must then observe the measurement's results. For example, a manager who wanted to measure the performance of janitors would first have to establish such units of measure as the number of floors to be swept or the number of lightbulbs to be changed. Then the manager would observe how many floors each of the janitors sweeps and how many lightbulbs each changes.

Comparing Performance to Standards

Standards are the criteria established by management to serve as a model for evaluating performance within the organization.

Standardization is the continual production of uniform goods and services.

Once a manager has taken a measurement of organizational performance, the next step is to compare this measured effort against some standard. **Standards** are the criteria established by management to serve as a model for evaluating performance within the organization. These criteria are often closely identified with the specific objectives of the organization. Setting and following an appropriate set of standards helps a company achieve **standardization**—the continual production of uniform goods and services

In essence, standards are the yardsticks that determine if organizational performance is adequate. They can be established in such diverse areas as productivity, profitability, and social responsibility. A performance standard applied to janitors might be twelve floors swept per day. Any janitor who did not sweep the full twelve would be performing at an inadequate level.

Identifying Deviations and Their Causes

When a measurable variation, or deviation, from the established standard is discovered, it must be noted and investigated. A deviation is a signal that performance

Conserve Paper Please Circulate

MANAGEMENT IN GENERAL

A Newsletter for Management from Corporate Personnel-Akron

MALICE IN BLUNDERLAND

Thomas L. Martin wrote a book published in 1973 called Malice in Blunderland. If you haven't read it, you might want to obtain it from your local library or the Corporate Research Library. The following are some excerpts:

"MURPHY'S LAWS"

First Law:	If something can go wrong, it will.
Second Law:	When left to themselves, things always go from bad to worse.
Third Law:	Nature always sides with the hidden flaw.

"REVISION OF MURPHY'S FIRST LAW"

If anything can go wrong (with a mechanical system), it will, and generally at the moment the system becomes indispensable.

"COROLLARIES TO MURPHY'S FIRST LAW"

It is impossible to make anything foolproof because fools are so ingenious.

Any wire or tube cut to length will be too short.

Interchangeable parts won't.

Identical units tested under identical conditions will not perform identically in the field.

After any machine or unit has been completely assembled, extra components will be found on the bench.

Components that must not and cannot be assembled improperly, will be.

All constants are variables.

In any given computation, the figure that is most obviously correct will be the source of the error.

The book goes on and on with other laws as well. The thought hit us that you might have your own contributions. So, if you have corollaries to "Murphy's First Law," send them to us and we will publish them in a later issue of Management in General.

Figure 6.2 Newsletter emphasizing the importance of managerial control.

Figure 6.3
The controlling process includes measuring performance, comparing performance to standards, and taking corrective action.

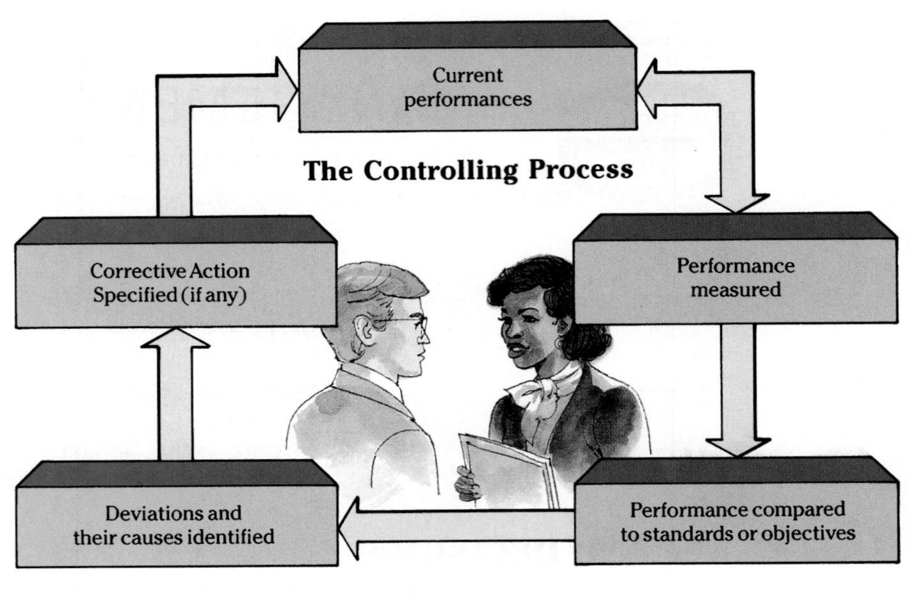

is not up to standard. An investigation into why a particular janitor is not sweeping twelve floors, for instance, may reveal an important reason for a slowdown in performance.

Taking Corrective Action

Once a manager has determined that there are deviations from performance standards and has analyzed the reasons, the next step is to take corrective action. This action is managerial activity aimed at bringing organizational performance up to the level of performance standards. In other words, corrective action focuses on correcting organizational mistakes that threaten organizational performance. Should the janitor be fired or retained? Should the janitor's job be redefined?

Reaching Objectives through Management Functions

We have examined the four functions of managers individually to clarify their use. In real life, however, planning, organizing, directing, and controlling are closely related (see Figure 6.4).

Organizing is based on well-thought-out plans developed during the planning process. Directing must be tailored to reflect both the plans and the organizational design used to implement them. Controlling proposes possible modifications to existing plans, organizing systems, or directing systems in order to help the organization succeed. Creative managers can blend the four functions so that performance successfully fits organizational objectives.

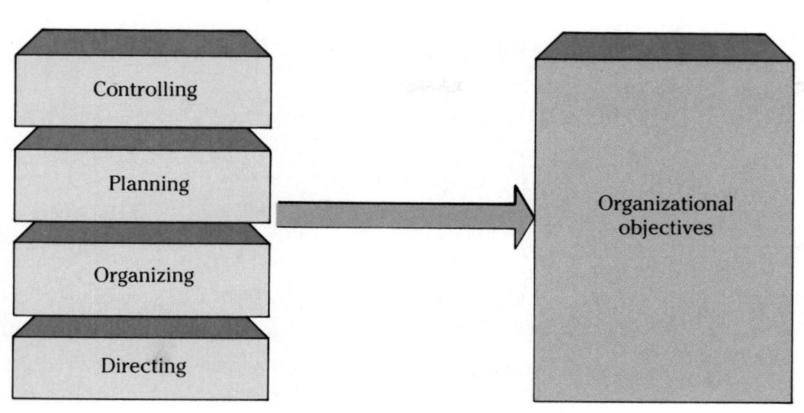

Figure 6.4
Managers reach goals by performing closely related activities.

MANAGEMENT AND DECISIONS

One of the most important managerial tasks is decision making. To a great extent, the quality of a manager's decisions will influence not only the success of the organization but also the success of the manager's career. The following sections explain what decisions are, discuss the different types of decisions, and describe the process managers follow in making decisions.

What Is a Decision?

A **decision** is a choice made between two or more available alternatives. Managers are forced to make many decisions each working day, whether they are planning, organizing, directing, or controlling. Some of the decisions may be critically important to the overall success of the company, affect many employees, and require a large amount of money. Others may be insignificant to the overall success of the company, affect only a few employees, and require little money.

A ***decision*** is a choice made between two or more available alternatives.

Types of Decisions

One of the most common methods for categorizing a decision is based on its uniqueness. With this method, the two categories of decisions are programmed and nonprogrammed.

A **programmed decision** is a decision made to apply to routine or recurring situations. Typically, managers develop policies or guidelines to handle such decisions. A programmed decision might involve determining how products should be arranged on a shelf or how much vacation time to give employees. The allocation of shelf space is routine for supermarkets, and decisions relating to it are generally made according to established guidelines. Similarly, managers set guidelines for vacation times.

A ***programmed decision*** is a decision made to apply to routine or recurring situations.

A **nonprogrammed decision** is a decision made about a complex, unique, or rarely occurring situation. Such decisions require individual consideration, since policies and guidelines do not exist for them. The decision of whether to enter into foreign markets is a nonprogrammed decision.

A ***nonprogrammed decision*** is a decision made about a complex, unique, or rarely occurring situation.

HIGHLIGHT IN BUSINESS PRACTICE

Buck Rodgers on Creating Customer Commitment

Buck Rodgers worked for thirty years for IBM, taking early retirement in 1984 to serve as a management consultant. His last ten years at IBM were spent as vice-president worldwide of marketing. Rodgers is a well-known and highly respected motivator and speaker on behalf of excellence in companies, who has spoken before countless groups of businesspeople across the United States eager to hear his message.

According to Rodgers, paying attention to the following will ensure that companies succeed in creating customer commitment—the key, according to Rodgers, to the success of any company.

1. *Companies Should Have Top-Down Commitment.* Companies should know what business they are in, pay attention to detail in all areas, and be market driven.
2. *Companies Should Provide Superior Service to Their Customers.* Rodgers advises managers to study companies that excel—across industries—and emulate them. "The customer is king," Rodgers admonishes. Respect for the customer provides purpose to the corporation. Thus, Rodgers says, companies should always be:
   - creating new customers
   - maintaining old customers
   - making people want to do business with you
3. *Communicate an operating philosophy company-wide that "everybody sells,"* including those in engineering, finance, development, manufacturing, research, and other departments. Every employee's single purpose, according to Rodgers, should be to provide a level of service beyond what anyone else can provide. "Differentiate yourself everyday," says Rodgers.
4. *Devote Resources to Training and Development.* The Japanese make people in companies feel important and raise their expectation levels very high, according to Rodgers. Everyone is told what is expected of him or her. "If you know what you are asked to achieve, it is easier to achieve it," Rodgers tells managers.
5. *Measurement and Feedback.* It is crucial that companies measure their performance. Rodgers advises managers to survey their sales forces every ninety days, for instance, regarding customer satisfaction. "Put in place the mechanism for market feedback," Rodgers says.

Many decisions can be clearly defined as either programmed or nonprogrammed. Others, however, may be more difficult to categorize.

The Decision-Making Process

The ***decision-making process*** is the steps the decision maker takes to choose one alternative from a set of available alternatives.

The steps the decision maker takes to choose one alternative from a set of available alternatives is the **decision-making process.** These steps are presented in Figure 6.5. As step 1 shows, the decision-making process is used primarily to solve organizational problems. A *problem* is any organizational issue that could hinder organizational success.

To visualize the decision-making process, assume that a manufacturer faces the problem that its products are of low quality. As a result, they are not being purchased in the marketplace. According to the decision-making process, management would (1) identify the factors causing poor quality, (2) list various ways of eliminating these factors, (3) choose the most desirable method of eliminating them, (4) implement this method, and (5) gather feedback to see if the implemented alternative is solving the quality problem. The steps of the decision-making process should be repeated until the problem is solved.

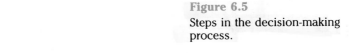

A non-programmed decision focuses on a complex or unique situation and requires the manager's individual consideration.

MANAGERS AND RESOURCES

A key characteristic of management is that it reaches the organization's goals by working with its resources. **Organizational resources** are all the assets available for the production process. There are four basic types of resources: people, money, materials, and equipment. As Figure 6.6 shows, organizational resources are combined and used during the production process to create goods or services. (The production process is examined in chapter 11.)

Managers must keep track of how the resources are used. The manager of a McDonald's restaurant, for example, keeps close watch on how the counter help (people), salaries (money), meat patties and buns (materials), and french fry cookers (equipment) blend together during the production process in order to provide desirable food to customers.

Organizational resources are all the assets available for the production process: people, money, materials, and equipment.

Managerial Effectiveness and Efficiency

Managers try to be effective in what they do. In a managerial context, **effectiveness** is the extent to which managers reach organizational objectives. The better

In a managerial context, ***effectiveness*** is the extent to which managers reach organizational objectives.

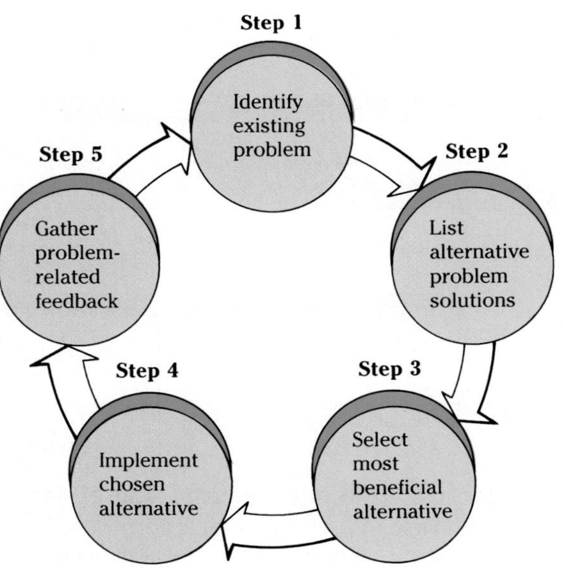

Figure 6.5
Steps in the decision-making process.

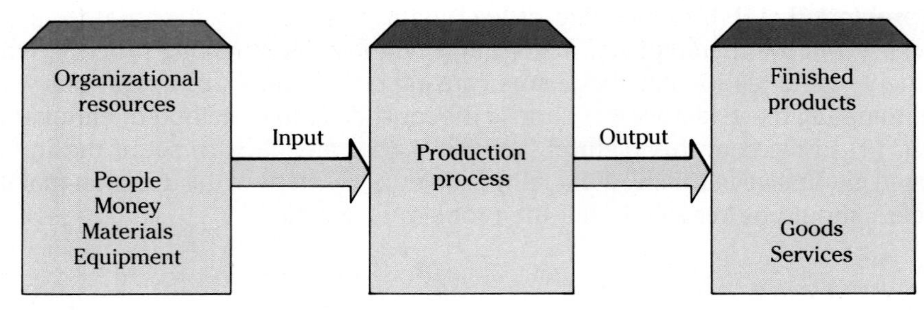

Figure 6.6
The production process turns organizational resources into finished products.

the objectives are met, the more effective is the manager. Of course, there are degrees of managerial effectiveness. The closer the organization comes to achieving its objectives, the more effective its managers are said to be.

In a managerial context, ***efficiency*** is using the optimum amount of organizational resources to help the organization reach its objectives.

In addition to being effective, managers also strive to be efficient. In a managerial context, **efficiency** means using the optimum amount of organizational resources to help the organization reach its objectives. The fewer the resources used to achieve objectives, the more efficient the manager. In other words, efficiency means using only what you need, without wasting any materials.

The effective manager, then, is one who achieves organizational objectives, while the efficient manager is one who conserves resources in production. However, as Figure 6.7 indicates, the two concepts are related. A manager could be ineffective *because* of being inefficient. For example, a newspaper may not be able to show a profit (its objective) because it is paying too much money (resources) to its reporters. On the other hand, a manager could be somewhat effective despite being inefficient. Some drug companies sell their products at such high prices that they can make a profit (objective) even if their equipment

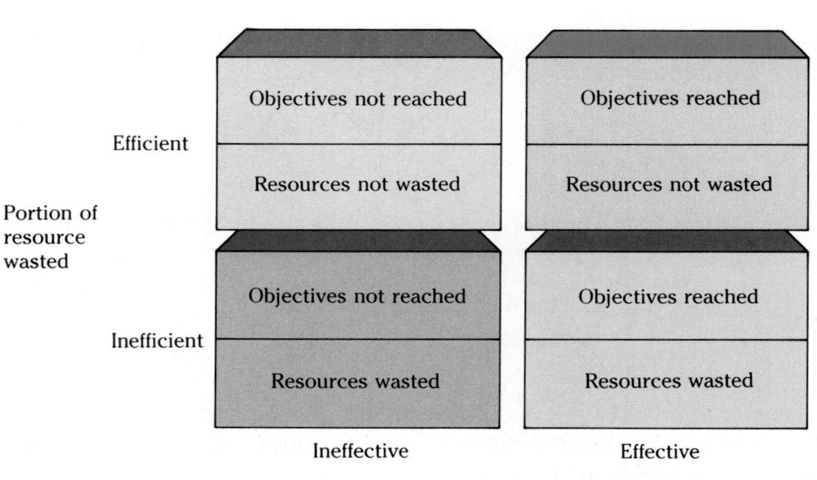

Figure 6.7
Successful managers are both effective and efficient.

BUSINESS PRACTICE EXAMPLE Continues

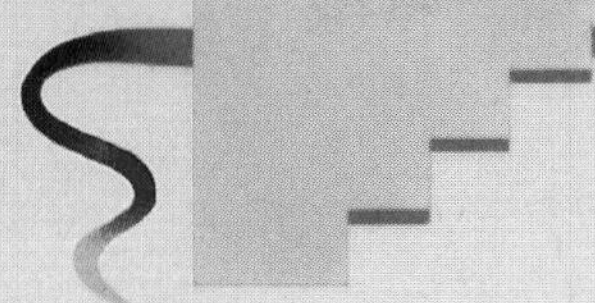

Although Merck has emphasized the importance of new products, it is also actively working to control costs. This will preserve profit margins, helping the company through sales fluctuations to achieve long-term success. "Companies can get fat, dumb, and happy when they're having as much success as Merck has had," says one business analyst. "The word we're getting is that Dr. Vagelos is as tight on expense control and cost efficiency as ever before. To me that is a sign of a great manager." An analyst at Prudential-Bache Securities called attention to the nearly 8% rise in manufacturing dollars spent in 1987; he was pleased to note that this was actually a gain in efficiency, since Merck had spent 4% less per dollar of sales than the year before. He called this performance "possibly a unique control of manufacturing costs for so large a company growing so rapidly."

is old-fashioned and it takes a great deal of time (resources) to produce the drugs. In other words, the selling price is high enough that managerial inefficiencies can be absorbed. In this situation, management has a chance of being somewhat effective despite its inefficiency.

Effective and efficient—a manager can be one without being the other. To maximize long-term organizational success, however, the manager must be both.

TYPES OF ORGANIZATIONAL OBJECTIVES

As we saw at the beginning of the chapter, the achievement of organizational objectives is an overall aim that dominates every managerial activity. Equally important, however, is for managers to have a clear idea about the kinds of objectives they should try to achieve to help the company succeed.

In his classic book *The Practice of Management,* management theorist Peter F. Drucker indicates that the very survival of an organization may be endangered if managers emphasize only the profit objective.[2] Managers who stress this one objective tend to take action designed to make money today, with little regard as to how the organization will make a profit tomorrow.

As we have seen, managers generally should strive to develop and emphasize the attainment of a variety of objectives in all areas where activity is critical to

HIGHLIGHT IN BUSINESS PRACTICE

Tips for Managerial Success

While it is true that successful managers must be knowledgeable and experienced in all four of the basic management activities of planning, organizing, directing, and controlling, there are additional qualities or skills managers must possess—or cultivate—to perform the four basic managerial functions successfully. As these are basic human qualities that most people expect in a leader of any group—a family, business, church—they may seem too obvious to warrant discussion. However, those who attempt to manage without these attributes will likely fail.

Building Trust. It is increasingly accepted that the most effective model for a business organization spreads responsibility "back down" into the ranks from the top where it has traditionally resided. But it is also recognized that this model cannot succeed if there is no mutual give-and-take of trust among employees within an organization, if employees do not feel that they are seen as capable of handling their responsibilities. As no one manager can possibly possess all the talent, skills, and expertise necessary to develop a company, there is a stubborn and fatal egomania behind a belief to the contrary. On the flip side, trusted employees often add value beyond management expectation. The Big Mac was born of such circumstances; it was developed by the manager of one of the chain's franchises, all of which are encouraged to operate independently.

Building Team Spirit. Communicating effectively with employees is an extension of a manager's ability to build an atmosphere of trust. Employees need to feel that they are part of a team with a long-range purpose, that their value is not short-lived, and that they are kept abreast of crucial changes in plans as they directly affect each employee. Managers who cannot share this information and sense of purpose with their employees risk not achieving their goals: they cannot do so without loyal employees behind them.

Capitalizing on Risk and Dissension. Little innovation or progress arises out of the status quo. However, there are many managers whose fear of failure prevents them from taking any risk or exploring new ideas—and therefore making any significant gains. Encouraging and assimilating employee risk-taking and dissension into company operations, and responding creatively to failures that result from risk-taking or dissension, can cause a company to flourish and move smoothly beyond most crises.

Adaptability. Insecure managers are threatened by the many internal and external changes they face daily; they choose to ignore change and thereby forfeit its benefits.

The development of managerial strength requires complex knowledge and skill. Those managers who learn to plan, organize, direct, and control in the style we've discussed above will win the battle.

organizational success. More specifically, Drucker advises managers to set organizational objectives in eight key areas:

1. *Market standing.* Managers should set objectives indicating where they would like the organization to be in relation to its competitors.
2. *Innovation.* Managers should set objectives concerning the development of new methods of operation.

3. *Productivity.* Managers should set objectives concerning levels of production.
4. *Physical and financial resources.* Managers should set objectives concerning equipment use and monetary resources.
5. *Profitability.* Managers should set objectives concerning a profit level they would like the organization to reach.
6. *Manager performance and development.* Managers should set objectives regarding both rates and levels of managerial productivity, and the personal competence of managers.
7. *Worker performance and attitude.* Managers should set objectives regarding both the rates and levels of worker productivity, and worker attitudes.
8. *Public or social responsibility.* Managers should set objectives concerning the organization's responsibilities to customers and society and how the organization plans to meet these responsibilities.

According to Drucker, most managers would probably agree that objectives should be set in the first five areas, which relate to tangible characteristics of organizational operation. The last three areas, however, are more personal and subjective. Regardless, an organization should generally have objectives in all eight areas to maximize its probability of success.

A Hierarchy of Objectives

An organization will always have an overall objective. A book publishing company, for example, may have the overall objective of providing high-quality educational materials and making a profit from their sale.

At the same time, organizations need more specific objectives. From the highest to the lowest, all the levels of a company's objectives are tied together in a pyramid arrangement termed a **hierarchy of objectives.** Below the broad objectives are **subobjectives**—lower-level, specific objectives that are developed from the broader objectives and that specify how they are to be carried out (see Figure 6.8).

The ***hierarchy of objectives*** is the entire set of objectives for an organization, from overall objectives to specific subobjectives.

Subobjectives are lower-level, specific objectives that are developed from broader objectives and that specify how they are to be carried out.

Subobjectives guide individuals in different parts of the organization toward doing things to help the organization reach its overall objective. A subobjective for the publisher's editorial department might be to choose the best books to publish and to ensure the quality of their content. A subobjective of the production department might be to use materials such as paper and ink efficiently and to manufacture the books on time. A subobjective of the marketing department might be to determine what types of books the customers want. A subobjective of the sales department might be to reach a certain sales quota. Subobjectives help each worker, each department, and each division of the organization contribute to overall success, even though the various people and units are all doing different things.

This supervisor must possess interpersonal skills, technical skills, and conceptual skills to manage the day to day operation of the laboratory.

LEVELS OF MANAGEMENT

In discussing business operations, managers typically use the phrase *levels of management.* This section will consider the meaning of the phrase. It will also examine the skills managers must possess at different levels and the time managers at various levels spend in planning, organizing, directing, and controlling.

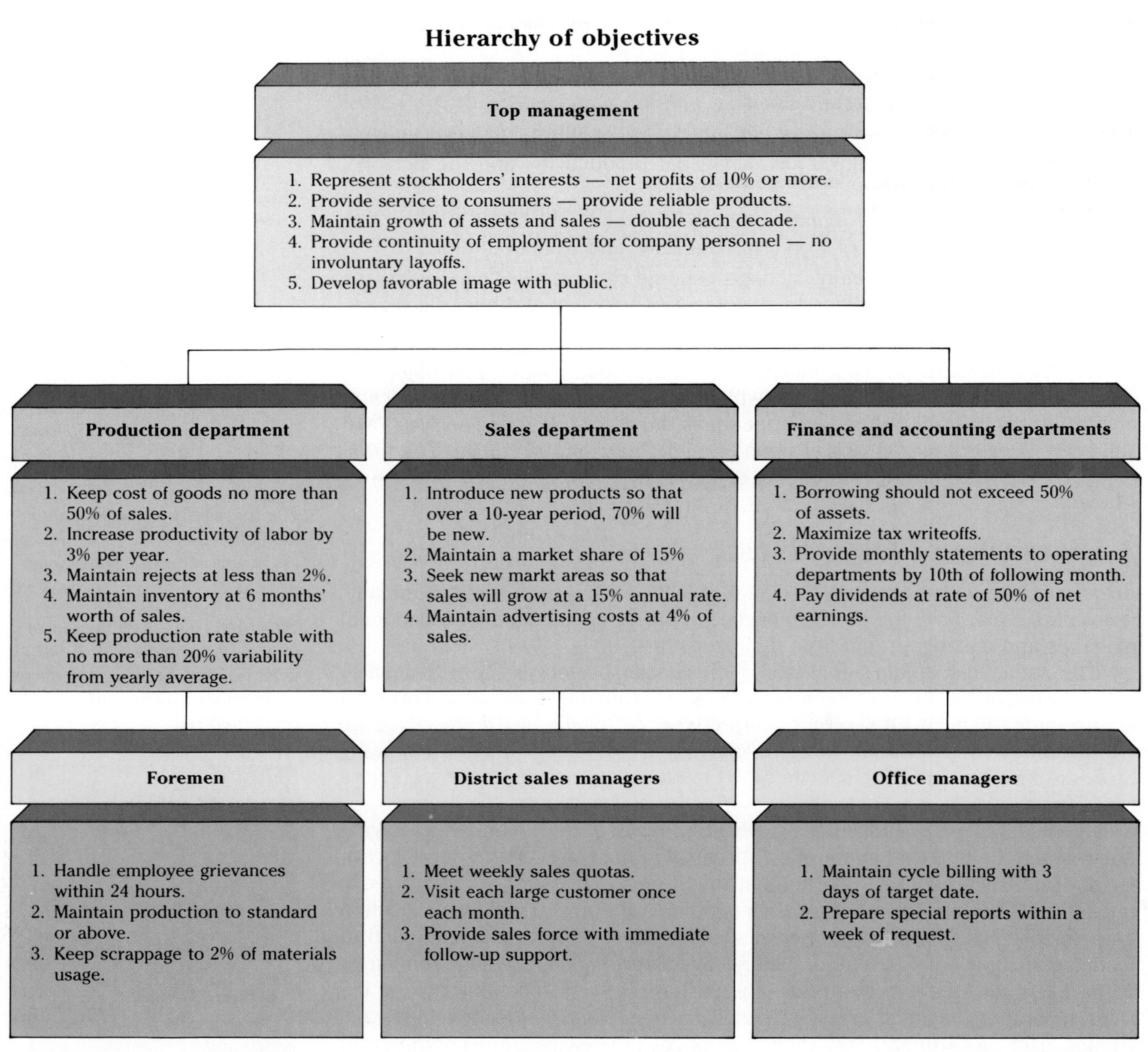

Hierarchy of objectives
Top management
1. Represent stockholders' interests — net profits of 10% or more.
2. Provide service to consumers — provide reliable products.
3. Maintain growth of assets and sales — double each decade.
4. Provide continuity of employment for company personnel — no involuntary layoffs.
5. Develop favorable image with public.
Production department
1. Keep cost of goods no more than 50% of sales.
2. Increase productivity of labor by 3% per year.
3. Maintain rejects at less than 2%.
4. Maintain inventory at 6 months' worth of sales.
5. Keep production rate stable with no more than 20% variability from yearly average.
Sales department
1. Introduce new products so that over a 10-year period, 70% will be new.
2. Maintain a market share of 15%
3. Seek new markt areas so that sales will grow at a 15% annual rate.
4. Maintain advertising costs at 4% of sales.
Finance and accounting departments
1. Borrowing should not exceed 50% of assets.
2. Maximize tax writeoffs.
3. Provide monthly statements to operating departments by 10th of following month.
4. Pay dividends at rate of 50% of net earnings.
Foremen
1. Handle employee grievances within 24 hours.
2. Maintain production to standard or above.
3. Keep scrappage to 2% of materials usage.
District sales managers
1. Meet weekly sales quotas.
2. Visit each large customer once each month.
3. Provide sales force with immediate follow-up support.
Office managers
1. Maintain cycle billing with 3 days of target date.
2. Prepare special reports within a week of request.

Figure 6.8 Overall objectives are divided into smaller subobjectives.

A ***management level*** is a particular horizontal segment of management; top management, middle management, and supervisory (operating) management are the three levels.

A **management level** is a particular horizontal segment of management. In general, large organizations have three levels of management: top, middle, and supervisory (or operating). These levels are collectively referred to as the **organizational hierarchy** (or **management pyramid**).

Top management is the highest level of management. Managers at this level typically are the president or chief executive officer, vice-president, and board of directors.

Middle management is the next-to-highest level of management. Managers at this level generally are plant managers, division managers, and department heads. These managers have more specific responsibilities than do top-level managers.

Supervisory (operating) management is the lowest level of management. Managers at this level are usually called supervisors. Their primary responsibility is managing workers involved in the day-to-day operations of the organization. Figure 6.9 illustrates the three management levels and lists the job titles typically associated with each level.

The ***organizational hierarchy (management pyramid)*** is the collective term for the three management levels: top, middle, and supervisory (operating).

Top management is the highest level of management.

Middle management is the next-to-highest level of management.

Supervisory (operating) management is the lowest level of management; managers at this level are usually called supervisors.

Management Levels and Skills

Managerial success depends on managerial skills. Generally, a manager should possess three basic skills: technical, conceptual, and human. **Technical skill** is the ability to use specialized knowledge about the mechanics of a job. **Conceptual skill** is the ability to see the organization as a series of parts and to

Technical skill is the ability to use specialized knowledge about the mechanics of a job.

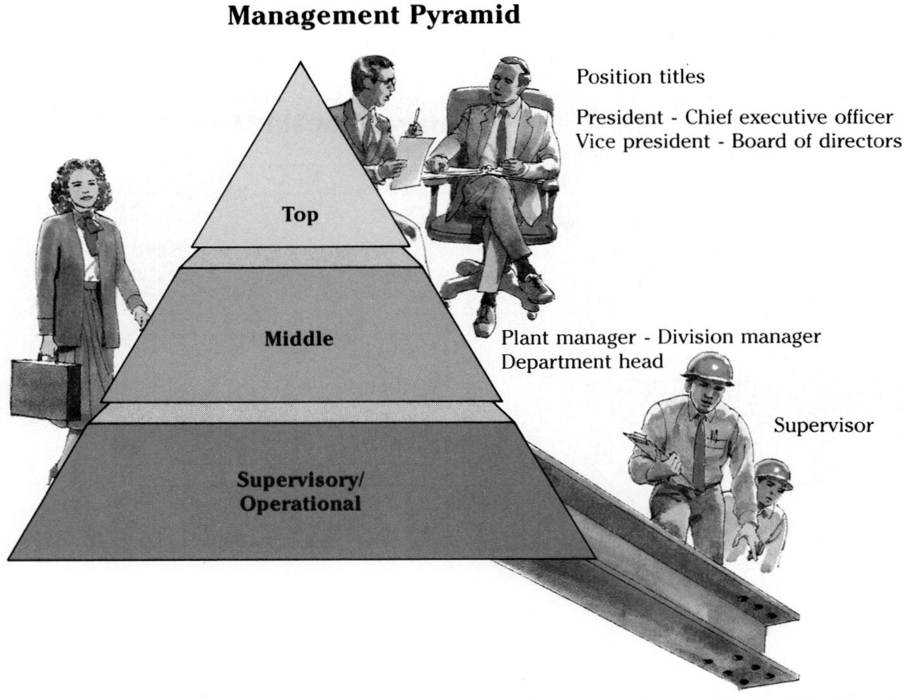

Figure 6.9 Organizations typically have three levels of management, with each level assuming different degrees of responsibility.

Conceptual skill is the ability to see the organization as a series of parts and to understand how the parts relate to one another.

Human skill is the ability to work well with people.

understand how the parts relate to one another. **Human skill** is the ability to work well with people. It includes leadership, motivation, and the ability to communicate, both verbally and in writing.

Figure 6.10 shows how important each of these skills is to managers at each level. Basically, as a person moves from lower management to upper management, conceptual skills become more important and technical skills become less important. Managers moving upward in the organization become less involved with the everyday production process (technical areas) and more involved with managing the organization as a whole. However, human skills are important at all levels, since the one constant at all management levels is people.

Management Levels and Functions

Managers at different levels in the organization spend different amounts of time performing the management functions of planning, directing, and controlling. Although there is some debate on this point, managers at all levels seem to spend equivalent amounts of time organizing. Research clearly indicates, however, that as managers are promoted from lower levels to upper levels, they spend less time directing and controlling and more time planning (see Figure 6.11).

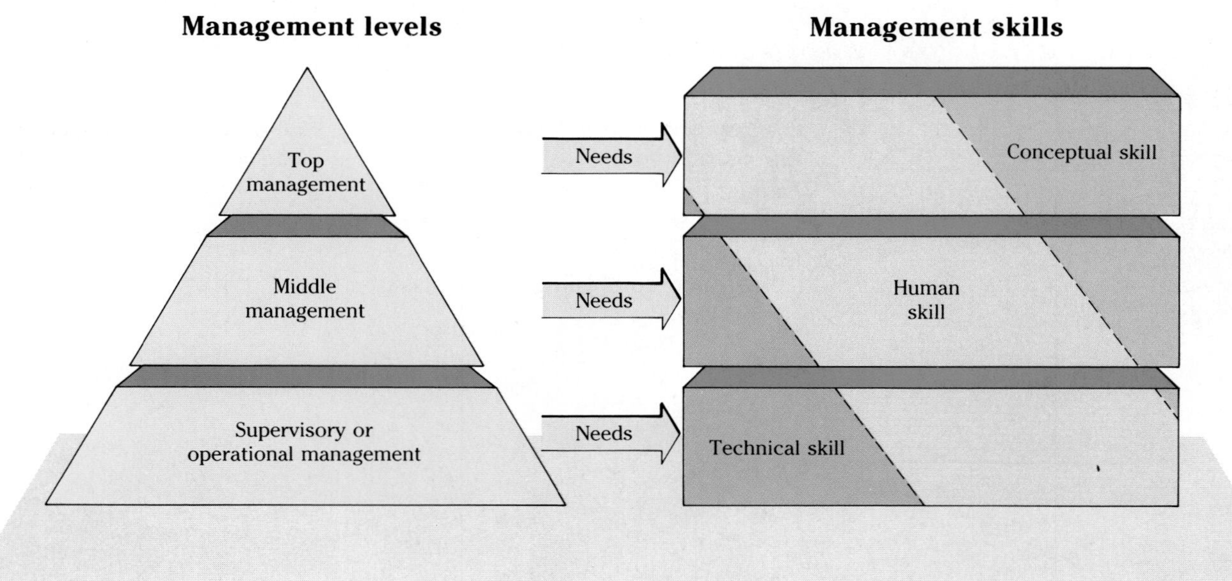

Figure 6.10 As a manager moves from the supervisory to the top management level, conceptual skills become more important than technical skills, but human skills remain equally important.

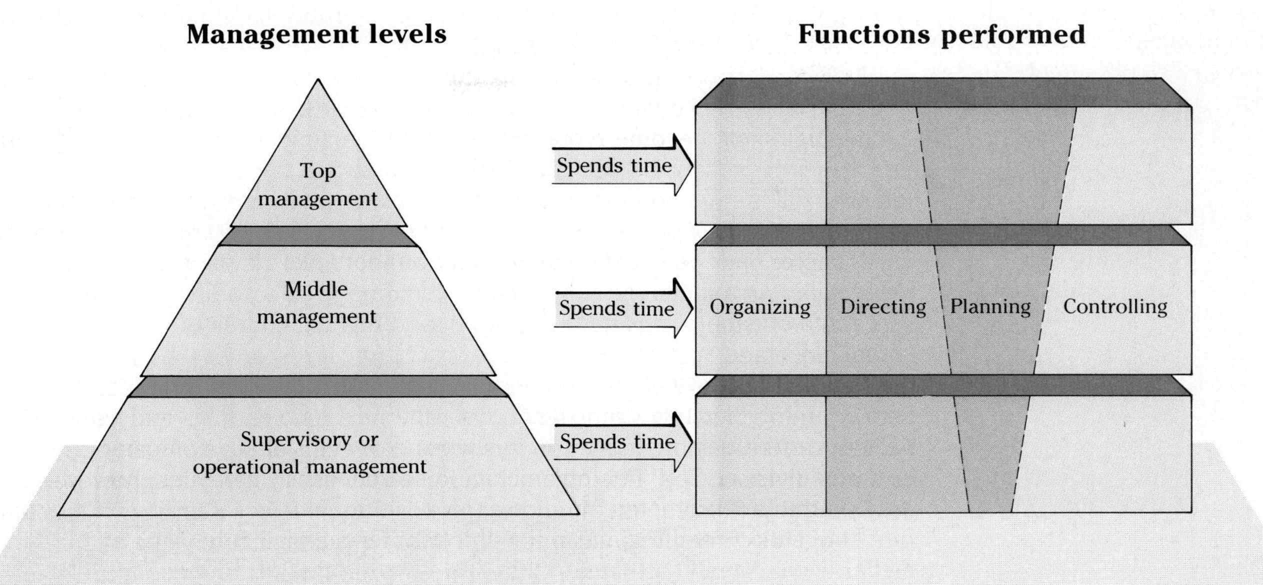

Figure 6.11 As managers move from lower levels to higher levels of management, they spend more time planning and less time controlling and directing. They spend about the same amount of time organizing.

THE UNIVERSALITY OF MANAGEMENT

The concept that management principles are relevant to all types and levels of organizations is called **universality of management.** These principles can be applied to businesses, churches, fraternities, athletic teams, and hospitals, for example. Naturally, managers' jobs will be different in each type of organization, since each requires the use of special knowledge, exists in a unique environment, and uses different technology. In certain basic ways, however, the jobs will be similar—because planning, organizing, directing, and controlling are necessary in all organizations.

Universality of management is the concept that management principles are relevant to all types and levels of organizations.

BUSINESS PRACTICE EXAMPLE Continues

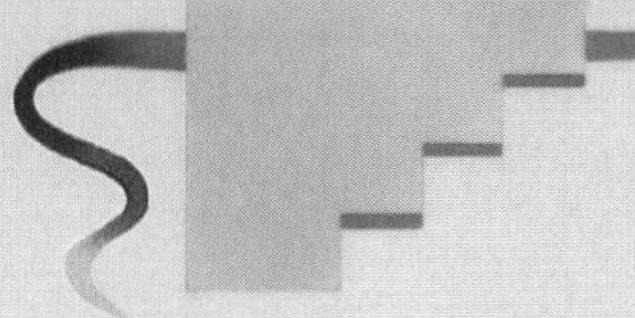

This chapter ends with a discussion of the importance of various management skills. As a manager, Roy Vagelos came up from a somewhat unusual route outside of business. He developed high standards of competence and supervisory skill as a biochemical researcher, both at the National Institute of Health and at Washington University in St. Louis, before joining Merck & Co. in 1975. Over the next ten years his managerial responsibilities broadened as he became director of the company's research division. The division's outstanding success in generating new drug products finally earned him the top position as Merck's CEO.

As Vagelos gained responsibility and broader management skills at higher levels, he still retained a firm grip on what it takes to make a project succeed. "He's a brilliant researcher in his own right," one industry analyst commented. "He's able to exercise hands-on judgment in R & D. . . . There's nobody better or more experienced to evaluate the direction of the overall corporate research program." Vagelos's ability to get the best from subordinates became clear when his hand-picked successor, Dr. Edward Scolnick, led the research division to produce several major new drug successes. The division soon outgrew the talent pool in the headquarters area, and developed new communities of researchers with labs built in Italy and England.

Most observers expected Vagelos to excel in the skills needed for product development. Yet he surprised many with his ability to extend his conceptual and human skills into unfamiliar areas. Said one analyst, "His background is not finance and marketing, but he's got very talented people in all those other areas." Another commented, "I guess what impresses me, because I would not necessarily have expected it from him, is his firm grasp of the financial affairs and his ability to control costs and foster productivity."

With so much success and such a hands-on style, Vagelos's methods were bound to raise a few doubts. "My only concern," an observer confessed, "would be . . . that probably almost too much power or too many parts of the company are reporting directly to Vagelos. It's a very large, complex company to be run ultimately by one person."

Issues for Discussion

1. Do the tactical plans and actions of Merck's management seem suited to implementing its strategy? Explain how levels of planning are matched at Merck.

2. Many drug companies can mask inefficiencies in production with increased revenues from selling costly products. How can you tell whether Merck has avoided this trap of inefficiency?
3. Where do you see conceptual skills, human skills, and technical skills at work in Vagelos' career as manager?

SUMMARY

Management is the process of reaching organizational goals by working with and through people and other organizational resources. There are four main steps in the management process: planning, organizing, directing, and controlling. Managers plan by outlining what must be done in the future to reach organizational objectives. They organize by combining people and other organizational resources in order to carry out plans. Directing is guiding people so that organizational objectives are accomplished. Controlling emphasizes evaluating organizational performance and making changes, if necessary, to achieve organizational objectives.

Managers are constantly making decisions (choices between alternatives). There are two general types of decisions: programmed (those commonly made) and nonprogrammed (those seldom made). The decisions are made through the process of identifying a problem, listing possible solutions to it, selecting the most beneficial solution, implementing the selected alternative, and gathering feedback to see if the problem has been solved.

In running organizations, managers use four basic types of resources: people, money, materials, and equipment. If managers use resources to attain organizational objectives, they are effective. If managers do not waste organizational resources in attaining organizational objectives, they are efficient. Managers strive to be both effective and efficient.

Organizational objectives are targets the organization is attempting to hit. Organizations generally have both short-term targets (those of about a year or less) and long-term targets (those of about three to five years). In addition, the objectives can be set in such different areas as market standing, innovation, and productivity. Organizational objectives are generally arranged in a hierarchy, or set. This set is composed of objectives for the organization as a whole and related subobjectives for various parts of the organization.

To be successful over the long term, managers must have technical skill, conceptual skill, and human skill. Technical skill is the ability to work with specific issues of a job situation, conceptual skill is the ability to deal with the organization as a whole, and human skill is the ability to work with people. Technical skill is more valuable to lower-level managers than to upper-level managers, and conceptual skill is more valuable to upper-level managers than to lower-level managers. Human skill is equally important to all levels of management.

The amount of time a manager spends performing most management functions may vary according to the level of management at which the manager is functioning. However, managers at all levels seem to spend equivalent amounts of time organizing. Managers moving from lower-level positions to upper-level positions seem to spend less time directing and controlling and more time planning. Management principles in regard to these functions and all others are considered universal, or applicable to all management levels in all organizations.

KEY TERMS

CHECK YOUR LEARNING

Reread the following learning objectives. Each objective is followed by a few questions. Answering these questions accurately will help you retain the most important concepts discussed in this chapter. After answering each question, check your answer with the key at the end of this chapter. (*Hint:* If you have doubt regarding the correct response, consult the page whose number follows the answer.)

Circle:

A. Define *management.*

a b c d — 1. Management is best described by the phrase: (a) a process; (b) reaching organizational goals; (c) working with people; (d) all of the above.

a b c d — 2. Listing tasks that must be performed to attain organizational goals is: (a) planning; (b) communicating; (c) evaluating; (d) supervising.

B. Explain the purpose of management.

T F — 1. Managers influence most phases of modern organizations.

C. List the four basic management functions and describe the relationships among them.

T F — 1. Organizing and directing are the two closely related management functions.

a b c d — 2. The main management functions include: (a) forecasting; (b) assisting; (c) controlling; (d) reprimanding.

D. Discuss the implications of decision making, effectiveness, and efficiency for managers.

a b c d e — 1. A decision is: (a) an opinion; (b) an attitude about a situation; (c) the outcome of planning; (d) a choice between two or more available alternatives; (e) none of the above.

a b c d e — 2. The first step of the decision-making process is: (a) listing available problem solutions; (b) selecting the most beneficial alternative; (c) gathering problem-related feedback; (d) identifying an existing problem; (e) implementing the chosen alternative.

T F — 3. A manager could be judged as efficient yet ineffective.

T F — 4. An inefficient manager wastes resources and does not reach organizational goals.

E. Discuss the role of objectives and the hierarchy of objectives in the management process.

1. Organizational objectives: (a) are targets; (b) are aimed at by managers; (c) reflect organizational purposes; (d) all of the above. a b c d
2. Objectives indicating where an organization would like to be in relation to competitors are found in the area of: (a) profitability; (b) market standing; (c) worker attitude; (d) physical resources. a b c d
3. In fact, management is the hierarchy of objectives. T F

F. Outline the skills and functions appropriate for various levels of management.

1. Human skills are important for all levels of management. T F
2. Supervisory managers generally plan more than middle managers. T F

G. Explain the term *universality of management.*

1. Management principles are universal, or taught throughout the world. T F
2. The basic planning task is similar in all organizations. T F

QUESTIONS FOR REVIEW AND DISCUSSION

1. Define the key terms listed at the end of the chapter.
2. What is the difference between planning and controlling?
3. What is the most important step of the decision-making process? Explain.
4. How can a manager be inefficient but effective? Explain.
5. Write a sample objective for an organization in each of the following areas: innovation, worker performance and attitude, and public responsibility.
6. For each of the objectives you wrote in the preceding question, develop three related subobjectives that could appear in a well-designed hierarchy of objectives.
7. If you were to begin working as a manager tomorrow, what skills would you probably need and what activities would you probably be performing? Explain.
8. Think about how you spent yesterday. List all the organizations with which you came into contact. What purposes do these organizations serve?
9. Think about the manager you respect the most. Why is this manager successful?
10. Think about a company whose advertising is familiar to you. Can you tell the company's strategy from its advertising? If so, give examples. If not, explain why.
11. Would a competent basketball coach at UCLA have a chance of being successful as a manager at Procter & Gamble? Explain.

CONCLUDING CASE

Managers of Large and Small Businesses—Some Differences

Studies by the National Federation of Independent Business and by *Business Week* have revealed some interesting demographic differences in the top managers of large and small companies. Among the most striking differences are that small business owners, compared to large corporate CEOs, tend to be younger, have less education, and are more likely to be women.

The study on the large corporate CEOs focused on the *Business Week* top 1000 companies, while the NFIB study surveyed nearly 5000 companies that were less than two years old. The *Business Week* study found that 98 percent of its top CEO respondents were 40 or older, whereas 65 percent of the small business owners responding to the NFIB study were under 40 years old.

Almost 90 percent of the large corporation CEOs in the *Business Week* top 1000 companies had college degrees, and almost half had graduate degrees. By contrast, of the 5000 small business owners, 40 percent had little or no formal education. This may perhaps have a relationship to the fact that 45 percent of the NFIB owners were themselves children of small business owners; a large number may have come from a self-taught family business tradition.

Only two women were in charge of the top 1000 large corporations survey by *Business Week*. Compared with this poor showing for women CEOs, the figure from the NFIB study shows that 22 percent of the new small business owners were women.

Issues for Discussion

1. From these studies on simple demographic characteristics of top management, what conclusions would you draw about why top managers have more education in a large corporation?
2. Since corporate CEOs are much older, their managers evidently take longer to get to the top. One reason is that they are less likely as young persons to inherit a top position from parents who own the company. What are some other reasons why corporate managers take longer to succeed?
3. How do you explain the high percentage of women owners in new small companies? Aside from inheriting the business, why are women's management skills more likely to make them owners or top managers in a smaller business?

NOTES

1. Samuel C. Certo, *Principles of Modern Management,* 4th ed. (Boston: Allyn and Bacon, 1989).
2. Peter F. Drucker, *The Practice of Management* (New York: Harper & Row, 1954), pp. 62–65, 126–29.

CHECK YOUR LEARNING ANSWER KEY

A. 1. d, *p. 167*
   2. a, *p. 168*
B. 1. F, *p. 165*
C. 1. F, *p. 167*
   2. c, *p. 167*
D. 1. d, *p. 175*
   2. d, *p. 177*
   3. T, *p. 178*
   4. F, *p. 179*
E. 1. d, *p. 179*
   2. b, *p. 180*
   3. F, *p. 181*
F. 1. T, *p. 184*
   2. F, *p. 184*
G. 1. F, *p. 185*
   2. T, *p. 185*

CHAPTER

7

MOTIVATION AND LEADERSHIP IN ORGANIZATIONS

LEARNING OBJECTIVES

After reading this chapter you should be able to:

1. Describe human relations in organizations and in the Hawthorne studies.
2. Discuss the human motivation process.
3. Draw a diagram of and discuss Maslow's hierarchy of needs.
4. Explain how managers motivate employees.
5. Describe Theory X, Theory Y, Theory Z, and behavior modification.
6. Discuss motivation through management by objectives, leadership, and the managerial grid.
7. Explain various job design strategies for motivating employees.

OUTLINE

Business Practice Example: Trying Harder at Avis
What Is Human Relations?
The Hawthorne Studies: The Beginning of Human Relations
The Motivation Process
- Maslow's Hierarchy of Needs
  - Physiological Needs
  - Security Needs
  - Social Needs
  - Esteem Needs
  - Self-Actualization Needs
  - Evaluating Maslow's Hierarchy of Needs
- Motivating Organization Members: Building Organizations People Like
  - Theory X and Theory Y
  - Theory Z
  - Behavior Modification
  - Management by Objectives

Leadership
- Leader Behavior and Leadership Styles
  - The Autocratic Leadership Style
  - The Democratic Leadership Style
  - The Laissez-faire Leadership Style
- Situational Leadership

Job Design and Employee Motivation
- Job Rotation and Job Enlargement
- Job Enrichment
- Flextime
- Job Sharing

The Managerial Grid
Summary
Key Terms
Check Your Learning
Questions for Review and Discussion
Concluding Case
- Americans Manage in Australia

Notes
Check Your Learning Answer Key
Highlight in Business Practice: Human Relations: Tom Peters' Principle
Highlight in Business Practice: Job Enrichment at Procter & Gamble

BUSINESS PRACTICE EXAMPLE

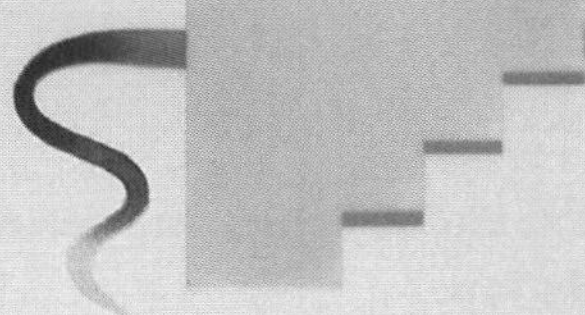

Trying Harder at Avis

"AVIS—Number 2—WE TRY HARDER!!" is the longstanding motto of the car rental company founded by Warren Avis in 1946. This famous saying and many clever ad campaigns have made the Avis name a household word for the tradition of working hard to come from behind. One memorable early television spot invited customers to clock the Avis woman filling out their order tickets: "If it takes her more than two minutes—rip off her badge!"

Over the years the Avis "Try Harder" attitude came to represent an expected level of performance, and the company settled into solid earnings as Number Two for a series of different owners. Then in the early 1980s a new corporate tax environment created a wave of price wars in the car rental industry. Suddenly in 1982 Avis earnings nosedived; they showed a loss nearly as big as the profit of the year before. The owners, Norton Simon Inc., reacted by moving in with a new management style under their CEO, David Mahoney.

Mahoney began a clampdown that was painful and demoralizing to the "Try Harder" company. According to Juergen Ladendorf, a Harvard Business School professor who served as a consultant to the new overseer, "Mahoney ruled by dictates and fear; he couldn't extend loving care to his children. The people at Avis hated us from the first day." An Avis manager retold how "teams of financial analysts were sent in to 'help us' with a lot of operating decisions" and sent out a barrage of uninformed questions. Mahoney next appointed his own financial officer, J. Patrick Barrett, as Avis CEO. Barrett promptly eased out 13 of Avis' 14 top managers and hundreds of employees.

Although Barrett, a self-described "mild-mannered upstate New Yorker," tried to soften this blow with generous severance packages and retraining assistance, everyone at Avis looked back on the firings as the low point in company morale. The first wave of relief actually came when Mahoney's overseers were replaced by another hard-nosed regime. The new owner's manager, Don Kelly, set strict sales and profit goals. "If you don't make your number . . ." Kelly was reported to have said, "I'll get somebody else to run the company." With that, however, he adopted a hands-off policy, leaving Barrett in place as CEO and the managers delighted to operate without the owners constantly looking over their shoulder.

Barrett continued the "make your number" policy, slowly bringing up profits and working to revive the "Try Harder" ethic. Gradually, while surviving erratic management from the Beatrice Food Co. owners, plus more tax shifts triggering new car-rental price wars, Avis began a steady climb back to profitability. Then, in a surge of merger activity, the company was sold in 1986 for a bargain price to yet another conglomerate, Wesray. This time the new owner, after selling off unwanted subsidiaries, unleashed new energy in Avis' ambitious employees. Within a year profits jumped 30% and the workers were in charge of their own company through an employee buyout. By the end of the 1980s the Avis people were ready to try for Number One in the car rental business.

WHAT'S AHEAD

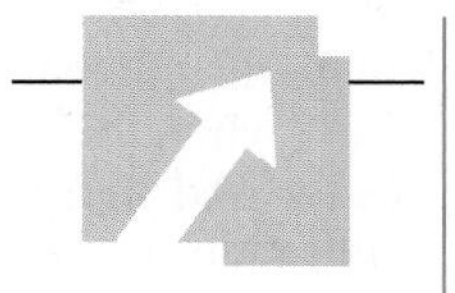

The introductory case focuses on human relations issues at Avis. This chapter will explain why management at a company like Avis should be concerned about human relations and will suggest steps management can take to deal positively with organization members. It will cover the history of human relations, the motivation process (including Maslow's hierarchy of needs; Theories X, Y, and Z; and management by objectives), and the important topics of leadership, job design, and the managerial grid.

WHAT IS HUMAN RELATIONS?

American executives consider the ability to get along with others an important factor in management success and the inability to understand others a primary reason for management failure.[1] **Human relations** is the area of study that is concerned primarily with finding the best way to work with and deal with people in organizations. Obviously, this area of study is extremely important.

Human relations is the area of study concerned primarily with finding the best way to work with and deal with people in organizations.

Managers study human relations to find out how to make their organizations more desirable to employees and thereby encourage employees to help reach organizational goals more efficiently and effectively. A central concern of human relations study is **morale**—the general attitudes workers have about their jobs. Not surprisingly, workers who like an organization and feel good about their jobs will work harder to achieve the organization's goals. In this chapter we will explore human relations and try to determine how managers can maximize employee performance.

Morale is the general attitudes workers have about their jobs.

Management writers Thomas Peters and Robert Waterman describe the importance of managers developing good relationships with their workers. The two studied numerous major companies, such as Frito-Lay and Maytag, over several years to find out what management characteristics existed at excellently run companies. These characteristics are the essence of their best-selling *In Search of Excellence.*

THE HAWTHORNE STUDIES: THE BEGINNING OF HUMAN RELATIONS

The ***Hawthorne studies*** are a series of pioneering human relations studies conducted between 1924 and 1932 at the Hawthorne Works Plant of the Western Electric Company.

A series of pioneering human relations studies conducted between 1924 and 1932 at the Hawthorne Works Plant of the Western Electric Company, in Cicero, Illinois, has become known as the **Hawthorne studies.** Most researchers agree that these studies, conducted by Elton Mayo of Harvard University, were the first systematic attempt to understand organizational human relations.

The original purpose of the studies was to determine what physical working conditions would make the employees most effective and efficient. The researchers varied such things as the level of lighting and the level of noise to determine their effects on worker productivity. The results were surprising and confusing. For example, productivity increased when the level of lighting was intensified, *and* it increased when the level of lighting was diminished. Regardless of the physical conditions, productivity increased. Mayo and his colleagues had to figure out why, so they asked the employees.

The employees replied that regardless of certain working conditions, their work groups were friendly and, during the experiments, their supervisors had asked for their help and cooperation rather than trying to motivate them with fear. The point is that when their feelings and needs were considered and when they were asked to help and cooperate, they responded by working faster and more efficiently. The experimenters concluded that human factors could significantly influence production.

The ***Hawthorne effect*** is the phenomenon, discovered in the Hawthorne studies, that worker productivity increases in response to positive feedback, even if other positive factors are lacking.

The Hawthorne investigations were important to the development of management theory because they opened up a new area of management study. Rather than being concerned solely with effectiveness and efficiency, management researchers began giving more attention to people. The **Hawthorne effect** is named after the phenomenon discovered by Mayo's investigators: that worker productivity increases in response to positive feedback, even if other positive factors (such as high compensation and good working conditions) are lacking. In general, managers can encourage workers to become more productive by making them feel valued and important.

THE MOTIVATION PROCESS

Motivation is the part of an individual that causes the person to behave in a way that will ensure the attainment of some goal.

A ***need*** is the lack of something desired or perceived as necessary, or the difference between what an individual has and what the person would like to have.

Goal-supportive behavior is any preliminary behavior that makes goal behavior possible.

Perhaps the most often discussed topic in human relations is employee motivation. **Motivation** is the part of an individual that causes the person to behave in a way that will ensure the attainment of some goal.

Probably the most fundamental model used to describe the motivation process is the needs-goal model of motivation. As its name implies, needs and goals are the two main parts of this model (see Figure 7.1). According to this model, motivation starts when an individual feels a **need**—the lack of something desired or perceived as necessary. A need can also be thought of as representing the difference between what an individual has and what the person would like to have.

Needs lead to **goal-supportive behavior**—any preliminary behavior that makes goal behavior possible. **Goal behavior** is behavior aimed specifically at reducing or eliminating a need. The individual continues to exhibit goal-supportive behavior and goal behavior until the felt need has been appropriately reduced or eliminated.

BUSINESS PRACTICE EXAMPLE Continues

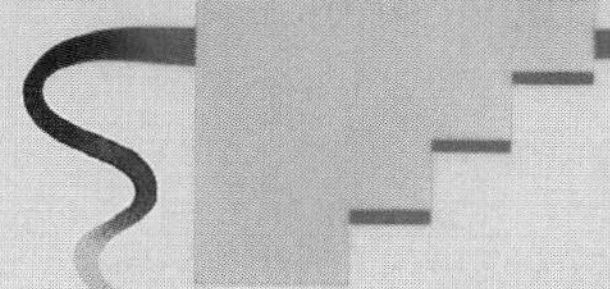

An important lesson that the Hawthorne studies taught us is that as people feel more valued and important, they tend to work harder. "Make your number!" was the key operating phrase that set Avis on the road to recovery. The Don Kelly regime under CEO J. Patrick Barrett's management was able to motivate Avis people to try harder, first by setting reasonable goals and making clear what was demanded from employees to reach them, and second by letting everyone know that their salaries would be dependent on their making good. At the same time, they were given responsibility to devise their own best ways to reach the goals. This approach quickly put Avis back in the black; but later, as the managers and employees worked together to set worker goals, Avis was able to increase profits to 30%. This "working together" clearly illustrated that management felt workers were an important and respected part of goal-setting and goal attainment at Avis.

To visualize this model, think about a person who is hungry. The desire for food (need) causes the individual to buy and prepare food (goal-supportive behavior). Next, the individual eats the food (goal behavior). The individual will continue to perform the goal-supportive and goal behaviors of buying, preparing, and eating whenever hunger arises. Although this example is simple and universal, it illuminates the basic process that must exist if any goal is to be attained.

Goal behavior is behavior aimed specifically at reducing or eliminating a need.

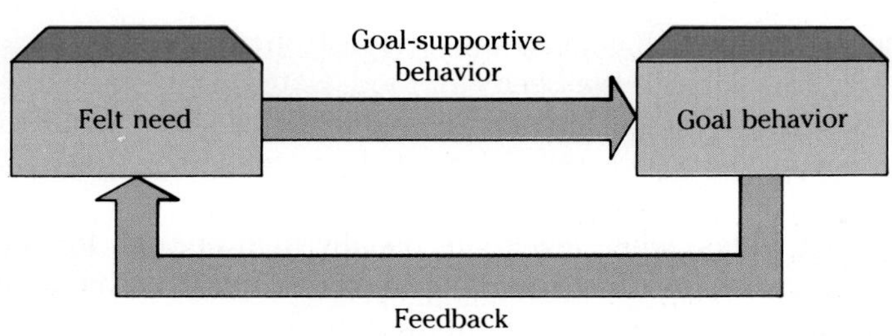

Figure 7.1
The needs-goal model of motivation—one of the fundamental models used to describe the motivation process.

Figure 7.2
Maslow theorized that humans possess five basic needs, which are arranged in a hierarchy of importance.

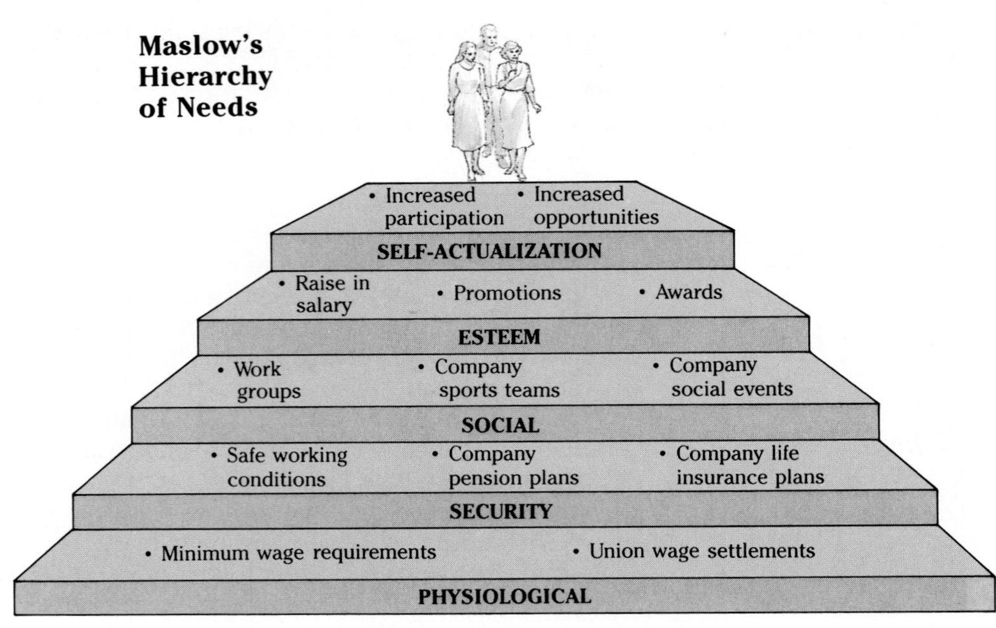

Maslow's Hierarchy of Needs

The ***hierarchy of needs*** is the concept, developed by Abraham Maslow, that humans have five basic needs arranged in a hierarchy of importance—from most basic to least basic: physiological needs, security needs, social needs, esteem needs, and self-actualization needs.

The motivation process involves human needs. Probably the most widely accepted description of these needs is the **hierarchy of needs** developed by the motivational psychologist Abraham Maslow.[2]

According to Maslow, humans have needs of five types: physiological, security, social, esteem, and self-actualization. Maslow has arranged these needs in a hierarchy of importance, in the order in which individuals generally strive to satisfy them. Figure 7.2 shows each need and its position in the hierarchy. An important aspect of Maslow's concept is that an individual will concentrate on satisfying basic needs before turning to the others.

Physiological Needs

Physiological needs are the needs involved in keeping the body functioning normally—the most basic survival needs in Maslow's hierarchy.

At the base of Maslow's hierarchy are **physiological needs**—the most basic survival needs; they include the needs for food, water, air, rest, clothing, and sex. Until these needs are met, a significant portion of an individual's behavior is aimed at satisfying them. Once they are satisfied, the person goes on to the next level of needs.

In the United States, wage levels are usually high enough for individuals to satisfy their basic needs. Thus, the other needs in Maslow's hierarchy normally have a more major role in worker motivation. This may not be the case for individuals in less developed countries, however.

Security Needs

Needs related to individuals keeping themselves free from harm are **security needs,** the second level in Maslow's hierarchy. The harm includes both bodily disaster (getting hit by a car, for example) and economic disaster (getting fired from a job, for example). Behavior aimed at satisfying security needs includes wearing protective clothing such as goggles or steel-toed shoes while working in a factory.

Security needs are needs related to keeping oneself free from harm; they are the second level of needs in Maslow's hierarchy.

Social Needs

The desire for love, companionship, and friendship—the desire to be accepted by others—is labeled **social needs.** To satisfy these needs in the workplace, a person might lunch or take breaks with certain people or join a committee.

Social needs are needs for love, companionship, and friendship—the desire to be accepted by others; they are the third level of needs in Maslow's hierarchy.

Esteem Needs

Needs for respect are **esteem needs.** These needs are generally divided into two basic types: the need for self-respect and the need to be respected by others. To satisfy esteem needs at work, an individual might try to achieve the honor of being chosen employee of the month or salesperson of the week.

Esteem needs are needs for respect; they are the fourth level in Maslow's hierarchy.

Self-Actualization Needs

Needs to maximize one's potential are **self-actualization needs.** As Figure 7.2 shows, they are at the final level of Maslow's hierarchy. A high school principal might attempt to become the best principal he possibly could be. An accountant might work hard to become the best in her field. Both are striving to satisfy their self-actualization needs.

Self-actualization needs are needs to maximize potential, to be the very best the person can be; they are the fifth and final level in Maslow's hierarchy.

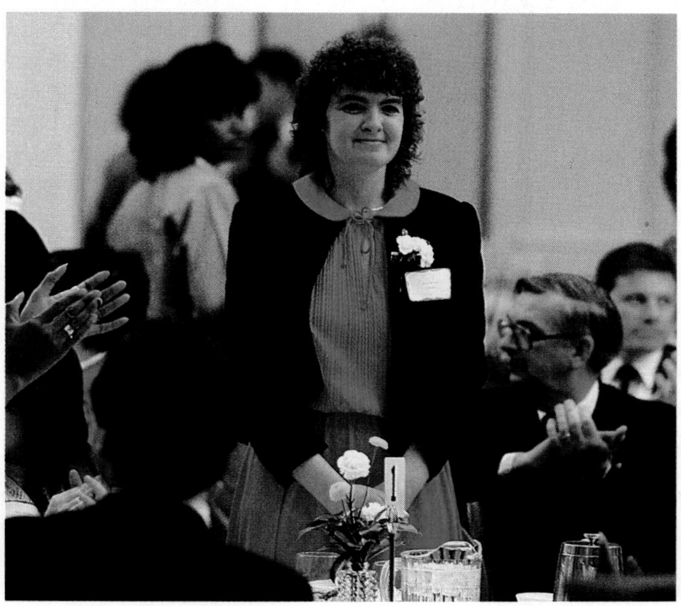

The psychologist Abraham Maslow termed the need for self-respect and respect from others *esteem needs.* This employee's esteem needs are being fulfilled by a formal recognition of outstanding achievement.

Evaluating Maslow's Hierarchy of Needs

Maslow's hierarchy has gained wide acceptance, and many management theorists readily admit that it can be useful in understanding human needs. Others, however, have reservations about it. They question whether Maslow has accurately pinpointed five basic needs and whether such needs really are arranged in a hierarchy. Because of these reservations, Maslow's hierarchy should be viewed more as a subjective statement about human needs than as an objective description of them.

Motivating Organization Members: Building Organizations People Like

To motivate employees, managers should provide them with opportunities to satisfy their needs by performing productive activities.

The following sections will cover several strategies for motivating organization members: Theory X, Theory Y, Theory Z, behavior modification, and management by objectives.

Theory X and Theory Y

One motivation strategy that is consistent with modern human relations thought focuses on the assumptions managers make about human nature. Douglas McGregor has identified two sets of these assumptions, which he has termed Theory X and Theory Y (see Figure 7.3).[3]

Theory X is the set of managerial assumptions that people dislike work, must be forced to work under threat of punishment, want to be controlled, and desire security above all else.

Theory Y is the set of managerial assumptions that work is natural, that people will work to achieve objectives to which they are committed, that commitment is tied to rewards, that many people want responsibility, and that people can use imagination and talent in solving problems.

Theory X is the set of managerial assumptions that people dislike work, must be forced to work under threat of punishment, want to be controlled, and desire security above all else. These assumptions present a rather dismal view of workers and the work situation. Managers who hold Theory X assumptions might constantly monitor and bully employees and intimidate them with threats of dismissal. Theory X focuses on the first two levels of needs in Maslow's hierarchy: physiological and security needs.

Theory Y is the set of managerial assumptions that work is as natural as play and rest, that people will work hard to achieve objectives to which they are committed, that commitment is tied to rewards, that many people want and seek responsibility, and that people can use imagination and talent in solving organizational problems. Managers who use Theory Y assumptions might give employees responsibilities, encourage them to come up with their own ways of fulfilling them, and reward them for jobs well done. Theory Y focuses on the higher levels of needs in Maslow's hierarchy: social, esteem, and self-actualization needs.

McGregor suggests that managers are better off using Theory Y assumptions than Theory X assumptions. The basic rationale for using Theory Y is that it is likelier than Theory X to satisfy the human needs of employees and therefore likelier to motivate employees to do their jobs well.

Theory Z is a management philosophy for motivating organization members through a combination of Japanese and American management practices.

Theory Z

Valuable insights about motivation have been gained through studying Japanese management methods and comparing them to American methods. One such comparison was made by management theorist William Ouchi, who developed what he called **Theory Z,** a management philosophy for motivating organization

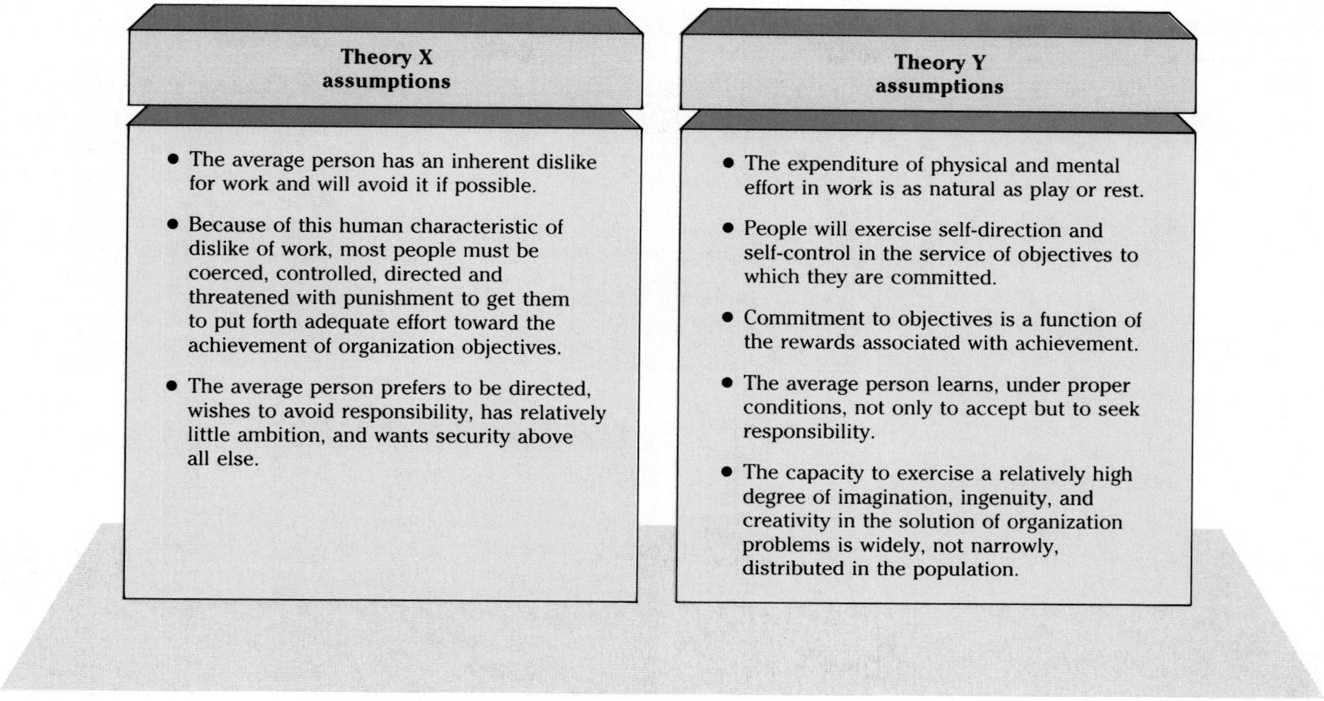

Theory X assumptions	Theory Y assumptions
• The average person has an inherent dislike for work and will avoid it if possible. • Because of this human characteristic of dislike of work, most people must be coerced, controlled, directed and threatened with punishment to get them to put forth adequate effort toward the achievement of organization objectives. • The average person prefers to be directed, wishes to avoid responsibility, has relatively little ambition, and wants security above all else.	• The expenditure of physical and mental effort in work is as natural as play or rest. • People will exercise self-direction and self-control in the service of objectives to which they are committed. • Commitment to objectives is a function of the rewards associated with achievement. • The average person learns, under proper conditions, not only to accept but to seek responsibility. • The capacity to exercise a relatively high degree of imagination, ingenuity, and creativity in the solution of organization problems is widely, not narrowly, distributed in the population.

Figure 7.3 McGregor's Theory X and Theory Y. McGregor believes managers should possess Theory Y assumptions about human nature.

members through a combination of Japanese and American management practices. Ouchi studied the following management practices in U.S. and Japanese firms:

- The length of time workers were employed.
- The way decisions were made.
- Where responsibility existed.
- The rate at which employees were evaluated and promoted.
- The control tools used.
- The concern shown for employees.

The results of his study are presented in Figure 7.4. As the figure shows, Ouchi believes that organization type Z (a modified American organization) is the best one for managing and maintaining employee motivation. This type of organization is a combination of organization type A (an American organization) and organization type J (a Japanese organization). Theory Z organization emphasizes motivating organization members by employing workers for the long term, making decisions in groups, encouraging individuals to assume responsibility, controlling informally, not making career paths too narrow, and being concerned for the whole worker—including the person's family.

Figure 7.4
Theory Z—American practices combined with Japanese practices.

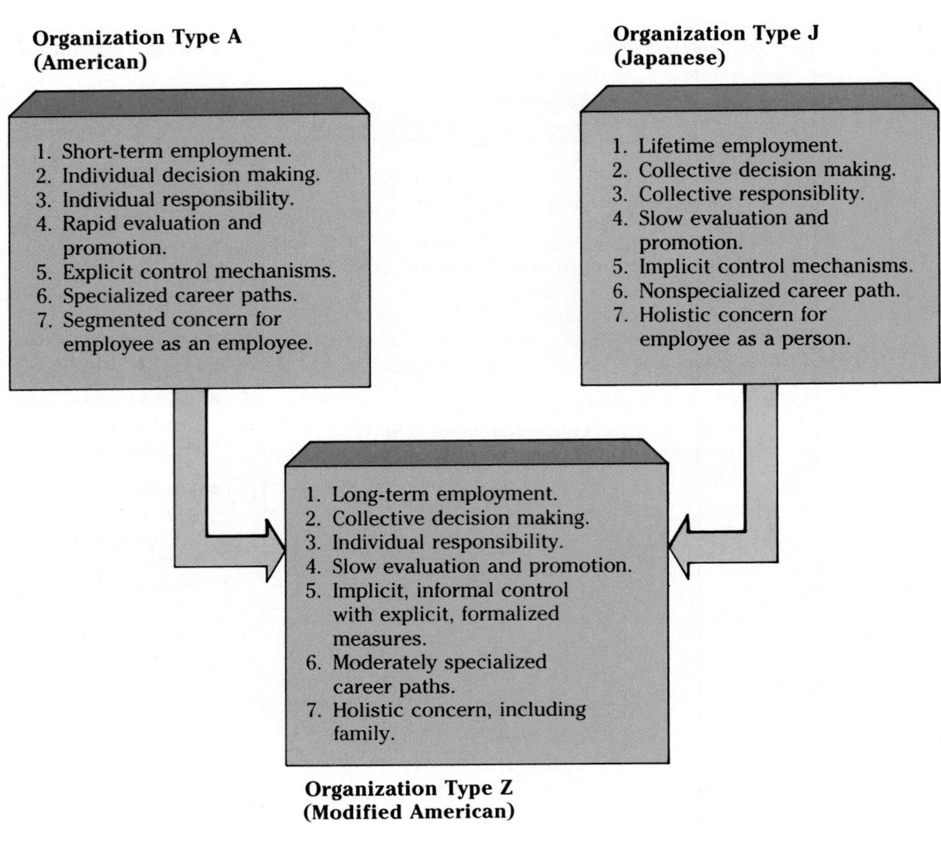

Organization Type A (American)
1. Short-term employment.
2. Individual decision making.
3. Individual responsibility.
4. Rapid evaluation and promotion.
5. Explicit control mechanisms.
6. Specialized career paths.
7. Segmented concern for employee as an employee.
Organization Type J (Japanese)
1. Lifetime employment.
2. Collective decision making.
3. Collective responsiblity.
4. Slow evaluation and promotion.
5. Implicit control mechanisms.
6. Nonspecialized career path.
7. Holistic concern for employee as a person.
1. Long-term employment.
2. Collective decision making.
3. Individual responsibility.
4. Slow evaluation and promotion.
5. Implicit, informal control with explicit, formalized measures.
6. Moderately specialized career paths.
7. Holistic concern, including family.
Organization Type Z (Modified American)

The Theory Z concept has gained much popularity. Many American managers, including some at companies like Chrysler, have reported that Theory Z works. Some caution should be exercised in applying the Theory Z concept, however. Differences between the American and Japanese cultures may place limits on the value of Theory Z. More research must be done to determine the true worth of Ouchi's theory.

Behavior Modification

Behavior modification is the process of encouraging desirable behavior through the use of rewards and punishments.

Another strategy that is consistent with modern human relations thought and that managers can use in motivating organization members is behavior modification. A concept developed by psychologist B. F. Skinner, **behavior modification** is the process of encouraging desirable behavior through the use of rewards and punishments.[4] It is based on the premise that behavior that is rewarded tends to be repeated and behavior that is punished tends to be eliminated. Although behavior modification programs typically involve the administration of both rewards and punishments, rewards are generally emphasized. They are typically considered to be more effective long-term influencers of behavior than are punishments.

BUSINESS PRACTICE EXAMPLE Continues

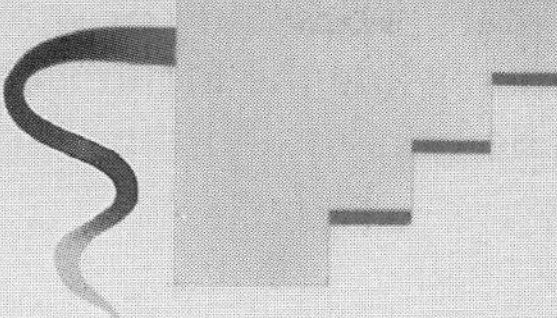

In the spring of 1987, J. Patrick Barrett explained in a CNN interview why Avis seemed poised for renewed takeoff: He felt the company had turned itself around, regaining self-respect after living through an interval of harsh—"Theory X"—management. As the owners permitted a new approach to take hold—a period of "Theory Y" management—the company recovered its pride in the "Try Harder" ethic. Also, Barrett felt the current owners' plan to give 24% equity in the firm to 50 top managers would serve as a fresh motivating force. In fact, the company that year delivered on its potential with a sharp rise of almost 30% in profits for the first time during the 1980s. By the fall of 1987, the employees had taken the initiative, buying out a controlling interest in Avis from the new conglomerate under an Employee Stock Ownership Plan. Now fully in control of their own destiny, company managers and workers have a good chance, in the opinion of industry analysts, to try for the Number One spot against Hertz in a new round of price wars.

A manager who wants to modify an employee's behavior must ensure that appropriate consequences occur as a result of the new behavior. Suppose, for example, an employee is constantly late. If the manager rewards the behavior of arriving on time, the worker will probably arrive on time more often. Conversely, if the worker is punished for arriving late, that person will probably be late less frequently.

Although punishment stops behavior quickly, it may be accompanied by unwanted side-effects, such as high turnover and absenteeism, if it is emphasized over the long term. These side-effects are signals that the organization does not reflect the principles of modern human relations.

One company that has taken steps to reward appropriate behavior in a way that is consistent with behavior modification theory is Nabisco Brands. The board of directors of Nabisco has endorsed a compensation program that allows management to reward productive employees in a special way:

> The program consists of two separate plans: an annual incentive award plan, under which annual cash awards may be made to key employees, and a long-term performance share plan, under which awards, payable in cash or shares of the company's common stock, may be made to a smaller group of key employees with payments contingent upon the achievement of pre-established company earnings growth goals over four-year performance periods. The program will be administered by the compensation committee, no member of which may participate in the program.

In the opinion of the board of directors, the program will benefit the company and its shareholders by (a) attracting, motivating and retaining executives of outstanding ability, (b) providing incentives based on pre-established performance objectives, and (c) with respect to the long-term performance share plan, increasing the identification of key executives with the company and its shareholders by affording increased ownership of company stock.[5]

Management by Objectives

Management by objectives (MBO) is the management philosophy in which the primary management tool is the process of setting and monitoring performance targets for organization members.

The management philosophy in which the primary management tool is the process of setting and monitoring performance targets for organization members is **management by objectives (MBO).** Some managers believe that management by objectives best motivates people, in a human relations–oriented fashion, to work productively. The idea is that employees will be more highly motivated if they participate in the process of setting goals and monitoring their progress toward them.

The MBO strategy, which has been popularized mainly through the writings of Peter Drucker, has three basic parts:

1. All individuals within an organization are assigned a specialized set of objectives, which they try to reach during a normal operating period, perhaps a three-month, six-month, or twelve-month period. In each case, these objectives are mutually set and agreed upon by the individual and the manager. A sales manager and a sales representative may decide, for example, that the rep's objective will be to increase sales in the assigned territory by 15 percent. Both the manager and the rep agree that this is a reasonable goal to shoot for.
2. Performance reviews are conducted periodically to determine how close individuals are to attaining their objectives. The sales rep may aim to produce the 15 percent increase in six months, for example. Periodically, at one-month or two-month intervals perhaps, the manager and the rep will review the sales in the territory to determine if the goal is being achieved.
3. At the end of the operating period rewards are given to organization members on the basis of how close they came to reaching their goals. For example, the sales rep may be paid a bonus if sales actually did increase by 15 percent.[6]

The MBO process contains five steps (see Figure 7.5):

1. *Reviewing organizational objectives.* The manager gains a clear understanding of the organization's overall objectives.
2. *Setting worker objectives.* The manager and worker meet to agree on worker objectives to be reached by the end of the normal operating period.
3. *Monitoring progress.* At intervals during the normal operating period, the manager and worker check to see if the objectives are being reached.
4. *Evaluating performance.* At the end of the normal operating period, the worker's performance is judged on the extent to which the worker reached the objectives.
5. *Giving rewards.* Rewards are given to the worker on the basis of the extent to which the objectives were reached.

MBO programs have been used extensively in organizations of various types. The Columbia Broadcasting System (CBS), for example, has used it in all of its companies and enterprises. Black and Decker has also used the program, with

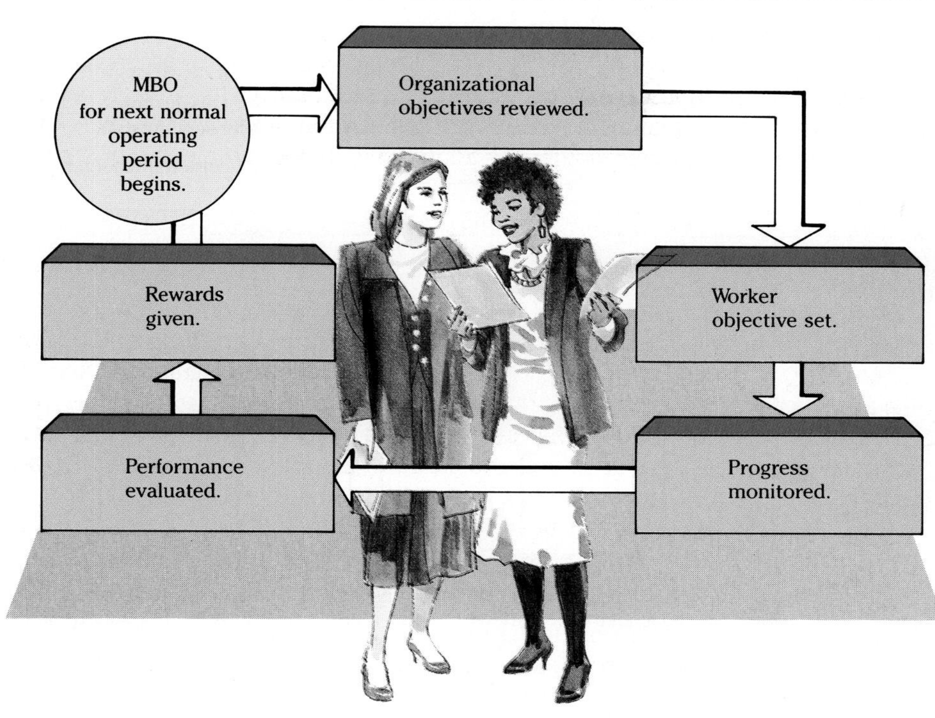
MBO for next normal operating period begins.
Organizational objectives reviewed.
Worker objective set.
Progress monitored.
Performance evaluated.
Rewards given.

Figure 7.5
The MBO process.

excellent results. There is no single kind of company in which the MBO program works best. Rather its success depends on how carefully and realistically the objectives are set. Managers indicate that MBO has the significant advantage of constantly emphasizing what must be done to achieve organizational objectives. MBO programs can, however, be time-consuming and costly. Managers must be careful to use them as a means to the end of organizational goal attainment, not as an end in themselves.

In any enterprise, leadership is critical to management success. The leadership style of the chief executive officer of Allen-Bradley will determine how the organizational goals will be implemented.

LEADERSHIP

Leadership is critical to management success in any enterprise. We can discuss the leadership of Billy Martin as the manager of the New York Yankees, George Bush as the president of the United States, or Lee Iacocca as the chief executive officer of Chrysler. This part of the chapter will examine leader behavior and leadership styles as well as situational leadership.

Leader Behavior and Leadership Styles

Robert Tannenbaum and Warren Schmidt conducted one of the first and most well known studies on leadership. Their study focused on how leaders make decisions.[7] Figure 7.6 presents the Tannenbaum/Schmidt model of leadership behavior.

The model is actually a continuum, or range, of leader behavior that is available to the manager who is making decisions. Each type of decision-making behavior

Figure 7.6

The Tannenbaum/Schmidt continuum of leader behavior. The behavior ranges from boss-centered to subordinate-centered.

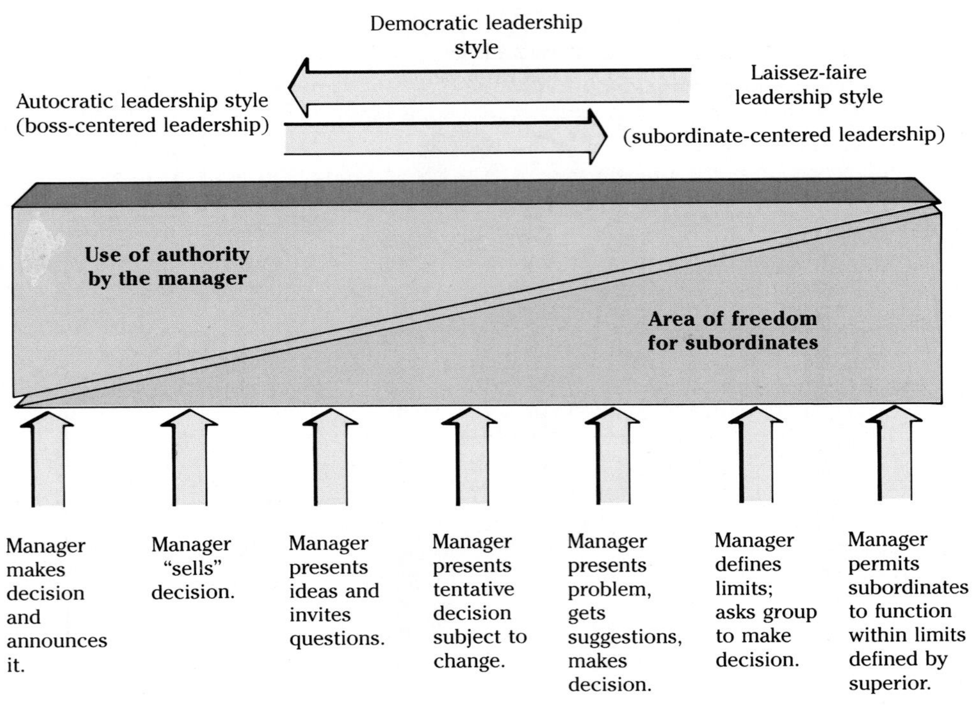
Democratic leadership style
Laissez-faire leadership style
Autocratic leadership style (boss-centered leadership)
(subordinate-centered leadership)
Use of authority by the manager
Area of freedom for subordinates
Manager makes decision and announces it.
Manager "sells" decision.
Manager presents ideas and invites questions.
Manager presents tentative decision subject to change.
Manager presents problem, gets suggestions, makes decision.
Manager defines limits; asks group to make decision.
Manager permits subordinates to function within limits defined by superior.

HIGHLIGHT IN BUSINESS PRACTICE

Human Relations: Tom Peters' Principle

In 1982, a management consultant named Tom Peters wrote a controversial book about success in the business community at large entitled *In Search of Excellence.* The book was an instant best-seller. In it, Peters identified eight characteristics of successful companies. According to the author, if you wanted to be a success, like IBM, 3M, or Hewlett-Packard (three of the companies Peters singled out) you needed to do the following:

1. *Create a bias for action.* Act immediately to solve problems and accommodate change and experiment to find solutions.

2. *Establish close customer contact.* Listen and incorporate customers' reactions to products and service into company operations. Learn to view customers as valuable sources for new product ideas or improvements.

3. *Promote autonomy and entrepreneurship.* Create an innovative work environment where risk and risk-takers are highly valued.

4. *Encourage productivity through people.* Respect your employees and give them an active role in company operations.

5. *Be hands-on and value driven.* Managers should establish and clearly communicate the company's corporate culture to all employees.

6. *Stick to the knitting.* Accomplish only that which is your company's mission to accomplish and give it your best shot.

7. *Stay simple and lean.* No matter what its size or mission, a company should enact an elegantly simple form of management.

8. *Stay simultaneously loose and tight.* Hold all employees strictly accountable to the organizational goals and, at the same time, set each employee free to solve problems in his or her own way.

That was what Tom Peters prescribed in 1982. In 1987, Peters' third book, *Thriving on Chaos,* was released. (Ironically, the exact date of publication was October 19, 1987, the day the stock market crashed.) *Thriving on Chaos* was written in response to managers' repeated and urgent requests for a more detailed program for attaining the level of excellence Peters described in *In Search of Excellence.* Peters produced forty-five prescriptions he says companies need, not even to excel, but to survive in today's rapidly-changing business environment. In *Thriving on Chaos,* Peters envisions the manufacturing floor as a hotbed of invention and improvement, where engineers work beside production workers. He urges that companies work with their suppliers as a team to determine and meet customers' needs. He urges executives to roam the company listening to employees' ideas and concerns.

Everyone in the organization should meet with and listen to customers—and then, Peters advises, act to implement customer suggestions by making use of small production runs aimed at specialized, even customized, niches in the market.

According to Peters, American businesses have never really focused on quality or customization in the marketplace. Instead they've concentrated on economies of scale through mass production. Similarly, American research has focused on big breakthroughs in technology rather than on smaller, consumer-oriented adaptations. Now Americans are watching the Japanese succeed with small, flexible production runs, a highly trained, non-specialized work force, and an orientation toward quality and customers' needs and desires.

Thus, Peters advocates sweeping changes in the way Americans do business. *Thriving on Chaos* is strong medicine indeed. It will be interesting to see who takes it.

in this model involves a certain degree of authority on the part of the manager and a related amount of freedom available to subordinates.

At the extreme left is the manager who makes a decision and announces it. This type of management behavior characterizes the leader who maintains tight control, allowing little freedom to subordinates. At the extreme right of the model is the manager who allows subordinates to help make decisions within certain limits. This type of management behavior characterizes the leader who exercises little control, allowing subordinates much freedom and self-direction. Between the extremes, the range of behaviors reflects a gradual change in the use of authority and the freedom of subordinates. Three leadership styles have been derived from this model: the autocratic style, the democratic style, and the laissez-faire style.

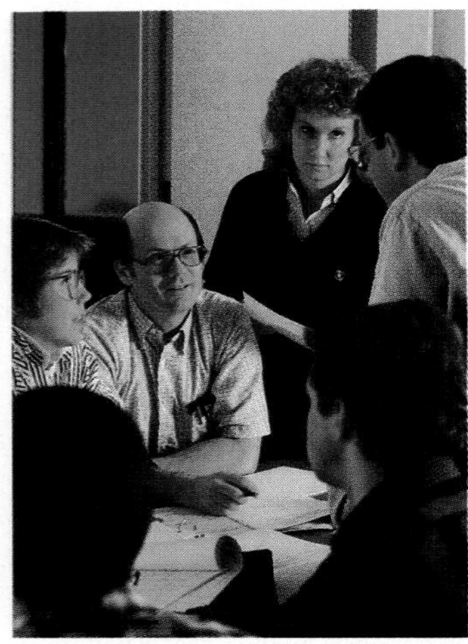

The democratic leadership style emphasizes allowing subordinates a voice in determining actions the leader will take. This leader is asking input for ideas and suggestions before taking action.

The ***autocratic leadership style*** is the pattern of leader behavior that emphasizes the use of authority in leading others.

The ***democratic leadership style*** is the pattern of leader behavior that emphasizes allowing others to have a voice in determining actions the leader takes.

The ***laissez-faire leadership style*** is the pattern of leader behavior that emphasizes autonomy for the workers.

Situational leadership is the leadership approach that recognizes that success in leading is determined by a leadership style appropriate to the followers being led and to the situation faced by the leader.

The Autocratic Leadership Style

The pattern of leader behavior that emphasizes the use of authority in leading others is the **autocratic leadership style.** This style is represented by the boss-centered leader in the Tannenbaum/Schmidt model. The autocratic leader issues orders telling people what to do, how to do it, and when to do it. This leadership style might be appropriate if the leader faces tight time constraints, but it could be a disaster if the leader is managing a group of highly qualified research scientists.

The Democratic Leadership Style

The pattern of leader behavior that emphasizes allowing others to have a voice in determining actions the leader takes is the **democratic leadership style.** This style appears at about the middle of the Tannenbaum/Schmidt model. The democratic manager presents subordinates with decisions that are subject to change. This type of leader commonly asks for input, ideas, and suggestions from subordinates and then takes action on the basis of the feedback. The style could be appropriate if the workers are highly experienced and able to analyze job-related problems. On the other hand, if workers have little experience and cannot analyze problems, such a leadership style could result in business failure.

The Laissez-faire Leadership Style

The pattern of leader behavior that emphasizes autonomy for the workers is the **laissez-faire leadership style.** This style is represented by the subordinate-centered leader in the Tannenbaum/Schmidt model. The laissez-faire leader allows followers much freedom in their work but must keep in touch to ensure that workers have clear ideas of the organizational goals and how to achieve them. This style is normally best suited for situations in which leaders know their workers well, the workers are able to perform their jobs well, and mutual trust exists between the leader and the workers. The style is also normally well suited for encouraging intrapreneurship (entrepreneurship within a large company).

Situational Leadership

The leadership approach that recognizes that success in leading is determined by a leadership style that is appropriate to the followers being led and to the situation faced by the leader is **situational leadership.** In formula form, situational leadership is SL = f(L, F, S). The equation means successful leadership (SL) is a function (f) of the leader (L), the follower (F), and the situation (S).

According to the situational approach to leadership, managers should not limit themselves to one leadership style. Instead, as changes occur in the characteristics of workers and of the situation, the leadership style should also change. Figure 7.7 makes this point by indicating that tomorrow's boss must be a leader/motivator who coaches teams as well as commanding them.

JOB DESIGN AND EMPLOYEE MOTIVATION

Another human relations–oriented strategy that a manager can use to motivate organization members relates to job design. The four main areas of job design are job rotation and job enlargement, job enrichment, flextime and job sharing.

Figure 7.7 Future managers must coach and command.

Job Rotation and Job Enlargement

There has been a movement in business to make jobs simpler and more specialized, thereby increasing worker productivity through greater efficiency.

Perhaps the best example of this movement is the development of the automobile assembly line. There is, however, a negative result of this simplicity. As work becomes simpler and more specialized, it typically becomes more boring and less satisfying. Thus productivity suffers.

Job rotation is moving a worker from job to job to keep the worker from becoming bored with doing a simple, specialized job over and over.

One major attempt to overcome boredom is **job rotation**—moving a worker from job to job to keep the person from having to perform one simple and specialized routine over and over. A gardener, for example, might be shifted from mowing lawns one day to trimming bushes, raking grass, or sweeping sidewalks on another day.

Job rotation programs have been known to increase organizational profitability in some cases. Over the long term, however, they tend to be ineffective because the worker eventually becomes bored with all the jobs. Job rotation is more effective for an individual who is being trained for a job that requires an overview of how various units of an organization function. A trainee in financial management, for example, will have a better understanding of how the finance division functions after working the accounts receivable, accounts payable, and payroll departments.

Job enlargement is adding operations or tasks to a job to keep the job from being boring.

Job enlargement—adding operations or tasks to a job—is another strategy to overcome the boredom of simple and specialized jobs. The theory is that jobs become more satisfying as the number of operations or tasks increases. The gardener, for example, might find the job more satisfying as trimming bushes, raking grass, and sweeping sidewalks are added to the initial job of mowing grass. As you might suspect, some research supports the notion that job enlargement makes jobs more satisfying, while some research does not. Generally, however, job enlargement programs have been more successful than job rotation programs in increasing employee satisfaction.

Job Enrichment

On the basis of extensive research, Frederick Herzberg[8] concluded that the degree of satisfaction and the degree of dissatisfaction felt by workers as a result of performing a job are two different variables and are determined by two different elements. The elements that influence the degree of job satisfaction are called **motivators.** Those that influence the degree of job dissatisfaction are called **hygiene factors.** Motivators relate to the work itself, and hygiene factors relate to the work environment. Table 7.1 describes the elements that make up Herzberg's motivators and hygiene factors.

According to Frederick Herzberg, ***motivators*** are elements that influence the degree of job satisfaction.

According to Frederick Herzberg, ***hygiene factors*** are elements that influence the degree of job dissatisfaction.

Hygiene factors include such things as company policy, salary, and relationships with other people, including supervisors. Herzberg claims that if hygiene factors are undesirable in a particular job situation, the organization member will become dissatisfied. If, for example, you do not get along with your boss and think that you are grossly underpaid, you will become dissatisfied with your job. Moreover, making these factors more desirable, perhaps by increasing your salary, will not motivate you to do a better job but merely will keep you from becoming dissatisfied. Generally, you will be motivated to do a better job only if motivators are high in the particular job situation.

Motivators include such things as the work, the responsibility it involves, the chances the worker has for achievement and recognition, and whether the job contributes to the worker's personal growth. In general, organization members tend to be more motivated and productive as more motivators are built into their

Table 7.1 Herzberg's hygiene factors and motivating factors.

Dissatisfaction: Hygiene or Maintenance Factors	Satisfaction: Motivating Factors
1. Company policy and administration.	1. Opportunity for achievement.
2. Supervision.	2. Opportunity for recognition.
3. Relationship with supervisor.	3. Work itself.
4. Relationship with peers.	4. Responsibility.
5. Working conditions.	5. Advancement.
6. Salary.	6. Personal growth.
7. Relationship with subordinates.	

Herzberg maintains that an employee's satisfaction or dissatisfaction with job performance is affected by motivation and hygiene factors.

job situation. Correspondingly, as motivators are added, human relations tend to become more positive.

The process of incorporating motivators into a job situation is called **job enrichment.** Enrichment is concerned not with such factors as salary, working conditions, and training, but rather with scope for personal achievement. Experience indicates that for job enrichment programs to be successful, they must be designed and administered carefully. An outline of a successful job enrichment program is presented in Table 7.2.

Job enrichment is the process of incorporating motivators into a job situation.

Flextime

A relatively recent job design strategy for motivating workers is based on the concept of flextime. **Flextime** (or flexible working hours) is a program that allows workers to complete their jobs within a workweek of a normal number of hours, which they schedule themselves. One of the most traditional characteristics of work performed in the United States is the workday of a fixed number of specified hours. Recently, however, this tradition has been challenged. Faced with the problems of absenteeism and lack of motivation, many managers are turning to time-scheduling innovations as a possible solution.

Flextime is a program that allows workers to complete their jobs within a workweek of a normal number of hours, which they schedule themselves.

These scheduling innovations are intended not to reduce the total number of hours worked but to provide greater flexibility in the exact hours worked. The choice of starting and finishing times can be as flexible as the organizational situation will allow. Workers may choose to come in at 6 o'clock in the morning and to leave early in the afternoon, for example. Or they may decide to arrive late and leave late. Most companies that are experimenting with flexible hours set a core time, maybe from 10 A.M. to 3 P.M., during which employees must be present. The typical flextime program is summarized in Figure 7.8.

Various kinds of organizational studies show that flextime programs seem to have positive effects. One researcher, for example, reported that flextime contributes to job satisfaction, which typically results in greater productivity. Other

Table 7.2 Successful job enrichment programs are carefully designed and administered.

Specific Changes Aimed at Enriching Jobs	"Motivators" Aimed at Increasing Satisfaction
1. Removing some controls while retaining accountability.	Responsibility and personal achievement.
2. Increasing the accountability of individuals for their own work.	Responsibility and recognition.
3. Giving a person a complete natural unit of work (module, division, area, and so on).	Responsibility, achievement, and recognition.
4. Granting additional authority to an employee in his or her activity; job freedom.	Responsibility, achievement, and recognition.
5. Making periodic reports directly available to the worker, rather than to the supervisor.	Internal recognition.
6. Introducing new and more difficult tasks not previously handled.	Growth and learning.
7. Assigning individuals specific or specialized tasks, enabling them to become expert.	Responsibility, growth, and advancement.

investigations conclude that flextime programs can motivate workers. Although many well-known companies—including Scott Paper, Sun Oil, and Samsonite—have decided to adopt flextime programs, further research must be conducted to assess their worth.

Job Sharing

Job sharing is a program through which two part-time employees hold the job of one full-time employee.

The last job design strategy to be discussed in this section is **job sharing**—a program through which two part-time employees hold the job of one full-time employee. Job sharing allows individuals who already have part of their time

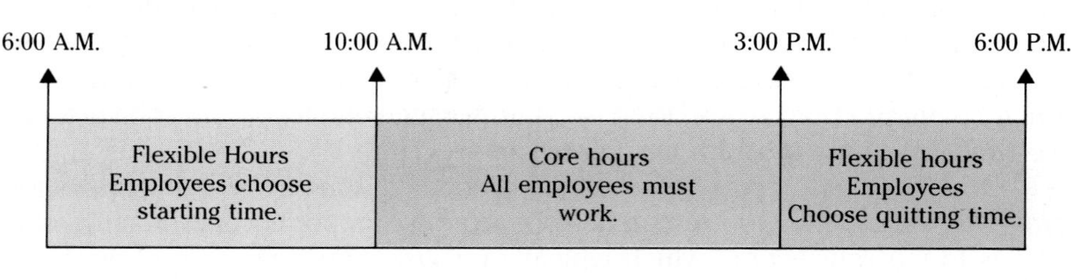

Figure 7.8
The typical flextime program requires employees to work core hours but allows them flexibility in starting and quitting times.

committed to hold a job. Job sharers are typically mothers with young children or students who can work only part time.

By allowing individuals to share jobs, organizations gain two advantages: (1) motivated workers, since employees are generally pleased with the opportunity to work this way; and (2) less tired workers, since job sharing employees work only about four hours a day. A potential disadvantage of job sharing is that because

HIGHLIGHT IN BUSINESS PRACTICE

Human Relations at Procter & Gamble

When John Smale was a young man, he joined a new venture that hoped to make a fortune, or at least a profit, from nose drops. An industrious sort, he had an ambitious program. As he tells it: "I put the thing together, got the packaging done, ran the test market, placed the advertising, and did the market research calls and all of that."

His method was sound. His financial backing was not, and that first company didn't last long. But when Smale answered a recruiting ad in the *Chicago Tribune,* he found a company that not only thinks his way, but was also financially sound. It was a union fortunate for both parties.

Procter & Gamble, the company that placed the ad, is now a $17 billion operation observing its sesquicentennial. And John G. Smale is now its seventh chief executive officer, about 38 years after he tried to sell nose drops in a way uncannily similar to Procter's fabled method.

Smale has been at Procter for 35 years. That sort of career is not a rarity, but the rule. The first P&G employee, a jack-of-all-trades named Barney Krieger, stayed 47 years. The company goes to great lengths to keep its good people. It pioneered shorter hours for workers, and profit sharing. Today, it offers extraordinary benefits and progressive personnel programs. It entrusts its young managers with great responsibility, pays them well, and makes a promise it hasn't broken in 150 years: all promotion will be from within. No one ever works hard for years only to see someone brought in from another company to take the job he or she covets.

All of which creates great loyalty to the company. "I think our people feel an identification with the company, and an affection," Smale says. "They like their fellow employees." When Procter asked its workers to suggest a motto for its sesquicentennial, over 8,000 responded. The winner was, "Excellence Through Commitment & Innovation."

That commitment comes from people Smale describes as: "Bright. Aggressive. Competitive. People who want to win. People who are comfortable with the character of the company. We don't put up with intellectual dishonesty.

"Our business is really a business of young people. The change is constant and you have to keep up with it. One important way you do it is with people who are in tune with it."

Under Smale, P&G has continued to respond to changes in the workplace. More women work at all levels of the company, and that created a need for child care. The company now has liberal maternity—and paternity—leave, and provided start-up funding for two daycare facilities located near the company headquarters. These programs cover adoptive parents as well. As more of its employees became concerned with fitness, Procter responded with a new corporate-fitness center and stress-reduction seminars.

the employees work part time, they may have less commitment to the job than would a full-time worker. Another disadvantage is that since two employees work the job of one, management may have to spend more time supervising and coordinating their work.

THE MANAGERIAL GRID

The ***managerial grid*** is a model that describes various combinations of concern for people and concern for production that managers can use to relate to their subordinates.

Another human relations–oriented area in motivating organization members is the **managerial grid.**[9] The grid is based on the idea that managerial styles can be described by means of two primary attitudes of managers: concern for people and concern for production. In the grid, each attitude is placed on an axis, is scaled 1 through 9, and is used to identify five major managerial styles. Figure 7.9 illustrates the managerial grid and lists the characteristics of each managerial style.

Figure 7.9
Managerial grid. Managers with an ideal style (9, 9 on the managerial grid) are equally concerned about people and production.

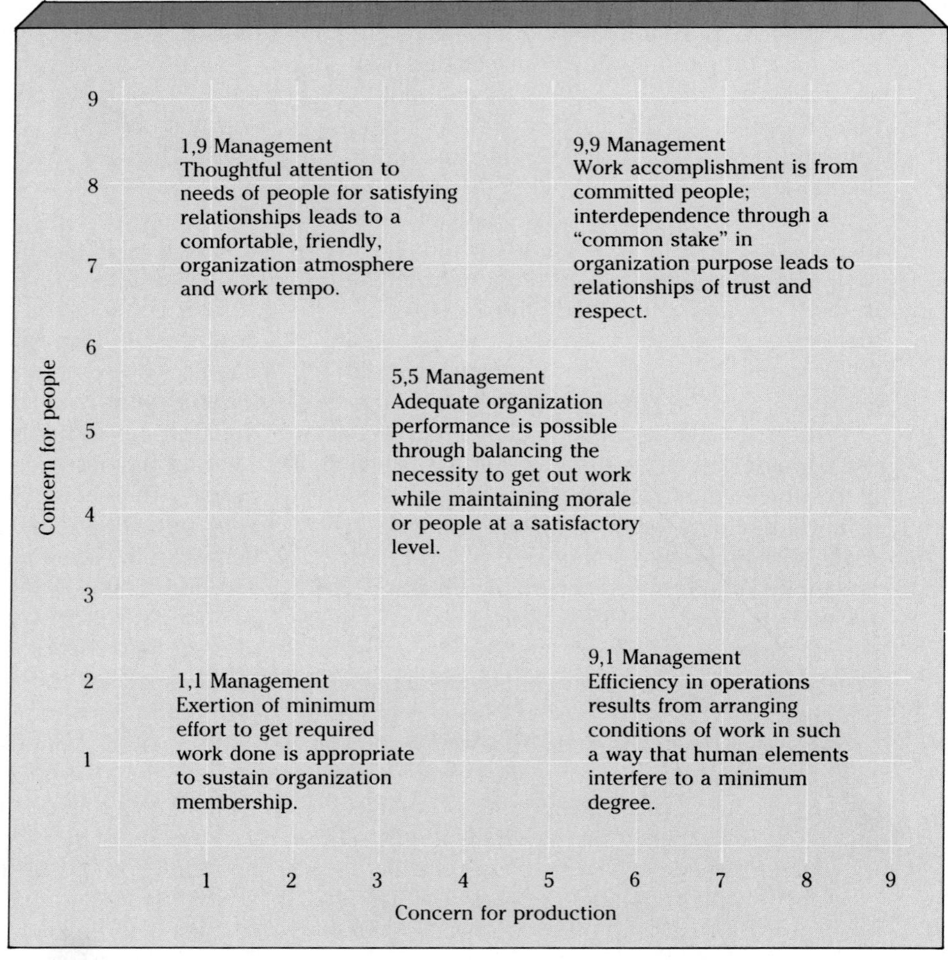

The main point of the managerial grid is that the 9, 9 management style is the ideal style. Managers having this style show high levels of concern for both people and production. They are generally seen as contributing to the development of positive human relations. Correspondingly, managers having any other style show lesser degrees of concern for people or production and are generally seen as contributing less to the development of positive human relations.

BUSINESS PRACTICE EXAMPLE Continues

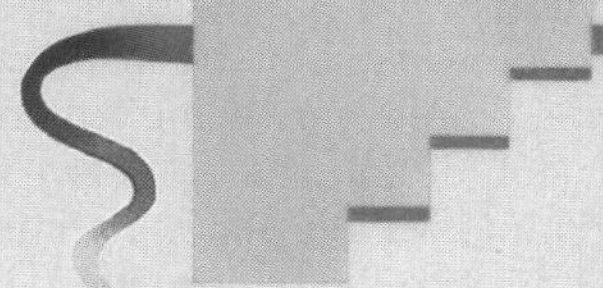

It is interesting to look back over the course of Avis's management history during the 1980s to see where they might fit in the "Managerial Grid" scheme.

In phase 1, before profits took a nosedive, Avis's "Try Harder" attitude had possibly softened to the point where concern for people had overcome concern for productivity, resulting in a lack of readiness for competitive pressure and eventually a loss of jobs and confidence.

During phase 2 in 1982, the pendulum swung to the opposite side; with David Mahoney looking over everyone's shoulder, concern for production seemed more apparent than concern for people.

In phase 3 under Kelly and Barrett, the "make your number" hands-off policy seems to have produced a balance in the center of the grid, with adequate levels of performance.

Finally in phase 4, new management seemed highly concerned for both people and production. Managers and employees became committed to their own goals and exceeded them, eventually achieving a "common stake" in good results through control of their own company.

Issues for Discussion

1. What elements in the basic human motivation process can be identified in the early phases of goal-setting at Avis? What needs were involved, how were goals set?
2. To what extent did David Mahoney's regime at Avis fit the "Theory X" model? In what ways did anyone later adopt a "Theory Y" approach? Do you see any evidence eventually of a "Theory Z" pattern at work? Explain.
3. What scores would you give on the "Managerial Grid" system for each of the four phases identified above in the history of Avis' management in the 1980s? Why?

SUMMARY

Human relations is the area of study that is concerned primarily with finding the best way to work and deal with people in organizations. It is generally agreed that the study of human relations began with the Hawthorne studies, which were conducted between 1924 and 1932 by Elton Mayo.

Human relations focuses on understanding the motivation process. Motivation is the part of an individual that causes behavior of a sort that will ensure the attainment of some goal. The needs-goal model of motivation describes the motivation process as a series of steps in which an individual feels a need, performs some behavior aimed at reducing this need, and then evaluates feedback to determine if the need has been satisfied and the behavior can stop or if the need has not been satisfied and the behavior should continue.

Maslow's hierarchy of needs theorizes that individuals have five basic needs, in the following order of importance: physiological needs, security needs, social needs, esteem needs, and self-actualization needs. According to Maslow's concept, as fundamental needs are satisfied, individuals tend to emphasize satisfying more advanced needs.

In order to motivate people in organizations, managers should provide them with opportunities to satisfy their individual needs through productive behavior. Appropriate assumptions about people (Theory Y), the use of rewards and punishments (behavior modification), a combination of American and Japanese business practices (Theory Z), and setting and monitoring performance objectives for people (management by objectives) are all tools that can help managers motivate workers.

Leadership is an important part of motivation. Autocratic leaders emphasize their authority in leading others, democratic leaders emphasize allowing followers to have a voice in what the leader does, and laissez-faire leaders emphasize worker autonomy. According to the situational theory of leadership, the leader should act according to the type of followers being led and the situation being faced.

Job design strategies give managers valuable insights into motivation. Job enrichment, which incorporates motivators into the job situation, is probably the most effective of such job design strategies for the long term. Job enlargement and job rotation can be effective in the short term but tend to be less effective in the longer term. Flextime tries to motivate people by allowing them to design their own work schedules. Job sharing attempts to motivate people by allowing two part-time workers to share the job of one full-time worker.

The managerial grid also furnishes insights into motivation. According to this concept, managers who stress both concern for production and concern for people will be successful not only in motivating workers but also in reaching organizational objectives.

KEY TERMS

Autocratic leadership style p. 208
Behavior modification p. 202
Democratic leadership style p. 208
Esteem needs p. 199
Flextime p. 211
Goal behavior p. 197
Goal-supportive behavior p. 196
Hawthorne effect p. 196
Hawthorne studies p. 196
Hierarchy of needs p. 198
Human relations p. 195
Hygiene factors p. 210
Job enlargement p. 210
Job enrichment p. 211
Job rotation p. 210
Job sharing p. 212
Laissez-faire leadership style p. 208
Management by objectives (MBO) p. 204
Managerial grid p. 214
Morale p. 195
Motivation p. 196
Motivators p. 210
Need p. 196
Physiological needs p. 198
Security needs p. 199
Self-actualization needs p. 199
Situational leadership p. 208
Social needs p. 199
Theory X p. 200
Theory Y p. 200
Theory Z p. 200

CHECK YOUR LEARNING

Reread the following learning objectives. Each objective is followed by a few questions. Answering these questions accurately will help you retain the most important concepts discussed in this chapter. After answering each question, check your answer with the key at the end of this chapter. (*Hint:* If you have doubt regarding the correct response, consult the page whose number follows the answer.)

Circle:

A. Describe human relations in organizations and in the Hawthorne studies.

T F 1. Human relations is an area of study that focuses mainly on technology and planning.

T F 2. The Hawthorne studies showed that how people are treated can influence how productive they are.

B. Discuss the human motivation process.

a b c d e 1. Perhaps the most fundamental model of motivation contains elements regarding: (a) needs; (b) feedback; (c) money; (d) a and c; (e) a and b.

T F 2. Goal behavior comes after goal-supportive behavior.

C. Draw a diagram of and discuss Maslow's hierarchy of needs.

T F 1. Physiological needs include the need for companionship.

T F 2. According to Maslow, esteem needs generally include the desire for both self-respect and respect from others.

T F 3. Maslow's hierarchy is an objective description of human needs.

D. Explain how managers motivate employees.

T F 1. Basically, managers motivate employees by giving them opportunities.

T F 2. People behave in certain ways to satisfy needs.

E. Describe Theory X, Theory Y, Theory Z, and behavior modification.

a b c d 1. Which of the following is a Theory X assumption: (a) work is like play; (b) most people must be threatened to work; (c) people learn quickly; (d) people are imaginative.

T F 2. Behavior modification emphasizes punishments more than rewards.

T F 3. Consequences influence behavior.

F. Discuss motivation through management by objectives, leadership, and the managerial grid.

T F 1. The MBO process entails little input from subordinates.

T F 2. Boss-centered and subordinate-centered are two different decision-making methods.

T F 3. The managerial grid recommends a 9, 9 management style for most situations.

G. Explain various job design strategies for motivating employees.

T F 1. Job enlargement has been successful in motivating employees.

T F 2. Job rotation and job enlargement are essentially the same.

T F 3. Job enrichment includes building an opportunity for employee growth into the job situation.

T F 4. Job sharing involves full-time employees sharing several jobs.

QUESTIONS FOR REVIEW AND DISCUSSION

1. Define the key terms listed at the end of the chapter.
2. Use the needs-goal model of motivation to explain why you are enrolled in this course.
3. How do students function in school when they are attempting to satisfy self-actualization needs?
4. Discuss the role of opportunity in motivating organization members.
5. Would you like to work for a manager who held Theory X assumptions? Explain.
6. Would you prefer to work in a Theory Z organization or a more traditional U.S. organization? Explain.
7. How might an MBO program and behavior modification be used together?
8. Evaluate a familiar organization by using Peters and Waterman's characteristics of excellently run companies.
9. Under what conditions should managers use boss-centered decision-making practices? Explain.
10. How would you try to enrich the job of a shoe salesperson?
11. Is flextime consistent with a 9, 9 management style? Explain.
12. Describe the policies that might be used in a human relations–oriented supermarket.

CONCLUDING CASE

Americans Manage in Australia

Are you a successful businessman with an urge for travel and new challenges? Or maybe an entrepreneur who's never quite managed to get that pet project off the drawing board? Then, mate, it may be time to take the plunge Down Under.

Australia is scouring the globe for business people willing to relocate—and bring their cash and expertise with them. "It's the last frontier," says Dennis Bramnick, a plucky resident of Los Angeles who plans to move to Sydney with his wife in June [1988] and begin life anew. He and three partners are betting a big chunk of their savings—$560,000—on his dream of opening a chain of Mexican restaurants in the land of barbecue and that bittersweet yeast paste known as Vegemite. The first restaurant will be located in a historic building on Sydney's waterfront, and Bramnick eventually plans to open 14 more eateries in other major cities over the next seven years. The fact that Mexican restaurants haven't fared well in Australia in the past doesn't deter him. "The quality of the food doesn't even come close to what we do in California," Bramnick says. "That's where we'll have a competitive edge."

Though businessmen have made up only a small share of Australia's total of 130,000 yearly immigrants, Canberra is doing its best to pave the way for the well-heeled wanderers. Last November the government licensed some 70 local "migration consultants" who trim the immigration process from as long as a year to as little as three months. These agents also help arrange inspection trips to Australia, line up business and government contacts, assist with market surveys and—not least—help arrange housing and schools.

Despite government help and a shared language, for Americans, adjusting to cultural differences can also be difficult. Even the most vaunted attribute of Australians—their easygoing nature—can be a drawback when it comes to opening a business. Aussies take things slowly, says Touche Ross's Diana Huang. "That lackadaisical attitude puts many migrants off." Adds Colin Cohen, a Sydney migration agent: "Business is handled differently here. Australians don't like to be pushed into a deal. They place more importance on personal relationships." Cohen advises his clients, especially Yanks, to tone down their characteristic aggressiveness. "Americans are used to the hard sell and getting a deal done and closed," he says. "They find it strange that the Australian is not out there just to make a buck." Even in business, as Hogan would say, if you want to succeed you have to relax and learn to say g'day.

Issues for Discussion

1. What needs in Maslow's hierarchy might motivate individuals like Dennis Bramnick to open businesses in Australia? Explain.
2. Do workers in the United States seem to have the same needs as workers in Australia? What does this tell you about managing workers in Australia?
3. Will Bramnick be able to use Theory Z in managing his business in Australia? Explain.

NOTES

1. Lyman W. Porter and Lawrence E. McKibbin, *Management Education and Development* (New York: McGraw-Hill, 1988), chapters 3 and 4.
2. Abraham Maslow, *Motivation and Personality* (New York: McGraw-Hill, 1970).
3. Douglas McGregor, *The Human Side of Enterprise* (New York: McGraw-Hill, 1960).
4. B. F. Skinner, *Contingencies of Reinforcement* (New York: Appleton-Century-Crofts, 1969).
5. "Proxy Statement of Nabisco Brands, Inc.," March 17, 1982, p. 13.
6. Peter Drucker, *The Practice of Management* (New York: Harper & Row, 1954).
7. Robert Tannenbaum and Warren H. Schmidt, "How to Choose a Leadership Pattern," *Harvard Business Review,* March–April 1957, pp. 95–101.
8. Frederick Herzberg, "One More Time: How Do You Motivate Employees?" *Harvard Business Review,* September–October 1987, pp. 109–120.
9. Robert R. Blake, Jane S. Mouton, Louis Barnes, and Larry Greiner, "Breakthrough in Organization Development," *Harvard Business Review,* November–December 1964.

CHECK YOUR LEARNING ANSWER KEY

A. 1. F, *p. 195*
   2. T, *p. 196*

B. 1. e, *p. 196*
   2. T, *p. 197*

C. 1. F, *p. 198*
   2. T, *p. 199*
   3. F, *p. 200*

D. 1. T, *p. 200*
   2. T, *p. 200*

E. 1. b, *p. 200*
   2. F, *p. 202*
   3. T, *p. 203*

F. 1. F, *p. 204*
   2. T, *p. 207*
   3. T, *p. 215*

G. 1. T, *p. 210*
   2. F, *p. 210*
   3. T, *p. 210*
   4. F, *p. 212*

CHAPTER

8

ORGANIZING A BUSINESS

LEARNING OBJECTIVES

After reading this chapter you should be able to:

1. Discuss organizing and the organizing process.
2. Describe the roles of structure and span of management in organizing.
3. Explain how responsibility, authority, and accountability are related.
4. Compare and contrast authority in line organizations, staff organizations, functional organizations, and matrix organizations.
5. Outline the relationships among delegation, decentralization, and centralization.
6. Describe structural change.
7. Explain why organization members resist change.

OUTLINE

Business Practice Example: Apple Changes Course

Organizing

- What Is Organizing?
- The Organizing Process

Organizational Structure

- Formal Structure
- Informal Structure
- Organizational Culture
- Departments and Departmentalization

Span of Management in Organizations

- Factors Determining Span of Management
- Tall versus Flat Organizations

Organizing Work Behavior

- Responsibility and Authority
  - Authority to Match Responsibility
- Forms of Organization and Authority
  - Line Authority
  - Staff Authority
  - Functional Authority
- Authority in Matrix Organizations
- Accountability and Delegation
  - Accountability
  - Delegation
  - Centralization and Decentralization

Changing an Organization

- Structural Change
- Resistance to Change

Summary

Key Terms

Check Your Learning

Questions for Review and Discussion

Concluding Case

- What's Next for DEC?

Notes

Check Your Learning Answer Key

Highlight in Business Practice: Organizational Culture at McDonald's

Highlight in Business Practice: Colgate Experiments with Matrix Groups in Product Development

BUSINESS PRACTICE EXAMPLE

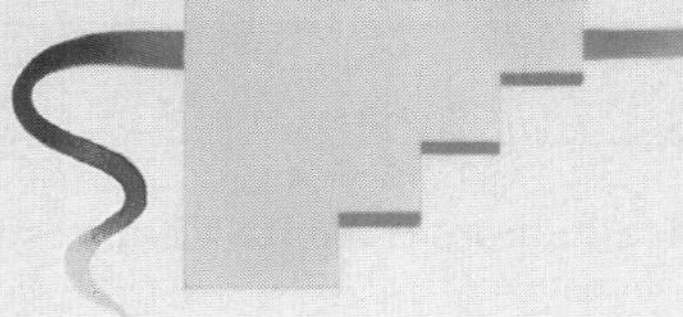

In 1977, the Apple Computer Company launched the microcomputer revolution with the introduction of a personal computer (PC) called the Apple II. Just three years later, the fledgling company in California, founded by computer geniuses Steve Wozniak and Steven Jobs, joined the ranks of the *Fortune* 500 companies, with over $300 million in sales.

Until the first Apple was introduced to the marketplace, individuals—versus companies equipped with large "number crunching" computing machines—did not own computers. The Apple II changed all that. Personal computer use took off, both in the home and in the office, and in the process altered much about the way we live today.

As often happens when a new technology is introduced, almost immediately more than fifty companies emerged with their own brands of personal computer. The Apple II remained the market leader, however, until November 1981, when IBM introduced its PC. By the beginning of 1983, Apple was sharing the spotlight with IBM as the industry leaders, each selling approximately $1 billion worth of personal computers.

But by the end of that same year, so many new products had flooded the market that buyers became confused, and the infant industry began to suffer heavy losses. By the close of 1983, total industry losses were greater than the combined earnings on PCs by both Apple and IBM. Apple was in trouble.

Steve Jobs, then 27, knew he needed management help to achieve his dream of selling millions of Apple computers worldwide. The company's acting president had just resigned, and Jobs began a search for a replacement. He ultimately settled on John Sculley, the president of Pepsi-Cola. Sculley was famous as the brilliant marketer who created the "Pepsi Generation" marketing campaign. Although he was reluctant to leave Pepsi, eventually Sculley was unable to pass up the opportunity to participate in the amazing computer revolution going on in Silicon Valley. "Do you want to spend the rest of your life selling sugared water," Jobs challenged Sculley after Sculley had turned the job down twice, "or do you want a chance to change the world?"

For nearly two years, Sculley and Jobs not only worked together—Jobs as chairman and co-founder and Sculley as president and chief executive officer—but they also became best friends. Forsaking his expensive suits and plush corner office, Sculley entered a world where young blue-jean clad computer wizards routinely worked at least until midnight—and sometimes around the clock—to perfect Apple products. The atmosphere at Apple was more like that of the most dynamic research unit within a university than a corporation, and Sculley loved it.

But by 1984 IBM was fast threatening to dominate the business market (the largest and most lucrative) in PCs. Apple's defensive strategy positioned its third product, the much-heralded Macintosh, against IBM. Unfortunately, the strategy failed. As a consequence, the company was faced with excess inventory, plummeting sales, and increasing friction between Jobs and Sculley about what to do next.

The outcome of this friction shocked many. By 1985, Apple's charismatic co-founder had resigned, and Sculley had completely reorganized the barely eight-year-old organization.

WHAT'S AHEAD

The first two chapters in this section focused on management fundamentals and human relations. In this chapter, we move into the management areas of organizing and change. An understanding of this material is very useful to a manager like John Sculley of Apple Computer in the introductory case. The organizing section will examine various organizational structures and will explain how to organize work behavior. The change section will discuss modifying the organization to make it more successful in the long term.

ORGANIZING

Every day the ordinary things in our lives have to be organized. We organize our efforts to study for an exam, we organize our budget to maximize our buying power, we organize our errands to cover the most ground in the least amount of time. And every day less ordinary events are being organized all around us. Factories organize to produce their products, airlines organize to get their planes off the ground, a newspaper organizes to put out its morning edition on time. We could not have built the first automobile, split the atom, or put an astronaut on the moon without organization.

What Is Organizing?

The process managers use to best combine people, equipment and materials, and all other resources in order to carry out plans and reach organizational objectives is **organizing.** Managers need to organize so as to focus on the most orderly and efficient ways to use resources for achieving objectives. Through organizing they are able to classify in detail both the objectives and the resources needed to achieve them.

Organizing is the process managers use to best combine people, equipment and materials, and all other resources in order to carry out plans and reach organizational objectives.

Organizing is important because it is a mechanism for putting plans into action. A thorough organizing effort by the manager will help minimize such costly weaknesses as duplication of effort and idle organizational resources.

The Organizing Process

The ***organizing process*** is the five steps managers follow in organizing: (1) reflecting on plans and objectives, (2) establishing major tasks, (3) dividing the tasks into subtasks, (4) allocating resources and directives for subtasks, and (5) evaluating the results of the implemented organizing strategy.

As Figure 8.1 shows, the **organizing process** is the five steps managers follow in organizing: (1) reflecting on plans and objectives, (2) establishing major tasks, (3) dividing major tasks into subtasks, (4) allocating resources and directives for subtasks, and (5) evaluating the results of the implemented organizing strategy. The manager should continually repeat these steps to obtain feedback that will help in improving the organization.

Consider Luigi Marco, who manages a restaurant that has been in his family for three generations. He begins his organizing process by reflecting on how to make a reasonable profit while continuing to provide the high-quality food the restaurant has become known for. His plan involves determining how the restaurant will reach its objective, and his organizing involves determining how the restaurant's resources will be used to activate the plan. Thus Marco must start to organize by planning. Marco's mother has supervised the cooking for the last ten years, but ill health is preventing her from working full time. Part of the plan, then, must be to hire an experienced chef. This will help ensure quality but may cut into the profit margin.

The second and third steps of the organizing process focus on tasks to be performed within the management system. The second step Marco must take in organizing is to designate the major jobs that must be done. Two of these jobs are waiting on customers and cooking food.

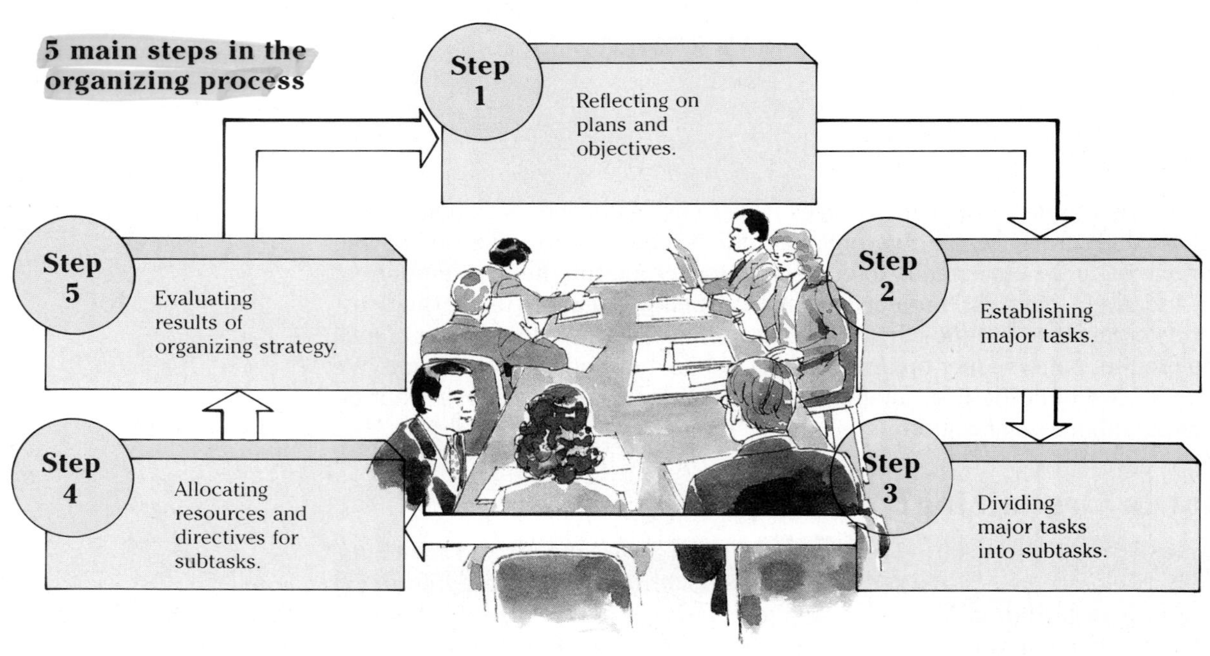
5 main steps in the organizing process
Step 1
Reflecting on plans and objectives.
Step 2
Establishing major tasks.
Step 3
Dividing major tasks into subtasks.
Step 4
Allocating resources and directives for subtasks.
Step 5
Evaluating results of organizing strategy.

Figure 8.1 Five main steps of the organizing process. Effective managers organize all resources in the management system as they work to achieve organizational objectives.

The third step Marco must take is to divide major tasks into subtasks. For example, he might divide waiting on customers into taking orders, serving meals, and clearing tables. And he might divide cooking into buying food, preparing it, cooking it, and arranging it on serving dishes.

The fourth organizing step allocates resources and directives to accomplish the subtasks. In this step, Marco will determine who is to take orders, who is to serve meals, who is to pour coffee, and who is to clear tables. He will also specify the relationships of the various subtasks. The result of the third and fourth steps is a *division of labor* into specialized tasks. When these tasks are organized and coordinated, a tremendously efficient use of resources can be achieved. By dividing the work into specialties, managers let each worker concentrate on a cluster of tasks that allows the most work to be done with the least distraction. The service in Marco's restaurant will be of better quality and greater speed and will cause less waste of the resources of space, equipment, and food.

The fifth step—evaluating the results—means that Marco must gather feedback on how well his implemented strategy is working. This feedback will furnish him with information to use in improving the organization. Marco may find, for example, that the meal servers and coffee pourers are getting in each other's way. He can then use this information to design better routines for them.

The end result of the organizing process is termed **organization**—the establishment of logical relationships of people and other resources to achieve organizational objectives. In their organizing efforts, managers must keep in mind three important considerations: structure, span of management, and the organizing of work behavior.

Organization is the result of the organizing process—the establishment of logical relationships of people and other resources to achieve organizational objectives.

ORGANIZATIONAL STRUCTURE

The specific pattern of relationships among the activities and resources of an organization is **structure.** It expresses the form and design that managers give to activities when they organize their resources. Its purpose is to promote efficient use of the individual and collective resources needed to attain objectives. In an organizing effort, managers must begin by developing the structure that is most appropriate for the specific situation. Structure is shaped by several influences, both formal and informal.

Structure is the specific pattern of relationships among the activities and resources of an organization.

Formal Structure

The structure in which the relationships among organizational resources are outlined by management is **formal structure.** An example is management's arranging people into separate work groups and subgroups.

An **organization chart** shows the main components of formal structure in diagram form. It indicates how the work is divided, where authority lies, what departments exist, and what the lines of formal communication are. (These topics will be discussed later in the chapter.) Traditionally, an organization chart is constructed in pyramid form, with individuals toward the top having more authority and responsibility than those toward the bottom. The relative positioning of the individuals (shown in boxes on the chart) indicates their broad working relationships. The lines between the boxes designate the formal lines of communication between the individuals.

Formal structure is the structure in which the relationships among organizational resources are outlined by management.

An ***organization chart*** is a diagram that shows the main components of formal structure.

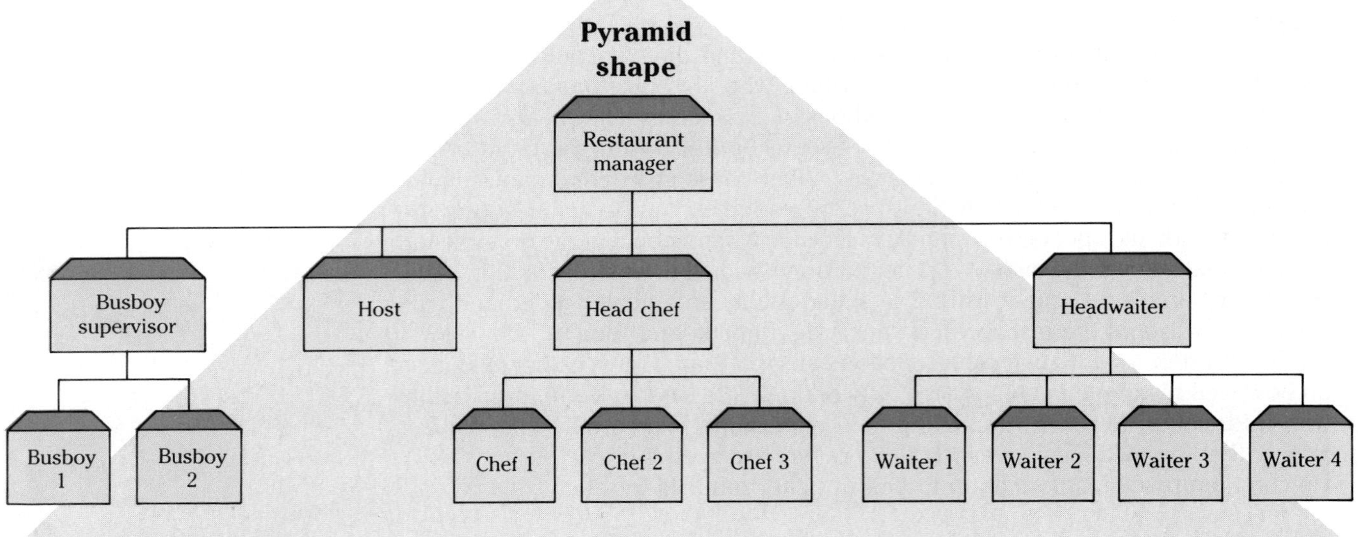

Figure 8.2 Sample organization chart for a small restaurant. An organization chart reveals a company's basic working relationship and its formal lines of communication.

Figure 8.2 is an organization chart for a small business—Marco's restaurant. The restaurant manager has the most authority and responsibility. The positioning of the head chef over the other chefs indicates that the head chef has authority over them and is responsible for their work. The lines between the individual chefs and the restaurant manager indicate that formal communication from the chefs to the restaurant manager (and back again) must go through the head chef.

Informal Structure

The patterns of relationships among workers and others that develop naturally as people interact are the **informal structure** of an organization (also termed *informal groups* and *informal organization*). An example of informal structure is a group of people in a company who become good friends as a result of working together, lunching together, having cultural similarities, or being interested in the same sports.

Informal structure is the patterns of relationships among workers and others that develop naturally as people interact.

The informal structure evolves over time and tends to be molded by the norms, interests, values, and social relationships of the people in it. Although this structure coexists with management's formal structure, it does not necessarily follow the same pattern.

Figure 8.3 builds on Figure 8.2 by showing how informal structure might coexist with formal structure at Marco's restaurant. In the figure, one of the informal groups is composed of busboy 2, the host, chef 1, and the head chef. The host exerts a dominant influence in this group—which does not match the setup in the formal structure. The other informal group is composed of chefs 2 and 3,

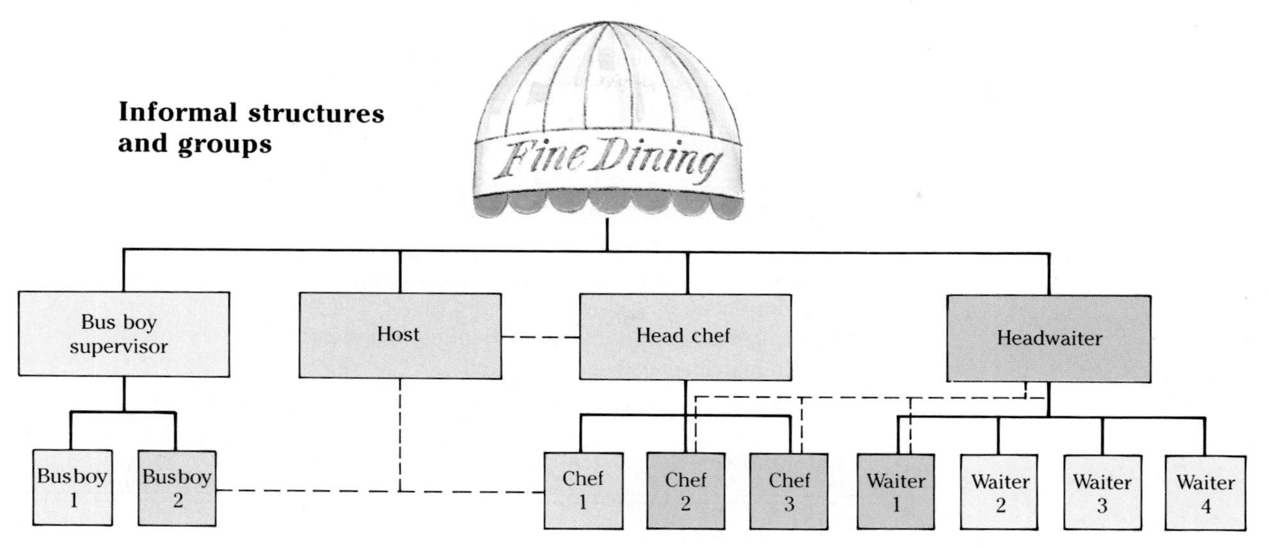

Figure 8.3 Informal structures and groups within the formal structure of an organization chart for a small restaurant.

waiter 1, and the headwaiter. Here the headwaiter exerts the dominant influence over people outside his sphere in the formal structure.

Communication in the informal structure is called *informal communication.* An example is chef 2, who is a friend of the headwaiter, giving the headwaiter information about events in the kitchen. The term **grapevine** is used to apply to networks of informal communication and to communication that doesn't follow the formal lines on the organization chart. For example, the headwaiter might get information about events in the kitchen from chef 2, then tell the restaurant manager that he heard it "through the grapevine."

Grapevine is a term used for networks of informal communication and for communication that doesn't follow the formal lines on the organization chart.

Since all organizations have some kind of informal structure, and since the informal structure can influence the organization's success, managers must stay aware of these informal links in the organization. In addition, managers must attempt to influence the informal structure in such a way that the organization can benefit from its advantages and avoid its disadvantages. Table 8.1 lists several potential advantages and disadvantages of informal structure.

Organizational Culture

In addition to maintaining a formal corporate structure, management exerts a powerful influence on relationships in an organization by expressing the attitudes and behavioral norms it expects from employees. In doing so, it promotes an **organizational culture,** the set of values and beliefs shared by all organization members. For example, the organizational culture of McDonald's Corporation

The ***organizational culture*** is the set of values and beliefs shared by all organization members.

Table 8.1 Potential advantages and disadvantages of informal structure.

Potential Advantages
Informal groups can ■ Help workers identify with the organization. ■ Help workers become more satisfied socially with their work environment. ■ Help spread important information through the organization quickly. ■ Help managers gather information.
Potential Disadvantages
Informal groups can ■ Develop the norm of fighting management rather than helping it. ■ Distort information, since messages are almost never in writing. ■ Disrupt lines of authority within or among formal work groups. ■ Become the primary vehicle for satisfaction within the company (in place of excellence in job performance).

strongly supports a positive attitude toward assembly line cooking, fast service, and a wholesome image—and "a near-religious devotion to hamburgers." Over the years, McDonald's organizational values grew strong enough to endure even the death of founder Ray Kroc. Companies with a strong organizational culture are able to get continuing employee support for organizational objectives, through both the formal and the informal structures.

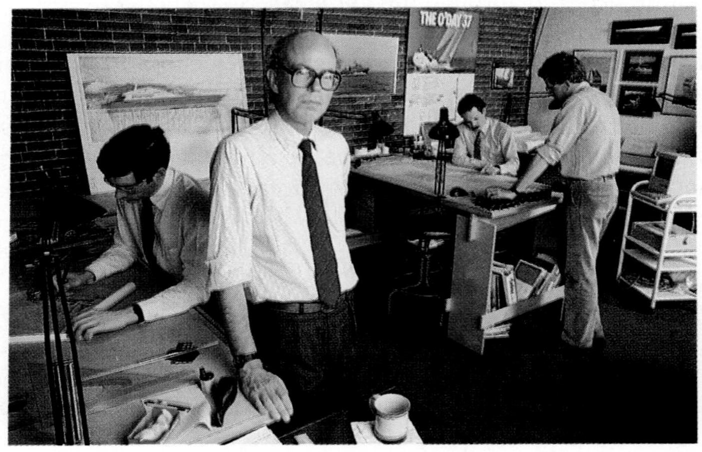

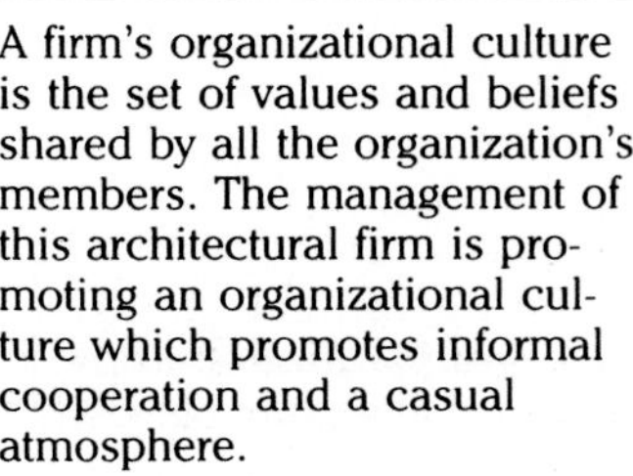
A firm's organizational culture is the set of values and beliefs shared by all the organization's members. The management of this architectural firm is promoting an organizational culture which promotes informal cooperation and a casual atmosphere.

HIGHLIGHT IN BUSINESS PRACTICE

Organizational Culture at McDonald's

In a room suitably dimmed for a seance, new employees of McDonald's Corp. gather to contact Ray A. Kroc, the fast-food company's founder.

Their voices hushed, half a dozen workers tap into rows of desktop computers offering 1½ hours of videotaped messages from the late Mr. Kroc. Wearing a sport coat and looking in the pink, the short, balding executive appears on their screens, barking pronouncements from telephones at each terminal.

On cleanliness: "If you've got time to lean, you've got time to clean." On the competition: "If they were drowning to death, I would put a hose in their mouth." On expansion: "When you're green, you grow; when you're ripe, you rot."

Ten years after Mr. Kroc stepped away from day-to-day operations at the world's largest fast-food chain, his ghost lives on. His office at McDonald's headquarters here is preserved as a museum, his reading glasses untouched in their leather case on the desk.

Mr. Kroc wasn't averse to new ideas. In fact, he encouraged them—and had his own, some of them awful. But McDonald's main strategy can be summed up in his three-decades-old philosophy of assembly-line cooking and preparation, fast service, a wholesome image and a near-religious devotion to the hamburger. Today a new generation of McDonald's executives cheers his axioms.

It is an odd corporate culture in an industry where products, promotions and strategies change at a dizzying pace. But its impact is growing. Defying a recent threat by competitors, McDonald's this year raised its share of hamburger restaurants' $25 billion fast-food market by two percentage points, whipping other chains into a frenzy of cost-cutting.

At the same time, the Kroc legacy is beginning to exert an almost Disneylike effect on American culture as the company spreads Mr. Kroc's platitudes and promotional characters through an ever-expanding network of restaurants, charities, sporting events and retail stores. Some critics see serious problems in McDonald's growing influence on youth.

Little has changed in the war rooms of McDonald's suburban headquarters since Mr. Kroc died in 1984. A photograph near his old office shows the former milkshake-machine salesman washing windows at his first McDonald's, the Des Plaines, Ill., hamburger stand he opened 32 years and 60 billion burgers ago.

Few departed corporate chiefs have left such an imprint. Today's executives at McDonald's cite Mr. Kroc so often that he still seems to be in charge. His photo smiles down on every desk. "When Ray died, people worried that his vision couldn't be kept alive," says Sharon Vuinovich, assistant vice president for accounting. "But we're doing that."

Departments and Departmentalization

As organizations grow, the most common method of establishing formal relationships is by setting up departments. Basically, a **department** is a subdivided part of an organization, which management has established as a distinct group of people and other resources working on a common task.

A ***department*** is a subdivided part of an organization, which management has established as a distinct group of people and other resources working on a common task.

Departmentalization is the process of setting up departments.

The process of setting up the departments is called **departmentalization.** This process creates departments based on the needs of the organization. The patterns of authority that develop within and among departments will be discussed in later sections. Here we will examine how departments are typically formed around such factors as work function, product, territory, target customer, and manufacturing process. Figure 8.4 is an organization chart for the hypothetical Greene Furniture Company. This figure will be referenced throughout the section to illustrate the various kinds of departments.

Function Perhaps the most widely used basis for establishing departments is work function—the type of activity performed. Typically, the activities are production, marketing, and finance. (See the assistant vice president boxes in Figure 8.4 for this type of departmentalization.)

Product As a company manufactures more and more products, it becomes difficult to coordinate the activities involved in producing them. Therefore, management may turn to the organization structure based primarily on product. With this type of structure, the resources necessary to produce each product can be grouped. (See the part of Figure 8.4 that deals with products—recliner chairs, beds, and kitchen tables.)

Territory As market areas and work locations expand, the physical space between them can make the management task cumbersome. When this happens, management is likely to departmentalize on the basis of territory—the place where the work is done or the geographic market area on which the organization is focusing. The territorial departments can be relatively near one another or in different cities, states, or even countries. (See the vice presidential boxes in Figure 8.4, which show departmentalization by country—Canada, the United States, and Europe.)

Customers Department structuring according to types of customers works when major kinds of customers can be identified and categorized. For example, one department may sell its products by mail order while another sells to wholesalers. (See the sales representative boxes in Figure 8.4, which show the division by educational sales, residential sales, and commercial sales.)

Manufacturing Process Many organizations departmentalize on the basis of the phases involved in the manufacturing process. (In Figure 8.4, this type of departmentalization results in boxes for the woodcutting department, the sanding department, the glueing department, and the painting department.)

SPAN OF MANAGEMENT IN ORGANIZATIONS

Span of management is the number of individuals a manager supervises.

The second main consideration of any organizing effort is **span of management**—the number of individuals a manager supervises (also termed *span of control, span of authority, span of supervision,* and *span of responsibility*). As the number of supervised employees increases, the span of management also increases.

The central concern of the span of management concept is the determination of how many individuals a manager can supervise effectively. To use human

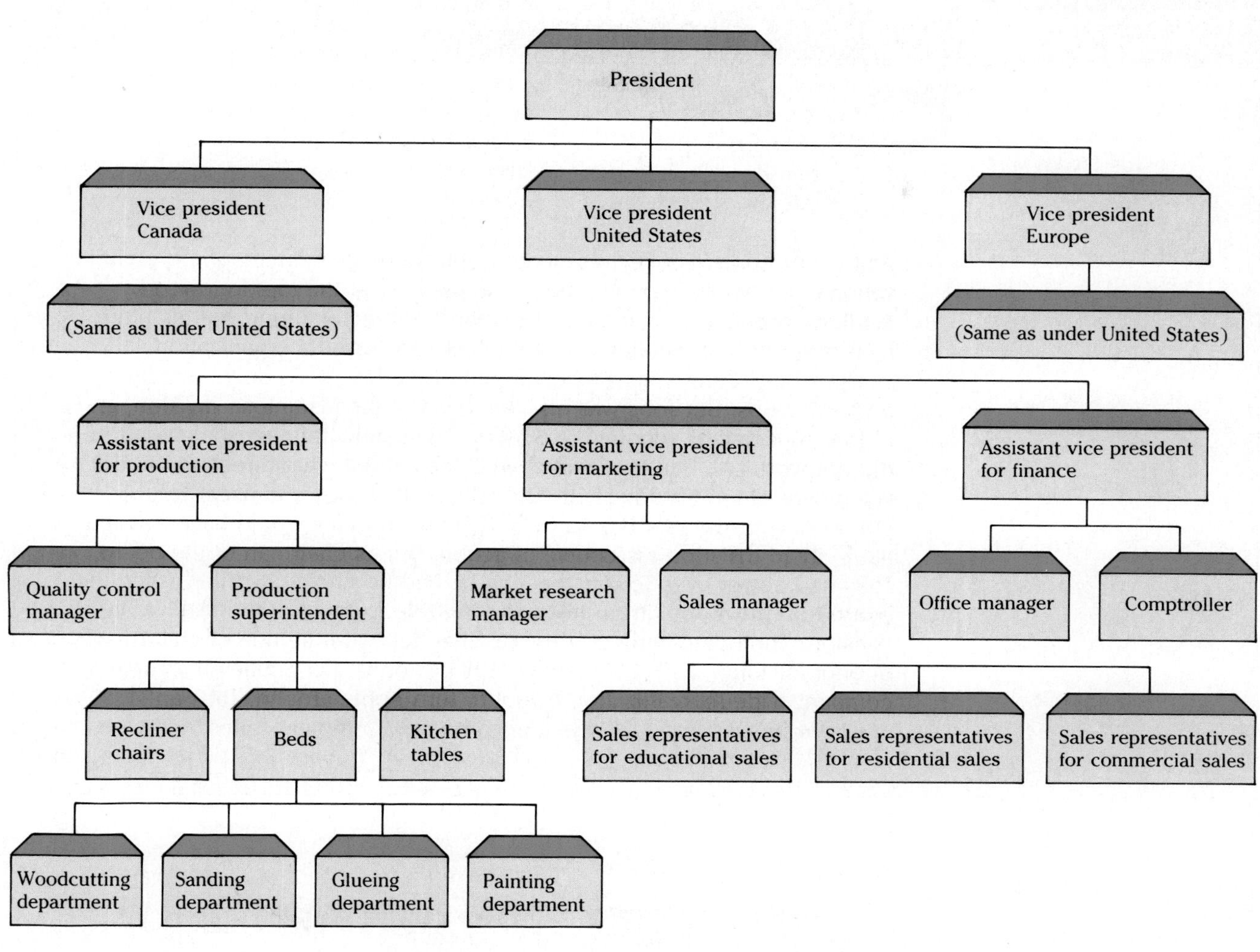

Figure 8.4 Sample organizational chart for Greene Furniture Company. Many organizations departmentalize according to function, product, territory, customers, or manufacturing process.

resources efficiently, managers should supervise as many people as they can best guide toward production quotas. Supervising too few people wastes productive capacity. Supervising too many leads to ineffectiveness and frustration.[1]

Factors Determining Span of Management

The span of management that is appropriate for each manager must be carefully worked out. Although there is no formula for determining it, several factors involving the work and the workers should be considered:

Likeness of jobs—the degree of similarity among the jobs workers are performing. In general, a manager can supervise more workers doing similar jobs than workers doing dissimilar jobs.

BUSINESS PRACTICE EXAMPLE Continues

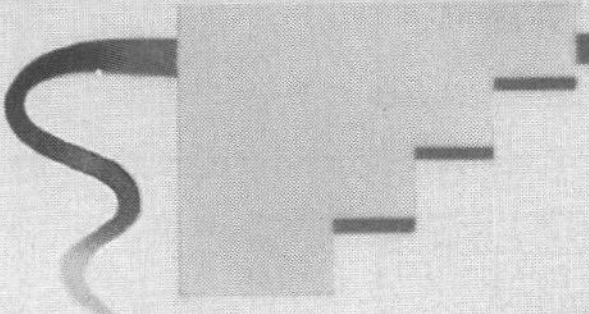

As CEO of Apple, Sculley reports to Apple's board of directors. An organization chart would show the board of directors at the top, followed by Sculley underneath. As long as the board of directors approves his plans by a majority vote, Sculley has the authority to run the organization.

Until 1985, Steve Jobs was chairman of the board. As such, Sculley reported to Jobs. But Jobs was also the head of the Macintosh division, and in that capacity, he reported to Sculley. Ultimately, this unusual situation did not work out. Sculley differed with Jobs about what direction the development of the Macintosh should take so that business users would choose it over the IBM PC. As CEO, Sculley normally would have had the authority to insist on his course of action. But as chairman of the board, Jobs had power over Sculley. Feeling he had no choice, Sculley asked the board to remove Jobs from his operating role as head of the Macintosh division. The board agreed. Jobs was then left with the title of chairman, but not for long. On September 17, 1985, shortly after Sculley instituted a company-wide reorganization meant to turn Apple around, Jobs announced he was leaving Apple to head a new company called Next.

Closeness of workers—how physically far apart the workers are. Over all, a manager can supervise more workers who are close to one another than who are great distances apart.

Difficulty of jobs. Jobs are difficult if they are complex, involved, and complicated. A manager can usually supervise a greater number of workers at relatively simple jobs than at relatively difficult jobs.

Coordination required. Jobs that require coordination involve synchronizing the efforts of workers. A manager usually can supervise more workers requiring little or no coordination than those requiring extensive coordination.

Flat organizations are organizations whose organization charts are short and whose spans of management are wide.

Tall organizations are organizations whose organization charts are high and whose spans of management are narrow.

Tall versus Flat Organizations

A clear relationship exists between span of management and height of the organization chart. In general, the taller the organization chart, the narrower the span of management. And, of course, the shorter the organization chart, the wider the span of management. **Flat organizations** are organizations whose organization charts are short and whose spans of management are wide. **Tall organizations** are organizations whose organization charts are tall and whose spans of management are narrow.

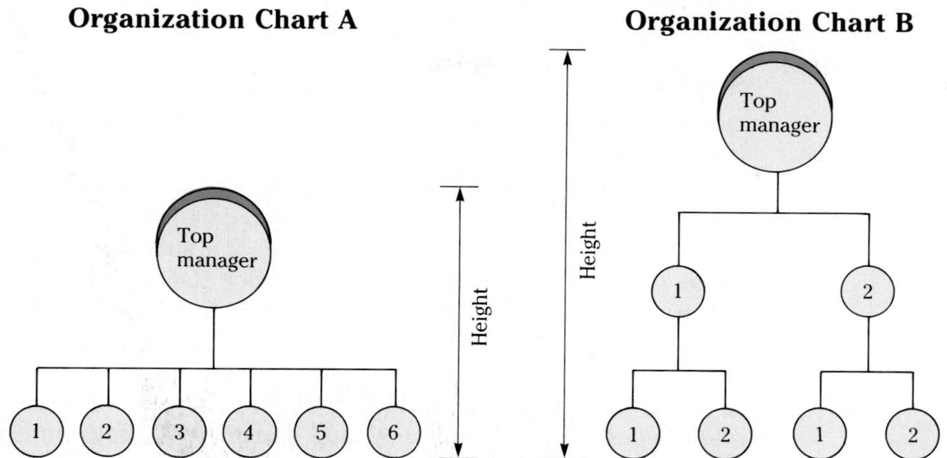

Figure 8.5 As span of management changes, organizational height also changes.

Figure 8.5 is a simple comparison of flat and tall organizations and their spans of management. Organization chart A has a span of management of six, and organization chart B has a span of management of two. Thus, although both organizations contain the same number of people, chart A is flatter than chart B.

ORGANIZING WORK BEHAVIOR

The third main consideration of any organizing effort is work behavior. The four variables involved in organizing work behavior are responsibility, authority, accountability, and delegation.

Responsibility and Authority

Perhaps the most fundamental ingredient in channeling the activity of individuals in the organization is **responsibility**—the obligation to perform an assigned activity. Responsibility is a commitment that people take upon themselves to handle their jobs to the best of their ability. The person who accepts a job is obligated to a superior to carry out a series of duties or activities or to see that someone else carries them out. A responsible worker is one who gets the job done. Since a person *accepts* responsibility, there is no way it can be passed on to a subordinate.

Responsibility is the obligation to perform an assigned activity.

A summary of the activities that go with a particular position is usually contained in the formal statement called a *job description.* (The process of working with job descriptions is discussed in chapter 9.)

Job activities are assigned by management to help accomplish organizational objectives. A manager analyzes objectives, decides which duties will lead to reaching them, and assigns the performance of those duties to workers. A sound organizing strategy includes specific job activities for each worker. However, as objectives and other conditions change, individual job activities may have to be changed.

Authority to Match Responsibility

Authority is the right to perform or command.

Any worker who has been given a job to do must also be given the authority with which to do it. **Authority,** in this situation, is the right to perform or command. It allows its holder not only to act in certain designated ways but also to directly influence the actions of others by issuing orders to them.

The relationship between responsibility and authority can be seen in the situation of Bill Myers, the manager of a service station. Bill is responsible for two primary tasks: pumping gasoline and repairing automobiles. He also has the authority necessary to perform both tasks. If Bill chooses, he can assign the repair activity to his assistant manager, who is a very responsible worker. Bill should also give his assistant the authority to order parts, to have certain attendants help when necessary, and to do anything else that will help him perform his job. Without this authority, it might be impossible for him to complete the delegated job activities, no matter how responsible he is.

Forms of Organization and Authority

Modern organizations have put the relationship of responsibility and authority into some common organizational forms, each with a characteristic pattern. The oldest and simplest pattern is line authority. An enlargement of the pattern is staff authority. Two more recent developments are functional authority and matrix-group authority.

Line Authority

Line authority is the right to make decisions and give orders concerning the production, sales, or finance areas of an organization.

The right to make decisions and give orders concerning the production, sales, or finance areas of an organization is **line authority.** This type of authority is the most fundamental one in any organization. It reflects the most basic superior-subordinate relationship—the right of superiors to give orders to subordinates.

Line authority is the right to make decisions and give orders in an organization. This manager has the authority to give orders to his subordinates regarding a production issue.

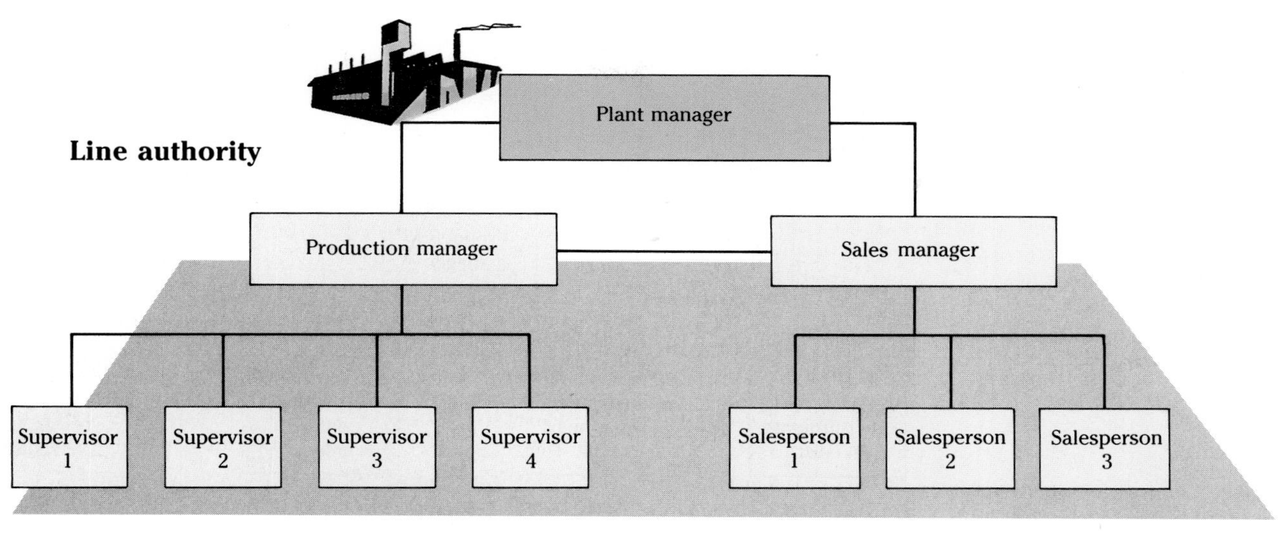

Figure 8.6 A partial organization chart emphasizing line authority.

Figure 8.6 is a partial organization chart depicting how an organization might structure its line authority. The plant manager has line authority over the production manager and the sales manager. The production manager, in turn, has line authority over four supervisors; and the sales manager has line authority over three salespeople.

Staff Authority

The right to advise or assist those who possess line authority is **staff authority.** It exists to enable those responsible for line personnel to perform their required tasks effectively. Members of the accounting and personnel departments, for example, have staff authority. Line and staff organization members must work closely together if the organization is to be run effectively and efficiently.

Staff authority is the right to advise or assist those who possess line authority.

Since staff authority cannot exist independently of line authority, Figure 8.7 builds on Figure 8.6 to illustrate how the two typically coexist. In this figure, the personnel manager advises the plant manager, the quality control manager advises the production manager, and the sales research specialist advises the sales managers. Within the personnel department, the personnel manager has line authority over the testing and recruitment specialist and over the management development specialist.

Functional Authority

The right to give orders within a segment of the organization in which this right is normally nonexistent is **functional authority.** It is usually assigned to individuals to complement the line or staff authority they already possess. Functional authority generally covers only specific task areas and only for designated amounts

Functional authority is the right to give orders within a segment of the organization in which this right is normally nonexistent.

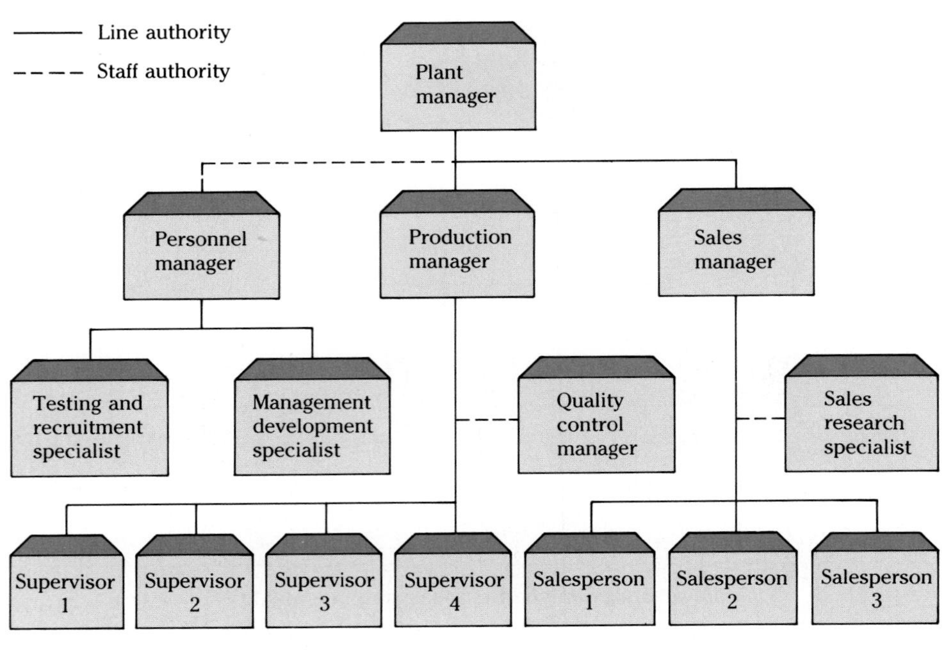

Figure 8.7
A partial organization chart showing how line authority and staff authority can complement each other.

of time. It is typically given to individuals who, in order to meet their responsibilities, must be able to exercise some control over organization members in other areas.

Consider, for example, an organization's vice president of finance. Among her basic responsibilities is that of monitoring the organization's financial situation. In order to accomplish this task, she must continually receive appropriate financial information from various segments of the organization. Therefore, she is delegated the functional authority to order various departments to furnish her with the kinds and amounts of information she needs to perform her analysis. Her functional authority allows her to give orders to people in departments over which she normally has no control.

Figure 8.8 builds on Figures 8.6 and 8.7 to illustrate how functional authority might complement both line and staff authority. In addition to having line and staff relationships, the testing and recruitment specialist has functional authority over the supervisors. For example, the specialist might want to determine if the company's employment tests are helpful in selecting people who can do well in actual job situations and thus might request information from the supervisors about how well workers are doing.

It is reasonable to conclude that although authority can exist in various forms, these forms should be used in the combinations that will best enable people to carry out their responsibilities and the organization to accomplish its objectives. Also, the manager who is trying to decide which form to use must keep in mind that each type of authority has both advantages and disadvantages. Figure 8.9 shows the advantages and disadvantages for all three types of authority.

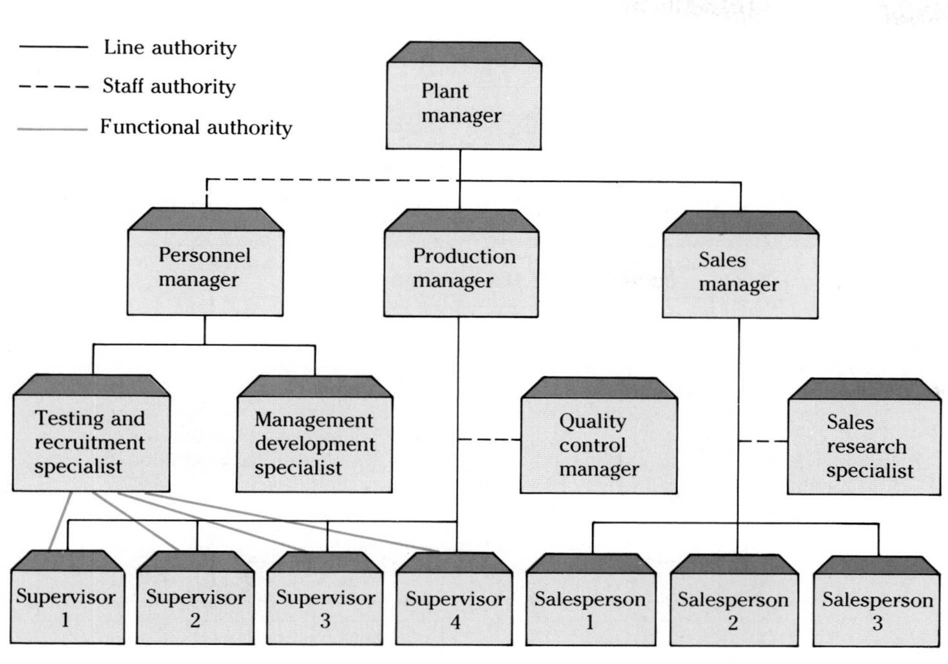

Figure 8.8
A partial organization chart showing a combination of line, staff, and functional authority.

Authority in Matrix Organizations

A more flexible and temporary form of authority is found in an organizational structure much used in project-centered, high-technology companies: the matrix organization. A **matrix organization** is an organizational structure in which specialists from different departments are brought together for a specific project and time period, while they are still functioning in the company's traditional structure. Thus matrix organizations are also called *project organizations.* The project may be long term or short term, and it is headed by a project manager, whose authority exists only for the duration of the project.

A ***matrix organization*** is an organizational structure in which specialists from different departments are brought together for a specific project and time period, while they are still functioning in the company's traditional structure.

The matrix organization is given authority to borrow employees from other organizational segments to complete the project. Once the project is finished, the borrowed employees return to their departments. This organizational structure allows for experiment and change. Its flexibility and temporary nature can be an advantage, but they can also create divided loyalties, since two forms of authority exist in parallel.

For an example of how a matrix organization is set up, consider Warfare Plus, a hypothetical corporation that manufactures military weapons and other products (see Figure 8.10). The first partial organization chart for Warfare Plus (Figure 8.10a), with its solid lines, shows the traditional form of line authority from the president to the department heads of the military division.

Although this structure is normally useful, the company has recently won two government contracts—one to build several hundred tanks and the other to build several thousand heat-sensitive missiles. Figure 8.10b, with its broken lines, il-

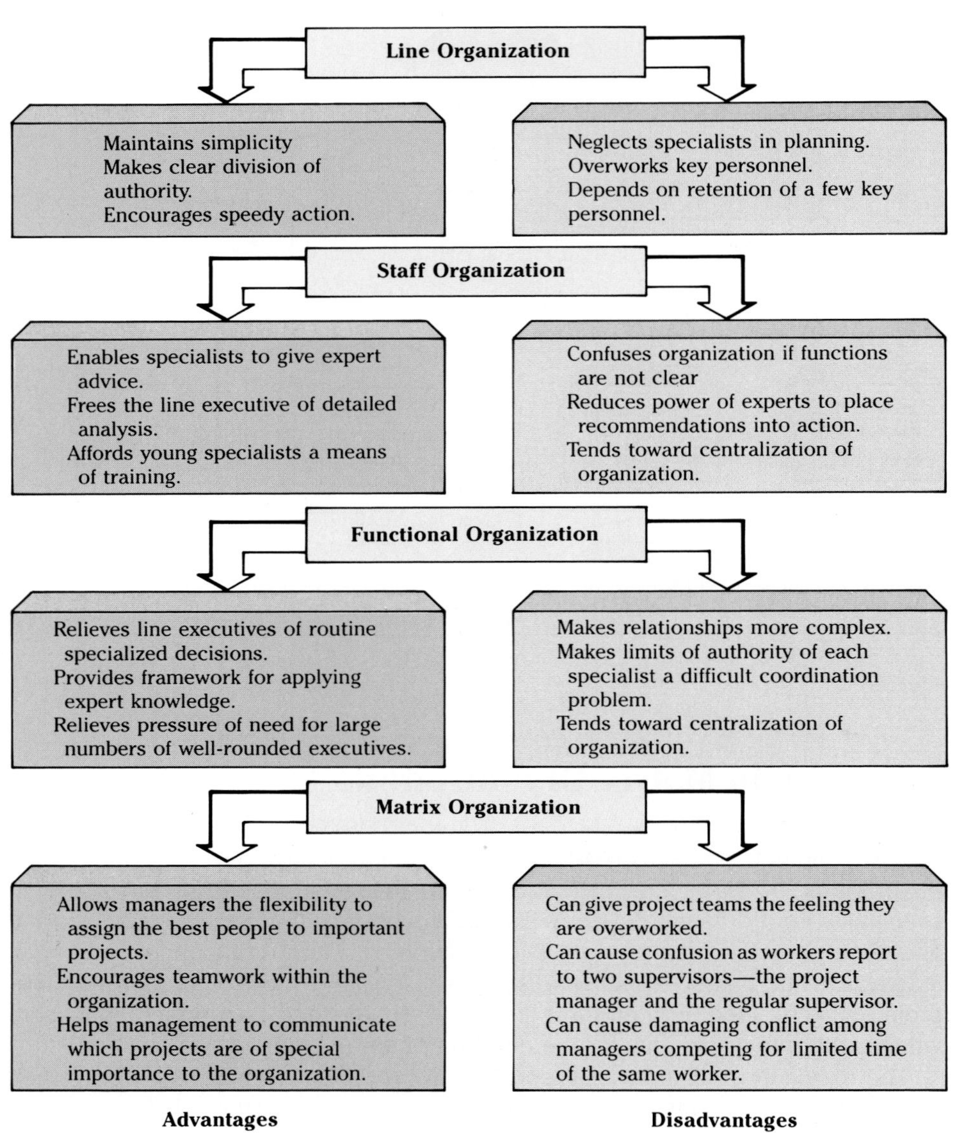

Line Organization
Maintains simplicity
Makes clear division of authority.
Encourages speedy action.
Neglects specialists in planning.
Overworks key personnel.
Depends on retention of a few key personnel.
Staff Organization
Enables specialists to give expert advice.
Frees the line executive of detailed analysis.
Affords young specialists a means of training.
Confuses organization if functions are not clear
Reduces power of experts to place recommendations into action.
Tends toward centralization of organization.
Functional Organization
Relieves line executives of routine specialized decisions.
Provides framework for applying expert knowledge.
Relieves pressure of need for large numbers of well-rounded executives.
Makes relationships more complex.
Makes limits of authority of each specialist a difficult coordination problem.
Tends toward centralization of organization.
Matrix Organization
Allows managers the flexibility to assign the best people to important projects.
Encourages teamwork within the organization.
Helps management to communicate which projects are of special importance to the organization.
Can give project teams the feeling they are overworked.
Can cause confusion as workers report to two supervisors—the project manager and the regular supervisor.
Can cause damaging conflict among managers competing for limited time of the same worker.
Advantages
Disadvantages

Figure 8.9
Comparison of authority in organizational forms. Managers must choose the types of authority they believe best fit their organization, recognizing that each type has advantages and disadvantages.

lustrates how Warfare Plus might alter its traditional organization chart to create a matrix organization structure that will enable it to give added attention to the two new projects.

In the new Warfare Plus matrix structure, a manager who reports directly to the president is appointed for each project. The two managers have the responsibility of ensuring that the projects will receive adequate attention and will be executed successfully. Also, each manager is given authority over a team of workers borrowed from other divisions because of their expertise. Individuals A, B, C, and D are the tank team, and individuals E, F, G, and H are the missile team.

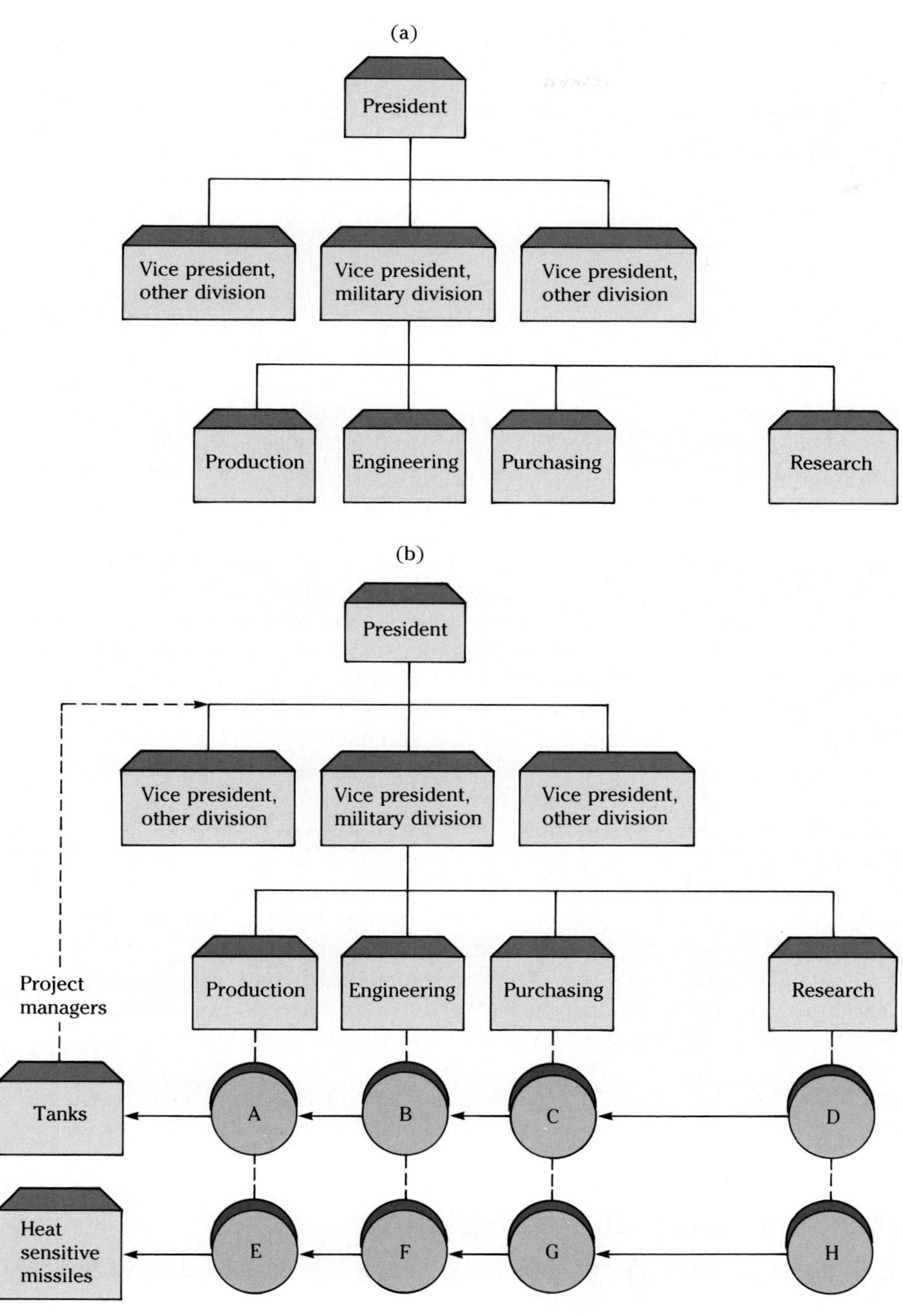

Figure 8.10 Partial organization charts for Warfare Plus, a hypothetical manufacturer of military weapons. (a) A traditional structure. (b) A matrix structure.

For the duration of the two projects, the teams will facilitate the manufacture of the new products. In addition, however, their members will maintain their former jobs, continuing to work within the line authority of the more traditional organization structure.

HIGHLIGHT IN BUSINESS PRACTICE

Colgate Experiments with Matrix Groups in Product Development

Colgate-Palmolive Co. isn't accustomed to thinking small. In a single year, it sells well over $3 billion of soaps and toothpaste world-wide. So why is one of the foremost mass marketers suddenly fooling around with a hodgepodge of small, specialized products—such as a deodorizing pad for cat litter boxes and a cleaning solution for teen-agers' retainers?

Well, it isn't Colgate the marketing Goliath that actually is launching these new products. The company directly behind them: Colgate Venture Co.

Insulated from its parent's regimented bureaucracy, Colgate Venture is proving to be an oasis for people with an entrepreneurial, risk-taking nature. "We move more quickly and we have the leeway to act on instinct, rather than wait for exhaustive market research," says Barrie Spelling, Colgate Venture's president. "That's a very major change from the mainstream marketing culture at Colgate."

Colgate Venture is trying to create entirely new product categories, as well, with such innovations as Fresh Feliners, a diaper-like pad for litter boxes. Another novel product is New Again, a menstrual bloodstain remover sold alongside tampons.

The company also is betting young people will go for Teen Clean. The retainer cleanser is being test marketed in California as an alternative to regular denture cleansers. Colgate Venture executives say teen-agers feel depressed enough about braces and retainers without having to buy a geriatric product.

"The real secret to making these projects work is having a small, closely knit team championing a product as if it were their own baby," says Mr. Spelling. "Psychologically, at least, they own the company." Colgate Venture's five operating divisions, which employ only 70 people, provide both annual bonuses tied to performance and long-term incentives to be paid either in cash or in equity interests in an operating group.

The entrepreneurial units usually struggle to keep a comfortable distance from the parent company. But there can be benefits from drawing on a well-known corporate name. "When we call on retailers and try to get a new product on the shelf, we do leverage our association with Colgate," Mr. Spelling says.

Accountability and Delegation

After responsibility and authority come accountability and delegation of authority.

Accountability is the management philosophy of holding individuals liable, or accountable, for how well they use their authority and how well they live up to their responsibility.

Accountability

The management philosophy of holding individuals liable, or accountable, for how well they use their authority and how well they live up to their responsibility is **accountability.** The implication of accountability is that if the required duties are performed well, a reward will be given—and if they are not performed well, a penalty will be forthcoming. As one executive said, "Individuals who do not perform well simply will not be around too long."

Delegation

The process of assigning job duties and related authority to specific organization members is **delegation.** The delegation process includes three steps: assigning specific duties, granting appropriate authority, and creating the obligation to perform the duties.[2] The steps in the process may be observable or implied.

Delegation is the process of assigning job duties and related authority to specific organization members.

In assigning duties, the manager must make sure the subordinate clearly understands what they entail. Whenever possible, the manager should state the required activities in operational terms, so the subordinate will know exactly what action must be taken. In granting appropriate authority, the manager must ensure that the subordinate will have the right and the power to accomplish the assigned duties. Finally, in creating the obligation to perform the duties, the manager must make the subordinate aware of the responsibility to complete the assigned and accepted duties.

Centralization and Decentralization

If you were to go from organization to organization, comparing the relative amounts of job activities and authority delegated to subordinates, you would find noticeable differences. It is not that delegation either exists or does not exist. It does exist in most organizations—but in varying degrees.

The terms *centralization* and *decentralization* are used to describe the degree of delegation in organizations. As Figure 8.11 shows, they can be viewed as being at opposite ends of a continuum. From the figure, it becomes apparent that **centralization** is the organizing practice in which minimal amounts of job

Centralization is the organizing practice in which minimal amounts of job activities and authority are delegated to subordinates.

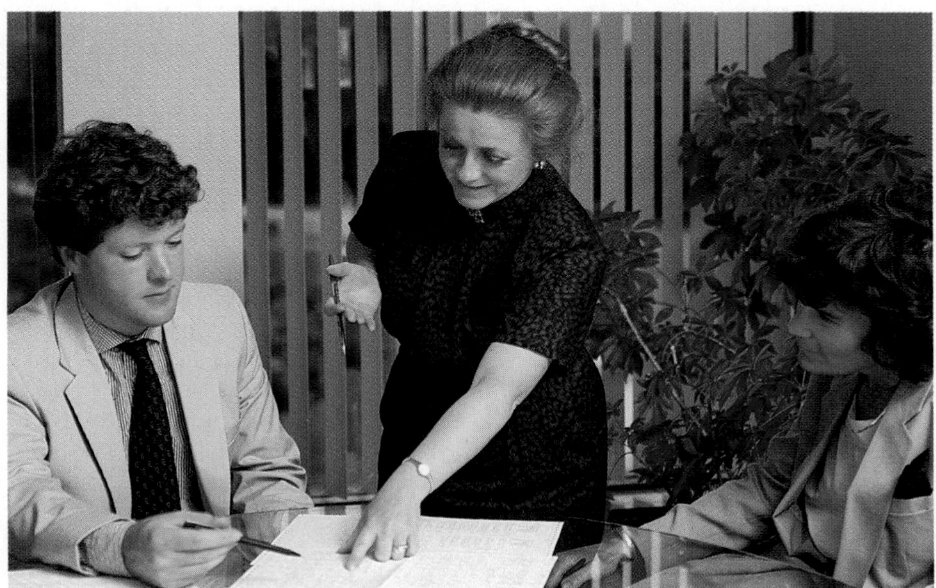

The delegation process involves assigning specific duties, granting appropriate authority, and creating the obligation to perform duties. Here, the manager is making sure that the subordinate clearly understands what action should be taken.

Figure 8.11
Delegation continuum. Organizations differ in regard to their amount of delegation.

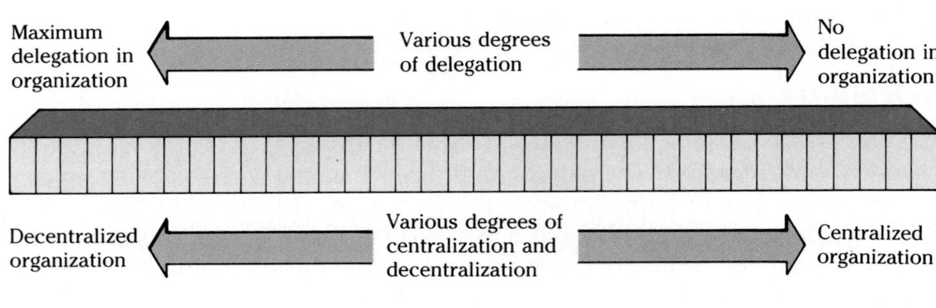

Decentralization is the organizing practice in which significant amounts of job activities and authority are delegated to subordinates.

activities and authority are delegated to subordinates. Conversely, **decentralization** is the organizing practice in which significant amounts of job activities and authority are delegated to subordinates.

BUSINESS PRACTICE EXAMPLE Continues

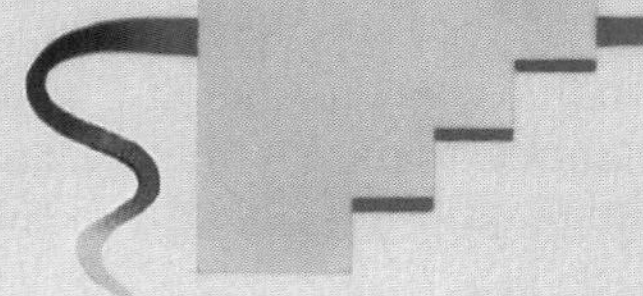

Until Sculley reorganized, Apple was a highly decentralized company, organized around product lines. There was a product division for the Lisa computer, one for the Apple II, and one for the Macintosh. Sculley felt that these divisions, however, were like "little fiefdoms," each competing against the other instead of working together for the good of the company as a whole. For instance, the employees in the Macintosh division, who considered the product they were developing superior to the other Apple products, called everybody else in the company "bozos." They even began wearing buttons with a line running through the face of a bozo clown.

Sculley felt it was imperative that he find a way to reorganize the divisions so that Apple products complemented, rather than competed, with one another. His solution was to move in the direction of centralization. He organized Apple into a more traditional functional organization. He appointed key people to be in charge of product development, manufacturing, and marketing efforts on a company-wide, versus product division, basis. These key people reported directly to Sculley. Previously each division had made its own decisions in these areas. Now such decisions would be centralized.

CHANGING AN ORGANIZATION

Organizational change is the process of modifying an existing organization. Thus far, the focus has been on how to organize. This section emphasizes how an established organization will need normal modifications to make it more efficient and effective.

Managers generally agree that if an organization is to have long-term success, it will have to be changed over time to reflect important developments in the environment of the organization. Such developments commonly include changing customer needs, changing educational backgrounds of employees, and changing technology. Organizational changes in response to such environmental developments could include the following: Existing products could be modified to meet changing customer needs. More efficient and sophisticated jobs might be developed to fit more educated employees. Robots could be introduced into manufacturing as a technological innovation.

The following sections provide some guidelines for successful change in organizations. They focus on three important topics: structural change, resistance to change, and stress and change.

Structural Change

Organizations can be changed in many different ways. Managers can change workers by providing different kinds of training. Managers can use changing technology by buying the latest equipment. Managers can change organizations by revising organizational structure.

Structural change is the modification of an existing organization structure. Its main emphasis is increasing organizational success by changing elements that influence how people perform their jobs. Such elements could include any organization variable discussed so far in this chapter. For example, structural change might involve changing the pattern of departmentalization to a functional basis rather than a manufacturing process basis, increasing the spans of management, or using functional authority more extensively.

Structural change is the modification of an existing organizational structure.

Matrix organization is a much-used vehicle for structural change. Because it is project centered and temporary, and because it does not need to disrupt established patterns of line authority, it is a flexible structure suited to experiment and change. When the accomplishments of the project and the matrix organization have been evaluated, modifications can be planned for further stages of organizational change.

Resistance to Change

Managers typically face resistance when they try to change organizations. Once a manager decides on a suitable change, it is common for other organization members to attempt to block the change. This resistance is usually the result of individuals fearing they will incur some personal loss as a result of the change. They may fear that the change will eventually result in a loss of prestige, a loss of values that were part of the corporate culture, the elimination of established working relationships with friends, or the elimination of certain jobs. Following are some safeguards that managers should take to reduce resistance to organizational change and to manage the change process successfully:

Avoid surprises. People need time to evaluate proposed change. Communicating openly and freely about changes under consideration can give organization members time to adjust to possible change.

Make sure people understand the change. A significant part of the resistance to organizational change is caused by a lack of understanding of what the change entails. This lack can magnify fears about the change. Some managers may also be able to encourage employee participation in planning and carrying out the change process.

Outline what workers can gain from the change. Management should show workers what positive things they will receive as a result of the change. In this way, workers will have an incentive for making sure that the change is successful.

Make the change tentative. Resistance can often be reduced or eliminated if a change is made on a temporary basis to see if it will work. Organization members typically view such change as an experiment aimed at bettering the work situation.

BUSINESS PRACTICE EXAMPLE Continues

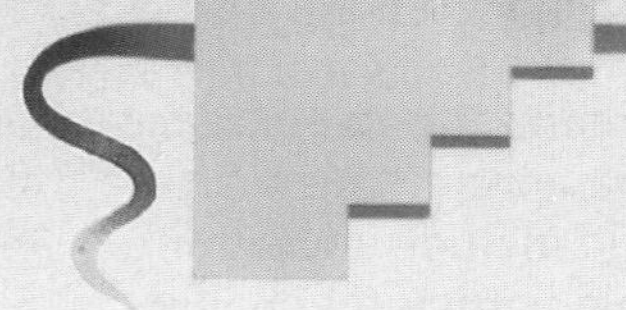

In order to reorganize Apple, Sculley was forced to eliminate 20 percent of Apple's workforce. Three factories were closed and 1,200 full-time and 1,500 temporary employees lost their jobs. Morale plunged. Disillusioned by the turn of events, Apple employees wondered if management had lost its ability to manage the company.

Fortunately, Sculley was ultimately able to convince employees that his reorganization plan was necessary for the survival and prosperity of Apple. He convinced them that the company's future lay with developing computers that could coexist with, rather than completely replace, business computers such as those made by IBM and Digital Equipment Co. He strongly believed in innovation as much as ever, but he persuaded employees that Apple had to adapt to the needs of the business marketplace, and his way was the way to do it. Events have proved Sculley correct. By 1990, Apple's sales had soared. The battle was on again between IBM and Apple, who together held a virtual lock on the business market for PCs. In addition, Apple continued to change the world with its pathbreaking desktop publishing systems.

Issues for Discussion

1. From the case, can you identify any matrix organizations within Apple? Discuss.
2. Can you tell whether Apple's organization was flat or tall? Discuss.
3. What are some actions Sculley might have taken to help Apple employees weather the reorganization?

SUMMARY

Organizing is the process managers use to best combine people, equipment and materials, and all other resources in order to carry out plans and reach organizational objectives. The process entails reflecting on plans and objectives, establishing major task areas, dividing major tasks into subtasks, allocating resources and directives for subtasks, and evaluating the results of implemented strategy.

Organization is the end result of the organizing process. One factor that managers must emphasize in organizing is structure—the specific pattern of relationships among resources. Structure can be either formal or informal. Formal structure is established by management and is represented mainly by an organization chart. Informal structure develops naturally over time as people interact with one another. Structure is reflected in the departments that management establishes.

Span of management, a second major factor that managers must emphasize in organizing, is the number of individuals a manager supervises. It must be established in response to specific organizational situations. A manager who supervises too few individuals wastes managerial time. A manager who supervises too many people cannot give them adequate direction and support.

Organizing work behavior is the last major factor that managers must emphasize in organizing. Three forms of organizational authority are common: line authority, staff authority, and functional authority. A more flexible and temporary form of authority is found in matrix organizations. Organizing work behavior appropriately requires that managers establish responsibilities—obligations people accept to perform certain work—and delegate the authority necessary to meet these obligations. Managers generally delegate the combination of authority that will best enable individuals to carry out their responsibilities. They also use accountability in organizing work behavior. Accountability holds people liable for performing the jobs they are responsible for and have been given authority to carry out.

Over time, the organizational pattern must be modified to become more useful. In such a situation, managers commonly make structural changes—modifications to an existing organizational structure. When planning for structural change of any type, managers should always consider how to cope with the resistance to change that workers commonly display.

KEY TERMS

Accountability p. 240
Authority p. 234
Centralization p. 241
Decentralization p. 242
Delegation p. 241
Department p. 229
Departmentalization p. 230
Flat organizations p. 232
Formal structure p. 225
Functional authority p. 235
Grapevine p. 227
Informal structure p. 226
Line authority p. 234
Matrix organization p. 237
Organization p. 225
Organizational culture p. 227
Organization chart p. 225
Organizing p. 223
Organizing process p. 224
Responsibility p. 233
Span of management p. 230
Staff authority p. 235
Structural change p. 243
Structure p. 225
Tall organizations p. 232

CHECK YOUR LEARNING

Reread the following learning objectives. Each objective is followed by a few questions. Answering these questions accurately will help you retain the most important concepts discussed in this chapter. After answering each question, check your answer with the key at the end of this chapter. (*Hint:* If you have doubt regarding the correct response, consult the page whose number follows the answer.)

Circle:

A. Discuss organizing and the organizing process.

T F 1. Organizing stresses objectives more than resources.

T F 2. Dividing tasks into subtasks is part of organizing.

B. Describe the roles of structure and span of management in organizing.

a b c d 1. The variable that influences structure the least is: (a) function; (b) resources ordered; (c) territory; (d) customer.

T F 2. Span of management and span of responsibility are the same thing.

C. Explain how responsibility, authority, and accountability are related.

T F 1. Responsibility and authority are similar in that both can be delegated.

T F 2. Accountability implies rewards for good work.

D. Compare and contrast authority in line organizations, staff organizations, functional organizations, and matrix organizations.

T F 1. Line authority includes the right to command production workers in the organization.

T F 2. All organizations should have both line and staff authority.

a b c d 3. An advantage of line authority is that it: (a) maintains simplicity; (b) enables specialists to give expert advice; (c) includes planning specialists; (d) frees staff people of routine decisions.

T F 4. One disadvantage of a matrix structure is that it can result in confusion because some workers may have more than one supervisor.

E. Outline the relationships among delegation, decentralization, and centralization.

1. Delegation does not include: (a) assigning specific duties to individuals; (b) assigning specific responsibility to individuals; (c) creating the obligation for subordinates to perform; (d) granting authority. — a b c d
2. Centralization and decentralization are different degrees of delegation. — T F

F. Describe structural change.

1. Structural change emphasizes changing the habits of people in the organization. — T F
2. A structure suited to experimenting with organizational change is: (a) top-heavy organization; (b) matrix organization; (c) line organization. — a b c

G. Explain why organization members resist change.

1. Organization members may resist change because they fear some personal loss as a result of the change. — T F
2. Managers can minimize resistance to change by: (a) avoiding surprises; (b) making sure people understand the change; (c) outlining what workers can gain from the change; (d) all of the above. — a b c d

QUESTIONS FOR REVIEW AND DISCUSSION

1. Define the key terms listed at the end of the chapter.
2. Draw an organization chart of the university department in which this course is being taught. Discuss the broad working relationships and the lines of communication in the chart.
3. Discuss the issue of departmentalization as it relates to the store in which you bought your last major piece of clothing.
4. Can responsibility be delegated? Explain.
5. Do you think there is a significant amount of potential for conflict between line and staff personnel? Explain.
6. Suppose you are a project manager in a matrix organization. What do you see as your most significant challenges?
7. Would you be more motivated to work in a highly centralized or a highly decentralized organization? Explain.
8. Do you think that it would be easier for managers to change people, technology, or organizational structure? Explain.
9. Describe the organizational culture that has evolved in this course. What possible changes could your instructor make that would be inconsistent with this culture and would result in student resistance to change?

CONCLUDING CASE

What's Next for DEC?

Ken Olsen [company president] saw it once before, in 1982. For several years before then, Digital Equipment Corp., the company he started in 1957, could do no wrong. Computer buyers and investors went overboard in their enthusiasm for DEC. Then, suddenly, they fell out of love. DEC became beset by management and product problems, and its earnings fell. Analysts, customers, and competitors began to find flaws in its strategy. And Olsen, hailed as a visionary during the flush times, was second-guessed and, occasionally, ridiculed.

On the surface, at least, it's starting again. After the company's longest-ever winning streak, four years in which its revenues more than doubled and it became a potent No. 2 to industry leader International Business Machines Corp., sentiment is turning away from DEC anew. With IBM's recovery finally under way, investors are betting more on Big Blue. DEC's stock, which dropped 25% in the October [1987] market crash, has since fallen about 25% more and now hovers several points below IBM's. Young upstarts and longtime competitors alike are eroding DEC's technological lead and chipping away at its markets. "The slowdown in DEC's momentum is becoming more obvious by the day," says Robert Randolph, an analyst at International Data Corp.

Part of the problem, as Olsen puts it, may be that "success can deteriorate a company." The addition of thousands of new employees in 1987, combined with a smaller-than-anticipated sales increase, has pushed overhead expenses 37% ahead of [1987]. So far in fiscal 1988, which ends on June 30, these swelling costs have pared DEC's pretax profit margin to 14.9% from 17.2% a year ago. Even though revenues jumped 17% in the third quarter, ended Mar. 26, earnings were about flat—and some 10% below analysts' estimates. For the full year, things may not look as bad. Wall Street expects an 18% profit increase, to $1.3 billion, on a 21% sales gain, to $11.6 billion.

But it's the long term that has DEC observers worried. The company has prospered since 1984 by expanding sales of its hugely successful VAX minicomputers from their customary scientific and technical niches into the broader commercial market. The key was a single computer design, or architecture, available in many sizes and easily linked into networks—a combination no other company offered. Now, for the first time, serious competition may be developing to DEC's approach. Dozens of computer makers are backing research efforts on so-called open systems—standardized software that would tie together all brands of computers and perhaps blunt DEC's selling edge.

Issues for Discussion

1. What is meant by the phrase *success can deteriorate a company?*
2. Has DEC made structural changes as a result of its success? Explain.
3. Will the situation depicted in the case eventually result in employees feeling more stress? Explain.
4. Name three factors in the case that could be stressors. How are they stressors?

NOTES

1. Harold Koontz, Cyril O'Donnell, and Heinz Weihrich, *Management* (New York: McGraw-Hill, 1984), pp. 236–250.

2. William H. Newman and E. Kirby Warren, *The Process of Management: Concepts,* 4th ed. (Englewood Cliffs, N.J.: Prentice-Hall, 1977), pp. 39–40.

CHECK YOUR LEARNING ANSWER KEY

A. 1. F, *p. 223*
   2. T, *p. 224*

B. 1. b, *p. 230*
   2. T, *p. 230*

C. 1. F, *p. 234*
   2. T, *p. 240*

D. 1. T, *p. 234*
   2. F, *p. 236*
   3. a, *p. 234*
   4. T, *p. 237*

E. 1. b, *p. 241*
   2. T, *p. 241*

F. 1. F, *p. 243*
   2. b, *p. 243*

G. 1. T, *p. 243*
   2. d, *p. 244*

CHAPTER

9

HUMAN RESOURCE MANAGEMENT

LEARNING OBJECTIVES

After reading this chapter you should be able to:

1. Define *human resource management.*
2. Define *human resource planning.*
3. Discuss the steps necessary to carry out human resource planning.
4. Outline how to provide appropriate human resources for an organization.
5. Discuss several activities involved in human resource management and who normally performs them.
6. Describe different types of financial and nonfinancial compensation.
7. Discuss how the law can influence the practice of human resource management.

OUTLINE

BUSINESS PRACTICE EXAMPLE

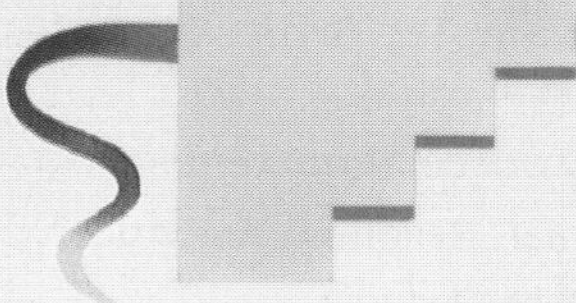

Toyota Manages Human Resources in Kentucky

Getting a job at the Toyota plant in Georgetown, Kentucky, is nothing like getting a job with most car manufacturers.

In fact, Toyota isn't hiring many people with auto experience at all. The theory is: no bad habits to "unlearn" while workers are taught Toyota's method of creating cars.

Toyota went through quite a process to fill some 3,000 jobs in Kentucky. A battery of tests was required for anyone who would attach a fender or spray paint a door. These tests included workplace simulations, long interviews, and sit-down tests. Kentuckians expecting to breeze on through were sorely disappointed. In a state where much of the adult population has not finished high school, many of those hired did have high school and college degrees.

Toyota opened the 1,300 acre Kentucky plant in May of 1988. The first Camry rolled off the line on May 26. By 1989, full production reached 200,000 Camrys. Other Japanese car manufacturers with plants in the United States include Honda Motor Co., in Marysville, Ohio, and Nissan Motor Co. in Smyrna, Tennessee. In terms of hiring, they're all pretty tough, although nowhere as tough as Toyota. Honda does not require tests but does demand three interviews. Nissan asks its final candidates to participate in 40 hours of "pre-employment" training—without pay. The training is a final check on whether the company and those in training are really right for each other.

Toyota's known talent for avoiding adversarial management-labor relations seems to be at work in the Kentucky facility. Even with what looked like a lack of educated workers, the company did not have to go outside of the state for its employees. For those who made the grade, the going is apparently very good indeed. "I saw this as an opportunity of a lifetime," said leader-in-training Sharon Busse, "of joining a company where no one has an unimportant job and where employee ideas are welcomed."

Another happy hire, Ron Raider, commented, "Job security has big appeal for me. Toyota has not laid off anyone for 30 years."

WHAT'S AHEAD

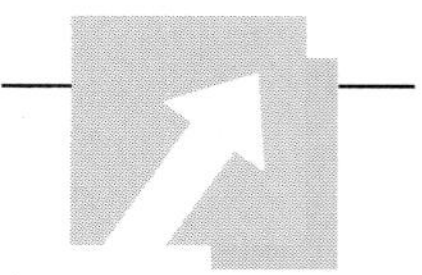

As Toyota management in Georgetown, Kentucky, would undoubtedly attest, human resource management is one of the most important concepts in management. This chapter discusses planning future employment needs, providing appropriate human resources (through recruitment, selection, training, and performance appraisal), and keeping employees by

offering them adequate financial and nonfinancial compensation. It also covers how various laws affect human resource management.

DEFINING *HUMAN RESOURCE MANAGEMENT*

The process of determining the kinds of people an organization needs to achieve its goals, hiring those people, and retaining them through an equitable compensation system and desirable work environment is **human resource management** (also termed *personnel management*). Although descriptions of the most desirable environment may differ, most employees would probably agree that it includes worker safety, fairness in performance appraisals, and opportunities for career growth. Table 9.1 presents several important concerns of human resource managers.

Who Performs Human Resource Activities?

The size of the organization is one of the most common factors in determining the responsibility for human resource management. In a small company, the president might assume the responsibility for human resource functions. Larger companies are likely to have an entire department of human resources, with its own director.

The organization of human resource departments differs by industry and by company. Figure 9.1, however, illustrates a common approach. The department is headed by a director, and individual managers are responsible for the major

Table 9.1 Several important concerns of human resource managers.

Personnel record maintenance.
Insurance benefit administration.
Wage/salary administration.
Pre-employment testing.
Hiring of new employees.
New-employee orientation.
Determination of promotions, transfers, and firings.
Retirement program administration.
Organization of company recreational programs.
Career counseling.
Employee surveys.
Performance appraisals.
Training of workers and managers.
Maintenance of community relations.
Maintenance of employee motivation programs.

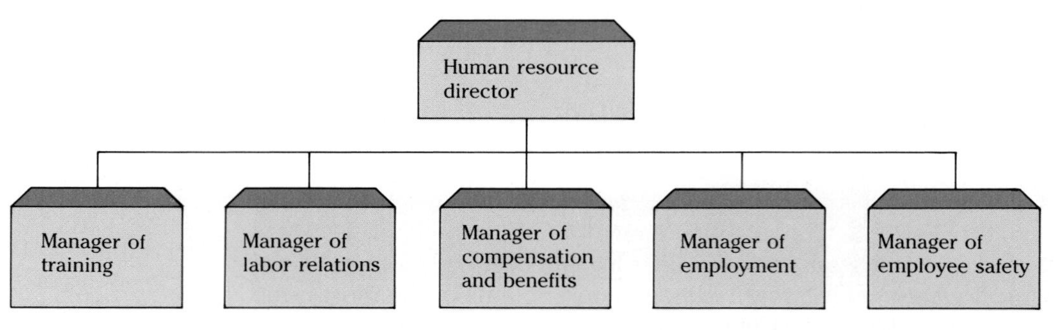

Figure 9.1 Organization of a typical human resource department.

areas: training, labor relations, compensation and benefits, employment, and employee safety. The director has line authority over the managers. (The director also has a staff position as adviser to line managers outside the department—for example, the president and the production manager.)

HUMAN RESOURCE PLANNING

Human resource management is the process of determining the kinds of people an organization needs, hiring them, and retaining them through an equitable compensation system and desirable work environment.

Human resource planning is strategic planning to meet the future human resource needs of the organization.

A ***job analysis*** is a detailed investigation of the task requirements of a job and the characteristics of the people needed to perform the tasks.

A ***job description*** is a listing of the specific activities the holder of a position must perform and the skill level the person will need.

All management activity normally begins with planning, and human resource management is no exception. **Human resource planning** is strategic planning to meet the future human resource needs of the organization. Although an organization may presently have adequate human resources, the human resource manager must ensure their future adequacy.

Human resource planning is a series of steps (illustrated in Figure 9.2):

Step 1: Reflecting on the strategic plans of the organization. Human resource planning starts with an examination of strategic plans (long-range plans for the organization as a whole). Human resource plans must flow from the strategic plans. For instance, assume that strategic plans developed by the management of a fast-food chain call for increasing the number of restaurants by 10 percent in each of the next five years. Certainly, a plan of this sort would influence what must be done to meet the chain's future human resource needs.

Step 2: Analyzing the jobs to be performed. This step means acquiring an understanding of the jobs that must be performed in the future in order to carry out the strategic plans. The understanding comes from the use of job analysis, job descriptions, and job specifications. A **job analysis** is a detailed investigation of the task requirements of a job and the characteristics of the people needed to perform the tasks. It is aimed at determining the **job description**—a listing of specific activities that the holder of a position must perform and the skill level the person will need. Job analysis also determines the **job specification**—a written document listing the characteristics required of an individual who is to perform a specific job.

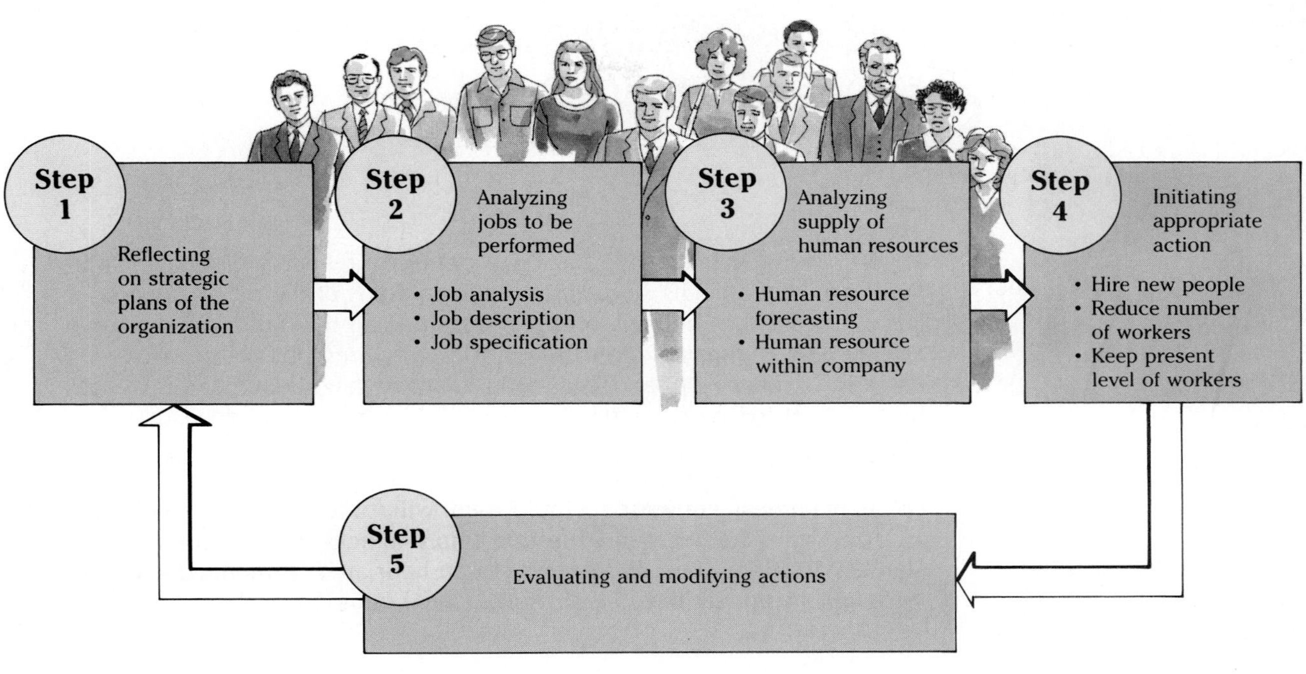

Figure 9.2 Steps in the human resource planning process.

Step 3: Analyzing the supply of human resources. Once the jobs to be performed are defined and analyzed, the manager must determine future personnel needs, focusing on both the projected numbers of employees and the skills they will need, through the process of **human resource forecasting.** Then the manager must analyze the present number of employees and their characteristics, including impending retirements, transfers, terminations, and promotions. The two sets of figures enable the manager to calculate the number and kinds of people who will be needed to staff the business.

A ***job specification*** is a written document listing the characteristics required of an individual who is to perform a specific job.

Human resource forecasting is the process of determining the extent of future personnel needs (both number of people and types of skills).

Step 4: Initiating appropriate action. The comparison of future personnel needs with available personnel will result in one of three conclusions: (1) If the company has just enough human resources to meet future needs, no action will be necessary. (2) If the company does not have enough human resources to meet future needs, it must begin hiring them. (3) If the company has more people than it will be able to use in the future, it may have to lay off or fire some of them.

Step 5: Evaluating and modifying actions. The action initiated in step 4 may be appropriate only for a given strategic plan or at a specific point in time. If the plan changes, human resource planning may have to be adjusted accordingly. In addition, such factors as individuals leaving a company or being hired by it can significantly change the results of the analysis of human resources. Therefore, human resource planning activities should be checked periodically and modified as needed.

BUSINESS PRACTICE EXAMPLE Continues

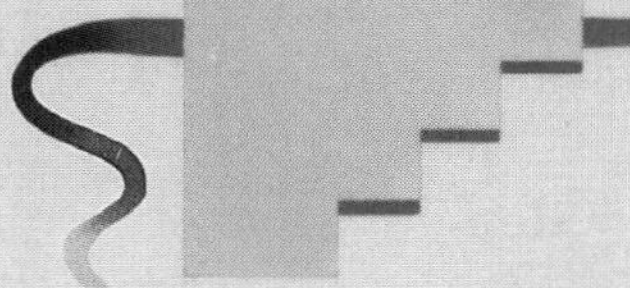

Toyota's hiring activities are the result of human resource planning. Only after company officials studied the strategic plans of the company, analyzed the jobs they needed to fill, and determined the human resources available, were they able to carry out focused hiring practices. Toyota carefully assessed the labor market in Kentucky, and concluded it would be sufficient for the company's needs well before the final decision to build the plant was made.

Toyota has done extremely careful human resource forecasting. The company already knows that employment will top out at 3,500 employees in 1991, with 70 percent hired from within Kentucky. Hourly workers will start at $10.50 an hour, and rise to $12 an hour after 18 months. The Kentucky plant's annual payroll will exceed $100 million.

WHAT ARE APPROPRIATE HUMAN RESOURCES?

Appropriate human resources are the people in an organization who make a valuable contribution to the attainment of organizational objectives.

Human resources are people. **Appropriate human resources** are the people in an organization who make a valuable contribution to the attainment of organizational objectives. This contribution, of course, is a result of their productivity. Inappropriate human resources are organization members who do not make a valuable contribution to the attainment of organizational objectives. Essentially, they are ineffective in their jobs.

Providing appropriate human resources is an important managerial task. Productivity is determined by how human resources interact and how they use all other management system resources. Such factors as background, age, job-related experience, and level of formal education all have some role in determining the degree of appropriateness of the individual to the organization. Although the process of providing appropriate human resources is complex and somewhat subjective, this chapter explains how to increase its success.

STEPS IN PROVIDING APPROPRIATE HUMAN RESOURCES

Appropriate human resources must be provided as various positions become open. The process involves four main steps: recruitment, selection, training, and performance appraisal (see Figure 9.3). It can be used for either managerial or nonmanagerial positions.

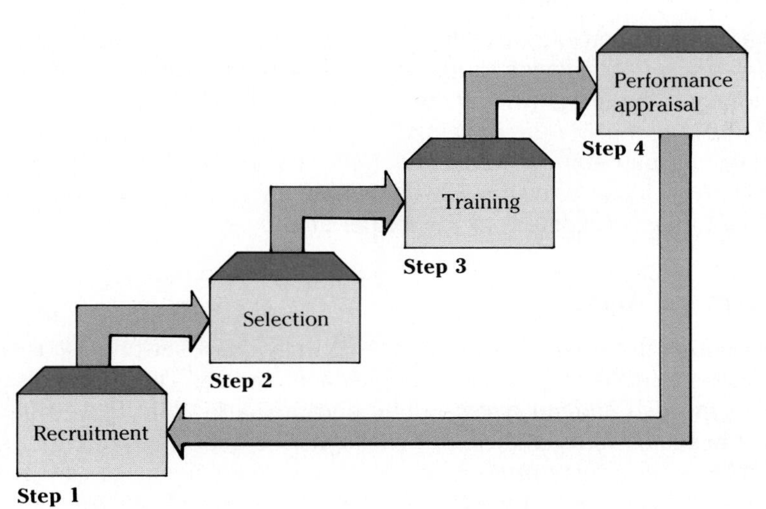

Figure 9.3 Four sequential steps in providing appropriate human resources. Organizations must be methodical in order to maintain an adequate level of appropriate human resources.

Recruitment

The first step in providing appropriate human resources is **recruitment**—the initial screening of the total supply of applicants for a position. The purpose of recruitment is to narrow a large field of prospective employees down to a relatively small number, from which one person can eventually be hired. An effective recruiter will know where potential employees can be located, how the law influences recruiting efforts, and what exactly is required in the job to be filled.

Recruitment is the initial screening of the total supply of applicants for a position.

Many companies try to fill positions with people who are already members of the organization. If a position cannot be filled from within, however, there are numerous sources of prospective employees outside the organization.

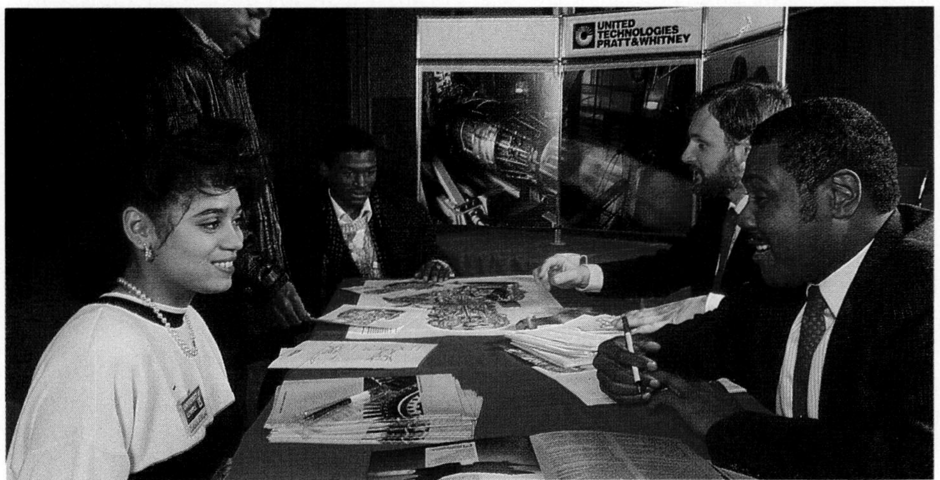

The purpose of recruitment is to narrow a large field of prospective employees down to a few from which one person can eventually be hired. The applicants at this job fair hope to pass the screening process and be chosen for a position.

Competitors

One commonly tapped external source of employees is competing organizations. There are several advantages to luring people away from competitors, and this type of piracy is common. Among the advantages are the following: (1) the competitor will have paid for the individual's training up to the time of hire, (2) the competitor will probably be weakened somewhat by the loss of the individual, and (3) the individual, once hired, will become a valuable source of information about how to best compete with the former employer.

Employment Agencies

An organization that specializes in matching individuals seeking a position with organizations in need of them is an employment agency. These agencies can be classified into two general types: public and private. Public (government) employment agencies were created by the Wagner-Peyser Act of 1933 to assist the public in the employment process. Private employment agencies exist to make a profit. They collect a fee, either from the person hired or from the organization, once a hiring has been completed.

Readers of Certain Publications

Perhaps the most widely addressed source of potential human resources is the readers of certain publications. To tap this source, the recruiter simply places an advertisement in a suitable publication. The advertisement should describe the position and announce that the organization is accepting applications. The type of position to be filled determines the type of publication in which the advertisement should be placed. Obviously, the objective is to advertise in a publication whose readers would likely be interested in filling the position. A top-level executive opening might be advertised in the *Wall Street Journal*, a training director opening might be advertised in the *Journal of Training and Development*, and an educational opening might be advertised in the *Chronicle of Higher Education*.

Educational Institutions

In their quest for employees, some recruiters go directly to educational institutions to interview graduating students. Liberal arts schools, business schools, engineering schools, junior colleges, and community colleges all offer potential employees. Recruiters should focus their efforts on the schools that offer the highest probability of providing appropriate human resources.

Selection

Selection is the process of choosing an individual to hire from all those who have been recruited.

After recruitment, the next major step in furnishing appropriate human resources is **selection**—the process of choosing an individual to hire from all those who have been recruited. The process is typically represented as a series of stages through which prospective employees must pass in order to be hired.

All prospective employees are screened. They may be asked about educational attainment or past job performance. They may be given intelligence tests or aptitude tests. An interviewer will talk to them and evaluate their personality and personal ambitions and the overall impression they make.

Each successive stage in the selection process reduces the total group of prospective employees, until, finally, only the one to be hired remains. Table 9.2 lists the stages of the process and gives reasons for eliminating candidates at each stage.

Training

After recruitment and selection comes **training**—the process of developing qualities in employees that will enable them to be more productive and, as a result, to contribute more to the attainment of organizational objectives. Virtually every organization in modern society is placing great emphasis on the need for training.

Training is the process of developing qualities in employees that will enable them to be more productive and, as a result, to contribute more to the attainment of organizational objectives.

Training can focus on workers or managers. **Management development programs,** for example, are training programs that focus on developing problem-solving and other skills needed by good managers. Both current and potential managers may participate.

Management development programs are training programs that focus on developing problem-solving and other skills needed by good managers.

The training process consists of determining training needs and then designing, administering, and evaluating the training program (see Figure 9.4).

Determining Training Needs

The first step of the training process is determining training needs—information or skill areas (of individuals or groups) that can be further developed to increase productivity. For example: Are deadlines being met? Are labor costs too high? Are products being rejected because they are not up to standard? Training must focus on such needs if it is to be of benefit to the organization.

Table 9.2 Stages in the selection process.

Stage	**Examples of Why Applicant Might Be Rejected**
Stage 1: Preliminary screening.	Applicant doesn't seem committed to career.
Stage 2: Application.	Applicant doesn't have enough experience.
Stage 3: Interview.	Applicant cannot communicate well orally.
Stage 4: Testing.	Applicant fails skills test.
Stage 5: Reference checks.	Applicant has questionable or negative references.
Stage 6: Physical exam (if applicable).	Applicant is physically unable to do job.
Stage 7: Final interview.	Applicant does not seem committed enough to the organization.

HIGHLIGHT IN BUSINESS PRACTICE

Training Program Design at Frito-Lay

When Frito-Lay Inc. changed its method of making corn chips, employees suddenly were called upon to operate a complex new machine that required some degree of reading skill to master.

And a number of workers fell short of the mark, recalls Regina Andrews, Frito-Lay's employee relations administrator. It had been years since many of the Orlando manufacturing employees had attended high school, and many then had not attained degrees. The result: Safety and productivity were threatened by workers who didn't understand how to operate the machine.

"We had some employees who were a little slow. Things are becoming more automated, and so more difficult to work with," Andrews said. "With things becoming more computerized, we wanted to work with employees to be sure they could keep up."

Frito-Lay is one of thousands of companies across the nation and dozens in Florida to find some of their employees lack basic reading and math skills. Such deficiencies become most apparent, education experts say, when companies automate the workplace, installing, as Frito-Lay did, sophisticated equipment. At such times, employees occasionally are found to lack the rudimentary reading, writing and comprehension skills to operate the machinery.

Frito-Lay took action when the installation of new equipment pointed up some of the educational deficiencies of its workers.

Beginning in August, the company will offer classes in conjunction with the Orange County Public Schools. The courses will be held at the plant and will cover two areas: training on machinery, and employee benefits. The goal is not only to teach employees specifics about the workplace, but also to foster better comprehension skills.

"We'll offer this to all employees on a voluntary basis," Andrews said. "The instructors will go over the information in a step-by-step way, so if it is difficult for the employee to read, there is someone to help them. A lot of times it is easier to accomplish those kinds of things as a group, rather than taking a book home and having distractions."

Frito-Lay, Andrews said, considered the courses a positive move, and if anything, felt pleased to be able to help employees help themselves. She said the company hoped the training might spur employees who do not have a high-school degree to obtain one, or encourage others to further their education with night college classes.

Designing the Training Program

Once training needs have been determined, the next step is to design a training program aimed at meeting them. Designing a program entails assembling various types of facts as well as information about activities that will help meet the training needs. Perhaps a supervisor should perform the work duties for a new employee, then watch the newcomer go through the work. Perhaps a lecture should be put

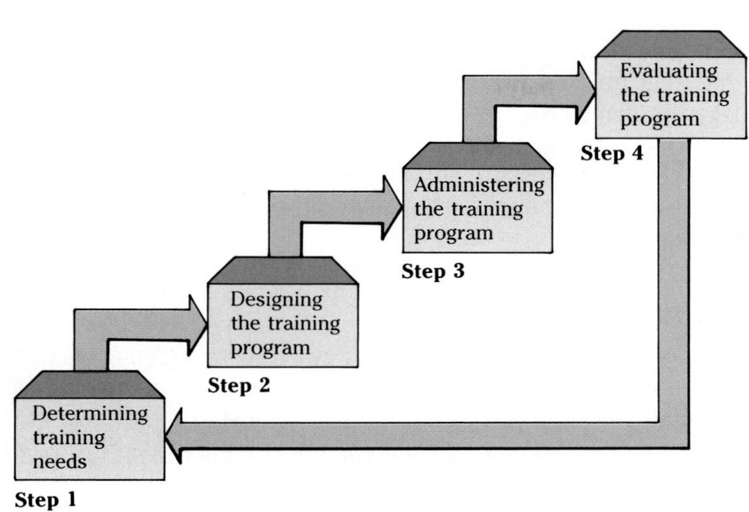

Figure 9.4
Steps in the training process. Training, which consists of four steps, must take place after the recruitment and selection process.

together to teach new employees the basics of their jobs. Perhaps a film should be shown. The design of the training program is highly dependent on the training needs. The Highlight in Business Practice illustrates how determining training needs resulted in a related training program at Frito-Lay.

Administering the Training Program

The next step of the training process is administering the training program—actually training people. Such techniques as lectures and case studies can be used to transmit information and develop skills.

On-the-job training is a training method through which workers learn job skills by performing appropriate tasks in the actual work situation, with the help of experienced employees. **Vestibule training** is a training method through which workers learn job skills by operating equipment similar to that used in the actual job situation in a setting similar to the actual job setting. This type of training is done in a room, or *vestibule,* away from the work location.

On-the-job training is a training method through which workers learn job skills by performing appropriate tasks in the actual work situation, with the help of experienced employees.

Vestibule training is a training method through which workers learn job skills by operating equipment similar to that used in the actual job situation in a setting similar to the actual job setting.

One tool commonly used in training and development is *assessment centers*—programs (not places) in which trainees engage in individual and group exercises that simulate important job activities. The exercises commonly include role playing, oral presentations, and group leadership. Assessment centers are also used to identify employees with management potential. The development of the technique is usually credited to AT&T. Other companies that saw its value and began using it for organizational training include IBM, Prudential Life, and General Electric.

Evaluating the Training Program

After the training program has been completed, it should be evaluated for effectiveness in meeting the needs for which it was designed. After all, training programs represent costs for which management should obtain some reasonable return. These costs include materials, the trainer's time, and production time lost because the trainee is not doing a job.

Answering questions such as the following can help determine whether the program has met training needs: Has a department's excessive reject rate for produced goods declined? Are deadlines being met more regularly? Are labor costs per unit decreasing? If the answer to such questions is yes, the training program is probably successful, although management might enhance its effectiveness through certain changes. If the answer is no, the program should probably be modified significantly.

Performance appraisal is the process of reviewing an individual's productive activity to evaluate the contribution made to the attainment of organizational objectives.

Performance Appraisal

After recruitment, selection, and training, the task of making an individual a productive member of the organization is still not finished. The fourth step in providing appropriate human resources is **performance appraisal** (also called *performance review* and *performance evaluation*)—the process of reviewing an

BUSINESS PRACTICE EXAMPLE Continues

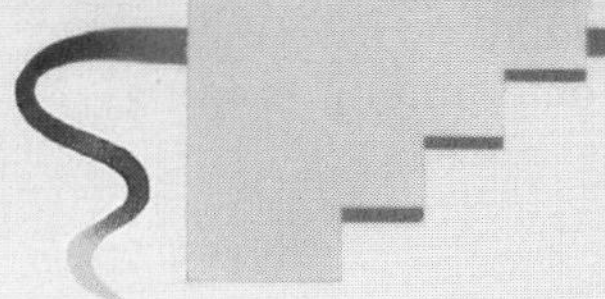

Toyota dedication to training is probably unsurpassed both within and outside of the automobile industry. "With most companies, training is a day—or a week if you're lucky," says leader-in-training Sharon Busse. "With Toyota, it's forever."

Ms. Busse joined 318 men and women, ranging in age from 22 to 55, selected by Toyota to travel to Japan for a four-week program for leaders-in-training. The program featured not only classroom lectures on management philosophy and Toyota's production process, but also 16 days of actually assembling cars in a local plant. The trainees will pass their knowledge on to work groups in Kentucky.

More than 100,000 people had applied to Toyota by August, 1988, just 3 months after the plant opened, and another 44,000 had been screened in a six-step process done in concert with state and local officials before Toyota's final testing. An estimated $50 million in training costs were picked up by the state, which worked hard to convince Toyota to build its plant in Kentucky.

Specific testing focused on technical, interpersonal, and leadership skills, as well as a health examination.

"I paid to go to college," said an obviously pleased new hire, Randy Sinkhorn, "and now they're paying me to learn."

Table 9.3 Sample methods of performance appraisal.

Appraisal Method	Description
Rating scale	Individuals appraising performance use a form containing several employee qualities and characteristics to be evaluated (e.g., dependability, initiative, leadership). Each evaluated factor is rated on a continuum or scale ranging, for example, from one to seven or more points.
Employee comparisons	Appraisers rank employees according to such factors as job performance and value to the organization. Only one employee can occupy a particular ranking.
Free-form essay	Appraisers simply write down their impressions of employees in paragraph form.
Critical-form essay	Appraisers write down particularly good or bad events involving employees as these events occur. Records of all documented events for any one employee are used to evaluate his or her performance.

individual's productive activity to evaluate the contribution made to the attainment of organizational objectives. (See Table 9.3 for a description of several methods of appraisal.)

As with training, performance appraisal is a continuing activity that focuses on both new and established organization members. It is used in determining compensation, promotions, transfers, and terminations.

EMPLOYEE COMPENSATION[1]

The wages, salaries, and other benefits employees receive for work accomplished is **compensation.** People are willing to work in exchange for these rewards, but only if they perceive that the level of compensation in relation to the amount of time and effort is fair.

Compensation is the wages, salaries, and other benefits employees receive for work accomplished.

To achieve a fair level, organizations can compensate employees in many different ways. Figure 9.5 describes several possible components of a total compensation package. As the figure shows, employees can receive compensation in one of two basic forms: financial or nonfinancial.

Financial Compensation

Financial compensation is the monetary reward employees receive for performing a job.

The monetary reward employees receive for performing a job is **financial compensation.** Employees give time and effort to the organization, and the organi-

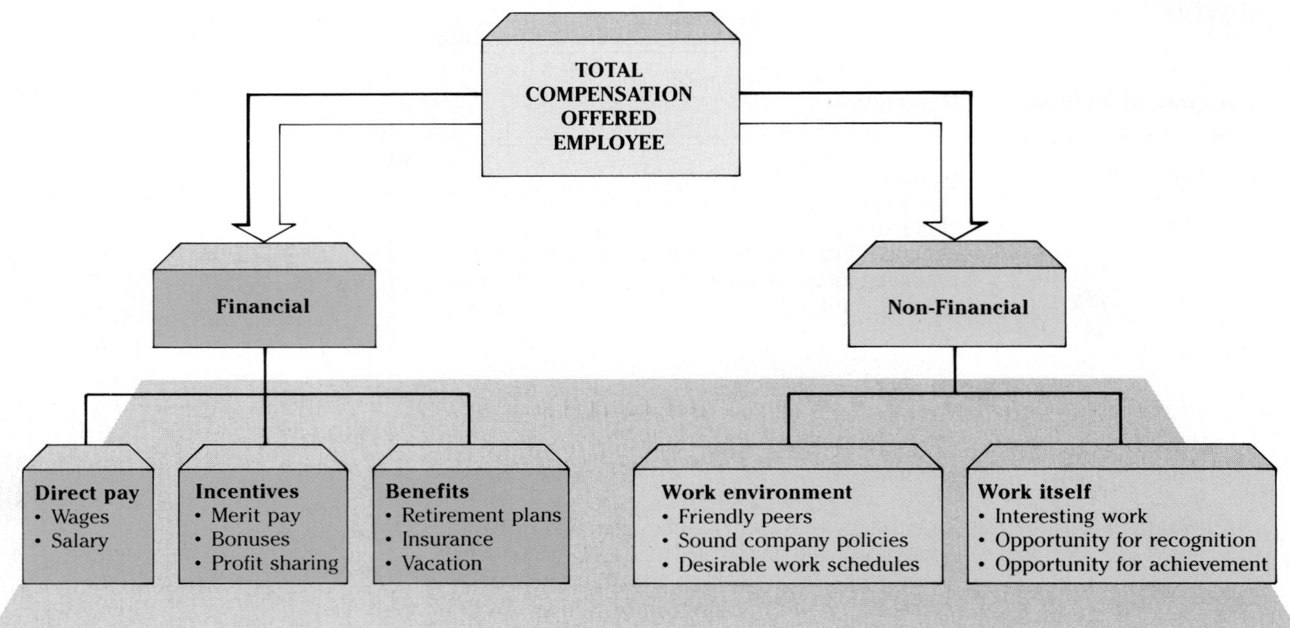

Figure 9.5 Possible components of a company's total compensation package.

zation gives them money in return. Financial compensation usually consists of direct pay, incentives, and fringe benefits.

Direct pay is money that employees receive according to the amount of time spent working or the number of units produced.

A ***wage*** is direct pay determined by the number of hours an employee works.

A ***piece-rate wage*** is direct pay determined by the number of units an employee produces.

A ***salary*** is direct pay based on an extended period of time worked, such as a week, a month, or a year.

An ***incentive*** is a type of financial compensation an individual receives in addition to a wage or salary because of outstanding performance in a job.

Direct Pay

Money that employees receive according to the amount of time spent working or the number of units produced is **direct pay.** It can be in the form of a wage or a salary. A **wage** (or time wage) is direct pay determined by the number of hours an employee works. A **piece-rate** wage is direct pay determined by the number of units an employee produces. The wage method of compensation is most often applied to nonmanagerial, lower-level positions—for example, assembly line worker and cashier.

A **salary** is direct pay based on an extended period of time worked, such as a week, a month, or a year. Middle and upper-level managers are generally compensated through salaries. Managers at these levels include division managers, plant managers, and department heads.

Incentives

A type of financial compensation an individual receives in addition to a wage or salary because of outstanding performance in a job is an **incentive.** Incentives can take the form of merit pay, bonuses, or profit sharing. **Merit pay** is incentive pay typically given to nonmanagement employees. The procedure is straightforward. Employee performance is rated periodically, and high performers are awarded merit pay increases.

Merit pay is a type of incentive pay typically given to nonmanagement employees.

A **bonus** is a type of incentive pay given to managers. It is intended to enhance departmental or divisional cooperation. The amount is usually based on the overall performance of the company. If the company does well, bonuses tend to be high. If it does poorly, bonuses may be low or nonexistent. Bonuses are often a major part of the total pay a manager receives from an organization. One study has indicated that the bonus of a typical chief executive officer can be as high as 46 percent of the person's total salary.

A ***bonus*** is a type of incentive pay typically given to managers.

Profit sharing is a type of incentive pay in which workers receive some portion of the profits that the organization earns. Profit-sharing programs encourage good relations between management and workers. The usual result is lower levels of absenteeism and turnover and therefore increased profits. Although profit-sharing programs are generally designed for nonmanagement employees, they can include managers as well.

Profit sharing is a type of incentive pay in which workers receive some portion of the profits that the company earns.

Fringe Benefits

Financial compensation that is generally not paid directly to employees is termed **fringe benefits** (or simply *benefits*). Benefits commonly provided by employers are retirement plans, life insurance, and vacations. Some of the more uncommon ones are IBM's two country clubs, which cost employees only $5 a year; Hewlett Packard's dozen vacation spots for employees, including ski chalets in the German alps and a lakeside resort in Scotland; and Hallmark's low-interest college loans for employees' children.

Fringe benefits are financial compensation that is generally not paid directly to employees.

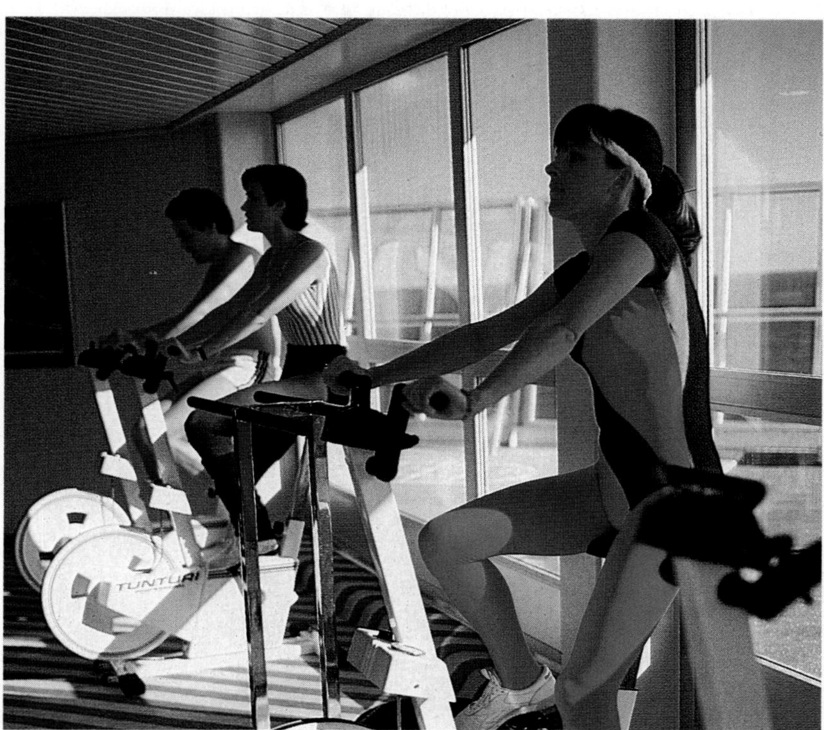

Fringe benefits are company-supplied benefits taking forms other than financial compensation. Membership in a health club is one of many benefits companies may choose to offer their employees.

According to a Department of Commerce study, the average U.S. company spends $6,627 a year in fringe benefits for an average salary of $17,911. Figure 9.6 shows the components of the fringe-benefit package as determined by the study.

A ***cafeteria fringe benefits program*** is a flexible benefits system in which employees are allocated an established total dollar amount to spend on any of several available benefits.

To better meet the financial needs of employees, many companies have adopted a **cafeteria fringe benefits program**—a flexible benefits system in which employees are allocated an established total dollar amount to spend on any of several benefits offered. Table 9.4 lists the types of benefits that could be offered through a cafeteria program. By choosing their own benefits, employees can obtain the combination that best suits their individual financial situations.

Day care is one fringe benefit that will probably receive increased attention from human resource managers. Many companies do not offer day care as a benefit. One that has—since 1971—is the Stride Rite Corporation. The Highlight in Business Practice illustrates how the company and its employees benefit from its day care program.

Nonfinancial Compensation

Nonfinancial compensation is a nonmonetary reward that an organization member receives for performing a job.

The second major type of compensation employees can receive from an organization is **nonfinancial compensation**—a nonmonetary reward that an organization member receives for performing a job. This type of compensation consists of factors in the job situation that employees find satisfying and motivating. For example, part of the compensation individuals receive for performing a job could be the social relationships they develop and enjoy while working. As Figure 9.5 indicates, individuals can receive nonfinancial compensation through desirable

Figure 9.6
Components of a typical fringe benefits package.

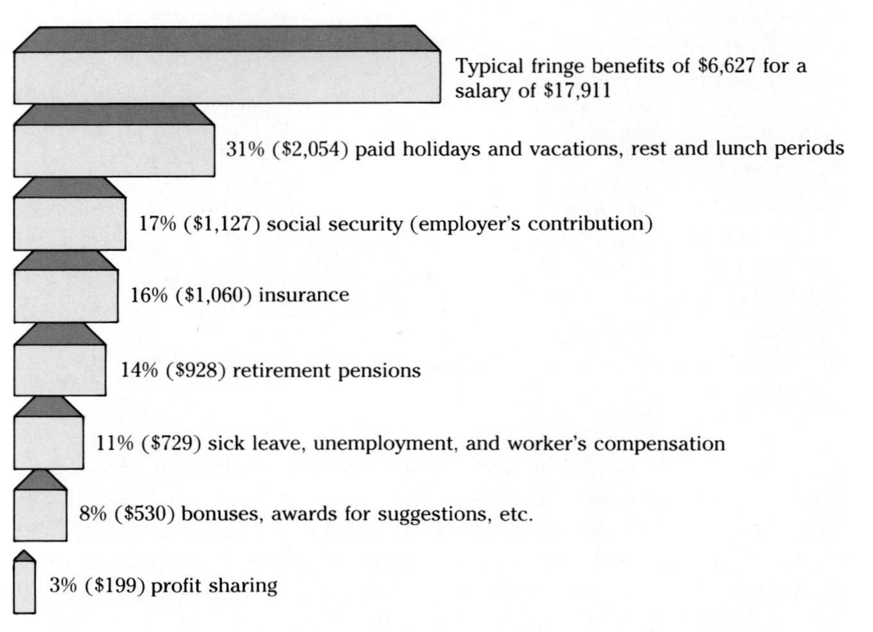

Table 9.4 Possible offerings in a cafeteria fringe benefits program.

Birthdays (vacation)
Club memberships
Company medical assistance
Company-provided automobile
Company-provided housing
Company-subsidized travel
Day-care centers
Deferred compensation plan
Dental and eye-care insurance
Discount on company products
Education costs
Free checking account
Free or subsidized lunches
Group automobile insurance
Group homeowner's insurance
Group life insurance
Home health care
Hospital-surgical-medical insurance
Interest-free loans
Loans of company equipment
Long-term disability benefits
Nursing-home care
Parking facilities
Personal counseling
Personal credit cards
Personal expense accounts
Physical examinations
Psychiatric services
Resort facilities
Retirement gratuity (gift at retirement)
Sabbatical leaves
Savings plan
Scholarships for dependents
Severance pay
Sickness and accident insurance
Social service sabbaticals
Vacations

features of either the work or the work environment. (See chapter 7 for more detail about job satisfaction and motivation.)

When compensation programs are evaluated, factors such as interesting work and a friendly environment are often overlooked. However, given that nonfinancial factors may provide an economical means for raising the compensation level of employees, human resource managers should emphasize them in the total compensation program.

HIGHLIGHT IN BUSINESS PRACTICE

Stride Rite Chief: Day Care Working

WASHINGTON—The head of Cambridge-based Stride Rite Corp., saying that early education programs are good for business and the community, told a Senate panel yesterday that his firm's day-care centers have strengthened the work force and saved the company thousands of dollars per employee.

After witnessing the failures of federal worker training programs, Stride Rite decided to "intervene earlier in the development cycle," and opened its first children's center on the company premises in Roxbury in 1971, said Arnold Hiatt, chairman and chief executive officer.

"While we did not initiate this program to reduce turnover and absenteeism, the children's centers have in fact enhanced the stability of the work force," Hiatt said. Recruiting and retaining high-caliber employees saves Stride Rite about $25,000 per employee that would otherwise be spent to train replacement workers, Hiatt said.

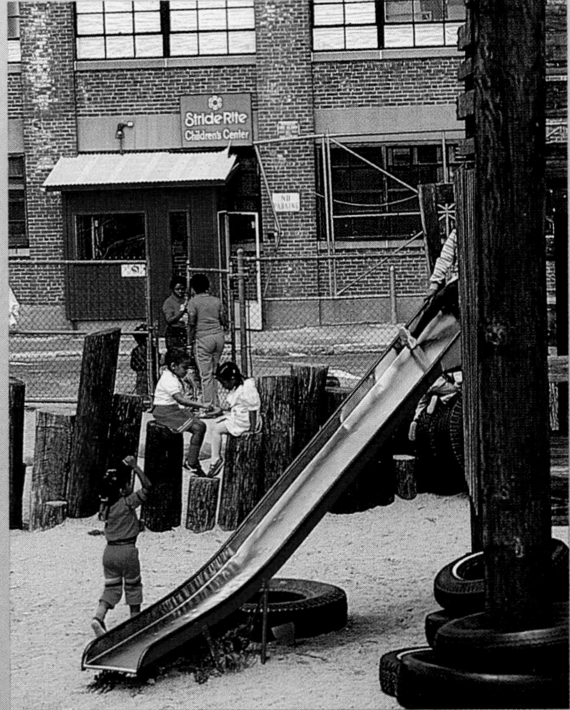

Hiatt testified before the Senate Labor and Human Resources Committee, chaired by Sen. Edward M. Kennedy, during a hearing on the link between early education and a skilled work force. He expressed support for Kennedy's "Smart Start" bill, which would provide federal grants to state and local governments to establish education programs for 4-year-olds.

Stride Rite's early child-care program has helped families move off welfare and has provided the company with educated employees, Hiatt said, explaining that some of the first students at the Roxbury children's center now work for Stride Rite.

"They were more fortunate in their earlier childhood than many of their peers who are now unemployed, or had become teen-age mothers, or worse, [are] in detention centers," Hiatt said.

He said it is less expensive to prevent social problems through such programs than to correct them later.

"The cost of providing good child care in our Cambridge or Roxbury facilities is $7,000 a year," he said. "The cost of maintaining a troubled adolescent in a residential group home is $50,000."

HUMAN RESOURCE MANAGEMENT AND THE LAW

Over the years, many laws affecting the practice of human resource management have been passed. Table 9.5 lists seven of these laws and describes their purposes. The rest of this section focuses on the Occupational Safety and Health Act (OSHA), the Civil Rights Act of 1964 and its 1972 amendment, and sex discrimination and comparable worth.

The Occupational Safety and Health Act

Passed in 1970, the **Occupational Safety and Health Act (OSHA)** is a federal law that requires employers to ensure as much as possible that every worker has a safe and healthy work environment and to keep all records necessary to judge how safe the work environments actually are. The law created the **Occupational Safety and Health Administration,** a federal agency charged with ensuring the safety of workers. The agency hires and trains inspectors, audits businesses to check on the safety of working conditions, and is empowered to fine employers for maintaining unsafe working conditions.

The ***Occupational Safety and Health Act (OSHA)*** is a 1970 federal law that requires employers to provide safe and healthy work environments and to keep records for judging safety.

The ***Occupational Safety and Health Administration*** is a federal agency charged with ensuring the safety of workers.

Reactions to OSHA have been varied. Initially, it was viewed as a controversial law that established safety standards that were too nitpicky and too expensive, thereby threatening the very existence of businesses. Since the major criticism of OSHA was its administration, not its purpose, President Ronald Reagan emphasized counseling employers into safer working conditions rather than imposing harsh penalties for unsafe conditions. Many of the nitpicky safety regulations were dropped. In addition, OSHA administrators began to focus more on accident-riddled industries such as the meatpacking and mobile home construction industries and to deemphasize industries reporting relatively few worker injuries.

The Occupational Safety and Health Act (OSHA) is a federal law that requires employers to ensure a safe and healthy environment. This OSHA inspector may fine an employer who does not correct unsafe working conditions.

Table 9.5 Some of the laws affecting human resource management.

1. *Workman's Compensation Act (1910).* Provides compensation for employees injured while working, regardless of who is at fault.
2. *Social Security Act (1935).* Established the social security program by placing a federal tax on wages to provide retirement and unemployment benefits.
3. *Equal Pay Act (1963).* Eliminates pay discrimination between employees on the basis of sex by establishing that employees should be paid the same wage, regardless of their sex, if they are performing the same job.
4. *Age Discrimination in Employment Act (1967).* Prohibits the unfair treatment of employees and prospective employees between the ages of forty and seventy on the basis of their age.
5. *Federal Wage Garnishment Law (1970).* In the situation where a creditor wins a court order to have an employer send the creditor an employee's wages because of an unpaid debt, this law limits the portion of the employee's pay that can be given to the creditor.
6. *Vietnam Era Veterans Readjustment Act (1974).* Prohibits discrimination against disabled veterans by federal contractors.
7. *Employee Retirement Income Security Act (ERISA) (1974).* Regulates the administration, funding, and investment of pension funds.

Recently, however, the OSHA administration has been calling itself a newly awakened giant and has been handing out some big fines to big companies for workplace safety and health violations.[2]

Critics of OSHA seem to have become more critical in recent times. They charge that because of limited resources OSHA administrators mostly pick out a few highly visible companies on which to impose headline-grabbing fines. In addition, critics say that the administrators have been judging companies on their safety record-keeping rather than on the safeness of the work environment.

The Civil Rights Act

The ***Civil Rights Act*** is a 1964 law that prohibits discrimination in employment on the basis of sex, race, color, religion, and national origin.

The ***Equal Employment Opportunity Commission (EEOC)*** is a government agency that has the right to file suit against employers if an acceptable resolution of job discrimination charges against them cannot be obtained within a reasonable time period.

Passed in 1964, the **Civil Rights Act** is a federal law that prohibits discrimination in employment on the basis of sex, race, color, religion, and national origin. This is one of the most far-reaching laws influencing the practice of human resource management today. Title VII of the law prohibits discrimination in hiring, compensation, terms of employment, working conditions, and any other privileges of employment.

The Equal Employment Opportunity Act of 1972 was passed as an amendment to Title VII. This act established the **Equal Employment Opportunity Commission (EEOC),** a government agency that has the right to file suit against employers if an acceptable resolution of job discrimination charges against them cannot be obtained within a reasonable time period.

In essence, the equal opportunity legislation protects the right of citizens to work and to get a fair wage rate based primarily on merit and performance. The EEOC seeks to maintain the existence of this right by holding labor unions, employers, educational institutions, and government bodies responsible for it. Figure 9.7 presents the four steps usually followed by the EEOC to gain compliance by organizations.

Human resource managers must understand the equal opportunity laws that relate to their companies and must make sure company practices are legal. The cost of not complying with these laws can be high. For example: After twelve years in a low-level position at State Farm Insurance Company, Muriel Kraszewski fought for two years for a sales job that would boost her pay to $80,000. Finally, she was denied the promotion on the grounds that she had no college degree and her husband had "too much control over her." She charged State Farm with discrimination and won one of the largest sex-bias awards ever: $443,000 for herself and hundreds of millions of dollars for other women in the company.[3]

Sex Discrimination and Comparable Worth

As Table 9.5 shows, in 1963 Congress passed the Equal Pay Act, which made pay discrimination based on sex illegal. The act mandated that men and women performing the same tasks and possessing the same skills should be paid the same, even if the employer assigned different titles to job positions. For example, some firms assigned the title *researcher* to female employees and *reporter* to male employees. Under the Equal Pay Act, many women successfully filed suits against employers, winning lost wages and other settlements.

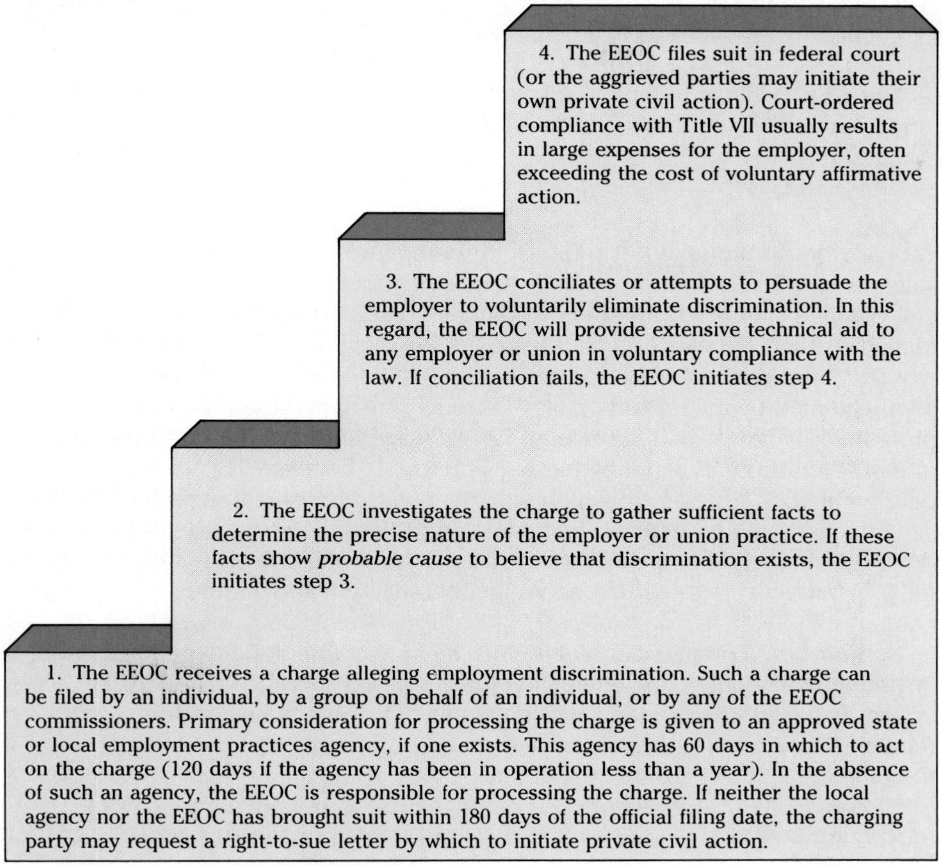

4. The EEOC files suit in federal court (or the aggrieved parties may initiate their own private civil action). Court-ordered compliance with Title VII usually results in large expenses for the employer, often exceeding the cost of voluntary affirmative action.

3. The EEOC conciliates or attempts to persuade the employer to voluntarily eliminate discrimination. In this regard, the EEOC will provide extensive technical aid to any employer or union in voluntary compliance with the law. If conciliation fails, the EEOC initiates step 4.

2. The EEOC investigates the charge to gather sufficient facts to determine the precise nature of the employer or union practice. If these facts show *probable cause* to believe that discrimination exists, the EEOC initiates step 3.

1. The EEOC receives a charge alleging employment discrimination. Such a charge can be filed by an individual, by a group on behalf of an individual, or by any of the EEOC commissioners. Primary consideration for processing the charge is given to an approved state or local employment practices agency, if one exists. This agency has 60 days in which to act on the charge (120 days if the agency has been in operation less than a year). In the absence of such an agency, the EEOC is responsible for processing the charge. If neither the local agency nor the EEOC has brought suit within 180 days of the official filing date, the charging party may request a right-to-sue letter by which to initiate private civil action.

Figure 9.7
Four steps followed by the EEOC in holding organizations accountable for following the equal rights laws.

In recent years, the concept of **comparable worth** has emerged as a means of addressing the continuing disparity between men's and women's earnings. Proponents of comparable worth argue that women should be paid wages equal to men's for jobs that are of comparable worth to a company. In other words, women in traditionally female jobs should be paid at the same rate as men in traditionally male jobs of equal value. Unfortunately, establishing which jobs are of comparable value is a task without established guidelines.

Comparable worth is the concept that women's pay should be equal to men's for jobs that are of comparable worth to a company.

Many federal legislators have opposed including comparable worth in any federal law. Several states, however, have passed laws favoring comparable worth. Thus, although its future is unclear, human resource managers need to be aware of its status and potential implications.

BUSINESS PRACTICE EXAMPLE Continues

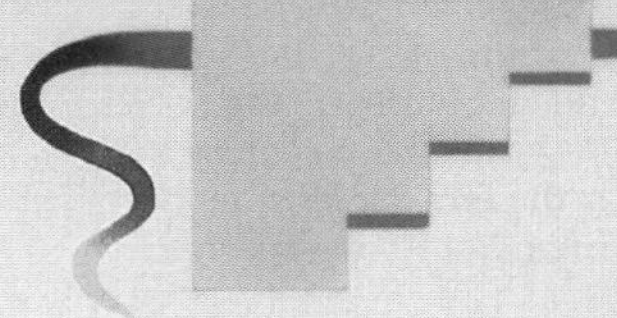

People work for companies in return for compensation. Toyota compensates its employees both financially and nonfinancially. In terms of financial compensation, Toyota offers workers a combination of direct pay, incentives, and benefits. Toyota has found, as many companies do, that workers can be motivated to produce more when salaries or wages are supplemented by incentive bonuses. Through this type of compensation program, Toyota workers receive an hourly wage but have the opportunity to earn even more by working harder. In terms of benefits, Toyota could offer a cafeteria program in which workers could choose among offerings such as medical and dental, educational, and life insurance benefits. Whatever financial compensation program Toyota offers to its workers must be attractive enough to encourage them to remain with the company.

Nonfinancial compensation at Toyota includes fair company policies, desirable work schedules, interesting jobs, and job security. "The Toyota system is based on not overworking people," explains manager Ron Raider. This kind of nonfinancial benefit encourages company loyalty at the plant.

Of course, as a Japanese-owned company in the United States, Toyota must comply with U.S. laws as they relate to human resource management. Managers must address issues in the U.S. that may be very different from those in Japan, including maintaining a safe working environment and avoiding discrimination in hiring. Additional issues include maintaining employees' rights of privacy and appropriately handling employees with AIDS. In order to be successful, Japanese human resource managers at Toyota in Kentucky must thoroughly understand the role that U.S. laws play in business.

Issues for Discussion

1. Does it sound like Toyota has spent some time in human resource planning? Explain.
2. Can a company like Toyota spend too much time screening job applicants? Do you think Toyota might be spending too much time? Explain.

SUMMARY

Human resource management is the process of determining the kinds of people the organization needs to achieve its goals, hiring those people, and retaining them through an equitable compensation system and desirable work environment. Important human resource management activities include maintaining personnel records, doing career counseling, hiring new employees, and training employees.

Human resource planning is the process of determining what must be done to meet the future human resource needs of an organization. It includes the following important steps: reflecting on strategic plans; analyzing future jobs; analyzing the supply of human resources to fill the jobs; increasing, decreasing, or maintaining the number of employees on the basis of the analyses; and evaluating and modifying actions.

Appropriate human resources are the organization members who help the organization achieve its goals. To acquire them, management must go through the process of recruitment, selection, training, and performance appraisal. Recruitment is the screening of the supply of prospective employees. Sources of prospective employees include competitors, employment agencies, readers of certain publications, and educational institutions.

Selection is choosing an individual to be hired from those recruited. Training is developing the qualities in employees that will make them more productive. It involves determining training needs, designing a training program to reflect those needs, administering the program, and evaluating the program.

Performance appraisal is reviewing an individual's productive activity to determine the person's contribution to the organization. Feedback is given to employees to help them improve, and training programs are evaluated against the results of performance appraisals to see how training can be improved.

An important part of human resource management is employee compensation—rewards for working. This compensation can be in the form of money distributed through direct pay, incentives, or benefits. It can also be nonfinancial, including interesting work and the desirability of the work environment.

Several laws influence the manner in which human resource management should be practiced. The Occupational Safety and Health Act of 1970 requires employers to provide a safe and healthy work environment and to keep records about it. The Civil Rights Act of 1963 prohibits workplace discrimination based on sex, race, color, religion, and national origin. Comparable worth is the idea that men and women should receive equal pay for jobs of equal worth to the organization. Some states have passed laws favoring comparable worth.

KEY TERMS

CHECK YOUR LEARNING

Reread the following learning objectives. Each objective is followed by a few questions. Answering these questions accurately will help you retain the most important concepts discussed in this chapter. After answering each question, check your answer with the key at the end of this chapter. (*Hint:* If you have doubt regarding the correct response, consult the page whose number follows the answer.)

Circle:

A. Define *human resource management.*

T F — 1. Human resource management tends to regard hiring the right people as slightly more important than paying them an appropriate wage.

T F — 2. *Human resource management* and *personnel* are two terms that mean basically the same thing.

B. Discuss several activities involved in human resource management and who normally performs them.

a b c d — 1. Activities commonly performed in human resource management include: (a) career counseling; (b) maintaining community relations; (c) training workers; (d) all of the above.

T F — 2. Regardless of the size of a business, the president normally performs human resource management activities.

C. Define *human resource planning.*

T F — 1. Human resource management normally begins with human resource planning.

T F — 2. Human resource planning involves meeting future personnel needs of the organization.

D. Discuss the steps necessary to carry out human resource planning.

T F — 1. In the human resource planning process, human resource forecasting normally comes before reflecting on strategic plans of the organization.

a b c d — 2. Job analysis is normally aimed at determining the: (a) job description; (b) job specification; (c) job demand; (d) a and b.

E. Outline how to provide appropriate human resources for an organization.

T F — 1. Training generally comes before performance appraisal.

T F — 2. Performance appraisal is a continuing activity.

a b c d — 3. The training process includes: (a) determining training needs; (b) designing a training program; (c) administering the training program; (d) all of the above.

F. Describe different types of financial and nonfinancial compensation.

T F — 1. A salary and a wage are two types of fringe benefits employees can receive from an organization.

a b c d — 2. Nonfinancial compensation employees can receive includes: (a) merit pay; (b) bonuses; (c) interesting work; (d) a and c.

G. Discuss how the law can influence the practice of human resource management.

T F — 1. Employers can be fined for not furnishing employees with a safe work environment.

T F — 2. The Employee Retirement Income Security Act (ERISA) prohibits discrimination in the workplace on the basis of sex, race, color, and religious belief.

QUESTIONS FOR REVIEW AND DISCUSSION

1. Define the key terms listed at the end of the chapter.
2. Discuss the importance of feedback for all the steps of the human resource planning process.
3. How important is human resource management to the organization? Explain.
4. Have you ever been recruited for any type of organization? Describe the experience and explain the recruiter's action at each step.
5. In which stage of the selection process do you think most people are eliminated from job consideration? Explain.
6. Which is the most important step of the training process? Explain.
7. List a number of guidelines you think managers should follow in appraising the performance of their subordinates.
8. Suppose a company wanted to offer employees extra compensation. Do you think the employees would prefer financial compensation or nonfinancial compensation? Explain.
9. What types of human relations problems might a merit pay program cause? Give an example of one such problem. Could this problem be avoided?
10. Do you think that the Occupational Safety and Health Act is good for the livelihood of American businesses in the short term? How about in the long term? Explain.
11. Does the Civil Rights Act force business to pay for the ills of society? Explain. Would you be in favor of repealing this law? Explain.

CONCLUDING CASE

The Aerospace Labor Crunch

Remember "The Life of Riley"? The popular 1950s TV series revolved around the adventures of Chester A. Riley, a hard hat with a soft heart who reacted to change of any sort by exclaiming, "What a revoltin' development this is!" For all his protestations, Riley enjoyed a pretty laid-back lifestyle—including plenty of snoozing in his hammock—thanks to his steady-paying job as a riveter in a southern California aircraft plant.

Life is no longer so laid back for today's Rileys. Aerospace and other defense-related companies have adopted computer-aided manufacturing and design techniques that have made assembly-line jobs far more complex. As the demands grow, the number of blue-collar workers skilled enough to meet them is shrinking. The shortage is particularly acute in southern California, the hub of the U.S. aerospace industry. "In the past you could prepare yourself for a job just by taking industrial-arts classes like woodshop and machine shop," says Saran Kruse, a Northrop executive on the Southern California Industry Education Council. Now "students coming out of high school [don't] have basic skills like math or an understanding of what manufacturing is all about."

What manufacturing is increasingly about is working with computers and other high-tech equipment. Riveters don't just bang bolts into sheet-metal wings anymore. At the plants where Stealth planes are produced, they drive "fasteners" with tolerances as close as a thousandth of an inch into contoured surfaces designed to elude radar. Machinists operate computerized tool-making devices. Other workers mold exotic composite materials like graphite to make fighter fuselages. Grease monkeys need not apply;

cleanliness and "foreign-object elimination" (FOE) are now the order of the day.

Workers who can perform the new tasks are in intense demand. Electric Boat, a Groton, Conn., unit of General Dynamics, needs specially skilled workers to build the nuclear-powered Trident submarine. When a nearby plant laid off 97 employees last fall, Electric Boat expected to hire 30 of its machinists. But the company managed to get only two because of a fierce bidding war among 50 firms in the area.

Issues for Discussion

1. Does this case involve a human resource management situation? Explain.
2. Does the labor shortage faced by Electric Boat reflect poor human resource planning? Explain.
3. What should Electric Boat do to better meet its human resource needs in the future?

NOTES

1. This section is based on David J. Cherrington, *Personnel Management: The Management of Human Resources,* 2d ed. (Dubuque, Iowa: Wm. C. Brown, 1987), pp. 338–459.
2. See Robb Deigh, "As OSHA Flexes Its Muscle, Critics Doubt Power of the Punch," *Insight,* October 5, 1987, pp. 42–43.
3. "State Farm Is Stuck with a Colossal Claim," *U.S. News & World Report,* February 1, 1988, p. 10.

CHECK YOUR LEARNING ANSWER KEY

A. 1. F, *p. 253*
   2. T, *p. 253*
B. 1. d, *p. 253*
   2. F, *p. 253*
C. 1. T, *p. 254*
   2. T, *p. 254*
D. 1. F, *p. 254*
   2, d, *p. 254*
E. 1. T, *p. 256*
   2. T, *p. 263*
   3. d, *p. 259*
F. 1. F, *p. 265*
   2. c, *p. 267*
G. 1. T, *p. 269*
   2. F, *p. 269*

CHAPTER

10

LABOR-MANAGEMENT RELATIONS

LEARNING OBJECTIVES

After reading this chapter you should be able to:

1. Explain what unions are and why they began.
2. Describe the major labor movements in American labor history.
3. Explain why workers join unions.
4. Summarize the major labor laws that have influenced the union movement.
5. Describe the collective bargaining process and explain assisted settlements.
6. List and describe the major collective bargaining tactics used by labor and management.
7. Project what the future of labor unions will be.

OUTLINE

Business Practice Example: The International Ladies' Garment Workers' Union

Basic Facts about Labor Unions

- Defining *Labor Union*
- Why Unions Began
- Labor Union History
  - Knights of Labor
  - American Federation of Labor
  - Congress of Industrial Organizations
  - AFL-CIO
- Why Workers Join Unions

Government Reactions to Unions: Labor Laws

- Norris-LaGuardia Act
- Wagner Act (National Labor Relations Act)
- Fair Labor Standards Act
- Taft-Hartley Act (Labor Management Relations Act)
- Landrum-Griffin Act

Collective Bargaining

- Preparation
- Bargaining
- Tentative Agreement
- Assisted Settlements
  - Conciliation
  - Mediation
  - Arbitration and Grievances
- Collective Bargaining Tactics
  - Labor Tactics
    - Strikes
    - Picketing
    - Boycotts
  - Management Tactics
    - Lockouts
    - Injunctions
    - Associations

Unions in the Future

Summary

Key Terms

Check Your Learning

Questions for Review and Discussion

Concluding Case

- Unions Lose at Safeway Stores and Chrysler

Notes

Check Your Learning Answer Key

Highlight in Business Practice: Membership and Demands Soar in Newly Formed South Korean Labor Unions

BUSINESS PRACTICE EXAMPLE

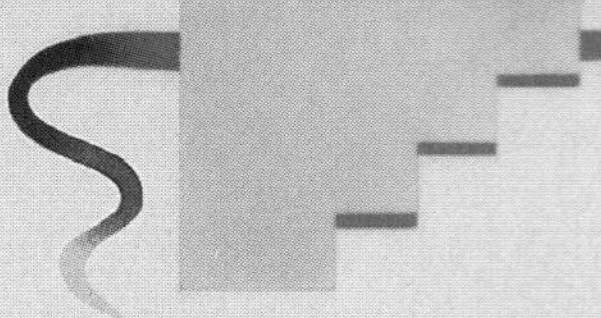

The International Ladies' Garment Workers' Union

Most people are familiar with the slogan "Look for the Union Label." The phrase belongs to the International Ladies' Garment Workers' Union (ILGWU), an AFL-CIO–affiliated union representing approximately 200,000 workers in the apparel industry in the United States, Canada, and Puerto Rico. Founded in 1900, the ILGWU has an illustrious history as a forceful and innovative union. It was the first union to set up a pension fund for workers (1943) and the first to win an employer-financed health insurance plan for its members (1944).

At the beginning of this century, garment workers toiled for fifteen or sixteen hours daily, every day of the week. The pay was rock bottom, and the benefits were nonexistent. Conditions inside the "sweatshops"—defined by the federal government as "establishments employing workers at low wages, for long hours, under poor conditions"—were dangerous and uncomfortable. Because most of the workers were recent immigrants, many of whom spoke little or no English, employers felt free to exploit their labor unfairly, even cruelly.

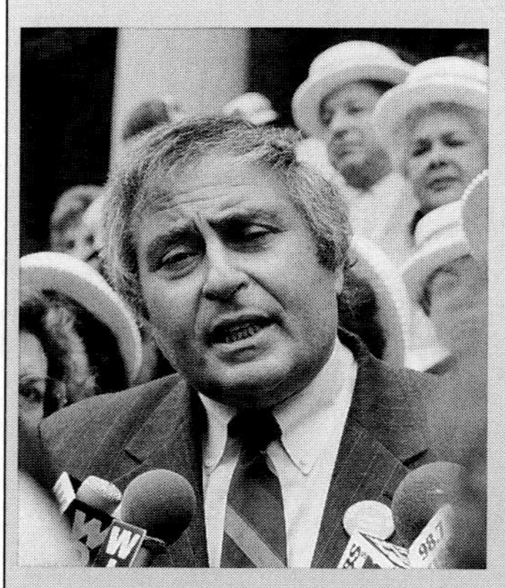

In 1909 and 1910, the ILGWU organized two major strikes. In the first, 20,000 shirtwaist makers, mainly women and young girls, struck for two months. Withstanding violence and the loss of income, the shirtwaist makers ultimately won a wage increase and a reduction in their workweek to fifty-two hours. In 1910, about 50,000 cloak makers, mainly men, also struck. Eventually they won uniform wages throughout their industry, a shorter workweek, and paid holidays.

On March 25, 1911, a devastating fire broke out in a garment shop called the Triangle Shirtwaist Company. The fire killed 146 garment workers and generated a public outcry for government safety regulations. The successful strikes and the Triangle tragedy drew thousands of garment workers to the ILGWU. The workers saw that by joining together they could win benefits from employers that alone, they had no chance of receiving.

The ethnic composition of the ILGWU has changed over the years, mirroring the successive waves of immigration to the United States during the twentieth century. Early members were largely Jewish and Italian, followed by Puerto Ricans, Portuguese, Slavs, and French Canadians. Today's membership includes many people arriving from Asia and Latin America.

The years from the 1930s to the 1960s were a time of steady growth for the ILGWU. By 1970, membership had reached an all-time peak of over 450,000 workers. But as the decade of the 1970s wore on, a terrible problem emerged for the entire apparel industry: The name of the problem was imports.

WHAT'S AHEAD

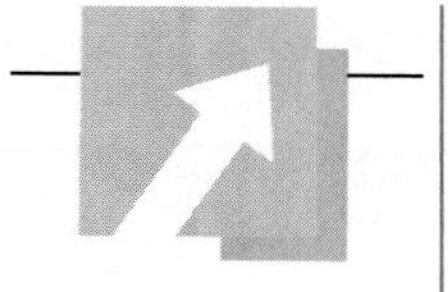

The introductory case about the International Ladies' Garment Workers' Union provides a powerful example of why people join unions. This chapter continues the discussion by examining the history of unions and of government legislation affecting them. It then goes on to collective bargaining, including the tactics used by both labor and management. It concludes with a forecast about unions in the future.

BASIC FACTS ABOUT LABOR UNIONS

The only time some people think about unions is when they are directly affected by a strike. Public transportation came to a halt in New York in 1980, for example, as the transit workers went on strike. Football disappeared from our television sets in the fall of 1982 when the players' association took strike action. The 1989 Eastern Airlines strike upset many plans for spring vacations in Florida.

Strikes such as these capture big headlines and are a dramatic reminder of the power of organized labor. Once they are over, however, and the headlines disappear, the public tends to forget about the unions. In fact, strikes are only one tactic that labor unions use in dealing with management, and they are a sign that negotiations have broken down.

The story of organized labor is an important and fascinating chapter in the history of this country. It's a story that has its beginnings in the late eighteenth century, when the workday started at sunrise and ended at sunset—for men, women, *and* children. This chapter discusses the basics of labor unions, focusing on their history and purpose and on why workers join them.

Defining *Labor Union*

An organization of employees formed to achieve common goals in the areas of wages, hours worked, and working conditions is a **labor union.** Basically, labor unions exist to influence employers to further the benefits of employees. Labor unions provide strength by numbers. One worker alone can have little effect on management; a majority of workers can exert far greater power.

A ***labor union*** is an organization of employees formed to achieve common goals in the areas of wages, hours worked, and working conditions.

There are two basic types of labor unions—craft and industrial. A *craft union* is an organization of workers with specific skills, such as carpentry and plumbing. An *industrial union* is an organization of all workers at all levels in a given industry. Two well-known industrial unions are the United Auto Workers and the United Mine Workers.

Why Unions Began

Workers have sought protection in numbers since the earliest days of this country. The Philadelphia printers' craft union, for instance, struck for a minimum wage of $6 per week in 1786. Early craft unions representing carpenters, bricklayers, and textile workers also actively sought better conditions by banding together and then bargaining collectively for improved conditions.

The rise of large-scale modern labor unions can be traced to America's Industrial Revolution, which took place during the nineteenth and early twentieth

The famed photographer Lewis Hine documented conditions of child laborers in the early part of this century. Twelve-year-old Addie Laird, a cotton mill spinner in North Pownal, Vermont, is shown here in the year 1910.

centuries. Factory systems were designed to accommodate ever-increasing production capacities. Worker comfort and even basic safety were largely ignored. While new technology was raising the standard of living for many people, the majority of workers toiled about eleven hours a day, six days a week, often in unsafe conditions and under abusive management.

The abuse of children and women has been well documented. In 1910, about 2 million young adults and children (as young as four years of age) worked in industries such as clothing and glass to help their families. They were paid from $2 to $3 a week, while women earned about $6, usually for a seventy-hour week. Industrial accidents and deaths were commonplace. Workers devised labor unions to protect themselves from exploitation and physical harm.

Labor Union History

Small craft unions and benevolent societies set up to protect workers' families were present in this country in the mid-1700s. In 1834, the National Trades Union (NTU) was founded in New York, but it fell apart only three years later when the economy weakened. Typographers and iron workers also formed national trade unions in the 1850s and 1860s.

The strength of labor unions has always been vitally connected to economic conditions. Labor, like other products, is a commodity. Unions demand a fair market price for their members. When the marketplace suffers from hard times, the price of labor generally falls. Thus the rise and fall of labor unions in many ways mirrors changing economic conditions.

Knights of Labor

The ***Knights of Labor,*** founded in 1869, was the first national labor union in America to represent workers of diverse occupations.

Founded in Philadelphia in 1869, the **Knights of Labor** was the first national labor union to represent workers of diverse occupations. At first it was a secret society, in response to antiunion pressures from Philadelphia employers. While the Knights of Labor initially was formed as a craft union for local garment workers, within fifteen years it represented well over 500,000 members of diverse occupations from across the nation. The union worked hard to improve the conditions of child workers and to establish an eight-hour workday. It also sought many socialist reforms, such as worker-owned factories.

In 1886, on the first day of May, Chicago police opened fire on a group of Knights of Labor strikers, killing four of them. Three days later, the union held a peaceful rally in Chicago's Haymarket Square to protest the shooting. Someone threw a small bomb that knocked down sixty policemen, killing eight of them. An enraged police force fired into the crowd.

In fact, the year 1886 was a peak year for strikes—with some 610,000 workers involved in strike action throughout the country. The New York City Public Transit Workers, for example, settled for $2 pay for a twelve-hour day, with an hour off for lunch.

The Haymarket Square incident, coupled with unfavorable reaction within the ranks to some of the socialist aims of the Knights of Labor, ultimately led to the dissolution of the Knights of Labor and the rise of the American Federation of Labor.

American Federation of Labor

Established in 1886, the **American Federation of Labor (AFL)** was the union resulting from a merger of the Federation of Organized Trades and Labor Unions, composed of several unions that had previously been associated with the Knights of Labor but had broken away because they did not agree with its socialist sentiments, and a group of unaffiliated craft unions. The AFL was composed chiefly of craft unions, although there were also some industrial union affiliates. Its first president, Samuel Gompers, an English-American cigar maker, headed the union for thirty-seven years. Gompers was thoroughly opposed to socialism. Under his leadership, the AFL grew in size and power. Membership reached the million mark in 1902. The AFL represented its members through strong collective bargaining programs and a flexible approach to union-management relations.

The ***American Federation of Labor (AFL)*** was a labor union established in 1886 as the result of a merger of the Federation of Organized Trades and Labor Unions.

Congress of Industrial Organizations

As industries grew increasingly automated, it became clear that the craft-union focus of the AFL did not meet the needs of a large number of industrial workers. Some AFL members began to advocate *industrial unionism*—unions organized by industry. The **Congress of Industrial Organizations (CIO)** was formed in 1937 by former members of the American Federation of Labor, who believed that the AFL was not meeting the needs of the growing numbers of industrial machine operators and other noncraft workers.

The ***Congress of Industrial Organizations (CIO)*** was a labor union formed in 1937 by noncraft workers who broke away from the American Federation of Labor.

The CIO organized workers by industries, including the automobile and the garment industries. In 1935, the United Auto Workers held its first convention, in Detroit, and received a charter from the AFL. The CIO organized the United Steel Workers of America the following year.

The increasing number of workers who were organizing during the 1930s was perceived as a threat by management, which often reacted by firing union organizers and breaking up union meetings with hired toughs. Many times the confrontations were violent. In 1931, in Harlan County, Kentucky, several people died in a shoot-out between coal miners and armed guards whose job it was to convince the miners to resist the organizing efforts of the United Mine Workers.

By the time the Great Depression had taken firm hold of the country, however, the balance of power had tipped toward the workers. During this time, industrial workers represented a massive 40 percent of the labor force. When the workers in one industry went on strike, the whole economy suffered. It became clear that if the country was to recover from the depression, it needed a stable work force. This realization prompted several pieces of pro-union government legislation, which will be examined shortly.

AFL-CIO

For many years, the AFL and CIO competed with each other for members. Eventually, however, leaders of both groups realized that they could better represent labor to management if they combined forces. In December 1955, the American Federation of Labor and the Congress of Industrial Organizations merged into a new and more powerful union called the **AFL-CIO.** The presidency of this union went to George Meany. Figure 10.1, an organization chart of the AFL-CIO, illustrates

The ***AFL-CIO*** is a union formed in 1955 as a result of a merger between the American Federation of Labor and the Congress of Industrial Organizations.

Figure 10.1
Organization chart of the AFL-CIO.

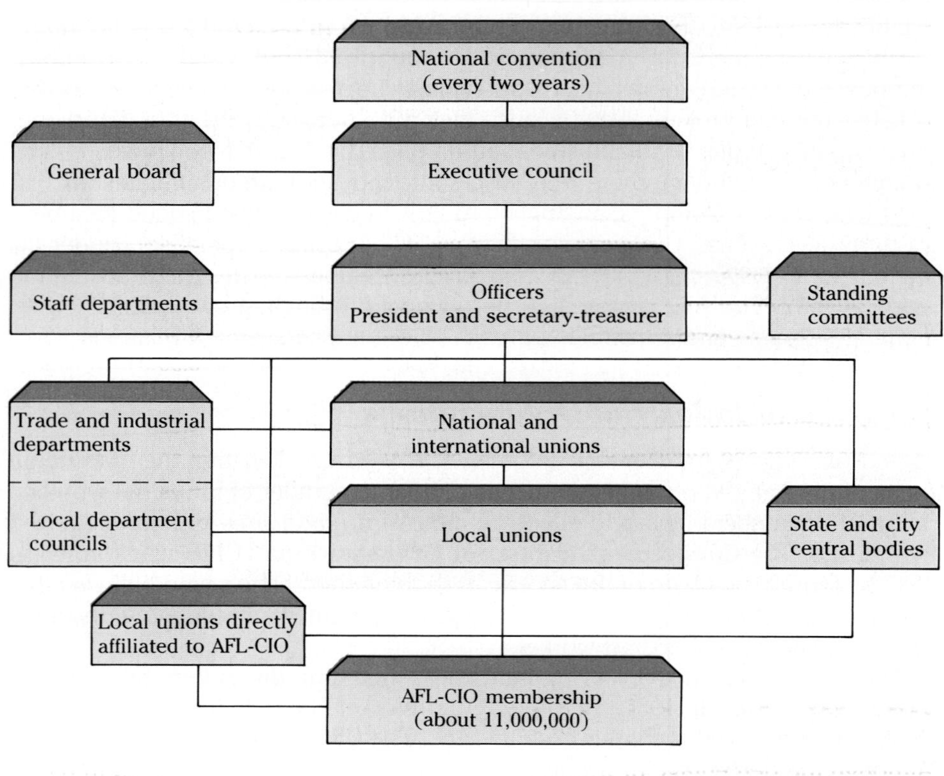

the end result of the merger. ~~Today, about 80 percent of all labor unions in America are affiliated with the AFL-CIO.~~ (The Teamsters union remains independent.) The ten largest unions in the AFL-CIO are listed in Table 10.1. Perhaps the purpose of the AFL-CIO is best stated in the preamble to its constitution, which is reprinted in Figure 10.2.

Figure 10.2
The preamble to the AFL-CIO constitution states the federation's purpose and goals.

Preamble to the AFL-CIO Constitution

The establishment of this Federation through the merger of the American Federation of Labor and the Congress of Industrial Organizations is an expression of the hopes and aspirations of the working people of America.

We seek the fulfillment of these hopes and aspirations through democratic processes within the framework of our constitutional government and consistent with our institutions and traditions.

At the collective bargaining table, in the community in the exercise of the rights and responsibilities of citizenship, we shall responsibly serve the interests of all the American people.

We pledge ourselves to the more effective organization of working men and women; to the securing to them of full recognition and enjoyment of the rights to which they are justly entitled; to the achievement of ever higher standards of living and working conditions; to the attainment of security for all the people; to the enjoyment of the leisure which their skills make possible; and to the strengthening and extension of our way of life and the fundamental freedoms which are the basis of our democratic society.

We shall combat resolutely the forces which seek to undermine the democratic institutions of our nation and to enslave the human soul. We shall strive always to win full respect for the dignity of the human individual whom our unions serve.

With Divine guidance, grateful for the fine traditions of our past, confident of meeting the challenge of the future, we proclaim this Constitution.

Table 10.1 The ten largest unions in the AFL-CIO.

Organization	Number of Members	Percent of Total AFL-CIO Membership
Local and State Government	1,032,000	9.34%
Food Workers	1,000,000	9.05
United Auto Workers	998,000	9.03
Electrical Workers	765,000	6.92
Service Employees	762,000	6.90
Carpenters	609,000	5.51
Communication Workers	515,000	4.66
Machinist and Aerospace	509,000	4.61
Teachers	499,000	4.52
Steel Workers	494,000	4.47

Why Workers Join Unions

Although the percentage of workers who belong to unions has declined in recent decades, the total number of union workers is substantial. There are several reasons for this substantial membership.

- *Unions are seen as helping workers get higher wages and fringe benefits.* This is probably the reason union members themselves would most often cite.
- *Unions are seen as helping workers improve working conditions.* Job safety is an important concern in this area. Through unions, workers can often influence management to invest in appropriate safety equipment.
- *Unions are seen as protecting workers from unfair management.* Certainly, many employees would like to be shielded from what they consider to be unfair decisions, rules, and rule enforcement. Through unions, workers have some such protection.
- *Unions are seen as possessing political power.* Employees may respond favorably to being members of an organization that can lobby for laws to affect such areas as minimum wage levels and worker safety.[1]

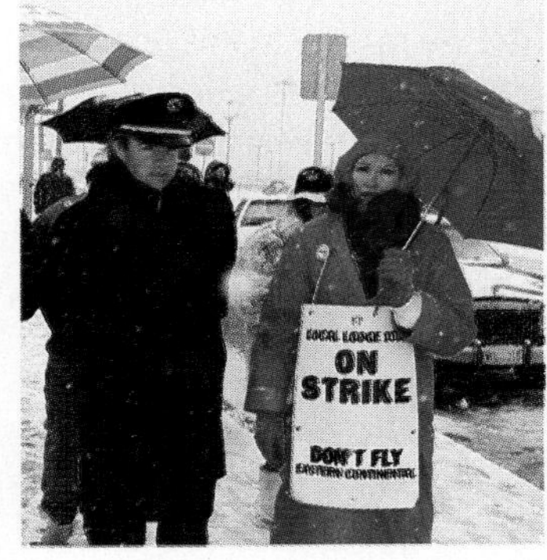

Unions are seen by supporters as helping workers get higher wages and benefits, improving working conditions, and protecting workers from unfair management practices. These striking Eastern Airline workers hope their union can address these issues for them.

GOVERNMENT REACTIONS TO UNIONS: LABOR LAWS

Thus far we have focused on the fundamentals of labor unions—why unions began, union history, and why workers join unions. This section summarizes the significant U.S. labor laws throughout union history.[2] Many of the major pro-union

HIGHLIGHT IN BUSINESS PRACTICE

Membership and Demands Soar in Newly Formed South Korean Labor Unions

The rules of the game used to be so clear: If South Korean workers went on strike to press for wage increases, the government of former President Chun Doo Hwan would send in riot police. Then last summer [1987] a wave of labor unrest pushed the nation into deep political crisis. Independent unions were born. And a new president, Roh Tae Woo, was elected in Korea's first democratic transition of power.

Now a new round of labor negotiations is beginning—but no one knows the rules. Union membership has soared, and the rank and file are demanding huge increases in compensation. New union leaders have neither been able to control their members nor bargain effectively with management. Korean managers, already concerned about the rising value of the South Korean won, are worried. So are U.S. companies that have joint ventures in Korea or depend on Korean manufacturers. "Labor is a big issue," says one U.S. executive involved in a joint venture with the Samsung group. "In fact, it is *the* issue in Korea."

Take the case of Daewoo Shipbuilding & Heavy Machinery Ltd. Its 11,000 workers now earn roughly $3 an hour, an average wage by Korean standards. The workers demanded a 55% increase in basic salary, and their union leaders negotiated a still-generous 20% hike. When the workers gathered on Apr. 10 [1988], however, they rejected the 20% offer by a 2-to-1 margin. The unprecedented rejection raised major questions as to whether other union leaders will be able to reach deals. Overall, as of Apr. 15, 256 wage disputes had been solved, but 83 were not settled, resulting in a handful of strikes. Further strikes are certain before the negotiations peak in June.

Although there is little likelihood of violence, the strikes are already having economic impact. Stoppages at Daewoo Motor Co., a 50-50 joint venture with General Motors Corp., have interrupted the supply of Daewoo-made LeMans autos to GM's Pontiac division. The Samsung subsidiary that makes forklifts for Clark Equipment has been hit by a strike. And Reebok International Ltd. is bracing for higher costs for its Korean-made footwear. "As Koreans become more prosperous, wages have to increase—there's not much we can do about that," says a Reebok spokesman. Some U.S. companies have begun shifting Korean operations to such lower-wage countries as China and Thailand.

The fact that Korean unions are turning down big pay offers suggests that radical members, some of them recent university graduates, are playing a more influential role than outsiders suspect. "Many of these workers are 'progressive' in their political orientation and are unwilling to compromise," says Kim Young Vae, a labor economist with the Korean Employers' Federation.

As a result, some bargaining sessions have been highly emotional. "When they come for negotiations, the workers have their minds made up to seek confrontation, not dialogue," says one U.S. attorney who advises American companies. "When the managers lose their own patience, then you know what to expect."

As long as there is no violence, Roh's government is likely to sit on the sidelines, allowing labor and management to work out their differences. Government planners are concerned, of course, about inflationary pressures and reduced Korean competitiveness. But they hope that Roh's ruling Democratic Justice Party will eke out a majority in the National Assembly elections on Apr. 26, dampening the demands of workers allied with opposition parties. In the longer term, Roh's camp believes that increases in labor costs will force Korea's *chaebol,* or conglomerates, to keep making big productivity gains while shifting away from labor-intensive activities.

Korean executives worry that a new round of labor-cost increases, coming on top of last year's average 17% increase, will confront them with painful competitive dilemmas. But they have little choice: South Korea's era of cheap labor is rapidly coming to an end.

labor laws were formulated during the 1930s and 1940s, a time of tremendous growth and activity for unions. The four-term Roosevelt administration was friendly to the labor movement, which made the passage of these laws possible.

By studying the content of union laws, we will see how public attitudes toward unions changed over the years. The laws are discussed in the order in which they were passed by Congress.

Norris-LaGuardia Act

Passed by Congress in 1932, the **Norris-LaGuardia Act** made "yellow dog" contracts—contracts requiring employees, as a condition of employment, not to join unions—illegal. This law also made it more difficult for management to obtain injunctions (court orders) preventing workers from participating in union activities. (Injunctions will be discussed in more detail later in the chapter.) The Norris La-Guardia Act was clearly aimed at protecting union rights. At the time of its passage, employers actively sought injunctions barring workers from participating in union activities. The Norris La-Guardia Act was the first federal law to protect union members' rights.

The ***Norris-LaGuardia Act*** of 1932 is the federal law that made "yellow dog" contracts—contracts requiring employees, as a condition of employment, not to join unions—illegal and made it difficult for management to obtain injunctions preventing workers from participating in union activities.

Wagner Act (National Labor Relations Act)

Passed by Congress in 1935, the **Wagner Act** identified and outlawed certain unfair labor practices; mandated secret ballot election procedures, which allowed employees to vote to unionize; and created the *National Labor Relations Board (NLRB)* to enforce fair practices and elections.

Like the Norris-LaGuardia Act, the Wagner Act regulated the actions of employers rather than employees. For the first time, employers were required to do such things as (1) bargain collectively with representatives chosen by employees, (2) treat union members fairly in both hirings and firings, and (3) refrain from attempting to influence union officials.

Clearly, the Wagner Act was aimed at supporting unions in their attempts to organize. It was so influential in establishing union rights that it has come to be known as organized labor's Magna Carta.

The ***Wagner Act*** of 1935 (also known as the *National Labor Relations Act*) is the federal law that identified and outlawed certain unfair labor practices, mandated secret ballot election procedures that allowed employees to vote to unionize, and created the National Labor Relations Board.

The ***Fair Labor Standards Act*** of 1938 is the federal law that set a minimum wage and maximum number of regular work hours for workers at companies involved in interstate commerce.

Fair Labor Standards Act

Passed in 1938, the **Fair Labor Standards Act** set a minimum wage and maximum number of regular work hours for workers at companies involved in interstate commerce. This law also favored employees more than employers. It established the first minimum wage at 25 cents an hour. (The minimum wage was increased to 40 cents per hour in 1945 and has continued to climb since then. Since 1981, it has been $3.35 per hour.) It was eventually amended to limit the workweek to forty hours, with overtime to be compensated at 1.5 times the regular work rate.

In addition to the minimum wage and number of hours worked, the Fair Labor Standards Act also focused on two other major issues. It prohibited child labor, and it prohibited pay discrimination on the basis of sex.

In 1942, the Fair Labor Standards Act was amended to prohibit industrial homework—home-based piecework employment—in seven industries: women's apparel, jewelry, gloves and mittens, buttons and buckles, handkerchiefs, embroideries, and knitted outerwear. Industrial homeworkers, many of them women and children, had been working for subminimum wages in hazardous tenements. During the Reagan administration, the U.S. Labor Department began attempts to lift the ban on industrial homeworkers. By 1989, it had succeeded in legalizing homework in all of the industries but apparel.

Taft-Hartley Act (Labor Management Relations Act)

The ***Taft-Hartley Act*** of 1947 (also known as the *Labor Management Relations Act*) is an employer-favoring federal law aimed at balancing the power of unions with that of management in union-related matters.

Also known as the *Labor Management Relations Act,* the **Taft-Hartley Act** was passed by Congress in 1947 to balance the power of unions with that of management in union-related matters. As with the Wagner Act, issues concerning the implementation of the Taft-Hartley Act are the domain of the National Labor Relations Board.

In contrast to the earlier acts discussed here, the Taft-Hartley Act favored employers over employees. The act was hotly debated in Congress, was vetoed by President Truman, and was finally passed over his veto. At that time, the prevailing sentiment toward unions seemed to be that they were too powerful. Reaction to strikes, many of which affected major industries, was negative.

A ***closed shop*** was an agreement between unions and businesses that required businesses to hire only union workers.

A ***union shop*** is a union and business agreement that allows the business to hire the most qualified employees, who then are required to join a union within a specified period.

Right-to-work laws are state laws that have made required union membership illegal.

Featherbedding is the practice by which unions force employers to contract for unnecessary workers or assign tasks that do not need to be performed.

The Taft-Hartley Act made several concessions to employers. First, it made closed shops illegal. A **closed shop** was an agreement between unions and businesses that required businesses to hire only union workers. Workers who were not union members at the time they were interviewed for a job were required to join a union and maintain membership in order to get and keep the job. Congress was sympathetic to employer arguments that a closed shop infringed on the rights of those who didn't want to be union members and interfered with hiring employees on the basis of merit.

In addition to outlawing closed shops, the Taft-Hartley Act contained a clause allowing states to outlaw union shops on an individual basis. A **union shop** is a union and business agreement that allows the business to hire the most qualified employees, who then are required to join a union within a specified period. Many states have passed **right-to-work laws**—laws that make mandatory union membership illegal (see Figure 10.3).

Finally, the Taft-Hartley Act outlawed **featherbedding**—the practice by which unions force employers to contract for unnecessary workers or assign tasks that do not need to be performed. Employers, however, must still be alert to the practice, since unions can legally bargain for work rules or conditions that are essentially unnecessary in producing a good or service. Examples of such "make-work" activities are shown in Figure 10.4.

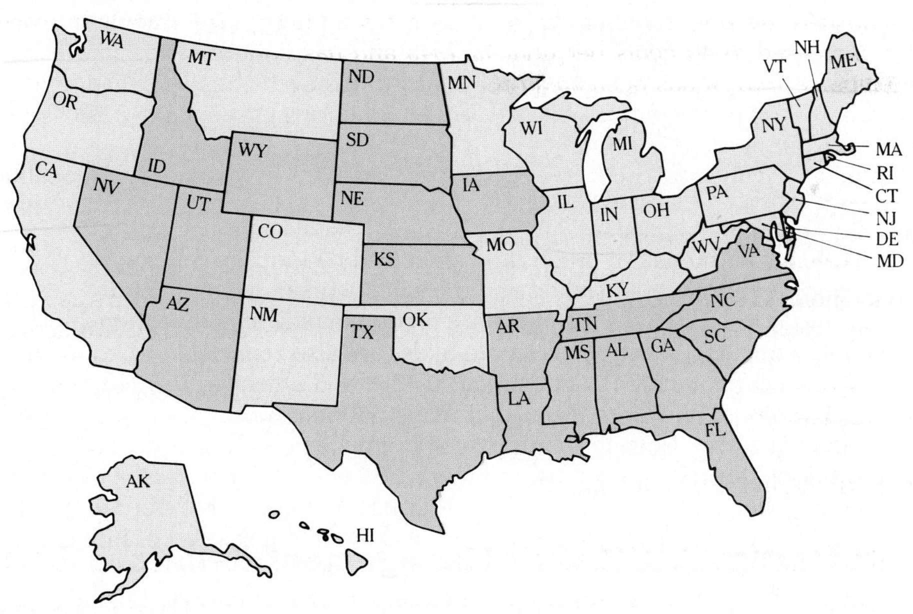

Figure 10.3
The twenty states that have passed right-to-work laws are highlighted in blue.

Electrical workers performing unnecessary rewiring on apparatus purchased from another manufacturer.	More brakemen riding trains in some states (the number written into law) than in others.	Meatcutters refusing to handle precut and prepackaged meats.
Compositors performing unnecessary resetting of advertisements run in another paper.	Unnecessary stagehands in theaters.	Union electricians required to replace lightbulbs.
Operating engineers employed to merely push buttons or turn switches.	Dockworkers refusing to use pallets that would increase loading and unloading efficiency.	Airline employees who can unload baggage, and some who can unload cargo, but not both.
		Thirteen separate crafts required to install bathrooms in a hotel or apartment house in New York City.

Figure 10.4 Featherbedding was declared illegal by the Taft-Hartley Act, but some elements of it have continued.

BUSINESS PRACTICE EXAMPLE Continues

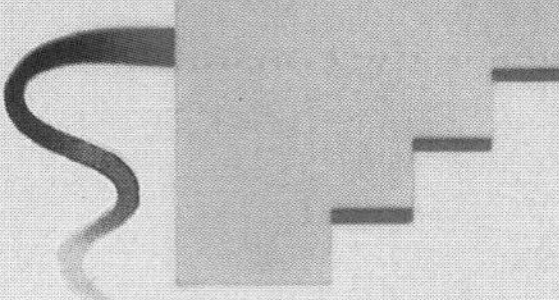

The ILGWU is an industrial union. It is organized by industry (e.g., apparel) and represents both skilled and unskilled workers within that industry. Today, the ILGWU's members are predominantly female, although cutters and truckers, most of whom are male, are also represented.

The Fair Labor Standards Act, passed in 1938 and amended in 1942, is receiving renewed attention because of industrial homework, or factory work done at home. Notwithstanding the ban imposed on industrial homework by the 1942 amendment, the practice never entirely disappeared. And beginning in the 1970s, in response to competition from imports, more manufacturers have adopted the cost-cutting strategy of hiring industrial homeworkers.

The ILGWU has vehemently opposed lifting the ban on the one remaining industry not already legalized—its own apparel industry—calling legalized industrial homework "a return to unchecked exploitation of desperate immigrant workers."[3] The ILGWU has conducted a large-scale public information campaign and lobbying effort against lifting the ban.

Landrum-Griffin Act

The ***Landrum-Griffin Act*** of 1959 (also called the *Labor Management Reporting and Disclosure Act*) is a federal law aimed at protecting individuals against the illegal activities of unions.

Passed by Congress in 1959 in response to corruption in labor unions, the **Landrum-Griffin Act** (also called the *Labor Management Reporting and Disclosure Act*) was an amendment to the Taft-Hartley Act aimed at protecting individuals against the illegal activities of unions. It required unions to report information to the U.S. Secretary of Labor on the following: (1) union constitutions and bylaws, (2) annual financial reports, (3) financial transactions made by union officials, and (4) the calling of union meetings. Employees of unions also were required to report to the Secretary of Labor various union-related financial expenditures.

COLLECTIVE BARGAINING

Collective bargaining is the process by which employees, through the union or association representing them, negotiate a labor agreement with their employer.

A ***labor contract*** is a legally enforceable agreement between labor and management regarding the employment responsibilities of both.

The process by which employees, through the union or association representing them, negotiate a labor agreement with their employer, is called **collective bargaining.**[4] The result of collective bargaining is a **labor contract,** a legally enforceable agreement between labor and management regarding the employment responsibilities of both.

Naturally, union negotiators attempt to include labor contract stipulations that benefit workers. In general, issues brought up by union negotiators include higher wages, more fringe benefits, and more flexible work hours. Following are examples of more specific issues commonly introduced by union negotiators:

COLAs. A stipulation in a labor contract designed to protect employees' real income by changing wage amounts according to changes in the consumer price index is a **cost-of-living adjustment (COLA)** clause. As the index rises, wages are increased accordingly, and thus the buying power of the wages is maintained.

A ***cost-of-living adjustment (COLA)*** is a clause in a labor contract designed to protect employees' real income by changing wage amounts according to changes in the consumer price index.

ESOPs. A program that enables employees to obtain company stock and therefore some degree of ownership in the company is an **employee stock ownership plan (ESOP).** Employees involved in ESOPs generally see themselves as contributing to the long-term success of the organization and want to participate in organizational profits.

An ***employee stock ownership plan (ESOP)*** is a program through which employees can obtain company stock and therefore some degree of ownership in the company.

Comparable worth. As chapter 9 explained, the concept of *comparable worth* holds that workers performing jobs of similar value to the organization should be paid the same wage even if the jobs are dissimilar. Unions often seek to apply the comparable worth principle in negotiations in response to perceived occupational or sex discrimination against members.

While union negotiators seek benefits for workers, management negotiators try to gain employment conditions that encourage the overall profitability of the business. As a result, management negotiators commonly try to limit the level of return that labor seeks. At times, management negotiators may pressure the union for *givebacks,* wage and benefit reductions that management thinks are necessary if the business is to remain competitive.

Despite their seemingly conflicting objectives, unions and management do manage to produce labor contracts as a result of the collective bargaining process. As Figure 10.5 indicates, the three main steps of this process are preparation, bargaining, and tentative agreement.

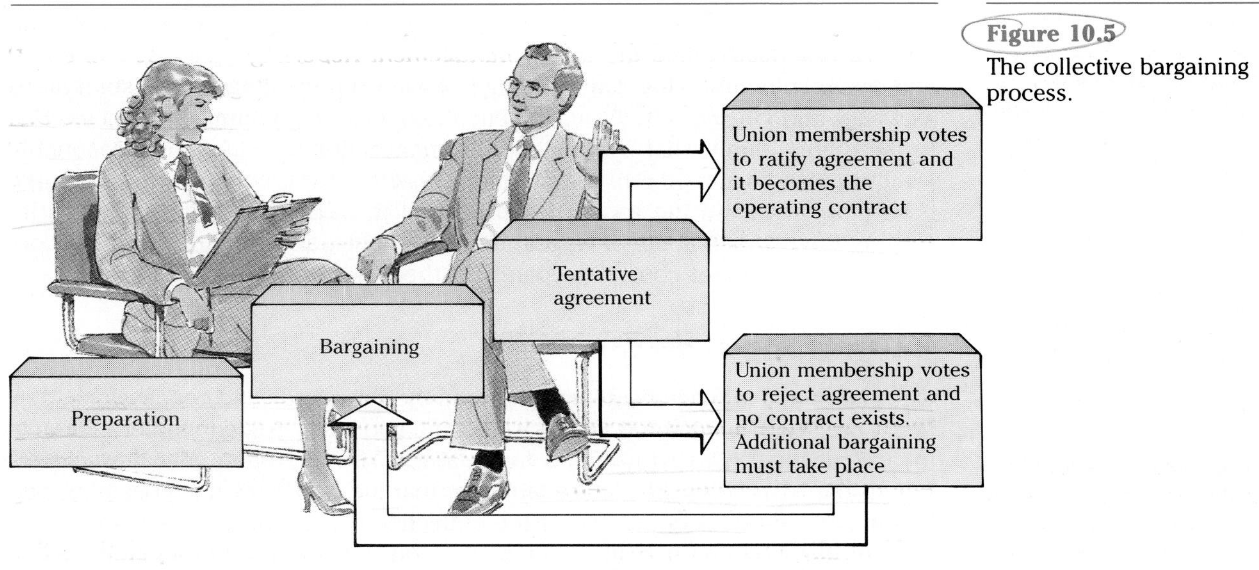
Preparation
Bargaining
Tentative agreement
Union membership votes to ratify agreement and it becomes the operating contract
Union membership votes to reject agreement and no contract exists. Additional bargaining must take place

Figure 10.5
The collective bargaining process.

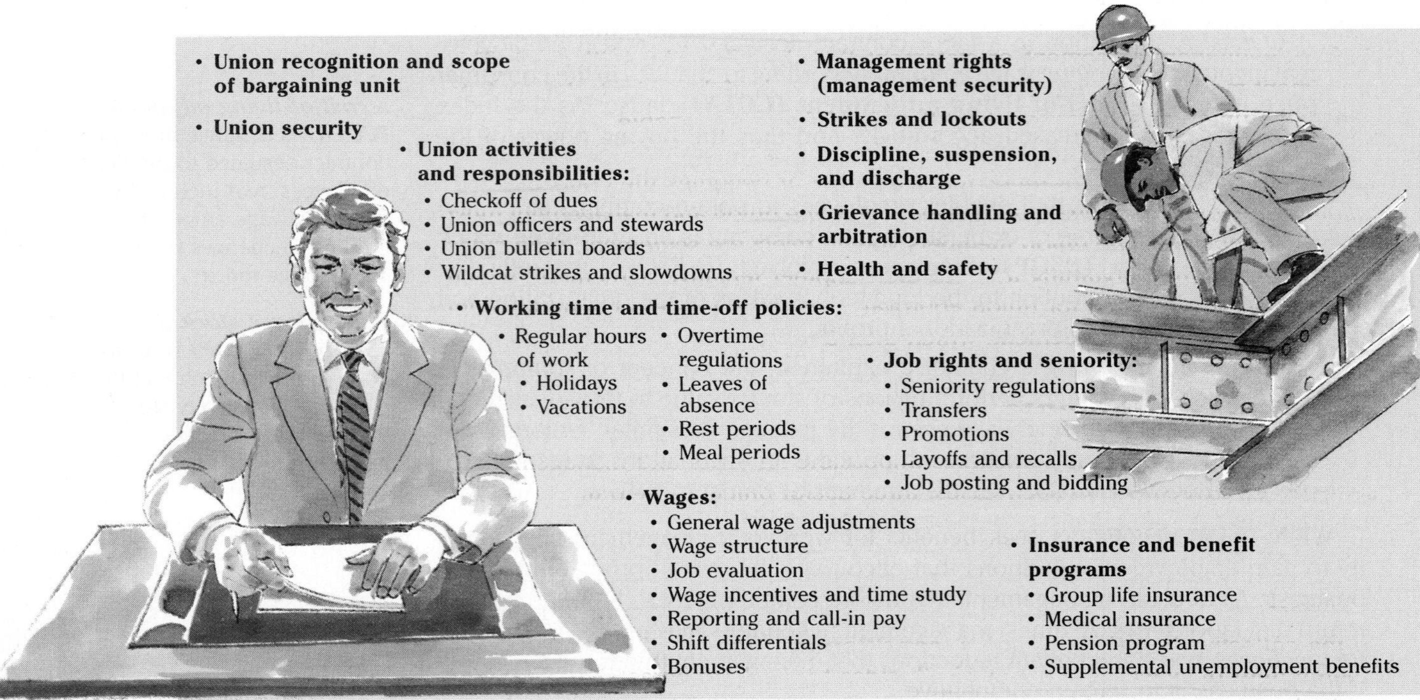

• Union recognition and scope of bargaining unit
• Union security
• Union activities and responsibilities:
• Checkoff of dues
• Union officers and stewards
• Union bulletin boards
• Wildcat strikes and slowdowns
• Working time and time-off policies:
• Regular hours of work
• Holidays
• Vacations
• Overtime regulations
• Leaves of absence
• Rest periods
• Meal periods
• Wages:
• General wage adjustments
• Wage structure
• Job evaluation
• Wage incentives and time study
• Reporting and call-in pay
• Shift differentials
• Bonuses
• Management rights (management security)
• Strikes and lockouts
• Discipline, suspension, and discharge
• Grievance handling and arbitration
• Health and safety
• Job rights and seniority:
• Seniority regulations
• Transfers
• Promotions
• Layoffs and recalls
• Job posting and bidding
• Insurance and benefit programs
• Group life insurance
• Medical insurance
• Pension program
• Supplemental unemployment benefits

Figure 10.6 Topics addressed in union-management negotiations.

Preparation

In the first step of the collective bargaining process, preparation, union and management negotiators formulate their demands and concessions. The union attempts to pinpoint what it would like to have from management in such areas as wages and job seniority. Management attempts to define limits in concessions to the union—limits that will enable the organization to maintain a reasonable level of profit. Figure 10.6 lists a number of issues that unions and management have emphasized in the past when preparing to bargain with one another, including the obvious areas of wages, hours, benefits, and safety of working conditions. Each side, of course, prepares for the negotiations independently.

Bargaining

Once labor and management have prepared their demands and concessions, they begin the actual bargaining. At this stage, the two sides come together in a face-to-face meeting, usually around a large table. (You will often hear newscasters report that both sides are "at the table" or that all the issues have been "put on the table.") In this second step of the collective bargaining process, both sides attempt to follow the bargaining plans they outlined during preparation. Essentially, they try to achieve their individual objectives, but in a spirit of compromise.

Tentative Agreement

If the bargaining during the initial bargaining phase is satisfactory, the negotiators draft a preliminary agreement or statement that describes the settlement. This agreement means that management will meet enough of the union's demands to satisfy the union negotiators while still maintaining a reasonable level of profit. The agreement must then be presented to the union members for a vote.[5] If the members vote to accept, or *ratify*, the settlement, it becomes the collective bargaining agreement or contract under which both the union and management must operate. If, however, the union members vote to reject the settlement, both sides must return to the bargaining table to draft another tentative agreement, which again must be presented for union approval. This basic process continues until the members ratify an agreement, which then becomes the contract.

Assisted Settlements

As you might suspect, it is sometimes impossible for labor and management to settle on an agreement. In such cases, three useful practices help the two sides reach agreement: conciliation, mediation, and arbitration.

Conciliation

In the collective bargaining process, **conciliation** is the practice of involving a neutral third party who encourages both sides to reach an agreement. The third party, known as a *conciliator*, has no formal power over either side but simply tries to get the two to bargain productively. Conciliators are provided by the *Federal Mediation and Conciliation Service*, an agency set up by the Taft-Hartley Act to serve in labor disputes. There is no charge for their service.

Conciliation is the practice of involving in the collective bargaining process a neutral third party who, although virtually powerless, encourages both sides to reach an agreement.

Mediation

In the collective bargaining process, **mediation** is the practice of involving a neutral third party who focuses primarily on proposing solutions to bargaining problems. The third party, known as the *mediator*, goes further than the conciliator. Whereas the conciliator encourages the two sides to arrive at their own solutions, the mediator proposes solutions. Like the conciliator, the mediator is furnished at no charge by the Federal Mediation and Conciliation Service and has no authority over either party.

Mediation is the practice of involving in the collective bargaining process a neutral third party who focuses primarily on proposing solutions to bargaining problems.

Arbitration and Grievances

In the collective bargaining process, **arbitration** is the practice of involving a neutral third party who can settle disputes. The third party, known as the *arbitrator*, actually decides how the disputes should be settled. The arbitrator's decision is legally binding and enforceable. Labor and management typically choose the person from a list supplied by the Federal Mediation and Conciliation service. The two sides generally split the costs of the arbitrator, who is usually paid a fee and reimbursed for expenses.

Arbitration is the practice in the collective bargaining process of involving a neutral third party who can settle disputes.

In addition to being used to settle the specifics of the contract, arbitration is commonly used to help implement it to the satisfaction of both parties. Although contracts are written to be comprehensive and clear, disagreements between labor and management concerning their respective rights under contracts are commonplace.

A ***grievance*** is a formal complaint made by a union member concerning an alleged violation of the labor contract by management.

A **grievance** is a formal complaint made by a union member concerning an alleged violation of the labor contract by management.[6] A sample written grievance is shown in Figure 10.7. Most organizations have a set of *grievance procedures,* which outline such things as how a grievance is to be initiated; whether it should be oral, written, or both; and which union and management people are to be involved at each step.

Naturally, the procedures vary somewhat from organization to organization. A common characteristic of most of them, however, is that the evaluation and settlement of a specific grievance begins with the employee who filed the grievance, the employee's supervisor, and a union official at an equivalent level—for example, a union steward. Most grievances are settled at lower organizational levels. But if these three individuals cannot settle the grievance, it continues up the organizational and union hierarchies simultaneously until it is settled, with or without an arbitrator.

Figure 10.8 illustrates where arbitrators can become involved in a typical grievance procedure. This figure also shows how grievances tend to start at the bottom of the organization and move upward if not settled. In addition to arbitrators, mediators and conciliators are also sometimes involved in settling grievances.

Collective Bargaining Tactics

Actions taken by either labor or management to pressure the other in a collective bargaining situation are collective bargaining tactics.

Figure 10.7
A sample written grievance. Most organizations have an established set of grievance procedures.

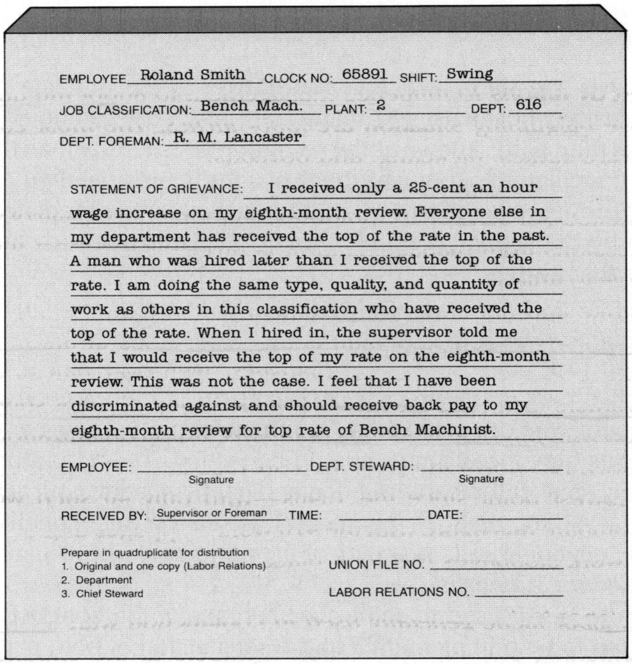

EMPLOYEE Roland Smith CLOCK NO: 65891 SHIFT: Swing
JOB CLASSIFICATION: Bench Mach. PLANT: 2 DEPT: 616
DEPT. FOREMAN: R. M. Lancaster

STATEMENT OF GRIEVANCE: I received only a 25-cent an hour wage increase on my eighth-month review. Everyone else in my department has received the top of the rate in the past. A man who was hired later than I received the top of the rate. I am doing the same type, quality, and quantity of work as others in this classification who have received the top of the rate. When I hired in, the supervisor told me that I would receive the top of my rate on the eighth-month review. This was not the case. I feel that I have been discriminated against and should receive back pay to my eighth-month review for top rate of Bench Machinist.

EMPLOYEE: ______ (Signature) DEPT. STEWARD: ______ (Signature)

RECEIVED BY: Supervisor or Foreman TIME: ______ DATE: ______

Prepare in quadruplicate for distribution
1. Original and one copy (Labor Relations)
2. Department
3. Chief Steward

UNION FILE NO. ______
LABOR RELATIONS NO. ______

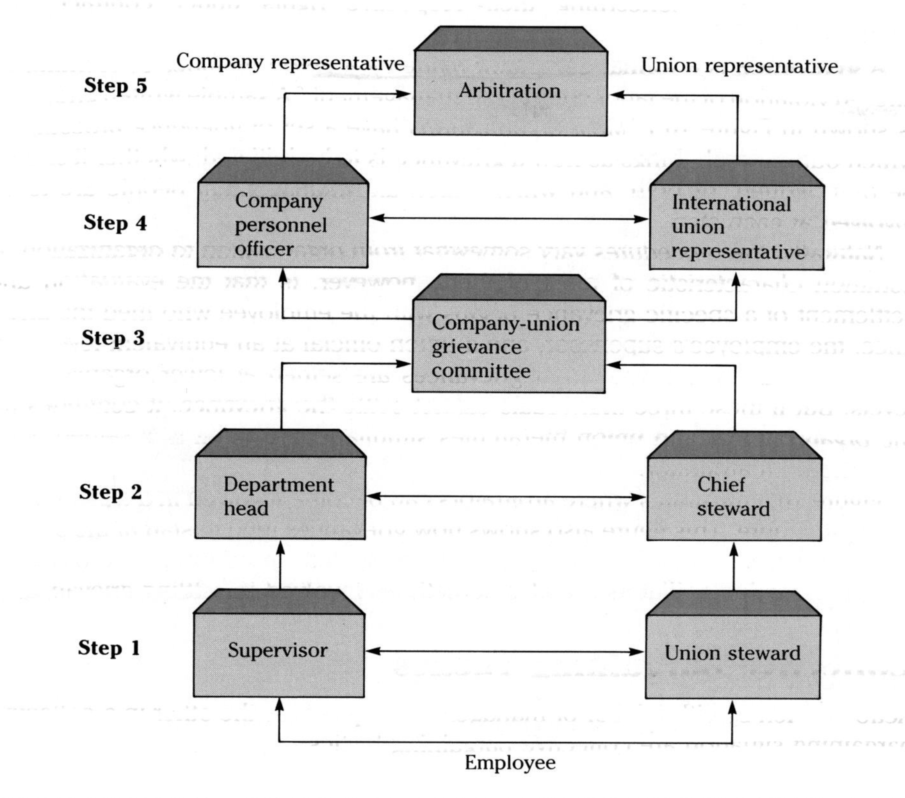

Figure 10.8
The grievance process. Grievances usually start at the bottom of the organization and move upward for a settlement, sometimes through arbitration.

The strike, a temporary stoppage of work by employees, is probably the most influential labor tactic available to unions. One sanitation workers' strike in a major U.S. city resulted in the alarming conditions depicted here.

Labor Tactics

Actions taken by unions to influence management to adopt the union viewpoint in a collective bargaining situation are *labor tactics.* The most commonly used labor tactics are strikes, picketing, and boycotts.

Strikes A walkout, or **strike,** is employees' temporary stoppage of work intended to win concessions from management.[7] It is probably the most influential labor tactic available to unions. The unions pay their members from special strike funds during the strike and hope that management will decide the halt in production is more harmful to the company than is the acceptance of union demands. According to the U.S. Bureau of Labor Statistics, well over half of all strikes are caused by workers' demands for higher wages. Other frequent spurs to strike are dissatisfaction with physical working conditions, union organization and security, and job security. As shown in Figure 10.9, in 1988 the number of work stoppages reached its lowest point since the 1940s—with only 40 such work stoppages occurring. Compare this figure with the 470 work stoppages that occurred in 1952, and the 424 work stoppages that took place in 1979.

A ***strike,*** or walkout, is employees' temporary stoppage of work intended to win concessions from management.

Picketing is a labor tactic, generally used in conjunction with a strike, that involves positioning one or more union members at the entrance of a struck workplace to stop or make difficult any entry to the workplace.

Picketing A labor tactic generally used in conjunction with a strike, **picketing** involves positioning one or more union members at the entrance of a struck workplace to stop or make difficult any entry to the workplace. Picketers inform

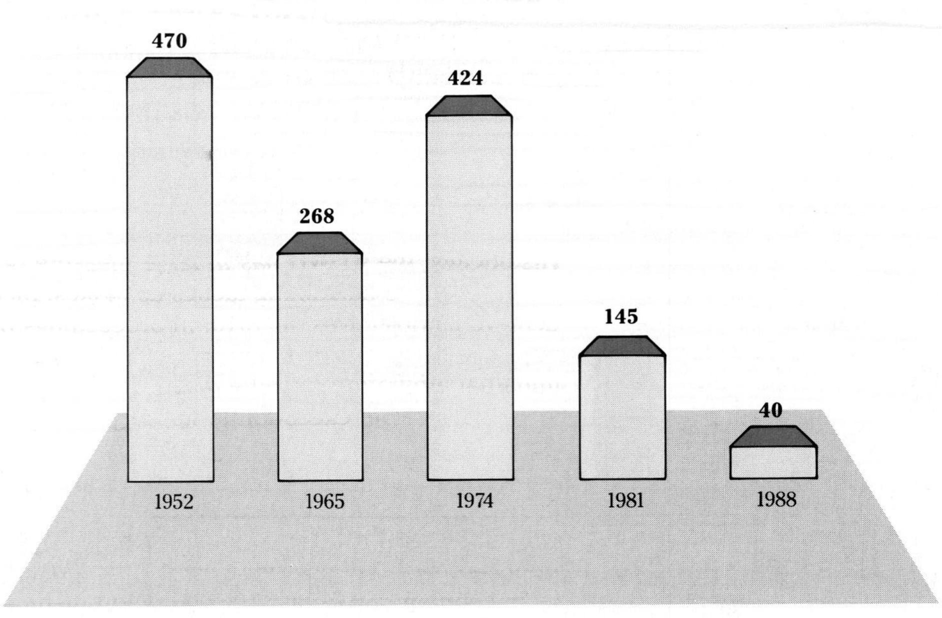

Figure 10.9 Work stoppages caused by strikes. Note that in 1988, the number of work stoppages reached its lowest point since the 1940s.

the public that a strike exists, make deliveries to the workplace difficult or impossible, and discourage other people from working their jobs.

A ***boycott*** is the labor tactic wherein union members refuse to purchase products from companies that are giving a union a difficult time.

Boycotts The labor tactic wherein union members refuse to purchase products from companies that are giving a union a difficult time is the **boycott.** Obviously, the purchasing power of unions can be a very influential tactic. In fact, the use of boycotts is on the rise.

One of the longest boycotts of this century was against the Adolph Coors Company. In 1977, the AFL-CIO initiated a consumer boycott of Coors beer to pressure the company to end discrimination against women and minorities. Ten years later, in 1987, Coors finally took the initiative in settling its dispute with the union. Management decided that the company's success at the national level would be impossible if its conflict with the union remained unresolved.[8]

A ***secondary boycott*** is an attempt by labor to force an employer to stop doing business with another employer who is in conflict with a union.

A recent court ruling has encouraged the use of secondary boycotts as a collective bargaining tactic. A **secondary boycott** is an attempt by labor to force an employer to stop doing business with another employer who is in conflict with a union.

Management Tactics

Actions taken by management in an attempt to influence unions to adopt the management viewpoint in a collective bargaining situation are *management tactics.* The most important of these tactics are lockouts, injunctions, and associations.

BUSINESS PRACTICE EXAMPLE Continues

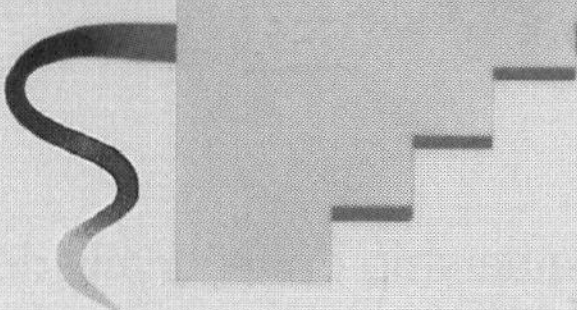

Historically, the ILGWU has in large measure been very successful using such collective bargaining tactics as strikes, picketing, and boycotts to achieve its objectives. In 1910, in proceedings presided over by the famed Supreme Court justice Louis D. Brandeis, the union pioneered the use of impartial arbitration to settle disputes.

In one notable exception to its long history of successes, in 1926, Communists, who had been gaining influence in the union, tried to take it over by staging a strike in the cloak industry. The strike failed, and the ILGWU went bankrupt in the process. Membership plummeted, from over 100,000 in 1920 to below 25,000 in 1932. But in the 1930s, the ILGWU bounced back, stronger than ever.

In February 1958, over 100,000 union members struck to gain a better contract agreement. This largest strike in the union's history led to higher wages, additional holidays, and the adoption of the union label.

Lockouts A refusal by management to allow workers to work, by keeping them out of the workplace, is a **lockout.**[9] Actually, a lockout is a sort of strike called by management. Through it, management hopes to financially pressure the union into adopting management's viewpoint. Although not often used by management, the lockout can be extremely effective.

A ***lockout*** is a refusal by management to allow workers to work, by keeping them out of the workplace.

Injunctions A court order prohibiting or requiring some specific action on the part of someone is an **injunction.** Before the Norris-LaGuardia Act, employers commonly used injunctions to prohibit various union-related activities within organizations. Since the passage of this act, however, injunctions are used primarily to restrict such actions as violence and physical damage to company property. They can also be used to force striking public employees back to work when such strikes are illegal. In addition, the president of the United States can obtain an injunction to prohibit a strike determined to be generally harmful to the nation.

An ***injunction*** is a court order prohibiting or requiring some specific action on the part of someone.

Associations Organizations formed by employers to help neutralize the influence of unions are known as **associations.** The National Association of Manufacturers is one example. Like employees, employers have found added strength in bargaining as a unit rather than individually. Assume, for an example, that a group of employers offered a union a maximum wage increase, as opposed to individual employers offering this same increase. It would be much harder for the union to apply pressure against all the employers collectively than against

Associations are organizations formed by employers to help neutralize the power and influence of unions.

one lone employer. Associations can also provide negotiators for employers. Thus, in the future, unions may find themselves facing better and more experienced management negotiators than they faced in the past.

UNIONS IN THE FUTURE

In the 1980s, U.S. union membership dramatically declined, to a low of about 19 percent in 1988. This decline is due in part to an economy in which the service sector is growing at a far greater pace than the manufacturing sector. Because the service sector tends to employ fewer blue-collar workers than the manufacturing sector, analysts project that there will be a lower growth rate for the blue-collar union jobs than for nonunion professional jobs.

This trend suggests that union membership in the United States will not increase significantly in the near future. As Figure 10.10 indicates, employment growth in

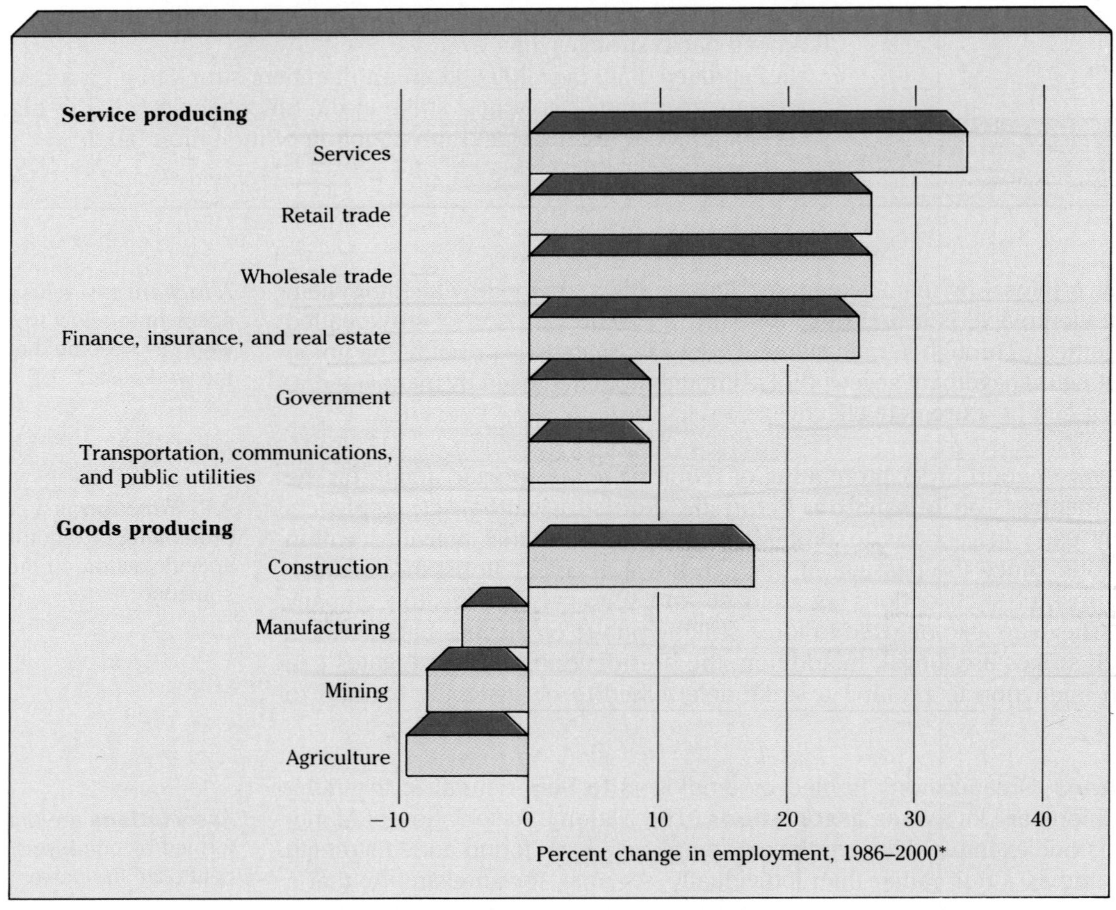

Figure 10.10 The service industry, which is typically not unionized, is expected to show the greatest increase in employment growth.

such industries as construction and mining, which historically have been heavily unionized, is expected to increase only moderately. Employment growth in service industries such as banking, insurance, and education, on the other hand, is expected to grow much more rapidly. As Figure 10.11 shows, about 80 percent of all jobs in the United States in the year 2000 will be created by service industries.

Today, unions are attempting to build membership in industries that have traditionally been nonunion. Whether they will achieve significant success is difficult to predict. Still, the total number of union members as a percentage of the labor force of tomorrow will no doubt remain significant.

Although union membership and the impact of unions on managing a business are declining in the United States, union trends in other countries may be significantly different. For example, labor unrest in South Korea has begun to cause General Motors serious problems. Perhaps more than at any other time in our history, managers of the future will need to keep informed of labor trends worldwide. They will want to avoid relationships with businesses in countries where labor movements seem likely to have a detrimental effect on them, and they will want to establish relationships in countries where labor trends seem advantageous to them.

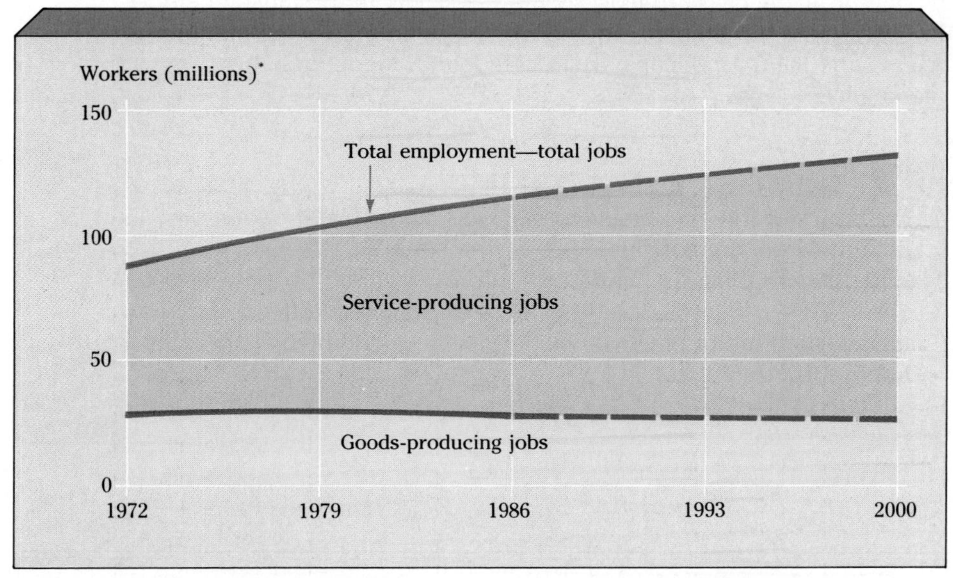

Figure 10.11
By the year 2000, about four of every five jobs will be in the service sector.

*Wage and salary employment except for agriculture, which includes self-employed and unpaid family workers.

BUSINESS PRACTICE EXAMPLE Continues

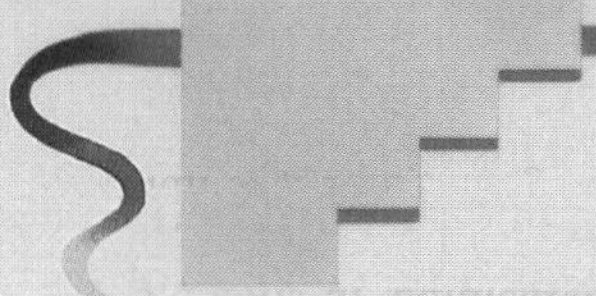

Beginning in the 1970s, the dominant concern of the ILGWU has been a sharp rise in imports. These imports are produced in countries where non-union workers earn just a fraction of what ILGWU members make. According to the U.S. Department of Labor, the United States has lost 300,000 textile and apparel jobs since 1980. In 1987, imports accounted for fully 58 percent of what Americans purchased.

The ILGWU has vigorously campaigned for legislation that would limit the amount of imports entering the United States. It claims that other countries control the amount of imports they allow into their countries, and it argues that the United States should follow suit.

The president of the ILGWU, Jay Mazur, has predicted that if the United States does not legislate a better balance of trade, the U.S. apparel industry will probably cease to exist by the year 2000. In the meantime, the ILGWU's current members, among which are an increasing number of Asians and Latin Americans, try to compete in the international marketplace.

Issues for Discussion

1. Can union workers compete with cheap labor in other countries? Explain how or why not.
2. What do you think the future of the ILGWU will be by the year 2000?
3. The ILGWU is fighting to keep industrial homework illegal. From a management point of view, what are some of the benefits of industrial homework?

SUMMARY

A labor union is an organization of employees that is formed to achieve common goals in the areas of wages, hours, and working conditions. Unions exist to influence employers to further the benefits of employees. There are two basic types of labor unions, craft and industrial. Craft unions consist of workers with specific skills, and industrial unions consist of workers at all levels in a given industry.

The Knights of Labor was the first national labor union to represent workers of various occupations. Conflict within the membership of this union eventually caused its dissolution and the subsequent rise of the American Federation of Labor (AFL), in 1886. As the AFL continued to grow, it became clear that its main focus, craft workers, was not broad enough to serve the needs of many industrial workers filling noncraft jobs. As a result, the Congress of Industrial Organizations (CIO) was founded, in 1937, to better serve the needs of noncraft workers. For many years, the AFL and CIO competed with each other for members. Eventually, the leadership of both groups realized that they could better serve labor's needs by combining forces. In 1955, the two unions merged into a new, dominant union called the AFL-CIO.

Many significant labor laws have been passed throughout the history of unions. The Norris-LaGuardia Act of 1932 made it difficult for management to obtain injunctions to prevent workers from participating in union activities. The Wagner Act (National Labor Relations Act) of 1935 regulated employer actions in areas of collective bargaining, hirings, firings, and treatment of union officials. The Fair Labor Standards Act of 1938 established a minimum wage and a forty-hour workweek. In 1947, the Taft-Hartley Act (Labor Management Relations Act) made closed shops illegal, gave states the right to outlaw union shops, and made featherbedding illegal. The Landrum-Griffin Act of 1959 (Labor Management Reporting and Disclosure Act) was aimed at protecting individual workers from the illegal activities that seemed to surround union situations.

Collective bargaining is the process by which employees, through the union or association representing them, negotiate a labor agreement with their employer. Bargaining can focus on issues such as cost-of-living adjustment clauses (COLAs), employee stock ownership plans (ESOPs), and comparable worth. The major steps in the collective bargaining process are preparation, bargaining, and tentative agreement.

Sometimes it is impossible for management and a union to settle on a labor agreement through collective bargaining. In such a situation, conciliation, mediation, or arbitration can help the two parties arrive at an agreement. Arbitration can also focus on settling grievances—formal complaints made by union members concerning alleged management violations of an existing labor contract. Tactics used by labor during collective bargaining include strikes, picketing, boycotts, and secondary boycotts. Tactics used by management during collective bargaining include lockouts, injunctions, and associations.

In recent times, there has been a decrease in the total number of U.S. workers belonging to unions. Labor trends in union membership as well as other union issues may be significantly different, however, in foreign countries.

KEY TERMS

AFL-CIO p. 283
American Federation of Labor (AFL) p. 283
Arbitration p. 293
Associations p. 297
Boycott p. 296
Closed shop p. 288
Collective bargaining p. 290
Conciliation p. 293
Congress of Industrial Organizations (CIO) p. 283
Cost-of-living adjustment clause (COLA) p. 291
Employee stock ownership plan (ESOP) p. 291
Fair Labor Standards Act p. 287
Featherbedding p. 288
Grievance p. 294
Injunction p. 297
Knights of Labor p. 282
Labor contract p. 290
Labor union p. 281
Landrum-Griffin Act p. 290
Lockout p. 297
Mediation p. 293
Norris-LaGuardia Act p. 287
Picketing p. 295
Right-to-work laws p. 288
Secondary boycott p. 296
Strike p. 295
Taft-Hartley Act p. 288
Union shop p. 288
Wagner Act p. 287

CHECK YOUR LEARNING

Reread the following learning objectives. Each objective is followed by a few questions. Answering these questions accurately will help you retain the most important concepts discussed in this chapter. After answering each question, check your answer with the key at the end of this chapter. (*Hint:* If you have doubt regarding the correct response, consult the page whose number follows the answer.)

Circle:

A. Explain what unions are and why they began.

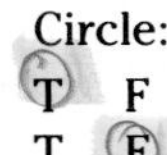

T F — 1. Labor unions are employee organizations formed to achieve common goals.

T F — 2. Unions began despite already fair treatment of employees by employers.

B. Describe the major labor movements in American labor history.

a b c d — 1. The first national labor union in the United States was the: (a) AFL; (b) CIO; (c) Federation of Organized Trades; (d) none of the above.

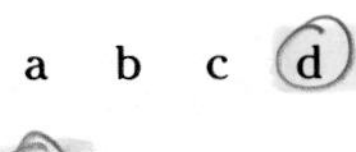

a b c d — 2. Samuel Gompers was president of the: (a) AFL; (b) CIO; (c) Knights of Labor; (d) none of the above.

C. Explain why workers join unions.

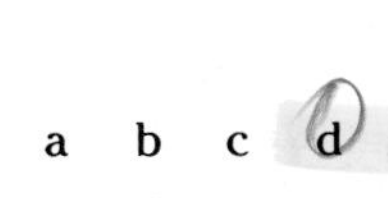

a b c d — 1. Workers join unions to get: (a) protection from employers; (b) better wages; (c) better working conditions; (d) all of the above.

T F — 2. Over the years, unions have been able to exert only an insignificant amount of political power.

D. Summarize the major labor laws that have influenced the union movement.

T F — 1. The Norris-LaGuardia Act outlawed the practice of hiring workers under the condition that they would not become union members.

T F — 2. The NLRB was established as part of the Taft-Hartley Act.

T F — 3. The Fair Labor Standards Act eventually became known as organized labor's Magna Carta.

E. Describe the collective bargaining process and explain assisted settlements.

T F — 1. An ESOP focuses on cost-of-living wage increases.

a b c d — 2. ________ is a document to be ratified by union membership: (a) the preparation; (b) the part; (c) the contract; (d) the tentative agreement.

a b c d — 3. The arbitrator: (a) mainly tries to prevent negotiations from breaking down; (b) suggests solutions to employers; (c) dictates a binding compromise; (d) none of the above.

T F — 4. Mediators can be used for grievance settlements.

F. List and describe the major collective bargaining tactics used by labor and management.

T F — 1. A strike is also commonly called a walkout.

a b c d — 2. Picketing involves: (a) not buying company products; (b) posting workers at work entryways; (c) sabotaging productivity; (d) b and c.

T F — 3. An injunction is essentially the same as a lockout.

G. Project what the future of labor unions will be.

T F — 1. Projections on the types of jobs that will exist in the future imply that union membership soon will be accelerating.

T F — 2. The percentage of our future unionized labor force will be relatively insignificant.

QUESTIONS FOR REVIEW AND DISCUSSION

1. Define the key terms listed at the end of the chapter.
2. What is your opinion about the union movement in contemporary society?
3. Why do you think people join unions today as opposed to in earlier times?
4. If you had the opportunity to write a new labor law that could influence the future direction of labor-management bargaining, what would be the essentials of the law? Why is this law needed?
5. Discuss the advantages and disadvantages of conciliation from both management and union viewpoints.
6. Which collective bargaining tactic do you see as labor's most influential tactic? Explain.
7. Which collective bargaining tactic do you see as management's most influential tactic? Explain.

CONCLUDING CASE

Unions Lose at Safeway Stores and Chrysler

Nineteen eighty-eight might have been a big year for organized labor. More than 700 contracts, covering nearly 40% of unionized workers in America, were up for negotiation. The unions, worried over inflation, frustrated by job losses and long outmaneuvered by their foes in industry, had been hoping to show a few people what they could do.

Instead, they started to understand how Michael Spinks must feel.

Take the United Rubber Workers. The union charged into talks with tire companies vowing to win a "meaningful" pay increase. What it got was two bits an hour. At one threatened plant, the union agreed to a *cut* in pay.

So did the union representing workers at Safeway Stores in Oklahoma and Kansas City. The United Food and Commercial Workers, fearing members would be left with no pay at all because of store closings or sell-offs, accepted a wage rollback of $2.50 an hour.

Even the mighty Teamsters union, while gaining modest wage and benefit increases, agreed to a plan permitting pay givebacks under some circumstances.

Companies claim they can no longer afford to be generous. Competitive pressures, domestic and international, are growing, they argue. And they say the current takeover climate could leave them vulnerable if they offered workers too much and ran up their costs. Many managers, fearing that their own jobs would be in jeopardy in a merger or takeover, are tougher than ever about labor costs. At the same time, the growing use of temporary workers helps ease fears of strikes and reduces unions' leverage.

Nowadays, strikes are risky. Employers' increasing use of temporary, part-time, and other so-called contingent workers means companies have a supply of willing help ready to replace union members who walk. "People never expected to lose their job completely when they went on strike," notes a federal mediation official. "They have to expect it now."

In return for all the concessions they have to swallow, unions are determined to make sure their members at least have a job. A new coal contract, which raised pay but weakened benefits, gave laid-off miners hiring preference at new mines. A Chrysler contract also has provisions meant to limit layoffs. Also getting attention this year is the idea of "employment security," in which a company that is laying off a worker would train him for another job and try to place him at another company.

Job-security clauses give unions something positive to take back to their members, at modest cost to employers. But they can look more generous than they are. Auto contracts provide for job security, but, because they limit the funds available for it, they haven't prevented sizable layoffs.

Says Richard Belous, an economist for the Conference Board: "It makes good headlines, but when you start reading the fine print, you find it doesn't cover you."

Issues for Discussion

1. Do we need more labor laws to give unions more bargaining power? Explain.

2. Can you think of any new bargaining tactics unions might be able to use to gain more leverage over management? How would these tactics be implemented?
3. How will union bargaining losses discussed in the case affect union membership in the future?
4. How will union bargaining losses discussed in the case affect the attitude of unions toward bargaining in the future?

NOTES

1. For more information on why workers join unions, see Donald P. Crane, *Personnel: The Management of Human Resources* (Boston: Kent Publishing, 1982), pp. 285–287.
2. This section is based on Bruce Feldacker, *Labor Guide to Labor Law* (Reston: Reston Publishing, 1980).
3. Testimony by Jay Mazur, president of the ILGWU, before the U.S. Department of Labor, Hearings on Industrial Homework in the Women's Apparel Industry, New York, New York, March 29, 1989.
4. H. J. Chruden and A. W. Sherman, Jr., *Personnel Management: The Utilization of Human Resources,* 6th ed. (Cincinnati, Ohio: South-Western Publishing, 1980), p. 375.
5. Robert L. Mathis and John H. Jackson, *Personnel: Contemporary Perspectives and Applications* (St. Paul, Minn.: West Publishing, 1982), p. 502.
6. E. Edward Herman and Alfred Huhn, *Collective Bargaining and Labor Relations* (Englewood Cliffs, N.J.: Prentice-Hall, 1981), p. 435.
7. William F. Glueck, *Personnel: A Diagnostic Approach* (Plano, Texas: Business Publications, Inc., 1982), p. 601.
8. James Cox, "New Guard Brews Beer's New Image," *USA Today,* August 21, 1987, p. B1.
9. Daniel Quinn Mills, *Labor-Management Relations* (New York: McGraw-Hill, 1982), p. 90.

CHECK YOUR LEARNING ANSWER KEY

A. 1. T, *p. 281*
2. F, *p. 281*

B. 1. d, *p. 282*
2. a, *p. 283*

C. 1. d, *p. 285*
2. F, *p. 285*

D. 1. T, *p. 287*
2. F, *p. 287*
3. F, *p. 287*

E. 1. F, *p. 291*
2. d, *p. 293*
3. c, *p. 293*
4. T, *p. 294*

F. 1. T, *p. 295*
2. b, *p. 295*
3. F, *p. 297*

G. 1. F, *p. 298*
2. F, *p. 299*

CHAPTER

11

PRODUCTION AND OPERATIONS MANAGEMENT

LEARNING OBJECTIVES

After reading this chapter you should be able to:

1. Define *production.*
2. Explain what is meant by productivity.
3. Discuss site selection and layout patterns as related to the production facility.
4. Explain the relationship between forecasting and production.
5. Describe how the process of coordinating production relates to operations management.
6. Discuss quality control and JIT inventory control as components of production control.

OUTLINE

BUSINESS PRACTICE EXAMPLE

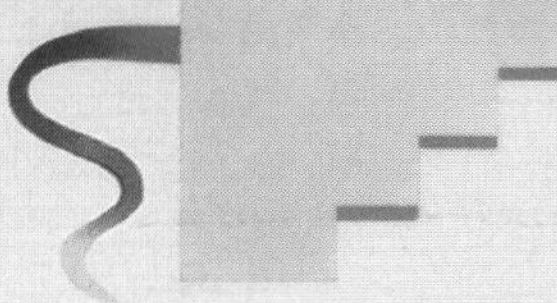

Keeping up the Quality at Maytag

"Ol' Lonely"—the Maytag repairman whose dependable products never need a service call—may be one of TV's most recognizable characters. Since 1966 the face of actor Jesse White has created worldwide impact and viewer empathy. Once, walking through the streets of ancient Athens, White was stopped by an astonished Greek who pointed at him: "Maytag!" said the Athenian, "You're Maytag!" The lonely repairman has become a symbol for the highest quality in American-made merchandise.

Behind this quality image, Maytag's top-line products are solidly supported by the reputation of their management team. "They're just a conservative, well-run company," said an analyst for the *Wall Street Transcript,* which gave Maytag's team a 1988 award for managerial excellence. Maytag was also rated by *Fortune* among the top 5 corporate management teams during the mid-1980s. The magazine's analysts admired more than the Maytag reputation for quality; they saw it as an exceptionally cost-effective company that "always paid their stockholders well." CEO Daniel Krumm, born and bred in Iowa, directs key players in the Newton, Iowa headquarters, including President Leonard Hadley and Vice Presidents for Manufacturing Sterling Swanger and Robert Faust. As Maytag's acquisitions kept expanding their product line beyond its "high-end" washing machines into dishwashers, stoves, floor cleaners, and recently refrigerators, the manufacturing group had a difficult job. They had to find a way to integrate the famous "Ol' Lonely" quality standards into more and more scattered and complex production operations.

With different plants and products located throughout the Midwest, Maytag needed some way to get all the new operations working together toward the company's time-honored standard of excellence. Maytag had up-to-date techniques, high technology robots, and well planned inventory systems, but these were only part of the picture. The management team needed good plans and effective models to bring all the technology together for top quality and efficiency in production.

Manufacturing Vice President Robert Faust thought Maytag's best point of departure should be the company's tradition of high standards and the Midwest work ethic. "Here at Maytag we are brought up in an atmosphere of producing quality products," he said. "The spirit emanates from the top to the bottom and from the bottom to the top. We just grew up with it as the right way to do things." This translated into a number of worker cooperation programs in place on the production line.

The Maytag team also felt they could build up new manufacturing systems with an employee reward plan that had enjoyed over 40 years' success in the Newton, Iowa plants, a program that brought employees and engineers together to focus on cost-savings. Manufacturing Vice President Swanger of the Newton, Iowa, plant stoutly maintained that cost-saving programs were not inconsistent with quality. "We have never sacrificed a quality principle or feature for a cost savings—but we have found that we often get improved quality when we install a cost-saving project."

WHAT'S AHEAD

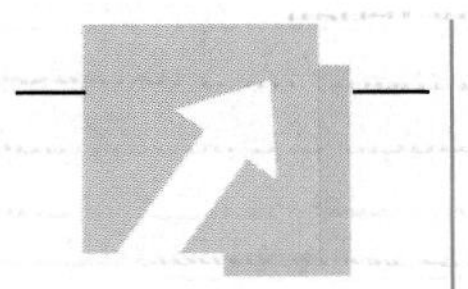

Maintaining product quality at Maytag involves both production and operations management. This chapter is divided into two sections: (1) production and (2) operations management. Production includes primarily processes used to produce goods and services, productivity, the production facility, and forecasts. Operations management includes coordinating production (through planning, routing, scheduling, dispatching, and materials requirements planning) and controlling production (through quality control and just-in-time inventory control).

WHAT IS PRODUCTION?

As Figure 11.1 shows, the production process turns organizational resources into finished products. There is scarcely a topic in this book—from management and finance to marketing and organizing—that does not have an impact on the pro-

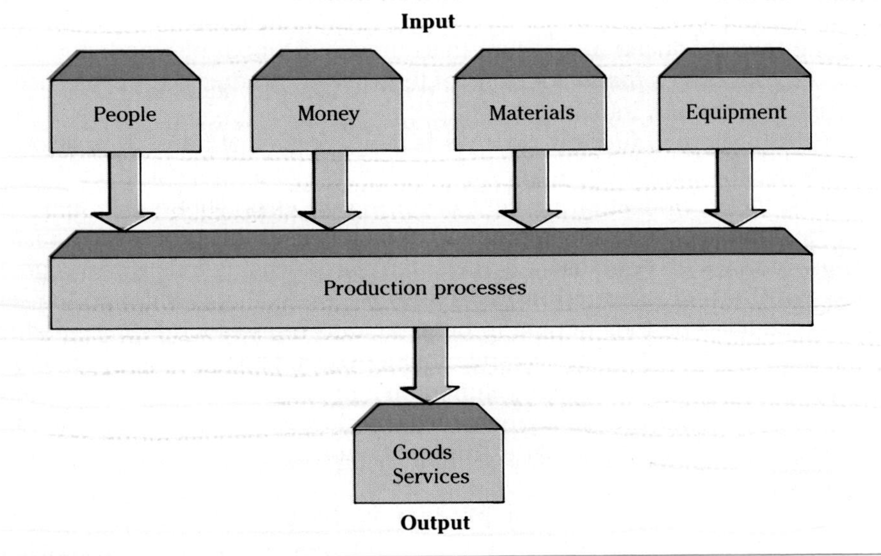

Figure 11.1
The production process turns organizational resources into finished products.

duction process. This section will examine production by first defining it, then discussing the production facility and the importance of forecasting in formulating effective production plans.

Defining *Production*

Production is the transformation of organizational resources into products.

There is a simple definition of **production:** the transformation of organizational resources into products. The whole story, however, is not quite so simple. Look again at each element in the definition. *Organizational resources* are all the assets (such as people, money, materials, and equipment) available to the manager to be used in generating products. *Transformation* is all the steps involved in the activities necessary to change organizational resources into products (for example, purchasing, manufacturing, and hiring). *Products* are the various commodities aimed at meeting human needs—soup, skirts, washing machines, cars, haircuts, courses, meals, even advice from an accountant. Obviously, the word *production* takes in a wide variety of things and activities: supplies that go in, processes that change them, and commodities or services that come out at the other end.

Utility is the quality of a product that makes it useful or desirable in satisfying customers' needs.

Transforming resources into products creates what is called **utility,** the quality of a product that makes it useful and desirable in satisfying customers' needs. As we will see in chapter 12, utility can be created in several ways.

Form utility is the usefulness resources gain after they are transformed into products.

The production process is concerned primarily with **form utility,** the usefulness resources gain after they are transformed into products. Silk, for example, gains form utility when it is transformed into clothing. Paper and ink gain form utility when they are transformed into a book.

Production Processes

Form utility can be created in many ways, each of which is a separate production process. Four production processes commonly used in modern businesses are analytic, synthetic, continuous, and intermittent.

The ***analytic production process*** is the process that transforms resources by breaking them down into one or more products.

The **analytic production process** is the process that transforms resources by breaking them down into one or more products. For example, an analytic production process is used to turn crude oil (raw material) into gasoline and kerosene (two products) and to turn trees into solid wood, plywood, and paper. Figure 11.2 illustrates the major steps of the analytic production process used at Kellogg's to turn corn into corn flakes.

The ***synthetic production process*** is the process that transforms resources into products by combining two or more materials into a single product.

The **synthetic production process** is the process that transforms resources into products by combining two or more materials into a single product. A bakery uses a synthetic production process to turn flour, eggs, shortening, and sugar (materials) into a cake (a single product). A factory uses this process to transform a variety of tubes and circuits, a screen, and plastic casing into a television.

The ***continuous production process*** is a process that is followed the same way for extended periods of time in order to transform resources into products.

The **continuous production process** is a process that is followed the same way for extended periods of time in order to transform resources into products. In this process, the equipment is rarely shut down; and adjustments, if any, barely interrupt production. For example, aluminum is produced the same way for weeks, months, or even years at a time. When iron is produced from ore, the blast furnaces are never shut down. Oil refineries run continuously as long as raw material is available.

The ***intermittent production process*** is the transformation of resources into products in relatively short production runs, between which machines are often shut down and retooled or prepared to perform a different function.

The **intermittent production process** is the transformation of resources into products in relatively short production runs, between which machines are

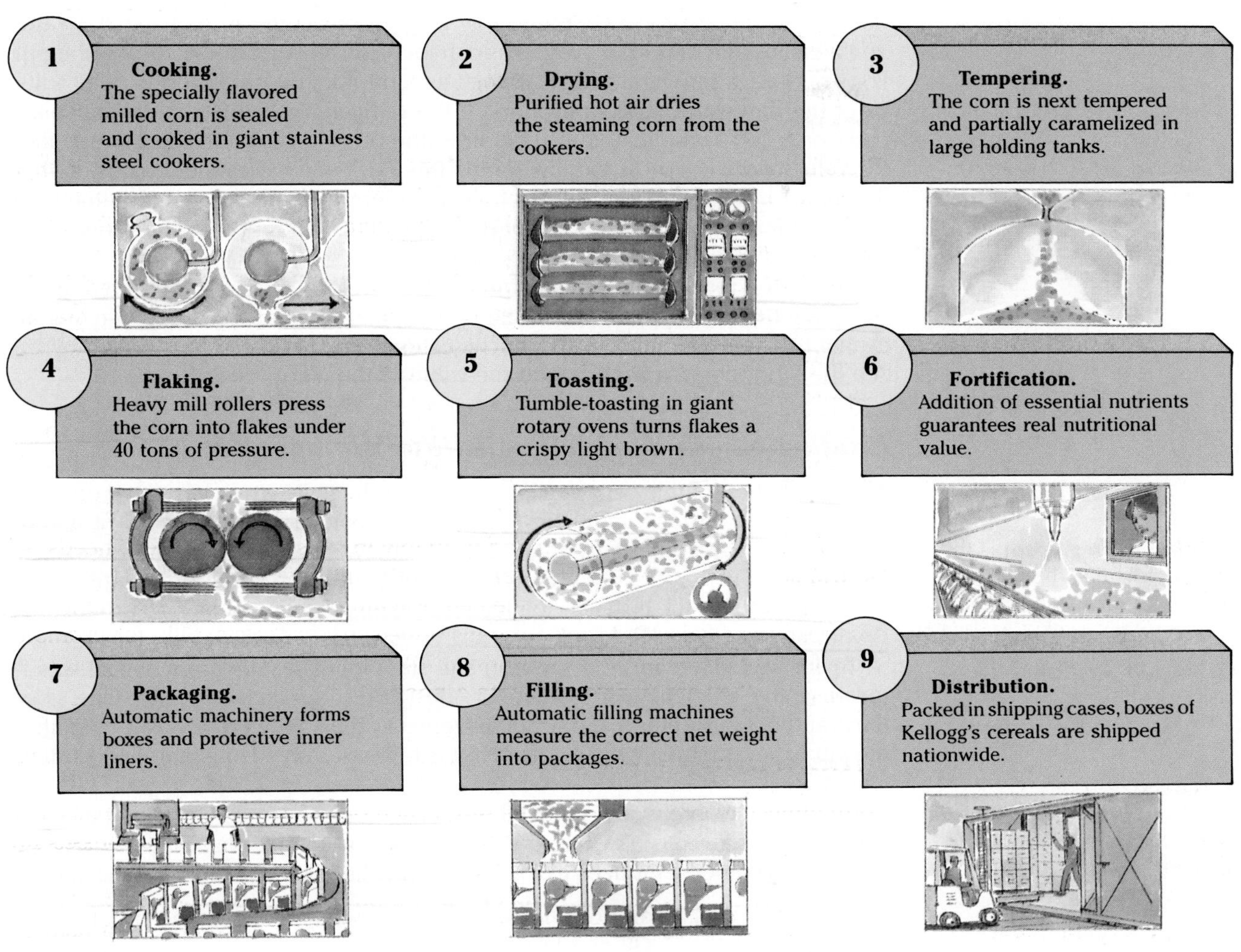

Figure 11.2 The analytic production process turns corn into cornflakes at Kellogg's.

often shut down and retooled or prepared to perform a different function. A good example is a foundry, where many different metal products can be produced through adjustment of existing equipment. An intermittent production process can be either analytic or synthetic.

Productivity

As chapter 2 showed, **productivity** is a measure of the relationship between the total amount of goods and services being produced (output) and the resources needed to produce them (input). This relationship can be expressed in the following equation:

Productivity is a measure of the relationship between the total amount of goods and services being produced and the resources needed to produce them.

$$\text{Productivity} = \frac{\text{Output}}{\text{Input}}$$

The higher the value of the ratio of output to input, the higher the productivity of the production process. Productivity is often measured in terms of this ratio, and a discussion of productivity rates can focus on any part of the output or input. For example, a refrigerator can be seen as a product output in terms of its value or of the hardware features it offers. If the refrigerator has too many expensive parts or is too complicated in relation to the price it brings in the market, then the value of the output is too low for the input. If the price cannot be raised, then the input should be examined carefully. Simpler parts and construction methods might be found; cutting the cost of these elements will improve the productivity ratio.

Any of the inputs can be examined in terms of the resources involved: Is the equipment efficiently matched to the production process? Are the right materials available when needed? Is the flow of finances enough to keep production moving? Are the labor costs appropriate to the value of the end product?

Productivity in the Past: Scientific Management

Scientific management is the process of finding the one best way to perform a task.

Around the turn of this century, the study of productivity emphasized the one best way to perform a task. Efficiency was a major concern. The process of finding the one best way to perform a task became known as **scientific management.** Frederick W. Taylor (1856–1915) is commonly called the father of scientific management. Perhaps the best way to illustrate the historical emphasis on productivity is with an account of his work.

Taylor was an engineer in the iron and steel industry. His primary goal was to increase the efficiency of workers by designing jobs scientifically. One good illustration of his method and his management philosophy is the way he modified the job of several men whose sole responsibility was shoveling materials at Bethlehem Steel.[1]

Taylor's basic premise was that there is one best way to do a job, and that way should be discovered and put into operation. Taylor first made the assumption that any job could be reduced to a science. Then he asked the following questions:

1. Will a first-class man do more work per day with a shovel load of 5 pounds, 10 pounds, 15, 20, 30 or 40 pounds?
2. Which kinds of shovels work best with which materials?
3. How quickly can each shovel be pushed into a pile of materials and pulled out properly loaded?
4. How much time is required to swing a shovel backwards and throw the load a given horizontal distance while achieving a given height?

Through observation and experimentation, Taylor answered these questions, in the process developing a "science of shoveling." He discovered how to increase the total amount of materials shoveled per day and then increased worker efficiency by matching shovel size with such factors as the man, the materials, and the height and distance the materials were to be thrown.

Three years after Taylor's shoveling efficiency plan was put into operation, records at Bethlehem Steel indicated that the total number of shovelers needed was reduced from about 600 to 140, the average number of tons shoveled per man per day rose from 16 to 59, the average earnings per man per day rose from \$1.15 to \$1.88, and the average cost of handling a ton of materials dropped from

HIGHLIGHT IN BUSINESS PRACTICE

Quality Control at McDonald's—A+ is the Only Passing Grade

You own a McDonald's franchise, and at any point of any day—you never know *when*—one of the company's 300 quality control inspectors will walk through the doors of your store. Merely anticipating that visit keeps you and your entire staff on your best behavior. God forbid that anything is found seriously out of order, out of place, or under par; the inspector is the one with the power to see that you lose your license.

This may sound like a nerve-wracking way to run a business, but if you work for McDonald's, it is the *only* way. The corporation's strict quality control is also the *reason* you are a success. The corporation's founder, Ray A. Kroc, required all of his employees to give their jobs a 100% effort. Therefore, that is also the way the quality inspectors approach their jobs.

McDonald's quality controllers focus on every detail of everything in your restaurant. If a store is being run according to Kroc's stringent standards, then it follows that there are no stray shirttails: storage areas are orderly, lids on cardboard boxes discarded for neatness's sake; the entire contents of refrigerators are completely up-to-date; hand-cut food must look appealing and is handled so as not to destroy its appearance; and *everything* must gleam. A quality controller's checklist is endless, the stores are under constant surveillance, and, as a result, they pull in an average of $1.5 million annually each.

If you do run a McDonald's franchise, it means you have graduated successfully from Hamburger University, McDonald's crash course in corporate culture. Establishing Hamburger University is an additional way management attempts to exert quality control: by ensuring that those in charge of each and every one of its stores know exactly how to run a McDonald's restaurant the *right* way, management builds quality control right into the production process at the labor level.

Enhancing certain aspects of the production process by using new technologies as they become available is yet another way to monitor quality. For instance, the restaurants are exploring the use of wireless headphones. A drive-through order-taker wearing a wireless headphone can do double-duty: he or she can take orders *and* fill the orders that have already been taken, shortening the customer's wait and improving the quality of the restaurant's service.

The entire food service industry fights an ongoing battle with labor shortages and a high rate of personnel turnover. This fact of life affects product quality and its control adversely. However, McDonald's strong sense of team at each individual restaurant and the powerful reach of its corporate culture has helped to counter both situations. People enjoy working in such a positive environment, and they are rewarded for meeting the company's high expectations. Some people believe that young McDonald's employees do not earn enough money; however, they earn points toward purchases at Sears or toward college tuition. Thorough and effective quality control is the reason McDonald's continues to earn an A+, both on paper and from the still-growing ranks of dedicated consumers around the world.

$0.072 to $0.033. This case is an impressive application of scientific management to the task of shoveling.

Labor Productivity

The wages paid to workers have been a significant portion of the inputs that organizations earmark for the production process. As Figure 11.3 indicates, over the years, U.S. manufacturing workers have been paid substantially more for an hour of their work than many of their foreign counterparts. From a cost of labor viewpoint, some foreign companies may be more productive than their U.S. competitors if they incur lower costs in producing the same or similar products.

This business practice has increased the difficulty U.S. manufacturers may face in competing with foreign manufacturers. Since some foreign companies incur lower labor costs in manufacturing products, they may be able to sell their products at lower prices than can U.S. competitors. To better compete on a worldwide basis, U.S. companies can attempt to increase productivity in two proven ways: by increasing the efficiency of the production system or by developing technological innovations that establish new ways of producing.

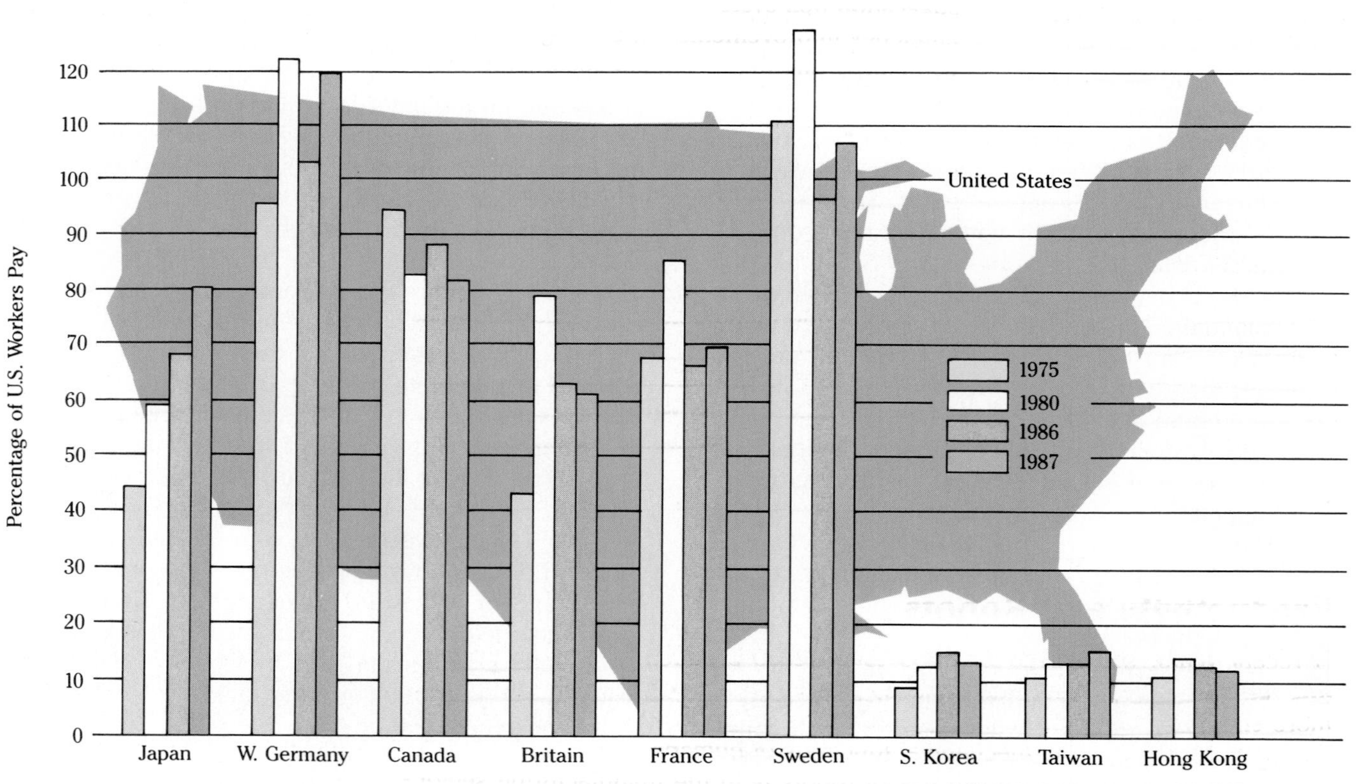

Figure 11.3 Pay practices around the world: International manufacturing workers' compensation as a percentage of U.S. manufacturing workers' pay. Note: Hourly compensation includes average hourly wages plus benefits computed on a per-hour basis.

BUSINESS PRACTICE EXAMPLE Continues

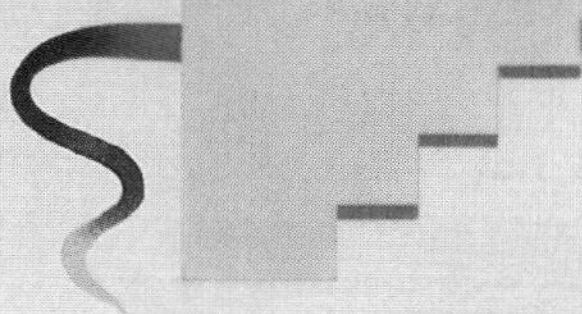

Maytag's top-line products, uniquely suited to American standards of living, have left the company without much foreign competition, in terms of either market share or labor productivity. Even with minimal challenge from offshore productivity pressures, Maytag's production people have long been committed to getting the most from workers and from machines. For over 40 years Maytag's "work simplification program" has practiced a home-grown approach to boosting productivity. The practice that works for Maytag doesn't fit the view that American managers should squeeze out more productivity by cutting wages or badgering workers for more effort. Successful productivity in Newton, Iowa and other Maytag plants came from good old American teamwork.

Maytag's program uses an Employee Idea Plan which is more than a suggestion box system. In a three-hour course, employees are shown how efficiency improvements—including robots—can benefit them and the company while improving job security. In the process employees gain confidence in their ability to make improvements. The program rewards participants with recognition and payments tied to actual cost savings, while giving workers channels for discussing and analyzing ideas with their superiors and with engineers to make them workable.

This approach, using teamwork up and down the levels of supervision, was credited by Manufacturing VP Swanger as helping Maytag to modernize the newly acquired stove-building plant at Jenn-Air in Indianapolis. Engineers and manufacturing workers from Maytag and Jenn-Air served together on a task force to set up a production line that included new robotics operations. Said Swanger, "We have used robotics for a number of years in those areas where it was effective to do so; this has allowed us to apply better techniques for improved quality at lower costs."

Productivity and Robots

In recent years, the search for ways to increase productivity has focused on **automation**—the process that replaces people with machines that can do jobs more effectively and more efficiently. Part of this focus is on **robots,** machines that perform some of the mechanical functions of humans.

Automation is the process that replaces people with machines that can do jobs more effectively and efficiently.

Perhaps the most well known use of robots is in the manufacturing sector.[2] Today the manufacturing of automobiles, computers, and vacuum cleaners, for example, commonly involves the use of robots.

Robots are machines that perform some of the mechanical functions of humans.

Robots have proved quite successful at improving production efficiency in certain manufacturing situations. They can repeatedly perform a single task, such

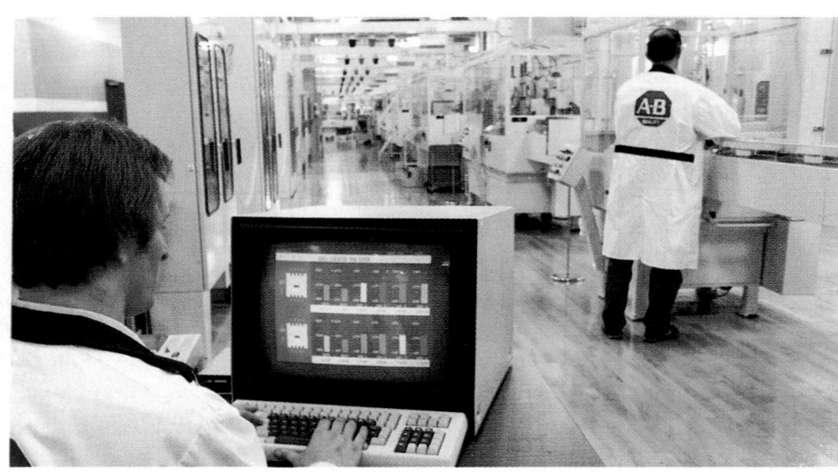

Automation replaces people with machines that can do the job more effectively, efficiently, and often more safely. At Allen-Bradley, automated robots are programmed and coordinated by computers to perform. Needless to say, robots do not suffer the boredom and fatigue that can affect human productivity.

A ***flexible manufacturing system*** is the production process that uses computer-controlled robots that can be adapted to perform various versions of the same task.

as welding, without the boredom and fatigue that reduce human production efficiency. In addition, some robots can be programmed and coordinated by a computer to perform different versions of a task. The production process that uses computer-controlled robots that can be adapted to perform various versions of the same task is called a **flexible manufacturing system.**

Robots in Service Industries

Robots are also being used successfully in the service sector.[3] They have proved adept at such diverse tasks as drilling during brain surgery and cleaning up hazardous materials at the Three Mile Island nuclear plant. In controlled conditions, robots drive vans, harvest oranges, and care for the disabled. Researchers have called some of these basic service uses "mops and cops" applications.[4] Regarding "cops," in Boston a robot security guard roams a specified area to sense intruders and notify police. Regarding "mops," several companies are working on robot cleaners that, equipped with brooms and floor plans, can sweep through office buildings.

The move toward using robots in production processes is still in its infancy. More useful and productive applications of robots in the manufacturing and service sectors will undoubtedly be developed in the future. To remain competitive, the modern manager must incorporate today's practical robot applications while watching for future developments that will upgrade manufacturing processes.

Naturally, there are both advantages and disadvantages in using robots. As already mentioned, one advantage is that they can take over boring factory jobs, thereby allowing people to perform more interesting and motivating jobs. One disadvantage is that if workers perceive robots as a threat to their jobs, the use of robots can strain labor-management relations.[5]

Productivity and Computers

Modern managers are using computers in several different ways to improve productivity. Three productive applications of the computer are value-added networks (VANs), computer-aided design (CAD), and computer-aided manufacturing (CAM).

Value-Added Networks (VANs)

A communication system that allows computers to coordinate production processes with other computers over long distances is a **valued-added network (VAN).**[6] From a production viewpoint, a VAN can link manufacturers electronically with suppliers and customers, helping to speed goods to market while lowering costs.

A ***value-added network (VAN)*** is a communication system that allows computers to coordinate production processes with other computers over long distances.

Figure 11.4 describes a sample VAN for an automobile manufacturer. It electronically links the auto company's dealers, parts makers, and other suppliers. When a customer orders a particular model or color, the dealer types the order into a terminal in the showroom. The VAN orders the parts needed for the order, schedules shipments from the suppliers to the factory, and orders the assembly line to adjust its routine to make the special order. The VAN also tracks the payment amounts for each supplier and indicates when each payment is due.

Computer-Aided Design and Computer-Aided Manufacturing

An exciting application of the computer involves product design. **Computer-aided design (CAD)** is interaction between a designer and a computer to produce a blueprint that meets established product specifications. The designer starts by developing a rough sketch of a proposed product, using a special pen and drafting table or drawing directly on the computer screen.

Computer-aided design (CAD) is interaction between a designer and a computer to produce a blueprint that meets established product specifications.

The computer helps the designer continually refine the rough sketch in an efficient manner until a detailed and acceptable product design evolves. The designer can then ask the computer to check for design weaknesses or strengths. On the basis of the computer's responses, the designer can use the computer once again to make design modifications quickly and simply. Naturally, the computer can generate a printed version of the final blueprint after the designer is satisfied that the product plan is acceptable.

Computer-aided design (CAD) lets this designer use a computer to produce design specifications. This designer began with a rough sketch which the computer refined until an acceptable design evolved.

Chrysler uses CAD to improve production efficiency. The company also follows another worthwhile business practice: Once an acceptable product design is generated, the company attempts to improve production efficiency even further by using the same basic design as the foundation for many different products.

The field of computer-aided design is merging with the field of **computer-assisted manufacturing (CAM)**—the computer analysis of a product design to determine the steps necessary for producing the product and to ready and control the equipment used in producing it. A manufacturer can take a product design generated by CAD and turn it into reality through a production system set up and monitored by CAM.

There are many benefits to using a CAD/CAM production system. First, using the computer for product design usually results in higher product quality because the designer is able to investigate many alternatives quickly and efficiently. Also, the design phase of production is usually shorter and therefore less costly than if it uses only human analysis. Finally, because the production process is monitored by computer, inventory is more easily kept at appropriate levels; the inefficiency of committing too much or too little money to inventory is minimized.[7]

Computer-aided manufacturing (CAM) is the computer analysis of a product design to determine the steps necessary for producing the product and to ready and control the equipment used in producing it.

The Production Facility

A place where goods and services are produced is a **production facility.** Two especially important issues regarding such facilities are where to locate them and how to lay them out.

A ***production facility*** is a place where goods and services are produced.

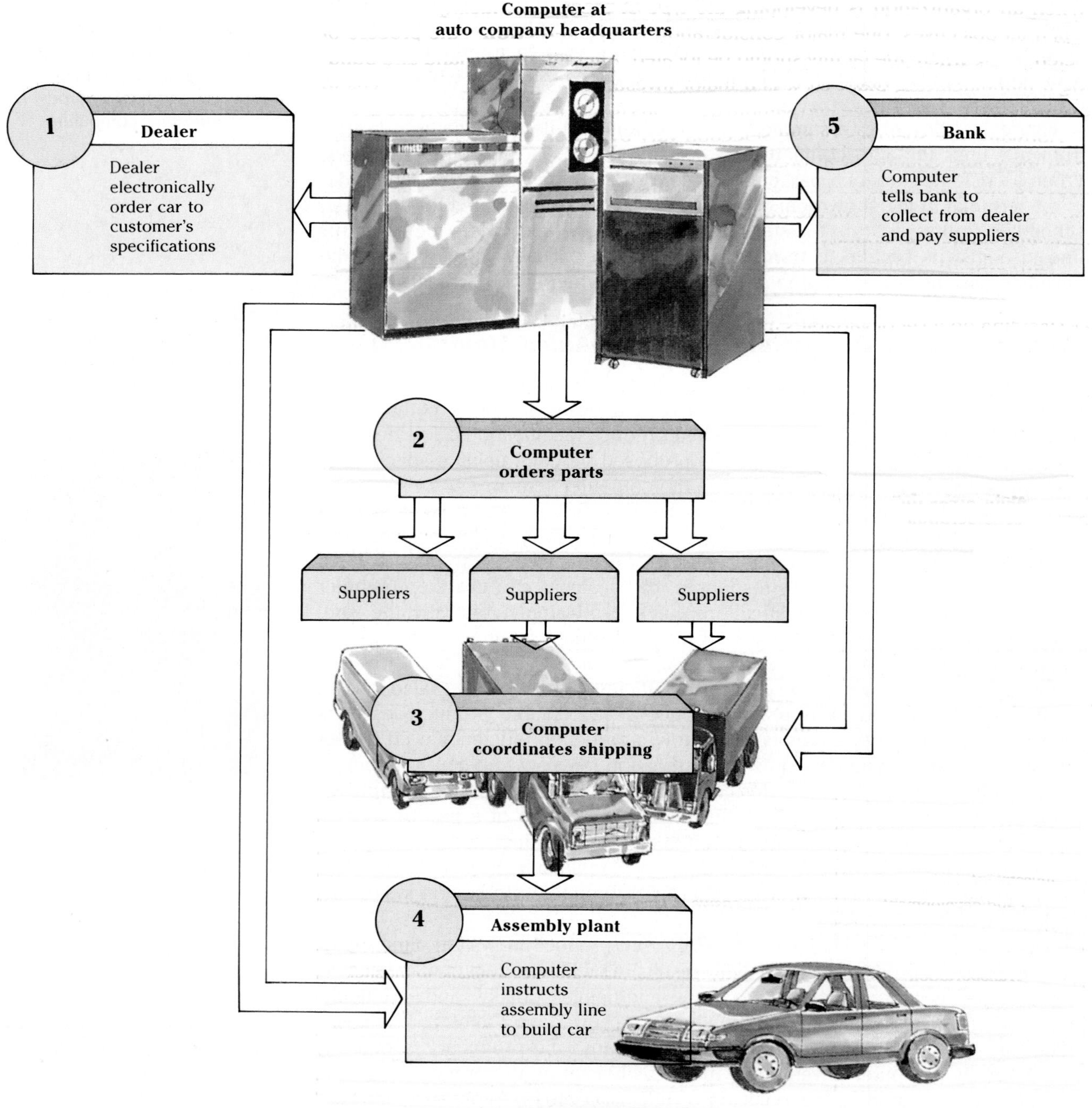

Figure 11.4 A sample value-added network for an automobile manufacturer.

Site Selection

When an organization is developing the type of production facility it needs to reach its objectives, one major consideration is **site selection**—the process of determining where the facility should be located. After all, buying land and building a manufacturing plant on it is a major investment. Figure 11.5 lists areas to consider in choosing a site and sample questions to ask when exploring the areas.

Site selection is the process of determining where a production facility should be located.

Normally, the specifics of site selection vary by region or by whether the site is in the home country or a foreign country. For example, governments tend to approve site purchases at different speeds, and political pressures—which can slow down or even prevent the purchase of a site—vary drastically from state to state and country to country.

Many organizations use a weighting process to compare potential sites in various countries. Basically, this process involves

1. Deciding on a set of variables that are critical to obtaining an appropriate site.

Major areas for consideration in site selection	Sample question to begin exploring major areas
Profit	
Market location	Where are our customers in relation to the site?
Competition	What competitive situation exists at the site?
Operating costs	
Suppliers	Are materials available near the site at reasonable cost?
Utilities	What are utility rates at the site? Are they sifficiently available?
Wages	What wage rates are paid in comparable organizations near the site?
Taxes	What are tax rates on income, sales, property, etc., to the site?
Investment costs	
Land/development	How expensive is land and construction at the site?
Others	
Transportation	Are airlines, railroads, highways, etc., available to the site?
Laws	What laws exist related to zoning, pollution, etc., which influence operations if the site is chosen?
Labor	Does an adequate labor supply exist aroung the site?
Unionization	What degree of unionization exists in the site area?
Living conditions	Are housing, schools, etc., appropriate around the site?
Community relations	Is the community supportive of the organization moving into the area?

Figure 11.5
Major areas of consideration and sample exploratory questions in selecting a plant site.

2. Assigning each variable a weight, or rank, of relative importance.
3. Ranking alternate sites according to how they reflect the different variables.

The ***layout pattern*** is the overall arrangement of machines, equipment, materials handling, aisles, service areas, storage areas, and work stations in a production facility.

Mass production is producing goods in large quantities.

Process layout is the layout pattern based primarily on the grouping together of similar types of equipment or materials.

Product layout is the layout pattern based primarily on the progressive steps required to make a particular product.

The ***assembly line*** is a type of product layout in which the product is moved past several different work groups, each of which performs one specific step in the progression.

Table 11.1 shows the results of such a weighting process for several site variables and countries. A number of points were given for each variable, depending on the importance of the variable and its existence in a country. With this set of weighted criteria, Japan, Mexico, and France proved to have more desirable sites than Chile, Jamaica, and Australia.[8]

Layout Patterns

Choosing an appropriate layout pattern can also be a major consideration in plant facilities planning. The **layout pattern** is the overall arrangement of machines, equipment, materials handling, aisles, service areas, storage areas, and work stations in a production facility. The primary objective of layout is to arrange these variables in a way that maximizes their total contribution to productivity. In modern industrial society, most layout patterns emphasize **mass production**—producing goods in large quantities.

There are three basic layout patterns: process, product, and fixed position. **Process layout** is the layout pattern based primarily on the grouping together of similar types of equipment or materials. A metal fabricating shop has a process layout. All the lathes are in one location, the drill presses in another, the welding equipment in another, and the finishing equipment in yet another. An organization that produces a service can also have a process layout. A department store provides the service of selling goods. Within the store, all goods of one kind are grouped together—clothing in one aisle, shoes in another, and gift items in another.

Product layout is the layout pattern based primarily on the progressive steps required to make a particular product. The **assembly line** is a type of product layout in which the product is moved past several different work groups, each of which performs one specific step in the progression. The automobile assembly

Table 11.1 Results of weighting seven site variables for six countries.

Criteria	Maximum Value Assigned	Sites* Japan	Chile	Jamaica	Australia	Mexico	France
Living conditions	100	70	40	45	50	60	60
Accessibility	75	55	35	20	60	70	70
Industrialization	60	40	50	55	35	35	30
Labor availability	35	30	10	10	30	35	35
Economics	35	15	15	15	15	25	25
Community capability and attitude	30	25	20	10	15	25	15
Effect on company reputation	35	25	20	10	15	25	15
Total	370	260	180	165	225	280	265

*Site names were arbitrarily added to this table to enhance clarity.

line and its conveyor belt are an example. Different workers assemble different parts of the car as it moves by conveyor belt on the assembly line. At the end of the line, a complete car has been assembled.

Fixed position layout is the layout pattern in which—because of the weight or bulk of the product being manufactured—workers, tools, and materials are brought in stages to a stationary product. Ships and airplanes are usually manufactured in a fixed position layout.

Fixed position layout is the layout pattern in which—because of the weight or bulk of the product being manufactured—workers, tools, and materials are brought in stages to a stationary product.

Figure 11.6 illustrates the three layout patterns. As this figure implies, appropriate plant layout reflects the process required to develop the goods or services

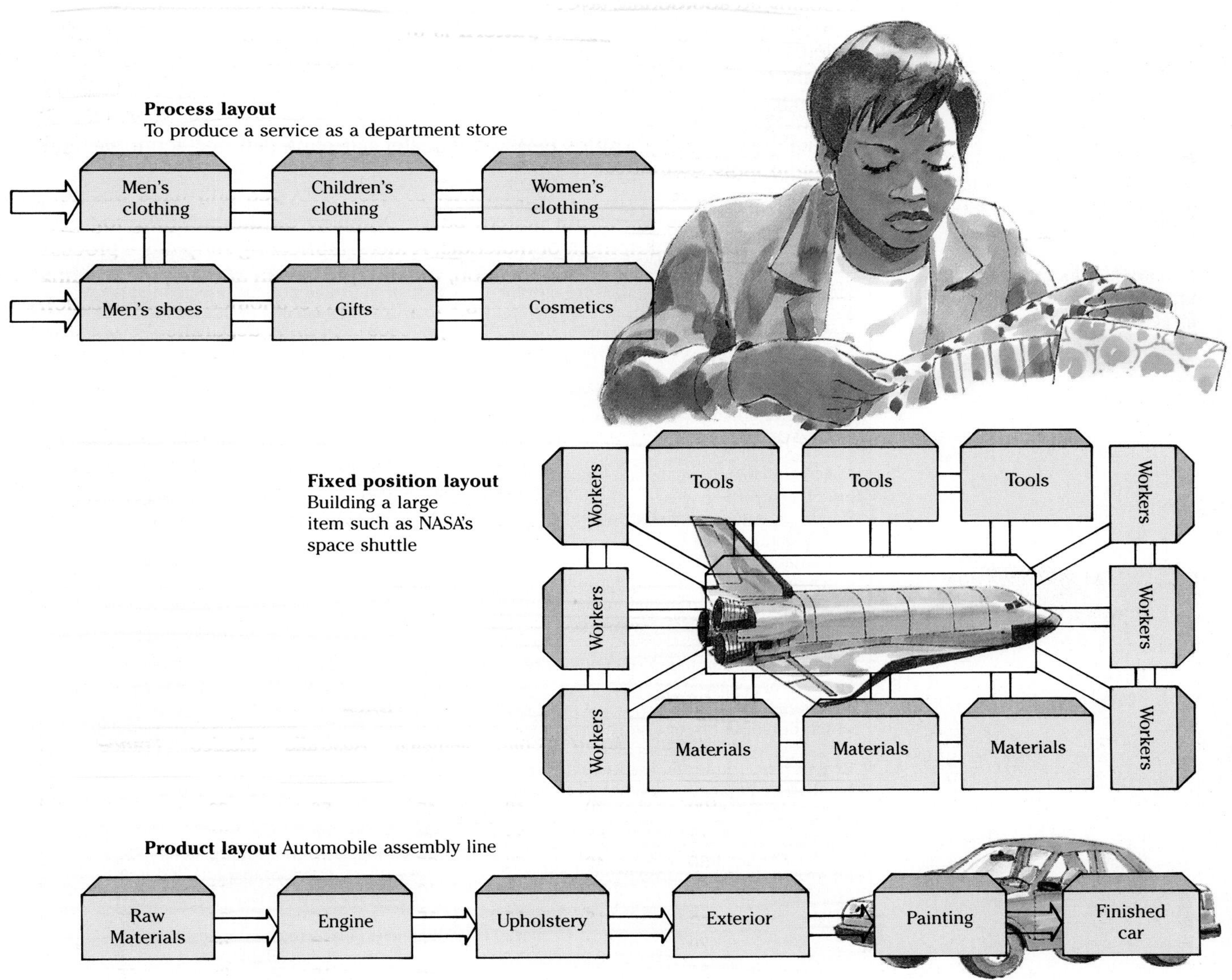

Figure 11.6 Three basic layout patterns. Clockwise from upper left, they are process layout, fixed position layout, and product layout.

the organization produces. In addition, an appropriate layout for any plant may be some combination of the three basic layout patterns.

Forecasting

Forecasting is the process of predicting future happenings that will likely influence the operation of the organization.

The process of predicting future happenings that will likely influence the operation of the organization is **forecasting.** This process is important because it helps the manager understand the future makeup of the organizational environment. On the basis of this understanding, the manager is able to formulate effective production plans and other types of plans. Of course, one danger in forecasting is that predictions of the future are based on the past. If conditions change, the forecast may be inaccurate.

In describing the Insect Control Services Company, William C. House has developed an excellent illustration of how forecasting works. Figure 11.7 lists the primary factors Insect Control Services attempts to measure in developing its forecasts. Generally, the company attempts to

1. Establish the relationships between industry sales and national economic and social indicators.

Figure 11.7
Primary factors measured during Insect Control Services' forecasting process.

Gross national product — Measure of total dollars available for industrial, commercial, institutional, and residential purchases of Insect Control units. Personal consumption expenditures — Measure of dollars available for consumer purchases of: Services — Affects potential contract of Insect Control Services. Durables — Affects market potential for residential units. Nondurables — Affects sales of food, drugs, and other products that influence expansion of industrial and commercial users of Insect Control equipment. Governmental purchases of goods, services — Measure of spending for hospitals, government food services, other institutions which purchase Insect Control equipment. Gross private domestic investment in new plant and equipment — A measure of business expansion which will indicate the size and nature of market potential for industrial and commercial purchases of Insect Control units in new or expanded existing establishments.	Industrial production for selected industries — Measure of expansion of industrial output for industries which are users, potential users of Insect Control units, or materials suppliers for Insect Control Services. Such expansion (or contraction) of output will likely affect: Industrial and commercial purchases of Insect Control units. Availability of materials used to manufacture Insect Control units. Employment and unemployment levels — Indicates availability or scarcity of manpower available to augment Insect Control Services manpower pool. Consumer, wholesale prices — Measure of ability, willingness of homeowners to purchase residential units and of the availability and cost of raw materials and component parts. Corporate profits — Indicates how trends in prices, unit labor costs, and productivity affect corporate profits. Size of total corporate profits indicates profit margins in present and potential markets and funds available for expansion. Business borrowings, interest rates — Measures of the availability and cost of borrowed funds needed to finance working capital needs and plant and equipment expansion.

2. Determine the impact of government restrictions concerning the use of chemical pesticides on the growth of chemical, biological, and electromagnetic energy pest control markets.
3. Evaluate sales growth potential, profitability, resources required, and risks involved in each market area (e.g., commercial, industrial, institutional, government, and residential).
4. Evaluate the potential for expansion of marketing efforts in certain geographical areas of the United States as well as in foreign countries.
5. Determine the likelihood of technological breakthroughs that would render existing product lines obsolete.

OPERATIONS MANAGEMENT

The first section of this chapter focused on production. The rest of the chapter will deal with **operations management,** the process of managing production. More specifically, operations management is the performance of the managerial activities entailed in selecting, designing, operating, controlling, and updating production systems.[9] These activities are basic to both manufacturing and service operations.

Operations management is the process of managing production, or, more specifically, the performance of the managerial activities entailed in selecting, designing, operating, controlling, and updating production systems.

Figure 11.8 categorizes the activities as being either periodic or continual, on the basis of how often they occur. For example, selecting and designing products

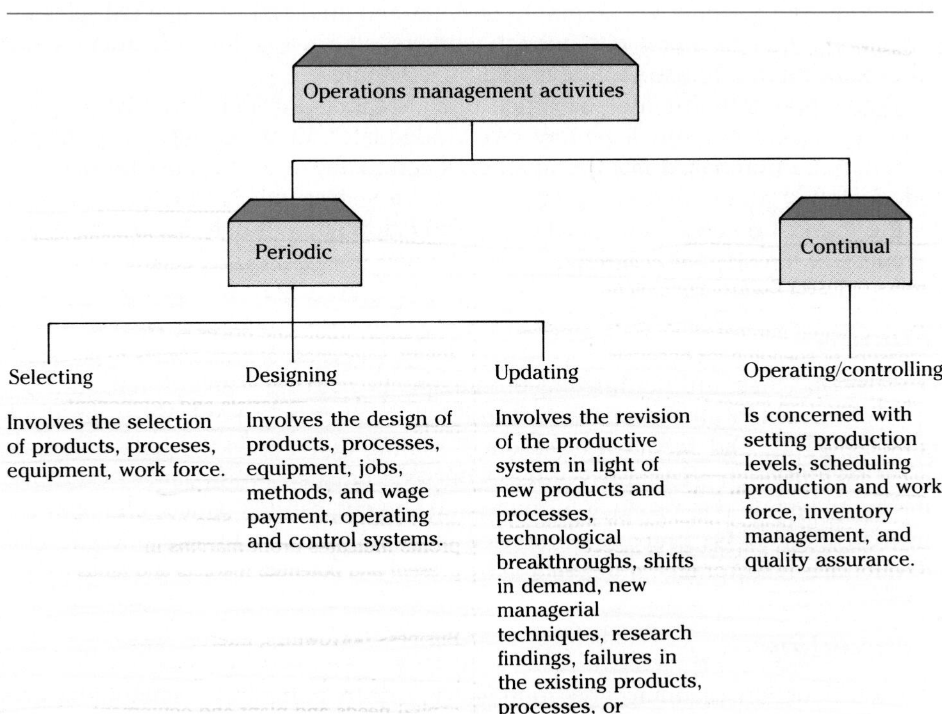
Operations management activities
Periodic
Continual
Selecting
Involves the selection of products, proceses, equipment, work force.
Designing
Involves the design of products, processes, equipment, jobs, methods, and wage payment, operating and control systems.
Updating
Involves the revision of the productive system in light of new products and processes, technological breakthroughs, shifts in demand, new managerial techniques, research findings, failures in the existing products, processes, or operating and control systems.
Operating/controlling
Is concerned with setting production levels, scheduling production and work force, inventory management, and quality assurance.

Figure 11.8
Major activities in managing production. Operations management involves five managerial activities—three on a periodic basis and two on a continual basis.

and updating production systems occur from time to time and are therefore categorized as periodic. Inventory management, however, never stops and is therefore categorized as continual.

What exactly is involved in operations management? The rest of this chapter will focus on this question by explaining how production is coordinated and controlled.

Coordinating Production

Production coordination is the performance of a series of four sequential steps needed to produce goods or services. The steps are production planning, routing, scheduling, and dispatching. An important technique is also involved in the coordination: materials requirements planning. (This topic will be discussed after the steps.)

Production Planning

Production planning is determining the types and amounts of resources needed to produce specified goods and services.

Purchasing is obtaining the raw materials needed to produce the product.

The first step in coordinating production is **production planning**—determining the types and amounts of resources needed to produce specified goods and services. The resources include people, money, materials, and equipment. One of the most important aspects of production planning is **purchasing**—obtaining the raw materials needed to produce the product. The purchasing department must locate a reliable supply of the materials, negotiate to buy them at a good price, and arrange to have them available when they are needed. Table 11.2 explains in detail the goals of the purchasing function. In a construction company, the production planner would aim to have the required amount of wood, plaster, bricks, and fittings, along with enough workers, all arrive at the construction site in time to build a house profitably and on schedule.

Production planning includes such other areas as the following: How much must be produced? Are inventory levels adequate? Must supplies or parts for products be purchased from a supplier? Each of these areas must be handled adequately if production coordination is to be successful. Production planning is the foundation step in production coordination since it determines the effectiveness of the steps that follow.

Routing

Routing is determining the sequence in which all the phases of production must be completed to produce specific goods and services.

The second step in coordinating production is **routing**—determining the sequence in which all the phases of production must be completed to produce specific goods and services. In essence, routing determines the path materials must take through a facility in order to become finished products. For example, the wood acquired to produce furniture must be cut, sanded, glued, and painted, in that order. A tax preparation service must tally the customers' income and deductions before making tax estimates.

Scheduling

Scheduling is listing in detail each activity that must be followed to produce goods or services and calculating how long each activity will take.

After production planning and routing have been completed, scheduling can begin. **Scheduling** is listing in detail each activity that must be followed to produce goods or services and calculating how long each activity will take. This section will examine two scheduling techniques: Gantt charts and network analysis.

Table 11.2 Purchasing-related goals. Through effective purchasing, an organization obtains the raw materials it needs.

1. To locate, evaluate, and develop sources of the materials, supplies, and services that the company needs.
2. To ensure good working relations with these sources in such matters as quality, delivery, payments, and exchanges or returns.
3. To seek out new materials and products and new sources of better products and materials so that they can be evaluated for possible use by the company.
4. To purchase wisely the items that the company needs at the best price consistent with quality requirements, and to handle the necessary negotiations to carry out this activity. The best value does not always represent the lowest initial cost, so products should also be evaluated for their expected lifetime, serviceability, and maintenance cost.
5. To initiate if necessary and to cooperate in cost-reduction programs, market analyses, and long-range planning. Purchasing should keep abreast of trends and projections in prices and availability of the inputs that a company must have.
6. To work to maintain an effective communication linkage between departments within the company and between the company and its suppliers or potential suppliers.
7. To keep top management aware of costs involved in the company's procurements and any market changes that could affect the company's profits or growth potential.

Gantt Charts One graphic scheduling device, a **Gantt chart,** uses a bar chart format to represent the time dimension on the horizontal axis and the resource to be scheduled on the vertical axis. Figure 11.9 is an example. The Gantt chart is named for the man who developed it, Henry L. Gantt. Possible resources to be scheduled include both human resources and machines.

A ***Gantt chart*** is a graphic scheduling device that uses a bar chart format to represent the time dimension on the horizontal axis and the resource to be scheduled on the vertical axis.

The completed Gantt chart in Figure 11.9 is for the period workweek 28. The resources scheduled over the five days on this chart are human resources: Wendy Reese and Peter Thomas. During workweek 28, both Reese and Thomas were scheduled to produce ten units a day for five days. Actual units produced, however, show a deviation from planned production. There were days when each worker produced more than ten units and days when each produced less than ten units. Cumulative production on the chart shows that Reese produced a total of forty units and Thomas a total of forty-five over the five days.

Network Analysis A second graphic scheduling technique is the **program evaluation and review technique (PERT).** This technique displays a network of separate project activities, showing the relationships among the activities and a time estimate for each activity. PERT was developed in 1958 for use in designing the Polaris submarine weapon system. The individuals involved in managing the Polaris project believed that Gantt charts and other existing scheduling tools were

The ***program evaluation and review technique (PERT)*** is a graphic scheduling technique that displays a network of separate project activities, showing the relationships among the activities and a time estimate for each activity.

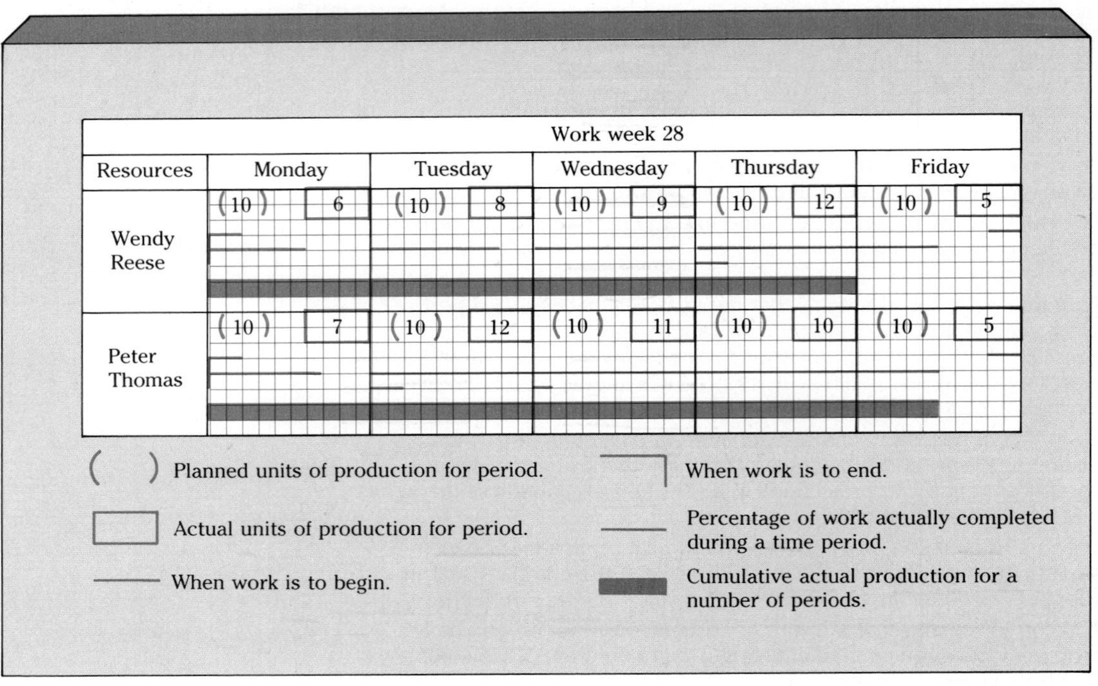

Figure 11.9 The Gantt chart, which schedules resources and time, is a planning tool for managers.

inadequate because of the complicated nature of the Polaris project and the interdependence of its tasks.

Figure 11.10 shows a sample PERT network designed for the building of a house. As the figure indicates, once the event "frame complete" (represented by a circle) has materialized, certain activities, such as completing the electrical work (represented by an arrow), can be performed. It is easy to see that PERT takes into account relationships that the Gantt chart does not.

Two other features of the network in Figure 11.10 must be emphasized. First, events are presented from left to right, showing how they interrelate or the sequence in which they should be performed. Second, the number in parentheses above each arrow indicates the units of time needed to complete each activity. These two features help the manager ensure that only necessary work is being done on a project and that no project activity is taking too long.

The ***critical path*** is the sequence of events and activities in a PERT network that requires the longest period of time to complete.

In using a PERT network, close attention should be given to the **critical path**—the sequence of events and activities in a PERT network that requires the longest period of time to complete. This path is "critical" because a delay in the time necessary to reach key stages of this sequence would result in a delay in the completion of the entire project. It also provides a way to focus attention on unnecessary delays or slack times at key points in the process. The critical path in Figure 11.10 is indicated by the thick arrow, while all other paths are indicated by thinner arrows. The manager tries to control a project by completing each step within the time frame designated by the critical path.

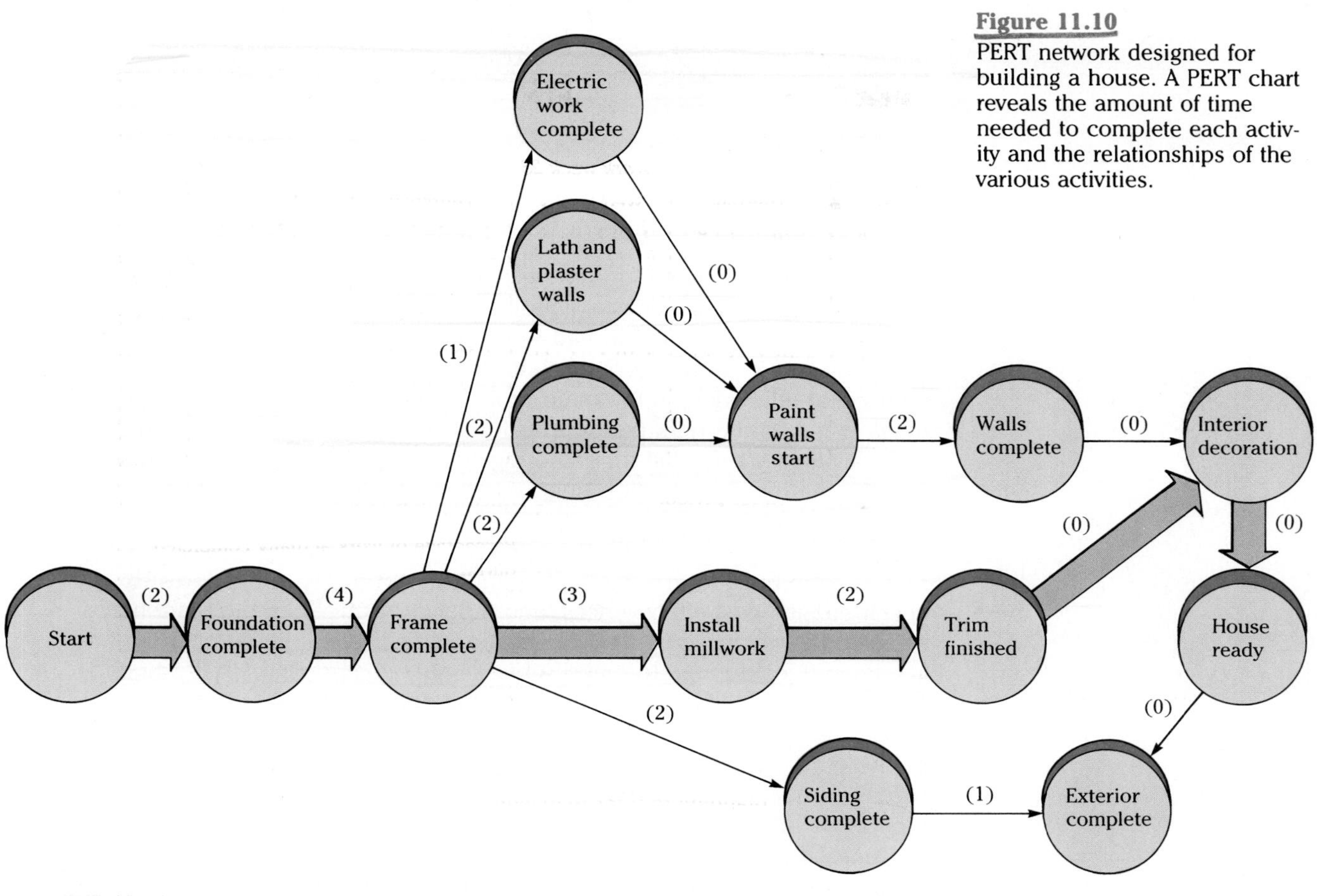

Figure 11.10
PERT network designed for building a house. A PERT chart reveals the amount of time needed to complete each activity and the relationships of the various activities.

Dispatching

Issuing detailed work orders based on the planning, scheduling, and routing needed for a coordinated production project is **dispatching.** This activity takes the results of production planning, routing, and scheduling and puts them into operation in the organization. A dispatch order might specify, for example, that the plumbers show up on the site on a certain day and complete their work within a certain period.

Dispatching is issuing detailed work orders based on the planning, scheduling, and routing needed for a coordinated production project.

Materials Requirements Planning

An important technique to help managers coordinate production is **materials requirements planning (MRP)**—a computer-based production coordination system that ensures that needed parts and materials are available for the production process at the right time and the right place.

Materials requirements planning (MRP) is a computer-based production coordination system that ensures that needed parts and materials are available for the production process at the right time and the right place.

BUSINESS PRACTICE EXAMPLE Continues

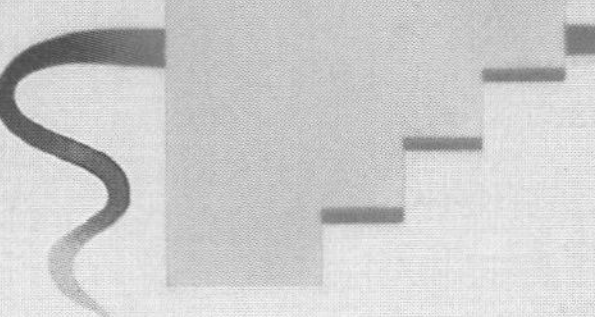

A new production layout for Maytag's Jenn-Air stove plant in Indianapolis required careful management planning, and teamwork from many areas of expertise. The layout plan had to locate sub-assembly processes, such as the making of oven doors or control panels, to be sure of optimum timing and efficiency on the main production line. This in turn required plans to get all the right building materials to the right place at the right time. A plan was needed for gathering steel, rubber, and other raw materials for the main production line as well as for the sub-assembly processes.

Some components, such as electronics for oven controls, might be bought from outside manufacturers, and these required procedures to check quality, cost-effectiveness, and timely arrival. When the plant had invested heavily in equipment, a decision was needed: Should Maytag adjust its own equipment to make sub-assembly components? According to President Hadley, "the demand for Maytag quality often required us to bring many jobs in-house to meet our standards." But the decision could go the other way. The company responded positively when a supplier of wire for a heating element suggested, "Why don't we make the element for you? It will cost you no more than the wire itself."

Until the late 1980s Maytag avoided dealing directly with foreign suppliers. As one production manager put it, "The last part quoted from an offshore source cost more than the same product bought here." But more recently compressor units were imported from Japan and Italy, and the company began to consider acquiring its own overseas parts manufacturers.

Figure 11.11 is a diagram of the major dimensions of an MRP system. Within this system, data from three main sources serve as input for the MRP computer: (1) orders from consumers, (2) engineering specifications of the products being manufactured, and (3) an inventory of raw materials and parts on hand. The computer gathers all three sets of data, considers them collectively, and generates a report about them. The MRP system may report on which raw materials and parts should be ordered, when they should be ordered, and which should be canceled, expedited, or put through different channels.

Production processes in some organizations are so complex that MRP has become invaluable. Consider the production of a farm tractor. This product requires hundreds of different parts, each of which must be in the right place at the right time if production is to work efficiently. Further complicating the situation is the fact that some portions of the tractor may be assembled at sites far from

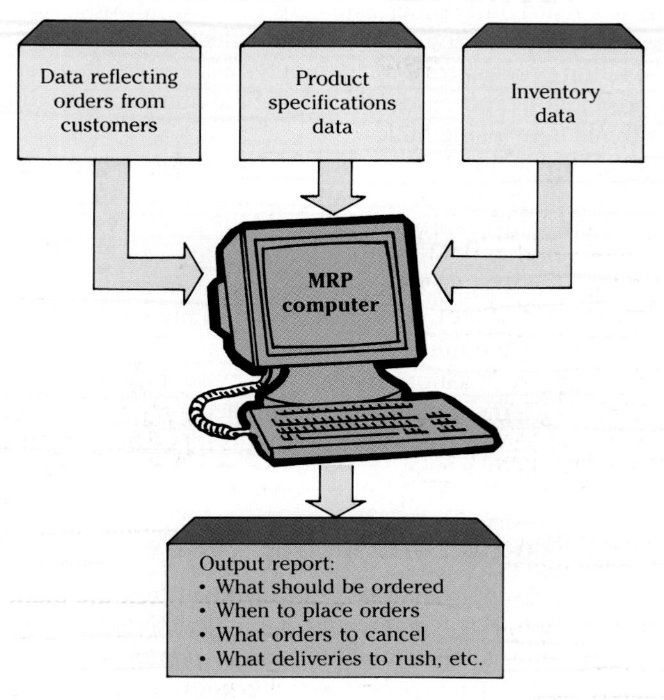

Figure 11.11
Major dimensions of an MRP system.

A materials requirements planning (MRP) system is a computerized production coordination system that ensures that these parts and materials are available when needed for the production process. Shown here is an industrial warehouse, in which parts and materials are stored.

the main plant. For example, at Massey-Ferguson, a manufacturer of farm tractors, transmissions are made in France, axles are made in Mexico, and sheet metal parts are made in Detroit. The efficient and effective coordination of such a complex production process requires computer assistance. In general, the more complex the production process and the greater the number of products, the more the company benefits by using MRP.

Downtime is the time when employees cannot work because the materials, parts, or equipment they need to perform their jobs are not available.

One benefit of MRP is the minimization of **downtime**—time when employees cannot work because the materials, parts, or equipment they need to perform their jobs are not available. A primary focus of MRP is to have parts and materials available for production at the time they are needed.

Another benefit of MRP is its ability to help management track which suppliers are reliable in their deliveries and which are not. Choosing suppliers who keep delivery promises helps minimize downtime.

MRP also can help organizations manage their cash flow. A well-designed MRP system can give management up-to-the-second accuracy regarding costs of purchases from various suppliers, possible discounts for paying bills early, and final dates at which payments are due.

Controlling Production in the 1990s

As chapter 6 indicated, controlling is a management function closely related to planning. Through control, a manager makes sure that things happen as planned. In operations management, the techniques for *coordinating* production are useful in implementing plans, checking on their execution, and controlling how production occurs.

However, in the 1990s, the *control function* will be one of the most critical areas of concern for American production. During much of the 1980s, U.S. markets have been inundated with high-quality and low-cost competing products from abroad. To meet this competition and rebuild a reputation for quality and cost-effectiveness, American production managers must learn to implement the latest techniques in two key control areas: quality control and inventory control.

Quality Control

Quality control is the process of making the quality of finished goods and services what it was planned to be.

The process of making the quality of finished goods and services what it was planned to be is **quality control.**[10] Managers compare the quality of goods or services being produced to organizational quality standards and take steps to increase, decrease, or maintain the level of product quality as dictated by the situation. The standards are controlled through a program of product inspection. Such a program may be limited to finished products or be extended to such areas as materials purchased for inventory, materials available from various suppliers, and progress at different stages of product assembly.

Statistical quality control is a quantitative tool for determining the acceptable number of units to inspect in order to maintain the quality of the entire batch of products being produced.

Regarding product inspection, managers must determine not only what products or components to inspect but also how many units to inspect. Although managers may limit inspection expenses by not examining all units, they must ensure that the number of units inspected gives an accurate measure of the quality of all the products being produced. **Statistical quality control** is a quantitative tool for determining the acceptable number of units to inspect in order to maintain the quality of the entire batch of products being produced.

In addition to inspecting products, managers have begun to involve employees in quality control by soliciting their ideas on how to improve quality in the pro-

HIGHLIGHT IN BUSINESS PRACTICE

Manufacturing Innovations at Harley-Davidson

The legendary "Harley" motorcycle wings have become more frequent fliers on America's highways. A new Harley-Davidson plant at York, Pennsylvania, is one of the reasons. The plant assembles two engine types in three displacement sizes; these propel 20 street bike models, available in 13 colors and two wheel options. This adds up to 95 total combinations. Such an array of motorcycles requires no fewer than 20,000 different pieces to be assembled on one production line. The old Harley manufacturing system could barely handle the job. When Harley's demand for the motorcycles increased from 23,000 to 52,000 units annually, it was time for sweeping manufacturing changes. Harley-Davidson adopted innovations and introduced some advanced manufacturing techniques to keep pace.

One of Harley's new manufacturing techniques uses the "quality circle" philosophy, which transfers much of the responsibility for quality control and production to the individual worker. Traditionally, inspectors examine the parts after certain steps in the production process as the part moves along the line or at the end of the process. At Harley, a "work cell"—a small team of workers—takes a part from the raw material to the finished state without it ever moving outside the cell. This insures a consistent quality with little variation because one team is responsible for the whole process. For instance, to make a frame gusset, the sheet metal arrives at the cell, is cut, shaped, stamped, and welded to a subassembly by only one worker. Each subassembly is then loaded onto a specially made container to protect and store the part until it is to be taken to the next work cell. Every production employee has the responsibility to track the quality of the product and monitor the production on the line. Any worker who spots a problem has the authority to stop the line until the problem has been corrected.

Another innovation Harley has adopted is the "just-in-time" concept, which allows inventory costs to be kept at a minimum. Before the innovations, the set-up times for the machinery to make each part was very long. Harley has been able to cut the set-up times by using standardized dies stored near the work cell. A machine operator simply rolls out the next die to be used and places it in the proper machine for the operation. The reduced set-up times allow smaller batches to run more frequently, thus keeping inventory stock costs down. Specially made parts containers also play a role in inventory reduction. They travel only between the work cell where the parts are made and the cell where the parts are to be used. After the inventory pieces have been removed at the assembly work cell, the container is returned to the originating cell as a message to build more parts. The containers serve as a signal at each end either to "feed me" or "empty me."

The new manufacturing philosophies in quality control, process control, and just in time have added up to big cost savings—enough to give Harley-Davidson the competitive edge.

Quality circles are small groups of workers who volunteer to meet regularly to discuss and help solve quality-related problems.

duction process. This idea was developed from a control system originating in Japan, called quality circles. **Quality circles** are simply small groups of workers who volunteer to meet regularly to discuss and help solve quality-related problems. Solutions to the problems are communicated directly to management at a formal presentation session, at which management analyzes and accepts, rejects, or modifies the group-developed solution. Figure 11.12 shows the roles of management and quality circle members.

Most quality circles are similar in the way they operate. Each circle is usually under twenty members in size, and leaders of the circles are not necessarily the members' supervisors. Members are generally from a common work site or task area, and their focus is operational problems rather than interpersonal ones. Although the problems are sometimes assigned by management, they can also be uncovered by the group itself. Generally, the members do not receive extra pay for participating in a quality circle on their own time.[11]

Quality control has become an important production issue. The failure of many U.S. firms to compete successfully with foreign firms has been blamed in part on the inferior quality of U.S. products. Ensuring high quality has thus become a major concern of U.S. businesses. As an example, Ford Motor Company has spent millions of dollars in recent years not only improving the quality of its vehicles but convincing consumers that quality has been improved. The slogan "At Ford, Quality is Job 1" has been heard over and over again by American consumers.

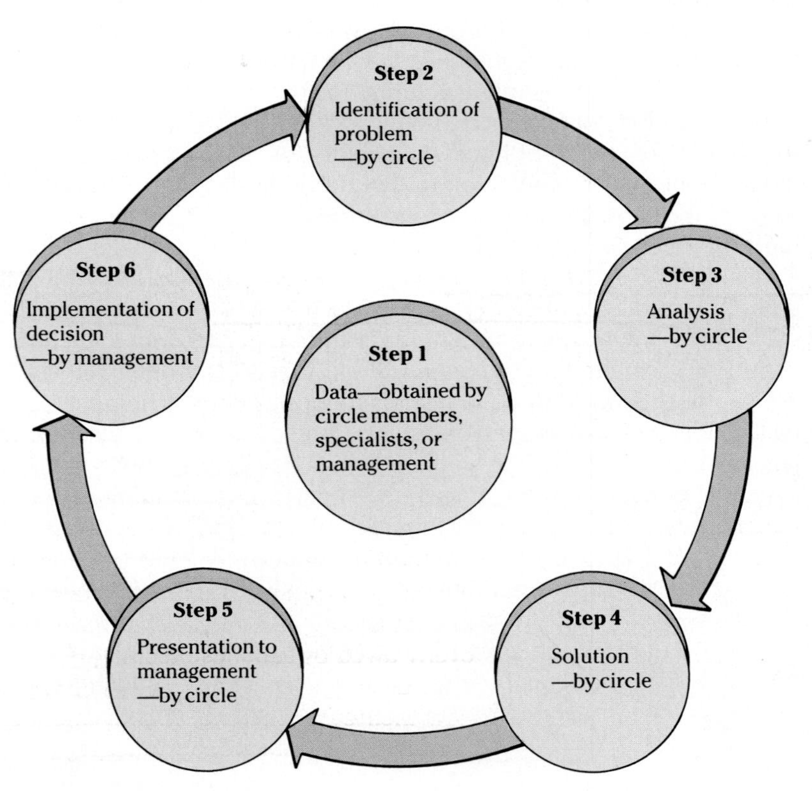

Figure 11.12
Quality circles and management have distinct roles in the quality circle problem-solving process.

Just-In-Time Inventory Control: Lessons from Japan

The technique that reduces inventories to a minimum by arranging for them to be delivered to the production facility just in time to be used in the manufacturing of a product is **just-in-time (JIT) inventory control.** To implement the JIT concept, a carefully coordinated system of control is required. *Kanban* (the name for a special dispatch order card) is the Japanese term for this complex system of implementation, which comes from Japan.[12] It requires every phase of the operation to coincide so the exact quantities of resources needed will be available at the precise moment they are to be used. All aspects of supply, transportation, and production processing must be coordinated with perfect timing through MRP systems and other techniques.

Just-in-time (JIT) inventory control is the technique that reduces inventories to a minimum by arranging for them to be delivered to the production facility just in time to be used in the manufacturing of a product.

A JIT system can be difficult to coordinate, and the critical details in operating it are different for each use and every industry. However, by minimizing the levels of raw-material and finished-goods inventories that are kept on hand, managers can gain huge benefits in cost-effectiveness.

Keeping inventory at the lowest level necessary to meet customer demand sharply reduces the amount of money invested in it. Thus inventory does not absorb unneeded cash, which can then be used for other purposes. Additionally, inventory-related costs, such as materials handling and storage, are normally reduced through JIT, resulting in less strain on cash reserves.

Many U.S. businesses are adopting JIT as a means of improving organizational performance.[13] General Motors, for example, has used JIT since 1980 and has slashed its annual inventory-related costs from $8 billion to $2 billion. One American Motors plant has cut its inventories to less than a day's supply, compared to the more usual six-day reserve. Some reports indicate that the use of JIT is spreading from the automotive industry to other industries, including the small-appliances industry. General Electric and RCA are two small-appliance firms seriously experimenting with JIT.[14] As JIT and other production control techniques become more widespread, American industry's cost efficiency and productivity will gradually become more competitive in the world markets of the 1990s.

BUSINESS PRACTICE EXAMPLE Continues

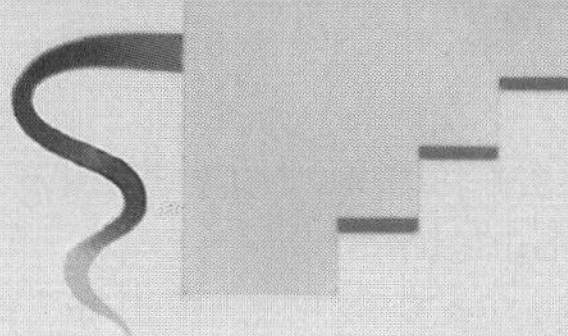

Production managers at Maytag show a clear awareness of the latest techniques in manufacturing from Japan, such as quality circles and just-in-time inventory and supply systems. Yet they have good reason not to be overly awed by Japanese techniques.

In describing how they operate, Maytag production managers stress how their own efficiency-improvement system, the work simplification program, has improved productivity for over forty years. Says Manufactur-

BUSINESS PRACTICE EXAMPLE Continues

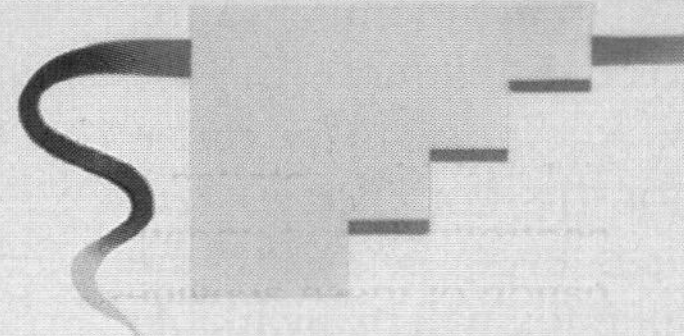

ing VP Robert Faust, "We promote a teamwork attitude, an environment that encourages a lot of contact between supervisors and workers. While we don't have quality circles here, we put strong emphasis on employee involvement."

Similarly, Maytag has a long-standing reputation with business analysts as conservative about keeping inventory to a minimum at all levels. The Maytag director of purchases, Dean Ward, is a careful man in checking out sources of supply for quality, cost, and convenience of access for short inventory orders. "In the past year," he said, "we've discovered some new vendors, some as close as 30 miles away," including a shipping crate manufacturer right in Newton, Iowa. This helps him make small-quantity but frequent orders, especially for bulky materials, from vendors in neighboring towns or in nearby Cedar Rapids; these materials arrive for "just-in-time" deliveries to production without a big inventory pile-up. On the other hand, he maintains a skeptical attitude: "Some vendors tell me that other users of components and materials are backing off of JIT. The cost of expediting shipments for JIT on the part of the user exceeds that of maintaining larger inventories."

In the area of quality control, Maytag managers feel they have lessons to teach others. Their procedures for sampling and testing, including extensive hard-wear and destructive testing, would be impressive anywhere in the world. Nevertheless, even Maytag will have to make some adjustments as it seeks to move into worldwide markets with lower-priced appliances. Maytag's record of maintaining quality top-of-the line goods will certainly help, if and when the company turns to a harder job—keeping good quality at even lower cost.

Issues for Discussion

1. What are the most important factors contributing to productivity in Maytag's manufacturing operations?
2. What seem to be the main reasons Maytag has not bought many materials from foreign suppliers?
3. In what ways could Maytag's record of manufacturing success put the company in danger of being unprepared for new competitive challenges?

SUMMARY

Production is the transformation of organizational resources into products. Through this transformation, resources gain form utility, their usefulness for some purpose after they are molded into a product. The four types of production processes used to achieve the transformation are analytic, synthetic, continuous, and intermittent.

Productivity is a measure of the relationship between the amount of goods and services being produced and the resources needed to produce them. The fewer resources needed in a particular production process, the more productive the process is said to be. Early emphasis on improving productivity focused on scientific management—finding the one best way to perform a task.

More recently, the focus has shifted to increasing productivity through the use of robots—machines that perform some of the mechanical functions of humans. The focus has also shifted to the use of computers in the production process. Value-added networks, computer-aided design, and computer-aided manufacturing are all examples of computers used to increase productivity.

The production facility—the place where goods and services are produced—is a critical part of production. Its site can influence such variables as profit and operating costs and can largely determine if a company can remain in business over the long term. In addition, the layout pattern of the production facility can be a major determinant of organizational success. Three major types of layout patterns are process layouts, product layouts, and fixed position layouts.

Operations management is the performance of managerial activities entailed in selecting, designing, operating, controlling, and updating production systems. The coordination of these activities is achieved through production planning, routing, scheduling, and dispatching. Production planning is determining the types and amounts of resources needed to produce specified goods or services. Routing is determining the sequence in which all phases of production must be completed. Scheduling is listing in detail each activity that must be followed in order to produce goods and services and calculating how long each activity will take. Gantt charts and network analysis are two practical scheduling tools available to managers. Dispatching is issuing work orders to the individuals involved in producing goods and services. Materials requirements planning is a computer-based technique managers can use to help coordinate complex production processes.

In addition to being coordinated, production processes must also be controlled. Controlling production is making sure that the process operates as planned. One part of production control is quality control, the process of making sure that the quality of finished goods or services is what it was planned to be. Statistical quality control and quality circles are two quality control tools available to managers.

Another part of production control is inventory control. Just-in-time (JIT) inventory control is a method for making sure that the amounts of materials kept in inventory for production do not get too high or too low.

KEY TERMS

Analytic production process p. 310
Assembly line p. 320
Automation p. 315
Computer-aided design (CAD) p. 317
Computer-aided manufacturing (CAM) p. 317
Continuous production process p. 310
Critical path p. 326
Dispatching p. 327
Downtime p. 330
Fixed position layout p. 321
Flexible manufacturing system p. 316
Forecasting p. 322
Form utility p. 310
Gantt chart p. 325
Intermittent production process p. 310
Just-in-time (JIT) inventory control p. 333
Layout pattern p. 320
Mass production p. 320
Materials requirements planning (MRP) p. 327
Operations management p. 323
Process layout p. 320
Production p. 310
Production facility p. 317
Production planning p. 324
Productivity p. 311
Product layout p. 320
Program evaluation and review technique (PERT) p. 325
Purchasing p. 324
Quality circles p. 332
Quality control p. 330
Robots p. 315
Routing p. 324
Scheduling p. 324
Scientific management p. 312
Site selection p. 319
Statistical quality control p. 330
Synthetic production process p. 310
Utility p. 310
Value-added network (VAN) p. 317

CHECK YOUR LEARNING

Reread the following learning objectives. Each objective is followed by a few questions. Answering these questions accurately will help you retain the most important concepts discussed in this chapter. After answering each question, check your answer with the key at the end of this chapter. (*Hint:* If you have doubt regarding the correct response, consult the page whose number follows the answer.)

Circle:

A. Define *production.*

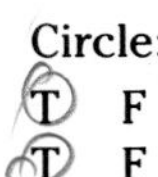

1. Production involves transformation. — T F
2. Products are aimed at human needs. — T F

B. Explain what is meant by productivity.

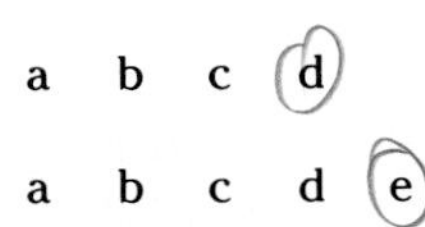

1. ________ is/are least closely associated with productivity: (a) Output; (b) Resources; (c) Input; (d) Standards. — a b c d
2. A recent trend in productivity improvement is: (a) the use of robots; (b) motion analysis; (c) scientific management; (d) the use of computers; (e) a and d. — a b c d e

C. Discuss site selection and layout patterns as related to the production facility.

1. Business climate studies can be a part of site selection. — T F
2. One of the basic types of layout pattern is: (a) process layout; (b) coordination layout; (c) specialization layout; (d) morale layout. — a b c d

D. Explain the relationship between forecasting and production.

1. Forecasting normally focuses mainly on consumers. — T F
2. Whether or not a plant should be expanded could depend largely on company forecasting. — T F

E. Describe how the process of coordinating production relates to operations management.

1. Which of the following is a continual operations management activity: (a) updating; (b) controlling; (c) selecting; (d) designing. — a b c d
2. Determining the sequence in which work must be completed in order to produce specified goods or services is called: (a) scheduling; (b) routing; (c) planning; (d) none of the above. — a b c d
3. Gantt charts show relationships between activities. — T F
4. MRP emphasizes buying the right materials but does not focus on when they should be delivered. — T F

F. Discuss quality control and JIT inventory control as components of production control.

1. JIT emphasizes having materials to be used in the production process delivered from suppliers as close as possible to the time when they are to be used in the production process. — T F
2. Quality control focuses primarily on setting the level of quality for products being manufactured. — T F
3. Quality circles generally involve: (a) small groups of volunteer workers; (b) solutions to problems being communicated by management to workers; (c) organizational problems being identified primarily by management; (d) data on organizational problems gathered by management and analyzed by volunteer workers. — a b c d

QUESTIONS FOR REVIEW AND DISCUSSION

1. Define the key terms listed at the end of the chapter.
2. Describe a production process with which you are personally familiar.
3. From a site selection viewpoint, discuss the advantages and disadvantages of the location of the school in which you are taking this course.
4. Would you forecast that the sale of video games will increase or decrease over the next five years? What factors most influenced your forecast?
5. How should production in a restaurant be coordinated? Explain. (Refer to production planning, routing, scheduling, dispatching, and MRP.)
6. Decide on a task that would be better scheduled by PERT than by a Gantt chart. Explain why you chose this task.
7. In what type of production situation would you advise management to use quality circles? Explain.
8. What problems might a manager face in using JIT inventory control? How can they be avoided or solved?

CONCLUDING CASE

Phoebe Putney Hospital Uses Computer to Improve Health Care Services

Hospitals that are using new software systems to evaluate their services are discovering that they can identify—and in some cases change—costly, inadequate or inappropriate medical practices.

"Although they won't admit it, doctors and hospitals already have an idea who is good and bad," says Dr. Sidney Wolfe, head of Health Research Group in Washington. "The new data will force them to do something about it because everyone is going to know what they know."

Officials at Phoebe Putney Memorial Hospital in Albany, Ga., are using MedisGroups—a data system developed by Medi-Qual Systems Inc. in Westborough, Mass.—to identify doctors who cost the hospital money by keeping patients longer than necessary or because their patients don't get well quickly. The system works by quantifying the severity of a patient's illness at admission and then tracking the illness throughout the hospital stay.

A recent computer search found, for example, that the hospital's pediatric ward was overcrowded. The reason: Three of the 13 pediatricians on staff were filling beds with children whose degree of illness, as defined by the computer, didn't require hospitalization, says Woody Sanders, a pediatrician and head of the hospital's quality assurance committee.

The three doctors were notified of the findings and soon afterward, beds opened up, allowing other, sicker children to be admitted, Dr. Sanders says. "Just knowing they were being watched encouraged them to practice differently," he says.

Another computer search found that premature infants were staying in the hospital's intensive-care unit for 20 days to 30 days on average, running up about $30,000 in bills. That worried hospital administrators because many of the parents were covered by Medicaid, the state health plan for the poor. The plan pays the hospital only $1,800 for each case—no matter how long an infant is hospitalized.

The hospital has since set up a program providing outside support services and education for parents to get the babies home sooner.

Such economic considerations are driving the new computer programs because "inappropriate care is more costly," says Greg Binns, an official at Lexecon Health Service Inc. in Chicago.

Many doctors, however, chafe at being held up to a computerized standard or scrutinized in great detail. At Phoebe Putney Hospital, the computer recently kicked out data that showed that a young surgeon's patients had extended stays in the hospital. When confronted by a peer committee, "he wasn't pleased," says Dr. Sanders. However, he adds, "most of us view this as a necessary evil" since the government and private insurers will soon have access to the same data.

Indeed, officials at Blue Cross-Blue Shield of Minnesota are already using MedisGroups to determine if hospitals ought to receive higher or lower insurance payments by measuring the severity of a patient's illness.

Susan Horn, a professor of health finance at Johns Hopkins University in Baltimore, says the data systems are so powerful that almost any deviation from norms will be identified. In a study at one hospital using a program she helped develop, researchers found that 41% of one physician's patients became sicker in the hospital vs. 23% for other doctors. Moreover, 10% of the one physician's patients died vs. 4% among his colleagues.

The physician was shown the data and "began to change his practice patterns after he was made aware of how differently he practiced from his colleagues," Mrs. Horn's study says. A study six months later found a sharp reduction in the proportion of the doctor's patients who died in the hospital.

Issues for Discussion

1. Explain how the activities at Phoebe Putney Hospital can be described as quality control activities.
2. Could quality circles be used by management in this situation to supplement the computer tracking? Explain.
3. List three other factors that you think the hospital should be monitoring as part of quality control. Why should each factor be monitored?

NOTES

1. Frederick W. Taylor, *The Principles of Scientific Management* (New York: Harper & Row, 1947), pp. 66–71.
2. Barry Render and Jay Heizer, *Production and Operations Management: Strategies and Tactics* (Boston: Allyn & Bacon, 1988), chaps. 6, 7.
3. Gene Bylinsky, "Invasion of the Service Robots," *Fortune,* September 14, 1987, pp. 81–88.
4. Michael Rogers, "Robots Find Their Place," *Newsweek,* March 28, 1988, pp. 58–59.
5. Joann S. Lublin, "As Robot Age Arrives, Labor Seeks Protection against Work Loss," *Wall Street Journal,* October 26, 1981.
6. Joel Dreyfuss, "Networking: Japan's Latest Computer Craze," *Fortune,* July 7, 1986, pp. 94–96.
7. "Software Slices Much Tooling from Design to Part," *Industry Week,* February 1, 1988, p. 58.
8. E. S. Groo, "Choosing Foreign Locations: One Company's Experience," *Columbia Journal of World Business,* September–October 1971, p. 77.
9. Richard B. Chase and Nicholas J. Aquilano, *Production and Operations Management,* 4th ed. (Homewood, Ill.: Richard D. Irwin, 1985), p. 5.
10. Samuel C. Certo, *Principles of Modern Management: Functions and Systems,* 4th ed. (Boston: Allyn & Bacon, 1989), p. 481.
11. John B. Miner, *Organizational Behavior: Performance and Productivity* (New York: Random House, 1988), pp. 308–316.
12. Lee J. Krajewski and Larry P. Ritzman, *Operations Management: Strategy and Analysis* (Reading, Mass.: Addison-Wesley, 1987), p. 573.
13. Jack R. Meredith, *The Management of Operations* (New York: Wiley, 1987), pp. 391–392.
14. Sumer C. Aggarwal, "MRP, JIT, OPT, FMS?" *Harvard Business Review,* September–October 1985, pp. 6–16.

CHECK YOUR LEARNING ANSWER KEY

A. 1. T, *p. 310*
   2. T, *p. 310*

B. 1. d, *p. 311*
   2. e, *p. 315*

C. 1. T, *p. 319-320*
   2. a, *p. 320*

D. 1. F, *p. 322*
   2. T, *p. 323*

E. 1. b, *p. 323*
   2. b, *p. 324*
   3. F, *p. 325*
   4. F, *p. 327*

F. 1. T, *p. 333*
   2. F, *p. 330*
   3. a, *p. 332*

PART

MARKETING FOR TODAY'S CONSUMER

CHAPTER 12

The Marketing Concept

CHAPTER 13

Developing and Pricing Products to Sell

CHAPTER

Distributing Goods and Services

CHAPTER 15

Promoting Goods and Services

CHAPTER

12

THE MARKETING CONCEPT

LEARNING OBJECTIVES

After reading this chapter you should be able to:

1. Explain the importance of the marketing concept and how marketing benefits our daily lives.
2. Discuss how time, place, and ownership utility are created by the marketing process.
3. List and describe each of the eight functions of marketing.
4. Explain how the marketing mix is used to develop a marketing strategy.
5. Explain how potential markets are selected by the use of market segmentation.
6. Discuss the four methods used to collect primary data.

OUTLINE

BUSINESS PRACTICE EXAMPLE

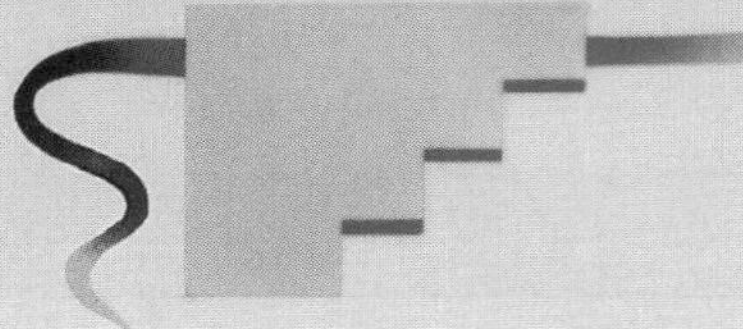

The Timberland Company—Marketing Made It Work

If rugged fashion and a preference for quality is high on your list, you've probably heard of the Timberland Company. Timberland is a popular maker of boots and handsewn boat shoes, casual shoes and dress shoes, and a limited selection of apparel and accessories. The New Hampshire-based company, which sells its products around the globe—in one recent year its boots were the biggest hit in Milan, Italy, the shoe-capital of the world—posted sales of more than $133 million in 1988. Timberland products are decidedly "upscale," with prices to match. Yet only 15 years earlier, the business run by the Swartz family since 1955 (then called Abington Shoes) was facing tiny profits and an ominous future.

Once one of the trades driving the U.S. industrial revolution, the shoe industry had faced increasingly adverse conditions since the early 1960s. Low-priced shoes imported from overseas had taken over the marketplace, forcing about two-thirds of American shoe factories to close by 1970. By the late 1980s, more than 80 percent of all shoes sold in the U.S. were made abroad. Most American shoe manufacturers struggled vainly to match foreign manufacturers' prices while trying to provide customers with up-to-date styles.

Abington Shoes sold inexpensive shoes and boots to discount retailers and army-navy stores. Like other shoe companies, Abington made its shoes the old fashioned way—it hand-stitched them. But good stitchers were becoming hard to find, and they were demanding higher wages. Ultimately, shoe manufacturers turned to injection molding, a process that chemically bonded soles and uppers. While injection molding lowered prices by eliminating the need to pay the stitchers, it also lowered the quality of the shoes.

But not entirely. Herman and Sidney Swartz discovered one important way in which injection molding was actually an improvement over hand-stitching: Abington's boots were now more waterproof than before. The Swartzes decided it was time to split off from the pack, stop chasing lower costs and lower profits, and start looking at the shoe and boot market from a new angle. They designed a top-quality, insulated, waterproof leather boot, taking full advantage of injection molding technology. They began using more expensive grades of leather and a new, extremely durable synthetic sole developed by Goodyear Tire. In 1973, the Swartzes formed an Abington subsidiary to manufacture the boot and called it, at a neighbor's suggestion, Timberland.

In less than ten years, Abington, a near-failing private-label company selling its shoes in army-navy stores, had become Timberland, a company selling tens of millions of dollars worth of boots and shoes in stores like

Bloomingdale's and Saks. The Swartzes had turned a rustic, partially rubberized boot into a highly desirable fashion item, something that had not been done before. What made that unique transformation possible can be attributed largely to one factor: marketing.

WHAT'S AHEAD

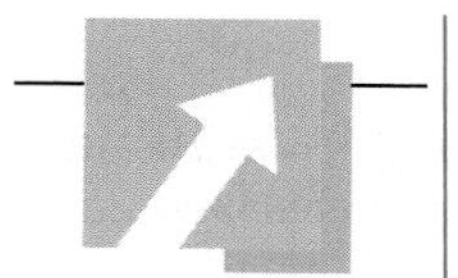

Marketing is a central part of all business activity, as the owners of The Timberland Company know. In this chapter, we explain the evolution of marketing, discuss the marketing concept, and describe the development of marketing strategies (especially with regard to the 4Ps of the marketing mix). We will also discuss market segmentation, analyze the elements of marketing research, and explain the marketing plan—all marketing activities at which The Timberland Company excels.

MARKETING DEFINED

Marketing is a central aspect of contemporary business practices. The American Marketing Association defines **marketing** as "the process of planning and executing the conception, pricing, promotion, and distribution of ideas, goods, and services to create exchanges that satisfy individual and organizational objectives."[1] Today, marketing has emerged as one of the most competitive organizational weapons. According to a study by Coopers and Lybrand and Yankelovich, Skelly, and White, more than half the polled executives at 250 corporations ranked marketing as the most important strategy for the 1980s and beyond.[2]

Marketing is the process of planning and executing the conception, pricing, promotion, and distribution of ideas, goods, and services to create exchanges that satisfy individual and organizational objectives.

HOW MARKETING EVOLVED

A **market** is a group of potential buyers for a good or service. Marketing in the United States has evolved through three eras: the production era, the sales era, and the marketing era.

A ***market*** is a group of potential buyers for a good or service.

Production Era Until the early part of this century, most companies were production oriented. Producers were concerned more with producing enough goods than with tailoring them to consumer preferences. Demand was high relative to supply for all types of quality products. Thus a wide variety of consumer goods were sold with relative ease. In such a seller's market, companies could afford to concentrate on production concerns.

Sales Era By the 1920s and 1930s, increased production capacity meant that in many industries production caught up with, or surpassed, demand. The result was a buyer's market. Because customers now had to be actively sought, companies adopted a sales orientation. For instance, during the Great Depression of the 1930s, when demand fell sharply, companies added sales forces to their payroll and increased advertising budgets. Two popular forms of promotion were company-produced and -sponsored radio shows and the traveling salesmen who crisscrossed America seeking new customers.

Marketing Era The beginning of the marketing era can be traced to 1952, when General Electric established as its managerial philosophy the idea that consumers' wants should be considered at each stage of the production cycle. Instead of designing a product and then seeking customers for it, the customers' preferences were sought and then built into the design.

THE MARKETING CONCEPT

The ***marketing concept*** is the concept that the decision-making process in production should begin with the customer.

The concept that the decision-making process in production should begin with the customer is the **marketing concept.** Modern businesspeople believe that profits can be maximized through the creation of products for which there is known demand. Thus companies today are constantly looking for creative ideas that will meet specific consumer needs and wants. For example, in the late 1970s and into the 1980s, consumers were paying escalating prices for the gas, oil, and coal used to heat their homes. They needed products that could decrease their costs. To meet this need, an industry that produced a variety of solar energy systems emerged. With the great demand for such products, profits were high for many of the companies willing to take the risk of entering a new product area.

Marketers now are faced with radical changes in the competitive environment. These changes are the result of deregulation, shifting consumer characteristics and values, and foreign competition. The net effect is a splintered mass market that has fewer brand loyalties. To achieve success in today's competitive environment, companies must find new products, new customers, and new ways of selling.

Today, the marketing concept is as much a part of nonprofit organizations, such as charities, hospitals, universities, and museums, as it is of profit-oriented businesses. Competition for consumers of health care and education is as fierce as and sometimes fiercer than competition for products. When marketing research showed that young people would be more likely to read a magazine than a brochure, for example, many colleges began producing lively publications to describe their offerings to prospective students. Thus, in today's marketplace, targeting services as well as products to known consumer preferences is essential.

Johnson & Johnson, a sponsor of Shelter Aid, paid for this ad insert. This form of social marketing promotes Shelter Aid and provides coupons on an accompanying page for Personal Products Company products. (Courtesy of Johnson & Johnson Personal Products Company.)

Societal Marketing Concept Some companies have broadened the marketing concept to include the *societal marketing concept,* which extends the company's focus on consumer wants and its own profitability to include consideration of society's long-term well-being. In an age of the greenhouse effect, worldwide pollution, and a host of other pressing social problems, the societal marketing concept attempts to factor social welfare considerations into the decision-making process.

Cause-Related Marketing Many companies have promoted philanthropic causes in connection with product campaigns. This *cause-related marketing* has added as much as $100 million annually to the coffers of U.S. charities. For example, Johnson & Johnson Personal Products Company, in support of the issue of domestic violence, established Shelter Aid, a cause-related marketing program to help victims of domestic violence. The Personal Products Company contributes up to $1 million annually, largely through coupon redemptions and a retailer support program, and at the same time has measurably increased its sales and profits for Personal Products Company products.[3]

How Marketing Produces Utility and Value

Every good or service must have utility for its consumers. Chapter 11 defined *utility* as the quality of a product that makes it useful or desirable in satisfying customers' needs. It went on to define *form utility* as the usefulness resources gain after they are transformed into products. Form utility is created by the production process. However, marketing inputs, such as research, guide and direct the design and creation of the products. Marketing also creates utility. In fact, time, place, and ownership utility are created solely by the marketing process.

Time utility means that products must be available when the consumer wants to purchase them. A Toro snowblower on sale in July has no time utility if the consumer doesn't need it then. *Place utility* is created by having a product conveniently located when the consumer is ready to buy it. A snowblower has place utility in January if it is in a store close to the consumer. It has no place utility if it is in a distant warehouse or on order. Finally, *ownership utility* is created when there are no obstacles to transferring title from seller to buyer. A consumer may face financial obstacles when purchasing an expensive product like a snowblower. However, good marketing techniques can create ownership utility by allowing the consumer to use a credit plan or credit card to make the purchase.

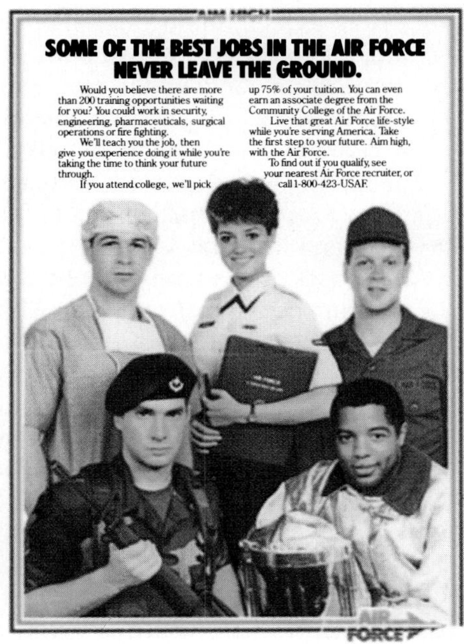

The military services, which are nonprofit organizations, use the marketing concept to attract new recruits. (United States Air Force Recruiting Service.)

HIGHLIGHT IN BUSINESS PRACTICE

SAS Makes Service a Potent Marketing Tool

In 1981, Scandinavian Airlines System was struggling with a severe downturn in business. The worldwide recession had cut deeply into the airline industry, and most airlines were experiencing financial problems. During that year SAS posted an $8 million loss.

The multinational board of directors of SAS was understandably concerned. The company president resigned and the board promoted Jan Carlzon, an energetic, flamboyant man of 39, who had been managing one of the company's subsidiaries. In a period of less than a year, Carlzon dramatically turned the company around and posted a gross profit of $71 million. The company was named "airline of the year" and laid claim to being the most punctual airline in Europe.

Just how did Jan Carlzon make SAS so successful in so short a time? Carlzon had a strong marketing orientation and this became the cornerstone of the turnaround. He did not relate his success to such conventional tactics as advertising, rate cutting, or cost reduction—or even his own leadership. Instead, he credited most of the improvement to the effects of a deceptively simple philosophy of marketing: make sure you're selling what the customer really wants to buy. By "turning on" the whole organization to the mission of service, he believed he could get the customer to recognize a significant difference between SAS and other airlines. This would bring the customer back in the future and generate goodwill, resulting in a significant level of word-of-mouth business.

With the help of his key executives, Carlzon began to apply this gospel of customer orientation energetically and persistently throughout the organization, taking it right down to the front lines. Here we find an interesting contrast between Carlzon's approach and the usual U.S. approach to such a program. The characteristic American way to bring a new theme down to grassroots level would involve putting the middle managers, and perhaps the first-line supervisors as well, through a training program, hoping that the word would trickle down through the ranks of the rest of the organization. (This usually doesn't happen, of course.)

Carlzon and his team put all 20,000 SAS managers and employees through a two-day training program designed to fill them with a new and dynamic sense of the organization's purposes. They hired one of the best-known training companies in Europe, Time Manager International, which made use of a high-energy, inspirational style of training. There was also an intensive internal program of employee communications, aimed at constantly reinforcing the message. In addition, the top 120 SAS managers and 30 labor leaders attended a three-week session to answer questions about the philosophy and strategic planning of the new approach.

The Exchange Process

Marketing provides many benefits to society. One of the more basic benefits is the *exchange process*. This process allows consumers to trade things of value. Thus they can purchase specific products to fit their needs and wants. Without the exchange process, they would be limited to the products they could make or provide for themselves.

When you set out to purchase a car, for example, you find out what is available through advertising. If you decide you would like a Chevrolet, you probably will not have to travel more than a few miles to your Chevrolet dealer, because marketing has transported the cars to the various dealers and provided showrooms in which to store them until you make your purchase.

At the dealer's, a salesperson will tell you about the features of each model on display. You will probably be amazed at the many colors, sizes, interiors, and styles available—all indicators that the consumer was put first in the development of this product. Finally, when you reach a price agreement, you will be offered a credit plan to overcome the obstacle of high cost. For example, when fewer people can purchase cars because of high sticker prices and high interest rates, dealers offer special financing. Once the automobile is purchased, your dealer will be able to provide warranty service and a supply of future repair parts.

Without the benefit of marketing, you would have to drive a great distance to the car manufacturer. Once there, you would receive little assistance in selecting your automobile, and probably you would have no choice of models. Obviously, marketing adds value to products.

This GTE ad illustrates this aspect of the marketing concept: find a need and fill (satisfy) it. (U.S. Sprint)

Value-Added Concept Some people frown on marketing activities because they believe that marketing adds to the cost of products. However, few people object to value being added to their purchases. Therefore, the value-added concept has become popular in marketing products. For example, the sale of a home has value added if the purchase price includes a warranty plan. The home buyer sees the warranty as value added, not as a marketing cost.

The Functions of Marketing

The marketing concept directly influences the eight traditional functions of marketing. Although all of the functions apply to the marketing of products, not all of them apply to the more modern concept of the marketing of ideas, issues, individuals, and organizations. The eight functions are as follows:

1. *Buying*—selecting suppliers and acquiring the raw materials, goods, and services for business, government, or consumer uses. Buying also includes inventory control.
2. *Selling*—finding prospective buyers; promoting goods and services through personal selling, advertising, sales promotion, and publicity; and providing postpurchase service. This function provides ownership utility.
3. *Transportation*—selecting vehicles, such as railroad cars or trucks, to get goods from the producer to the customer at an acceptable speed and cost. Transportation provides time utility.
4. *Storage*—providing a place to locate goods until the final sale can be made. Storage provides place utility.
5. *Finance and credit*—obtaining the necessary cash or credit to conduct operations. Financing also provides customers with the funds to purchase and own products (see chapter 17).
6. *Marketing research*—the systematic gathering, recording, and analyzing of data about problems related to the marketing of goods and services.[4] (This topic will be discussed later in the chapter.)
7. *Risk taking*—using marketing research to avoid possible product or business failures and shifting that risk to insurance companies for such areas as fire, theft, and flood.
8. *Standardization and grading*—providing uniform specifications so that the quality and quantity of products can be controlled and compared.

Two of the eight traditional marketing functions are buying and selling. Trade shows such as the one depicted here provide an excellent opportunity for buyers and sellers to come together.

DEVELOPING A MARKETING STRATEGY

Figure 12.1 shows how a marketing strategy for an actual product was developed and implemented. A **marketing strategy** is an organization's selection of target markets and development of a marketing mix of activities to accomplish its objectives. **Target markets** are segmented groups of potential buyers. The marketing mix is explained in the next section.

A ***marketing strategy*** is an organization's selection of target markets and development of a marketing mix of activities to accomplish its objectives.

Target markets are segmented groups of potential buyers.

The Marketing Mix

The integration of product, pricing, place (distribution), and promotion is the **marketing mix,** or the "4Ps" (see Figure 12.2). Each element affects the others. Hence marketing managers must be careful to develop a mix that reflects the total marketing strategy.

The ***marketing mix*** is the integration of product, pricing, place (distribution), and promotion (the 4Ps).

Product

Every business must have goods or services to sell. A manufacturer must develop products the consumer will demand from local retailers. Product development

Marketing Strategy for a Major Cola Drink

Target Market	• Cola drinkers • Younger drinkers
Product Strategy	• Offers a sweeter cola • Strategy based on premise a sweeter cola is better
Distribution Strategy	• Sell cola extract to independent bottlers • Distribute through supermarkets, convenience stores, and vending machines
Promotional Strategy	• Heavy television and newspaper advertising • Free samples and coupons
Pricing Strategy	• Use discounting and special sale prices • Price close to other colas • Obtain market share of 5%

COLA

12 FL. OZ.

Figure 12.1 The marketing strategy for Coke utilized the four marketing activities: product, distribution (place), promotion, and pricing.

Figure 12.2
The marketing mix consists of four unique activities, each related to the others.

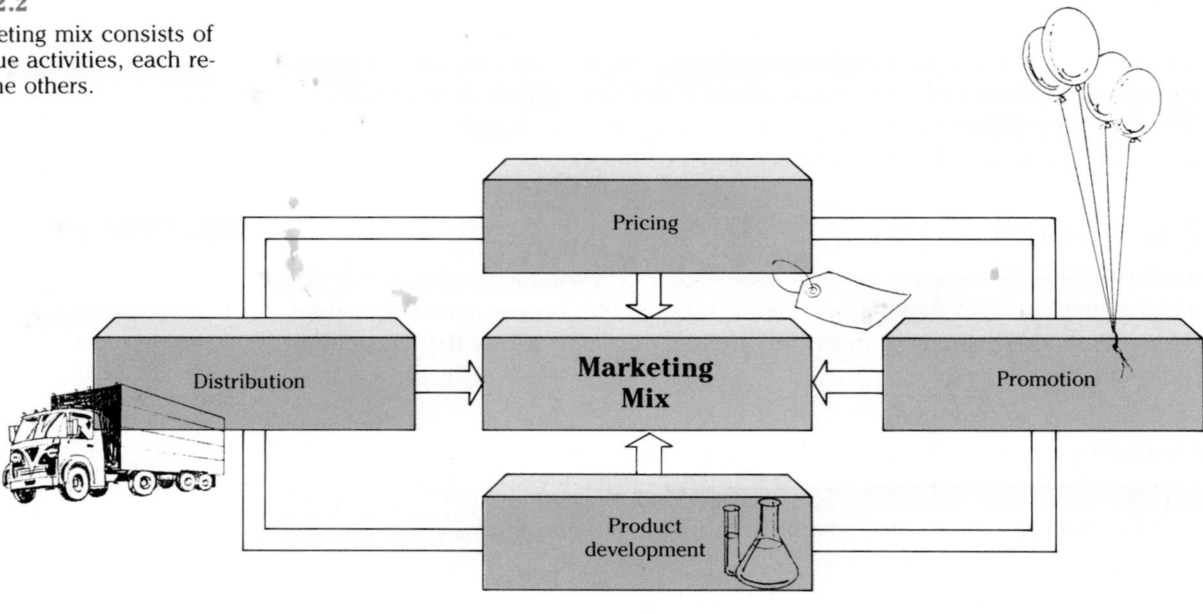

includes many things, among them design, package, color, warranties and guarantees, and branding or naming of the product.

Wholesalers and retailers must also select the right mix and quantity of products to sell. This includes deciding which brands to offer, what and how much service to include, which products to eliminate, and how much variety to allow.

Pricing

Once a product is developed, it must be priced to sell. Many factors influence the pricing of a product. For example, manufacturers must consider government regulations, discounts, and present and predicted economic conditions. Retailers consider some or all of these factors and pay special attention to markups, the competition, sales (markdowns), and the product image.

Place (Distribution)

Products must be stored, transported, and eventually sold, either directly to consumers or indirectly through wholesalers or retailers. Some products can be sold in several ways. For example, Burpee seed can be sold from a catalog or in retail stores. Other products are sold only door-to-door (for example, Mary Kay cosmetics). Wrigley's gum is sold through a series of wholesalers and eventually by a retailer. How a product is distributed can affect how much of it is sold.

Promotion

Most of us are familiar with the many ways marketers make us aware of their products. Selecting the proper promotional mix of advertising, personal selling, sales promotion, and publicity is very important. The mix will often depend on whether the product is new or has been around for a while. New products are usually advertised heavily on TV and radio and in newspapers and magazines. More mature products rely more on sales promotion. By contrast, personal selling is the most important element in the promotional mix for industrial products.

Potential Markets

As indicated earlier in the chapter, a market is a group of potential buyers. Consumers, buyers for retail stores, government procurement officers, industrial purchasing agents—each of these groups of buyers constitutes a market. Markets are classified into two major categories: consumer and organizational. For each, marketing managers must carefully plan for all phases of the marketing strategy.

BUSINESS PRACTICE EXAMPLE Continues

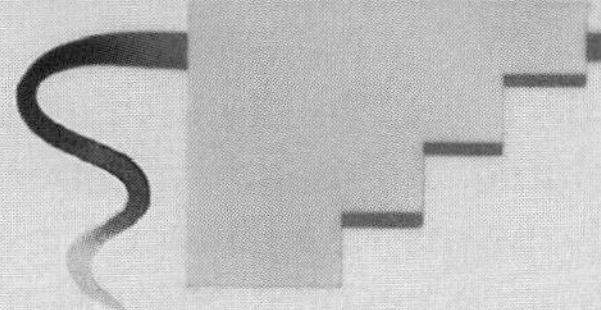

Timberland boots were initially sold through the L.L. Bean catalogue, where they quickly sold out to college students and backpackers. While they were obviously happy with this turn of events, the Swartzes realized that it was just a matter of time before another manufacturer used the same technology and honed in on their market. What would they do then?

Unsure of how to capitalize on the boot's early success, they turned to a professional advertising firm. The agency told them that it was time to abandon the shoemaking industry's traditional marketing strategies. No longer should the Swartzes think of themselves as selling reasonably priced, sturdy work boots that just happened to appeal to college kids; it would only be a matter of time before imitators would come along and Timberland would once again be locked in a price battle. Instead, they should make Timberland boots a fashion item, if an unusual one. They should raise the boots' *price, distribute* them through top-drawer retailers, and *promote* them in upscale magazines such as the *New Yorker* (note that a marketing strategy involves developing a specific marketing mix). The Swartzes decided to follow the agency's advice and to gamble on a marketing strategy emphasizing their product's quality and performance. The agency then designed a series of print advertisements humorously portraying the adventures of fictional Timberland-shod characters. Each ad ended with the tag-line, "A whole line of fine leather boots that cost plenty, and should."

Soon Timberland's earnings soared.

The ***consumer market*** is the market composed of individuals who buy products for their personal use—the market of end users.

The Consumer Market

The market composed of individuals who buy products for their personal use—the market of end users—is the **consumer market.** It contains the largest number of potential buyers. In the United States, there are 248 million consumers, but worldwide there are 5.2 billion potential consumers. (As discussed in chapter 1, the world's population is increasing rapidly.) Products sold to consumers are marketed primarily through retailers. (Consumer products will be discussed in detail in chapter 13.)

The ***organizational market*** is the market composed of buyers from industry, wholesaling and retailing (resellers), and government.

The ***industrial market*** is the market composed of buyers in manufacturing, agricultural, transportation, communications, mining, construction, utility, and service industries.

The Organizational Market

The market composed of buyers from industry, wholesaling and retailing (resellers), and government is the **organizational market.** The market composed of buyers in manufacturing, agricultural, transportation, communications, mining, construction, utility, and service industries is the **industrial market.** This market, the largest and most diverse of the three organizational markets, is characterized by derived demand. *Derived demand* means that organizations purchase products only if their own products are in demand. For instance, there would be little need for plastic, an industrial product, if there were no demand for such consumer goods as records and plastic forks. The industrial market is also characterized by a greater total sales volume, a smaller number of buyers, greater primary demand inelasticity—which means less chance for demand to be stimulated by price cuts—more complex price negotiation, and more direct purchasing than exist in the other parts of the organizational market.

Resellers (wholesalers and retailers) make a profit primarily by creating time, place, and ownership utility. They buy products and make them available to other buyers at the right time, place, price, and quantity.

The government market is large. In the United States, approximately 20 percent of the gross national product is purchased by the federal government, making it the country's single biggest customer. This market also includes the many local and state governments.

The marketing manager for this dress shop in Coconut Grove, Florida, hopes to attract shoppers in the high-income segment of the market. These high-income shoppers are her *target market.*

ANALYZING MARKET OPPORTUNITIES: MARKET SEGMENTATION

Market segmentation is the process of dividing the total market of potential buyers into homogeneous groups (groups with similar characteristics).

Many opportunities exist within consumer and organizational markets to sell products to a wide variety of customers. It is the marketer's responsibility to identify homogeneous groups of buyers and to develop special appeals to them. This section examines market segmentation and identification of market opportunities.

In working with any market, consumer or organizational, the marketing manager must divide the total market into homogeneous groups (groups with similar characteristics). This process is called **market segmentation.** Each segment is a target market.

To grasp the concept of marketing segmentation, examine the AARP ad on the opposite page. It is an ad targeted to older people, a growing segment of the population. Another example of market segmentation is the American Express ad, which reflects the use of income and lifestyle as segmentation variables.

In the United States, there are many minority target markets, including blacks,

Hispanics, Asians, and women. A new wave of immigration is changing the complexion of the American consumer market, and several of today's minority markets will be tomorrow's majority markets (see Figure 12.3). A study by the Population Reference Bureau predicts that if current immigration (legal and illegal) remains high, the non-Hispanic white population will drop to under 50 percent of the total U.S. population by 2080.

Many smart companies are actively marketing to blacks, Hispanics, and Asians because of their market size and spending potential. For example, when Chinese-Americans celebrated the Year of the Tiger, Metropolitan Life Insurance sent them a greeting. In the company's first-ever Asian language advertisement, Metropolitan Life congratulated the Chinese on their accomplishments in the United States and wished them a prosperous New Year.[5]

Positioning is an approach to market segmentation that identifies current or proposed marketing segments and indicates where they perceive the product in relation to competing products. The market segments are identified through market research (discussed later in the chapter). Then the product is differentiated from the competition's and promoted with the appropriate market image. **Product differentiation** is the technique used to distinguish the characteristics of one product from those of another. Among the characteristics are brand name, package design, product capabilities, color, taste, and price. One industry that uses positioning is the computer industry. For example, Atari and Commodore computers are positioned as game and home-use computers. Compaqs were originally perceived as executive computers designed specifically for travel. The Apple Macintosh is viewed as ideal for desktop publishing and graphic arts. The computers are also differentiated by memory capacity, speed, monitor size, resolution, and other characteristics.

Positioning is an approach to segmenting that identifies current or proposed marketing segments and indicates where the segments perceive the product in relation to competing products.

Product differentiation is the promotional technique used to distinguish the characteristics of one product from those of another.

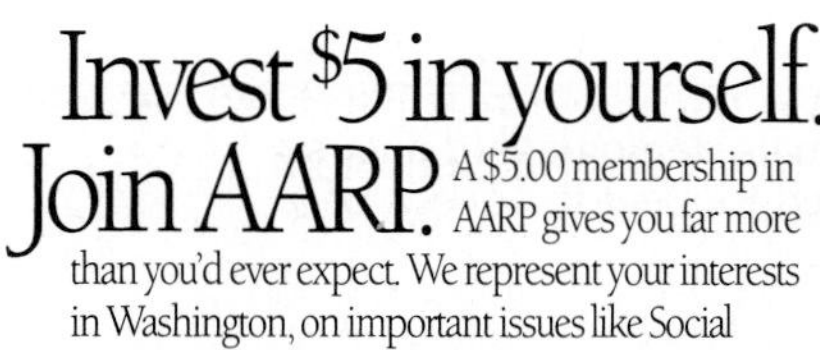

Invest $5 in yourself.
Join AARP.
A $5.00 membership in AARP gives you far more than you'd ever expect. We represent your interests in Washington, on important issues like Social Security, long term care, and taxes. You get the award-winning Modern Maturity Magazine, and timely AARP News Bulletins. You can save on hotels, motels and car rentals nationwide. Plus qualify for quality health, home and auto insurance. Even save on prescriptions through the mail with our pharmacy service.
AARP American Association of Retired Persons
12345678
10/24/89
Ronald C. Wilson
1234 Main Street
Kragertown, USA 99999
Help yourself to a better life for just $5.00.
Become a member today. You don't have to be retired, just 50 or over. To join, call:
1-800-345-8600
AARP
Or write: AARP Membership Processing Center, P.O. Box 199, Long Beach, CA 90801.

This AARP ad reflects the use of age as a segmentation variable. (© 1988, American Association of Retired Persons. Reprinted with permission.)

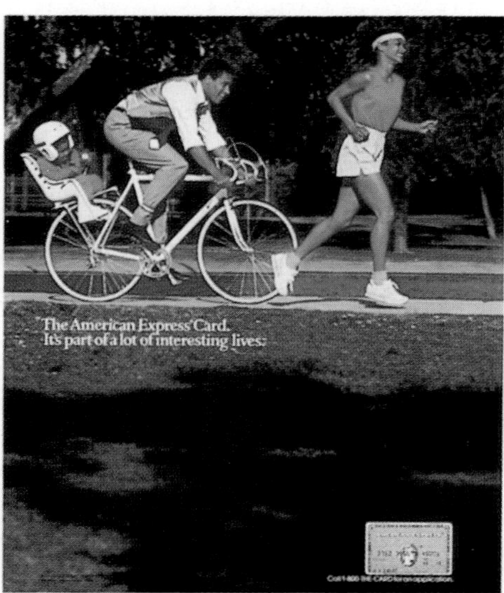

This American Express ad reflects the use of income and lifestyle as segmentation variables. (Courtesy of the American Express Travel Related Services Company, Inc. Copyright 1986.)

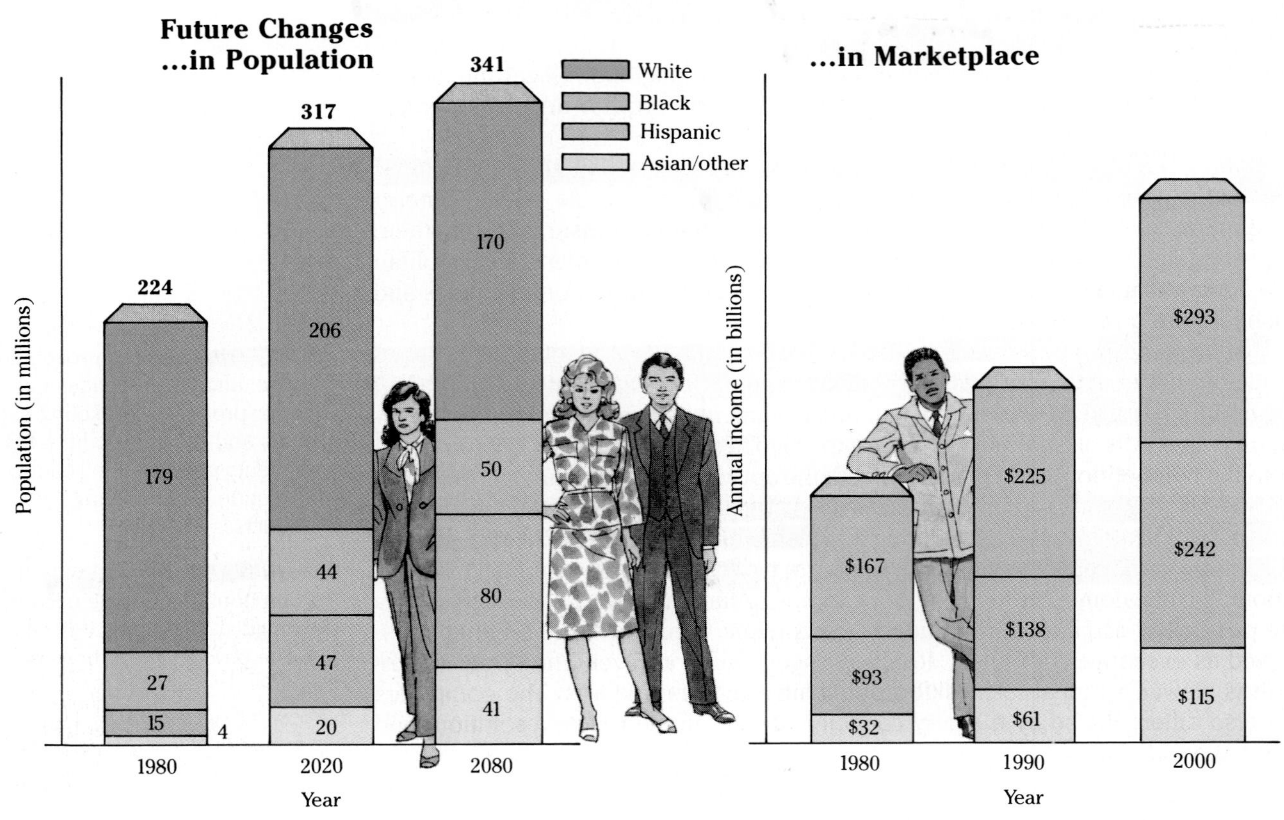

Figure 12.3 Marketers need to continually evaluate demographic data so that new products can be developed to meet the needs of a changing population.

Markets can also be segmented according to three major consumer characteristics: geographic, demographic, and psychographic characteristics (see Table 12.1). The first two characteristics have to do with the consumer's state of being. The last one is related to the consumer's state of mind.

Table 12.1 Consumer markets can be segmented into many groupings.

Variable	Typical Breakdowns
Geographic	
Region	Pacific, Mountain, West North Central, West South Central, East North Central, East South Central, South Atlantic, Middle Atlantic, New England

Variable	Typical Breakdowns
Geographic	
County size	A, B, C, D
City or SMSA size	Under 5,000; 5,000–20,000; 20,000–50,000; 50,000–100,000; 100,000–250,000; 250,000–500,000; 500,000–1,000,000; 1,000,000–4,000,000; 4,000,000 or over
Density	Urban, suburban, rural
Climate	Northern, southern
Demographic	
Age	Under 6, 6–11, 12–19, 20–34, 35–49, 50–64, 65+
Sex	Male, female
Family size	1–2, 3–4, 5+
Family life cycle	Young, single; young, married, no children; young, married, youngest child under 6; young, married, youngest child 6 or over; older, married, with children; older, married, no children under 18; older, single; other
Income	Under \$5,000; \$5,000–\$10,000; \$10,000–\$15,000; \$15,000–\$20,000; \$20,000–\$25,000; \$25,000–\$30,000; \$30,000–\$50,000; \$50,000 and over
Occupation	Professional and technical; managers, officials, and proprietors; clerical, sales; craftsmen, foremen; operatives; farmers; retired; students; housewives; unemployed
Education	Grade school or less; some high school; high school graduate; some college; college graduate
Religion	Catholic, Protestant, Jewish, other
Race	White, black, Oriental
Nationality	American, British, French, German, Scandinavian, Italian, Latin American, Middle Eastern, Japanese
Psychographic	
Social class	Lower lowers, upper lowers, working class, middle class, upper middles, lower uppers, upper uppers
Lifestyle	Straights, swingers, longhairs
Personality	Compulsive, gregarious, authoritarian, ambitious
Behavioral	
Occasions	Regular occasion, special occasion
Benefits	Quality, service, economy
User status	Nonuser, ex-user, potential user, first-time user, regular user
Usage rate	Light user, medium user, heavy user
Loyalty status	None, medium, strong, absolute
Readiness stage	Unaware, aware, informed, interested, desirous, intending to buy
Attitude toward product	Enthusiastic, positive, indifferent, negative, hostile

BUSINESS PRACTICE EXAMPLE Continues

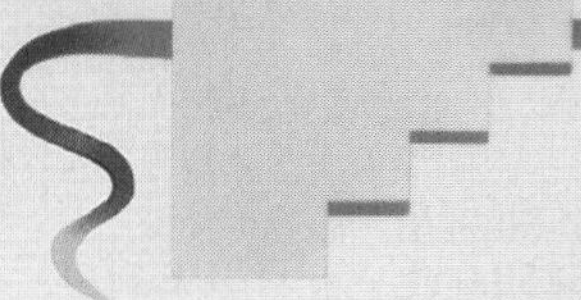

Timberland positioned its product—first boots, and later various styles of casual and dress shoes—to appeal to several target markets. Its boots were positioned to appeal to serious hikers, climbers, and other outdoorspeople, as well as to those consumers who might not need all of the protection the boot provided, but who purchased it for its quality performance and looks anyway. By placing the boot in upscale department stores, and by advertising it in upscale magazines, Timberland was able to differentiate its product from other sturdy boots sold in army-navy stores and sporting goods stores. Thus Timberland very successfully made its products stand out from the pack.

Geographic Segmentation

Geographic variables are useful in determining marketing strategies because they help establish potential sales possibilities. Several sources of data can be used to calculate the sales potential for a geographic region, county, or city.

One of the most popular sources is the U.S. Census. Census statistics indicate that in 1977, for the first time in America's history, more people lived in the South and West than in the North and East. Furthermore, on the basis of the 1980 Census, the Census Bureau projected that for the first time in our history the population center lies west of the Mississippi River.

Does this mean that the hottest retail markets are emerging in the South and West? Absolutely not. Population *density* is what retailers seek the most. For now and the near future, the highest density is in a pocket of ten states east of the Mississippi River and north of the Mason-Dixon line (see Figure 12.4).

Information such as this is invaluable to marketing planners. When the object is to get the product to the people, you have to know where the people are.

Census Bureau information can be used in a variety of ways to determine market characteristics. For example, on a smaller geographic scale, the Jewel Company of Chicago once used a certain type of census data to collect market characteristics at a cost of just a few thousand dollars. Jewel first recorded the license plate numbers of cars parked in Jewel Food Store parking lots. For $2 apiece, the names and addresses of the car owners were obtained from the Illinois Secretary of State. The names and addresses were then fed into a Census Bureau computer, which supplied the census tract in which each of the customers lived. Using this information, Jewel was able to determine exactly who shopped at its stores, how far the shoppers traveled, and in which neighborhoods they lived.

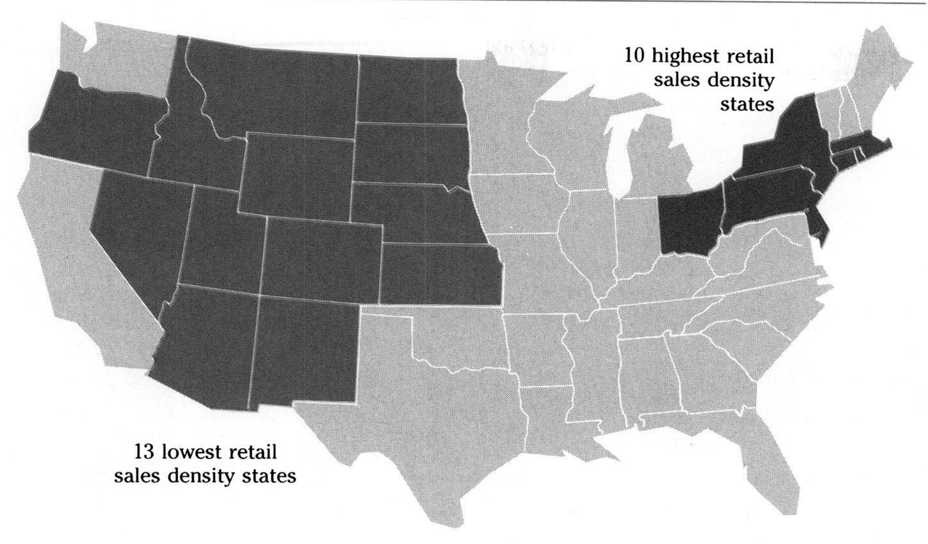

Figure 12.4
The ten states with the highest retail sales density and the thirteen states with the lowest density.

Demographic Segmentation

Demographics is the study of human population statistics.

Demographics is the study of human population statistics. Demographic variables include age, income, family size and life cycle, occupation, religion, race, nationality, and social class. This section will examine some of these variables to show why it is important for marketing managers to consider their influence on consumer behavior and motives.

In the United States, there was a baby boom between 1946 and 1961. As these babies grew up, they slowly and inexorably rearranged the country's entire marketing structure. The effect on the various market segments was a little like the effect on a snake of swallowing a football. First, there was an increased demand for toys and children's clothes, then for schools and colleges, and lately for furniture, cars, and housing.

Just as this age group created a demand for some products, it also caused large drops in demand for others as it moved through the various stages of its life cycle. For example, Gerber Products Company did a large amount of business in baby food prior to 1961. As the birthrate began to decline, so did Gerber's sales. Declining sales forced Gerber to diversify its product line to include toys, life insurance for young couples, clothes, and other related products. This diversification was necessary to prevent lost earnings and to attempt to capture a larger share of the total dollars spent by young families. Even the Gerber slogan, "Babies are our business . . . our only business," was dropped. Gerber read the changing demographic variables accurately and responded to them correctly.

The baby boomers are still with us. They are now in their late twenties, thirties, and early forties. They still represent a challenge for any marketing manager.

Another segment of the market that has been increasing in influence is that of senior citizens. Some marketing managers describe their influence as the "graying of America." Because of better health care, people are living longer. According

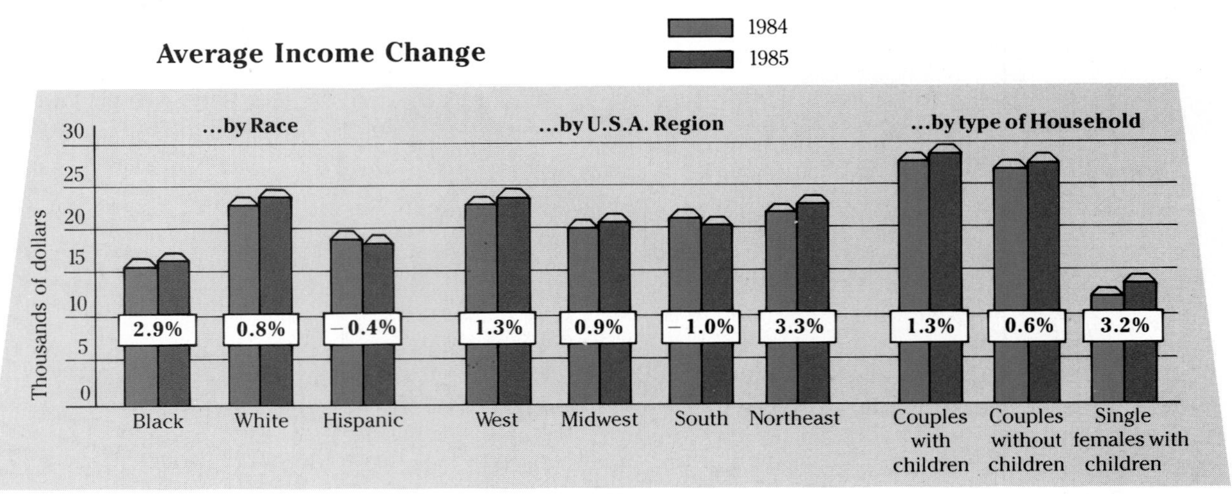

Figure 12.5 Rising after-tax income. In 1985, for the fourth consecutive year, average household income rose, this time from $22,333 to $22,646—an increase of 0.9 percent.

Purchasing power is the ability of consumers to purchase goods and services.

to the Census Bureau, the age group of sixty-five and older is expected to increase by 23% by the year 2000. With social security benefits and other pensions and retirement plans, senior citizens should be able to increase their **purchasing power**—the ability of consumers to purchase goods and services. What are the implications for marketing? There should be increased demands for travel services, medical care, and gifts for younger relatives. Remember, demand plus purchasing power plus authority (the legal right and mental competence) to buy are necessary for a sale to take place.

This discussion of the baby boomer and senior citizen market segments tells us that spending patterns vary with the stages of the life cycle. Several other demographic variables also influence spending. One of them is *social class.* Occupation and income group play important roles in determining an individual's social class. According to sociologists, the majority of Americans are middle class, largely because of the increase in two-income families. During the first part of the 1980s, the tremendous growth of office occupations created more white-collar jobs than blue-collar jobs. Census data indicate that white-collar jobs traditionally pay $7,000 to $14,000 a year more than blue-collar and farm jobs.

Studies show that even if individuals in the lower class had the same amount of money to spend as do middle-class individuals, the purchases of the two groups would be quite different. Knowledge about consumers' social classes is useful to marketing managers because from it they can predict spending patterns. These patterns also vary with other measurable factors, such as geographic region and rural versus urban or suburban location of households. Suburban families, for example, have substantially higher median (average) incomes than rural or urban families. Figure 12.5 illustrates average income by race or origin, region of the United States, and type of household.

Average household incomes are higher in the Northeast, the North Central region, and the West than in the South.[6] However, according to a Conference

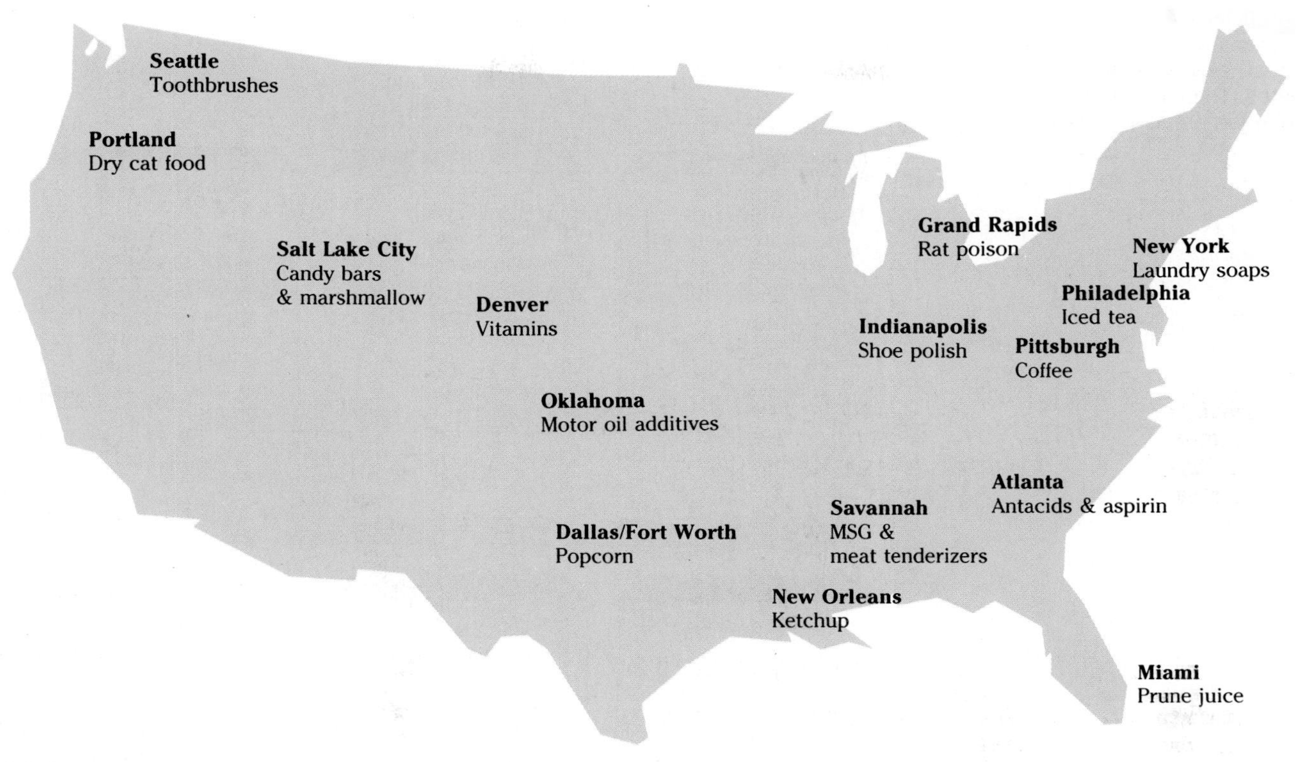

Figure 12.6 Number 1 markets for selected products.

Board report, the Northeast has the lowest standard of living of any region. Consumer purchasing power in the Northeast has been drastically eroded by high living costs and taxes.

Generally, consumers in the South have more **discretionary income**—the income that remains after the necessities of life, such as food, housing, clothing, transportation, and similar needs, are paid for. Because discretionary income is hard to pinpoint, marketing managers find disposable income more useful in determining spending patterns. **Disposable income** is all the personal income that remains after taxes and any other required payments are made.

Discretionary income is the income that remains after the necessities of life are paid for.

Disposable income is all the personal income that remains after taxes and other required payments are made.

By using geographic and demographic data, marketing managers can predict the sales potential for a product in a particular locality (see Figure 12.6) and can identify the market segments that are likely to purchase it. They can determine the relative dimensions, size, and location of their target market.

Psychographic Segmentation

Geographic and demographic data make it possible to predict basic trends in spending patterns. However, they are of relatively little value in predicting *which* products and brands consumers will purchase. For this, marketing managers must examine "state of mind" variables. They must find out why consumers purchase particular products and brands and reject others.

Figure 12.7
Psychographics has been used to sell everything from beer to autos. The categories and distribution are shown here.

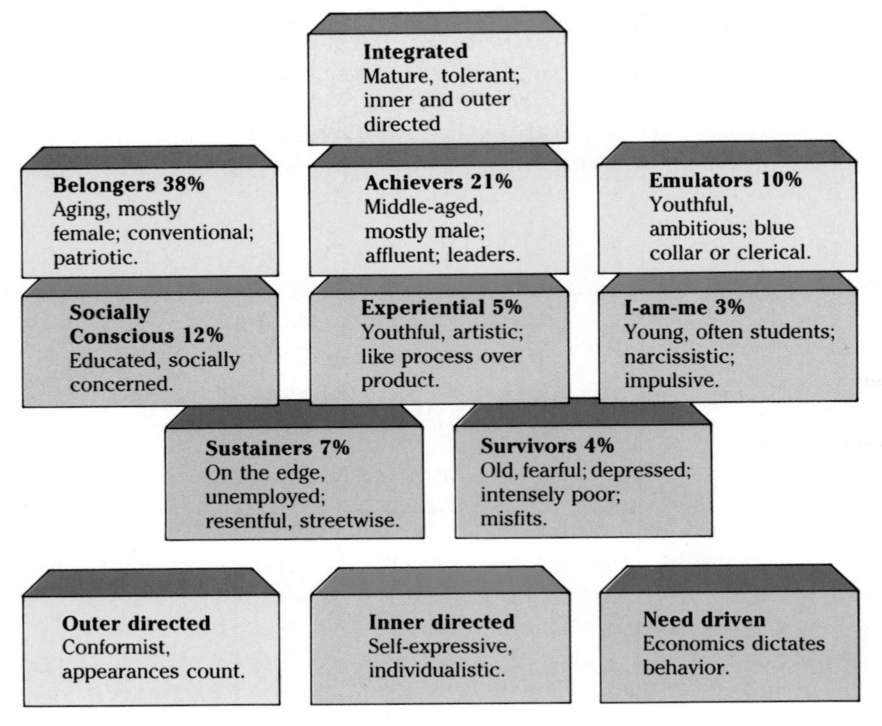

Psychographics is the study of consumers' values, interests, attitudes, personalities, and lifestyles.

The basis for this type of segmentation is **psychographics**—the study of consumers' values, interests, attitudes, personalities, and lifestyles. The information about consumers tells marketing researchers what consumers value; how they spend their time; and what opinions they hold about education, products, and other variables, including themselves. Once the information is collected, it can be used to develop profiles of the typical users of products. Figure 12.7 describes and gives percentages for the psychographic categories marketers often use.

Psychographics is commonly used in the automobile industry, which often targets customers according to such lifestyle variables as living arrangements and marital status, occupation, recreation, and achievement. For example, the Ford Bronco is targeted primarily at men who perceive themselves as rugged outdoorsmen.

While values and lifestyles are important psychological characteristics, consumers must still be motivated to make a purchase. As chapter 7 explained, the motivation process involves human needs, and the most widely accepted description of needs is that of Abraham Maslow. According to Maslow, needs are arranged in a hierarchy, from physiological, to security, to social, to esteem, and finally to self-actualizing needs.[7] The lower-level needs must be satisfied before the needs on the next level can be.

Maslow's hierarchy provides one explanation of consumer behavior. Consumers must satisfy their basic physical needs for food, clothing, shelter, and medical care before they move up to the needs for safety, belongingness, esteem, love, and self-actualization. For example, a consumer must have a place to live before considering the purchase of a smoke alarm (to satisfy safety needs) or a swimming pool (to satisfy self-actualization needs).

A purchase could, of course, satisfy more than one need. For instance, a Liz Claiborne sweater might satisfy both the lower need for clothing and the higher need for status and esteem. Everyone has basic needs. Marketing managers concentrate their efforts on the higher needs and focus their strategies on persuading consumers to purchase specific products and brands.

Most consumers purchase or reject products on the basis of emotional or rational motives. **Emotional motives** are motives related to feelings about something. On Valentine's Day, for example, people are motivated to purchase cards, candy, and other gifts for those they love. Hallmark Cards and Fannie May Candies concentrate their marketing efforts on special and appealing gift items related to that day.

Emotional motives are motives related to feelings about something.

An emotion at the opposite extreme is fear. Many individuals fear mice and therefore purchase mouse traps and the services of exterminators. Those who fear they may die and leave their families unprotected purchase life insurance.

Rational motives also play a compelling part in product and brand selection. The **rational motives** are the motives that evolve from the reasoning process. They are often related to the most economical purchases. For example, when the rational motive is at work, consumers look for sale items, bargains, durable and long-lasting goods, and dependable and efficient products. A rationally motivated consumer might purchase a $100 pair of Rockport Prowalkers over other, less expensive brands of walking shoes because of Rockport's reputation for well-made, long-lasting, and comfortable shoes. Often consumers are willing to pay more for items because the rational thought process tells them that longer-lasting products will save money in the long term.

Rational motives are the motives that evolve from the reasoning process.

The integration of emotional and rational motives influences where consumers will purchase goods and services. This integration is called the **patronage motive.** Consumers patronize stores for a number of reasons, including location, price, service, loyalty, product variety, and friendliness and competence of personnel. Many consumers patronize shopping centers because of free parking and climate control.

The ***patronage motive*** is a combination of emotional and rational motives that influences where a consumer will purchase goods and services.

MARKETING RESEARCH

Marketing managers want to identify the characteristics of target markets so they can develop a unique marketing strategy for each one. They isolate the characteristics of each segment through **marketing research,** the systematic gathering, recording, and analyzing of data about issues related to the marketing of goods and services.[8] The research is used to generate, refine, and evaluate marketing actions; monitor marketing performance; and improve the understanding of marketing as a process. It specifies the information required to address these issues, designs the method for collecting information, manages and implements the data collection process, analyzes the results, and communicates the findings and their implications.[9]

Marketing research is the systematic gathering, recording, and analyzing of data about problems related to the marketing of goods and services.

Some companies do their own marketing research, and others hire it out to marketing research firms or advertising agencies. Often companies identify and develop marketing strategies for several target markets. For example, the car companies provide a model for virtually every conceivable preference.

A ***marketing information system*** is a computer-based framework for the continuous processing and management of marketing information.

When combined with marketing research, an information system can provide the insight for carrying out the marketing concept. A **marketing information system** is a computer-based framework for the continuous processing and management of marketing information (gathered from both internal and external sources). It is used to store research information so marketing decisions can be made on present and future problems. Examples of such information include advertising and distribution expenses, prices of the company's and competing products, inventory levels, and sales figures.

Types of Data Collected

Primary data are data gathered through original research for a specific purpose.

Secondary data are data previously gathered and made available in journals, newspapers, computer data bases, and other sources.

A major classification scheme divides business data into primary and secondary data. **Primary data** are data gathered through original research for a specific purpose. A research analyst who surveys teenagers about their opinion of alcohol use is gathering primary data. **Secondary data** are data previously gathered and made available in journals, newspapers, computer data bases, and other sources. Secondary data often serve as a source against which to compare primary data. Researchers usually start with a library search for secondary data and then gather their own primary data to answer their research question.

Methods for Collecting Primary Data

Library information is classified as external secondary data. Most business researchers review the available literature regarding a problem facing the company. After this preliminary work, the company may decide to gather first-hand information of its own. Four common methods used to collect primary data are observation, interviewing, questionnaires, and experimentation.

Observation Method

Trained researchers are needed for the observation method of acquiring data. Among these researchers are time-and-motion-study engineers, who may observe the work flow of employees. As a result of their research, wasted motion may be minimized and productivity improved. Consumer research specialists are another example. They frequently observe flow of customers entering and moving through a store. Retailers use this information to determine product location and general store layout. Real estate specialists are yet another example. They record traffic flow patterns for certain commercial properties. This information is helpful in selling such properties, especially if franchises or retail stores are interested in them.

Although the observation technique is a pragmatic and useful tool for gathering data, some caution must be exercised. For example, if this method is used to observe human behavior, the trained researcher should remain as unnoticeable as possible. If individuals are aware they are being observed, their reactions may not be normal. Toy companies such as Fisher-Price often test new toys by observing children's reactions to the toys through a one-way mirror. The observation method is labor-intensive and can be a costly way of collecting a small amount of data.

Interview Method

Interviewing involves a verbal exchange between the data gatherer and the person being interviewed. The two most common types of interviews are face-to-face and telephone. Face-to-face interviews are often used by management consultants to assess the morale of the work force. They are also used by market researchers, who interview customers leaving a store to find out why they purchased a particular brand. Although face-to-face interviews can be expensive, they allow the researcher to obtain a candid reaction. Telephone interviewing is less expensive but also less reliable. Most people resent being asked information by an unidentified caller. In addition, people without a phone or those with unlisted numbers are often omitted from the research.

Another form of interview is the **focus group,** an informal group of about six to twelve consumers led by a moderator, who guides them through a session that deals with their likes and dislikes of a product. These sessions are often taped (audio or video), and some are viewed through one-way mirrors. This allows market researchers to observe the total reaction of consumers in a group dynamics process. After the session, researchers analyze comments for meaningful and useful ideas.

A ***focus group*** is an informal group of about six to twelve consumers led by a moderator, who guides them through a session that deals with their likes or dislikes of a product.

Focus groups have been used to develop many new products and advertising campaigns. For example, the idea for Arm and Hammer's promotion of increased use of baking soda was born in a focus group. The theme the group supplied was that baking soda could be used to clean the air in refrigerators. That theme was then used in a most successful campaign.[10]

Questionnaires

A third method of gathering data uses questionnaires. For example, consumers may be asked to complete questionnaires dealing with product satisfaction. Most, often businesses solicit this information through the mail by polling a large number of consumers. Any effort to gather data that contacts every possible source is called a *census.* The most obvious example is the United States census of the population, which the government conducts every ten years.

It would be expensive, however, to poll every consumer in the United States. To minimize the cost, most companies select a **sample,** a representative part of a larger group. The entire group is called the universe, or population. For the sample to reflect accurately the entire group of consumers being studied, it must be chosen at random. A **random sample** is a sample for which each person in the population being studied has an equal chance of being selected. For example, the dean of students at your college may want to study the attitudes of freshmen toward drug use. A random selection of names of freshmen from the registrar's record would provide a sample that would be representative of all first-year students on campus.

A ***sample*** is a representative part of a larger group.

A ***random sample*** is a sample for which each person in the population being studied has an equal chance of being selected.

The random sample is the most common type of sampling procedure used by researchers. Sampling is most frequently used in questionnaire surveys, but it can also be used in interviews. (Although random sampling is commonly used with the questionnaire method, it can also be incorporated into the other methods used for getting primary data.)

Mail questionnaires offer certain advantages. They are cost-effective because they can be distributed and returned with a minimum of expense. This is especially important if the sources being surveyed are spread out geographically. Another advantage is that the respondent can remain anonymous. This may encourage straightforward and truthful answers. There is one major disadvantage, however. The rate of return of mail questionnaires is usually low, although a self-addressed, stamped envelope may increase the response rate.

Experimentation

Most experiments are conducted in a laboratory environment. You have probably done scientific experiments, for example, in a chemistry or physics lab. In an experiment, researchers begin with two equivalent groups: the experimental group and the control group. The researchers measure the groups, subject the experimental group to an outside element, then measure the two groups again. Any difference between the two should be due to the outside element.

The experimental method is often used by advertising agencies to test the effectiveness of promotional campaigns. Usually, two cities with similar demographic makeup are chosen for comparison. One city is the experimental group and the other is the control group. If Fort Wayne had a sales increase of 12 percent compared to 3 percent in Indianapolis, strong justification would exist to introduce the promotional package in all similar cities.

As you can see, experiments attempt to show a causal relationship. Unfortunately, this method is costly and time-consuming. More importantly, researchers cannot control all of the significant variables during a promotional program. Uncontrollable variables must be examined when experimentation occurs in a nonlab environment.

THE MARKETING PLAN

The ***marketing plan*** is the program that outlines the specific actions necessary to implement the marketing strategy.

In order to implement strategies for each of the marketing mix elements, a **marketing plan** must be developed. This plan outlines the specific actions necessary to implement the marketing strategy. The marketing plan also includes a market or situational analysis, an overall strategy, a budget, and provisions for control and measurable market feedback. It is essential that the marketing plan be compatible with the organization's goals and resources.

The elements and activities of the marketing mix are controllable. However, the marketing manager must also be aware of uncontrollable elements in its marketing environment. Among them are economic forces, societal changes, the competition, legal and political forces, and technological changes. Each of these forces can have an impact on a company's marketing strategy.

Some examples of the effects of external forces follow:

Economic forces. The 1987 stock market crash caused a slowdown in the sale of many luxury products, such as second homes, private aircraft, and yachts.

Societal changes. The use of birth control pills and the legalization of abortion have greatly reduced the average size of the American family.

The competition. The use of price wars or heavy discounting can force companies to cut their prices in order to meet the competition. Often this shrinks or eliminates a profit.

Legal and political forces. In 1983, Congress passed a law requiring that Medicare hospital reimbursements be based on diagnosis, rather than treatment or length of stay. Seventy percent of hospitals now lose money on Medicare patients, once the lifeline for small or rural hospitals. Hospitals now advertise, use market research to identify and attract likely patients, and may use sales forces to sell hospitalization plans to industry.

Technological changes. The advent of computers, robots, and other devices that increase production forced auto manufacturers to develop all new production and distribution systems in order to meet the Japanese challenge.[11]

BUSINESS PRACTICE EXAMPLE Continues

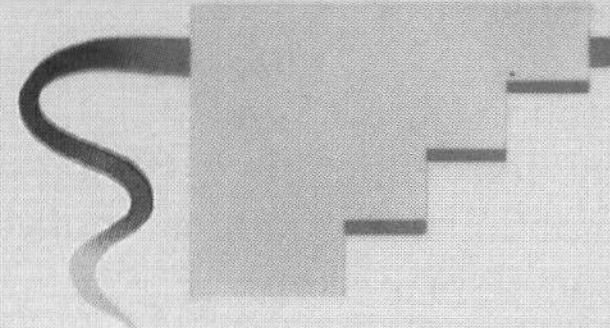

Timberland's marketing research department carefully studies the purchasing behavior of its various target markets. Information on geographic, demographic, and psychographic data is used in creating and marketing Timberland's products.

In 1988 Timberland branched out for the first time into apparel and accessories, introducing the new line, called the Signature Collection, with a large national print ad campaign in September. Much like Timberland's shoes and boots, the line of sweaters, shirts, shearling coats, backpacks, duffel bags, and high-performance weather gear featured waterproof construction and rugged styling. To promote the Signature Collection, as well as Timberland's shoes and boots, the company planned to open its own "concept shops" and "concept corners" within prestigious retail stores across the country. The interiors of these shops would suggest turn-of-the-century hunting and fishing camps and lodges.

By 1987, almost a third of Timberland's sales were made in foreign countries. "Quality American products are in great demand all over the world," said Swartz. "We especially go out of our way to have 'Made in the U.S.A.' put on our product. It is an enormous selling vehicle."

"There's a very special thing in the United States and, I've found, all over the world, and that's brand recognition. If there's anything we have, it's brand recognition, and quality is associated with that brand. So I think we can—again, carefully, and again, with testing—do quality apparel well."

Issues for Discussion

1. Describe Timberland's marketing strategy for its original Timberland boot. Include the "4Ps" in your discussion.
2. How can Timberland use psychographic data to sell shoes?
3. Suggest several kinds of market research Timberland may have used to test both domestic and foreign markets. Discuss.

SUMMARY

Marketing is the process of planning and executing the conception, pricing, promotion, and distribution of ideas, goods, and services to create exchanges that satisfy individual and organizational objectives. It evolved through three eras—the production era, the sales era, and the marketing era.

The marketing concept means consumers' needs and wants are considered even before production begins. The marketing concept has been broadened to include the societal marketing concept and sometimes, cause-related marketing.

Marketing creates three types of utility: time, place, and ownership. It also provides the benefit of the exchange process, which allows consumers to trade things of value for the products they need and want.

Marketing has eight functions: buying, selling, transportation, storage, finance and credit, marketing research, risk taking, and standardization and grading. It also uses the value-added concept.

An organization's marketing strategy is its selection of target markets and development of a marketing mix of activities. The marketing mix is also known as the 4Ps: product, pricing, place (distribution), and promotion.

There are two major categories of markets: the consumer market (the market of individual end users) and the organizational market (the market of buyers from industry, wholesaling and retailing, and government).

Market segmentation is the division of the total market into homogeneous groups. Each segment is a target market. One approach to segmentation is positioning (indicating where segments perceive the product in relation to competing ones). Product differentiation distinguishes the characteristics of one product from those of another.

Markets can also be segmented according to three characteristics: geographic (regions, counties, and cities, for example), demographic (age, income, family size, occupation, and so on), and psychographic (values, interests, attitudes, personality, and lifestyle).

The motivation process involves human needs. According to Abraham Maslow, these needs are arranged in a hierarchy: physiological, security, social, esteem, and self-actualization needs. The lower-level needs must be satisfied first.

Three consumer motives are emotional (those related to feelings about something), rational (those that evolve from the reasoning process), and patronage (the integration of emotional and rational motives to determine where consumers will shop).

Marketing research is the systematic gathering, recording, and analyzing of data about problems related to the marketing. Marketing information systems are computer-based frameworks to process and manage marketing information.

The data collected are either primary (gathered through original research) or secondary (available in journals, newspapers, data bases, and the like). Primary data are collected through four methods: observation, interviewing, questionnaires, and experimentation.

The marketing plan outlines the actions needed to implement the marketing strategy. Some elements in the marketing environment cannot be controlled but must be considered and addressed in the formation of a marketing plan. Among them are economic forces, societal changes, the competition, legal and political forces, and technological changes.

KEY TERMS

Consumer market p. 354
Demographics p. 359
Discretionary income p. 361
Disposable income p. 361
Emotional motives p. 363
Focus group p. 365
Industrial market p. 354
Market p. 345
Marketing p. 345
Marketing concept p. 346
Marketing information system p. 364
Marketing mix p. 351
Marketing plan p. 366
Marketing research p. 363
Marketing strategy p. 351
Market segmentation p. 354
Organizational market p. 354
Patronage motive p. 363
Positioning p. 355
Primary data p. 364
Product differentiation p. 355
Psychographics p. 362
Purchasing power p. 360
Random sample p. 365
Rational motives p. 363
Sample p. 365
Secondary data p. 364
Target markets p. 351

CHECK YOUR LEARNING

Reread the following learning objectives. Each objective is followed by a few questions. Answering these questions accurately will help you retain the most important concepts discussed in this chapter. After answering each question, check your answer with the key at the end of this chapter. (*Hint:* If you have doubt regarding the correct response, consult the page whose number follows the answer.)

Circle:

A. Explain the importance of the marketing concept and how marketing benefits our daily lives.

T F — 1. The marketing concept is consumer oriented.

a b c d — 2. All of the following are benefits of marketing except: (a) innovative products; (b) lower costs; (c) immediate availability; (d) credit plans.

B. Discuss how time, place, and ownership utility are created by the marketing process.

T F — 1. Time utility is created by having the right product produced in the right place.

T F — 2. Ownership utility is created when there are no obstacles to transferring title from seller to buyer.

C. List and describe each of the eight functions of marketing.

a b c d — 1. All of the following are functions of marketing except: (a) production; (b) risk taking; (c) transportation and storage; (d) buying and selling.

T F — 2. Postpurchase service is a primary marketing function because it is part of the selling process.

D. Explain how the marketing mix is used to develop a marketing strategy.

a b c d e — 1. All of the following are part of the marketing mix except: (a) product; (b) policy; (c) distribution; (d) price; (e) promotion.

T F — 2. Each of the four elements of the marketing mix is independent of the other.

E. Explain how potential markets are selected by the use of market segmentation.

T F — 1. A market is the geographic location of buyers.

T F — 2. Market segmentation is the dividing of the total market into homogeneous groups (groups with similar characteristics).

a b c d — 3. Market segmentation is based on all of the following except: (a) geographic variables; (b) demographic variables; (c) psychographic variables; (d) sociographic variables.

T F — 4. Purchasing power varies from region to region.

a b c d — 5. All of the following are major motives for purchasing a product except: (a) emotional; (b) rational; (c) sexual; (d) patronage.

F. Discuss the four methods used to collect primary data.

a b c d — 1. Collecting data over a wide geographic area is usually achieved by using: (a) face-to-face interviews; (b) experimentation; (c) mail questionnaires; (d) telephone interviews.

a b c d — 2. Which of the following methods attempts to establish a causal relationship between two variables? (a) questionnaires; (b) telephone interviews; (c) surveys; (d) experimentation.

T F — 3. Using questionnaires is advantageous if you want the respondent to remain anonymous.

QUESTIONS FOR REVIEW AND DISCUSSION

1. Define the key terms listed at the end of the chapter.
2. Select a product and describe how marketing creates utility for it.
3. Choose a product that you are familiar with and describe the flow of that product from producer to consumer. Try to include as many marketing functions as possible in your example.
4. Explain the differences in the ways consumer products and industrial products are marketed.
5. Select another product and demonstrate market segmentation by isolating as many potential target markets for it as you can.
6. Explain why purchasing power might be higher or lower in some geographic regions.
7. Explain the relationship between Maslow's hierarchy of needs and explanations of consumer behavior.
8. Discuss how marketing research and marketing information systems provide the necessary insight for carrying out the marketing concept.
9. Develop a brief marketing plan for a product of your choice.

CONCLUDING CASE

What You Watch Does Make A Difference

General Foods Corporation spends $243 million a year on television advertising during such programs as "Family Ties" and "The Cosby Show." Overall business expenditures for commercials amount to $27 billion annually.

As a result of this huge promotional investment, corporations are demanding accurate profiles of network viewing audiences. Traditionally, the national networks have relied on the ratings provided by the A. C. Nielsen Company. Nielsen collects data from 1,700 carefully selected American households regarding the viewing habits of the occupants. Audimeters are attached to the TV sets to electronically record the viewing patterns of each household. In addition to the audimeter, Nielsen collects viewing diaries from a national sample of 2,600 homes.

Critics of the Nielsen ratings contend that cable network viewing is grossly understated in most diaries. With dozens of channel selections available, ratings analysts claim that people are less apt to remember and record their viewing decisions accurately. Analysts have further questioned the value of the audimeter since it does not record *who* is watching TV.

Ratings agencies such as A. C. Nielsen have responded by experimenting with new data-gathering devices. The "people meter" is a small keypad on which viewers punch a code to indicate their presence in front of a television. The meter keeps a computerized tally of channel selections. Each time a viewer leaves or enters the room, he is expected to punch the keypad. People meters should provide more detailed data about viewers.

A second device is the "data scan wand," a tool that helps determine the effectiveness of commercials. The wand attaches to the people meter. When families complete their shopping, they are asked to wave the wand above the universal product code on all new purchases. After the wand is reconnected to the people meter, the purchases are transmitted to a central computer and correlated with viewing patterns.

Issues for Discussion

1. In what types of demographic statistics would corporations be especially interested in regard to their viewing audience?
2. Do you foresee any problems with the people meter device? The data scan wand? Explain.
3. How will the use of home satellite systems and videocassette recorders affect the accuracy of the Nielsen ratings?

NOTES

1. American Marketing Association, *Marketing News,* March 1, 1985, p. 1.
2. "To Market, to Market," *Newsweek,* January 9, 1984, p. 70.
3. Zachary Schiller, "Doing Well by Doing Good," *Business Week,* December 5, 1988, p. 53.
4. American Marketing Association, Committee on Definitions, *Marketing Definitions: A Glossary of Marketing Terms* (Chicago: American Marketing Association, 1963), p. 16.
5. Joel Kotkin, "Selling to the New American," *Inc.,* July 1987, pp. 44–52.
6. Sam Allis, "South Leads, Northeast Lags in New Living Standard Measure," *Wall Street Journal,* November 25, 1980, p. 29.
7. Abraham H. Maslow, *Motivation and Personality* (New York: Harper & Bros., 1954).
8. American Marketing Association, Committee on Definitions, *Marketing Definitions,* p. 16.
9. Personal Communication from Leonard Berry, president, American Marketing Association, May 4, 1987.
10. Jack Honomickl, "The Ongoing Saga of Mother Baking Soda," *Advertising Age,* September 20, 1982, p. n–3.
11. Thomas Bossé and John E. Swan, "Strategic Marketing Planning by Product Managers—Room for Improvement?" *Journal of Marketing,* Summer 1983, pp. 92–95.

CHECK YOUR LEARNING ANSWER KEY

A. 1. T, *p. 346*
   2. b, *p. 349*

B. 1. F, *p. 347*
   2. T, *p. 347*

C. 1. a, *p. 350*
   2. F, *p. 350*

D. 1. b, *p. 351*
   2. F, *p. 351*

E. 1. F, *p. 353*
   2. T, *p. 354*
   3. d, *p. 356*
   4. T, *p. 360*
   5. c, *p. 363*

F. 1. c, *p. 365*
   2. d, *p. 366*
   3. T, *p. 366*

CHAPTER

13

DEVELOPING AND PRICING PRODUCTS TO SELL

LEARNING OBJECTIVES

After reading this chapter you should be able to:

1. Differentiate between consumer and industrial products and describe the strategies used to market them.
2. List and explain the six stages of product development.
3. Discuss the product life cycle in relation to market strategy planning.
4. Explain the importance of brands and trademarks.
5. Distinguish among profit-oriented, sales-oriented, and status quo pricing objectives.
6. Compare and contrast demand-based pricing, cost-based pricing, and competition-based pricing.
7. Discuss the significance and interpretation of key pricing legislation.

OUTLINE

BUSINESS PRACTICE EXAMPLE

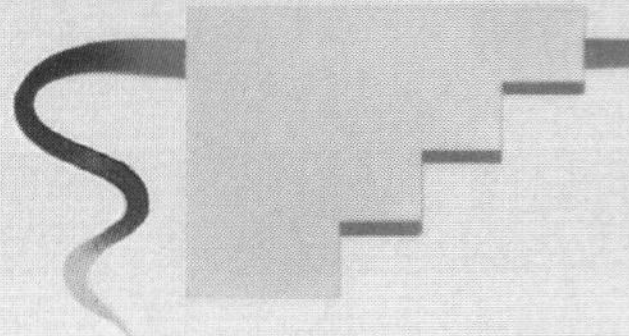

Ford's New Marketing Tool . . . Product Design

The Ford Motor Company, founded in 1903 by Henry Ford, has grown to be the world's second largest automobile manufacturer and the third largest company in America. Using his garage as his first plant, Henry Ford worked for seven years at night (in the day he worked for Detroit's Edison Illuminating Co.) developing his first automobile. Today Ford operates plants in the U.S. and in Germany, England, Canada, Spain, Brazil, Australia, Argentina, and Mexico. The Ford Motor Company is truly a multinational business.

The company has a long history of innovation in production and marketing, beginning with its founder. For example, Ford was convinced that the future of the automobile industry lay in turning out inexpensive cars for the mass market. To enable his employees to afford his cars, Ford introduced a $5 day minimum wage (double the existing minimum). With the successful introduction of the Model A and the Model T, Ford became the largest automobile maker by 1921.

Along the way, Henry Ford and his company lost touch with its consumers. During the 1930s, the company slipped to the number two spot behind General Motors. While there were occasional moments of glory, such as the introduction of the popular Mustang, there were also classic failures such as the Edsel. Many attribute these hot and cold spells to Ford's "seat-of-the pants" management style.

By 1980, the company was losing $1 billion annually while continuing to build bland and stodgy cars. Finally, Ford executives concluded that the old way of doing business was dead. The automobile industry was no longer a comfortable shared monopoly: OPEC and Toyota had seen to that. To survive, Ford would have to jump ahead of the market. In order to accomplish this goal, Ford had to find new ways to build cars.

Ford decided to hang its banner on quality. Indeed, Ford's new slogan became "Ford, Where Quality Is Job One." With this in mind, Ford designers set out to develop a superior new car that would be simple to manufacture, reliable, and easy and economical to operate and service. The result was the award-winning Taurus and its twin, the Lincoln Sable.

WHAT'S AHEAD

This chapter discusses how products are developed and priced and explains the importance of services as products. A major example of product development will be Ford Motor Company's design and development of its new line of automobiles. The chapter will also introduce many new

marketing concepts: the stages of product development, the product life cycle, and various pricing strategies.

THE DEVELOPMENT OF PRODUCTS

A *product* is any good or service that provides tangible or intangible attributes that satisfy a customer's needs and wants. Some of these attributes are brand name, package, guarantee or warranty, service agreement, and reputation.

The particular assortment of related products that a company offers is the company's **product line**. For example, Kodak produces a product line of various camera models. When a company manufactures a variety of product lines or items, its total offering is called its **product mix.** Kodak's product mix is several different product lines consisting of cameras, films, photographic development chemicals and papers, and other related photographic products.

A ***product line*** is an assortment of related products that a company sells.

The ***product mix*** is the total of different products or product lines that a company sells.

Products can be tangible, with definite physical characteristics—for example, an Oster electric mixer. Or they can be intangible—for example, a termite exterminating service. In addition, many tangible products offer intangible benefits. An expensive Brooks Brothers suit is tangible because it is physical and it may keep you warm, but it also offers intangible benefits because it makes you feel good and perhaps important. Thus, we can see that satisfaction comes from the total product.

Services

In contrast to goods, which are tangible, **services** are the intangibles that we purchase. It is possible to purchase a service that can never be touched or even defined clearly, as in the case of life insurance and inoculation against disease.

Services are the intangible activities that are purchased by customers and provide benefits and some form of satisfaction.

Like tangible goods, services provide benefits and satisfaction. Whereas goods are produced, however, services are performed. The mechanic who repairs your car, the hotelier who provides you with a comfortable room, the physician who diagnoses your illness, and the hairdresser who cuts your hair all provide services. (See Table 13.1 for ten types of service businesses.)

This hotelier offers a perishable service; if a room goes unoccupied for a night, the opportunity to rent it is lost.

Table 13.1 Types of service businesses.

1. Housing (includes rentals of hotels, motels, apartments, houses, and farms).
2. Household operations (includes the purchase of utilities, house repairs, repair of equipment, and household cleaning).
3. Personal business (includes legal, financial, accounting, and advertising).
4. Recreation (includes rental and repairs of recreation equipment, food service, entertainment activities, clubs and organizations).
5. Personal care (includes laundry, dry cleaning, and beauty care service).
6. Medical care (includes medical, dental, and nursing services; hospitalization; eye care; and health care).
7. Transportation (includes car repair, insurance, leasing, and passenger service).
8. Insurance and financial (includes personal and property insurance, tax service, and investment advice).
9. Private education (includes teaching personal skills such as driving, sewing, crafts, art, typing, and many more).
10. Communications (includes telephone systems, telegraph systems, broadcasting companies, and special business communication systems).

The market for services is increasing. Today, purchases for services total nearly 50 percent of the U.S. consumer's dollar. Services also constitute a large proportion of expenditures made by industrial buyers. For example, waste management has become a big service business. Many firms provide for the disposal of chemical and solid wastes for a growing number of companies. In international trade, expenditures on services are estimated to be in the range of $400 billion to $500 billion annually, about 25 percent of the amount of world trade in goods.

In recent years, there has been a dramatic shift in the types of services exported. The traditional services of transportation and tourism remain important, but business services such as banking, insurance, consulting, franchising, and communications have gained significantly in sales. Sales abroad in the business service sector would be even larger if legal regulations and tariff, embargo, and quota barriers were removed.

Services are different from goods in several ways. Service sales tend to be less affected by economic booms and recessions than are goods sales. The production of services tends to require more labor and less capital than the production of goods. As a result (at least in part), increases in productivity have been lower in the service sector.

Four characteristics set services apart from goods:

1. *Services are intangible*. The fact that services often cannot be seen, heard, smelled, touched, or tasted makes them hard to choose. In most cases, quality can be judged only after the purchase. Therefore, the marketer must help the purchaser imagine the benefits.
2. *Services are inseparable*. You can't separate the service from the provider. Services are produced and consumed at the same time.

3. *Services are perishable.* Services have value at the time they are purchased. They cannot be stored and used at another time. For instance, if you purchase football tickets and can't use them, you can't sell them to someone else after the game.
4. *Services are not standardized.* The quality of service purchased will be different from seller to seller and even from the same seller at different times. For example, while it is obvious that different golf courses vary, it is also possible that if you play the same course three weeks later, you may find the grass shorter, the greens faster, or even the holes changed. Similarly, airline flights are subject to delays caused by bad weather.

It is necessary to classify services in order to make it easier to develop a marketing strategy for them. There are several ways to do so. One easy way considers whether they depend on equipment or people (see Figure 13.1). *Equipment-based services* require equipment for their production or delivery. A taxicab driver, for instance, requires a car. A movie theater requires a projector. *People-based services* can be produced and delivered without the aid of equipment. Legal and educational services are an example. Within the primary categories of equipment- and people-based services, there are secondary categories based on the skill level of the people involved: unskilled, skilled, or professional. Another way of classifying services is by purchaser. This method will be discussed later in the chapter.

The development of a marketing mix for services requires the answers to many questions. These questions are similar to the ones that marketing managers for goods must ask. They include the following:

What services should be offered? The service mix to be developed must list all the services the supplier can offer. Then the supplier should make a

An international long-distance phone call is a perishable service. (AT&T)

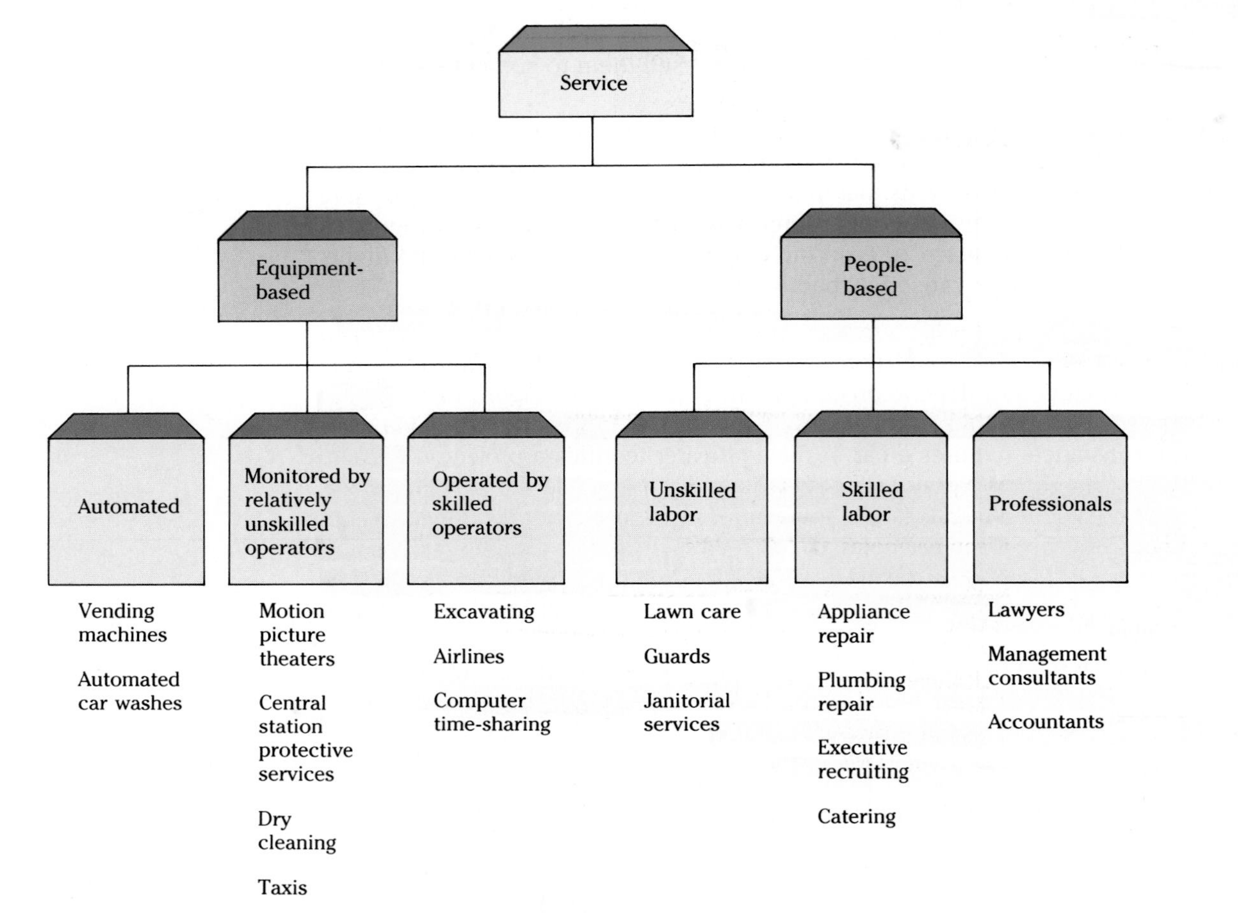

Figure 13.1 Equipment- and people-based services.

clear attempt to select the mix that satisfies its organizational goals. Sometimes this attempt requires the addition or deletion of services. For example, hospitals have recently been adding outpatient care, infant car-seat loaners, mobile CAT scanners, and birthing rooms. Services that might be deleted include the prospective-fathers' waiting room, multiple-patient wards, and free telephone and TV service.

What attributes of services should be emphasized to encourage a purchase? In order to answer this question, the marketer should understand what the consumer is buying when a service is purchased. Service attributes such as security, consistency, and completeness may be important factors in the purchase decision (see Table 13.2). Correctly identified attributes can become the foundation for a customer-oriented service ethic throughout the firm. The attributes can be advertised, promoted, and marketed to customers.

What price should be charged? The marketer should consider the following factors in establishing price: demand for service; production, marketing, and administrative costs; and competitive influences. Furthermore, if the service

Table 13.2	Examples of service attributes.
Security	Confidence in the airline pilot. Double locks on hotel room doors. Confidentiality of records by a tax preparation firm.
Consistency	TWA's on-time airline strategy. Same flavor or quality of food at each visit to a restaurant.
Attitude	Recognition of regular customers at a restaurant. Airline VIP rooms. Restaurant manager asking guests about the quality of their meals.
Completeness	American Airline's introduction of curbside check-in service. Acceptance of credit cards at a restaurant. Holiday Inn's policy of providing a swimming pool at all hotels. Airport parking facilities. Salad bar at a restaurant.
Condition	Clean restrooms at McDonald's. Decor in theme restaurants. Nonsmoking seating at Victoria Station restaurants.
Availability	Easy access of race track to public transportation. Locations of service stations. Convenient and frequent airline departures.
Timing	Serving of a meal at the "right" psychological moment in the dining experience. Fast completion of tax reports by tax preparation firms.

industry is regulated (as are utilities), the price is likely to be one of the features regulated.

How should the service be distributed and promoted? Distribution channels for services tend to be shorter than those for goods. When intermediaries do exist in the channel, they focus on stimulating and leveling demand rather than on controlling inventory, transportation, or storage. Promotional strategy may focus on increasing the tangibility of services. One technique is to highlight a particular feature of the firm, such as the employees. For example, Kroger features an employee of the week. Personal selling and contact with the customer are important parts of promotional programs for service firms. Courtesy, diplomacy, and the resolution of customer problems by employees are usually desired features. In addition, publicity plays an important role, often in the form of sponsoring a local team or event.

The Stetson hats produced in this factory are specialty goods. Buyers of this item are willing to make a special effort to purchase it.

Types of Products

Products are classified into two major categories: consumer and industrial (see chapter 12 for a discussion of consumer and organizational markets). For each, marketing managers must carefully plan for all phases of a marketing strategy. This section will examine the differences in the types of products sold in consumer versus organizational markets.

Consumer Products

Consumer products are the goods and services designed for use by the consumer.

Goods and services destined for use by the consumer are **consumer products.** These are the products with which we're all familiar—for example, food, automobiles, clothes, carpeting, furniture, lawn mowers, housecleaning services, painting services, carpet cleaning services, and appliance repair services. In examining this brief list, you probably have recognized that many of these items can also be classified as industrial goods or services, since they can be destined for use by industrial and organizational customers.

On the basis of consumer buying behavior, consumer products can be further classified into three major categories: convenience goods and services, shopping goods and services, and specialty goods and services (see Figure 13.2).

Convenience goods and services are the products that consumers purchase immediately, frequently, and with little effort.

Shopping goods and services are the products that consumers buy after taking the time to compare quality, price, style, and other competitive factors.

Specialty goods and services are products that have unique characteristics and brand identification and are in demand by buyers willing to make a special effort to purchase them.

Convenience goods and services are the products that consumers purchase immediately, frequently, and with little effort. Newspapers, flashlight batteries, razor blades, most food items, and other staples are all convenience goods. Pay telephones, tire repairs, and shoeshines are all convenience services. Often, convenience goods and services are purchased on impulse or in an emergency.

Shopping goods and services are the products that consumers buy after taking the time to compare quality, price, style, and other competitive factors. Furniture, automobiles, major appliances, clothing, carpeting, long-distance telephone service, and car repair are shopping goods. Price usually plays an important part in the selection process for shopping goods and services.

Specialty goods and services are products that have unique characteristics and brand identification and are in demand by buyers willing to make a special effort to purchase them. Antiques, high-performance sports cars, fur coats, and yachts are specialty goods. Services provided by heart surgeons and stock brokers are specialty services. Price is normally not a factor in the purchase. For example, some consumers are willing to pay much more for a Rolls Royce than they would for another luxury automobile.

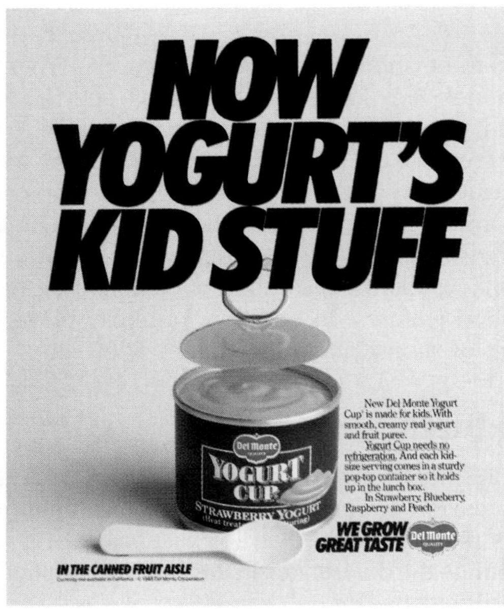

Del Monte sells consumer products, for example, canned yogurt. (Advertisement reproduced with permission of Del Monte Corporation.)

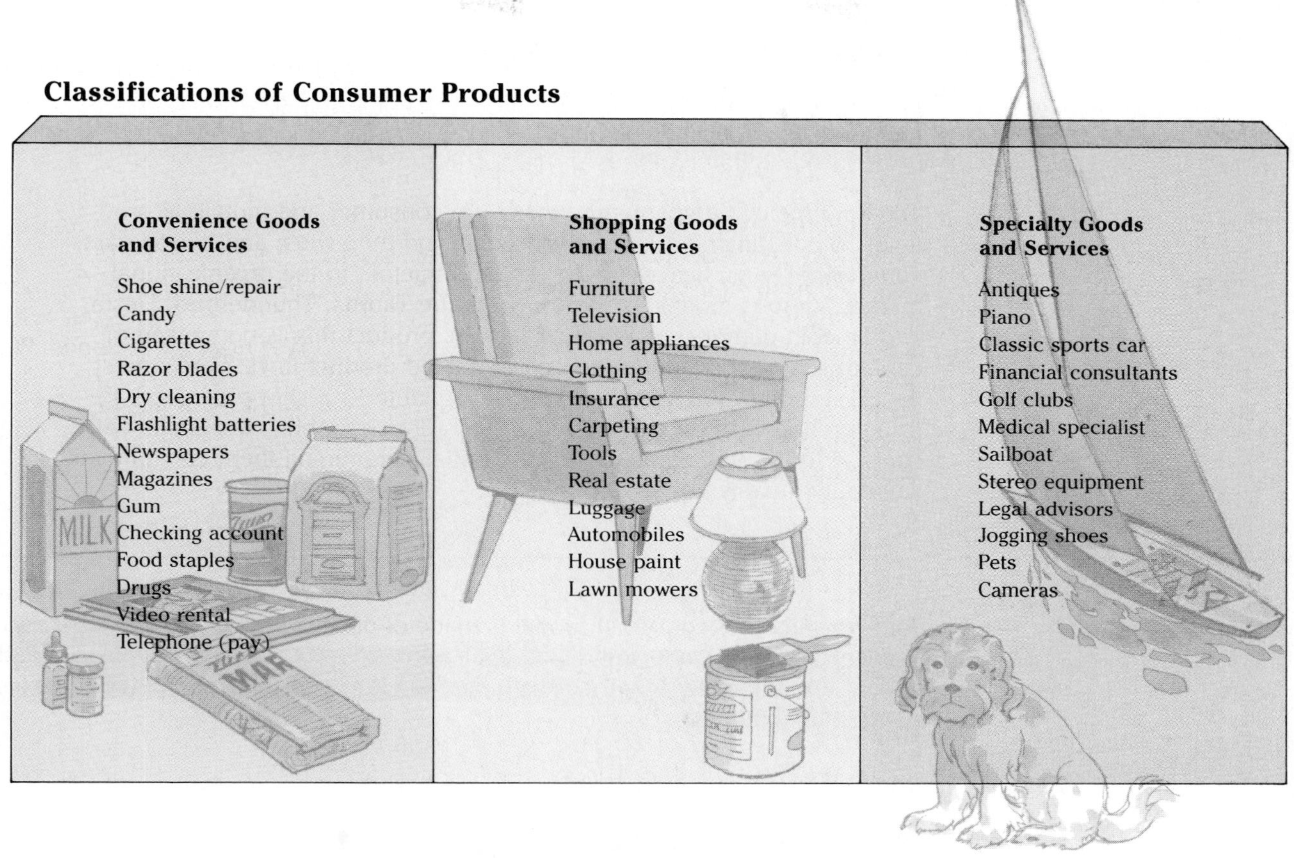

Classifications of Consumer Products
Convenience Goods and Services
Shoe shine/repair
Candy
Cigarettes
Razor blades
Dry cleaning
Flashlight batteries
Newspapers
Magazines
Gum
Checking account
Food staples
Drugs
Video rental
Telephone (pay)
MILK
Shopping Goods and Services
Furniture
Television
Home appliances
Clothing
Insurance
Carpeting
Tools
Real estate
Luggage
Automobiles
House paint
Lawn mowers
Specialty Goods and Services
Antiques
Piano
Classic sports car
Financial consultants
Golf clubs
Medical specialist
Sailboat
Stereo equipment
Legal advisors
Jogging shoes
Pets
Cameras

Figure 13.2 Classifications of consumer products. Consumer products can appear in more than one classification, depending on consumers' motives for purchase.

Industrial Products

The goods and services that are sold directly to businesses for their operational use or for use in producing other goods are **industrial products.** Industrial services include such intangible tasks as the preparation of accounting records for a small business and the delivery of packages and important papers by an express delivery service.

Industrial products are the goods and services that are sold directly to businesses for their operational use or for use in producing other goods.

The market for industrial products differs in several significant ways from the consumer market. Industrial goods buyers usually do less shopping; thus the seller often goes to the buyer. Like consumer products, industrial products can be classified according to buying behavior. Buying motives are essentially economic and are concerned with the development of sales over a long period of time.

In addition, the demand for most industrial goods is derived from the demand for consumer goods. There would be little need for plastic if there were no demand

BUSINESS PRACTICE EXAMPLE Continues

The Ford Motor Company produces both consumer and industrial products. To consumers, it sells cars, trucks, and mini-vans; and it sells cars, commercial vans, heavy-duty trucks, and tractors to the organizational market. Various models of cars such as the Taurus, Thunderbird, Fiesta, and Lincoln comprise its product line. Its product mix is composed of cars, trucks, vans, tractors, and other related product lines. Ford's most successful consumer product, the Taurus/Sable, is a shopping good. Before purchasing an automobile like the Taurus or Sable, consumers will spend a lot of time comparing automobiles, examining them carefully for suitability, quality, price, and style.

for toys and other consumer products made of plastic. In the situation of derived demand, there are also fewer potential customers for industrial markets, larger purchases, and better-informed customers that are more likely to react to changing economic conditions.

Stages of Product Development

All good products spring from new creative ideas (see Figure 13.3). In the first stage of product development, ideas often come from an analysis of the products

Nodrips.Nodrabs.
Thanks to our unique washerless construction, chances are you'll never have to worry about a Delta® faucet distracting you with drips. And thanks to our dazzling designs, you'll never have to worry about a Delta faucet being drab. You see, we won't sell you a Delta faucet unless it's beautiful. Inside and out.
©1988 Masco Corporation of Indiana

This ad for Delta faucets shows that product design is important. (© 1988 Masco Corporation of Indiana. Courtesy of Delta.)

1. Wheel	2. Bow and arrow	3. Telegraph	4. Electric light	5. Plow	6. Steam engine	7. Vaccine	8. Telephone	9. Paper	10. Flush toilet

Figure 13.3 Three hundred fifty research and development executives named the wheel as the most creatively developed idea of all time.

the company already offers or from thinking of other uses for technology it already possesses (see Figure 13.4). To copy another firm's ideas can spell lost profits. For that matter, so can introducing products that have not been fully developed

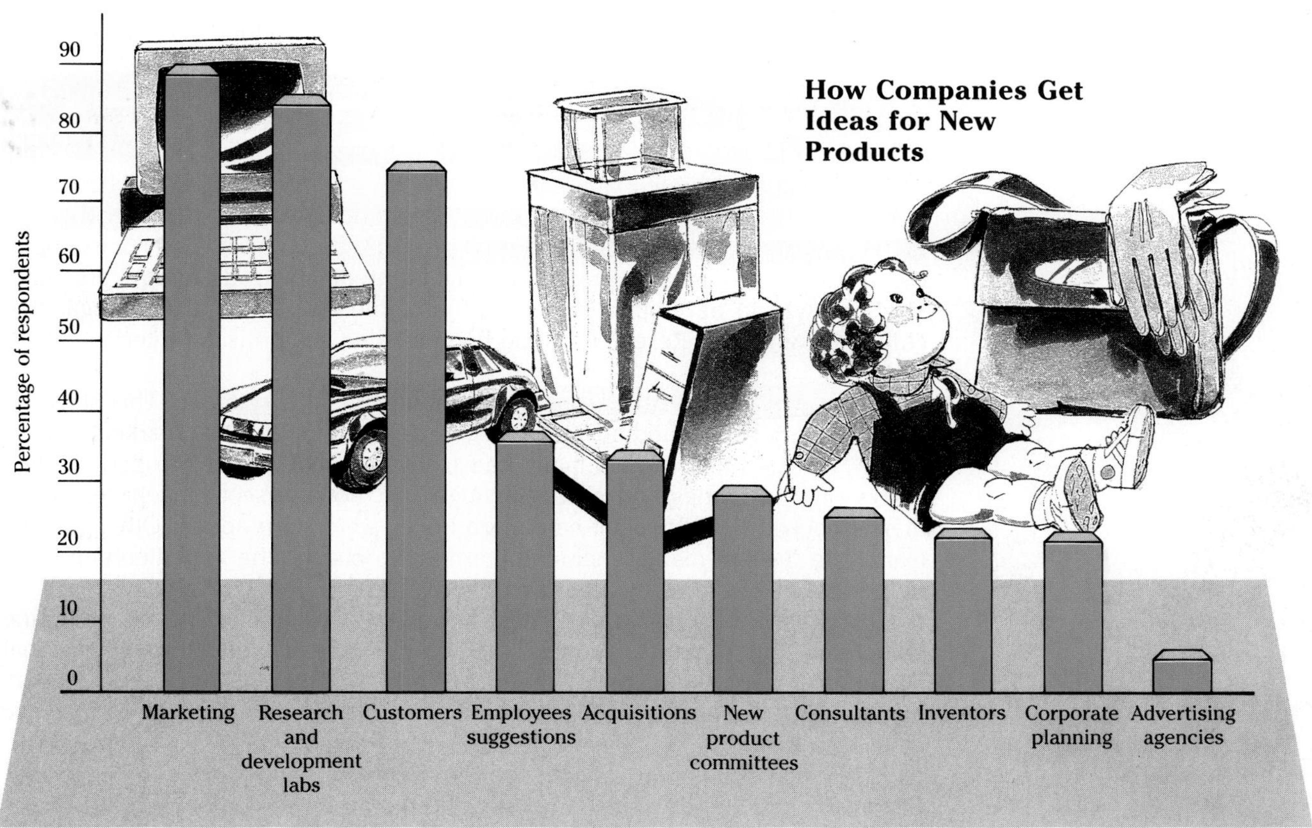

Figure 13.4 New-product ideas. According to a study of 179 companies, most get their ideas for new products from these sources.

and tested. Companies that are well managed and that root themselves in the research and development of creative new ideas and products usually succeed.

A good example is the Campbell Soup Company. From 1972 to 1982, Campbell had only two major new product successes: Chunky soups and Hungry Man dinners. However, all this changed when R. Gordon McGovern became Campbell's new leader. Wanting to generate creative new product ideas, McGovern divided Campbell's four divisions into fifty business groups. Each group was given the responsibility for marketing, manufacturing, and the profits and losses of their units. The result was an astounding 500 new products introduced in the next seven years.[1]

The next stage of product development is to screen the collection of product ideas and related thoughts that result from the first stage. Of Campbell's first 334 product ideas, only 10 became major market entries. These included Le Menu frozen dinners, Prego spaghetti sauce, Chunky New England Clam Chowder, Great Starts Breakfasts, Prego Plus, Pepperidge Farm Star Wars cookies, Pepperidge Farm Delis, and the Juice Works. Of the ten major introductions, six have been commercial successes.

One leading product development firm, Arthur D. Little, claims that of some four hundred product inventories screened in one year, only fifteen were chosen for further development. And of those fifteen, only five succeeded commercially.[2] Because much of the success of product development is due to the marketing effort, most new development is done by marketing personnel. Since this is such a high-risk area, its potential rewards are also the highest.

Once an idea is accepted for further development, research is conducted to analyze the best methods of development and to project expected costs and revenues. This stage is an ongoing one, and only the products with the best profit potential will be commercialized.

The next stage represents many hours of laboratory work to discover the best formula, design, or other necessary components for product success. For example, Campbell spent years trying to find the right ingredients for its Juice Works line. The idea was to develop a line of fruit juice blends without added sugar that children would like. Research on the line included six thousand interviews with children.

Products are next test marketed under commercial conditions. This stage includes testing names and advertising strategies. Campbell's test markets, for example, revealed that the company had made the costly error of offering Juice Works only in bottles and single-serving cans, not in aseptic packages. Juice blends packed in lightweight cardboard boxes were soon added. Other lessons learned in the test market included the need to change the ingredients in three of the flavors and to revamp the ad campaign.

Commercialization is the final step in product development. At this point, the company decides to mass-produce the item for quantity sales through regional or national distribution. Although Juice Works was delayed approximately six months, Campbell did offer it nationally when the changes created an increase in sales.

The result of Campbell's product development thrust was a revision in strategy. Campbell's product drive proved costly and did not meet company goals. Therefore, McGovern sought a balanced strategy of production cost control and a slower pace of national product introductions.

Product Life Cycle

Each product that is finally commercialized will normally pass through four stages during its life. These stages are called the **product life cycle.** Figure 13.5 illustrates the typical path of a product and the relationship of product stage to sales and profits.

The ***product life cycle*** is the four stages that a typical product passes through.

Introductory Stage During the first stage, a product is introduced to the market. At this stage, the company rarely shows a profit, because large sums of money are spent to promote the product. (It is essential that the consumer become aware of the product and accept it as a possible purchase item.) According to the Conference Board, one of every three major new products fails at this stage.[3]

Growth Stage Once a product enters the growth stage, it can begin earning substantial profits as a result of sharply increasing sales. It is during this period that competitors may copy the successful product. As competition enters the market, promotion centers on brand awareness.

Maturity Stage During the maturity stage, competition becomes much more intense as more competitors enter the market. Sales reach a peak during this period, and profits per unit may decline. Often, companies will change their marketing strategies during this stage. For example, a company may try to improve

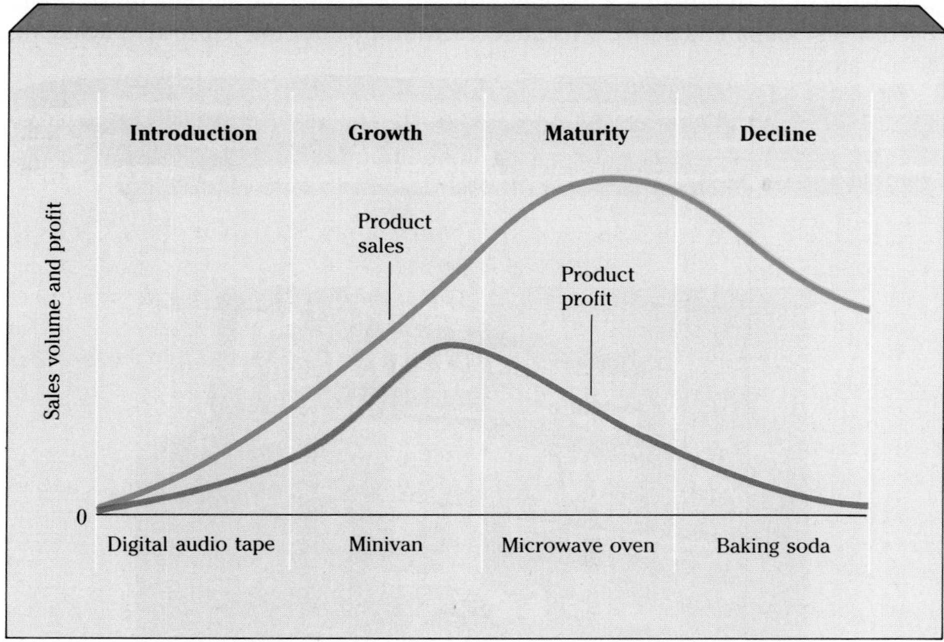

Figure 13.5
Life cycle of typical products. As a product enters the maturity stage of its life cycle, sales reach a peak, but profits can decline because intense competition forces changes in marketing strategies.

its product, drop the price, or change promotional techniques. Tough competition may force many companies to drop from the market.

Decline Stage In the decline stage, sales decline and the product attracts only the most loyal of consumers. Some products will earn a profit right to their end but will eventually be replaced by newer products. Others, however, refuse to die. For example, Jell-O has been around since 1897. Ovaltine, Pet Evaporated Milk, and Arm & Hammer baking soda are other old brands that have been saved from the graveyard. One reason these products remain profitable is that few competitors have survived and they have filled a consumer demand economically and effectively. As retailers grow more sophisticated they are learning to extract maximum profit from every inch of shelf space, and that means many products in the decline stage will be withdrawn from the shelf faster than in the past.

Importance of Brands and Trademarks

A ***brand name*** is a product's identification by use of word, letter, or group of words that can be spoken.

National brands are brand names owned by the manufacturer of a product.

One method of cutting the risk of new products is to exploit proven brand names. A **brand name** is a product's identification by use of a word, letter, or group of words that can be spoken. Consumers place tremendous value on the name, often associating product attributes with a particular brand. Brand names represent the image of a company. EverReady, Marlboro, RC Cola, Coppertone, Arrow, Taurus, Big Mac, and Pampers are all brand names. (These examples are also **national brands** because they are owned by the manufacturers.)

Since Frank Perdue proved that brand name chicken sells, there has been a growing trend to expand brand names to beef, pork, and lamb and to fresh produce. Campbell Soup Company was one of the first companies to attempt the marketing of fresh produce. Campbell's began by selling the surplus mushrooms used in its soups and sauces. Its success with mushrooms led to its packaging of tomatoes.

Good brand names are used to communicate important facts about a company and its products. The name should be short, simple, and easy to remember; easy to recognize; inoffensive; and positive. In addition, it should not include certain generic words (common usage words that describe a type of product).

Brand names and trademarks are used universally to represent the image of a product or a company. Familiar brand names are in abundance on this London street corner.

HIGHLIGHT IN BUSINESS PRACTICE

The Life Cycle of NutraSweet

The story of the development, marketing, and rise and decline of the sale of NutraSweet provides a good demonstration of the life cycle of a new product. It remains to be seen if the NutraSweet Company can reposition their product for long-term sales.

NutraSweet was discovered by chance. In 1965, James M. Schlatter, a research chemist for the drug company G.D. Searle, was working with a compound of two amino acids, phenalyanine and aspartic acid. He happened to lick his finger and discovered the compound was extremely sweet. Although neither amino acid alone is sweet, combined they provide a taste 180–200 times sweeter than sugar. Schlatter's observation led to the development of a sweetener, based on these two amino acids, called aspartame. Aspartame has some striking advantages over both sugar and saccharine. It can reduce calories by up to 95%. It tastes like sugar, and, unlike saccharine, has no aftertaste. It has also been proved to be safe for use by the general population, and it does not promote tooth decay.

It took 16 years and an investment of $70 million for G.D. Searle to complete product development and initial safety testing for aspartame. After repeated challenges, the sweetener was finally granted FDA approval in 1981. It is now used in over 1700 food products, including soft drinks, cereal, and breath mints.

A revolutionary marketing strategy, aggressively supported by NutraSweet CEO Robert Shapiro, has played a large part in the commercial success of the sweetener. The company decided to give the sweetener a brand name, NutraSweet, and a logo, and to advertise it directly to consumers. They also persuaded their customers to feature the NutraSweet logo prominently on food products. This strategy had been used with substances like Teflon and Scotchguard, but it had never been used before in the food industry. The company also engaged in a revolutionary pricing strategy, basing its price on the value NutraSweet added to a customer's products.

In the four years following its introduction on the market, sales of NutraSweet rose dramatically. In 1986 and 1987, the NutraSweet Co., now a subsidiary of Monsanto, reported sales of over $700 million. But by late 1987, profits had already begun to decline. The company insists overall consumer demand for NutraSweet products is continuing to grow; the drop in sales, they say, largely reflects a build-up in customers' inventories. However, the company does face major challenges in the next three years. Its Canadian patent expired last year, and its U.S. patent expires in 1992. In addition, the company's pricing strategy has angered some of its customers, who feel the company has exploited its monopoly. To prepare for increased competition, the company has been actively trying to improve its relations with customers.

The company believes its low production costs and strong brand name will carry it safely through its patent expirations. "Anyone can make aspartame who wants to," says Nick Rosen, NutraSweet's vice-president of international sales. "But our brand name stands for a lot more than a marketing ploy—our experience, security of supply and our knowledge of food technology."

NutraSweet has also come up with a new marketing strategy in an attempt to reposition the product and extend its life cycle. Their new strategy is to expand the role of the sweetener in non-diet products, to compete on taste rather than calories. "I feel a personal kind of pressure to do everything possible to take full advantage of the product's potential," says CEO Robert Shapiro. "Basically we represent about 1 percent of the sweetness in the world—there's a lot of sugar out there, most of it consumed in the Third World. We've got a better product than sugar."

Private brands are brand names owned by the retailer.

Generic products are products that do not carry a brand name.

A ***trademark*** is a name, word, symbol, or other device that has been registered by the owner for the purpose of identifying its product line.

Some retailers and distributors have their own brand names. These are called **private brands.** Many retail chains have private brands for a variety of product lines. For instance, Sears offers Kenmore appliances and Craftsman tools. A&P offers Ann Page canned products and Jane Parker bakery goods. The use of private brands is growing rapidly. However, the use of **generic products**—products that carry no brand name—is decreasing, as consumers place more value on brand loyalty. This is especially true with grocery items.

In order to prevent a brand name from becoming generic, the company must register it as a **trademark**—a name, word, symbol, or other device that has been registered by the owner for the purpose of identifying a product line. Trademarks are protected indefinitely by the Landham Act of 1946. Companies go to great lengths to protect their trademarks. The Coca-Cola Company seeks legal action against hundreds of companies each year. The company has never lost a trademark case.

Packaging and Labeling

According to the marketing research director of Container Corporation of America, *packaging* is a medium for communicating information about and changes in products, especially through the use of graphics.[4] In today's segmented market, packaging is becoming more and more important in influencing the purchasing decision, as the Tylenol scares of 1982 and 1986 (created by product tampering) illustrate. The 1982 scare prompted Tylenol to drastically redesign its packages in order to fight the difficult battle to regain its once-commanding market share. Finally, the company was forced to abandon the capsule in favor of tamper-proof caplets.

Other companies are also redesigning their packages to keep up with market demands. Besides protecting the product, the packaging can "improve" or even "create" a new product by reinforming, repeating, reinforcing, or specifically targeting advertising messages and images.

The *label* is an important part of the package. It provides such product information as ingredients, instructions for the use and care of the product, and the product's benefits. Much of this information is required by federal laws, including the Food, Drug, and Cosmetics Act (1938), the Fair Packaging and Labeling Act (1966), the Wool Products Labeling Act (1939), the Fur Products Labeling Act (1952), the Textile Fiber Products Identification Act (1960), and the Federal Hazardous Substances Labeling Act (1960), and more recent changes to these laws. For example, a 1985 change to the Fair Packaging and Labeling Act required sodium content be listed on packages.

PRICING THE PRODUCT

Consider a coat that sells for $100 in a store. Certainly it cost the manufacturer much less than $100 to make the coat. Consumers know, of course, that the goods they purchase cost the manufacturer much less than the retail price, and prices are therefore a constant subject of conversation and controversy.

As goods move through the channels of distribution, they are priced according to their value. (See chapter 14.) Because channel members—product distributors such as wholesalers and retailers—provide a variety of services for the manufacturer, the value of a product is increased each time a new channel member is involved. This section will examine how and why goods are priced as they are.

BUSINESS PRACTICE EXAMPLE Continues

Like all products, the Taurus/Sable brands pass through the product life cycle; the models are presently in the growth stage. Prior to the introduction stage, designers spent considerable time working on a design that would yield a quality product with form utility. To accomplish this, Ford engineers tore apart 50 comparable midsize cars and adapted 400 of their best features for the Taurus/Sable. Ford claims 80 percent of these features are met or exceeded in the Taurus/Sable models. For example, Ford spent two years studying ways to make car seats more comfortable. Using seats from twelve different cars, Ford test drove them for more than 100,000 miles. Drivers of all ages were quizzed on their likes and dislikes. In addition, Ford asked its customers, internal and external, detailed questions about what they wanted. By talking to consumers, dealers, and service people, Ford developed a list of 1401 "wants" for the new product. In all, the Taurus/Sable incorporates 700 of these ideas. Listening to the customer pays off. Ford was able to increase sales and capture market share from its rival, General Motors.

The Importance of Pricing and Its Objectives

Price, one of the four basic elements of the marketing mix, is the exchange value of a good or service. In developing a marketing strategy, it is essential that the marketing manager use specific pricing policies that coincide with the firm's overall objectives. These policies and objectives often determine the success of a good or service. Thus it is important that pricing be integrated with all product decisions.

Price is the exchange value of a good or service.

As chapter 6 pointed out, ideally objectives for both short-term and long-term periods should be specified in writing. Following are three common pricing objectives: profit-oriented objectives, sales-oriented objectives, and status quo objectives.

Profit-Oriented Objectives

For profit-oriented objectives, a company may set a target return. This target is usually expressed as a percentage of sales, and it is often based on the level of competition. For example, a company expecting little competition might set a long-term target of 10 to 20 percent after taxes.

Another profit-oriented objective is **profit maximization,** the strategy under which a company charges what the market will bear in order to increase profits.

Profit maximization is the pricing strategy under which a company charges what the market will bear in order to increase profits.

As prices rise, however, sales may drop off. This dropoff can continue until it is no longer profitable to produce the product.

Sales-Oriented Objectives

Market share is the percentage of a company's sales in relation to total industry sales.

Market share is the percentage of a company's sales in relation to total industry sales (see Figure 13.6). For example, if a tire company has a market share of 22.4 percent, this means that 22.4 percent of all tires sold in the country are sold by that company. Maintaining or increasing market share is very important to some companies. Unsatisfied with its market share for baking soda, for example, Arm & Hammer promoted new uses for the product in order to increase its share. But increased sales can lead to increased costs—for example, in promotion and selling. Therefore, by setting sales-oriented objectives, many companies increase their market share but decrease their profits. This usually occurs when a company sells a product at near cost and miscalculates the potential number of sales.

Status Quo Objectives

The object of some pricing policies is simply to maintain the status quo. Many companies seek simply to meet the competition, to stabilize prices or even to

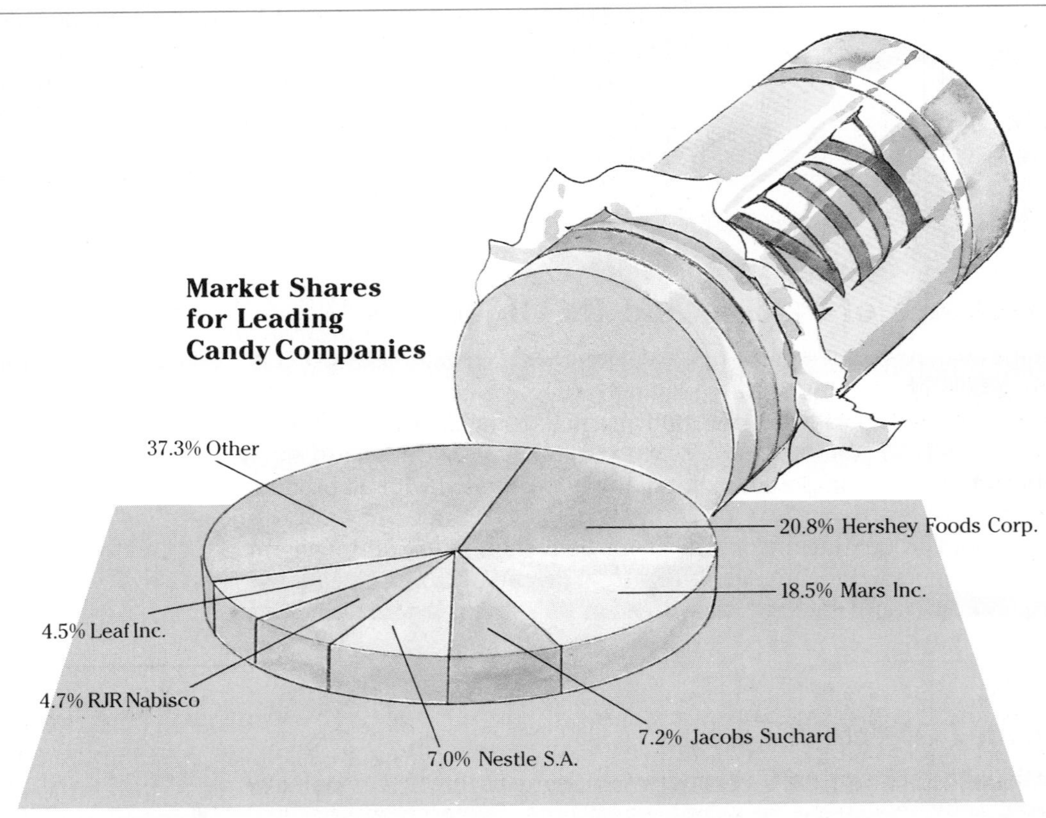

Figure 13.6 Market shares for leading candy companies.

avoid competition. For example, the owner of a small business may desire more free time and thus may not want to increase sales. The most common status quo strategy is to follow the price leader. The **price leader** is usually a leading producer or channel member that has substantial market share and therefore can set the going price for a product.

A ***price leader*** is a leading producer or channel member that has substantial market share and can therefore set the going price for a product.

For example, when IBM slashed prices on its popular PC, many producers of IBM clones, including Leading Edge, ITT, and Corona Data Systems, responded with price cuts of their own. The same happened in the famous "burger wars." Burger King dropped the price of its hamburger, and McDonalds immediately met the lower price. On the other hand, a company that stabilizes prices and avoids price competition is free to put more emphasis on the other three elements of the marketing mix.

Other Objectives

In addition to status quo objectives, social and ethical considerations may be used to set prices. It may be socially unacceptable, for example, to charge extremely high prices for health insurance premiums; and this may be factored into the pricing decision. For firms facing a crisis in operations, survival may be the immediate objective. Finally, the image a business wishes to convey can be used as a consideration in setting price. If Gucci—a maker of high-priced purses, wallets, and men's and women's clothing—sold its women's wallets for $10 instead of $180, the company's image would be altered.

Several methods of pricing are available to the marketer. The method selected should be one that will be used regularly and will be consistent with pricing objectives. The three most common methods of pricing are demand-based pricing, cost-based pricing, and competition-based pricing.

Demand-Based Pricing

Marketers selecting a *demand-based pricing method* are choosing a method based on the level of demand for a product rather than on such factors as cost, profit, and competition. Demand-based methods require an estimate of the quantities that can be sold at various prices, the elasticity of demand (sensitivity to price changes), the existence of market segments, and the buyer's ability to buy. The result is a high price when demand is strong and a low price when demand is weak.

Skimming Pricing

As products move through their life cycle, different pricing strategies are often used. The most common pricing strategy for a new product is skimming. **Skimming pricing** is a strategy in which the price of a new product is set high during the introduction stage and reduced as the product gains acceptance. Skimming has been used for videocassette recorders, calculators, home computers, and video games. Companies use this strategy to recover their development and promotional costs quickly.

Skimming pricing is a strategy in which the price of a new product is set high during the introductory stage and reduced as the product gains acceptance.

Penetration Pricing

Penetration pricing is a strategy that introduces a new product at a low price with the aim of recovering the initial investment through high sales volume.

A second pricing strategy is **penetration pricing,** in which a new product is introduced at a low cost with the aim of recovering the initial investment through high sales volume. When the airlines were deregulated, many companies initiated passenger service on new routes at highly publicized low fares. For example, New York Air introduced a weekend flight between New York and Washington, D.C., for $29. This fare was only 55 cents more than the Greyhound bus fare and was much less than the $60 fare offered by Eastern Airlines.[5] Penetration pricing may discourage competitors because it involves low profits. However, it often includes raising the price once buyers accept the product.

Price Lining

Price lining is a pricing strategy that occurs when a store offers its products at a limited number of prices.

A pricing strategy commonly found in retailing is **price lining,** which occurs when a store offers its products at a limited number of prices. A shoe store, for example, may offer all of its lowest-quality shoes at $25 a pair, its middle-quality shoes at $35 a pair, and its highest-quality shoes at $45 a pair. Price lining is best illustrated by Sears' pricing policy of "good-better-best," offering the same item in each of the quality levels. This policy is designed to make buying decisions easier and to produce faster stock turnover.

Psychological Pricing

Psychological pricing is a pricing technique designed to make the price of a product look right.

The practice of offering prices that look right to consumers is called **psychological pricing.** Two forms of this practice are odd pricing and prestige pricing.

Many retail stores use *odd pricing*—ending prices with uneven numbers. For example, stores may price items at $4.98 or $2,995. Marketers know that the emotional response of the buyer is to think of the items in terms of $4 or $2,000 rather than $5 or $3,000. The practice of odd pricing was originally used by Marshall Field to force his salespeople to open the register and make change rather than pocketing the money.

Another example of psychological pricing is *prestige pricing*—setting an artificially high price to signify prestige or quality. A good example is found at Boston Celtic Larry Bird's MVP Club restaurant. A private club, the restaurant charges corporate members a $1333.33 initial membership fee and a $33.33 monthly charge. The number 33, Bird's jersey number since high school, "looks right" to Bird's many fans. The high cost of membership adds prestige to those who want to eat with celebrities and local CEOs and their families.

Cost-Based Pricing

The pricing method based on an item's production cost or purchase price is cost-based pricing. This method stresses the supply side of the pricing problem rather than the demand side. A specified dollar amount or percentage is added to what the dealer paid to determine the price. This is one of the simplest and easiest to use pricing methods.

HIGHLIGHT IN BUSINESS PRACTICE

Air Fare Pricing Strategies

The deregulation of the airline industry in 1978 changed the way that airlines structured their prices and resulted in a decade of cheap travel for some Americans. Before deregulation, routes and prices were set by the government. With deregulation came competition-based pricing; many new airlines sprang up offering inexpensive travel. In order for the large airlines to stay competitive and entice travelers, they too were forced to offer discount tickets and extra lures such as frequent flyer programs. Many analysts believe that because of this competition, the cost of air travel has increased at only half the rate of the consumer price index and that the traveling consumer is the big winner.

Demand pricing also helps to set the fares for air travel. There will always be slack periods when demand for travel is slow. The airlines try to fill the empty seats by offering discounts to travelers able to meet such restrictions as advance sale or flying on off-peak times. The tourist can often take advantage of these low fares. The last-minute business traveler, with an inflexible schedule, is usually forced to pay the higher prices. The larger airlines use a computerized yield management system to allocate their discount tickets. They are able to pinpoint the number of seats to set aside for last-minute business travelers and discount only those seats that would otherwise go unfilled. This way a big carrier can match any discounts offered by another airline and still maximize profits.

Some analysts believe that the cost of travel may be leveling off because the number of airlines competing for business is decreasing. The smaller, more financially troubled airlines are gradually being swallowed up by the larger, stronger airlines. In 1978 there were 30 airlines in the U.S. After deregulation had been in effect for a few years, the number jumped to 200. By 1989, there were about 125 airlines, and most analysts believe that number will continue to decline. The industry's growing concentration is likely to continue to push the fares higher. The very cheap fares generated by the airline price wars of the early 1970s may be a thing of the past.

Standard Markups

The difference between the cost of an item and its selling price is the **standard markup.** The markup must cover all business expenses and a planned profit. There are two types of standard markup: markup in cost and markup in retail price.

The ***standard markup*** is the difference between the cost of an item and its selling price.

First, let us take an example of a markup based on cost. If a dealer buys a crystal dish for \$30 and sells it for \$50, the markup is \$20 and the percentage of markup is 66 percent. This is calculated as follows:

$$\begin{aligned}\text{Markup percentage} &= \frac{\text{Markup}}{\text{Cost}}\\ &= \frac{\$20}{\$30}\\ &= 66 \text{ percent}\end{aligned}$$

Markup expressed as a percentage of cost is a simple approach to pricing. However, it does not adjust for cost variations at different levels of output. If allowances are not made for the variety of costs and changes in costs, this method of markup will fail.

Markup can also be expressed as a percentage of the retail price. If a retailer pays $5.50 for a record album and sells it for $8.98, the markup is $3.48 and the markup percentage is 38.7 percent. This form of markup is the more common because it roughly equals the gross margin (gross profit before expenses and taxes are deducted), which is important to every business. It is calculated in this way:

$$\text{Markup percentage} = \frac{\text{Markup}}{\text{Selling price}} = \frac{3.48}{8.98} = 38.7 \text{ percent}$$

Stock turnover is the number of times the average inventory is sold in a given time period.

Companies can use either type of markup. In both cases, however, the key to determining markups is often **stock turnover**—the number of times the average inventory is sold in a given time period (usually annually). If turnover is high, markups can be lower. If turnover is low, markups should be higher. A related factor to consider is the type of goods sold and thus the kind of accounting procedures used.

Breakeven Analysis

Breakeven analysis is a method of evaluating possible prices for a product by considering the costs and quantities ordered.

A method of evaluating possible prices for a product by considering the costs and quantities ordered is **breakeven analysis.** A breakeven chart shows marketers the amount of sales volume needed to cover a product's variable and fixed costs. Variable costs can include utilities, advertising, supplies, and wages; fixed costs include rent, insurance, and equipment. The total of these costs is called the *breakeven point.* Beyond the breakeven point, profit will be earned. Each price will have its own breakeven chart.

Breakeven points are calculated by the following formula:

$$\text{Breakeven point (in units)} = \frac{\text{Total fixed costs}}{\text{Fixed cost contribution per unit}}$$

Assume that crystal dishes are selling for $50 each, with the variable cost at $30 per unit and total fixed costs of $35,000. The fixed cost contribution is $20 ($50 − $30). Thus:

$$\text{Breakeven point (in units)} = \frac{\$35{,}000}{20} = 1{,}750 \text{ units}$$

As the formula indicates, the manufacturer must sell 1,750 units ($50 × 1,750 = $87,500) to break even at the unit price of $50. Any sales over 1,750 units will generate a profit. Marketing personnel will usually compare several different breakeven points and then use this information in conjunction with marketing research to determine the most realistic price. (This example is illustrated in Figure 13.7.)

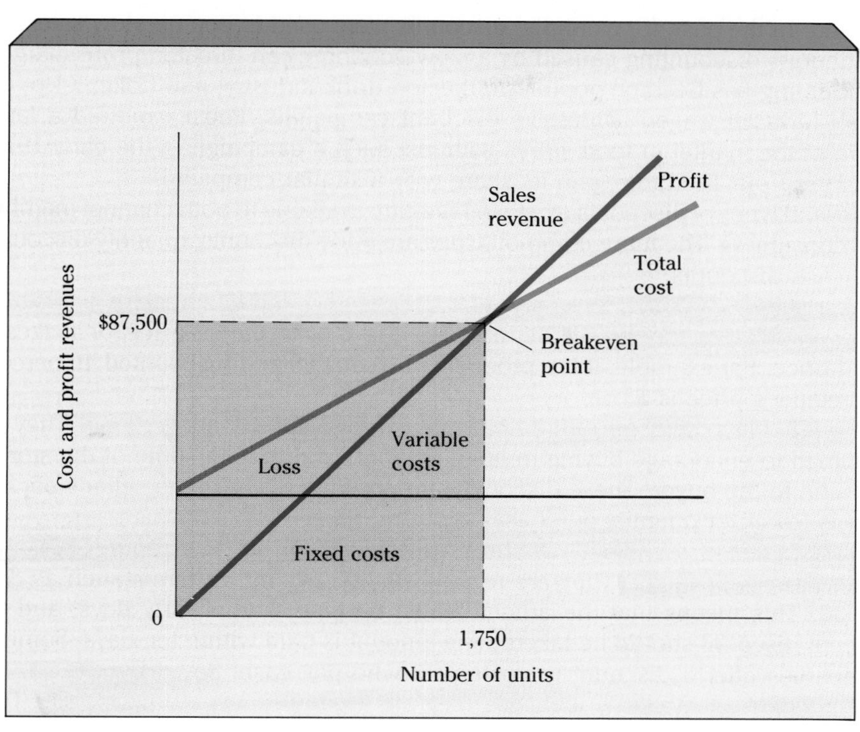

Figure 13.7
A breakeven chart showing the amount of sales volume needed to cover the variable and fixed costs for a product.

Competition-Based Pricing

Primary consideration in *competition-based pricing* is given to competitors' prices rather than supply or demand. This method is compatible with a sales-oriented pricing strategy and allows the marketer to price below, at, or above competitors' prices, depending on the image of the business or the class of products sold. For example, Wal-Mart is known as a discount merchandiser and thus tries to price its products below the price asked by competitors in the immediate area.

Leader Pricing

One type of competition-based pricing is **leader pricing,** a technique designed to offer high-demand products at or below cost in order to attract customers to a store. Items priced this way are called *loss leaders*. One Richway discount department store in Atlanta offered approximately ten loss leaders at a grand opening celebration. So many people were attracted that the local fire marshall had to be called to keep out additional customers. Loss leader prices are cut substantially, but the loss on these items is more than made up by the successful sale of a large volume of other goods to the people attracted by the loss leader.

Leader pricing is a technique designed to offer high-demand products at or below cost in order to attract customers to a store.

Discounts

A reduction in the regular price of an item is a **discount.** Discounts are made by the seller to the buyer.

A ***discount*** is a reduction in the regular price of an item.

Some marketing experts believe that promotional discounting has gotten out of hand. In the past, for example, discounts were used to pep up slow sales. But continuous discounting caused by a slow economy can threaten profit margins. Discounting has become popular in the soft drink industry, and Coke, 7-Up, and Crush have all waged aggressive discount campaigns. Pepsi captured a larger share of the market in food stores with just such a campaign in the early 1970s, and later Coke tried to regain its share with a similar campaign.

Several types of discounts exist, and they are available to both channel members and consumers. The more common types are trade discounts, quantity discounts, and cash discounts.

Trade discounts are price reductions offered to middlemen for performing various marketing functions. They are usually based on the list price, or suggested retail price. For example, if the product is listed at $5 and discounted 40 percent, the retailer's price is $3.

Quantity discounts are price reductions offered for quantity buying. They are designed to encourage buying in large amounts and to shift some of the storage function to the buyer. These discounts are possible because the seller's per unit cost is lower for quantity purchases.

Cash discounts are price reductions offered by sellers to encourage buyers to make prompt payment. They are usually stated on a bill in terms such as 3/10, net 30. This means that the amount must be paid within thirty days, and a 3 percent discount should be taken if the amount is paid within ten days. Some oil companies offer a discount to customers who pay cash. Smart buyers take advantage of cash discounts because they are a good financial opportunity. (Discounts will be discussed further in chapter 18.)

Pricing Legislation

Predatory pricing is a practice whereby a company deliberately tries to damage or destroy a competitor by cutting prices below cost.

When developing a pricing strategy, a marketing manager must consider both federal and state laws. For example, **predatory pricing,** a practice whereby a company deliberately tries to damage or destroy a competitor by cutting prices below cost, was ruled illegal by the Supreme Court in the 1960s. However, in 1987, the chairman of the Federal Trade Commission said:

> More recently, the Supreme Court has recognized that predatory pricing is rarely tried and even more rarely successful. This view has risen from the general perception that low prices enhance consumer welfare, whether or not competing firms find them distasteful.[6]

In the mid-1970s, Congress passed legislation designed to eliminate *fair trade laws.* These laws, which were passed in the 1930s, allowed manufacturers to sue retailers that did not adhere to their set retail prices. The 1970s legislation stated that manufacturers and wholesalers could no longer force retailers to sell goods at set prices. Today, suggested retail prices appear on the labels of many products—for example, books and clothing—but these prices are used strictly as guides.

The ***Robinson-Patman Act*** is a federal law forbidding certain types of price discrimination between buyers and sellers of goods of "like grade and quality," when the effect may be to decrease competition or create a monopoly.

The major federal law governing pricing policy is the **Robinson-Patman Act,** passed in 1936. This act generally forbids certain types of price discrimination between buyers and sellers of goods of "like grade and quality," when the effect may be to decrease competition or create a monopoly. Specifically, the act forbids quantity discounts unless the buyer reduces vendor costs by performing such marketing functions as advertising or storage. The discount must be offered to all buyers who perform the same functions.

BUSINESS PRACTICE EXAMPLE Continues

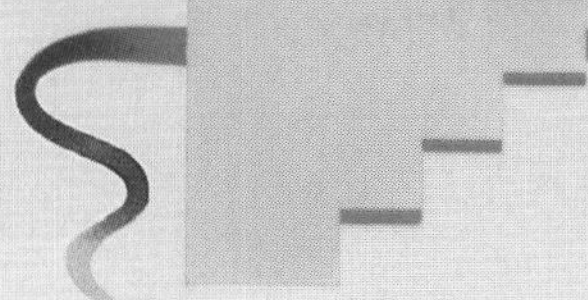

General Motors has been unable to halt or recapture recent gains made by Ford. Apparently using a profit-oriented objective, GM continued to alienate its customers by announcing further price increases despite the success of the Taurus and Sable. Experts calculate that GM made the decision based on a breakeven point that had drifted upwards to 5.3 million cars by 1986 (from 5 million in 1984).

In addition, the auto manufacturers, led by Ford, pleaded with Congress to lower the exchange rate of the dollar, which in turn would drive up the price of Japanese imports. Once the rates were lowered in 1986, the Big Three automakers, rather than keep prices down and go for an increased market share, decided to aggressively raise prices by adding previously high markup options to the base price; thus gambling that profits would likewise increase. This gamble is based on the theory that price elasticity for cars is so low that it would take an enormous and highly unlikely sales drop over a 12-month period to offset the revenue generated by the hike.

The results were mixed. In the short run the Big Three's profits climbed 25 percent in 1987, to a near-record $9.5 billion. Ford's profit in 1987 set a one-year record for the industry. In the long run, many experts feel that Ford and the other U.S. automakers should have kept prices down and gone for sales-oriented objectives rather than status quo objectives. They cite as evidence the fact that the Japanese increased their market share from 20.7 percent to 21.3 percent during that time. U.S. automakers have countered these claims by charging the Japanese were successful because they sold cars for less in the U.S. than they did in Japan (a practice called dumping).

Issues for Discussion

1. Why is product design becoming such an important marketing tool?
2. In order to build a quality product, what ingredients do you believe are necessary?
3. How is the final consumer price for automobiles determined?

Most state pricing laws identify *unfair trade acts*. These laws forbid producers and channel members from selling goods at less than their cost plus expenses. State laws and their applications vary by product. For example, New Mexico passed a law forbidding brewers to sell beer to New Mexico wholesalers at a price higher than the lowest price it charged anywhere in the country. Brewers reacted to the law in different ways. Anheuser-Busch switched from twelve-ounce containers to ten-ounce containers while keeping the same price. Its competitor, Schlitz, increased the amount of beer in its containers by an ounce. As might be expected, the Anheuser-Busch pricing strategy flopped.[7]

SUMMARY

A product is a good or service that provides tangible or intangible attributes that satisfy a customer's needs and wants. Related products may appear in a product line or a product mix.

Services provide benefits and satisfaction to customers. They are performed rather than manufactured. They differ from goods in that they are intangible, inseparable, perishable, and nonstandardized. They can be equipment-based or people-based.

A marketing mix for services should be based on the answers to a number of questions: What services should be offered? What attributes should be emphasized? What price should be charged? How should the service be distributed and promoted?

Products can be either consumer or industrial. Consumer products are goods and services destined for use by consumers. They can be divided into three categories: convenience goods and services, shopping goods and services, and specialty goods and services. Industrial products are sold directly to businesses for either operational use or use in producing other goods.

The stages in product development are (1) research and development of creative new ideas, (2) screening of the collection of product ideas, (3) analysis of development methods and projected costs and revenues, (4) discovery of the best formula or design, (5) test marketing, and (6) commercialization. The product life cycle consists of four stages: introductory, growth, maturity, and decline.

Brand names are a product's identification by use of a word, letter, or group of words that can be spoken. The two types of brand names are national brands and private brands. Generic products carry no brand name. A trademark is a name, word, symbol, or other device that has been registered by the owner to identify a product line.

Packaging communicates information about a product, usually graphically. Labels also provide information about the product, including ingredients, use and care instructions, and benefits.

Price is the exchange value of a good or service. There are three common pricing objectives: profit-oriented objectives, sales-oriented objectives, and status quo objectives. A few other objectives are social and ethical objectives, survival objectives, and image objectives.

The three most common methods of pricing are demand-based pricing, which includes skimming pricing, penetration pricing, price lining, and psychological pricing; cost-based pricing, which includes standard markups and breakeven analysis; and competition-based pricing, which includes leader pricing and discounts. The three most common types of discounts are trade discounts, quantity discounts, and cash discounts.

Legislation affecting pricing has changed over the years. Predatory pricing, for example, used to be outlawed but now seems to be accepted. Fair trade laws have been eliminated. The Robinson-Patman Act of 1936 forbids certain types of price discrimination and is still in effect. Most state pricing laws oppose unfair trade acts.

KEY TERMS

Brand name p. 386
Breakeven analysis p. 394
Consumer products p. 380
Convenience goods and services p. 380
Discount p. 395
Generic products p. 388
Industrial products p. 381
Leader pricing p. 395
Market share p. 390
National brands p. 386
Penetration pricing p. 392
Predatory pricing p. 396
Price p. 389
Price leader p. 391
Price lining p. 392
Private brands p. 388
Product life cycle p. 385
Product line p. 375
Product mix p. 375
Profit maximization p. 389
Psychological pricing p. 392
Robinson-Patman Act p. 396
Services p. 375
Shopping goods and services p. 380
Skimming pricing p. 391
Specialty goods and services p. 380
Standard markup p. 393
Stock turnover p. 394
Trademark p. 388

CHECK YOUR LEARNING

Reread the following learning objectives. Each objective is followed by a few questions. Answering these questions accurately will help you retain the most important concepts discussed in this chapter. After answering each question, check your answer with the key at the end of this chapter. (*Hint:* If you have doubt regarding the correct response, consult the page whose number follows the answer.)

Circle:

A. Differentiate between consumer and industrial products and describe the strategies used to market them.

a b c d
1. All of the following are categories of consumer products except: (a) expensive goods; (b) convenience services; (c) shopping goods; (d) specialty services.

T F
2. The demand for industrial goods is derived from the demand for consumer goods.

B. List and explain the six stages of product development.

a b c d
1. Which of the following stages best describes the process of projecting expected cost and revenues: (a) screening; (b) limited tests; (c) analysis; (d) commercialization.

T F
2. Most ideas are turned into marketable products, which are eventually commercialized.

C. Discuss the product life cycle in relation to market strategy planning.

a b c d e
1. All of the following are product life cycle stages except: (a) introduction; (b) growth; (c) maturity; (d) peak; (e) decline.

T F
2. During the maturity stage, profits will likely begin to decline.

T F
3. During the introduction stage, profits are usually nonexistent because of high production and promotion costs.

D. Explain the importance of brands and trademarks.

a b c d
1. Which of the following best describes a product such as Craftsman tools: (a) national brand; (b) individual brand; (c) private brand; (d) local brand.

T F
2. Trademarks are protected by the Landham Act of 1946.

E. Distinguish among profit-oriented, sales-oriented, and status quo pricing objectives.

T F
1. Profit maximization does not necessarily bring on higher prices.

T F
2. Companies with sales-oriented objectives often try to increase their market share.

T F
3. Following the price leader is an example of a profit-oriented objective.

F. Compare and contrast demand-based pricing, cost-based pricing, and competition-based pricing.

T F
1. The two major pricing strategies for new products are skimming and penetration.

T F
2. The standard markup is always based on the retail price.

a b c d
3. Which of the following is an example of competition-based pricing? (a) price lining; (b) breakeven analysis; (c) leader pricing; (d) odd pricing.

G. Discuss the significance and interpretation of key pricing legislation.

T F
1. Leader pricing and predatory pricing are the same.

a b c d
2. Which federal law is the primary legislation governing pricing policy? (a) Clayton Act; (b) Robinson-Patman Act; (c) Sherman Act; (d) Roosevelt-Wilson Act.

QUESTIONS FOR REVIEW AND DISCUSSION

1. Define the key terms listed at the end of the chapter.
2. Research a new product and discuss how it progressed through the stages of product development.
3. Make a list of products (minimum of five each) that are currently in each of the four product life cycle stages.
4. Explain how a company such as Coca-Cola protects its trademark.
5. Discuss the importance of packaging. Make a list of different forms of packaging found around your home, apartment, or dorm room and explain why each form of packaging is used.
6. What are some techniques used by manufacturers to increase their market share? Why is having a large market share often not enough?
7. Explain how supply and demand affect prices.
8. What noneconomic price considerations does a local retailer have to consider when pricing an item?
9. Make a list of several new products on the market and determine whether a skimming or penetration pricing strategy was used.
10. Explain why breakeven analysis is so important to the manufacturer and retailer.

CONCLUDING CASE

Should the Clayton and Robinson-Patman Acts Be Repealed?

Section 2 of the Clayton Act, written in 1914, states that it is unlawful for a seller to discriminate in price among different customers when the discrimination tends to limit competition. This law is often associated with price fixing (when competitors agree to a set price for a given item). The Robinson-Patman Act, intended to protect small businesses, was signed into law in 1936. This act was passed to encourage competition and to stop quantity discounts given by manufacturers to large chain stores.

After fifty-plus years, some experts believe it is time to repeal both acts. The reasons given are varied. However, antitrust experts cite a trend by a majority of the federal appeals courts and the Supreme Court to ease the application of the antitrust laws as a major reason to eliminate the acts. These laws in many instances have become obsolete.

A good example occurred in a 1988 Supreme Court decision. The Court, in *Business Electronics v. Sharp Corporation,* ruled that a manufacturer's decision to cut off a retailer who is selling goods at less than the suggested retail price isn't automatically illegal, unless it involves an effort to fix prices. In 1911, the Supreme Court had ruled that agreements between manufacturers and independent retailers fixing the retail price of goods were so likely to be anticompetitive that they automatically violated antitrust laws. When a violation occurred, a lawsuit needed to show only the existence of an agreement, without having to prove that it was anticompetitive or caused injury. The 1988 decision did not overrule the 1911 decision, but it did narrow it.

The practical effect of the ruling, antitrust experts say, "is to limit this antitrust standard, giving manufacturers more freedom to persuade retailers to follow suggested retail prices. This may be done in a variety of ways not directly related to price, such as awarding exclusive territories or insisting that retailers offer set service levels."

Issues for Discussion

1. What is price discrimination?
2. Discuss at least four arguments for repealing the Clayton and Robinson-Patman acts.
3. Offer at least four reasons for strictly enforcing the antitrust laws.
4. In light of 1970s legislation regarding fair trade and of recent Supreme Court rulings, how should retailers handle the suggested retail prices on merchandise?

NOTES

1. Francine Schwadel, "Burned by Mistakes, Campbell Soup Co. Is in Throes of Change," *Wall Street Journal*, August 14, 1985, p. 1.
2. Roger Rocklefs, "Success Comes Hard in Tricky Business of Creating Products," *Wall Street Journal*, August 23, 1978, p. 1.
3. "New Product Failures One in Three, Study Says," *Advertising Age*, February 4, 1980, p. 74.
4. "Research, Packaging, and Graphics: A Winning Team for Marketing Pros," *Marketing News*, February 20, 1981, p. 7.
5. "A New Air War," *Time*, September 22, 1980, p. 72.
6. Christopher Elias, "Scales Tip against Antitrust Statutes," *Insight*, June 15, 1987, p. 13.
7. Kate Pound, "Anheuser-Busch's 'Baby Beer' Flops as Brewers in New Mexico Fight a Law Meant to Cut Prices," *Wall Street Journal*, September 9, 1980, p. 48.

CHECK YOUR LEARNING ANSWER KEY

A. 1. a, *p. 380*
   2. T, *p. 381*

B. 1. c, *p. 384*
   2. F, *p. 384*

C. 1. d, *p. 385*
   2. T, *p. 385*
   3. T, *p. 385*

D. 1. c, *p. 388*
   2. T, *p. 388*

E. 1. T, *p. 389*
   2. T, *p. 390*
   3. F, *p. 391*

F. 1. T, *pp. 391–392*
   2. F, *p. 393*
   3. c, *p. 395*

G. 1. F, *pp. 395–396*
   2. b, *p. 396*

CHAPTER

14

DISTRIBUTING GOODS AND SERVICES

LEARNING OBJECTIVES

After reading this chapter you should be able to:

1. Explain the importance of selecting the proper channels of distribution and how channels should be evaluated for selection.
2. Distinguish between merchant wholesalers and agents/brokers.
3. Distinguish among different types of retail stores and discuss possible future retail trends.
4. Discuss the different degrees of target market coverage.
5. Compare and contrast consumer and industrial channels.
6. Distinguish between a traditional channel system and a vertical marketing system.
7. Discuss the factors that the physical distribution manager must consider in selecting the best materials handling techniques, storage facilities, and modes of transportation.

OUTLINE

BUSINESS PRACTICE EXAMPLE

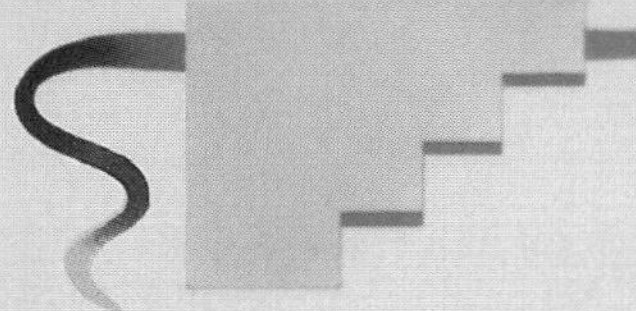

Compaq Packs a Wallop in Distribution Channels

Most people expect a story about computer-whiz entrepreneurs to read something like this: a little shop starts small and creates an irresistible new product; it succeeds because the founder has vision and faith that the public's need for a new machine will lead someone to buy it, somewhere, somehow. Who ever heard of a startup computer company worrying primarily about how to do their distribution? In fact, computer entrepreneur Rod Canion was ready to follow the usual story for his startup Gateway Technology—until a survey of the market changed his strategy. His plunge into the swirling personal computer business of the early 1980s developed into a two-part plan: The product was to be based on a standard, almost "me too" personal computer that could run nearly everybody's business software, but the channels of selling and distributing it would be completely new and aggressively built. The new computer company would be called Compaq.

The key influence in forming Canion's two-part strategy came not from hi-tech consultants but from contacts with the retailers he hoped to work with. They convinced him that any machine sold in retail outlets must offer the customer lots of serious business software, which meant the standardized software being developed for the new IBM-PC. Following this advice, Canion developed a product strategy around software compatibility. He developed equipment and software systems built to a standard allowing them to run the most-used business programs. IBM, as the dominant player in the market, would set the standard; Compaq's machine needed programs using standard operating software closely tracked on the trend-setting IBM-PC system without violating copyright. The Compaq product came out with total "IBM compatible" power to run the newly standardized business programs better than a dozen sizzling new competitors.

Compaq's takeoff succeeded beyond all expectations. Analyst Peter Drucker and others called Canion's approach "creative imitation, or entrepreneurial judo," exploiting giant-elephant IBM's strength in establishing a standard, while adroitly shadowing the elephant's moves to develop rich specialty markets. A Wall Street analyst was said to have called this "sticking your head up the behind of a fast-moving elephant—and when the elephant turns, you get your head snapped off." In fact, Compaq itself soon became a very healthy adult elephant. But at the startup, with a product basically standardized to assure them of a decent demand, the young Compaq firm was free to concentrate on its new and primary focus of innovation—which lay in distribution.

Canion's first challenge was to identify the sales channels he wanted—

the computer store retailers; then he needed to attract them to his product's software compatibility, yet offer just enough convenient extra features—compact portable size, more speed, more memory, bigger screens. These conveniences assured retailers that Compaq would not have to compete nose-to-nose with cheaper machines on price alone. The stage was set for the right selling channels to give Compaq spectacular sales growth beyond all projections in their first two years. How did they find the best ways to distribute, and how did they capture enough loyalty to come out on top?

WHAT'S AHEAD

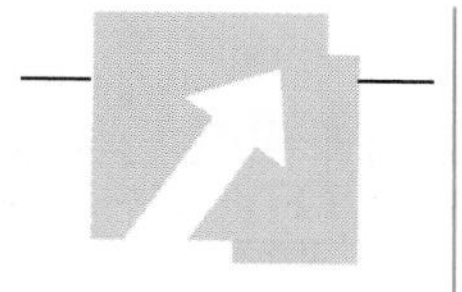

Chapter 14 describes the problems that product managers at Compaq and other companies face when they have to select the right middlemen to distribute their products. More specifically, the chapter covers both wholesalers and retailers, including the types of retail businesses and projected retail trends for the 1990s. It then goes on to the channel systems, including distribution strategies and consumer, industrial, and vertical channels. Finally, it explains the importance and types of physical distribution, including the types of carriers and the modes of transportation.

THE DISTRIBUTION MIX

As we've seen in the previous chapter, distribution is an important activity in the marketing mix. Once products are manufactured or produced, they must be distributed to buyers. Manufacturers and service producers have many choices when they are considering how to move their products to buyers. These choices are what make up the distribution mix, and they consist of the functions or services performed by middlemen in the channels of distribution.

The ***channels of distribution*** are the various routes a product can take in getting from the producer to the final buyer.

The **channels of distribution** are the various routes a product can take in getting from the producer to the final buyer. There are hundreds of possible routes, and each requires the cooperation of middlemen in the channel.

The Need for Middlemen

Middlemen are agents or merchants who specialize in performing marketing functions directly related to the purchase of products in the course of their flow from producer to consumer.

Middlemen are agents and merchants (such as wholesalers and retailers) who specialize in performing marketing functions directly related to the purchase of products in the course of their flow from producer to consumer. Middlemen reduce the number of exchange transactions needed between producer and consumer and thus increase channel efficiency. The two major categories of middlemen are wholesalers and retailers. Both perform valuable marketing functions (as discussed in chapter 12). For example, they provide sales forces, market information, credit, promotion, storage, inventory control, and transportation for the producer and consumer.

Each middleman in the channel adds value to a product by creating utility. As chapter 12 showed, there are four major types of utility: form, time, place, and ownership. All four are created by middlemen. The following examples illustrate how each type of utility can be created.

Form Utility Suppose you are building an addition to your house. If you go to the lumberyard for 2 by 4s (boards approximately 2 inches deep and 4 inches wide), you'll probably find them in varying lengths that do not exactly fit your measurements. As a special service, many lumberyards will cut lumber to your specifications, thus creating form utility.

Time Utility If you had to write a report and needed a special piece of software to produce the graphics, how could you quickly purchase the software if it was not available locally? For one thing, you could call, toll free, to one of the many retail mail-order houses that carry a full line of software. These retailers can send you the software overnight. They are creating time utility by getting you the product when you need it.

Place Utility Suppose that while you are driving on the expressway, you discover that the gas tank is just about empty. After an instant of horror, you start looking for a nearby gas station. Much to your relief, there are two of them at the next exit, and you are able to fill up. These stations are providing place utility by having gas where you need it.

Ownership Utility Many of us dream of owning a new car. Of course, the cost of new cars is higher than most of us can pay instantly. However, with the use of a loan from a car dealer, a bank, a credit union, or some other financial institution, we can purchase the car. The auto dealer and the financial institutions make the transfer of ownership possible, and thus they create ownership utility.

Wholesalers

Wholesalers are middlemen who buy and resell merchandise to retailers, commercial and industrial users, and institutions.

Merchant wholesalers are wholesalers who take legal title to merchandise and provide a variety of services.

Middlemen who buy and resell merchandise to retailers, commercial and industrial users, and institutions are **wholesalers.** Few of a wholesaler's sales are made to the ultimate consumer. Although most wholesale operations are relatively small, over 400,000 wholesale establishments generated nearly $2 trillion in sales in a recent year. As Figure 14.1 shows, their major role is to collect orders from numerous smaller retailers and to act as the retailers' buyer with manufacturers. Selling to wholesalers is much less costly for manufacturers than dealing directly with thousands of small retailers. In addition, it greatly simplifies the distribution process.

Merchant wholesalers are wholesalers who take legal title to merchandise and provide a variety of services. They can be either full-service or limited-function wholesalers, depending on the range of services they provide. *Full-service wholesalers* provide a full range of services to both the manufacturer and the retailer. Possible services include promotion and sales force support, credit plans, delivery, postpurchase service, and storage. Full-service wholesalers often handle hardware supplies, groceries, pharmaceuticals, and dry goods. *Limited-function wholesalers* do not offer the range of services provided by full-service wholesalers. Often

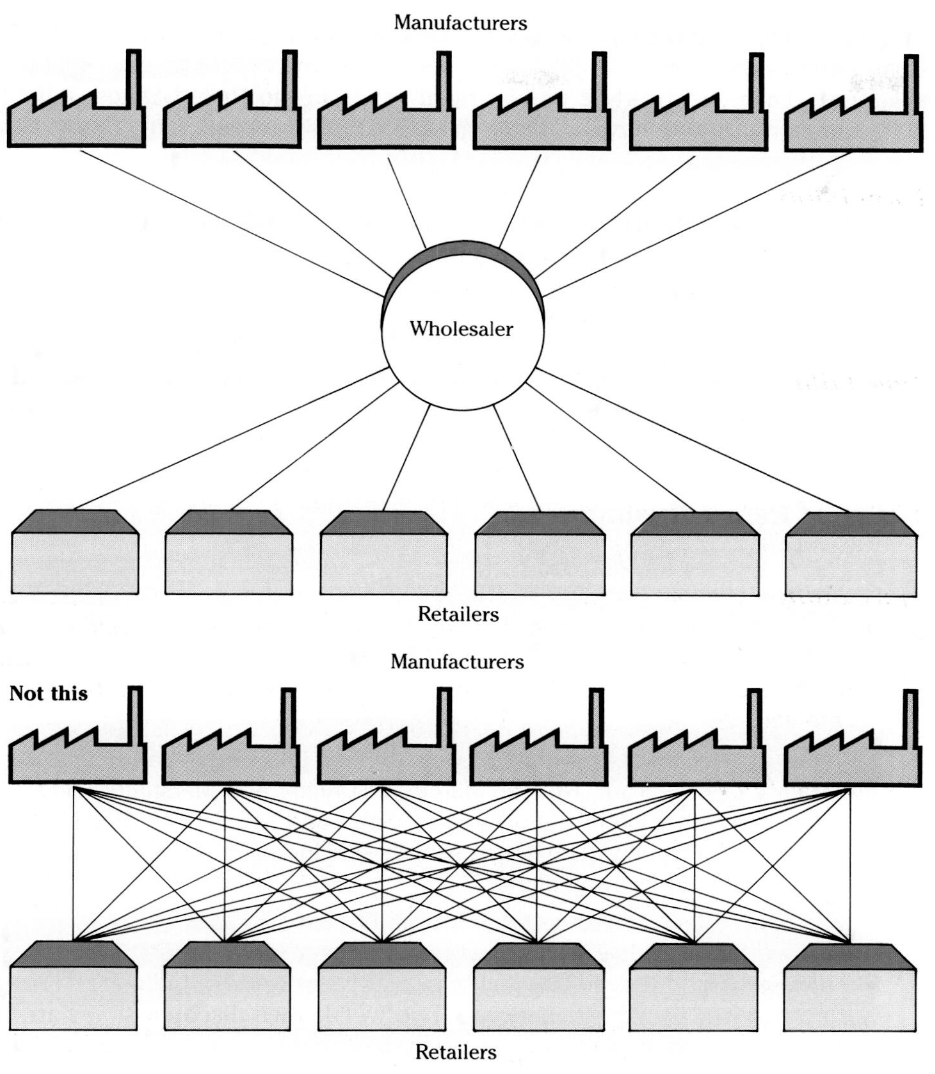

Figure 14.1
Wholesalers provide manufacturers with a simplified and less costly method of distribution to retailers.

this is because of the nature of the merchandise—for example, perishable items such as fruits and vegetables or large, bulky items such as lumber and steel. Limited-function wholesalers take orders from their customers, make arrangements with manufacturers, and have merchandise shipped directly to the customers.

Brokers (or **agents**) are wholesalers who do not take title to the goods they sell. Instead they often act as a sales force for manufacturers and are paid a percentage commission on their sales. Examples include sales agents, manufacturing representatives, real estate agents, and stockbrokers. Brokers can work for either the buyer or seller and can be involved in a wide variety of marketing functions.

Brokers (or **agents**) are wholesalers who do not take title to the goods they sell.

Retailers

Retailers are middlemen who sell directly to the consumer.

Middlemen who sell directly to the consumer are **retailers.** Most of us are familiar with retail stores because they are the final link between the producer and the consumer. There are nearly 2 million retail stores in the United States, selling both merchandise and service. Retail establishments vary from small specialty shops and supermarkets to large department and discount stores.

Chain stores are corporations that usually operate two or more retail stores in different geographical areas.

Voluntary chains are independently owned stores that band together under a common name to gain the advantages of chain stores.

Most retail stores are independently owned, but 20 percent of them are chains. **Chain stores** are corporations that usually operate two or more retail stores in different geographical areas. J. C. Penney, K mart, 7-Eleven, and Kroger are all chain stores. Chains are normally operated by centralized management, which purchases merchandise for all the stores and provides warehousing, advertising, and other marketing functions. Another form of chain is **voluntary chains**—independently owned stores that band together under a common name to gain the advantages of chain stores—for example, volume purchasing and cooperative advertising. Ace Hardware and IGA supermarkets are voluntary chains.

Types of Retail Businesses

There are several categories of retail stores. Major categories include department stores, discount houses, supermarkets, and specialty stores. Minor categories include mail-order houses, convenience stores, discount warehouse outlets, catalog showrooms, variety stores, and hypermarkets. A final category is retail service businesses.

Department stores are large retail stores that departmentalize a wide assortment of merchandise under one roof. Some well-known department stores are Macy's of New York, Nieman-Marcus of Dallas, and Marshall Field's of Chicago. Two other giants in this area are Sears and J.C. Penney. Department stores offer a full variety of customer services, including credit plans, delivery, gift wrapping, and layaway plans.

Discount houses are large retail stores that feature mass merchandising, high stock turnover, low prices, and few customer services. First introduced shortly after World War II, discount houses have grown in popularity and now are a major segment of retail stores. Two well-known discount stores are K mart, and Zayre. K mart is now the nation's second largest nonfood retailer.

Supermarkets are large retail businesses that specialize in a wide variety of food and grocery items. They operate on a low margin (profits often average less than 1 percent) and are characterized by high volume and self-service. Large supermarket chains include Kroger, Safeway, and Jewel. Safeway and Cub, among others, have introduced "super warehouse" stores that are twice the size of typical stores. Unlike "no-frill" stores, they offer a wide variety of brand name goods, fresh produce, and fresh bakery items, as well as discount prices.

Specialty stores are smaller retail stores whose product assortment is limited to one type of shopping good. Furniture stores, sporting goods shops, clothing stores, bakeries, computer stores, and camera shops are all specialty stores. Some well-known specialty stores are B. Dalton (books), Spencer Gifts (gift items), and Radio Shack (electronic products). Consumers often shop at specialty stores because their selection is good and their salespeople are knowledgeable.

BUSINESS PRACTICE EXAMPLE Continues

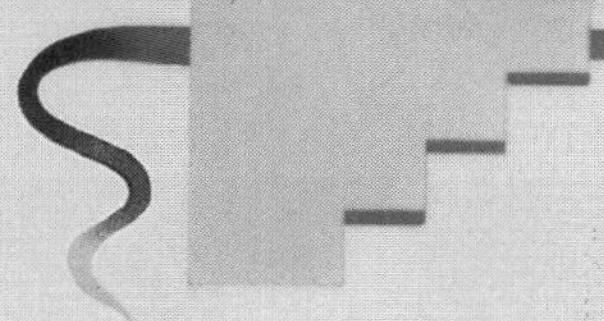

Compaq entered the market for business personal computers at a time when a formerly wide-open market was about to be dominated by the giant marketing efforts of IBM's new PC desktop business machine. The selling and retailing of personal computers, too, was about to mature. Big national chains of specialized computer stores were forming to retail an assortment of computers to a population of newly computer-literate and informed business people. From the start Compaq realized that computer store retailers were to be the key factor in rivaling IBM, and that convincing retailers to put Compaq prominently on display would be critical to success.

Compaq targeted one of the largest chains, Computerland, as an important retailer to sign up. At a three-day series of big national conventions for dealers and retailers, Compaq's co-founder William Murto trotted out a fragile prototype of the new company's machine. In one meeting he cornered a group of five dealers who were the product review committee for Computerland. The only three-hole electric outlet for running the new computer in their hotel room was for bathroom appliances; so Murto propped up the fledgling Compaq on the toilet seat while the five dealers squeezed around it for a demonstration. Fortunately, they liked the new machine and Compaq was on its way to competing successfully for shelf space.

A currently successful type of specialty store is the *category killer.* Its name comes from its marketing strategy: carry such a large amount of merchandise that you destroy the competition. Although the first category killer, Toys R Us, has been around for years, other retailers are just beginning to adopt the strategy. Among them are Tower Records and Ikea (furniture and housewares). At Sportmart, a sporting goods store in Chicago, customers can find 70 models of sleeping bags, 265 styles of socks, 12,000 pairs of shoes, and 15,000 fishing lures.[1]

Mail-order houses are retail businesses that offer a wide variety of merchandise from catalogs. Mail-order sales have skyrocketed in the past decade. The Direct Marketing Association estimates that over 7 billion catalogs are stuffed in mailboxes each year. That averages out to over eighty per family for this nearly $50 billion industry.[2] Consumers usually order merchandise by phone or by mail. Mail-order houses are uniquely positioned to appeal to working women who have little time for shopping. L. L. Bean of Freeport, Maine, and Spiegel's of Chicago are two of the better-known mail-order houses. Sears and J. C. Penney also offer mail-order services. (Table 14.1 shows which

THE
CHILDREN'S MUSEUM
TOUCH
Holiday Gift Mail-Order Catalog
see page 2 for cover story
All orders intended for holiday delivery must be received by December 1, 1988.
$2

Nonprofit organizations are also making use of mail-order retailing. (© 1989 The Children's Museum of Indianapolis.)

Table 14.1 Shopping by catalog.

When asked which items they would prefer to buy through catalogs and which items they would never buy through catalogs, these percentages of surveyed shoppers said:

Prefer to Buy		**Never Buy**	
Books, records, tapes	33%	Expensive jewelry	84%
Casual clothing	20	Expensive dresses	72
Undergarments	19	Major appliance	71
Sports equipment	16	Woman's/man's suit	71
Small kitchen appliances	16	Shoes	68

types of goods people prefer to buy by catalog and which types they prefer not to buy that way.)

Convenience stores are small retail stores that offer a limited assortment of high-priced grocery and fast-moving impulse items such as gasoline, beer, candy, and cigarettes. Today the average convenience store sells over three thousand items and has captured 8 percent of all retail food sales. Southland Corporation's 7-Eleven is the country's largest retail chain of convenience stores. In order to compete with supermarkets and with the growing number of gas stations that sell grocery items, convenience stores are cutting prices, adding products, and experimenting with delivery.[3]

Discount warehouse outlets are a European fad that is catching on in America. They are large, members-only operations that combine wholesale features with discount retailing. The Wholesale Club, Sam's Wholesale Club, and The Price Club, for example, sell a wide variety of goods to businesses and individuals for a small membership fee and about 5 percent over marked prices. The marked prices are as much as 50 percent off regular retail prices. Warehouse outlets ignore nearly every marketing principle. They do little advertising, operate on a cash-and-carry basis, offer a limited number of name brands, have poor locations and decor, and do not provide customer services such as delivery.

Catalog showrooms are large retail stores that provide an assortment of sample merchandise for display, but sell from stock in a large attached warehouse. These showrooms offer low prices and few services. Merchandise is also available by mail or phone. Service Merchandise and Best Products Company are two of the largest catalog showrooms.

Variety stores are a dying breed of retail stores that offer a wide variety of inexpensive merchandise. Many variety store chains are closing their smaller stores, yet some chains—Woolworth's, Ben Franklin, Murphy's, and Roses, for example—are still profitable, especially in smaller cities and rural areas.

Hypermarkets are superlarge retail stores that offer a variety of food and general merchandise. This form of retailing started in Europe and was introduced into the United States by chains such as Jewel Companies of Chicago, Biggs of Cincinnati, and Meijer of Grand Rapids, Michigan. Hypermarkets can be as large as 267,000 square feet (about one football field length by three lengths) and can have as many as fifty checkout lanes. The average store occupies approximately 160,000 square feet. The hypermarket's main attraction is prices that are often 15 percent below regular retail levels.

Retail service businesses are the fastest growing segment of our economy. Because there are so many types of retail services, it is difficult to categorize them. All of the following are examples: Embassy Suites (hotels and motels), BankOne (banks), Merrill, Lynch (brokerage firm), Lincoln National (insurance company), Delta (airline), Burger King (fast-food chain), Disney World (entertainment complex), Federal Express (express delivery service), Coldwell Banker (real estate agency), and H&R Block (accounting services).

Retail Trends for the 1990s

The field of retailing is always changing. Following are some retailing innovations that may be commonplace by the mid-1990s.

Theme Plazas As more and more people look for unique shopping environments, a greater number of small outdoor shopping centers that feature Old World, international, or colonial village atmosphere are appearing. These plazas usually provide unique specialty shops and restaurants. For example, in Tampa's Ybor City (Latin Quarter), an old cigar factory has been converted into a shopping and eating facility. Other plazas are Union Stations in St. Louis and Indianapolis and Jackson Brewery in New Orleans.

Downtown Malls City officials are beginning to realize that it will take much more than redevelopment and remodeling to lure shoppers back to downtown areas. Many cities are therefore building retail malls downtown. Among the cities providing such malls are Philadelphia, Boston, St. Louis, and Milwaukee. Even small cities now have downtown malls—for example, Huntington, West Virginia; Evansville, Indiana; and Duluth, Minnesota.

Specialty Shops within Department Stores Some large department stores—including Macy's and Bloomingdale's—have converted large open floors into clusters of self-contained specialty shops, each of which is designed to attract certain segments of shoppers. For example, food boutiques are gaining in popularity. They feature wine and cheese; choice beef, fish, and poultry; and other expensive foods.

Electronic Kiosks Interactive video systems are being used by several major manufacturers and retailers to sell products. For example, at Express Shop USA's *electronic kiosks,* found at airports around the nation, shoppers can insert a major credit card and choose from ninety-two items sold by twenty vendors. Purchases are shipped anywhere in the country. J. C. Penney stores and Monsanto Company have used kiosks to provide information on 2,500 carpets, and Sears has used them to help customers select and measure their draperies and to provide printed orders for salespeople.

Home Video Shopping Encouraged by the success of cable TV's Home Shopping Club and other imitators, Sears and J. C. Penney have started to use interactive cable systems to sell goods instantly to consumers who are not flocking to their stores. Some cable networks are offering the Real Estate Channel, which provides twenty-four-hour viewing of homes for sale in their area. Other retailers—for example, Home-Video Marketplace—are distributing video-tape catalogs to homes, libraries, and video clubs. After viewing the tapes, customers can order merchandise by calling a toll-free number.

In-Office Shopping As more and more women join the work force, they have less and less time to shop. In the past, some companies (Avon and Tupperware, for example) sold their goods to women in their homes. The market for this type of selling service became saturated, however; and direct sales companies were forced to seek new ways to sell their products. The most recent trend is to sell them in the office. For example, Avon, which once sold only door-to-door, now picks up 25 percent of its sales from buyers at businesses. Products for men are also finding their way into the workplace. Alfred Dunhill, a London tailoring firm, has found a lucrative market in selling to executives who shop in-office at lunch time.

Mini Discount Houses in Rural Communities National discount chains such as K mart and Wal-Mart are bringing small stores to smaller communities as the larger cities become saturated with big stores. These stores (under 40,000 square feet) are being met with head-on competition from regional chains and local stores, which could result in lower costs in rural communities.

Vending Machines An increasingly popular method of selling consumer goods is vending machines. Besides the traditional offerings of candy, soda pop, and cigarettes, vending machines in hotels and similar establishments sell magazines, razors, and other travel items. Some machines "talk" to customers, and Coca-Cola's electronic vending machine allows customers to play video games and receive discounts on multiple purchases.

Factory Outlet Malls Factory and off-price discount stores sell surplus and irregular goods (manufacturer's seconds, overruns, and off-season products) at a discount. These outlets, which include the Burlington Coat Factory, Loehmann's, T. J. Maxx, and Marshall's, run on limited budgets and offer reduced prices. A trend in some large metropolitan areas is to join several outlets together into one exclusive outlet, such as the largest outlet mall, Potomac Mills (140 stores), in Dalecity, Virginia. Factory outlet malls are especially popular in vacation areas such as Orlando, Florida; Williamsburg, Virginia; and Myrtle Beach, South Carolina. Over four hundred such malls now exist.

Some of these retail trends illustrate the idea of the wheel of retailing. Introduced by Malcom McNair in 1958, the **wheel of retailing** is the concept that retailers go through their own life cycle—entering a market as price leaders with few services and then gradually increasing prices and services as competition stiffens and the market matures.[4] For example, K mart originally entered the market offering low prices, but in 1981 the corporation began a massive facelift of store interiors

The ***wheel of retailing*** is the concept that retailers go through their own life cycle—entering a market as price leaders with few services and then gradually increasing prices and services as competition stiffens and the market matures.

THE GUERLAIN BOUTIQUE
AT
BERGDORF GOODMAN
754 FIFTH AVENUE
NEW YORK CITY 10019
(212) 753-7300
EXCLUSIVE
FRAGRANCE
SKIN CARE
MAQUILLAGE

The Guerlain boutique at Bergdorf Goodman is an example of a self-contained specialty shop within a department store. (Guerlain, Inc.)

to upgrade its image and set itself apart from other price leaders. And in 1988 it hired Martha Stewart, a noted author and caterer to the rich and royal, to be the store's "entertaining and lifestyle consultant." Stewart has appeared in K mart ads that attempt to give K mart a classier image. In other words, K mart has come almost full circle in the wheel of retailing.

Scrambled merchandising is the retailer's diversification of a product mix to increase sales volume.

These retail trends also illustrate **scrambled merchandising**—the retailer's diversification of a product mix to increase sales volume. Kroger, for example, opened many super stores featuring flowers, cameras, restaurants, alcohol, financial services, and small appliances. And Sears offers legal, optical, insurance, accounting, and dental services.

HOW DO CHANNEL SYSTEMS WORK?

Clearly, cooperation between producers and middlemen is essential. The marketing manager must therefore select the channels of distribution carefully. If the wrong channels are used, products can sit on shelves indefinitely, limited numbers of customers may be reached, local product promotion may be ignored, and postpurchase service may be nonexistent. A bad choice will prevent a product from reaching its maximum sales potential.

Thus, every marketing manager must ask the following questions before making a channel decision:

1. Who are the potential users of this product? The target market can be either consumers or industrial buyers, and they can be spread out geographically or concentrated in one large city. Generally, fewer middlemen are needed for industrial products than for consumer products.
2. What services can channel members or middlemen provide to make the producer's job easier? For example, will middlemen take title to goods, provide promotion (including sales force support), assure credit risks, offer credit plans, furnish delivery and postpurchase service to buyers, provide sufficient storage and inventory, and perform many other support activities?
3. Do the product's characteristics have a bearing on channel selection? Perishable items and large or bulky merchandise require shorter channels. Smaller goods may use longer channels or several middlemen.
4. What characteristics of the producer affect channel selection? For example, if a company is small or vulnerable to the effects of a poor economy, the marketing manager may choose to limit the number of middlemen. Or a federal tax credit for energy-saving devices could result in a tremendous increase in demand for those goods and cause the producer to increase the number of middlemen.

Target Market Coverage: Distribution Strategies

The characteristics of the product and the target market determine the intensity of market coverage. Thus various distribution strategies are used in selecting the type of wholesaler or retailer and the number of outlets needed. These strategies include exclusive, intensive, and selective distribution.[5] The strategies chosen vary from product to product and from region to region.

Exclusive distribution is the strategy of giving a wholesaler or retailer the exclusive right to sell a line of products in a specific geographic region or territory.

Exclusive distribution gives a wholesaler or retailer the exclusive right to sell a line of products in a specific geographic region or territory. This type of arrangement is often made for automobiles, boats, cleaning services, and computers, for example. Retailers selected to distribute products under exclusive arrangements often receive a great deal of promotional support from the producer but have little control over pricing.

Intensive distribution is the strategy of placing a product at as many wholesale or retail outlets as possible. This strategy is usually used for convenience goods and services such as candy, pay telephones, soft drinks, automatic teller machines, newspapers, and cigarettes. Producers usually have little control over local marketing practices.

Intensive distribution is the strategy of placing a product at as many wholesale or retail outlets as possible.

Selective distribution is the strategy of selecting a limited number of wholesalers or retailers in a geographic area to carry a product. This strategy, which lies between the other two, is the most common strategy used. It works best with shopping goods and services—for example, clothing, furniture, appliances, and sporting goods.

Selective distribution is the strategy of selecting a limited number of wholesalers or retailers in a geographic area to carry a product.

Consumer Channels

The four primary consumer channels used in distributing consumer products are manufacturer to consumer, manufacturer to retailer to consumer, manufacturer to wholesaler to retailer to consumer, and manufacturer to agent/broker to wholesaler to retailer to consumer (see Figure 14.2).

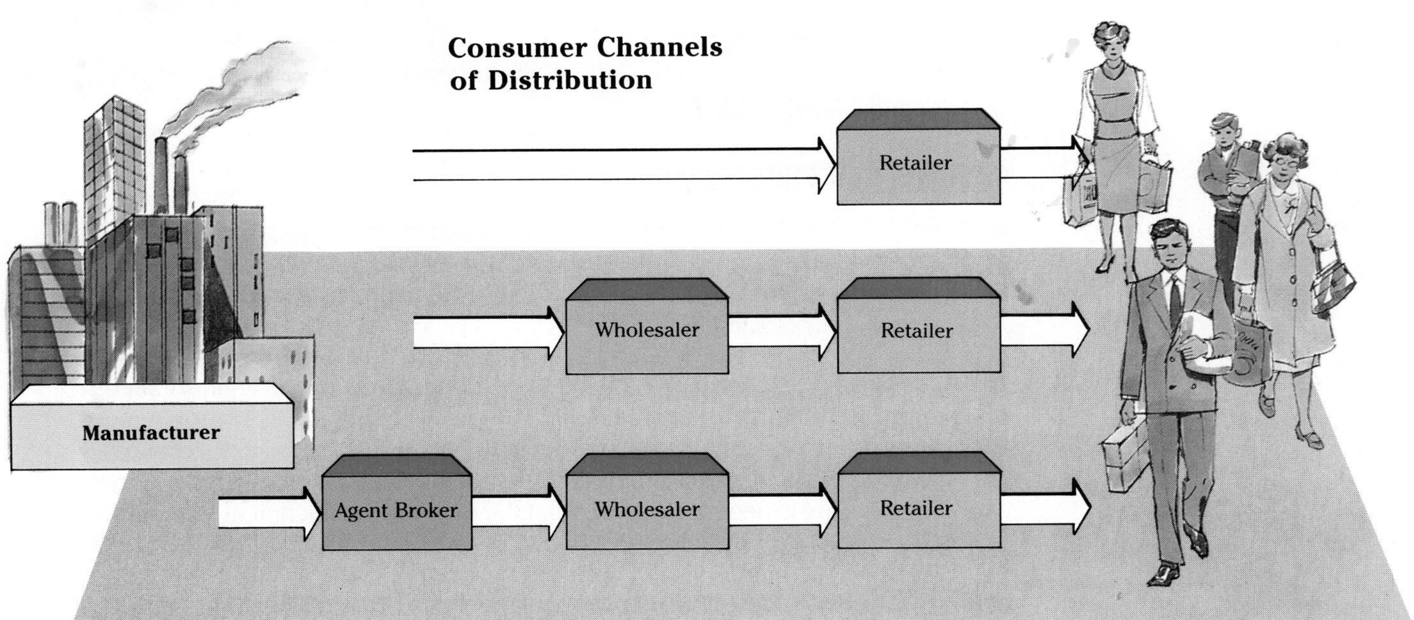

Figure 14.2 Consumer channels of distribution. Marketing managers must decide if their company will assume all marketing functions or if they should work through other channels of distribution.

Manufacturer to Consumer The most direct route, involving no middlemen, is manufacturer to consumer. This approach forces manufacturers to assume all marketing functions. For example, Burpee Seed Company sends catalogs to the target market of home gardeners. Consumers then order their seeds directly from Burpee. Burpee assumes the responsibility for the catalog and other product promotion; storage, handling, and transportation costs; and other marketing functions. Because of high marketing costs, less than 5 percent of all products are distributed through this channel. Often, artisans offer their products directly to consumers at fairs and flea markets or in small shops and galleries. Among the manufacturers that use this channel are Avon, Mary Kay Cosmetics, Columbia House Record Club, Tupperware, Electrolux, Amway, and various encyclopedia companies.

Manufacturer to Retailer to Consumer Because of large product size or quantity buying, some manufacturers sell directly to retailers, who in turn sell directly to consumers. Automobiles, furniture, tires, boats, TV equipment, and other large products often are sold through this channel. Frequently, large stores such as Macy's and chains such as K mart order their merchandise directly from manufacturers.

Manufacturer to Wholesaler to Retailer to Consumer The most commonly used channel of distribution is manufacturer to wholesaler to retailer to consumer. This channel is most often used by smaller manufacturers and in markets where there are many small retailers. Among the most suitable items are records, sporting goods, and convenience goods.

Manufacturer to Agent/Broker to Wholesaler to Retailer to Consumer The multiple wholesaler channel is used extensively for smaller products—especially in agricultural and other seasonal areas. Often, the first wholesaler is an agent who does not take title to the goods but represents the manufacturer when selling to merchant wholesalers.

Industrial Channels

The two primary channels for distributing industrial products are manufacturer to industrial user and manufacturer to wholesaler to industrial user (see Figure 14.3). Because neither involves a retailer, the channels are usually shorter than the channels for consumer goods.

Manufacturer to Industrial User The most commonly used channel for industrial products is the direct marketing approach of manufacturer to industrial user. Most machinery, equipment, and raw materials are sold through this channel. For example, NCR and Xerox sell directly to industrial users through their branch sales offices. This is necessary because of the high level of technical information required.

Manufacturer to Wholesaler to Industrial User The indirect marketing approach of manufacturer to wholesaler to industrial user is used for small accessory equipment and operating supplies. This channel is popular for office supplies and for building and construction materials.

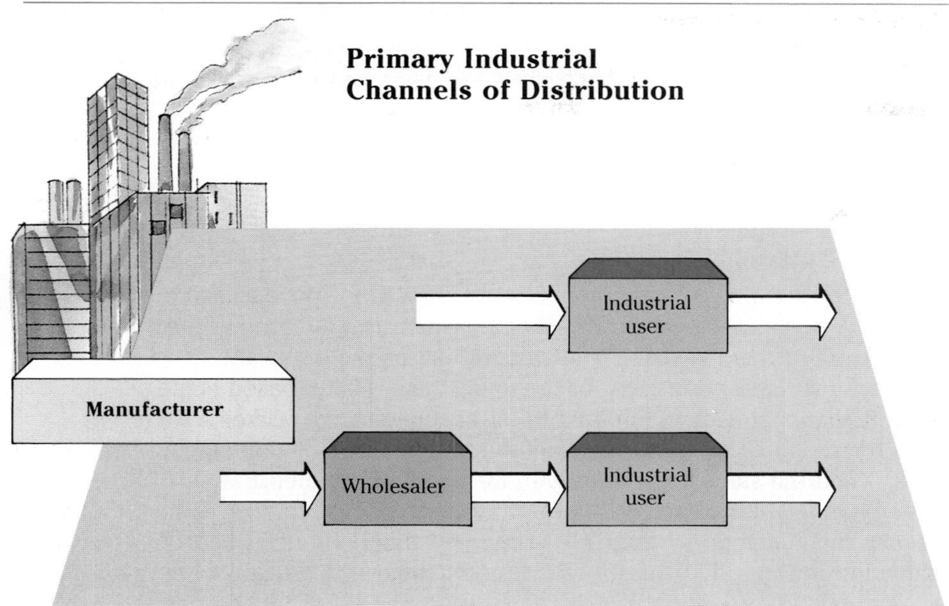

Figure 14.3
Primary industrial channels of distribution. Because industrial markets do not require retailers, their marketing channels are usually less complicated than those for consumer goods.

Vertical Channel Systems

Thus far, we have looked at the traditional marketing channels for consumer and industrial products. As more effort is placed on exchange efficiency and the addition of value to products, the number of new channel arrangements will increase. The major nontraditional channel arrangement is the **vertical marketing system (VMS)**—a centrally controlled and managed distribution system. The objective of most vertical marketing systems is to improve distribution by integrating two or more stages in the marketing channel under one company. The three most common vertical marketing systems are the corporate system, the contractual system, and the administered system.

A ***vertical marketing system (VMS)*** is a centrally controlled and managed distribution system.

In a **corporate system,** successive stages of production and distribution are combined under one owner. For example, Porter Paints manufactures and sells its paints in company-owned stores. Firestone and Goodyear both produce and then sell tires at their own retail outlets.

A ***corporate system*** is the type of vertical marketing system in which successive stages of production and distribution are combined under one owner.

Commonly used in franchising, a **contractual system** is a type of VMS in which the producer and an independent distributor integrate their efforts. Car dealerships, soft drink bottlers, fast-food restaurants, and hotels are among the many companies that use this arrangement, which is the most popular vertical marketing system.

A ***contractual system*** is a type of vertical marketing system in which the producer and an independent distributor integrate their efforts.

An **administered system** is a type of VMS that relies on the dominant channel member to plan and take responsibility for the marketing effort. The channel member could be the producer, wholesaler, or retailer, depending on the firm's size and reputation. For example, Procter & Gamble can set its own image, price range, and method of selling. Companies with this type of marketing clout can often obtain significant cooperation from other channel members.

An ***administered system*** is a type of vertical marketing system that relies on the dominant channel member to plan and take responsibility for the marketing effort.

BUSINESS PRACTICE EXAMPLE Continues

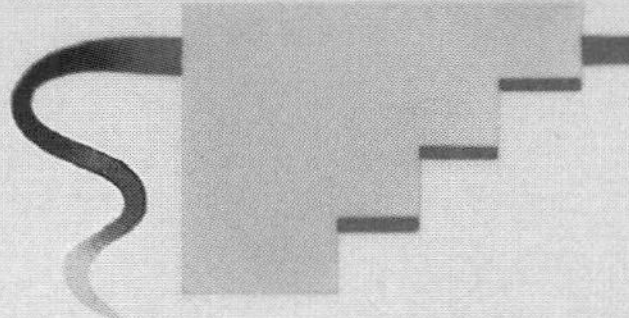

Peter Drucker called it "entrepreneurial judo" when Compaq used the IBM elephant's product weight to work in their favor. But the real judo maneuver was in the way they used IBM's traditional marketing channels to work against IBM and in favor of Compaq's new retailer-based strategy. Since IBM was already committed to big machines and worked a large sales force effectively for a manufacturer-to-consumer marketing channel, it also used the sales force to help move the new, smaller IBM-PC's in the same channels. IBM also had its PC in retail stores for small-volume sales: a manufacturer-to-retailer-to-consumer channel much like Compaq's. But the Big Blue sales force was actually working against the retailers, depriving them of any large orders of the IBM personal computers.

Compaq, on the other hand, made an exclusive commitment to retail store sales and was very generous in its support of the retailers. They hired a former IBM sales executive to give dealers support and promotional help, and most significantly, offered them a 3% higher profit margin than IBM. One analyst summed it up: "Unlike many of its competitors, including Apple and IBM, Compaq never tried to compete with retailers by selling its machines directly to large customers. Compaq offered key dealers exclusive franchises and attractive margins and won the distribution battle." These early high-margin offers cost Compaq dearly in profits, and their stock price dropped in the first two years, despite spectacular sales, to half its opening value. But eventually the investment paid off; by 1989 Compaq had gained an eightfold increase over its opening value and was considered on the way to becoming a Fortune 500 company.

PHYSICAL DISTRIBUTION

Physical distribution is the movement and handling of goods from the producer to the point of consumption.

Today, up to 30 percent of total marketing costs are for **physical distribution**—the movement and handling of goods from the producer to the point of consumption. Included in this type of distribution is materials handling and storage, inventory control, order processing, protective packaging, and transportation. All these activities, which take place in the chosen channel of distribution, must be coordinated and integrated into a total physical distribution system. The purpose of such a system is to lower overall costs and maximize customer service satisfaction (see Figure 14.4).

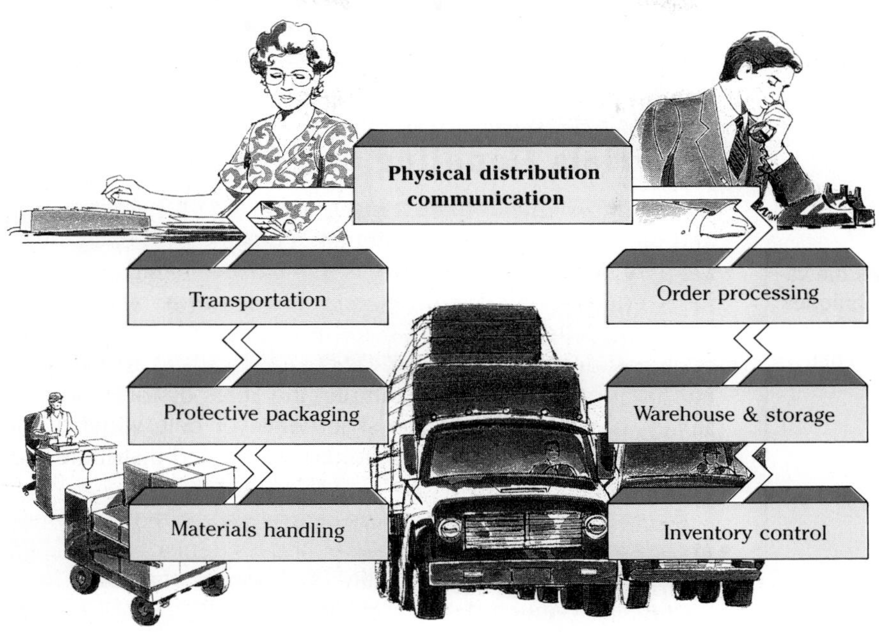

Figure 14.4
The physical distribution system includes seven major activities that help create place utility in the products we purchase.

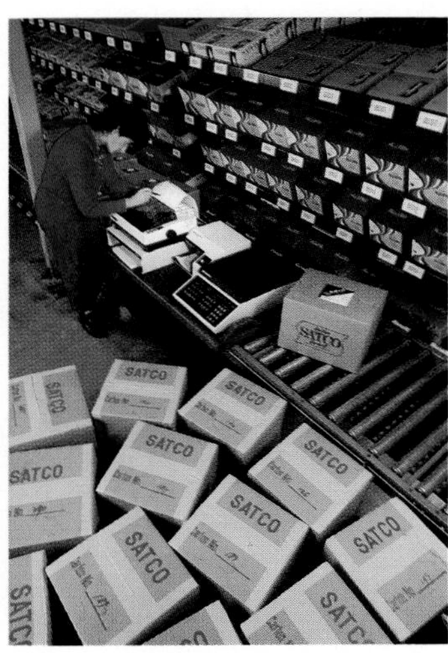

Physical distribution of a product involves many types of materials handling. Here a shipment is unloaded, stored, and reshipped to the ultimate customer. A specialized conveyor belt is used in this warehouse to facilitate the loading of cartons.

Importance of Physical Distribution

A product has little value if it stays on the assembly line, at the farm, or in any other place of production. Physical distribution is important because it creates place utility (convenient location at the time the consumer wants to buy something).

Many consumers complain about the high cost of food. Many farmers complain that they barely earn a living, and often they don't. This discrepancy is a problem of the physical distribution process. Farm commodities that remain unprocessed have no value to the consumer. Middlemen add the costs of transportation, sorting and grading, processing, handling and storage, and other physical distribution activities. Each area is labor-intensive, and many are also energy-intensive. Thus, when a loaf of bread, a package of frozen vegetables, or a pound of sirloin steak arrives at the consumer's home, the extra value added by the middlemen will result in a price far higher than what the farmer receives.

To increase product value, it is essential to choose the best channel of distribution. But that's not the whole story. Who will transport and store the goods, and who will pay for these services? Some middlemen, for example, demand a transportation allowance for using their trucks or rail cars for transportation; others may want the goods delivered to them. The number of physical distribution possibilities can be endless. To reduce costs and improve delivery efficiency, it is important that the best choices be made. Choosing who should haul, handle, and store goods is an essential task of the marketing manager or the physical distribution manager.

Materials Handling and Storage

Materials handling is the variety of specialized techniques and equipment designed for moving goods in a terminal, warehouse, or store.

Once a shipment has been transported to a customer, it must be unloaded, stored, and often reshipped to the ultimate consumer. At each step, the goods must be handled. **Materials handling** is the variety of specialized techniques and equipment designed for moving goods in a terminal, warehouse, or store. Forklifts, conveyor belts, chain-driven trollies, and cranes are examples of this type of equipment. Each piece of equipment is adapted to the type of goods being handled and the plant layout. For example, the Sears distribution center in Newark, New Jersey, has a clothes-hanger-style conveyor belt, which uses a network of belts at different ceiling heights to unload trucks and distribute the clothes throughout the center.

Many types of *storage facilities* are available for goods once they are unloaded. Among them are stockrooms, warehouses, tanks, refrigerated areas, and outdoor areas. Each serves the marketing function of physically holding goods between the time they are produced and the time they are finally used. Storage helps create time utility (the quality of having products available when the customer wants them).

A ***warehouse*** is a facility used to store goods for a relatively long period of time.

The most common type of storage facility is the **warehouse,** which is used to store goods for a relatively long period of time. This type of facility can be private (owned by the manufacturer) or public (leased). In either case, the purpose is to hold goods until they are needed by customers or until market conditions are favorable. For example, snowblowers manufactured by Toro in the summer months are warehoused until the winter months. Corn may be warehoused until farmers can get a price better than the currently offered one.

A ***distribution center*** is a type of warehouse created to speed the flow of goods and eliminate unnecessary storage.

Often, storage is not justified, because time utility is not crucial to making the sale. In such a case, **distribution centers** are used. They are a type of warehouse created to speed the flow of goods and eliminate unnecessary storage. Goods are shipped in bulk directly to the centers, where they are combined (in smaller quantities) with orders for other goods and then shipped to the customer. This system of distribution increases stock turnover and reduces cost. Sears has large distribution centers in seven cities. Its goods are shipped to the centers by rail, then transported by truck to customers.

Transportation

The largest part of the total physical distribution cost is usually transportation. Transportation costs are high and are being driven higher by the expense of fuel and by inflation. However, cost should not be the only factor in selecting a mode of transportation. For example, a *traffic manager* (the person who manages transportation in and out of production or warehouse facilities) who selects railroad transportation because it is cheap may incur additional warehouse and distribution expenses, thereby increasing the total cost. These days, so many variables are involved in transportation that a computer is essential to help the manager make wise decisions.

Several factors besides cost should be considered. Speed of delivery: How fast will it get to the user? Flexibility: Will it reach the user directly, or will other modes of transportation also be required? Bulk size of shipment: Which mode of transportation is best suited for the bulk size of the product? Speed of delivery is especially important for time-sensitive items such as perishable fruits and vegetables, cut flowers, periodicals, and livestock or pets. Bulk size is a major concern in transporting coal, sand, and grain.

Basic Types of Carriers

Carriers are classified legally as common, contract, or private carriers. **Common carriers** are transportation companies that offer regular services to the general public. They haul the vast majority of small shipments in the United States and will carry just about anything along specified routes. Common carriers include airlines, railroads, truck lines, and bus lines. In the early 1980s, the rates and competitive practices of the transportation industry were deregulated. In general, deregulation has meant more competitive rates and the creation of large multimodal (using more than one mode of transportation) companies.

Common carriers are transportation companies that offer scheduled or regular service to the public.

Contract carriers are transportation companies that offer their services for hire by independent contract. Chartered planes and buses and independent truckers are examples. Because contract carriers are subject to fewer regulations on hours drivers can work and weight of loads, price rates vary according to individual circumstances.

Contract carriers are transportation companies that offer their services for hire by independent contract.

Private carriers are companies that provide their own transportation fleets to move their products. Exxon, for example, owns huge oil supertankers and trucks to move petroleum products to the market. This form of transportation is economical for large companies, which can afford to buy and maintain their own transportation equipment.

Private carriers are companies that provide their own transportation fleets to move their products.

Modes of Transportation

Goods can be distributed in five major ways: by railroads, trucks, pipelines, ships and barges, and airways. Each offers unique advantages (see Figure 14.5).

Railroads The backbone of America's transportation system is the railroads. They offer low-cost rates for hauling heavy, bulky freight such as merchandise shipped in large quantities. Railroads have a good record of transporting goods over long distances with minimum damage.

Manufacturers that ship goods in *full carloads (CLs)* get much cheaper rates than do those that ship in *less-than-carload lots (LCLs).* Shippers of LCLs find that goods take much longer to reach markets because of increased handling.

One problem with railroad shipping is that railroads no longer service small communities. Goods destined for areas not serviced by rail must be transferred to another mode of transportation at the end of the rail line. This can cause delays in delivery.

To be competitive, railroads offer a variety of innovative services. In response to competition from trucking, for example, they introduced *piggyback service*—hauling truck trailers on rail flatcars to locations close to customers. On delivery, truck tractors haul the trailers a short distance to the customer. For many routes, this service provides the flexibility of trucking at a lower cost.

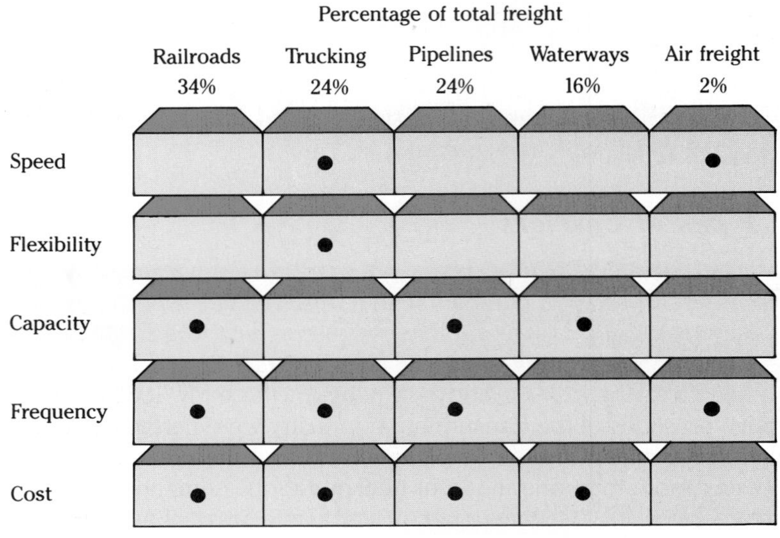

Figure 14.5
The decision to use one of the five major modes of transportation depends on the requirements of the goods being shipped.

Trucks The second largest mode of transportation and the fastest growing is trucks. They have the advantage of being able to deliver goods quickly almost anywhere there are roads. They are relatively inexpensive and indeed can deliver at costs lower than rail's LCL rates. Trucks are limited only by the weather and the size of shipments.

Although special trucks have been designed to hold liquids, perishable goods, and livestock, trucks have problems delivering heavy, bulky items. Each state has strict laws regulating the weight of loads that trucks can transport on their highways. Many people also object to trucks because they add to congestion, safety

Trucks, second only to railroads, are able to deliver goods quickly almost anywhere. Trucks are relatively inexpensive and are limited only by the weather and size of shipments.

HIGHLIGHT IN BUSINESS PRACTICE

Flying Cars to Market: A Global Assembly Line

Global manufacturing has created new ways for airlines to tailor their capabilities to the needs of industrial customers. It is rapidly becoming a way of life as many companies take advantage of the lowest-cost production methods. Henry W. Kluck, cargo manager in New York for KLM Royal Dutch Airlines, describes one typical routing: Glass for liquid crystal displays manufactured in Michigan is flown to Zurich for processing, flown to Singapore for further processing, and then flown back to the United States to be installed in watches.

In 1986, Lufthansa German Airlines joined with Italy's Alitalia in a unique air bridge to become an integral part of the assembly line for a new Cadillac model being produced by General Motors. Underbodies and components for the new Allante are manufactured and assembled in Detroit. They are loaded onto specially equipped 747 freighters and flown directly to Turin, Italy, where they are mated with the new Pininfarina-built bodies. The subassemblies are then loaded onto 747s and flown back to Detroit, where engines and transmissions are installed and final assembly work performed.

Alitalia operates one round trip each week, and Lufthansa flies two loads of subassemblies westbound weekly, giving Cadillac a production capability of more than 8,500 Allantes a year. Each air freighter holds 56 Cadillac bodies, 45 of them in two-level racks on the main deck and 11 on specially designed pallets in the two lower cargo compartments.

Lufthansa and Alitalia provide the transportation, working with freight forwarders in Romulus, Michigan and Turin. Like most of its international airline competitors, Klaus Zimmerman, general manager cargo, North and Central America for Lufthansa, says his company has a policy to offer its service through the forwarder. "We don't see them as competitors," he says. "We've had a tradition of labor-sharing between forwarders and us."

Even though inflation has slowed dramatically in the U.S. and interest rates have been at their lowest for a decade, cost reductions have become a way of life. Many companies determined that air shipment and faster delivery of goods can lead to faster payments as well as shorter, less costly supply lines. Other savings are realized because packaging costs are lower and exposure to in-transit damage is reduced when shipping by air. These savings often offset the higher cost of air shipment and are at the heart of the total cost concept. The cost for air shipping Cadillac's Allante averages between $2500 and $2800 per car.

hazards, and road damage. However, in March 1981, the Supreme Court ruled that states could not forbid hauling of double trailers. This ruling made trucks more flexible in their ability to haul large quantities of goods.

Pipelines Relative newcomers to the field of transportation are pipelines. The best-known one is the Alaskan pipeline, which transports millions of barrels of oil annually to waiting ships for transport to American and international markets. Pipelines were specifically designed to transport liquids and natural gas. Later, the increased importance of coal as an energy source led to the development of

Slurry pipelines are pipelines that carry powdered coal in liquid form to areas of major usage and to port cities for export.

slurry pipelines, which carry powdered coal in liquid form thousands of miles to areas of major usage and to port cities for export. Pipelines lack flexibility and speed, but when linked with other modes of transportation they offer continuous delivery unaffected by weather.

Ships and Barges Water was around long before rails and roads, and it would be hard to overestimate the historical importance of waterways as a mode of transportation. Today, ships and barges are the major vehicles of water transport, and together they offer the cheapest method of transportation. The 2,342-mile St. Lawrence Seaway, completed in 1959, enables 80 percent of all ships that enter the Great Lakes to serve the American industrial and agricultural heartlands. Barges are used primarily on internal waterways such as the Ohio and Mississippi rivers. Ships and barges are slow and are affected by freezing conditions.

Containerized freight is small packages transported from shipper to receiver in a larger sealed container.

The early 1970s witnessed a major advance in coastal and transoceanic shipping. Ships were redesigned to handle **containerized freight**—small packages transported from shipper to receiver in a larger sealed container. These containers enable ships and barges to link more efficiently with trucks and railroads. Ships that link with trucks provide what is called *fishyback service.* Those that link with railroads are known as *seatrains.* Containerized freight cuts down on damage and pilferage of goods—both major disadvantages of water transportation. In addition, containerized ships can stack this freight on deck, which increases the load capacity.

Airways The global economy would not be possible on a massive scale if modern jetliners did not exist. The airways offer a fast but expensive means of transportation. Air freight accounts for less than 2 percent of all goods shipped. But with the use of wide-body planes and increased exporting (35 percent of the value of international commerce moves by air), the tonnage is slowly growing. Most freight is carried by passenger airlines. The rest is carried by all-cargo airlines, such as Flying Tiger, Seaboard, World Airlines, and Airlift International. The passenger and all-cargo airlines, however, are being challenged by such companies as Federal Express, UPS, and Airborne Express, which specialize in overnight delivery of small packages.

BUSINESS PRACTICE EXAMPLE Continues

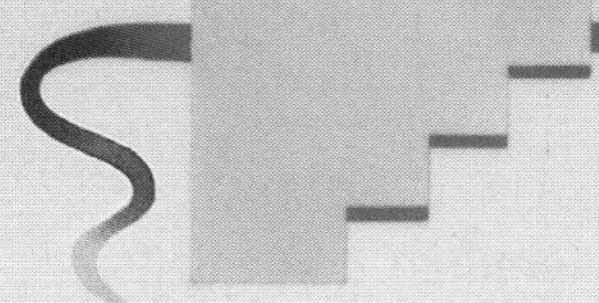

By the end of the 1980s, Compaq was a large company, with strong dealership alliances that brought its increasingly sophisticated machines to full rivalry with IBM and Digital. No longer bearing the image of IBM-imitator, Compaq was big enough to act as industry standard-setter for a new generation of microcomputer machine and software systems called Industry Standard Architecture, or ISA. As Compaq Vice President Gary Stimac put it, "Whoever delivers the largest quantity of machines to the marketplace and whoever the customers vote for with their dollars will set the standard. Compaq is in the position to be the leader and set that standard."

The success of Compaq remained strongly based on communicating with retailers and dealers, as well as with suppliers of software and equipment. Stimac observed, "Very few people have the strong relationships with major players that we have." In the view of a Dallas-based chain-store dealer, "Compaq's success isn't from the latest technology or a lot of razzle-dazzle, but from coming out with what dealers want."

By the late 1980s, Compaq was beginning to deal with the complex problems of distribution and sales abroad. According to Canion in a CNN Business News interview, "We have subsidiaries in five countries in Europe and we'll be expanding . . . our sales in the European market. . . . We're also expanding our manufacturing facilities for the first time overseas with a plant in Scotland that will build most of our PC line and support the European market."

Issues for Discussion

1. How did tiny Compaq manage to put itself on an almost equal footing with IBM in the product and pricing arenas? Did this leave Compaq free to do something different in distribution and placement?
2. In what ways did retail dealers get more from Compaq's exclusively retailer channel systems, as compared with IBM's combination of direct sales plus retailer distribution?
3. Compaq is launching into new markets and distribution channels in Europe. What will they need to do, in order to duplicate their successful strategy in European retailing channels?

SUMMARY

Once a product has been manufactured, it must be distributed. The channels of distribution are the routes it can take in getting from the producer to the final buyer.

Essential to this process are the middlemen—the agents and merchants who perform marketing functions related to the purchase of products in the course of their flow from producer to consumer. Each middleman creates form utility, time utility, place utility, or ownership utility.

Wholesalers are middlemen who buy and resell merchandise. They include merchant wholesalers, who take title to goods and can be either full-service or limited-function wholesalers. They also include brokers (or agents), who do not take title to goods.

Retailers are middlemen who sell directly to the consumer. Many retail stores are chain stores, and some are voluntary chains. There are many types of retail businesses, including department stores, discount houses, supermarkets, specialty stores (a particular type of which is category killers), mail-order houses, convenience stores, discount warehouse outlets, variety stores, hypermarkets, and retail service businesses.

Among the retail trends for the 1990s are theme plazas,

downtown malls, specialty shops within department stores, catalog showrooms, electronic kiosks, home video shopping, in-office shopping, mini discount houses in rural communities, vending machines, and factory outlet malls. Some of these trends illustrate the wheel of retailing, the concept that retailers go through a life cycle. And some illustrate scrambled merchandising—diversification of the product mix to increase sales volume.

Cooperation between producers and middlemen is essential if channel systems are to work. A manager who is selecting a marketing channel should ask who the potential users of the product are, what services the channel members or middlemen provide, whether the product's characteristics affect the selection, and which characteristics of the producer affect the selection.

Three major distribution strategies are used: exclusive, intensive, and selective.

The four primary consumer channels are manufacturer to consumer, manufacturer to retailer to consumer, manufacturer to wholesaler to retailer to consumer, and manufacturer to agent/broker to wholesaler to retailer to consumer. The two primary industrial channels are manufacturer to industrial user and manufacturer to wholesaler to industrial user.

Another type of channel arrangement is a vertical marketing system (VMS), which is used for both consumer and industrial products. The three most common systems of this sort are the corporate system, the contractual system, and the administered system.

Physical distribution is the movement and handling of goods from the producer to the point of consumption. It includes materials handling and storage, inventory control, order processing, protective packaging, and transportation. The two basic types of carriers are contract carriers and private carriers. The modes of transportation are railroads, trucks, pipelines, ships and barges, and airways.

KEY TERMS

Administered system p. 417
Brokers (or agents) p. 407
Chain stores p. 408
Channels of distribution p. 405
Common carriers p. 421
Containerized freight p. 424
Contract carriers p. 421
Contractual system p. 417
Corporate system p. 417
Distribution center p. 420
Exclusive distribution p. 414
Intensive distribution p. 415
Materials handling p. 420
Merchant wholesalers p. 406
Middlemen p. 405
Physical distribution p. 418
Private carriers p. 421
Retailers p. 408
Scrambled merchandising p. 414
Selective distribution p. 415
Slurry pipelines p. 424
Vertical marketing system (VMS) p. 417
Voluntary chains p. 408
Warehouse p. 420
Wheel of retailing p. 413
Wholesalers p. 406

CHECK YOUR LEARNING

Reread the following learning objectives. Each objective is followed by a few questions. Answering these questions accurately will help you retain the most important concepts discussed in this chapter. After answering each question, check your answer with the key at the end of this chapter. (*Hint:* If you have doubt regarding the correct response, consult the page whose number follows the answer.)

Circle:

A. Explain the importance of selecting the proper channels of distribution and how channels should be evaluated for selection.

T F — 1. Among other things, improper selection of channels can result in poor local product promotion and nonexistent customer postpurchase service.

a b c d — 2. When selecting channels, marketing managers must evaluate: (a) potential users; (b) middlemen support; (c) product characteristics; (d) all of the above.

B. Distinguish between merchant wholesalers and agents/brokers.

T F 1. Agents/brokers are wholesalers who take title to the goods they sell.

a b c d 2. Merchant wholesalers can be: (a) agents; (b) limited-function; (c) full-function; (d) b and c.

C. Distinguish among different types of retail stores and discuss possible future retail trends.

T F 1. Voluntary chains are independently owned retail stores banded together under a common name to gain chain store advantages.

T F 2. Supermarkets operate on an average profit margin of 5 percent.

T F 3. Zayre is the largest discount house chain.

T F 4. Mail-order houses are the fastest growing retail industry, whereas variety stores are decreasing in numbers.

D. Compare and contrast consumer and industrial channels.

T F 1. There are four primary consumer channels.

T F 2. The most common consumer channel is manufacturer to wholesaler to retailer to consumer.

T F 3. Products are marketed the same way in consumer channels as in industrial channels.

E. Discuss the different degrees of target market coverage.

a b c d 1. All of the following are distribution strategies except: (a) mass; (b) intensive; (c) exclusive; (d) selective.

a b c d 2. Products such as cigarettes, candy, and soft drinks should be sold using which type of distribution strategy: (a) mass; (b) intensive; (c) exclusive; (d) selective.

F. Distinguish between a traditional channel system and a vertical marketing system.

T F 1. Most traditional marketing systems are centrally planned and controlled.

a b c d 2. Which of the following vertical marketing systems is commonly used in franchising? (a) corporate; (b) managed; (c) administered; (d) contractual.

G. Discuss the factors that the physical distribution manager must consider in selecting the best materials handling techniques, storage facilities, and modes of transportation.

a b c d 1. All of the following are types of carriers except: (a) private; (b) public; (c) common; (d) contract.

a b c d 2. All of the following modes of transportation offer a frequency advantage except: (a) waterways; (b) railroads; (c) trucks; (d) airways.

a b c d 3. Storage is provided for goods in all of the following except: (a) tanks; (b) warehouses; (c) outdoors; (d) distribution centers.

QUESTIONS FOR REVIEW AND DISCUSSION

1. Define the key terms listed at the end of the chapter.
2. Why is it important that product managers select the best channels for product distribution? What would be the best possible channels for a set of golf clubs? A minicomputer?
3. Explain the difference between merchant wholesalers and agents/brokers. Give some examples of each in your community.
4. Interview a retail store manager from each of three categories mentioned in the text, and ask each of the managers to make some predictions about retail trends.

5. What types of retail trends have you noticed in your community or in a nearby large city? Explain.
6. Make a list of products commonly sold in each distribution strategy category.
7. Make a list of marketing functions that can be performed by consumer and industrial channel members.
8. Explain the advantages and disadvantages of using a vertical marketing system.
9. Select the best materials handling techniques, storage facilities, and mode of transportation for each of the following: tomatoes from Florida for shipment to New York, a yacht from California for shipment to Missouri, and coal for shipment from St. Louis to New Orleans.

CONCLUDING CASE

Italy's Benetton Sells Shirts to America

From a small town near Venice, Italy, Luciano Benetton and his three siblings started a fashion empire in 1965 that extends around the globe. Today there are over 4,500 Benetton stores worldwide. Approximately 1,000 of them are in the United States, Canada, and the Caribbean. The U.S. stores were started in 1980 and now account for 15 percent of the company's $1 billion in annual sales. Profits on worldwide sales in 1987 were reported to be $108 million.

In order to achieve fast growth, Benetton's relies mainly on independent licensees to sell its merchandise. (The company owns only a few stores.) Benetton's licensees pay no fees or royalties. Instead, they agree to sell only Benetton-made goods through one of several standard store formats. Startup costs can top $200,000, and a store can earn a nice profit if sales exceed $200,000 a year. Licensees are selected by one of Benetton's fourteen U.S. agents. The company representatives show new collections to store owners every six months and earn a 4 percent commission on orders placed.

By targeting their customers by age and income, Benetton can respond quickly to changing trends, plugging in knocked-off designer looks and pumping them for all they're worth. For example, a Benetton factory in Rocky Mount, North Carolina, produces 20 percent of the company's U.S. merchandise. Sweaters are made there in gray wool and are dyed to match the colors in demand each season. If mauve is hot in Chicago and Boston, then mauve is what the stores will stock.

Unfortunately, success is not without its problems. Several Benetton licensees have sued the company because the chain has located stores too close to one another. For example, it is not uncommon to find competing Benetton stores right across the street from one another. Benetton clusters stores on the theory that the more there are, the larger the market they create. Despite licensees' claims that Benetton agents do not support store owners and are greedy, the credit loss rate for the company is said to be less than 1 percent.

Realizing that the company had stretched itself thin, Benetton hired management consultant Federico Minoli to head U.S. operations and organize Benetton USA as an autonomous New York company. Minoli's first goals were consolidation and licensee service. He hoped to convert some stores to larger United Color of Benetton superstores, which carry the full line of products. The company planned to open fewer traditional shops and to concentrate instead on its children's division.

Issues for Discussion

1. What are some of the problems that companies such as Benetton have when they try to manage their retail operations from overseas locations? How do these problems relate to the marketing concept?
2. Identify the type of retail distribution strategy used by Benetton and explain how it works. In addition, identify the type of channel system used by Benetton.
3. How does Benetton promote its stores and products in the U.S. market? How might this be different from trying to sell products in Europe?

NOTES

1. Steve Weiner, "With Big Selection and Low Prices, 'Category Killer' Stores Are a Hit," *Wall Street Journal,* June 17, 1986, p. 33.
2. Bill Abrams, "Entrepreneur's Slick Catalogue for Affluent is Pacing the Growing Direct Mail Business," *Wall Street Journal,* March 1, 1984, p. 25.
3. Karen Blumenthal, "Convenience Stores Try Cutting Prices and Adding Products to Attract Women," *Wall Street Journal,* July 13, 1987, p. 11.
4. Malcolm P. McNair, "Significant Trends and Developments in the Postwar Period," in *Competitive Distribution in a Free High-Level Economy, and Its Implications for the University,* ed. A. B. Smith (Pittsburgh, Pa.: University of Pittsburgh Press, 1958).
5. William M. Pride and O. C. Ferrell, *Marketing: Basic Concepts and Decisions,* 5th ed. (Boston: Houghton Mifflin, 1987), pp. 277–282.

CHECK YOUR LEARNING ANSWER KEY

A. 1. T, *p. 414*
   2. d, *p. 414*

B. 1. F, *p. 407*
   2. d, *p. 406*

C. 1. T, *p. 408*
   2. F, *p. 408*
   3. F, *p. 408*
   4. T, *pp. 409, 411*

D. 1. T, *p. 415*
   2. T, *p. 416*
   3. F, *p. 416*

E. 1. a, *pp. 414–415*
   2. b, *p. 415*

F. 1. F, *p. 417*
   2. d, *p. 417*

G. 1. b, *p. 421*
   2. a, *p. 422*
   3. d, *p. 420*

CHAPTER

15

PROMOTING GOODS AND SERVICES

LEARNING OBJECTIVES

After reading this chapter you should be able to:

1. Discuss the importance of promotional strategy in the overall marketing mix.
2. Distinguish between product advertising and institutional advertising.
3. Compare and contrast the characteristics, advantages, and disadvantages of the major advertising media.
4. Describe the role of the advertising agency in developing a promotional strategy.
5. Discuss the major criticisms of advertising and explain how industry and the government attempt to regulate advertising.
6. List the various types of sales promotion and describe the characteristics of each.
7. Distinguish between publicity and public relations and explain how each can be an important part of the promotional strategy.
8. Describe the importance of personal selling as a form of interpersonal communication.
9. List and explain the steps in the sales process.
10. Explain why the assignment of territories is key to managing a successful sales force.

OUTLINE

Business Practice Example:
Pepsi-Cola Co.—A Premier Promoter

The Promotional Mix
- Promotional Objectives
- Importance of Promotion
- Promotional Strategies

Advertising
- Types of Advertising
  - Product Advertising
  - Institutional Advertising
- Types of Advertising Media
  - Newspapers
  - Television
  - Direct Mail
  - Radio
  - Magazines
  - Outdoor Advertising
- Advertising Agencies
- Ethical Issues in Advertising
- Regulation of Advertising

Sales Promotion
- Point-of-Purchase Displays
- Specialty Advertising
- Premiums, Trading Stamps, and Samples
- Coupons
- Contests and Sweepstakes
- Trade Shows

Publicity

Personal Selling
- Types of Personal Selling
  - Retail Selling
  - Business Selling
  - Telemarketing
- The Sales Process
  - Prospecting
  - The Pre-approach
  - The Approach
  - The Sales Presentation
  - Meeting Objections
  - The Close
  - The Follow-up
- Managing the Sales Force

Summary

Key Terms

Check Your Learning

Questions for Review and Discussion

Concluding Case
- Minority Advertising Agencies Have Arrived

Notes

Check Your Learning Answer Key

Highlight in Business Practice:
Humor Used to Promote Popular College

Highlight in Business Practice: Advertising with an International Flavor Can Be Embarrassing

BUSINESS PRACTICE EXAMPLE

Pepsi-Cola Co.— A Premier Promoter

The Pepsi-Cola Co., a division of Pepsico Corp., spends about $150 million annually on advertising and another $75 million on promotions. In the eternal "cola wars," promotion is the sword arch-rivals Pepsi and Coca-Cola use to win the battle for market share. Although Pepsi is the best-seller in food-store sales, Coca-Cola remains number one in total market share (including food stores, fountain, and vending), with 40 percent of the entire soft-drink industry versus Pepsi's 30.9 percent.

But if Coca-Cola remains number one overall, Pepsi may well take the first spot when it comes to advertising. Pepsi consistently creates memorable advertisements. According to an ad recall survey conducted in 1988 by the industry newsweekly *Advertising Age,* more people remembered Pepsi ads than any others. Coca-Cola stood behind Pepsi as number two in ad recall.

Some recent hot Pepsi ads have included singer Robert Palmer's "Simply Irresistible" commercial and Michael J. Fox's "Two Michaels" spot. In 1989, Pepsi turned to comedy in its efforts to fight Coca-Cola's attempt to position Diet Coke against Pepsi. One commercial poked fun at the Diet Coke 3-D spot shown during the 1989 Super Bowl. (The Coke commercial, which received a great deal of hype, was widely perceived to be a dud.) With ads such as these, Pepsi keeps the huge population of aging "sixties kids" in its fold while continually picking up a new "Pepsi Generation" among the teen and young adult set.

Pepsi must promote its products not only to the ultimate consumer but to its bottlers as well. These bottlers are the sales force that persuades the food-store and vending operators to stock their shelves with Pepsi. The bottlers want to know that the product they're selling is getting the right promotional push. The more confident they are that the promotional program is strong, the harder they'll push Pepsi into outlets.

Alan Pottasch, senior vice president, worldwide creative services, is Pepsi's head of promotion. Pottasch has earned rave reviews from just about everyone, including Pepsi's bottlers. One bottler praised him as "without a doubt the genius of soft drink advertising."

Another commented, "I don't envy the person that ever follows in his shoes. It's going to be like trying to follow Mickey Mantle. Arguing against Pepsi advertising is like arguing against Santa Claus. You can love or hate Pepsi, but you always know that they're going to have probably the best soft drink advertising in the business."

WHAT'S AHEAD

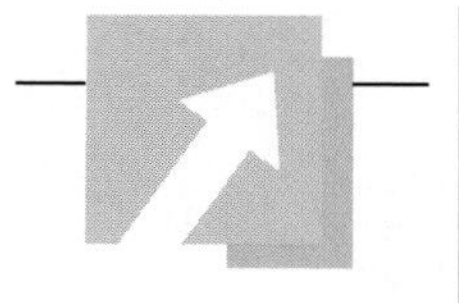

This chapter will show how companies such as the Pepsi-Cola Co. use the four elements of the promotional mix: advertising, personal selling, sales promotion, and publicity. It will discuss the types of advertising and of advertising media, advertising agencies, ethical issues in advertising, and regulation of advertising. It will then go on to the various types of sales promotion and will continue with a discussion of publicity. The final part of the chapter will deal with personal selling, including the sales process and managing the sales force.

THE PROMOTIONAL MIX

Chapter 12 described the marketing mix—the specific way an organization combines the "4Ps" of product, price, promotion, and place for a given good or service. **Promotion** is the communications means used by sellers to persuade or remind potential buyers that a product or service exists. Put another way, promotion is a form of marketing communication that attempts to reach a target audience with a persuasive message. Promotion consists of four major elements: advertising, personal selling, sales promotion, and publicity. The combination of two or more of these elements to reach a target audience is called the **promotional mix.**

Promotion is the form of marketing communication that attempts to reach a target audience with a persuasive message through advertising, personal selling, sales promotion, and publicity.

The ***promotional mix*** is the combination of two or more of the following to reach a target audience: advertising, personal selling, sales promotion, and publicity.

Companies differ considerably in terms of how they design their promotional mix, which varies according to the objectives for the promotion and how the market is segmented. Some promotional mixes concentrate on advertising and personal selling. Others combine advertising, sales promotion, and publicity. Some companies rely almost entirely on telemarketing, a form of personal selling. Each of the promotional elements will be examined later in the chapter.

Promotional Objectives

Every day we are bombarded by promotional messages. The morning paper promotes sales through advertisements, the television promotes new products, and the car radio broadcasts spots promoting a company's image. Each of these messages is part of a promotion designed to *inform, persuade,* or *influence* us to purchase a good or a service. Following are examples of how some prominent organizations achieve the promotional objectives of informing, persuading, and influencing:

Informing Pepsi, MCA Home Video, Amblin Entertainment, and local video stores took out magazine and newspaper ads to inform consumers that the movie *ET* was available in the video stores. In addition, as part of their "cause" marketing effort, they informed consumers that a contribution from the sale of *ET* tapes would go to the Special Olympics.

Persuading The Republican and Democratic parties aired local and national advertising campaigns to persuade people to vote for their presidential candidate and for others running on their tickets.

AN OPEN LETTER TO THE PUBLIC

On March 24, in the early morning hours, a disastrous accident happened in the waters of Prince William Sound, Alaska. By now you all know that our tanker, the Exxon Valdez, hit a submerged reef and lost 240,000 barrels of oil into the waters of the Sound.

We believe that Exxon has moved swiftly and competently to minimize the effect this oil will have on the environment, fish and other wildlife. Further, I hope that you know we have already committed several hundred people to work on the cleanup. We also will meet our obligations to all those who have suffered damage from the spill.

Finally, and most importantly, I want to tell you how sorry I am that this accident took place. We at Exxon are especially sympathetic to the residents of Valdez and the people of the State of Alaska. We cannot, of course, undo what has been done. But I can assure you that since March 24, the accident has been receiving our full attention and will continue to do so.

L. G. Rawl
Chairman

This Exxon ad is an example of influencing as a promotional objective. (Exxon Corporation.)

Influencing Exxon, in response to the disastrous oil spill in Prince William Sound, Alaska, used an advertisement in the form of an open letter from the chairman of Exxon. This letter explained that Exxon was sorry for the accident and was giving it its full attention.

Importance of Promotion

The promotion of products, ideas, and organizations serves many valuable purposes. For example, how would you know that a new product or service was available if you did not see an ad or display or have a salesperson tell you about it? **Sales promotion**—any promotional activity that is not advertising, personal selling, or publicity—can build goodwill, presell products and ideas, increase sales, reduce sales fluctuations, reach inaccessible prospects, and introduce new products. Each of these purposes makes promotion an important part of the marketing mix. In addition, promotion helps stimulate the American economy. It is a multibillion-dollar industry that employs thousands of workers (as copywriters, account executives, photographers, and models, among others) as well as creating jobs in manufacturing and distribution.

Sales promotion is any promotional activity that is not advertising, personal selling, or publicity.

Promotional Strategies

A promotional strategy is an action plan that specifies how the promotional mix of advertising, sales promotion, personal selling, and publicity will be used. The strategy is usually designed to be used more than once and may consist of a number of promotional campaigns for one or more products. For example, Chrysler's promotional strategy for its Caravan and Voyager minivans was implemented by different promotional mixes and separate campaigns, each with its own theme.

Promotional strategies push or pull products through the marketing channels. A **push strategy** is a promotional effort that persuades middlemen to sell a product aggressively. It relies heavily on personal selling to wholesalers and retailers and attempts to influence them by providing promotional allowances for displays, special discounts, brochures, pamphlets, posters, and **cooperative advertising** (an arrangement whereby the manufacturer shares the cost of local advertising). This type of advertising is especially important to companies competing for space in food stores, where the amount of shelf space is very restricted.

A ***push strategy*** is a promotional effort that persuades middlemen to sell a product aggressively.

Cooperative advertising is an arrangement whereby the manufacturer shares the cost of local advertising.

A **pull strategy** is a promotional effort designed to stimulate consumer demand for products through the use of advertising and sales promotion. The idea is to persuade consumers to request a specific product from retailers so that middlemen will be forced to carry it. This strategy is commonly used for health care products, books, records, and most supermarket products.

A ***pull strategy*** is a promotional effort designed to stimulate consumer demand for products through the use of advertising and sales promotion.

Although a company may focus on one strategy, push and pull strategies can be implemented simultaneously. Such is the case for many supermarket products.

BUSINESS PRACTICE EXAMPLE Continues

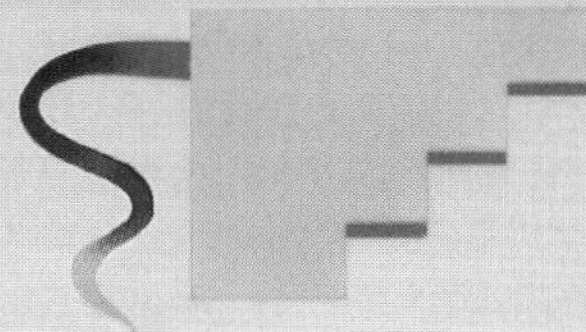

Pepsi must use both push and pull promotional strategies to move its products. One rather controversial *push strategy* the company uses involves marketing agreements, or arrangements, between wholesale distributors and retailers that guarantee a product exclusive advertising and display rights for a specific calendar period in exchange for a cash payment. In many markets, the Coca-Cola Co. and Pepsi have divided up the year between themselves. For instance, for 26 weeks each, participating retailers agree to promote Coke, and to sell it at a lower price than other brands. The remaining weeks, they do the same with Pepsi. This practice has come under some fire from the Federal Trade Commission, which has investigated charges that in certain markets Coke and Pepsi conspired to control prices.

Obviously, Pepsi makes tremendous use of many pull strategies through advertising and sales promotion campaigns, as we'll see in the pages ahead.

ADVERTISING

Advertising is any paid form of nonpersonal presentation of ideas, goods, or services by an identified sponsor.

The American Marketing Association defines **advertising** as "any paid form of nonpersonal presentation of ideas, goods, or services by an identified sponsor."[1] According to *Advertising Age,* American companies spend more money per person per year on this form of promotion than does any other country in the world. By the age of twenty-one, each U.S. resident has been exposed to between 1 and 2 billion advertising messages. Advertising is persuasive and ever-present, and it has a potent influence on our socialization process.

Types of Advertising

Product advertising is advertising designed to promote a product or product line.

Institutional advertising is advertising designed to promote an image or goodwill message of a company, industry, organization, or government.

There are two basic types of advertising. **Product advertising** is designed to promote a product or product line. **Institutional advertising** is designed to promote an image or goodwill message of a company, industry, organization, or government.

Product Advertising

Product advertising can be used to stimulate either primary or selective demand. When used to stimulate primary demand, it tries to increase sales for established products without regard to brand. Trade associations and unions often try to stimulate primary demand. One example is the International Ladies' Garment Workers' Union, which ran a "Buy America" campaign featuring a series of TV commercials that encouraged Americans to "Look for the Union Label" when shopping for women's or children's clothing.

Selective demand can be stimulated by advertisements for a specific product. The ads can make individuals aware of a new product *(pioneer advertising),* ensure they are aware that a product is still around *(reminder advertising),* or point out the benefits, uses, and features of a product in relation to competitors' products *(comparative advertising).* Ads stimulating selective demand account for the largest share of advertising dollars spent. They are commonly found in newspapers and magazines and on radio and television. The ad for Acuvue contact lenses (p. 438) is an example of an ad for a new product.

Institutional Advertising

Advertisers use institutional advertising for several purposes. For example, to promote a new store in Terre Haute, Indiana, J. C. Penney took out ads in the local newspapers that announced the closing of the old store and invited people to shop at the new one. To convey a message of goodwill, Anheuser-Busch ran a campaign to promote the responsible consumption of alcoholic beverages. Public service campaigns encourage responsible behavior in society (see Figure 15.1, p. 439).

Cities, states, and nations often use institutional advertising to promote their image and to attract businesses and tourists to their region. For example, Louisville, Kentucky, featured an ad touting Louisville as "a city on the move."

Types of Advertising Media

In advertising, the term *medium* refers to any avenue used to persuade the consumer to make a purchase, including newspapers, television, direct mail, radio,

IBM CONNECTED ("AIRPLANE") :30

SUNG: YOU WISH YOUR DATA WERE BETTER DIRECTED,
THAT ALL YOUR DEPARTMENTS WERE INTERCONNECTED.
HOW'RE YOU GONNA DO IT?
WELL, YOU'RE GONNA PS/2 IT!
WITH THE IBM PS/2.
YOU WANT TO NETWORK UP… NETWORK DOWN.
EXCHANGE INFORMATION WITH OTHER TOWNS.
WHEN YOU'RE ALL LINKED UP…
YOU CAN SHARE IDEAS FROM BOTTOM TO TOP.
HOW'RE YOU GONNA DO IT?
WELL, YOU'RE GONNA PS/2 IT!
THE SOLUTION IS IBM.

The television medium accounts for a large share of advertising expenditures. This ad for a 30-second IBM commercial promotes the networking capabilities of IBM's PS/2 computers.

magazines, and outdoor ads. Newspapers get the largest share of advertising expenditures, but television, direct mail, and radio also account for a large percentage. Figure 15.2 (p. 439) offers a summary of media expenditures, characteristics, advantages, and disadvantages. Figure 15.3 (p. 440) gives the percentages of adults reached by the major media in an average day.

Newspapers

Most adults read one of America's 7,600 weekly and 1,657 daily newspapers. Studies indicate that 108 million adult Americans read a paper at least once a week.[2] Newspapers are thus the most popular advertising medium, and because

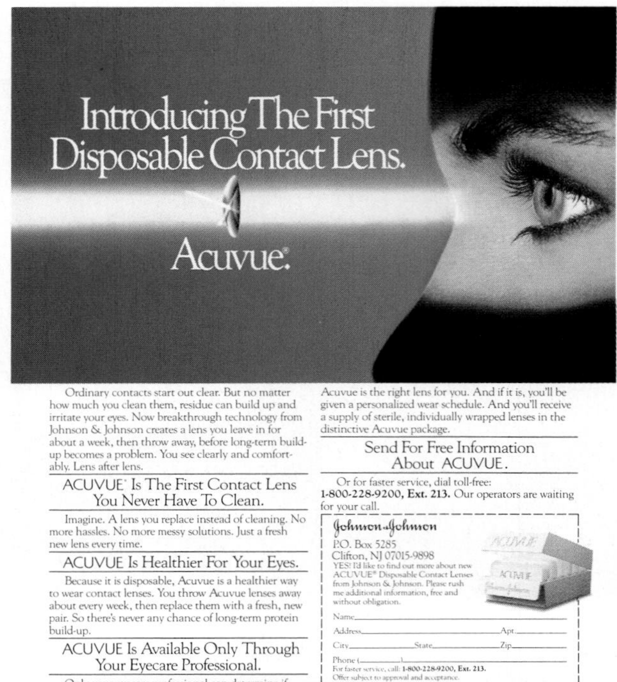

This product ad is an example of pioneer advertising, which attempts to stimulate selective demand by making people aware of a new product. (Courtesy of Johnson & Johnson.)

Institutional ads, such as this one by Anheuser-Busch, promote an image of goodwill. (Anheuser-Busch)

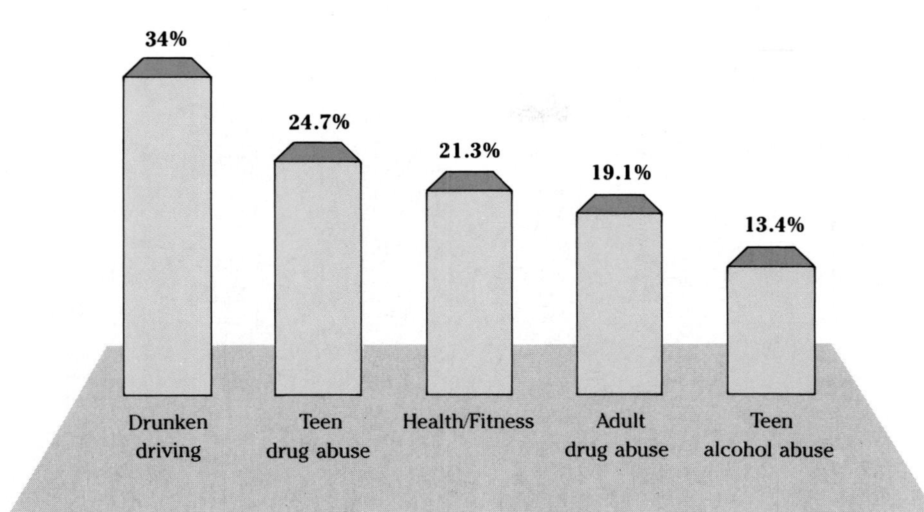

Figure 15.1 The most extensive public service campaigns conducted by TV stations in 1987. Public service campaigns attempt to persuade us to be a responsible society. Note: Respondents could choose more than one answer.

	Newspapers	Television	Direct mail	Radio	Magazine	Outdoor
	Advertising media					
Expenditures (% of total advertised)	26.4%	21.8%	17.9%	6.6%	5.1%	0.9%
Characteristics	Most popular mass medium used heavily by retailers.	Fastest growing medium.	Includes letters, catalogs, postcards, folders.	Experienced strong comeback in the 1960s and 1970s.	Renewed popularity as alternate medium, designed for special markets.	Oldest medium; includes billboards, skywriting, and portaboards.
Advantages	General appeal; lowest cost per thousand; short placement lag time.	Maximum reach and frequency selectivity; product demonstration ability.	Can be personalized; very selective.	Low cost for spots and production; demographic selectivity; universal availability.	Demographic and geographic selectivity; long life; color pictures; inserts.	Low cost; geographic selectivity; long life.
Disadvantages	Expensive for advertisers; short life span; possible clutter.	High absolute cost; high clutter and noise level; long production time.	Very expensive per thousand; limited reach.	High level of clutter; low reach; short file of messages.	Delayed reach and frequency; early closing dates; high level of clutter.	Lack of reach and frequency.

Figure 15.2 Advertising media and their expenditures, characteristics, advantages, and disadvantages.

of their local emphasis they are used heavily by retailers. In late 1982, the United States witnessed the birth of the nation's first national newspaper, *USA Today*, whose circulation is now over 1.3 million. This newspaper, designed as an alternative to magazines for national advertisers and readers, is now the third largest daily in the United States. Although the number of daily newspapers has declined over the last decade (since many cities no longer have both a morning and an evening paper), the number of weekly newspapers published specifically to advertise local products has grown.

Figure 15.3
The percentages of adults reached each day by television, radio, newspapers, and magazines.

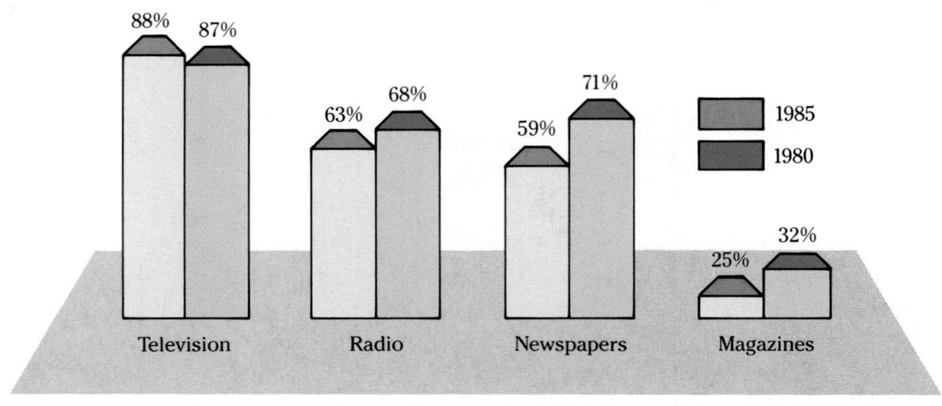

Television is the most popular advertising medium after newspapers. The average price for a 30-second prime-time spot, like the commercial this family is watching, is now over $121,860.

Television

The most popular advertising medium after newspapers is television. According to the A. C. Nielsen Company (a marketing research firm), the average American family has more television sets than ever but watches less network and cable TV than in the past. It is likely that many people are using their sets for viewing video tapes. In response, some companies—for example, Pepsi—have placed ads on videos.

Television advertising is classified as either network, local, or spot. Network time is purchased by national advertisers that sponsor shows alone or with other advertisers. Their message is seen nationally on hundreds of local stations. Locally, time can be purchased by national or local companies on a single station. Either network or local time can also be purchased as single spots—for instance, 10-, 20-, 30-, or 60-second commercials shown during or between programs. (Figure 15.4 is the storyboard—a series of illustrations showing key scenes—for a New England telephone commercial.)

The demand for and cost of prime network time has become so great that many advertisers are pushing for a fourth network. The average price for a 30-second prime-time spot is now over $121,860, and average production costs exceed $125,000. One response to the high demand is Ted Turner's national cable "Super Station," which was established in Atlanta and is beamed by satellite to other parts of the country. Other responses include compressed 24-second TV spots and the introduction of more ads during each hour of programming. One alternative open to advertisers, of course, is switching to other media. (For the top ten advertisers in all media, see Table 15.1, p. 442.)

Other promotional uses of television include in-store videos to promote new fashions or other goods and thereby increase sales. As noted earlier, companies are also beginning to promote their products in movie videos. (For a discussion of direct marketing uses of television, see chapter 14.)

Direct Mail

The third most commonly used advertising medium is direct mail. It includes letters, catalogs, postcards, folders, and other forms of mail. The purpose is to

1988 NEW ENGLAND TELEPHONE ADVERTISING RESIDENCE USAGE CAMPAIGN

"FAMILY IV" **:60**

(SFX: PHONE RING)
MOM: Can you get that?

DAD: Hello?
JILL: Hi, Dad . . . this is Jill.

DAD: Hello
JILL: How are you?

DAD: I'm good.

JILL: I'm good too . . . I . . . uh . . . wanted to call you many times. It's been two years now.

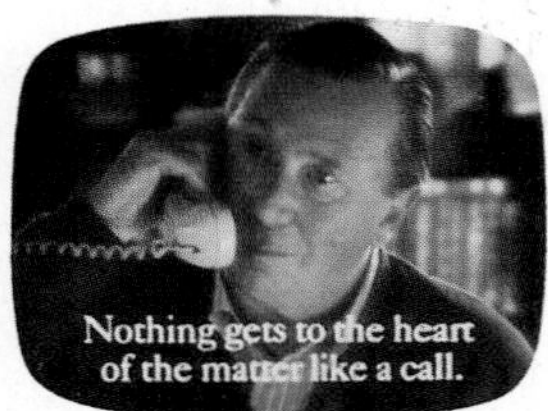

DAD: Jill . . . I was wrong . . . I had no right to interfere in your life like that.
JILL: Oh, Dad.
DAD: I'm sorry.

JILL: I've missed you so much, Dad.

New England Telephone
A NYNEX Company

SINGERS: WE'RE THE ONE FOR YOU NEW ENGLAND. NEW ENGLAND TELEPHONE.

DATE: AUGUST 26, 1988

Figure 15.4
A TV storyboard.

obtain immediate orders or inquiries from consumers. Generally, the greater the frequency or number of mailings, the greater the number of orders.

Direct mail is expensive. Postage costs are high, as are the costs of purchasing mailing lists (which are $25 to $50 per 1,000 names for one-time use). However, direct mail is also very effective on a cost-per-unit basis and therefore continues to grow at a fast pace. Another form of direct mail is electronic mail. New technology using facsimile machines allows companies to send ads over telephone lines and into offices.

Table 15.1 Top ten advertisers in all media.

	Company	Ad Spending (in millions)
1	Philip Morris	$1,557.8
2	Procter & Gamble	1,386.7
3	General Motors	1,024.9
4	Sears, Roebuck	886.5
5	RJR Nabisco	839.6
6	PepsiCo	704.0
7	Eastman Kodak	658.2
8	McDonald's	649.5
9	Ford Motor	639.5
10	Anheuser-Busch	635.1

Specialized mailing lists have limited reach but can yield many eager buyers for new products. For example, a mail-order video cassette company may get good results with a mailing list purchased from *Video Magazine.*

Every month, new magazines appear for a specific market segment. This ad is targeted at business people. (© Newsweek Inc., 1988.)

Radio

Radio has made a strong comeback after a sharp decline in popularity during the 1950s. Today there are approximately 4,863 AM and 3,944 FM stations, and they take in over $7.5 billion a year in advertising revenues. Part of the popularity of radio is its change from "top 40" songs to soap operas, "talk lines," and other special features.[3] AM stations can broadcast at greater distances and are most suitable for car radios. FM stations feature clearer reception and fuller tones and are most suitable for stereo.

Many advertisers believe radio is undervalued for the size of audience it can reach. Because there are so many local radio stations in existence that are all competing for the same advertising dollars, local spot times are rarely sold out. Cost benefits have made radio especially attractive to local advertisers, who account for two-thirds of radio advertising revenues. This results not only because of the low cost for spots but also because of negligible production costs.

Magazines

As more advertisers switch to alternate media to escape the increasing costs of television time, magazines are getting a new lease on life. Also helping this medium is the indication that fewer viewers are watching TV commercials. As "zappers" (VCR owners who skip ads when playing back tapes) become more numerous, advertisers are running more consecutive-page magazine ads.[4] The

HIGHLIGHT IN BUSINESS PRACTICE

Humor Used to Promote Popular College

The Rose-Hulman Institute of Technology is a private, all-male engineering and science college in Terre Haute, Indiana. If you are like most students, you've probably never heard of "Rose," as the college is better known. With a name like "Rose," something unusual is needed to promote the college of 1,350 students. This is especially true when the average student admitted is in the top 5 percent of his class and averages 1220 on the SAT. This type of student will typically receive as many as 200 direct mail pieces from colleges and universities.

According to the Rose-Hulman dean of admissions, Chuck Howard, humor is the key ingredient to a very successful promotional effort. During the students' junior year in high school, they are mailed a black and white brochure designed to attract their attention and to tell them how good the college actually is. One recent brochure was dubbed the "Tinkertoy" brochure after an introductory phrase that states, "Rose-Hulman Institute of Technology: a college for students who take their tinkertoys seriously." Other lines in the brochure also poke fun at the college: "With a name like Rose-Hulman you have to be tough," or "82% of our faculty take a bath each day, whether they need it or not."

Other Rose-Hulman publications also serve as marketing ploys. Probably the all-time favorite is a "Ski Terre Haute" poster belittling the local area, which is nowhere near a ski slope. The poster reads: "Ski conditions (on fictitious Mt. Wabash) are described as being mellow-wet corn on a 72-inch packed dirt base," and "Terre Haute is conveniently located between three major ski resorts: Aspen, Colo.; Boyne Mt., Mich.; and Lake Placid, N.Y."

Results of this less than highbrow direct mail approach are outstanding. Howard claims the college has never failed to fill its 350-student freshman class and each year breaks records for the number of students applying (over 3,000). Furthermore, the publications sent by the college generate a 20 percent response rate compared to the national average of 5 percent.

new popularity of magazines is obvious at the news stands, where every month new magazines designed for specific market segments are showing up. Furthermore, special geographic and demographic editions are being published by *Time*, *Newsweek*, and *Business Week*, among others.

Outdoor Advertising

The \$1 billion industry that includes billboards, portaboards (inflatable portable billboards), skywriting, placards, sails, neon signs, and a new technique using lasers is outdoor advertising. (Don't confuse outdoor advertising with signs or on-premises advertising by proprietors to identify their business. The two are different.)

Poster panels are the billboards we are most used to seeing. They are the ones that dot the interstate routes. They measure 12′ 3″ × 24′ 6″ and are designed to accommodate sales messages printed on posters by the advertiser. They are distributed by outdoor agencies—agencies that specialize in outdoor advertising.

The $1 billion outdoor advertising industry makes use of vehicles such as this truck as an advertising medium, as well as billboards, portaboards, skywriting, neon-signs, and even lasers.

Manufacturers of beer, cigarettes, automobiles, and soft drinks commonly use this type of billboard. Politicians also use them in their election campaigns. Many billboards along interstate routes inform travelers about local restaurants, motels, and gas stations.

Advertising Agencies

An ***advertising agency*** is an independent company that specializes in all phases of preparation and execution of client advertising.

A ***full-service advertising agency*** is an agency that offers a wide range of services.

A small company will usually employ an advertising manager to plan and direct its advertising program. Often, this individual will write the advertising message, place it in the appropriate media, and perform any other related tasks. In larger companies, however, the advertising manager will work with an **advertising agency**—an independent company that specializes in all phases of preparation and execution of client advertising.

An advertising agency that offers a wide range of services is called a **full-service agency.** Young & Rubicam, the nation's largest ad agency, provides market research, media planning, package design, account management, copy and art layout, media placement and monitoring, and many other services. Young & Rubicam's clients have included Kentucky Fried Chicken, Sanka, Xerox, and Band-Aid. Often, an agency will work with a client from the time of product conception through each stage in the product life cycle.

Approximately 43 percent of all agencies charge the traditional 15 percent media commission. For example, if the J. Walter Thompson agency buys $120,000 worth of advertising on *L. A. Law* for a client, it will pay NBC $102,000. (The $18,000 difference is the 15 percent commission granted by NBC to the agency.) It will charge the client $120,000 and keep the difference as compensation. In addition, the client will be charged for expenses incurred for such outside services as production and photography. Some agencies charge expenses plus a standard 17.65 percent markup and a fee for agency staff time spent on non-media-related work. The billing process can vary, and advertisers must be sure what services their percentage commission covers.

BUSINESS PRACTICE EXAMPLE Continues

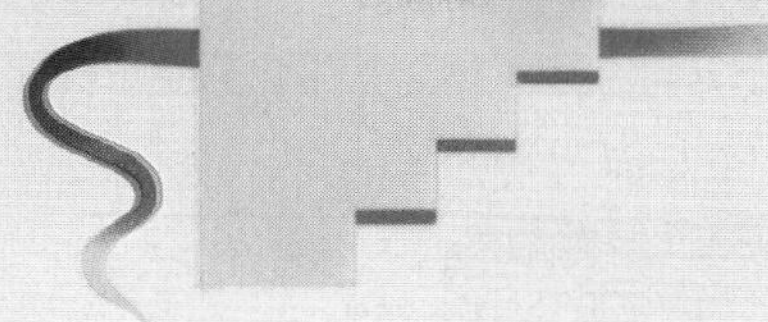

Pepsi uses product advertising to create selective, rather than primary, demand. The company most emphatically wants consumers to buy Pepsi instead of any cola of their choosing!

In addition to virtually all other advertising media, Pepsi uses television extensively as an advertising vehicle. Pepsi's massive advertising efforts have long featured such memorable campaigns as the creation of the "Pepsi Generation" and spectacular events such as the simultaneous broadcast on the "Big Three" television networks of a two-minute Madonna video accenting Pepsi tie-ins.

Pepsi's use of television advertising is not restricted to the U.S. In the Soviet Union, for instance, during the May 1987 Moscow Goodwill Games, Pepsi and Visa became the first American companies to broadcast ads on Soviet TV. In Japan, where Coca-Cola strongly overshadows Pepsi, a series of ads featuring Michael Jackson contributed to a doubling of sales.

Pepsi also makes use of outdoor advertising. During the 1989 Superbowl games in Miami, Pepsi brightened the Miami skyline with lighted 100-to-200 foot tall graphics carrying Diet Pepsi logos and depicting football players in action. A Diet Pepsi blimp was also in view throughout the festivities.

Pepsi's advertising agency—BBDO Worldwide—is one of the largest and most successful in the world. They're the ones who plot and plan to sign up celebrities for the increasingly clever ad campaigns the agency's personnel dream up.

Ethical Issues in Advertising

Since the early days of print and radio advertising, people have questioned unethical practices in mass advertising. In 1929, in reaction to consumer complaints about exaggerated claims made for products, the National Association of Broadcasters urged broadcasters to prohibit advertising "making false, deceptive, or grossly exaggerated claims."[5] Since advertising is an advocate for products, it is not easy to determine exactly what constitutes an exaggerated claim.

Today, many consumers protest the proliferation of suggestive advertising, particularly in the jeans and perfume industries. Calvin Klein's ad for *Obsession* perfume, consisting of three naked young men kissing a nude woman, caused an outpouring of complaints. (Nonetheless, the campaign paid off. Klein's worldwide retail sales are close to $1 billion a year.[6])

Critics of advertising also complain that television commercials trivialize women as stupid creatures whose lives are filled with washing machines that talk, mar-

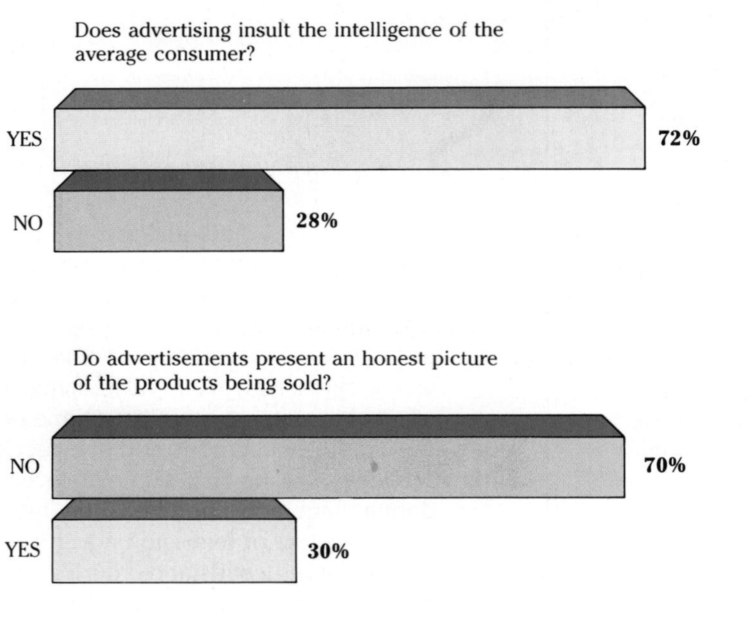
Does advertising insult the intelligence of the average consumer?
YES
72%
NO
28%
Do advertisements present an honest picture of the products being sold?
NO
70%
YES
30%

Figure 15.5
Attitudes toward advertising. A strong 72 percent of Americans believe that advertisements insult the intelligence of the average consumer. Only 30 percent believe ads present an honest picture of the products being sold.

garine that whispers, and soaps that shout.[7] Others argue that white Americans are disproportionately represented in ads.

A major charge leveled against the industry is that it persuades people to want products they don't need. This is a slippery issue. It is difficult to measure at what point a desire becomes a need, since there are no agreed-upon criteria of what constitutes either category. In addition, it has always been difficult to separate advertising's function of facilitating exchange from its function of fostering desires.

Regulation of Advertising

The criticism of advertising through the years has led to two types of regulation of the industry: self-regulation and government regulation. *Self-regulation* is a healthy attempt by the advertising industry to keep its act clean and to avoid further government regulation. At the local level, over 250 Better Business Bureaus throughout the country act as watchdogs to spot misleading ads. At the national level, in 1971 the Council of Better Business Bureaus established the National Advertising Division (NAD) and a court of appeals, the National Advertising Review Board (NARB), to hear complaints.[8] Each NARB panel consists of three advertisers, one agency representative, and one consumer.

The media associations have also established their own advertising codes. The National Association of Broadcasters (NAB), the Direct Mail Advertising Association (DMAA), and the Outdoor Advertising Association of America are all active in self-regulation. In addition, the American Advertising Federation and the American Association of Advertising Agencies have waged truth-in-advertising campaigns and have issued codes for advertising.

Government regulation of the advertising industry is controlled by the Federal Trade Commission (FTC). Prior to the 1970s, the FTC mostly issued cease and desist orders to stop unfair or deceptive ads. In the 1970s, stricter enforcement saw the FTC suing advertisers for up to $10,000 per day for false claims about product benefits and seeking redress for consumers or businesses damaged by the offenders. In the 1980s, however, the Reagan administration supported government deregulation and stressed self-regulation and voluntary cooperation with federal standards. A 1983 ruling adopted by the FTC reduces the amount of evidence required for some advertising claims and puts a greater burden on the consumer for determining the merits of the ad.

Other federal agencies that regulate advertising include the Food and Drug Administration (FDA), the Federal Communications Commission (FCC), the U.S. Postal Service, and the Alcohol and Tobacco Tax Division of the Treasury Department. At the state level, all but four states have adopted the 1911 ***Printer's Ink code,*** a model statute that provides punishment for unethical advertising practices. (The holdouts are Arkansas, Delaware, Mississippi, and New Mexico.)

The ***Printer's Ink code*** is a model statute which provides punishment for unethical advertising practices.

HIGHLIGHT IN BUSINESS PRACTICE

Advertising with an International Flavor Can Be Embarrassing

Every year there are new examples of how companies failed to take their international advertising effort seriously enough to guarantee that no embarrassing mistakes occurred in their ads. The most common mistakes include poor translations and cultural ignorance. Recent domestic examples with an international flavor include:

Frank Perdue, the chicken entrepreneur, decided to sell his chickens to Hispanics. His ad agency got sloppy and translated his popular slogan, "It takes a tough man to make a tender chicken" to "It takes a sexually excited man to make a chicken affectionate." Obviously they forgot about double meanings and slang.

Budweiser became the "queen of beers" while another brewery boasted that it sold "beer that would make you more drunk." One light beer boasted of being "Filling. Less delicious." One food company advertised a huge burrito as a "burrada." Colloquially, it means "a big mistake."

Translations aren't the only problem. Florsheim, the shoe company, apparently needed a history lesson, when in 1988 it ran an ad in a woman's magazine that featured a close-up of a woman's feet in wooden sandals. The headline read, "Some women have to bind their feet. But you don't." The ad copy further states, "In Japan they used to bind women's feet for tradition's sake. In America, women still do it for fashion's sake." The problem: the custom of binding feet was a Chinese custom, not Japanese. Furthermore, the feet in the ad weren't bound.

SALES PROMOTION

As explained earlier in the chapter, sales promotion is any promotional activity that is not advertising, personal selling, or publicity. It includes point-of-purchase displays, specialty advertising, premiums, trading stamps, samples, coupons, contests, sweepstakes, and trade shows. The importance of these activities is continually increasing. Sales promotion expenditures now exceed $100 billion a year and are growing at twice the rate of advertising.[9]

Point-of-Purchase Displays

Point-of-purchase (POP) displays are a type of sales promotion designed to display or demonstrate a product at or close to where a purchase takes place.

Once consumers have entered a store, **point-of-purchase (POP) displays** (a type of sales promotion designed to display or demonstrate, a product at or close to where a purchase takes place) and other forms of visual merchandising can be effective in making them aware of a product or reminding them of its existence. One study has revealed that 80.7 percent of all supermarket buying decisions are made at the point of purchase.[10]

Around Christmas, manufacturers of small appliances (such as popcorn poppers) often employ people to demonstrate the effectiveness of their products and to offer free samples of any food prepared in the demonstration (this is useful in getting customers to try a new product). POP displays can also take the form of windows, counters, walls, and hanging displays. Gaining in popularity are computerized information stations, which dispense coupons and product information.

Specialty Advertising

Specialty advertising is useful articles of merchandise imprinted with an advertiser's message and distributed without obligation to the recipient.

According to Specialty Advertising Association International, **specialty advertising** is "useful articles of merchandise imprinted with an advertiser's message and distributed without obligation to the recipient."[11] First used in 1845 by an insurance agent who distributed calendars to his clients, specialty advertising has grown to annual billings of over $3 billion, and now represents an estimated 15,000 articles of merchandise. These articles include baseball hats, glasses, and playing cards carrying a company's name; business gifts such as a set of golf balls bearing a company's logo; and advertising calendars.

The repeated exposure of the advertising message without added cost is just one of the major advantages of specialty advertising. Imprinted calendars, for example, keep the advertiser's name before the client throughout the year, as do litter bags for cars.

Unlike advertising that uses the mass media, specialty advertising is aimed at small target groups trying to solve specific internal or external client problems. Some basic marketing objectives of specialty advertising include introducing new goods and services, opening new accounts, building an image, motivating employees, and promoting new facilities. The merchandise is distributed by a network of 3,300 specialty advertising counselors, or distributors, some of whom hold exclusive franchise rights to specialty items.

Premiums, Trading Stamps, and Samples

A ***premium*** is a piece of merchandise that is either offered to a consumer as a free gift or sold for a small sum to cover costs.

A **premium** is a piece of merchandise that is either offered to consumers as a free gift or sold to them for a small sum to cover costs. This type of promotion is designed to encourage a change in consumers' purchasing behavior. Towels in boxes of laundry soap and toys in boxes of cereal are examples of premiums. Banks may offer premiums to customers who open new accounts or deposit large sums of money. A California bank once offered free luxury cars to customers who deposited a million dollars.

Trading stamps, such as those offered by S&H Green Stamps, are similar to premiums. Consumers collect the stamps from a retailer when they purchase merchandise and can redeem them for additional merchandise. Trading stamps have traditionally been used to build customer loyalty to a retailer; the customer keeps coming back to accumulate more stamps.

Trading stamps are a sales promotion method used by retailers that provides stamps or similar credits to consumers for the redemption of merchandise.

Seeking alternatives to actual stamps, S&H now provides a "Gift Saver Card" that works with computerized cash registers. When an order is totaled, the clerk inserts the card into a specially designed terminal and the correct number of stamps is electronically added to the total. This system requires no more pasting of stamps.[12]

Samples are free products given to potential customers to induce them to make a purchase. Often, samples are made available in small trial sizes and are sent directly to consumers through the mail or given out by the sales force at a trade show or during a product demonstration. For example, many soft drink companies and food companies give out samples in supermarkets when they are introducing new products.

Samples are free products given to potential customers to induce them to make a purchase.

Coupons

The major way in which a manufacturer can offer the consumer a price break is through **coupons**—advertising clippings or tearoffs used by producers to encourage consumers to take advantage of a small price reduction. Commonly distributed by newspapers and magazines, coupons offer cents off the retail price and are redeemed at the point of purchase. Approximately 375 billion coupons were issued by 1989.[13] A current trend to increase coupon usage is to offer in-store coupons and packages with attached coupons. These techniques are appealing to people who have little time to clip coupons. The redemption rate for coupons is 4 percent. (See Figure 15.6 for more details about coupons.)

Coupons are advertising clippings or tearoffs used by producers to encourage consumers to take advantage of a small price reduction.

Contests and Sweepstakes

Two popular sales promotion activities are contests and sweepstakes, which involve the customer in games of chance or skill. *Reader's Digest* and Publisher's Clearing House are famous for their annual sweepstakes. Nestlé Crunch's "Go One-on-One with Larry Bird" contest paid cash and other prices to the contest winners.

Although contests and sweepstakes attract many new customers, they must be open to everyone, meaning you do not have to buy something in order to participate. Also, many professional contestants enter, and some have sued companies for nonpayment. In Pepsi's "Spell Pepsi Spirit" contest, for example, people advertised in newspapers for key letters. In some cases, Pepsi refused payment, claiming that some of the key letters were obtained outside the contestant's region—which was against the rules. The unpaid winners countered that Pepsi dealers had not displayed the contest rules. Needless to say, the lack of contest pretesting can cause legal and marketing problems.

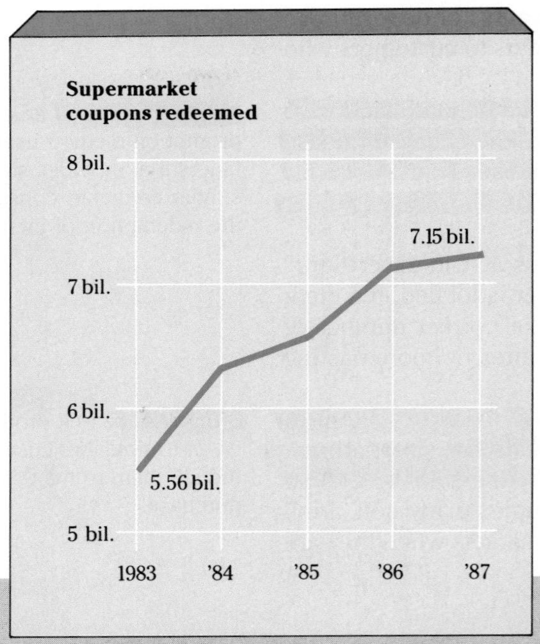

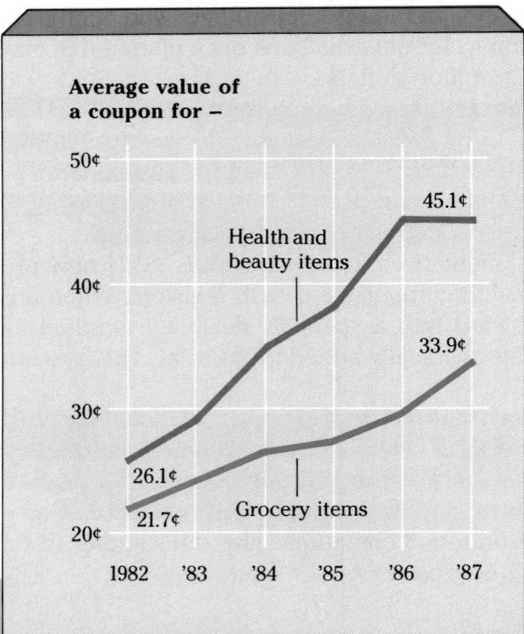

Figure 15.6 The use of coupons continues to increase, as does the value of each coupon.

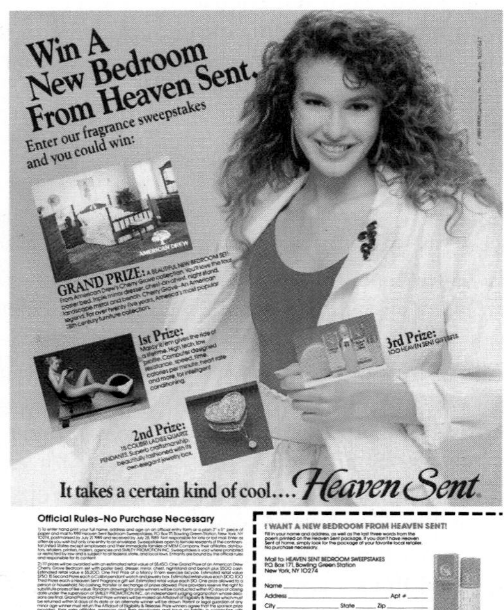

This magazine ad illustrates a sweepstakes sponsored by Heaven Sent. (Heaven Sent®, MEM Company, Inc., Northvale, NJ.)

Trade Shows

A fast-growing, relatively low-cost promotional method used as a pushing strategy aimed at channel middlemen is **trade shows.** Here, manufacturers or wholesalers display their products to other wholesalers or retailers. A sale generated by a trade show is estimated to cost an average $290, compared with $1,263 for a sale generated by a traditional sales call.[14]

Trade shows are a relatively low-cost sales promotion method used as a pushing strategy to display products to channel middlemen.

Trade shows offer manufacturers the opportunity to exhibit and sell their various lines. One of the most popular trade shows is the annual Detroit Auto Show. Other industries that make use of these shows include agriculture, publishing, furniture, fashion, and toys.

PUBLICITY

The fourth type of promotion in the promotional mix is **publicity**—a "nonpaid commercially significant news or editorial comment about ideas, products, or institutions."[15] In other words, publicity cannot be purchased. If 7-Up buys space in a newspaper to tout the thirst-quenching qualities of the soft drink, that is advertising. If the same newspaper reports the story of a miner who has been rescued after two days of being trapped underground, and quotes the victim as claiming that he got so thirsty all he could think of was opening a can of 7-Up, that is publicity.

Publicity is a nonpaid commercially significant news or editorial comment about ideas, products, or institutions.

This form of nonpersonal promotion serves to stimulate demand for a product or business. It can be generated by the company or by word of mouth. When Frito-Lay created a flashy new commercial for its Doritos snack chips, the company produced a "news video"—a backstage look at how commercials are made. For authenticity, a reporter from a Dallas TV station narrated the story. The tape mentioned Doritos only once. However, the package was shown several times. Fifteen stations picked up the spot for viewing on local news programs. All of this was free publicity for Frito-Lay.[16]

Publicity can be good or bad. McDonald's received negative word of mouth publicity in the late 1970s, when rumor had it that the hamburgers contained worms. Procter & Gamble received negative publicity when a rumor circulated that the P&G logo was a symbol of witchcraft. Eventually, the company was forced to drop its 103-year-old trademark from its products. Of course, both rumors were false and both required good public relations efforts on the part of the companies to prevent decreasing sales.

Public relations is the process by which an organization obtains goodwill and promotes a positive image of itself. Public relations and publicity are often combined. Together they can contribute substantially to mass selling at relatively low costs and in some cases can be more effective than advertising. For example, Burger King annually promotes the Denver Children's Museum Halloween campaign. Purchasers of Burger King items are given coupons to visit the special Halloween exhibits at the museum. Burger King publishes and pays for promotional materials and gives the Children's Museum a percentage of the profits on sales. This public relations effort generates thousands of dollars for the museum and promotes a positive image of Burger King.

Public relations is the process by which a business obtains goodwill and promotes a positive image of itself.

PERSONAL SELLING

Thus far, we have examined advertising, sales promotion, and publicity. All three are conveyed through the mass media. **Personal selling** is different. It is a form

Personal selling is a form of interpersonal communication designed to inform a prospective customer and induce the person to make a purchase.

of interpersonal communication designed to inform a prospective customer and induce the person to make a purchase. Approximately 8 million people, or 7 percent of the work force, is involved in the selling profession. This includes retail clerks, account executives, manufacturer's representatives, sales consultants, and sales managers.

The major advantage of personal selling over the use of mass media is its flexibility. Personal selling allows the salesperson to demonstrate, answer questions, overcome objections, and predict possible customer problems. Its major disadvantage is cost. Companies spend more money on personal selling than they do on any other form of promotion. Including salaries, commissions, travel expenses, and training, this cost is often at least twice the cost of advertising.[17]

Types of Personal Selling

Personal selling is often divided into retail selling, business selling, and telemarketing.

Retail Selling

The one-to-one selling that takes place in retail stores is *retail selling.* Retail clerks, who are responsible for selling to the consumer, are often nothing more than cashiers and are the lowest-paid personnel in the selling profession.

Retail selling is declining in importance because of an increase in advertising, which presells merchandise; a lack of knowledgeable and motivated salespeople willing to work for low wages; and the consumer's lack of confidence in a sales clerk's ability to provide competent assistance. Retailers claim that shopping in the future will be "characterized by price and value promotion, smaller selections of merchandise, store layouts designed to increase sales and signs and displays instead of salespeople."[18] The end result is more self-service characterized by fast, efficient central or area checkouts. Even such masters of merchandising as Sears, Penney's, and Ward's are moving in this direction.

As service declines, however, direct in-home selling is growing. Related to the old door-to-door selling practice, in-home selling relies on a sales force of neighbors and friends who sell products for companies such as Mary Kay Cosmetics, Tupperware, and Avon. In-house selling is successful because salespeople are invited into homes at convenient times and because the sales presentation often resembles a social event, with friends and neighbors gathered together for fun and refreshment. People don't seem to mind buying from friends, but hesitate at the high-pressure techniques often used by strangers operating door-to-door.

Business Selling

In contrast to retail selling, *business selling* is one of the highest-paid professions in America today. Business salespeople sell products to business and industry. Examples include merchandise for resale, such as Sperry-docksiders sold to shoe stores; and the leather for the shoes, sold to Sperry.

Technical selling is a technique used by experienced scientists to convince customers of an industrial product's superiority.

Two unique classifications of business selling are technical and missionary selling. **Technical selling** is often done by experienced scientists, who work with potential customers or their technical staffs. Their function is not to take orders but rather to convince customers of a product's superiority. For example,

International Minerals and Chemicals Corporation employs technical salespeople with Ph.D.'s in animal science to sell feed and pharmaceuticals to farmers.

The second type of business selling is **missionary selling.** Missionary salespeople employed by the manufacturer are used to supplement the personal selling activities of the middlemen. Their job is to periodically contact wholesalers and retailers to check their stocks, arrange displays, provide advice on selling, and inform customers of new products. Usually, any orders that result are given to wholesalers for filling. For its cereals and various other lines, General Mills needs aggressive selling far beyond what wholesalers can provide. Therefore, the company employs a sales force of missionary salespeople to call on wholesalers and retailers.

Missionary selling is the use of salespeople to supplement the personal selling activities of middlemen.

Telemarketing

A type of selling used in both retail and business settings is telemarketing. *Telemarketing* magazine defines **telemarketing** as "the discipline that puts advanced telecommunications technology to work as a well-organized and well-managed marketing program.[19] In this field, sales representatives use the telephone as the medium for the marketing message. Telemarketing is used to screen and qualify incoming sales, generate sales leads, and call present customers on a regular basis. It allows sales representatives to contact many prospective customers and thus lowers total selling costs. Personal selling costs for business calls average over $250 per contact, while the average range for telemarketing to business is $7 to $15 per contact.

Telemarketing is the discipline that puts advanced telecommunications technology to work as a well-organized and well-managed marketing program.

The Sales Process

In business selling, the sales process consists of seven stages (see Figure 15.7). The stages are (1) prospecting, (2) the pre-approach, (3) the approach, (4) the sales presentation, (5) meeting objections, (6) the close, and (7) the follow-up. The stages may vary in their application, but they are normally used by every salesperson in business selling.

Prospecting In the first stage of the selling process, the salesperson attempts to locate potential customers. **Prospecting** is the systematic approach to developing new sales leads. Many salespeople rely on friends to find new sales leads. Others use **cold canvasing**—finding new sales leads from public announcements. This sales method is popular in the insurance business, where agents may devise lists of prospects from wedding, birth, promotion, and other announcements found in the newspaper.

Prospecting is the systematic approach to developing new sales leads.

Cold canvasing is a sales method used to find new sales leads from public announcements.

The Pre-approach Once prospective customers have been located, they must be qualified. That is, the salesperson must determine if they have the financial ability and authority to purchase. This can be done in person, although it is often done by telephone. If the prospect looks good, the salesperson will try to arrange an appointment. Another purpose of the pre-approach is to gather other information on a prospect in order to make the approach more effective.

The Approach The first official meeting between the customer and the salesperson is usually the approach. It is important to plan this stage carefully so the

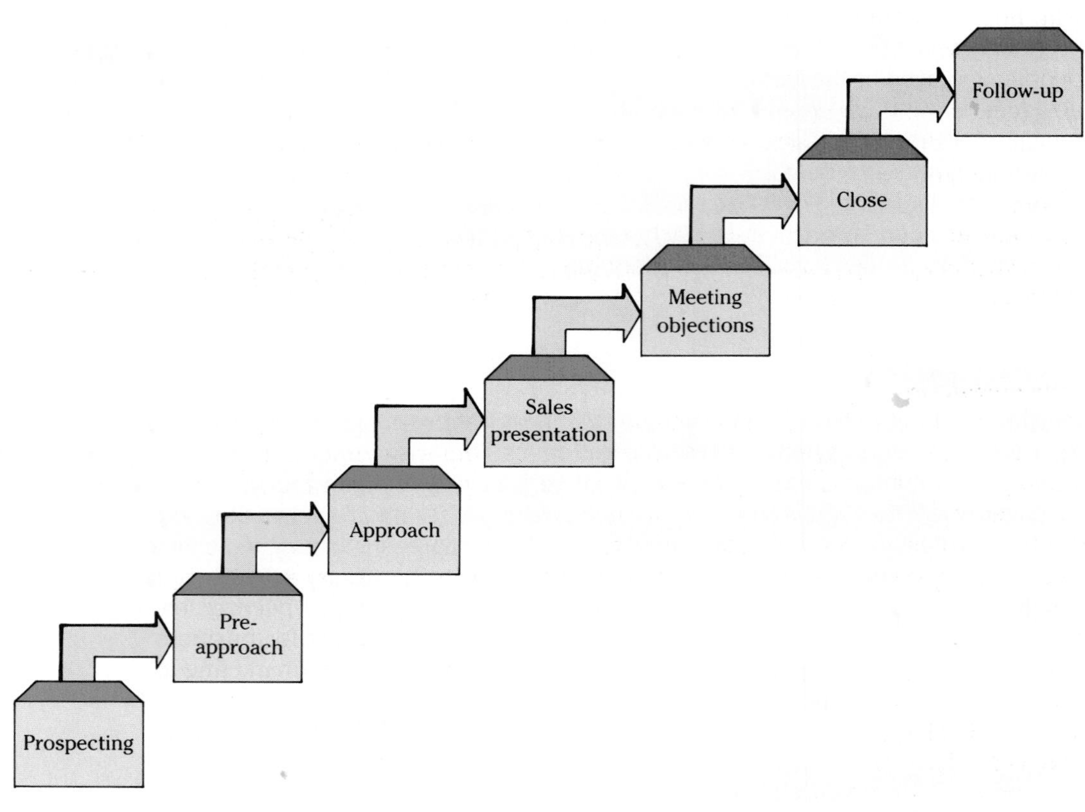

Figure 15.7 The seven stages of the sales process.

interest and attention of the prospect can be secured and the salesperson can make a good impression.

The Sales Presentation The salesperson communicates the product's attributes and benefits in the sales presentation stage. This stage is crucial. The salesperson must gain the confidence of the customer and, through a series of questions, identify a problem that the product can solve. If possible, the product is demonstrated and the customer is given the opportunity to test it.

Meeting Objections Closely tied to the presentation is meeting objections. This stage requires skill and a sound knowledge of the product. Objections from customers often reveal additional points that can be made for the product. The best method of meeting objections is to anticipate them and to handle them as clarifications of information already given or as opportunities to give additional information.

The Close The opportunity to bring the customer to a decision occurs at the close. Part of the skill is in knowing when the customer is ready to buy. Often, a salesperson will attempt a trial close, such as asking, "Will this be cash or charge?" This and similar techniques can often lead to a sale. Once it becomes apparent that a customer desires a product, it is also a good idea to suggest additional items that go with the product. This is called **suggestion selling.** For example, a salesperson may suggest a tie to go with a shirt, or batteries with a radio.

Suggestion selling is a sales technique used to suggest additional items of merchandise that go with the product being purchased.

The Follow-up A good salesperson is never satisfied with one sale. If a customer is to remain a customer, it is essential that the salesperson check to see if the product is working correctly. This activity serves to remove any possible negative feelings that the buyer may have and to assure the buyer that the product was a wise choice. The follow-up often leads to additional sales of accessories and perhaps a later step-up product investment. Home buyers, for example, might return to the same real estate agent when they decide to buy a newer and bigger house.

Managing the Sales Force

Successful salespeople often find themselves promoted to the position of sales manager. This position can be found at many different levels—from district, to regional, to national. At each level, sales managers must recruit, select, train, compensate, motivate, and evaluate the sales force they supervise. They must also solve a variety of similar problems at each level in order to implement the company's promotional strategy.

Each salesperson is assigned a territory by the sales manager. Salespeople are usually given a car, samples, displays, expense accounts, and any other tools necessary to do their job successfully. The assignment of territories is especially important to the sales force because the number of potential customers in a territory will often determine how much a salesperson will earn. For example, some salespeople have huge geographic territories with few customers. Much of their time is spent in traveling. Other salespeople have large metropolitan areas for their territories. They have little long-distance driving to do and often have the potential for making large sales because they can spend most of their time selling.

Most salespeople are paid a *commission,* or percentage of their profit volume, usually combined with a salary. However, some salespeople make a straight salary and others make a straight commission. Normally, the better the territory, the higher the compensation. Sales managers often promote salespeople by assigning them to better territories.

BUSINESS PRACTICE EXAMPLE Continues

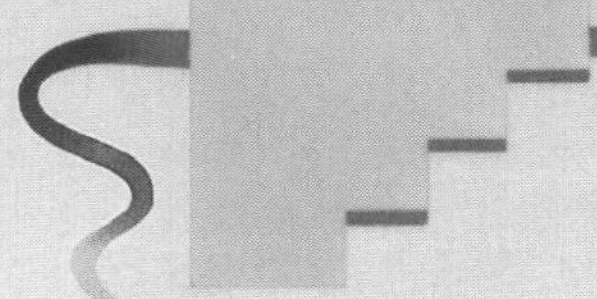

To promote its various beverages, Pepsi regularly offers coupons and sponsors contests and sweepstakes. Pepsi also often offers free samples when it introduces new brands such as Slice, Mug, and Mountain Dew.

Over 300 bottlers act as Pepsi's sales force. These are the people who deliver the products to the customers, bargain for shelf space, set up the point-of-purchase displays, and line the shelves with Pepsi products. The bottlers eagerly await news of each and every promotion that Pepsi sponsors, since these promotions could make or break a sale with a retailer.

Since Pepsi relies on its bottlers to get its products into the marketplace, the company has a vested interest in providing the best promotional effort possible. It must convince its middlemen that it is providing the best possible sales support to their efforts. Poor promotional campaigns could convince some bottlers to switch accounts to other companies, something Pepsi obviously wants to avoid.

Issues for Discussion

1. Can you think of any instance in which Pepsi would want to create primary demand for its product? Discuss.
2. How many different types of advertising media used by Pepsi can you recall? Were they successful in generating demand for their products? Discuss.
3. If you were a bottler for Pepsi, what kinds of promotions would you most like to see?

SUMMARY

Promotion attempts to reach target audiences with persuasive messages. It consists of four elements: advertising, personal selling, sales promotion, and publicity. The combination of any two or more of these elements to reach a target audience is the promotional mix.

The three promotional objectives are informing, persuading, and influencing consumers to buy goods or services. Promotional strategies specify how the promotional mix will be used. There are two major strategies. Push strategies persuade middlemen to market products aggressively. Pull strategies try to stimulate consumer demand. The two types of advertising are product advertising, which promotes products or product lines; and institutional advertising, which promotes an image or goodwill message.

Advertising media are the avenues used to persuade consumers to make purchases. They include newspapers, television, direct mail, radio, magazines, and outdoor ads.

Advertising agencies are independent companies that

specialize in all phases of preparation and execution of client advertising. Those that offer a wide range of services are full-service agencies.

Some of the ethical issues in advertising involve exaggerated claims made for products, suggestive advertising, the trivializing of women, a lack of minority representation, and the persuading of people to buy things they don't need. Criticisms of advertising have led to self-regulation and government regulation of the industry.

Sales promotion includes point-of-purchase displays, specialty advertising, premiums, trading stamps, samples, coupons, contests and sweepstakes, and trade shows.

Publicity—commercially significant news or editorial comment about ideas, products, or institutions—serves to stimulate demand for a product or business. Public relations is the process by which an organization obtains goodwill and promotes a positive image of itself.

Personal selling is a form of interpersonal communication designed to inform a prospective customer and induce the person to make a purchase. It is categorized into retail selling, business selling, and telemarketing.

Retail selling is one-on-one selling that takes place in retail stores. Business selling is selling products to business and industry. Telemarketing is using the telephone as the medium for the marketing message.

The sales process consists of seven stages: prospecting, the pre-approach, the approach, the sales presentation, meeting objections, the close, and the follow-up.

Sales force management includes recruiting, selecting, training, compensating, motivating, and evaluating the sales force. Salespeople are assigned territories and usually are paid commissions.

KEY TERMS

Advertising p. 436
Advertising agency p. 444
Cold canvasing p. 453
Cooperative advertising p. 435
Coupons p. 449
Full-service advertising agency p. 444
Institutional advertising p. 436
Missionary selling p. 453
Personal selling p. 451
Point-of-purchase (POP) displays p. 448
Premium p. 448
Printer's Ink code p. 447
Product advertising p. 436
Promotion p. 433
Promotional mix p. 433
Prospecting p. 453
Publicity p. 451
Public relations p. 451
Pull strategy p. 435
Push strategy p. 435
Sales promotion p. 434
Samples p. 449
Specialty advertising p. 448
Suggestion selling p. 455
Technical selling p. 452
Telemarketing p. 453
Trade shows p. 451
Trading stamps p. 449

CHECK YOUR LEARNING

Reread the following learning objectives. Each objective is followed by a few questions. Answering these questions accurately will help you retain the most important concepts discussed in this chapter. After answering each question, check your answer with the key at the end of this chapter. (*Hint:* If you have doubt regarding the correct response, consult the page whose number follows the answer.)

Circle:

A. Discuss the importance of promotional strategy in the overall marketing mix.

a b c d — 1. All of the following are examples of basic promotional objectives except: (a) inform; (b) suggest; (c) persuade; (d) influence.

T F — 2. A pull strategy is designed to stimulate customer demand for goods and services by heavy use of advertising and sales promotion.

B. Distinguish between product advertising and institutional advertising.

T F 1. Product advertising can be used to stimulate primary or selective demand.

a b c d 2. All of the following are examples of institutional advertising except: (a) Procter & Gamble's commercial for Crest toothpaste; (b) McDonald's commercial for the Ronald McDonald house; (c) Virginia's commercial "Virginia Is for Lovers"; (d) the Bahamas' commercial "Nassau Has It All."

C. Compare and contrast the characteristics, advantages, and disadvantages of the major advertising media.

a b c d 1. The most popular mass medium for advertising is: (a) radio; (b) television; (c) magazines; (d) newspapers.

T F 2. The biggest disadvantage of television is cost.

a b c d 3. All of the following are advantages of magazines except: (a) long life; (b) production quality; (c) lack of clutter; (d) precise market segmentation.

a b c d 4. All of the following are disadvantages of radio except: (a) clutter; (b) selectivity; (c) low reach; (d) short life.

T F 5. Catalogs are a form of direct-mail advertising.

T F 6. Signs and billboards are both forms of outdoor advertising.

D. Describe the role of the advertising agency in developing a promotional strategy.

T F 1. J. Walter Thompson and other large agencies are examples of full-service agencies.

a b c d e 2. Which of the following is an appropriate role for an advertising agency: (a) marketing research; (b) account management; (c) copy and art layout; (d) media placement and monitoring; (e) all of the above are correct.

E. Discuss the major criticisms of advertising and explain how industry and the government attempt to regulate advertising.

a b c d 1. All of the following are major criticisms of advertising except: (a) high cost; (b) unnecessary; (c) poor taste; (d) misleading.

a b c d e 2. Which of the following is responsible for federal regulation of advertising: (a) FTC; (b) NARB; (c) NAB; (d) DMMA; (e) *Printer's Ink*.

F. List the various types of sales promotion and describe the characteristics of each.

T F 1. Premiums are useful articles of merchandise that are imprinted with an advertiser's message and distributed without obligation to the recipient.

T F 2. An Izod alligator banner hanging above La Coste clothing is an example of a point-of-purchase display.

T F 3. The use of contests has come under attack from consumers.

G. Distinguish between publicity and public relations and explain how each can be an important part of the promotional strategy.

T F 1. Public relations is any nonpaid, commercially significant news or editorial comment about ideas, products, or institutions.

T F 2. Publicity and public relations are often used together as an important part of promotional strategy.

H. Describe the importance of personal selling as a form of interpersonal communication.

T F 1. Personal selling offers the advantage of flexibility and the disadvantage of relatively high cost.

T F 2. Personal selling is worthless when selling highly technical goods, because most sales personnel don't have the background to sell it.

I. List and explain the steps in the sales process.

T F 1. There are seven stages in the sales process.

T F 2. Prospecting is the key element in the sales process.

J. Explain why the assignment of territories is key to managing a successful sales force.

a b c d

1. Sales managers are often found at which level: (a) national; (b) regional; (c) district; (d) all of the above are correct.

T F

2. Smaller geographic territories are reserved for new salespeople because they yield fewer sales.

a b c d

3. Most sales personnel are paid by: (a) salary; (b) commission; (c) salary and commission; (d) bonus.

QUESTIONS FOR REVIEW AND DISCUSSION

1. Define the key terms listed at the end of the chapter.
2. Why do advertisers spend large sums of money on institutional advertising in addition to promoting specific products? Select three examples of recent institutional advertising that you have observed and explain what you think is the motive behind each.
3. If you were a local sporting goods store owner, in which media would you advertise your merchandise? Explain.
4. Why has radio shown a strong comeback as an advertising medium after a previous sharp decline?
5. Explain why the magazines you purchase are filled with ads of products you are likely to purchase. Give specific examples.
6. Explain the difference between the traditional ad agency commission-only system and the fee-basis system.
7. Find two recent articles, each dealing with a specific case of truth in advertising. Explain why you think the advertiser was or was not guilty.
8. What are the recent trends in visual merchandising in the stores in which you shop? What kind of aisles, displays, and so on are used?
9. Make a list of specialty advertising items that you currently have.
10. Visit an advertising agency and record your observations about how different departments of the agency cooperate to produce successful advertisements.
11. Interview a technical salesperson, asking how the person's job differs from the jobs of other company sales personnel, such as missionary salespeople and manufacturers' representatives.

CONCLUDING CASE

Minority Advertising Agencies Have Arrived

For years, the focus of mass marketing was an amorphous general population, with advertisers trying to reach everyone with mass media. Today the focus is changing to segments of the population. The two major segments are blacks and Hispanics. Companies are rushing to reach these markets by using minority agencies that are familiar with them.

There are many examples of advertising campaigns designed for and by minorities. For instance, do you remember the catchy Kentucky Fried Chicken jingle "We do chicken right" or the Wendy's commercials for Crispy Chicken Nuggets that encouraged consumers to "celebrate the good times" (sung by Cool & The Gang)? Both of these television ads were specifically produced for the black market by black advertising agencies.

According to some experts, minority agencies are on the cutting edge of segmentation marketing. Industry experts believe that as more companies enter the global marketplace, they'd better learn how to market to blacks in New York before attempting to market to Brazil or other faraway segmented markets.

McDonald's is a leader in segmentation marketing. This fast-food chain has hired minority actors to focus on minority themes and has even designed ads focusing on the handicapped and senior citizens. According to *Hispanic*

Business Magazine, McDonald's spent $7 million on the Hispanic market alone in 1987. However, several other firms spent even more: Philip Morris, $13.3 million; Procter & Gamble, $12 million; Coors, $9.8 million; and Anheuser-Busch, $8 million. Recognizing that Anglos drink more beer than Latins, Coors attempted to improve its image among Hispanics. The effort included launching an ad blitz, hiring more Hispanics, and contributing to Latino charities.

Issues for Discussion

1. Give some reasons why advertisers have spent so much money to advertise to Hispanics for the following products: cigarettes, fast food, soft drinks, and movies.
2. Why do some companies ignore or refuse to specifically advertise to minorities? Give examples.
3. Discuss why minority advertising agencies are on the leading edge of segmentation marketing.

NOTES

1. American Marketing Association, Committee on Definitions, *Marketing Definitions: A Glossary of Marketing Terms* (Chicago: American Marketing Association, 1963), p. 9.
2. Louis Rukeyser, *Louis Rukeyser's Business Almanac* (New York: Simon and Schuster, 1988, p. 548).
3. "Radio's Wacky Road to Profit," *Newsweek,* March 25, 1985, p. 70.
4. "Why TV Zappers Worry Ad Industry," *U.S. News & World Report,* November 12, 1984, pp. 66–67.
5. Edward Jay Whetmore, *MediaAmerica,* Third Ed., Belmont, CA: Wadsworth, 1987, p. 261.
6. "A Kinky New Calvinism," *Newsweek,* March 11, 1985, p. 65.
7. Greer Litton Fox, "Sex Roles," in *Sociology,* ed. R. Hagedorn (Dubuque, Iowa: Wm. C. Brown, 1983).
8. "The Industry Gets a Controversial Watchdog," *Business Week,* May 12, 1973, pp. 130–133.
9. Joe Agneu, "Burgeoning Sales Promotion Spending to Top $100 Billion," *Marketing News,* May 22, 1988, p. 8.
10. Russ Bowman, "Sales Promotion," *Marketing and Media Decisions,* January 25, 1987, p. 78.
11. "The Case for Specialty Advertising," *SAAI,* 1980, p. 1.
12. Kathryn Hudson, "Trading Stamps Alive and On-line," *Insight,* January 25, 1988, p. 43.
13. Ronald Alsop, "Companies Seek Ways to Put Coupons Where They'll Count," *Wall Street Journal,* August 8, 1985, p. 25.
14. "Trade Shows Keep Growing, Spawning a Slew of New Convention Centers," *Wall Street Journal,* August 21, 1986, p. 1.
15. James F. Engle, Martin R. Warshaw, and Thomas C. Kinnear, *Promotional Strategy* (Homewood, Ill.: Richard D. Irwin, 1979), p. 30.
16. Ronald Alsop, "When Is a TV Ad Not an Ad? When It's Hyped as an Event," *Wall Street Journal,* March 21, 1985, p. 31.
17. Kenneth R. Davis and Frederick E. Webster, Jr., *Sales Force Management* (New York: Ronald Press, 1968), p. 10.
18. Steve Weinter, "Many Stores Abandon 'Service with a Smile,' Rely on Signs, Displays," *Wall Street Journal,* March 16, 1981, p. 1.
19. Ernan Roman, "Telemarketing Rings in New Business Era," *Advertising Age,* January 27, 1986.

CHECK YOUR LEARNING ANSWER KEY

A. 1. b, *pp. 433–434*
2. T, *p. 435*

B. 1. T, *p. 436*
2. a, *p. 436*

C. 1. d, *p. 437*
2. T, *p. 440*
3. c, *p. 439*
4. b, *p. 439*
5. T, *p. 440*
6. F, *p. 443*

D. 1. T, *p. 444*
2. e, *p. 444*

E. 1. b, *pp. 445–446*
2. a, *p. 447*

F. 1. F, *p. 448*
2. T, *p. 448*
3. T, *p. 449*

G. 1. F, *p. 451*
2. T, *p. 451*

H. 1. T, *p. 452*
2. F, *p. 452*

I. 1. T, *p. 453*
2. F, *p. 454*

J. 1. d, *p. 455*
2. F, *p. 455*
3. c, *p. 455*

PART 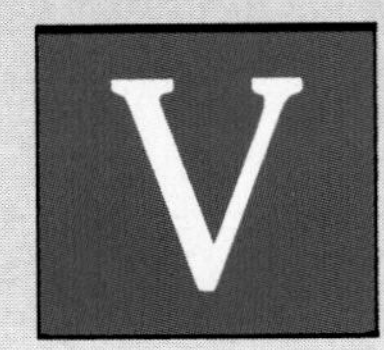

FINANCING BUSINESS VENTURES

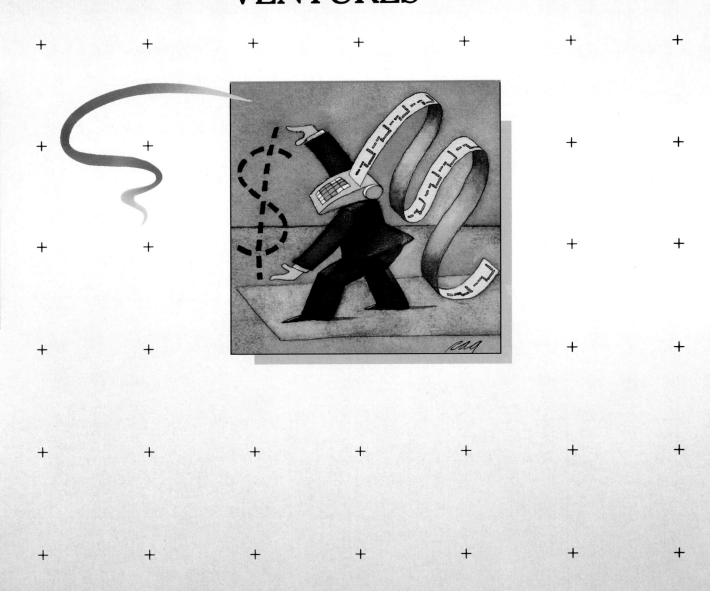

CHAPTER

16

Money and the Banking System

CHAPTER

17

Accounting: Understanding the Language of Business

CHAPTER

18

Managing the Firm's Financing

CHAPTER

19

Investments and Securities

CHAPTER

20

Insurance and Risk Management

CHAPTER

16

MONEY AND THE BANKING SYSTEM

LEARNING OBJECTIVES

After reading this chapter you should be able to:

1. Explain the role of money in America prior to the development of the modern capitalistic system.
2. List and discuss the three basic functions of money.
3. Describe the characteristics of sound money.
4. Distinguish between the basic money supply (M1) and near money.
5. Compare and contrast the changing role of depository financial institutions following deregulation.
6. Describe the structure and organization of the Federal Reserve System.
7. Discuss the tools of monetary policy used by the Federal Reserve System.
8. Describe the role of foreign exchange rates in international business.

OUTLINE

BUSINESS PRACTICE EXAMPLE

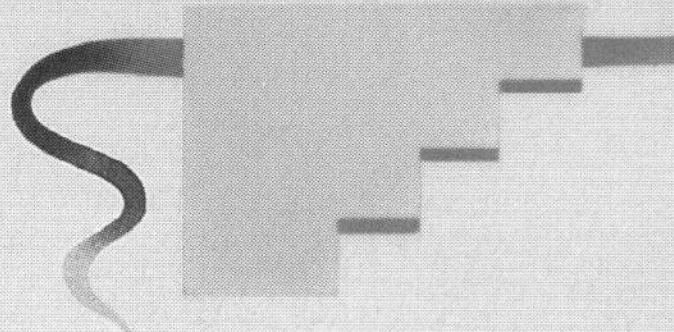

Banking on Innovation at Dollar Dry Dock

In one sense, banks never change. Their lifeblood is the flow of money in the community they serve. But if American banking once ran cautiously and conservatively on a slow track, it has been moving since the 1980s more like a wild roller-coaster on a track of risk and adventure. Many a comfortable neighborhood bank has been pushed out or taken over in the competitive and deregulated environment of the 1980s, and banking giants seem to loom larger on every corner.

Even in New York, as world-class giants such as Citibank, Chase Manhattan, and Chemical Bank have grown bigger, many old banks have had to reorganize and scramble to survive in the unstable and competitive new environment. The story of two smaller New York firms, Dollar Savings Bank and Dry Dock Savings Bank, is typical. Both were nearly driven under, squeezed by the fluctuating cost of new money against the fixed income from old loans, before they combined resources under CEO Robert Steele to become today's Dollar Dry Dock Bank. Unlike some high-risk banks of the early 1980s, they undertook a disciplined program. They worked at cost cutting, restructuring, and, above all, developing and marketing innovative new banking services.

By 1988, Dollar Dry Dock Bank was being described in the media as a "turnaround story." The praise was based in large part on the bank's ambitious program to become a "financial supermarket" offering a fresh mix of services to a new and growing community of customers. Aiming to become a one-stop banking service, Dollar Dry Dock succeeded well enough in 1988 to attract an 1100 percent gain in new deposits in one year and an 82 percent gain in customers.

The new business was generated partly by careful attention to the needs of hurried New Yorkers. Supporting the one-stop banking concept was a new idea in helping customers—a professional banker in a central location directing people to the financial specialists they needed. To gain customers from untouched groups, the bank launched new marketing programs aimed at Spanish, Asian, and Russian immigrants looking for home loans.

Business analysts were impressed with Dollar Dry Dock's performance, its new business, and its relatively low level of risk. The bank's new services had gained business without a large and risky outlay of funds. Its loans seemed to be evenly balanced in commercial and real estate lending, spreading the risk to cope with New York's up-and-down economic climate. Dollar Dry Dock Bank seemed to have found new ways to live with the flow of money in its community.

WHAT'S AHEAD

Innovations in banking services helped Dollar Dry Dock deal with rapid changes in the banking environment during the 1980's. Competitive pressures in the United States and from abroad have focused attention on the value of U.S. money and on the many new demands on U.S. financial institutions. Much of the change began in the early 1980s, when deregulation created greater competition between banks and other depository financial institutions. The differences in the services offered by commercial banks, savings and loan associations, mutual savings banks, and credit unions are rapidly vanishing. Competition among depository financial institutions has been further enhanced by the deregulation of interest rates paid on savings and checking accounts. Instability and change continue to be part of the economic pattern of the United States. This chapter will first trace the role money played in the past. Next, it will emphasize the characteristics and functions of sound money. The rest of the chapter will cover the modern money supply, depository and nondepository financial institutions, the Federal Reserve System, and international finance.

THE ROLE OF MONEY IN A GROWING SOCIETY

Money is anything that is widely accepted as a medium for the buying and selling of goods and services. Every society whose members exchange things needs to have some medium to make the process work. Early America, even though it began as a tiny and primitive colony, was no exception.

Money is anything that is widely accepted as a medium for the buying and selling of goods and services.

The simplest form of exchange, still practiced by many people at the neighborhood level, is swapping, or **barter**—the direct exchange of one thing for another, without the need for money. In early America, the colonists exchanged goods with one another and with the home country. The goods included tobacco, furs, and food supplies.

Barter (or swapping) is the direct exchange of one thing for another, without the need for money.

Exchanging furs, tobacco, timber, or a side of beef is an awkward and inefficient way to do business. European coin was scarce in the colonies, and for a while Native American wampum was used as a compact, convenient way to measure the value of the tobacco and furs that were originally bartered among the Native Americans and the colonists. This medium did not serve for long, however, since colonial goods often had to be exchanged for European goods. Colonists had to operate in a wider market, where the value of and demand for their tobacco, furs, and timber were never stable. They needed a more reliable form of money.

As the flow of American goods grew steadier, merchants and traders took a central role. They began to write out paper promises to pay for goods in return for scarce gold or silver. This helped the flow of exchange with very little need for anyone to see the gold. However, the value of the paper promises depended on merchants' ability to deliver the goods. For over two hundred years, Americans worried about the merchants, bankers, and eventually governments that promised to deliver silver or gold in exchange for paper money used to pay for goods and services.

What was needed as the country's trade grew stronger was a paper currency that would be widely used because its value and acceptability could be reliably controlled. A firm step toward stable currency came with the establishment of a truly central banking system in the Federal Reserve Act of 1913. The next step was the 1933 establishment of the Federal Deposit Insurance Corporation, which protects people's savings. These key developments will be discussed later in the chapter.

FUNCTIONS OF MONEY

To survive the test of time, money must serve certain purposes for society. Modern money must function as a medium of exchange, a measure of value, and a liquid store of value (see Figure 16.1).

Medium of Exchange

The primary function of money is to provide a *medium of exchange*—a commonly accepted unit of value used to complete economic transactions. Regardless of the name attached to this medium, the important point is that it facilitates transactions as an alternative to the cumbersome barter system.

Measure of Value

Money also serves as a *measure of value*—a common standard used to determine the value of goods and services. This function facilitates comparison shopping.

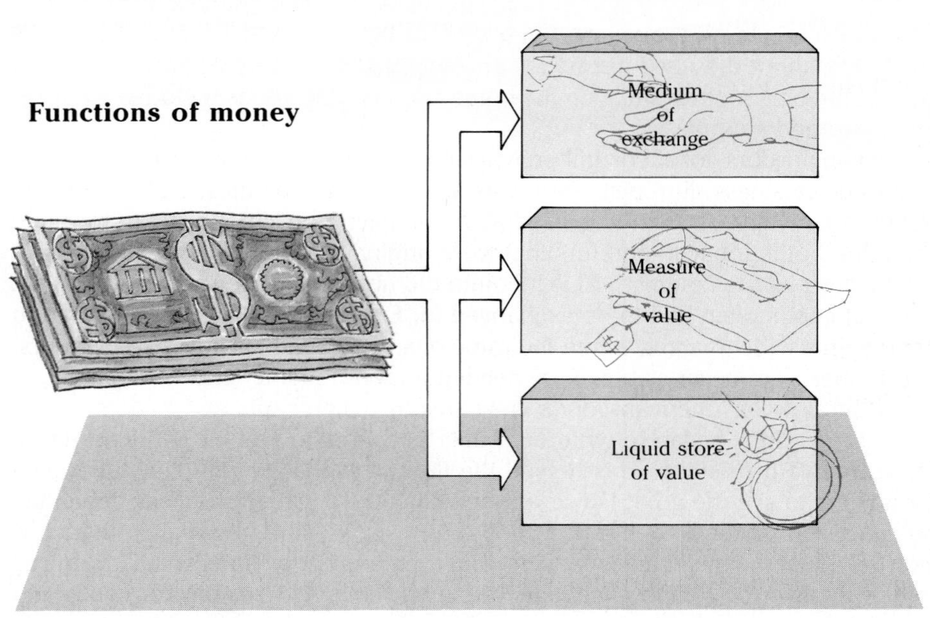

Figure 16.1
Functions of money. Money has outlived the barter system because its efficiency fulfills the needs of society.

The primary function of money is to provide a medium of exchange to help facilitate transactions.

Establishing prices through a common denominator allows consumers and businesses to make better decisions about the allocation of their money.

Liquid Store of Value

A third function of money is as a *liquid store of value*—a medium for storage of value that can be quickly converted to purchase something. We often accumulate or store money so we can purchase items in the future. Money can be saved (invested) in many ways, each of which has different degrees of **liquidity**—the ease and predictability with which an asset can be converted into cash. The ultimate form of liquidity is cash (currency, coins, and checking accounts).

Liquidity is the ease and predictability with which an asset can be converted into cash.

Everyone should maintain a reasonable level of liquidity to meet daily expenses and pay for unforeseen emergencies. However, in times of excessive inflation, holding money in the form of cash can be unprofitable. The purchasing power of the uninvested funds declines. Most people therefore attempt to establish a comfortable liquidity level by maintaining sufficient funds in cash and investing excess funds. (Although stocks are often recommended as investments, during an economic downturn shareholders who wish to liquidate them may have to sell them at a loss.)

CHARACTERISTICS OF SOUND MONEY

Money should be portable and durable, acceptable and consistent in value, and divisible and difficult to counterfeit.

Portability and Durability

For maximum utility, money must be small in bulk but large in face value. Often, the commodities used for money during the colonial period were just the opposite. (Livestock, for example, is not very portable.) Modern U.S. currency (paper money) is lightweight and available in eleven denominations, ranging in value from $1 to $10,000. Checking accounts are more portable yet. Figure 16.2 shows the dollar value of currency presently in circulation.

A key advantage to currency, coins, and checking accounts is the length of time they are useful for repeated transactions. Commodities often lacked this quality because of their bulk or spoilage. The average life of all paper currency

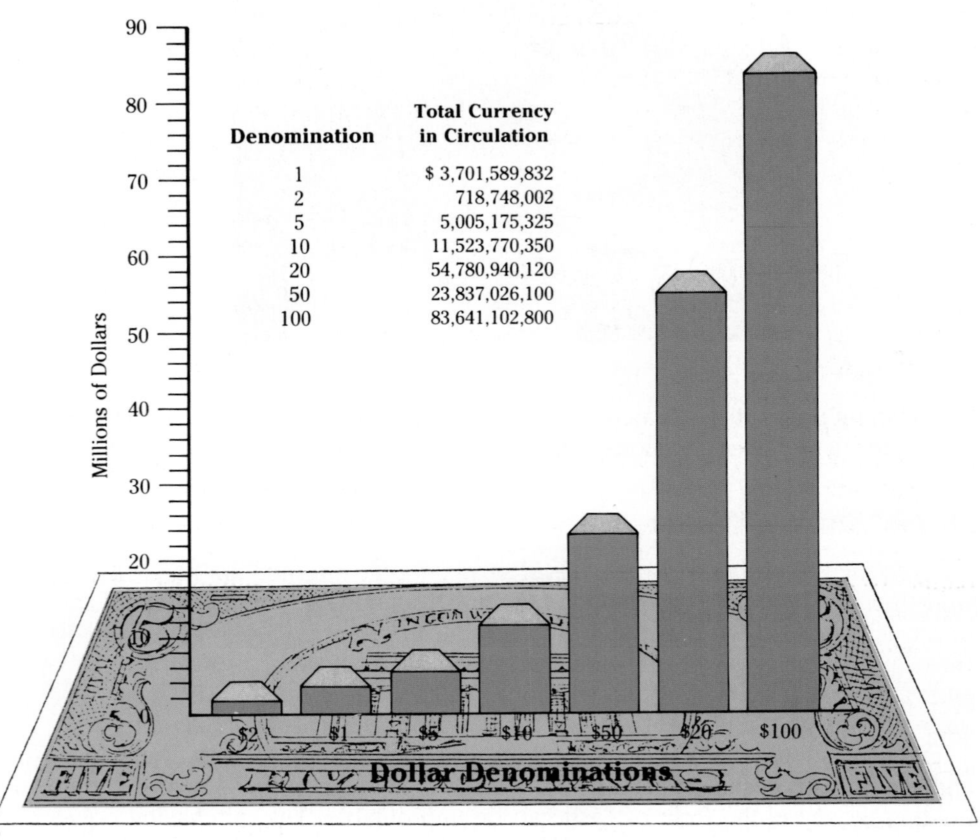

Denomination	Total Currency in Circulation
1	$ 3,701,589,832
2	718,748,002
5	5,005,175,325
10	11,523,770,350
20	54,780,940,120
50	23,837,026,100
100	83,641,102,800

Figure 16.2
Dollar value of currency in circulation (in billions of dollars, by denomination). In 1969, the Treasury stopped issuing denominations higher than $100, but some larger bills still circulate.

in the United States is just over five years. U.S. dollar bills have an average life of eighteen months.[1]

The printing of currency and the minting of coins are the sole responsibility of the federal government. Shown here is a *plate* for one-dollar bill.

Acceptability and Consistency in Value

If a currency is to survive as a medium of exchange, the public must trust it and must therefore maintain faith in the agency issuing it. Consumers are more likely to hold money if they believe their currency has a stable value. The main threat facing most economic systems today is inflation. If inflation continues for a long time, consumers lose confidence in their currency.

Divisibility and Difficulty of Counterfeiting

In order to facilitate exchange, money must be divisible into subunits. Since prices vary for different products, transactions can be most easily completed with a wide range of currency values. The U.S. monetary system provides currency and coins in multiple denominations in order to promote the exchange of goods and services between business and consumers. A check can be written for any amount.

The type of paper and chemicals used in U.S. paper currency makes counterfeiting extremely difficult, although criminals continue to attempt it. The printing of the currency and the minting of the coins are the sole responsibility of the federal government. This centralization has helped maintain a high-quality currency that is not very susceptible to counterfeiting. The staffs of the Federal Reserve System regularly sort currency and remove any counterfeit bills from circulation. (The Federal Reserve System—Fed—will be discussed later in the chapter.)

THE SUPPLY OF MONEY IN THE AMERICAN ECONOMY

Modern society needs a currency whose value can be trusted. Trust is based in part on the circulation of a steady and reliable amount of money. Some governments in debt have tried to create the illusion of value by printing paper without gold or commodities behind the promise of payment. In effect, they have used their authority to create counterfeit value. When this happens, the exchange process quickly reveals that there are no goods behind the paper. People then lose faith in the value of their money and tend to limit themselves to exchange by barter. To avoid such a slowdown of commerce and to keep faith in the value of currency, modern governments must monitor and make public the total amount of money circulating.

A number of money supply measures are used by the U.S. government. However, it is not easy to determine precisely which funds—apart from currency and coin—can be used in transactions. The government's measures are an attempt to make useful distinctions between funds that are immediately available and funds that are used to earn interest but that can be quickly converted into cash.

The most basic measure of the money supply is **M1**—all circulating cash and any funds readily convertible into cash, such as those available in checking accounts. Figure 16.3 shows the different categories of funds in M1. (These categories will be described later in the chapter.) Notice that checking accounts make up almost three-quarters of this measure of the money supply.

M1 is all circulating cash and any funds readily convertible into cash, such as those available in checking accounts.

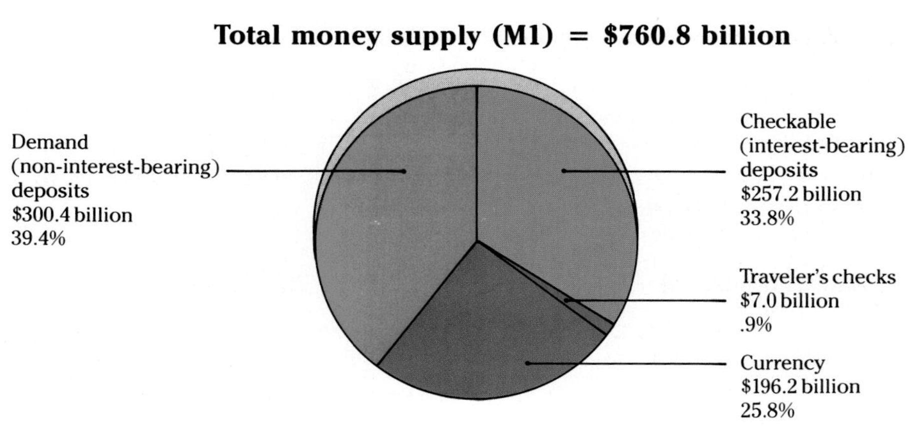

Figure 16.3
The components of the money supply (M1).

M2 is M1 plus near money (funds that are almost as liquid as those in checking accounts).

A broader measure of money available to circulate is **M2,** which is M1 plus *near money* (funds that are almost as liquid as the funds in checking accounts), including interest-bearing savings accounts and money market accounts. Table 16.1 lists these measures of the money supply as well as broader measures. Such measures are part of the U.S. government's effort to monitor the amount of money that is ready to be spent and the amount of value that is stored in various ways. The U.S. government tries to keep too many funds from flowing into circulation at once, since a too-large flow could put the value of money at risk. People who have their money in banks want assurance that its value is safe when they write checks or make plans for their savings. Without this assurance, they would feel safe only in exchanging gold or barter.

Table 16.1 Measures of the money stock and liquid assets.

M1
Currency
Traveler's checks of nonbank issuers
Demand deposits
Other checkable deposits at all depository institutions

M2
M1
Overnight repurchase agreements issued by commercial banks
Overnight Eurodollars held by U.S. residents at overseas branches of U.S. banks
Money market mutual fund shares (general-purpose and broker/dealer, taxable and nontaxable)
Savings deposits at all depository institutions
Money market deposit accounts at all depository institutions
Small-denomination time deposits at all depository institutions

M3
M2
Large time deposits at all depository institutions
Money market mutual funds (institution-only)
Term repurchase agreements at all depository institutions
Term Eurodollars held by U.S. residents

L
M3
Banker's acceptances
Commercial paper
Savings bonds
Short-term Treasury obligations

DEPOSITORY FINANCIAL INSTITUTIONS

The 1980s may go down in history as the decade of financial revolution. The "revolution" is a major increase in competition and innovation in the financial services industry. Much of the increase stems from deregulation of this industry during the early 1980s (which will be discussed in the next section).

Deregulation has blurred the differences among commercial banks, other depository financial institutions, and nondepository financial institutions. The long-term result has been a greater variety of consumer services offered at more competitive prices.

Differences among Depository Financial Institutions

Commercial Banks

For-profit institutions that accept deposits in the form of checking and savings accounts and use them to lend money to businesses and individuals are **commercial banks.** While commercial banks are operating in a more and more competitive environment, they continue to play a dominant role in the U.S. financial community.

Commercial banks are for-profit institutions that accept deposits in the form of checking and savings accounts and use them to lend money to businesses and individuals.

Nearly a third of all commercial banks are *national banks*—banks chartered and regulated by the federal government and required to be members of the Federal Reserve System. The remaining two-thirds are *state banks*—banks incorporated under the laws of the states in which they are located. State banks can join the Federal Reserve System if they meet certain criteria. Figure 16.4 shows how the top four U.S. banks compare with some of the world's largest banks.

Chase-Manhattan Bank is a commercial bank—a for-profit institution that accepts deposits and uses them to lend money to businesses and individuals.

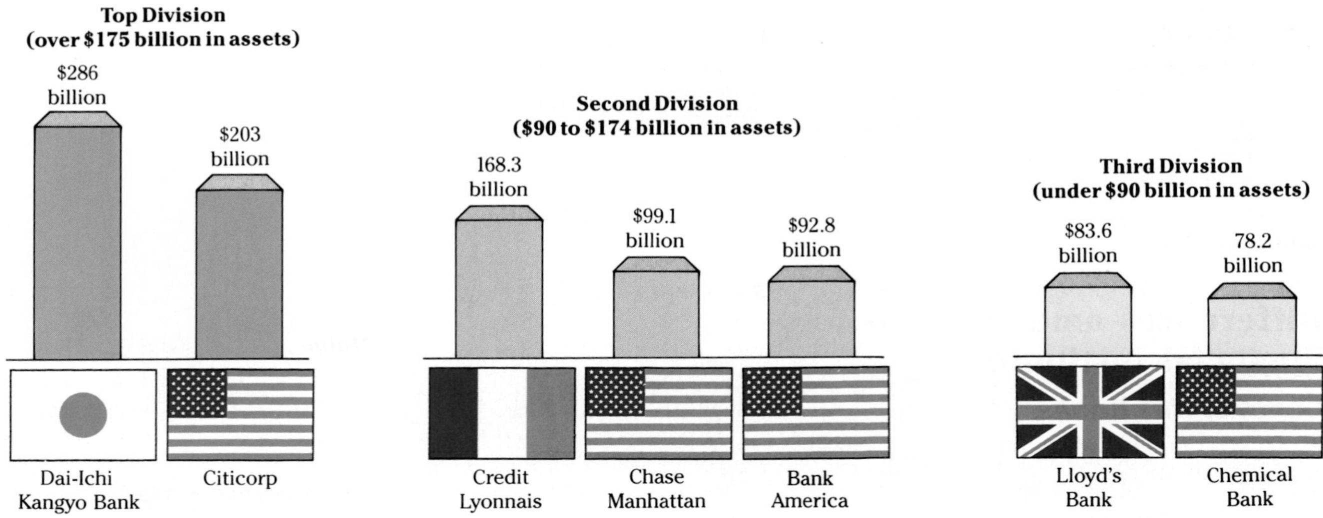

Figure 16.4 How the top four U.S. banks compare with some world giants. The banks are measured by the size of their assets.

In addition to supplying a variety of checking account services, commercial banks typically offer consumer and business loans, a wide selection of savings accounts, investment counseling, discount brokerage services, and tax deferred **Individual Retirement Accounts (IRAs)**—a category of savings account, investment, or pension fund that sets aside money and its earnings for deferment of tax until retirement.

The ***Individual Retirement Account (IRA)*** is a category of investment or pension fund that sets aside tax-deferred money and its earnings for retirement needs.

Credit Unions

Cooperative financial institutions organized by people associated with a particular group—usually an employer or a union—are **credit unions.** There are over 16,000 credits unions in the United States. About 60 percent are chartered under federal law and the rest under the laws of various states. Credit union membership is approaching 60 million.[2]

Credit unions are cooperative banks organized by people associated with a particular group—usually an employer or a union.

Credit unions are organized solely to meet the needs of their members. The members pool their savings and make loans to other members. From 1970 to 1988, the total savings deposits in credit unions (called shares) grew from $15 billion to over $170 billion.[3] Many credit unions offer a wide variety of financial services at reasonable cost. Included are credit and debit cards, interest-bearing checking accounts, automatic teller machines, and discount brokerage services. (These services will be described in more detail in the next major section of the chapter.) Credit unions are a growing source of competition for commercial banks and other depository financial institutions.

Savings and loan associations (S&Ls) are depository financial institutions that accept savings and provide mortgage loans for local housing.

Savings and Loan Associations

Depository financial institutions that accept savings and provide mortgage loans for local housing are **savings and loan associations (S&Ls).** There are 3,500

S&Ls in the United States, and over 60 percent of their savings deposits are invested in mortgages.[4]

Since deregulation, these associations also offer financial services that parallel those of commercial banks. And like commercial banks, they have a dual system of chartering. State S&Ls are chartered under state laws and are supervised by state authorities. Federal S&Ls are chartered under federal law and are supervised by the Federal Home Loan Bank Board.

Mutual Savings Banks

Only sixteen states charter **mutual savings banks**—depository financial institutions that are owned by their depositors; like S&Ls, they use their savings deposits mainly to make housing loans. The majority of the mutual savings banks are located in New York, New Jersey, and the New England states.[5]

Mutual savings banks are depository financial institutions that are owned by their depositors and that, like S&Ls, use their savings deposits mainly to make housing loans.

These institutions have also been changing their product mix to compete in the deregulated environment. They offer consumer loans, NOW accounts (see next section for details), and other financial services.

Services of Depository Financial Institutions

Depository financial institutions provide some or all of the following services: demand deposits, checkable deposits, traveler's checks, credit and debit cards,

BUSINESS PRACTICE EXAMPLE Continues

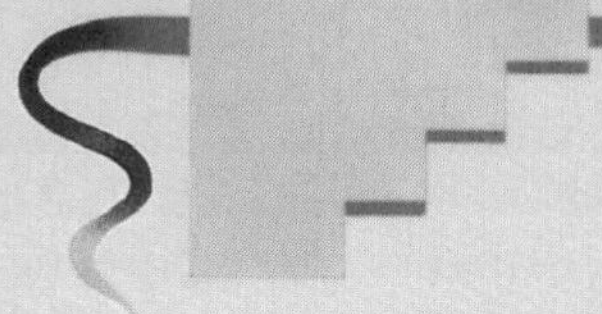

As part of the changing scene of depository banking in America, Dollar Dry Dock depends on a mix of traditional bank services and new services suited to the community. Among the services are commission sales of financial services that other banks do not usually offer (including insurance and securities), credit cards, foreign exchange, and a new approach to real estate mortgages.

A major part of the bank's outreach is toward people who have never felt comfortable in the world of American finance. For example, Dollar Dry Dock instituted a marketing and information service to deal with New York's Spanish-speaking, Korean, Southeast Asian, and Russian immigrant population. At the same time, it launched a credit card program that offered benefits to the previously neglected Vietnam veterans. With regard to the immigrant groups, the bank has been using unconventional criteria to evaluate credit prospects for home loans. Through all its new services, Dollar Dry Dock Bank has kept pace with the changing banking environment by establishing new bonds with the community.

time deposits, money market deposit accounts, and consumer lending and other services.

Demand Deposits

Demand deposits are non-interest-bearing checking account funds held in commercial banks.

Non-interest-bearing checking account funds held in commercial banks are **demand deposits.** Only banks can offer these deposits. When depositors write checks, they are ordering the bank to withdraw money from their accounts and make payments to third parties.

Checkable Deposits

Checkable deposits are interest-bearing checking accounts offered by commercial banks, savings and loan associations, mutual savings banks, and credit unions.

Interest-bearing checking accounts offered by commercial banks, savings and loan associations, mutual savings banks, and credit unions are **checkable deposits.** Most checking account plans require that a minimum balance be maintained in order to avoid a monthly service charge.

As part of the deregulation of the banking system, the federal government has allowed all the depository financial institutions except credit unions to offer a special interest-bearing checking account called a *negotiable order of withdrawal (NOW) account.* A spinoff of the NOW account is the *Super NOW account,* which usually pays higher interest than NOW accounts but requires a larger minimum balance. Holders of NOW and Super NOW accounts usually can write unlimited numbers of checks.

A popular feature of many checking accounts is an overdraft option. This arrangement provides automatic low-interest loans to customers to cover checks that exceed the account balance.

Traveler's Checks

Traveler's checks are checks issued by large financial institutions and sold through depository institutions such as banks and credit unions.

The difficulty of cashing personal checks in distant cities led to the offering of **traveler's checks**—checks issued by large financial institutions and sold through depository institutions such as banks and credit unions. Among the companies offering traveler's checks are American Express, VISA, and Citicorp.

The checks, which usually are available in denominations ranging from $10 to $100, are readily accepted all over the world. Lost or stolen traveler's checks can usually be replaced once the serial numbers are given to the company.

Credit and Debit Cards

The service that most consumers are best acquainted with is *plastic money*—credit cards and debit (access) cards that are issued mainly through commercial banks. *Credit cards* provide a temporary loan to their users by allowing them to purchase items and pay for them later. The monthly bill can be paid in full on the due date or paid off over a period of months. An interest rate (often 1.5 percent per month) is charged on bills not paid on the due date.

VISA and MasterCard are the most popular bank credit cards. In the early 1980s, over 45 percent of U.S. families used either VISA or MasterCard. More than 100 million cards from these companies are in effect worldwide.[6]

Electronic funds transfer systems (EFTSs) are computerized networks that transfer funds from one party to another.

Debit cards (also called access cards) allow customers access to their accounts through **electronic funds transfer systems (EFTSs)**—computerized networks that transfer funds from one party to another. A common example is *automatic* *teller machines (ATMs)*—twenty-four-hour-a-day electronic banking stations. The customer inserts the debit card into the machine, punches in a personal identification code, and transacts bank business. Most people use ATMs to withdraw cash from their accounts. The machines are typically located outside banks and in shopping centers.

Time Deposits

The different forms of insured savings accounts offered by depository financial institutions are **time deposits.** They pay interest and usually have restrictions on the withdrawal of funds. Unlike checking accounts, savings accounts are referred to as near money, because the funds often cannot be used immediately as a medium of exchange.

Time deposits are the different forms of insured savings accounts offered by depository financial institutions.

A popular form of time deposit is the *certificate of deposit (CD)*—a savings deposit made for a fixed term, usually from thirty-two days to eight years. Financial institutions usually pay higher interest rates on these fixed-term accounts because the deposits are locked in for the indicated time period. (Usually, the longer the maturity, the higher the interest rate.) The assurance of having the money for a specific period of time gives the institutions flexibility in making investment decisions. If money is withdrawn early from a CD, there is a monetary penalty, usually in the form of a lower interest rate.

Money Market Deposit Accounts

In order to compete with money market funds (discussed later in the chapter), depository financial institutions now offer **money market deposit accounts (MMDAs).** These accounts pay competitive interest rates and have no minimum maturity, and depositors can withdraw funds from them at any time. However, depositors are allowed only a limited number of monthly transactions—three checks and three automatic transfers is typical.

Money market deposit accounts (MMDAs) are accounts at depository financial institutions that pay competitive interest rates, have no minimum maturity, allow the withdrawal of funds at any time, and limit transactions to six a month.

Lending and Other Services

Depository financial institutions are the major lenders of money to all kinds of borrowers—individuals, companies, and governments, at home and abroad. Their lifeblood is the use of depositors' funds to earn interest income through loans that are as profitable as possible.

They have designed a number of ways to protect their loans in case borrowers cannot repay them promptly. **Secured loans** are protected by a pledge from borrowers to forfeit to lenders something of value if the loans are not repaid. Frequently, loans are secured by the value of what is being purchased. For example, a car loan is secured by the value of the car, which may be sold to recover the amount of the loan. The same principle is applied to many other loans, including those for agricultural equipment and supplies, business inventory, commercial buildings, and home mortgages.

Secured loans are loans protected by a pledge from borrowers to forfeit to lenders something of value if the loans are not repaid.

Mortgages—long-term loans specifically for the purchase of real estate—are usually secured by the value of the real estate itself. Depository financial institutions are heavily involved in lending money for residential mortgages, which amounted in late 1988 to a total of $2.1 trillion.

Mortgages are long-term loans specifically for the purchase of real estate.

Through mortgages and other types of lending, these institutions are tied to the fortunes of the communities they serve. They are betting their depositors'

Depository financial institutions, like this bank in Tokyo, are major lenders of money to all kinds of borrowers including individuals, companies, and governments.

money on their borrowers' ability to repay the loans. If hard times come to a community, as they did to the oil-based economy of the Southwest in the mid-1980s, banks may be unable to recover the money owed on defaulted loans. When businesses do not thrive and laid-off employees cannot make the payments on their mortgage loans, the homes or farms sold for nonpayment will not usually bring in enough money to cover the loans. Thus successful depository financial institutions try to keep in touch with the business prospects of their communities.

Some of the other services found at depository financial institutions are trust departments, safe deposit boxes, foreign exchange trading, and discount brokerage.

Deposit Insurance Protection

Between 1930 and 1933, over nine thousand commercial banks failed. To restore the confidence of Americans in the banking system, the federal government created the *Federal Deposit Insurance Corporation (FDIC)*—the government agency charged with protecting customers' deposits in the event of bank failures. The FDIC began operation on New Year's Day in 1934.

Today, the FDIC insures depositors' accounts up to a maximum of $100,000 per account. It also examines and supervises the operations of many national and state banks. If a bank fails, the FDIC liquidates its assets in an efficient and orderly manner.

All commercial banks that are members of the Federal Reserve System must carry FDIC coverage. Nonmember banks and mutual savings banks may join if they qualify. Banks pay an insurance premium for FDIC protection.

Two other agencies provide similar insurance for deposits. They are the *Federal Savings and Loan Insurance Corporation (FSLIC),* which insures accounts in federal savings and loan associations; and the *National Credit Union Administration (NCUA),* which covers federal credit union deposits. Both agencies insure accounts to the same maximum as the FDIC's.

Some depository institutions choose not to be insured by any of these agencies. Most, however, are privately insured.

HIGHLIGHT IN BUSINESS PRACTICE

Crisis in the S&L Industry

The S&L industry faced a severe crisis in 1989. The FSLIC was bankrupt, with annual losses in excess of $8 billion. Five hundred S&Ls—16 percent of the industry—were insolvent, and five hundred more were failing. The figure shows the rise in bank failures during the 1980s. Estimates of the cost of closing insolvent S&Ls ran to over $60 billion, and shoring up the failing ones was estimated to cost another $25 billion. Many feared the cost could go even higher.

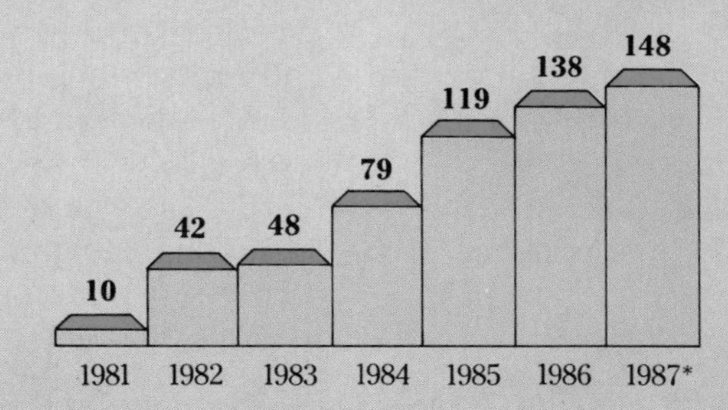

Bank failures in the 1980s. The number of banks that could not be bailed out increased during the 1980s.
**As of mid-October 1987.*

The lack of adequate government monitoring after deregulation is thought to have been a major cause of the crisis. S&Ls were originally established to accept short-term deposits and to provide long-term fixed-rate mortgage loans for local housing. However, in the late 1970s and early 1980s, many S&Ls faced financial problems because they were locked into investments that paid less than it cost to carry them. In response, Congress and many states deregulated the S&Ls to allow them to invest in riskier nonhousing ventures—from hamburger franchises to junk bonds. In California and Texas, particularly, state charters granted S&Ls extraordinary freedom to enter new fields.

Even though they were investing in riskier ventures, the S&Ls were able to amass almost unlimited funds by raising interest rates on deposits guaranteed by the FSLIC. In Texas, for example, from 1982 to 1986, S&Ls were able to increase their assets from $36 billion to $100 billion despite the badly faltering economy. All of this S&L activity went almost completely unmonitored because the Reagan administration and Congress had decided to reduce supervision of the S&Ls in an attempt to reduce the federal budget deficit.

They thought the S&Ls would be regulated by the market. However, the S&Ls were not subject to standard market constraints because of their unlimited ability to raise money by raising interest rates on deposits. In effect, they were borrowing without limit on the deposit insurance offered by the FSLIC. By the time regulators stepped in, the S&Ls were in such bad shape the FSLIC did not have the money needed to bail them out. In 1988, the FSLIC's obligations to depositors in insolvent S&Ls exceeded its assets by roughly $11.6 billion.

The means the FSLIC used to bail out S&Ls were criticized for depleting the FSLIC without resolving the crisis. Bailout schemes led to "prop-up" tactics, with financial giveaways guaranteed by the FSLIC. Individual investors like William Simon, William Howard Beasely, and Robert Bass snapped up these deals, although many companies turned them down. Ford Motor Company, for example, decided it couldn't risk accepting the "wallpaper" promissory notes offered by the FSLIC, which aren't backed by collateral.

With minimal personal investment, private investors were allowed to buy, at extremely low prices, "good" S&Ls—ones that held only profitable mortgages. All the bad loans were put in a separate collecting S&L managed by the FSLIC. The major criticism of the bailouts was that they would eventually force taxpayers to

(continued on next page)

HIGHLIGHT IN BUSINESS PRACTICE

Crisis in the S&L Industry
(Continued)

shoulder the burden of the bad loans, while the current owners of the S&Ls were enjoying unencumbered profit.

Legislation to resolve the S&L crisis was one of the first priorities of the Bush administration. All parties were aware of the need to preserve confidence in the banking system and in deposit insurance and of the need to institute major reforms in the S&L industry, particularly in relation to the insurance program.

NONDEPOSITORY FINANCIAL INSTITUTIONS

Nonbanking companies that provide a range of financial services that used to be the domain of depository financial institutions are known as *nonbanking financial institutions.* Generally, these companies do not accept direct deposits or offer standard checking accounts. Instead they hold individual or corporate funds for investment.

However, some nonbanking institutions act very much like banks. These institutions are often called *financial supermarkets.* The best-known example is Sears Financial Network. Sears takes deposits through Allstate Savings and Loan, writes insurance through Allstate Insurance, sells stocks and bonds through Dean Witter Reynolds, markets real estate through Coldwell Banker, and distributes a credit card—the Discover card—to compete with VISA, MasterCard, and American Express. The card can be used not only at Sears but at many other retail stores and for travel and entertainment.

Money Market Funds

Money market funds are institutions that pool contributions from a large number of investors who wish to put their money into a variety of short-term securities and loans.

Institutions that pool contributions from a large number of investors who wish to put their money into a variety of short-term securities and loans are **money market funds.** Like the depository financial institutions that offer money market deposit accounts, these funds have a limited check-writing capability.

Most money market funds invest in high-quality debt from sound corporate borrowers or governments. They offer a high degree of safety and a competitive interest rate. Since the late 1970s, many people have moved their money out of savings accounts and into money market funds. Investors can withdraw their money from these funds on very short notice. Hence, in many respects, the funds are like time deposits.

Investment Companies and Mutual Funds

There are a variety of other investment company formats, all designed to pool the savings of a large number of individual investors seeking professional management and diversified investments to spread their risk. Some of these companies—for example, Merrill Lynch, American Express, and Fidelity—have broadened their investment services into a network of specialized funds. Investment companies propose financial objectives and strategies to make money for their investors.

Mutual funds, which put most of the pooled funds into stocks, bonds, and other securities, are a common type of investment company. Characteristically, they are willing to let investors sell shares back to them at a prescribed market price. Today, there is a vast array of mutual funds to choose from, depending on investors' taste for risk, tax savings, and willingness to tie up funds for a long or short period.

Mutual funds are investment companies that pool investors' funds to buy stocks, bonds, and other securities.

Investment companies and other nonbanking financial institutions commonly offer IRAs for long-term investment. Under the professional management of an investment company or pension fund, IRAs can grow enough to provide some financial security during retirement.

Pension Funds

Financial institutions designed to provide retirement benefits to employees of various organizations (including the government) are **pension funds.** Billions of dollars are contributed to these funds each year.

Pension funds are financial institutions designed to provide retirement benefits to employees of various organizations.

Given the normal time lag of several years between the cash inflow from contributions and the cash outflow for benefits, pension fund managers have ample opportunity to earn investment income on the accumulated contributions. Consequently, pension funds invest in a variety of financial instruments. As a matter of fact, they are the largest class of investors in the stock market. The largest pension fund is the social security system run by the U.S. government.

Insurance Companies

In exchange for protecting the lives, homes, autos, and so on of policy holders, insurance companies collect billions of dollars in premiums each year. Since the premiums are usually received well in advance of claims payments, the accumulated funds of each company can be invested in loans and securities.

Life insurance companies hold huge amounts of mortgages and bonds. Property and casualty insurance companies are large investors in corporate stocks and municipal bonds. Insurance companies are regulated by state-level insurance commissions. (See chapter 20 for more detail on insurance.)

Finance Companies

Nonbanking companies in the business of making loans to individuals, businesses, or both are **finance companies.** There are three major types of finance companies: consumer, sales, and commercial.

Finance companies are nonbanking companies in the business of making loans to individuals, businesses, or both.

Consumer finance companies, such as Household Finance Corporation (HFC), make secured loans directly to consumers for the purchase of such goods and services as boats, cars, and vacations. Sales finance companies specialize in financing certain types of business—for example, auto and appliance dealers. They are distinguished by the close, long-term relationships they have with their clients. Commercial finance companies make only secured short-term business loans.

Finance companies obtain funding through the sale of short-term unsecured loans to financially sound companies. As a rule, the interest rates they charge are higher than those charged by banks.

REGULATION AND DEREGULATION OF FINANCIAL INSTITUTIONS

The financial revolution of the 1980s has blurred the differences among the many kinds of depository financial institutions and between these institutions and the nondepository financial institutions. Most of the blurring has occurred because government regulations, which once gave each type of institution a separate role, were severely modified by landmark legislation in 1980 and 1982. Table 16.2 provides the key provisions of these laws.

There are compelling reasons, however, for the government to maintain basic forms of regulation of financial institutions. First, the government wishes to help small savers and investors by protecting them from major losses caused by poor managers and unscrupulous professionals. Second, the government wishes to

Table 16.2 Deregulatory legislation affecting banking industry.

Key Provisions of the Monetary Control Act of 1980

1. The Fed was granted the power to establish reserve requirements for all commercial banks and thrift institutions instead of just for Fed member banks.
2. All depository institutions are allowed to offer interest-bearing checking accounts, or negotiable order of withdrawal (NOW) accounts. Interest paid on these accounts was limited.
3. Federally chartered savings and loans and mutual savings banks are allowed to offer consumer loans, serve as agents for credit cards, and invest in a wider variety of debt instruments than before.
4. All interest rate ceilings on time accounts have been eliminated.

Key Provisions of the Garn–St. Germain Depository Act of 1982

1. Banks and thrifts are allowed to offer money market deposit accounts that are directly equal to and competitive with money market mutual funds.
2. Interest rate differentials between banks and savings and loan associations were eliminated.
3. Federally chartered savings and loan associations are allowed to expand their loan portfolios to include nonresidential real estate, commercial loans, and consumer loans.

BUSINESS PRACTICE EXAMPLE Continues

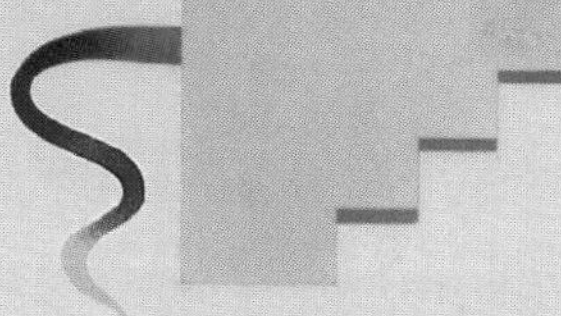

Dollar Dry Dock Bank has been careful to cut costs and reduce risk by avoiding large outlays of funds in its quest for new business. However, it remains vulnerable to the ups and downs of the local economy. Like every bank, its money is tied up largely in loans for community businesses and real estate. Some analysts are worried that too many loans may be out on property with inflated New York prices. If so, the bank is vulnerable to sudden changes in the local economy.

In the southwestern United States, where the oil industry is a major economic factor, a sudden downturn in oil prices affected the entire community, especially the banks. As people were laid off and businesses closed, commercial and real estate loans went unpaid and banks often took big losses. Similar misfortunes occurred with many high-risk loans held by savings and loans during the crisis of the late 1980s.

Unfortunately, many of the S&Ls needing bailout had not been carefully monitored by federal and state regulatory agencies, and irresponsible loan managers were allowed to farm out even riskier loans in an attempt to cover losses. As the FSLIC took a hand with some of these dying S&Ls, it became clear that many bankers had exceeded the limits of good management and safe banking. The federal government had to step in to restore faith in responsible banking and the safety of deposits.

insulate the nation's economy from the shock effect of massive financial institution failures, such as those that helped touch off the Great Depression of the 1930s.

These aims guide the activities of various federal and state agencies, which regularly examine bank records, set up requirements for banks to maintain adequate supplies of capital, and restrict certain kinds of competition and some management practices. They also provide operating rules for securities brokers and insurance companies.

How much government regulation is enough or too much is constantly debated. Many think that the collapse of hundreds of savings and loan associations in the 1980s was due to insufficient supervision or regulation. The *Wall Street Journal*, surveying 162 savings and loans institutions that failed in the decade before 1988, revealed that inadequate controls for key financial officers or departments were responsible for nearly two-thirds of the failures.[7]

On the other hand, critics of regulation claim that the savings and loan losses were speeded up by the actions of regulators. They point out that high-risk bailout schemes, approved by government regulators and backed by the Federal Savings and Loans Insurance Corporation, multiplied losses fivefold or more, giving guaranteed bonanza profits to bailout investors.[8]

Regardless of the debate, the landscape of banking and finance will continue to change rapidly, as institutions adjust to less regulation and more pressure from international competition.

THE FEDERAL RESERVE SYSTEM

The ***Federal Reserve System (Fed)*** is the central banking system of the United States.

As mentioned earlier, the American banking system during the nineteenth century was marked by financial panics and unstable currency. In response to an epidemic of bank failures, Congress passed the Federal Reserve Act in 1913. This legislation established the framework for our central banking system, the **Federal Reserve System (Fed).** The Fed has two traditional functions: to monitor the growth and stability of commercial banking and to regulate the nation's supply of money and credit. Both functions were considerably expanded by the 1980 Monetary Control Act. This law broadened the regulatory powers of the Fed to cover nonmember banks, mutual savings banks, savings and loan associations, and credit unions.

Organizational Makeup of the Fed

The Federal Reserve Act divided the United States into twelve Federal Reserve districts, each with a Federal Reserve Bank (see Figure 16.5). Each Federal Reserve Bank is owned by member commercial banks in its district. A board of directors and officers are responsible for coordinating the day-to-day activities of each branch bank. In practice, the Federal Reserve Banks are banker's banks.

The coordination of the Fed's twelve banks is relegated to a seven-member Board of Governors. Each member is appointed by the president of the United States, subject to the confirmation of the Senate, to a fourteen-year term. The chairperson of the Federal Reserve Board plays a crucial role in deciding U.S. monetary policy.

An important spinoff of this board is the Federal Open Market Committee, which is composed of the seven members of the board plus five of the twelve Federal Reserve Bank presidents. The decisions of this committee have a tremendous impact on the supply of money and credit.

Managing the Money Supply

The key function of the Federal Reserve System, as discussed early in this chapter, is to provide adequate amounts of money to foster economic growth as well as stability. It is generally accepted that too much money in the economy will lead to inflation—the loss of buying power; too little money, however, can mean insufficient funds for investing in growth, which could lead to a recession.

Monetary policy is the set of policies the Fed uses to manage the money supply.

The set of policies the Fed uses to manage the money supply is called **monetary policy.** The Fed's three tools for controlling the money supply are open market operations, the reserve requirement, and the discount rate.

Open Market Operations

The most regularly used tool of monetary control is *open market operations*—the buying and selling of government securities by the Federal Open Market Committee. The securities are usually Treasury bills and notes issued to finance

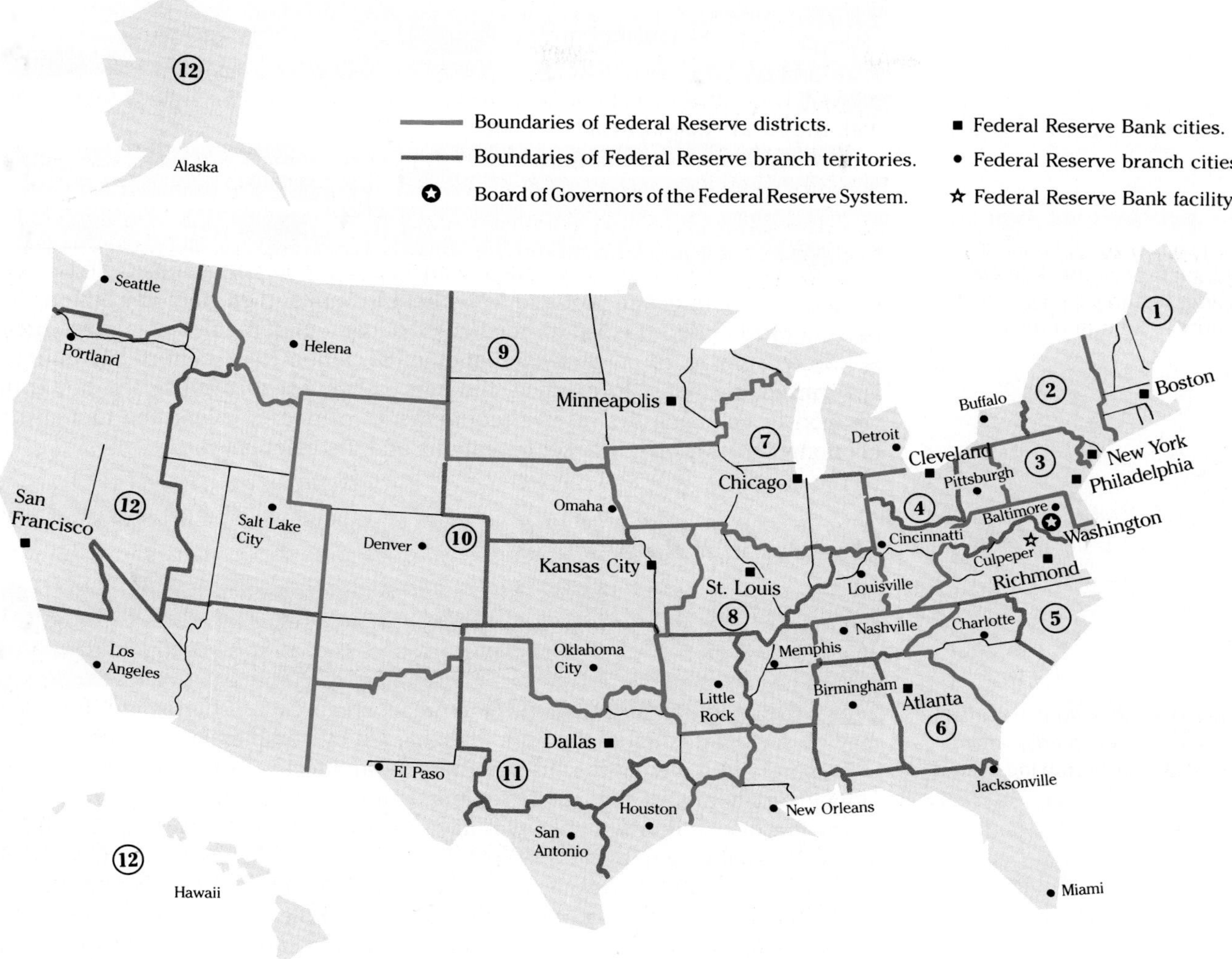

Figure 16.5 The Federal Reserve System and its divisions.

the federal debt. The Fed serves as an agent for the government in the buying and selling process.

If the Fed wants to increase the money supply, it purchases government securities. For example, the Fed might purchase $5 million worth of Treasury bills from Prudential Insurance, paying Prudential with a check. Prudential would deposit the check in its commercial bank, thereby increasing the money supply. This increase should result in lower interest rates and increased economic activity.

Reserves and the Reserve Requirement

The Federal Reserve System gets its name from the fact that it can require depository financial institutions to keep a certain percentage of their savings and checking deposits "on reserve." The reserve funds cannot be loaned out to customers. They must be kept on hand as currency, held in bank vaults or on deposit with the local Federal Reserve Bank.

The Federal Reserve Bank in each district has the power to set the percentage of total funds that must be held in reserve. The percentage established at any point in time is called the **reserve requirement.** Controlling this percentage gives the Fed the power to release money into the economy or to draw it back.

The ***reserve requirement*** is the percentage of funds the Federal Reserve Bank in each district requires banks in that district to hold in reserve.

Consider a district banking system with $40 billion in total deposits. If, say, 15 percent of the funds are required to be held in vaults, then only $34 billion (85 percent of $40 billion) is left for the banks to loan out. If the percentage required is lowered, say to 10 percent, then another $2 billion (5 percent of $40 billion) is released for loans. In practice, the Fed prefers not to overuse the powerful weapon of changing the reserve requirement. Instead, it favors fine tuning the economy through open market operations and the discount rate.

The Discount Rate

An advantage to banks participating in the Federal Reserve System is that they can borrow from their local Federal Reserve Bank—often to create the required reserves. This gives each participating bank access to a large backup fund to draw against if necessary. The interest rate that member banks are charged for borrowing from the Fed is the **discount rate.** To discourage excess borrowing, this rate may be set slightly higher than the rate charged by commercial sources.

The ***discount rate*** is the interest rate the Fed charges member banks for borrowing from it.

Raising and lowering the discount rate is an effective way of controlling the money supply and of influencing interest rates—the cost of money. If the Fed raises the discount rate, banks will have to pay more to borrow money. Since they will usually try to avoid this cost, they will have to be more cautious about lending money, and the result will be an overall decrease in the money supply. As the supply drops, the continuing demand for money will cause interest rates to rise. If higher interest rates discourage a large number of businesses from borrowing the money they need to expand, a widespread economic slowdown can result.

For example, during the inflationary spiral of the early 1980s, the discount rate was raised several times. The overall effect was to slow down borrowing by making it more expensive. As less money was loaned out, companies became more cautious about spending, the economy slowed, and further inflation was avoided. The Fed's efforts to create this kind of economic contraction are called *tight money policy.*

The Fed's decrease in the discount rate has the opposite effect. Money becomes cheaper to borrow, and businesses can afford to take more risks in expanding their activities. Thus a lower discount rate can stimulate the economy. As you can see, the governing board of the Federal Reserve System has a major influence on balancing economic activity in the United States. Table 16.3 summarizes how each of the Fed's regulatory tools can be used to curb or stimulate the economy.

Table 16.3 The tools of the Federal Reserve System.

Federal Reserve Decision	Effect on the Money Supply	Change in Interest Rates	General Economic Impact
Open Market Operations			
1. Fed buys government securities.	Money supply increases.	Interest rates decrease.	Economic activity increases.
2. Fed sells government securities.	Money supply decreases.	Interest rates increase.	Economic activity decreases.
Reserve Requirement			
Fed increases reserve requirement.	Money supply decreases.	Interest rates increase.	Economic activity decreases.
Fed decreases reserve requirement.	Money supply increases.	Interest rates decrease.	Economic activity increases.
Discount Rate			
1. Fed increases discount rate.	Money supply decreases.	Interest rates increase.	Economic activity decreases.
2. Fed decreases discount rate.	Money supply increases.	Interest rates decrease.	Economic activity increases.

The Fed as Fiscal Agent for the U.S. Treasury

As fiscal agent for the U.S. Treasury, the Fed conducts sales of Treasury securities, maintains the government's checking account, and helps administer the official gold stock. It also prints the nation's currency (known officially as Federal Reserve notes) and distributes it to depository financial institutions. The Fed also serves as an agent for the government in buying and selling its securities in the open market.

Check Clearing

Checking accounts are the major payment mechanism in the U.S. economy. In other words, most bills are paid with checks. Since millions of checks are written every day, a system for processing or clearing checks is essential.

The simplest situation involves a check writer and a check recipient whose checking accounts are with the same depository institution. All the institution has to do in order to clear such a check is raise the recipient's checking account balance by the amount of the deposited check while simultaneously lowering the check writer's account balance.

When two depository institutions are involved and they are located in the same community, clearing a check is somewhat more involved. The affected institutions must transfer funds from one to the other. *Clearinghouses* have been set up in most communities to facilitate this matter, and they often compete with the Fed in efficiency and price.

When the check writer's and check recipient's checking accounts are with institutions in different communities, check clearing is normally handled by the Federal Reserve Bank. The Fed clears a check simply by adjusting the reserve accounts of the two institutions. (The Fed charges a fee for this service.) As you can imagine, such a process can be time-consuming. (See Figure 16.6.)

Since most checking accounts are maintained in computers, it is now possible to pay bills electronically with checking account money. Electronic payment leads to electronic clearing of checking accounts, since most depository institution computers are linked together in various ways. Many experts believe electronic payments will someday eclipse checks as the principal means of payment.

INTERNATIONAL FINANCE

A ***monetary system*** is a country's money and banking system, embodied in a central bank.

Each country has its own **monetary system** (money and banking system, embodied in a central bank) and currency. The United States has the Federal Reserve

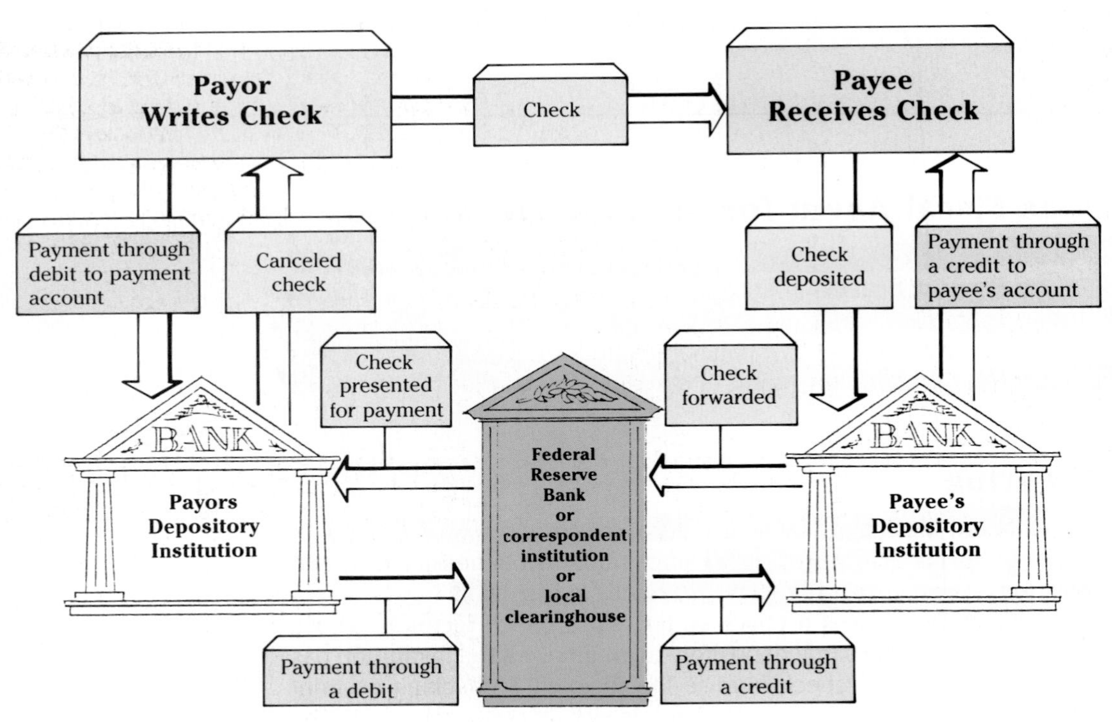

Figure 16.6 Elements of the check-clearing system. Transactions are settled at a Federal Reserve Bank or a correspondent institution or local clearinghouse by crediting the deposit account of the payee's depository institution and debiting the deposit account of the payor's depository institution.

System and the dollar, West Germany the Bundesbank and the mark, and Great Britain the Bank of England and the pound. As a group, all of the various monies are referred to as foreign currencies. Since each country controls its money supply independently of other countries, the various currencies tend to have different values. For example, one dollar does not equal one pound or one yen. This situation gives rise to the need for exchange rates between foreign currencies. **Foreign exchange** is the trading of one country's currency for funds of equal value in another country's currency.

Foreign exchange is the trading of one country's currency for funds of equal value in the currency of another country.

Most international business transactions require the exchanging of currency. For example, Americans exchange dollars for pounds in order to buy British stocks, and Germans exchange marks for francs in order to acquire French wine. Sometimes, the value of something priced in one currency must be translated into another currency. All foreign currency exchanging and translating is carried out at specified rates; hence the term *foreign exchange rates* (or *exchange rates*). An **exchange rate** is the price of one currency in terms of another currency.

An ***exchange rate*** (or foreign exchange rate) is the price of one currency in terms of another currency.

Table 16.4 shows some foreign exchange rates in terms of the U.S. dollar. Take, for example, the exchange rate between the German mark and the U.S. dollar: 1.9395. This means that at the time indicated in the table, 1.9395 marks equaled 1 dollar. The dollar to mark exchange rate is the inverse of 1.9395 (1 divided by 1.9395), or .5155. Notice the variation in exchange rates displayed in the table. At one extreme is the British pound–U.S. dollar exchange rate of .6307. At the other extreme is the Italian lira–U.S. dollar rate of 1,389.00.

From an economic standpoint, the wide disparity in exchange rates is not nearly as important as the fact that rates can change over time. For instance, the Japanese yen–U.S. dollar exchange rate went from over 250 in 1985 to under 125

Table 16.4 Foreign exchange rates as of September 1989.

Country/Currency	Currency Units per U.S. Dollar
Australia/dollar	1.3003
Canada/dollar	1.1760
China, P.R./yuan	3.7214
France/franc	6.5200
Germany/deutsche mark	1.9395
Hong Kong/dollar	7.8075
India/rupee	16.61
Italy/lira	1389.00
Japan/yen	143.10
Malaysia/ringgit	2.6950
Netherlands/guilder	2.1810
Singapore/dollar	1.9655
South Korea/won	670.70
Sweden/krona	6.5525
Switzerland/franc	1.6705
Taiwan/dollar	25.43
United Kingdom/pound	.6307

Since every country controls its money independently of other countries the various currencies have different values. The foreign exchange rate determines the price of one currency in terms of another.

in 1987. (The implications of such a change will be addressed in chapters 18 and 23.)

The rate of exchange between one nation's currency and another's is determined largely by supply and demand in the *foreign exchange market*—a loosely knit system of exporters, importers, speculators, investors, and bankers from around the world. Most currency trading is handled by large banks located in financial centers such as Paris, New York, Tokyo, London, and Zurich. These financial centers are tied together electronically to form a global foreign exchange market with around-the-clock trading.

A number of factors underlie the supply of and demand for a particular country's money in relation to another's. Chief among these factors is the relative price level of goods and services in the two countries. Another important factor is the countries' relative interest rates. Governments and their central banks also intervene in foreign exchange markets from time to time in an effort to alter exchange rates.

BUSINESS PRACTICE EXAMPLE Continues

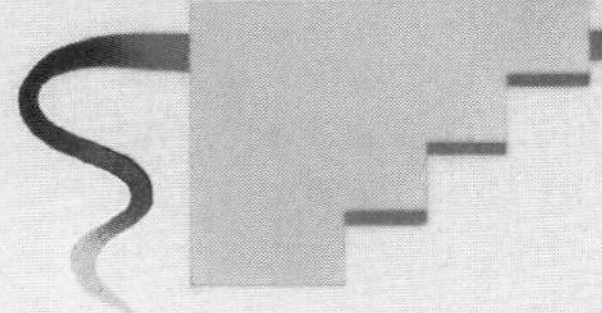

Dollar Dry Dock Bank's survival in the cutthroat competition of banking in the 1980s depended on its ability to set new trends for innovative customer services. One innovation was a different approach to the credit rating of newcomer immigrants applying for mortgage loans. The bank backed the credit of immigrant homeowners on the basis of their work records. Said CEO Robert Steele, "The first generation always works harder than the next will. If we help them buy a home, they'll do everything they can to keep that home."

Dollar Dry Dock's major innovation was the "supermarket," or "department store," idea—offering insurance and investment services along with loans, checking, foreign exchange, and so on. But the most surprising part of the bank's innovation was the addition of a simple ingredient—a real person. The bank created a position for an information officer—a well-informed professional who understood all the bank's offerings and could explain them in ways that would help a variety of customers, including non-English-speaking immigrants new to American banking. Positioned at a centrally located desk, the information officer was able to route customers efficiently to the banks brokers, insurance agents, loan officers, or agents to help with foreign currency exchange or traveler's checks.

Issues for Discussion

1. How much of Dollar Dry Dock's financial service offering goes beyond the normal limits of services from a depository financial institution? Explain.
2. How much risk does the individual savings account depositor take if the bank makes unsound mortgage loans that lose money?
3. In what areas of Dollar Dry Dock's operation would the public benefit from careful monitoring by government regulators?

SUMMARY

Money is anything widely accepted as a medium for the buying and selling of goods and services. The simplest form of exchange is barter, which doesn't need money. The American colonists used barter locally but were forced to use paper promises (of gold and silver) to pay for goods abroad.

Money must function as a medium of exchange, a measure of value, and a liquid store of value. It should be portable, durable, acceptable, consistent in value, divisible, and difficult to counterfeit.

Modern society needs a currency whose value can be trusted. The U.S. government uses several measures of the money supply. The two most basic are M1 (cash and funds readily convertible to cash) and M2 (M1 plus near money).

The United States has a variety of depository financial institutions. In the past, their functions were different, but since deregulation in the early 1980s they do many of the same things. The four major types of these institutions are commercial banks (which are either national or state banks), credit unions, savings and loan associations (S&Ls), and mutual savings banks.

Commercial banks offer demand deposits. All the depository financial institutions offer checkable deposits, and all but credit unions can offer negotiable order of withdrawal (NOW) accounts. Other services of depository financial institutions are traveler's checks, credit and debit cards (debit cards are used with the electronic funds transfer systems of automatic teller machines and point-of-sale terminals), time deposits (including certificates of deposit), money market deposit accounts, and consumer lending and other services (including secured loans and mortgages).

The Federal Deposit Insurance Corporation (FDIC) insures bank deposits to a maximum of $100,000 per account. The Federal Savings and Loan Insurance Corporation (FSLIC) does the same for savings and loans, and the National Credit Union Administration (NCUA) covers credit union deposits.

Interstate banking is a growing trend since restrictions against it were removed.

Nonbanking financial institutions supply a number of financial services. Among these institutions are money market funds, investment companies and mutual funds, pension funds, insurance companies, and finance companies.

Although the banking industry was deregulated to a large degree in the early 1980s, some regulations are still needed to protect consumers and the economy.

The Federal Reserve System (Fed) is the central banking system of the United States. It is made up of twelve districts, each with a Federal Reserve Bank, and it is coordinated by a Board of Governors. A spinoff of the board is the Federal Open Market Committee.

The Fed's key function is to manage the money supply, for which it uses three tools: open market operations, the reserve requirement, and the discount rate. The Fed is also the fiscal agent for the Treasury and plays a role in check clearing.

Each country has its own monetary system and currency. As a group, all of the various monies are called foreign currencies, or foreign exchange. The price of one currency in terms of another is the exchange rate (or foreign exchange rate). The currencies are traded in the foreign exchange market.

KEY TERMS

Barter p. 467
Checkable deposits p. 476
Commercial banks p. 473
Credit unions p. 474
Demand deposits p. 476
Discount rate p. 486
Electronic funds transfer systems (EFTSs) p. 476
Exchange rate p. 489
Federal Reserve System (Fed) p. 484
Finance companies p. 481
Foreign exchange p. 489
Individual Retirement Accounts (IRAs) p. 474
Liquidity p. 469
M1 p. 471
M2 p. 472
Monetary policy p. 484
Monetary system p. 488
Money p. 467
Money market deposit accounts (MMDAs) p. 477
Money market funds p. 480
Mortgages p. 477
Mutual funds p. 481
Mutual savings banks p. 475
Pension funds p. 481
Reserve requirement p. 486
Savings and loan associations (S&Ls) p. 474
Secured loans p. 477
Time deposits p. 477
Traveler's checks p. 476

CHECK YOUR LEARNING

Reread the following learning objectives. Each objective is followed by a few questions. Answering these questions accurately will help you retain the most important concepts discussed in this chapter. After answering each question, check your answer with the key at the end of this chapter. (*Hint:* If you have doubt regarding the correct response, consult the page whose number follows the answer.)

Circle:

A. Explain the role of money in America prior to the development of the modern capitalistic system.

T F 1. During the colonial period, all money was in the form of either gold or silver.
T F 2. Early forms of money were stable in value and small in bulk.
a b c d 3. An exchange process based on commodities is known as (a) bartering; (b) auctioning; (c) catering; (d) collective bargaining.
T F 4. The exchange of goods and services is easier in a money economy as compared to a barter system.

B. List and discuss the three basic functions of money.

a b c d 1. The store of value of money is most affected by: (a) bond prices; (b) stock prices; (c) currency size; (d) inflation.
T F 2. All money serves as a medium of exchange.

C. Describe the characteristics of sound money.

T F 1. Livestock was a good form of money because of its liquidity.
T F 2. Unlike earlier forms of money, America's paper currency is difficult to counterfeit.
T F 3. A checking account has less divisibility than gold.

D. Distinguish between the basic money supply (M1) and near money.

a b c d 1. All the following are included in the basic money supply except: (a) traveler's checks; (b) checkable deposits; (c) money market funds; (d) currency.
T F 2. Checking accounts are considered to be part of the basic money supply (M1).
a b c d 3. Which one of the following items makes up the greatest percentage of M1? (a) currency; (b) time deposits; (c) checkable deposits; (d) demand deposits.

E. Compare and contrast the changing role of depository financial institutions following deregulation.

1. All of the following are called depository financial institutions except: (a) insurance companies; (b) credit unions; (c) mutual savings banks; (d) savings and loan associations. a b c d
2. The Monetary Control Act of 1980 paved the way for more government control in the banking industry. T F
3. Credit union checking accounts are called: (a) debit accounts; (b) NOW accounts; (c) shares; (d) bank drafts. a b c d
4. Deposit insurance of $100,000 per account is provided by: (a) NCUA; (b) FDIC; (c) FSLIC; (d) all of the above. a b c d

F. Describe the structure and organization of the Federal Reserve System.

1. All national banks must belong to the Federal Reserve System. T F
2. The decision-making process used by the Fed to manage the money supply is called: (a) monetary policy; (b) hedging; (c) fiscal policy; (d) discounting. a b c d

G. Discuss the tools of monetary policy used by the Federal Reserve System.

1. Select one of the following that is *not* a tool of monetary control: (a) legal reserve requirement; (b) electronic funds transfer; (c) discount rate; (d) open market operations. a b c d
2. A decrease in the reserve requirement usually increases the money supply. T F
3. An increase in the discount rate results in a: (a) decrease in credit demanded; (b) increase in credit demanded; (c) decrease in interest rates; (d) increase in money supply. a b c d

H. Describe the role of foreign exchange rates in international business.

1. A mark to franc exchange rate of 5 would correspond to a franc to mark exchange rate of 1. T F
2. The most significant thing about foreign exchange rates is that they are: (a) easy to calculate; (b) quoted in terms of international currency; (c) susceptible to change; (d) unrelated to foreign trade patterns. a b c d

QUESTIONS FOR REVIEW AND DISCUSSION

1. Define the key terms listed at the end of the chapter.
2. What is the relationship between money and the bartering process?
3. Money serves three basic functions. Name them and explain how each facilitates the working of our economy.
4. Do you agree or disagree with the following statement: Inflation has a minimal impact on money's store of value. Explain.
5. Compare and contrast commercial banks and the other depository financial institutions.
6. Interview the marketing director of a bank or another bank officer. Ask about the types of checking and savings accounts offered and about whether you qualify for a NOW account. Do your findings agree with the information in the text?
7. How are nonbanking financial institutions competing with depository financial institutions?
8. Explain why financial institutions should be regulated.
9. List the Fed's three tools for controlling the money supply and explain how they are used.
10. In cooperation with your instructor, form a committee and design a talk about money, specifying the topics and the professionals you would like to have address them. Invite a couple speakers or a panel to talk about these topics.

CONCLUDING CASE

Bank's New Services Cost More

The deregulation of financial institutions has spawned a vast array of new accounts and services at our nation's banks and savings institutions. Customers receive promotional brochures offering NOW accounts and Super NOW accounts, automatic tellers are on every corner, and multiple options for savings accounts are readily available. Many consumers are confused and often pay service fees needlessly.

These fees, or penalties, are charged when balances for regular checking, savings, and NOW accounts fall below prescribed levels. Charges for insufficient funds in a checking account (bounced check) are also common. These hidden fees have risen greatly and vary among financial institutions. One survey found that penalties for bounced checks ranged from $7 to $20. The minimum balance to avoid charges on NOW accounts varied from a low of $50 to a high of $2,500. The Fed estimated that deregulation has resulted in the doubling of service charges on deposit accounts. In one year, banks collected $10 billion in service fees on deposit accounts. Banks claim they must impose the fees and set account minimums because deregulation has forced them to pay higher interest rates on deposits.

Issues for Discussion

1. Should banks be required to inform consumers about service fees? Explain.
2. What advice would you give consumers to help them avoid charges on deposit accounts?
3. Should the Fed impose limits on fees charged for bounced checks or for balances below the minimum?

NOTES

1. "Fundamental Facts about United States Money," (Atlanta: Federal Reserve Bank of Atlanta, 1988), p. 11.
2. *Credit Union Magazine,* Credit Union National Association, Inc., Madison, Wisconsin, May 1989, p. 8.
3. Ibid.
4. *Savings Institution Sourcebook* (U.S. League of Savings Institutions, 1984), p. 9.
5. Ibid., p. 5.
6. Laurie P. Cohen, "Prestige Cards: For Big Bucks and Big Egos," *Wall Street Journal,* April 17, 1985, p. 31.
7. *Wall Street Journal,* February 25, 1988, p. 23.
8. Gary Schilling, "Let the Government Make You Rich," *Fortune,* October 10, 1988, pp. 167–168; and William Sheeline, "Big Names in S&L Buyouts," *Fortune,* September 26, 1988, p. 10.

CHECK YOUR LEARNING ANSWER KEY

A. 1. F, *p. 467*
   2. F, *p. 467*
   3. a, *p. 467*
   4. T, *p. 467*

B. 1. d, *p. 469*
   2. T, *p. 468*

C. 1. F, *p. 469*
   2. T, *p. 471*
   3. F, *p. 470*

D. 1. c, *p. 471*
   2. T, *p. 471*
   3. d, *p. 471*

E. 1. a, *pp. 473-474*
   2. F, *p. 482*
   3. c, *p. 474*
   4. d, *p. 478*

F. 1. T, *p. 484*
   2. a, *p. 484*

G. 1. b, *p. 484*
   2. T, *pp. 486, 487*
   3. a, *pp. 486, 487*

H. 1. F, *p. 489*
   2. c, *p. 489*

CHAPTER

17

ACCOUNTING: UNDERSTANDING THE LANGUAGE OF BUSINESS

LEARNING OBJECTIVES

After reading this chapter you should be able to:

1. Explain the purpose and scope of accounting.
2. Distinguish between the roles of public and private accountants.
3. List and discuss three outside groups that use information generated by financial accountants.
4. Chart the flow of information in the accounting cycle.
5. Define the two basic accounting equations.
6. Create a simple example of a balance sheet and an income statement.
7. Compare and contrast the different accounts in financial statements.
8. Calculate and interpret the meaning of selected financial ratios.
9. Explain the role of accountants in the processes of budgeting and cost analysis.

OUTLINE

Business Practice Example: Accountant Sleuths Uncover Phony Money in California

The Nature of Accounting

- Defining *Accounting*
- Sorting Out Accounting Titles

Users of Accounting Information

- Managers
- Owners and Investors
- Creditors
- Government

The Accounting Cycle

Key Accounting Equations

- Balance Sheet Equation
- Profit Equation

Financial Statements: Company Scorecards

- Balance Sheets
  - Assets
  - Liabilities
  - Owner's (Stockholders') Equity
- Income Statements

Ratios: The Heart of Financial Analysis

- Liquidity Ratios
- Activity Ratios
- Leverage Ratios
- Profitability Ratios
- Time Series Analysis

Internal Uses of Accounting

- Budgeting
- Cost Analysis

Summary

Key Terms

Check Your Learning

Questions for Review and Discussion

Concluding Case: The Annual Report: A Medium of Fluff?

Notes

Check Your Learning Answer Key

Highlight in Business Practice: Price Waterhouse Covers the Waterfront in Business

BUSINESS PRACTICE EXAMPLE

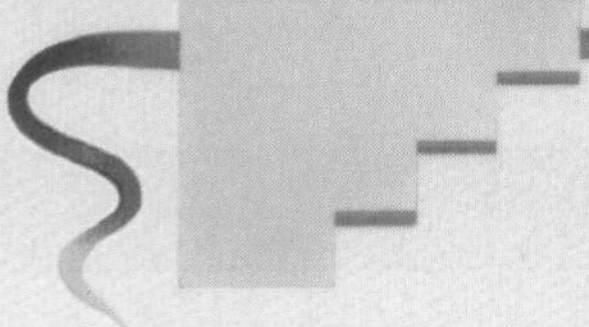

Accountant Sleuths Uncover Phony Money in California

The forensic accounting firm John Murphy and Associates Inc. specializes in investigating the financial records of firms suspected of fraud. Murphy and Associates was hired in early 1988 to unravel the tangled affairs of ZZZZ Best, a Reseda, California, carpet cleaning company. Their efforts in that case revealed the difference between a routine audit of the books and an in-depth analysis to uncover fraud.

After declaring bankruptcy, ZZZZ Best was reported to have left its investors holding over $70 million in losses. The firm's founder, Barry J. Minlow, was put in prison to await trial on charges of fraud, money laundering, and racketeering.

Murphy and Associates initiated the audit with a thorough investigation into the backgrounds of ZZZZ Best's top officers. The forensic accountants then began their work in earnest, examining ZZZZ Best's ledgers, contracts, and bank statements. Company checks were particularly suspect, because they tended to be written by hand, in large round numbers, and often payable to cash. The checking account analysis was performed on computer.

The accounting firm concentrated on the checking account transactions between ZZZZ Best and two other firms: Interstate Appraisal Services, which supposedly gave ZZZZ Best the building refurbishing jobs that accounted for nearly 90 percent of its business; and Marbil Management Company, a contractor that was allegedly working for ZZZZ Best.

Murphy accountants said the checking account information indicated that the same money was going round and round: from ZZZZ Best to Marbil, back to Interstate, and apparently back again to ZZZZ Best. A member of the accounting team said it was still trying to determine how much money was siphoned off during the transfers. The purpose of all this money movement was to make ZZZZ Best look like a legitimate business, the auditors said. Probably the most unsettling discovery made by the Murphy accountants was that ZZZZ Best's major source of revenue—the building refurbishing contracts—appeared to be bogus.

The accounting firm Ernst & Whinney, ZZZZ Best's regular auditor, resigned after it began to suspect that one of the company's major contracts did not exist. The firm was sued by ZZZZ Best's investors over alleged violations of federal and state securities laws. Ernst & Whinney denied any wrongdoing.

WHAT'S AHEAD

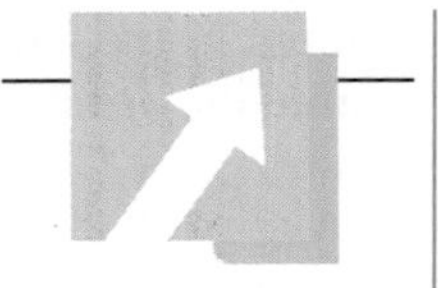

Someone once said that accounting is the language of business. As a matter of fact, accounting is even more. It is also responsible for the development, organization, and synthesis of business information. In the case of ZZZZ Best, a clear statement of business information was needed as a test for fraud. In the following pages, we will look into the basics of accounting and examine some of the duties of accountants. We will also become familiar with the construction and meaning of two financial statements, the balance sheet and the income statement, and of how they are analyzed by investors. Finally, we will view some of the major functions of accounting in company management.

THE NATURE OF ACCOUNTING

The goal of every business is to achieve and maintain financial fitness. Just as individuals must eat a balanced diet to be physically fit, a business must take in sufficient funds to be financially fit. Many doctors recommend keeping records documenting progress toward specific fitness goals. Business transactions must also be recorded and evaluated regularly. In a business setting, the accountant often plays the role of doctor—recording financial information and diagnosing the results.

Defining *Accounting*

The process of collecting, analyzing, and reporting information that reflects the financial condition of a company is **accounting.** More specifically:

Accounting is the process of collecting, analyzing, and reporting information that reflects the financial condition of a company.

> Accounting focuses on the measurement and reporting, in monetary terms, of the flows of resources into and out of an organization, of the resources controlled by the organization, and of the claims against those resources. In doing this, accounting collects, processes, evaluates, and reports certain information. In addition, accounting involves broad judgemental and interpretative roles in the reporting and use of financial results.[1]

As this explanation implies, the first step of the accounting process involves the accurate recording of all the financial transactions that occur in an organization. This step is called **bookkeeping.** However, the role of a bookkeeper and that of an accountant are vastly different. Bookkeeping involves the routine and clerical side of accounting and requires only a minimal knowledge of the entire accounting process. In fact, many bookkeeping procedures are now computerized. Accounting calls for a more analytical perspective. Indeed, a professional accountant is challenged with complex decisions involving ratio analysis, tax preparation, information systems, and management consulting.

Bookkeeping, the initial step in the accounting process, is the accurate recording of all the financial transactions that occur in an organization.

Sorting Out Accounting Titles

One basic way to distinguish between accountants is to refer to them as either public or private accountants. *Public accountants* offer professional services to the general public for a fee and are not employees of any one client. A public accountant serves clients by inspecting, or auditing, their accounting records, preparing company and individual tax returns, and offering management assistance. Many public accountants achieve the status of **certified public accountant (CPA).** Over one-fourth of the nearly 1 million accountants in the United States have achieved this status by passing a rigorous state examination and completing certain residency and field experience requirements. Although a CPA license is not required to practice public accounting, only a CPA can officially attest to whether an organization's financial statements represent a fair and accurate picture of the financial condition.

A ***certified public accountant (CPA)*** is a public accountant who has passed a rigorous state examination and completed certain residence and field experience requirements.

In contrast to public accountants, *private accountants* are salaried employees of the firms they serve. Often referred to as corporate or industrial accountants, private accountants may be comptrollers, internal auditors, treasurers, or business managers (see Table 17.1). Although private accountants are often involved in the key decisions affecting the financial status of a company, their professional status has traditionally been lower than that of CPAs.

Public accountants offer professional services to the general public for a fee; they are not employees of any one client. This certified public account (CPA) inspects and audits accounting records for his clients.

To deal with the issue of professional qualifications, the National Association of Accountants developed the *certified management accountant (CMA)* program in 1972. The CMA program is geared specifically to private accountants engaged in accounting for management decision making. To achieve a CMA designation, an accountant must meet specific educational and professional standards, pass a series of tests written by the National Association of Accountants, and be awarded the Certificate in Management Accounting. Approximately 4,200 private accountants are CMAs.[2] Table 17.2 (p. 502) compares the CPA and CMA requirements.

USERS OF ACCOUNTING INFORMATION

Accountants compile financial data that serve the needs of both management and outside groups that have an interest in the company. (Figure 17.1 illustrates the accounting process both within and outside the company.) What are the groups that use accounting information, and why do they want it?

Table 17.1 Functions of private accountants.

Organizational Title	Functions (Using Accounting Information)
Comptroller	Oversees all financial record-keeping; serves as chief accounting officer.
Internal auditor	Inspects and evaluates accounting and other financial records to determine their accuracy.
Treasurer	Oversees financing and financial management planning decisions.
Business manager	Oversees both accounting and financial management planning, usually for a corporate subdivision.

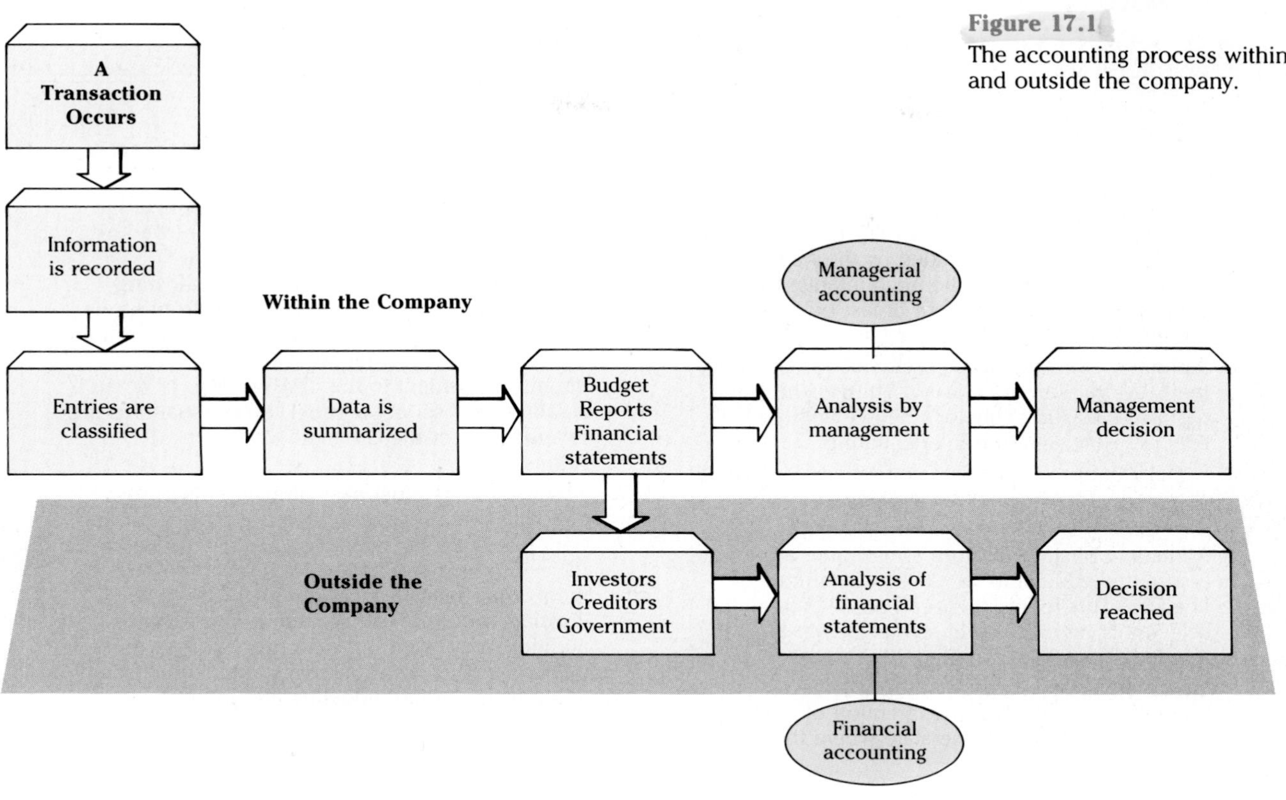

Figure 17.1
The accounting process within and outside the company.

Managers

Managers constantly need reports of financial information to determine organizational efficiency in the areas of costs, profit margins, and resource use, as well as to plan for the money and resources needed for the future.

Accounting that focuses on helping managers inside the organization is called *managerial accounting.* (It will be discussed in detail at the end of the chapter.) Accounting that focuses on financial statements for those outside the organization is called *financial accounting.* The information provided by financial accounting is also important to internal managers, who measure financial progress and stability in periodic financial reports.

Owners and Investors

All businesses rely on investments made by their owners (stockholders in the case of corporations). Anyone interested in investing in a partnership, for example, would want to see basic information on the firm's track record of profitability and financial stability. Whether these potential owners were considering investing in a small firm or in a large corporation, they would rely heavily on accounting data. Since most stockholders are not active in the daily management of corporations, the accounting information included in the annual report (the report to investors

Table 17.2 Comparison of CPA and CMA requirements.

CPA Requirements	CMA Requirements
1. All states require that the prospective CPA obtain a passing score on the Uniform CPA Examination, which is prepared and graded by the American Institute of Certified Public Accountants. CPA candidates are tested in four areas: practice, theory, auditing, and business law. 2. Minimum educational requirements for sitting for the CPA exam are increasing. Thirty-eight states require at least a bachelor's degree with an effective concentration in accounting. 3. A majority of states require some degree of public accounting or equivalent experience before granting a CPA license. 4. A majority of states require a minimum amount of continuing education for CPAs to retain their licenses. This requirement forces CPAs to attend selected conferences and seminars over a given period of time, usually one to three years. 5. Most states require that the test applicant be a U.S. citizen (or declare the intention of becoming one) and a resident of the state where the test is taken.	1. The CMA program requires the test applicant to be of good moral character, to be employed or expect to be employed in management accounting, and to meet one of the following conditions: hold a bachelor's degree from an accredited college or university, be a CPA or hold a professional designation issued in a foreign country equivalent to the CPA or CMA, or achieve a satisfactory score on either the Graduate Record Examination or the Graduate Management Admission test. 2. Test applicants must pass all five parts of the certificate examination within a three-year period. Candidates are tested in these areas: (a) economics and finance; (b) organization theory and behavior, including ethical considerations; (c) public reporting standards, auditing, and taxes; (d) periodic reporting for internal and external purposes; and (e) decision analysis, including modeling and information systems. 3. Test applicants must have two years of professional experience in management accounting before the examination is taken or must acquire this experience within seven years of completing the examination before the certificate is awarded. 4. Individuals must complete ninety hours of continuing education in each three-year period following the successful writing of the exam.

about the economic status of the firm) is most significant. Likewise, the potential investor often wishes to examine past financial performance as well as the current status of the business. Such information is usually published widely for the benefit of the investing public. Many corporations encourage consumers to write for a copy of their annual report.

Creditors

Most businesses rely on creditors for part of their financial funding. As we will see in chapter 18, securing credit is a complex and challenging task. Accountants must be able to provide accurate and up-to-date financial statements to lenders. Lending agencies such as banks carefully examine the financial position of the applicant in order to judge growth potential, profitability, liquidity, and solvency.

Reliable accounting information greatly increases the borrowing capability of businesses.

Government

The federal government and state and local governments tax company income. In order to file accurate tax returns, accountants must generate financial statements. The Internal Revenue Service has strict specifications on how revenues and expenses are to be classified and summarized for computing the federal income tax of a company. Many other government agencies also request information periodically. The Federal Trade Commission, for example, frequently analyzes the profit patterns of various industries. And the Securities and Exchange Commission requires special reports from public corporations on a regular basis.

THE ACCOUNTING CYCLE

The comptroller serves as the scorekeeper for the business. Just as a scorekeeper for a basketball tournament must have a prescribed way to document the results of each game, so too must a financial accountant have a defined set of procedures and books to record the business's activities. Since most of the initial work of the comptroller involves the recording of financial events, this section will examine the nature of transactions and accounts.

Modern accounting practices are composed of accepted procedures that accountants must follow over a specific period of time. The sequence of procedures is referred to as the **accounting cycle.** These procedures usually involve recording and classifying all transactions in a set of accounts. An **account** is a register of financial value. For example, cash is an asset account having a specific dollar balance. A **transaction** is an event that increases or decreases the value of an account. Spending cash to pay off a loan is a transaction that must be recorded to reflect the changes in account balances. The entire collection of all the dollar values in all the accounts is referred to as the firm's *books.*

The ***accounting cycle*** is the sequence of accepted procedures that accountants must follow over a specific period of time.

An ***account*** is a register of financial value.

A ***transaction*** is an event that either increases or decreases the value of an account.

Journals are a special set of books in which all transactions affecting account values are first recorded.

Posting is the procedure of transferring the transactions in journals to the respective accounts.

Most businesses use the following five basic types of accounts: asset accounts, income accounts, expense accounts, liability accounts, and equity accounts. The role of the comptroller is to ensure that all transactions that affect the values in these accounts are recorded properly. Usually, the daily transactions are recorded in a special set of books called **journals.** Journals are referred to as books of original entry because all transactions affecting account values are recorded in them first. **Posting** is the procedure of transferring the transactions in the journals to the respective accounts. Today, much of this bookkeeping is done by computer. However, in smaller businesses, it is still done manually.

Eventually, a business must tally up the accounts so that the financial status of the firm can be evaluated. The accounts are totaled and then accounts are *closed,* so that no further transactions are recorded, and the totals are transferred to the financial statements. With this step, the accounting cycle is complete. Figure 17.2 (p. 505) depicts this process graphically. Later, ratios may be calculated and used to determine the financial condition of the firm.

Accountants are concerned with analyzing the end product of the accounting cycle, which consists of the balance sheet and the income statement. The balance sheet equation and the profit equation are needed for an understanding of these financial statements.

HIGHLIGHT IN BUSINESS PRACTICE

Price Waterhouse Covers the Waterfront in Business

The Big Eight accounting firm Price Waterhouse has been described as the Tiffany of accounting firms—not the biggest but the best. It has been ranked the number 1 auditor of financial records of Fortune 500 companies and Forbes 100 U.S. multinationals. An old firm, Price Waterhouse was founded in London in 1849 and opened its first U.S. office in 1890. It now has a hundred offices across the country. It is also profitable, with revenues of $1.7 billion in a recent year. As part of a network of twenty firms with approximately four hundred offices in ninety-nine countries and territories, Price Waterhouse's scope is global.

Half the work the firm does is direct accounting and auditing. Because of its emphasis on an in-depth understanding of each business and its management philosophy, goals, and operating environment, Price Waterhouse's audits can assist a company in its financial management. "We audit your business, not just your books," the firm claims. "I think it's going too far to say that we know more than the chairman," says Joseph Connor, chairman of Price Waterhouse, "but we have valuable insights for that chairman as well as for the directors or other levels of management as a result of an audit."

Consulting services are the faster-growing half of Price Waterhouse's work. What kind of consulting? "Almost without limit I would say is the best description," Connor replies. "Tax consulting, employee benefit consulting, pension consulting, valuation consulting, EDP [electronic data processing] consulting."

Among Price Waterhouse's consulting services are services for small-business entrepreneurs and a special office of government services, which provides information on pending tax legislation and conducts economic studies for businesses, industries, the federal government, and state governments. Through its network, Price Waterhouse and Partners, a separate firm composed of Price Waterhouse representatives and bankers from various countries, the firm can provide financial, trade, and management advice to multinational corporations and governments around the world.

The real product of Price Waterhouse is, according to Connor, "intellectual deliveries. We are in the business of selling credibility, objectivity, believability." He continues, "The people skills in the business are much more important than the technical skills, because you have to convince and you have to hear. That's the Latin root of the word auditor, to hear, and I think the successful accountant and auditor has to listen first before he decides what professional advice he's going to give."

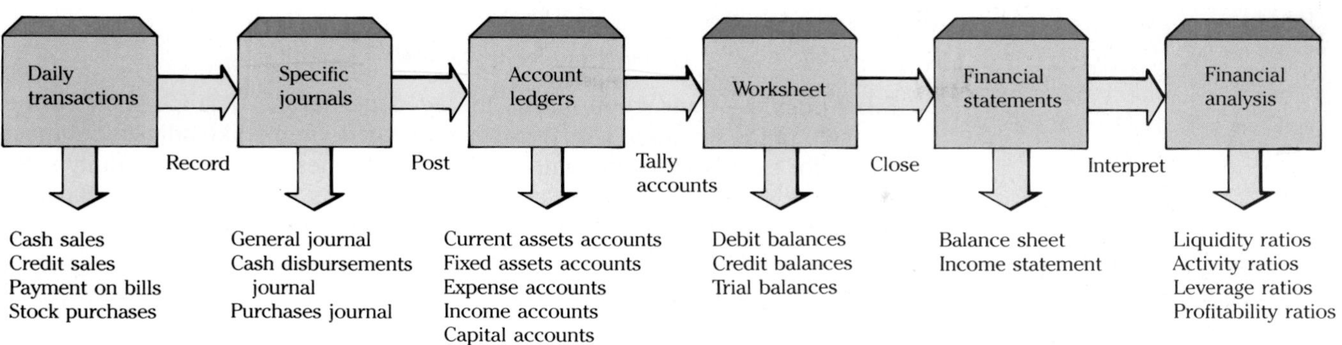

Figure 17.2 Steps in the accounting cycle. Each business must tally its individual accounts so the firm's financial status can be established.

KEY ACCOUNTING EQUATIONS

To help ensure that accounting procedures have been followed, accountants depend on a set of basic equations that define the relationships among the five common types of accounts. These equations are the balance sheet equation and the profit equation.

Balance Sheet Equation

The first basic accounting equation focuses on the mathematical relationship of the accounts that make up the balance sheet: assets, liabilities, and equity. The **balance sheet equation** is

The ***balance sheet equation*** is assets equal liabilities plus owner's equity.

Assets = Liabilities + Owner's equity

Assets are items of value owned by a business, including such things as buildings, inventory, cash, and equipment. The owner's investment in the business is the **owner's (stockholders') equity,** or net worth. Borrowed funds and delayed payments make up the **liabilities** of a business. (*Debt* is another term used to describe borrowed funds.) Those who lend a business money or agree to accept delayed payments are *creditors.* (Delayed payments go by such names as payables and accruals.)

Assets are items of value owned by a business.

Owner's (stockholders') equity is the owner's investment in a business (also called net worth).

Liabilities are borrowed funds (debt) and delayed payments (such as payables and accruals) of a business.

The major difference between liabilities and owner's equity rests in the fact that a firm has a legal obligation to pay its creditors but no such obligation toward its owners. For example, a business that fails to make scheduled interest or principal payments on its debt can be sued for breach of contract.

It is often said that liabilities represent the creditors' claims on the assets of a firm, whereas owner's equity represents the owner's claim. For example, if you started a lawn care service and purchased $9,000 worth of equipment with $5,000 from your savings and $4,000 borrowed from a bank, your balance sheet equation would look like this:

Assets (equipment) = Liabilities (bank loan) + Owner's equity (savings)

$9,000 = $4,000 + $5,000

It is sometimes useful to rearrange the balance sheet equation in order to highlight the owner's equity position, as follows:

Owner's equity = Assets − Liabilities

Every business transaction affects the accounts on the balance sheet. If the assets side of the equation is increased or reduced, then a like adjustment must be made for exactly the same amount on the liabilities and owner's equity side. The balance sheet is simply an amplification of this basic equation. (Balance sheets will be discussed in the next major section of the chapter.)

Profit Equation

Revenues are the funds received by a business, mainly from the sales of goods and services.

Expenses are the costs incurred in the generation of revenue.

The ***profit equation*** is profits equal revenue minus expenses.

The second significant accounting equation—the profit equation—focuses on the accounts that make up the income statement: revenues and expenses. (Income statements will be discussed shortly.) **Revenues** are the funds received by a business, mainly from the sale of goods and services. Additional sources of funds are rental income, interest income, and royalties. **Expenses** are the costs incurred in the generation of revenues. A manufacturing firm, for example, must spend money on wages, materials, advertising, equipment, and energy in order to produce goods for sale.

The major objective of businesses is to generate a profit. The achievement of this objective is reflected in the **profit equation:**

Profit = Revenues − Expenses

When revenues exceed expenses, a profit is earned. (Other common accounting names for *profit* are *net income* and *earnings.*) When expenses are greater than revenues, a loss is incurred. As chapter 1 pointed out, some profits are paid to owners in the form of dividends, and some are reinvested in the business. The profit that is reinvested in the firm—*retained earnings*—is added to the owner's equity account.

FINANCIAL STATEMENTS: COMPANY SCORECARDS

A company's chief accounting officer must periodically evaluate the past performance and current standing of the firm in order to judge its financial fitness. Much of this information is contained in the company's basic financial statements: the balance sheet and the income statement. Both are usually included in some form in the annual report to stockholders.

Financial statements should be prepared in accordance with *generally accepted accounting principles (GAAP).* These principles, which are formulated by the professional accounting association known as the Financial Accounting Standards Board (FASB), serve as formal guidelines and rules to provide objectivity, relevance, and accuracy to financial statements.

Balance Sheets

The ***balance sheet*** is the statement of financial position that reports the dollar amounts for a company's assets, liabilities, and owner's (stockholders') equity at a specific point in time.

The statement of financial position that reports the dollar amounts for a company's assets, liabilities, and owner's (stockholders') equity at a specific point in time is the **balance sheet.** An evaluation of balance sheets over a period of years can provide important insights about the growth and stability of a firm.

BUSINESS PRACTICE EXAMPLE Continues

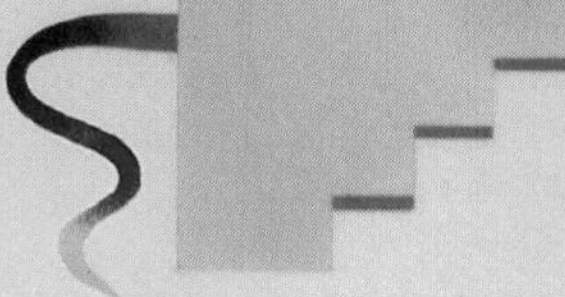

As the ZZZZ Best case reveals, a company's financial dealings can be quite complex, and the need for firms to observe generally accepted accounting practice becomes especially obvious when fraud is suspected. Accordingly, the job of external auditing, as performed by a public accounting firm, demands highly trained and professional individuals, schooled not only to analyze what goes into generally accepted accounting principles and practice, but also to know computer usage in accounting. The CPA designation is designed to provide such people.

One might ask why ZZZZ Best's regular external auditor, Ernst & Whinney, did not uncover the fraudulent activities of the firm. After all, Ernst & Whinney is staffed by CPAs. However, regular external audits traditionally have been limited in scope and depth, relying extensively on spot check samplings of financial information. In addition, there are those who claim that a company's regular public accounting firm is not truly independent of the company because it is paid by the company.

The practice of external auditing is changing, though, in large part because of cases such as ZZZZ Best's. Public accounting firms are being sued for negligence much more often than in the past, which causes liability insurance premiums to rise. Not only that, the outside auditors are now required to look behind accepted practices to discover and report fraudulent practices by clients. There have even been calls for government regulation of the auditing profession.

Figure 17.3 is a balance sheet for a hypothetical chain of specialty stores selling clothing for men over six feet tall—the Tall Men's Shop, Inc. Using this figure, we will examine the classes of accounts that make up the balance sheet.

Assets

Any asset that will change form in a year or less is a **current asset.** Examples are cash, marketable securities, accounts receivable, merchandise inventory, and prepaid insurance. *Cash*—currency and checking account money—is the most liquid form of current assets. **Marketable securities** are interest-earning investments that are highly liquid (can be sold readily) partly because an active resale market with quoted prices exists for them. They are so liquid, in fact, that many firms lump them in with cash.

Accounts receivable are debts owned to the business by customers who buy products on credit. For the Tall Men's Shop, the $42,000 in accounts receivable reflects the amount that credit customers owed the firm on the day the books

A ***current asset*** is any asset that will change form in a year or less.

Marketable securities are interest-earning securities that are highly liquid (can be sold readily) because a market with quoted prices exists for them.

Accounts receivable are debts owned to a business by customers who buy products on credit.

Current assets			
Cash		$ 15,000	
Accounts receivable		42,000	
Merchandise inventories		110,000	
Prepaid insurance		3,500	
Total current assets			$170,500
Fixed assets			
Land		$ 79,500	
Buildings & equipment	$150,000		
Less accumulated depreciation	50,000	100,000	
Total fixed assets			179,500
Total assets			$350,000
Current liabilities			
Accounts payable		$45,000	
Notes payable		18,000	
Accrued wages		4,000	
Taxes due		8,000	
Total current liabilities			$ 75,000
Long-term liabilities			
First mortgage bonds			$ 75,000
Stockholder's equity			
Common stock			$170,000
Retained earnings		30,000	200,000
Total equities + liabilities			$350,000

Figure 17.3 Balance sheet for the Tall Men's Shop, Inc. (December 31, 1989).

Merchandise inventory is all the goods on hand for sale.

were closed. However, some of these accounts may never be collected, in which case they will be reclassified as *bad debts*.

Merchandise inventory is all the goods on hand for sale. In the case of the Tall Men's Shop, it is clothing purchased for resale but not yet sold, and its value is $110,000. (Inventory goods held by a manufacturer are raw materials, finished goods, and work-in-process.)

Prepaid insurance, the last current asset, is insurance premiums that have been paid but are for coverage during a period in the future. If the Tall Men's Shop pays its insurance premiums once a year, and the year is half over on the date of the balance sheet, half the premiums are listed as a current asset.

As a group, cash, accounts receivable, and inventory are often referred to as a firm's *working capital*. As the name implies, working capital assets are always changing in form and substance as they turn over, or cycle, in the course of business activity. Figure 17.4 shows how these assets cycle in a retail business. The process is called the *cash conversion cycle*.

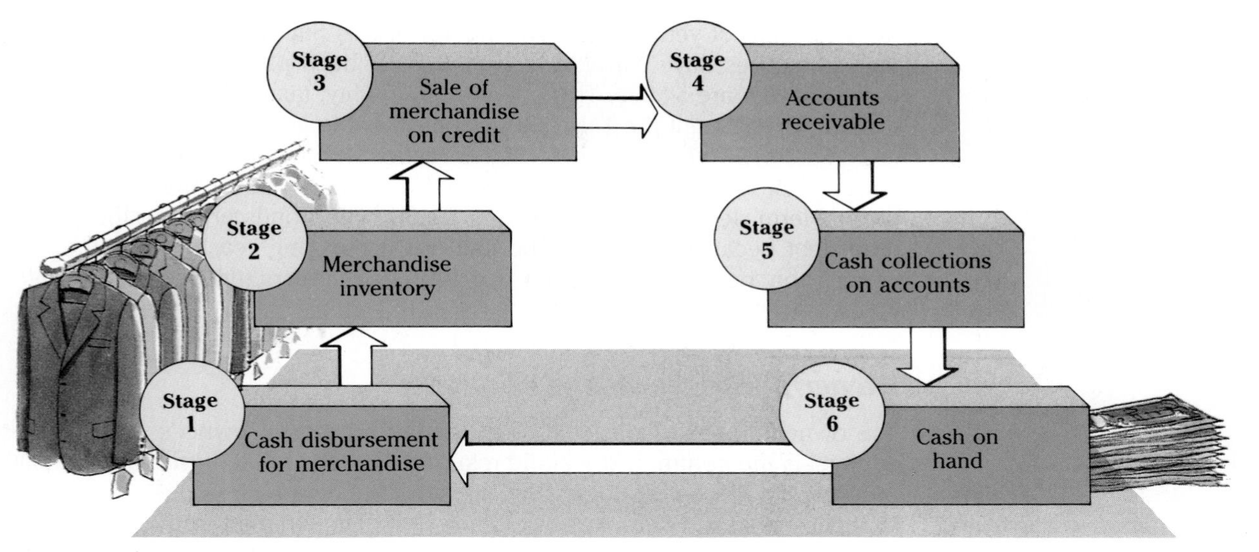

Figure 17.4 The cash conversion cycle.

Fixed assets (or capital assets) are permanent assets used in the operation of the business.

Fixed assets are permanent assets used in the operation of the business. These resources normally have a useful life in excess of one year and are not offered for sale in the general course of business. Examples are solid, tangible goods such as land, buildings, and equipment. For the Tall Men's Shop, a cash register would be an example.

Depreciation is the reduction in value allowed by law for long-lived tangible assets.

As a fixed asset loses its productive value, accountants say it depreciates. **Depreciation** is the reduction in value allowed by law for long-lived tangible assets. In order to encourage and provide for the replacement of fixed assets, a generally accepted accounting principle allows firms to charge off (i.e., depreciate) a portion of a fixed asset's original cost as an expense. (No such charge is allowed on land, as it is assumed not to lose value over time.) The expense does not involve an outlay of cash each year, but claiming this long-term loss of value reduces income taxes. *Accumulated depreciation* (the sum of prior years' depreciation expenses) is shown on the balance sheet as a negative account. It is usually deducted from the original cost of capital assets before their final (or net) value is recorded. The deduction for the Tall Men's Shop is $179,500. This deduction is allowed on the assumption that cash saved by depreciation allowances will be available as a reserve fund for new equipment. The allowances are to provide an incentive for businesses to maintain the most up-to-date fixed assets. The buildings and equipment of the Tall Men's Shop are approximately one-third used up.

Liabilities

Debts of a firm that must be paid within one year are *current liabilities*. The $45,000 in the *accounts payable* account of the Tall Men's Shop represents money owed to the firm's clothing suppliers. The firm also has a short-term loan with a commercial bank, which is represented by the $18,000 in the *notes payable* account.

The *accrued wages* account illustrates an accrued expense—one the firm has used up but not yet paid for. For the Tall Men's Shop, *accrued wages*—wages that employees have earned but have not yet been paid at the time the books were closed—are $4,000. The last current liability, taxes, is common to all businesses. The amount the Tall Men's Shop owes the government is $8,000.

Long-term liabilities are debts that are scheduled to mature in the distant future. For the Tall Men's Shop, they consist of $75,000 in bonds. Other common types of long-term debt are mortgages and leases. The bonds are classified as long-term debt because they won't be paid off within one year. In fact, they could conceivably be on the books for over twenty-five years, drawing interest all the while.

Owner's (Stockholders') Equity

The owner's claim against the assets of the business—owner's (stockholders') equity—is the common stock and retained earnings of the firm. The $170,000 in the *common stock* account of the Tall Men's Shop represents the money secured by the issuance of common stock to investors. The retained earnings are $30,000.

An examination of the totals will demonstrate that the balance sheet is an amplification of the first basic accounting equation:

$$\text{Assets} = \text{Liabilities} + \text{Equity}$$

$$\$350{,}000 = \$150{,}000 + \$200{,}000$$

Income Statements

The ***income statement*** is the summary of a firm's revenues and expenses for a specific period of time.

The summary of a firm's revenues and expenses for a specific period of time is the firm's **income statement.** The time period is usually a month, a quarter, or a year. The format of the income statement follows the second basic accounting equation—the profit equation. Expenses are deducted from income to determine the net profit or loss. Net profit retained in a business is likely to increase future revenues and profits, because the reinvested funds can be used to purchase additional productive assets.

As Figure 17.5 shows, the Tall Men's Shop sold $485,000 worth of clothing during the year. (A portion of these sales must have been on credit, as the accounts receivable entry in the balance sheet indicates.) Some of the customers returned their purchases, however; the returns and allowances were $15,000. Net sales revenue (gross sales revenue minus returns and allowances) was therefore $470,000. Tall Men's gross profit was $170,000 (net sales revenue of $470,000 minus the cost of goods sold of $300,000).

The ***cost of goods sold*** is the total of all costs directly required for the acquisition and preparation of goods for sale during a given time period.

The **cost of goods sold** is the total of all costs directly required for the acquisition and preparation of goods for sale during a given period. Specifically, it is the value of inventory on hand at the beginning of the year (for the Tall Men's Shop, assume this amount to be $125,000), plus the cost of all merchandise acquired during the year (assume $285,000), minus the value of inventory still on hand at the end of the year (assume $110,000). The income statement for the Tall Men's Shop shows $300,000 as the cost of goods sold:

$$(\$125{,}000 + \$285{,}000) - \$110{,}000 = \$300{,}000$$

Operating expenses are the normal expenses of operating a business, not including the cost of goods sold.

Next on the income statement is **operating expenses**—the normal expenses of operating a business, not including the cost of goods sold. For the Tall Men's

Gross sales revenue	$485,000	
Less returns & allowances	15,000	
Net sales revenue		$470,000
Less cost of goods sold		300,000
Gross profit		170,000
Less operating expenses		
Wages & salaries	$ 85,000	
General & administrative expenses	35,500	
Interest expenses	4,000	125,000
Net profit before taxes		45,000
Taxes paid and accrued		10,000
Net profit		35,000
Less cash dividends		15,000
Amount added to retain earnings		$ 20,000

Figure 17.5
Income statement for the Tall Men's Shop, Inc. (year ended December 31, 1989).

Shop, these expenses are $125,000: wages and salaries of $85,500, general and administrative expenses of $35,500 (including depreciation calculated as lost value, utilities, office expenses, and insurance), and interest expenses of $4,000 (interest paid to bondholders and other creditors).

Subtracting the total operating expenses of $125,000 from the gross profit of $170,000 leaves a net profit before taxes of $45,000. Once taxes are subtracted (income taxes, here), the net profit is $35,000.

The board of directors of the Tall Men's Shop decided to pay $15,000 in cash dividends to the company's shareholders. This left $20,000 in retained earnings.

RATIOS: THE HEART OF FINANCIAL ANALYSIS

Now that we've examined the financial statements that are part of the annual report, we will look at how investors and others use this information to analyze a company's financial health. In this analysis, certain **ratios**—fractional or percentage relationships between two or more variables—in the financial statements will be particularly helpful.

Ratios are fractional or percentage relationships between two or more variables.

Traditionally, ratio analysis has been the core procedure for determining financial fitness. However, ratios are of use primarily as clues for further analysis. And they should be used with care, since they do have limitations. For one thing, they are only as good as the data that go into them. If financial statement figures are inaccurate, so too will be the associated ratios. Another problem is that it might not be possible to find satisfactory industrywide averages with which to compare them.

BUSINESS PRACTICE EXAMPLE Continues

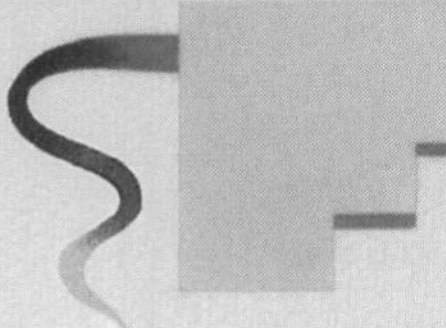

Financial statements are important sources of information for management, investors, and others who make financial decisions based on the ratios and relationships among critical parts of the stated information. The information must be based on accurate data and follow generally accepted accounting principles. If financial statements are not drawn up in this manner, the consequences could be serious. For example, users of the statements could be duped, through their ratio analyses based on misleading information, into making financially disastrous decisions.

This appears to be what happened in the ZZZZ Best case. Investors in ZZZZ Best seem to have had no idea that the reports they were receiving were based not only on questionable financial practices but also on apparently illegal transactions, such as money laundering and bogus sales contracts.

Companies must maintain good internal accounting controls in order to prevent not only illegalities but also serious accounting errors. A rigorous use of financial ratios is one way to uncover unsound relationships in key aspects of a company's business.

Liquidity Ratios

Liquidity ratios are ratios used to determine if a firm can pay its current debts.

Ratios used to determine if a firm can pay its current debts are **liquidity ratios.** For example, can the Tall Men's Shop generate sufficient funds to pay its $75,000 worth of short-term obligations? Normally, the flow of funds in a firm depends heavily on the turnover of accounts receivable and inventories. Although a complete liquidity analysis would include more detailed kinds of analysis, two ratios can be used to determine the liquidity position of the Tall Men's Shop: the current ratio and the quick ratio.

The *current ratio* is calculated by dividing current assets by current liabilities:

$$\text{Current ratio} = \frac{\text{Current assets}}{\text{Current liabilities}} = \frac{\$170{,}500}{\$75{,}000} = 2.27$$

The current ratio is very important. It tells us that the Tall Men's Shop has $2.27 worth of current assets for every $1 worth of short-term indebtedness. The claims of short-term creditors are covered more than twice by the assets that are expected to be converted into cash in less than a year. Creditors are concerned with this short-term solvency ratio because it reflects the potential flow of funds with which short-term debts will be paid.

Most firms also compare their current ratio to the industrywide averages published by Dun & Bradstreet or other trade organizations. Table 17.3 compares Tall

Table 17.3 Industrywide averages for retail clothing stores compared to the averages for the Tall Men's Shop.

Type of Ratio	Industrywide Averages	Tall Men's Averages
Liquidity Ratios		
Current ratio	2.5/1	2.27/1
Quick (acid-test) ratio	1.45/1	.81/1
Activity Ratios		
Inventory turnover ratio	4.55 times	2.73 times
Average collection period	30.2 days	32 days
Leverage Ratios		
Debt ratio	37.2%	42.9%
Times interest earned ratio	7.4 times	12.25%
Profitability Ratios		
Return on total assets	9.4%	10%
Return on net worth	11.7%	17.5%

Men's current ratio to a sample of industrywide ratios. It shows that Tall Men's current ratio is slightly below the industrywide average (2.5) but is not low enough to cause concern.

Another well-known liquidity ratio is the *quick ratio,* or acid-test ratio. This ratio is calculated by deducting inventory from current assets (any assets that will change form in a year or less) and dividing the remainder by current liabilities (any debts that must be paid in one year):

$$\text{Quick ratio} = \frac{\text{Current assets} - \text{Inventory}}{\text{Current liabilities}} = \frac{\$170{,}500 - \$110{,}000}{\$75{,}000} = .81$$

The equation tells us that the Tall Men's Shop has 81 cents' worth of cash, accounts receivable, and prepaid insurance for every dollar's worth of current liabilities.

The quick ratio measures a firm's dependence on inventory—that is, it shows whether a firm is liquid without having to depend on inventory. Since inventory can become obsolete or difficult to liquidate, it is important not to have excessive funds tied up in it. As Table 17.3 indicates, the industrywide average is 1.45, which tells us that the Tall Men's Shop needs better inventory management. The apparent imbalance needs to be evaluated so the liquidity position of the firm is not further jeopardized.

Activity Ratios

Ratios that measure how effectively a company uses its resources are **activity ratios.** They are especially useful in tracking the performance of operations

Activity ratios are ratios that measure how effectively a company uses its resources.

managers in charge of such specific functions as inventory management, cash management, and credit policy. The two most common activity ratios are the inventory turnover ratio and average collection period.

The *inventory turnover ratio* shows how many times inventory was sold during a particular time period. The higher the turnover, the greater the profits, assuming that the items are sold at proper markup. Inventory turnover is calculated as follows:

$$\text{Inventory turnover} = \frac{\text{Cost of goods sold}}{\text{Inventory}} = \frac{\$300{,}000}{\$110{,}000} = 2.73$$

This means that, on the average, all items of inventory at the Tall Men's Shop were sold, or turned over, almost three times during the accounting period under study. Many stores use a computer to generate inventory turnover information by brand, product, size, and so on. This type of detailed information is useful in determining the most profitable product mix. The inventory turnover ratio of 2.73 indicates that the Tall Men's Shop needs to manage its inventory more judiciously, since the industrywide average is 4.55.

The *average collection period* relates to credit management. Retail stores must maintain a cash flow that is adequate to meet daily operating expenses. Ensuring that accounts receivable are paid on time is one way to minimize cash flow problems. Two steps are needed to calculate the average collection period. The first is to calculate the sales per day:

$$\text{Sales per day} = \frac{\text{Net sales revenue}}{\text{Days in business year}} = \frac{\$470{,}000}{360} = \$1{,}306$$

The second is to divide the accounts receivable by the sales per day:

$$\text{Average collection period} = \frac{\text{Accounts receivable}}{\text{Sales per day}} = \frac{\$42{,}000}{\$1{,}306} = 32 \text{ days}$$

This ratio tells us that the credit manager for the Tall Men's Shop seems to be doing an adequate job, since the industrywide average collection period is just over 30 days. Some collection managers also periodically "age" their accounts; that is, they categorize the accounts receivable according to how long they have been outstanding. Aging the accounts ensures that no overdue indebtedness is hidden by the average collection period.

Leverage Ratios

Leverage ratios are ratios that measure the equity contribution of stockholders as compared with the debt funds provided by a firm's creditors.

Ratios that measure the equity contribution of stockholders as compared with the debt funds provided by a firm's creditors are **leverage ratios.** Usually, a firm carries a certain amount of long-term and short-term debt on the books. We say that a firm with a high proportion of debt to equity is highly leveraged. Since borrowing costs money in terms of interest payments, the leverage position of a firm is important to creditors and owners. If a company's debt cost 10 percent but the company earns 15 percent on its assets, then the owners' leverage is usually considered favorable. The 5 percent difference may be paid to stockholders in the form of extra dividends.

Trans World Airlines and Ramada Inns were highly leveraged during the mid-1980s. That is, they used a high percentage of bonds or notes to raise capital. Just the opposite was true for Eastman Kodak, General Motors, and Levi Strauss.

Two key ratios are used to determine the extent to which borrowed funds are being used to finance the firm: the debt ratio and the times interest earned ratio. The *debt ratio* measures the percentage of total funds provided by creditors. Using the balance sheet of the Tall Men's Shop, we can calculate this ratio as follows:

$$\text{Debt ratio} = \frac{\text{Total liabilities}}{\text{Total assets}} = \frac{\$150{,}000}{\$350{,}000} = 42.9\%$$

At 42.9 percent, the Tall Men's Shop has a slightly higher debt ratio than the 37.2 percent industrywide average. However, the difference may be considered negligible.

The second leverage measure is the *times interest earned ratio.* Interest expense is a legal obligation that is paid regularly. Using data from the income statement of the Tall Men's Shop, we can calculate this ratio:

$$\text{Times interest earned ratio} = \frac{\text{Net profit before taxes} + \text{Interest charges}}{\text{Interest charges}}$$

$$= \frac{\$45{,}000 + \$4{,}000}{\$4{,}000} = 12.25$$

The Tall Men's Shop earned over 12 times the annual interest cost on its indebtedness. This ratio compares very favorably with the industrywide ratio of 7.4 times.

Profitability Ratios

The ratios used by management and owners to determine if the firm's resources are being utilized in the best manner are **profitability ratios.** The two ratios commonly employed to measure profitability are return on total assets and return on net worth.

Profitability ratios are the ratios used by management to determine if the firm's resources are being employed in the best manner.

The *return on total assets* compares net profit to total assets. It is calculated as follows:

$$\text{Return on total assets} = \frac{\text{Net profit}}{\text{Total assets}} = \frac{\$35{,}000}{\$350{,}000} = 10\%$$

At 10 percent, the Tall Men's Shop return on total assets compares favorably to the industrywide average of 9.4 percent.

The *return on net worth* measures the relationship of net profit to stockholders' equity. The ratio is calculated as follows:

$$\text{Return on net worth} = \frac{\text{Net profit}}{\text{Stockholders' equity}} = \frac{\$35{,}000}{\$200{,}000} = 17.5\%$$

At 17.5 percent, the Tall Men's Shop shows a very favorable return on stockholders' investment compared to the industrywide average of 11.7 percent.

Time Series Analysis

In addition to comparing a firm's ratios with industry averages, it is often helpful to trace the behavior of a ratio or set of ratios over time. This process is commonly referred to as *time series analysis.* Suppose we have at our disposal ten years' worth of inventory turnover ratios for both the Tall Men's Shop and the retail clothing industry. A time series analysis can be performed from this information by plotting a graph of the ratio figures for Tall Men's versus the industry for the same period (see Figure 17.6). It is easy to compare not only the firm's ratio with the industry average but also the ratio's behavior over time. The inventory turnover ratio for the Tall Men's Shop has clearly been on a downward trend over the ten years being compared.

INTERNAL USES OF ACCOUNTING

Much of a firm's accounting activity is concerned with the preparation of internal financial reports that are useful in managerial decision making. In particular, managerial accounting is used to develop an internal system of data gathering, reporting, and analysis. A good system is one designed so that individual decision

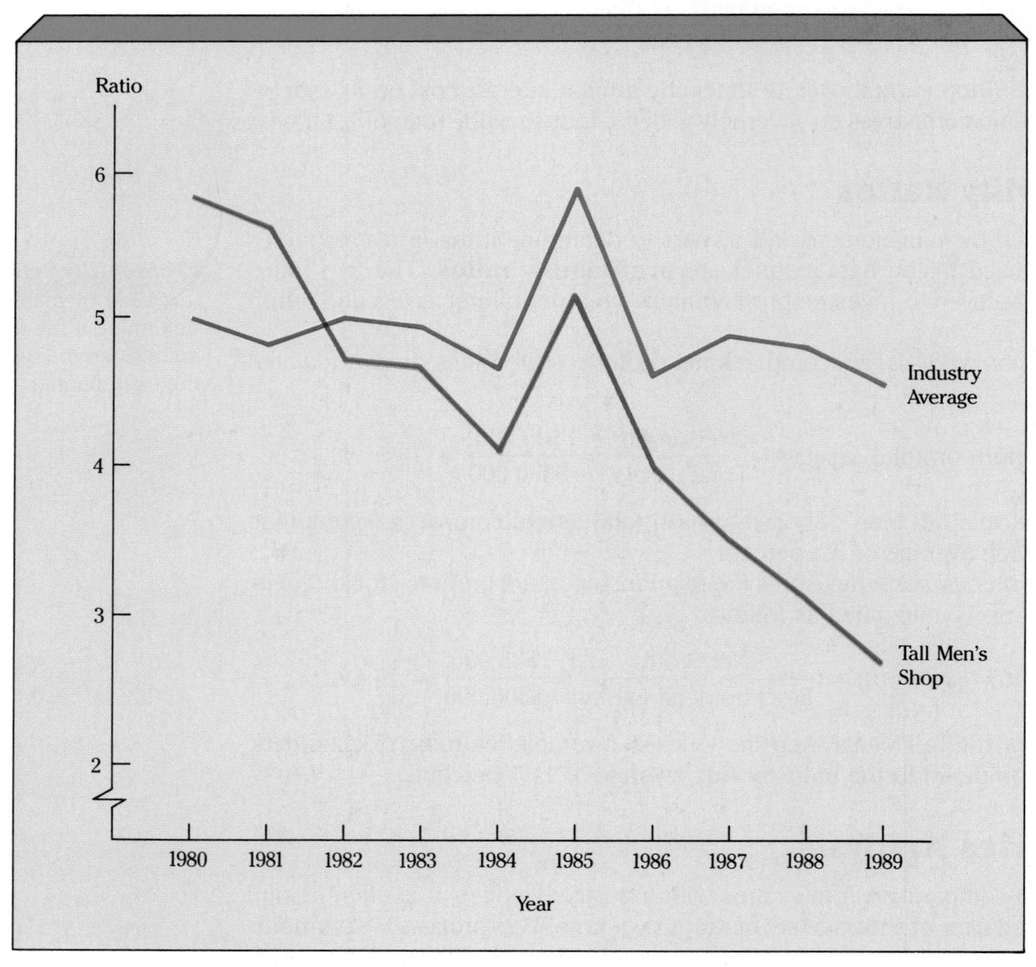

Figure 17.6 Inventory turnover ratios for the Tall Men's Shop, Inc., and the retail clothing industry, 1980–1989.

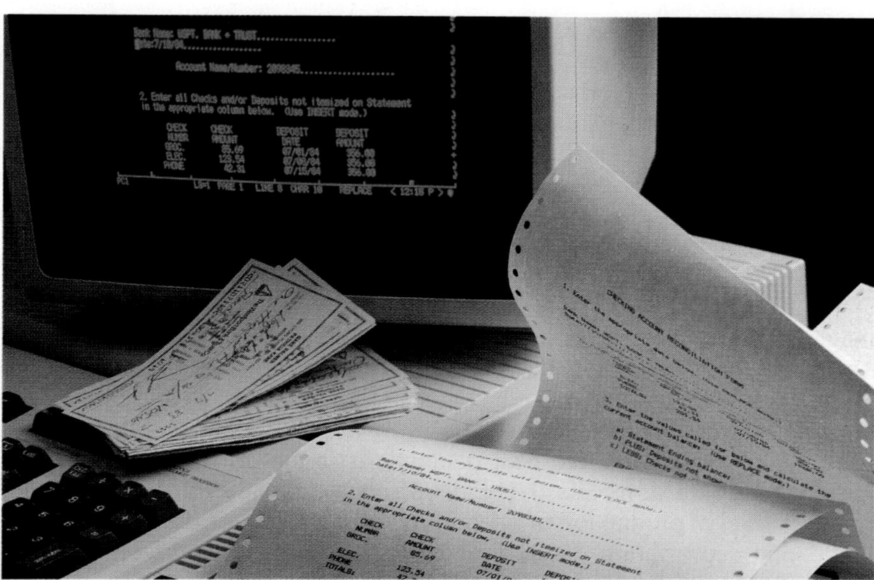

Much of a firm's accounting activity is concerned with preparation of internal reports. This system is designed so that individual decision makers will have access to the information they need.

makers not only have access to timely and relevant information but also are able to make decisions that are in the interest of the entire organization. Data from internal accounting systems are particularly critical in two common types of business responsibilities: budgeting, and cost analysis.

Budgeting

The word *budget* has acquired a number of meanings over the years. In general, **budgets** are the internal financial forecasts of expected income and expenditure for a specific period of time. Here we will deal with appropriations budgets and operating budgets.

Budgets are the internal financial forecasts of expected income and expenditure for a specific period of time.

Appropriations budgets are used extensively by governments. They typically specify the amount of money a government unit has the authority to spend during some future period of time.

Operating budgets are a set of guidelines regarding the estimated income or expenses of a business unit for a specific period of time, usually a year. A *master budget* is the operating budget for an entire company. It is a comprehensive financial forecast for all departments and subunits of the company.

Each department and subunit works with a detailed operating budget; all the individual budgets are incorporated into the master budget. The smaller the subunit, the more detailed the budget. The income and expense figures that go into a budget are expected to refer to and be based on a realistic standard assessment of some kind, such as historical or industry data, engineering estimates, or customer surveys.

Operating budgets are useful in planning and coordinating the activities of a business. They can also be used to assign responsibility for various activities. For instance, a sales budget can be used to assign the marketing department responsibility for next year's sales. When used in this way, budgets can be guides to performance evaluation.

Finally, budgets can be used to control or monitor the actual income and expenses of a business unit. This use of budgets helps identify problem areas and opportunities at an early stage, so appropriate action can be taken.

Table 17.4 is a comparison of budgeted amounts versus actual amounts for a restaurant. The column on the right shows the variance (difference) between budgeted and actual figures for each item. Balancing income items and expenses allows the manager to see if the restaurant is behind or ahead of the forecast.

Cost Analysis

Fixed costs are costs that remain relatively stable no matter what the company's level of production or operations.

Variable costs are costs that are directly tied to the level of business activity, rising as volume picks up and declining as volume slacks off.

Managerial accountants put considerable effort into various kinds of cost analysis. Here we will focus on cost analysis as used to support business decisions. Since most business decisions are affected by costs, accountants need to provide managers with relevant and timely cost data.

One of the most important cost distinctions is that of fixed versus variable costs. **Fixed costs** are costs that remain relatively stable no matter what the company's level of production or operations. Examples are rent, equipment maintenance, and depreciation. **Variable costs** are costs that are directly tied to the level of business activity, rising as volume picks up and declining as volume slacks off. Examples are wages and materials expenses.

Table 17.4 1990 budget variance analysis for Lucille's Restaurant.

Budgeted Item	Budgeted Amount	Actual Amount	Variance*
Income			
Sales revenue	$420,000	$445,000	$25,000 (F)
Expenses			
Wages and benefits	105,000	120,000	15,000 (U)
Food and beverages	90,000	83,500	6,500 (F)
Utilities	6,000	4,800	1,200 (F)
Maintenance	3,000	5,500	2,500 (U)
Management salaries	65,000	65,000	0
Advertising	6,500	7,250	750 (U)
Insurance	3,000	8,000	5,000 (U)
Taxes and license	6,750	6,750	0
Supplies	10,000	5,800	4,200 (F)
Depreciation	8,000	8,000	0
Rent on building	36,000	36,000	0
Janitorial service	11,000	13,000	2,000 (U)
Accounting service	15,000	12,000	3,000 (F)
Miscellaneous expenses	18,000	30,000	12,000 (U)

**F* indicates a favorable variance and *U* an unfavorable variance.

By knowing which costs are fixed and which are variable, a manager can make reasonable decisions about cost control for the appropriate level of business activity.

BUSINESS PRACTICE EXAMPLE Continues

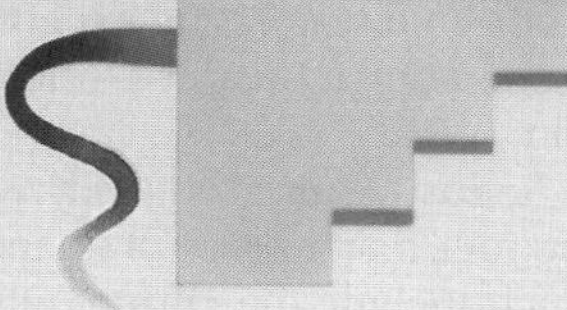

The accountant sleuths at John Murphy and Associates could not find much reliable information from management budgets in the poorly kept ZZZZ Best records. However, by conducting a form of cost analysis, the Murphy accountants traced the flow of bogus income and expenses in the company's checks. With the bulk of income recorded as coming from one firm, Interstate Appraisal, and the bulk of costs booked as general expenses to one alleged contractor, Marbil Management, the investigators were able to "smell a rat."

On the expense side, ZZZZ Best showed no indication of whether costs were variable or fixed. The Murphy investigators were forced to conclude that no normal firm could survive with such uncontrolled costs, showing only a "slush fund" account of expenses. Looking further, they discovered that the "expenses" were just another part of a money laundering operation. From there they went to the income side and found it even more suspicious. As the phony income and expenses went round and round, ZZZZ Best's profit equation always seemed to come up less than 0 in the carpet cleaning business. In fact the company's loss cleaned out the owners for $70 million.

Issues for Discussion

1. Why didn't ZZZZ Best's regular accounting firm identify the illegal financial transactions?
2. Since the investors had a chance to look at ZZZZ Best's annual reports and key financial statements, to what extent should they be held responsible for not uncovering problems? Explain.
3. What arguments can be made in favor of the idea that accounting firms such as Ernst & Whinney should be regulated by the government? What arguments can be made against the idea?

SUMMARY

Accounting is the process of collecting, analyzing, and reporting information that reflects the financial condition of a company. The initial step in the process is bookkeeping.

Public accountants offer their services to the general public. Private accountants are salaried employees of the firms they serve. Many public accountants become certified public accountants (CPAs), and many private accountants become certified management accountants (CMAs).

The major groups that use accounting information are managers, owners and investors, creditors, and the government. Managerial accounting focuses on internal decision making; financial accounting focuses on financial statements for groups outside the firm.

The accounting cycle is the sequence of procedures accountants must follow over a specific period of time. It involves recording transactions in journals and then posting them to accounts.

The key accounting equations are the balance sheet equation and the profit equation. The balance sheet equation is assets equal liabilities plus equity. The profit equation is profit equals revenues minus expenses.

The main financial statements are the balance sheet and the income statement. Balance sheets report the dollar amounts for a company's assets, liabilities, and owner's (stockholders') equity at a specific point in time. They include current assets such as cash, marketable securities, accounts receivable, merchandise inventory, and prepaid insurance. Fixed assets are depreciated over time.

Liabilities include current liabilities (such as accounts payable, notes payable, accrued wages, and taxes) and long-term liabilities. Owner's (stockholders') equity is the common stock and retained earnings of the firm.

Income statements are the summary of a firm's revenues and expenses for a specific period of time. They include gross sales, net sales, gross profit, operating expenses, net profit, and taxes. Gross profit is net sales minus the cost of goods sold. Operating expenses are the normal expenses of operating a business—not including the cost of goods sold.

Ratios are used to analyze a company's financial health. The four major types of financial ratios are liquidity ratios, which include the current ratio and the quick (acid-test) ratio; activity ratios, which include the inventory turnover ratio and the average collection period; leverage ratios, which include the debt ratio and the times interest earned ratio; and profitability ratios, which include the return on total assets and the return on net worth. Time series analysis is used to trace the behavior of ratios over time.

Managerial accounting is used to develop an internal system of data gathering, reporting, and analysis. It is involved in budgeting and cost analysis. Budgets are internal financial forecasts of income and expenses for a specific period of time. They include appropriations budgets (used by governments) and operating budgets (used by businesses).

Cost analysis is used in making business decisions. The most important cost distinction is fixed costs (those that remain stable) versus variable costs (those that are tied to the level of business activity).

KEY TERMS

CHECK YOUR LEARNING

Reread the following learning objectives. Each objective is followed by a few questions. Answering these questions accurately will help you retain the most important concepts discussed in this chapter. After answering each question, check your answer with the key at the end of this chapter. (*Hint:* If you have doubt regarding the correct response, consult the page whose number follows the answer.)

Circle:

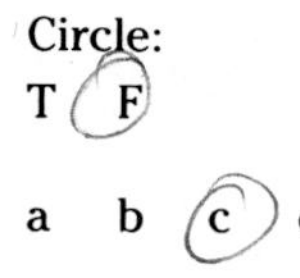

A. Explain the purpose and scope of accounting.

1. Today's accountants usually report financial data but seldom interpret the results. T F
2. Which term refers to the initial phase of the accounting process? (a) posting; (b) ratio analysis; (c) bookkeeping; (d) internal auditing. a b c d

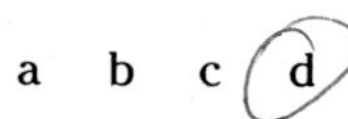

B. Distinguish between the roles of public and private accountants.

1. Private accountants are more likely to be CPAs than are public accountants. T F
2. A professional designation for industrial accountants is: (a) chartered financial accountant; (b) certified public accountant; (c) chartered financial analyst; (d) certified management accountant. a b c d

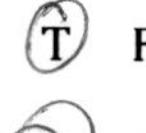

C. List and discuss three outside groups that use information generated by financial accountants.

1. Annual reports are of special interest to stockholders. T F
2. Banks frequently require extensive accounting information before granting a loan to a company. T F

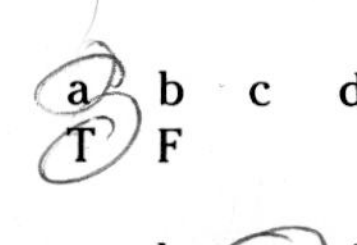

D. Chart the flow of information in the accounting cycle.

1. Posting to the accounts usually occurs before transactional data are entered into the journals. T F
2. The first step in the accounting cycle is: (a) recording transactions; (b) closing the account; (c) posting to ledgers; (d) using ratios to determine the firm's financial condition. a b c d
3. A transaction results in changes in account balances. T F
4. A firm's books include all the following types of accounts except: (a) asset; (b) income; (c) liquidity; (d) equity. a b c d

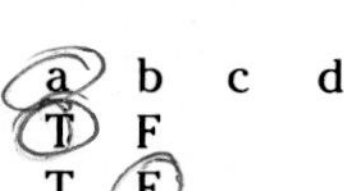

E. Define the two basic accounting equations.

1. If total assets are $500,000 and total liabilities are $250,000, then owner's (stockholders') equity is: (a) $250,000; (b) $750,000; (c) $1,000,000; (d) $500,000. a b c d
2. Assets equal liabilities plus equity is known as the balance sheet equation. T F
3. Revenues minus expenses equal stockholders' equity. T F

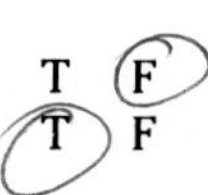

F. Create a simple example of a balance sheet and an income statement.

1. Accounts receivable are an example of fixed assets. T F
2. Retained earnings appear on the balance sheet. T F

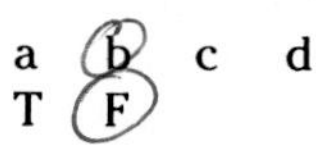

G. Compare and contrast the different accounts in financial statements.

1. The most liquid current asset is: (a) inventory; (b) cash; (c) machinery; (d) accounts receivable. a b c d
2. Cost of goods sold is a minor expense item for most retail firms. T F

H. Calculate and interpret the meaning of selected financial ratios.

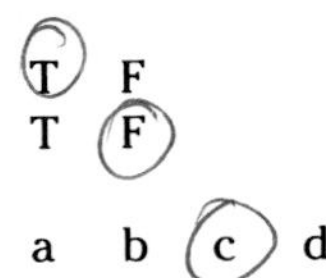

1. If current assets are $580,000 and current liabilities are $240,000, then the current ratio is 2.42/1.
2. Leverage ratios are used to determine the liquidity position of a firm.
3. Inventory turnover is an example of a (an): (a) profitability ratio; (b) liquidity ratio; (c) activity ratio; (d) debt ratio.

I. Explain the role of accountants in the processes of budgeting and cost analysis.

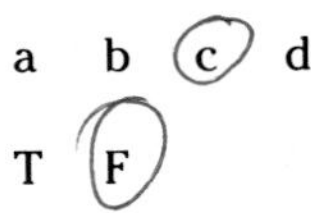

1. The primary role of accountants in the budgeting process is to maintain accurate standards of: (a) bookkeeping; (b) forensics; (c) expense forecasts; (d) closing the accounts.
2. The role of accountants in cost analysis is to help managers reduce or eliminate fixed costs.

QUESTIONS FOR REVIEW AND DISCUSSION

1. Define the key terms listed at the end of the chapter.
2. Draw a chart that shows each step of the accounting cycle in sequence.
3. Create a numerical example of each of the two basic accounting equations.
4. Differentiate between current assets and fixed assets. How do they relate to liabilities and stockholders' equity?
5. What are some of the types of expenses incurred by businesses? How do they affect net profit?
6. How does the retained earnings account increase?
7. Examine a copy of an annual report of a well-known company, and calculate some financial ratios using the financial statements in it.
8. Give three general reasons for a financial statement being wrong.
9. Give some possible reasons for the budget variances shown in Table 17.4.
10. Visit with a CPA or a CMA and ask about the challenges of the accounting profession. Describe them.

CONCLUDING CASE

The Annual Report: A Medium of Fluff?

For years, the corporate annual report has been a slick, voluminous edition of company highlights, complete with color photographs and footnotes. However, a 1986 Securities and Exchange Commission ruling involving General Motors now permits corporations to file "summary" annual reports. These reports are expected to be approximately half the size of conventional annual reports. Thus far, few companies have adopted the summary version. One of the first companies to adopt the new format was McKesson. Its annual report dropped twelve pages of financial notes, which helped reduce the size from forty pages in 1986 to twenty-six in 1987.

Experts seem to agree that the current trend in annual reports is the "antiannual" look. Many annual reports mailed to shareholders look and read like news magazines. These snappy editions include headlines, teasers, and two-page spreads. For example, one Reynolds Metals Company annual report looks very much like *Business Week* magazine. General Motors even ran sixteen pages of color photos of its newest cars and trucks. These pages resemble magazine ads more than strictly informative pieces for stockholders to use in evaluating the company's progress. Although General Motors' performance was not something to boast about, CEO Roger Smith nevertheless chose to include a surprisingly upbeat letter to stockholders in that report.

Many investors are worried that corporations will use the new report format to engage in puffery (favorable and often exaggerated publicity) and to bury bad financial news. For example, Procter & Gamble dispensed with the normal, up-front summary of financial results and instead included six paragraphs of good news before telling readers that the company incurred an $805 million restructuring charge that cut net income by 54 percent. Other companies are even omitting embarrassing events. A classic example can be found in the low number of annual reports that mention the stock market crash of 1987. Most companies elected to pretend it never happened, even though it had a dramatic impact on them. Another example involves the Home Shopping Network, which went public in 1986. This company failed to mention in its maiden annual report that it had a 17 percent return rate (three times the industry rate) for merchandise sold.

Issues for Discussion

1. Explain the purpose of the annual report.
2. Explain why improperly reported financial statements in the annual report reflect on the credibility of the report and the company generally.
3. Examine several annual reports (usually available in the reference department of your school library) and cite examples of puffery. Why do companies engage in puffery? Have you noticed any embarrassing events or facts being downplayed in a report? Explain.

NOTES

1. Glenn A. Welsch and Robert N. Anthony, *Fundamentals of Financial Accounting,* rev. ed. (Homewood, Ill.: Richard D. Irwin, 1977), p. 3.
2. Marilyn Vasquez and Daniel T. Simon, "Industry Attitudes toward the CMA and CPA Certificates," paper presented at Midwest Business Administration Conference, Chicago, March 1985, p. 1.

CHECK YOUR LEARNING ANSWER KEY

A. 1. F, *p. 499*
2. c, *p. 499*

B. 1. F, *p. 500*
2. d, *p. 500*

C. 1. T, *p. 501*
2. T, *p. 502*

D. 1. F, *p. 503*
2. a, *p. 503*
3. T, *p. 503*
4. c, *p. 503*

E. 1. a, *p. 505*
2. T, *p. 505*
3. F, *p. 506*

F. 1. F, *p. 507*
2. T, *p. 510*

G. 1. b, *p. 507*
2. F, *p. 510*

H. 1. T, *p. 512*
2. F, *p. 514*
3. c, *p. 514*

I. 1. c, *p. 517*
2. F, *p. 518*

CHAPTER

18

MANAGING THE FIRM'S FINANCING

LEARNING OBJECTIVES

After reading this chapter you should be able to:

1. Describe the duties of a financial manager and the significance of asset and financing decisions.
2. Discuss issues involved in cash management.
3. Define *accounts receivable,* and describe the four *C*s of credit.
4. Explain the characteristics of inventory and its carrying cost.
5. Discuss the forms and suppliers of short-term financing.
6. Define *fixed asset management* and *capital budgeting,* and explain the steps in capital budgeting.
7. Distinguish between equity financing and long-term debt.
8. Appreciate some problems of fluctuating foreign exchange rates.

OUTLINE

Business Practice Example: Liquid Assets Shape Up to Solid Profits at Bethlehem Steel

What Financial Managers Do

Managing Current Assets

- Cash Management
  - Money and Checking Assets
  - Earning Interest in Marketable Securities
- Accounts Receivable Management
  - Credit Standards: The 4 *C*s of Credit Analysis
  - Credit Terms and Collection Programs
- Inventory Management

Managing Short-Term Financing

- Payables and Accrued Liabilities
- Bank Commercial Loans and Commercial Paper
- Finance Companies and Factoring

Long-Term Financial Decisions

- Fixed Assets and the Capital Budgeting Process
- Looking for Long-Term Funds
  - Equity versus Debt
  - Raising Long-Term Funds

International Financial Management

Summary

Key Terms

Check Your Learning

Questions for Review and Discussion

Concluding Case: Getting a New Venture off the Ground

Notes

Check Your Learning Answer Key

Highlight in Business Practice: Money in Cold Storage

BUSINESS PRACTICE EXAMPLE

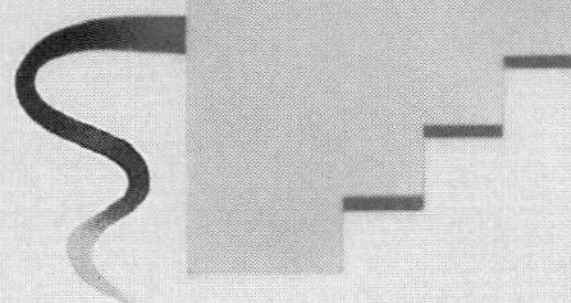

Liquid Assets Shape Up to Solid Profits at Bethlehem Steel

"It's sort of a . . . stigma that we in the industrial base have been carrying around for four or five years," said Walter Williams, CEO at Bethlehem Steel. He was referring to media perceptions of "financially troubled Bethlehem Steel" as a "rust belt" manufacturer among America's "aging smokestack industries." When Williams took over as chief in 1986, such phrases were more than justified by Bethlehem's all-time record loss of $2 billion, earning the firm a description in a *Fortune* magazine survey as the company with "one foot in a blast furnace and the other on a banana peel." This figure of speech summed up Bethlehem's rating as a long-term investment value—near the bottom of major U.S. corporations. Financially, the firm was ready to go under.

How did a major industrial giant fall into such a financial trap? According to Williams, American steel companies from the 1950s to the 1970s became "fat, dumb, and happy" as the world's sole suppliers, seeing no need to prepare for competition. By the 1980s, fully modernized competitors emerged into the market from Japan, Korea, and Europe, many with the help of heavy subsidies from their national governments. Bethlehem and other American steel makers lost foreign markets to efficiently produced and lower-priced competing products. Yet, for a while, their steel was priced competitively for U.S. customers. Transport costs were low. There was also low maintenance on the same plants, equipment, and work procedures that had served the industry of the previous generation.

As Bethlehem gradually lost customers to foreign competitors, it faced smaller profits, loss of cash, and less opportunity to modernize equipment. With both revenues and overall corporate value drifting downward, the firm finally nosedived into its record loss year. Fortunately for Bethlehem, in early 1986 this disaster produced new management—including Williams—and a new financial plan. Williams's first objective was to free some of the money tied down by inefficient equipment and outmoded production processes. The aim was to convert this value into the liquid cash needed for modern operations and investment in more current steel-making technology. Unfortunately, the first moves were the most painful—layoffs, shutdowns, and selloffs.

"I have to give a lot of credit to our steel workers," said Williams to a *Fortune* interviewer in late 1987. "Our shutdowns and cutbacks have hurt a lot of people, but our production workers responded very well to our retraining and quality programs." As Williams told a CNN interviewer shortly afterward, "We have scaled back from about 80,000 people in 1982 to about 33,000. . . . In that period of time our capacity reduced from about 22 million tons a year down to 16, . . . and we think that it's a good solid base that we have now."

In fact, by the time of these interviews, in early 1988, Williams's cutbacks and redirection of resources had achieved a dramatic turnaround for Bethlehem. Williams combined scaled-down operations, strategically planned selloffs of some divisions, and acquisitions of divisions better fitted to streamlined production. The result was a better supply of cash and another Bethlehem record at the end of 1988—as the biggest profit gainer in corporate America, with profits up almost 39 percent from the previous year.

WHAT'S AHEAD

Financially troubled Bethlehem Steel had to take a hard look at its downward drift into near bankruptcy. With the help of a new financial plan, they were able to control short-term costs and rebuild long-term value in a new mix of plant and equipment. Their comeback clearly shows the power of strong financial management.

This chapter discusses the role of financial managers like those at Bethlehem Steel in meeting the challenges of risk and profitability. It outlines the need for assets, identifies the major sources of funds, and explains the various types of financing arrangements. The material in this chapter will provide a broad understanding of the risk-profitability tradeoff faced by financial managers.

WHAT FINANCIAL MANAGERS DO

Financial managers are responsible for monetary decisions and for their effect on the firm's "report card," its annual report. As described in chapter 17, the company's monetary transactions are reflected in the annual *balance sheet*—the statement of assets versus liabilities. Consequently, monetary decisions must be planned and approved by the chief financial officer and other financial managers.

The firm's accountants are responsible for properly recording the asset, liability, and equity transactions. However, the financial managers are the people expected to analyze or approve those transactions. For example, a financial manager might recommend that the firm sell some property to raise money for other operations. The firm's private accountant would see that the sale of the property is correctly transacted and the funds are correctly credited to the company.

The vice president for finance is a company's chief financial officer, reporting directly to the president. This person is responsible for all the firm's monetary planning and may also have a special responsibility for fundraising, unless this is delegated to the treasurer. Working under these top money managers in a large company are other financial managers, including the comptroller, or chief accountant. The others may be called budget managers, financial analysts, cash managers, credit managers, and cost analysts, among other titles. Figure 18.1 shows the relationships of the financial managers in a typical company.

The firm's financial managers, even more than its accountants, must constantly ask: How will the balance sheet add up? They are concerned with how the company will achieve balance in the accounting equation (described in chapter 17). All the things of value to the firm—its assets—must add up to an amount equal to its combined liabilities (debts) plus its equity (the value held by the owners).

The logic of that equation cannot be avoided. If the value of the assets is reduced by heavy costs and bad sales, and the liabilities remain the same, then the value held by the owners will be less. If their ownership is in shares of stock, the value of the stock will be less, and the owners will start asking angry questions when they analyze the balance sheet in the annual report. Under the same con-

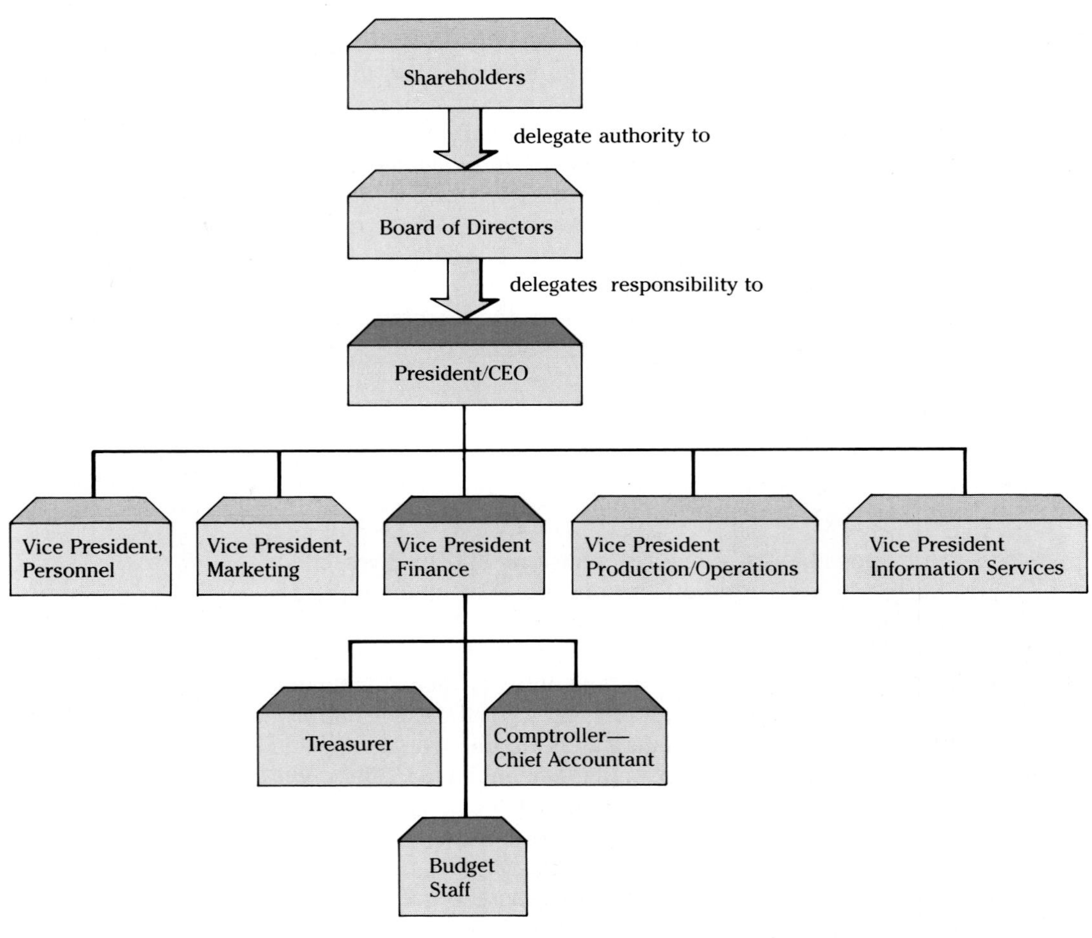

Figure 18.1 The organization of the financial management staff.

ditions, if owners buy new shares to put more money into the firm, they expect to see better performance and asset growth over time. If this happens, there will be more value and profit in their shares.

One way to visualize a financial manager's responsibility is shown in Figure 18.2. The assets appear on top. The assets that are turned over quickly are the short-term assets, or *current assets.* They include (1) cash on hand, (2) money owed the firm as accounts receivable, and (3) goods on hand, or inventory. These will be examined in detail in the next section of the chapter. The assets that change less often are the long-term assets, or *fixed assets.* They include property, plant, and equipment. Companies vary a great deal in the amount of fixed assets they need.

A financial manager must monitor the relationship between current and fixed assets to be sure the company does not have the wrong mix. For example, financial problems at Bethlehem Steel grew almost out of control when too much of the company's value was tied up in property, plant, and equipment. Too many fixed assets and not enough current assets left the company unable to make the changes needed to meet the challenge of lower-cost imported steel from Japan and Korea.

Balanced against all of its assets is the company's **financing**—the funding an enterprise receives by borrowing or by selling ownership shares. As shown in Figure 18.2, financing includes all liabilities and owners' equity. A basic concern

Financing is the funding an enterprise receives by borrowing, by selling shares, or from personal resources.

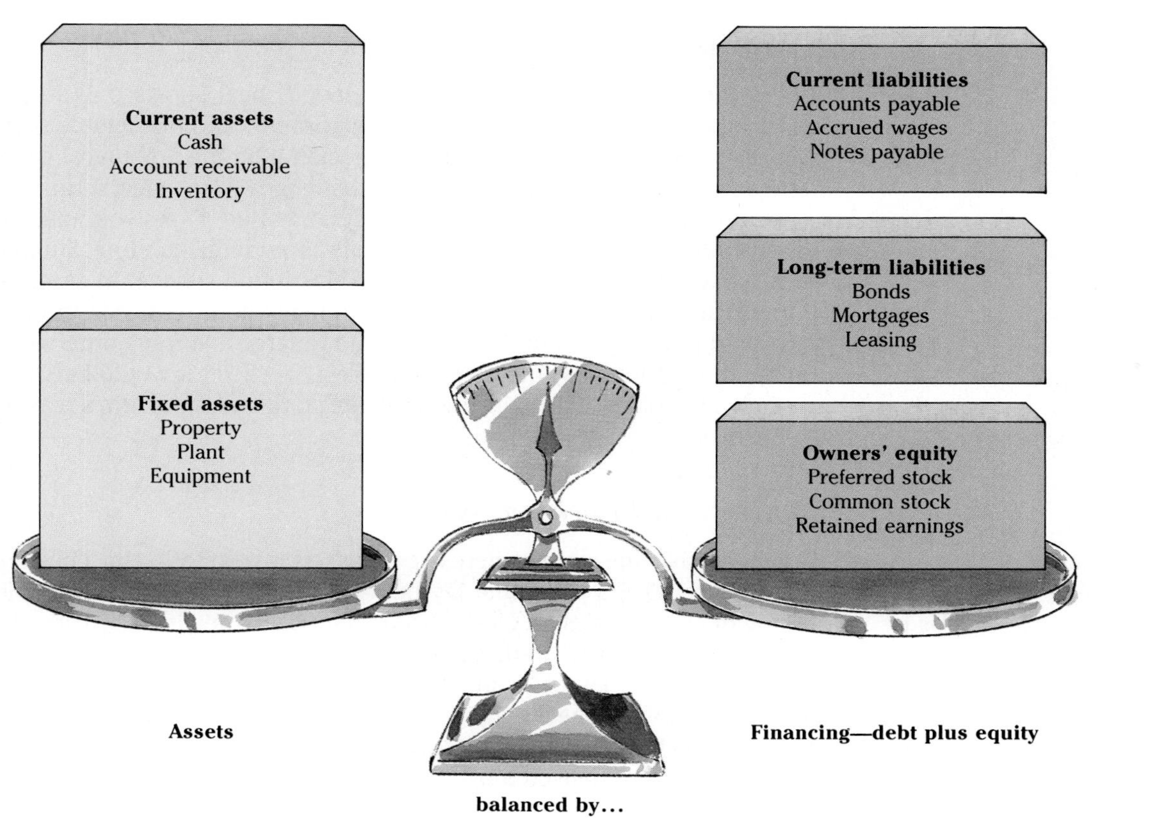

Figure 18.2 Areas of responsibility for the firm's financial managers.

for financial managers is the firm's *current liabilities,* the funds the company owes on a short-term basis. These funds include (1) all purchases on credit due, called *accounts payable;* (2) short-term obligations such as *accrued wages;* and (3) short-term loans, called *notes payable.*

Assets include everything of value that a business owns. This Italian deli holds a wide variety of food products in its inventory of current assets.

MANAGING CURRENT ASSETS

Everything of value that a business has is part of its assets. The nature of the business determines what its assets are. Companies differ greatly in the way they hold their assets. A seasonal retailer may have a large inventory before Christmas and hold a great deal of cash afterward. A beauty shop may hold only a few goods on hand as inventory but may offer credit to many customers whose money will not come in until next payday.

Later sections will discuss how managers deal with long-term assets such as buildings and equipment. This section will focus on how managers handle current assets in the short term—from day to day and week to week, usually over the course of a single year.

The management of current assets is likely to take up a large part of a financial manager's time. Keeping such assets under control and regulating their flow help keep the company solvent. The current assets requiring the most managerial attention are cash, accounts receivable, and inventory.

Cash Management

Under the category of *cash,* a firm's balance sheet shows only its most liquid assets: money in currency or in checking accounts and marketable securities that can be quickly converted into money. Deciding on the amount of cash assets to hold at any point can pose interesting challenges to managers. Businesses need a certain amount of cash to pay bills that come due. Firms with insufficient cash to pay bills on time will suffer losses from poor credit standing. Suppliers whose bills remain unpaid will be unwilling to give future service. In an extreme case, a low-cash company may be forced to sell something it needs in order to raise money to pay bills. On the other hand, if too large a surplus of money were kept on hand, the money would earn no interest. In effect, it would be sitting in dead storage and not be performing the valuable work that is the firm's reason for being in business.

Money and Checking Assets

Check float is the time lag between the issuing of checks and the completed processing of them.

Another area in the management of cash assets is monitoring the checking account to take advantage of the time lag between the issuing and the completed processing of checks—called **check float.** A manager needs to be sure of not losing interest-earning power during this period.

As we saw in chapter 16, most large money payments are made through checking accounts. The checks must be cleared, usually through the Federal Reserve System, and this processing and record-keeping takes time. Moreover, in many cases, checks are delivered by mail. Each activity is time-consuming. Combined, they can take several days, and sometimes weeks, to complete. A check that is caught up in this sequence of events is said to be floating. Because of float, checks are a less desirable payment mechanism than cash or immediate credit for the party on the receiving end. However, they are ideal for the bill payer looking to buy time.

Financial managers have become adept at maximizing float on check payments (thus keeping cash in interest-bearing securities) and minimizing float on check collections. Consumers often play this game too. For example, they may write checks for groceries on Friday, knowing there will be no need for money in their accounts to cover the checks until Monday morning.

Figure 18.3 shows the main elements of check float. There is no doubt that the time lag in float creates an opportunity that can be unfairly exploited. From time to time, state legislatures investigate charges that firms, banks, or individuals deliberately create extra time lags in the float process in order to collect more interest in their accounts. However, since firms or banks can lose as much as they would gain by creating a longer float period, businesses in general benefit from moving funds as promptly as possible.

Earning Interest in Marketable Securities

A manager of current assets must keep the firm's current funds earning as much as possible. An important part of this responsibility is to keep a profitable rela-

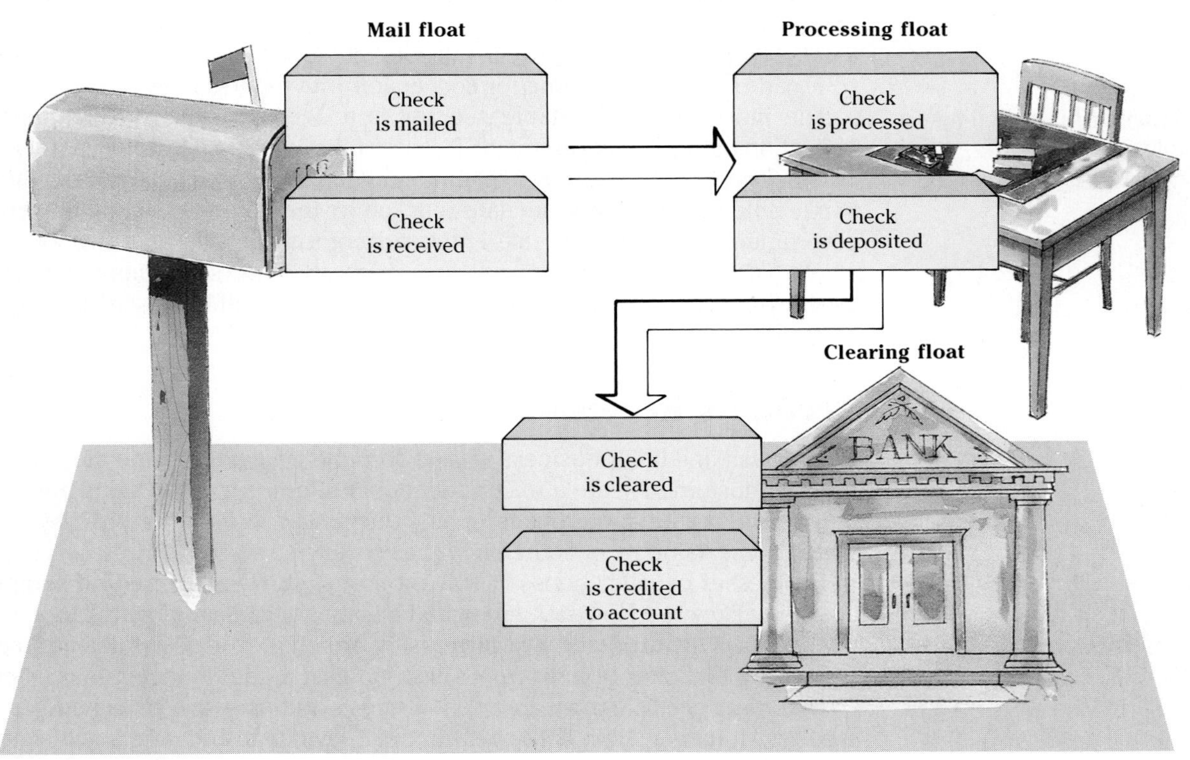

Figure 18.3 Elements of check float.

tionship between money balances and marketable securities. Businesses cannot usually collect interest on checking account balances. Since a financial manager must avoid holding assets in dead storage with no earning, checking account money must be moved whenever possible into investments in which it can earn interest.

An ***Electronic Funds Transfer System*** is a bank's computerized service that allows almost instant transfer of funds between checking accounts and marketable securities.

Many banks make this effort easier by offering computerized **electronic funds transfer systems.** These systems move surplus cash electronically—and almost instantly—debiting checking accounts and crediting marketable securities accounts, or vice versa, when bills must be paid.

For a large firm, it is worthwhile for money left at the end of a business day to be put into securities to earn interest overnight and then back into checking accounts for the next day's business. Large cash assets can usually earn enough interest in a few hours to overcome the costs charged by banks for such transactions. A smaller business must be more cautious. The manager must decide when the amount of money is large enough and when the time it can be invested long enough so that its interest income will be sufficient to exceed the bank's charge for moving it.

Marketable securities are short-term investments that are low-risk, maturing within one year, and can be readily sold on the market.

When the decision to put money into marketable securities is made, the manager must choose the best securities for the company. To be considered a **marketable security,** a security must be safe, profitable, and liquid—quickly convertible to cash in the market. (Chapter 19 will discuss how safety and risk are traded off for investment profitability.) A security in an institution not backed by solid assets is too risky to be a marketable security.

At the same time, the interest rate to be earned should reflect the going rate of the current market for money. Hence it should be a very short-term investment. Finally, there must be an active resale market (secondary market) for the security, so it can be sold at any time for conversion into money.

A ***Treasury bill*** is a short-term debt obligation of the U.S. government.

The most basic marketable security is a **Treasury bill,** a short-term debt obligation of the U.S. government. Treasury bills are issued by the Federal Reserve System every week and have maturities of up to one year. They are the ideal marketable security. They are safe (backed by the unlimited taxing power of the government), their interest rate is the current market rate, and they are easy to resell. They are the standard against which all other securities are measured. (Marketable securities issued by commercial banks will be described in the next section.)

Accounts Receivable Management

Unlike cash and other business assets, *accounts receivable*—the money owed to firms by customers—are a major by-product of a firm's credit sales policies and practices. They are a current asset as money owed to the firm, but they can also create some value by encouraging more customers to buy.

Businesses usually choose to sell goods and services on credit if competitors are doing likewise. However, credit can also be used as a marketing tool in much the same way that pricing and advertising are employed. Car sales are regularly boosted by the offer of low-cost or even no-cost credit financing for customers.

Unfortunately, selling on credit entails costs and risks as well as benefits. Some credit customers will be delinquent in their payments, and others will simply not pay at all. This behavior gives rise to bad debt expense. Credit programs are also costly to administer, with expenses for such things as staff, credit reports, and collection agencies. Last, but not least, a business must contend with the costs of financing, particularly the interest expense for costs of goods and services delivered to customers before they have paid.

Managing accounts receivable effectively requires the establishment of policies in three areas: credit standards, credit terms, and collection programs.

Credit Standards: The 4 Cs of Credit Analysis

Credit standards are guidelines or standards for evaluating the creditworthiness of potential credit customers.

The ***four Cs of credit analysis*** are the criteria by which creditworthiness is judged: character, capacity, capital, and conditions.

Credit standards are the guidelines or standards for evaluating the creditworthiness of potential credit customers (much as financial institutions evaluate loan applicants). Credit managers try to minimize the risk of bad debt losses. Their decision-making process is often difficult and subjective. The most common criteria they use in the process of judging the creditworthiness of both businesses and consumers are the **four *C*s of credit analysis:** character, capacity, capital, and conditions:

Character. The probability that a customer will make an earnest effort to pay its bills is termed *character.* Credit managers may evaluate the past payment record in making this determination. This record is important because every credit transaction implies a *promise to pay.* Some corporations interview credit applicants to determine character.

Capacity. The capability of the credit applicant to pay its short-term debts is termed *capacity.* Credit managers often examine customers' projected cash-flow budgets to determine the likelihood that the customer can pay future bills.

Capital. The credit applicant's equity base is *capital.* Credit analysts often calculate the applicant's net worth by subtracting liabilities from selected assets. If the applicant doesn't receive a high rating in this area, the credit manager may require that selected assets be pledged as collateral.

Conditions. The impact of the economy on the credit applicant is termed *conditions.* Credit managers must examine each applicant to determine its position in the economy.

Information about the four *C*s of credit analysis is frequently obtained by evaluation of the seller's previous experience with the customer. However, many credit managers supplement this information with external evaluations provided by various credit rating agencies and credit bureaus. The best-known commercial credit agency is Dun & Bradstreet, which provides its subscribers with a reference book and written credit reports on most businesses.

Credit Terms and Collection Programs

Credit terms are the specific arrangements under which credit will be extended. All credit programs must designate a *credit period*—the number of days customers are given to pay their bills. Unfortunately, long credit periods are associated with large and costly accounts receivable balances. Another common credit term is *cash discounts* for early payment. On occasion, one can also find collateral requirements and finance charges. A seller's credit terms are dictated by a number of factors, including (1) credit terms offered by competitors, (2) level of interest rates, (3) bargaining position of the customer, and (4) industry tradition.

A credit program would be incomplete without a policy on collections. A collection effort is necessary when customers fail to pay their bills on the scheduled due date. However, collection policies vary considerably in both intensity and formality. A very aggressive collection policy may end in expensive lawsuits. An easy policy may leave too many bad debts to write off. Most companies design collection policies somewhere between these two extremes to avoid losing money. Some firms even sell their accounts receivable in order to avoid collection costs, as we will see later in the chapter.

Inventory Management

Inventory is the supply of goods that firms hold on hand and expect to turn over within a year.

Every kind of business has a somewhat different reason for carrying current assets as **inventory,** the supply of goods that firms hold on hand and expect to turn over within a year. Businesses in the service sector, such as barbershops and tax services, need little inventory. Publishers have to hold supplies of printed books. Steel companies must be constantly watchful of the great size of their unsold supplies of ore, fuel, and processed steel.

Inventory carrying costs are the costs of carrying inventory for a year.

Underlying the financial manager's concern in monitoring inventory assets is the fact that whatever inventory goods cost to purchase, they do not earn anything for the firm until they are sold. But the manager also has another important concern: Inventory goods are the ultimate form of "dead storage." Not only do they earn nothing until some time in the future; they also cost the firm money. (**Inventory carrying costs** are the costs of carrying inventory for a time period.) As long as the goods are stored, the firm is giving up the opportunity to put the cash value of the goods into interest-earning marketable securities such as Treasury bills. If the firm has borrowed money to pay for the inventory goods, its costs are in the form of interest paid for the loan. Thus the financial manager is constantly making production and marketing people aware that their inventory goods, because they have a substantial interest cost as well as other carrying costs, are temporarily losing the firm money. And for this reason, the financial manager is always asking other managers for commitments as to when the inventory goods will be sold.

One of the financial manager's greatest concerns is that inventory, such as this supply of lumber, does not earn anything for the firm until it is sold.

HIGHLIGHT IN BUSINESS PRACTICE

Money in Cold Storage—A Management Consultant's Story

We proceed as follows. First look for a five-by-five-by-three-foot bin of gears or parts that looks like it has been there a while. Pick up a gear and ask, casually, "How much is this worth?" You then ask, "How many of these are in the bin?" followed by, "How long has this bin been here?" and, "What's your cost of money [interest cost] for this company?" I recall one case in a nameless South American country where the unit cost times the number of parts times the time it had been there times the interest rate resulted in a cost-per-day figure that would insure a comfortable retirement for the plant manager on the bank of the Rio de la Plata at one of the better resorts to be found there. The plant manager suddenly realized that what he was holding was not just a chunk of high-test steel, but was *real money*. He then pointed out that *he* now understood the value of the inventory but could I suggest a way to drive the point home to upper management? I suggested that he go to the accounting department and borrow enough money to be equal to the bin's value for as long as it had been sitting there, and pile it on the top of the bin. I further suggested that he do that for every bin on the production line. We rapidly figured out that by the time we had the money piled up on the bin, you would not even be able to *see* the bin. My opinion was that if the upper managers were given a tour of the line with the money piled up, they would *never forget it*.

Manufacturers hold inventory goods of three kinds: raw materials, partially completed manufactured goods (called work-in-process inventory), and fully completed goods ready for sale. The cost of keeping inventory on hand includes the following considerations: physical storage and transport costs, spoilage or deterioration, insurance and property tax costs, and the cost of lost interest as well as the possible cost of money borrowed to buy the goods. Table 18.1 is a report that lists an auto dealership's categories of costs for carrying cars in inventory along with total inventory carrying costs for one month at different quantities of inventory.

All company managers are responsible for achieving inventory cost efficiency. Chapter 11 described some manufacturing techniques designed to cut down inventory—notably the just-in-time inventory system. Operations managers are expected to determine the most economical quantities to order when planning their inventory stocks.

For example, there can be cost benefits in ordering large amounts of seasonal raw materials when the market cost is lowest or when a shortage can be predicted. In a seasonal sales business, there can also be benefits to building up more finished goods than will be sold in one month. This often allows a more economical, smooth, and steady rate of production for manufactured goods. In a retail business, if large wholesale purchases are made on good credit terms, the

Table 18.1 Inventory cost categories for Rex's Auto Dealership.

Unit Carrying Cost per Month		**Total Carrying Cost per Month**				
Expense Category	Cost per Auto	Number of Autos in Stock		Unit Carrying Cost		Total Carrying Cost
Interest expense	$105	25	×	$165	=	$ 4,125
Lot storage	25	50	×	165	=	8,250
Casualty insurance	12	75	×	165	=	12,375
Property tax	15	100	×	165	=	16,500
Record-keeping	3	150	×	165	=	24,750
Maintenance	5	200	×	165	=	33,000
Unit carrying cost	$165	300	×	165	=	49,500

savings may be greater than the carrying costs. It is the financial manager's job to help other managers work out these trade-offs realistically in order to maximize the company's current asset value.

MANAGING SHORT-TERM FINANCING

Regardless of a financial manager's efficiency, there are intervals during the year when cash inflows cannot exactly match cash outflows. At some time during a year, almost every company needs to seek *short-term financing*—funds to be put into the firm in order to fund ongoing operations. These short-term funding arrangements make up a firm's *current liabilities*—the money it owes during the course of a year.

One of the most common reasons for needing short-term financing is seasonal variations in current assets. Many businesses provide products or services whose peak demand is at specific times of the year. Toy manufacturers such as Mattel and Fisher Price generate 80 percent of their sales during the Christmas season. Retailers such as Sears, J. C. Penney, and K mart often have to borrow to obtain huge inventories for Christmas demand. Construction companies may find that the demand for their services peaks from April to October.

These temporary fluctuations in product demand cause an erratic cash flow for many businesses. Short-term interim financing is a common way to bridge the gap between the investment in inventory and receivables and the eventual receipt of money from customers.

Special circumstances also create a need for temporary funds. Projecting funding needs in the short term is a key role of the financial manager. *Cash-flow budgets* are used to project receipts and expenditures of cash, usually for a period of a year or less. Figure 18.4 is a quarterly cash budget for the hypothetical Creative

BUSINESS PRACTICE EXAMPLE Continues

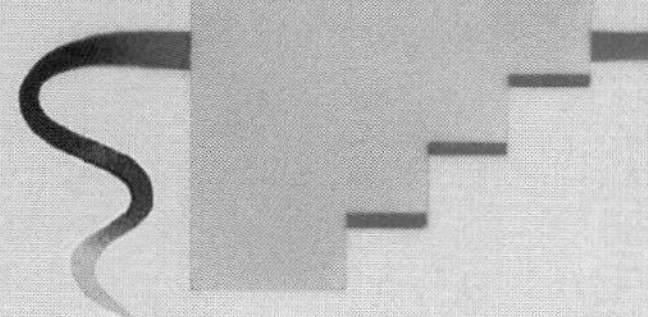

As foreign competition took away Bethlehem Steel's markets, the firm's loss of income caused it to suffer from low liquidity, or lack of cash. Financially, Bethlehem was operating on slimmer profit margins every year, squeezing equipment harder, leaving itself with too much of its value tied up in the fixed assets of the aging plants. Management seemed to be caught in a dilemma: On the current asset side, the smaller market for the firm's steel production meant declining cash, or accounts receivable. In current liabilities, the cost of ongoing salaries and production remained much the same. As for long-term assets, the outmoded equipment had begun to decline in value, yet there was no cash to reinvest in new equipment.

As Walter Williams decided in 1986, Bethlehem would have to get rid of heavy financial burdens and raise cash; in financial terms, his goal was more liquidity. The crucial steps would be getting a better balance between current assets and liabilities while unlocking fixed assets tied up with inefficient factories. Only then could Bethlehem use its own resources to rebuild its future with a more efficient mix of plant and equipment.

Williams saw no way to do this except by scaling back the entire Bethlehem operation to a more basic level. This meant shutting down operations and laying off employees in divisions that were not a good fit in Bethlehem's markets. The immediate effect was reduced current liabilities, with lower salary and pension outlays.

By 1988, Bethlehem had lost approximately 55,000 employees, or nearly 60 percent of the number it had in 1982. According to Williams, about half that number was the result of shutting down or selling off businesses. "The other half was through just plain slimming down and trimming down our forces," he said, referring to retraining workers and streamlining operations to fit a different mix of steel-making facilities. Bethlehem was beginning to redirect its valuable resources into a smaller, more flexible production capability.

Playtime, Inc. It projects cash shortages in August and October. Therefore, Creative Playtime must arrange to cover the projected shortages for those months.

To balance cash-flow needs, the company's financial manager may resort to a number of different funding arrangements. Sources of credit—whether for Sam's Pizza Parlor or International Harvester—are very similar. We will now examine them.

	July	August	September	October
Receipts/collections	$12,000	$31,000	$35,000	$22,000
Cash payments				
Purchases	13,500	26,000	25,000	25,000
Wages & salaries	2,000	3,500	3,000	3,000
Utilities	400	500	500	500
Payment to creditors	300	3,400	4,000	1,000
Taxes			2,000	
Total payments	$16,200	$33,400	$34,500	$29,500
Net cash gain (loss) during month	(4,200)	(2,400)	500	(7,500)
Initial cash at start of month	6,200	2,000	(400)	100
Cash balance	$ 2,000	($400)	$ 100	($7,400)

Figure 18.4 Quarterly cash budget for Creative Playtime, Inc. Organizations need to monitor cash flow to ensure a sufficient amount of working capital.

Payables and Accrued Liabilities

Among the short-term financial obligations that a firm acquires during the year are bills that come due for the services or goods it buys—its *accounts payable.* In addition to bills are regularly accumulated *accrued expenses,* such as wages, insurance, and pension fund payments, which the firm is using up but has not yet paid for in full.

Trade credit is informal short-term credit granted directly to the buyer of goods or services by the seller.

Probably the most common kind of payable expense is **trade credit,** an informal short-term credit granted directly to the buyer of goods or services by the seller. The sale is completed on the basis of mutual trust, since no formal credit instruments are used in the transaction. For example, a wholesaler may sell a hundred cans of Wilson tennis balls to a sporting goods store, granting the store thirty days to make payment. In essence, the wholesaler is financing the retailer for a thirty-day period.

Trade credit represents accounts receivable to the seller and accounts payable to the buyer. It is estimated that this open-book credit is used in more than 85 percent of the business transactions involving merchandise.

The buyer of merchandise is usually granted a certain number of days in which to pay for the goods. However, a cash discount may be offered to motivate early payment. For example, K mart may receive an invoice for $10,000 that has cash discount terms of 2/10, net 30. This means that K mart must pay the full amount in thirty days but may deduct $200 (2% × $10,000 = $200) if it pays the bill within ten days. If K mart takes the discount, the seller will receive $9,800 for its goods. However, if K mart fails to meet the discount deadline, it must pay the full $10,000 within thirty days.

Often, the discount period is interpreted quite liberally by many businesses, and the discount is deducted regardless of the payment date. Creditors must police such actions so that abuse of credit terms does not become routine.

Should a buyer take advantage of cash discount terms? At first glance, the 2 percent discount may seem like a small amount. However, it actually is quite substantial. To see this, we will translate the discount into an annual percentage rate. We will then determine whether forgoing the discount and using other sources of credit is cheaper. The steps are as follows:

1. The buyer must pay the bill within ten days to take the cash discount. If the discount isn't taken, the additional 2 percent must be included at the end of thirty days. It would cost K mart 2 percent interest to use the money ($200) for this twenty-day period (thirty days minus ten days). The twenty-day period is called the credit period.
2. How many twenty-day periods are there in a business year? Eighteen (360/20 = 18).
3. Multiply 2 percent by eighteen periods to arrive at an annual interest rate of 36 percent. This represents the annual interest charged for ignoring the discount.

Obviously, passing up cash discounts can result in large annual interest costs. Since many financial institutions lend money at much less than 36 percent, it is often to the buyer's advantage to borrow and take the cash discount. Table 18.2 shows the annual interest equivalents of selected cash discounts.

Accrued wages are by far the largest current expense item for a business. They are a major source of short-term funding for certain kinds of businesses, and for the most part, there is no interest cost associated with this financing. Accrued wages result from the fact that employees are normally willing to work a certain number of days before getting paid. The longer they are willing to wait for their paychecks, the greater the firm's accrued wages financing.

Bank Commercial Loans and Commercial Paper

The most common supplier of short-term commercial credit is commercial banks. Lending officers in the larger banks manage hundreds of accounts, often lending millions of dollars to a single firm. Some of these loans are granted under a regular line of credit to the firm, and others are loans for special circumstances.

A ***line of credit*** is a formal loan agreement with a bank that allows a specific maximum amount of credit at specific rates.

A **line of credit** is a formal loan agreement with a bank that allows a specific maximum amount of credit at specific rates. A bank line of credit for $250,000

Table 18.2 Cost of trade credit.

Terms	Credit Period (Days)	Annual Rate
3/10, net 60	50	21.6%
2/10, net 20	10	72
1/10, net 30	20	18
2/10, net 30	20	36

means that the client firm can borrow up to this amount. Usually, lines of credit are granted for one-year periods. Each year, the commercial bank officer reviews the performance and financial position of the firm to determine whether to renew the line of credit.

A line of credit provides considerable flexibility in financial planning, since firms are able to draw on the funds as needed, much as consumers use credit cards. Interest is paid only on the funds actually borrowed, and loans can be paid off at any time during the year. Gibson Greetings Inc., a maker of greeting cards and gift wrap, arranged for a $250 million line of credit with a group of banks headed by Bankers Trust Company. The short-term borrowings were used to finance inventory purchases for the holiday season.[1]

A ***promissory note*** is a written promise from a borrower to make future payment to the lender at a specified rate of interest.

The ***prime rate*** is the interest rate that banks routinely charge their most financially sound business borrowers.

Commercial paper is short-term unsecured promissory notes issued by corporations for a period usually ranging from 30 to 270 days.

Every commercial bank loan is documented by means of a **promissory note**—a written promise on the part of a borrower that future payment will be made to the lender at a specified rate of interest. Figure 18.5 shows a typical promissory note. Interest rates on bank commercial loans are tied in various ways to the **prime rate**—the interest rate that banks routinely charge their most financially sound business borrowers.

Over the past two decades, the commercial paper market has provided one of the major sources of short-term funds for American firms. **Commercial paper** is short-term unsecured promissory notes issued by corporations for a period usually ranging from 30 to 270 days. These IOUs are normally purchased by large institutional investors (banks, pension funds, and insurance companies) that are looking to put their idle cash into a marketable security.

Who sells commercial paper? Normally, big corporations such as General Motors Acceptance Corporation (GMAC) and Phillip Morris issue large amounts of commercial paper. Since these notes are not backed by specific collateral, the issuing corporation must usually be well known and financially stable for investors to buy its IOUs.

If GMAC issues $2 million in face value of ninety-day paper, it means that GMAC must repay this debt in ninety days. Commercial paper is discounted, which means it sells for less than face value. (This process is described in detail in chapter 19.) If $2 million of GMAC paper sold for a discounted price of $1.95 million, then the amount of interest would be $50,000—the face value minus the sales proceeds.

Figure 18.5

A promissory note. Notes formally bind a customer to pay for certain goods or services.

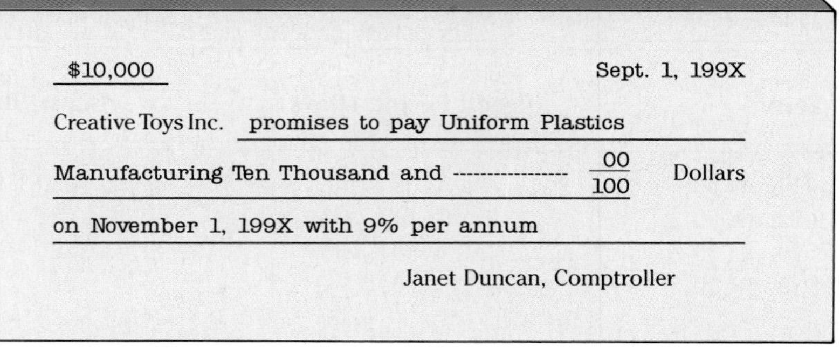

$10,000 Sept. 1, 199X

Creative Toys Inc. promises to pay Uniform Plastics

Manufacturing Ten Thousand and ---------------- 00/100 Dollars

on November 1, 199X with 9% per annum

Janet Duncan, Comptroller

Some 900 companies issue commercial paper to raise short-term funds.[2] Many corporations sell their commercial paper to dealers known as commercial paper houses. These dealers act as wholesalers, selling the issues of commercial paper to ultimate investors such as insurance companies and pension funds. Some of the better-known commercial paper houses are First Boston Corporation, Salomon Brothers, Merrill Lynch, and Goldman Sachs. An estimated 25 percent of all commercial paper is sold through dealers.[3]

Finance Companies and Factoring

Sales finance companies specialize in financing the customers of certain types of retail businesses. For example, suppose you purchase a Pioneer amplifier from a stereo store and sign an installment contract to pay for it over a twenty-four-month period. The store needs cash, however, so it sells (discounts) the contract to a sales finance company. The store receives immediate cash, and you pay the sales finance company. Of course, the store remains liable if you fail to pay what you owe. In short, retailers sell installment contracts to convert credit sales into cash sales, thereby improving their available cash.

Sales finance companies are companies that specialize in financing the customers of certain types of retail businesses.

In **factoring,** another method of increasing liquidity, a firm sells its accounts receivable at a discount to a commercial finance company or bank (the factor). The factor provides credit and collection services for businesses that do not wish to bear the cost of these functions themselves. Usually, the accounts receivable are sold to the factor without recourse. This means that the factor assumes the risk of loss if an account goes unpaid. It is also common practice to sell the accounts on a notification basis. Under this arrangement, customers make payments directly to the factor, not to the firm that sold the merchandise.

Factoring is selling one's accounts receivable at a discount to a commercial finance company or bank (the factor).

A company that factors its accounts receivable is technically not raising funds on loan. Instead of paying direct interest for financing, it sells its accounts receivable, often for less than their full value. The factoring makes money on the difference, and the selling company avoids having to take on short-term liabilities.

LONG-TERM FINANCIAL DECISIONS

Assets are the lifeblood of businesses. There must be enough of them to cover payments for all liabilities and to provide profits and benefits to the owners—their equity. However, unless a company can find owners who can supply money or other resources or get loans from lenders, there will be no funding to run the company—and thus no development of assets.

To keep these basic factors in balance, it is important for financial managers to find time to look at the big issues behind the company's long-term decisions: Who will put money into the firm? How much control will they want? How much money will the firm need to raise in order to buy new equipment? How will the company know what equipment to buy or whether it will pay off and make a profit?

Fixed Assets and the Capital Budgeting Process

Fixed assets (or capital assets) such as machinery, land, and buildings are necessary parts of most businesses. They are often called the company's *capital assets.* If properly planned, they allow employees to do their jobs fast, efficiently,

BUSINESS PRACTICE EXAMPLE Continues

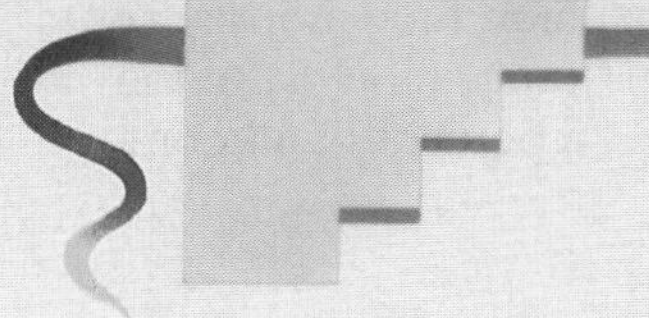

Bethlehem Steel's aggressive program of reshaping its fixed assets was particularly active in 1988. Through a series of major capital budgeting projects, the company radically rearranged its plants, property, and equipment. As with all such projects, financial managers at Bethlehem kept a careful watch on expenses as well as incomes as they planned for new operations.

For example, Bethlehem senior vice president Roger Penny announced in late summer 1988 that the firm would use funds from other sales to invest $45 million in three remaining plants in the Buffalo, New York, area over the next five years. This decision represented a comeback, since almost all the Buffalo plants had been closed in 1983.

To accomplish the renewal, Bethlehem would need to be assured of a critical margin of cost-effectiveness in the future, namely a guaranteed low rate for the cost of hydroelectric power generated from Niagara Falls. To back the demand for low-cost power, the steel maker launched a lawsuit against the Niagara Mohawk Power Company and the state of New York for $23 million in damages, based on overcharging for power in past years. If the capital budgeting project to invest in the plants could recover this amount, almost half its cost would be repaid. Bethlehem managers argued that continued investment in the plants and employment for 1,400 workers would depend on the steel maker getting power at lower cost in the future.

To pay for this investment and others, Bethlehem took on another capital budgeting project at the same time—selling its wire-making division in Williamsport, Pennsylvania. Bethlehem management claimed that "pressure from unfairly traded imports" was one reason for leaving the business but also said wire making was not consistent with its basic strategic steel-making mission. The customer was a British wire-making firm, Bridon, which found the facility more central to its business.

Earlier in the year, Bethlehem's shipbuilding facilities in Texas and Singapore were put up for sale, and another facility on Chesapeake Bay was scaled down. Again, foreign competition had made this business a distraction to Bethlehem's new strategic plan—to gain financial strength through more efficient steel-making facilities.

cheaply, and well. Managers must constantly make decisions about the acquisition, repair, sale, or replacement of fixed assets. Such decisions are part of **capital budgeting** (or fixed asset management)—the process of planning how to buy, sell, and develop fixed assets. Overseeing this process is a major function of financial management.

Capital budgeting (also termed fixed asset management) is the process of planning how to buy, sell, and develop fixed assets.

Financial decisions about fixed assets must consider both profit and risk. Why should managers consider risk in addition to profit? Primarily because the owners of a business are, as a rule, unwilling to expose their holdings to unpredictable risks unless there is some additional reward in prospect.

The capital budgeting process normally begins with a proposal to buy, sell, or develop a particular fixed asset. The recommendation usually comes initially from a manager or department within the company. However, it can also come from an outsider—a government agency, for example, or a salesperson for a capital goods manufacturer. Consider the following fixed asset proposals:

> A consulting firm hired by Depco Enterprises recommended to Depco's top management that the company increase plant production capacity by 20 percent to prepare for a significant increase in demand that was expected to materialize within the next two years.
>
> The industrial engineering division of a large Midwest aluminum manufacturer proposed replacing all the company's smelters with two new models that required 40 to 60 percent less electrical energy and 20 to 30 percent lower labor cost.
>
> Topco Industries was told by the Environmental Protection Agency that it must install pollution control equipment in order to reduce air pollutants coming from the firm's main factory.
>
> The treasurer of Safeco Corporation recommended the sale of the company's six-year-old private jet because of much reduced fares for commercial air travel.

The financial manager's initial response to a fixed asset proposal is a *feasibility study*—a cursory examination to determine if the proposal holds sufficient promise to merit an in-depth financial analysis. Feasibility studies also filter out proposals that are illegal, excessively risky, or unsuitable. Once a major proposal passes the feasibility review, it undergoes an intensive analysis by a financial manager.

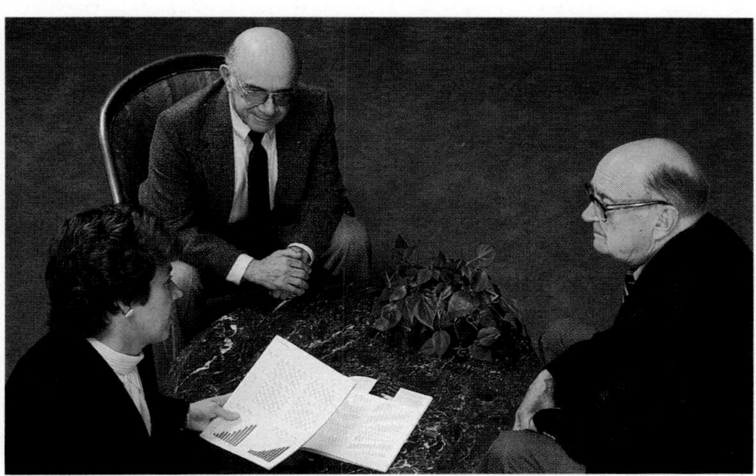

Assets are the lifeblood of businesses. This financial manager hopes that the two potential owners will invest their money to create assets in her firm, in return for their opportunity to earn a profit on the investment.

The most crucial aspect of any fixed asset proposal concerns the risk and predictability factors involved in it and the probable impact the investment will have on the business's future profits. Each contributing factor is analyzed by the financial management staff, which pays special attention to all risk factors.

Generally speaking, a fixed asset proposal should be accepted if its lifetime projected benefits (cash inflows) profitably exceed its lifetime projected costs (cash outflows). Prominently included among the projected costs are the costs of getting funds for the investment as well as a variety of special income tax rules. The most detailed aspect of the benefit analysis will be attempts to measure what is predictable and what is risky.

Most businesses consider several fixed asset proposals at the same time. The acceptable proposals are grouped together in a capital budget, such as the one for an amusement park shown in Table 18.3.

Table 18.3 Summary capital budget form for an amusement park.

Proposal	Sponsor	Investment Outlay	Payback Period (in Years)	Cost of Funding (Percent)	Net Benefit	Benefit/ Cost Ratio	Rate of Return	Comments
Replace ferris wheel	Maintenance department	$190,000	5	14%	$100,000	1.53	24%	Cannot be postponed.
Purchase water slide	Sales representative	175,000	3	18	120,000	1.69	25	All competing parks have one.
Restore roller coaster	Maintenance department	260,000	7	13	125,000	1.48	18	
Enlarge parking lot	Grounds keeper	115,000	6	12	35,000	1.30	18	
Install gourmet restaurant	Marketing manager	350,000	8	18	150,000	1.42	22	This will add prestige to the park.
Convert dance pavillion into haunted house	Park general manager	90,000	4	20	10,000	1.11	22	
Replace parachute jump with moon walk (Option A)	Park general manager	75,000	5	16	60,000	1.80	33	
Replace parachute jump with pirate ship (Option B)	Marketing manager	140,000	8	18	90,000	1.64	24	

Once accepted, a fixed asset proposal must be implemented. That is, all of the necessary arrangements must be made to acquire, install, document, and raise funds for the proposal. Lastly, a financial manager should audit each of the accepted proposals from time to time, in order to evaluate their on-the-job performance. This completes the capital budgeting process.

Looking for Long-Term Funds

As we have seen, all businesses must have some sort of funding to operate normally and build up valuable assets for the owners. In the search for long-term financing, the most basic choice for managers is between funding from equity and funding from debt. Both have costs and benefits.

Equity versus Debt

The starting point for funding any business must be the owners' equity. At the simplest level, an independent consultant puts up owner equity in the form of cost-of-living and business expenses to make services available. In exchange for the cost of equity, the owner expects a profit and whatever value and benefit comes with the business—including the right to control it.

Owners and managers usually find that building up more value in the business requires financing beyond the owners' money. One option, described in chapter 4, is to form a partnership or corporation to bring in funding from the equity of other owners. For the company, the cost of this source of funding is giving up some control, profit, and value to new owners. As we saw in chapter 4, a new mix of owners in a partnership or small corporation can have disadvantages. These include the potential for unexpected owner conflicts, which could become severe enough to create a "freeze" of the operations and assets in a small business. The major alternative to the cost of equity is borrowing funds from someone willing to take a chance on the success of the company. That is, the company can take on debt. In doing this, the company assumes funding costs in the form of two basic obligations.

The first obligation of debt is that the company and its owners must pay back lenders (called *creditors*) as part of basic business expenses, or liabilities, before they can claim profits or any other value for themselves. In short, the owners get paid last. As a second obligation, the company must compensate creditors for losing their own use of the money. At the same time, the creditors must be persuaded that the risk of losing their money is either very small or worth some extra compensation. The second obligation adds up to an interest expense as the cost of funding.

In spite of these disadvantages, most businesses get a large part of their funding by means of debt. Of course, there are a number of advantages in using debt funding. First, under U.S. tax laws, the cost of borrowing funds is a liability to the company and is therefore a tax-deductible cost of doing business. The interest paid on loans is deducted every year from the firm's declared earnings. Funds obtained from selling equity shares do not carry interest and do not produce a tax deduction.

Perhaps the most important benefit in raising funds from debt, however, is using the power of borrowed funds to multiply the owners' earnings. **Financial leverage** is the firm's use of borrowing to increase its earnings per share and

Financial leverage is a firm's use of borrowing to increase its earnings per share and return on owners' equity.

return on owners' equity. It works this way: Suppose a company borrows $1,000 at an interest rate of 10 percent, planning to use the money in its own operations, which it calculates will earn a return of 15 percent. The company thus expects to earn $150 for each $1,000 of debt and to pay $100 for the use of the money. This means the company expects to gain 5 percent, or $50, for each $1,000 it borrows. The risk, however, is that the company's operations may *not* produce a 15 percent return. If the operations earn less than the 10 percent cost of borrowing funds, the firm loses money.

In making decisions between equity and debt financing, financial managers must continue to balance the trade-offs described earlier. They must calculate how the funding will add to the value of the company and make sure that its value will at least equal the money to be put into the company. The accounting equation from chapter 17 still holds. Profits and value produced from the firm's assets must exactly balance debt liabilities and owners' equity. Managers must therefore be sure that the company's assets will substantially exceed the total costs of all financing, in order to produce the increased value in equity and profit potential that owners expect. Financial managers always look for long-term financing funds that will be well balanced against the firm's investment in long-term assets. Where do they find long-term funds, and how do they make choices?

Raising Long-Term Funds

In the section on short-term financing, we examined how businesses borrow money for a year or less to meet current costs. When managers need money for fixed assets, they need financing for a longer span of time (from five to forty years). These funds are normally used to purchase expensive equipment and to underwrite plant expansions. Financial managers rely on several sources of funding to purchase these types of fixed assets. Figure 18.6 depicts the key sources of long-term funds for most firms.

The first source is internal funds from *retained earnings.* Most corporations keep a portion of their profits (retained earnings) to plow back into the business. Large corporations such as General Motors, Sears, and Textron often retain 40 percent or more of their profits for reinvestment.

The second source is internal funds generated from the sale of assets. Managers often evaluate each of the firms's assets to see if its continued operation is its greatest value to the long-term plan. If not, and if funds are needed to pursue alternatives—as at Bethlehem Steel in 1987—then selling the asset may be the best plan.

Externally, the firm acquires long-term funding through long-term debt and through equity financing. Most long-term debt is issued in the form of bonds (which will be discussed in detail in chapter 19). In equity financing, the company sells stock to investors, thereby making them owners.

Corporate bonds are interest-bearing debt instruments issued by corporations and promising to pay specific amounts at specific times.

Long-Term Debt Financing The three major forms of long-term business debt financing are corporate bonds, mortgages, and leasing. **Corporate bonds**—the largest single category of long-term corporate debt—are interest-bearing debt instruments issued by corporations and promising to pay specific amounts at specific times. Interest is usually paid in installments and principal in a lump sum. Bonds are described in more detail in chapter 19.

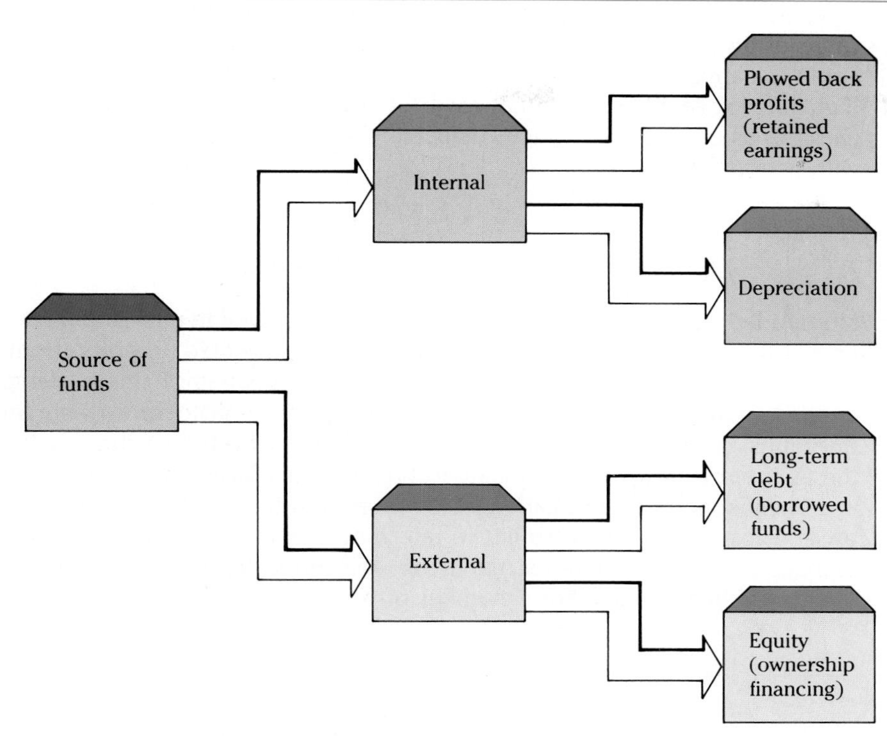

Figure 18.6
Key sources of long-term funds.

Mortgages, as chapter 16 indicated, are long-term secured loans usually for the purchase of real estate. They are documented by means of promissory notes. Mortgage loans are installment loans. That is, the loan payments are equal, with each containing portions of principal and interest. Mortgages are particularly well suited for funding the purchase or construction of commercial buildings and manufacturing plants. They are also used extensively in residential home financing. Banks and insurance companies are major mortgage lenders.

Today, many firms choose to lease rather than buy such fixed assets as warehouses, airplanes, computers, and land. **Leasing** is renting fixed assets for a specified period of time. It may not seem like financing, but it is. Leasing allows for the use of an asset without the need to acquire funds to purchase it. By being an alternative to financing, leasing is a form of fundraising. In fact, it is debt financing because of the rental payment obligations. Leasing is often selected over other forms of debt because of certain tax advantages.

Leasing is renting fixed assets for a specified period of time.

Owners' Equity Decisions Financial managers have a basic choice to make regarding the common stocks that are the main part of owners' equity. They can declare dividends or keep retained earnings as part of the firm's assets. This decision becomes an issue mainly when the company needs additional funds for long-term financing. To raise the money, should the company sell more stock, increasing the number of owners who have a piece of the profits? Or should it retain earnings to cover the financing and pay the current owners less?

In theory, the decision could go either way without much effect on the overall value of the company. In practice, managers must consider what owners have come to expect in the way of dividends. If the company is making an unusually high rate of profit, management will strongly consider retaining some of the earnings as a source of financing, since the firm seems to be able to make money with its funding.

INTERNATIONAL FINANCIAL MANAGEMENT

More American companies than ever before are involved in international business activities. Regardless of whether the activity is trade oriented (imports and exports) or finance oriented (foreign investment and foreign financing), financial managers are major participants in the proceedings. They must consider long-term financial questions about whether to undertake new fixed asset ventures abroad or whether foreign companies may be looking to buy the fixed assets of American firms.

Foremost among the challenges of short-term financial planning is the ever-present reality of foreign exchange rate movements (see chapter 16). Financial managers are responsible for managing their firms' exposure to risk in regard to foreign exchange rates. For a number of years, the exchange rates between the

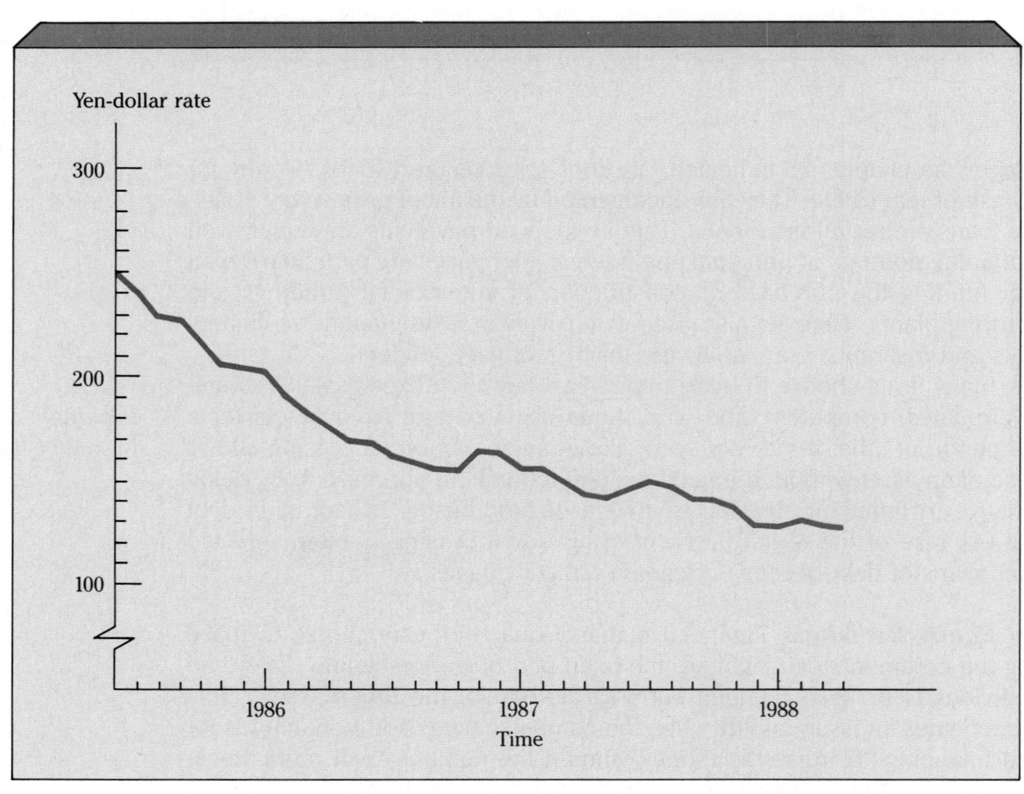

Figure 18.7 The yen-dollar exchange rate, June 1985 to April 1988.

U.S. dollar and the monies of most other major industrial countries have been anything but stable. Consider, for example, the recent experience of the Japanese yen–U.S. dollar exchange rate, as shown in Figure 18.7. Within a period of only about two and a half years, the yen-dollar exchange rate fell by 50 percent (from 250 yen to the dollar to 125 yen to the dollar). Although some experts consider the 1985–1988 period to be abnormal, most financial managers would be uncomfortable even with far smaller exchange rate movements.

Corporations and financial institutions with international business dealings are troubled by large exchange rate movements for the simple reason that they don't know what to expect from their endeavors. For instance, let's say an American wine importer agrees to buy 20,000 cases of expensive French champagne. The price has been set at 1,500 French francs per case, and payment is to be made in ninety days. Accordingly, the importer is obligated to pay a French company 1,500 francs × 20,000 cases = 30,000,000 francs in ninety days. The question is: How many U.S. dollars will it take to acquire 30,000,000 francs on the foreign exchange market in ninety days? It all depends on the franc-dollar exchange rate at that time, which may bear little resemblance to the exchange rate at the time the agreement was entered into. Depending on the direction of movement, the American firm could be injured or aided. Fortunately, several techniques for a company to cover itself against market movements have been developed over the years to distribute the risks and reduce the uncertainty of exchange rate movements.

BUSINESS PRACTICE EXAMPLE Continues

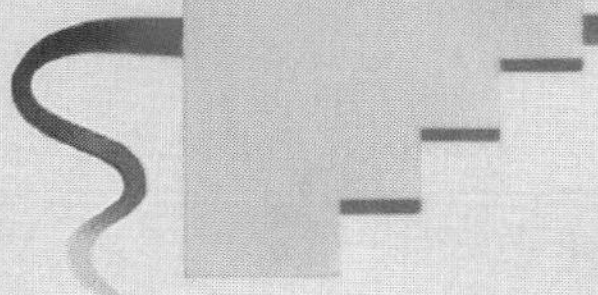

For Bethlehem Steel, the record loss of $2 billion in 1986 was preceded by a number of unfavorable circumstances. One critical factor that made the difference by the mid-1980s was the high value of the dollar relative to other world currencies, because of foreign capital attracted to American investments and because of a high volume of goods—including steel—imported into the United States. For Bethlehem Steel, this meant that the exchange rates favored foreign imported steel; customers paid fewer dollars for Japanese and Korean steel. Any American steel product bought in Japan would cost more yen than would an identical product made of Japanese steel. Partly as a result of this imbalance, by 1984 foreign steel had captured 26 percent of the American market.

On the other hand, a weaker dollar in 1987 and 1988 gave a major assist to Bethlehem. As foreign imports and investments in the United States became fewer, the prices of Bethlehem's steel in world markets came closer to those of imports. By 1987, because of this factor and foreign

(continued)

trade agreements, steel imports dropped to 22 percent of the U.S. market. By mid-1988, the share for imports had dropped even lower, to about 20.5 percent. Walter Williams, Bethlehem's CEO, thought that would be a baseline market share for imports until other competitive factors were made more equal.

Williams's chief complaint about competition from abroad was that, in spite of efforts at international trade agreements, steel makers in Europe as well as in the Orient were receiving heavy subsidies from their governments. Williams believed that without such subsidies for foreign competition, American steel makers could hold their own and gain competitively in world markets.

Issues for Discussion

1. How did a reduction in the workforce and in pension payments affect Bethlehem's current assets and liabilities?
2. How did capital budget projects for selling wire-making and shipbuilding plants and investing in Buffalo steel-making plants fit into Williams's long-range financial plan for Bethlehem Steel?
3. How do you account for the fact that a smaller production volume at Bethlehem—down to 16 million tons a year from a previous 22 million tons—could make the firm more valuable?

SUMMARY

Financial managers are responsible for monetary decisions and their effects. The vice president for finance is the chief financial officer.

Balanced against company assets (short-term and long-term) is the company's financing—funding through borrowing, by selling shares, or from personal resources.

Everything of value to a business is its assets. Current assets (or short-term assets) requiring a good deal of managerial attention are cash, accounts receivable, and inventory.

Cash management involves deciding the amount of cash assets to hold at any point. It includes taking advantage of check float and earning interest in marketable securities.

Accounts receivable management deals with credit standards, credit terms, and collection programs. The four *C*s of credit analysis are character, capacity, capital, and conditions. Credit terms are the arrangements under which credit is extended, including cash discounts for early payment. Collection policies should be between aggressive and easy.

Inventory management involves inventory carrying costs. A firm doesn't earn any income on its inventory of goods until the goods are sold.

Almost every firm needs to seek short-term financing to see it through temporary slowdowns in product demand. Cash-flow budgets are used to help determine when cash shortages are likely to occur.

Accounts payable and accrued expenses are short-term financial obligations. The most common type of payable is trade credit—informal short-term credit granted to buyers by sellers. Accrued wages are the largest current expense item.

Commercial banks are the most common supplier of short-term commercial credit. Some of the loans made by banks are under lines of credit—formal agreements that specify the maximum amount of credit a firm will receive in a year. Bank loans are documented with promissory notes—the borrowers' written promises to pay the lenders. Commercial paper is short-term unsecured promissory notes issued by corporations.

Sales finance companies finance the inventories and customers of certain types of retailers, thereby increasing the retailers' liquidity. Factoring is another method of increasing liquidity. A firm sells its accounts receivable at a discount to a finance company or bank, which then collects the payments.

Fixed assets such as machinery, land, and buildings are the subject of long-term financing. Capital budgeting, or fixed asset management, is the process of planning how to buy, sell, and develop these assets. Feasibility studies are used to determine if a fixed asset proposal has merit. Once a proposal is accepted, it must be implemented and later on audited.

The starting point for long-term funding is owners' equity. Then comes borrowing. An advantage of borrowing is that interest on business loans is tax deductible. Borrowing also can give firms financial leverage.

Long-term funds are raised internally from retained earnings and sales of assets. They are raised externally through long-term debt and equity financing. The three major forms of long-term business debt financing are corporate bonds, mortgages, and leasing.

American companies are heavily involved in international business activities. If a company agrees to buy goods from a foreign country and must pay for them at some point in the future, it is important for it to be able to know approximately what the exchange rate will be at that time.

KEY TERMS

Capital budgeting p. 543
Check float p. 530
Commercial paper p. 540
Corporate bonds p. 546
Credit standards p. 533
Electronic Funds Transfer System p. 532
Factoring p. 541
Financial leverage p. 545
Financing p. 529
Four *C*s of credit analysis p. 533
Inventory p. 534
Inventory carrying costs p. 534
Leasing p. 547
Line of credit p. 539
Marketable securities p. 532
Prime rate p. 540
Promissory note p. 540
Sales finance companies p. 541
Trade credit p. 538
Treasury bill p. 532

CHECK YOUR LEARNING

Reread the following learning objectives. Each objective is followed by a few questions. Answering these questions accurately will help you retain the most important concepts discussed in this chapter. After answering each question, check your answer with the key at the end of this chapter. (*Hint:* If you have doubt regarding the correct response, consult the page whose number follows the answer.)

Circle:

A. Describe the duties of a financial manager and the significance of asset and financing decisions.

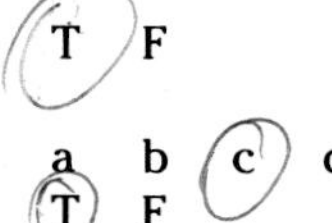

T F — 1. Financial managers can hold a number of different titles in an organization.

a b c d — 2. Financial managers are generally not involved in which of the following decisions: (a) credit standards; (b) capital budgeting; (c) pricing; (d) dividends.

T F — 3. A firm's total assets must equal its total financing.

B. Discuss the issues involved in cash management.

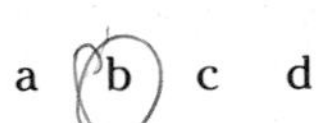

1. One of the following is not a cash management issue: (a) selection of marketable securities; (b) setting credit standards for customers; (c) determining the minimum cash balance; (d) playing the float.

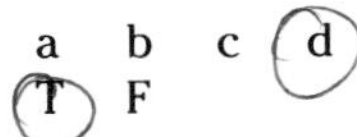

2. In terms of cash management, a security is marketable if it: (a) is actively traded in the secondary market; (b) is free of default risk; (c) has a maturity of a year or less; (d) all of the above.
3. Corporations do not collect interest on checking accounts.

C. Define *accounts receivable,* and describe the four *C*s of credit.

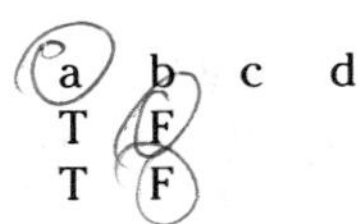

1. Which of the following is *not* one of the four *C*s of credit: (a) cosigners; (b) conditions; (c) capital; (d) capacity.
2. *Capacity* normally refers to the equity, or net worth, of a credit applicant.
3. Dun & Bradstreet guarantees payments to creditors.

D. Explain the characteristics of inventory and its carrying cost.

1. As a company's inventory balance rises, the carrying cost should decline proportionately.

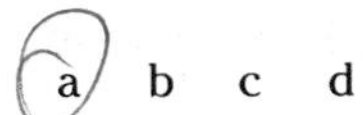

2. The amount of inventory on hand can be influenced by all but one of the following: (a) financial leverage; (b) order size; (c) sales volume; (d) safety stocks.

E. Discuss the forms and suppliers of short-term financing.

1. Businesses use lines of credit much like consumers use credit cards.
2. One firm's accounts payable is another firm's accounts receivable.

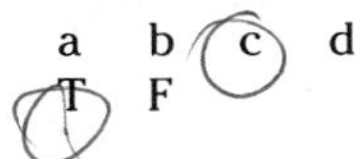

3. Which of the following is *not* a common form of short-term financing: (a) trade credit; (b) commercial paper; (c) mortgages; (d) accrued wages.
4. The most common lenders of short-term funds are commercial banks.

F. Define *fixed asset management* and *capital budgeting,* and explain the steps in capital budgeting.

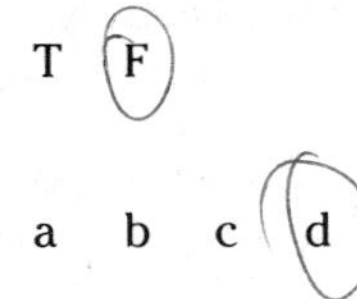

1. Feasibility studies should be conducted within one year after a capital asset is acquired.
2. Which of the following is the first step in the capital budgeting process: (a) profitability and risk analysis; (b) postaudit; (c) implementation; (d) proposal submission.

G. Distinguish between equity financing and long-term debt.

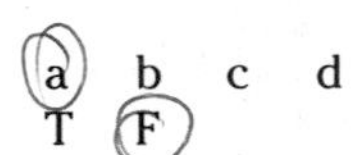

1. One of the following represents debt financing: (a) bonds; (b) common stock; (c) preferred stock; (d) retained earnings.
2. Leasing is not a common form of long-term debt financing.

H. Appreciate some problems of fluctuating foreign exchange rates.

1. An American business would be exposed to exchange rate risk if it: (a) contracted to pay for imported goods with dollars; (b) contracted to pay for imported goods with a foreign currency; (c) contracted to be paid for exports with dollars; (d) a and c.

QUESTIONS FOR REVIEW AND DISCUSSION

1. Define the terms listed at the end of the chapter.
2. Discuss why and how businesses use short-term financing.
3. How does trade credit differ from selling on a note basis?
4. Explain through an arithmetic example why a firm should take a 2/10, net 60 cash discount even if it must borrow from a bank at 10 percent interest to do so.
5. In what ways are notes and drafts similar? In what ways are they different?
6. Define *commercial paper.* What types of corporations normally sell this type of short-term debt instrument?
7. Do you agree or disagree with the following statement: Using factors often reflects poorly on the past credit management of the firm. Explain.
8. Discuss the main difference between equity financing and long-term debt.
9. Most successful corporations rely on retained earnings as a main source of growth capital. Since plowing back earnings reduces the amount of cash available for dividends to stockholders, how do shareholders benefit?
10. How are industrial bonds used to finance long-term needs of corporations?
11. Visit the reference room of your campus library and examine a copy of the Dun & Bradstreet reference book. Pick three businesses in your college community and see if they are listed in the directory. Report your findings to the class.
12. Businesses often depend on certain financial institutions as sources of short-term money. Name the financial institutions mentioned in this chapter, and discuss the role of each in raising short-term funds.

CONCLUDING CASE

Getting a New Venture off the Ground

Maxwell's, a neighborhood bar, was started by Jake L. Frantz and his partners, Jeff Palmer and Dennis Seaman. Unfortunately, the neighbors haven't moved in yet. Jake and his partners are banking on Cleveland's downtown renaissance to lure young professionals to the warehouse district that is home to Maxwell's, a three-tiered club. The basement and the first floor in the refurbished century-old building feature a jazz club, a video music hall, a deli, and a restaurant. When completed, the third tier will house a disco and champagne lounge.

Frantz anticipates that a condominium will be opening up across the street providing a captive market for Maxwell's. An estimated 5,000 workers are within a two-minute walk.

According to the partners, weekend traffic has been exceptional. Weekly revenues are running between $10,000 and $17,000; overhead expenses are around $10,000. Frantz, who has three years of experience as operations manager of several New York discos, expects the disco traffic to nearly double the weekly revenues.

Initially, Maxwell's was capitalized with $93,000 of the partners' funds and a $55,000 bank loan. Palmer, an active manager of the complex, contributed $35,000 worth of sound equipment from his audio equipment business. Seaman, an attorney, is a silent partner.

The partnership is hoping to raise $100,000 in additional funds to help complete renovation. Ultimately, the partners want to add a health club on the third floor.

Issues for Discussion

1. What types of short-term financing are available to Maxwell's?
2. Complete the following chart regarding the credit analysis of Maxwell's.
3. Would you lend money or extend trade credit to Maxwell's? What additional information might be helpful?

Four *Cs*	Poor	Average	Good	Excellent	Reason(s)
Character					
Capacity					
Capital					
Conditions					

NOTES

1. "Gibson Greeting Sets Agreement on Credit," *Wall Street Journal,* July 2, 1985, p. 39.
2. David Hertzberg, "Bypassing Banks," *Wall Street Journal,* May 8, 1980, pp. 1, 18.
3. *Federal Reserve Bulletin,* June 1985, p. A23.

CHECK YOUR LEARNING ANSWER KEY

A. 1. T, *pp. 527-528*
   2. c, *p. 529*
   3. T, *p. 529*

B. 1. b, *pp. 530-532*
   2. d, *p. 532*
   3. T, *p. 530*

C. 1. a, *p. 533*
   2. F, *p. 533*
   3. F, *p. 533*

D. 1. F, *p. 534*
   2. a, *p. 535*

E. 1. T, *p. 540*
   2. T, *p. 538*
   3. c, *pp. 538-539*
   4. T, *p. 539*

F. 1. F, *p. 543*
   2. d, *p. 543*

G. 1. a, *p. 546*
   2. F, *p. 546*

H. 1. d, *p. 000*

CHAPTER

19

INVESTMENTS AND SECURITIES

LEARNING OBJECTIVES

After reading this chapter you should be able to:

1. Discuss how saving, speculation, risk, and diversification relate to investing.
2. Discuss the differences and similarities of bonds, preferred stocks, and common stock, and identify the role of the investment banker.
3. Discuss the functions of a stock exchange and identify steps taken by brokers to purchase securities.
4. Identify key features of financial news reports, and discuss how markets are influenced by corporate takeover activity.
5. Discuss the information that is considered in selecting investment securities and explain the role of mutual funds and other investment companies.
6. Identify major agencies and legislation designed to protect investors and discuss how investing is changing in the global marketplace.

OUTLINE

Business Practice Example: Reginald Lewis—Venture Capitalist and Investor

What Is Investing?

Types of Corporate Securities

- Corporate Bonds
  - General Features of Bonds
  - Special Features of Bonds
  - Bond Valuation
  - Junk Bonds
- Preferred Stock
  - General Features of Preferred Stock
  - Special Features of Preferred Stock
- Common Stock
- Offering Securities: Investment Bankers

The Investor's Perspective

- Stock Exchanges
- Over-the-Counter Markets
- A Typical Stock Exchange Transaction
- Reading the Financial News
  - Interpreting Stock Quotes
  - Interpreting Bond Quotes
  - Interpreting Stock Indexes
- Corporate Takeover Activity in the Market
- Stocks as an Investment
- Mutual Funds—A Place for Individuals to Invest

Protecting the Investor

- State and Federal Legislation
- Organizations That Help Protect Investors
  - National Association of Securities Dealers
  - Securities Investors Protection Corporation

The Global Investment Marketplace

Summary

Key Terms

Check Your Learning

Questions for Review and Discussion

Concluding Case: The Crash of '87

Notes

Check Your Learning Answer Key

Highlight in Business Practice: Insider Trading

BUSINESS PRACTICE EXAMPLE

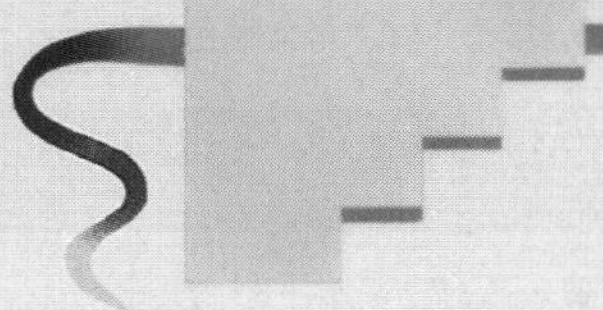

Reginald Lewis—Venture Capitalist and Investor

What does it take to be a successful player in the most serious of investment games—the fast-moving field of buying and selling businesses? The media show us high-rolling, colorful figures playing this game. We get the impression that a third of them are from Texas, another third apparently under indictment for some kind of illegal trading, and the rest perhaps brash newcomers from Britain or Australia. A calm, low-profile African-American lawyer from Harvard who grew up in Baltimore may not seem the usual type for the role of corporate takeover artist, but Reginald Lewis, chairman of the TLC Group, is one of the most successful.

In fact, Lewis does not even describe his fast-moving buying and selling of a huge corporate conglomerate as risky. "I think we never take risks," he says. "We take calculated steps that really are designed to mitigate against any risks that we have." Lewis claims that his venture capital business is not so much looking for problems or exploiting weakness as trying to accent the positive—looking for opportunity and for ways to give good managers another chance. To play in the arena of buying and selling control of giant companies, Lewis has had to develop two kinds of expertise.

First, as a potential corporate takeover buyer, he has to be able to size up the potential of a target company and estimate how it could do better under optimal business conditions. Analyzing the company's current market value, he must discover more value in it than other owners have seen. Lewis's success at doing this has often been notable for getting turnaround performance without the usual move of firing the original managers.

Venture capitalists need a second type of expertise to find sources of purchase money that no one else has readily available. They must start with the money they own or control and go on to convince other people that it will be profitable to buy the target company. Using these two types of skills, Lewis became the successful bidder in a major buyout, paying nearly a billion dollars for Beatrice International Food Company, which operates in thirty-one countries.

Lewis's background for this kind of investing was not from money, or even at first from financial expertise, but from the law. Within five years of graduating from Harvard Law School, Lewis founded his own firm, Lewis & Clarkston, devoted to raising venture capital in New York for small-business people. Lewis described his apprenticeship leading up to the Beatrice purchase as "fifteen years of doing fifteen deals a year" in buyouts and venture capital work. Lewis's first large deal was the 1983 purchase of declining McCall's Pattern, a sewing trade company that he bought for $1 million of his own money and $24 million in borrowed funds. Keeping original management and investing in new products and market channels, Lewis doubled McCall's profits in three and a half years to a yearly $14 million before selling in 1987 for $95 million—almost quadruple the company's earlier value.

Lewis immediately put the proceeds into play for a much bigger fish, angling for the Beatrice Group—a bloated conglomerate that had already begun breaking up. After a shrewd analysis of what could be done with the Beatrice international food division, Lewis went to some of America's most inventive money raisers at Drexel Burnham Lambert and to Manufacturers Hanover Bank, seeking funds for the purchase.

Persistently reexamining all the best sources of value in the target company, Lewis pushed his offer to what he described as the outer perimeter of possibility. He won the Beatrice purchase with a $985 million offer: his own funds and $450 million in credit from Manufacturers Hanover, plus a similar amount in Drexel Burnham's high-yield bonds and a share of their ownership. Some of this was paid back when Lewis sold over $430 million in Beatrice international subsidiaries. The rest of the recovery was earned when Lewis kept the original managers on the job, helping them gain better profits by focusing on the company they knew best.

WHAT'S AHEAD

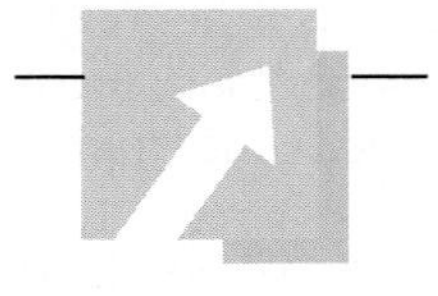

Like all investors in corporate securities, Reginald Lewis bought companies in order to profit from their endeavors. This chapter will explore the key aspects of the corporate securities that are involved in funding and purchasing ownership of companies like Lewis's. Special attention will be focused on common stock—both the securities and the market for them. The role of preferred stock and corporate bonds will also be examined. The chapter will conclude with a glimpse of two current financial phenomena: corporate takeovers and the global investment marketplace.

WHAT IS INVESTING?

Investing has an important role in the business world—one that differs from saving and from speculating. As discussed in chapter 16, placing money into savings instruments is an easy, convenient, and safe undertaking. This business is handled mostly by banks and other depository financial institutions through insured time deposits, money market funds, and government savings bonds. At the opposite extreme is **speculation**—putting money into very risky ventures in the hope of making a large profit quickly.

Speculation is putting money into very risky ventures in the hope of making a large profit quickly.

Investing is putting money into ventures expected to make a reasonable profit given the level of risk; it usually refers to buying stocks and bonds.

Risk is the degree of uncertainty surrounding an investment's payoff.

Risk aversion is the preference for investments with good potential profit and little risk.

Diversification is investing in a group *(portfolio)* of unrelated securities, so that losses on some securities will be offset by profits on others.

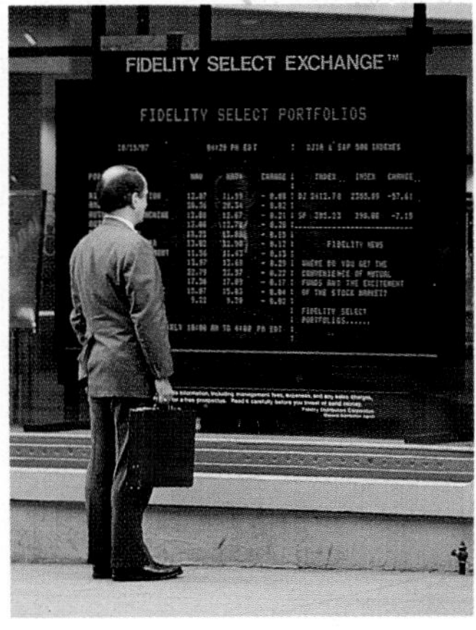

Risk is the degree of uncertainty of pay-off from an investment. This investor plans to reduce his risk by diversification—investing in a portfolio or group of securities in different industries.

Investing is putting money into ventures expected to make a reasonable profit at a given level of risk. It usually refers to buying stocks and bonds. In the areas of both risk and return, investing is somewhere between saving and speculation. Investors should be guided by the principle that risk and return are related. That is, one who seeks a greater profit, or return, must be prepared to shoulder greater risk.

In investment terms, **risk** is the degree of uncertainty surrounding an investment's payoff. Most investors are **risk averse**—preferring investments with good potential profit and little risk. One common means of reducing risk in investment is **diversification**—investing in a group *(portfolio)* of unrelated securities, so that losses on some securities will be offset by profits on others. For example, an investor might buy stocks of firms in different industries.

Individuals can diversify by investing in several different markets or funds (such as bonds, options, real estate, etc), thus avoiding risks from forces operating in any one market. In the stock market, for example, massive and nearly unpredictable shifts (up and down) are often caused by large investment organizations, called *institutional investors.* On any given day in the New York Stock Exchange, for example, the large pension funds, insurance companies, and mutual funds can account for over 70 percent of the transactions. Acting together, such investors can move the entire market, perhaps downward as they did on "Black Monday," October 19, 1987, to destroy any individual's diversification in stocks alone.

TYPES OF CORPORATE SECURITIES

The three most common corporate securities are bonds, preferred stock, and common stock. Many corporations rely on all three for funding.

Corporate Bonds

Bonds are long-term interest-bearing debt instruments issued by corporations with commitments to specifically timed payments.

As chapter 18 pointed out, corporations issue **bonds,** which are long-term interest-bearing debt instruments issued by corporations and promising to pay specific amounts at specific times. They are basically IOUs for money loaned to businesses. Most bonds are paid off many years after they are issued—often from twenty to forty years but sometimes earlier.

For example, if General Motors sold $10 million worth of bonds in 1990 with a due date (maturity date) in 2010, the bonds could be in the hands of investors for twenty years. In the year 2010, GM would be obligated to pay back the entire $10 million.

General Features of Bonds

Most corporate bonds are sold in denominations of $1,000 (the face value, or *par value,* of the bonds). Since they represent loans to the corporation, investors are paid interest on them. If the interest rate is 9 percent, the corporation will pay $90 per year (9 percent × $1,000) for every bond sold. If 10,000 bonds are sold, the corporation must pay $900,000 ($90 × 10,000 bonds) each year in interest.

How do corporations know where to send the interest payments? In the past, investors would clip interest "coupons" from the bond at the appropriate times and present them to the issuer for payment. Most bonds sold today, however, are *registered bonds*—bonds whose owners' names are listed on the books of the issuing corporation. When the interest payments come due, the corporation mails checks to the bondholders whose names appear on the corporate roster. (The interest rate is still referred to as the coupon interest rate.)

Most corporations pay interest twice a year. Usually, they hire commercial banks to take care of these payments.

If a corporation fails to pay interest on the due date, the investor should contact the *trustee* supervising the bond issue. Trustees, which often are banks, administer the formal agreements *(indentures)* between the corporations and the bondholders and act on behalf of the bondholders when problems arise. The names of the transfer agent and trustee usually are printed on the face of the bond. See Figure 19.1 for a sample bond.

Special Features of Bonds

Bonds are often sold with special features. For example, they may be secured by specific collateral of the issuing corporation. Bonds backed by the fixed assets of the corporation, such as real estate, are called *mortgage bonds.* Those that have no specific collateral pledged against them are **debenture bonds,** often referred to as general credit bonds. Debentures can be higher risks than other

Debenture bonds (or general credit bonds) are bonds that have no specific collateral pledged against them.

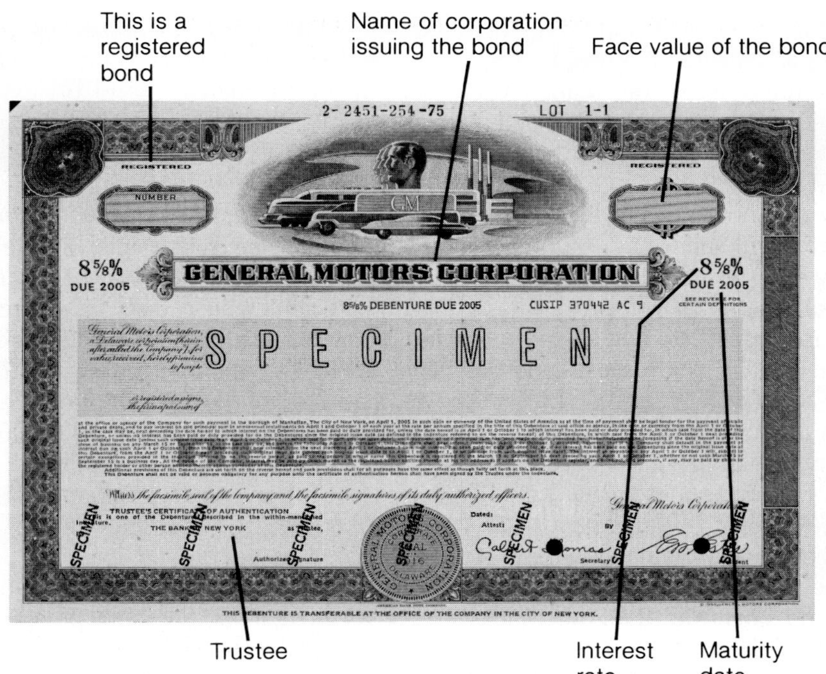

Figure 19.1
A corporate bond.

bonds, since their owners' inveestments are not backed by specific fixed assets of the issuing corporation.

Callable bonds are bonds that can be redeemed before maturity.

A second important feature of bonds is that they may be callable. **Callable bonds** are bonds that can be redeemed before maturity. For example, suppose Black & Decker had a callable bond due in 2015. The firm has the right to retire the bond and pay off the bondholders anytime between the issue date and 2015.

Almost all bonds are callable bonds, because corporations want to be able to take advantage of falling interest rates. Suppose a corporation sold a bond in 1989 at an 11 percent interest rate and with a maturity date of 2009. Then suppose that market interest rates fell to 9.5 percent in 1991. The company would likely issue a new bond at the 9.5 percent rate and use the money it received for the new issue to pay off the 11 percent bond issue. By doing so, it would save 1.5 percent interest a year.

A ***convertible bond*** is a bond that can be exchanged for the common stock of the issuing corporation.

A third feature of bonds—one that also affects the interest rate—is convertibility. A **convertible bond** is a bond that can be exchanged for the common stock of the issuing corporation. A clause in the bond might allow the holder of a $1,000 bond to exchange it for twenty shares of common stock. If the market value of the stock advances to more than $50 a share, the bondholder may want to exercise the conversion privilege. Convertible bonds usually pay less interest than other bonds because of this feature.

A ***sinking fund*** is a special fund into which a corporation must put money regularly so it can pay back bondholders when the bond reaches maturity.

Yet another feature of bonds is the **sinking fund.** This is a special fund into which a corporation must put money regularly so it can pay back bondholders when the bond reaches maturity.

Bond Valuation

Most bonds have a market value in addition to a face value. The *market value* of a bond is the price it brings on the open market. Unlike the face value, which is contractually fixed, the market value can and does change. Bond prices are affected most by market interest rate movements. A bond's market price will deviate from its face value whenever the bond's fixed coupon interest rate differs from the market interest rate.

A ***discount price*** for bonds is a lower price than the face value so as to bring the bond's market value in line with current market interest rates.

A ***premium price*** for bonds is a higher price than the face value so as to bring the bond's market value in line with current market interest rates.

For instance, a $1,000 face value 8 percent coupon bond (worth $80 in interest per year) will sell for $1,000 on the market whenever the market interest rate for this type of security is 8 percent. If the market interest rate rises to 10 percent, the bond's market value will fall by an amount sufficient to turn an 8 percent coupon interest rate into a 10 percent market interest rate. Otherwise no one will buy it. That is, there must be a **discount price**—a price lower than the face value—that will bring the bond's value in line with current market rates. As a rough approximation, a discount price of $800 should do the trick ($80/$800 = 10 percent). By the same token, if market interest rates fall to, say, 6 percent, the 8 percent bond should rise in value. In this case, the bond will sell for a **premium price**—an addition to its face value that will reflect its increased value in the market—of approximately $1,250 ($80/$1,250 = 6 percent).

These figures are only approximations because we have not taken into account the bond's maturity. If all other factors (such as interest and company prospects) are equal, the longer the maturity, the greater the price change (see Figure 19.2). This discussion introduces a fundamental rule of investment: *Bond prices and market interest rates are inversely related.*

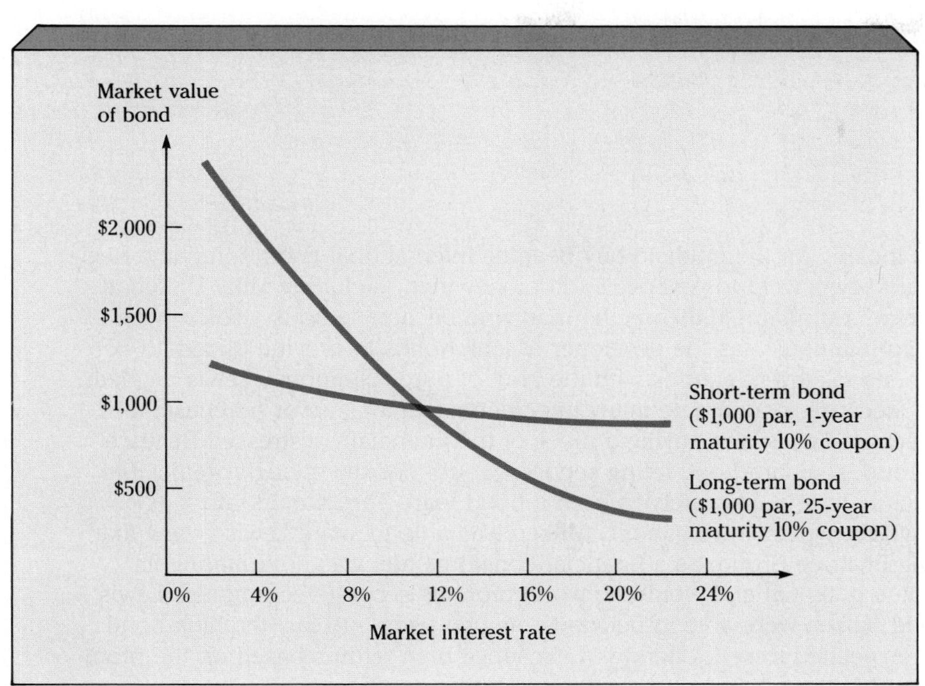

Figure 19.2
Relationship between market values of bonds and market interest rates.

Junk Bonds

An influential development in bonds during the 1980s has been the appearance of an unconventional loan instrument, commonly called the *junk bond,* whose widespread currency was pioneered by the Drexel Burnham Lambert company. The term originates from the fact that these bonds are given a "speculative" grade, indicating very high risk from established bond rating services. The Standard & Poor's Corporation and Moody's Investors Service are highly respected firms that assign bond ratings from AAA (least risk) to C (highly speculative) or D (in default).

In keeping with the basic concept of risk and return, these bonds offer a high interest rate to compensate for the high risk. Junk bonds are often sold by venture capitalists and financiers seeking to raise money quickly. Often, they want the money to pay for taking over a company whose assets they claim they know how to resell for a quick profit. The chances for profit are usually difficult to predict, and the proposed resale of assets may actually lose money. Thus, many such bonds lose their original value, living up to the high-risk "junk" rating they get.[1] Nevertheless, the high interest offered for junk bonds can attract a large number of buyers who believe they can stand the risk. For this reason, well-connected financiers in the late 1980s found it much easier to raise money to buy a company than they would have earlier.

BUSINESS PRACTICE EXAMPLE Continues

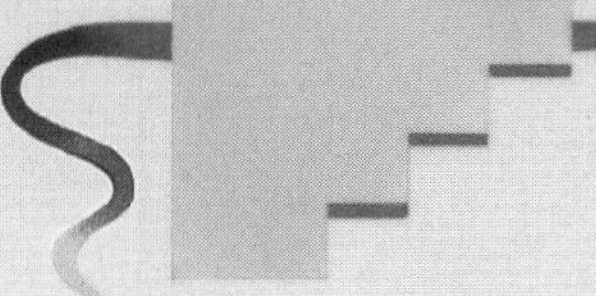

In looking for the funds to buy Beatrice International Food Company, Reginald Lewis went to America's top money men, including Mike Milken at Drexel Burnham. Milken is the man who became famous—some have said infamous—as the developer of junk bonds to provide uncertain corporate takeover ventures with the kind of purchase money Lewis needed.

Because there are so many uncertainties in a takeover purchase, and because Lewis was buying a piece of the financially distressed Beatrice Group, standard bond-rating services would not see enough predictable factors to find any safety in such a bond loan. They would rate it as a high-risk speculative gamble. Milken was able to share Lewis's view that the Beatrice Group, as a financial conglomerate, was not fulfilling its value potential and would be worth more as separate companies. Lewis and Milken were able to persuade enough people to buy the junk bonds they needed to sell, offering in exchange high returns based on the promise of better future value resulting from the purchase.

For Lewis, the promised value was delivered with sales of Beatrice international subsidiaries and a turnaround in company profits. However, Milken's dealings led to too many promises based on questionable inside information about target companies. Charged by the federal government with illegal dealing, he was indicted in 1989.

Preferred stock is stock whose owners receive dividends (if any are declared) in stated amounts before dividends can be distributed to owners of common stock.

Preferred Stock

Like bonds, preferred stock is sold by corporations to raise funds. However, preferred stock confers ownership on the holders. Specifically, **preferred stock** is stock (shares of ownership in a corporation) whose owners receive dividends (if any are declared) in stated amounts before dividends can be distributed to owners of common stock. Also, if a corporation liquidates (sells) its assets and goes out of business, the holders of preferred stock are paid back their investment before any money is distributed to the holders of common stock.

General Features of Preferred Stock

Par stock is stock that has a stated value printed on the face of the stock certificate.

Preferred stock can be par or no-par, as can common stock. **Par stock** is stock that has a stated value printed on the face of the stock certificate. No par stock is stock that doesn't have a stated value on the face of the certificate.

Most preferred stock has a face value (par value) of $100 a share. The dividends paid to preferred stockholders are usually stated as a percent of par value. For example, a 5 percent dividend would mean the corporation could pay $5 on a

$100 share of preferred stock. If the stock has no par value, the dividend rate is given in terms of dollars, such as $5 per share. There is little difference between par and no-par preferred stock.

Preferred stock can be cumulative or noncumulative—terms that apply to the dividends. Suppose a corporation's board of directors fails to declare a dividend for a quarter or more. What happens to the owners of preferred stock? Do they lose the chance for any dividends for the missing quarters?

It depends on whether the stock is cumulative or noncumulative. For *cumulative preferred stock,* any dividends not paid must eventually be declared and distributed to the holders of this stock before dividends can be paid to common stockholders. For *noncumulative preferred stock,* dividends for missed quarters do not have to be paid. Of course, when dividends are declared once again for a particular quarter, the preferred stockholders must be paid before the common stockholders.

Special Features of Preferred Stock

Like bonds, preferred stock can be callable. *Callable preferred stock* may be redeemed at the option of the issuing corporation. The holder of this stock is legally obligated to return the preferred stock certificates in exchange for the call price value of each share. This feature allows the corporation the option of calling in any outstanding preferred stock issue. Since preferred stock has no maturity date, noncallable preferred stock can remain in the hands of investors as long as the corporation exists.

Preferred stock can also be convertible. Like convertible bonds, convertible preferred stock can be exchanged for common stock of the issuing corporation. The value of the exchange privilege depends on the exchange ratio and the market value of the common stock. The conversion clause is often included in preferred stock agreements as a lure for investors who want the safety of preferred stock while still having the chance to benefit from the potential of common shares.

Preferred stock is similar to bonds in many ways. However, preferred stock is a form of ownership, while bonds represent debt. Although dividends on preferred stock are sometimes stated as a percent of par value, the dividends are not owed until they are declared by the board of directors. Interest, on the other hand, is a legal debt that must be paid to bondholders. Finally, bondholders are creditors and therefore are paid before preferred stockholders if liquidation occurs.

Common Stock

Selling common stock is the way most corporations initially raise capital. **Common stock** is stock whose owners (often called residual owners) receive dividends only after bondholders receive their interest and preferred stockholders receive their dividends. In essence, common stockholders receive the residue—what's left over. Sometimes, the residue is large and common stockholders receive large dividends. Usually, common stock is considered riskier than bonds and preferred stock because dividend rates fluctuate according to the corporation's profitability. See Figure 19.3 for a common stock certificate.

Common stock is a company's primary trading stock, whose owners receive dividends only after bondholders receive their interest and preferred stockholders receive their dividends.

Like preferred stock, common stock can be par or no-par. Par stock has the par value printed on the face of the stock certificate. No-par stock usually has a stated value included in the articles of incorporation. But par values and stated values seldom reflect the true worth of common stock. The true value of common stock is the market value—what the public will pay for it.

Figure 19.3
A common stock certificate.

Another key feature of common stock is that its owners have certain voting rights. They vote at the annual meeting to elect the board of directors and often vote on key policy and organizational changes, such as mergers and employee stock option programs (see chapter 4). Preferred stockholders usually do not have the right to vote.

Table 19.1 highlights the major differences between bonds and stocks.

Table 19.1 Major differences between bonds and stocks.

Bonds	**Stocks**
1. Bonds represent debt.	1. Stocks represent ownership.
2. Interest is a legal debt that must be paid to bondholders on a regular schedule.	2. Dividends do not have to be declared and paid to stockholders.
3. Bonds must be purchased back (retired) at a future time.	3. Stock can remain outstanding indefinitely.
4. Interest is an expense of doing business.	4. Dividends are a distribution of net profits.
5. Bonds are sold in denominations of $1,000.	5. Stock is sold in shares.

Offering Securities: Investment Bankers

Investment bankers are specialists that help corporations sell new issues of securities. They can be thought of as wholesalers. They purchase merchandise (common stock, preferred stock, and bonds) for resale to the public (investors).

Investment bankers are specialists that help corporations sell new issues of securities.

Assume, for example, that McDonald's wishes to sell $50 million worth of 11 percent interest bonds due in 2010. McDonald's financial executives would contact one or more investment bankers and negotiate the terms of the sale. Fifty million dollars is a large amount of capital. To handle it, investment bankers will form an *underwriting syndicate*—a group of investment bankers that temporarily creates a joint venture for the purpose of buying and selling a new issue of securities. Each participant will purchase a portion of the McDonald's bond issue, then through brokers and security dealers will resell the individual bonds to the public. Some underwriting syndicates consist of thirty to forty investment bankers. The process of distributing new issues of securities through investment bankers is called *public placement*.

The public market for U.S. corporate securities is no longer limited to American stock exchanges. Many of these securities are now in the major markets of foreign countries as well. At the same time, a large proportion of corporate bonds are sold in *private placements*. In financing of this sort, the issuing firm sells securities directly to a large investor in face-to-face negotiations.

Like all businesses, investment bankers need to make a profit. Just like any other wholesaler, they purchase the securities for less than the amount the public will be charged. For example, if investment bankers determined that the McDonald's bonds could be sold at face value ($1,000 per bond, for a total of $50 million), they would buy the bonds at a discount, paying $48.5 million. The $1,500,000 difference is gross profit for the underwriting syndicate. Figure 19.4 charts the investment banking process.

One key point to remember is that the securities sold through investment bankers are *new* issues—they have never been in the hands of investors. New

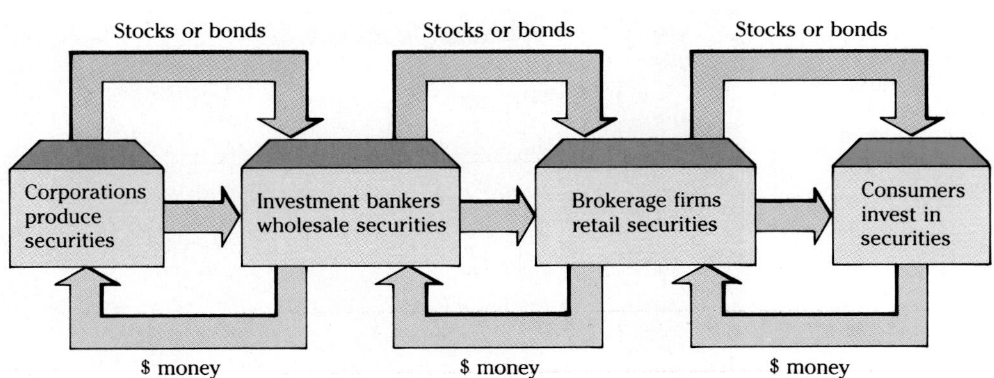

Figure 19.4 The investment banking process. A corporation sells its securities to investment bankers, who resell them to a brokerage house, which sells them to the public.

The ***primary market*** is the market in which new shares of stocks or bonds are sold.

The ***secondary market*** is the market in which previously issued stocks and bonds are bought and sold.

shares of stocks or bonds are sold in the **primary market.** Once these securities are sold, their market value fluctuates according to complex economic variables. We say that previously issued stocks and bonds are sold in the **secondary market.**

The market value of stocks and bonds in the secondary market is important to investors. Thus far in the chapter, we have examined stocks and bonds from the viewpoint of the corporation. In the next section, we will switch to the viewpoint of the investor.

THE INVESTOR'S PERSPECTIVE

Although the relationship between corporation and investor is based on mutual gain, investors tend to view securities in a slightly different light than do corporations. Investors, for example, view dividends as income and return on their investment, whereas corporations view dividends as distributions of net profits. Interest may be a large expense to the corporation, but it represents a source of income to a bondholder.

Although investors can purchase new securities from brokers in the primary market, many choose to purchase them in the secondary market. These stocks and bonds are frequently traded on stock exchanges or sold in the over-the-counter market.

Stock Exchanges

Stock exchanges are the marketplaces in which securities are bought and sold.

The marketplaces in which securities are bought and sold (traded) are **stock exchanges.** In the United States, there are seven regional and two national stock exchanges. The two national exchanges are located in New York City. The bigger and more well known is the *New York Stock Exchange (NYSE),* often referred to as the *Big Board.* It is located on Wall Street, a street often considered the center of financial activity in the United States. The second largest exchange is the

Stock exchanges are the marketplaces in which securities are bought and sold. The busy New York Stock Exchange shown here is often considered the center of financial activity in the United States.

Table 19.2 Minimum listing requirements for the New York Stock Exchange.

Demonstrated earning power, under competitive conditions, of $2.5 million annually before taxes for the most recent year and $2 million for each of the two preceding years.

Net tangible assets of $16 million, but greater emphasis placed on the aggregate market value of the common stock.

A total of $18 million in market value of publicly held common stock (subject to change depending on market conditions).

A total of 1.1 million common shares publicly held.

Either 2,000 holders of 100 shares or more or 2,220 total shareholders, together with an average monthly trading volume of 100,000 shares.

American Stock Exchange (Amex). These two national exchanges account for 88 percent of the volume of all exchange-based trading activity. With some minor differences, most exchanges function in basically the same way as the New York Stock Exchange.

Like all organized stock exchanges, the New York Stock Exchange facilitates the trading of listed securities. A *listed security* is a corporate stock or bond that has been approved for trading on the exchange. The minimum requirements for being listed on the Big Board are shown in Table 19.2. Examples of NYSE-listed stocks are IBM, General Motors, Sears, and McDonald's.

Only members can transact business on an exchange. A membership on the New York Stock Exchange is called a *seat.* Because the number of seats on the Big Board is limited to 1,366, gaining membership is not easy. Prices for seats have varied from a predepression high of $625,000 to a World War II low of $17,000, and back up again.

Brokerage companies can and normally do buy their own seats on the New York Stock Exchange. Brokerage companies that own a seat on the exchange or that employ one or more exchange seatholders are known as member firms.

Over-the-Counter Markets

Securities transactions for companies not listed on any U.S. stock exchange take place in the **over-the-counter (OTC) markets.** Although there are exceptions, most of the securities traded in the OTC markets are issued by small to mid-sized companies.

Over-the-counter (OTC) markets are markets for securities not listed on any U.S. stock exchange.

Unlike stock exchanges, where brokers meet on the exchange floor to transact business, the OTC business is usually transacted by telephone, wire service, or computer network. Large brokerage houses usually have inventories of most OTC stocks. This is called *making a market* for the stock. OTC stocks are quoted on a bid and ask basis. For example, a company may be bid at 7¼ ($7.25) and ask at 7¾ ($7.75). Dealers will buy shares at the bid price and sell them to investors at the ask price. The difference between the bid and ask prices (known as the spread) represents the dealer's gross profits.

BUSINESS PRACTICE EXAMPLE Continues

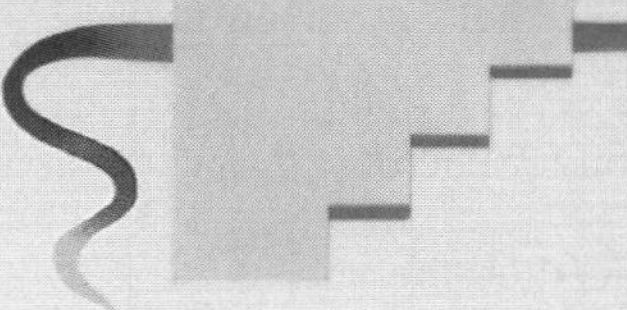

Before venture capitalist Reginald Lewis was able to enter the buyout game for Beatrice Group, a giant financially distressed conglomerate, its publicly exchanged stock had already been bought, and the shares had been taken off the New York Stock Exchange. This maneuver was arranged in 1986 by the giant takeover firm Kohlberg Kravis Roberts (KKR), guided by a former Beatrice divisional CEO, Donald Kelly.

Knowing Beatrice from the inside, Kelly understood what many analysts later said—that the Beatrice Group was an overblown conglomerate of unrelated financial interests. Its management was too busy watching the combined profit numbers go up and down and did not really attend to the business of any one of its divisions. Kelly and KKR decided the conglomerate was ripe for the auction block. Through junk bonds and other securities, they made an offer to buy all the public stocks of the Beatrice Group. When the purchase was complete, they took the shares off the open market.

Over the next year, exercising total private control over Beatrice assets, they sold entire subsidiary corporations, such as Avis and Playtex, without using stock shares. In 1987, they sold Beatrice International Food Company to Lewis's TLC Group. By 1988, after selling nearly $7 billion of the old Beatrice Group's value, they still controlled about $3 billion in assets.

The sales made a huge profit for Kelly and KKR, even though most companies went at bargain prices to buyers who could raise the money. In the process, entrepreneurs such as Lewis were able to create more value in selling subsidiaries and in letting company managers run the companies they were hired to run.

Statistics pertaining to both OTC and listed securities are reported in the financial section of many large newspapers, especially the *Wall Street Journal.* During the trading day, most brokers rely on computerized information. In 1971, the National Association of Securities Dealers, a trade group to which most brokerage houses belong, began operating a vast automated trading network known as NASDAQ (National Association of Securities Dealers Automated Quotations). Of the nearly 30,000 securities traded in the OTC market, over 4,700 have been accepted for trading over the NASDAQ system. This computerized set of statistics is readily available to all members by way of a desktop terminal. Dealers simply enter certain stock symbols on the keyboard and information regarding the security is flashed on a video screen.

A Typical Stock Exchange Transaction

Most investors purchase stocks and bonds through retail brokerage houses. You have probably seen commercials promoting such companies as Merrill Lynch, Shearson Lehman Hutton, and Dean Witter Reynolds.

Suppose you have decided to purchase some General Electric stock. What should you do? First of all, you should talk to a broker at a brokerage firm. These professionals are also called *account executives.* Your broker will open an account for you and may ask if you wish to purchase a round lot or odd lot of stock. A *round lot* is a hundred shares or any multiple thereof. Less than a hundred shares is called an *odd lot.*

If you decide to buy, your broker will wire your order directly to the house's floor representative on a stock exchange. Figure 19.5 highlights the details of this procedure, which takes only a few minutes. The representative will go to the specific post at which General Electric stock is traded, will execute the market order at the best possible price, and then will electronically transmit the completed transaction to your broker's branch office. The data for the transaction will be entered into a computer and appear on a ticker tape. A *ticker tape* is a composite register of all round lot transactions that occur on the exchanges and in the OTC market. Many brokerage offices display the ticker tape on large electronic screens. The data eventually appear in the financial news.

Brokers charge a commission to buy and sell securities. In addition to processing orders, your account executive may provide you with investment tips and market research regarding specific companies. After you invest your money in the stocks or bonds of specific corporations, you will want to follow the market value of these securities. If you purchase stock, you will hope for a **bull market**—a market characterized by rising stock prices. The opposite is a **bear market,** which is characterized by declining stock prices. So that we can track the value of your investment, we will now examine the common statistics regarding stock and bond quotes.

A ***bull market*** is a securities market characterized by rising stock prices.

A ***bear market*** is a securities market characterized by falling stock prices.

Reading the Financial News

The most popular daily report of market activity is found in the *Wall Street Journal.* Many large newspapers also report selected stock and bond statistics. Two crucial sets of statistics in these reports are stock quotes and bond quotes.

Most investors purchase stocks or bonds through a broker, such as the one shown at this Salomon Brothers brokerage firm. The broker can wire an order for stocks directly to the firm's floor representative on a stock exchange.

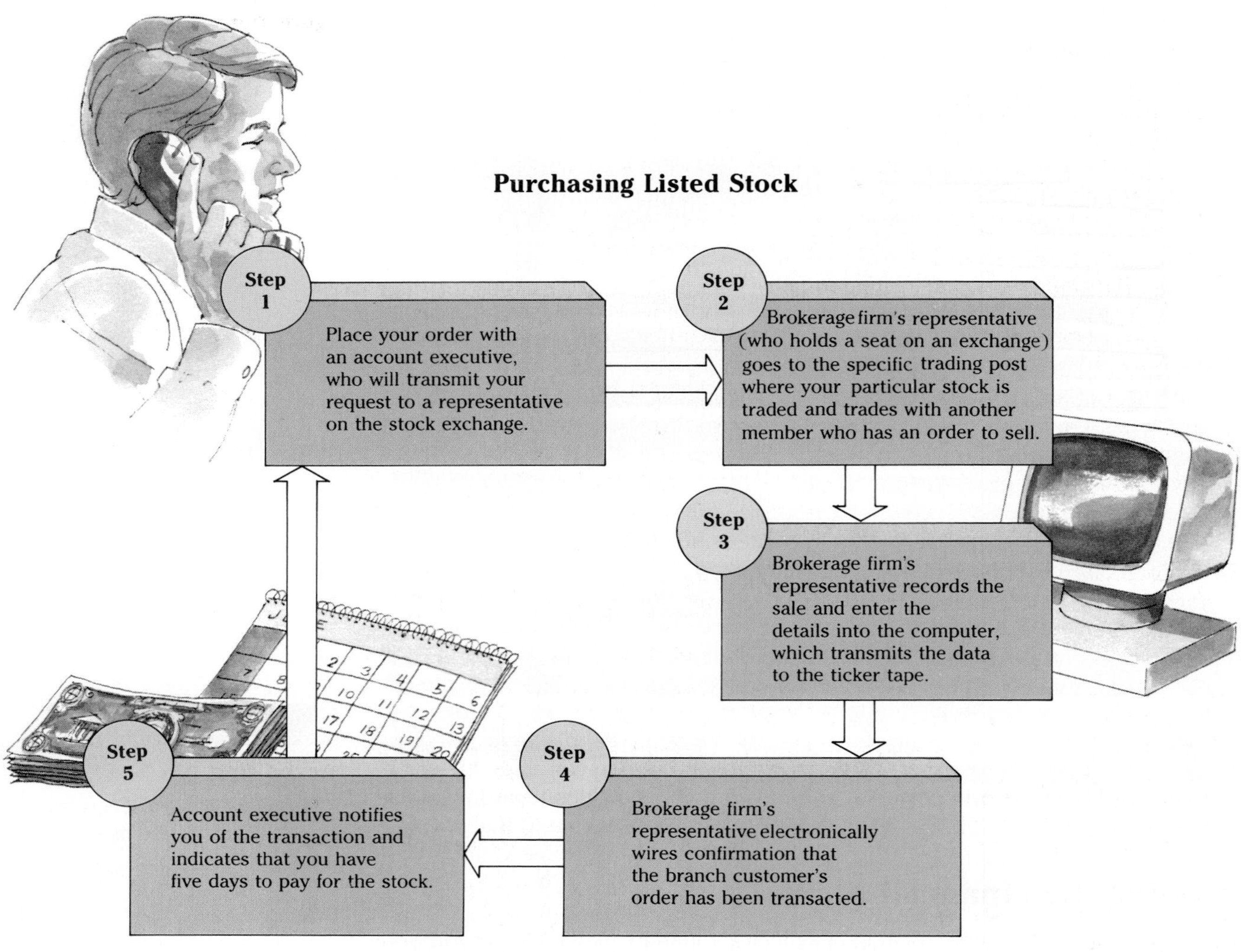

Purchasing Listed Stock
Step 1
Place your order with an account executive, who will transmit your request to a representative on the stock exchange.
Step 2
Brokerage firm's representative (who holds a seat on an exchange) goes to the specific trading post where your particular stock is traded and trades with another member who has an order to sell.
Step 3
Brokerage firm's representative records the sale and enter the details into the computer, which transmits the data to the ticker tape.
Step 4
Brokerage firm's representative electronically wires confirmation that the branch customer's order has been transacted.
Step 5
Account executive notifies you of the transaction and indicates that you have five days to pay for the stock.

Figure 19.5 The five steps in purchasing listed stock.

Interpreting Stock Quotes

Stock values are quoted in points. One point equals one dollar. Usually, every newspaper will quote the value of a stock in fractions. For example, a stock quoted at 28⅛ has a market value of $28.125. One quoted at 62½ has a market value of $62.50.

Figure 19.6 shows a set of stock market quotes from the *Wall Street Journal.* The highlighted line is for General Motors common stock. Using the headings above each column, let's interpret each of these numbers. The first two numbers, 65⅞ and 39½, show that the highest price of GM common stock during the preceding fifty-two weeks was $65.875 and the lowest price was $39.50. GMot is the abbreviated name of the stock. The next number, $3.85, is the annual dividend paid on each share of common stock, based on the last quarterly dividend.

Figure 19.6
Sample stock quotes.

52 Weeks High	Low	Stocks	Div.	Yld. %	P.E. Ratio	Sales 100s	High	Low	Close	Net Chg.
30⅝	19	GnMills	1.48	5.1	8	166	29¼	28⅞	28⅞	− ⅛
65⅞	39½	GMot	3.85	6.8	9	6538	57⅝	56¼	56¼	−1½
44½	32	GMot	pf3.75	10.		7	36¼	36¼	36¼	
59⅝	43¼	GMot	pf 5	10.		14	49	48½	48½	− ½
22⅞	12⅛	GnPort	.80	3.5	5	498	23⅜	22¾	23⅛	+ ⅝
9⅝	3⅜	GPU		..	7	3466	6	5⅛	5¾	+ ½
13½	6¾	GnRefr		..	6	87	9⅛	8¾	8¾	− ¼
45¼	28¼	GnSignal	1.28	2.8	12	153	46¾	45¼	45¼	+ ⅜
9⅞	6¾	GnSteel	.44	5.0	7	104	9⅛	8⅞	8⅞	− ⅛
29¼	23	GTE	2.72	10.	8	2971	26¼	26	26	− ¼
28⅜	22⅛	GTE	pf2.50	10.		1	24⅞	24⅞	24⅞	
24½	17¾	GTE	pf2.48	12.		9	20⅛	20	20	

(Remember, dividends are not guaranteed and the amount declared may change each quarter. Dividends are paid quarterly but reported on an annual basis in the financial news.)

In the next column, the number 6.8 indicates the dividend yield. This is calculated automatically by the computer, which divides the annual dividend ($3.85) by the closing price on a specific day ($56.25).

The next column shows a price/earnings ratio of 9. This figure reflects the ratio of the market price of GM stock to the firm's latest earnings per share. Usually, the higher the P/E ratio, the riskier the stock.

How many shares of GM were traded today? This is answered in the seventh column, which shows that the volume of GM stock traded this day was 653,800 shares. Don't forget to add the zeroes, as the column is reported in hundreds. You should be able to see that 6,538 round lots of GM exchanged hands during this trading day.

The next three columns report the high, low, and closing prices for the day. During this day, GM stock sold at a high of $57.625 and a low of $56.25 and closed at $56.25. The last column shows the net change between today's closing price ($56.25) and that of the previous day. Today, GM investors lost 1½ points, or $1.50 per share. It is interesting that even blue chip stocks such as those of GM can lose value. *Blue chip stocks* are stocks offered by companies known for quality products and stable dividends.

Interpreting Bond Quotes

Bond quotes are also reported in points, but with bonds one point equals 1 percent of the face value. Here we will assume that the face value is $1,000, so one point is equal to $10. The key thing to remember is that bond quotes are a percent of face value. For example, a bond quote of 97½ means 97½ percent × $1,000 (.975 × $1,000), or a market value of $975.

The highlighted line in Figure 19.7 contains bond quotes for American Airlines. AAirl is the abbreviated name for the company. The second column shows the

Figure 19.7
Sample bond quotes.

AlldC	zr05	. .	20	10¾	10¾	10¾	−1¼
AlldC	zr09	. .	5	8	8	8	+ ¼
AlldSt	10⅜90	10.	10	101	101	101	− ¾
AlldSt	8¾09	cv	16	119	118½	119	+ ¾
AlsCha	12s90	12.	110	97⅝	97⅜	97⅜	+ ⅞
AlsCha	16s91	15.	20	108⅛	107	108⅛	+1⅛
Alcoa	9s95	10.	23	89½	89⅛	89⅛	− ⅝
Amax	14¼90	14.	99	101	100¼	100¾	+ ½
Amax	14½94	15.	61	99½	99⅜	99½	+ ⅛
AFoP	4.8s87	5.1	8	93⅞	93⅞	93⅞	.....
AFoP	4.8s87r	5.1	10	94	94	94	.....
AAiri	4¼92	6.3	52	68	67½	67½	+ ¼
ABrnd	11⅛89	11.	11	104	104	104	+1½
ABrnd	9¾87	9.6	35	101¾	101¾	101¾	.....
ACan	4¾s90	6.2	3	77	77	77	.....
AExC	11¼00	11.	15	101⅞	101	101	−1
AExC	12⅞91	12.	1	106⅝	106⅝	106⅝	− ⅜
AHoist	5½93	cv	15	75½	75¼	75¼	+ ¾
AmMed	9½01	cv	13	124	124	124	+1
AmMed	8¼08	cv	37	96½	95	95	+ ½

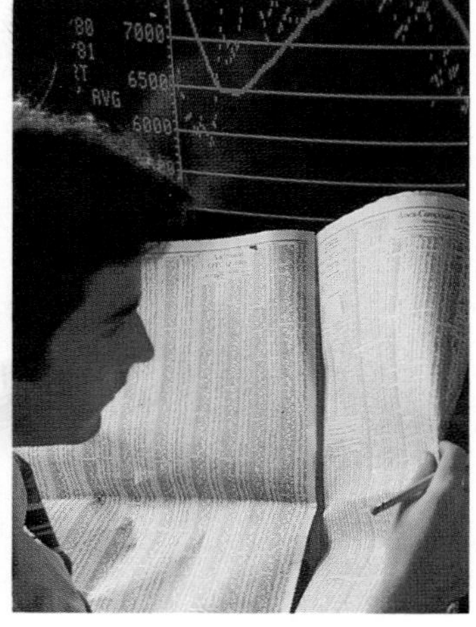

The Dow Jones Industrial Average is one index that can help inform investors about how well the securities market is doing. This stock broker checks the daily report of *The Wall Street Journal* to follow the market's activity.

coupon interest rate on the bond and the maturity date. Here, 4¼ means that American Airlines must pay 4¼ percent interest on each bond per year (4¼ percent × $1,000), and the entire bond debt must be paid back in 1992, the year it matures. The next column shows the current yield. This number, 6.3, is calculated by dividing the dollar amount of interest per bond (4¼ percent × $1,000 = $42.50) by the closing price ($675). This calculation gives us the current yield column, in this case 6.3 percent.

How many bonds of this issue were traded? This is answered in the volume column. In this case, only 52 bonds were traded, which translates into a dollar volume of $52,000. Don't forget to add the three zeroes to find the dollar volume. The $52,000 is the maturity value of the bonds.

The next three columns show the high for the day, the low for the day, and the closing price. To translate these quotes into dollars and cents, multiply each one by $1,000. The high for this trading day was $680. The low and the closing price are the same: $675 (.675 × $1,000). The last column indicates the bond value has risen ¼ point from the value the previous day. Remember that this is ¼ percent of the face value of the bond (.0025 × $1,000), or $2.50 per bond.

Interpreting Stock Indexes

The ***Dow Jones Industrial Averages (DJIA)*** are stock averages based on thirty high-quality stocks in well-established firms.

When investors ask how the market is doing, they're normally asking about the **Dow Jones Industrial Averages (DJIA).**

In 1884, Charles Henry Dow proposed that the overall performance of the securities market could be measured by computing a daily average of representative stocks. Dow's first stock market index was composed of eleven key stocks. In 1928, the average was broadened to the present thirty stocks. These stocks represent high-quality securities in well-established firms. Changes in their combined value generally reflect overall market activity. Although the Dow Jones Industrial Averages are the most widely quoted stock averages, Dow Jones has formulated more specialized indexes also. Indexes covering twenty transportation stocks and fifteen utility stocks, along with a composite index of all sixty-five stocks, have been added.

Some corporate executives consider the Dow Jones averages too narrow in scope and not always an accurate measure of stock market trends. A broader-based index has been designed by Standard & Poor's Corporation. The S&P 500 index covers 500 stocks made up of 400 industrial, 20 transportation, 40 utility, and 40 financial stocks. Broader still is the Wilshire index, which combines some 5,000 corporate issues from both stock exchanges and the OTC markets. All of these indexes are used as a general measure of market activity and represent an estimate of investor interest.

Corporate Takeover Activity in the Market

Normal stock market activity involves the buying and selling of very small fractions of businesses. For the average corporation, the buying of hundreds or even thousands of shares of stock may represent just a tiny fraction of 1 percent of company ownership. However, as soon as any one group or corporation starts to increase its percentage of ownership of a company to as much as 3 percent, other stockholders and management begin to react.

Typically, current owners suspect a possible **corporate takeover**—an attempt by a group of special-interest owners, who are usually not part of the target company's management, to acquire control of the company's assets. They start by trying to accumulate the largest single block of shareholder votes. The usual effect is to create stockholder uncertainty about the future value of their company. One effect of such uncertainty is that the company's stock prices may rise temporarily as stockholders anticipate a takeover group's higher-priced offer to buy total control. If the takeover effort falls short, however, the stock may lose its attractiveness and plummet in value.

A ***corporate takeover*** is an attempt by a group of special-interest owners, who usually are not part of the target company's management, to purchase a controlling interest in a company's voting stock.

For example, in 1986, the Kohlberg Kravis Roberts investors and entrepreneur Donald Kelly successfully bought enough stock to take away control of the conglomerate Beatrice Group from existing management—what management termed a "hostile" takeover.

With its controlling votes, the takeover group succeeded in buying out all the stockholders and soon took Beatrice out of the public stock exchange. This allowed the takeover group to make huge profits selling off parts of the Beatrice conglomerate. During the course of the takeover, large junk bond issues were floated as the takeover group looked for money for the purchase.

Sometimes, a target company's management tries to fight the takeover by buying stockholders' shares with its own higher-priced offer. If it succeeds, it too may have to take out large loans in the bond market and risk large debts for the company.

Not every takeover move has such revolutionary effects, but most takeovers are motivated by the desire to make more money than is paid for the company's assets. In effect, the new owners claim there are more profits to be gained than current management is making for the stockholders. Although this claim sounds like good news for stockholders, sometimes the uncertainty that results from a takeover is bad news. Takeover side effects—sold companies, lost contracts, and lost jobs—can cause company profits to lose momentum and stocks to lose value.

Stocks as an Investment

Careful selection of stocks for investment is a job mostly for professionals or the well informed. There is a huge selection of common stocks to choose from, American as well as foreign, all with distinctive differences in prospective value. A typical investor buys a common stock because it has prospects for strong earnings in the future and because, if the stock is known to have good earning prospects, its price will rise. For example, if rumors circulate that the Merck company has developed a new drug, the prospect of profits from the new product will increase demand for the stock and raise its price. The investor can either be paid those earnings as strong future dividends or collect the gain in value when the stock's price rises.

Well-informed investor analysts are always evaluating companies for promising signs of their chances for strong future earnings. Analysts look in detail at how the general economic forecast will affect a particular company. (Is the company recession-proof?) They check how changes in the industry will affect it. (What if there is a price war?) They examine in detail its management, market share, and company history, and they do the kind of ratio analysis that was described in chapter 17.

Another approach is statistical analysis of a stock's price movements over time. Here analysts are looking for any pattern of change that might suggest favorable openings for buying or selling. Part of an investment analysis page from Standard & Poor's, a prominent stock analyst, is shown in Figure 19.8.

Mutual Funds—A Place for Individuals to Invest

Because investments in stocks and other securities require well-informed professional attention, individuals have turned more and more to companies that specialize in knowing how to invest. Among the nonbanking financial institutions described in chapter 16 were *investment companies*—incorporated groups of investment professionals who acquire funds by selling ownership shares to individual investors.

The most popular kind of investment company, the *mutual fund,* has grown throughout the 1980s. As the number of mutual funds increases, so does the variety of areas in which these funds invest. It is possible to join such a fund for virtually any kind of investment—from highly speculative junk bonds and gold to agricultural commodities, high-growth common stocks, safe money market funds, and U.S. government securities.

Mutual funds allow individuals to sell or buy proportional shares at any time. Investors are drawn to mutual funds because their large sizes offer efficiency, professional knowhow, and diversification.

PROTECTING THE INVESTOR

During one period in American history, the Roaring Twenties, investors perceived the stock market as a guaranteed way to instant wealth. But the stock market crashed on October 24, 1929, when the Dow Jones Industrial Averages dropped

Figure 19.8
Standard & Poor's stock report for General Electric, May 2, 1989.

General Electric

966

NYSE Symbol GE Options on CBOE (Mar-Jun-Sep-Dec) In S&P 500

Price	Range	P-E Ratio	Dividend	Yield	S&P Ranking	Beta
Apr. 24'89	1989					
48	49-43½	12	1.64	3.4%	A+	1.10

Summary

A diversified technology, services and manufacturing company, General Electric's major businesses include aerospace, medical systems, financial services, broadcasting, appliances and lighting. An active program of acquisitions and divestitures is being pursued primarily to boost its market share in various operations. While restructuring charges caused earnings to decline in 1987, higher profits were reported for 1988 due primarily to strength in financial services, broadcasting and materials, as well as medical systems. A further earnings gain is likely in 1989.

Current Outlook

Earnings for 1989 should approximate $4.30 a share, up from the $3.75 reported for 1988.

An increase in the $0.41 quarterly dividend is likely in 1989.

Revenues in 1989 are expected to increase approximately 7%, assuming moderate economic growth. The gain should continue to be led by financial services, plastics and medical systems. Somewhat restraining will be a likely decline in broadcasting and aerospace revenues, as well as essentially flat appliance sales. Margins should expand due to the higher volume, well contained costs, and absence of restructuring charges. Long-term prospects should benefit from GE's strong management, its leading market positions, and an ongoing restructuring of operations. Its extremely strong financial condition should also continue to give the company operating flexibility.

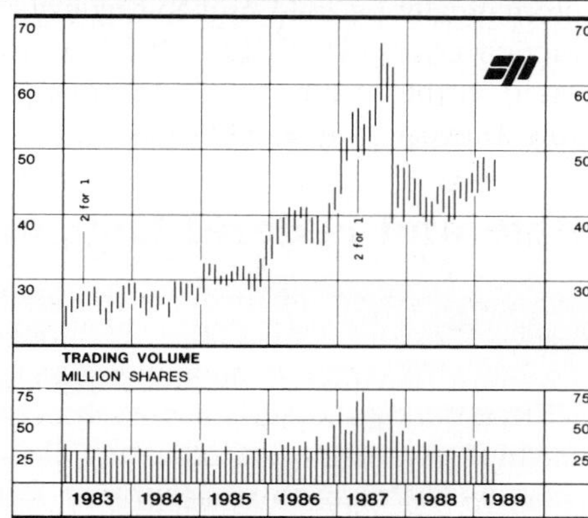

[1]Total Revenues (Billion $)

Quarter:	1989	1988	1987	1986
Mar.	11.90	10.53	8.32	5.88
Jun.	---	11.71	9.56	7.79
Sep.	---	12.02	9.40	9.28
Dec.	---	15.83	12.04	12.27
	---	50.09	39.32	35.21

Revenues for the three months ended March 31, 1989 advanced 13%, year to year, led by plastics, appliances, industrial and power systems and broadcasting. Plastics and appliances were helped by the Borg-Warner and Roper acquisition. Margins widened on the higher volume, and pretax income increased 20%. After taxes at 32.6%, versus 31.0%, net income was up 17%.

Common Share Earnings ($)

Quarter:	1989	1988	1987	1986
Mar.	0.94	0.80	0.35	0.59
Jun.	E1.07	0.93	0.74	0.68
Sep.	E1.15	0.90	0.73	0.66
Dec.	E1.14	1.12	0.51	0.80
	E4.30	3.75	2.33	2.73

Important Developments

Apr. '89— GE said that its operating margin on sales of goods and services for the first three months of 1989 was 10.7%, a five-tenths of a point improvement over the year earlier quarter and the best first quarter margin in the company's history. It added that productivity improvements were across the company.

Next earnings report expected in mid-July.

Per Share Data ($)

Yr. End Dec. 31	[2]1988	[3]1987	[3]1986	1985	[3]1984	1983	1982	1981	1980	1979
Tangible Bk. Val.	**10.99**	13.35	12.65	15.01	13.55	12.02	10.78	9.66	8.92	8.02
Earnings[4]	**3.75**	2.33	2.73	2.57	2.52	2.23	2.00	1.82	1.67	1.55
Dividends	**1.46**	1.32½	1.18½	1.11½	1.02½	0.93⅞	0.83⅞	0.78⅞	0.73⅞	0.68⅞
Payout Ratio	**39%**	56%	43%	44%	41%	42%	42%	43%	44%	44%
Prices—High	**47⅞**	66⅜	44½	36⅞	29¾	29½	25	17½	15⅞	13⅞
Low	**38⅜**	39	33⅜	27⅞	24	22¾	13⅞	12⅞	11	11⅜
P/E Ratio—	**13-10**	28-17	16-12	14-11	12-10	13-10	13-7	10-7	9-7	9-7

Data as orig. reptd. Adj. for stk. div(s). of 100% May 1987, 100% Jun. 1983. **1.** Sales prior to 1988. **2.** Reflects acctg. change. **3.** Reflects merger or acquisition. **4.** Bef. spec. item(s) of +0.87 in 1987. E-Estimated.

Standard NYSE Stock Reports
Vol. 56/No. 84/Sec. 9

May 2, 1989

Standard & Poor's Corp.
25 Broadway, NY, NY 10004

30.57 points—a severe drop for that time. Some popular stocks plunged 100 points or more in less than a week of trading. During the Great Depression that followed, investors faced the stark reality that purchasing securities involves risks.

One result of this financial disaster was the passage of state and federal legislation to protect and inform the buying public. Prior to the stock market crash, unethical promoters were selling shares in ventures that had little chance of success. Speculation in the stock market was rampant. The desire for instant money was reinforced in part by a procedure known as **buying on the margin,** which allowed investors to purchase securities by making a cash down payment often as small as 10 percent of the market value of the stock and then borrowing the rest from the broker. If the price of the margined stock dropped below a specific value, brokers were legally obligated to request more money from the investor. If the investor could not come up with additional money, the stock would automatically be sold and the investor would bear a heavy financial loss. This practice, coupled with the public's get rich quick mood, led to the worst economic period in the history of capitalism. State and federal legislation was passed to protect investors in the future.

Buying on the margin is making a small cash down payment on a stock and then borrowing the rest of the cost of the stock from the broker.

State and Federal Legislation

Concern for securities fraud and investor exploitation existed even before the market crashed. Many states attempted to prevent fraudulent security sales by passing what came to be known as *blue sky laws.* This nickname reflected the fact that during the early twentieth century, some promoters would sell stock in the "blue sky" itself. Unfortunately, these state laws could not adequately control interstate distribution of securities. This inadequacy led to the passage of the federal Securities Act in 1933 and Securities Exchange Act in 1934.

The Securities Act of 1933 required that corporations fully disclose pertinent financial information, including extensive information about the corporation and the proposed issue of securities. These facts were to be contained in a *registration statement,* to be filed with the Securities and Exchange Commission. Furthermore, a shortened version of the registration statement, called a *prospectus,* was to be made available to all investors prior to the corporation's offering the stocks and bonds for sale. A large majority of for-profit corporations fell under the jurisdiction of this act.

The Securities Exchange Act of 1934 established the **Securities and Exchange Commission (SEC),** which monitors and controls dealings in interstate securities. Specifically, this act empowered the SEC to enforce the following major reforms:

The ***Securities and Exchange Commission (SEC)*** is the federal agency empowered to regulate the interstate distribution of listed securities.

1. Ensure that every corporation listed on a national exchange files registration statements with the SEC as well as annual reports documenting the financial condition of the corporation.
2. Monitor the sales on all national stock exchanges.
3. Restrict the practice of buying stock on the margin. (The Federal Reserve System has established a current margin requirement of 50 percent.)
4. Require the registration of all securities, brokers, and dealers with the SEC.
5. Evaluate proxy statements for the purpose of eliminating ambiguous material.
6. Supervise the holdings of corporate officers who own 10 percent or more of their company's listed stock.

Many of these regulatory powers have been modified and amplified since 1934, but the original mission of the SEC remains intact: to regulate the interstate distribution of listed securities.

These acts did not cover the OTC market, however. This regulatory gap was eventually closed in 1938 with the establishment of the National Association of Securities Dealers.

Organizations That Help Protect Investors

National Association of Securities Dealers

In 1938, the Maloney Act was passed. This federal law established the *National Association of Security Dealers (NASD),* a self-regulating association composed of most of the broker-dealer firms in the securities business. At first, the primary purpose of the NASD was to screen brokers and dealers and require them to uphold a set of fair practice rules.

HIGHLIGHT IN BUSINESS PRACTICE

Insider Trading

The laws of the United States forbid what is called "insider trading"—trading corporate securities on the basis of critical market-related "insider" information that is not available to the public. Anyone passing or trading on such information who has a relationship of trust with the company or its shareholders can be prosecuted. In fact, anyone receiving and acting on such confidential information can also be prosecuted.

Although insider trading regulations have been on the books of the Securities and Exchange Commission for many years, the late 1980s witnessed a number of dramatic prosecutions for insider trading. The most famous were the cases of Dennis Levine and Ivan Boesky, whose evidence led to the identification of complex insider dealings by other financiers, among them Mike Milken at Drexel Burnham Lambert, developer of the junk bond as a way to raise money for corporate takeovers. A leading prosecutor of insider traders, U.S. Attorney Rudolph Giuliani, became famous enough from these cases to consider running for mayor of New York.

Uncovering insider trading abuses can be complex and difficult. In a simple case, a corporate official or employee, learning of a significant research discovery at a drug company before it becomes public, would be guilty if it were proved that he or she immediately bought company stock on the basis of that information. More complexities might arise in corporate takeover or buyout situations, where competitors look for undiscovered indicators of a company's value. In such cases, it is difficult to prove when key people had critical information or whether their actions were based solely on this kind of knowledge.

Some prosecutions for insider trading drag on for years. Others get nowhere because evidence gathering is too expensive or time-consuming for U.S. Attorneys.

Later, however, the power of the NASD increased. A 1964 amendment gave the SEC and the NASD disciplinary authority over brokers and securities dealers. This meant that the fair practice rules would be strictly enforced. The key provision of the amendment was that any publicly held company trading in the OTC market now had to file a registration statement and provide a prospectus. Again, the purpose of the legislation was to protect investors by giving them access to pertinent information before they invested their money.

Securities Investors Protection Corporation

Just because information is available does not guarantee that people will read it. Neither does the existence of a law guarantee that investors will not lose money. The late 1960s and early 1970s were painful times for brokerage firms. Many large brokerage houses, such as Francis I. Dupont and Hayden Stone, were forced to merge or go out of business. Investors lost large amounts as a result of these failures. Small investors were especially hurt.

In 1970, the *Security Investors Protection Corporation (SIPC)* was formed. This corporation protects investors' assets in the event that a brokerage company fails. If an investor leaves cash and securities on deposit with a brokerage firm and the firm goes bankrupt, the SIPC will reimburse the investor up to $500,000. However, claims for cash are limited to $100,000 per customer.

The SIPC provides some investor protection and thereby promotes confidence in the securities market. The financial base of the SIPC is derived from assessments of ¼ of 1 percent of each member's gross revenues from its securities business. SIPC's membership generally consists of all persons registered under the Securities Exchange Act and all persons who are members of a national securities exchange.

THE GLOBAL INVESTMENT MARKETPLACE

Finance is now a truly global enterprise. Corporations and governments, in search of lower interest rates, regularly raise funds overseas through primary security offerings. Investors, individual as well as institutional, can buy and sell securities on numerous secondary markets around the world. A U.S. investor, for example, can readily buy British securities on the London Stock Exchange or French securities on the Paris Bourse.

As a matter of fact, a number of large corporations have chosen to list their stocks and bonds on major security exchanges around the globe so as to give them wider investor exposure. Large money center commercial banks and investment bankers now commonly have branch offices, or at least correspondent relations with foreign financial institutions, in major cities throughout the free world. For instance, one is likely to find branch offices of Chase Manhattan Bank and Merrill Lynch in such cities as Paris, Bombay, London, Hong Kong, Zurich, and Melbourne.

Joint ventures are currently being formed between some of the world's major stock and futures exchanges. These ventures are intended to provide the exchange members' customers with twenty-four hour, around-the-clock trading. As trading closes in North America it opens in Asia, only to be followed by Europe several hours later. A U.S. investor will be able to call a broker in Des Moines, Iowa, at 2:00 A.M. and place an order to buy Japanese bonds or sell IBM common stock. The trade will be carried out immediately in another country.

The global financial marketplace has been driven to its current status by the almost simultaneous arrival of four elements: improvement in satellite communications, widespread use of computers, deregulation of the financial systems of most industrialized countries, and the development of several new and appealing financial instruments.

The globalization of every nation's securities markets has had a number of repercussions. In the first place, competition among foreign financial institutions has risen considerably. One result of this has been a consolidation of competing firms through mergers and joint ventures in an effort to achieve economies of scale. Secondly, far-flung financial markets are now more likely to behave as if they were one market. The worldwide stock market crash of October 1987 is evidence of this. Thirdly, there has been a call for worldwide uniformity in the regulation of financial institutions and markets. Lastly, foreign exchange markets have become more volatile. It is not clear at this point how the global market will eventually develop. However, no one seriously doubts that it is here to stay.

BUSINESS PRACTICE EXAMPLE Continues

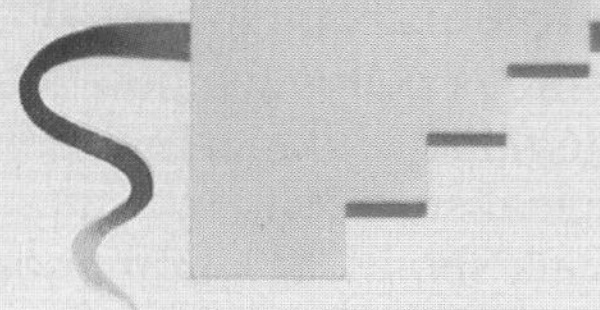

Observers in Congress as well as on Wall Street watched in amazement while the pieces of the giant Beatrice Group were picked up and sold. They saw how entrepreneurs such as Reginald Lewis unlocked hidden value in such pieces of the original as Beatrice International Food Company.

Congressman John Dingell (a Democrat from Michigan), chairman of the House Energy and Commerce Committee, was concerned about such huge corporate buyouts, with their profits for fast-moving financiers. If the assets of a publicly traded company such as Beatrice had proved so valuable in the hands of its entrepreneur purchasers, why hadn't the original stockholders received a higher price? Had the original buyers, Donald Kelly and the Kohlberg Kravis Roberts firm, concealed information about Beatrice's value—information that should have been available to stockholders on the public exchange?

Since the stock exchanges are public and subject to oversight by the U.S. government, Congressman Dingell was concerned that secret information, and possibly illegal insider trading confidentialities, had figured in the deal. Though this particular investigation did not proceed very far, some related investigations by the U.S. Attorney's office involved such participants as Mike Milken of Drexel Burnham. He was among those indicted for violation of SEC regulations on illegal insider trading information.

(continued)

The underlying issue for the congressman was the rights of owners in a publicly owned corporation. Dingell was concerned about the effects of secret transactions surrounding a formerly public company. With Beatrice off the market and trading privately, the owners' rights to full financial information and a fair price might have been suppressed.

Although this kind of concern is never easy to put to rest, most Wall Street analysts believed that the original lower value had been due to poor management at the Beatrice Group. Once managers in separate companies were freed from the stranglehold of the conglomerate, they were able to unleash new value in such companies as Avis and Beatrice International Food Company. This potential value, not visible to Beatrice Group shareholders or top officers, needed uncovering by well-informed or venturesome entrepreneurs. Investors such as Reginald Lewis were able to see possibilities in what managers could do if they were given the chance to make things work.

Issues for Discussion

1. When companies or entrepreneurs try to borrow money through bond offerings, what considerations determine how risky the loan is?
2. What considerations determine how much value was really available in the Beatrice Group's original stock?
3. Whose claims do you think should be given priority—those of the investors in publicly owned stocks or those of managers who know how to create value in a company?

SUMMARY

Investing is somewhere between saving and speculating. It means putting money into ventures expected to make a reasonable profit given the level of risk. Risk can be reduced through diversification.

The three most common types of corporate securities are bonds, preferred stock, and common stock. Bonds are long-term interest-bearing debt instruments of corporations. They are sold in denominations of $1,000. Bonds are often callable. That is, they can be redeemed before maturity. They may also be convertible—exchangeable for common stock. Bond prices and market interest rates are inversely related. Junk bonds are speculative bonds that offer a high interest rate to compensate for their high risk.

Preferred stock is stock whose owners receive dividends (if any are declared) before common stockholders do. Preferred stock and common stock can be par (with a stated value printed on the face of the stock certificate) or no-par (with no stated value). Preferred stock can also be cumulative or noncumulative—terms that refer to dividend distribution. Callable preferred stock may be redeemed at the option of the issuing corporation. Convertible preferred stock can be exchanged for common stock.

Common stock is stock whose owners receive dividends only after bondholders receive interest and preferred stockholders receive dividends. The owners of common stock have voting rights.

Investment bankers help corporations sell new issues of securities. They may form underwriting syndicates—joint ventures for the purpose of buying and selling new issues of securities. New securities issues are sold in the primary market. Previously issued securities are bought and sold in the secondary market.

The marketplaces in which securities are bought and sold (traded) are stock exchanges. Many small and mid-sized companies are traded instead in over-the-counter (OTC) markets. Statistics about securities are reported in financial sections of newspapers. Most investors purchase securities through retail brokerage houses. A bull market is characterized by rising stock prices and a bear market by falling stock prices.

Stock values are quoted in points, with each point equaling a dollar. Bond values are also quoted in points, but each point equals 1 percent of the face value of the bond. The Dow Jones Industrial Averages (DJIA) reports on thirty stocks of well-established firms.

Corporate takeovers cause upheavals in the stock market. Even successful takeovers may have side effects that cause company profits to lose momentum and stocks to lose value.

It is difficult for individual investors to make careful selections of stocks for investment. Some investor analysts evaluate companies for their potential. Others use statistical analysis of stock price movements over time to determine whether a stock should be bought or sold. Many individual investors choose to put their money into mutual funds, which offer efficiency, professional knowhow, and diversification.

Before the 1929 stock market crash, many states had passed laws to prevent fraud in securities sales. After the crash, the federal government passed the Securities Act of 1933 and the Securities Exchange Act of 1934 to protect investors. The latter act established the Securities and Exchange Commission, which monitors and controls interstate securities dealings. Other protectors of investors are the National Association of Securities Dealers (NASD) and the Securities Investors Protection Corporation (SIPC).

Finance has become a global enterprise. U.S. investors can now buy foreign securities on foreign exchanges twenty-four hours a day. Among the repercussions of this globalization is increased competition among foreign financial institutions and volatility in foreign exchange markets.

KEY TERMS

Bear market p. 571
Bonds p. 560
Bull market p. 571
Buying on the margin p. 578
Callable bonds p. 562
Common stock p. 565
Convertible bond p. 562
Corporate takeover p. 575
Debenture bonds p. 561
Discount price p. 562
Diversification p. 560
Dow Jones Industrial Averages (DJIA) p. 574
Investing p. 560
Investment bankers p. 567
Over-the-counter (OTC) markets p. 569
Par stock p. 564
Preferred stock p. 564
Premium price p. 562
Primary market p. 568
Risk p. 560
Risk aversion p. 560
Secondary market p. 568
Securities and Exchange Commission (SEC) p. 578
Sinking fund p. 562
Speculation p. 559
Stock exchanges p. 568

CHECK YOUR LEARNING

Reread the following learning objectives. Each objective is followed by a few questions. Answering these questions accurately will help you retain the most important concepts discussed in this chapter. After answering each question, check your answer with the key at the end of this chapter. (*Hint:* If you have doubt regarding the correct response, consult the page whose number follows the answer.)

Circle:

A. Discuss how saving, speculation, risk, and diversification relate to investing.

T F — 1. The purchase of an insured commercial bank deposit is an illustration of investing.

a b c d — 2. Which of the following organizations is *not* usually considered an institutional investor: (a) mutual fund; (b) U.S. Treasury; (c) life insurance company; (d) pension fund.

T F 3. All other things being equal, as one increases the total number of investments in a portfolio, the element of investment risk should decline.

B. Discuss the differences and similarities between bonds, preferred stocks, and common stock, and identify the role of the investment banker.

T F 1. Dividends are paid quarterly to bondholders.

T F 2. A debenture bond is backed up by specific collateral of the issuing corporation.

a b c d 3. Which one of the following securities cannot have a call feature: (a) bonds; (b) debentures; (c) preferred stock; (d) common stock.

T F 4. Cumulative is a feature that can be attached to preferred stock.

T F 5. Investment bankers have a role very similar to that of investment companies.

C. Discuss the functions of a stock exchange and identify steps taken by brokers to purchase securities.

T F 1. The New York Stock Exchange is commonly referred to as the Big Board.

T F 2. Stock exchanges provide a marketplace where members can buy and sell securities.

T F 3. A membership on the stock exchange is called a "blue chip."

a b c d 4. The fourth step when purchasing listed stock through a broker is: (a) placing the order; (b) deciding the amount of stock to be purchased; (c) visiting the exchange to pick up the stock; (d) receiving confirmation of the purchase from the floor broker.

T F 5. Over-the-counter stock is usually purchased on a bid and ask basis.

D. Identify key features of financial news reports, and discuss how markets are influenced by corporate takeover activity.

a b c d 1. A bond with a market value of 103½ would be quoted at: (a) $10.35; (b) $103.50; (c) $1,035; (d) none of the above.

T F 2. If a share of stock has a closing price of 25¼ and the annual dividend is $2, then the investor's yield is about 8 percent.

T F 3. If a share of stock lost five points in value and you have 100 shares, you lost $500.

a b c d 4. Choose the stock market index that is composed of thirty blue chip industrial stocks: (a) Wilshire index; (b) Value-Line index; (c) Dow Jones Industrial Averages; (d) Standard & Poor's 500 index.

E. Discuss the information that is considered in selecting investment securities and explain the role of mutual funds and other investment companies.

T F 1. Investors select securities for investment on the basis of past performance.

T F 2. Investors have little interest in trying to estimate how securities may perform in the future.

a b c d 3. Individual investors are drawn to mutual funds because of the funds': (a) professional management; (b) diversification properties; (c) low operating costs; (d) all of the above.

F. Identify major agencies and legislation designed to protect investors and discuss how investing is changing in the global marketplace.

a b c d 1. State laws passed to protect the investor from unethical security sales practices were known as: (a) margin laws; (b) kiting codes; (c) blue sky laws; (d) freedom of information laws.

a b c d 2. Small investors are protected against losses from brokerage firm bankruptcies by the: (a) SEC; (b) NASD; (c) FDIC; (d) SIPC.

T F 3. The Securities and Exchange Act of 1934 established the National Association of Securities Dealers for the purpose of monitoring dealings in interstate securities.

T F 4. American investors can now purchase common stocks of foreign corporations on stock exchanges outside the United States.

QUESTIONS FOR REVIEW AND DISCUSSION

1. Define the terms listed at the end of the chapter.
2. How are bonds and preferred stock alike? How are they different?
3. Compare common stock to preferred stock. Why are common shareholders viewed as residual owners?
4. How do investment bankers help market new issues of securities to investors?
5. What's the difference between a listed stock and an unlisted stock?
6. Secure a recent copy of the *Wall Street Journal.* Practice reading and interpreting bond and stock quotes from the following industries: auto, computer technology, fast-food franchising, general retailing, and utilities. Which industry seems to rely most heavily on bonds? Which industries have higher P/E ratios? Which industries are paying the highest dividends? Are there any particular companies that you would suggest for an investment? Explain.
7. Translate the following bond quotes into dollars and cents: 87⅛; 105½; 79⅞; 11⅜.
8. Explain how a stockbroker can help an investor purchase securities.
9. In cooperation with your instructor, invite a stockbroker to visit your class. Ask each class member to submit at least two questions for the guest speaker.
10. Do you agree or disagree with the following statement: The SEC "polices" the securities market. Explain.
11. Small investors have frequently been hurt financially by investing in the stock market. How does the Securities Investor Protection Corporation help protect small investors?
12. Visit your library's reference room and secure a recent copy of *Moody's Handbook of Common Stocks.* Look up specific information about the following companies: Avon Products, Chrysler Corporation, the New York Times Company, Pinkerton, and Time. For each company, answer the following questions:
    a. What is the current product line or service provided by the company? What markets does it serve? Have you ever purchased any of its products?
    b. Is the corporation listed or unlisted? If listed, on which stock exchange?
    c. How many stockholders does the company have? How many shares are held?
    d. Have quarterly dividends been consistent? Are dividends increasing?
    e. What is Moody's investment rating of this stock? Do you think the rating is fair?
    f. What other interesting data did you discover about this company?
13. Given the following data, translate the closing stock prices and compute the investor's yield for each company.

Corporation	**Closing Price**	**Div.**	**Investor's Yld.**
Textron	27⅛	2.50	________
General Motors	58¼	2.35	________
Standard Oil (OH)	103⅝	6.75	________
Tandy	120½	5.60	________

14. Write or visit a local brokerage office and secure a copy of a prospectus. What types of information does the prospectus contain? Would you recommend purchasing the security highlighted in the prospectus? Explain.

CONCLUDING CASE

The Crash of '87

There were telltale signs of trouble brewing in the weeks and days leading up to Black Monday, October 19, 1987. But no one, certainly not the experts, envisioned anything like what happened on that historic day. As the New York Stock Exchange opened for business, most investors and traders were well aware of the fact that the Japanese stock market had fallen substantially the night before. The market was also in the process of digesting several negative economic reports just out of Washington. Furthermore, the Dow Jones Industrial Averages had already fallen in fits and starts some 17 percent from their all-time high of 2722.42 on August 25, 1987, to the close of trading on the preceding Friday. Last, but not least, the stock market had been experimenting with a number of new investment vehicles and trading strategies. The stage was set.

At the opening bell for the start of trading, the DJIA stood at 2246.74. Stock prices began falling immediately. With the exception of a short-lived rally around midmorning, the market headed straight down. When trading on the Big Board finally shut down, the DJIA stood at 1738.42. It had fallen a record 508.32 points on a panic-driven record volume of 604,801,000 shares.

On a percentage basis, the one-day decline came to 22.6 percent, nearly double the previous record of 12.8 percent, which occurred on Black Tuesday, October 28, 1929. Volume had also doubled the previous record. Other stock market gauges collapsed as well. It has been estimated that the one-day market collapse wiped out over $1,000,000,000,000 of investor wealth.

The Standard & Poor's 500 stock index, for example, dropped by 20.4 percent. European and Asian markets followed suit. It was nothing short of a panic atmosphere as investors tried to unload their shares on an overburdened trading system. Government and stock exchange officials helplessly watched as the stock market turned in its worst day ever. In the aftermath, there were widespread predictions of a "financial meltdown," not to mention a 1930s style depression.

The key financial questions of the late 1980s were: Why did the U.S. stock market collapse in value by some 36 percent in the summer and fall of 1987? How could this happen in a modern, sophisticated economy? A number of explanations were offered: (1) Foreign investors decided to get out of the U.S. stock market, fearing a declining dollar. (2) Computer program trading by institutional investors created a vicious, uncontrolled price spiral. (3) Many investors came to a sudden realization that the burgeoning budget and trade deficits could not be sustained. (4) Profit taking became widespread.

Although all of these reasons have merit, they somehow don't seem to be enough of an answer. Could it be that the wrong question was asked? A better question might be: Why did the stock market rise so far and so fast during the mid-1980s? Is it possible that many individual stocks and the market were vastly overvalued, and that sooner or later the bubble had to burst? It would not be the first speculative excess in our country's history.

Issues for Discussion

1. Should the government be given the tools to prevent or at least minimize volatile stock market behavior? Explain.
2. Why is it that stock markets in different countries seem to move up and down together? Should they? Explain.
3. Is there anything individual investors can do to protect themselves against stock market crashes such as the one on Black Monday?

NOTE

1. David Warsh, "Buy This Junk Bond! Don't Break the Chain," *Boston Globe,* April 16, 1989, pp. A-1, A-5.

CHECK YOUR LEARNING ANSWER KEY

A. 1. F, *p. 560*
 2. b, *p. 560*
 3. T, *p. 560*

B. 1. F, *p. 560*
 2. F, *p. 561*
 3. d, *p. 565*
 4. T, *p. 565*
 5. F, *p. 567*

C. 1. T, *p. 568*
 2. T, *p. 568*
 3. F, *p. 569*
 4. d, *p. 571*
 5. T, *p. 569*

D. 1. c, *p. 573*
 2. T, *p. 573*
 3. T, *p. 572*
 4. c, *p. 574*

E. 1. T, *p. 576*
 2. F, *p. 576*
 3. d, *p. 576*

F. 1. c, *p. 578*
 2. d, *p. 580*
 3. F, *p. 578*
 4. T, *p. 580*

CHAPTER

20

INSURANCE AND RISK MANAGEMENT

LEARNING OBJECTIVES

After reading this chapter you should be able to:

1. Discuss the different methods used by business to manage risks.
2. Distinguish between a pure risk and a speculative risk.
3. List the requirements for an insurable risk.
4. Compare and contrast mutual and stock insurance companies.
5. Discuss the roles of selected government insurance programs.
6. Explain the differences among the basic types of life insurance.
7. List four examples of how businesses use life insurance and describe them.
8. Provide a brief explanation of the common forms of health insurance.
9. Compare and contrast the various types of property and liability insurance.

OUTLINE

Business Practice Example: Flight from the Boardroom

Managing Business Risks
- Avoiding Risks
- Assuming Risks
- Reducing Risks
- Transferring Risks

Determining Insurable Risks
- Pure versus Speculative Risks
- Insurable Interest
- Requirements for Insurable Risks

Shifting Risks to Insurance Underwriters
- Private Insurance Companies
  - Mutual Companies
  - Stock Companies
- Public Insurance: Government Programs
  - Social Security
  - Worker's Compensation
  - Unemployment Insurance
  - Other Government Programs

Basics of Life and Health Insurance
- Life Insurance Policies
  - Term Insurance
  - Whole Life Insurance
  - Universal Life Insurance
- Business Uses of Life Insurance
  - Key Executive Life Insurance
  - Credit Life Insurance
  - Group Life Insurance
  - Retirement Programs
- Health Insurance

Property and Liability Insurance
- Fire Insurance
- Automobile Insurance
- Theft Insurance
- Fidelity and Surety Bonds
- Liability Insurance
- Other Business Coverages
- Insurance Needs in Service Industries

Internationalization of the Insurance Industry

Summary

Key Terms

Check Your Learning

Questions for Review and Discussion

Concluding Case: Run for Your Life—Insurance

Notes

Check Your Learning Answer Key

Highlight in Business Practice: Lloyd's of London: Insurer to the World

BUSINESS PRACTICE EXAMPLE

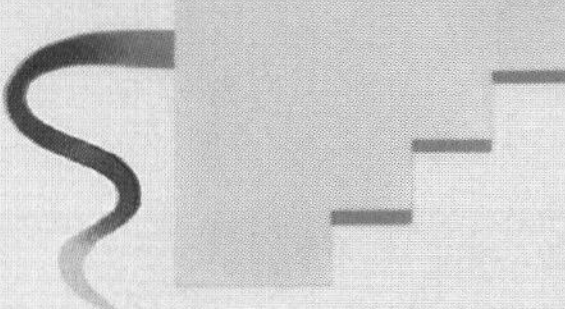

Flight from the Boardroom

Traditionally, executives willingly have accepted appointments to serve as members of corporate boards of directors. In fact, many continue to serve in multiple assignments. Corporations are pleased to have the expertise of outside directors, and the executives enjoy the prestige and recognition attached to their role.

This trend of corporate governance may be changing. Suits filed against directors and company officers by unhappy shareholders are on the increase. Most directors and officers have been protected by directors' and officers' liability insurance, known as D & O coverage. However, recent claims have skyrocketed, and insurance companies are canceling policies and/or raising premiums. In a landmark 1985 Delaware Supreme Court decision, the court ruled against the directors of Trans Union Corporation after they approved a takeover in an unusually brief meeting. Company shareholders argued that the board's brief meeting denied them a potentially higher bid from another company. This court decision made directors extremely vulnerable to shareholder suits.

This risk exposure has forced mass exits of outside directors. When Verna Corporation, a Houston-based oil and gas drilling company lost its $2 million D & O coverage, four of its five outside directors quit. One outside Verna director stated, "I just can't afford to expose my personal assets to the risk."

In a study by Touche Ross & Co., 93 percent of the directors polled believed that increased liability will make it more difficult for companies to recruit and retain talented and experienced people to serve on boards. The reasons are fairly clear. Over 18 percent of companies reporting had claims against directors and officers (thirty-five claims per hundred companies responding). The average cost per claim was $1,044,000, including an average payment of $583,000 and an average $461,000 defense cost per claim.

Large insurance firms such as the Hartford Insurance Group and CNA Insurance Companies argue that D & O coverage has been abused. For example, the FDIC and the FSLIC have routinely filed suits against directors and officers of failed banks and thrifts hoping to collect on D & O policies. Most companies have retaliated by writing D & O policies that exclude claims stemming from government agencies. Another cancellation of insurance resulted from an unprecedented charge in which two major banks sued their own employees under D & O policies. Chase Manhattan Bank sued six former officers for $175 million for negligence in decision making. Bank of America sued one current and six former employees for their role in a securities scam that cost the bank $95 million. D & O insurance underwriters cite that these atypical claims have contributed to the rising premiums and withdrawal of companies from the market.

Clearly, the crises in providing D & O coverage could change the long-term performance of numerous corporations. Fewer outside directors will be willing to serve on boards, which could possibly lead to "tunnel vision." Walter B. Wriston, former chairman of Citicorp and currently a director of nine companies stated, "I don't know of anybody who would join a board without D & O insurance."

WHAT'S AHEAD

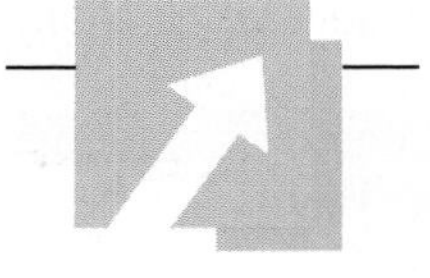

Stockholders' suits reflect one of the many risks faced by business today. Most enterprises rely on various types of insurance as part of their risk management program. This chapter presents a number of ways to manage business risks and explains how some risks can be transferred to insurance companies. The basic kinds of insurance available and the coverage each provides are explained. The material in this chapter should help you appreciate the challenging roles of risk managers and insurance underwriters.

MANAGING BUSINESS RISKS

An inherent part of our capitalist system, **risk** is uncertainty about exposure to possible losses or injuries. People face risks every day. If you commute to school, you run a greater risk of having a car accident than do students who live on campus. If you do not exercise or eat wisely, you run a greater risk of heart failure and high blood pressure than do people who are more health conscious.

Risk is uncertainty about exposure to possible losses or injuries.

Businesses face similar uncertainties. Fire, theft, bad debts, and death are common risks that businesses must face. Less common, but just as real, is the risk that products will have to be recalled because of customer complaints, faulty parts, or product design. For example, Honda, Suzuki, Kawasaki, and Yamaha agreed in 1987 to stop marketing three-wheel all-terrain vehicles (ATVs) in the United States because of the high number of injuries reported. ATVs in dealer inventories were recalled in a buyback program.

It is impossible to avoid all types of risks, so businesses attempt to deal with them through effective management. First, they usually try to identify all potential losses. Once a company is aware of the various losses to which it is exposed, it will normally consider the following strategies: risk avoidance, risk assumption, risk reduction, and risk transfer.

Avoiding Risks

One sure way to eliminate the possibility of loss is to avoid the risk. For example, a manufacturer may avoid the risk of bad debts by having a no-credit policy. Of course, this policy may at the same time cut into potential sales. A key executive can avoid the risk of an airplane crash by choosing to travel by train. The long-term impact of this decision, however, may not be in the best interests of the company. Usually, businesses accept some risk because of the chance for gain. In short, the very nature of the capitalist system forces businesses to take many risks rather than avoid them.

Assuming Risks

Self-insurance is a risk-bearing method whereby a company makes a regular deposit into a fund to pay for potential losses.

Once a business has identified the unavoidable risks to which it is exposed, a decision must be made about them. A risk manager may decide that certain contingencies should be assumed by the company through **self-insurance**—a risk-bearing method whereby a company makes a regular deposit into a fund to pay for potential losses.

It is common for large corporations to self-insure their property. A retail chain with hundreds of stores may find self-insurance much cheaper than commercial insurance. J. C. Penney, for example, would have to buy insurance coverage on each of its many stores, although it is unlikely that several of them would be damaged or destroyed at the same time.

Usually, self-insurance means raising the regular insurance deductible to the point where the business is taking a significant risk and placing an "excess" policy with an outside insurer to cover catastrophic risks. Occasionally, however, a business must self-insure because no commercial insurance coverage is available. Not many companies are eager to insure property located in a high-crime district, for example.

Whether the decision is to insure or to assume the risk, all businesses should monitor their environments so as to reduce risks. Figure 20.1 shows a business risk checklist commonly used to evaluate firms.

Reducing Risks

Perhaps the most logical alternative to assuming risks is reducing them, usually through a well-designed loss prevention and control plan. An example is safety programs that attempt to make employees aware of hazards. Sprinkler systems, smoke alarms, and well-located fire extinguishers are all part of a safety program. In addition, some buildings are constructed with fire-resistant materials. Some industrial plants even have their own fire departments.

Ultimately, however, risk reduction does not prevent the possibility of losses. And since losses usually result in financial hardship, many companies share the burden of this hardship by shifting risks to insurance companies.

Transferring Risks

A ***premium*** is a cash payment to an insurance company for an insurance policy.

Most businesses cannot afford to pay for large losses that might occur, so they transfer the risk to an insurance company. Insurance companies issue policies that specify the terms and conditions under which certain risks are covered. For this coverage, the insured pays a **premium** (a cash payment to an insurance company for an insurance policy) based on the type of risk and the degree of

	No need for action	Look into this
Boiler and machinery accidents		
Burglary		
Business interruption		
Cargo loss		
Computer coverages		
Contractual obligations		
Directors' and officers' liability		
Earthquake		
Employee dishonesty		
Flood		
Glass breakage		
Maritime workers' injuries		
Motor vehicle accidents		
Pollution liability		
Product liability		
Product recall		
Professional liability		
Robbery		
Vacant/unoccupied buildings		
Vandalism		
Workers' accidents and injuries		

Figure 20.1
Business risk checklist. Recognizing hazards and areas of potential loss is a critical aspect of risk management.

exposure. If a loss does occur, the insurance company compensates the insured according to the stipulations in the policy. Before managers can shift risks to an insurance company, however, they must determine which risks are insurable.

DETERMINING INSURABLE RISKS

Before an insurance company accepts a risk, it evaluates the type and possibility of loss. This procedure for screening risks is called the **underwriting process.** The financial success of any insurance company depends greatly on underwriting.

The ***underwriting process*** is the procedure insurance companies use for screening risks.

Pure versus Speculative Risks

First, the insurance company decides if the risk is pure or speculative. As a general rule, pure risks are insurable and speculative risks are not. A **pure risk** offers no chance for gain—only loss. For a doctor, a malpractice suit is a pure risk. If the doctor carries malpractice insurance and is never sued, the policy is not a source of gain. A **speculative risk** offers an opportunity for both gain and loss. Investing in a new business venture and purchasing stocks are examples of speculative risks. Once the insurance company has determined that a risk is pure, it examines the issue of insurable interest.

A ***pure risk*** is a risk that offers no chance for gain—only loss.

A ***speculative risk*** is a risk that offers an opportunity for both gain and loss.

Insurable Interest

An ***insurable interest*** is the right to insure property or life if the loss of or damage to it would cause the person or company financial loss.

If your car is wrecked in a collision, you will suffer a financial loss. If a Safeway Corporation plant is destroyed by fire, the company will suffer a financial loss. Individuals and companies have an **insurable interest** in owned property when damage to it would result in their suffering a financial loss. The same principle extends to people. A family may carry a life insurance policy on its main wage earner because the person's death would impose financial hardship on the family.

Requirements for Insurable Risks

If the risk is pure and the applicant has an insurable interest, the insurance company will evaluate the risk according to the following requirements:

1. *The loss must be predictable.* Insurance companies will not insure a loss that cannot be predicted. To predict loss accurately, insurance companies must be able to calculate the likelihood, or probability, of a loss occurring. The likelihood is based on a large number of similar cases. The *law of large numbers* is a statistical rule of thumb stating that the larger the number of cases, the more accurate the predictions. This law is used to develop a special set of tables for predicting the number of fires, auto accidents, or deaths that will occur under given conditions in a given year.

   In life insurance, the table is called a *mortality table,* and it indicates the number of deaths per thousand persons that will occur in a given year. It also shows the number of years people are expected to live after reaching a certain age. Table 20.1 is an abbreviated mortality table for American males. Using it, we can predict the following: for eighteen-year-old males, only 2 per 1,000 (1.78) are expected to die in the year the table was made up. The others should live a further 54.18 years, or to the age of 72.
2. *The loss must be accidental.* Insurance companies base their charges on accidental losses. Planned fires (arson) are not accidental losses. (Insurance experts estimate that arson costs up to $1.6 billion per year in direct property damage.[1]) Many large casualty companies have full-time arson squads that investigate all property losses caused by fire. Life insurance policies have an exclusionary clause that prevents payment if the insured person commits suicide during the initial year of coverage. In short, losses must occur by chance, not by the intention of the insured.
3. *The risk must be geographically spread out.* Most insurance companies will not concentrate all of their coverage in one or two regions. California mudslides and forest fires have frequently destroyed millions of dollars worth of property. For this reason, an insurance company will insure only a certain percentage of property located in a specific geographical location.
4. *Losses must be measurable.* Methods exist to estimate the cost of medical care and the financial loss caused by death. Sentimental losses—family pictures or pets, for example—are seldom insurable. Companies will accept only risks that are measurable in dollars.
5. *Costs of insuring losses must be economically sound.* Although a person's life is generally an acceptable risk, sometimes a life can be uninsurable. An individual with heart disease or one who races cars professionally is often considered too high a risk. A property located in a flood-prone district may be considered an unsound risk from an underwriting viewpoint. Companies will either charge these applicants more or simply deny them coverage. As we will

Table 20.1 Abbreviated mortality table for males.

Age	Deaths per 1,000	Life Expectancy (Years)	Age	Deaths per 1,000	Life Expectancy (Years)
0	4.18	70.83	19	1.86	53.27
1	1.07	70.13	20	1.90	52.37
2	.99	69.20	25	1.77	47.84
3	.98	68.27	30	1.73	43.24
4	.95	67.34	35	2.11	38.61
5	.90	66.40	40	3.02	34.05
6	.86	65.46	45	4.55	29.62
7	.80	64.52	50	6.71	25.36
8	.76	63.57	55	10.47	21.29
9	.74	62.62	60	16.08	17.51
10	.73	61.66	65	25.42	14.04
11	.77	60.71	70	39.51	10.96
12	.85	59.75	75	64.19	8.31
13	.99	58.80	80	98.84	6.18
14	1.15	57.86	85	152.95	4.46
15	1.33	56.93	90	221.77	3.18
16	1.51	56.00	95	329.96	1.87
17	1.67	55.09	99	1,000.00	.50
18	1.78	54.18			

see later in the chapter, the federal government is sometimes called on to insure high-risk property and lives.

SHIFTING RISKS TO INSURANCE UNDERWRITERS

Most business risks are underwritten by private insurance companies. Certain risks, however, cannot be insured by a private company because they need regulation or are too large. In these cases, the federal government often fills the gap.

Private Insurance Companies

Most private insurance companies are classified as *legal reserve companies*. This means that a certain percentage of the premiums they receive from customers must be set aside for payment of future claims. These reserves provide a margin of safety for all consumers who purchase policies. An estimated 2,265 legal reserve companies account for nearly 98 percent of the life insurance in force in the United States.[2]

Mutual Companies

One of the important categories of private insurers is mutual insurance companies, which issue no stock. The policyholders are the owners. Mutual companies are

BUSINESS PRACTICE EXAMPLE Continues

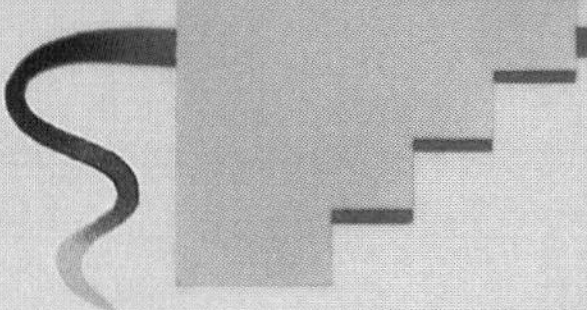

Cancellation of D & O coverage has left many companies vulnerable to stockholders' liability suits. Certain depository financial institutions have been blacklisted because the risk exposure is so high. To restore coverage, a few banks have decided to use self-insurance. Bank of America established its own insurance company and pays premiums to itself. If a claim occurs, the bank draws on this fund to pay it.

Other companies also are establishing their own insurance companies. For example, thirty-three corporations, including Ford Motor Company, General Electric, and USX, formed American Casualty Excess Insurance Co. Ltd. to handle their claims. The formation of such insurance companies was caused by a jump of some 900 percent in premiums for D & O insurance from 1985 to 1987.

managed by boards of directors elected by the policyholders. They earn no profit for their owners. If surplus funds exist, they are distributed to policyholders in the form of cash dividends or premium reductions.

Stock Companies

Over 93 percent of private insurance companies in the United States are stock companies. They are corporations owned by stockholders and managed by elected boards of directors. Like most other corporations, they attempt to provide the best selection of policies and services to their customers at the lowest possible costs. Stock companies earn profits from premiums collected in excess of claims and operational expenses and from investments of surplus cash in stocks, bonds, and real estate.

Are mutual companies more efficient than stock companies? There is much debate about this, but no clear-cut evidence exists to show that the cost of stock insurance policies is higher than that of mutual insurance companies. Table 20.2 shows that most of the ten largest life insurance companies are mutuals. Traditionally, mutual companies have dominated the life insurance field, whereas most other types of insurance have been underwritten by stock companies.

Public Insurance: Government Programs

Government at all levels offers a variety of insurance programs to individuals and organizations. In fact, the U.S. government is the single largest source of insurance

Table 20.2 The ten largest U. S. life insurance companies in 1988. Asterisk indicates mutual life insurance companies.

Rank by Assets 1988	Company	Assets $ Millions	Premium and Annuity Income $ Millions	Net Investment Income $ Millions
1	Prudential of America, Newark, N.J.*	116,197.0	14,396.7	7,436.9
2	Metropolitan Life, New York*	94,232.0	15,487.1	7,261.0
3	Equitable Life Assurance, New York*	50,415.5	4,917.3	3,130.0
4	Aetna Life, Hartford[8]	48,884.9	8,266.1	3,345.0
5	Teachers Insurance & Annuity, New York	38,631.4	3,064.9	3,641.3
6	New York Life, New York*	35,153.8	6,929.3	2,758.2
7	Connecticut General Life, Bloomfield[9]	31,095.5	2,732.3	2,011.4
8	Travelers, Hartford[10]	30,672.2	4,200.9	2,185.1
9	John Hancock Mutual Life, Boston*	28,315.2	4,865.9	2,216.7
10	Northwestern Mutual Life, Milwaukee*	25,349.0	3,542.1	1,829.4

in America. Coverage includes not only life insurance, disability benefits, and some medical insurance but also flood insurance, deposit insurance and pension plans.

Social Security

Perhaps the greatest risk borne by American society as a whole is that of guaranteeing that the aged and disabled, regardless of their ability to pay for insurance, are not left without care and protection. To handle this concern, the social security system was created in 1935 as a nationwide insurance system, with participants paying today for tomorrow's guaranteed retirement or disability benefits. The system currently covers 90 percent of all jobs and provides three types of insurance: (1) old age and survivor's insurance, (2) disability insurance, and (3) health insurance in the form of Medicare.

Old age and survivor's insurance is what is often referred to as social security. It provides pension payments to 38 million Americans. Under new regulations, the retirement age for benefits, which used to be sixty-five, will gradually increase to 67 by the year 2000. The benefits are subject to income tax for incomes over a specific base amount. Funds for social security benefits come from taxes on earned income. The maximum amount of social security taxes a person can pay each year is reviewed annually by the Treasury Department. Figure 20.2 shows the variations over the years in the tax rate, the maximum tax collected, and the maximum amount of earned income taxed. For example, the maximum social security tax an individual wage earner could pay in 1989 was $3,604.80.

The second type of insurance under social security—disability insurance—provides monthly payments to workers who are unable to pursue gainful employment. To complete this package of coverage, the federal government added

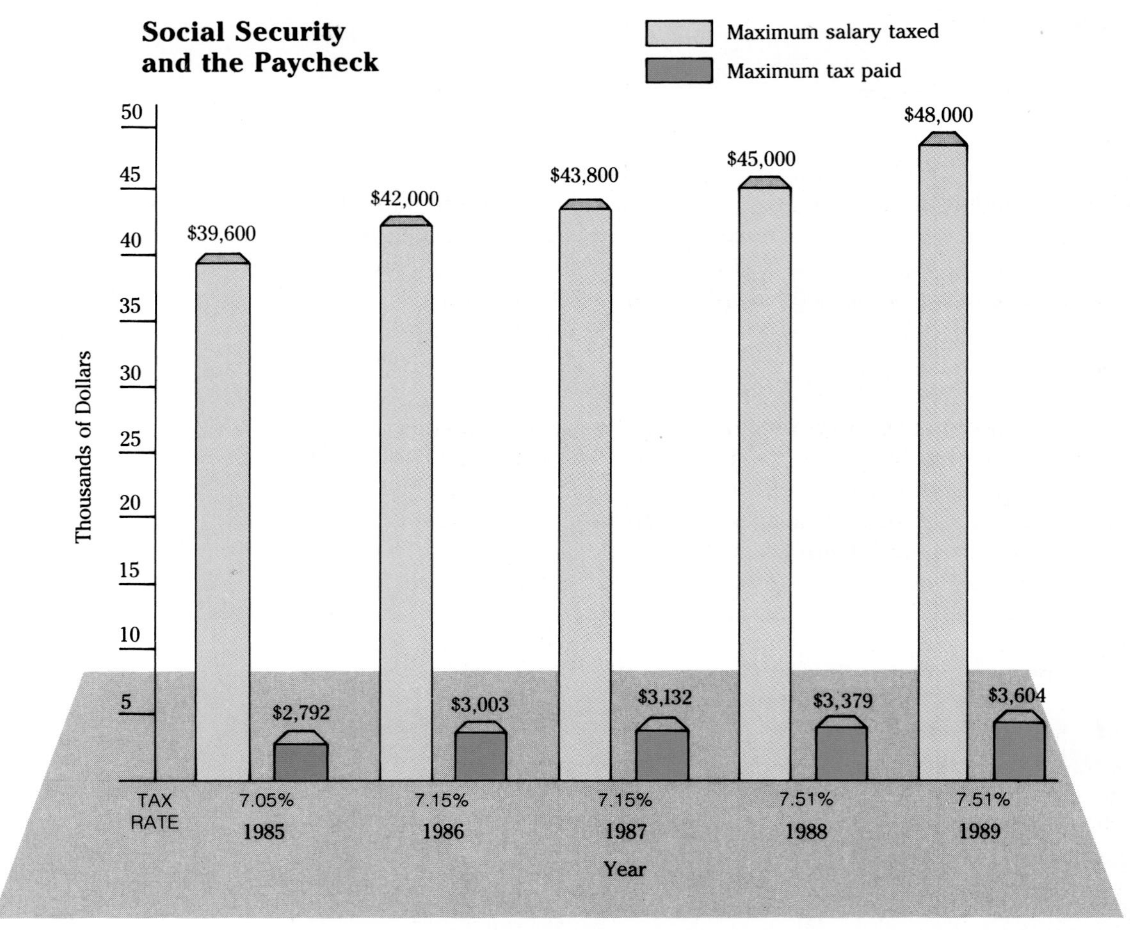

Figure 20.2 Social security and the paycheck.

Medicare is a supplemental health insurance program provided to retirees sixty-five years of age and older who are covered by social security.

hospitalization insurance called **Medicare**—a supplemental health insurance program provided to retirees sixty-five years of age and older who are covered by social security. Social security is one of the main underwriting ventures of the federal government.

Worker's Compensation

Worker's compensation is a state-mandated insurance that every employer must provide to employees for job-related injuries and illnesses.

Every employer is required by state law to provide **worker's compensation** to employees for job-related injuries and illnesses, regardless of who, if anyone, is at fault. Benefits received normally do not exceed two-thirds of the weekly wage; however, they are tax-free. Coverage includes lost income, medical care, rehabilitation, and survivor's benefits. Organizations insure against this risk by purchasing coverage from the state or from a private company. Premiums vary according to the risks within each industry. Large corporations may be allowed to self-insure if their financial condition is sound.

Unemployment Insurance

Regardless of where you live, U.S. employers have certain financial responsibilities to you if you are laid off from work. Benefits, job counseling, and placement services are provided to workers for a period that does not normally exceed thirty-nine weeks. However, the amount of benefits and the time allowed depend on the state, the unemployment rate, and other factors. Benefits are financed from a state payroll tax and are sometimes supplemented by the federal government.

Other Government Programs

Among the other government programs developed to underwrite specific risks are GI life insurance for all military personnel. During World War II, private insurers had inserted clauses in their policies stating that the proceeds would not be paid if death occurred in a war zone. War clauses reappeared during the Korean and Vietnam wars but are not in general use today.

The Federal Deposit Insurance Corporation is another example of government underwriting. As chapter 16 pointed out, the FDIC insures your depository institution deposits for up to $100,000 per account. The Federal Crime Insurance Program provides burglary and robbery protection to businesses located in high-crime districts. Recently, the amount of coverage in force was $286.8 million.[3] Still another type of public insurance is flood insurance, provided by the National Flood Insurance Association. It protects properties against flooding and mudslides in flood-prone areas.

Regardless of the existence of government insurance, however, the overwhelming majority of underwriting is still provided by private companies. The main areas of underwriting are life insurance, health insurance, and property and liability insurance.

BASICS OF LIFE AND HEALTH INSURANCE

Most people buy life insurance to protect someone else from financial loss if the insured person dies unexpectedly. The someone is usually a spouse or other family member. It could also be a business partner or a corporation.

The legal contract that stipulates the terms and conditions under which benefits will be paid is the *policy.* The individual designated to receive the cash proceeds from the policy if the insured party dies is the **beneficiary.**

A ***beneficiary*** is an individual designated to receive the cash proceeds from an insurance policy if the insured party dies.

Life Insurance Policies

Life insurance is one of the most frequently purchased and least understood commodities sold today. Nearly 86 percent of American families and over two-thirds of individuals currently have some form of life insurance coverage. In 1987, the amount of life insurance per family averaged $82,800.[4] One of the more useful approaches to understanding life insurance is to examine the basic types of coverage: term, whole life, and universal life.

Term Insurance

Term insurance is a type of life insurance that is issued for a specific period of time, from one to thirty years, and pays a benefit only if the insured dies during that period.

Insurance that provides protection for the insured for a specific period of time, from one to thirty years, is **term insurance.** This type of policy pays benefits only if the insured dies during the period covered by it. At the end of the term, the protection ends, but the insured can continue for another term if the policy is renewable.

A renewable policy does not require the insured to take a medical exam. However, the premium will be higher because the insured is older. For example, a twenty-five-year-old father may purchase a $100,000 renewable term policy for a ten-year period. If the father dies during the coverage period, the beneficiary receives $100,000. If he lives, the coverage ceases after ten years. Of course, he has the option to renew the term insurance at a higher premium.

Another feature that many term policies offer is convertibility. If you have a term policy that is convertible, you can exchange it for a whole life policy without a medical exam but at a higher premium. (Whole life insurance is permanent in that the insureds have coverage for the rest of their lives with no increase in premium.)

Term insurance is also sold in a form in which the face amount of coverage decreases gradually over time. This type of coverage is often purchased to protect a long-term decreasing debt obligation such as a home mortgage.

Term insurance normally does not build up cash value. Its premiums are initially lower than those for other types of policies for the same amount of coverage. It provides the insured with the largest immediate coverage at the lowest dollar cost. For this reason, it is popular with individuals who need high amounts of protection for a limited period of time, such as home buyers, parents of young children, and people with high credit obligations.

Whole Life Insurance

Whole life insurance is a type of permanent life insurance in which the insured agrees to pay a regular premium for the rest of the insured's life in return for a guaranteed specific amount of coverage.

Life insurance that continues for the insured's lifetime and cannot be canceled as long as the premium is paid is **whole life insurance.** Policyholders never need to renew the coverage or prove their insurability again. The premiums usually remain unchanged during the life of the insured. If a policyholder dies, the face amount of coverage is paid to the beneficiary. Whole life insurance is often referred to as straight life or ordinary life insurance.

Whole life insurance is one form of cash value life insurance. This means that a portion of the premium is used to buy death payment protection and a portion is allocated to savings. Over the life of the policy, the cash value (savings element) grows in value. Many policyholders use this accumulation for retirement. Policyholders may also borrow against it or cash in the policy.

Critics have claimed that the cash value in whole life policies has been based on a low rate of return and that the policies have lacked flexibility. The result of these charges has been the development of several variations in whole life policies:

1. *Modified life policies* are whole life policies with lower premiums in the early years and higher premiums thereafter.
2. *Limited-payment life policies* are whole life policies that allow the insured to pay premiums for a stated period, say twenty years. After this period, no more premiums are paid, but the coverage continues for life. (See Figure 20.3.)
3. *Variable life policies* are whole life policies in which the cash values fluctuate according to yields earned by a separate investment account. Policyholders

Figure 20.3
The opening page of a limited-payment life insurance policy.

STATE FARM LIFE
Insurance Company

STATE FARM INSURANCE

INSURED	CENNIS LECN BAUMHCVER	36	AGE
POLICY NUMBER	4,380,277	$100,CCC	AMOUNT OF BASIC PLAN
POLICY DATE	JANUARY 19, 1978	$100,CCC	TOTAL INITIAL AMOUNT

HOME OFFICE: ONE STATE FARM PLAZA, BLOOMINGTON, ILLINOIS 61701

Guide to policy provisions

	PAGE
Assignment	13
Beneficiary	7
Cash Value	13
Credits to Avoid Lapse	10
Definitions	2
Dividends	11
Extended Term Insurance	13
Grace Period	10
Ownership	7
Payment of Premiums	10
Policy Loans	12
Reduced Paid-Up Insurance	14
Reinstatement	12
Schedules of Benefits and Premiums	3
Schedule of Insurance and Values	5
Settlement Methods	8
Waiver of Premium Disability	15

The Application and Additional Benefits Provisions, if any, are found following page 16.

The Owner and the Beneficiary of this policy are as named in the application unless changed.

State Farm Life Insurance Company will pay the insurance proceeds under this policy to the Beneficiary upon receipt of satisfactory proof of the Insured's death.

The insurance provided by this policy, beginning on the Policy Date, is granted in consideration of the application and of the payment of the specified premiums during the lifetime of the Insured. The first premium is due on the Policy Date.

If not satisfactory, this policy may be returned to State Farm Life Insurance Company, or to an agent of the company within ten days of its receipt. All premiums paid on this policy will be refunded.

State Farm Life Insurance Company has issued this policy on the Issue Date.

This policy is a conversion of term insurance under policy 4,003,857.

Secretary President Registrar

PLAN DESCRIPTION

Basic Plan provides a Limited Payment Whole Life Benefit with Waiver of Premium for Disability. Schedules of Benefits and Premiums on page 3. Amounts of Insurance on page 5. Insurance payable on death. Annual Dividends. Premiums payable for premium paying period or until Insured's prior death.

FORM 7802 PAGE 1 770318

are often viewed as investors and control the types of investments made with their premiums. These policies have a minimum guaranteed death benefit.

4. *Endowment life policies* are whole life policies that provide for payment of the face amount on the insured's death or at a previously agreed-upon date, whichever comes first.

As this list implies, the policies sold by life insurance companies have been revised to meet the needs of consumers. The most popular revision of whole life insurance has been universal life. The radical differences in this form of life insurance deserve special discussion.

Universal Life Insurance

Universal life insurance is a flexible premium life insurance that allows the insured to change the death benefit from time to time or to vary the amount or timing of premium payments.

A flexible premium life insurance that allows the insured to change the death benefit (face value of coverage) from time to time or to vary the amount or timing of premium payments is **universal life insurance.** Universal life policies essentially combine renewable term insurance with a savings account that represents an investment fund. Part of the premium payment is used to pay for term insurance and part (after deductions for sales commissions and expenses) is invested in a side fund composed of low-risk financial instruments. Within limits, the purchaser can usually select the amount of premium that goes for insurance and the amount that is placed in savings.

Universal life insurance policies are normally sold only in face amounts of $100,000 or more. The rate paid on the insured savings is usually tied to the interest rates prevailing in the financial markets. The rates of return on universal life policies have been much higher than those commonly paid on whole life policies. Policyholders usually have access to the savings portion of their policy without a major penalty. They receive annual reports showing the amount of protection, cash value, costs of insurance, company fees, amount credited to savings from premium payments, and rate of return paid on savings.

Business Uses of Life Insurance

Businesses frequently purchase life insurance policies to insure their key people and pay their creditors and to provide a fringe benefit for employees.

Key Executive Life Insurance

Key executive life insurance is life insurance for certain executives, naming the corporation as beneficiary, to minimize the impact of the loss of leadership by these executives in the event of their death.

The untimely death of a key executive may reduce the stability and profits of a company. To minimize the impact of this loss of leadership, companies purchase **key executive life insurance** for certain executives, naming the corporation as beneficiary. If the executive dies, the firm receives money to help it through the adjustment period. Partnerships are also subject to transition problems if a partner dies unexpectedly. Usually, partnerships buy insurance policies for each partner, naming the other partners as beneficiaries. This provides money to the surviving partners to buy out the deceased partner's interest and continue operating the firm.

Credit Life Insurance

Credit life insurance is a form of term insurance that lenders purchase on the lives of borrowers for the amount of the loan.

A special form of term insurance is **credit life insurance,** which lenders usually purchase on the lives of borrowers for the amount of the loan. The premium is normally transferred to the borrower as part of the loan costs. If the borrower dies before the loan is paid back, the money from the life insurance policy is used to pay off the remaining debt. Usually, credit life insurance decreases in value as the loan is repaid. At the end of 1987, the amount of credit life insurance in force in the United States totaled $243 billion.[5]

Group Life Insurance

A growing number of people depend on their employers for a good portion of their life insurance protection. Usually, a firm purchases **group life insurance,** which covers all its employees for a specified amount, say $15,000 each. In some cases, the amount of coverage is based on the income level of the employee. Those in the higher income brackets receive more protection.

Group life insurance is a form of life insurance that covers all the employees of a firm for a specified amount.

Group insurance is usually term and builds no cash value for employees. Some companies pay the entire premium, and others require the employees to share the costs. Group rates are usually lower than those for individual coverage from a private insurance company. At the end of 1987, group life insurance in the United States amounted to $3,043.8 billion—40.8 percent of the life insurance in force.[6]

Retirement Programs

In the United States, nearly half of all workers in commerce and industry participate in retirement plans in addition to social security. Businesses often rely on a trust arrangement, whereby the employer deposits an annual amount with an insurance company to cover all the employees. When an individual retires, the insurance company takes a lump sum from the pension fund and purchases an annuity for the employee. An *annuity* provides monthly payments to the employee for as long as the individual lives. The amount of each payment is usually determined by the length of service and wage level. In some plans a spouse continues to collect after the insured's death; in others this is not the case.

Health Insurance

Insurance that covers financial losses resulting from sickness, injury, or disability is **health insurance.** The most common form of health insurance is hospitalization insurance, which pays the charges an individual incurs during hospitalization.

Health insurance is insurance that covers financial losses resulting from sickness, injury, or disability.

Most hospitalization plans pay for room and board, routine lab work, X-rays, basic supplies, medication, common surgical procedures, and general nursing care. If an illness is prolonged or requires an expensive specialist, basic coverage may not be enough. Most people carry **major medical insurance** to supplement basic hospitalization insurance. For example, if the basic policy will pay up to $15,000 for open-heart surgery but the operation costs $30,000, major medical insurance will cover a large percentage of the additional $15,000.

Major medical insurance is health insurance that supplements basic hospitalization insurance.

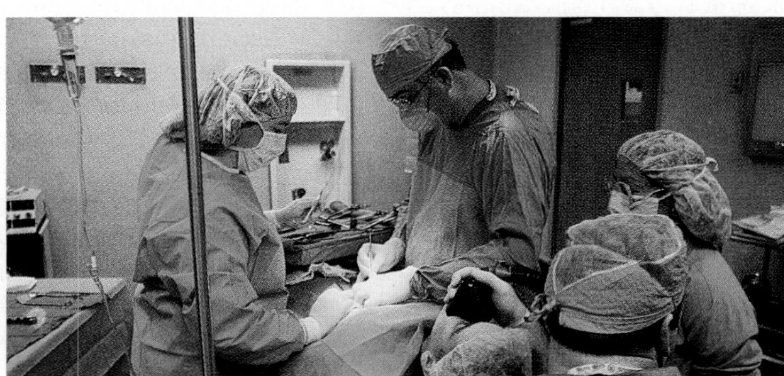

Health insurance covers financial losses resulting from sickness, injury, or disability. Most people carry major medical insurance to supplement their basic hospitalization in order to cover expensive medical procedures, such as this operation.

Approximately 80 percent of all Americans are protected by hospitalization insurance. Most coverage is provided through group plans by employers, although private plans frequently supplement group plans. One of the better-known providers of hospitalization insurance to individuals and employers is Blue Cross/Blue Shield. The Blue Cross and Blue Shield Association coordinates ninety Blue Cross and Blue Shield plans that operate statewide or regionally across the nation as nonprofit hospital and medical service corporations. Recently, Blue Cross/Blue Shield and other insurers have introduced *preferred-provider plans* to cut medical costs. The plans reimburse individuals for medical expenses only if they go to hospitals on their list of approved low-cost providers.

Health maintenance organizations (HMOs) are companies that offer medical care that is paid for in advance in the form of monthly fees and that is given, usually at certain locations, by member doctors.

Other health insurance providers are private insurance companies such as the independent **health maintenance organizations (HMOs).** These companies offer medical care that is paid for in advance in the form of monthly fees and that is given, usually at certain locations, by member doctors. HMOs are a recent cost-cutting measure. The insured's monthly premium covers a variety of medical services.

In addition to hospital insurance, other forms of health insurance are available. *Disability income insurance* replaces income lost when the insured is unable to work because of sickness or injury. *Dread disease insurance* pays medical expenses resulting from the occurrence of a specific illness. The most common form of dread disease policy is cancer insurance. Many group health insurance packages are providing employees with dental and eye-care insurance. Table 20.3 summarizes the basic types of health insurance coverage.

PROPERTY AND LIABILITY INSURANCE

Several types of risk are covered under the general insurance category of property and liability. The more common examples are fire insurance, automobile insurance, theft insurance, fidelity and surety bonds, and liability insurance.

Fire Insurance

Property losses such as the one resulting from this fire in First Interstate Bank building, amount to billions of dollars annually. Most businesses protect themselves from property loss by purchasing fire insurance policies.

Ever since Mrs. O'Leary's cow kicked over the lamp and started the great Chicago fire of 1871, businesses have been worried about property damage caused by fire. The Chicago fire destroyed 17,340 buildings, resulting in an estimated loss of $175 million. The most costly fire in the United States followed the San Francisco earthquake of 1906. In current dollars, the estimated loss from that fire was more than $3.5 billion.[7]

Fire risk is still common. Experts claim that a fire involving a building starts somewhere in the country every fifteen seconds. Property losses by fire amount to billions of dollars annually. The 1980 MGM Grand Hotel fire in Las Vegas resulted in 1,357 death and injury claims. MGM corporate officials and the sixty-three insurance companies involved in the case reached a final settlement of $76 million.[8]

Most businesses protect their property by purchasing a standard fire insurance policy. This policy is usually written for a three-year period and covers losses caused by fire or lightning. Other types of perils may be covered if the insured adds endorsements (extra coverage) to the basic policy. Examples are windstorms, hail, explosion, aircraft collision, smoke, and vandalism. Such all-inclusive coverage may appear in a *multiple-peril policy.*

Table 20.3 Basic forms of health insurance.

Type of Health Insurance	Range of Coverage
Hospitalization insurance	Reimburses the insured for the following expenses arising out of a hospital stay: room and board charges, operating-room costs, general nursing services, X-ray and lab expenses, routine supplies and drugs, and common surgical procedures.
Major medical insurance	Usually provides supplementary coverage for specific medical expenses that exceed the limits of normal hospital insurance. Most plans pay for 80 percent of the additional cost after the insured pays a small initial amount called a deductible.
Disability income insurance	Provides for reimbursement of income loss resulting from accident or illness. Most policies will pay 50 to 75 percent of insured's predisability income.
Dread disease insurance	Provides protection for medical expenses resulting from catastrophic illness such as cancer.
Dental expense insurance	Provides payment for dental-care expenses such as routine hygiene checkups, orthodontia, and oral surgery. Most coverages have deductibles, coinsurance requirements, and maximum payments allowed for specific procedures.
Eye-care insurance	Reimburses the insured for expenses related to the purchase of glasses and contact lenses. Eye exams, special screening tests, lens fitting, and the cost of lenses and frames are usually covered.

It is rare for a building to be completely destroyed as a result of fire. For this reason, property owners often bear part of the loss through coinsurance. The **coinsurance clause** states that the insured party is required to have fire insurance protection equal to some percentage of the replacement value of the property (usually 80 percent). This means that a property owner whose insurance coverage is less than 80 percent of the replacement value will have to bear part of the loss. For example, suppose the replacement value of a clothing store is $100,000, the owner has coverage of $60,000, and fire causes $10,000 in property damage. How much will the insurance company pay? The formula for the insurance company's share of the loss is this:

The ***coinsurance clause*** is the clause in fire insurance policies that requires the insured to have protection equal to some percentage of the replacement value of the property or to pay some of the replacement costs.

$$\text{Insurance company's share of the loss} = \frac{\text{Amount of insurance carried}}{\text{80\% of replacement value}} \times \text{loss}$$

$$= \frac{\$60{,}000}{80\% \times \$100{,}000} \times \$10{,}000 = \$7{,}500$$

In this example, the amount of insurance coverage is only three-fourths of the coinsurance requirement ($60,000 divided by $80,000). Therefore, the insurance company is responsible for 75 percent of the loss, or $7,500. The property owner bears the remaining 25 percent, or $2,500. Coinsurance clauses are more common in industrial coverage than in residential coverage.

Automobile Insurance

Bodily injury liability insurance is automobile insurance that pays claims against the insured that result from injuries to others, including pedestrians, people in the other cars involved in the accident, and passengers in the insured's car.

Medical payments insurance is automobile insurance that pays the medical expenses of the policyholder and passengers in the event of an accident, regardless of liability.

Property damage liability insurance is automobile insurance that pays for damage to others' property caused by the insured car.

Collision insurance is automobile insurance that pays for damage to the policyholder's car, even if the driver is at fault.

If you own a car, you need automobile insurance, which comes in a variety of coverages. The most common coverage is **bodily injury liability insurance.** If a taxicab plows into the back of your car and injures you and your passengers, the owner's insurance company is liable for damages up to a certain amount. Bodily injury coverage stated as 20/40 means that the insurance will pay a maximum of $40,000 per accident and up to $20,000 for the injury or death of one person. If you sue for more than the maximum amounts in the policy, the taxicab owner is liable for the remainder.

One option that many people take is **medical payments insurance,** which pays the medical expenses of the policyholder and passengers in the event of an accident—without regard to liability. This type of policy also covers the policyholder and family members who are hit by a car either while walking or as passengers in someone else's car.

What about the physical damage to the cars? **Property damage liability insurance** covers damage to others' property caused by the insured car. Again, amounts vary according to the degree of risk exposure. In our example, each taxi driver may have property damage protection of up to $50,000. This coverage would pay for the damage to your car, not to the cab. If the owner of the taxi fleet wanted protection for the cars in the fleet, **collision insurance** would be necessary. It pays for damage to the policyholder's car, even if the driver is at fault. Most collision clauses carry a deductible, ranging from $50 to $250. If the taxi fleet owner has a $150 deductible, then the insurance company will pay for damages over this amount. If $1,150 worth of damage was done to the cab that rear-ended your car, for example, the cab owner could collect $1,000 from the insurance company ($1,150 − $150).

Car owners insure themselves against the financial risks of driving by purchasing automobile insurance. With bodily injury liability insurance, the most common coverage, the owner and passengers are covered for damages due to injuries from an accident.

The coverages just discussed are often packaged together in one policy. In addition, people can purchase protection against other types of damage, such as fire, theft, windstorm, hail, and riot, through **comprehensive coverage.** With car thefts on the rise, this type of coverage is becoming more common.

Lastly, **uninsured motorist coverage** is offered as part of many auto policies. This means that the insured can collect damages for bodily injury (and sometimes for auto damage) from the insured's own insurance company if the person's car is hit by the car of an uninsured motorist who is judged to be at fault.

In most states, the burden of payment after a car accident rests with the party judged to be at fault. However, twenty-four states, Washington, D.C., and four provinces in Canada have turned to **no-fault insurance** (see Figure 20.4). This type of insurance is intended to lower insurance premiums by having injured individuals receive payment from their own insurance companies, regardless of which driver is at fault. (See Figure 20.5 for a comparison of no-fault insurance with traditional automobile liability insurance.) If medical costs or property damage exceed a certain amount—which varies by state—then the traditional determinations of fault and the accompanying lawsuits would be permitted.

Comprehensive coverage is automobile insurance that pays for automobile damage other than that caused by collision—for example, fire, theft, windstorm, hail, and riot damage.

Uninsured motorist coverage is automobile insurance that pays for the insured's bodily injury (and sometimes damage to the car as well) if the person's car is hit by the car of an uninsured motorist who is judged to be at fault.

No-fault insurance is automobile insurance under which injured individuals receive payment from their own insurance companies, regardless of which driver is at fault.

Theft Insurance

Property owners are protected against losses from burglary and robbery by **theft insurance.** *Burglary* is defined as breaking into a property for the purpose of stealing. Evidence of forcible entry must be present to prove burglary. *Robbery* is defined as the unlawful taking of property from another person. If it involves the use of weapons, it is termed *armed robbery.* For businesses, burglary is

Theft insurance is insurance that protects property owners against losses caused by burglary and robbery.

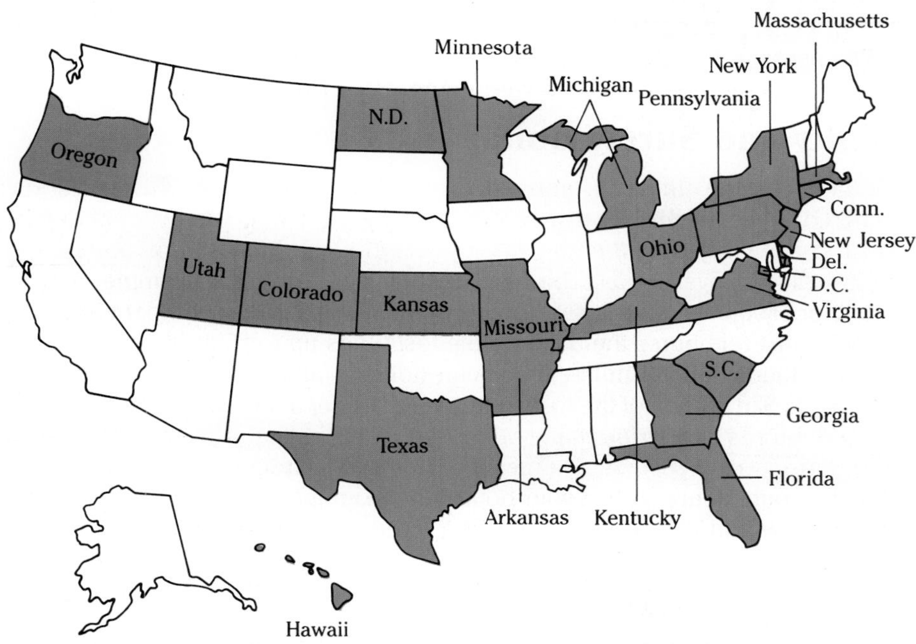

Figure 20.4
States having no-fault automobile insurance systems.

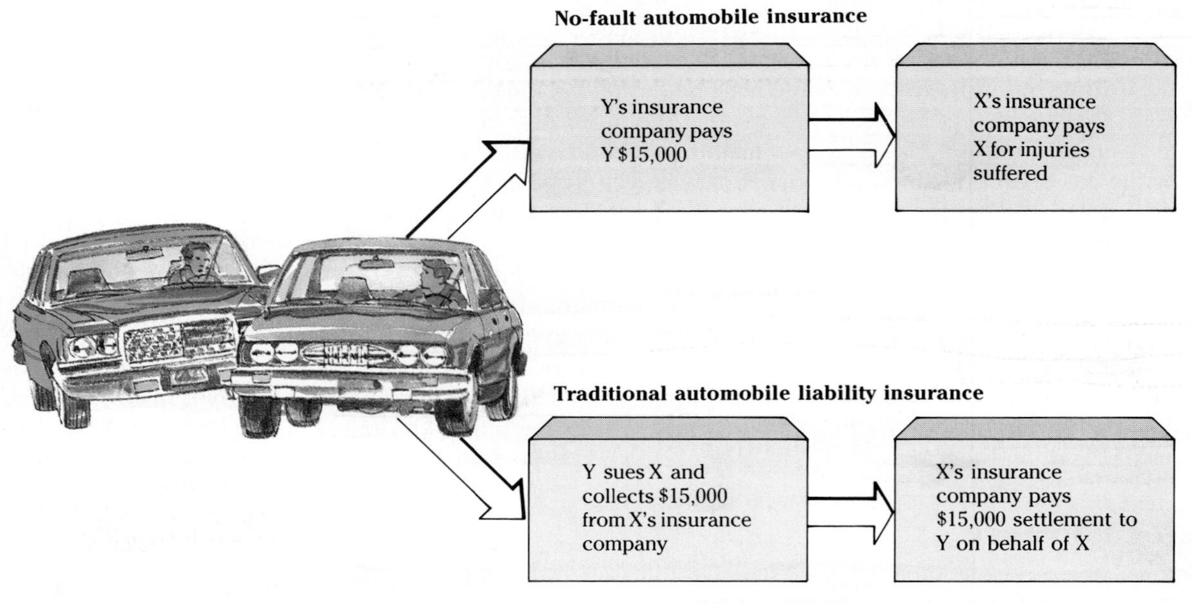

Figure 20.5 No-fault versus traditional automobile liability insurance.

assumed to occur after normal business hours and robbery during normal business hours. The combination of coverages available with theft insurance is complex and varied. The most common business package protects retailers against burglary or robbery from the safe or from inventory.

Fidelity and Surety Bonds

A ***fidelity bond*** is a form of insurance that protects companies against losses caused by theft by employees who occupy positions of trust and have jurisdiction over funds.

Surety bonds are performance bonds—guarantees that a job will be finished within a reasonable period of time or that payment will be made to another company to complete the work.

Liability insurance is insurance that covers the policyholder's liability for injuries to others or for damage to their property.

What happens if an employee embezzles funds from a company? This type of risk is covered by a **fidelity bond,** a form of insurance that protects companies against losses caused by theft by employees who occupy positions of trust and have jurisdiction over funds. The head cashier of a bank, for example, may be bonded for $500,000. If the cashier steals funds, the insurance company that sold the bond must reimburse the bank for the lost funds up to $500,000. Wells Fargo Bank once found that $21 million had been stolen by an inside officer. Fortunately for the bank, $20 million of the loss was covered under a fidelity bond agreement.[9]

Surety bonds are performance bonds—guarantees that a job will be finished within a reasonable period of time. If a home construction company fails to complete a remodeling job on your house, the insurance company that holds the surety bond would pay another contractor to complete the project.

Liability Insurance

Corporations, nonprofit organizations, and individuals alike are often forced to have **liability insurance** (if they can get it). This form of insurance covers

HIGHLIGHT IN BUSINESS PRACTICE

Lloyd's of London: Insurer to the World

For nearly three hundred years, Lloyd's of London has been the largest and most influential insurance market in the world. Lloyd's is not a company but an association of 26,000 member investors from over sixty countries who form syndicates and accept insurance business. Membership, once restricted to the British, was opened to foreigners in 1969. Currently, there are over 2,000 American members (70 percent of Lloyd's business is done in the United States).

The tradition started in the booths of Edwin Lloyd's coffeehouse, when shipowners and others would negotiate face to face. Today, just as then, those seeking insurance visit underwriter "boxes," offering the underwriter a slip of paper that outlines the desired coverage and provides details that might influence the coverage. If the underwriter agrees, he or she initials the slip, indicating how much coverage the syndicate is willing to risk. For these risks, investors can earn large yearly returns. Each day, millions of dollars' worth of insurance is sold without contracts or lawyers.

The insurers do not always make a profit. In 1985, syndicates managed by the Richard Beckett Underwriting Agencies lost $165 million. Beckett investors (over four hundred) were heavily insuring Americans in the areas of medical malpractice, product liability, and pollution. Liability claims on such policies were skyrocketing. The result was payouts that were greater than earned revenues. Because the investors in the Beckett syndicate have unlimited liability, they are responsible for paying off

the entire amount of any claims. Many of these investors believed their syndicate was mismanaged and threatened legal action.

Examples of Lloyd's insurance policies are often spectacular. For instance, eager to cut potential losses of $285 million for three satellites that went astray in 1984, Lloyd's commissioned the space shuttle *Discovery* to recover the $105 million Western Union Westar 6 and the $75 million Indonesian communications Palapa B-2 satellites. The cost to Lloyd's was $5.5 million. In addition, despite losses of well over $525 million, Lloyd's continued to insure thousands of ships sailing the Persian Gulf during the Iran-Iraq War. In total, Lloyd's keeps tabs on over 21,000 ships. And Lloyd's was the first, in 1909, to offer auto insurance and the first to provide insurance on professional athletes such as Larry Bird of the Boston Celtics and Magic Johnson of the Los Angeles Lakers.

policyholders' liability for injuries to others or for damage to their property. Some of the types of auto insurance are liability insurance. Over the past decade, the number of liability suits and the size of awards by juries have rapidly escalated.

Thus there is a greater need than ever for liability insurance. (More on this topic appears in chapter 22.)

Product liability insurance is insurance that covers manufacturers and suppliers of products whose proper use results in personal injury.

Product liability insurance covers manufacturers and suppliers of products whose proper use results in personal injury. Food companies and drug producers are prime candidates for this type of liability insurance. If a canned soup causes botulism or a medication has serious side effects, the victims will probably sue. If current trends continue, manufacturers and retailers may soon be paying annual premiums totaling over $3 billion for product liability insurance.

Other Business Coverages

Ocean marine insurance is transportation insurance that protects against the loss of merchandise transported on the high seas.

Inland marine insurance is transportation insurance that protects against the loss of merchandise shipped by rail, airplane, truck, or barge and on inland waterways.

Business interruption insurance is insurance that provides regular payments to the insured when the business is temporarily shut down because of a catastrophe.

The types of risks faced by businesses are so extensive that a complete explanation of all types of insurance is impossible here. However, a few more deserve at least some mention.

Transportation insurance is used to protect goods in transit. **Ocean marine insurance** protects against the loss of merchandise transported on the high seas. **Inland marine insurance** protects against the loss of merchandise shipped by rail, airplane, truck, or barge and on inland waterways. A popular extension to the traditional inland marine insurance is the *personal property floater.* This insurance covers all perils to goods regardless of location. If you have a personal property floater on your household insurance policy, your personal property may be covered if damaged in transit to campus or stolen from your college residence.

Another type of business coverage worth having is **business interruption insurance,** which provides regular payments to the insured when the business is temporarily shut down because of a catastrophe, such as a fire. The insurance covers lost profits as well as paying for ongoing expenses.

Businesses face many types of risk for which they need insurance. Ocean marine insurance protects the insurance holder against the loss of merchandise, such as this boatload of fish, being transported on the high seas.

Insurance Needs in Service Industries

Small businesses in service industries often have special liability insurance needs. Among these businesses are bars, restaurants, liquor stores, day-care centers, and nursing homes. Their owners need to carry **public liability insurance,** which covers against suits initiated by parties injured on the owner's premises. For instance, if a bartender serves too many drinks to a customer, and the customer then causes a car accident that kills or seriously injures someone, the resulting claims are shifted to underwriters. Because small business owners and others have so many liability insurance needs, they usually purchase an *umbrella policy,* which provides coverage beyond other liability policies.

Public liability insurance is liability insurance that provides protection to organizations and individuals against claims caused by personal injuries or damage to the property of others when the insured is responsible.

Professionals, including midwives, physicians, accountants, architects, and lawyers, are being hard hit by malpractice suits. **Malpractice insurance,** which is closely related to product and personal liability insurance, protects professionals from the risk of being faulted for negligence. For example, famed defense attorney Melvin Belli used malpractice insurance to protect him in the event of suits by clients who believed he lost their cases because of such negligence as not gathering all the evidence needed to clear them. Belli gave up his malpractice insurance (a practice called "going bare or naked") in 1986, when the quote he received for $1 million in coverage was $600,000.[10]

Malpractice insurance is liability insurance that protects professionals from the risk of being faulted for negligence.

Most physicians cannot afford the luxury of "going naked." Many obstetricians have been forced to give up their practices because of the high number of medical malpractice suits in their specialty and the consequent high insurance rates. Often, obstetricians are sued for the consequences of possible improper delivery of a baby, especially if this may be shown as causing brain damage or some other permanent handicap to the child.

Hospitals also purchase special liability insurance. A hospital could be sued for giving responsibility to incompetent nurses or physicians. If a nurse gives the wrong dose of a medication, this could be considered the cause of death or serious injury to a patient. The same accusation could result if a physician did not isolate a patient with a highly contagious disease quickly enough to prevent others from contracting it.

INTERNATIONALIZATION OF THE INSURANCE INDUSTRY

Insurance companies are part of the increasing internationalization of financial services. In 1986, twenty-two U.S. insurance companies were owned by foreign-based corporations, a trend that is expected to continue.[11]

U.S. companies are also finding vast markets overseas. In 1985, U.S. life insurance companies received income exceeding $1.2 billion from overseas operations, and the U.S. insurance industry is currently seeking insurance opportunities in the Middle East. These opportunities range from insuring shippers, to providing life insurance to royalty in oil-rich countries, to insuring a full line of other risks.[12] Of course, companies must take a long-term approach to this market and be especially sensitive to local conditions before they develop a customer base.

BUSINESS PRACTICE EXAMPLE Continues

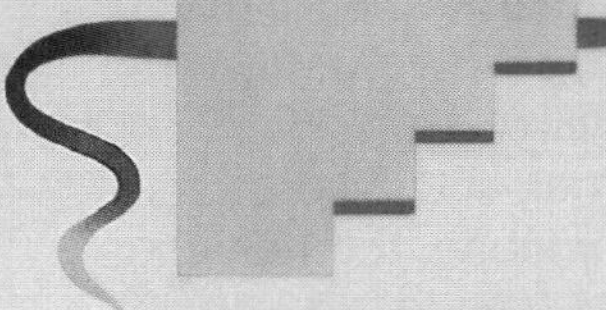

The amount of D & O coverage is shrinking, and the premium costs are skyrocketing. Most companies are limiting coverage to $50 million, and premiums of more than $1 million a year are common.

In response to this tightening market, Marsh & McLennan Inc., the world's largest insurance broker, started a company that is owned by its policyholders. Each corporate policyholder receives $50 million of D & O coverage. The catch, however, is that there is a big deductible. The coverage is only for claims in excess of $50 million. On a $70 million claim, the policy will pay $20 million. The policyholder will be responsible for the first $50 million or will need another policy to pay it.

Issues for Discussion

1. Some insurance executives believe that the tighter market for D & O coverage could lead to an improvement in corporate boards. Do you agree? Explain.
2. Should a company be entitled to a thirty-day notice before a D & O policy is canceled? Explain.
3. Would you assume the risk of serving on a board of directors without liability insurance? Explain.

SUMMARY

Risk is uncertainty about exposure to possible losses or injuries. Businesses deal with risks through avoidance, assumption, reduction, and transfer.

The requirements for an insurable risk are the following: (1) the loss must be predictable, (2) it must be accidental, (3) it must be geographically spread out, (4) it must be measurable, and (5) the costs for insuring it must be economically sound.

Most business risks are underwritten by mutual companies (which earn no profits for their owners) and stock companies (which do earn profits).

The government also offers insurance programs. Among them are social security (which includes old age and survivor's insurance, disability insurance, and Medicare), worker's compensation, and unemployment insurance.

Life insurance comes in three basic forms: term insurance, which provides protection for a specific period of time; whole life insurance, which continues for the insured's lifetime and cannot be canceled as long as the premiums are paid; and universal life insurance, which is a revision of whole life insurance that allows the insured to change the death benefit from time to time or to vary the amount or timing of premium payments.

Life insurance is used in business in several ways. Key executive life insurance covers losses caused by the death of important executives. Credit life insurance is obtained by borrowers to pay off their creditors if they die before their loans are paid back. Group life insurance is purchased as a fringe benefit for employees. Companies also offer employee retirement plans in the form of pension funds that purchase annuities for retiring employees.

Health insurance covers financial losses resulting from sickness, injury, or disability. It includes hospitalization insurance and major medical insurance. Health maintenance organizations (HMOs) are providers of prepaid medical care given by member doctors, usually at certain locations. Some other types of health insurance are disability income insurance, dread disease insurance, dental insurance, and eye-care insurance.

Some common examples of property and liability insurance are fire insurance, automobile insurance, theft insurance, fidelity and surety bonds, and liability insurance. Fire insurance includes multiple-peril policies and coinsurance clauses.

Automobile insurance comes in the forms of bodily injury liability insurance, medical payments insurance, property damage liability insurance, collision insurance, comprehensive coverage, and uninsured motorist coverage. Some states have turned to no-fault insurance, which has injured individuals compensated by their own insurance companies if the costs involved are not very high.

Theft insurance protects against losses from burglary and robbery. Fidelity bonds protect against theft by trusted employees. Surety bonds guarantee that jobs will be finished on time.

Liability insurance covers injuries to others or damage to their property. It includes product liability insurance. Other business coverages include ocean marine insurance, inland marine insurance (and the personal property floater), and business interruption insurance.

Small businesses in service industries may need personal liability insurance, and professionals often need malpractice insurance. Hospitals require their own liability insurance.

Many U.S. insurance companies are owned by foreign-based corporations, and many American-owned insurance companies do business abroad.

KEY TERMS

Beneficiary p. 599
Bodily injury liability insurance p. 606
Business interruption insurance p. 610
Coinsurance clause p. 605
Collision insurance p. 606
Comprehensive coverage p. 607
Credit life insurance p. 602
Fidelity bond p. 608
Group life insurance p. 603
Health insurance p. 603
Health maintenance organizations (HMOs) p. 604
Inland marine insurance p. 610
Insurable interest p. 594
Key executive life insurance p. 602
Liability insurance p. 608
Major medical insurance p. 603
Malpractice insurance p. 611
Medical payments insurance p. 606
Medicare p. 598
No-fault insurance p. 607
Ocean marine insurance p. 610
Premium p. 592
Product liability insurance p. 610
Property damage liability insurance p. 606
Public liability insurance p. 611
Pure risk p. 593
Risk p. 591
Self-insurance p. 592
Speculative risk p. 593
Surety bonds p. 608
Term insurance p. 600
Theft insurance p. 607
Underwriting process p. 593
Uninsured motorist coverage p. 607
Universal life insurance p. 602
Whole life insurance p. 600
Worker's compensation p. 598

CHECK YOUR LEARNING

Reread the following learning objectives. Each objective is followed by a few questions. Answering these questions accurately will help you retain the most important concepts discussed in this chapter. After answering each question, check your answer with the key at the end of this chapter. (*Hint:* If you have doubt regarding the correct response, consult the page whose number follows the answer.)

Circle:

A. Discuss the different methods used by business to manage risks.

T F 1. Risk refers to certainty regarding the predictability of losses.

a b c d 2. The most common method used in managing business risks is: (a) risk avoidance; (b) risk assumption; (c) risk reduction; (d) risk transfer.

B. Distinguish between a pure risk and a speculative risk.

T F 1. Betting on a horse race is a type of speculative risk.

T F 2. A pure risk has no chance for gain—only loss.

C. List the requirements for an insurable risk.

a b c d 1. In order for a risk to be insurable, it must be: (a) predictable; (b) geographically concentrated; (c) accidental; (d) both a and c.

a b c d 2. The law of large numbers is best exemplified by a(an): (a) mortality table; (b) present value table; (c) annuity table; (d) conversion table.

T F 3. Before purchasing any type of insurance, an individual must have an insurable interest in the item or person being insured.

D. Compare and contrast mutual and stock insurance companies.

T F 1. Over 90 percent of the private insurance companies in the United States are mutual companies.

T F 2. Mutual companies earn profits for their shareholders.

a b c d 3. Most private insurance companies in the United States are classified as: (a) legal reserve; (b) stock; (c) mutual; (d) fractional reserve.

E. Discuss the roles of selected government insurance programs.

a b c d 1. Which one of the following government insurance programs is funded by a payroll tax: (a) federal deposit insurance; (b) GI life insurance; (c) federal crime insurance; (d) social security.

T F 2. The retirement age for maximum Social Security benefits will be 70 by 2000.

F. Explain the differences among the basic types of life insurance.

T F 1. Term insurance seldom builds cash value.

a b c d 2. Which form of life insurance offers the greatest amount of control and flexibility to the policyholder: (a) universal life; (b) limited-pay life; (c) variable life; (d) term.

a b c d 3. All other things being equal, which one of the following types of life insurance initially offers the most protection at the least premium cost: (a) endowment; (b) twenty-payment life; (c) term; (d) whole life.

G. List four examples of how businesses use life insurance and describe them.

T F 1. Credit life insurance is usually a form of whole life insurance.

T F 2. Partnerships are fortunate not to have the need for life insurance.

a b c d 3. Most employees rely heavily on: (a) key-executive insurance; (b) credit life insurance; (c) group insurance; (d) permanent insurance.

H. Provide a brief explanation of the common forms of health insurance.

a b c d 1. Which type of health insurance replaces income lost when sickness or injury prevents a person from working: (a) major medical; (b) hospitalization; (c) disability income; (d) term insurance.

T F 2. The most common form of health insurance is hospitalization insurance.

a b c d 3. Fee-for-service medical systems are facing growing competition from: (a) health maintenance organizations; (b) Medicare; (c) visiting nurse associations; (d) Blue Cross/Blue Shield.

I. Compare and contrast the various types of property and liability insurance.

T F 1. Auto insurance usually contains a collision clause.

T F 2. Fire insurance for businesses is normally written with a coinsurance feature.

a b c d 3. Which one of the following types of insurance covers ships at sea: (a) inland marine insurance; (b) personal property floater insurance; (c) ocean marine insurance; (d) surety bonds.

a b c d 4. Which type of insurance has been affected by the no-fault principle: (a) malpractice insurance; (b) theft insurance; (c) business interruption insurance; (d) auto insurance.

QUESTIONS FOR REVIEW AND DISCUSSION

1. Define the key terms listed at the end of the chapter.
2. Do you agree or disagree with the following statement: You can forget about risk management once you purchase insurance. Explain.
3. Lloyd's of London insures speculative risks. Is this normal underwriting procedure? Explain.
4. List the characteristics of an insurable risk and give some examples of such risks. Can an insurable risk become uninsurable? Explain.
5. Would you expect to find any significant differences between the premium rates of mutual and stock companies? Talk to a representative of each kind of company and ask both to quote premiums for certain kinds of life insurance. Are there any significant differences in the actual quotes?
6. What role does the federal government play in providing insurance? Should this role be expanded or curtailed? Explain.
7. George is thirty-three years old, married, and has two children. His salary as a foreman is $24,800 per year. George believes his group life insurance (twice his annual salary) is enough coverage. Should George have a personal life insurance policy? Should he carry protection on his family? Are there any possible losses for which George is not covered? Is there any other coverage you would advise him to get?
8. Discuss some specific business uses of life insurance.
9. Ask an insurance salesperson if no-fault auto insurance reduces costs for individual companies. Explain.
10. Distinguish between a surety bond and a fidelity bond.
11. Do you agree or disagree with the following statement: Malpractice insurance results in higher settlements for all consumers of this insurance. Explain.
12. Find four articles dealing with property damage caused by fire. What types of losses and coverages were involved?
13. Talk to the owner of a gas station. Ask the owner to explain the types of risks faced by the business. Does the station have self-service pumps? If so, have the owner's insurance rates increased as a result?

CONCLUDING CASE

Run for Your Life—Insurance

Staying physically fit has many benefits, one of which is lower life insurance premiums. Insurance industry analysts have determined that fitness is not a fad but has become a permanent part of many American life-styles. Actuaries can predict that fitness keeps policyholders healthier. These physically fit individuals live longer so their premium payments continue over longer spans.

In response to this trend, ITT Life Insurance Corporation of Minneapolis has offered the physically fit nonsmoker insurance protection that is often 50 percent lower than the norm for average sedentary policyholders at other companies. To qualify for the fit-nonsmoker policies that ITT and other companies offer, applicants must take a thorough examination. Physical and medical standards are applied to determine that the applicant has been following a schedule of vigorous physical exercise. Cholesterol, blood pressure, and heart and pulse rates are measured before and after exercise.

According to the president of ITT Life, Robert W. McDonald, too many insurance companies "are getting fat on America's longer lives." McDonald emphasizes that many companies find themselves paying out fewer death claims because premium rates were determined on pre-1960 actuarial data. The experts did not anticipate that life expectancy would increase as much as it has. It appears that policies for physically fit nonsmokers may create a substantial financial incentive for a more healthful American life-style.

Issues for Discussion

1. Given the criteria used for risk analysis, should fit-nonsmokers be given lower rates for life insurance? Why or why not?
2. Should the standards for physical fitness be adjusted for age? Sex? Physically handicapped? Why or why not?
3. List three questions you would ask an agent about the fit-nonsmoker policy.

NOTES

1. *1988–1989 Property/Casualty Fact Book* (New York: Insurance Information Institute, 1988), p. 71.
2. *Life Insurance Fact Book* (Washington, D.C.: American Council of Life Insurance, 1988), pp. 88, 100.
3. *1987–1988 Property/Casualty Fact Book,* p. 48.
4. *Life Insurance Fact Book,* p. 15.
5. Ibid., p. 19.
6. Ibid., p. 30.
7. *1984–1985 Property/Casualty Fact Book* (New York: Insurance Information Institute, 1984), p. 62.
8. "Hotel Insurance Told," *The Tribune-Star,* November 30, 1980, p. 8.
9. Jim Drinkall, "Amount in Alleged Fraud at Wells Fargo Doesn't Rate High on List of Bank Cases," *Wall Street Journal,* March 4, 1981, p. 14.
10. Carol J. Loomis, "Naked Came the Insurance Buyer," *Fortune,* June 10, 1988, pp. 67–72.
11. Louis Rukeyser, *Business Almanac* (New York: Simon & Schuster, 1988), p. 333.
12. Josh Martin, "Middle East Big Market for U.S. Insurance Companies," *Tribune-Star,* 1988.

CHECK YOUR LEARNING ANSWER KEY

A. 1. F, *p. 591*
   2. d, *p. 592*
B. 1. T, *p. 593*
   2. T, *p. 593*

C. 1. d, *p. 594*
   2. a, *p. 594*
   3. T, *p. 594*
D. 1. F, *p. 596*
   2. F, *p. 596*
   3. a, *p. 595*

E. 1. d, *p. 597*
   2. F, *p. 597*
F. 1. T, *p. 600*
   2. a, *p. 602*
   3. c, *p. 600*

G. 1. F, *p. 602*
   2. F, *p. 602*
   3. c, *p. 603*
H. 1. c, *p. 604*
   2. T, *p. 603*
   3. a, *p. 604*

I. 1. T, *p. 606*
   2. T, *p. 605*
   3. c, *p. 610*
   4. d, *p. 607*

PART

A NEW WORLD OF BUSINESS OPPORTUNITY

CHAPTER

21

Computers and Information Management

CHAPTER

22

The Legal Environment of Business

CHAPTER

23

Business in a Global Environment

CHAPTER

21

COMPUTERS AND INFORMATION MANAGEMENT

LEARNING OBJECTIVES

After reading this chapter you should be able to:

1. Describe the five generations of computers.
2. Differentiate between hardware and software.
3. Give examples of input and output devices and mass storage devices.
4. Describe the functions of the central processing unit.
5. Discuss the primary uses for BASIC, COBOL, and FORTRAN.
6. Discuss various computer applications in business.
7. Describe the functions of word processing, spreadsheet, and database management software.
8. Discuss three problems of the computerized workplace: information privacy; computer security; and automation, robotics, and unemployment.

OUTLINE

Business Practice Example: Can Technology Bring the Apparel Industry Back Home?

Computers and Information

Information Processing

The Evolution of Computers

- Five Generations of Computers
- Mainframes, Micros, and Minis

Computer Hardware—How Computers Work

- The Central Processing Unit
- Mass Storage Devices

Software and Computer Programming

- Computer Programs
- Programming Languages
  - Machine Languages
  - BASIC
  - COBOL
  - FORTRAN

Management Information Systems

Computer Applications in the Business Environment: Key Areas

- Accounting
- Finance
- Marketing
- Manufacturing

Popular Business Software

- Word Processing Software
- Spreadsheets
- Database Management Systems

Office Automation

- Problems of the Computerized Workplace
  - Information Privacy
  - Computer Security
  - Automation, Robotics, and Unemployment
- Trends and Developments

Summary

Key Terms

Check Your Learning

Questions for Review and Discussion

Concluding Case: Computers Change Restaurants

Notes

Check Your Learning Answer Key

Highlight in Business Practice: Managing People with Computers at Visible Changes, Inc.

BUSINESS PRACTICE EXAMPLE

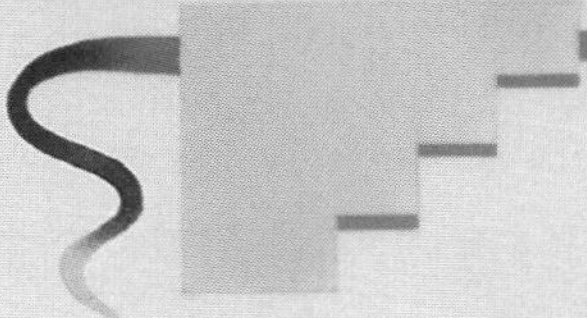

Can Technology Bring the Apparel Industry Back Home?

Computer-aided technology is bringing the U.S. apparel-making industry back to life. The manufacturing of clothing is one of the most difficult of all factory operations and among the least susceptible to automation—which is why nearly half the $125 billion worth of garments purchased in this country are made largely by hand in relatively low-wage countries such as Korea and Taiwan, despite tall trade barriers.

New technological breakthroughs in the cutting and sewing of fabrics, however, are giving U.S. manufacturers reason for hope—and encouraging them to bring more of their overseas business back home. The switch to U.S. manufacturing reflects economic factors such as the weak dollar, tougher quotas, and rising Far East wages. But at the heart of this revival in domestic apparel manufacture is new technology, from new automated sewing assembly lines to computer-aided design systems.

Take VF Corp. as an example. The giant jeans-maker has managed to keep most of its production here by spending up to 4 percent of sales on automation and equipment upgrading—$110 million in 1988 alone. Its Vanity Fair division uses computers to design new styles of bras and panties, to turn the designs into patterns to suit all sizes, and to configure layouts on fabric for minimum waste. The data are sent to the factory floor, where mechanical cutters (lasers are used in other plants) slice thick bolts of fabric into parts for assembly. These steps, when performed manually, require weeks of painstaking labor. Now, computer-aided design and manufacturing technology, which is just starting to make its way into apparel plants, has shortened the process to a few days. Labor unions, already decimated by Asian imports, are going along with the automation.

The new technology is giving domestic apparel makers an important advantage over their Asian competitors. Because of fickle fashion trends and the practice of changing styles as often as six times a year, retailers want to be able to keep inventories low. This calls for quick responses from apparel makers that can offer fast turnaround on smaller lots in all styles, sizes, and colors. Asian suppliers, half a world away, typically require three months or more in advance.

Meanwhile, Haggar Apparel, the Dallas-based pants maker, uses a computer network to receive up-to-date sales information from electronic cash registers at its 2,500 retail outlets. Haggar is now able to restock slacks covered by the network every three days, instead of about every seven weeks. This type of service is marginally more expensive, admits Bernard Olsoff, president of the marketing co-op Frederick Atkins, but he adds, "I'm willing to pay that extra buck to reduce my inventory risk."

Does all of this mean U.S.-made apparel will one day again be exported in quantity? Just possibly. "I think there is tremendous potential," says James High, Sr., chief executive officer of Seminole Manufacturing. "Technology became an issue of survival. We're a quick-turning industry today. Give it five years."

WHAT'S AHEAD

This chapter discusses a number of computer-related issues that modern businesspeople like those at Haggar Apparel must understand and appreciate in order to apply computers to the best advantage of their organizations. Topics include the evolution of computers, computer hardware and software, programming, computer applications in business, problems of computerization, and trends and developments in computers.

COMPUTERS AND INFORMATION

The rapid growth of the use of computers in organizations in the past twenty years has been nothing short of revolutionary. The computer's power to manage information is unprecedented. Organizations of all kinds, including businesses, government agencies, and hospitals, now depend on computers as an integral part of their operations. Companies use computers to become or remain competitive, and new applications are constantly being created. By now, the following examples of computer use are standard operating procedure:

- In financial management, computer links are established among offices worldwide so that current information on cash flow is instantly available to the investing company.
- In marketing, the computer is used for market research, giving users access to a tremendous range of information on customers, competitors, and the environment.
- In advertising and promotion, desktop publishing technology lets workers design, write, edit, and publish promotional pieces of all types in a fraction of the time it took just several years ago.
- In customer service, employees instantly determine the availability and location of products and shipments, thereby building customer satisfaction.

Computers give a boost to virtually every industry. As Figure 21.1 shows, Frederick Transportation uses computers and a shared U.S.-French satellite to track the progress of its trucks nationwide and internationally. Through this tracking, the company is able to plan efficient return trips, offer help in breakdowns, and even discourage the theft of trucks and their shipments.

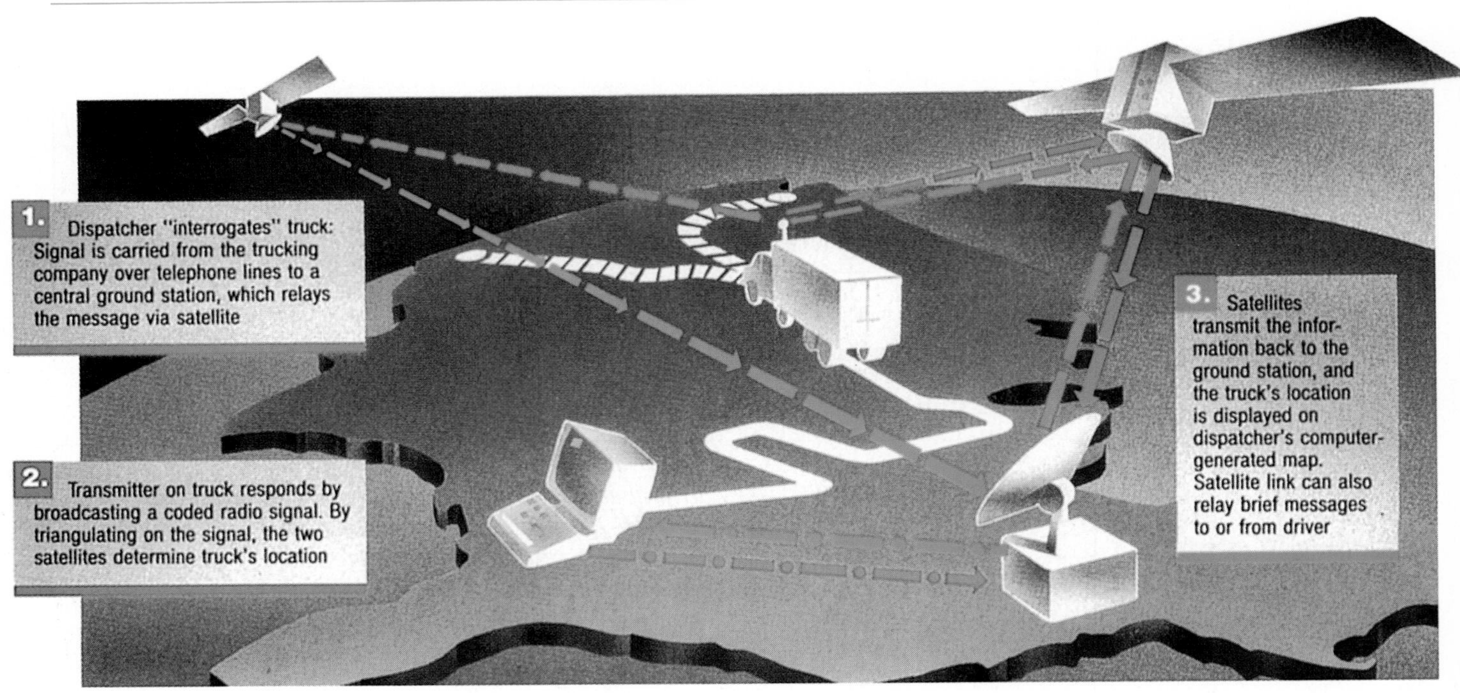

1. Dispatcher "interrogates" truck: Signal is carried from the trucking company over telephone lines to a central ground station, which relays the message via satellite
2. Transmitter on truck responds by broadcasting a coded radio signal. By triangulating on the signal, the two satellites determine truck's location
3. Satellites transmit the information back to the ground station, and the truck's location is displayed on dispatcher's computer-generated map. Satellite link can also relay brief messages to or from driver

Figure 21.1 How Frederick Transportation uses computers and a U.S.-French satellite to monitor its fleet of trucks.

Computers are an essential business tool with a fascinating range of applications, some of which we'll see in the sections ahead. Basic to all computer applications are *information* and *data,* the building blocks of any system.

Information is processed data used for business planning and decision making.

Data are raw facts and figures that relate to the functioning of an organization.

Batch processing is a method of handling computer-processed data in which the data are stored and then processed in batches.

INFORMATION PROCESSING

Information is processed data used for business planning and decision making. **Data** are raw facts and figures that relate to the functioning of an organization. Although a tremendous amount of data are generated in an organization, the data must be processed before they become information. *Processing* includes reading, sorting, calculating, storing, and reporting the data.

The electric company, for example, gathers data from each customer once a month: account number and kilowatt-hours used. This data must be processed. Using the account number, the computer can determine the customer's name and mailing address by checking a stored file of sorted account numbers. The computer calculates the monthly charge for the kilowatt-hours consumed, according to a formula, and adds the taxes, which it also calculates according to a formula. It computes late charges and adds them to the total amount. Finally, the computer combines all of this information and prints it in the appropriate places on a billing statement. Only then, after the data have been processed, can the electric bills be mailed.

HIGHLIGHT IN BUSINESS PRACTICE

Managing People with Computers at Visible Changes, Inc.

One of the last places you might expect to find a ground-breaking computer system is in a hair salon. But that's exactly where John McCormack of Visible Changes, Inc. has used computers to put his innovative management theories into practice. In an industry in which mom-and-pop establishments eke out the most meager of profits, McCormack's Houston-based chain of sixteen hair salons generates revenues three to four times the industry average.

Visible Changes, Inc. uses a computer to track the amount of business done by each employee. Every Monday, the computer gives reports to the haircutters about how they did the previous week: the number of customers they did and the number who requested them. And they also get a report on how they did for the same week the year before—and each of the previous five years, if they've been with the company that long. The master computer also pulls out the name of any cutter who has had three recuts in a given month—when the customer doesn't like a cut and comes back in. A list ranking of the amount of business done by each employee is posted for everyone to see. Everybody is shooting at everybody else, in a friendly way, to do better. So even if you yourself don't have the drive to want to be in the top 100 people in the company, people in your salon are going to push you.

McCormack creates a positive atmosphere using the computer generated data by showing employees what their earning potential is. When people can do three or four times the industry average, they get excited by it. In the salon industry, if stylists do $30,000 a year gross after four or five years, they're doing well. Visible Changes, Inc. is averaging twice that for any stylist who has been with the company for more than three years.

If the numbers indicate that a problem has occurred, such as too many recut requests, McCormack can find out right away where it is happening. More than likely, it's in one particular salon, and the stylists in that salon have a problem with the salon management. McCormack sits down, talks with the manager, and has meetings with the salon staff to resolve the problem.

McCormack believes that although most people do not know how to use a computer to help them manage people, it is really just a matter of going right to the basics. If you want to break an industry record, every haircutter in the salon is in a key role.

Most data processing can be categorized as **batch processing**—a method of handling computer-processed data in which the data are stored and then processed in batches. Utilities such as electric and gas companies use batch processing. **Online processing** is a method of handling computer-processed data in which the data are processed as they are entered into the computer. An automatic teller machine, for example, processes banking transactions as they occur.

Online processing is a method of handling computer-processed data in which the data are processed as they are entered into the computer.

THE EVOLUTION OF COMPUTERS

We have used computing and counting devices throughout history. Fingers and toes were probably the first such devices. They are convenient for counting and adding. The decimal number system is based on the fact that most people have ten of each. Among the earliest computers were the ancient Babylonian abacus and calculating sticks.

Five Generations of Computers

Thus far, there have been five generations of computers, the first starting in the 1940s during the intense war effort.

The first generation of modern computers used the *vacuum tube* and mechanical relays as major circuit elements and punched cards as the primary storage medium. These early computers were massive in size and generated considerable heat. Thus they required large rooms and extra cooling. They also broke down frequently. An example of this generation was the ENIAC (electronic numerical integrator and calculator) computer, developed in 1946.

In the 1950s, businesses began to acquire and use computers. This next generation of computer technology used *transistors,* a miniaturized version of vacuum tubes, which required considerably less power to operate and gave off much less heat. The primary storage medium was magnetic tape, developed in the early 1950s. The IBM 1401, one of the early commercial computers, was a second-generation model.

Third-generation computers, developed in the mid-1960s, were smaller, faster, and more powerful than ever before. Their *integrated circuits* placed thousands of transistors on a tiny sliver of silicon. This new circuit device was called a "chip." Magnetic disks replaced tape as the primary storage medium, and computers became much less expensive. The IBM 370 and DEC PDP 11/34 were third-generation computers.

In the fourth generation, during the late 1970s, computers became even smaller, combining many thousands of transistors on a single quarter-inch-square integrated circuit. This led to the development of the **microprocessor**—one or more computer chips containing the basic functions of arithmetic, logic, and storage necessary for the computer to process data. Magnetic disks remained the primary storage medium, but memory became much less costly as manufacturers squeezed more and more transistors onto each chip. Fourth-generation computers were much smaller and much less expensive than previous computers. The microprocessor became part of many noncomputer devices, such as automobile engines, stereo equipment, and the talking Coke machine.

A ***microprocessor*** is one or more computer chips containing the basic functions of arithmetic, logic, and storage necessary for the computer to process data.

The fifth generation of computers, the generation being designed today, focuses on computer "thinking." **Artificial intelligence (AI)** is the segment of computer science that focuses on developing computers with capabilities similar to those of the human mind. The ultimate goal of artificial intelligence is to build a computer that can simulate the human's abilities to reason and make decisions.[1]

Artificial intelligence (AI) is the segment of computer science that focuses on developing computers with capabilities similar to those of the human mind.

Expert systems are among the most useful and marketable products that have evolved from artificial intelligence research. An **expert system** is a computer program based on expert human knowledge and designed to help people solve technical problems in well-defined areas such as engineering, law, and medicine. Individual expert systems are developed by a computer programmer, who extensively "picks the brains" of a real expert in a particular field. The resulting program

An ***expert system*** is a computer program based on expert human knowledge and designed to help people solve technical problems in well-defined areas such as engineering, law, and medicine.

is based on the highly detailed information the expert has provided on the field of expertise.

For example, an expert system was created for an oil company. An engineer who had been with the company for fifty years and who knew virtually every problem—and its solution—that could occur at an oil-drilling site, announced plans for retirement. The company hired a computer programmer to interview the engineer and create an expert system. Thus, while the engineer was getting set to leave the company, the company was working to retain much of his knowledge in the system.

Expert systems are helpful in many areas of endeavor. They are, however, expensive to create. Artificial intelligence research has not yet resulted in a computer that can think. Although many look forward to the development of such a computer, others doubt that a truly intelligent machine will ever come to pass.

Mainframes, Minis, and Micros

Modern computers can be classified into three categories: mainframes, minis, and micros. **Mainframe computers** are the largest and most powerful computers, with price tags in the hundreds of thousands to over a million dollars. These computers are able to handle hundreds of simultaneous users. They often occupy entire rooms and require special power, cooling, and environmental equipment. Mainframe computers are used in airline reservation systems, government agencies, banks, universities, and anywhere else high levels of computing power are needed.

Mainframe computers are the largest and most powerful computers.

Advanced mainframe computers are called supercomputers. A **supercomputer** is a computer with an extremely large memory, the most advanced processing capabilities, and the highest possible performance speeds.[2] Supercomputers are being designed with state-of-the-art features, including unique cooling systems, the ability to execute several programs simultaneously rather than sequentially, and excellent graphics capabilities.[3] Prices of these computers can exceed $10 million.

A ***supercomputer*** is a mainframe computer with an extremely large memory, the most advanced capabilities, and the highest possible performance speeds.

The market for supercomputers is limited because only a few organizations can justify or afford the advanced uses such computers offer. The National Weather Service uses supercomputers for calculating complex mathematical simulations. Oil companies use them to process large amounts of geological and production data. The military uses them for complex planning, logistics, and code-breaking functions.

A **minicomputer** is a computer that is larger than a microcomputer but smaller and less powerful than a mainframe computer. Minicomputers require about the space of a file cabinet and do not need a special computer room environment. They typically cost from $20,000 to $40,000. They are used by smaller businesses and for *distributed data processing* in larger businesses. In this type of processing, departments or remote plants have their own minicomputers, each linked to the others and to a central mainframe computer. Distributed processing allows each unit to do the bulk of its own data processing locally but provides the power of a single large computer when the individual machines are linked together in a network.

A ***minicomputer*** is a computer that is larger than a microcomputer but smaller and less powerful than a mainframe computer.

Microcomputers, also called personal computers (PCs), are computers that are smaller and generally less powerful than either mainframes or minicomputers. They occupy about as much space as a notebook (the laptop computer) to a large typewriter. In some cases, the entire circuitry resides in a single circuit board

Microcomputers are computers that are smaller and generally less powerful than either mainframes or minicomputers. They are also called personal computers (PCs).

less than one square foot in size. The costs of micros range from only a few hundred dollars to over $10,000, and their performance, considering their size and cost, is remarkable. Apple computers and the IBM PCs are only two of many brands of microcomputers.

Various parts of microcomputers and an explanation of what each part does are presented in Figure 21.2. The performance of some high-end microcomputers approaches that of minicomputers at a fraction of the cost.

Hardware is all of the physical equipment related to computers, such as keyboard, monitor, and printer.

Software is the computer programs or instructions that tell the computer what to do.

Input and output (I/O) devices are the hardware used to get information into or out of the computer, including keyboard, voice activator, monitor, mouse, disk drive, modem, and printer.

The ***central processing unit (CPU)*** is the working part of the computer, where calculations are done and control of the computer is maintained.

COMPUTER HARDWARE—HOW COMPUTERS WORK

Hardware is all of the physical equipment related to computers, such as the keyboard, monitor, and printer. **Software** is the computer programs or instructions that tell the computer what to do.

Although computers vary in size and performance, they all have the same functional parts: an input device, a central processing unit, a storage device, and an output device. **Input and output (I/O) devices** are the hardware used to get information into or out of the computer, including keyboard, voice activator, monitor, mouse, disk drive, modem, and printer.

The Central Processing Unit

The working part of the computer, where the calculations are done and control of the computer is maintained, is the **central processing unit (CPU)** (see Figure 21.3). It consists of three parts: (1) the control unit, (2) the arithmetic/

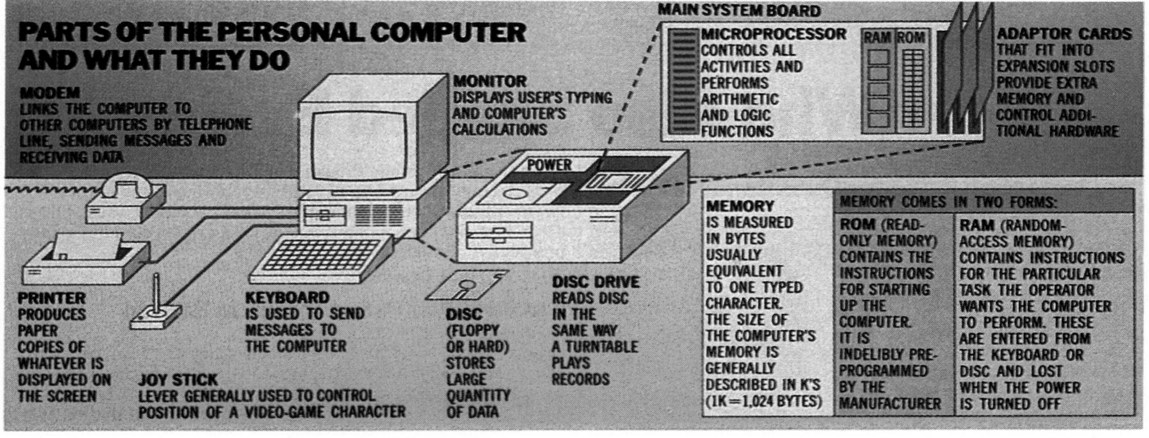

Figure 21.2 Parts of the personal computer and what they do.

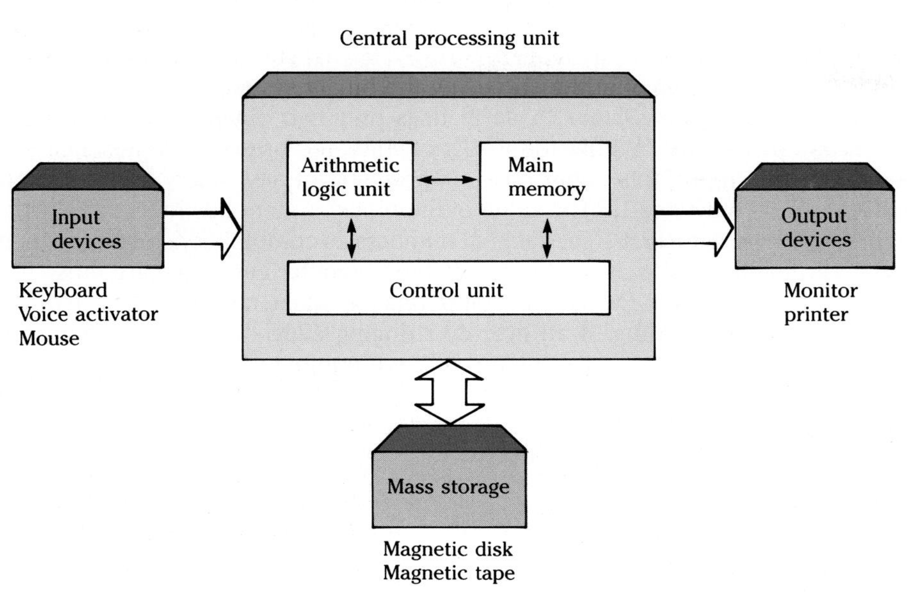

Figure 21.3
Functional diagram of a computer. Although computers vary in size and performance, they all have the same functional parts: an input unit, a storage device, and an output device.

logic unit (ALU), and (3) the main memory. The *control unit* manages the CPU and monitors the flow of data and information through the computer. The *ALU* performs the arithmetic calculations while executing the computer program. The *main memory* holds the program currently being executed and some of the data used by that program.

BUSINESS PRACTICE EXAMPLE Continues

The apparel industry puts many different types of computer hardware and software components to use, depending on the purpose. A microcomputer with an advanced graphics software program can be effectively used in the design process. A minicomputer linked to the various work stations in a manufacturing plant can run the automated machines. A mainframe computer with linkage terminals in all areas of the business can be the backbone of a company's information system. The data generated from the different processes (such as retail sales, inventory control, and manufacturing) are integrated with all the other data, creating an information system that can be used to make intelligent business decisions and maintain the competitive advantage.

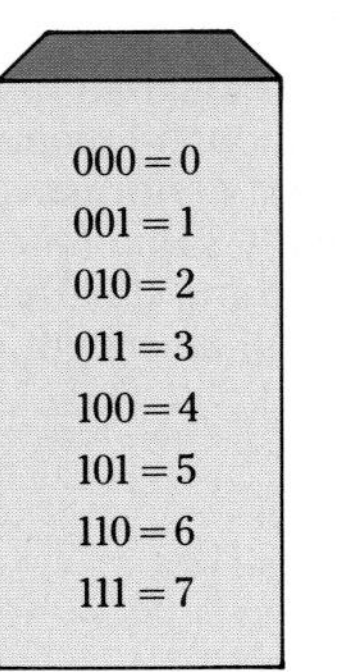

Figure 21.4
Circuits in the CPU perform arithmetic with the binary system, which uses only two digits: 0 and 1.

The CPU's power is often measured by the amount of main memory the CPU can use and by the number of instructions it can execute per second (usually given in millions of instructions per second, or MIPS). The circuits within the CPU perform a special kind of arithmetic using the binary system.

The *binary number system* (base 2) uses only two digits, 0 and 1, each of which is termed a **bit.** Within the CPU's circuits, the presence or absence of a certain voltage represents either 0 or 1. The result of any binary arithmetic operation can be only 0 or 1. (The value of the binary system lies in its simplicity.) Figure 21.4 shows the first eight decimal numbers as combinations of three binary digits, or three bits. The only "decisions" the computer can make are those that involve either yes or no. Even small computers can make millions of these binary decisions in the twinkling of an eye. By stringing eight or sixteen or thirty-two bits together, the computer can represent large numbers and can perform arithmetic operations on them very quickly. A group of adjacent digits, letters, or other characters that are often shorter than a word and that are processed as a unit are a **byte.** Each byte is usually eight bits.

A ***bit*** is the digit 0 or 1 in the binary numbering system.

A ***byte*** is a group of adjacent digits, letters, or other characters that are often shorter than a word and that are processed as a unit—usually eight bits.

Mass Storage Devices

The part of the computer that holds the programs and data until the CPU is ready to process them is the **mass storage device.** The most common media for mass storage are magnetic tape and magnetic disks.

The ***mass storage device*** is the part of the computer that holds the programs and data until the central processing unit is ready to process them.

Magnetic tape is a magnetized metal-coated ribbon on which data are stored. It follows the same recording principles as audio tape. Once magnetized, the tape retains the data indefinitely, even when it is removed from the computer or when the electricity is turned off. The much smaller main memory within the CPU is temporary—it "forgets" its contents as soon as power is removed. Magnetic tape is less expensive than magnetic disks per character stored.

Magnetic tape is a magnetized metal-coated ribbon on which data are stored.

Magnetic tape is used primarily in mainframes and minicomputers and for backing up data. Data files are copied from the disk onto reels of tape, which are then stored. Large amounts of data are saved for archival purposes on magnetic tape. Microcomputer users sometimes use standard cassette tapes for storage.

A **magnetic disk** is a thin, metal-coated circular magnetic surface on which data are stored. The *read-write head,* a device similar to a phonograph tone arm, is used to store the data on the disk and to recover it from the disk. There are two kinds of magnetic disks: floppy disks and hard disks. **Floppy disks**—flexible magnetic disks in protective envelopes—are the most convenient and portable medium for storing and transporting data. The disks come in three formats: 3½ inch, 5¼ inch, and 8 inch. **Hard disks**—magnetic disks on a rigid base—are high-capacity storage disks that can hold up to thousands of times more data than typical floppy disks. Hard disks can be installed either inside or outside the computer.

A ***magnetic disk*** is a thin, metal-coated circular magnetic surface on which data are stored.

Floppy disks are flexible magnetic disks in protective envelopes, used mainly with microcomputers.

Hard disks are high-capacity magnetic disks on a rigid base that can hold up to thousands of times more data than typical floppy disks.

SOFTWARE AND COMPUTER PROGRAMMING

We have to tell the computer what to do. Without proper instructions, it is no more useful than a record player without records.

Applications software tells the computer how to solve specific problems for the organization. There are thousands of different applications software programs available, including inventory, payroll, and other general ledger software; as well as word processing and spreadsheet applications programs. Applications software is not a part of the computer's operating system.

Systems software, usually written by the computer's manufacturer, provides internal instructions that permit the computer to operate, and to run applications software. The systems software that controls the CPU's resources and provides communication between parts of the computer is called the *operating system.*

Computer Programs

The detailed description of the precise steps the computer is to follow in order to solve a problem is a **computer program.** Most programs follow the same pattern of logic that you would use to solve the problem yourself. An **algorithm** is the procedure of solving a problem by a finite series of steps. Algorithms serve as the basis of computer programs.

There are several steps in writing a program. The first step is to *analyze the problem* to determine what needs to be done. The second step is to *design the program.* A **flowchart**—a schematic diagram of the steps necessary to solve a problem—is often used at this stage. After the design has been approved, the next (third) step is to *write the program,* using a **programming language**—a set of symbols, with rules for how to combine and interpret them, that is the basis for writing computer programs.

After the program is written, it is entered into the computer's memory. At this point, the program might contain errors, or bugs. The fourth step, therefore, is to *test and debug the program.* It is not unusual for this step to take a great deal of time, particularly for large, complex programs. For example, to rewrite a payroll program according to new tax laws might take a week, but debugging it could take an additional two weeks. Generally, however, the more time spent in analyzing the problem and designing the program, the less time spent fixing errors. The final step in developing the program is to *prepare the program's documentation,* the instructions on how to use the program.

Once the program is installed and working, however, it is not considered finished. As the organization gains experience with the program, suggestions for changes or enhancements are often made. In addition, errors may still exist, and they must be fixed. Program changes such as these are called *program maintenance.*

Computer programming is part science, part art. It involves creativity and a sense of logic and organization. Testing and debugging requires curiosity and patience. Some experts predict that in the future many managers will do their own programming.

A ***computer program*** is the detailed description of the precise steps the computer is to follow in order to solve a problem.

An ***algorithm*** is the procedure of solving a problem by a finite series of steps.

A ***flowchart*** is a schematic diagram of the steps necessary to solve a problem.

A ***programming language*** is a set of symbols, with rules for how to combine and interpret them, that is the basis for writing computer programs.

Programming Languages

Computers have two broad categories of programming languages: low-level and high-level. The computer can execute programs written in low-level languages directly, without substantial translation. These programs execute very quickly, so they are useful for systems software and certain applications software that involves many calculations. However, low-level programs are difficult to write and take longer to debug than high-level programs.

Programs written in high-level languages are significantly easier to write and test, but at a penalty of slower execution. There are explicit standards for most high-level languages, which allow programs to be transported between computers, often without change. Most applications software is written in high-level languages. With the exception of machine language, all the languages described next are high-level languages.

Machine Languages

Machine language is the most elementary programming language for processing instructions and data; it is expressed as a string of 0s and 1s.

The most elementary programming language for processing instructions and data is **machine language,** which is expressed as a string of 0s and 1s. Machine language programs are the binary codes that are directly executed by the CPU. These programs are difficult to write and especially difficult to modify.

BASIC

BASIC—Beginner's All-purpose Symbolic Instruction Code—is an easy-to-learn programming language that is used with both minicomputers and microcomputers.

A programming language that is comparatively easy to learn but still possesses significant capabilities for solving complex problems is **BASIC**—Beginner's All-purpose Symbolic Instruction Code. Used with both minicomputers and microcomputers, BASIC typically is one of the first languages people learn. It was developed in part to help science and engineering students learn FORTRAN but quickly became a useful tool on its own. Most microcomputers come with BASIC as the standard language. Some versions of BASIC have been used for sophisticated business applications. However, large business programs are difficult to write in it.

COBOL

COBOL—Common Business Oriented Language—is a programming language specifically designed to solve business problems that require a significant amount of file processing.

A programming language specifically designed to solve business problems that require a significant amount of file processing is **COBOL**—Common Business Oriented Language. It handles large amounts of character data, such as names and addresses, and its programs can have 10,000 or more instructions. The vast majority of mainframe business applications use COBOL.

FORTRAN

FORTRAN—FORmula TRANslation—is a programming language that focuses on solving scientific problems.

A programming language, developed in the early 1960s, that focuses on solving scientific problems is **FORTRAN**—FORmula TRANslation. Once the most popular computer language, FORTRAN is now used primarily for "number crunching." It is most widely employed in engineering and mathematical applications. FORTRAN has a number of weaknesses, and its popularity has diminished somewhat.

MANAGEMENT INFORMATION SYSTEMS

A ***management information system (MIS)*** is a formalized procedure for collecting, storing, and retrieving information to help managers make decisions.

A formalized procedure for collecting, storing, and retrieving information to help managers make decisions is a **management information system (MIS).** It typically uses computers to organize past, current, and projected information on the total environment (both inside and outside the company). The MIS determines information needs, then collects, sorts, summarizes, and analyzes data and outputs information in usable form (see Figure 21.5).

The primary purpose of the MIS is to assess the overall information needs of the organization and furnish this information to the three levels of management—

Figure 21.5
How a management information system works.

top, middle, and lower-level—by the most efficient and effective means possible.

MIS systems vary from company to company. Some organizations have large, formally designated MIS departments, with one or more MIS managers and personnel to operate the system. Large MIS departments are most likely to be found in large corporations. As organizations get smaller, MIS systems tend to be more unstructured and informal.

MIS systems are used differently by different levels of management. As we saw in chapter 6, as managers move upward in an organization, they are less involved with the everyday production process (technical areas) and more involved with managing the organization as a whole. As you go from lower-level to top management, information focuses on broader issues in larger segments of the organization. For example, top management might need information relating to one or more divisions or subsidiaries of the company and to overall financial performance. Lower-level managers might need information regarding operational procedures, policies, and plans.

An MIS includes one or more databases. A **database** is a collection of all the data stored in one or more files. A **corporate database** contains facts regarding all important facets of company operations. It typically includes financial as well as nonfinancial information. A **user database** is a database developed by an individual user. User databases may be derived from but are not necessarily limited to a corporate database. For example, a production manager who is interested in lowering production costs might build a user database that includes departmental performance facts regarding reject rates and materials purchased from various suppliers. Such a database might help the manager lower costs by indicating which materials typically result in high reject rates.

This police department uses a management information system (MIS) to collect, store, and retrieve information from their 911 telephone log. The data is quickly accessible when needed.

A ***database*** is a collection of all the data stored in one or more files.

A ***corporate database*** is a database containing facts regarding all important facets of company operations.

A ***user database*** is a database developed by an individual user.

BUSINESS PRACTICE EXAMPLE Continues

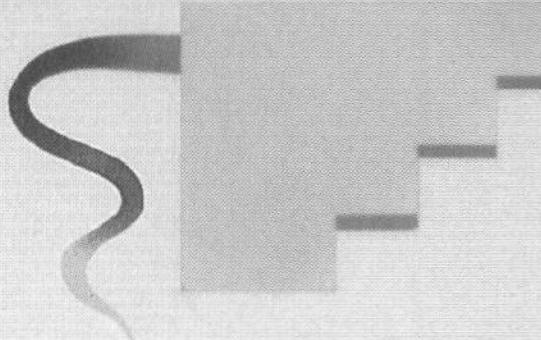

The garment industry is finding that the use of management information systems can save significant amounts of money by allowing for reduced inventory stocks. The data generated by retail sales is fed into a computerized storage and processing system. The manufacturing plants can read this information and determine which items are the hottest selling and which are not moving.

Plans to increase or decrease production on certain items can be made in a matter of days rather than the months it would take to convey the information to and plan the changes for a foreign operation halfway around the globe. Inventories can be kept low by making small runs of popular items. The industry can then keep up with fickle, fashion-conscious consumers without having to maintain huge inventories of products that may never be sold.

Accounting is the most common business computer application. This accountant uses a wide variety of software to keep track of every activity in the accounting process.

COMPUTER APPLICATIONS IN THE BUSINESS ENVIRONMENT: KEY AREAS

Accounting

Gone are the days of pencil, ledger, and journal. The most common business application for computers is in accounting. There is an abundance of software available to keep track electronically of almost every activity in the accounting process, as described in chapter 17. Below we describe the general tasks performed by software programs available for key business functions.

Basic bookkeeping tasks are handled by *general ledger software.* These programs maintain accurate account information, and prepare income statements, balance sheets, and funds flow statements. An important benefit is the speed with which the reports can be prepared at the end of an accounting period.

Billing software generates customer statements, and *accounts-receivable software* stores customer credit sales and helps firms track overdue accounts. Reports list the accounts by age, highlighting those whose balances have not been paid on time. Potential bad debts may be avoided by the use of this tool.

Accounts-payable software is used by businesses to pay their own bills. These programs can display accounts by due date, highlighting those that offer discounts for early payment. By reminding a firm of coming deadlines, the programs can save firms a good deal of money. Most accounts-payable programs also have the capability of printing checks automatically.

Payroll software calculates gross pay and determines the various deductions automatically. The information is stored, and paychecks are printed every pay period. At the end of the quarter and the year, the computer generates any required reports, such as social security reports. It also prints W2 forms for the employees. Payroll is often one of the first functions for which a company will use a computer.

Inventory control software accounts for issues and receipts of inventory, keeping an accurate count of the balance on hand. Many inventory control programs track demand for each item over a period of time, which is an aid to planning production quantities. The programs can notify the purchasing department to reorder an item when the quantity drops to a certain level. They can also value the stock on hand for tax or other purposes.

Finance

Financial planning, analysis of capital expenditures, and cash management activities can be managed by *financial software.* Financial software programs manage organizational funds.

Capital expenditure analysis software is used by persons responsible for capital budgeting, in which projects that involve large sums of money are evaluated. These programs can help determine if such investments are worthwhile. The analyst can use the computer to do several types of analyses in a short time, allowing greater consideration of all aspects of the decision.

Financial personnel often project their short-term cash requirements by using *cash management software.* High interest rates have made short-term cash borrowing very expensive. By anticipating cash needs in advance, a company can arrange financing more economically. If excess cash is predicted, these funds can be profitably invested, even if only for a few days. One local government body set up an arrangement with a bank to invest its excess funds for Saturdays and Sundays. On Monday morning the funds were returned to city coffers. Over several months, the interest amounted to more than $100,000.

Marketing

Market research, product and competitor analysis, advertising effectiveness, pricing and promotion studies, and a host of other applications are accomplished by different *sales and marketing software.* The computer can analyze sales data to discover trends in demand and to reveal information about the marketplace.

Software can be used to determine the efficiency of each salesperson by product or geographic territory. Sales managers can use these studies to plan sales quotas and to allocate salespeople for specific products or customers.

Many companies use *tracking software* to maintain the status of customer orders. Thus a customer can receive accurate information on production, shipment, and delivery. Overnight delivery services such as Federal Express have developed highly sophisticated computerized systems to track packages in order to guarantee overnight delivery.

Manufacturing

As we saw in chapter 10, computer aided design and manufacture (CAD/CAM) is used by designers of machine parts and other items—such as the garments described in the Business Practice Example—to sketch designs on a screen, with the computer determining precise measurements (CAD). Computer-aided manufacturing (CAM) maps out in a program the process involved in producing a product.

POPULAR BUSINESS SOFTWARE

Word Processing Software

Word processing is a method of using computers to create, edit, store, and print documents.

A major labor-saving advance in document management, **word processing software** electronically creates, edits, stores, and prints documents. Until the advent of word processing programs, typists spent hours manually correcting, cutting and pasting, and otherwise arranging documents. Errors often meant that whole pages had to be retyped. Word processing programs such as WordPerfect and MicroSoft Word allow users to create documents to specification in just a fraction of the time it took to do the same tasks on a manual typewriter, and to revise documents as often as is needed. Many word processing programs allow charts and tables to be merged into the document. Different typefaces can be selected, and the margins can be aligned to give a typeset look. Dictionary programs—usually called "spell-checkers"—can be used to check documents for accuracy. (See Figure 21.6 for an example of a word processing program display.)

Spreadsheets

Spreadsheets are computer programs that accept data in the form of columns and rows, which the user can then manipulate.

Computer software that accepts data in the form of columns and rows, which the user can then manipulate, are **spreadsheets.** They are used by managers at all levels to organize, analyze, and run what-if analyses. A what-if analysis is a simulation of a business situation using different data for selected decision areas. For example, a manager might first determine the profitability of the company under present conditions. The manager might then ask "what if" materials costs increased by 5 percent, "what if" products were sold at different prices, and so on. Popular spreadsheet software such as Lotus 1-2-3 and Interactive Financial Planning System (IFPS) allow managers to ask many what-if questions.

Database Management Software

Database management software is computer programs that allow individuals to define, manipulate, and output database information.

Computer programs that enable individuals to define, manipulate, and output database information are **database management software.** For example, assume that a database contains hourly wage rates for all employees in all divisions of an organization, along with other data such as age, length of service, and five-year wage rate histories. Database management software allows management to generate individual reports, such as a listing of the present average hourly wage for each job in each division. Examples of popular database management programs are DBase IV and RBase System V.

OFFICE AUTOMATION

Computers have had a dramatic impact on white-collar workers, both clerical and managerial. In addition to placing computers on desktops to increase the productivity of these employees, many organizations have installed computerized telephone systems, electronic mail systems, and fax machines.

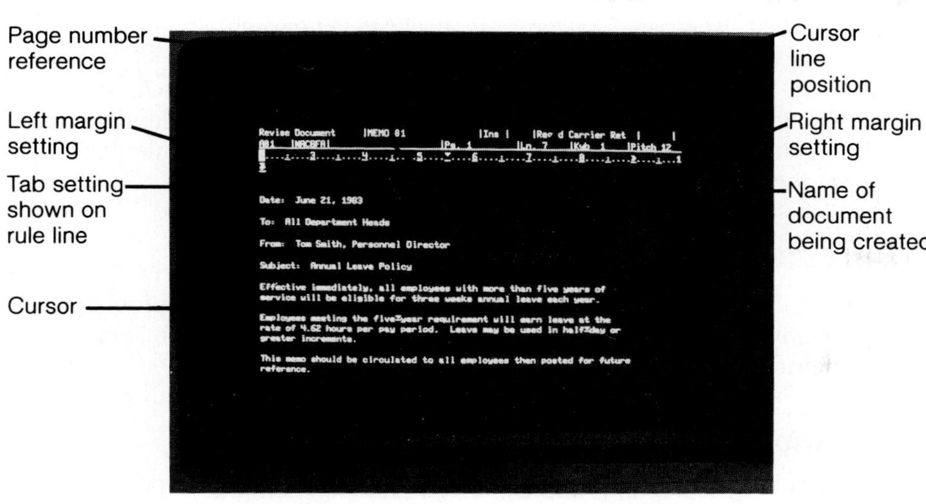

Figure 21.6
A word processor display.

In many offices, telephones have been transformed into sophisticated communications systems, which improve productivity with features such as call forwarding, call waiting, and speed dialing of frequently called numbers. Additional capabilities include automatic conference calls, programmed calling with prerecorded messages, and computerized switchboards. Some new phone systems even allow voice messages to be digitized and stored in the computer's disk, so the recipient can retrieve them at will. A single verbal memo can be electronically sent to dozens of individuals.

To reduce the flow of paper, many offices have adopted *electronic mail systems*—usually called "electronic mail" or "electronic mailbox." Managers can use the computer to send out messages, reports, charts, and graphs electronically to a single individual or to a selected group. Messages coming in can be read on monitors or printed on paper. Replies can be issued immediately. All messages

Some people fear that the increasing use of automation, such as that shown in this factory, will result in widespread unemployment. Evidence indicates just the opposite; many service and support industries have grown up around computer operations.

can be transferred as soon as the senders complete them, thus cutting delivery time by days. Electronic mail systems are as effective between offices in different cities as they are between floors in one building.

One of the latest additions to the electronic office is the *fax machine.* ("Fax" is short for "facsimile.") Fax machines transport documents via telephone lines to their targeted destination, providing a copy of the document in minutes to the receiver at the other end.

Problems of the Computerized Workplace

As useful as computers are, their progress has not been without problems. Invasions of privacy, computer fraud, and the fear of being replaced by computers have combined to slow the progress of information systems.

Information Privacy

Invasion of privacy is not new, nor is it linked only with computers. But computer databases have become the focus of a measure of fear and suspicion. The fear is that unauthorized people can easily access private information. In fact, there have been a sizable number of such abuses, both intentional and accidental.

The accuracy and validity of the stored data is sometimes also suspect. The local credit bureau, for example, maintains a valuable source of financial data about most families in the area. When you apply for credit, your credit history is usually checked by the bureau. If there are errors in your file, you may be unfairly denied credit.

It is necessary, then, to program controls into the system to ensure data integrity and privacy. Care should be taken to store only the data that are necessary and to delete unneeded data regularly. Access to data should be controlled, and the utmost care should be taken to ensure that the data collected are accurate.

Fortunately, efforts are being made to safeguard computer information. Legislative actions have affirmed the need to maintain data security. The *Privacy Act of 1974* provides guidelines for federal agencies in handling data. Other legislation established procedures for data maintained by the IRS, by banks and other financial institutions, and for electronic funds transfer systems, through which funds are exchanged between computers. In addition to Congress and the courts, certain industrial associations promote privacy measures. The Data Processing Management Association regularly sponsors seminars in this area, and the American Civil Liberties Union has worked to protect personal data.

Computer Security

The rapid increase in the numbers of computers and people with access to databases has led to a tremendous increase in breaches in computer security. Some experts place the cost as high as $1 billion a year. Until recently, however, incidents of data piracy, sabotage, and theft of high-technology secrets have not received widespread publicity. Most companies would prefer not to publicize their computer break-ins for fear that it would only encourage others.

Computer "criminals" include disgruntled employees, mischievous students, professional criminals, and even international terrorist rings. Industrial espionage is becoming more common as companies try to catch up with rapidly changing technologies or try to gain a competitive edge.

Automation, Robotics, and Unemployment

Some people fear that the increasing use of automation and robots will result in widespread unemployment. The fact is that some unskilled jobs, particularly those that are unpleasant or dangerous, have indeed been eliminated. But it is not at all clear that computers will cause a reduction in the total number of jobs. In fact, evidence indicates just the opposite. A host of service and support industries have grown up around computer operations, in addition to the companies that manufacture the hardware and software.

However, some experts paint a bleak picture for workers who lack the skills necessary to do the jobs created by the new technology. Education and retraining will play an important role in preparing workers for these changes. The short-term effect may be severe in certain industries, but the long-term benefits of increased productivity may include more jobs for American workers. (For more information on robotics see chapter 11.)

Trends and Developments

In the past ten years, technology has dramatically changed the ways in which companies operate. Many futurists believe that technology will change the workplace even more significantly in the next ten years than in the last ten. According to these people, within the next ten years, the following will occur:[6]

1. *More and more organization members will be using microcomputers.* The number of microcomputers in offices is expected to quadruple, to 46 million by the year 2000. Figure 21.7 illustrates the expected rise in the use of these computers from 1990 to 2000. The challenge facing workers will be to take the microcomputer beyond its word processing and spreadsheet applications to even more useful and more powerful business applications.
2. *Computers that use voice capabilities will become more commonplace.* Workers will be able to enter data into a computer simply by speaking. For example, a manager tracking the number of products sold in various sales territories could simply dictate relevant data into a computer rather than using the key-

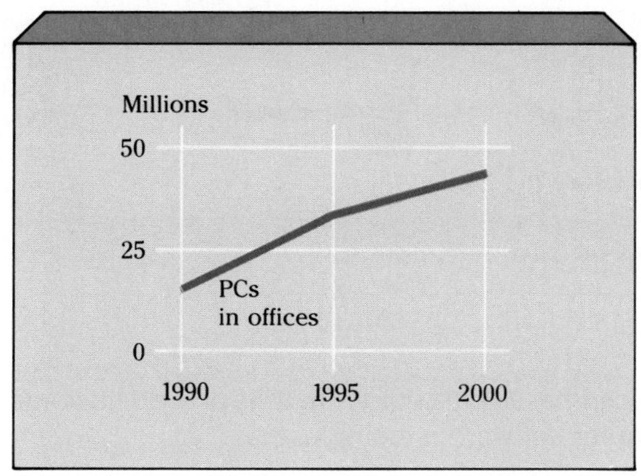

Figure 21.7
The expected growth of personal computers in offices from 1990 to 2000.

Figure 21.8
How groupware works.

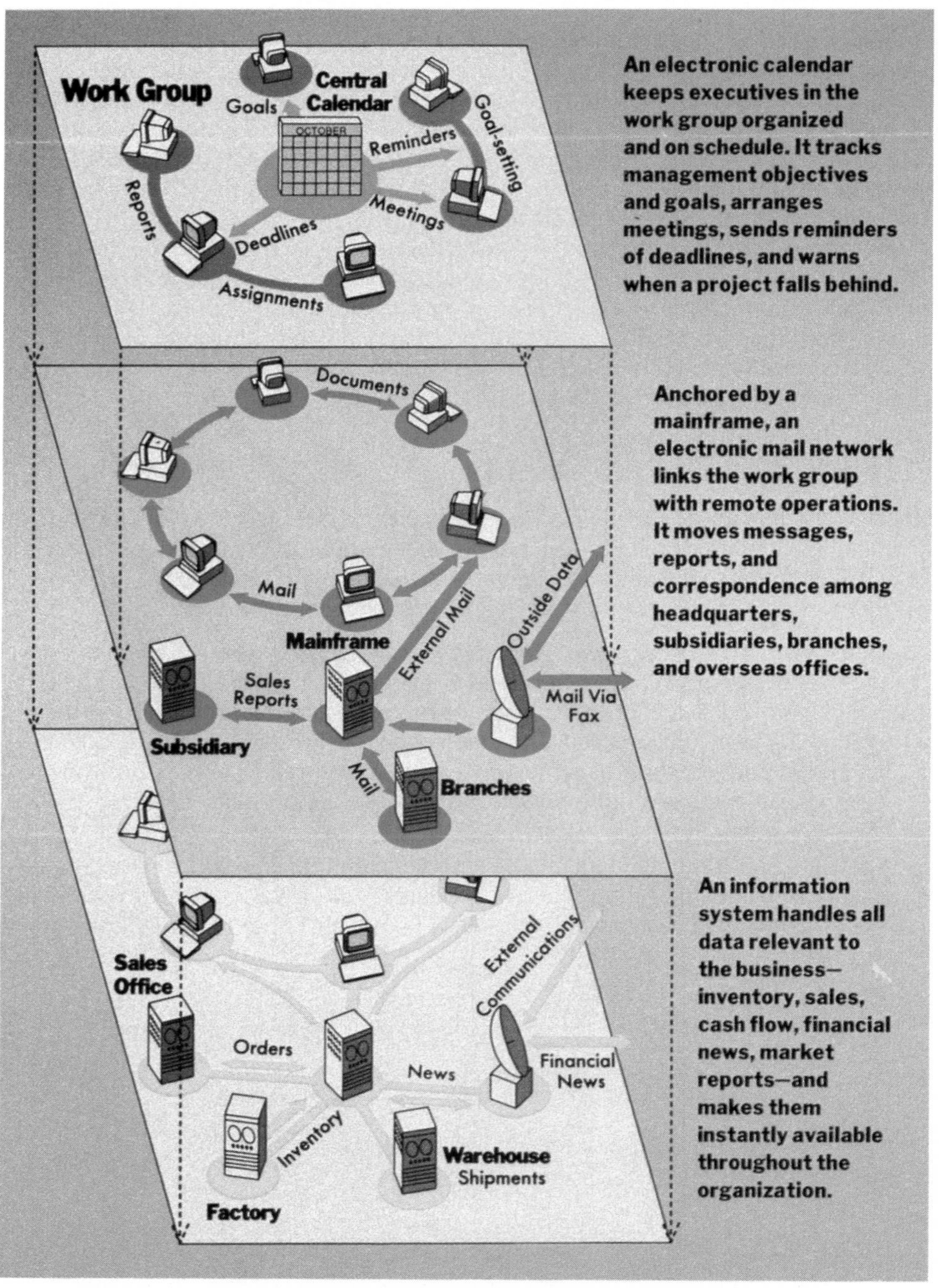
Work Group
Goals
Central Calendar
OCTOBER
Reminders
Goal-setting
Meetings
Deadlines
Reports
Assignments
An electronic calendar keeps executives in the work group organized and on schedule. It tracks management objectives and goals, arranges meetings, sends reminders of deadlines, and warns when a project falls behind.
Documents
Mail
Mainframe
External Mail
Outside Data
Sales Reports
Mail Via Fax
Subsidiary
Mail
Branches
Anchored by a mainframe, an electronic mail network links the work group with remote operations. It moves messages, reports, and correspondence among headquarters, subsidiaries, branches, and overseas offices.
Sales Office
External Communications
Orders
News
Financial News
Inventory
Warehouse
Shipments
Factory
An information system handles all data relevant to the business—inventory, sales, cash flow, financial news, market reports—and makes them instantly available throughout the organization.

board. After voiced-based data entry, analysis of the data could proceed through whatever computer software is being used.

3. *More management oriented computer software will become prevalent.* A type of computer software currently being developed to help coordinate the daily

tasks of management is *groupware* (see Figure 21.8). One groupware software package, called *The Coordinator,* arranges meetings, sorts electronic mail, keeps track of organizational objectives and who is to achieve them, monitors the progress of individuals and groups in achieving objectives, and sends organization members updates about their success in reaching the objectives for which they are responsible. Software of this sort increases the speeds at which data are accumulated and decisions are made, which gives managers more time to spend on other company matters.

4. *Managers will be spending more time trying to keep abreast of technological innovations.* Perhaps more than at any other time in our history, we are in the midst of an information-technology revolution. As a result, a critical challenge for managers of the future will be to keep up with technological advances and to implement them so as to ensure an advantage over the competition.

BUSINESS PRACTICE EXAMPLE Continues

Computer-aided design and computer-aided manufacturing (CAD/CAM), discussed in chapter 11, has proved its value in the design and manufacture of many products. Its use in automobile design is particularly well known. Recently, the garment industry has found that CAD/CAM can also be applied to the design and manufacture of clothing. A designer begins by developing a rough sketch or idea, then uses a computer graphics display as a drawing board to construct the design. When the design is completed, a sophisticated CAD system will allow the designer to ensure that the parts will fit together and that there will be no interferences when other parts are subsequently assembled. One size and style of garment can be turned into all the patterns and variations required to make a complete line of the article.

Issues for Discussion

1. In what way has the garment industry been able to make use of CAD/CAM capabilities?
2. How can information help a manager reduce inventory stocks?
3. What types of computer equipment are required for the various processes in the apparel industry?

SUMMARY

The rapid growth of computer use has been overwhelming. Organizational areas in which computers are being used include marketing, financial management, and customer service. In general, computers use either batch processing or online processing to manipulate data and provide managers with critical information.

For all of our history, we have used computing and counting devices. Key events in the evolution of computers include the use of vacuum tubes during the 1940s, transistors in the 1950s, integrated circuits in the 1960s, microprocessors in the 1970s, and artificial intelligence and expert systems in the 1980s.

Modern computers can be classified into three categories. The first category, mainframe computers, contains the largest computers, with the highest price tags. Advanced mainframes are called supercomputers. Minicomputers, the second category, are about the size of a file cabinet and cost far less than mainframes. Microcomputers, the smallest computers, occupy about as much space on an office desk as a typewriter. For any of these categories, computer equipment is generally known as hardware. Programs, or instructions, that tell the computer what to do are called software.

In general, the functional parts of the computer are an input device, a central processing unit (CPU), a storage device, and an output device. The CPU is the working part of the computer, where calculations are done and control of the computer is maintained. Input and output devices respectively represent vehicles for getting data and programs into the computer and for getting processed data out of the computer. A mass storage device is where the programs and data are kept until the computer processes the data. Devices include magnetic tape and magnetic disks.

A computer program is a detailed description of the precise steps the computer is to follow in order to solve a problem. Writing a program entails analyzing the problem to be solved, designing a program to solve the problem, writing the program, debugging the program, and preparing the program's documentation. Commonly used languages for writing programs are BASIC, COBOL, and FORTRAN.

Computer applications in business include accounting programs, financial programs, and marketing programs.

A management information system (MIS) is a formalized procedure for providing managers with information that will assist them in decision making.

Some business applications for computer software are in the areas of spreadsheets, database management software, and office automation.

There are many advantages to using computers in the workplace. There are also potential problems. The problems are in the areas of information privacy; computer security; and automation, robotics, and unemployment.

Computer technology and use will change substantially in the next ten years. Some of the changes include greater use of microcomputers, voice capabilities in computers, groupware, and more managerial time devoted to keeping up with technological innovation.

KEY TERMS

Algorithm p. 631
Artificial intelligence (AI) p. 626
BASIC p. 632
Batch processing p. 624
Bit p. 630
Byte p. 630
Central processing unit (CPU) p. 628
COBOL p. 632
Computer program p. 631
Corporate database p. 633
Data p. 624
Database p. 633
Database management software p. 636
Expert system p. 626
Floppy disks p. 630
Flowchart p. 631
FORTRAN p. 632
Hard disks p. 630
Hardware p. 628
Information p. 624
Input and output (I/O) devices p. 628
Machine language p. 632
Magnetic disk p. 630
Magnetic tape p. 630
Mainframe computer p. 627
Management information system (MIS) p. 632
Mass storage device p. 630
Microcomputer p. 627
Microprocessor p. 626
Minicomputer p. 627
Online processing p. 625
Programming language p. 631
Software p. 628
Spreadsheets p. 636
Supercomputer p. 627
User database p. 633
Word processing p. 636

CHECK YOUR LEARNING

Reread the following learning objectives. Each objective is followed by a few questions. Answering these questions accurately will help you retain the most important concepts discussed in this chapter. After answering each question, check your answer with the key at the end of this chapter. (*Hint:* If you have doubt regarding the correct response, consult the page whose number follows the answer.)

Circle:

A. Describe the five generations of computers.

1. A primary characteristic of early computers was the lack of reliability due to excess heat generation.

T F

2. As computers have evolved, each generation's machines have become faster but more expensive than those of the previous generation.

3. Integrated circuits have meant a tremendous size reduction of the computer.
4. The fifth generation of computers involves artificial intelligence.

B. Differentiate between hardware and software.

T F

1. Computers cannot "think" for themselves—software is necessary to provide directions.

2. Minicomputers were developed for businesses that didn't need all the power of a mainframe computer.

C. Describe the functions of the central processing unit.

T F

1. Data and information are essentially the same thing.

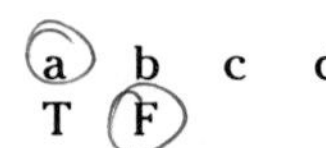

2. The ALU is responsible for: (a) calculations; (b) input; (c) controlling the CPU; (d) mass storage.
3. Mass storage is used to temporarily hold programs and data until needed.

4. Despite size differences, all computers have these functional parts: (a) some input device; (b) CPU; (c) dot matrix printer; (d) mass storage; (e) main memory. (Circle all that apply.)

D. Give examples of input and output devices and mass storage devices.

T F

1. The floppy disk is an output device.

T F

2. Hard disks are low-capacity storage disks.

T F

3. The read-write head is used to store and recover data from disks.

4. The following can be considered mass storage devices: (a) magnetic tape; (b) dot matrix printer; (c) floppy disk; (d) monitor; (e) plotter. (Circle all that apply.)

E. Discuss the primary uses for BASIC, COBOL, and FORTRAN.

1. BASIC is the primary commercial language.
2. FORTRAN is used primarily for scientific data processing.

a b c d e

3. Which of the following languages is the CPU's own internal language: (a) BASIC; (b) COBOL; (c) FORTRAN; (d) machine language; (e) none of the above.

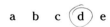

F. Discuss various computer applications in business.

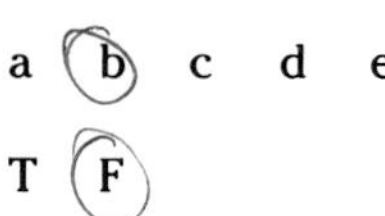

1. As discussed in the chapter, the application of the computer to cash management is most closely related to: (a) marketing; (b) finance; (c) management performance appraisal; (d) none of the above; (e) all of the above.
2. The MIS is used mainly to store company performance records and is only rarely used for managerial decision making.

G. Describe the functions of word processing, spreadsheet, and database management software.

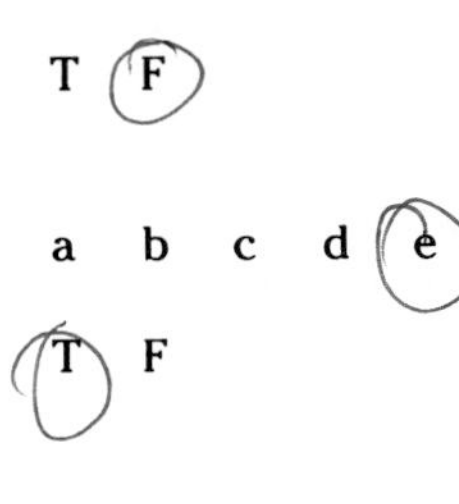

1. Word processing software is used to create databases.
2. Spreadsheets are valuable for: (a) creating edited documents; (b) defining management decisions; (c) creating designs for products; (d) creating production schedules; (e) running "what if" simulations.

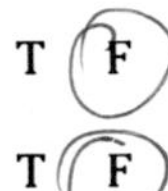

3. Examples of popular database management software include WordPerfect and MicroSoft Word.

H. Discuss three problems of the computerized workplace: information privacy; computer security; and automation, robotics, and unemployment.

1. T F Computer crime has not been a serious problem in the United States.
2. T F Most experts believe computers will replace workers and result in widespread unemployment.

QUESTIONS FOR REVIEW AND DISCUSSION

1. Define the key terms listed at the end of the chapter.
2. Describe the differences between batch and online systems. In which situations would each be more appropriate?
3. Compare and contrast mainframes, minicomputers, and microcomputers.
4. Why do computers use the binary number system? Explain what is meant by the terms *bit* and *byte*.
5. Discuss the advantages and disadvantages of using a floppy disk for mass storage.
6. What are the differences between applications and systems software? Which would a beginning programmer be more likely to create?
7. Describe the steps in developing a computer program. Which step is likely to be the most time-consuming?
8. Why is BASIC generally the first programming language taught?
9. How can what-if planning help managers make decisions?
10. Describe office automation and explain why it is so important.
11. How can a business avoid computer crime?

CONCLUDING CASE

Computers Change Restaurants

Computers in the kitchen and other technological innovations are changing the way restaurants serve their customers.

More and more, restaurants are using computer systems to link the dining room with the kitchen so that waiters and waitresses can place orders without leaving their service area. The server simply takes down the order, goes to a computer station and enters the order into a terminal that provides instant printouts to the kitchen staff or to bartenders.

A portable system now makes that process even easier. The Electronic Service Pad uses radio signals to let waiters transmit orders directly from the table to the kitchen. The device, small enough to fit inside an apron pocket, holds up to 120 menu items in its program, including such specifications as how a meat entree should be cooked.

Ordering by electronics provides faster service, cuts down on preparation time and gives servers more time to tend to customers, says a spokesman for Remanco Systems

Inc., a company in Danvers, Mass., that specializes in computer systems for restaurants.

Another advantage, says the spokesman, is more accurate billing because the customer's check is tabulated by the system. After a yearlong test, Remanco introduced the electronic ordering device last month and expects to have several hundred units in use by the end of the year.

On the drawing board elsewhere is a computer that would put the ordering in the hands of the customer. Under the newly patented system, each table would be equipped with a touch-screen computer terminal that diners would use to order food and play video games while they wait to be served, says television program producer Daniel Dubno, who invented the system with his brother, a computer consultant.

Will diners put up with this? Industry experts are divided. "Self-service has been accepted in all areas, from banks to hotels. Diners entering their own order will one day be fairly commonplace," says Michael Kasavana, acting director at the School of Hotel, Restaurant and Institutional Management at Michigan State University. Angelos Vlahakis, a lecturer at the school, disagrees: "People dining out want other people taking care of them. Computers are best used in back-room operations to better run the restaurant."

Issues for Discussion

1. Are there any possible disadvantages to using the Electronic Service Pad? Explain.
2. What factors should a restaurant manager consider in deciding whether to use a system that would equip each table with a touch-screen for ordering food and playing video games? Why should each factor be considered?
3. Name three other applications of a computer to managing a restaurant. Explain the significance of each application.

NOTES

1. Catherine Harris, "Information Power," *Business Week,* October 14, 1985, pp. 108–114.
2. Mark G. Simkin, *Introduction to Computer Information Systems for Business* (Dubuque, Iowa: Wm. C. Brown, 1987), p. 31.
3. William J. Cook and Daniel P. Wiener, "Steve Jobs's NeXT Frontier," *U.S. News & World Report,* April 18, 1988, pp. 56–57.
4. "The Retailing Boom in Small Computers," *Business Week,* September 6, 1982, p. 94.
5. "Executive Guide: How to Conquer Fear of Computers," *Business Week,* March 29, 1982, pp. 176–178.
6. This section is based on Joel Dreyfuss, "Catching the Computer Wave," *Fortune,* September 26, 1988, pp. 78–82.

CHECK YOUR LEARNING ANSWER KEY

A. 1. T, *p. 626*
 2. F, *p. 626*
 3. T, *p. 626*
 4. T, *p. 626*

B. 1. T, *p. 630*
 2. T, *p. 627*

C. 1. F, *p. 624*
 2. a, *p. 629*
 3. F, *p. 630*
 4. a,b,d,e, *p. 628*

D. 1. F, *p. 630*
 2. F, *p. 630*
 3. T, *p. 630*
 4. a,c, *p. 630*

E. 1. F, *p. 632*
 2. T, *p. 632*
 3. d, *p. 632*

F. 1. b, *p. 635*
 2. F, *p. 632*

G. 1. F, *p. 636*
 2. e, *p. 636*
 3. F, *p. 636*

H. 1. F, *p. 638*
 2. F, *p. 639*

CHAPTER

22

THE LEGAL ENVIRONMENT OF BUSINESS

LEARNING OBJECTIVES

After reading this chapter you should be able to:

1. Explain the difference between common law and statutory law.
2. Discuss the basic purpose of the Uniform Commercial Code.
3. Discuss the federal laws that promote fair trade and competition.
4. Explain the five elements necessary for a legal contract and the meaning of *breach of contract.*
5. List the requirements for negotiability.
6. Write out and label four types of endorsements.
7. Discuss how title is passed for personal property.
8. Compare express warranties and implied warranties.
9. Discuss the impact of agency law and the law of torts on business activities.
10. Differentiate among trademarks, copyrights, and patents.
11. Discuss the basic aspects of bankruptcy law and proceedings.

OUTLINE

Business Practice Example: Products Can Be Liabilities

A Framework for Studying Business Law
- Common Law
- Statutory Law
- The Uniform Commercial Code
- Separating Business Law

Laws Promoting Fair Trade and Competition
- Sherman Antitrust Act of 1890
- Clayton Act of 1914
- Federal Trade Commission Act of 1914
- Robinson-Patman Act of 1936
- Pure Food and Drug Act of 1906
- Fair Packaging and Labeling Act of 1966

Law of Contracts
- Requirements for a Legal Contract
  - Lawful Purpose
  - Competency of Parties
  - Voluntary Agreement
  - Consideration
  - Form of Contract
- Breach of Contract

Negotiable Instruments
- Requirements for Negotiability
- Types of Endorsements
  - Blank Endorsements
  - Restrictive Endorsements
  - Special Endorsements
  - Qualified Endorsements

Property law
- Transfer of Title
- Warranties

Agency Law

Law of Torts
- Product Liability Law

Trademarks, Copyrights, and Patents
- Trademarks
- Copyrights
- Patents

Business Bankruptcy
- Bankruptcy Law
- Bankruptcy Procedures

Summary

Key Terms

Check Your Learning

Questions for Review and Discussion

Concluding Case: Buyer Protection for Used Cars

Notes

Check Your Learning Answer Key

Highlight in Business Practice: California Voters Influence Insurance Laws

BUSINESS PRACTICE EXAMPLE

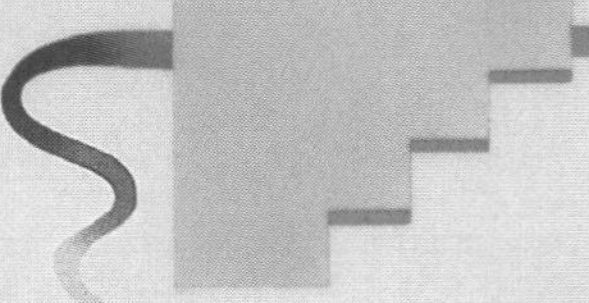

Products Can Be Liabilities

Every industry has its risks. One of the most vulnerable to legal risks is the health industry. Both the goods and the services used in this industry are under the constant scrutiny of the public and the legal profession.

For example, over 2 million American women have used the intrauterine contraceptive devise (IUD) for birth control. However, that option is no longer available to women in the United States. Why? Because it was proved in court that the IUD designed and manufactured by A. H. Robins Co.—the Dalkon Shield—had left hundreds of women sterile.

Another company, G. D. Searle & Co., quickly withdrew its Copper 7 and Tatun T IUDs. The withdrawal came about because of the fear of further product liability suits and increasing insurance rates.

Even withdrawing a product from the marketplace does not solve a company's problems. U.S. product liability law holds manufacturers liable as long as the products are in use. This gives foreign competitors an advantage. Their products usually have not been on the U.S. market as long.

Manufacturers of suspect products have three options. They can redesign the products and increase the price to cover increased insurance rates and production costs. They can declare bankruptcy. Or they can quit producing the products. For most, the threat of lawsuits is enough to push them out of the business.

For example, Merck & Co. is the only manufacturer still producing vaccines for measles, mumps, and rubella (MMR). Only two manufacturers still produce diphtheria, tetanus, and pertussis (DTP) vaccine. And only one manufacturer still produces oral polio vaccine.

Products do not have to be at fault to land a company in court. In one case, Bendectin, the only prescription drug available to help pregnant women who suffer from severe nausea, was found *not* to cause birth defects. In numerous courtroom trials, Merrell Dow, the manufacturer, never lost a lawsuit. However, publicity given to allegations that the drug was dangerous kept lawsuits coming by the score. When the costs of legal fees and insurance premiums threatened to exceed the product's $13 million a year revenues, the company quit making the product.

WHAT'S AHEAD

The introductory case reflects the problems that occur when products are the target of legal claims. Many of those situations can also cause a company to seek legal counsel or to be affected by business law. For example, when a business accepts a check for payment, sells merchandise

through a catalog, or markets real estate through an agency system, business law regulates these transactions. This chapter discusses the basic elements of business law: law of contracts, negotiable instruments, property law, agency and tort law, new-product protection, and bankruptcy. Although the chapter will not make you a legal expert, it should increase your understanding of legal terms.

A FRAMEWORK FOR STUDYING BUSINESS LAW

Law can be defined as a process of thinking that is often reflected by court decisions, statutes, and regulations promulgated by government agencies. However, most legal decisions are not clear-cut. The law is not black and white but gray. Since businesses must function within this cloudy legal environment, it is imperative that we understand the basics of commercial law.

Common Law

Law made by judges, not legislators, is **common law**—the unwritten laws that have evolved through custom and legal precedents rather than through the action of legislative bodies. This judge-made form of law developed in England and was carried to America by the immigrating colonists. Under a system of common law, judges rule case by case. In order to ensure consistency, they review previous decisions in cases of a similar nature. This process relies on legal precedents and is often referred to as the doctrine of **stare decisis** (to stand on decided cases).[1]

Common law is the unwritten laws that have evolved through custom and legal precedents rather than through the action of legislative bodies.

Stare decisis (to stand on decided cases) is the doctrine of basing legal decisions on decisions in previous cases.

Statutory Law

Much of our common-law heritage has been incorporated into **statutory law**—laws written and enacted by government bodies. Laws adopted by Congress and state legislatures are called *statutes,* and rules of municipalities and towns are called *ordinances.* Volumes of laws passed by government bodies are usually codified into books so judges can refer to the laws during court procedures.

If a conflict exists between common law and statutory law, statutory law takes precedence. All laws, common or statutory, must comply with the United States Constitution. The Constitution is the supreme law of the land.

Statutory law is laws written and enacted by government bodies.

The Uniform Commercial Code

Laws can vary from state to state, which makes business transactions difficult for companies engaged in interstate commerce. To encourage and facilitate exchange among businesses in different states, the *Uniform Commercial Code (UCC)* was developed. This code attempts to make business laws more consistent among the states. All fifty states, the District of Columbia, and the Virgin Islands have adopted the UCC, although Louisiana has yet to accept a few sections. The UCC covers a broad spectrum of commercial law in such areas as sales contracts, negotiable instruments (such as checks), and warranties.

Separating Business Law

Mercantile law was developed during the Middle Ages to help settle disputes among merchants, especially those engaged in commerce between countries in Western Europe and England. Since England was still an agrarian society, common-law courts were not overly concerned with the practices of traders. To overcome this legal gap, merchant courts were formed and a system of private commercial law evolved. This body of law serves as a basis for modern contracts, the law of negotiable instruments, and other business-law transactions. Although many legal scholars claim that business law is not a separate body of information, it is possible to define the term. **Business law** is the complex system of rules, statutes, codes, and regulations that form the legal environment in which businesses operate.

Business law is the complex system of rules, statutes, codes, and regulations that form the legal environment in which businesses operate.

LAWS PROMOTING FAIR TRADE AND COMPETITION

The U.S. government has enacted many laws to encourage fair trade and competition and to regulate specific business practices. The government's role, as we saw in chapters 1 and 2, is to provide enough guidelines so that every business can compete equally in a free-market atmosphere.

Sherman Antitrust Act of 1890

The American economy operated for nearly a century under the free-market economic system described in chapter 1, with minimal government regulation. The first law to protect the public against the potential abuses in a free-market system was aimed at trusts. **Trusts** are a combination of a few companies in a tight monopolistic network. One company would own the controlling stock of a competing company for the purpose of reducing competition and creating near-monopoly conditions. Before legislation was passed, corporations such as John D. Rockefeller's Standard Oil Company had enough economic power to charge whatever they wanted for their products. Trusts were common in the oil, steel, railroad, and rubber industries.

Trusts are a combination of a few companies in a tight monopolistic network.

After years of this monopolistic activity, farmers in the Midwest lobbied against fixed railroad shipping prices. The result was the **Sherman Antitrust Act of 1890,** which declared trusts and other forms of monopoly illegal. (Several years passed, however, before most trusts were eliminated.)

The ***Sherman Antitrust Act of 1890*** is federal legislation that declared trusts and other forms of monopoly illegal.

Specifically, the Sherman Act declared illegal "every contract, combination . . . , or conspiracy in restraint of trade or commerce." The law prohibits companies from price fixing, allocating markets among competitors, boycotting competitors, and creating monopolies. Today, its primary focus is illegal business practices that tend to eliminate competition. For example, the federal government has warned physicians and lawyers against establishing standard prices for services. This practice is considered an attempt at price fixing, which restricts competition.

The ***Clayton Act of 1914*** is federal legislation that forbade tying contracts, interlocking directorates, and the purchase of a competitor's stock to lessen competition.

Clayton Act of 1914

Because the Sherman Act was not breaking up monopolies as fast as the public demanded, Congress passed the **Clayton Act of 1914** to clarify and broaden the scope of the Sherman Act. The Clayton Act specifies the activities that are thought to lead to monopolies or to significantly lessen competition. The forbidden activities include (1) creating tying contracts, through which customers agree not to purchase or lease the goods of the vendor's competitors; (2) forming interlocking directorates, which include the same board members in directly competing corporations; and (3) purchasing the stock of a competitor if the purpose is to lessen competition or to create a monopoly.

In 1950, the **Celler-Kefauver Antimerger Act** was passed as an amendment to the Clayton Act to broaden its power. The amendment restricts mergers to the acquisition of companies in different lines of business. Unlike the Clayton Act, it also forbids the acquisition of a company's capital or assets, as well as its stock; and it requires prior approval of all planned mergers by the Federal Trade Commission (FTC).

The ***Celler-Kefauver Antimerger Act of 1950*** is federal legislation that amended the Clayton Act to restrict mergers to the acquisition of companies in different lines of business.

Many mergers are approved by the FTC because they will not lessen competition—for example, the Coca-Cola and Columbia Pictures merger and the PepsiCo and Taco Bell merger. Other proposed mergers are rejected because they would give the resulting companies too great a share of their market (a monopoly). Two examples of rejections are the proposed mergers of Coca-Cola and Dr. Pepper and of PepsiCo and 7-Up—because they would have given the resulting companies an 80 percent share of the soft drink market. (Pepsi *was* allowed to purchase the European division of 7-Up.)

Federal Trade Commission Act of 1914

Congress also enacted the **Federal Trade Commission Act of 1914,** which created the FTC, the regulatory agency that monitors unfair methods of competition and penalizes companies for using them. What constitutes unfair competition is not precisely defined in the legislation. Thus the FTC has the right to investigate complaints by other businesses or to probe on its own. The FTC is most noted for its cases involving deceptive advertising and false or deceptive warranties.

The ***Federal Trade Commission Act of 1914*** is federal legislation that created the Federal Trade Commission, a government regulatory agency that monitors unfair methods of competition and penalizes companies for using them.

The Federal Trade Commission Act was amended in 1938 by the *Wheeler-Lea Act,* whose creation was spurred by the *Raladam* case (1931). In that case, the Supreme Court held that a "producer's misrepresentation of an obesity cure was not unfair competition because the firm's action did not injure competition." The Wheeler-Lea Act prohibits unfair and deceptive practices regardless of whether they injure competition; thus it protects the public. In addition, the act placed the advertising of food and drugs under the jurisdiction of the FTC.

Robinson-Patman Act of 1936

The federal legislation that prohibits price discrimination is the *Robinson-Patman Act of 1936.* As chapter 13 explained, this act prohibits manufacturers and other nonretail sellers from selling goods of like grade and quality at different prices when the effect may be to decrease competition or create a monopoly. Thus discounts given to chains and other large retailers must also be offered to smaller retailers. Price differentials are legal only if the supplier can prove either of two things: (1) that there is a cost savings arising from quantity purchases, or (2) that different prices are necessary to meet competition in good faith. It is illegal to knowingly ask for or receive discriminatory prices.

HIGHLIGHT IN BUSINESS PRACTICE

California Voters Influence Insurance Laws

November 7, 1988, Election Day, will be remembered by California voters, but not because we elected a new president. That's the day California citizens, led by consumer activist Ralph Nader, voted to pass Proposition 103, a tough insurance reform measure requiring that California overhaul its insurance laws. The measure calls for a minimum 20 percent rate reduction in property and casualty insurance policies—including auto, homeowner's and business liability—from the rates in effect on November 8, 1987.

Other provisions of the measure include the following:

1. The rate freeze is effective until November 8, 1989, unless an insurer is threatened with insolvency.
2. Every eligible insured driver must be offered a good-driver policy that is 20 percent cheaper than the standard policy.
3. An insurance commissioner charged with reviewing property and casualty rate changes must be elected.
4. Automobile insurance premiums must be determined primarily by driving record.
5. Discrimination, price fixing, and unfair practices by the insurance industry are prohibited.
6. The insurance industry is stripped of its exemption from state antitrust laws.

The insurance industry wasted no time in mounting a counteroffensive. One day after the election, nine insurance companies filed suits against the measure. A tenth suit was filed the following day. The attorney handling the industry lawsuits claims that arbitrary rate slashing amounts to an unconstitutional taking of property without due process of law. He also argues that "the cut is so onerous as to constitute an illegal interference with insurers' contracts with policyholders."

In May 1989, the California Supreme Court ruled to uphold Proposition 103. The decision holds, in essence, that voters can give themselves huge reductions in rates for all kinds of property and casualty insurance—as long as insurers aren't deprived of due process or forced to accept "inadequate" profit. It is estimated that seventy-five companies will be driven to insolvency or forced to curtail insurance operations. Over sixty companies temporarily suspended writing new property and casualty insurance in California.

Pure Food and Drug Act of 1906

The ***Pure Food and Drug Act of 1906*** is federal legislation prohibiting the adulteration and misbranding of food and drugs; it was amended in 1938 to include the healthfulness, safety, and labeling of foods, drugs, and cosmetics and was renamed the Food, Drug, and Cosmetic Act.

Federal legislation prohibiting the adulteration and misbranding of food and drugs is the **Pure Food and Drug Act of 1906.** The act was amended in 1938 and is now the Food, Drug, and Cosmetic Act. It calls for the Food and Drug Administration (FDA) to monitor the healthfulness and safety of these products, and it requires basic testing standards for drugs. This act was further strengthened by the Kefauver-Harris drug amendments of 1962. Companies are also required to supply truthful branding and labeling of all foods, drugs, and cosmetics. The act prohibits the use of large containers that deceptively conceal smaller goods. For example, the labels on boxes of crackers and potato chips state that the boxes were full at shipment but that their contents may have settled in shipping. This type of explanation is required by the act.

Fair Packaging and Labeling Act of 1966

Do you shop for high-fiber cereals in the hope of lessening your chance of developing colon cancer? Do you need to avoid dairy products in the foods you eat? If so, you benefit from the **Fair Packaging and Labeling Act of 1966,** which gives the FDA the authority to require lists of ingredients on packages, including their quantities. In addition, the act requires the name and address of the producer or distributor on each product sold.

The ***Fair Packaging and Labeling Act of 1966*** is federal legislation that gives the Food and Drug Administration the authority to require lists of ingredients on packages, including their quantities.

LAW OF CONTRACTS

Anyone who has purchased an insurance policy or bought a car on installment has signed a **contract**—an agreement between two or more persons or companies that is enforceable in court. (See Figure 22.1 for an example.) Contracts play a significant role in practically every major business transaction.

A ***contract*** is an agreement between two or more persons or companies that is enforceable in court.

Requirements for a Legal Contract

Unfortunately, the question of what constitutes a legal contract often surfaces after a dispute arises. To minimize this risk, the content and circumstances of an

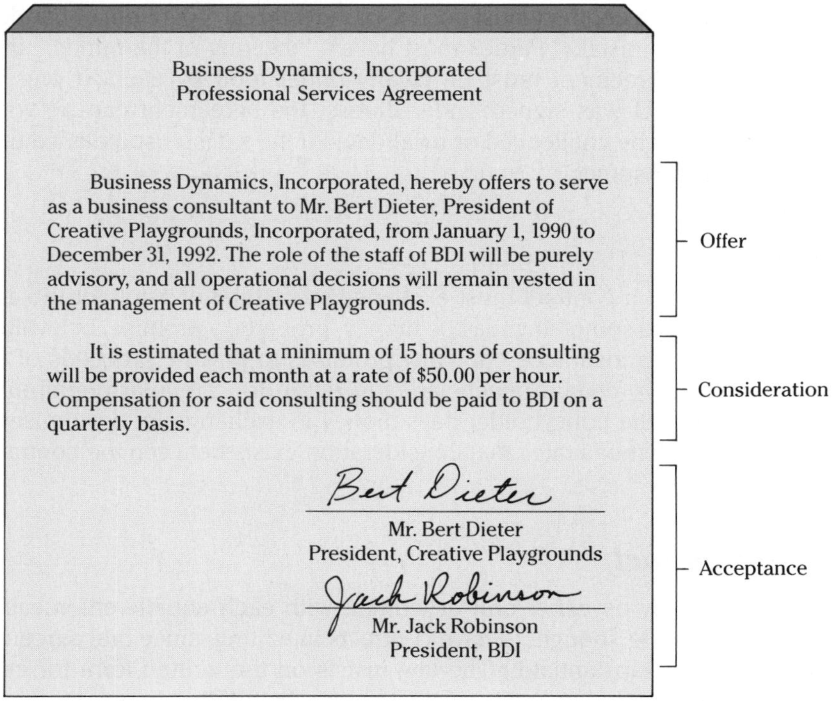

Business Dynamics, Incorporated
Professional Services Agreement

Business Dynamics, Incorporated, hereby offers to serve as a business consultant to Mr. Bert Dieter, President of Creative Playgrounds, Incorporated, from January 1, 1990 to December 31, 1992. The role of the staff of BDI will be purely advisory, and all operational decisions will remain vested in the management of Creative Playgrounds. — Offer

It is estimated that a minimum of 15 hours of consulting will be provided each month at a rate of $50.00 per hour. Compensation for said consulting should be paid to BDI on a quarterly basis. — Consideration

Bert Dieter
Mr. Bert Dieter
President, Creative Playgrounds

Jack Robinson
Mr. Jack Robinson
President, BDI
— Acceptance

Figure 22.1
A sample business contract.

agreement should be evaluated before any signature is put on paper. Five key elements are required for a valid contract: lawful purpose, competency of parties, voluntariness of agreement, consideration, and specific form of the contract.

Lawful Purpose

A contract cannot require performance of an act that is in violation of a law. If a state statute declares that gambling is illegal, promises to pay gambling debts are not legally enforceable in that state. If a county has an ordinance prohibiting the sale of liquor, a contract to supply liquor would not be valid. Some lenders demand interest in excess of that allowed under state laws. Contracts of this nature are illegal, although the lenders are usually entitled to collect the principal.

Competency of Parties

The capacity to enter into a valid contract is often restricted by age and mental stability. For example, minors (usually persons under eighteen years of age) can contract for a limited number of necessities, such as clothing, food, and housing, and can be held liable for these items (but not others) if a reasonable price was charged. Similar contractual limitations apply to intoxicated people and individuals who have been declared legally incompetent. If a contract is signed by any of these people, the person or relatives can cancel it. A minor who cancels a contract must return the merchandise or other consideration to the seller. Parties with limited contractual ability are often required to have a cosigner.

Voluntary Agreement

Parties entering into a contract must not do so under threat, coercion, or fraudulent manipulation or by mistake. Parties must have a "meeting of the minds," in that the terms of the agreement must be clearly understood by each. If one party believes the contract was signed under duress, the agreement can be voided. Sales contracts may be challenged or invalidated if the salesperson placed undue pressure on the consumer.

Consideration

Parties entering into a contract must exchange something of value for the agreement to be legal. The something may be money, property, a promise, or a valuable act. For example, an insurance company promises to pay the proceeds of a life insurance contract to certain beneficiaries in return for a regular premium payment. In this case, the policyholder pays money in exchange for a promise. The mutual exchange demonstrates that consideration exists between the contracting parties.

Form of Contract

Some contracts may be either oral or written, with each equally enforceable in court. (It is preferable, though, to have contracts in writing, since oral agreements can be difficult to substantiate.) The law insists on the written form for certain types of contracts, including contracts that cannot be fulfilled in less than a year, those involving the sale of real estate, and those dealing with the sale of personal goods valued in excess of a certain dollar amount, usually $500.

Breach of Contract

When one party fails to perform one of the duties or meet one of the conditions of the agreement, a **breach of contract** occurs. The individual who does not perform according to the stipulations of the contract is said to be guilty of breach of contract. The injured party may rescind the contract (consider that the agreement never existed), sue for damages, or solicit a court order forcing the other party to carry out the terms of the contract.

A ***breach of contract*** is the failure of one party to a contract to perform one of the duties or meet one of the conditions of the contract.

For example, an attorney who agrees to handle a client's case enters into a contract with the client. In recent years, a number of attorneys have been challenged for nondelivery on a promise and have been sued for breach of contract. Many attorneys take out liability insurance to protect themselves.

NEGOTIABLE INSTRUMENTS

Any form of business paper used in commercial transactions as a substitute for money is a **negotiable instrument.** Checks, certificates of deposit, promissory notes, and drafts are examples of negotiable instruments used to facilitate the exchange of goods and services.

A ***negotiable instrument*** is any form of business paper used in commercial transactions as a substitute for money.

BUSINESS PRACTICE EXAMPLE Continues

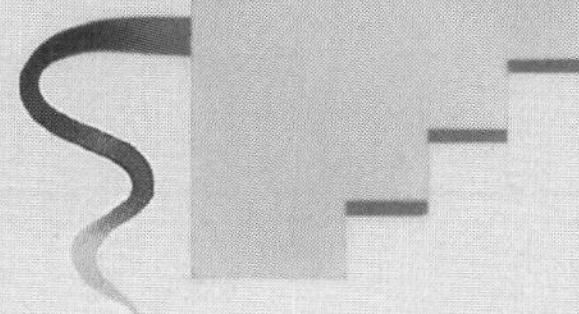

The reform of our complex civil justice system, based on U.S. common and statutory law, is a key goal of the Product Liability Alliance, a coalition of over three hundred businesses that wants to ease the liability crisis. A second goal is adoption of a federal product liability law to replace the present patchwork of individual state laws requiring manufacturers and retailers to comply with many different and often conflicting statutes.

An attorney who agrees to handle a client's case enters into a contractual agreement with the client. In recent years, a number of attorneys have been sued for breach of contract. Many attorneys therefore take out liability insurance to protect themselves. Settlements for clients and payments to attorneys are normally made by check, a negotiable instrument that must be endorsed to be cashed.

Requirements for Negotiability

The Uniform Commercial Code specifies the characteristics of a negotiable instrument:

1. The instrument must be in writing and signed by the maker or drawer.
2. The instrument must contain an unconditional promise or order to pay a specific amount of money.
3. Payment must be made on demand or at a definite future date.
4. The instrument must be payable *to order* or *to bearer.*

Figure 22.2 demonstrates that a personal check meets these four criteria for negotiability.

Types of Endorsements

Title to (ownership of) negotiable instruments can be transferred by *endorsement,* by signing the back of the instrument. A 1988 law requires that endorsements be made within the top inch (back side) of the negotiable instrument. The endorser of an instrument pledges certain things. For example, when Max E. Douglas endorsed the check in Figure 22.2, he pledged the following: that he was transferring ownership, that the instrument was genuine, that he had title to the instrument, and that he assumed the liability to pay the amount on the face of the instrument in the event the maker defaulted. For anyone who receives an endorsed instrument as part of a business transaction, it is important to understand the four principal types of endorsements: blank, restrictive, special, and qualified (see Figure 22.3).

Figure 22.2
A personal check.

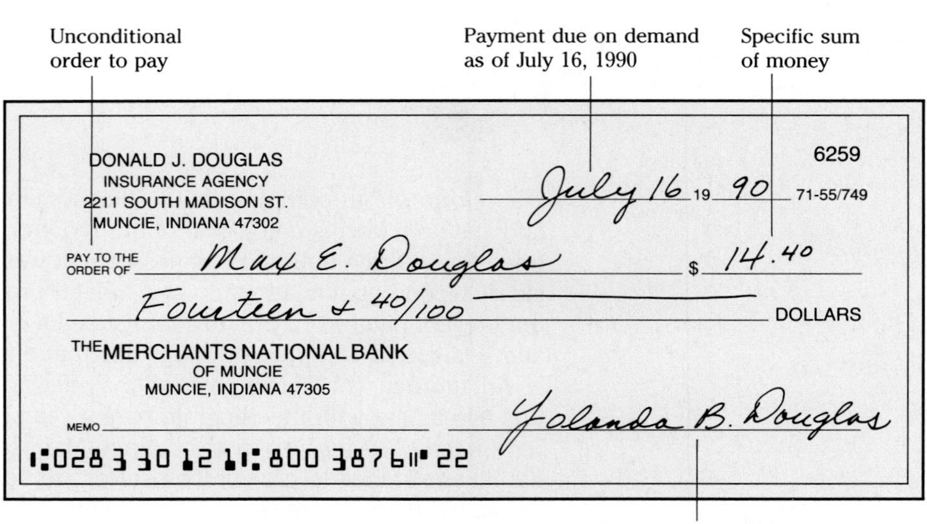

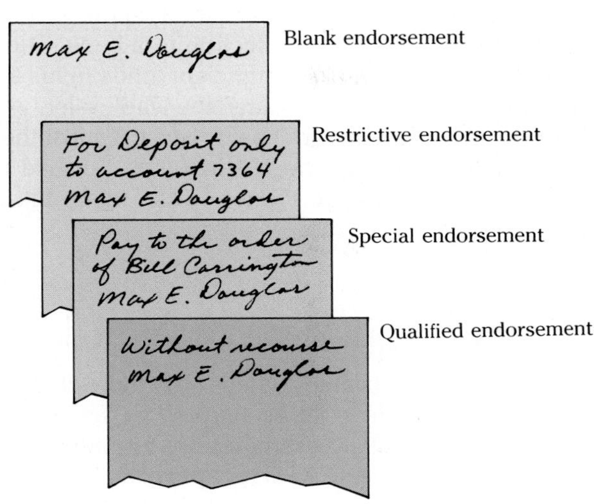

Figure 22.3
Types of endorsements. All endorsements must be made within the top inch of the negotiable instrument.

Blank Endorsements

The most frequently used endorsement is a blank endorsement, which requires nothing more than the signature of the payee (the person to be paid) on the reverse side of the instrument. Once the payee signs, however, anyone holding the endorsed instrument may cash it. For this reason, you should never endorse a check or any other instrument until you are ready to cash it. If you endorse your paycheck and then lose it on your way to the bank, the finder can cash it.

Restrictive Endorsements

To overcome the problem with blank endorsements, businesses may use a restrictive endorsement, which limits further negotiation of an instrument. When retail stores accept checks, they usually stamp them immediately *for deposit only.* This type of endorsement ensures that if the check is cashed, it will be deposited only into the store's account. The restrictive endorsement provides a safeguard against loss or theft of negotiable instruments.

Special Endorsements

A special endorsement transfers ownership of an instrument to a specific individual. Such instruments usually read "pay to the order of," followed by the signature of the payee. Like the restrictive endorsement, this form of transfer offers protection against loss or theft.

Qualified Endorsements

As indicated earlier, the endorser of an instrument accepts liability for the face value of the instrument in the event the maker does not pay. For instance, assume that Carlson's Appliance Store accepts a check from a customer named Smith. Carlson's endorses the check and uses it to pay a wholesaler. The wholesaler endorses the check and presents it for collection to a bank. The bank finds out that the maker of the check, Smith, has insufficient funds in his account to cover the check. The bank then has recourse against the wholesaler, which in turn has recourse against Carlson's, which in turn has recourse against the customer. The appliance store's liability could have been eliminated if it had used the words *without recourse* above the signature. These words make the endorsement a qualified endorsement.

PROPERTY LAW

Property is an item (or items) of value owned by an individual or business.

Personal property is all property other than real estate.

Real property is real estate, including buildings, land, and anything permanently part of the land.

Property is an item (or items) of value owned by an individual or business. Two types of property, personal and real, are recognized by law. **Personal property** is all property other than real estate; examples are furniture, stocks and bonds, automobiles, food, and appliances. **Real property** is real estate; it includes buildings, land, and anything permanently part of the land, such as oil deposits, minerals, and trees. The transfer of property is governed by a complex contractual relationship, which has many legal ramifications. Two of the most important aspects of property transfer are title transfer and warranties.

Transfer of Title

The most basic question underlying any exchange of property is: When does ownership (title) pass from seller to buyer? If goods are lost, damaged, or destroyed, the party holding title suffers the loss; disputes involving this issue of law are numerous.

Following are rules that govern the transfer of title to *personal property:*

1. If you purchase goods on a trial or approval basis, ownership passes to you if you pay for the goods or if you keep them for longer than a reasonable period of time. Some companies encourage you to try a certain product for a free trial period of a specified time. If you don't return the item within that time, the company will most likely bill you for it.
2. If you contract to have goods delivered to a specific place, title passes when the goods are delivered. For instance, if you order from a Sears catalog and designate home delivery, title passes to you when the goods reach your home. If the goods are delivered by mistake to the local warehouse, you have not assumed ownership.
3. If you purchase an item COD (cash on delivery), title passes to you when the goods are delivered by the seller to the carrier. You assume title while the goods are in transit.
4. Goods can be purchased FOB (free on board) shipping point (transportation paid by the buyer) or FOB destination (transportation paid by the seller). If you purchase an item FOB shipping point, title passes to you when the goods are delivered to that point. You are responsible for the item during transit. Just the opposite is true if you buy items FOB destination; you assume title when the goods arrive.
5. Sellers usually agree to provide goods in satisfactory condition. If you purchase a table that is supposed to be repaired as part of the purchase agreement, title will not pass to you on delivery unless the repair has been made satisfactorily.

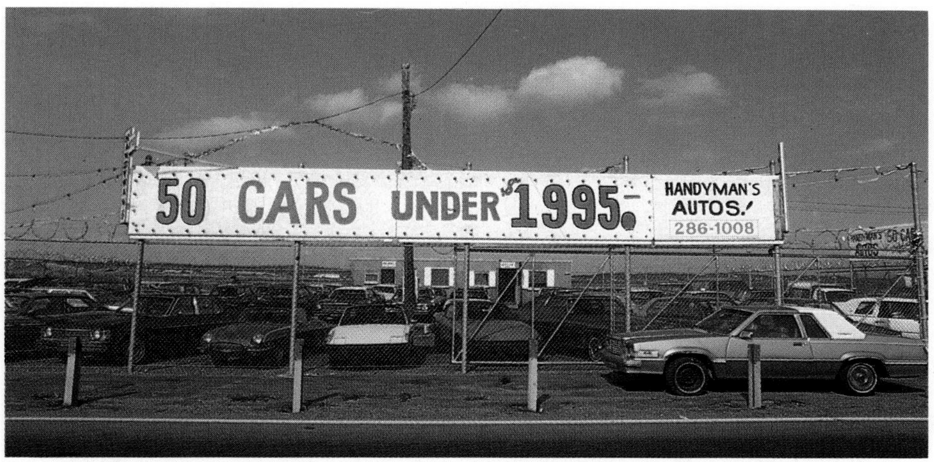

The transfer of property items of value owned by an individual or business is governed by a complex contractural relationship. The customer receiving one of these autos is therefore assured of a reasonable standard of performance of the auto purchased.

The transfer of title to *real property* is governed by two legal documents: deeds and leases. *Deeds* are documents that denote the legal owners of real property. To transfer real property, you must pass the deed to the new owners. Real property can also be leased. A *lease* is a contract that allows a party the right to use property for a specified time period. It is a common practice for retailers to lease their buildings or mall stores from property owners.

Warranties

To help ensure that consumers receive products that meet reasonable standards of performance, companies may back up their products with warranties. A **warranty** is a promise by a manufacturer or seller to stand behind its product. However, the history of consumer complaints regarding warranties demonstrates that the promises have often been misunderstood or not honored.

A ***warranty*** is a promise by a manufacturer or seller to stand behind its product.

There are two basic types of warranties: express and implied. **Express warranties,** sometimes called written warranties, spell out facts about the product's characteristics and how the manufacturer or seller will deal with defects in the product. Consumers must be careful in analyzing these warranties, because some are full warranties and others are limited. Table 22.1 compares full and limited express warranties. You can see that full warranties offer more extensive protection.

Express warranties, sometimes called written warranties, are warranties that spell out specific representations by the seller regarding the product.

Implied warranties are unwritten guarantees that automatically come with the product. They are created by state law, not by sellers. The most common implied warranty is the *warranty of merchantability*—the promise by the seller that the product is fit for its intended purpose. A reclining chair must recline, and a pen must write. If they don't, the buyer has the right to a refund or an exchange without charge.

Implied warranties are unwritten guarantees that automatically come with the product.

Congress attempted to clarify warranty law by passing the *Magnuson-Moss Warranty Act of 1975.* This act required that all warranties contain a simple, complete, and straightforward statement, including the name and address of the warrantor, what is covered, and to what degree it is covered. In addition, warranties must contain detailed procedures for processing claims, spell out how disputes between parties will be resolved, and state the warranty's duration.

Table 22.1 Comparison of full and limited warranties.

Full Warranties	Limited Warranties
A defective product will be fixed or replaced free, including removal and reinstallation if necessary.	The cost of labor is not covered; only the cost of parts is covered.
The defect will be repaired within a reasonable time after the complaint is registered.	The warranty allows for a prorated credit or refund based on usage, such as for auto tires.
The seller cannot impose unreasonable demands on the buyer. For example, the seller cannot demand that a grandfather clock be shipped to the factory for repair under the warranty.	The consumer is required to return the product to the store for service, even if it is heavy.
The warranty is extended to secondary buyers who acquire the product during the warranty period.	The warranty covers only the original purchaser.
If a product cannot be or has not been fixed after a reasonable number of attempts, the consumer gets the choice of a new item or a refund.	The customer is charged handling costs if the product must be shipped.

As a result of this legislation, warranties on consumer products costing more than $15 must be available to the buyer at the point of purchase. This allows the buyer to read the warranties of competing products before making a final decision. The act also requires that the language of the document be easy to read and understand. Legalese and fine print are not permissible. In addition, the act makes it easier for consumers to hold companies to their promises after the sale has been made.

AGENCY LAW

In the world of sport, *free agent* is a common term. It means that a player is no longer obligated by contract to the present team. Most likely, however, the player will use the law of agency in employing a lawyer to help negotiate a new contract.

The *law of agency* is a common legal arrangement whereby one party, called the principal, authorizes a second party, the agent, to act on his or her behalf. The principal creates the formal relationship by granting authority to the agent.

Many common business transactions are executed under agency arrangements. Real estate agents act on behalf of home sellers. Insurance agents represent the companies that employ them. Stockbrokers act as agents for investors. In fact, with the exceptions of voting, making a will, and executing an affidavit, almost any legal transaction can be handled by an agent. Sometimes, the relationship between the principal and the agent is more formal. **Power of attorney** is the document by which a principal-agent relationship is established. Disabled people and the elderly often use this type of document.

Power of attorney is the document by which a principal-agent relationship is established.

LAW OF TORTS

One of the major risks of doing business today is the possibility of being involved in a lawsuit. A customer at a retail store accidentally slips and injures her back while shopping and sues the store for damages. A registered nurse is charged with negligence for improperly caring for a patient after open-heart surgery. A corporation is charged by a competitor with advertising misleading statistics about the competitor's products. These examples reflect the type of wrongful conduct covered by tort law.

Just what is a tort? A **tort** is a civil, or private, wrongful act by one party that injures another party. Torts normally involve one party suing another for monetary damages. The injury must have resulted because of one of the following elements: negligence (the offending party failed to exercise due care in his or her actions) or deliberate intent to cause harm.

A ***tort*** is a civil, or private, wrongful act by one party that injures another party.

Rock star Elton John charged the London *Sun* with deliberately attempting to malign his name with headlines and articles that were not true. A large monetary settlement was eventually agreed upon. This example is of a deliberate tort, which includes fraud, slander, assault, invasion of privacy, and even trespass.

The law of torts is complex and covers a wide range of human activity. Some common torts are slander, libel, assault, battery, and defamation of character.

Product Liability Law

A critical area of tort law is **product liability law**—law that holds businesses liable for negligence in the design, production, or sale of defective products. Courts across the country are being tied up in long trials involving businesses that are sued because of alleged negligence involving their products.

Product liability law is law that holds businesses liable for negligence in the design, production, or sale of defective products.

In some cases, liability suits are brought based on a claim of company negligence. Several toy manufacturers have been sued for features of dolls, guns, or other products that proved dangerous to children. In other cases, liability suits may be brought against companies that were not negligent.

For example, the Will Burt Co. of Orville, Ohio, was found liable for $6.2 million as the result of a 1980 accident. The accident, caused by a collapsed scaffold, killed one Florida worker and left another a quadriplegic. The company made parts for the scaffold. Although the parts were not defective and the scaffold itself was designed by another company, Will Burt was sued because the manufacturer went bankrupt.[2]

Current legal theory holds that all companies involved in the production and sale of a defective product are liable for any injury it causes. Some business groups, including the National Association of Manufacturers, the Product Liability Alliance, and the U.S. Chamber of Commerce, are pushing for the establishment of a national standard for product liability law. Their hope is that a move to standardize parts of state liability laws will make court judgments more moderate and will stabilize insurance rates.[3]

In some cases, liability suits are brought based on a claim of company negligence. Some people believe that because cigarette smoking has been shown to be harmful or fatal, cigarette manufacturers are liable for injury under the product liability laws.

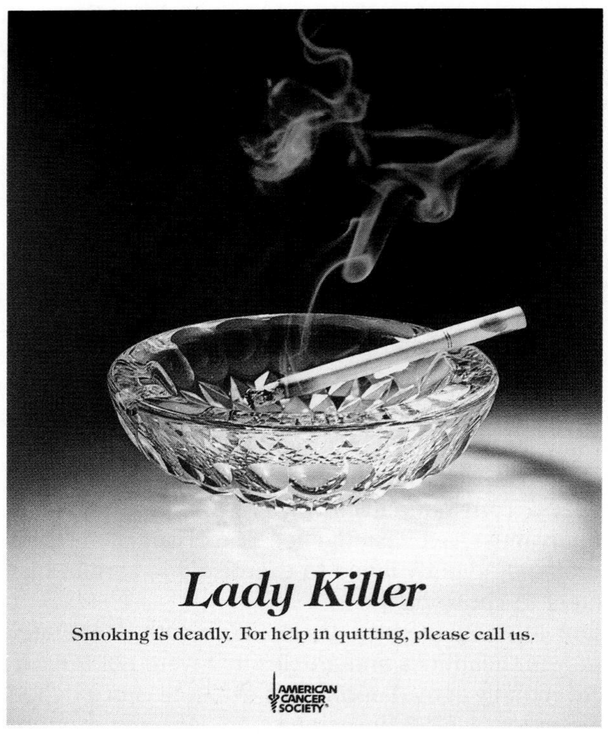

BUSINESS PRACTICE EXAMPLE Continues

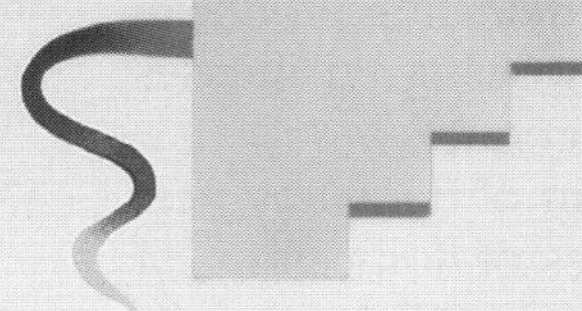

Sometimes companies that manufacture products are at risk for liability even when they are not actually at fault for negligence. One instance involved the Amigo Co., a family-owned business that manufactures motorized wheelchairs. The company, which has never lost a lawsuit, saw its insurance premiums increase from $30,000 annually to $150,000. This happened in part because the company was targeted for lawsuits aimed more at a defendant's ability to pay than at actual negligence.

In one case, Amigo was sued because a woman in a wheelchair, who was crossing a street with her husband, was hit by a car that had run a red light. The driver had no insurance, so the husband sued Amigo. The case dragged on for two years before Amigo won. The cost of its legal fees was $120,000. According to the company owner, if premiums and legal costs keep going up, the firm will be forced to close its doors.

TRADEMARKS, COPYRIGHTS, AND PATENTS

Competition forces companies to develop new products and to improve old ones. The federal government tries to encourage entrepreneurship by granting exclusive rights to the new product's owner. The areas of focus of the government's protective laws are trademarks, copyrights, and patents.

Trademarks

A ***trademark*** is a name, word, symbol, or other device that has been registered by the owner for the purpose of identifying its product line.

A name, word, symbol, or other device that has been registered by the owner for the purpose of identifying its product line is a **trademark.** The Pontiac chieftain, the Westinghouse W, and the Coke bottle are trademark symbols. Coca-Cola, 7-Up, Kleenex, and Chevrolet are trademarked words. Often, the symbol ® appears after a brand name or symbol. This means that the trademark has been registered with the United States Patent and Trademark Office and cannot be used by other companies. Although registered trademarks are subject to challenge, they remain the exclusive property of the owner forever. In 1987, 47,500 new trademarks were registered with the Patent and Trademark Office.[4]

Certain trademarks have become generic; that is, the trademarked term is used to describe an entire class of products (such as aspirin, linoleum, escalator) rather than one specific brand. To keep this from happening, companies are constantly on the lookout for improper use of their trademarks. Vaseline, for example, has been known to write to a newspaper that lowercased *vaseline* to insist that in the future *petroleum jelly* be the generic term and Vaseline be capitalized.

A trademark is a name, word, symbol, or other device that has been registered by the owner for the purpose of identifying its product line. McDonald's says that it has more than 5,000 product and service marks, such as the one shown on this sign in Hong Kong, registered in 110 foreign countries.

McDonald's says it has more than five thousand product and service marks registered in 110 foreign countries and about five hundred marks registered in the United States, including about one hundred that begin with "Mc" or "Mac." Since 1975, McDonald's has taken about fifty companies to court for trademark infringement. One infringement was Quality Inns' "McSleep" lodgings. The court ruled that Quality Inns could no longer use "Mc."[5]

Copyrights

Copyrights are the rights granted to owners of creative works to control any reproduction or distribution of these works.

The sole purpose of **copyrights** is to grant the owners of creative works the right to control any reproduction and distribution of these works. Copyrights cover creative efforts in areas ranging from books and music to television programs and video games. In the late 1970s, a heated debate developed over home videocassette recording. Some claimed that people who recorded a television program on a home recorder were violating copyright laws. The question was finally resolved by a 5 to 4 Supreme Court decision that the use of video recorders to tape TV programs at home doesn't violate federal copyright law.[6]

Normally, copyrights exist for the life of the author plus fifty years. Under this provision, families may benefit from texts, records, and other creative works long after the death of the originator. Works can be registered with the Copyright Office for $10.

Two international treaties that pertain to copyright are the Berne Convention of 1886, which established the International Union for the Protection of Literary and Artistic Works, and the Universal Copyright Convention (UCC), which came into force in 1955. The United States is a member of the UCC, but for a variety of legal and political reasons, it has not been a signatory to the Berne Union. Passage of the 1976 Copyright Act removed most of the legal barriers to U.S. entry into the Berne Union. Finally, Congress passed the Berne Convention Implementation Act of 1988 which allowed the U.S. to become a signatory to the threaty.[7]

Patents

A ***patent*** is a nonrenewable exclusive legal right to a product or process granted for seventeen years by the Patent and Trademark Office.

Our history is rich with stories of inventions that contributed to the betterment of industry and society. Thomas Edison, Eli Whitney, and Henry Ford are prime examples of American creativity. Modern inventors are less well known because many of their ideas are created in the labs of corporations. Nevertheless, if you ever invent something that has marketable potential, you may want to secure a patent. A **patent** is a nonrenewable exclusive legal right to a product or process granted for seventeen years by the Patent and Trademark Office. During this time period, the patent holder has complete control of the invention and can sue any person or company that attempts to duplicate the idea. Patent holders often license the use of their products in return for a fee and royalty payments.

As competition in certain markets has intensified, patent infringements and attempts to pirate new technology have become more common. A recent case, in which respected Japanese companies tried to steal business secrets from International Business Machines, reflects the nature of patent competition. Often, a company will change a minor part of a product or process and claim that a new product has been invented

BUSINESS BANKRUPTCY

Bankruptcy is the legal nonpayment of financial obligations.

Bankruptcy is the legal nonpayment of financial obligations. In 1970, the Penn Central Railroad suddenly went bankrupt, listing liabilities of over $3 billion. Penn Central was one of the largest corporations in the United States. Prior to its collapse, most people assumed that certain corporate giants would never have to bother with bankruptcy laws and procedures. This myth has been further put to rest by the bankruptcies of Manville Corporation, Texaco, LTV Corporation, Continental Airlines, and Wickes. Table 22.2 shows that during the 1980s bank-

Table 22.2 Number of business bankruptcy petitions filed in U. S. courts.

Year	Bankruptcies
1982	56,423
1983	69,818
1984	65,520
1985	66,651
1986	76,281
1987	88,278

ruptcies increased at an alarming rate. Many of the companies continue to operate under bankruptcy status, and many—Continental and Texaco, for example—resume normal operations after reorganizing or settling their debts.

Bankruptcy Law

The United States Constitution grants Congress the right to establish uniform bankruptcy laws. In 1898, Congress enacted the *Federal Bankruptcy Act.* The original act has been revised periodically. The most substantive update occurred in 1978 in what is now known as the *Bankruptcy Reform Act.* The intent of the revised law is to provide for a more orderly discharge of financial obligations for honest debtors who cannot pay their bills.

The most commonly cited provisions of the Bankruptcy Reform Act are Chapters 7 and 11. Chapter 7 outlines the procedures to be followed for liquidating a bankrupt firm. Sometimes a company can be reorganized to avoid complete liquidation; Chapter 11 specifies the procedures to be used for developing the reorganization plan. In 1987, 17,142 companies sought protection from creditors. Of these firms, 6,722 have survived with the same ownership under Chapter 11. However, the chances of a small or medium-size company surviving bankruptcy are less than one in ten.[8]

Bankruptcy Procedures

Bankruptcy is initiated by the filing of a petition with the appropriate court. **Voluntary bankruptcy** occurs when a company files a petition for bankruptcy of its own accord. If bankruptcy proceedings are initiated by creditors and the court declares the company bankrupt, the process is called **involuntary bankruptcy.** Both voluntary and involuntary petitions can place the debtor into bankruptcy under Chapter 7 (liquidation) or Chapter 11 (reorganization).

Voluntary bankruptcy is bankruptcy that occurs when a company files a petition for bankruptcy of its own accord.

Involuntary bankruptcy is bankruptcy that occurs when bankruptcy proceedings are initiated by creditors and the court declares the company bankrupt.

Under Chapter 7, the bankruptcy judge usually appoints a referee, who meets with creditors to elect a trustee. The trustee must liquidate all assets and use the resulting cash to pay necessary expenses and creditors' claims. Chapter 7 bankruptcy procedures are outlined in Figure 22.4.

Of great importance to creditors is the priority of payments following liquidation. In general, the trustee will distribute the assets of the firm according to the following priorities:

1. *Secured claims.* An example is the claim of a creditor who holds a loan backed by collateral (something of value).
2. *Unsecured claims.* Examples are court costs, unpaid wages, taxes, and trade credit outstanding.
3. *Equity interests.* An example is the stock held by the shareholders of the debtor corporation, with priority given to the holders of preferred stock (see chapter 19).

It is unusual for all creditors to receive full payment. Most creditors accept partial payment of the debt and write the remainder off as a bad debt expense. Although many creditors claim that the debtor has a moral obligation to pay, the owners of a bankrupt firm can legally start another venture without the obligation to pay back debts associated with the bankruptcy.

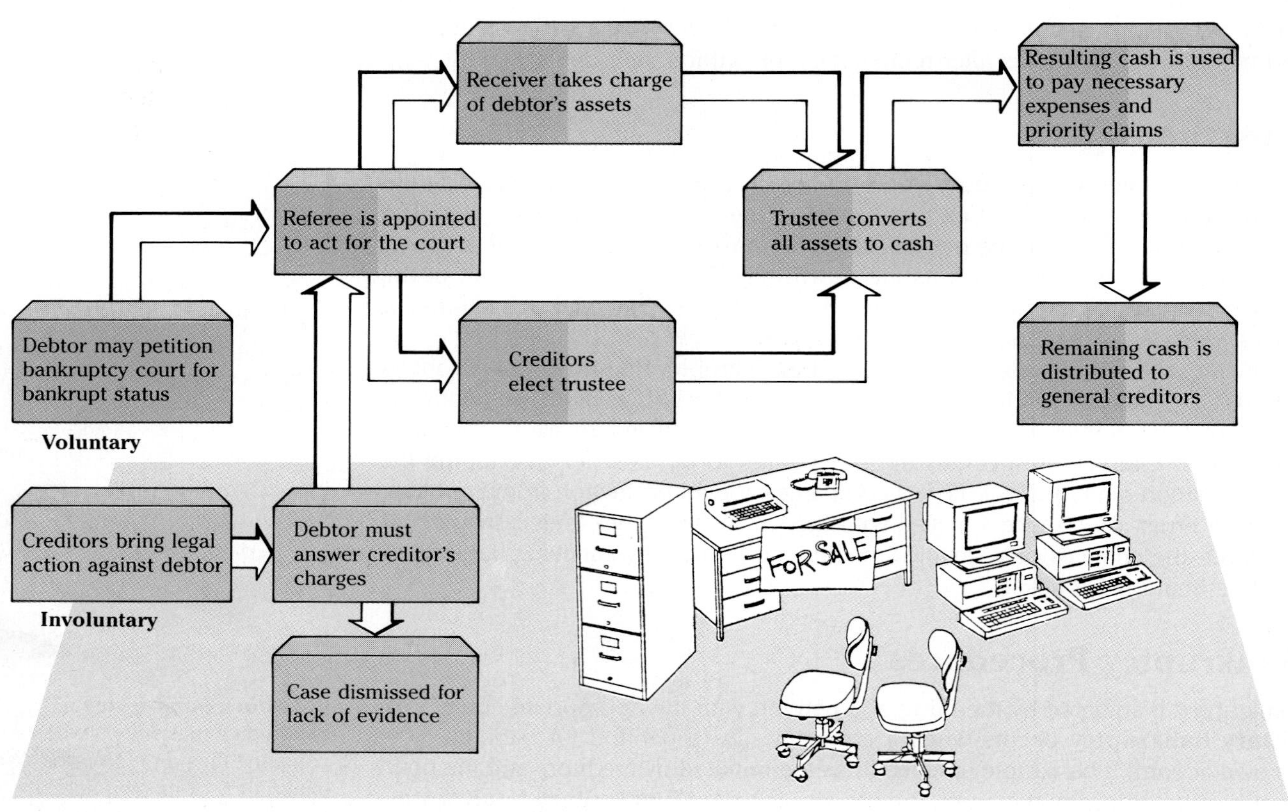

Figure 22.4 Chapter 7 bankruptcy procedures. Bankruptcy allows debtors to liquidate their assets, pay off creditors, and start over with a debt-free record.

BUSINESS PRACTICE EXAMPLE Continues

Alarmed by soaring commercial and municipal insurance rates and the disappearance of some types of coverage (see chapter 20), many state legislatures have tried to protect businesses by restricting plaintiffs' rights and opportunities for exploitation through liability suits. In addition to caps on jury awards, restrictions include the elimination of punitive damages, cutbacks in lawyer contingency fees, and shorter periods for bringing suits.

Recently attorneys have challenged these state-initiated tort reform laws, claiming they are infringements of such constitutional guarantees as equal protection of the law and access to jury trials. Thus far, they are having some success. Alaska, Kansas, Oklahoma, Texas, and Wyoming have struck down some state reform laws, despite the fact that the Supreme Court has ruled that state tort reform laws do not violate the Constitution.

The Dalkon Shield case is typical of the ongoing conflict between courts and legislatures trying to establish reformed guidelines for claims, versus attorneys doing their utmost for claimants. Company bankruptcy is the most extreme consequence of product liability claims. A. H. Robins declared bankruptcy after its Dalkon Shield was proved faulty. In a massive Chapter 11 case that lasted from August 1985 through November 1987, the U.S. District Judge told lawyers in the case that their fees bordered on "being utterly ridiculous." The fees to that point amounted to $12.2 million for work done. In an effort to limit what he saw as exploitation of the claim suit, the judge then ordered an end to all attorney payments until the conclusion of the case. Eventually, he awarded those injured $2.4 billion. The sum was to be paid on behalf of the bankrupt company from a trust fund established by A. H. Robin's insurer, Aetna Life & Casualty, to the estimated 200,000 Dalkon Shield users.

Issues for Discussion

1. Should companies be allowed to declare bankruptcy when faced with large product liability claims? Explain.
2. Do you believe consumers should be allowed to sue a company in a product liability case when the company is clearly not at fault? Explain.
3. What are the likely consequences of the increased numbers of product liability cases?

SUMMARY

Law is the process of thinking that is often reflected by court decisions, statutes, and regulations. Common law is judge-made, and statutory law is written and enacted by government bodies.

The Uniform Commercial Code is a collection of laws to make the conduct of business more consistent among the states. Mercantile law is the predecessor to modern business law.

A number of laws have been enacted to encourage fair trade and competition and to regulate certain business practices. Among the more important are the Sherman Antitrust Act of 1890, which declared trusts and other forms of monopoly illegal; the Clayton Act of 1914, which clarified and broadened the scope of the Sherman Act; the Celler-Kefauver Antimerger Act of 1950, which broadened the power of the Clayton Act; the Federal Trade Commission Act of 1914, which created the Federal Trade Commission and gave it the power to monitor unfair methods of competition and to penalize companies for using them; the Wheeler-Lea Act of 1938, which prohibited unfair and deceptive practices even if they didn't injure competition; the Robinson-Patman Act of 1936, which prohibited price discrimination; the Pure Food and Drug Act of 1908, which prohibited the adulteration and misbranding of food and drugs (and was later amended and renamed the Food, Drug, and Cosmetic Act of 1938); and the Fair Packaging and Labeling Act of 1966, which required the listing of ingredients on packages.

A contract is an agreement between two or more parties that is enforceable in court. The requirements for a contract are lawful purpose, competency of the parties, voluntary agreement, consideration, and form of contract. A breach of contract occurs when one party fails to perform the required duties or to meet one of the conditions of the agreement.

A negotiable instrument is any form of business paper used in commercial transactions as a substitute for money. The Uniform Commercial Code specifies its characteristics. The types of endorsements of negotiable instruments are blank endorsements, restrictive endorsements, special endorsements, and qualified endorsements.

Property is an item (or items) of value owned by an individual or business. There are two types of property: personal (anything other than real estate) and real (real estate). Ownership of property is passed through the title.

Warranties are promises by manufacturers or sellers to stand behind their products. Express warranties are written and spell out specific representations by the seller regarding the product. They can be full or limited. Implied warranties are unwritten and automatically come with the products. The Magnuson-Moss Warranty Act of 1975 required that warranted products contain straightforward language about how claims would be handled and other information.

Agency law is a legal arrangement whereby one party authorizes another to act on his or her behalf.

The law of torts is civil law dealing with wrongful acts by one party that injure another party, through negligence or deliberate intent. Product liability law holds businesses liable for negligence when their products cause injury.

Trademarks protect the name, word, symbol, or other device registered by owners for the purpose of identifying their product lines. Copyrights protect the owners of creative works against illegal reproduction of those works. Patents protect owners' inventions.

Bankruptcy is the legal nonpayment of financial obligations. In 1978, Congress passed the Bankruptcy Reform Act, whose Chapters 7 (liquidation) and 11 (reorganization) are the most important. Voluntary bankruptcy occurs when a company files for bankruptcy itself. Involuntary bankruptcy occurs when creditors force a company into bankruptcy.

KEY TERMS

CHECK YOUR LEARNING

Reread the following learning objectives. Each objective is followed by a few questions. Answering these questions accurately will help you retain the most important concepts discussed in this chapter. After answering each question, check your answer with the key at the end of this chapter. (*Hint:* If you have doubt regarding the correct response, consult the page whose number follows the answer.)

Circle:

A. Explain the difference between common law and statutory law.

1. Legal decisions based on previously decided cases reflect the use of: (a) substantive law; (b) tort law; (c) statutory law; (d) common law.

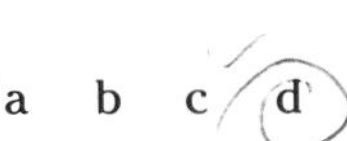
a b c d

2. Codified laws are known as: (a) statutory laws; (b) civil laws; (c) regulations; (d) common law.

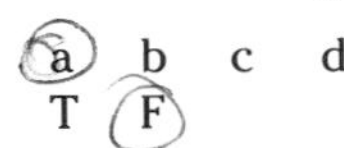
a b c d

3. *Stare decisis* is a term associated with merchant law.

T F

B. Discuss the basic purpose of the Uniform Commercial Code.

1. Which state has yet to accept all provisions of the UCC? (a) Louisiana; (b) California; (c) Mississippi; (d) New York.

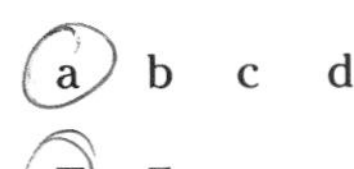
a b c d

2. The Uniform Commercial Code attempts to make business laws more consistent among states.

T F

C. Discuss the federal laws that promote fair trade and competition.

1. Which act forbade interlocking directorates: (a) Robinson-Patman Act; (b) Clayton Act; (c) Federal Trade Commission Act; (d) Sherman Antitrust Act.

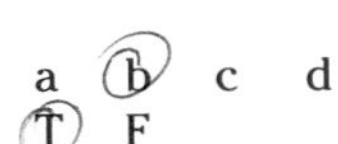
a b c d

2. The Sherman Antitrust Act prohibits price fixing.

T F

3. The Pure Food and Drug Act was amended and strengthened in 1962 by the: (a) Clayton Act; (b) Robinson-Patman Act; (c) Fair Packaging and Labeling Act; (d) Kefauver-Harris Act.

a b c d

D. Explain the five elements necessary for a legal contract and the meaning of *breach of contract.*

1. Contracts that cannot be performed in a year or less must be in writing.

T F

2. Money is a common form of consideration.

T F

3. Select one of the following that is *not* a requirement for a legal contract: (a) stipulations are written out; (b) consideration is exchanged; (c) parties are competent; (d) agreement is voluntary.

a b c d

E. List the requirements for negotiability.

1. A personal check is an example of a negotiable instrument.

T F

2. Negotiable instruments must be made payable to order or to bearer.

T F

3. Which one of the following is *not* a requirement for negotiability: (a) instrument must be in writing and signed by maker or drawer; (b) instrument must be made payable to order; (c) payment must be made on demand or at a specific time designated in the future; (d) all of the above are requirements.

a b c d

F. Write out and label four types of endorsements.

1. A lone signature on the back of a check is a blank endorsement.

T F

2. "For deposit only" represents a qualified endorsement.

T F

3. The words *without recourse* usually indicate a: (a) restrictive endorsement; (b) blank endorsement; (c) qualified endorsement; (d) special endorsement.

a b c d

G. Discuss how title is passed for personal property.

1. If you purchase merchandise FOB shipping point, you own the goods while they are in transit.

T F

2. Merchandise sent to you on a trial basis becomes your property immediately upon receipt.

T F

H. Compare express warranties and implied warranties.

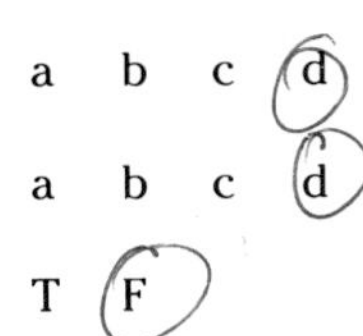

1. A limited warranty is a type of: (a) implied warranty; (b) guarantee; (c) de facto warranty; (d) express warranty. — a b c d
2. Guaranteeing that a typewriter will type is an example of a(an): (a) express warranty; (b) written warranty; (c) limited warranty; (d) implied warranty. — a b c d
3. Most consumers desire limited warranties because the prices of the items are much less. — T F

I. Discuss the impact of agency law and the law of torts on business activities.

1. Realtors are most frequently employed as principals by consumers to sell their homes. — T F
2. An agent may vote for you in a national election. — T F
3. Torts seldom involve lawsuits for monetary damages. — T F

J. Differentiate among trademarks, copyrights, and patents.

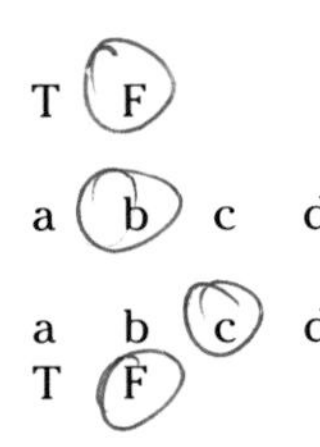

1. Copyrights are granted for a period of seventeen years. — T F
2. An inventor of a unique process would try to secure a: (a) trademark; (b) patent; (c) copyright; (d) both b and c. — a b c d
3. The name *Levis* is an example of a: (a) patent; (b) copyright; (c) trademark; (d) patent pending. — a b c d
4. Registered patents ensure that competitors will not infringe on your product area. — T F

K. Discuss the basic aspects of bankruptcy law and proceedings.

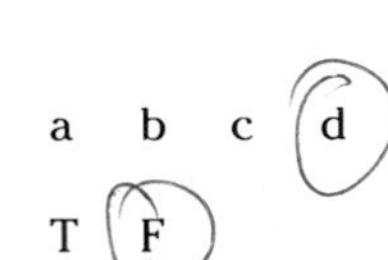

1. Involuntary bankruptcy occurs after creditors bring suit against the debtor. — T F
2. If a company files bankruptcy under Chapter 7 of the Bankruptcy Reform Act, which individual would most likely be paid last: (a) trade creditor; (b) preferred stockholder; (c) secured creditor; (d) common stockholder. — a b c d
3. After bankruptcy proceedings have been concluded, the debtor continues to have a legal obligation to pay past-due amounts associated with the bankruptcy. — T F

QUESTIONS FOR REVIEW AND DISCUSSION

1. Define the key terms at the end of the chapter.
2. Explain the difference between common law and statutory law.
3. How has the Uniform Commercial Code improved the exchange of goods and services among states?
4. List and discuss the major federal laws that promote fair trade and competition.
5. Do you agree or disagree with the following statement: It is best to get a contract in writing. Explain.
6. Jack Cahill verbally agreed to accept a summer job for the city park department. Afterwards, he decided to attend summer school and informed the city that he would not be working. Can Jack be sued for breach of contract?
7. Why is it important for a bank teller or cashier to be aware of the different endorsement procedures?
8. Do you agree or disagree with the following statement: Companies are taking warranty service more seriously in recent years. Explain.
9. How would a consumer use the agency principle to complete a business transaction?
10. List at least six trademark names that you consider to be generic in nature. Should the companies that trademarked the names continue to be protected? Explain.
11. What is the difference between voluntary and involuntary bankruptcy? List the steps normally followed during a bankruptcy procedure.

CONCLUDING CASE

Buyer Protection for Used Cars

Federal Trade Commission regulations require that buyer's guide stickers be attached to all used cars offered for sale by dealers. An estimated 10.5 million vehicles are sold through the nation's 89,000 used-car dealers. This law, covering $60 billion in sales, comes after a decade of investigation into the used-car business.

Traditionally, used-car dealers have sold cars "as is" but verbally promised to fix any problems that arose. These verbal agreements were often hard to enforce. The stickers must clearly state whether a warranty is offered and, if so, what systems are covered and for how long. Savings to consumers could range from $500 to $1,500 in repairs on cars with an average price of $3,000 to $4,000.

The rule covers all dealers who sell at least six vehicles a year. The 7 million individuals who sell their own used vehicles privately are not covered by the law. Dealers who fail to comply with the FTC ruling face fines up to $10,000 per day for each violation.

Carol T. Crawford, director of the FTC's Bureau of Consumer Protection, warns consumers that the stickers are not a replacement for good shopping judgment. Consumers should require promises in writing. Also, it is suggested that a used car be inspected by an independent mechanic before buying. It may also be a plus factor if the dealer has his own service repair shop.

Some states have passed laws guaranteeing used-car buyers a minimum warranty on specified parts. In Massachusetts, the law covers vehicles that cost $700 or more and have less than 125,000 miles at the time of sale. In Minnesota, a similar law applies to vehicles less than eight years old that have been driven less than 75,000 miles and that have sticker prices of at least $3,000.

Issues for Discussion

1. Do you agree with Crawford's suggestions in regard to purchasing a used car? Would you add any guidelines?
2. Will the FTC sticker rule reduce the number of warranty disputes between dealers and buyers?
3. Will the FTC sticker rule increase the cost of used vehicles? Explain.

NOTES

1. Joseph L. Frascona, *Business Law* (Dubuque, Iowa: Wm. C. Brown, 1981), pp. 36–37.
2. Harry Bacas, "Liability: Trying Times," *Nation's Business,* February 1986, pp. 22–25.
3. Paul M. Barrett, "Tort Reform Fight Shifts to State Courts," *Wall Street Journal,* September 9, 1988, p. 27.
4. Ronald Alsop, "It's Slim Pickings in Product Name Game," *Wall Street Journal,* November 24, 1988, p. B1.
5. "Burger Chain Charges Trademark Violation," *Tribune-Star,* July 26, 1988, p. A7.
6. Stephen Wermiel, "Home Taperecording of T.V. Shows Is Approved 5–4 by Supreme Court," *Wall Street Journal,* January 18, 1984, p. 3.
7. "U.S. Adherence to the Berne Convention," *Imprint,* Fall 1988, p. 4.
8. Buck Brown, "For Small Firms, Perils Lie in Chapter 11," *Wall Street Journal,* July 14, 1988, p. 25.

CHECK YOUR LEARNING ANSWER KEY

A. 1. d, *p. 649*
   2. a, *p. 649*
   3. F, *p. 649*
B. 1. a, *p. 649*
   2. T, *p. 649*
C. 1. b, *p. 651*
   2. T, *p. 650*
   3. d, *p. 652*
D. 1. T, *p. 654*
   2. T, *p. 654*
   3. a, *p. 654*
E. 1. T, *p. 655*
   2. T, *p. 656*
   3. b, *p. 656*
F. 1. T, *p. 657*
   2. F, *p. 657*
   3. c, *p. 658*
G. 1. T, *p. 658*
   2. F, *p. 658*
H. 1. d, *p. 659*
   2. d, *p. 659*
   3. F, *p. 659*
I. 1. F, *p. 660*
   2. F, *p. 660*
   3. F, *p. 661*
J. 1. F, *p. 663*
   2. b, *p. 664*
   3. c, *p. 663*
   4. F, *p. 664*
K. 1. T, *p. 665*
   2. d, *p. 665*
   3. F, *p. 665*

CHAPTER

23

BUSINESS IN A GLOBAL ENVIRONMENT

LEARNING OBJECTIVES

After reading this chapter you should be able to:

1. Explain why international trade is important to all nations, and how each can best utilize the principles of absolute and comparative advantage.
2. Distinguish between balance of payments and balance of trade, and explain what has caused the United States to have a trade deficit in recent years.
3. Discuss the various trends that indicate the world is entering a period of protectionism.
4. Distinguish among different types of trade barriers, such as tariffs, quotas, and embargoes.
5. Explain why it is important to understand cultural differences when marketing products internationally.
6. List and explain the role of various types of international assistance programs available to promote world trade.
7. Describe the differences among the primary methods of organizing for international markets.
8. Explain the role of multinational corporations and their importance to the American economy.
9. Discuss the growing implications of nationalism as it affects multinational corporations.
10. Explain how cartels and common markets can improve a country's bargaining position in the world market.

OUTLINE

Business Practice Example: The McDonnell Douglas Company

The Importance of International Trade

- Exports and Imports
- Principle of Absolute Advantage
- Principle of Comparative Advantage

Problems and Opportunities in International Trade

- Balance of Payments and Trade
- Shifting Currencies
- Trade Barriers
  - Tariffs
  - Quotas
  - Embargoes
- Cultural Differences
- Legal Barriers

Promotion of International Trade

- Export Trading Companies Act
- GATT
- Eximbank
- Foreign Sales Corporations
- Foreign Trade Zones
- World Bank and International Monetary Fund

Organizing for Global Markets

- Country-Centered and Global Marketing Strategies
- Exporting
- Licensing
- Contract Manufacturing
- Direct Investment
- Countertrade

Multinationals and Nationalism

- Role and Importance of Multinational Corporations
- Nationalism
- Cartels
- Common Markets

Summary

Key Terms

Check Your Learning

Questions for Review and Discussion

Concluding Case: Unilever Targets the U.S. Market

Notes

Check Your Learning Answer Key

Highlight in Business Practice: Heinz Plans a European Food Fight

BUSINESS PRACTICE EXAMPLE

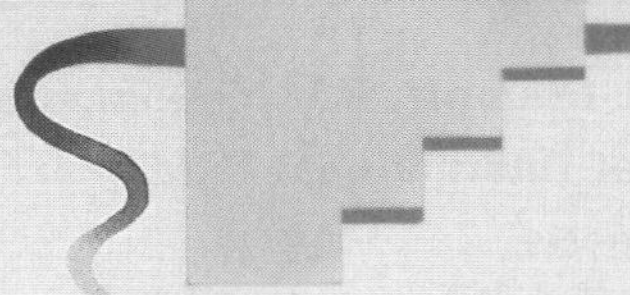

The McDonnell Douglas Company

The McDonnell Douglas Company, part of the aerospace and defense industry, produces commercial and military aircraft, ranging from the wide-body DC-10 and the MD-80 jet to the F-12 Eagle fighter plane. In 1989, *Fortune* magazine ranked McDonnell Douglas as the third largest U.S. company in its industry category, just behind Boeing and United Technologies. *Fortune* also ranked McDonnell Douglas as the twenty-fifth largest U.S. industrial corporation in sales. McDonnell Douglas is a multinational company, selling its fighters to the air forces of Japan, Israel, and Saudi Arabia, among other countries, and its commercial aircraft to Europe, Asia, and some Eastern bloc countries.

Like all successful companies, McDonnell Douglas must constantly monitor the environment and make adjustments to remain competitive. In 1987 and 1988, several important domestic and international events occurred; in all likelihood, they will have long-term global repercussions. First, the drastic stock market plunge, citizen concern, and our international trading partners made it very clear that Congress had to take more drastic measures to reduce the federal deficit and balance the budget. This meant a tightening of the federal pocketbook, including funds for defense. Second, sensing that the timing was right in the United States and in the Soviet Union, Soviet leader Mikhail Gorbachev announced before the United Nations Assembly in New York that the Soviet Union would soon begin withdrawing 500,000 troops from Eastern Europe. The message was obvious for armament companies such as McDonnell Douglas. They must be alert to survive in this new era of disarmament.

In addition, countries belonging to the European Community (EC) decided to dissolve many of their internal trade barriers by 1992. Thus, changes in McDonnell Douglas's current business and marketing strategies will no doubt occur. These changes will be made to protect and enhance the company's position as a leading multinational firm.

As the company's history shows, McDonnell Douglas knows how to succeed at difficult tasks and challenges. The present company was created in 1967, when two of the oldest family-owned aviation companies merged. The Douglas Company, founded in 1920 by Donald W. Douglas, made the famous D series planes that included the workhorse of World War II, the DC-3 (also used as a commercial aircraft). After Boeing introduced its 707 in 1959, Douglas was never able to keep up financially or in production.

By 1966, the Douglas Company was ripe for a merger offer by the McDonnell Company. McDonnell was founded in 1939 by James S. McDonnell. With the need for additional aircraft during World War II, the company became a major industry in its home city, St. Louis. The McDonnell Company was the first to manufacture commercial jets for aircraft carriers and to make famous military jets, such as the Demon, the Voodoo, and the Phantom. Today, the McDonnell Douglas Company is run by John F. McDonnell, who holds the position of CEO.

WHAT'S AHEAD

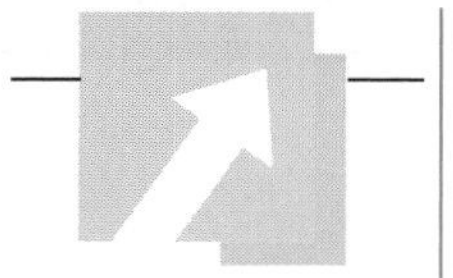

McDonnell Douglas is truly a multinational company. Not only does it import parts from around the world for its planes, but it also exports the finished product. This chapter explains why it is important that companies such as McDonnell Douglas become involved in international trade, the problems involved in international trade, the role of multinational companies, and the role of such organizations as the European community and OPEC. After reading this chapter, you should understand the basic considerations for evaluating international trade potential.

THE IMPORTANCE OF INTERNATIONAL TRADE

The United States has engaged in international trade since its earliest days. At no time in history, however, has international trade been as important to the economic health of nations as it is today. The world economy is now truly interdependent. What occurs in one part of the world is inevitably felt in another. As the world population grows, there is pressure for all nations to trade and work together to survive. As we will see, no single nation can efficiently create all the goods and services its citizens want and need. Self-sufficient economies are a thing of the past.

For U.S. companies of every size, the global marketplace offers much appeal. While the U.S. population is maintaining a steady growth, the world population is exploding (over 1 billion new people since 1977). Worldwide, there are 5 billion people. Demographers have predicted that if present birthrates continue, the world will have 8 billion people to feed, clothe, and provide shelter for by 2020. All these people will have many needs and wants that businesses across the globe will attempt to meet.

U.S. industries must remain competitive or lose business to countries such as Japan, Germany, Canada, and Korea. Today, nearly 20 percent of our industrial production is exported; 70 percent of the goods we produce compete with merchandise from abroad.[1] Despite the trade problems of the 1980s, caused by a strong dollar and a low U.S. productivity rate, the United States is finally beginning to recapture lost market share from foreign competitors.

In the late 1980s, a weaker dollar and years of cost cutting made U.S. products a bargain in world markets. Some companies even set their sights on a bigger piece of the pie at the expense of larger profits. This strategy has paid off for

At no time in history has international trade been as important to the economic health of nations as it is today. In our truly interdependent world economy, what happens on the streets of Moscow can have an economic impact on the rest of the world.

manufacturers of machinery, aircraft, paper, medical equipment, and chemicals. These industries have been successful at stopping the erosion of their markets. On the other hand, the U.S. automotive, textile and apparel, electronics, steel, and machine tool industries have been relative losers in world competition.

Although some skeptics argue that the boomlet for U.S. products is a temporary phenomenon created by the 50 percent drop in the dollar's value, others believe there is evidence that the new export strength will endure. During 1988, the volume of exports was growing at almost four times the rate of imports. This jump in exports may be attributed to three causes. First, thousands of smaller businesses (those of less than $400 million a year in sales) are now exporting. Second, America's larger multinationals (companies operating in several nations) are making a commitment to buy more U.S. parts and to build more U.S. plants. Finally, much growth is coming from the foreign industrial giants that have purchased ailing U.S. manufacturing plants and exported their goods abroad.

Exports and Imports

Exports are goods and services sold to other countries.

Imports are goods and services purchased from other countries.

Any nation can export or import products. **Exports** are goods and services sold to other countries. **Imports** are goods and services purchased from other countries. The exchange of products among countries is called *international trade.* Once a minor element in the U.S. economy, international trade now plays a major and rapidly expanding role. Between 1960 and 1987, imports and exports rose from 10 percent of GNP to an estimated 21 percent.

Since the United States is the world's largest exporter and importer, international trade has a significant impact on the employment of American workers. Some 5.4 million workers (more than twice the number in the 1960s) hold down jobs created by exports. Each billion dollars' worth of products sold overseas generates 25,000 new jobs. However, the Labor Department estimates that some 1.1 million U.S. job opportunities are lost yearly as a result of the products we import rather than manufacture. As Table 23.1 reveals, aircraft, chemical, and motor vehicle–related companies are America's leading exporters. Of all U.S. exports, 85 percent are attributed to only 250 corporations.[2]

Table 23.1 America's leading exporters.

Rank 1988	Rank 1987	Company	Products	Export Sales (Millions of Dollars)	Total Sales (Millions of Dollars)	Exports as Percent of Sales: Percent	Exports as Percent of Sales: Rank
1	1	General Motors (Detroit)	Motor vehicles and parts	$9,392.0	$121,085.4	7.8	41
2	2	Ford Motor (Dearborn, Mich.)	Motor vehicles and parts	8,822.0	92,445.6	9.5	35
3	3	Boeing (Seattle)	Commercial and military aircraft	7,849.0	16,962.0	46.3	1
4	4	General Electric (Fairfield, Conn.)	Jet engines, generators, medical systems	5,744.0	49,414.0	11.6	29
5	5	International Business Machines (Armonk, N.Y.)	Computers and related equipment	4,951.0	59,681.0	8.3	39
6	8	Chrysler (Highland Park, Mich.)	Motor vehicles and parts	4,343.9	35,472.7	12.2	28
7	6	E.I. Du Pont de Nemours (Wilmington, Del.)	Specialty chemicals, energy products	4,196.0	32,514.0	12.9	26
8	7	McDonnell Douglas (St. Louis)	Commercial and military aircraft	3,471.0	15,072.0	23.0	5
9	10	Caterpillar (Peoria, Ill.)	Heavy machinery, engines, turbines	2,930.0	10,435.0	28.1	4
10	11	United Technologies (Hartford)	Jet engines, helicopters, cooling equipment	2,848.1	18,087.8	15.8	20

Principle of Absolute Advantage

Some countries enjoy an **absolute advantage** in trading. A country achieves an absolute advantage when either it is the only country that provides a product or it can produce the product at a lower cost than any other country. Hong Kong, for example, has an absolute advantage in producing toys. Because of inexpensive labor, Hong Kong can produce toys at a cost lower than that of any other country. An absolute advantage can result from a nation's resources, labor, technology, or climate. It can also result when a country enjoys a monopoly in the world market.

Absolute advantage is the advantage a country has when it is the only one producing a product or when it produces the product at the lowest cost.

The United States, for example, has an absolute advantage in oil-drilling parts, because it is the only nation that produces them. Even the Soviet Union has to purchase these parts from us, because it does not have the advanced technology to produce them itself. Theoretically, each nation should specialize in and export the products for which it has an absolute advantage and import the products it needs.

Principle of Comparative Advantage

Comparative advantage is the advantage a country achieves when it specializes in the products it can supply more efficiently and at a lower cost than other items.

Most nations do not have unique natural resources, such as Saudi Arabia's oil, or specialized production capabilities. That is, they do not have any absolute advantages. However, they can and do engage in international trade. These countries use their **comparative advantage,** which means they specialize in the products they can supply more efficiently and at a lower cost than other items. By concentrating on what they can do best, countries are better able to utilize their natural resources, technology, labor, and climate to produce more efficiently.

Because the United States is rich in resources, for example, it has a comparative advantage in the manufacture of automobiles, electrical machinery, aircraft, and weapons. However, comparative advantage is not constant, and there is evidence that the United States is losing its comparative advantage in some manufacturing industries. Experts believe this long-term decline is due to diminished investment in research and development and the sluggish growth of American investment.

PROBLEMS AND OPPORTUNITIES IN INTERNATIONAL TRADE

Balance of Payments and Trade

The ***balance of payments*** is the difference between the expenditures made to other nations and receipts taken in from other nations during a given time.

The ***balance of trade*** is the difference between sales of exports and purchases of imports.

Although the global marketplace is now a fact of life, those engaged in international trade face problems as well as opportunities. A major concern for any country is its **balance of payments**—the difference between the expenditures made to other nations and the receipts taken in from other nations during a given time. This balance consists of eight major categories, five for expenditures *(outflows)* and three for receipts *(inflows)*. Outflows include imports, tourism, investment, foreign aid, and military expenditures. Inflows include exports, tourism, and investment income.

Recently Americans have focused on another balance: the U.S. balance of trade. The **balance of trade** is the difference between sales of exports and

Figure 23.1
The U.S. balance of trade, 1981–1988. The United States has experienced trade deficits off and on since 1971.

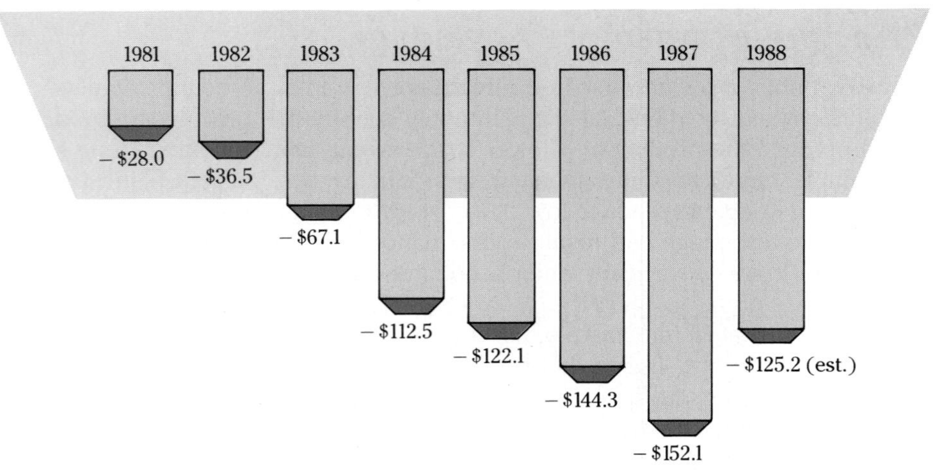

purchases of imports. Despite being the world's leading exporter, the United States began to experience periodic trade deficits in 1971. A **trade deficit** is a negative, or unfavorable, balance of trade. Figure 23.1 illustrates the U.S. trade deficits since 1981. Following are some of the many reasons economists have given for this downturn:

A ***trade deficit*** is a negative, or unfavorable, balance of trade.

1. A deep-rooted disinterest in exporting by many American businesses.
2. The sharp rise in the price of imported oil.
3. The prevalence of quality imports at cheaper prices.
4. The fact that America's economic growth has required more imports to meet demands.
5. Slow economic growth in Europe and Japan, which has resulted in a weak demand for American goods in those countries.
6. The strength of the dollar against competing currencies.

Some of these reasons are no longer valid. For instance, by 1989, responding to new opportunities created by the decline in the dollar, well over 100,000 U.S. companies were exporting to foreign markets, with small and medium-size companies most aggressively gaining sales.[3] Table 23.2 illustrates the percentage of exports to total sales by leading exporting industries. Table 23.3 gives the numbers of "infrequent," "growing," and "frequent" U.S. exporters today.

Although exporting activity has heated up considerably since 1981, U.S. demand for quality foreign consumer and industrial products continues to be strong—in spite of increased prices of most imports since 1986.

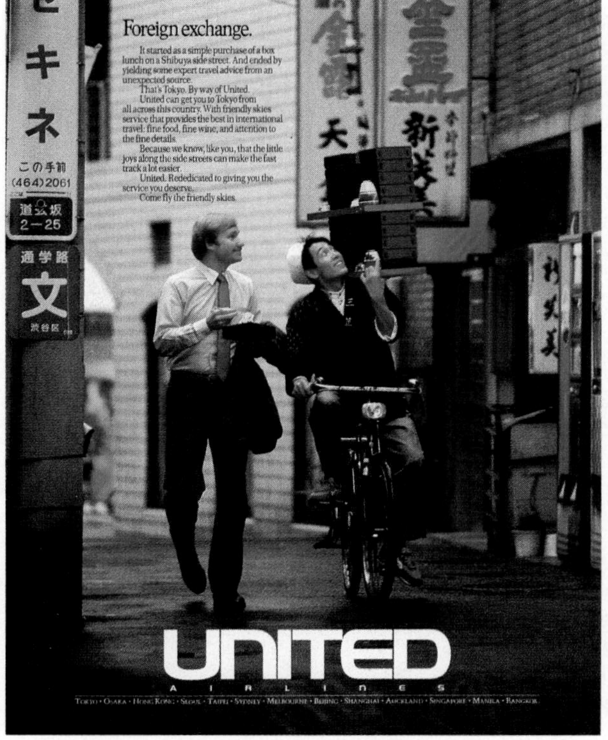

International travel and tourism is a major balance of payments category.

Table 23.2 Small business revs up exports.

Industry Company	1988 Sales (Millions of Dollars)	1988 Exports (Percent of Sales)	1989 Exports* (Increase over 1988)
Medical Technology			
Lectec (Minnetonka, Minn.)	$7.0	15%	100%
Lixi (Downers Grove, Ill.)	3.5	55	20
Medrad (Pittsburgh)	35.0	21	35
Scientific & Testing Equipment			
Koehler Instrument (Bohemia, N.Y.)	4.1	24	32
Lecroy (Chestnut Ridge, N.Y.)	37.0	28	10
SLM Instruments (Urbana, Ill.)	8.0	30	30
Specialized Industrial Machinery			
Ambrose (Redmond, Wash.)	1.5	10	300
Econocorp (Randolph, Mass.)	4.0	44	50
Pollution Control Equipment			
Aeration Industries Intl. (Chaska, Minn.)	15.0	25	100
Aqua-Aerobic Systems (Rockford, Ill.)	18.4	4	33
Environmental Control (Maple Shade, N.J.)	60.0	5	100
Computer-Related Products			
Clearpoint Research (Hopkinton, Mass.)	51.0	20	100
Progress Software (Bedford, Mass.)	15.5	45	60
Sequent Computer Systems (Beaverton, Ore.)	75.0	37	73
Homebuilding Products			
Lindal Cedar Homes (Seattle)	49.0	4	100
Marvin Windows (Warroad, Minn.)	250.0	10	30
Nectar Pacific Homes (Capitola, Calif.)	3.0	20	400

*Projected.

Table 23.3 Most U.S. exporters aren't in the big leagues yet.

Category	Number of Companies
Infrequent exporters (averaging 9 shipments a year)	86,500
Growing exporters (averaging 116 shipments a year)	9,900
Frequent exporters (averaging 4,410 shipments a year)	3,600

BUSINESS PRACTICE EXAMPLE Continues

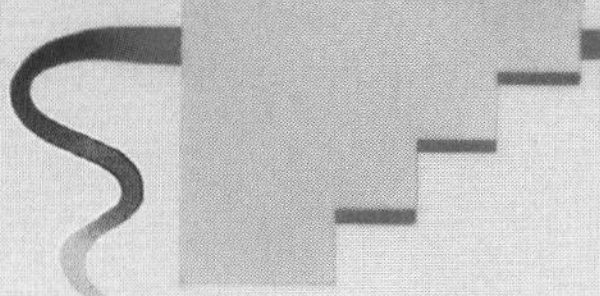

The United States has long held a comparative advantage in the manufacture of aircraft, but companies such as McDonnell Douglas are facing increasing competition from European manufacturers. For example, Airbus Industrie, a powerful French-led consortium of European aerospace manufacturers heavily subsidized by several governments, has directly competed with McDonnell Douglas. Thus McDonnell Douglas must compete not only against U.S. firms such as Boeing and United Technologies but against foreign firms as well.

Fortunately, McDonnell Douglas is part of an industry that enjoys an international trade surplus. In 1988, the aerospace industry's surplus was $13.2 billion. This stands in sharp contrast to the situation of the U.S. electronics industry, which in 1988 had a trade deficit of $2 billion.

Shifting Currencies

Prior to August 1971, differences in the balance of payments between countries were usually paid by transferring gold from the country with the deficit to the country with the surplus. In 1971, however, the United States accumulated deficit payments that were greater than the supply of gold the country held. In that year, president Richard Nixon took the United States off the gold standard of $35 per ounce (the Bretton Woods system). In so doing, he altered the entire international monetary system.

Previously, world currency had been based on the American dollar, which was tied to a fixed rate for gold. A new system, the free-floating exchange rate system, was devised in 1973. In the **free-floating exchange rate system,** market forces, not a country's gold reserve holdings, determine appropriate exchange rates. **Exchange rates** are the rates at which one country's currency is exchanged for the currency of another country. They vary with supply and demand.

The watchdog of international exchange is the *International Monetary Fund (IMF),* the United Nations agency that works to ensure that countries do not manipulate exchange rates to gain unfair competitive advantage over trade rivals. In addition, the IMF covers short-term differences in payment balances among its 147 members, secures international cooperation, stabilizes exchange rates, and expands international liquidity. (The IMF will be discussed again later in the chapter.)

Devaluation is a reduction in the value of currency in relation to gold or some other standard. During the 1970s, dollar devaluation made U.S.-made products cost-competitive in international markets. In the first half of the 1980s, the opposite

The ***free-floating exchange rate system*** is the exchange rate system under which market forces, not a country's gold reserve holdings, determine appropriate exchange rates.

Exchange rates are the rates at which one country's currency is exchanged for the currency of another country.

Devaluation is a reduction in the value of currency in relation to gold or some other standard.

occurred. Foreign currencies were devalued, and the American dollar became stronger. The result was fewer U.S. exports and a flood of imports into the United States. The strong dollar made U.S. products more expensive abroad and lowered the price of foreign products in the United States. In 1986, the U.S. dollar was once again devalued, and the United States began to increase its volume of exports.

Trade Barriers

Nations trade for many reasons. They also restrict trade for many reasons. In the U.S. Congress there is a growing belief that America's position on free trade has allowed Asia and Europe to become stronger at our expense. Many American industries and labor unions are pressing Congress for tougher trade barriers. The belief that trade should be restricted for the protection of domestic industries is called **protectionism.**

Protectionism is the belief that free trade should be restricted for the protection of domestic industries.

The use of trade barriers to improve the trade deficit was tried in the 1930s without success. Instead, attempts to cut foreign products from U.S. markets started a trade war and deepened the worldwide recession. Today, protectionist legislation costs consumers almost $50 billion a year. Figure 23.2 illustrates the hidden costs of protectionism.

Several methods are used by governments to restrict trade, including tariff and nontariff barriers.

Tariffs

Tariffs are taxes or duties placed on imported products.

Taxes or duties placed on imported goods are **tariffs.** For instance, Canada, the largest trading partner of the United States, currently uses a tariff on U.S.-made wire and cable that is three times the U.S. rate. The effect is that fewer units are sold in Canada, and thus fewer are imported into Canada. In addition, this tariff earns revenue for the Canadian government. Thus, we can see that tariffs are popular because they are both flexible and selective in nature. They can be aimed at any type of good or country and can provide both protection and revenue.

Quotas

Quotas are quantitative limits on the amounts of goods that can be legally imported into a country.

Dumping is the practice of selling a product in another country for less than it is sold in the producing country.

Quantitative limits on the amount of goods that can be legally imported into a country are **quotas.** A landmark case involving quotas in the United States occurred in 1968. American TV manufacturers complained to the United States Treasury that Japanese TV makers were dumping color TVs in the United States. **Dumping** is the practice of selling a product in another country for less than it is sold in the producing country. It allows a country to make a quick entry into a foreign market and to capture a large market share with low product costs. Economist Edward Bernstein, an architect of the Bretton Woods agreement, explained the situation this way: "Let's accept that the Japanese are very efficient. But by the definition of comparative advantage a nation can't have a comparative advantage in everything. Yet the Japanese can outsell us in steel, ships, TV sets, automobiles, and business machines. That can't be comparative advantage. That's dumping."[4]

Zenith sued in United States Customs Court to have a quota placed on Japanese color TVs. The result was a three-year accord signed by the United States and

Annual cost to consumers

	Total Cost	Cost per Job Saved
Textiles, apparel	**$27.0 billion**	$42,000
Steel	**$6.8 billion**	$750,000
Automobiles	**$5.8 billion**	$105,000
Dairy products	**$5.5 billion**	$220,000
Maritime industries	**$3.0 billion**	$270,000
Sugar	**$930 million**	$60,000
Book manufacturing	**$500 million**	$100,000
Rubber footwear	**$230 million**	$30,000
Glassware	**$200 million**	$200,000

Note: Protectionism is defined as exceptional restraints on imports implemented through high tariffs, quota limits or other limitations that go beyond normal tariff or border restrictions.
USN&WR—Basic data: *Trade Protection in the United States, 31 Case Studies* by Gary C. Hufbauer, Diane T. Berliner, and Kimberly A. Elliot

Figure 23.2
The hidden costs of protectionism. Copyright 1988, *U.S. News & World Report.*

Japan in mid-1977 that limited Japan's annual export of TVs to the United States to 1,560,000 sets—some 60 percent of the 1976 level. In 1984, the United States and Japan reached a voluntary agreement to limit the annual importing of Japanese-made cars into the United States to 1.7 million.

Embargoes

An ***embargo*** is an order that prohibits a particular good from entering or leaving the country.

An **embargo** is an order that prohibits a particular good from entering or leaving the country. Embargoes can be directed at specific goods or countries and can be ordered by the government or by unions. Usually, they are ordered for reasons of politics, health, or morality.

Politically Based Embargoes During the 1980s, the United States used political embargoes several times. In 1988, for instance, it imposed economic sanctions including embargoes against Panama. The purpose was to force Gen. Manuel A. Noriega out of power because of reported drug dealings and racketeering.

In 1985, the U.S. government ordered an embargo on goods shipped to and from Nicaragua because of that nation's continuing attempt to export communism to neighboring Central American countries. In late 1981, the U.S. government announced a cutoff of $300 million in annual sales of high-technology products, including computers and oil and gas equipment, to the Soviet Union in response to the Soviet military crackdown in Poland. This embargo caused many diplomatic problems with our European allies when, in 1982, the United States enforced the embargo and penalized two French firms for exporting gas-line equipment to the Soviets.

Another embargo occurred in 1980, this one against foreign automobiles in New Jersey. Smarting from the closing of Ford's giant Mahwah, New Jersey, assembly plant, New Jersey representatives rammed a "Buy American" law through the state legislature. The law, which applies only to cars and trucks, orders the state government to buy American-made vehicles unless the purchase is "inconsistent" with the public interest or the cost is "unreasonable."

Health-Based Embargoes Because of health reasons, various pharmaceuticals, animals, plants, chemicals, fruits, and vegetables cannot be imported into the United States. United States Customs is authorized to embargo any goods that might be harmful to Americans. For example, some toys from Hong Kong cannot be imported because of their possibly toxic paint content. Similarly, in 1986 Canada and the United States refused to accept some fruits and vegetables from Italy because of radiation contamination caused by the Chernobyl nuclear power plant disaster in the Soviet Union.

Morality-Based Embargoes What is considered acceptable or moral in one country may not be considered so in another. For example, the United States does not allow certain pornographic materials to be imported. But *Playboy* magazine is not considered pornographic and thus is not prohibited in the United States. In Australia, however, *Playboy* and other sexually oriented magazines are considered immoral, and importing them is illegal. Similarly, Americans of legal age can purchase alcoholic beverages; however, in Saudi Arabia and other Muslim nations, alcoholic beverages cannot be imported or sold for moral and religious reasons. Iran and some other nations, both Muslim and non-Muslim, banned the import of the book *The Satanic Verses* by British writer Salman Rushdie, which they deemed blasphemous or otherwise unacceptable.

Cultural Differences

A country's *culture* is composed of its distinct beliefs, social forms, and material traits. Many businesspeople engaged in international trade have failed to appre-

Business people involved with international trade should learn all that they can about the cultures in which they do business. This American business man greets a Japanese company official in a much different manner than he would greet an American official.

ciate the importance of understanding the culture in which they do business. Increasingly, however, to remain ignorant of cultural traditions is to put the business enterprise at risk.

By now, Americans are accustomed to hearing about Japanese culture—how the Japanese value loyalty to the group and place great emphasis on not losing face. Japan, like every country, has countless beliefs and customs that are uniquely its own.

Although it is unfair to expect people involved in international trade to become instant experts on every aspect of another culture, it is important that business-people learn what they can. Symbols of all kinds carry very different meanings from one culture to another. How do the officers of a company in India, Japan, or Pakistan, for instance, expect to be greeted and addressed? When negotiating business arrangements, what tactics are permissible and what tactics are culturally offensive? When staffing an office in a foreign country, how long do the workers expect the workday to be? What are their work habits?

Legal Barriers

Legal principles vary throughout the world. For example, in the United States, a foreign company can buy or establish a company. However, in China and Japan, the law requires a *joint venture* with a Chinese or Japanese partner before a foreign company can operate. The Chinese joint venture law is deliberately vague so that the Chinese can control multinationals by slow growth and, thus, negotiate details to their advantage as the need arises. According to a Conference Board survey, more than a third of surveyed corporations involved in international joint ventures had to meet laws mandating local participation.[5] (Joint ventures will be discussed again later in the chapter.)

Many nations have strict laws governing advertising. For example, in France, children cannot be used in TV spots unless the product applies to them, and

HIGHLIGHT IN BUSINESS PRACTICE

Heinz Plans a European Food Fight

Anthony J.F. O'Reilly, chairman of H.J. Heinz Co., is planning a European food fight. Although his $5.2 billion company is about one-sixth the size of big rivals Nestlé and Unilever, it has strong positions in ketchup, baby food, canned soups, and beans. To survive in a single Europe, O'Reilly plans to spend up to $1 billion on acquisitions, plant modernization, and marketing by 1992. A major goal: to push his frozen Weight Watcher meals across Europe.

That pits Heinz against Nestlé's Lean Cuisine. The two have been slugging it out in the U.S. for years. Now they are taking their gloves off in Europe, where O'Reilly expects rising ranks of working women to double the diet meal market to $1 billion in sales annually by 1992.

Nestlé is No. 1 in frozen diet meals thanks to strong positions in Britain and France. But Heinz is using its broad local distribution networks to push Weight Watchers into Britain and Italy. Both have just begun to face off in Germany, the big prize. There, Nestlé has the edge, but Heinz is gaining by introducing dishes such as beef stroganoff and apple strudel. "It's going to be hand-to-hand combat," says O'Reilly.

Heinz also plans to transform itself into Europe's low-cost ketchup producer by extending its reach into markets beyond Britain, the Netherlands, and Belgium, where it's the ketchup king. That means going after BSN in France and

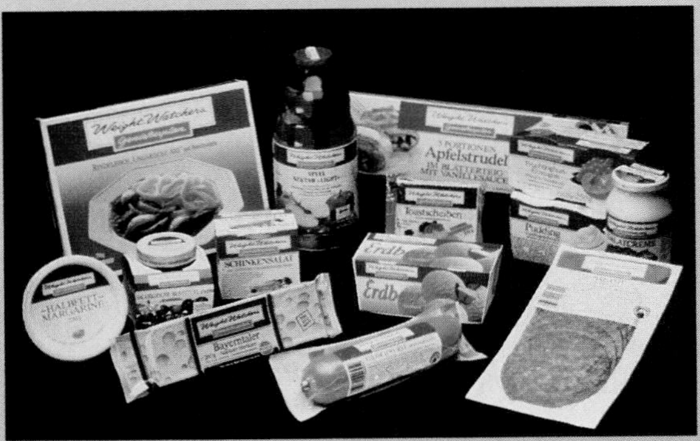

tackling Nestlé and Kraft across the rest of Europe. To do that, Heinz may turn its British and Iberian plants into regional production centers. O'Reilly has spent $250 million in Spain and Portugal, mainly on ketchup-related acquisitions and plant expansion. The goal "is to make Heinz ketchup as ubiquitous a product as Coca-Cola," says O'Reilly.

Europe-oriented rivals such as BSN aren't as international but can be tough in specific markets. BSN has bought 14 foodmakers across the Continent since mid-1987 and is driving against Heinz in ketchup, mustard, and pickles. Nestlé and Unilever, on the other hand, so dominate Europe that a U.S. company such as Heinz has to tread softly. When Nestlé focuses on a specific product, O'Reilly quips the best thing to do is: "Duck." Heinz will clearly be doing a lot of bobbing and weaving as 1992 approaches.

even then a child cannot give anything resembling a sales pitch. Twenty-four nations do not recognize U.S. trademarks or copyrights. Thus, the copying of movies, books, records, and brand names cannot be controlled by law. Furthermore, gifts to government employees (or bribes, as they are called in the United

States) are acceptable and encouraged in some nations. In other nations, such as the United States, they are illegal.

PROMOTION OF INTERNATIONAL TRADE

Most nations try to promote trade, in the belief that it efficiently allocates the world's economic resources. Governments and multinational corporations are constantly involved in activities to promote the cooperation and organization necessary to overcome trade problems.

The United States is no exception. The U.S. Department of Commerce, for example, utilizes a worldwide computer network to match prospective American exporters with buyers in key importing nations. The program, called "Matchmaker," invites U.S. business representatives to other countries to demonstrate their products at trade shows. In 126 U.S. embassies around the world, staff commercial officers represent American companies. In addition, the Department of Commerce publishes a catalog called *Commercial U.S.A.* ten times a year. This publication provides product descriptions and photos and is distributed to 110,000 foreign agents, distributors, and other interested buyers of U.S. products.

U.S.-Canada Agreement Despite the growing calls for protectionist measures from some, in 1988 the United States and Canada signed a trade agreement ending all tariffs between the two countries by January 1, 1999. This agreement will also reduce many nontariff barriers. Included in the terms are exemptions from quotas for meat importers by both nations, the easing of border crossings for business purposes, and the elimination of many restrictions that require government agencies to buy only products made within their own country. When the agreement is implemented, the United States and Canada will form the world's largest free trade zone and will serve as a major competitor to the European trading bloc.

In the following sections, we will look at some major laws and institutions that promote international trade.

Export Trading Companies Act

In 1982, Congress passed the **Export Trading Companies Act,** which grants U.S. companies the right to use export trading companies (ETCs) to set prices in concert abroad, provides access to government financing and guarantees, and allows banks the right to own and operate their own ETCs. Export trading companies are organizations whose purpose is to gain export markets.

The ***Export Trading Companies Act of 1982*** is federal legislation that grants U.S. companies the right to use export trading companies and gives them access to government financing and guarantees.

GATT

During the depression of the 1930s, a trade war broke out. So many countries had so many tariffs that not many could afford to sell their products abroad. This helped deepen the depression. In 1948, in order to prevent further trade wars caused by increasing tariffs, twenty-three nations formulated the treaty known as the **General Agreement on Tariffs and Trade (GATT).** A code of rules covering four-fifths of world trade, GATT encourages trade relations through the reduction and elimination of tariffs. Today, ninety-six nations abide by the treaty.

The ***General Agreement on Tariffs and Trade (GATT)*** is an international trade accord that encourages better trade relations among nations.

However, the organization that administers the agreement has no power to enforce it.

Eximbank

The ***Export-Import Bank (Eximbank)*** is an independent U.S. agency that finances loans to exporters and to foreign countries to purchase U.S. products.

The **Export-Import Bank (Eximbank),** established in 1934, is an independent U.S. agency that was designed to create jobs at home during the depression. Today, it finances loans to exporters who cannot find funds through commercial sources and to foreign countries that need money to purchase U.S. products. Big-ticket items such as aircraft, steel mills, and nuclear power plants are examples of items that have been financed.

Recently, the Eximbank has experienced difficulty in collecting as much as $3.5 billion in unpaid loans. (As a matter of diplomatic policy, the bank does not write off bad loans to other governments.) In 1981, the Congressional Budget Office tried to measure the benefits created by the Eximbank in jobs and exports. It could not find any.[6]

Foreign Sales Corporations

Foreign sales corporations (FSCs) are tax-sheltered subsidiaries that qualify eligible U.S. exporters for a 15 to 32 percent tax exemption on foreign income.

In 1985, the Tax Reform Act of 1984 replaced Domestic International Sales Corporations (DISCs) with **Foreign Sales Corporations (FSCs).** DISCs were tax-sheltered subsidiaries that allowed U.S. exporters to defer federal income tax on half of their export profits if the proceeds were invested in facilities making goods for U.S. export. Unlike DISCs, FSCs are required to maintain a foreign presence to qualify for a 15 to 32 percent tax exemption on foreign income. In addition, at least one non-U.S. resident must be employed as a director.[7]

Foreign Trade Zones

Foreign trade zones are designated areas set aside to allow businesses to store, process, assemble, and display products from abroad without first paying a tariff.

Designated areas set aside to allow businesses to store, process, assemble, and display products from abroad without first paying a tariff are **foreign trade zones.** Once a product leaves the zone and is delivered within the United States, a tariff must be paid, but not on the cost of assembly or on the profits. Foreign trade zones in the United States were established in 1934 by the *Foreign Trade Zones Act.* New York City opened the first zone, but few other localities followed suit. By 1970, only ten zones had been created.

Today, however, because of the competition for foreign trade zones in other countries and because of increased labor costs, foreign trade zones are booming in the United States. By federal law, every customs port of entry (place where goods enter the country) is entitled to a general-purpose trade zone. Requirements for subzones (smaller entry points) are tougher. Zones are generally run by states or port authorities. In 1987, there were 247 operating general-purpose zones and subzones in the United States (up from 55 in 1985).[8] Over fifty more applications for trade-zone status were being considered.

Two companies that use foreign trade zones in the United States are the Berg Steel Pipe Co. and the Olivetti typewriter company. Berg, a jointly owned German-French venture, avoids a 6 percent duty on the steel plates it converts into pipes at the Panama City, Florida, trade zone. With trade-zone status, Berg can move the pipe into the U.S. market at the rate for finished products, 1.9 percent, or export it free of tariffs.[9] Olivetti would normally pay an average duty of 92 percent on typewriter parts. By assembling the typewriters inside a foreign trade zone in

Harrisburg, Pennsylvania, however, the company pays no duty.[10] Thus, it is easy to see why over $40 billion in products are processed in U.S. foreign trade zones each year.[11]

World Bank and International Monetary Fund

The **World Bank,** an organization of 149 member nations, was established in 1946 to make loans to less developed countries (LDCs). Its loans are for "hard" development projects such as roads and factories and for "soft" projects such as health care and educational facilities. The International Monetary Fund (IMF) also makes loans to countries that need assistance in international trade. But in the past, the IMF has been accused by some LDCs of imposing stricter and less realistic conditions on their borrowing than on that of other countries, with the funding going primarily to private enterprise projects.[12] In 1986, plans were implemented to funnel $29 billion over three years to fifteen major debtors (mostly in Latin America). The IMF's goal was to boost all but dried-up capital flows to LDCs. Funding would be used for policy-based loans to encourage a better mix of economic policies within debtor nations.

The ***World Bank*** is an organization of 149 member nations whose purpose is to make loans to the less developed countries.

Today the World Bank and the IMF are faced with the difficult problem of increasing LDC loans without risking a wave of defaults that could cause an international depression. In 1983, the developing and Eastern bloc countries of the world had a staggering debt of $706 billion.

ORGANIZING FOR GLOBAL MARKETS

Country-Centered and Global Marketing Strategies

Several methods are used to market products around the globe. Before a method is selected, however, it is helpful for a company to determine its marketing approach. The traditional marketing approach uses a **country-centered strategy.** With this approach, a company examines its existing marketing plan and determines whether it needs to modify the parts of the marketing mix for each country in which it plans to do business. If so, a new marketing plan is tailored to the specific country and its various segments.

A ***country-centered strategy*** is a nonstandardized marketing approach to global markets in which firms create different strategies and expect different returns for individual countries or world regions.

For example, Kellogg's had to alter its promotional mix in France to include new labels instructing consumers to use cold milk on their corn flakes. The company advertised heavily, using "Tony le tigre" to promote this way of eating cereal. The modification was necessary because breakfast (especially cereal) is not a French custom and because milk usually is not served cold in France. In other cases, a company might have to modify the product itself. Kentucky Fried Chicken, for instance, used smoked chicken in Japan to satisfy consumers.

Another approach to marketing products internationally is to treat the world as *one* global market, producing standardized products that can be manufactured and marketed the same way for any country. This approach is called the **global marketing approach.** Companies credited by experts as being successful global marketers include Seiko, Boeing, Whirlpool, Coca-Cola, Sony, Panasonic, Westinghouse, Ford, and General Electric. A 1985 survey of 120 senior marketing executives concluded that soft drinks, cars, TVs, and appliances were suitable for global marketing, and beer, household cleaners, toiletries, food, and clothing were the least suitable.[13]

Global marketing is the use of a standardized approach to marketing a product in international markets.

After a company has decided to sell its products in another country, it must then decide which method of entry to use into that market. Choices include exporting, licensing, contract manufacturing, direct investment, and countertrade.

Exporting

The simplest method of entering a foreign market is through exporting. Companies can use either direct or indirect exporting. *Direct exporting* is the more expensive and riskier of the two, but the potential rewards are also greater. It allows the company to sell products directly to middlemen in other countries. Thus, the exporter has greater control over the distribution of the product. *Indirect exporting* uses the services of international middlemen such as export trading companies to export products. For example, Sears, and K mart Trading Services export brand name goods to wholesalers and retailers worldwide.

Licensing

Licensing is the practice of allowing foreign companies to use trademarks, patents, copyrights, or manufacturing processes of a domestic company.

The practice of allowing foreign companies to use the trademarks, patents, copyrights, or manufacturing processes of a domestic company is **licensing.** The domestic company receives a fee or royalty from each licensee. Licensing has been used by Calvin Klein, Gloria Vanderbilt, and Jordache to enter the Brazilian market. A form of licensing is *international franchising.* This technique has proved popular in the fast-food industry. (Franchising is discussed in chapter 5.)

Contract Manufacturing

Contract manufacturing is the arrangement in which a domestic company contracts with a foreign manufacturer to produce goods to the domestic firm's specifications and with its label.

The arrangement in which a domestic company contracts with a foreign manufacturer to produce goods to the domestic firm's specifications and with its label is **contract manufacturing.** This method is cost-effective in that it avoids investment costs and often takes advantage of inexpensive labor. Ford makes Escorts in Mexico, and Johnson & Johnson makes first-aid products in Argentina.

Direct Investment

Direct investment is a domestic firm's ownership and operation of a manufacturing plant in a foreign country.

For companies seeking maximum involvement in international markets, **direct investment** is a good entry method. It offers a company the opportunity to own and operate manufacturing plants in foreign countries. For example, Singapore attracted Micro Peripherals to build an exact duplicate of its Chatsworth, California, plant. One type of direct investment is *joint ventures,* through which foreign and domestic corporations enter into partnerships and split any profits. (See chapter 4.) In 1987, Ford and Volkswagen formed a joint venture to oversee both companies' automotive and credit operations in Brazil and Argentina.

Countertrade

Countertrade is a trading arrangement between countries or companies in which something other than money is exchanged for goods and services.

Another way of marketing products overseas is through **countertrade.** This method of trading involves transactions in which something other than money is exchanged for goods and services. Countertrade has grown rapidly in the past ten years and now accounts for 20 to 40 percent of all trade transactions. It is very popular in Third World and communist bloc countries. Many companies, especially those in the United States, do not like the concept but have little choice if they want to expand their global markets to countries that have little cash or credit.

Among the many U.S. companies engaging in some form of countertrade are Goodyear, Occidental Petroleum, Coca-Cola, Levi-Strauss, McDonnell Douglas, General Motors, Chrysler, Westinghouse, Union Carbide, and Navistar. Goodyear, for example, provided China with materials and training for a printing plant in exchange for finished labels and packing materials. Occidental Petroleum shipped a million tons of phosphate in exchange for half a million tons of Polish molten sulfur. Even the U.S. government is engaging in countertrade. In 1984, we traded 14,000 tons of surplus dairy products to Jamaica for 400,000 tons of bauxite valued at $13.6 million.

Table 23.4 Top twenty-five multinational corporations.

Rank		Company	Headquarters	Industry	Sales	Profits
1988	'87				$ Millions	$ Millions
1	1	General Motors	Detroit	Motor vehicles	121,085.4	4,856.3
2	4	Ford Motor	Dearborn, Mich.	Motor vehicles	92,445.6	5,300.2
3	3	Exxon	New York	Petroleum refining	79,557.0	5,260.0
4	2	Royal Dutch/Shell Group	London/The Hague	Petroleum refining	78,381.1	5,238.7
5	5	International Business Machines	Armonk, N.Y.	Computers	59,681.0	5,806.0
6	8	Toyota Motor	Toyota City (Japan)	Motor vehicles	50,789.9	2,314.6
7	10	General Electric	Fairfield, Conn.	Electronics	49,414.0	3,386.0
8	6	Mobil	New York	Petroleum refining	48,198.0	2,087.0
9	7	British Petroleum	London	Petroleum refining	46,174.0	2,155.3
10	9	IRI	Rome	Metals	45,521.5	921.9
11	11	Daimler-Benz	Stuttgart	Motor vehicles	41,817.9	953.1
12	16	Hitachi	Tokyo	Electronics	41,330.7	989.0
13	21	Chrysler	Highland Park, Mich.	Motor vehicles	35,472.7	1,050.2
14	18	Siemens	Munich	Electronics	34,129.4	757.0
15	17	Fiat	Turin	Motor vehicles	34,039.3	2,324.7
16	19	Matsushita Electric Industrial	Osaka	Electronics	33,922.5	1,177.2
17	15	Volkswagen	Wolfsburg (W. Ger.)	Motor vehicles	33,696.2	420.1
18	12	Texaco	White Plains, N.Y.	Petroleum refining	33,544.0	1,304.0
19	14	E.I. Du Pont de Nemours	Wilmington, Del.	Chemicals	32,514.0	2,190.0
20	20	Unilever	London/Rotterdam	Food	30,488.2	1,485.6
21	24	Nissan Motor	Tokyo	Motor vehicles	29,097.1	463.0
22	22	Philips' Gloeilampenfabrieken	Eindhoven (Neth.)	Electronics	28,370.5	477.1
23	27	Nestlé	Vevey (Switzerland)	Food	27,803.0	1,392.7
24	32	Samsung	Seoul	Electronics	27,386.1	464.3
25	25	Renault	Paris	Motor vehicles	27,109.7	1,496.7

BUSINESS PRACTICE EXAMPLE Continues

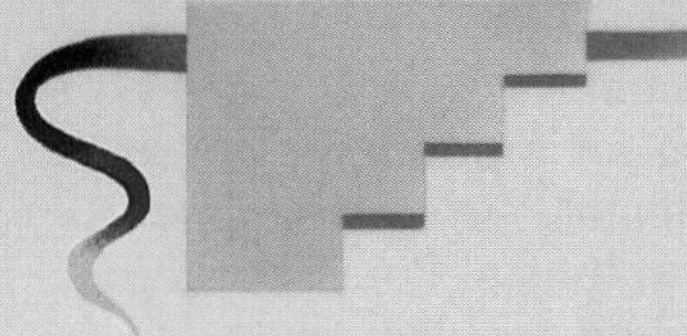

Companies such as McDonnell Douglas have several choices when deciding how to market their products abroad. McDonnell Douglas uses exporting and direct investment. In addition to its U.S.-based plants in St. Louis and in Long Beach, California, the company has plants in Japan, Canada, and China.

In 1985, China and McDonnell Douglas completed six years of negotiations to form an unprecedented alliance beneficial to both parties. The agreement they reached was to coproduce aircraft in a Shanghai factory. In this complex foreign coproduction agreement, McDonnell Douglas agreed to train Chinese workers to build planes. In exchange, the company achieved its goal of establishing a commercial aircraft manufacturing base in China—a huge potential market. The benefits for China included badly needed technological and management expertise.

The McDonnell Douglas–China deal was for cash plus "significant portions" of goods. It included McDonnell Douglas's agreement to accept parts supplied by China for U.S.-built MD-80s.

MULTINATIONALS AND NATIONALISM

Multinational corporations are corporations that operate in several countries and have a substantial part of their assets, sales, or labor force in foreign subsidiaries.

Multinational corporations are corporations that operate in several countries and have a substantial part of their assets, sales, or labor force in foreign subsidiaries. Corporations engaging in multinational trade must key their production and marketing strategies to the world market (see Table 23.4, p. 641).

Role and Importance of Multinational Corporations

Multinational corporations invest their money in manufacturing plants and other facilities in foreign countries. Many of them began originally as exporters but later found themselves hampered by trade restrictions, foreign exchange, mortgages, and high transportation costs. Eventually, they put down manufacturing roots in order to compete. Their activities are coordinated by the host country. The local management staff is supervised by parent company officials. There is no stereotypical multinational corporation. The multinationals are different in size, philosophy, investment, motive, locality, and many other variables.

As we face the questionable economic times of the 1990s, multinationals are expected to do well, because they have access to growing markets. Companies

Many multinational corporations, as illustrated by this foreign McDonald's restaurant, invest a substantial portion of their assets in facilities in countries all over the world and must therefore key their production and marketing strategies to the world market.

with products in the maturity stage, such as Coca-Cola and Polaroid, are finding real advantages in foreign economic strength.[14] Procter & Gamble and Bristol Myers get as much as 50 percent of their revenue from foreign sales.

Of course, many foreign multinationals also exist in the United States. For example, in 1988, foreign companies accounted for 2 percent of U.S. corporate profits and 6 percent of the U.S. GNP. Foreigners also own 12.5 million acres of U.S. farmland (1 percent of the total). Figure 23.3 is a short list of multinationals that manufacture products in the United States.

Foreign purchases of U.S. businesses accelerated in the 1980s. Figure 23.4 illustrates the ownership of businesses found in a typical American mall in the 1970s versus 1990. As you can see, "American" companies such as Burger King, Saks Fifth Avenue, and Baskin-Robbins are now foreign-owned. A number of these companies are owned by British firms. Great Britain is the largest foreign investor in the United States. It is followed by Holland and then Japan.

Nationalism

Initially, foreign nations may welcome multinationals. But a time usually comes when citizens of the host country begin to suspect them of having ulterior motives. For example, people in some less developed countries may view multinationals suspiciously because in their countries the entire GNP is lower than the gross sales of one multinational. Eventually, people begin to wonder what kind of political influence a multinational may enjoy when it has so much economic power. Such was the case during the 1970s, when people began to question the role of International Telephone & Telegraph (ITT) in the internal politics of Chile, of the United Brands Fruit Company in Central American nations, and of Bell Helicopter in Iran.

Suspicion and fear may build up slowly, or it may erupt violently, as it did in Iran, Cuba, and El Salvador. It is not uncommon for multinational executives to be held for ransom. For example, violence broke out in Argentina when Coca-Cola reportedly refused to pay the $1 million demanded by leftist guerillas for a kidnapped executive. Often, the end result of such violence is the nationalization of multinational industries. America's first exposure to the nationalization of Amer-

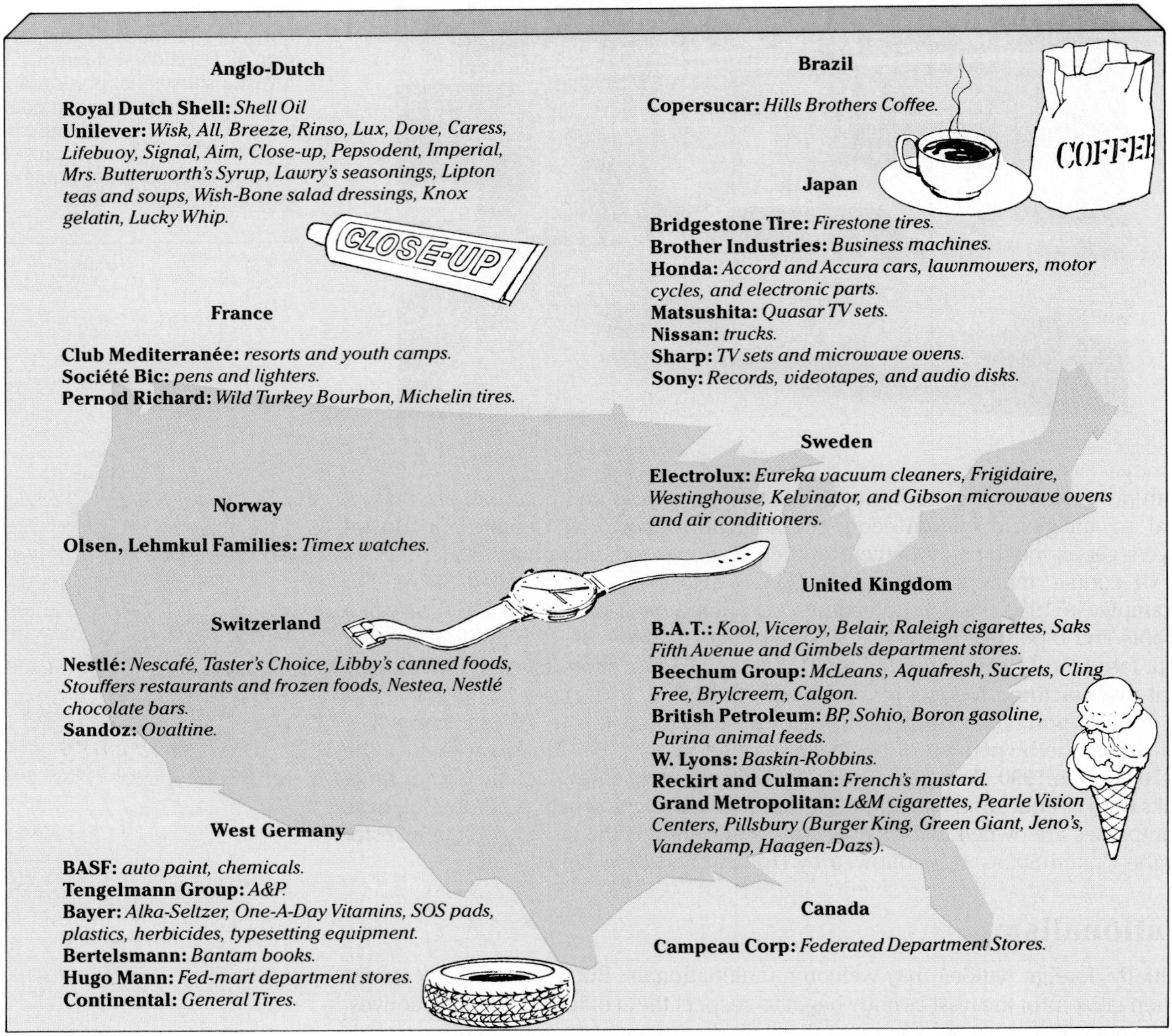

Anglo-Dutch

Royal Dutch Shell: *Shell Oil*
Unilever: *Wisk, All, Breeze, Rinso, Lux, Dove, Caress, Lifebuoy, Signal, Aim, Close-up, Pepsodent, Imperial, Mrs. Butterworth's Syrup, Lawry's seasonings, Lipton teas and soups, Wish-Bone salad dressings, Knox gelatin, Lucky Whip.*

France

Club Mediterranée: *resorts and youth camps.*
Société Bic: *pens and lighters.*
Pernod Richard: *Wild Turkey Bourbon, Michelin tires.*

Norway

Olsen, Lehmkul Families: *Timex watches.*

Switzerland

Nestlé: *Nescafé, Taster's Choice, Libby's canned foods, Stouffers restaurants and frozen foods, Nestea, Nestlé chocolate bars.*
Sandoz: *Ovaltine.*

West Germany

BASF: *auto paint, chemicals.*
Tengelmann Group: *A&P.*
Bayer: *Alka-Seltzer, One-A-Day Vitamins, SOS pads, plastics, herbicides, typesetting equipment.*
Bertelsmann: *Bantam books.*
Hugo Mann: *Fed-mart department stores.*
Continental: *General Tires.*

Brazil

Copersucar: *Hills Brothers Coffee.*

Japan

Bridgestone Tire: *Firestone tires.*
Brother Industries: *Business machines.*
Honda: *Accord and Accura cars, lawnmowers, motor cycles, and electronic parts.*
Matsushita: *Quasar TV sets.*
Nissan: *trucks.*
Sharp: *TV sets and microwave ovens.*
Sony: *Records, videotapes, and audio disks.*

Sweden

Electrolux: *Eureka vacuum cleaners, Frigidaire, Westinghouse, Kelvinator, and Gibson microwave ovens and air conditioners.*

United Kingdom

B.A.T.: *Kool, Viceroy, Belair, Raleigh cigarettes, Saks Fifth Avenue and Gimbels department stores.*
Beechum Group: *McLeans, Aquafresh, Sucrets, Cling Free, Brylcreem, Calgon.*
British Petroleum: *BP, Sohio, Boron gasoline, Purina animal feeds.*
W. Lyons: *Baskin-Robbins.*
Reckirt and Culman: *French's mustard.*
Grand Metropolitan: *L&M cigarettes, Pearle Vision Centers, Pillsbury (Burger King, Green Giant, Jeno's, Vandekamp, Haagen-Dazs).*

Canada

Campeau Corp: *Federated Department Stores.*

Figure 23.3 Goods made in the United States by foreign companies.

ican-owned companies occurred in Mexico in the 1930s. In the 1970s, American bauxite companies in Jamaica were nationalized or taken over by the government.

Problems caused by the employment practices, profit margins, investment policies, market positions, and political influence of multinationals are far from resolved. The United States faces similar problems with foreign companies at home. A typical example is Michelin, the French radial tire maker. The company's

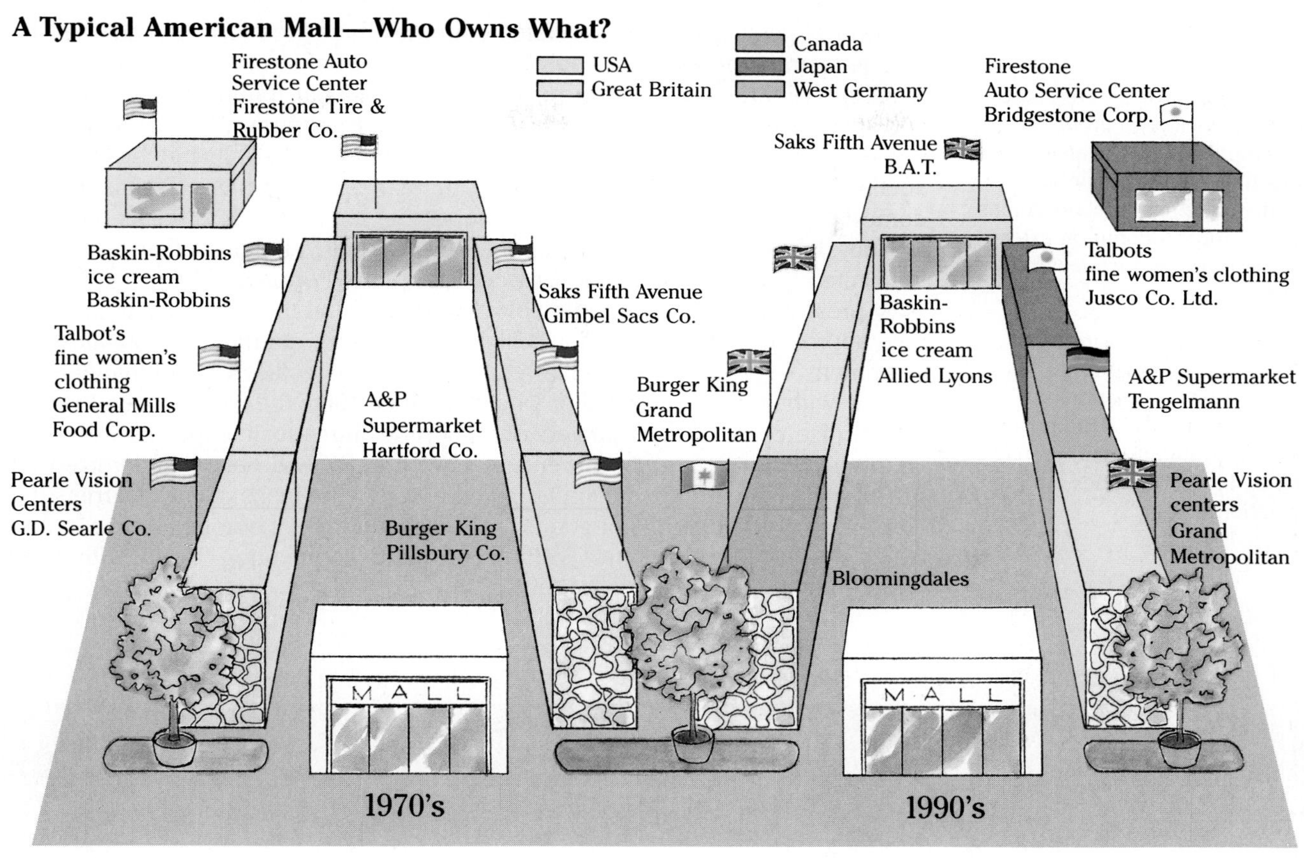

Figure 23.4 In the 1970s, all of the companies shown above were U.S.-owned. By 1990, none were.

four plants in South Carolina are staffed with so many technicians and managers from France that they've opened their own French school for employees' children. Local South Carolinians are beginning to understand how foreign nationals feel when they are employed by American multinationals.

Cartels

To combat their poorer bargaining position against the multinationals, some LDCs have developed **cartels**—groups of foreign firms or countries that agree to act as a monopoly. The most famous cartel is the *Organization of Petroleum Exporting Countries (OPEC),* which was founded in 1960. The purpose of OPEC is to raise the cost of petroleum throughout the world. By limiting production in its thirteen member countries, OPEC managed to increase its export revenues from approximately $20 billion in the early 1970s to a peak of $200 billion in 1982. It dipped significantly after 1982 and is now rising again. Another famous cartel, DeBeers Central Selling Organization, markets industrial and gem diamonds from South Africa, the Soviet Union, Zaire, and Botswana.

Cartels are groups of foreign firms or countries that agree to act as a monopoly.

Common Markets

A ***common market*** (or global trading block) is a group of geographically associated countries that agree to limit trade barriers among member nations and to apply a common external tariff on products entering member countries.

The ***European Community (EC)*** is an association of twelve European nations banded together for the purpose of promoting and protecting trade opportunities among member nations.

A group of geographically associated countries that agree to limit trade barriers among member nations and apply a common external tariff on products entering member countries is a **common market,** or regional trading block. The best-known common market is the twelve-member **European Community (EC),** founded in 1958 (and better known as the Common Market). It stretches from the Shetland Islands to Crete, includes 300 million people, and has a combined gross domestic product (similar to GNP) comparable to America's GNP. Its members are Italy, the Netherlands, Luxembourg, West Germany, Belgium, France, Ireland, the United Kingdom, Denmark, Greece, Spain, and Portugal.

At present, eleven other trading blocks exist around the world, each having its own approach and each playing a significant role in international business development. There is evidence that common markets will force multinationals to comply with strict standards. For example, since 1968, the EC has been trying to standardize corporate law and accounting procedures for companies with operations in EC countries. By the end of 1992, the EC will have standardized approximately three hundred such laws and dropped the maze of trade barriers that currently impede the flow of goods, services, and capital among members. As a result, American companies will find tougher competition along with more opportunity.[15]

BUSINESS PRACTICE EXAMPLE Continues

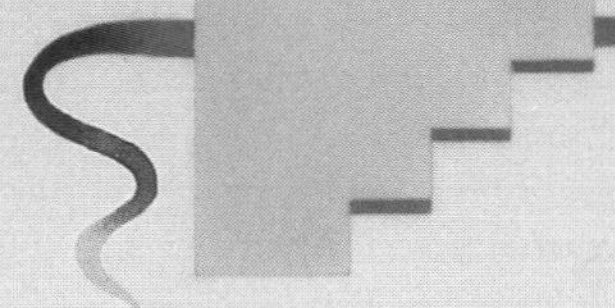

McDonnell Douglas is a multinational corporation that invests its money in manufacturing plants and other facilities in countries around the world—as we saw in the coproduction agreement the company reached with China. Along with other Western aircraft manufacturers, McDonnell Douglas has also sought sales opportunities for the first time in Eastern bloc countries such as Hungary, Romania, East Germany, and Czechoslovakia. According to industry analysts, Eastern bloc governments know that with modern Western carriers, their countries' airlines will be more attractive to foreign passengers, who will then travel to these countries and spend much-needed foreign currency there.

Of course, sales to these countries must comply with U.S. legal restrictions on technology transfers. U.S. law prohibits certain high-technology products from going to the East.

In Western Europe, McDonnell Douglas will soon face a single market of 320 million people, perhaps a common currency, and, some fear, increased trade barriers to those outside the community. This new single-market Europe could create many political as well as financial hurdles for U.S.-based multinationals. On the negative side, trade wars are a possibility. On the positive side, U.S.-based multinationals that are firmly entrenched in Europe stand to gain tremendous sales from a common market that buys billions of dollars' worth of goods and services manufactured by U.S. multinationals. IBM, Coca-Cola, Kellogg, Ford, and General Motors, for instance, are top sellers of their types of products in Europe.

Issues for Discussion

1. How does McDonnell Douglas benefit the people of the world?
2. What special types of problems does McDonnell Douglas encounter when selling its products overseas?
3. How can the U.S. government assist other nations in purchasing McDonnell Douglas aircraft?

SUMMARY

At no time in history has international trade been as economically important as it is now. International trade is the exchange of products among countries through exports (products sold to other countries) and imports (products purchased from other countries).

A country with an absolute advantage in trade is the only one producing a product or produces the product at the lowest cost. A country with a comparative advantage specializes in the products it can supply more efficiently and at a lower cost than other items.

A major concern for any country is the balance of payments—the difference between the expenditures made to other countries and the receipts taken in from others during a given time. Another concern is the balance of trade—the difference between sales of exports and purchases of imports. A negative trade balance is a trade deficit.

Soon after the United States went off the gold standard, a new system for determining exchange rates was instituted: the free-floating exchange rate system. Under this system, market forces determine the exchange rate—the rate at which one country's currency is exchanged for another's. Devaluation is a reduction in the value of currency.

Many countries impose trade barriers to protect domestic industries (protectionism). Among these barriers are tariffs (taxes or duties), quotas (limits on the amounts of imports), and embargoes (orders prohibiting goods from entering or leaving a country). Embargoes are often based on politics, health, or morals. Two other barriers are cultural differences and legal barriers.

Most nations try to promote trade. The United States and Canada, for instance, signed a trade agreement that will end all tariffs between them. Several other laws as well as institutions exist to promote trade. Among them are the Export Trading Companies Act of 1982, the General Agreement on Tariffs and Trade (GATT), the Export-Import Bank (Eximbank), foreign sales corporations (FSCs), foreign trade zones, the World Bank, and the IMF.

Two approaches to organizing for global marketing are country-centered strategies, under which marketing plans are tailored to specific countries; and the global marketing approach, under which countries produce standardized products that can be sold in any country without changes.

Foreign markets can be entered in several ways: through exporting (either direct or indirect), licensing, contract manufacturing, direct investment, and countertrade.

Multinational corporations operate in several countries with foreign subsidiaries. Many U.S. multinationals are doing well in other countries, and many foreign multinationals are doing well in the United States. Often, foreign countries welcome multinationals at first but then grow suspicious of them.

markets—regional trading blocks that limit trade barriers among their members and apply a common tariff on outsiders' products. The European Community (EC) is a major common market.

Some less developed countries have developed cartels—groups of firms or countries that act as monopolies—to increase their bargaining position against multinationals. Other countries have developed common markets—regional trading blocks that limit trade barriers among their members and apply a common tariff on outsiders' products. The European Community (EC) is a major common market.

KEY TERMS

Absolute advantage p. 677
Balance of payments p. 678
Balance of trade p. 678
Cartels p. 695
Common market p. 696
Comparative advantage p. 678
Contract manufacturing p. 690
Countertrade p. 690
Country-centered strategy p. 689
Devaluation p. 681
Direct investment p. 690
Dumping p. 682
Embargo p. 684
European Community (EC) p. 696
Exchange rates p. 681
Export-Import Bank (Eximbank) p. 688
Exports p. 676
Export Trading Companies Act of 1982 p. 687
Foreign sales corporations (FSCs) p. 688
Foreign trade zones p. 688
Free-floating exchange rate system p. 681
General Agreement on Tariffs and Trade (GATT) p. 687
Global marketing p. 689
Imports p. 676
Licensing p. 690
Multinational corporations p. 692
Protectionism p. 682
Quotas p. 682
Tariffs p. 682
Trade deficit p. 679
World Bank p. 689

CHECK YOUR LEARNING

Reread the following learning objectives. Each objective is followed by a few questions. Answering these questions accurately will help you retain the most important concepts discussed in this chapter. After answering each question, check your answer with the key at the end of this chapter. (*Hint:* If you have doubt regarding the correct response, consult the page whose number follows the answer.)

Circle:

A. Explain why international trade is important to all nations, and how each can best utilize the principles of absolute and comparative advantage.

1. International trade has always been important to the American economy.
2. Hong Kong currently has an absolute advantage in producing toys.

3. Most nations utilize comparative advantage to specialize in products they can make best.

B. Distinguish between balance of payments and balance of trade, and explain what has caused the United States to have a trade deficit in recent years.

T F 1. The balance of payments is a part of a country's balance of trade.

a b c d 2. All of the following are reasons for recent American trade deficits except: (a) strong dollar; (b) disinterest in exporting; (c) cheaper imports; (d) tariffs.

C. Discuss the various trends that indicate the world is entering a period of protectionism.

1. America's labor unions are pressing for tougher trade barriers to protect American products from foreign competition.

2. Europe and Japan have not dropped trade barriers sufficiently to allow most American products to compete fairly in their markets.

D. Distinguish among different types of trade barriers, such as tariffs, quotas, and embargoes.

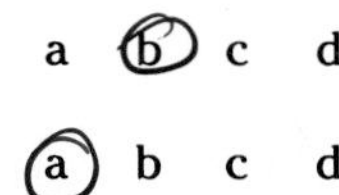

1. Dumping has caused the United States to use which type of trade barrier to curb color TV imports from Japan: (a) political; (b) quotas; (c) tariffs; (d) embargoes.
2. Which type of embargo on products did the United States use against Nicaragua: (a) political; (b) athletic; (c) health; (d) morality.

E. Explain why it is important to understand cultural differences when marketing products internationally.

1. Using correct colors is very important when marketing products in many foreign nations.
2. Small gifts to a trading partner are acceptable in all countries.

F. List and explain the role of various types of international assistance programs available to promote world trade.

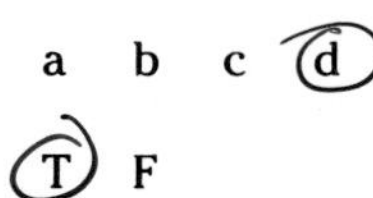

1. All of the following are examples of international assistance programs except: (a) GATT; (b) FSC; (c) IMF; (d) LDC.
2. The Eximbank makes loans to exporters who can't find commercial financing and to foreign countries that need money to purchase America's big-ticket items.

G. Explain the role of multinational corporations and their importance to the American economy.

1. Multinational corporations invest their capital in manufacturing and other facilities in a host country.
2. Few foreign multinationals operate in the United States.
3. Many American multinationals earn a large percentage of their total profits from overseas profits.

H. Describe the differences among the primary methods of organizing for international markets.

1. Licensing allows companies to enter partnerships with other companies.
2. Direct exporting is the simplest method of entering a foreign market.

I. Discuss the growing implications of nationalism as it affects multinational corporations.

1. Often, multinationals earn more than the entire GNP of some LDCs.
2. American multinational properties have been expropriated in Mexico.

J. Explain how cartels and common markets can improve a country's bargaining position in the world market.

1. OPEC is an example of a common market.
2. Cartels such as OPEC operate as monopolies.
3. Common markets such as the EC eliminate trade barriers among member nations.

QUESTIONS FOR REVIEW AND DISCUSSION

1. Define the key terms listed at the end of the chapter.
2. Prior to 1971, when the world used the Bretton Woods system of exchange, did the United States have an advantage or disadvantage in international trade? Explain.
3. After researching the event, discuss the effectiveness of the 1985 U.S. embargo of products to and from Nicaragua.
4. What is the purpose of the General Agreement on Tariffs and Trade?
5. How are FSCs being used by American multinationals to combat unfair foreign trade advantages?
6. What is the purpose of foreign trade zones? Is there likely to be a large increase in foreign trade zones?
7. How do the World Bank and the IMF work to improve the standard of living in LDCs?
8. Has the presence of foreign multinationals in the United States noticeably affected our economy?
9. Explain why multinationals are often viewed with fear and suspicion by host countries.
10. What safeguards can multinationals take to protect themselves from the growing trend of nationalism?
11. Make a list of American industries that are currently cost-competitive in international markets.
12. Graph America's balance of trade since the first major OPEC oil increases in 1974. Analyze your results and determine if we are making any progress in improving our balance of trade.

CONCLUDING CASE

Unilever Targets the U.S. Market

Unilever, the world's largest packaged goods company, does over $25 billion in sales a year. Although the Anglo-Dutch giant is number 1 in world markets for such products as deodorants, shampoo, and other personal care products, the company has yet to capture the U.S. market. Tired of seeing its market share eroded by Procter & Gamble and other U.S. companies, Unilever is setting into action a plan to attack the U.S. market.

One part of the plan is to acquire existing U.S. firms. In 1986, Unilever tried to purchase Richardson-Vicks, a big marketer of toiletries and home remedies. Its bid was too low, however, and the company was sold to Procter & Gamble. Unilever was more successful in 1987, when it was able to purchase Chesebrough-Ponds for $3.1 billion. This acquisition was Unilever's largest purchase in company history. Chesebrough-Ponds doubled the size of Unilever's U.S. personal products line to $700 million in annual sales.

Unilever's management team looks at the U.S. market with great anticipation. Unilever sees the United States as superior to Europe as a place to do business. The per capita consumption of packaged goods is high, production volumes can be huge, and unit costs are low. Another reason the United States looks good is Unilever's experience with culturally segmented Europe. The company hopes to capitalize on its international experience by appealing to the increasingly segmented U.S. market. By acquiring Chesebrough-Ponds, the company now has well-known global products such as Vaseline petroleum jelly and Vaseline Intensive Care skin creams, which give it a quick, well-established entry into this market.

Although Unilever has been in the U.S. market for almost a century, first with its U.S. subsidiary Lever Bros. and then with Thomas J. Lipton, the company has historically maintained a passive relationship with Lever Bros. This was due to the constant threat of antitrust action by the U.S. Justice Department, which did sue Lever Bros. in 1962. By being passive, Unilever failed to provide Lever Bros. with highly skilled European managers who knew and understood Unilever products and their European successes. Strong leadership was needed to give Unilever a greater foothold in the United States.

Before now, the U.S. market was a string of failures for Unilever's personal products. For example, Timotei shampoo is the best seller in Holland. This product never made it out of the test market in the United States (Americans couldn't pronounce the name). In addition, the product's daily-use concept hit the United States about five years too late. The idea that shampoo should be used daily is newer to Europeans than to Americans, so the marketing strategy was outdated in the U.S. This illustrates that the U.S. and European markets are very different. Europeans are more steeped in conservative consumer trends than are their American counterparts and thus they are less likely to use personal products on a regular basis. Toothpaste offers another example. In Belgium, consumers use an average of one and a half 150-milliliter tubes of toothpaste a year, about one-fourth the U.S. average. Thus, Americans are not very impressed that a Unilever brand is number 1 in France.

Issues for Discussion

1. How has Unilever decided to organize its effort for the expansion of its U.S. market share?
2. In your opinion, why has Unilever decided to no longer allow the threat of antitrust action to inhibit its drive to increase market share?
3. How can Unilever apply lessons learned from segmenting the European market to the United States?

NOTES

1. Louis Rukeyser, *Business Almanac* (New York: Simon & Schuster, 1988), p. 265.
2. William S. Hampton, "The Long Arm of Small Business," *Business Week,* February 29, 1988, pp. 63–66.
3. William Holstein and Brian Bremmer, "The Little Guys Are Making It Big Overseas," *Business Week,* February 27, 1989, p. 66; Christopher Elias, "Big Plans for Small Business: Firms Try to Boost Exports," *Insight,* July 13, 1988, pp. 40–42.
4. Lawrence Minard, "Is Free Trade Dead?" *Forbes,* May 14, 1979, p. 65.
5. "The U.S. Lags in Trade Zones," *Business Week,* November 17, 1980, p. 82.
6. Holman Jenkins, Jr., "Export-Import Bank Survives on Making Credit, Not a Profit," *Insight,* January 18, 1988, pp. 42–43.
7. Terrence Roth, "Small Firms Try to Master Export Plan," *Wall Street Journal,* January 24, 1985, p. 9.
8. Ken Slocum, "Foreign-Trade Zones Aid Many Companies but Stir Up Criticism," *Wall Street Journal,* September 3, 1987, p. 1.
9. Ibid.
10. "Behind Fresh Interest in Duty-Free Zones," *U.S. News & World Report,* November 24, 1980, p. 46.
11. Ken Slocum, "Foreign-Trade Zones Aid Many Companies but Stir Up Criticism," *Wall Street Journal,* September 30, 1987, p. 1.
12. "Worried Banks for the Poor," *Newsweek,* October 6, 1980, p. 78.
13. "Global Marketing Candidates," *Wall Street Journal,* June 20, 1985, p. 31.
14. William M. Bulkeley, "As U.S. Economy Falters, Multinationals Put Increased Stress on Overseas Business," *Wall Street Journal,* November 11, 1979, p. 40.
15. Shawn Tully, "Europe Gets Ready for 1992," *Fortune,* February 1, 1988, pp. 81–84.

CHECK YOUR LEARNING ANSWER KEY

A. 1. F, *p. 675*
2. T, *p. 677*
3. T, *p. 678*

B. 1. F, *p. 678*
2. d, *p. 679*

C. 1. T, *p. 682*
2. T, *p. 682*

D. 1. b, *p. 682*
2. a, *p. 684*

E. 1. T, *p. 684*
2. F, *p. 687*

F. 1. d, *p. 689*
2. T, *p. 688*

G. 1. T, *p. 692*
2. F, *p. 693*
3. T, *p. 693*

H. 1. F, *p. 690*
2. T, *p. 690*

I. 1. T, *p. 693*
2. T, *p. 694*

J. 1. F, *p. 695*
2. T, *p. 695*
3. T, *p. 696*

APPENDIX
Career Information: An Annotated Bibliography and Guide

Compiled by
O. Gene Norman
Reference Department
Indiana State University Library
Terre Haute, Indiana

OCCUPATIONAL OUTLOOK FOR THE 1990s BY INDUSTRY

Service-Producing Industries

The growth field of the 1990s will continue to be the service industries. Before 2000, more than half the nation's economic activity will center on industries that provide services rather than products. Furthermore, services employ more than twice the number of people working in the goods-producing and agricultural sectors. By 2000, four of every five jobs will be in the service industries. Employment for college graduates is expected to increase more rapidly than other groups in the service-producing industries.

The service industries reach into every area of the economy—from cutting hair to waiting on tables to the professional jobs in accounting, law, and medicine. Also included are governmental jobs. The demand for people in these areas is fueled by the increase in personal spending in these areas. It is estimated by the *U.S. News & World Report*'s Economic Unit that consumer spending for services will reach 49 percent of personal income by 1990. This increase is expected by analysts because despite the economic ups and downs since World War II, increased demand for services has been uninterrupted.

In the area of trade, some 5 million new jobs are projected by 2000 in retailing—primarily in eating and drinking establishments, pet shops, and general merchandise stores. Wholesale trade is not expected to provide as many jobs, but combined, a 27 percent increase in jobs is expected. Most of this could result in part-time workers replacing full-time workers; however, the number of college graduates needed should increase greatly as more computer technology is used.

Of the services, transportation and public utilities is the slowest growth area. An estimated 9 percent growth is expected. The best bets are in trucking, public utilities, and the airlines. Communications employment is expected to decline.

The finance, insurance, and real estate sector showed tremendous growth in the 1960s and 1970s, and should show about a 26 percent increase in the 1990s. Banking and credit are the fastest growing industries in this sector. The demand for these services will be greater as the population continues to increase; however, like real estate, high interest rates could have a major impact on this sector. College graduates compose approximately 21 percent of the workers in these industries.

The service sector has not only the greatest variety of occupations, but also the fastest growing employment rate. Between 1965 and 1978, this sector grew 77 percent. In the 1990s, this growth is expected to slow down to around 34 percent. High demand areas are in health care, legal and business services, accounting, advertising, commercial cleaning services, and lodging. Approximately 25 percent of workers in these areas are college graduates.

Presently one of every six workers is employed by federal, state, or local governments, and an increase of 9 percent is projected for the 1990s. The greatest area of increase will be by state and local governments. Furthermore, government will continue to be a major source of jobs for college graduates. Nearly a third of government employees are college graduates.

Goods-Producing Industries

Employment in the goods-producing industries—agriculture, manufacturing, construction, and mining—is expected to remain constant. Employment in this sector peaked in the late 1970s. Prospects will vary from industry to industry.

Manufacturing is the largest industry within the goods-producing sector. The current employment level of 19 million is expected to decrease to 18.2 million. While jobs in production will continue to decline, the number of professional, technical, and managerial positions in manufacturing will actually increase. Many of these positions are held by college graduates (9 percent).

As the worldwide demand for food increases, the technological advances needed in the agricultural area will demand more college graduates, but about 14 percent fewer workers overall. College graduates comprise only 5.9 percent of all agricultural workers.

Increased energy needs have caused a resurgence of demand for workers in the area of mining. This trend should continue through the 1980s. Nearly 12 percent of the 30,000 mining workers are college graduates. The biggest demand in those occupations is for geologists and petroleum engineers.

Contract construction is the only goods-producing industry expected to show an increase. Much of the expected 18 percent (4.9 to 5.8 million) increase this decade, will come from nonresidential construction. Growth will be especially strong in construction and renovation of health facilities.

Selected careers in management and related fields.*

Occupation	Job Description	Educational Requirements	Estimated Employment, 1986	Employment Prospects through 2000	Salary	Related Occupations**
Hotel managers and assistants	Hotel managers are responsible for operating their establishment profitably and satisfying guests. They determine room rates and credit policy, direct the operation of food services, manage housekeeping, accounting, security, and maintenance.	Experience is very important in selecting managers. A bachelor's degree in hotel and restaurant administration is also very useful.	78,000	Employment expected to grow more rapidly than average. Best opportunities for persons with degree in hotel administration.	$21,000–$87,000	Apartment building manager Store manager Office manager
Personnel and labor relations workers	These workers provide the link of assisting management in making effective use of employees' skills and helping employees find satisfaction in their jobs and working conditions. People who specialize in labor relations work in unions-management relations and are mainly found in unionized businesses and government agencies. Personnel specialists focus on the recruitment, selection, and training of new employees. In addition, personnel is normally involved in evaluating job performance.	Beginning positions normally filled by college graduates. Relevant degrees focus on personnel, administration, labor relations, as well as liberal arts majors.	381,000	Employment expected to grow faster than average as new standards in such areas as equal employment opportunity stimulate demand. But most opportunities are with state and local governments.	$14,400–$52,000	Industrial psychologists Placement counselors Health inspectors

*Based upon information in *Occupational Outlook Handbook,* 1988–1989 edition.
**Occupations requiring similar aptitudes, interests, and education and training.

Selected careers in management and related fields,* *continued*

Occupation	Job Description	Educational Requirements	Estimated Employment, 1986	Employment Prospects through 2000	Salary	Related Occupations**
Health service administrators	These administrators direct the various functions and activities that make a health organization work. They do this personally where the organization is small, or direct a staff of assistant directors in larger organizations. Health administrators make many kinds of management decisions, such as review budget proposals, make personnel decisions, and negotiate for expansion of facilities.	Mainly master's degree in health or hospital administration for most associate or assistant administrator positions. MBA (master's of business administration) may also qualify.	274,000	Employment expected to grow much faster than average as quantity of patient services increases and health services management becomes more complex. Advanced degree required for best position in hospitals.	$ 22,500–$132,000	Social welfare administrators College or university department heads Recreation superintendents
Counselors, employment, etc.	Employment counselors provide people with career information and other kinds of help in getting a job. Most employment counselors work in state employment service offices or in community agencies. These agencies offer career planning and placement programs for special groups such as women and minorities. In addition, such agencies counsel school dropouts and drug abusers and help direct young people toward meaningful roles in society.	Required educational background ranges from a high school diploma to a master's degree in counseling or a related field. Experience in counseling, interviewing, and job placement also may be required.	75,000	Employment growth is expected to grow more slowly than the average for all occupations and is highly dependent on the level of federal and state funding. Applicants are expected to face some competition in both public and private employment agencies.	$ 9,800–$24,000	Training specialists Affirmative action II Occupational therapists

*Based upon information in *Occupational Outlook Handbook,* 1988–1989 edition.
**Occupations requiring similar aptitudes, interests, and education and training.

Selected careers in management and related fields,* *continued*

Occupation	Job Description	Educational Requirements	Estimated Employment, 1986	Employment Prospects through 2000	Salary	Related Occupations**
Secretaries and stenographers	Secretaries relieve managers of certain duties so that they can work on other matters. Most secretaries schedule appointments, deal with callers, type, and take shorthand. The time spent on these duties, however, varies with different types of organizations.	Generally, a high school diploma is required. Many employers prefer applicants who have had additional secretarial training at a college or private business school.	3,234,000	Skilled persons seeking secretarial positions should find numerous opportunities. Part-time secretarial jobs should also remain plentiful.	\$11,802–\$28,051	Bookkeepers Receptionists Legal assistants
Blue-collar worker supervisors	For millions of workers who assemble television sets, service automobiles, lay bricks, unload ships, or perform any of thousands of other activities, a blue-collar worker supervisor is the boss. This supervisor tells employees what jobs to do and makes sure they are done correctly. In addition, this supervisor does such things as: (1) tell workers about company plans and policies; (2) recommend workers for wage increases and promotions; and (3) meet with union representatives to discuss problems and grievances.	Minimum of high school diploma, and one or two years of college or technical training can be very helpful.	1,800,000	Employment expected to increase at an average rate. Large part of increase to occur in manufacturing industries. The best opportunities are for workers with leadership ability and some college.	\$210–\$630 per week	Retail department managers Head nurses Head tellers

*Based upon information in *Occupational Outlook Handbook*, 1988–1989 edition.
**Occupations requiring similar aptitudes, interests, and education and training.

Selected careers in management and related fields,* *continued*

Occupation	Job Description	Educational Requirements	Estimated Employment, 1986	Employment Prospects through 2000	Salary	Related Occupations**
Programmers	Since computers cannot think for themselves, programmers write detailed instructions called programs that list, in logical order, the steps the machine must follow to organize data, solve a problem, or do some other tasks.	Most programmers are college graduates; others have taken special courses in computer programming at public and private vocational schools, community and junior colleges, or universities.	479,000	Employment expected to grow much faster than average as computer usage expands. The need for programmers will increase as business, government, schools, and scientific organizations seek new computer applications. The field of data communications, linking computers so they can talk to one another, will provide many openings.	\$14,800–\$33,900	Systems analysts Operations research analysts Financial analysts
Occupational safety and health workers	People in the occupational safety and health field have the challenging job of insuring a safe and healthful environment for workers and safe products for consumers. Safety and health workers, in a number of different occupations work with management to control occupational accidents and diseases, property losses, and injuries from unsafe products.	Entry-level positions generally require at least a bachelor's degree in engineering or science. Other helpful degrees include: safety management, industrial safety, fire protection.	125,000	Employment expected to grow faster than average as new safety and health programs are started and existing ones are upgraded.	\$15,400–\$46,000	Revenue agents Construction inspectors Game wardens

*Based upon information in *Occupational Outlook Handbook,* 1988–1989 edition.
**Occupations requiring similar aptitudes, interests, and education and training.

Selected careers in marketing and related fields.

Occupation	Job Description	Educational Requirements	Estimated Employment, 1986	Employment Prospects through 2000	Salary	Related Occupations**
Administrative and related occupations						
Retail buyers	Purchasing merchandise for resale by retailers; know what motivates consumers by studying marketing research; must be able to assess resale value of merchandise after a brief inspection and make a purchase decision quickly; work with budgets and understand store's profit ranges and many other related duties.	Associate or bachelor's degree in marketing and/ or purchasing.	192,000	Automation and centralization of purchasing will result in slower than average growth. But keen competition anticipated because merchandising attracts large numbers of college graduates.	$14,600–$29,000 Much higher salaries for those who advance to merchandise manager.	Sales managers Comparison shoppers Manufacturers' sales reps Wholesale sales reps
Purchasing agents/ industrial buyers	Maintaining an adequate supply of necessary items in market forecasting, production planning, and inventory control are all part of the job.	Bachelor's degree in business administration, science, or engineering; MBA preferred; less rigid requirements for smaller companies.	418,000	Employment expected to increase more slowly than average rate. Good job opportunities expected, especially for persons with two-year degrees in purchasing.	$15,100–$50,000; average starting salary $21,200 in private sector.	Retail and wholesale buyers Procurement services manager Traffic manager Livestock commission agent
Marketing research workers	Analyzing the buying public and its wants and needs in order to provide information on which these marketing decisions are made; collection of data and information about goods, services, and people likely to produce them; direct telephone, mail or personal interview surveys and many other related duties.	Bachelor's degree in marketing or advertising; MBA or other specialized degree often needed for advancement.	29,000	Employment expected to grow faster than average as demand for new products stimulates marketing activities. Best opportunities for applicants with graduate training in marketing research or statistics.	$12,000–$50,000	Telemarketing representative Political pollster Statistician Census worker Demographer Psychologist Sociologist

*Based upon information in *Occupational Outlook Handbook*, 1988–1989 edition.
**Occupations requiring similar aptitudes, interests, and education and training.

Selected careers in marketing and related fields, *continued*

Occupation	Job Description	Educational Requirements	Estimated Employment, 1986	Employment Prospects through 2000	Salary	Related Occupations**
Design occupations						
Retail display managers	Creating settings that enhance merchandise; supervise construction of props; coordinate displays with other store promotions and many other related activities.	Associate degree in marketing and design, or visual merchandising degree and experience as display worker preferred.	26,000	Employment expected to grow at average rate because of the popularity of visual merchandising, the use of merchandise to decorate stores.	$15,000–$25,000	Window dresser Prop set designer
Commercial and industrial photographers	Photographing a wide variety of subjects for use in commercials, magazines, brochures, annual reports, billboards and other promotional media.	Associate and bachelor's degree programs in photography or journalism available but not required.	109,000	Employment expected to grow faster than average. Good opportunities in areas such as law enforcement and scientific and medical research photography.	$16,600–$35,100	Commercial artist Floral designer Illustrator Industrial designer
Communications-related occupations						
Public relations workers	Preparing and presenting information about a company's policies, activities and accomplishments; maintain contacts with media representatives and other related duties.	Bachelor's degree in journalism, communications, or public relations preferred.	87,000	Employment expected to grow faster than average as corporations, associations, and other large organizations expand public relations efforts to gain public support. Competition for jobs likely to be keen during economic downturns.	$15,000–$50,000	Fundraiser Account executive Lobbyist Promotion manager Advertising manager
Sales occupations						
Real estate agents and brokers	Selling and leasing of homes, land, and buildings; arrange financing, promotions, multiple listings, title searches and many other related duties.	Associate or bachelor's degree in real estate preferred; however, most states only require a minimum of thirty hours of classroom instruction and the passing of state written exam; must have license.	376,000	Employment expected to rise much faster than average in response to growing demand for housing and other properties. However, field is highly competitive. Best prospects for college graduates and transfers from other sales jobs.	$19,000–$50,000 (Median salary was $17,000)	Auto sales worker Security sales worker Insurance agent Yacht broker

*Based upon information in *Occupational Outlook Handbook,* 1988–1989 edition.
**Occupations requiring similar aptitudes, interests, and education and training.

Selected careers in marketing and related fields, *continued*

Occupation	Job Description	Educational Requirements	Estimated Employment, 1986	Employment Prospects through 2000	Salary	Related Occupations**
Services sales representative	Selling services such as hotel convention space, non-profit fundraising, advertising, auto leasing and educational services.	Associate degree or bachelor's degree preferred in marketing or related area.	419,000	Employment expected to grow much faster than average as demand for services increases.	$ 20,000–$100,000 (Median salary for advertising was $23,600); depends on area of sales.	Security sales worker Insurance agent Yacht broker
Manufacturers' sales workers	Selling of technical and nontechnical products to all types of firms; often requires considerable travel and paperwork, including reports on sales prospects, "credit rating," sales reports, correspondence, and many other related duties.	College degree preferred (type usually depends on the products sold; however, marketing degree widely accepted).	543,000	Employment expected to grow more slowly than average. Good opportunities for persons with product knowledge and sales ability.	$16,300–$44,000 (Median salary $24,000)	Buyer Field-contact technician Wholesale trade worker Real estate sales worker Insurance agent
Retail store managers	Planning, organizing, directing and controlling daily retail store operations; resolve customer complaints; assist buyers; coordinate displays and advertising and many other related duties.	Associate degree in marketing, marketing education or retailing often required; however, large department chains prefer bachelor's degree in marketing, business administration, economics, or retailing.	971,000	Employment expected to grow faster than average. High turnover should create excellent opportunities for full-time, part-time, and temporary work.	$ 13,000–$125,000	Assistant manager Management

*Based upon information in *Occupational Outlook Handbook*, 1988–1989 edition.
**Occupations requiring similar aptitudes, interests, and education and training.

Selected careers in marketing and related fields, *continued*

Occupation	Job Description	Educational Requirements	Estimated Employment, 1986	Employment Prospects through 2000	Salary	Related Occupations**
Travel agents	Making travel arrangements for pleasure and business trips; sells tickets, leases cars, reserves lodging accommodations and many other related duties.	Associate or bachelor's degree in hospitality; marketing preferred, but not required.	105,000	Employment expected to grow much faster than average. Because travel expenditures often depend on business conditions, job opportunities are very sensitive to economic changes, however, many new agencies are expected to open.	$12,000–$21,000	Tour guides Rental car agent Airline reservationist Travel counselor
Retail trade sales workers	Selling a variety of merchandise to consumers; write sales checks, receive payment, demonstrate goods, handle returns and exchanges.	College degree not required, but marketing, retailing and sales courses would be helpful. Post-secondary marketing education program very useful.	4,266,000	Employment expected to grow faster than average. High turnover occupation.	$3.35 per hr., to $30,000 per yr. if on commission	Demonstrator Route driver Telephone solicitor Buyer Manufacturers' rep
Wholesale trade sales workers	Selling of products to retail, industrial, and commercial firms; perform many other tasks such as checking a store's stock and ordering items; advise about advertising, pricing, and displays; record-keeping and many other related activities.	Associate or bachelor's degree preferred (area depends on products sold).	1,217,000	Employment expected to grow faster than average as wholesalers sell wider variety of products and improve customer services. Good opportunities for persons with product knowledge and sales ability.	$13,000–$52,000 (Median salary was $23,000)	Buyer Sales-service promoter Demonstrator Manufacturers' salesworker

*Based upon information in *Occupational Outlook Handbook,* 1988–1989 edition.
**Occupations requiring similar aptitudes, interests, and education and training.

Selected careers in marketing and related fields, *continued*

Occupation	Job Description	Educational Requirements	Estimated Employment, 1986	Employment Prospects through 2000	Salary	Related Occupations**
Transportation occupations						
Commercial airline pilot/ business pilot	Flying of passengers and cargo to national and international designations.	Airlines require two years of college, and most prefer bachelor's degree; must have proper FAA license.	76,000	Employment expected to grow at faster than average rate, but applicants are likely to face keen competition for available jobs. Best opportunities for recent college graduates with flying experience.	$16,000–$120,000 for commercial pilots; $36,000–$54,000 for corporate pilots.	Helicopter pilot Air traffic controller Dispatcher
Flight attendants	Making airline passengers' flights safe, comfortable, and enjoyable; serve meals and beverages; administer first aid; supervise emergency evacuations and other related duties.	Some college preferred; foreign language fluency required of international flights.	80,000	Employment expected to grow faster than average. Competition for jobs likely to be keen.	$16,000–$32,000 (Average $21,000)	Tour guide Gate agent Waiter/waitress Host/hostess
Merchant marine officers	Directing navigation of the ship and supervising the cleaning and maintenance. Responsibilities depend on the nature of title, such as deck officer, radio officer, chief engineer, purser, etc.	B.S. degree from the Merchant Marine Academy or one of six state academies. Must pass Coast Guard exam.	13,000	Little change in employment expected as size of nation's fleet remains fairly constant.	$17,316–$69,632 (Base pay)	Naval or Coast Guard officer

*Based upon information in *Occupational Outlook Handbook*, 1988–1989 edition.
**Occupations requiring similar aptitudes, interests, and education and training.

Selected careers in finance and related fields.*

Occupation	Job Description	Educational Requirements	Estimated Employment, 1986	Employment Prospects through 2000	Salary	Related Occupations**
Bank officers and managers	Make decisions within a framework of policy set by the board of directors and existing laws and regulations. Specific assignments include the evaluation of credit and collateral of individuals and businesses applying for a loan. Other responsibilities may include branch supervision, trust administration, financial planning and investment research, and systems analysis.	Bachelor's degree in business administration, finance, or liberal arts curriculum; MBA preferred.	638,000	Employment expected to grow about as fast as average as banking services expand. Job opportunities should be good, especially for persons skilled in using computers and other data processing equipment.	\$30,000–\$52,000 (Experienced bank officers make several times starting salaries)	Business representatives, industrial relations director, safety council directors, purchasing agents, city managers, and export managers
Bank tellers	Spend most of their time providing services for bank customers. Common activities include cashing customer's checks and handling deposits and withdrawals from checking and savings accounts. Must be capable of typing and using selected business machines. May be required to use computer terminals to record transactions.	Minimum of high school diploma; prefer some college background—especially for promotional consideration.	539,000	Employment expected to increase more slowly than the average for all occupations through the year 2000. Employment growth among bank tellers is not expected to keep pace with overall employment growth in bank and other credit and savings institutions because of the increasing use of automatic teller machines and other electronic equipment.	\$ 8,500–\$18,700	Cashiers, toll collectors, post office clerks, auction clerks, and ticket sellers

*Based upon information in *Occupational Outlook Handbook,* 1988–1989 edition.
**Occupations requiring similar aptitudes, interests, and education and training.

Selected careers in finance and related fields,* *continued*

Occupation	Job Description	Educational Requirements	Estimated Employment, 1986	Employment Prospects through 2000	Salary	Related Occupations**
Accountants	Prepare and analyze financial reports that are used in the decision-making process. Other specialized activities performed by accountants include auditing, tax preparation, estate planning, budget administration, and cost analysis.	Bachelor's degree in accounting or a closely related field; larger companies prefer master's degree; professional certification such as CPA or CMA becoming extremely valuable.	945,000	Employment expected to increase faster than average as managers rely more on accounting information for decision making. Most openings will result from the need to replace workers who leave the occupation or retire.	\$21,000–\$80,000	Budget officers, loan officers, financial analysts, revenue agents, security sales workers
Bookkeepers	Maintain a record of business transactions using journals, ledgers, and other accounting forms. Prepare periodic billing statements pertaining to accounts receivable and accounts payable. Disburses and monitors payments of funds so as to insure a balanced cash budget. Use of computer terminals for data entry and retrieval becoming more common.	Associate degree in business administration preferred; high school graduates who have completed business math, bookkeeping, and principles of accounting meet minimum requirements.	2,100,000	Employment is expected to remain steady. Computers will be used to perform many functions previously done manually.	\$11,190–\$18,800	Bank tellers, collection agents, insurance clerks, and statistical clerks
Underwriters	Appraise and select the risks their company will insure. This process includes an intensive evaluation of insurance applications, medical reports, actuarial studies, and loss-control records.	Bachelor's degree in business administration or liberal arts.	99,000	Employment expected to rise faster than the average for all occupations as insurance sales continue to expand.	\$21,300–\$46,800	Auditors, loan officers, credit managers, real estate appraisers

*Based upon information in *Occupational Outlook Handbook,* 1988–1989 edition.
**Occupations requiring similar aptitudes, interests, and education and training.

Selected careers in finance and related fields,* *continued*

Occupation	Job Description	Educational Requirements	Estimated Employment, 1986	Employment Prospects through 2000	Salary	Related Occupations**
Insurance agents and brokers	Sell policies that protect individuals and businesses against future losses and financial pressures; provide clients with information about estate planning; frequently assist policyholders in processing claims.	Bachelor's degree in business administration or insurance preferred; license required by most states; CLU and CPCU are common professional designations.	463,000	Employment expected to grow about as fast as average as insurance sales continue to expand. Turnover is high because many beginners are unable to etablish a sufficiently large clientele in this competitive business.	$ 16,800–$100,000	Real estate agents and brokers, securities sales workers, estate planning specialists, and financial advisors
Economists	Study how society utilizes scarce resources (such as land, labor, raw materials, and capital) to produce goods and services. Gather statistics regarding energy costs, inflation, business cycles, unemployment tax policies, and farm prices. Present economic data and statistics in various governmental and corporate reports.	Bachelor's degree in economics; master's and Ph.D. preferred—especially for research positions.	37,000	Employment expected to grow faster than the average. Opportunities should be best in manufacturing, financial services, advertising agencies, research organizations, and consulting firms.	$19,000–$54,000	Financial analysts, bank officers, underwriters, actuaries, credit analysts, securities sales workers, appraisers
Securities sales workers	Main responsibility is to buy and sell stocks, bonds, and other securities for individual and institutional customers. Often provide investment advice and counseling to clients. Regularly provide up-to-date price quotes to the public over the telephone.	Bachelor's degree in business administration, economics, or finance; must pass specific examinations given by an exchange or the NASD.	197,000	Employment expected to grow much faster than average. Job opportunities fluctuate with economic conditions.	$ 12,000–$227,000	Insurance agents, broker floor representatives, commodities brokers

*Based upon information in *Occupational Outlook Handbook*, 1988–1989 edition.
**Occupations requiring similar aptitudes, interests, and education and training.

Selected careers in finance and related fields,* *continued*

Occupation	Job Description	Educational Requirements	Estimated Employment, 1986	Employment Prospects through 2000	Salary	Related Occupations**
Actuaries	Assemble and analyze statistics to calculate probabilities of death, sickness, injury, disability unemployment, retirement, and property loss resulting from accident, theft, fire, and other hazards. Composite information is used by the actuary to determine premium rates for different types of insurance policies offered.	Bachelor's degree in mathematics or statistics; a major in actuarial science preferred.	9,400	Employment expected to rise much faster than average as the volume of insurance sales and pension plans increases. As people live longer, they draw health and pension benefits longer and more actuaries are needed to recalculate the probability of factors like death, sickness, and length of retirement.	$19,000–$60,000	Statisticians, economists, financial analysts, engineering analysts

*Based upon information in *Occupational Outlook Handbook,* 1988–89 edition.
**Occupations requiring similar aptitudes, interests, and education and training.

GLOSSARY

Absolute advantage (p. 677)
The advantage a country has when it is the only one producing a product or when it produces the product at the lowest cost.

Account (p. 503)
A register of financial value.

Accountability (p. 240)
The management philosophy of holding individuals liable, or accountable, for how well they use their authority and how well they live up to their responsibility.

Accounting (p. 499)
The process of collecting, analyzing, and reporting information that reflects the financial condition of a company.

Accounting cycle (p. 503)
The sequence of accepted procedures that accountants must follow over a specific period of time.

Accounts receivable (p. 507)
Debts owed to a business by customers who buy products on credit.

Acquisition (p. 114)
The purchase of a controlling share in a corporation by another corporation.

Active Corps of Executives (ACE) (p. 147)
An SBA sponsored volunteer group of active business executives who give advice and consultation to small businesses.

Activity ratios (p. 513)
Ratios that measure how effectively a company uses its resources.

Administered system (p. 417)
A type of vertical marketing system that relies on the dominant channel member to plan and take responsibility for the marketing effort.

Advertising (p. 436)
Any paid form of nonpersonal presentation of ideas, goods, or services by an identified sponsor.

Advertising agency (p. 444)
An independent company that specializes in all phases of preparation and execution of client advertising.

The AFL-CIO (p. 283)
A union formed in 1955 as a result of a merger between the American Federation of Labor and the Congress of Industrial Organizations.

Agents (or brokers) (p. 407)
Wholesalers who do not take title to the goods they sell.

Air pollution (p. 86)
The contamination of the air we breathe.

Alien corporations (p. 109)
Corporations organized in a foreign country but operating in the United States.

Amalgamation (p. 116)
The merger of two corporations that creates a third corporation in which neither company is dominant.

American Federation of Labor (AFL) (p. 283)
A labor union established in 1886 as the result of a merger of the Federation of Organized Trades and Labor Unions.

Analytic production process (p. 310)
The process that transforms resources by breaking them down into one or more products.

Appropriate human resources (p. 256)
The people in an organization who make a valuable contribution to the attainment of organizational objectives.

Arbitration (p. 293)
The practice in the collective bargaining process of involving a neutral third party who can settle disputes.

Articles of incorporation (p. 109)
A legal document explaining the purpose of the corporation, the number of shares issued, the names of the officers and directors, the bylaws, and so on.

Articles of partnership (p. 105)
A legal document containing the provisions of ownership for a partnership, including an outline of the monetary and managerial responsibilities of each partner.

Artificial intelligence (AI) (p. 626)
The segment of computer science that focuses on developing computers with capabilities similar to those of the human mind.

Assembly line (p. 320)
A type of product layout in which the product is moved past several different work groups, each of which performs one specific step in the progression.

Assets (p. 505)
Items of value owned by a business.

Associations (p. 297)
Organizations formed by employers to help neutralize the power and influence of unions.

Authority (p. 234)
The right to perform or command.

Autocratic leadership style (p. 208)
The pattern of leader behavior that emphasizes the use of authority in leading others.

Automation (pp. 20, 315)
The process that replaces people with machines that can do jobs more effectively and efficiently.

Balance of payments (p. 678)
The difference between the expenditures made to other nations and receipts taken in from other nations during a given time.

Balance of trade (p. 678)
The difference between sales of exports and purchases of imports.

Balance sheet (p. 506)
The statement of financial position that reports the dollar amounts for a company's assets, liabilities, and owner's (stockholders') equity at a specific point in time.

Balance sheet equation (p. 505)
Assets equal liabilities plus owner's equity.

Bankruptcy (p. 664)
The legal nonpayment of financial obligations.

Barter (or swapping) (p. 467)
The direct exchange of one thing for another, without the need for money.

Basic—Beginner's All-purpose Symbolic Instruction Code—(p. 632)
An easy to learn programming language that is used with both minicomputers and microcomputers.

Batch processing (p. 624)
A method of handling computer-processed data in which the data are stored and then processed in batches.

Bear market (p. 571)
A securities market characterized by falling stock prices.

Behavior modification (p. 202)
The process of encouraging desirable behavior through the use of rewards and punishments.

Beneficiary (p. 599)
An individual designated to receive the cash proceeds from an insurance policy if the insured party dies.

Bit (p. 630)
The digit 0 or 1 in the binary numbering system.

Board of directors (p. 110)
The people elected by the stockholders to govern a corporation.

Bodily injury liability insurance (p. 606)
Automobile insurance that pays claims against the insured that result from injuries to others, including pedestrians, people in the other cars involved in the accident, and passengers in the insured's car.

Bonds (p. 560)
Long-term interest-bearing debt instruments issued by corporations with commitments to specifically timed payment.

Bonus (p. 265)
A type of incentive pay typically given to managers.

Bookkeeping (p. 499)
The initial step in the accounting process, the accurate recording of all the financial transactions that occur in an organization.

Boycott (p. 296)
The labor tactic wherein union members refuse to purchase products from companies that are giving a union a difficult time.

Brand name (p. 386)
A product's identification by use of word, letter, or group of words that can be spoken.

Breach of contract (p. 655)
The failure of one party to a contract to perform one of the duties or meet one of the conditions of the contract.

Breakeven analysis (p. 394)
A method of evaluating possible prices for a product by considering the costs and quantities ordered.

Brokers (or agents) (p. 407)
Wholesalers who do not take title to the goods they sell.

Budget (p. 171)
A financial plan that covers a specified period of time.

Budgets (p. 518)
The internal financial forecasts of expected income and expenditure for a specific period of time.

Bull market (p. 571)
A securities market characterized by rising stock prices.

Business (p. 8)
An organization that is created to earn a profit for providing needed goods and services to society.

Business cycles (p. 48)
Alternating periods of prosperity and recession.

Business interruption insurance (p. 610)
Insurance that provides regular payments to the insured when the business is temporarily shut down because of a catastrophe.

Business law (p. 650)
The complex system of rules, statutes, codes, and regulations that form the legal environment in which businesses operate.

Business plan (p. 131)
A comprehensive written proposal that describes a business and its specific goals and objectives.

Buying on the margin (p. 578)
Making a small cash down payment on a stock and then borrowing the rest of the cost of the stock from the broker.

Byte (p. 630)
A group of adjacent digits, letters, or other characters that are often shorter than a word and that are processed as a unit—usually eight bits.

Cafeteria fringe benefits program (p. 266)
A flexible benefits system in which employees are allocated an established total dollar amount to spend on any of several available benefits.

Callable bonds (p. 562)
Bonds that can be redeemed before maturity.

Capital (p. 12)
The funds used to modernize and expand businesses and to purchase machinery and other resources.

Capital budgeting (also termed fixed asset management) (p. 543)
The process of planning how to buy, sell, and develop fixed assets.

Capitalism (p. 50)
The economic system in which the bulk of capital is owned by individuals and corporations.

Cartels (p. 695)
Groups of foreign firms or countries that agree to act as a monopoly.

Celler-Kefauver Antimerger Act of 1950 (p. 651)
Federal legislation that amended the Clayton Act to restrict mergers to the acquisition of companies in different lines of business.

Central processing unit (CPU) (p. 628)
The working part of the computer, where calculations are done and control of the computer is maintained.

Centralization (p. 241)
The organizing practice in which minimal amounts of job activities and authority are delegated to subordinates.

Certified public accountant (CPA) (p. 500)
A public accountant who has passed a rigorous state examination and completed certain residence and field experience requirements.

Chain stores (p. 408)
Corporations that usually operate two or more retail stores in different geographical areas.

Channels of distribution (p. 405)
The various routes a product can take in getting from the producer to the final buyer.

Charter (p. 109)
A document authorizing a corporation to operate in a given state.

Check float (p. 530)
The time lag between the issuing of checks and the completed processing of them.

Checkable deposits (p. 476)
Interest-bearing checking accounts offered by commercial banks, savings and loan associations, mutual savings banks, and credit unions.

Chief executive officer (CEO) (p. 110)
The corporate officer who runs the day-to-day operations of a corporation.

Civil Rights Act (p. 270)
A 1964 law that prohibits discrimination in employment on the basis of sex, race, color, religion, and national origin.

Clayton Act of 1914 (p. 650)
Federal legislation that forbade tying contracts, interlocking directorates, and the purchase of a competitor's stock to lessen competition.

Closed shop (p. 288)
An agreement between unions and businesses that required businesses to hire only union workers.

COBOL—Common Business Oriented Language—(p. 632)
Programming language specifically designed to solve business problems that require a significant amount of file processing.

Coinsurance clause (p. 605)
The clause in fire insurance policies that requires the insured to have protection equal to some percentage of the replacement value of the property or to pay some of the replacement costs.

Cold canvasing (p. 453)
A sales method used to find new sales leads from public announcements.

Collective bargaining (p.290)
The process by which employees, through the union or association representing them, negotiate a labor agreement with their employer.

Collision insurance (p. 606)
Automobile insurance that pays for damage to the policyholder's car, even if the driver is at fault.

Commercial banks (p. 473)
For-profit institutions that accept deposits in the form of checking and savings accounts and use them to lend money to businesses and individuals.

Commercial paper (p. 540)
Short-term unsecured promissory notes issued by corporations for a period usually ranging from 30 to 270 days.

Common carriers (p. 421)
Transportation companies that offer scheduled or regular service to the public.

Common law (p. 649)
The unwritten laws that have evolved through custom and legal precedents rather than through the action of legislative bodies.

Common market (or global trading block) (p. 696)
A group of geographically associated countries that agree to limit trade barriers among member nations and to apply a common external tariff on products entering member countries.

Common stock (p. 565)
A company's primary trading stock, whose owners receive dividends only after bondholders receive their interest and preferred stockholders receive their dividends.

Communism (p. 55)
The term used to describe a totally planned economy, ruled by a single political party, whose industries and resources are all owned by the government.

Comparable worth (p. 271)
The concept that women's pay should be equal to men's for jobs that are of comparable worth to a company.

Comparative advantage (p. 678)
The advantage a country achieves when it specializes in the products it can supply more efficiently and at a lower cost than other items.

Compensation (p. 263)
The wages, salaries, and other benefits employees receive for work accomplished.

Comprehensive coverage (p. 607)
Automobile insurance that pays for automobile damage other than that caused by collision—for example, fire, theft, windstorm, hail, and riot damage.

Computer program (p. 631)
The detailed description of the precise steps the computer is to follow in order to solve a problem.

Computer-aided design (CAD) (p. 317)
Interaction between a designer and a computer to produce a blueprint that meets established product specifications.

Computer-aided manufacturing (CAM) (p. 317)
The computer analysis of a product design to determine the steps necessary for producing the product and to ready and control the equipment used in producing it.

Conceptual skill (p. 184)
The ability to see the organization as a series of parts and to understand how the parts relate to one another.

Conciliation (p. 293)
The practice of involving in the collective bargaining process a neutral third party who, although virtually powerless, encourages both sides to reach an agreement.

Conglomerate merger (p. 116)
The joining together of unrelated corporations.

Congress of Industrial Organizations (CIO) (p. 283)
A labor union formed in 1937 by noncraft workers who broke away from the American Federation of Labor.

Consumer market (p. 354)
The market composed of individuals who buy products for their personal use—the market of end users.

Consumer products (p. 380)
The goods and services designed for use by the consumer.

Consumerism (p. 81)
The social movement that seeks to strengthen the rights and powers of buyers in relation to sellers.

Consumers (p. 35)
The ultimate users of products.

Containerized freight (p. 424)
Small packages transported from shipper to receiver in a larger sealed container.

Continuous production process (p. 310)
A process that is followed the same way for extended periods of time in order to transform resources into products.

Contract (p. 653)
An agreement between two or more persons or companies that is enforceable in court.

Contract carriers (p. 421)
Transportation companies that offer their services for hire by independent contract.

Contract manufacturing (p. 690)
The arrangement in which a domestic company contracts with a foreign manufacturer to produce goods to the domestic firm's specifications and with its label.

Contractual system (p. 417)
A type of vertical marketing system in which the producer and an independent distributor integrate their efforts.

Controlling (p. 172)
The process of evaluating the organization's performance and taking corrective action, where necessary, to ensure that objectives are met.

Convenience goods and services (p. 380)
The products that consumers purchase immediately, frequently, and with little effort.

Convertible bond (p. 562)
A bond that can be exchanged for the common stock of the issuing corporation.

Cooperative advertising (p. 435)
An arrangement whereby the manufacturer shares the cost of local advertising.

Cooperatives (p. 118)
Groups of individuals who voluntarily act together for a common benefit.

Copyrights (p. 663)
The rights granted to owners of creative works to control any reproduction or distribution of these works.

Corporate bonds (p. 546)
Interest-bearing debt instruments issued by corporations and promising to pay specific amounts at specific times.

Corporate database (p. 633)
A database containing facts regarding all important facets of company operations.

Corporate system (p. 417)
The type of vertical marketing system in which successive stages of production and distribution are combined under one owner.

Corporate takeover (p. 575)
An attempt by a group of special-interest owners, who usually are not part of the target company's management, to purchase a controlling interest in a company's voting stock.

Corporation (p. 108)
A state-chartered legal entity with the authority to act on its own and with liability separate from that of its owners.

Cost of goods sold (p. 510)
The total of all costs directly required for the acquisition and preparation of goods for sale during a given time period.

Cost-of-living adjustment (COLA) (p. 291)
A clause in a labor contract designed to protect employees' real income by chang-

ing wage amounts according to changes in the consumer price index.

Cost-push inflation (p. 48)
Inflation caused by increased production expenses.

Cottage industries (p. 19)
Industries that rely on most items being made in homes.

Countertrade (p. 690)
A trading arrangement between countries or companies in which something other than money is exchanged for goods and services.

Country-centered strategy (p. 689)
A nonstandardized marketing approach to global markets in which firms create different strategies and expect different returns for individual countries or world regions.

Coupons (p. 449)
Advertising clippings or tearoffs used by producers to encourage consumers to take advantage of a small price reduction.

Creativity (p. 20)
Another term for innovation.

Credit life insurance (p. 602)
A form of term insurance that lenders purchase on the lives of borrowers for the amount of the loan.

Credit standards (p. 533)
Guidelines or standards for evaluating the creditworthiness of potential credit customers.

Credit unions (p. 474)
Cooperative banks organized by people associated with a particular group—usually an employer or a union.

Critical path (p. 326)
The sequence of events and activities in a PERT network that requires the longest period of time to complete.

Current asset (p. 507)
Any asset that will change form in a year or less.

Data (p. 624)
Raw facts and figures that relate to the functioning of an organization.

Database (p. 633)
A collection of all the data stored in one or more files.

Database management software (p. 636)
Computer programs that allow individuals to define, manipulate, and output database information.

Davis model of social responsibility (p. 73)
Five propositions that describe why and how business should take corrective action that protects and improves its welfare and the welfare of society as well.

Debenture bonds (or general credit bonds) (p. 561)
Bonds that have no specific collateral pledged against them.

Decentralization (p. 242)
The organizing practice in which significant amounts of job activities and authority are delegated to subordinates.

Decision (p. 175)
A choice made between two or more available alternatives.

Decision-making process (p. 176)
The steps the decision maker takes to choose one alternative from a set of available alternatives.

Delegation (p. 241)
The process of assigning job duties and related authority to specific organization members.

Demand (p. 17)
The quantity of a product that consumers are willing to purchase at different prices.

Demand curve (p. 36)
Illustrates graphically the relationship between price and quantity demanded at each price for a specific period of time.

Demand deposits (p. 476)
Non-interest-bearing checking account funds held in commercial banks.

Demand-pull inflation (p. 48)
A decline in the purchasing power of money.

Demographics (p. 359)
The study of human population statistics.

Democratic leadership style (p. 208)
The pattern of leader behavior that emphasizes allowing others to have a voice in determining actions the leader takes.

Department (p. 229)
A subdivided part of an organization, which management has established as a distinct group of people and other resources working on a common task.

Departmentalization (p. 230)
The process of setting up departments.

Depreciation (p. 509)
The reduction in value allowed by law for long-lived tangible assets.

Depression (p. 48)
An extended economic slump with very high unemployment.

Deregulation (p. 44)
The removal or softening of government regulation of industries.

Devaluation (p. 681)
A reduction in the value of currency in relation to gold or some other standard.

Direct investment (p. 690)
A domestic firm's ownership and operation of a manufacturing plant in a foreign country.

Direct pay (p. 264)
Money that employees receive according to the amount of time spent working or the number of units produced.

Directing (p. 171)
Guiding the actions of organization members toward the attainment of organizational goals.

Discount (p. 395)
A reduction in the regular price of an item.

Discount price (p. 562)
A lower price for bonds than the face value so as to bring the bond's market value in line with current market interest rates.

Discount rate (p. 486)
The interest rate the Fed charges member banks for borrowing from it.

Discretionary income (p. 361)
The income that remains after the necessities of life are paid for.

Dispatching (p. 327)
Issuing detailed work orders based on the planning, scheduling, and routing needed for a coordinated production project.

Disposable income (p. 361)
All the personal income that remains after taxes and other required payments are made.

Distribution center (p. 420)
A type of warehouse created to speed the flow of goods and eliminate unnecessary storage.

Diversification (p. 560)
Investing in a group (*portfolio*) of unrelated securities, so that losses on some securities will be offset by profits on others.

Domestic corporations (p. 109)
Corporations that do business in the state in which they are chartered.

Dow Jones Industrial Averages (DJIA) (p. 574)
Stock averages based on thirty high-quality stocks in well-established firms.

Downtime (p. 330)
The time when employees cannot work because the materials, parts, or equipment they need to perform their jobs are not available.

Dumping (p. 682)
The practice of selling a product in another country for less than it is sold in the producing country.

Economic function area (p. 79)
The part of measuring a company's social responsibility activity that gauges the economic impact on society.

Economics (p. 35)
The study of how economic systems allocate scarce resources in the production and distribution of goods and services for consumption.

Effectiveness (p. 177)
The extent in a managerial context to which managers reach organizational objectives.

Efficiency (p. 178)
Using in a managerial context the optimum amount of organizational resources to help the organization reach its objectives.

Electronic Fund Transfer System (EFT) (pp. 476, 532)
A bank's computerized service that allows almost instant moving of funds between checking accounts and marketable securities.

Embargo (p. 684)
An order that prohibits a particular good from entering or leaving the country.

Emotional motives (p. 363)
Motives related to feelings about something.

Employee stock ownership plan (ESOP) (p. 291)
A program through which employees can obtain company stock and therefore some degree of ownership in the company.

Entrepreneurial teams (p. 25)
Groups of experienced business managers and professionals who join together to create new companies.

Entrepreneurs (pp. 10, 129)
Individuals who assume the risk of starting their own businesses.

Environmental protection (p. 84)
The conducting of business in a fashion that assists the company in reaching its objectives but does not damage the natural surroundings.

Equal Employment Opportunity Commission (EEOC) (p. 270)
A government agency that has the right to file suit against employers if an acceptable resolution of job discrimination charges against them cannot be obtained within a reasonable time period.

Equilibrium price (p. 38)
The price at which the quantity supplied during a specific time period is equal to the quantity demanded during that period.

Esteem needs (p. 199)
Needs for respect; they are the fourth level in Maslow's hierarchy.

Ethics (p. 80)
A code of behavior that a society considers moral and appropriate for guiding the way in which its members deal with one another.

European Community (EC) (p. 696)
An association of twelve European nations banded together for the purpose of promoting and protecting trade opportunities among member nations.

Exchange rate (or foreign exchange rate) (pp. 489, 681)
The price of one currency in terms of another currency.

Exclusive distribution (p. 414)
The strategy of giving a wholesaler or retailer the exclusive right to sell a line of products in a specific geographic region or territory.

Expenses (p. 506)
The costs incurred in the generation of revenue.

Expert system (p. 626)
A computer program based on expert human knowledge and designed to help people solve technical problems in well-defined areas such as engineering, law, and medicine.

Export Trading Companies Act of 1982 (p. 687)
Federal legislation that grants U.S. companies the right to use export trading companies and gives them access to government financing and guarantees.

Export-Import Bank (Eximbank) (p. 688)
An independent U.S. agency that finances loans to exporters and to foreign countries to purchase U.S. products.

Exports (p. 676)
Goods and services sold to other countries.

Express warranties (sometimes called written warranties) (p. 659)
Warranties that spell out specific representations by the seller regarding the product.

Factoring (p. 541)
Selling one's accounts receivable at a discount to a commercial finance company or bank (the factor).

Fair Labor Standards Act of 1938 (p. 287)
The federal law that set a minimum wage and maximum number of regular work hours for workers at companies involved in interstate commerce.

Fair Packaging and Labeling Act of 1966 (p. 653)
Federal legislation that gives the Food and Drug Administration the authority to require lists of ingredients on packages, including their quantities.

Featherbedding (p. 288)
The practice by which unions force employers to contract for unnecessary workers or assign tasks that do not need to be performed.

Federal deficit (p. 48)
The negative difference between the government's revenues and spending.

Federal Reserve System (Fed) (p. 484)
The central banking system of the United States.

Federal Trade Commission Act of 1914 (p. 651)
Federal legislation that created the Federal Trade Commission, a government regulatory agency that monitors unfair methods of competition and penalizes companies for using them.

Fidelity bond (p. 608)
A form of insurance that protects companies against losses caused by theft by employees who occupy positions of trust and have jurisdiction over funds.

Finance companies (p. 481)
Nonbanking companies in the business of making loans to individuals, businesses, or both.

Financial compensation (p. 263)
The monetary reward employees receive for performing a job.

Financial leverage (p. 545)
A firm's use of borrowing to increase its earnings per share and return on owners' equity.

Financing (p. 529)
The funding an enterprise receives by borrowing, by selling shares, or from personal resources.

Fiscal policy (p. 47)
The government's use of spending or taxation to influence the economy according to a national economic plan.

Fixed assets (or capital assets) (p. 509)
Permanent assets used in the operation of the business.

Fixed costs (p. 518)
Costs that remain relatively stable no matter what the company's level of production or operations.

Fixed position layout (p. 321)
The layout pattern in which—because of the weight or bulk of the product being

manufactured—workers, tools, and materials are brought in stages to a stationary product.

Flat organizations (p. 232)
Organizations whose organization charts are short and whose spans of management are wide.

Flexible manufacturing system (p. 316)
The production process that uses computer-controlled robots that can be adapted to perform various versions of the same task.

Flextime (p. 211)
A program that allows workers to complete their jobs within a workweek of a normal number of hours, which they schedule themselves.

Floppy disks (p. 630)
Flexible magnetic disks in protective envelopes, used mainly with microcomputers.

Flowchart (p. 631)
A schematic diagram of the steps necessary to solve a problem.

Focus group (p. 365)
An informal group of about six to twelve consumers led by a moderator, who guides them through a session that deals with their likes or dislikes of a product.

Forecasting (p. 322)
The process of predicting future happenings that will likely influence the operation of the organization.

Foreign corporations (p. 109)
Corporations that do business outside their chartered state.

Foreign exchange (p. 489)
The trading of one country's currency for funds of equal value in the currency of another country.

Foreign sales corporations (FSCs) (p. 688)
Tax-sheltered subsidiaries that qualify eligible U.S. exporters for a 15 to 32 percent tax exemption on foreign income.

Foreign trade zones (p. 688)
Designated areas set aside to allow businesses to store, process, assemble, and display products from abroad without first paying a tariff.

Form utility (p. 310)
The usefulness resources gain after they are transformed into products.

Formal structure (p. 225)
The structure in which the relationships among organizational resources are outlined by management.

Fortran—FORmula TRANslation— (p. 632)
A programming language that focuses on solving scientific problems.

Four Cs of credit analysis (p. 533)
The criteria by which creditworthiness is judged: character, capacity, capital, and conditions.

Franchisee (p. 149)
The purchaser of a franchise.

Franchising (p. 149)
The creation of an agreement under which the owner-franchisor of a product, service, or method grants a license to a buyer-franchisee to distribute the owner's product or service or to use the owner's method.

Franchisor (p. 149)
The owner-supplier of a franchise who provides the license, training, merchandise, and managerial assistance necessary for a franchisee to do business.

Free-floating exchange rate system (p. 681)
The exchange rate system under which market forces, not a country's gold reserve holdings, determine appropriate exchange rates.

Free-market concept (p. 17)
The economic concept that how consumers spend their money determines which products and businesses will survive in the market.

Fringe benefits (p. 265)
Financial compensation that is generally not paid directly to employees.

Full employment (p. 48)
The point where further declines in unemployment would unleash steep inflation.

Full-service advertising agency (p. 444)
An agency that offers a wide range of services.

Functional authority (p. 235)
The right to give orders within a segment of the organization in which this right is normally nonexistent.

Gantt chart (p. 325)
A graphic scheduling device that uses a bar chart format to represent the time dimension on the horizontal axis and the resource to be scheduled on the vertical axis.

General Agreement on Tariffs and Trade (GATT) (p. 687)
An international trade accord that encourages better trade relations among nations.

General partnership (p. 105)
A partnership owned by general partners, who are usually active in the business and who must assume unlimited liability of all business debts.

Generic products (p. 388)
Products that do not carry a brand name.

Global marketing (p. 689)
The use of a standardized approach to marketing a product in international markets.

Goal behavior (p. 197)
Behavior aimed specifically at reducing or eliminating a need.

Goal-supportive behavior (p. 196)
Any preliminary behavior that make goal behavior possible.

Grapevine (p. 227)
A term used for networks of informal communication and for communication that doesn't follow the formal lines on the organization chart.

Grievance (p. 294)
A formal complaint made by a union member concerning an alleged violation of the labor contract by management.

Gross national product (GNP) (p. 15)
The sum of all goods and services produced per year.

Group life insurance (p. 603)
A form of life insurance that covers all the employees of a firm for a specified amount.

Guaranty loans (p. 149)
Loans made by banks or other private lenders that are guaranteed up to 90 percent by the SBA.

Hard disks (p. 630)
High-capacity magnetic disks on a rigid base that can hold up to thousands of times more data than typical floppy disks.

Hardware (p. 628)
All of the physical equipment related to computers, such as keyboard, monitor, and printer.

Hawthorne effect (p. 196)
The phenomenon, discovered in the Hawthorne studies, that worker productivity increases in response to positive feedback, even if other positive factors are lacking.

Hawthorne studies (p. 196)
A series of pioneering human relations studies conducted between 1924 and 1932 at the Hawthorne Works Plant of the Western Electric Company.

Hierarchy of needs (p. 198)
The concept, developed by Abraham Maslow, that humans have five basic needs arranged in a hierarchy of importance—from most basic to least basic: physiologi-

cal needs, security needs, social needs, esteem needs, and self-actualization needs.

Hierarchy of objectives (p. 181)
The entire set of objectives for an organization, from overall objectives to specific subobjectives.

Health insurance (p. 603)
Insurance that covers financial losses resulting from sickness, injury, or disability.

Health maintenance organizations (HMOs) (p. 604)
Companies that offer medical care that is paid for in advance in the form of monthly fees and that is given, usually at certain locations, by member doctors.

Horizontal merger (p. 115)
The combining of competing companies performing the same functions.

Human relations (p. 195)
The area of study concerned primarily with finding the best way to work with and deal with people in organizations.

Human resource forecasting (p. 255)
The process of determining the extent of future personnel needs (both number of people and types of skills).

Human resource management (p. 254)
The process of determining the kinds of people an organization needs, hiring them, and retaining them through an equitable compensation system and desirable work environment.

Human resource planning (p. 254)
Strategic planning to meet the future human resource needs of the organization.

Human skill (p. 184)
The ability to work well with people.

Hygiene factors (p. 210)
According to Frederick Herzberg, elements that influence the degree of job dissatisfaction.

Implied warranties (p. 659)
Unwritten guarantees that automatically come with the product.

Imports (p. 676)
Goods and services purchased from other countries.

Incentive (p. 264)
A type of financial compensation an individual receives in addition to a wage or salary because of outstanding performance in a job.

Income statement (p. 510)
The summary of a firm's revenues and expenses for a specific period of time.

Individual Retirement Account (IRA) (p. 474)
A category of investment or pension fund that sets aside tax-deferred money and its earnings for retirement needs.

Industrial market (p. 354)
The market composed of buyers in manufacturing, agricultural, transportation, communications, mining, construction, utility, and service industries.

Industrial products (p. 381)
The goods and services that are sold directly to businesses for their operational use or for use in producing other goods.

Industrial Revolution (p. 19)
The shift, originating in England, to a factory system of manufacturing.

Informal structure (p. 226)
The patterns of relationships among workers and others that develop naturally as people interact.

Information (p. 624)
Processed data used for business planning and decision making.

Injunction (p. 297)
A court order prohibiting or requiring some specific action on the part of someone.

Inland marine insurance (p. 610)
Transportation insurance that protects against the loss of merchandise shipped by rail, airplane, truck, or barge and on inland waterways.

Input and output (I/O) devices (p. 628)
The hardware used to get information into or out of the computer, including keyboard, voice activator, monitor, mouse, disk drive, modem, and printer.

Inside directors (p. 111)
Board members employed by the corporation.

Institutional advertising (p. 436)
Advertising designed to promote an image or goodwill message of a company, industry, organization, or government.

Insurable interest (p. 594)
The right to insure property or life if the loss of or damage to it would cause the person or company financial loss.

Intensive distribution (p. 415)
The strategy of placing a product at as many wholesale or retail outlets as possible.

Intermittent production process (p. 310)
The transformation of resources into products in relatively short production runs, between which machines are often shut down and retooled or prepared to perform a different function.

Intrapreneurship (p. 25)
The concept of allowing those with entrepreneurial skills to operate separate units within companies for the purpose of producing innovative new products.

Inventory (p. 534)
The supply of goods that firms hold on hand and expect to turn over within a year.

Inventory carrying costs (p. 534)
The costs of carrying inventory for a year.

Investing (p. 560)
Putting money into ventures expected to make a reasonable profit given the level of risk; it usually refers to buying stocks and bonds.

Investment bankers (p. 567)
Specialists that help corporations sell new issues of securities.

Involuntary bankruptcy (p. 665)
Bankruptcy that occurs when bankruptcy proceedings are initiated by creditors and the court declares the company bankrupt.

Job analysis (p. 254)
A detailed investigation of the task requirements of a job and the characteristics of the people needed to perform the tasks.

Job description (p. 254)
A listing of the specific activities the holder of a position must perform and the skill level the person will need.

Job enlargement (p. 210)
Adding operations or tasks to a job to keep the job from being boring.

Job enrichment (p. 211)
The process of incorporating motivators into a job situation.

Job rotation (p. 210)
Moving a worker from job to job to keep the worker from becoming bored with doing a simple, specialized job over and over.

Job sharing (p. 212)
A program through which two part-time employees hold the job of one full-time employee.

Job specification (p. 255)
A written document listing the characteristics required of an individual who is to perform a specific job.

Joint venture (p. 119)
Two or more people or companies who have joined together to undertake a specific, limited, usually short-term project.

Journals (p. 503)
A special set of books in which all transactions affecting account values are first recorded.

Just-in-time (JIT) inventory control (p. 333)
The technique that reduces inventories to a minimum by arranging for them to be delivered to the production facility just in time to be used in the manufacturing of a product.

Key executive life insurance (p. 602)
Life insurance for certain executives, naming the corporation as beneficiary, to minimize the impact of the loss of leadership by these executives in the event of their death.

Knights of Labor (p. 282)
Founded in 1869, the first national labor union in America to represent workers of diverse occupations.

Labor contract (p. 290)
A legally enforceable agreement between labor and management regarding the employment responsibilities of both.

Labor union (p. 281)
An organization of employees formed to achieve common goals in the areas of wages, hours worked, and working conditions.

Laissez faire (p. 19)
A hands off approach to business by government.

Laissez-fair leadership style (p. 208)
The pattern of leader behavior that emphasizes autonomy for the workers.

Land pollution (p. 87)
The contamination of the ground.

Landrum-Griffin Act of 1959 (also called the *Labor Management Reporting and Disclosure Act*) (p. 290)
A federal law aimed at protecting individuals against the illegal activities of unions.

Layout pattern (p. 320)
The overall arrangement of machines, equipment, materials handling, aisles, service areas, storage areas, and work stations in a production facility.

Leader pricing (p. 395)
A technique designed to offer high-demand products at or below cost in order to attract customers to a store.

Leasing (p. 547)
Renting fixed assets for a specified period of time.

Leverage ratios (p. 514)
Ratios that measure the equity contribution of stockholders as compared with the debt funds provided by a firm's creditors.

Leveraged buyout (LBO) (p. 118)
An acquisition technique that involves the use of large amounts of borrowed funds to purchase a company.

Liabilities (p. 505)
Borrowed funds (debt) and delayed payments (such as payables and accruals) of a business.

Liability insurance (p. 608)
Insurance that covers the policyholder's liability for injuries to others or for damage to their property.

License agreement (p. 169)
A right granted by one company to another to use its brand name or technology.

Licensing (p. 690)
The practice of allowing foreign companies to use trademarks, patents, copyrights, or manufacturing processes of a domestic company.

Limited partnership (p. 105)
A partnership in which at least one general partner must assume unlimited liability for all business debts and one or more other partners have liability limited to their investment.

Line authority (p. 234)
The right to make decisions and give orders concerning the production, sales, or finance areas of an organization.

Line of credit (p. 539)
A formal loan agreement with a bank that allows a specific maximum amount of credit at specific rates.

Liquidity (p. 469)
The ease and predictability with which an asset can be converted into cash.

Liquidity ratios (p. 512)
Ratios used to determine if a firm can pay its current debts.

Lockout (p. 297)
A refusal by management to allow workers to work, by keeping them out of the workplace.

M1 (p. 471)
All circulating cash and any funds readily convertible into cash, such as those available in checking accounts.

M2 (p. 472)
M1 plus near money (funds that are almost as liquid as those in checking accounts).

Machine language (p. 632)
The most elementary programming language for processing instructions and data; it is expressed as a string of 0s and 1s.

Macroeconomics (p. 35)
The study of the behavior of entire economies.

Magnetic disk (p. 630)
A thin, metal-coated circular magnetic surface on which data are stored.

Magnetic tape (p. 630)
A magnetized, metal-coated ribbon on which data are stored.

Mainframe computers (p. 627)
The largest and most powerful computers.

Major medical insurance (p. 603)
Health insurance that supplements basic hospitalization insurance.

Malpractice insurance (p. 611)
Liability insurance that protects professionals from the risk of being faulted for negligence.

Management (p. 167)
The process of working with and through people and other organizational resources to reach organizational objectives.

Management by objectives (MBO) (p. 204)
The management philosophy in which the primary management tool is the process of setting and monitoring performance targets for organization members.

Management development programs (p. 259)
Training programs that focus on developing problem-solving and other skills needed by good managers.

Managerial grid (p. 214)
A model that describes various combinations of concern for people and concern for production that managers can use to relate to their subordinates.

Management information system (MIS) (p. 632)
A formalized procedure for collecting, storing, and retrieving information to help managers make decisions.

Management level (p. 182)
A particular horizontal segment of management; top management, middle management, and supervisory (operating) management are the three levels.

Market (p. 345)
A group of potential buyers for a good or service.

Market segmentation (p. 354)
The process of dividing the total market of potential buyers into homogeneous groups (groups with similar characteristics).

Market share (p. 390)
The percentage of a company's sales in relation to total industry sales.

Marketable securities (pp. 507, 532)
Short-term investments that are low-risk, maturing within one year or less, and readily resold on the market.

Marketing (p. 345)
The process of planning and executing the conception, pricing, promotion, and distribution of ideas, goods, and services to create exchanges that satisfy individual and organizational objectives.

Marketing concept (p. 346)
The concept that the decision-making process in production should begin with the customer.

Marketing information system (p. 364)
A computer-based framework for the continuous processing and management of marketing information.

Marketing mix (p. 351)
The integration of product, pricing, place (distribution), and promotion (the 4Ps).

Marketing plan (p. 366)
The program that outlines the specific actions necessary to implement the marketing strategy.

Marketing research (p. 363)
The systematic gathering, recording, and analyzing of data about problems related to the marketing of goods and services.

Marketing strategy (p. 351)
An organization's selection of target markets and development of a marketing mix of activities to accomplish its objectives.

Mass production (p. 320)
Producing goods in large quantities.

Mass storage device (p. 630)
The part of the computer that holds the programs and data until the central processing unit is ready to process them.

Materials handling (p. 420)
The variety of specialized techniques and equipment designed for moving goods in a terminal, warehouse, or store.

Materials requirements planning (MRP) (p. 327)
A computer-based production coordination system that ensures that needed parts and materials are available for the production process at the right time and the right place.

Matrix organization (p. 237)
An organizational structure in which specialists from different departments are brought together for a specific project and time period, while they are still functioning in the company's traditional structure.

Mediation (p. 293)
The practice of involving in the collective bargaining process a neutral third party who focuses primarily on proposing solutions to bargaining problems.

Medical payments insurance (p. 606)
Automobile insurance that pays the medical expenses of the policyholder and passengers in the event of an accident, regardless of liability.

Medicare (p. 598)
A supplemental health insurance program provided to retirees sixty-five years of age and older who are covered by social security.

Mercantilism (p. 19)
An economic system based on colonization and the exploitation of natural resources.

Merchandise inventory (p. 508)
All the goods on hand for sale.

Merchant wholesalers (p. 406)
Wholesalers who take legal title to merchandise and provide a variety of services.

Merger (p. 114)
The combining of two companies.

Merit pay (p. 265)
A type of incentive pay typically given to nonmanagement employees.

Microcomputers (p. 627)
Computers that are smaller and generally less powerful than either mainframes or minicomputers. Also called personal computers (PCs).

Microeconomics (p. 35)
The study of the behavior of organizations or individuals.

Microprocessor (p. 627)
One or more computer chips containing the basic functions of arithmetic, logic, and storage necessary for the computer to process data.

Middle management (p. 183)
The next-to-highest level of management.

Middlemen (p. 405)
Agents or merchants who specialize in performing marketing functions directly related to the purchase of products in the course of their flow from producer to consumer.

Minicomputer (p. 627)
A computer that is larger than a microcomputer but smaller and less powerful than a mainframe computer.

Minority Business Development Agency (MBDA) (p. 148)
A Commerce Department agency that conducts surveys, provides credit assistance, and awards grants to organizations sponsoring minority enterprises.

Missionary selling (p. 453)
The use of salespeople to supplement the personal selling activities of middlemen.

Mixed economy (p. 57)
An economy that combines socialism and private enterprise.

Monetary policy (pp. 46, 484)
The process used by the Federal Reserve System to manage the money supply.

Monetary system (p. 488)
A country's money and banking system, embodied in a central bank.

Money (p. 467)
Anything that is widely accepted as a medium for the buying and selling of goods and services.

Money market deposit accounts (MMDAs) (p. 477)
Accounts at depository financial institutions that pay competitive interest rates, have no minimum maturity, allow the withdrawal of funds at any time, and limit transactions to six a month.

Money market funds (p. 480)
Institutions that pool contributions from a large number of investors who wish to put their money into a variety of short-term securities and loans.

Monopolistic competition (p. 17)
Competition occurring in industries where there are a large number of businesses but where the products are often differentiated from those of competitors by nonprice factors.

Monopoly (p. 17)
A market situation in which there is no competition.

Morale (p. 195)
The general attitudes workers have about their jobs.

Mortgages (p. 477)
Long-term loans specifically for the purchase of real estate.

Motivation (p. 196)
The part of an individual that causes the person to behave in a way that will ensure the attainment of some goal.

Motivators (p. 210)
According to Frederick Herzberg, elements that influence the degree of job satisfaction.

Multinational corporations (p. 692)
Corporations that operate in several countries and have a substantial part of their assets, sales, or labor force in foreign subsidiaries.

Multiplier effect (p. 12)
The change in the rate of spending that causes a chain reaction throughout the economy.

Mutual funds (p. 481)
Investment companies that pool investors' funds to buy stocks, bonds, and other securities.

Mutual savings banks (p. 475)
Depository financial institutions that are owned by their depositors and that, like S&Ls, use their savings deposits mainly to make housing loans.

National brands (p. 386)
Brand names owned by the manufacturer of a product.

Negotiable instrument (p. 655)
Any form of business paper used in commercial transactions as a substitute for money.

Need (p. 196)
The lack of something desired or perceived as necessary, or the difference between what an individual has and what the person would like to have.

No-fault insurance (p. 607)
Automobile insurance under which injured individuals receive payment from their own insurance companies, regardless of which driver is at fault.

Nonfinancial compensation (p. 266)
A nonmonetary reward that an organization member receives for performing a job.

Nonprogrammed decision (p. 175)
A decision made about a complex, unique, or rarely occurring situation.

Norris-LaGuardia Act of 1932 (p. 287)
The federal law that made "yellow dog" contracts—contracts requiring employees, as a condition of employment, not to join unions—illegal and made it difficult for management to obtain injunctions preventing workers from participating in union activities.

Occupational Safety and Health Act (OSHA) (p. 269)
A 1970 federal law that requires employers to provide safe and healthy work environments and to keep records for judging safety.

Occupational Safety and Health Administration (p. 269)
A federal agency charged with ensuring the safety of workers.

Ocean marine insurance (p. 610)
Transportation insurance that protects against the loss of merchandise transported on the high seas.

Oligopoly (p. 17)
An industry in which there are few competitors.

Online processing (p. 625)
A method of handling computer-processed data in which the data are processed as they are entered into the computer.

On-the-job training (p. 261)
A training method through which workers learn job skills by performing appropriate tasks in the actual work situation, with the help of experienced employees.

Operating expenses (p. 510)
The normal expenses of operating a business, not including the cost of goods sold.

Operations management (p. 323)
The process of managing production, or, more specifically, the performance of the managerial activities entailed in selecting, designing, operating, controlling, and updating production systems.

Organization (p. 225)
The result of the organizing process—the establishment of logical relationships of people and other resources to achieve organizational objectives.

Organization chart (p. 225)
A diagram that shows the main components of formal structure.

Organizational culture (p. 227)
The set of values and beliefs shared by all organization members.

Organizational hierarchy (management pyramid) (p. 183)
The collective term for the three management levels: top, middle, and supervisory (operating).

Organizational market (p. 354)
The market composed of buyers from industry, wholesaling and retailing (resellers), and government.

Organizational objectives (p. 167)
The targets an organization is attempting to hit.

Organizational resources (p. 177)
All the assets available for the production process: people, money, materials, and equipment.

Organizing (pp. 171, 223)
The process managers use to best combine people, equipment and materials, and all other resources in order to carry out plans and reach organizational objectives.

Organizing process (p. 224)
The five steps managers follow in organizing: (1) reflecting on plans and objectives, (2) establishing major tasks, (3) dividing the tasks into subtasks, (4) allocating resources and directives for subtasks, and (5) evaluating the results of the implemented organizing strategy.

Outside directors (p. 111)
Board members who are not employed by the corporation.

Over-the-counter (OTC) markets (p. 569)
Markets for securities not listed on any U.S. stock exchange.

Owner's (stockholders') equity (p. 505)
The owner's investment in a business (also called net worth).

Par stock (p. 564)
Stock that has a stated value printed on the face of the stock certificate.

Parent company (p. 116)
A corporation that owns all or the majority of stock in another company.

Partnership (p. 101)
An association of two or more individuals to carry on as co-owners of a business.

Patent (p. 664)
A nonrenewable exclusive legal right to a product or process granted for seventeen years by the Patent and Trademark Office.

Patronage motive (p. 363)
A combination of emotional and rational motives that influence where a consumer will purchase goods and services.

Penetration pricing (p. 392)
A strategy that introduces a new product at a low price with the aim of recovering the initial investment through high sales volume.

Pension funds (p. 481)
Financial institutions designed to provide retirement benefits to employees of various organizations.

Performance appraisal (p. 262)
The process of reviewing an individual's productive activity to evaluate the contribution made to the attainment of organizational objectives.

Personal property (p. 658)
All property other than real estate.

Personal selling (p. 451)
A form of interpersonal communication designed to inform prospective customer and induce the person to make a purchase.

Philanthropy (p. 88)
The active effort to help humanity that typically is demonstrated by donations of money, property, or labor.

Physical distribution (p. 418)
The movement and handling of goods from the producer to the point of consumption.

Physiological needs (p. 198)
The needs involved in keeping the body functioning normally—the most basic survival needs in Maslow's hierarchy.

Picketing (p. 295)
A labor tactic, generally used in conjunction with a strike, that involves positioning one or more union members at the entrance of a struck workplace to stop or make difficult any entry to the workplace.

Piece-rate wage (p. 264)
Direct pay determined by the number of units an employee produces.

Planning (p. 168)
Determining the tasks to be performed in achieving organizational objectives, setting guidelines on how to perform them, and indicating when they should be performed.

Point-of-purchase (POP) display (p. 448)
A type of sales promotion designed to display or demonstrate a product at or close to where a purchase takes place.

Policy (p. 171)
A planning tool that furnishes broad guidelines for channeling management thinking in certain directions.

Pollution (p. 85)
The contamination of the environment caused by human activities.

Positioning (p. 355)
An approach to segmenting that identifies current or proposed marketing segments and indicates where the segments perceive the product in relation to competing products.

Posting (p. 503)
The procedure of transferring the transactions in journals to the respective accounts.

Power of attorney (p. 661)
The document by which a principal-agent relationship is established.

Predatory pricing (p. 396)
A practice whereby a company deliberately tries to damage or destroy a competitor by cutting prices below cost.

Preferred stock (p. 564)
Stock whose owners receive dividends (if any are declared) in stated amounts before dividends can be distributed to owners of common stock.

Premium (for insurance) (p. 592)
A cash payment to an insurance company for an insurance policy.

Premium (for merchandising) (p. 448)
Piece of merchandise that is either offered to a consumer as a free gift or sold for a small sum to cover costs.

Premium price (p. 562)
A higher price for bonds than the face value so as to bring the bond's market value in line with current market interest rates.

Price (p. 389)
The exchange value of a good or service.

Price leader (p. 391)
A leading producer or channel member that has substantial market share and can therefore set the going price for a product.

Price lining (p. 392)
A pricing strategy that occurs when a store offers its products at a limited number of prices.

Primary data (p. 364)
Data gathered through original research for a specific purpose.

Primary market (p. 568)
The market in which new shares of stocks or bonds are sold.

Prime rate (p. 540)
The interest rate that banks routinely charge their most financially sound business borrowers.

Printer's Ink code (p. 447)
A model statute which provides punishment for unethical advertising practices.

Private brands (p. 388)
Brand names owned by the retailer.

Private carriers (p. 421)
Companies that provide their own transportation fleets to move their products.

Private enterprise system (p. 50)
A free-market system.

Problem-solving area (p. 80)
The part of measuring a company's social responsibility activity that gauges the degree to which the company actively solves social problems.

Process layout (p. 320)
The layout pattern based primarily on the grouping together of similar types of equipment or materials.

Procurement Automated Source System (PASS) (p. 147)
A computerized system for matching small businesses and federal government contracts.

Product advertising (p. 436)
Advertising designed to promote a product or product line.

Product differentiation (p. 355)
The promotional technique used to distinguish the characteristics of one product from those of another.

Product layout (p. 320)
The layout pattern based primarily on the progressive steps required to make a particular product.

Product liability insurance (p. 610)
Insurance that covers manufacturers and suppliers of products whose proper use results in personal injury.

Product liability law (p. 661)
Law that holds businesses liable for negligence in the design, production, or sale of defective products.

Product life cycle (p. 385)
The four stages that a typical product passes through.

Product line (p. 375)
An assortment of related products that a company sells.

Product mix (p. 375)
The total of different products or product lines that a company sells.

Production (p. 310)
The transformation of organizational resources into products.

Production facility (p. 317)
A place where goods and services are produced.

Production planning (p. 324)
Determining the types and amounts of resources needed to produce specified goods and services.

Productivity (pp. 40, 311)
A measure of the relationship between the total amount of goods and services being produced and the resources needed to produce them.

Profit (p. 8)
Revenue that exceeds expenses in a business.

Profit equation (p. 506)
Profits equal revenue minus expenses.

Profit maximization (p. 389)
The pricing strategy under which a company charges what the market will bear in order to increase profits.

Profit sharing (p. 265)
A type of incentive pay in which workers receive some portion of the profits that the company earns.

Profitability ratios (p. 515)
The ratios used by management to determine if the firm's resources are being employed in the best manner.

Program evaluation and review technique (PERT) (p. 325)
A graphic scheduling technique that displays a network of separate project activities, showing the relationships among the activities and a time estimate for each activity.

Programmed decision (p. 175)
A decision made to apply to routine or recurring situations.

Programming language (p. 631)
A set of symbols, with rules for how to combine and interpret them, that is the basis for writing computer programs.

Promissory note (p. 540)
A written promise from a borrower to make future payment to the lender at a specificed rate of interest.

Promotion (p. 433)
The form of marketing communication that attempts to reach a target audience with a persuasive message through advertising, personal selling, sales promotion, and publicity.

Promotional mix (p. 433)
The combination of two or more of the following to reach a target audience: advertising, personal selling, sales promotion, and publicity.

Property (p. 658)
An item (or items) of value owned by an individual or business.

Property damage liability insurance (p. 606)
Automobile insurance that pays for damage to others' property caused by the insured car.

Prospecting (p. 453)
The systematic approach to developing new sales leads.

Protectionism (p. 682)
The belief that free trade should be restricted for the protection of domestic industries.

Proxy (p. 110)
A written authorization that transfers a stockholder's voting rights to a corporate board member or other appointed person.

Psychographics (p. 362)
The study of consumers' values, interests, attitudes, personalities, and lifestyles.

Psychological pricing (p. 392)
A pricing technique designed to make the price of a product look right.

Public liability insurance (p. 611)
Liability insurance that provides protection to organizations and individuals against claims caused by personal injuries or damage to the property of others when the insured is responsible.

Public relations (p. 451)
The process by which a business obtains goodwill and promotes a positive image of itself.

Publicity (p. 451)
A nonpaid commercially significant news or editorial comment about ideas, products, or institutions.

Pull strategy (p. 435)
A promotional effort designed to stimulate consumer demand for products through the use of advertising and sales promotion.

Purchasing (p. 324)
Obtaining the raw materials needed to produce the product.

Purchasing power (p. 360)
The ability of consumers to purchase goods and services.

Pure competition (p. 17)
The competition that results when there are so many small businesses in an industry that no single business can influence the price charged on a fairly uniform product.

Pure Food and Drug Act of 1906 (p. 652)
Federal legislation prohibiting the adulteration and misbranding of food and drugs; it was amended in 1938 to include the healthfulness, safety, and labeling of foods, drugs, and cosmetics and was renamed the Food, Drug, and Cosmetic Act.

Pure risk (p. 593)
A risk that offers no chance for gain—only loss.

Push strategy (p. 435)
A promotional effort that persuades middlemen to sell a product aggressively.

Quality-of-life area (p. 79)
The part of measuring a company's social responsibility activity that gauges the improvement or maintenance of a desirable quality of life for individuals or society.

Quality circles (p. 332)
Small groups of workers who volunteer to meet regularly to discuss and help solve quality-related problems.

Quality control (p. 330)
The process of making the quality of finished goods and services what it was planned to be.

Quotas (p. 682)
Quantitative limits on the amounts of goods that can be legally imported into a country.

Random sample (p. 365)
A sample for which each person in the population being studied has an equal chance of being selected.

Rational motives (p. 363)
The motives that evolve from the reasoning process.

Ratios (p. 511)
Fractional or percentage relationships between two or more variables.

Real income (p. 14)
The value of a person's income in terms of its purchasing power.

Real property (p. 658)
Real estate, including buildings, land, and anything permanently part of the land.

Recession (p. 48)
A decline in total national spending for two consecutive quarters.

Recruitment (p. 256)
The initial screening of the total supply of applicants for a position.

Reserve requirement (p. 486)
The percentage of funds the Federal Reserve Bank in each district requires banks in that district to hold in reserve.

Responsibility (p. 233)
The obligation to perform an assigned activity.

Retailers (p. 408)
Middlemen who sell directly to the consumer.

Revenues (p. 506)
The funds received by a business, mainly from the sales of goods and services.

Right-to-work laws (p. 288)
State laws that have made required union membership illegal.

Right to be heard (p. 83)
The right to be listened to by business.

Right to be informed (p. 83)
The right to know what a product is, what precautions must be taken during its use, and what ingredients it contains.

Right to choose (p. 83)
The right to select a product from a number of competing ones in the marketplace.

Right to safety (p. 83)
The right to purchase products that are not dangerous.

Risk (pp. 560, 591)
The degree of uncertainty about exposure to possible losses or injuries in an investment or an insurance policy.

Risk aversion (p. 560)
The preference for investments with good potential profit and little risk.

Robinson-Patman Act (p. 396)
A federal law forbidding certain types of price discrimination between buyers and sellers of goods of "like grade and quality," when the effect may be to decrease competition or create a monopoly.

Robots (p. 315)
Machines that perform some of the mechanical functions of humans.

Routing (p. 324)
Determining the sequence in which all the phases of production must be completed to produce specific goods and services.

Rule (p. 171)
A planning tool that designates a specific required action.

S corporations (p. 113)
Small corporations with a limited number of stockholders; they are taxed as partnerships.

Salary (p. 264)
Direct pay based on an extended period of time worked, such as a week, a month, or a year.

Sales finance companies (p. 541)
Companies that specialize in financing the customers of certain types of retail businesses.

Sales promotion (p. 434)
Any promotional activity that is not advertising, personal selling, or publicity.

Sample (p. 365)
A representative part of a larger group.

Samples (p. 449)
Free products given to potential customers to induce them to make a purchase.

Savings and loan associations (S&Ls) (p. 474)
Depository financial institutions that accept savings and provide mortgage loans for local housing.

Scheduling (p. 324)
Listing in detail each activity that must be followed to produce goods or services and calculating how long each activity will take.

Scientific management (p. 312)
The process of finding the one best way to perform a task.

Scrambled merchandising (p. 414)
The retailer's diversification of a product mix to increase sales volume.

Secondary boycott (p. 296)
An attempt by labor to force an employer to stop doing business with another employer who is in conflict with a union.

Secondary data (p. 364)
Data previously gathered and made available in journals, newspapers, computer data bases, and other sources.

Secondary market (p. 568)
The market in which previously issued stocks and bonds are bought and sold.

Secured loans (p. 477)
Loans protected by a pledge from borrowers to forfeit to lenders something of value if the loans are not repaid.

Securities and Exchange Commission (SEC) (p. 578)
The federal agency empowered to regulate the interstate distribution of listed securities.

Security needs (p. 199)
Needs related to keeping oneself free from harm; they are the second level of needs in Maslow's hierarchy.

Self-actualization needs (p. 199)
Needs to maximize potential, to be the very best the person can be; they are the fifth and final level in Maslow's hierarchy.

Self-insurance (p. 592)
A risk-bearing method whereby a company make a regular deposit into a fund to pay for potential losses.

Selection (p. 258)
The process of choosing an individual to hire from all those who have been recruited.

Selective distribution (p. 415)
The strategy of selecting a limited number of wholesalers or retailers in a geographic area to carry a product.

Service Corps of Retired Executives (SCORE) (p. 147)
An SBA-sponsored volunteer group of retired business executives who give advice and consultation to small businesses.

Services (p. 375)
The intangible activities that are purchased by customers and provide benefits and some form of satisfaction.

Sherman Antitrust Act of 1890 (p. 650)
Federal legislation that declared trusts and other forms of monopoly illegal.

Shopping goods and services (p. 380)
The products that consumers buy after taking the time to compare quality, price, style, and other competitive factors.

Sinking fund (p. 562)
A special fund into which a corporation must put money regularly so it can pay back bondholders when the bond reaches maturity.

Site selection (p. 319)
The process of determining where a production facility should be located.

Situational leadership (p. 208)
The leadership approach that recognizes that success in leading is determined by a leadership style appropriate to the followers being led and to the situation faced by the leader.

Skimming pricing (p. 391)
A strategy in which the price of a new product is set high during the introductory stage and reduced as the product gains acceptance.

Skunkworks (p. 25)
Entrepreneurial units operating within a company.

Slurry pipelines (p. 424)
Pipelines that carry powdered coal in liquid form to areas of major usage and to port cities for export.

Small business (p. 129)
An independently owned and managed business that serves a limited geographic area and is not dominant in its industry.

Small Business Administration (SBA) (p. 130)
A federal agency whose main purpose is to provide financial and managerial assistance to small American firms.

Small Business Development Centers (SBDCs) (p. 147)
University-managed centers that provide faculty and others to give small businesses research, technical, and managerial assistance.

Small Business Institutes (SBIs) (p. 147)
SBA- and university-sponsored programs that allow qualified seniors and graduate students in business schools the opportunity to provide on-site managerial consulting to small businesses.

Small Business Investment Companies (SBICs) (p. 148)
Licensed by the SBA to lend money to small business ventures.

Social audit (p. 80)
A summary of an organization's social responsibility activities.

Social investment area (p. 80)
The part of measuring a company's social responsibility activity that gauges the contribution of money and other resources to help solve community social problems.

Social needs (p. 199)
Needs for love, companionship, and friendship—the desire to be accepted by others; they are the third level of needs in Maslow's hierarchy.

Socialism (p. 53)
The general term for any economic system that depends heavily on the government to make economic planning decisions and to own and control key resources and industries.

Socially responsible business practices (p. 80)
Actions taken by managers that contribute to the attainment of organizational objectives while enhancing the welfare of society.

Social responsibility (p. 69)
The managerial obligation to take action that will protect and improve not only the interests of the organization but also the welfare of society as a whole.

Software (p. 628)
The computer programs or instructions that tell the computer what to do.

Sole proprietorship (p. 101)
A business owned by one person.

Span of management (p. 230)
The number of individuals a manager supervises.

Specialty advertising (p. 448)
A kind of advertising that uses articles of merchandise imprinted with an advertiser's message and distributed without obligation to the recipient.

Specialty goods and services (p. 380)
Products that have unique characteristics and brand identification and are in demand by buyers willing to make a special effort to purchase them.

Speculation (p. 559)
Putting money into very risky ventures in the hope of making a large profit quickly.

Speculative risk (p. 593)
A risk that offers an opportunity for both gain and loss.

Spreadsheets (p. 636)
Computer programs that accept data in the form of columns and rows, which the user can then manipulate.

Staff authority (p. 235)
The right to advise or assist those who possess line authority.

Standard markup (p. 393)
The difference between the cost of an item and its selling price.

Standard of living (p. 14)
The quality of living in a nation.

Standardization (p. 172)
The continual production of uniform goods and services.

Standards (p. 172)
The criteria established by management to serve as a model for evaluating performance within the organization.

Stare decisis (to stand on decided case) (p. 649)
The doctrine of basing legal decisions on decisions in previous cases.

Statistical quality control (p. 330)
A quantitative tool for determining the acceptable number of units to inspect in order to maintain the quality of the entire batch of products being produced.

Statutory law (p. 649)
Laws written and enacted by government bodies.

Stock exchanges (p. 568)
The marketplaces in which securities are bought and sold.

Stock turnover (p. 394)
The number of times the average inventory is sold in a given time period.

Stockholders (p. 109)
The owners of a corporation. They are also referred to as shareholders.

Strategic planning (p. 168)
Long-range planning that focuses on the organization as a whole.

Strategy (p. 168)
A set of actions designed to help a company outperform the competition and reach its long-range objectives.

Strike, or walkout (p. 295)
Employees' temporary stoppage of work intended to win concessions from management.

Structure (p. 225)
The specific pattern of relationships among the activities and resources of an organization.

Structural change (p. 243)
The modification of an existing organizational structure.

Subobjectives (p. 181)
Lower-level, specific objectives that are developed from broader objectives and that specify how they are to be carried out.

Subsidiaries (p. 116)
Companies owned by corporations.

Suggestion selling (p. 455)
A sales technique used to suggest additional items of merchandise that go with the product being purchased.

Supercomputer (p. 627)
A mainframe computer with an extremely large memory, the most advanced capabilities, and the highest possible performance speeds.

Supervisory (operating) management (p. 183)
The lowest level of management; managers at this level are usually called supervisors.

Supply (p. 17)
The amount of a product for sale at a specific price.

Supply curve (p. 37)
Illustrates graphically the quantities of a product that will be offered at each price for a specific period of time.

Surety bonds (p. 608)
Performance bonds—guarantees that a jobs will be finished within a reasonable period of time or that payment will be made to another company to complete the work.

Synthetic production process (p. 310)
The process that transforms resources into products by combining two or more materials into a single product.

Tactical planning (p. 169)
Short-range planning that focuses on current operations of various parts of the organization.

Taft-Hartley Act of 1947 (also known as the Labor Management Relations Act) (p. 288)
An employer-favoring federal law aimed at balancing the power of unions with that of management in union-related matters.

Tall organizations (p. 232)
Organizations whose organization charts are high and whose spans of management are narrow.

Target markets (p. 351)
Segmented groups of potential buyers.

Tariffs (p. 682)
Taxes or duties placed on imported products.

Technical selling (p. 452)
A technique used by experienced scientists to convince customers of an industrial product's superiority.

Technical skill (p. 183)
The ability to use specialized knowledge about the mechanics of a job.

Telemarketing (p. 453)
The discipline that puts advanced telecommunications technology to work as a well-organized and well-managed marketing program.

Term insurance (p. 600)
A type of life insurance that is issued for a specific period of time, from one to thirty years, and pays a benefit only if the insured dies during that period.

Theft insurance (p. 607)
Insurance that protects property owners against losses caused by burglary and robbery.

Theory X (p. 200)
The set of managerial assumptions that people dislike work, must be forced to work under threat of punishment, want to be controlled, and desire security above all else.

Theory Y (p. 200)
The set of managerial assumptions that work is natural, that people will work to achieve objectives to which they are committed, that commitment is tied to rewards, that many people want responsibility, and that people can use imagination and talent in solving problems.

Theory Z (p. 200)
A management philosophy for motivating organization members through a combination of Japanese and American management practices.

Time deposits (p. 477)
The different forms of insured savings accounts offered by depository financial institutions.

Top management (p. 183)
The highest level of management.

Tort (p. 661)
A civil, or private, wrongful act by one party that injures another party.

Trade credit (p. 538)
Informal short-term credit granted directly to the buyer of goods or services by the seller.

Trade deficit (p. 679)
A negative, or unfavorable, balance of trade.

Trade show (p. 451)
A relatively low-cost sales promotion method used as a pushing strategy to display products to channel middlemen.

Trademark (pp. 388, 663)
A name, word, symbol, or other device that has been registered by the owner for the purpose of identifying its product line.

Trading stamps (p. 449)
A sales promotion method used by retailers that provides stamps or similar credits to consumers for the redemption of merchandise.

Training (p. 259)
The process of developing qualities in employees that will enable them to be more productive and, as a result, to contribute more to the attainment of organizational objectives.

Transaction (p. 503)
An event that either increases or decreases the value of an account.

Traveler's checks (p. 476)
Checks issued by large financial institutions and sold through depository institutions such as banks and credit unions.

Treasury bill (p. 532)
A short-term debt obligation of the U.S. government.

Trusts (p. 650)
A combination of a few companies in a tight monopolistic network.

Underwriting process (p. 593)
The procedure insurance companies use for screening risks.

Uninsured motorist coverage (p. 607)
Automobile insurance that pays for the insured's bodily injury (and sometimes damage to the car as well) if the person's car is hit by the car of an uninsured motorist who is judged to be at fault.

Union shop (p. 288)
A union and business agreement that allows the business to hire the most qualified employees, who then are required to join a union within a specified period.

Universal life insurance (p. 602)
A flexible premium life insurance that allows the insured to change the death benefit from time to time or to vary the amount or timing of premium payments.

Universality of management (p. 184)
The concept that management principles are relevant to all types and levels of organizations.

Unlimited liability (p. 103)
The condition that allows both the business and personal assets of a sole proprietor or a partner to be subject to the claims of creditors.

User database (p. 633)
A database developed by an individual user.

Utility (p. 310)
The quality of a product that makes it useful or desirable in satisfying customers' needs.

Value-added network (VAN) (p. 317)
A communication system that allows computers to coordinate production processes with other computers over long distances.

Variable costs (p. 518)
Costs that are directly tied to the level of business activity, rising as volume picks up and declining as volume slacks off.

Venture capital (p. 132)
Start-up money used to finance a new business or expand one that shows potential.

Venture capitalists (p. 132)
Investment specialists seeking to invest in potentially high-growth new companies.

Vertical marketing system (VMS) (p. 417)
A centrally controlled and managed distribution system.

Vertical merger (p. 115)
A merger that occurs when a major corporation purchases one of its suppliers or the supplier purchases the major corporation.

Vestibule training (p. 261)
A training method through which workers learn job skills by operating equipment similar to that used in the actual job situation in a setting similar to the actual job setting.

Voluntary bankruptcy (p. 665)
Bankruptcy that occurs when a company files a petition for bankruptcy of its own accord.

Voluntary chains (p. 408)
Independently owned stores that band together under a common name to gain the advantages of chain stores.

Wage (p. 264)
Direct pay determined by the number of hours an employee works.

Wagner Act of 1935 (also known as the National Labor Relations Act) (p. 287)
The federal law that identified and outlawed certain unfair labor practices, mandated secret ballot election procedures that allowed employees to vote to unionize, and created the National Labor Relations Board.

Warehouse (p. 420)
A facility used to store goods for a relatively long period of time.

Warranty (p. 659)
A promise by a manufacturer or seller to stand behind its product.

Water pollution (p. 87)
The contamination of lakes, rivers, and oceans.

Wheel of retailing (p. 413)
The concept that retailers go through their own life cycle—entering a market as price leaders with few services and then gradually increasing prices and services as competition stiffens and the market matures.

Whole life insurance (p. 600)
A type of permanent life insurance in which the insured agrees to pay a regular premium for the rest of the insured's life in return for a guaranteed specific amount of coverage.

Wholesalers (p. 406)
Middle men who buy and resell merchandise to retailers, commercial and industrial users, and institutions.

Word processing (p. 636)
A method of using computers to create, edit, store, and print documents.

Worker's compensation (p. 598)
A state-mandated insurance that every employer must provide to employees for job-related injuries and illnesses.

World Bank (p. 689)
An organization of 149 member nations whose purpose is to make loans to the less developed countries.

NAME INDEX

SUBJECT INDEX

Boldfaced entries in this index indicate key terms presented in the text and the page numbers on which they are defined.